THE HYMNS OF THE ṚGVEDA

THE HYMNS OF THE
ṚGVEDA

Translated with a Popular Commentary by
RALPH T. H. GRIFFITH

Edited by
PROF. J. L. SHASTRI

MOTILAL BANARSIDASS PUBLISHERS
PRIVATE LIMITED • DELHI

New Revised Edition: Delhi, 1973
Reprint: Delhi, 1976, 1986, 1991, 1995

ISBN: 81-208-0046-x

Also available at:

MOTILAL BANARSIDASS

41 U.A. Bungalow Road, Jawahar Nagar, Delhi 110 007
120 Royapettah High Road, Mylapore, Madras 600 004
16 St. Mark's Road, Bangalore 560 001
Ashok Rajpath, Patna 800 004
Chowk, Varanasi 221 001

PRINTED IN INDIA

BY JAINENDRA PRAKASH JAIN AT SHRI JAINENDRA PRESS,
A-45 NARAINA, PHASE I, NEW DELHI 110 028
AND PUBLISHED BY NARENDRA PRAKASH JAIN FOR
MOTILAL BANARSIDASS PUBLISHERS PRIVATE LIMITED,
BUNGALOW ROAD, DELHI 110 007

CONTENTS

PREFACE TO THE FIRST EDITION

"What can be more tedious than the Veda, and yet what can be more interesting, if once we know that it is the first word spoken by the Aryan man?"

"The Veda has a two-fold interest: it belongs to the history of the world and to the history of India. . . . As long as man continues to take an interest in the history of his race, and as long as we collect in libraries and museums the relics of former ages, the first place in that long row of books which contains the records of the Aryan branch of mankind, will belong for ever to the Ṛgveda."

—F. Max Müller

This work is an attempt to bring within easy reach of all readers of English a translation of the Hymns of the Ṛgveda which while aiming especially at close fidelity to the letter and the spirit of the original, shall be as readable and intelligible as the nature of the subject and other circumstances permit.

Veda, meaning literally knowledge, is the name given to certain ancient works which formed the foundation of the early religious belief of the Hindus. These are the Ṛgveda, the Sāmaveda, the Yajurveda, and the Atharvaveda; and of these the Ṛgveda—so called because its Saṁhitā or collection of mantras or hymns consists of Ṛcas or verses intended for loud recitation—is the oldest, the most important, and the most generally interesting, some of its hymns being rather Indo-European than Hindu, and representing the condition of the Aryans before their final settlement in India. These four Vedas are considered to be of divine origin and to have existed from all eternity, the Ṛṣis or sacred poets to whom the hymns are ascribed being merely inspired seers who saw or received them by sight directly from the Supreme Creator. In accordance with this belief these sacred books have been preserved and handed down with the most reverential care from generation to generation and have accompanied the great army of Aryan immigrants in their onward march from the Land of the Seven Rivers to the Indian Ocean and the Bay of Bengal. Each of these four Vedas is divided into two distinct parts, one the Mantra containing prayer and praise, the other the Brāhmaṇa containing detailed directions for the performance of the ceremonies at which the Mantras were to be used, and explanations of the legends connected with them, the whole forming a vast body of sacred literature in verse and in prose, devotional, ceremonial, expository and theosophic.

The Saṁhitā of the Ṛgveda is a collection of hymns and songs brought by the remote ancestors of the present Hindus from their ancient homes on the banks of the Indus where they had been first used in adoration of the Father of Heaven, of the Sun, of Dawn, of Agni or the God of fire, in prayers for health, wealth, long life, offspring, cattle, victory in battle, and freedom from the bonds of sin; and celebration of the ever-renewed warfare between the beneficent thunder-wielding Indra, the special champion of the Aryans, and the malevolent powers of darkness and the demons of drought who withheld the rain of heaven.

Of these hymns there are more than a thousand, arranged in ten Maṇḍalas, Circles or Books in accordance with an ancient tradition of what we should call authorship, the hymns ascribed to the same Ṛṣi, inspired poet or seer or to the same school or family of Ṛṣis being placed together. Within these divisions the hymns are generally arranged more or less in the order of the deities to whom they are addressed. Agni and Indra are the Gods most frequently invoked. Hymns to Agni generally come first, next come those addressed to Indra, and after them those in honour of other deities or deified objects of adoration. The ninth Book is devoted almost entirely to Soma, the deified juice used in pouring libations to the Gods, and the tenth forms a sort of appendix of peculiar and miscellaneous materials. Independently of the evidence afforded by Indian tradition, there can be no reasonable doubt of the great antiquity of the Ṛgveda Saṁhitā which with the exception of the Egyptian monumental records and papyrus rolls, and the recently discovered Assyrian literature, is probably the oldest literary document in existence. But it seems impossible to fix, with anything approaching to certainty, any date for the composition of the hymns. In the first Hymn of Book I, ancient and recent or modern Ṛṣis or seers are spoken of, and there is other internal evidence that some hymns are much older than others. Colebrooke came to the conclusion from astronomical calculations, that a certain Vedic calendar was composed in the fourteenth century before the Christian era; from which it would follow, that as this calendar must have been prepared after the arrangement of the Ṛgveda and the inclusion of the most modern hymn, the date of the earliest hymn might be carried back perhaps, some thousand years. The correctness of Colebrooke's conclusion, however, has been questioned, and some recent scholars consider that his calculations are of a very vague character and do not yield any such definite date. In the absence of any direct evidence, the opinions of scholars vary and must continue to vary with regard to the age of the Hymns of the Ṛgveda. "The reasons, however", (to quote Professor Weber[1]) "by which we are fully justified in regarding the literature of India as the most ancient literature of which written records of an extensive scale have been handed down to us are these:—In the more ancient parts of the Ṛgveda Saṁhitā, we find the Indian race settled on the north-western borders of India, in the Panjāb, and even beyond the Panjāb, on the Kubhā, or Kophen in Kabul. The gradual spread of the race from these seats towards the east, beyond the Sarasvatī and over Hindustān as far as the Ganges, can be traced in the later portions of the Vedic writings almost step by step. The writings of the following period, that of the epic, consist of accounts of the internal conflicts among the conquerors of Hindustān themselves, as, for instance, the Mahābhārata; or of the farther spread of Brāhmanism towards the south, as for instance, the Rāmāyaṇa. If we connect with this the first fairly accurate information about India which we have from a Greek source, viz., from Megasthenes,[2] it becomes clear that at the time of this writer the Brāhmanising of Hindustān was already completed, while at the time of the Periplus (see Lassen, *I. AK.*, ii. 150, n; *I. St.*, ii. 192) the very southern-most point of the Dekhan had already become the seat of the worship of Gaurī, the wife of Śiva. What a series of years, of centuries, must necessarily have elapsed before this boundless tract of country, inhabited by wild and vigorous tribes, could have been brought over to Brāhmaṇism!"

I must beg my European readers not to expect to find in these hymns and songs the sublime poetry that they meet with in Isaiah or Job, or the Psalms of David. "To me", says Professor Wilson, "the verses of the Veda, except in their rhythm, and in a few rare passages, appear singularly prosaic for so early an era as that of their probable composition, and at any rate their chief value lies not in their fancy but in their facts, social and religious." Professor Cowell, also, says: "The poetry of the Ṛgveda is singularly deficient in that simplicity and natural pathos or sublimity which we naturally look for in the songs of an early period of civilisation. The language and style of most of the hymns is singularly artificial. . . . Occasionally we meet with fine outbursts of poetry, especially in the hymns addressed to the dawn, but these are never long sustained, and as a rule we find few grand similes

1 *The History of Indian Literature*, by Albrecht Weber, Trübner's Oriental Series, 1878.

2 Who as ambassador of Seleucus resided for some time at the court of Chandragupta. His reports are preserved to us chiefly in the Indica of Arrian who lived in the second century A.D.

or metaphors." The worst fault of all, in the Collection regarded as a whole, is the intolerable monotony of a great number of the hymns, a monotony which reaches its climax in the ninth Book which consists almost entirely of invocations of Soma Pavamāna, or the deified Soma juice in process of straining and purification. The great interest of the Ṛgveda is, in fact, historical rather than poetical. As in its original language we see the roots and shoots of the languages of Greek and Latin, of Kelt, Teuton and Slavonian, so the deities, the myths, and the religious beliefs and practices of the Veda throw a flood of light upon the religions of all European countries before the introduction of Christianity. As the science of comparative philology could hardly have existed without the study of Sanskrit, so the comparative history of the religions of the world would have been impossible without the study of the Veda.

My translation, which follows the text of Max Müller's splendid six-volume edition, is partly based on the work of the great scholiast Sāyaṇa who was Prime Minister at the court of the King of Vijaynagar—in what is now the Madras District of Bellary—in the fourteenth century of our era. Sāyaṇa's Commentary has been consulted and carefully considered for the general sense of every verse and for the meaning of every word, and his interpretation has been followed whenever it seemed rational, and consistent with the context, and with other passages in which the same word or words occur. With regard to Sāyaṇa's qualifications as an interpreter of the Veda there is, or was, a conflict of opinion among European scholars. Professor Wilson—whose translation of the Ṛgveda is rather a version of Sāyaṇa's paraphrase—was firmly persuaded that he had a "knowledge of his text far beyond the pretensions of any European scholar, and must have been in possession of all the interpretations which had been perpetuated by traditional teaching from the earliest times." Yet, as Dr. J. Muir has pointed out, Professor Wilson in the notes of his translation admits that he "occasionally failed to find in Sāyaṇa a perfectly satisfactory guide", that "the scholiast is evidently puzzled", and that his explanations are obscure. On the other hand, Professor Roth—the author of the Vedic portion of the great St. Petersburg Lexicon—says in his preface to that work: "so far as regards one of the branches of Vedic literature, the treatises on theology and worship, we can desire no better guides than these commentators, so exact in all respects, who follow their texts word by word, who so long as even the semblance of a misconception might arise, are never weary of repeating what they have frequently said before, and who often appear as if they had been writing for us foreigners rather than for their own priestly alumni who had grown up in the midst of these conceptions and impressions. Here. . . . they are in their proper ground. The case, however, is quite different when the same men assume the task of interpreting the ancient collections of hymns. . . . Here were required not only quite different qualifications for interpretation but also a greater freedom of judgment and a greater breadth of view and of historical intuitions. Freedom of judgment, however, was wanting to priestly learning, whilst in India no one has ever had any conception of historical development. The very qualities which have made those commentators excellent guides to an understanding of the theological treatises, render them unsuitable conductors on that far older and quite differently circumstanced domain. As the so-called classical Sanskrit was perfectly familiar to them, they sought its ordinary idiom in the Vedic hymns also. Since any difference in the ritual appeared to them inconceivable and the present forms were believed to have existed from the beginning of the world, they fancied that the patriarchs of the Indian religion must have sacrificed in the very same manner. As the recognized mythological and classical systems of their own age appeared to them unassailable and revealed varieties, they must necessarily (so the commentators thought) be discoverable in that centre point of revelation, the hymns of the ancient Ṛṣis, who had, indeed, lived in familiar intercourse with the Gods, and possessed far higher wisdom than the succeeding generations. . . .It has never occurred to any one to make our understanding of the Hebrew books of the Old Testament depend on the Talmud and the Rabbins while there are not wanting scholars who hold it as the duty of a conscientious interpreter of the Veda to translate in conformity with Sāyaṇa, Mahīdhara, etc. Consequently, we do not believe like H.H. Wilson, that Sāyaṇa, for instance, understood the expressions of the Veda better than any European interpreter; but we think that a conscientious European interpreter may understand the Veda far better and more correctly than Sāyaṇa. We do not esteem it our first task to arrive at that understanding of the Veda which was current in India some centuries ago, but to search out the sense which the poets themselves have put into their hymns and utterances. Hence we are of opinion that the writings of Sāyaṇa and the other commentators do not form a rule for the interpreter, but are merely one of those helps of which the latter will avail himself for the execution of his undoubtedly difficult task, a task which is not to be accomplished at the first onset, or by any single individual. . . . We have, therefore, endeavoured to follow the path prescribed by philology to derive from the texts themselves the sense which they contain, by a juxtaposition of all the passages which are cognate in diction or contents:—a tedious and laborious path, in which neither the commentators nor the translators have preceded us. The double duty of exegete and lexicographer has thus devolved upon us. A simple etymological procedure, practised as it must be by those who seek to divine the sense of a word from the sole consideration of the passage before them without regard to the ten or twenty other passages in which it recurs, connot possibly lead to a correct result."[1]

Professor Max Müller says: "As the authors of the Brāhmaṇas were blinded by theology, the authors of the still later Niruktas were deceived by etymological fictions, and both conspired to mislead by their authority later and more sensible commentators, such as Sāyaṇa. Where Sāyaṇa has no authority to mislead him, his commentary is at all events rational; but still his scholastic notions would never allow him to accept the free interpretation which comparative study of these venerable documents forces upon the unprejudiced scholar. We must therefore discover ourselves the real vestiges of these ancient poets."

Professor Benfey says: "Every one who has carefully studied the Indian interpretations is aware that absolutely no continuous tradition extending from the composition of the Veda to their explanation by Indian scholars, can be assumed; that, on the contrary, between the genuine poetic remains of Vedic antiquity and their interpretations a long-continued break in tradition must have intervened, out of which at most the comprehension of some particulars may have been rescued and handed down to later times by means of liturgical usages and words, formulae, and perhaps, also, poems connected therewith. Besides these remains of tradition, which must be estimated as very scanty, the interpreters of the Veda had, in the main, scarcely any other helps than those which, for the most part, are still at our command, the usage of the classical speech, and the grammatical and etymological-lexicographical investigation of words. At the utmost, they found some aid in materials preserved in local dialects; but this advantage is almost entirely outweighed by the comparison which we are able to institute with the Zend, and that which we can make (though here we must of course proceed with caution and prudence) with the languages cognate to the Sanskrit,—a comparison which has already supplied so many helps to a clearer understanding of the Vedas. But quite irrespectively of all particular aids, the Indian method of interpretation becomes in its whole essence an entirely false one, owing to the prejudice with which it chooses to conceive the ancient circumstances and ideas which have become quite strange to it, from its own religious stand-point, so many centuries more recent, whilst, on the other hand, an advantage for the comprehension of the whole is secured to us by the acquaintance (drawn from analogous relations) with the life, the conceptions, the wants, of ancient peoples and

1 *On the Interpretation of the Veda*, by J. Muir.

popular songs, which we possess,—an advantage which, even if the Indians owed more details than they actually do owe, to tradition, would not be eclipsed by their interpretation."[1]

A very different opinion of the value of the Indian commentators was held and expressed by Professor Goldstücker. "Without the vast information", he says, "which those commentators have disclosed to us,—without their method of explaining the obscurest text,—in one word, without their scholarship, we should still stand at the outer doors of Hindu antiquity." He ridicules the assertion that a European scholar can understand the Veda more correctly than Sāyaṇa, or arrive more nearly at the meaning which the Ṛṣis gave to their own hymns, and yet even this staunch champion of the Indian commentators "cannot be altogether acquitted (as Dr. J. Muir says and shows) of a certain heretical tendency to deviate in practice from the interpretations of Sāyaṇa."

The last quotation which I shall make in connexion with this question is from Professor E.B. Cowell's Preface to his edition of Vol. V of Wilson's *Translation of the Ṛg-Veda Saṁhitā* : "This work does not pretend to give a complete translation of the Ṛg-Veda, but only a faithful image of that particular phase of its interpretation which the medieval Hindus, as represented by Sāyaṇa, have preserved. This view is in itself interesting and of an historical value; but far wider and deeper study is needed to pierce to the real meaning of these old hymns. Sāyaṇa's commentary will always retain a value of its own,—even its mistakes are often interesting,—but his explanations must not for a moment bar the progress of scholarship. We can be thankful to him for any real help; but let us not forget the debt which we owe to modern scholars, especially to those of Germany. The great St. Petersburg Dictionary is indeed a monument of triumphant erudition, and it has inaugurated a new era in the interpretation of the Ṛg-Veda."

My translation, then, is partly based on the commentary of Sāyaṇa, corrected and regulated by rational probability, context, and intercomparison of similar words and passages. For constant and most valuable assistance in my labour I am deeply indebted to the works of many illustrious scholars, some departed, and some, happily, still flourishing. I am thankful to Sāyaṇa, my first guide to the hymns of the Ṛgveda; to my revered Master, Professor H. H. Wilson; to Professors Roth, Benfey, Weber, Ludwig, Max Müller, Grassmann, and Monier Williams, and Dr. John Muir and Mr. Wallis. I have also consulted, and shall probably make more use hereafter of, the works of M. Bergaigne and Dr. Oldenberg; nor can I omit to mention the *Siebenzig Lieder des Ṛgveda* by Geldner and Kaegi, *Der Ṛgveda,* by Kaegi, and *Hymns from the Ṛgveda* by Professor Peterson of Bombay, all of which I have read with pleasure and profit.

But it must not be supposed that European students and interpreters of the Veda claim anything like infallibility, completeness, or finality for the results to which their researches have led them. All modern scholars will allow that many hymns are dark as the darkest oracle, that, as Professor Max Müller says, there are whole verses which, as yet, yield no sense whatever, and words the meaning of which we can only guess. As in the interpretation of the more difficult books of the Old Testament and the Homeric poems, so in the explanation of the Veda complete success, if ever attainable, can be attained only by the labours of generations of scholars.

The Hymns are composed in various metres, some of which are exceedingly simple and others comparatively complex and elaborate, and two or more different metres are frequently found in the same Hymn; one Hymn, for instance, in Book I shows nine distinct varieties in the same number of verses. The verses or stanzas consist of three or more—generally three or four—*Pādas,* semi-hemistichs or lines, each of which contains eight, eleven or twelve syllables, sometimes, but rarely, five, and still less frequently four or more than twelve. As regards quantity the first syllables of the

1 Ibid.

line are not strictly defined, but the last four are regular, the measure being iambic in the eight and twelve syllable verses and trochaic in those of eleven syllables. Partly by way of safeguard against the besetting temptation to paraphrase and expand, and partly in the hope of preserving, however imperfectly, something of the form of the Hymns, I have translated each verse by a verse syllabically commensurate with the original and generally divided into corresponding hemistichs.

The verses consisting of three or four octosyllabic lines are tolerably well represented by the common octosyllabic or dimeter iambic metre which I have employed. In other verses I have not attempted to reproduce or imitate the rhythm or metre of the original: such a task, supposing its satisfactory completion to be possible, would require more time and labour than I could spare for the purpose. All that I have done, or tried to do, is to show to some extent the original external form of the Hymns by rendering them in syllabically commensurate hemistichs and verses, as Benfey and the translators of the *Seventy Hymns* have done for a portion of the Ṛgveda, and Grassmann for nearly the whole of the Collection.

For further information regarding the Ṛgveda the English reader is referred to Max Müller's *History of Ancient Sanskrit Literature,* Muir's *Original Sanskrit Texts,* and Weber's *History of Indian Literature;* or if a simpler and more popular exposition be required, to Mrs. Manning's *India, Ancient and Medieval,* or to Kaegi's *Der Ṛgveda,* of which an English translation has recently appeared. The student who reads German and French will, as a matter of course, consult Ludwig's great work *Der Ṛgveda* and Bergaigne's *Etudes sur la Religion Vedique.*

To conclude, my reasons for publishing this work are chiefly these; there is at present no complete translation of the Ṛgveda in English, Professor Wilson's version—of which the last two volumes have only lately appeared—being "only a faithful image of that particular phase of its interpretation which the mediaeval Hindus, as represented by Sāyaṇa, have preserved," and, moreover, the price of Wilson's six volumes—upwards of ninety rupees—puts the work beyond the reach of the great majority of readers in India.

I can hardly hope that my work will find acceptance with Pandits and Indian scholars inasmuch as I venture to deviate both widely and frequently from Sāyaṇa whom they have been taught to regard as infallible. No arguments are likely to shake this belief. Nothing short of a course of study similar to that to which the leaders of the modern school of Vedic interpretation have devoted half their lives will enable them to see with our eyes and accept our views. I trust, however, that they will at any rate give the leaders and the followers of this modern school credit for deep devotion to ancient Indian literature and due admiration of the great Indian scholars who have expounded it, and will acknowledge that these modern scholars—however mistaken their views may appear to be—are labouring sincerely and solely to discover and declare the spirit and the truth of the most ancient and venerated literary records that are the heritage of Aryan man.

R. T. H. GRIFFITH.

KOTAGIRI, NILGIRI:
May 25th, 1889.

NOTE.

This Second edition of my translation is in the main a reprint in compacter and cheaper form, with some corrections and other improvements in text and commentary, of the original four volume edition.

R. T. H. G.

KOTAGIRI:
15th October, 1896.

PUBLISHER'S NOTE TO THE PRESENT EDITION

This edition incorporates some new characteristics. Following the suggestions of eminent Vedic scholars we have romanized Greek letters if there were references in the footnotes from Greek language. We have modernized the system of transcription not only in regard to Vedic but even in respect of Avestan words, following the system of Bartholomae. We have replaced the two-Volume edition by a single Volume edition for the convenience of our reader. We have checked Reference Numbers in Index and revised if they were found incorrect. We hope, the improvements which in no way disturb the original but add to the value of the work shall be welcomed by the reader.

THE HYMNS OF THE ṚGVEDA

THE HYMNS OF THE RGVEDA

BOOK THE FIRST

HYMN I. *Agni.*

1 I LAUD Agni, the chosen Priest, God, minister of sacrifice,
The hotar, lavishest of wealth.

2 Worthy is Agni to be praised by living as by ancient seers.
He shall bring hitherward the Gods.

3 Through Agni man obtaineth wealth, yea, plenty waxing day by day,
Most rich in heroes, glorious.

4 Agni, the perfect sacrifice which thou encompassest about
Verily goeth to the Gods.

5 May Agni, sapient-minded Priest, truthful, most gloriously great,
The God, come hither with the Gods.

6 Whatever blessing, Agni, thou wilt grant unto thy worshipper,
That, Aṅgiras, is indeed thy truth.

7 To thee, dispeller of the night, O Agni, day by day with prayer
Bringing thee reverence, we come ;

8 Ruler of sacrifices, guard of Law eternal, radiant One,
Increasing in thine own abode.

9 Be to us easy of approach, even as a father to his son :
Agni, be with us for our weal.

HYMN II. *Vāyu.*

1 BEAUTIFUL Vāyu, come, for thee these Soma drops have been prepared :
Drink of them, hearken to our call.

2 Knowing the days, with Soma juice poured forth, the singers glorify
Thee, Vāyu, with their hymns of praise.

The first two hymns of this Book are ascribed to the Ṛṣi or seer Madhucchandas Vaiśvāmitra, a son or descendant of the famous Viśvāmitra. The deity to whom this hymn is addressed is Agni, the God of fire, the most prominent, next to Indra, of the deities of the Ṛgveda. Agni is the messenger and mediator between earth and heaven announcing to the Gods the hymns, and conveying to them the oblations of their worshippers, inviting them with the sound of his crackling flames and bringing them down to the place of sacrifice. As concentrating in himself the various sacrificial duties of different classes of human priests, Agni is called the *Purohita* or chosen priest, the *proepositus* or *proeses*. He is a *Ṛtvij*, a priest or minister who sacrifices at the proper seasons, and a *Hotar*, an invoking priest, a herald who calls the Gods to enjoy the offering. All riches are at his disposal, and he is the most bountiful rewarder, both directly and indirectly, of the pious whose oblations he carries to the Gods.

2 *Ancient seers* : said by Sāyaṇa to be Bhṛgu, Aṅgiras, and others. The expression indicates the existence of earlier hymns.

3 *Most rich in heroes* : the heroes here spoken of, who accompany the acquisition and increase of wealth, are brave sons and dependents.

4 *Perfect* : uninterrupted by Rākṣasas or fiends, who are unable to mar a sacrifice which Agni protects on all sides.

6 *Aṅgiras* : here a name of Agni. The Aṅgirases appear to have been regarded as a race of higher beings between Gods and men, the typical first sacrificers, whose ritual is the pattern which later priests must follow.

8 *Law eternal*. The word used to denote the conception of the order of the world is *ṛtá*. Everything in the universe which is conceived as showing regularity of action may be said to have the *ṛtá* for its principle. In its most general application the conception expressed by the word occupied to some extent the place of natural and moral law, fate, or the will of a supreme God. See Wallis, *The Cosmology of the Ṛgveda*, p. 92.

In thine own abode : *své dáme*, *suā domo*, in the sacrificial hall or chamber in which fire-worship is performed, and in which the fire (*Agni*) increases as the oblations of clarified butter are poured upon it by the priest.

---

1 *Vāyu* : God of the wind.

Soma drops : libations of the juice of the Soma, or Moon-plant, said to be the Acid Asclepias or Sarcostema Viminalis. The plant was gathered by moonlight on certain mountains, stripped of its leaves, and then carried to the place of sacrifice; the stalks having been there crushed by the priests were sprinkled with water and placed on a sieve or stainer, whence, after further pressure, the acid juice trickled into a vessel called Droṇa; after which it was mixed with flour etc., made to ferment, and then offered in libations to the Gods or drunk by the Brāhmans, by both of whom its exhilarating qualities were supposed to be highly prized. This famous plant has remained unidentified till recently (see Max Müller, Biographies of Words, Appendix III.) 'Dr. Aitchison has lately stated that Soma must be the *Ephedra pachyclade*, which in the Harirud valley is said to bear the name of *hum*, *huma*, and *yahma*. This supposition is confirmed by Dr. Joseph Bornmüller, a botanist long resident in Kerman, who identifies the Soma plant with some kind of Ephedra, probably *Ephedra distachya*, but who remarks that different varieties of Ephedra are to be found from Siberia to the Iberia peninsula, so that we must give up the hope of determining the original home of the Aryas by means of the habitat of the Soma plant' (Quarterly Review, No. 354, October 1894, p. 455).

2 *Knowing the days* : knowing the proper days for sacrifices; or perhaps, knowing or marking the time of daybreak, the exact time for the commencement of sacrificial rites.

3 Vāyu, thy penetrating stream goes forth unto the worshipper,
Far-spreading for the Soma draught.
4 These, Indra-Vāyu, have been shed ; come for our offered dainties' sake :
The drops are yearning for you both.
5 Well do ye mark libations, ye Vāyu and Indra, rich in spoil !
So come ye swiftly hitherward.
6 Vāyu and Indra, come to what the Soma-presser hath prepared :
Soon, Heroes, thus I make my prayer.
7 Mitra, of holy strength, I call, and foe-destroying Varuṇa,
Who make the oil-fed rite complete.
8 Mitra and Varuṇa, through Law, lovers and cherishers of Law,
Have ye obtained your mighty power.
9 Our Sages, Mitra-Varuṇa, of wide dominion, strong by birth,
Vouchsafe us strength that worketh well.

HYMN III. *Aśvins.*

1 YE Aśvins, rich in treasure, Lords of splendour, having nimble hands,
Accept the sacrificial food.
2 Ye Aśvins, rich in wondrous deeds, ye heroes worthy of our praise,
Accept our songs with mighty thought.
3 Nāsatyas, wonder-workers, yours are these libations with clipt grass :
Come ye whose paths are red with flame.
4 O Indra, marvellously bright, come, these libations long for thee,
Thus by fine fingers purified.
5 Urged by the holy singer, sped by song, come, Indra, to the prayers,
Of the libation-pouring priest.
6 Approach, O Indra, hasting thee, Lord of Bay Horses, to the prayers.
In our libation take delight.
7 Ye Viśvedevas, who protect, reward, and cherish men, approach
Your worshipper's drink-offering.
8 Ye Viśvedevas, swift at work, come hither quickly to the draught,
As milch-kine hasten to their stalls.
9 The Viśvedevas, changing shape like serpents, fearless, void of guile,
Bearers, accept the sacred draught !

3 *Hymns of praise* : *ukthas*, lauds recited or spoken, in opposition to verses that are chanted or sung.

4 Indra and Vāyu are here conjointly addressed in a dual compound, Indravāyū. Indra was the favourite national deity of the Āryan Indians in the Vedic Age, and more hymns are dedicated to his honour than to the praise of any other divinity. He is the God who reigns over the intermediate region or atmosphere; he fights against and conquers with his thunderbolt the demons of drought and darkness, and is in general the type of noble heroism.

7 According to Sāyaṇa, Mitra presides over the day as Varuṇa over the night; hence the closest connexion subsists between these two deities who are more frequently invoked together than Varuṇa is invoked singly; together they uphold and rule the earth and sky, together they guard the world, together they promote religious rites, avenge sin, and are the lords of truth and light.

Oil-fed : performed with *ghṛtam* (the modern *ghī*), and clarified butter, or butter which has been boiled gently and then allowed to cool. The butter is then used for culinary purposes and also offered in sacrifice to the Gods. *Complete* : by granting the worshipper's prayer.

8 *Through Law* : i.e. in accordance with *ṛtá*, the eternal law or everlasting order of the universe. See I. 1. 8.

---

1 'The Aśvins seem to have been a puzzle even to the oldest Indian Commentators. Yāska thus refers to them in the Nirukta, XII. 1 :—'Next in order are the deities whose sphere is the heaven; of these the Aśvins are the first to arrive...Who then are these Aśvins ? 'Heaven and Earth', say some; 'Day and Night', say others; 'The Sun and Moon', say others; 'Two Kings, performers of holy acts,' say the legendary writers'. Professor Roth thus speaks of these Gods: 'The two Aśvins, though, like the ancient interpreters of the Veda, we are by no means agreed as to the conception of their character, hold nevertheless, a perfectly distinct position in the entire body of the Vedic deities of light. They are the earliest bringers of light in the morning sky, who in their chariots hasten onward before the dawn, and prepare the way for her.'—J. Muir, *O. S. Texts*, V. 234.

Nimble hands : hands outstretched and quick to seize the offerings.

2 *Rich in wondrous deeds* : some of these deeds for the protection and benefit of those who craved the aid of the Aśvins are mentioned in Hymns CXII., CXVI., and the three following, of this Book.

3 *Nāsatyas*, derived by Indian Commentators from *na+asatya* 'not untrue,' is a name of common occurrence applied jointly to the two Aśvins. *Nāsatya* is said to be specially the name of one of the Aśvins, the other being then called Dasra, 'wonder-worker', or perhaps 'destroyer' (of the wicked).

With clipt grass. The sacred *Kuśa* grass (Poa cynosuroides), after having the roots cut off, is spread on the *vedi* or altar; and upon it the libation of Soma juice, or oblation of clarified butter is poured out. It is also spread over the sacrificial ground or floor to serve as a seat for the Gods and the sacrificers.

4 *Thus by fine fingers purified* : carefully strained by the priests.

6 *Lord of Bay Horses* : Harivān and Haryaśva, 'having bay or tawny horses', are frequently occurring epithets of Indra.

7 *Ye Viśvedevas* : Viśve devāḥ may have originally denoted 'all the Gods collectively,' though the introduction of the Viśvas under the name *viśvadevāḥ* or *viśvedevāḥ* as a separate troop of deities seems to have taken place at an early period. It is sometimes difficult to decide whether the expression *viśvedevāḥ* refers to all the Gods or the particular troop.

9 *Ehimāyāsaḥ* appears to be another form of *ahimāyāsaḥ* which is explained by Bohtlingk, and Roth as 'multiform or versatile like a snake, showing the same variety of colour and shape.' Sāyaṇa explains it as 'those who have obtained knowledge universally'. It is more than probable, says Professor Wilson, that the origin and import of the term were forgotten when Sāyaṇa wrote.

10 Wealthy in spoil, enriched with hymns, may bright Sarasvatī desire,
With eager love, our sacrifice.

11 Inciter of all pleasant songs, inspirer of all gracious thought,
Sarasvatī accept our rite !

12 Sarasvatī, the mighty flood,—she with her light illuminates,
She brightens every pious thought.

HYMN IV. *Indra.*

1 As a good cow to him who milks, we call the doer of fair deeds,
To our assistance day by day.

2 Come thou to our libations, drink of Soma, Soma-drinker thou !
The rich One's rapture giveth kine.

3 So may we be acquainted with thine innermost benevolence :
Neglect us not, come hitherward.

4 Go to the wise unconquered One, ask thou of Indra, skilled in song,
Him who is better than thy friends.

5 Whether the men who mock us say, Depart unto another place,
Ye who serve Indra and none else;

6 Or whether, God of wondrous deeds, all our true people call us blest,
Still may we dwell in Indra's care.

7 Unto the swift One bring the swift, man-cheering, grace of sacrifice,
That to the Friend gives wings and joy.

8 Thou, Śatakratu, drankest this and wast the Vṛtras' slayer ; thou
Helpest the warrior in the fray.

9 We strengthen, Śatakratu, thee, yea, thee the powerful in fight,
That, Indra, we may win us wealth.

10 To him the mighty stream of wealth, prompt friend of him who pours the juice,
Yea, to this Indra sing your song.

HYMN V. *Indra.*

1 O COME ye hither, sit ye down : to Indra sing ye forth, your song,
Companions, bringing hymns of praise.

2 To him the richest of the rich, the Lord of treasures excellent,
Indra, with Soma juice outpoured.

3 May he stand by us in our need and in abundance for our wealth :

Bearers, of riches, according to Sāyaṇa.

10 *Sarasvatī* 'is a goddess of some, though not of very great importance in the Ṛgveda. As observed by Yāska (Nirukta ii, 23) she is celebrated both as a river and as a deity...She was, no doubt, primarily a river deity, as her name, "the watery", clearly denotes, and in this capacity she is celebrated in a few separate passages. Allusion is made in the Hymns, as well as in the Brāhmaṇas...to sacrifices being performed on the banks of this river and of the adjoining Dṛṣadvatī; and the Sarasvatī in particular seems to have been associated with the reputation for sanctity, which according to the well-known passage in the Institutes of Manu, was ascribed to the whole region, called Brahmāvartta, lying between these two small streams, and situated immediately to the westward of the Jumna. The Sarasvatī thus appears to have been to the early Indians what the Ganges (which is only twice named in the Ṛgveda) became to their descendants...When once the river had acquired a divine character, it was quite natural that she should be regarded as the patroness of the ceremonies which were celebrated on the margin of her holy waters, and that her direction and blessing should be invoked as essential to their proper performance and success. The connection into which she was thus brought with sacred rites may have led to the further step of imagining her to have an influence on the composition of the hymns which formed so important a part of the proceedings, and of identifying her with Vāc, the goddess of speech.'—J. Muir, *O. S. Texts*, V. 338.

12 'Sāyaṇa explains : "the Sarasvatī by her act (of flowing) displays a copious flood." Roth in his Illustrations of the Nirukta (xi. 26). p. 152, translates, "a mighty stream is Sarasvatī; with her light she lightens, illuminates, "all pious minds," He, however, regards the commencing words as figurative, and not as referring to the river. Benfey renders : "Sarasvatī, by her light, causes the great sea to be known; she shines through all thoughts." He understands the "great sea" as the universe, or as life...The conceptions of Sarasvatī as a river, and as the directness of ceremonies, may be blended in the passage.'—Muir, *O. S. T.*, V. p. 339.

1 *The doer of fair deeds* : Indra.

2 Indra is especially the lord of Soma and its chief drinker. The exhilaration produced by drinking the fermented juice offered in libations stimulates his warlike energies and disposes him to give out of his boundless riches liberal rewards in the shape of cattle and other wealth to those who worship him.

6 The general meaning of this and the two preceding verses seems to be : Indra is the best friend and protector, and so long as we enjoy his friendship and protection we care nothing for the revilings of the ungodly who mock at our faithful worship.

7 *The swift One* : Indra. The Soma juice which exhilarates men or heroes and accompanies or graces the sacrifice is also called swift both because it flows quickly and because it makes Indra hasten to the solemnity. *The Friend*, is Indra whom the juice, exhilarates and sends quickly to the sacrifice.

8 *Śatakratu*, a name of Indra, 'is explained by Sāyaṇa, he who is connected with a hundred (many) acts, religious rites (*bahukarmayukta*), either as their performer or their object : or it may be rendered 'endowed with great wisdom;' *kratu* implying either *karma*, act, or *prajñā*, knowledge.'—Wilson. *The Vṛtras*, the enemies, the oppressors, or obstructors, are 'the hostile powers in the atmosphere who malevolently shut up the watery treasures in the clouds. These demons of drought, called by a variety of names, as Vṛttra, Ahi, Suṣṇa, Namuci, Pipru, Śambara, Uraṇa, etc., etc., armed on their side, also, with every variety of celestial artillery, attempt, but in vain, to resist the onset of the gods.'—Muir, *O.S. Texts*, V. 95.

1 *Companions*. The call is addressed to the ministering priests.

3 'Two separate cases appear to be meant: *yoge*, where the God must recognize the necessity of his intervention, and *purandhyām*, where he may deem it superfluous'.—Ludwig.

May he come nigh us with his strength.
4 Whose pair of tawny horses yoked in battles foemen challenge not :
To him, to Indra sing your song.
5 Nigh to the Soma-drinker come, for his enjoyment, these pure drops,
The Somas mingled with the curd.
6 Thou, grown at once to perfect strength, wast born to drink the Soma juice,
Strong Indra, for preëminence.
7 O Indra, lover of the song, may these quick Somas enter thee :
May they bring bliss to thee the Sage.
8 Our chants of praise have strengthened thee, O Śatakratu, and our lauds :
So strengthen thee the songs we sing.
9 Indra, whose succour never fails, accept these viands thousandfold,
Wherein all manly powers abide.
10 O Indra, thou who lovest song, let no man hurt our bodies, keep
Slaughter far from us, for thou canst.

HYMN VI. *Indra.*

1 THEY who stand round him as he moves harness the bright, the ruddy Steed :
The lights are shining in the sky.
2 On both sides to the car they yoke the two bay coursers dear to him,
Bold, tawny, bearers of the Chief.
3 Thou, making light where no light was, and form, O men : where form was not,
Wast born together with the Dawns.
4 Thereafter they, as is their wont, threw off the state of babes unborn,
Assuming sacrificial names.
5 Thou, Indra, with the Tempest-Gods, the breakers down of what is firm,
Foundest the kine even in the cave.
6 Worshipping even as they list, singers laud him who findeth wealth,
The far-renowned, the mighty One.
7 Mayest thou verily be seen coming by fearless Indra's side :
Both joyous, equal in your sheen.
8 With Indra's well beloved hosts, the blameless, hastening to heaven,
The sacrificer cries aloud.
9 Come from this place, O Wanderer, or downward from the light of heaven:
Our songs of praise all yearn for this.
10 Indra we seek to give us help, from here, from heaven above the earth,
Or from the spacious firmament.

HYMN VII. *Indra.*

1 INDRA the singers with high praise, Indra reciters with their lauds,
Indra the choirs have glorified.
2 Indra hath ever close to him his two bay steeds and word-yoked car,
Indra the golden, thunder-armed.
3 Indra hath raised the Sun on high in heaven, that he may see afar:
He burst the mountain for the kine.

4 At the sight of whose chariot and horses all enemies flee.

9 *Wherein all manly powers abide.* The oblations of worshippers, as well as their hymns of praise, stimulate and strengthen the Gods for deeds of heroism.

---

1 *They who stand round* : *lokatrayavartinaḥ prāṇinaḥ*, 'the living beings of the three worlds,' is Sāyaṇa's explanation. Probably the Maruts, Indra's constant companions are intended.

The bright, the ruddy Steed, (*bradhnám aruṣám*), is probably the Sun, with whom Indra is frequently connected.

2 *On both sides* : *vipakṣasā* : harnessed on different sides.

3 *Thou*, i.e. the Sun. *O men* ! is perhaps merely an exclamation expressive of admiration. If *maryāḥ*, men, be taken to mean the Maruts, the words *thou, making, wast born*, although in the singular number, may apply to these Gods regarded as one host or company and born at one birth.

4 *Threw off the state of babes unborn* : according to Prof. M. Muller 'assumed again the form of new-born babes.' 'The idea that the Maruts assumed the form of a garbha, lit. of an embryo or a new-born child, is only meant to express that the storms burst forth from the womb of the sky as soon as Indra arises to do battle against the demon of darkness. As assisting Indra in this battle, the Maruts, whose name retained for a long time its purely appellative meaning of storms, attained their rank as deities by the side of Indra, or as the poet expresses it, they assumed their sacred name. This seems to be the whole meaning of the later legend that the Maruts, like the Ṛbhus were not originally gods, but became deified for their works.' M. Muller. *Ṛgveda Saṃhitā*, i. p. 25.

5 *The Tempest-Gods* : the Maruts, the friends and helpers of Indra.

The kine : are streams of water and the beams of light which follow their effusion. *The cave* is the thick dark cloud which holds the imprisoned waters and which Indra cleaves asunder with his thunderbolt or lightning.

7 *Thou* : the host of Maruts. According to Benfey, the Sun.

8 *The sacrificer cries aloud.* This is the interpretation proposed by Professor Max Muller, but it is only conjectural and not altogether satisfactory. Benfey translates : Mightily shines the sacrifice; and Ludwig : The warrior sings triumphantly.

9 *From this place* : from earth.

Wanderer : (*parijman*) here applied to Indra.

10 *The spacious firmament* : the expanse between earth and heaven.

---

1 *The choirs* : (*vāṇī*) referring perhaps to both singers and chanters.

2 *The golden* : i.e. richly decorated (*sarvābharaṇa-bhūṣitaḥ*) according to Sāyaṇa.

3 *The mountain* : is the mountain-shaped mass of thick cloud, and the *kine* are the waters as in I. 6, 5. The words *ádri* and *párvata* mean both mountain and cloud, these being constantly seen in close juxtaposition and being often indistinguishable one from the other.

4 Help us, O Indra, in the frays, yea, frays, where thousand spoils are gained,
With awful aids, O awful One.

5 In mighty battle we invoke Indra, Indra in lesser fight,
The Friend who bends his bolt at fiends.

6 Unclose, our manly Hero, thou for ever bounteous, yonder cloud,
For us, thou irresistible.

7 Still higher, at each strain of mine, thunder-armed Indra's praises rise:
I find no laud worthy of him.

8 Even as the bull drives on the herds, he drives the people with his might,
The Ruler irresistible :

9 Indra who rules with single sway men, riches, and the fivefold race
Of those who dwell upon the earth.

10 For your sake from each side we call Indra away from other men :
Ours, and none others', may he be.

HYMN VIII. *Indra.*

1 INDRA, bring wealth that gives delight, the victor's ever-conquering wealth,
Most excellent, to be our aid;

2 By means of which we may repel our foes in battle hand to hand,
By thee assisted with the car.

3 Aided by thee, the thunder-armed, Indra, may we lift up the bolt,
And conquer all our foes in fight.

4 With thee, O Indra, for ally with missile-darting heroes, may
We conquer our embattled foes.

5 Mighty is Indra, yea supreme; greatness be his, the Thunderer :
Wide as the heaven extends his power ;

6 Which aideth those to win them sons, who come as heroes to the fight,
Or singers loving holy thoughts.

7 His belly, drinking deepest draughts of Soma, like an ocean swells,
Like wide streams from the cope of heaven.

8 So also is his excellence, great, vigorous, rich in cattle, like
A ripe branch to the worshipper.

9 For verily thy mighty powers, Indra, are saving helps at once
Unto a worshipper like me.

10 So are his lovely gifts; let lauds and praises be to Indra sung,
That he may drink the Soma juice.

HYMN IX. *Indra.*

1 COME, Indra, and delight thee with the juice at all the Soma feasts,
Protector, mighty in thy strength.

2 To Indra pour ye forth the juice, the active gladdening juice to him
The gladdening, omnific God.

3 O Lord of all men, fair of cheek, rejoice thee in the gladdening lauds,
Present at these drink-offerings.

4 Songs have outpoured themselves to thee, Indra, the strong, the guardian Lord,
And raised themselves unsatisfied.

5 Send to us bounty manifold, O Indra, worthy of our wish,
For power supreme is only thine.

6 O Indra, stimulate thereto us emulously fain for wealth,
And glorious, O most splendid One.

7 Give, Indra, wide and lofty fame, wealthy in cattle and in strength,
Lasting our life-time, failing not.

8 Grant us high fame, O Indra, grant riches bestowing thousands, those
Fair fruits of earth borne home in wains.

9 Praising with songs the praise-worthy who cometh to our aid, we call
Indra, the Treasure-Lord of wealth.

9 *The fivefold race* : Benfey explains this as 'the whole inhabited world.' But the expression seems to mean the Āryan settlements or tribes only, and not the indigenous inhabitants of the country. The five tribes or settlements were probably the confederation of the Turvaśas, Yadus, Anus, Druhyus, and Purus. Sāyaṇa's explanation is 'those who are fit for habitations,' and the phrase is said to imply the four castes and Niṣādas or indigenous barbarians. But there were no such distinctions of caste when the hymn was composed.

---

2 *With the car* : *árvatā*, literally, with a horse, is explained by Sāyaṇa to mean fighting on horseback. But horses seem to have been used in war as drawers of chariots only, and *árvatā* here stands for *rathena*, with a car or chariot.

3 *May we lift up the bolt*. The thunderbolt here spoken of is sacrifice which, when employed against enemies, is as powerful a weapon as the bolt of Indra.

10 *Let lauds and praises be to Indra sung* : more exactly, 'be lauds, spoken and sung, to Indra given; *uktha* being properly the laud that is recited, and *stoma* the hymn of praise that is sung.

---

4 *And raised themselves unsatisfied* : *ájoṣāḥ*, not contented, that is, with prayers ever new. Ludwig observes that the Sāmaveda has preserved the correct reading *sajoṣāḥ*, 'with one accord.'

8 *Those fair fruits of earth brought home in wains*. 'The original of this hymn, as of many others, is so concise and elliptical as to be unintelligible without the liberal amplification of the Scholiast. We have in the text simply "those car-having viands," *tā rathinīr iṣaḥ*, meaning, Sāyaṇa says, those articles of food which are conveyed in cars, carts, or waggons, from the site of their production; as rice, barley, and other kinds of grain.'—Wilson.

The meaning of *rathinīr* is not clear.

10 To lofty Indra, dweller by each libation, the pious man
Sings forth aloud a strengthening hymn.

HYMN X. *Indra.*

1 THE chanters hymn thee, they who say the word of praise magnify thee.
The priests have raised thee up on high, O Śatakratu, like a pole.

2 As up he clomb from ridge to ridge and looked upon the toilsome task,
Indra observes this wish of his, and the Ram hastens with his troop.

3 Harness thy pair of strong bay steeds, long-maned, whose bodies fill the girths,
And, Indra, Soma-drinker, come to listen to our songs of praise.

4 Come hither, answer thou the song, sing in approval, cry aloud.
Good Indra, make our prayer succeed, and prosper this our sacrifice.

5 To Indra must a laud be said, to strengthen him who freely gives,
That Śakra may take pleasure in our friendship and drink-offerings.

6 Him, him we seek for friendship, him for riches and heroic might.
For Indra, he is Śakra, he shall aid us while he gives us wealth.

7 Easy to turn and drive away, Indra, is spoil bestowed by thee.
Unclose the stable of the kine, and give us wealth O Thunder-armed

8 The heaven and earth contain thee not, together, in thy wrathful mood.
Win us the waters of the sky, and send us kine abundantly.

9 Hear, thou whose ear is quick, my call; take to thee readily my songs
O Indra, let this laud of mine come nearer even than thy friend.

10 We know thee mightiest of all, in battles hearer of our cry.
Of thee most mighty we invoke the aid that giveth thousandfold.

11 O Indra, Son of Kuśika, drink our libation with delight.
Prolong our life anew, and cause the seer to win a thousand gifts.

12 Lover of song, may these our songs on every side encompass thee :
Strengthening thee of lengthened life, may they be dear delights to thee.

1 'The concluding phrase, *tvā...ud vaṁśam iva yemire,* "they have raised thee, like a bamboo," is rather obscure. The Scholiast says, they have elevated Indra, as tumblers raise a bamboo—on the summit of which they balance themselves; a feat not uncommon in India: or, as *vaṁśa* means, also, a family, it may be rendered, as ambitious persons raise their family to consequence.'—Wilson.

2 The text has only; mounting from ridge to ridge, or from height to height, which the scholiast completes by observing that this is said of the Yajamāna, the person who institutes or performs a regular sacrifice and pays the expenses of it, who goes to the mountain to gather the Soma-plant, fuel, etc. Ludwig thinks that Indra is meant, rising higher and higher, and yet not delaying to come to the sacrifice.

The Ram, (*vṛṣṇiḥ*) is Indra, and his flock or troop are the Maruts.

Hastens : comes quickly to the sacrifice.

5 *Śakra,* a common name of Indra, used in the next stanza as an epithet='the powerful', from *śak,* to be able.

7 *Easy to turn* : The Booty spoken of in the Ṛgveda consists chiefly of cattle, which with Indra's assistance are easily turned and driven away from the enemy who possesses them.

Unclose the stable of the kine : Open the thick cloud that holds the water imprisoned, and fertilize our fields with rain.

9 *Thy friend* : probably the *vájra* or thunderbolt which is Indra's inseparable associate and ally.

11 *Son of Kuśika* : Kuśika was the father or the grandfather of Viśvāmitra who was the father of the poet or seer of this hymn. This epithet Kauśika, son of Kuśika, is here applied to Indra as being the chief or special God of the seer's family.

12 *Of lengthened life*=immortal.

HYMN XI. *Indra.*

1 ALL sacred songs have magnified Indra expansive as the sea,
The best of warriors borne on cars, the Lord, the very Lord of strength.

2 Strong in thy friendship, Indra, Lord of power and might, we have no fear.
We glorify with praises thee, the never-conquered conqueror.

3 The gifts of Indra from of old, his saving succours, never fail,
When to the praise-singers he gives the boon of substance rich in kine.

4 Crusher of forts, the young, the wise, of strength unmeasured, was he born
Sustainer of each sacred rite, Indra, the Thunderer, much-extolled.

5 Lord of the thunder, thou didst burst the cave of Vala rich in cows.

1 This hymn is ascribed to Jetar the son of Madhucchandas the seer of the preceding hymn.

Expansive as the sea : cf. I. 8, 7. Or the expression may be, as Wilson says, 'a vague mode of indicating the universal diffusion of Indra as the firmament.

4 *Crusher of forts* : destroyer or breaker-down of the clouds that withhold the rain, which are regarded as the forts or strongholds of Vṛtra and the other hostile powers of the air.

5 *The cave of Vala* : Vala is the brother of Vṛtra, or Vṛtra himself under another name, who stole the cows of the Gods and hid them in a cave, that is, kept the light and waters imprisoned in dark clouds.

The Gods came pressing to thy side, and free from terror aided thee.

6 I, Hero, through thy bounties am come to the flood addressing thee.

Song-lover, here the singers stand and testify to thee thereof.

7 The wily Śuṣṇa, Indra ! thou o'erthrewest with thy wondrous powers.

The wise beheld this deed of thine : now go beyond their eulogies.

8 Our songs of praise have glorified Indra who ruleth by his might,

Whose precious gifts in thousands come, yea, even more abundantly.

HYMN XII. *Agni.*

1 We choose Agni the messenger, the herald, master of all wealth,

Well skilled in this our sacrifice.

2 With callings ever they invoke Agni, Agni, Lord of the House,

Oblation-bearer, much beloved.

3 Bring the Gods hither, Agni, born for him who strews the sacred grass :

Thou art our herald, meet for praise.

4 Wake up the willing Gods, since thou, Agni, performest embassage :

Sit on the sacred grass with Gods.

5 O Agni, radiant One, to whom the holy oil is poured, burn up

Our enemies whom fiends protect.

6 By Agni Agni is inflamed, Lord of the House, wise, young, who bears

The gift : the ladle is his mouth.

7 Praise Agni in the sacrifice, the Sage whose ways are ever true,

The God who driveth grief away.

8 God, Agni, be his strong defence who, lord of sacrificial gifts,

Worshippeth thee the messenger.

9 Whoso with sacred gift would fain call Agni to the feast of Gods,

O Purifier, favour him.

10 Such, Agni, Purifier, bright, bring hither to our sacrifice,

To our oblation bring the Gods.

11 So lauded by our newest song of praise bring opulence to us,

And food, with heroes for our sons.

12 O Agni, by effulgent flame, by all invokings of the Gods,

Show pleasure in this laud of ours.

HYMN XIII. *Agni.*

1 Agni, well-kindled, bring the Gods for him who offers holy gifts.

Worship them, Purifier, Priest.

2 Son of Thyself, present, O Sage, our sacrifice to the Gods today.

Sweet to the taste, that they may feast.

3 Dear Narāśaṁsa, sweet of tongue, the giver of oblations, I

Invoke to this our sacrifice.

4 Agni, on thy most easy car, glorified, hither bring the Gods :

Manu appointed thee as Priest.

5 Strew, O ye wise, the sacred grass that drips with oil, in order due,

Where the Immortal is beheld.

6 *To the flood* : i. e. to Indra, the river or sea of bounty.

7 *The wily Śuṣṇa* : Śuṣṇa is described as a demon slain by Indra. The word means drier up; *bhūtānāṁ śoṣaṇahetu*, cause of the drying up of beings, the excessive heat and drought before the Rains, which Indra puts an end to.

Now go beyond their eulogies : i. e. do deeds worthy of still higher praise. Or it may mean, make their eulogies endure.

---

1 The Hymns from XII to XXIII inclusive are ascribed to Medhātithi, son of Kaṇva.

The messenger : the mediator between men and Gods. *The herald* : *devānām āhvātāram*, the inviter of the Gods, is Sāyaṇa's explanation.

3 *Born* : newly produced by attrition for the man who has prepared and spread the sacrificial grass as a seat for the expected deities.

6 *By Agni Agni is inflamed* : The fire into which the oblation is poured is lighted by the application of other fire.

Young : as newly born each time the fire is produced. *The ladle* : used for pouring the sacrificial butter into the fire.

8 *Lord of sacrificial gifts* : the wealthy patron or institutor of the sacrifice.

9 *O Purifier* : *pāvaka*, purifying is in later Sanskrit a common word for fire.

This is one of the Āpri or propitiatory hymns, consisting of invocations to a series of deified objects, and said to be introductory to the animal sacrifice. All the deified objects addressed in this hymn are said by Sāyaṇa to be forms of Agni.

1 *For him who offers holy gifts* : for the institutor of the sacrifice.

2 *Son of Thyself*. Tanūnapāt, son or descendant of oneself, is a frequently recurring name of Agni so called because fire is sometimes self-generated, as in the lightning, or produced by attrition, and not necessarily derived from other fire. Other fanciful derivations are given.

3 *Narāśaṁsa* : 'Praise of Men' is one of Agni's mystical nam s.

4 *Manu* : is the man *par excellence*, or the representative man and father of the human race, regarded as the first institutor of sacrifices and religious ceremonies.

5 *The immortal* : according to Sāyaṇa either the clarified butter or Agni the God.

6 Thrown open be the Doors Divine, unfailing, that assist the rite,
For sacrifice this day and now.
7 I call the lovely Night and Dawn to seat them on the holy grass
At this our solemn sacrifice.
8 The two Invokers I invite, the wise, divine and sweet of tongue,
To celebrate this our sacrifice.
9 Iḷā, Sarasvatī, Mahī, three Goddesses who bring delight,
Be seated, peaceful, on the grass.
10 Tvaṣṭar I call, the earliest born, the wearer of all forms at will :
May he be ours and ours alone.
11 God, Sovran of the Wood, present this our oblation to the Gods,
And let the giver be renowned.
12 With Svāhā pay the sacrifice to Indra in the offerer's house :
Thither I call the Deities.

HYMN XIV. *Viśvedevas.*

1 To drink the Soma, Agni, come, to our service and our songs.
With all these Gods; and worship them.
2 The Kaṇvas have invoked thee; they, O Singer, sing thee songs of praise :
Agni, come hither with the Gods;
3 Indra, Vāyu, Bṛhaspati, Mitra, Agni, Pūṣan, Bhaga,
Ādityas, and the Marut host.
4 For you these juices are poured forth that gladden and exhilarate,
The meath-drops resting in the cup.
5 The sons of Kaṇva fain for help adore thee, having strewn the grass,
With offerings and all things prepared.
6 Let the swift steeds who carry thee, thought-yoked and dropping holy oil,
Bring the Gods to the Soma draught.
7 Adored, the strengtheners of Law, unite them, Agni, with their Dames :
Make them drink meath, O bright of tongue.

6 *The Doors Divine* : the doors of the chamber in which the oblation is offered.

Unfailing : the signification of *asaścátaḥ* in the text is uncertain. Sāyaṇa explains the word variously in various places.

8 *The two Invokers.* It seems uncertain who these two invokers or priests (*hotārā*) are, whether Agni and Āditya, or Agni and Varuṇa, or Varuṇa and Āditya See M. Müller's *A. S. Literature*, p. 464.

9 *Iḷā* : the Goddess of sacred speech and action.

Sarasvatī : see I. 3. 10.

Mahī : 'the great' (Goddess), said to be identical with Bhāratī, also a Goddess of speech.

10 *Tvaṣṭar*, is the Hephaistos, or Vulcan, of the Indian pantheon, the ideal artist, the divine artisan, the most skilful of workmen, versed in all wonderful and admirable contrivances.

11 *God, Sovran of the Wood* : *vanaspati*, lord of the wood; usually, a large tree; here said to be an Agni,—as if the fuel and the burning of it were identified. Or the Sacrificial Post may be intended, which is enumerated among the Āpri deities or deified objects.

12 *Svāhā* is the sacred word or exclamation (Hail ! Blessing !) used in pouring the oblation on the fire. According to Sāyaṇa, Svāhā also may be identified with Agni.

---

2 *The Kaṇvas* : sons or descendants of Kaṇva, men of the same family as the seer of the hymn.

3 *Indra, Vāyu*, etc. The names of these Gods are in the accusative case, governed by 'they (the Kaṇvas) have invoked.' or 'worship them,' understood.

Bṛhaspati, 'alternating with Brahmaṇaspati is the name of a deity in whom the action of the worshipper upon the Gods is personified. He is the suppliant, the priest who intercedes with the Gods for men, and protects them against the wicked. Hence he appears as the prototype of the priests and the priestly order, and is also designated as the Purohita of the divine community. The essential difference between the original idea represented in this God and those expressed in most of the other and older deities of the Veda consists in the fact that the latter are personifications of various departments of nature, or of physical forces, while the former is the product of moral ideas and an impersonation of the power of devotion.' Muir, *O. S. Texts*, V. 272.

Pūṣan is a God who protects and multiplies cattle and human possessions generally. In character he is a solar deity, beholds the entire universe, and is a guide on roads and journeys.

Bhaga, the gracious Lord and protector, is regarded as the bestower of wealth.

Ādityas. 'There (in the highest heaven) dwell and reign those Gods who bear in common the name of Ādityas. We must, however, if we would discover their earliest character, abandon the conceptions which in a later age, and even in that of the heroic poems, were entertained regarding th se deities. According to this conception they were twelve Sun-gods, bearing evident reference to the twelve months. But for the most ancient period we must hold fast the primary signification of their name. They are the inviolable, imperishable, eternal beings. Aditi, eternity or the eternal, is the element which sustains them and is sustained by them...The eternal and inviolable element in which the Ādityas dwell, and which forms their essence, is the celestial light...The Ādityas, the Gods of this light, do not therefore by any means coincide with any of the forms in which light is manifested in the universe. They are neither sun, nor moon, nor stars, nor dawn, but the eternal sustainers of this luminous life, which exists, as it were, behind all these phenomena'. Roth, quoted by Muir, *O.S. Texts*, V. p.56.

The Marut host : the Maruts are the Gods of the winds and storms, the companions and friends of Ind a. They are said in the Veda to be the sons of Rudra and Pṛśni, the latter being explained by Sāyaṇa as 'the many-coloured earth,' but regarded by Professor Roth as a personification of the speckled clouds.

7 *Unite them with their Dames* : *pátnīvatas kṛdhi* : make them (come) with their consorts.

8 Let them, O Agni, who deserve worship and praise drink with thy tongue
The meath in solemn sacrifice.

9 Away, from the Sun's realm of light, the wise invoking Priest shall bring
All Gods awaking with the dawn.

10 With all the Gods, with Indra, with Vāyu, and Mitra's splendours, drink,
Agni, the pleasant Soma juice.

11 Ordained by Manu as our Priest, thou sittest, Agni, at each rite :
Hallow thou this our sacrifice.

12 Harness the Red Mares to thy car, the Bays, O God, the flaming ones :
With those bring hitherward the Gods.

HYMN XV. *Ṛtu.*

1 O INDRA drink the Soma juice with Ṛtu; let the cheering drops
Sink deep within, which settle there.

2 Drink from the Purifier's cup, Maruts, with Ṛtu; sanctify
The rite, for ye give precious gifts.

3 O Neṣṭar, with thy Dame accept our sacrifice; with Ṛtu drink,
For thou art he who giveth wealth.

4 Bring the Gods, Agni; in the three appointed places set them down :
Surround them, and with Ṛtu drink.

5 Drink Soma after the Ṛtus, from the Brāhmaṇa's bounty : undissolved,
O Indra, is thy friendship's bond.

6 Mitra, Varuṇa, ye whose ways are firm—a Power that none deceives—,
With Ṛtu ye have reached the rite.

7 The Soma-pressers, fain for wealth, praise the Wealth-giver in the rite,
In sacrifices praise the God.

8 May the Wealth-giver grant to us riches that shall be far renowned.
These things we gain among the Gods.

9 He with the Ṛtus fain would drink, Wealth-giver, from the Neṣṭar's bowl.
Haste, give your offering, and depart.

10 As we this fourth time, Wealth-giver, honour thee with the Ṛtus, be
A Giver bountiful to us.

11 Drink ye the meath, O Aśvins bright with flames, whose acts are pure, who with
Ṛtus accept the sacrifice.

12 With Ṛtu, through the house-fire, thou, kind Giver, guidest sacrifice :
Worship the Gods for the pious man.

HYMN XVI. *Indra.*

1 LET thy Bay Steeds bring thee, the Strong, hither to drink the Soma draught—
Those, Indra, who are bright as suns.

2 Here are the grains bedewed with oil : hither let the Bay Coursers bring
Indra upon his easiest car.

3 Indra at early morn we call, Indra in course of sacrifice,
Indra to drink the Soma juice.

4 Come hither, with thy long-maned Steeds, O Indra, to the draught we pour :
We call thee when the juice is shed.

5 Come thou to this our song of praise, to the libation poured for thee :
Drink of it like a stag athirst.

9 *The wise invoking Priest* : Agni, who calls the Gods.
10 *All the Gods* : or Viśvedevas; see I.3.7.
11 *Manu* : see I.13.4.

---

1 *Ṛtu* : meaning generally a season, a sixth part of the Indian year, is here personified and addressed as a deity.

2 *The Purifier's cup* : the sacrificial vessel of the Potar, or Purifier, who pours into the fire the libation for the Maruts.

3 *O Neṣṭar* : the Neṣṭar is one of the chief officiating priests, who leads forward the wife of the institutor of the sacrifice. In this place Neṣṭar is said to be another name for the God Tvaṣṭar from his having on some occasion assumed the function of a Neṣṭar priest.

4 *The three appointed places* : by the three sacrificial fires.

5 *The Brāhmaṇa's bounty*. The Brāhmaṇa here is said to be the Brāhmaṇācchaṁsī, one of the sixteen priests employed in sacrifices; and perhaps his office may have been to hold some ladle or vase in which the offering is presented.

7 *The Soma-pressers* : *grāvahastāsaḥ*, men having stones in their hands with which to bruise the Soma plant. *The Wealth giver* is Agni.

In the rite, In sacrifices : 'in the *adhvara* and in the *yajñas*, the first is said to be the primary or essential ceremony, such as the Agniṣṭoma; the second, the modified ceremonies, such as the Ukthya which is elsewhere termed an offering with Soma juice.' Wilson.

10 *As we this fourth time* : Agni, as Draviṇodās or Wealth-giver, has now been celebrated in four stanzas instead of the usual *tṛca* or triad; or we may translate with Ludwig, 'As we in fourth place,' Agni being fourth in the invocation (Indra, Maruts, Tvaṣṭar, Agni).

12 *Through the house-fire*. The *gārhapatya* is the sacred fire perpetually maintained by the householder; the fire from which fires for sacrificial purposes are lighted.

---

1 *Bright as suns* : *sūracakṣasaḥ*. Sāyaṇa understands this to refer to the priests, and Wilson renders accordingly: may (the priests), radiant as the sun (make thee manifest).

2 *Easiest car*; *sukhátame ráthe* : that is, most easily moving, swiftest.

3 *Indra at early morn we call*. Although not more particularly named, the specification implies the morning, mid-day, and evening worship.

5 *Like a stag athirst* : like a *gaura* (Bos Gaurus) a kind of buffalo.

'Drink like a thirsty buffalo,' would perhaps be a more strictly accurate rendering.

6 Here are the drops of Soma juice expressed on sacred grass : thereof
Drink, Indra, to increase thy might.

7 Welcome to thee be this our hymn, reaching thy heart, most excellent :
Then drink the Soma juice expressed.

8 To every draught of pressed-out juice Indra, the Vṛtra-slayer, comes,
To drink the Soma for delight.

9 Fulfil, O Śatakratu, all our wish with horses and with kine :
With holy thoughts we sing thy praise.

HYMN XVII. *Indra-Varuṇa.*

1 I CRAVE help from the Imperial Lords, from Indra-Varuṇa; may they
Both favour one of us like me.

2 Guardians of men, ye ever come with ready succour at the call
Of every singer such as I.

3 Sate you, according to your wish, O Indra-Varuṇa, with wealth :
Fain would we have you nearest us.

4 May we be sharers of the powers, sharers of the benevolence
Of you who give strength bounteously.

5 Indra and Varuṇa, among givers of thousands, meet for praise,
Are Powers who merit highest laud.

6 Through their protection may we gain great store of wealth, and heap it up :
Enough and still to spare, be ours.

7 O Indra-Varuṇa, on you for wealth in many a form I call :
Still keep ye us victorious.

8 O Indra-Varuṇa, through our songs that seek to win you to ourselves,
Give us at once your sheltering help.

9 O Indra-Varuṇa, to you may fair praise which I offer come,
Joint eulogy which ye dignify.

HYMN XVIII. *Brahmaṇaspati.*

1 O BRAHMAṆAPSATI, make him who presses Soma glorious,
Even Kakṣīvān Auśija.

2 The rich, the healer of disease, who giveth wealth, increaseth store,
The prompt,—may he be with us still.

3 Let not the foeman's curse, let not a mortal's onslaught fall on us :
Preserve us, Brahmaṇaspati.

4 Ne'er is the mortal hero harmed whom Indra, Brahmaṇaspati,
And Soma graciously inspire.

5 Do, thou, O Brahmaṇaspati, and Indra, Soma, Dakṣiṇā,
Preserve that mortal from distress.

6 To the Assembly's wondrous Lord, to Indra's lovely Friend who gives
Wisdom, have I drawn near in prayer.

7 He without whom no sacrifice, e'en of the wise man, prospers; he
Stirs up the series of thoughts.

8 He makes the oblation prosper, he promotes the course of sacrifice :
Our voice of praise goes to the Gods.

---

1 Indra the Hero and Varuṇa the King are addressed conjointly as a dual deity, Indrāvaruṇa. The most prominent of the other dual deities are Agni-Soma, Indra-Vāyu, Indra-Agni, Indra-Bṛhaspati, Indra-Soma, Mitra-Varuṇa, Indra-Pūṣan, Indra-Vṣṇu, Dyaus-Pṛthivī and Soma-Rudra.

Brahmaṇaspati. See I. 14, 3. Professor Wilson says : 'The Scholiast furnishes us with no account of the station or functions of this divinity. The etymology will justify Dr. Roth's definition of him as the deity of sacred prayer, or rather, perhaps, of the text of the Veda; but whether he is to be considered as a distinct personification or as a modified form of one of those already recognized, and especially of Agni, is doubtful, His giving wealth, healing disease, and promoting nourishment, are properties not peculiar to him; and his being associated with Indra and Soma, while it makes him distinct from them, leaves him Agni as his prototype. His being, in an especial manner, connected with prayer appears more fully in a subsequent passage, Hymn XL. Agni is, in an especial degree, the deity of the Brahman ; and, according to some statements, the Ṛgveda is supposed to proceed from him; a notion, however, which according to Medhātithi, the commentator on Manu, was suggested by its opening with the hymn to Agni, *Agnim īḷe*.'

Kakṣīvān, called Auśija, or son of Uśij, was a renowned Ṛṣi or seer, of the family of Pajra, and the author of several of the hymns of the Ṛgveda.

2 *The rich, the healer of disease* : Brahmaṇaspati.

4 *Soma* : the God who represents and animates the juice of the Soma plant. He was in former times the Indian Dionysus or Bacchus. 'The simple minded Aryan people,' says Professor Whitney, 'whose whole religion was a worship of the wonderful powers and phenomena of nature, had no sooner perceived that this liquid (Soma juice) had power to elevate the spirits, and produce a temporary frenzy, under the influence of which the individual was prompted to and capable of, deeds beyond his natural powers, than they found in it something divine : it was to their apprehension a God, endowing those into whom it entered with godlike powers; the plant which afforded it became to them the king of plants; the process of preparing it became a holy sacrifice. The high antiquity of this cultus is attested by the references to it found occurring in the Persian Avesta.' See Muir, *O. S. Texts*, V. 258.

5 *Dakiṣnā* : properly the present made to the priests at the conclusion of a sacrifice, here personified as a Goddess.

6 *The Assembly's wondrous Lord* : Sadasaspati, the master or protector of the assembly of priests, is here a title of Agni.

9 I have seen Narāśaṁsa, him most resolute, most widely famed,
As 'twere the Household Priest of heaven.

HYMN XIX. *Agni, Maruts.*

1 To this fair sacrifice to drink the milky draught thou art invoked :
O Agni, with the Maruts come.

2 No mortal man, no God exceeds thy mental power, O Mighty one :
O Agni, with the Maruts come :

3 All Gods devoid of guile, who know the mighty region of mid-air :
O Agni, with those Maruts come.

4 The terrible, who sing their song, not to be overcome by might :
O Agni, with those Maruts come.

5 Brilliant, and awful in their form, mighty, devourers of their foes :
O Agni, with those Maruts come.

6 Who sit as Deities in heaven, above the sky-vault's luminous sphere :
O Agni, with those Maruts come.

7 Who scatter clouds about the sky, away over the billowy sea :
O Agni, with those Maruts come.

8 Who with their bright beams spread them forth over the ocean in their might :
O Agni, with those Maruts come.

9 For thee, to be thine early draught, I pour the Soma-mingled meath :
O Agni, with the Maruts come.

HYMN XX. *Ṛbhus.*

1 For the Celestial Race this song of praise which gives wealth lavishly
Was made by singers with their lips.

2 They who for Indra, with their mind, formed horses harnessed by a word,
Attained by works to sacrifice.

3 They for the two Nāsatyas wrought a light car moving every way :
They formed a nectar-yielding cow.

4 The Ṛbhus with effectual prayers, honest, with constant labour, made
Their Sire and Mother young again.

5 Together came your gladdening drops with Indra by the Maruts girt,
With the Adityas, with the Kings.

6 The sacrificial ladle, wrought newly by the God Tvaṣṭar's hand—
Four ladles have ye made thereof.

7 Vouchsafe us wealth, to him who pours thrice seven libations, yea, to each
Give wealth, pleased with our eulogies.

8 As ministering Priests they held, by pious acts they won themselves,
A share in sacrifice with Gods.

HYMN XXI. *Indra-Agni.*

1 Indra and Agni I invoke ; fain are we for their song of praise :
Chief Soma-drinkers are they both.

2 Praise ye, O men, and glorify Indra-Agni in the holy rites :
Sing praise to them in sacred songs.

3 Indra and Agni we invite, the Soma-drinkers, for the fame
Of Mitra, to the Soma-draught.

4 Strong Gods, we bid them come to this libation that stands ready here :

9 *Household Priest* : *sádmamakhasam* ; according to Sāyaṇa, 'radiant as heaven,' according to Ludwig, 'as one who fought to win heaven's seat.'

Narāśaṁsa has already occurred as a name of Agni (I. 13. 3.) The meaning appears to be : through my invocation and praise I have reached the Gods, and with the eye of the spirit have looked on Agni in heaven.

---

1 *For the Celestial Race* : *devāya janmane*, the divine class or race of the Ṛbhus, the three sons of Sudhanvan who is said to have been a descendant of Aṅgiras. They were named severally Ṛbhu, Vibhvan, and Vāja and styled collectively Ṛbhus from the name of the eldest. 'Through their assiduous performance of good works they obtained divinity and became entitled to receive praise and adoration. They are supposed to dwell in the solar sphere, and there is an indistinct identification of them with the rays of the sun; but, whether typical or not, they prove the admission, at an early date of the doctrine that men might become divinities.' Wilson.

3 *The two Nāsatyas* : the Aśvins. See I. 3. 3. The Ṛbhus may have been the first to attempt the bodily representation of the horses of Indra and the chariot of the Aśvins.

4 *Sire and Mother* : Heaven and Earth, which they, as deities of the seasons, refresh and restore to youth.

5 'According to Āśvalāyana, as quoted by Sāyaṇa, the libations offered at the third daily (or evening) sacrifice are presented to Indra along with the Ādityas, together with Ṛbhu, Vibhvan, and Vāja, with Bṛhaspati and the Viśvadevas.' Wilson.

6 'Tvaṣṭar, in the Paurāṇik mythology, is the carpenter or artisan of the Gods; so Sāyaṇa says of him, he is a divinity whose duty, with relation to the Gods, is carpentry...Sāyaṇa also calls the Ṛbhus the disciples of Tvaṣṭar.....The act ascribed to them in the text, of making one ladle four, has, probably, rather reference to some innovation in the objects of libation than to the mere multiplication of the wooden spoons used to pour out the Soma juice. The *Nīti-Mañjarī* says that Agni, coming to a sacrifice which the Ṛbhus celebrated, became as one of them, and, therefore, they made the ladle fourfold, that each might have his share.' Wilson.

7 Or the 'thrice seven' may refer to *rátnāni*, grant thrice seven rich treasures.

---

1 *Indra and Agni* : addressed conjointly as a dual deity, Indrāgni, that is, Indra-Agni, See. I. 17. 1.

3 *For the fame of Mitra* : the meaning is not clear. Mitra appears to be regarded as the guardian of the world. Sāyaṇa takes Mitra in the sense of friend, and refers it to the institutor of the sacrifice.

Indra and Agni, come to us.

5 Indra and Agni, mighty Lords of our assembly, crush the fiends :
Childless be the devouring ones.

6 Watch ye, through this your truthfulness, there in the place of spacious view :
Indra and Agni, send us bliss.

HYMN XXII. *Aśvins and Others*

1 WAKEN the Aśvin Pair who yoke their car at early morn : may they
Approach to drink this Soma juice.

2 We call the Aśvins Twain, the Gods borne in a noble car, the best
Of charioteers, who reach the heavens.

3 Dropping with honey is your whip, Aśvins, and full of pleasantness :
Sprinkle therewith the sacrifice.

4 As ye go thither in your car, not far, O Aśvins, is the home
Of him who offers Soma juice.

5 For my protection I invoke the golden-handed Savitar:
He knoweth, as a God, the place.

6 That he may send us succour, praise the Waters' Offspring Savitar :
Fain are we for his holy ways.

7 We call on him, distributer of wondrous bounty and of wealth,
On Savitar who looks on men.

8 Come hither, friends, and seat yourselves ; Savitar, to be praised by us,
Giving good gifts, is beautiful.

9 O Agni, hither bring to us the willing Spouses of the Gods,
And Tvaṣṭar, to the Soma draught.

10 Most youthful Agni, hither bring their Spouses, Hotrā, Bhāratī,
Varūtrī, Dhiṣaṇā, for aid.

11 Spouses of Heroes, Goddesses, with whole wings may they come to us
With great protection and with aid.

12 Indrāṇī, Varuṇānī, and Agnāyī hither I invite,
For weal, to drink the Soma juice.

13 May Heaven and Earth, the Mighty Pair, bedew for us our sacrifice,
And feed us full with nourishments.

14 Their water rich with fatness, there in the Gandharva's steadfast place,
The singers taste through sacred songs.

15 Thornless be thou, O Earth, spread wide before us for a dwelling-place :
Vouchsafe us shelter broad and sure.

16 The Gods be gracious unto us even from the place whence Viṣṇu strode
Through the seven regions of the earth !

5 *Crush the fiends* : the Rākṣasas, demons who go about at night, ensnaring and even devouring human beings, disturbing sacrifices and devout men, and generally hostile to the Āryan race.

6 *In the place of spacious view* : Sāyaṇa explains 'in the station which preëminently makes known the experience of results (of actions) that is in heaven (*Svarga*).' In the place where what is hidden will be made known.

---

3 *Your whip* : the *madhukaśā* or Honey-whip of the Aśvins is perhaps the stimulating morning breeze. See Atharva-veda IX. 1, the whole of which hymn is a glorification of this wondrous whip.

5 *Savitar* : the generator or vivifier, is a name of the Sun, in the Veda sometimes identified with and sometimes distinguished from Sūrya.

6 *The Waters' Offspring Savitar* : son or offspring of the Waters, *apām napāt*, is an epithet more frequently applied to Agni. Sāyaṇa explains it otherwise as 'one who does not cherish (na pālakam) the water, but dries it up with his heat.'

10 *Hotrā* is called the wife of Agni, or the personified invocation; *Bhāratī* is Holy Speech or Prayer; *Varūtrī* is explained as 'she who is' to be chosen, the excellent; and *Dhiṣaṇā* is said to be a synonym of Vāk or Vāgdevī, the Goddess of Speech.

11 *With whole wings* : literally, with unclipped wings; that is, swift as birds whose wings have not been cut.

12 *Indrāṇī, Varuṇānī, and Agnāyī* : are respectively the consorts of Indra, Varuṇa, and Agni.

14 *Their water rich in fatness* : the fertilizing rain sent by Heaven and Earth. The meaning appears to be : the holy singers enjoy, as guerdon for their hymns, the kindly rain and other good gifts which are sent down from the reigons above by the great parents Heaven and Earth.

The Gandharva's steadfast place : Though in later times the Gandharvas are regarded as a class, in the Ṛgveda more than one is seldom mentioned. He is commonly designated as 'the heavenly Gandharva,' whose habitation is the sky, and whose especial duty is to guard the heavenly Soma, which the Gods obtain through his permission.

16 *Viṣṇu* : This God, 'the all-pervading or encompassing,' is not placed in the Veda in the foremost rank of deities, and, though frequently invoked with Indra, Varuṇa, the Maruts, Rudra, Vāyu and the Ādityas, his superiority to them is never stated, and he is even described in one place as celebrating the praise of Indra and deriving his power from that God. The point which distinguishes him from the other Vedic deities is chiefly his striding over the heavens, which he is said to do in three paces, explained as denoting the threefold manifestation of light in the form of fire, lightning and the sun, or as designating the three daily stations of the sun, in his rising, culminating and setting.

The meaning of the stanza is obscure : Wilson, after Sāyaṇa, translates : 'May the Gods preserve us (from that portion) of the earth whence Viṣṇu, (aided) by the seven metres, stepped,' and notes : 'According to the Taittirīyas, as cited by the scholiast, the Gods with Viṣṇu at their head subdued the invincible earth, using the seven metres of the Veda as their instruments. Sāyaṇa conceives the text to allude to the *Trivikrama Avatāra*, in which Viṣṇu traversed the three worlds in three steps.

17 Through all this world strode Viṣṇu; thrice his foot he planted, and the whole
Was gathered in his footstep's dust.

18 Viṣṇu, the Guardian, he whom none deceiveth, made three steps; thenceforth
Establishing his high decrees.

19 Look ye on Viṣṇu's works, whereby the Friend of Indra, close-allied,
Hath let his holy ways be seen.

20 The princes evermore behold that loftiest place where Viṣṇu is,
Laid as it were an eye in heaven.

21 This, Viṣṇu's station most sublime, the singers, ever vigilant,
Lovers of holy song, light up.

HYMN XXIII. *Vāyu and Others.*

1 Strong are the Somas; come thou nigh; these juices have been mixt with milk:
Drink, Vāyu, the presented draughts.

2 Both Deities who touch the heaven, Indra and Vāyu we invoke
To drink of this our soma juice.

3 The singers, for their aid, invoke Indra and Vāyu, swift as mind,
The thousand-eyed, the Lords of thought.

4 Mitra and Varuṇa, renowned as Gods of consecrated might,
We call to drink the Soma juice.

5 Those who by Law uphold the Law, Lords of the shining light of Law,
Mitra I call, and Varuṇa.

6 Let Varuṇa be our chief defence, let Mitra guard us with all aids:
Both make us rich exceedingly.

7 Indra, by Maruts girt, we call to drink the Soma juice: may he
Sate him in union with his troop.

8 Gods, Marut hosts whom Indra leads, distributers of Pūṣan's gifts,
Hearken ye all unto my cry.

9 With conquering Indra for ally, strike Vṛtra down, ye bounteous Gods:
Let not the wicked master us.

10 We call the Universal Gods, and Maruts to the Soma draught,
For passing strong are Pṛśni's Sons.

11 Fierce comes the Maruts' thundering voice, like that of conquerors, when ye go
Forward to victory, O Men.

12 Born of the laughing lightning. may the Maruts guard us everywhere:
May they be gracious unto us.

13 Like some lost animal, drive to us, bright Pūṣan, him who bears up heaven,
Resting on many-coloured grass.

14 Pūṣan the Bright has found the King, concealed and hidden in a cave,
Who rests on grass of many hues.

15 And may he duly bring to me the six bound closely, through these drops,
As one who ploughs with steers brings corn.

16 Along their paths the Mothers go, Sisters of priestly ministrants,
Mingling their sweetness with the milk.

17 May Waters gathered near the Sun, and those wherewith the Sun is joined,
Speed forth this sacrifice of ours.

18 I call the Waters, Goddesses, wherein our cattle quench their thirst;
Oblations to the Streams be given.

19 Amrit is in the Waters; in the Waters there is healing balm:
Be swift, ye Gods, to give them praise.

20 Within the Waters—Soma thus hath told me—dwell all balms that heal,

The phrase "preserve us from the earth" implies according to the commentary, the hindrance of the sin of those inhabiting the earth.'

17 *The whole was gathered in his footstep's dust* : This is the meaning according to Sāyaṇa. Viṣṇu was so mighty that the dust raised by his footstep enveloped the whole world, or the earth was formed from the dust of his strides.

20 *The Princes* : the Sūris, the wealthy patrons of sacrifice.

21 *Light up* : glorify with their praises.

This hymn is addressed to Vāyu, Indra, Mitra, Varuṇa, the Viśve Devas, Pūṣan, the Waters, Agni.

3 *Lords of thought* : *dhī*, thought, means especially in the Veda holy thought, devotion, prayer, a religious rite, a sacrifice.

8 *Pūṣan* is the guardian of flocks and herds and of property in general.

10 *Pṛśnimātaraḥ* : Pṛśni's sons, those who have for their mother Pṛśni, the many-coloured earth or the speckled cloud; the Maruts.

11 *O Men* : O heroic Maruts.

13 *Him who bears up heaven* : Soma, the juice which prompts the world-sustaining deeds of the Gods.

14 *The King* : Soma.

Concealed and hidden in a cave : in a place difficult of access; the reference is to the flight of Agni. See III. 9. 4.

15 *The six* : the six seasons, spring, summer, the rains, autumn, winter, the dews. *Through these drops* : May this libation induce him to bring etc.

16 *The Mothers* : the Waters, regarded as the close allies of the priests, as they are mingled with the ingredients of the Soma libation.

19 *Amrit* : nectar, the drink that confers immortality; the Greek Ambrosia.

20 *Soma thus hath told me* : Soma is especially lord of medicinal plants.

And Agni, he who blesseth all. The Waters hold all medicines.

21 O Waters, teem with medicine to keep my body safe from harm,
So that I long may see the Sun.

22 Whatever sin is found in me, whatever evil I have wrought.
If I have lied or falsely sworn, Waters, remove it far from me.

23 The Waters I this day have sought, and to their moisture have we come :
O Agni, rich in milk, come thou, and with thy splendour cover me.

24 Fill me with splendour, Agni ; give offspring and length of days ; the Gods
Shall know me even as I am, and Indra with the Ṛṣis, know.

HYMN XXIV. *Varuṇa and Others.*

1 WHO now is he, what God among Immortals, of whose auspicious name we may bethink us ?
Who shall to mighty Aditi restore us, that I may see my Father and my Mother ?

24 *Indra with the Ṛṣis* : Perhaps the seven great Ṛṣis are intended,—Marīci, Atri, Aṅgiras, Pulastya, Pulaha, Kratu, and Vasiṣṭha.

This hymn, addressed to Varuṇa, Prajāpati, Agni, Savitar, and Bhaga, is the first of a series attributed to Sunaḥśepa, the son of Ajīgarta. The legend is told in full detail in the *Aitareya Brāhmaṇa*. A king, named Hariścandra, worships Varuṇa in order to obtain a son, promising to sacrifice to him his first-born. A son is born, named Rohita; but the king delays the sacrifice until Rohita grows up, when his father communicates to him his intended fate. Rohita refuses submission, and spends several years in the forest away from home. There, at last, he meets with Ajīgarta, a Ṛṣi in great distress, and persuades him to part with his second son Śunaḥśepa to be offered, as a substitute to Varuṇa. Śunaḥśepa is about to be sacrificed, when, by the advice of Viśvāmitra, one of the officiating priests, he appeals to the Gods, and is liberated. See Wilson, *Ṛgveda*, i. p. 60., Muir, *O. S. Texts*, i. 355, 407, 413, and M. Müller, *A. S. Literature*, p. 408.

1 *Mighty Aditi* : Professor Müller (*Trans. of the Ṛgveda*, 1. 230) says that 'Aditi, an ancient god or goddess, is in reality the earliest name invented to express the Infinite; not the Infinite as the result of a long process of abstract reasoning, but the visible Infinite, the endless expanse beyond the earth, beyond the clouds, beyond the sky.'

'These words (Who shall to mighty Aditi restore us?) may be understood as spoken by some one in danger of death...who prayed to be permitted again to behold the face of nature...If we should understand the father and mother whom the suppliant is anxious to behold, as meaning heaven and earth, it would become still more probable that Aditi is to be understood as meaning nature.' Muir, *O. S. Texts*, v. 45.

Sāyaṇa explains Aditi in the text as Earth; Roth, as freedom or security; Benfey, as sinlessness.

2 Agni the God the first among the Immortals,—of his auspicious name let us bethink us.
He shall to mighty Aditi restore us, that I may see my Father and my Mother.

3 To thee, O Savitar, the Lord of precious things, who helpest us
Continually, for our share we come—

4 Wealth, highly lauded ere reproach hath fallen on it, which is laid,
Free from all hatred, in thy hands.

5 Through thy protection may we come to even the height of affluence
Which Bhaga hath dealt out to us.

6 Ne'er have those birds that fly through air attained to thy high dominion or thy might or spirit ;
Nor these the waters that flow on for ever, nor hills, abaters of the wind's wild fury.

7 Varuṇa, King, of hallowed might, sustaineth erect the Tree's stem in the baseless region.
Its rays, whose root is high above, stream downward. Deep may they sink within us, and be hidden.

8 King Varuṇa hath made a spacious pathway, a pathway for the Sun wherein to travel.
Where no way was he made him set his footstep, and warned afar whate'er afflicts the spirit.

9 A hundred balms are thine, O King, a thousand ; deep and wide-reaching also be thy favours.
Far from us, far away drive thou Destruction. Put from us e'en the sin we have committed.

10 Whither by day depart the constellations that shine at night, set high in heaven above us ?

5 *Which Bhaga hath dealt out to us* : the riches which the distributer of wealth, Bhaga, Fate or Fortune, has allotted to us.

7 *Vánasya stūpam* in the text appears to mean 'the stem of the tree,' and Sāyaṇa's explanation 'the mass or pile of light' seems forced and unnatural The phrase is not clear, but perhaps the ancient myth of the world-tree, the source of life. may be alluded to.

9 *Nirṛti* is Decay or Destruction personified, the Goddess of death and corruption. Sāyaṇa calls her *pāpadevatā*, the deity of sin.

10 *Varuṇa's holy laws* : Varuṇa is the chief of the lords of natural order. His activity displays itself preëminently in the control of the most regular phenomena of nature. See Wallis, *Cosmology of the Ṛgveda*, p. 97 f. The connexion appears to be: Fear not: the laws of Varuṇa are inviolable, and the constellations will duly reappear.

Varuṇa's holy laws remain unweakened, and through the night the Moon moves on in splendour.

11 I ask this of thee with my prayer adoring; thy worshipper craves this with his oblation.

Varuṇa, stay thou here and be not angry ; steal not our life from us, O thou Wide-Ruler.

12 Nightly and daily this one thing they tell me, this too the thought of mine own heart repeateth.

May he to whom prayed fettered Śunaḥśepa, may he the Sovran Varuṇa release us.

13 Bound to three pillars captured Śunaḥśepa thus to the Āditya made his supplication.

Him may the Sovran Varuṇa deliver, wise, ne'er deceived, loosen the bonds that bind him.

14 With bending down, oblations, sacrifices, O Varuṇa, we deprecate thine anger :

Wise Asura, thou King of wide dominion, loosen the bonds of sins by us committed.

15 Loosen the bonds, O Varuṇa, that hold me, loosen the bonds above, between, and under.

So in thy holy law may we made sinless belong to Aditi, O thou Āditya.

HYMN XXV. *Varuṇa.*

1 Whatever law of thine, O God, O Varuṇa, as we are men,
Day after day we violate.

2 Give us not as a prey to death, to be destroyed by thee in wrath,
To thy fierce anger when displeased.

3 To gain thy mercy, Varuṇa, with hymns we bind thy heart, as binds
The charioteer his tethered horse.

4 They flee from me dispirited, bent only on obtaining wealth,
As to their nests the birds of air.

5 When shall we bring, to be appeased, the Hero, Lord of warrior might,
Him, the far-seeing Varuṇa ?

6 This, this with joy they both accept in common : never do they fail
The ever-faithful worshipper.

7 He knows the path of birds that fly through heaven, and, Sovran of the sea,
He knows the ships that are thereon.

8 True to his holy law, he knows the twelve moons with their progeny:
He knows the moon of later birth.

9 He knows the pathway of the wind, the spreading, high, and mighty wind :
He knows the Gods who dwell above.

10 Varuṇa, true to holy law, sits down among his people ; he,
Most wise, sits there to govern all.

11 From thence perceiving he beholds all wondrous things, both what hath been,
And what hereafter will be done.

12 May that Āditya, very wise, make fair paths for us all our days :
May he prolong our lives for us.

13 Varuṇa, wearing golden mail, hath clad him in a shining robe :
His spies are seated round about.

14 The God whom enemies threaten not, nor those who tyrannize o'er men,
Nor those whose minds are bent on wrong.

15 He who gives glory to mankind, not glory that is incomplete,
To our own bodies giving it.

16 Yearning for the wide-seeing One, my thoughts move onward unto him,
As kine unto their pastures move.

13 *Three pillars,* or trees, apparently the sacrificial post, a sort of tripod.

The Āditya is Varuṇa, one of the sons of Aditi. See I. 14. 3.

14 *Asura* : an incorporeal, spiritual, divine being; the Zend Ahura.

15 *The bonds* : according to Sāyaṇa, the ligatures fastening the head, the waist and the feet. But the bonds of sin are here intended.

May we belong to Aditi: May we be restored to freedom and the enjoyment of nature.

4 *They flee* : apparently, my enemies; but the passage is very obscure.

6 *Both* : Varuṇa and Mitra. Why Mitra is thus suddenly introduced is not clear. The stanza breaks the connexion between stanzas 5 and 7; and is probably an interpolation.

7 Varuṇa is King of the air and of the sea, the latter being often regarded as identical with the former.

8 *The twelve moons with their progeny* the twelve months with the days which are their offspring.

The moon of later birth : the thirteenth, the supplementary or intercalary month of the luni-solar year.

13 *His spies* : Varuṇa's spies, messengers or angels, are probably the rest of the Ādityas. See M. Müller, *A. S. Literature,* p. 536.

17 Once more together let us speak, because my meath is brought: priest-like
Thou eatest what is dear to thee.

18 Now saw I him whom all may see, I saw his car above the earth :
He hath accepted these my songs.

19 Varuṇa, hear this call of mine : be gracious unto us this day
Longing for help I cried to thee.

20 Thou, O wise God, art Lord of all, thou art the King of earth and heaven :
Hear, as thou goest on thy way.

21 Release us from the upper bond, untie the bond between, and loose
The bonds below, that I may live.

HYMN XXVI. *Agni.*

1 O WORTHY of oblation, Lord of prospering powers, assume thy robes,
And offer this our sacrifice.

2 Sit ever to be chosen, as our Priest, most youthful, through our hymns,
O Agni, through our heavenly word.

3 For here a Father for his son, Kinsman for kinsman worshippeth,
And Friend, choice-worthy, for his friend.

4 Here let the foe-destroyers sit, Varuṇa, Mitra, Aryaman,
Like men, upon our sacred grass.

5 O ancient Herald, be thou glad in this our rite and fellowship:
Hearken thou well to these our songs.

6 Whate'er in this perpetual course we sacrifice to God and God,
That gift is offered up in thee.

7 May he be our dear household Lord, Priest, pleasant and choice-worthy : may
We, with bright fires, be dear to him.

8 The Gods, adored with brilliant fires, have granted precious wealth to us :
So, with bright fires, we pray to thee.

9 And, O Immortal One, so may the eulogies of mortal men
Belong to us and thee alike.

10 With all thy fires, O Agni, find pleasure in this our sacrifice,
And this our speech, O Son of Strength.

HYMN XXVII. *Agni.*

1 WITH worship will I glorify thee, Agni, like a long-tailed steed,
Imperial Lord of sacred rites.

2 May the far-striding Son of Strength, bringer of great felicity,
Who pours his gifts like rain, be ours.

3 Lord of all life, from near; from far, do thou, O Agni evermore
Protect us from the sinful man.

4 O Agni, graciously announce this our oblation to the Gods,
And this our newest song of praise.

5 Give us a share of strength most high, a share of strength that is below,
A share of strength that is between.

6 Thou dealest gifts, resplendent One; nigh, as with waves of Sindhu, thou
Swift streamest to the worshipper.

7 That man is lord of endless strength whom thou protectest in the fight,
Agni, or urgest to the fray.

8 Him, whosoever he may be, no man may vanquish, mighty One :
Nay, very glorious power is his.

9 May he who dwells with all mankind bear us with war-steeds through the fight,
And with the singers win the spoil.

10 Help, thou who knowest lauds, this work, this eulogy to Rudra, him

17 *My meath* : or honey (*mádhu*), the libation of Soma juice.

18 *Now saw I him* : I saw Varuṇa, visible to the mental eye of his worshippers.

21 *Release us from the upper bond* : see I.24. 15.

---

1 *Assume thy robes* : clothe thyself in thy vesture of flames.

2 *Most youthful* : continually renewed for sacrifice, either from the household fire or by repeated attrition.

3 *For here a Father for his son* : Agni, who stands in the place of father, kinsman, and friend to his worshipper.

4 *Aryaman* : the name of an Āditya commonly invoked together with Varuṇa and Mitra. He is said to preside over twilight.

Like men : or, according to Sāyaṇa, as they sate at the sacrifice of Manus, who is the same as Manu.

10 *Son of Strength* : the appellation is of frequent occurrence, and is sometimes applied to Indra also as a specially mighty God. The expression, applied to Agni, alludes to the strength employed in rubbing together the two pieces of wood to generate fire.

1 *Like a long-tailed steed* : Agni, or Fire, is likened to a horse, probably, on account of his impetuosity ; and his long flames, curled and driven by the wind, are compared to the horse's flowing tail. Sāyaṇa explains : scattering our foes with thy flames as a horse brushes away the flies that trouble him.

6 *Sindhu* : the Indus; or the word may stand for any river, and the expression mean, with great abundance.

9 *With the singers* : the priests who sing hymns of praise at the sacrifice.

10 *Thou who knowest lauds* : (*jarābodha* seems to refer to the Ṛṣi or poet of the hymn, not to Agni.

Rudra : the Roarer, or Howler, is here a name of Agni, on account of the loud crackling or roaring of his flames. Or the word may signify red, bright. See Pischel, Vedische Studien, 1, pp. 55 sqq.

Adorable in every house.
11 May this our God, great, limitless, smoke-bannered, excellently bright,
Urge us to strength and holy thought.
12 Like some rich Lord of men may he, Agni, the banner of the Gods,
Refulgent, hear us through our lauds.
13 Glory to Gods, the mighty and the lesser, glory to Gods the younger and the elder!
Let us, if we have power, pay the Gods worship : no better prayer than this, ye Gods, acknowledge.

HYMN XXVIII. *Indra, Etc.*

1 THERE where the broad-based stone is raised on high to press the juices out,
O Indra, drink with eager thirst the droppings which the mortar sheds.
2 Where, like broad hips, to hold the juice, the platters of the press are laid,
O Indra, drink with eager thirst the droppings which the mortar sheds.
3 There where the woman marks and learns the pestle's constant rise and fall,
O Indra, drink with eager thirst the droppings which the mortar sheds.
4 Where, as with reins to guide a horse, they bind the churning-staff with cords,
O Indra, drink with eager thirst the droppings which the mortar sheds.
5 If of a truth in every house, O Mortar, thou art set for work,
Here give thou forth thy clearest sound, loud as the drum of conquerors.
6 O Sovran of the Forest, as the wind blows soft in front of thee,
Mortar, for Indra press thou forth the Soma juice that he may drink.
7 Best strength-givers, ye stretch wide jaws, O Sacrificial Implements,
Like two bay horses champing herbs.
8 Ye Sovrans of the Forest, both swift, with swift pressers press to-day
Sweet Soma juice for Indra's drink.
9 Take up in beakers what remains : the Soma on the filter pour,
And on the ox-hide set the dregs.

HYMN XXIX. *Indra.*

1 O SOMA DRINKER, ever true, utterly hopeless though we be,
Do thou, O Indra, give us hope of beauteous horses and of kine,
In thousands, O most wealthy One.
2 O Lord of Strength, whose jaws are strong, great deeds are thine, the powerful :
Do thou, O Indra, give us hope of beauteous horses and of kine,
In thousands, O most wealthy One.
3 Lull thou asleep, to wake no more, the pair who on each other look :
Do thou, O Indra, give us hope of beauteous horses and of kine,
In thousands, O most wealthy One.
4 Hero, let hostile spirits sleep, and every gentler genius wake :
Do thou, O Indra, give us hope of beauteous horses and of kine,
In thousands, O most wealthy One.
5 Destroy this ass, O Indra, who in tones discordant brays to thee :

12 *The banner of the Gods* : who like a banner brings the Gods together ; or it may be rendered 'the herald of the Gods,' he who notifies to them, as Sāyaṇa explains it.

13. These distinctions of greater and lesser, older and younger Gods, or as we should say, angels, are nowhere further explained. Śunaḥśepa, it is said, by the advice of Agni, worships the Viśvedevas or the Universal Gods. The Viśvedevas, as a separate troop or class of Gods, are ten in number, especially worshipped at funeral obsequies, and moreover, according to the laws of Manu, entitled to daily offerings.

This hymn—a song sung during the preparation of the Soma juice—is said to be addressed to Indra, and to the pestle and mortar and other utensils used in the work.

2 *Platters* : two shallow plates, one being used as a receiver and the other as a cover.

4 *They bind the churning-staff with cords* : the churning stick is moved by a rope passed round its handle and round a post used as a pivot.

5 *O Mortar* : according to Sāyaṇa the divinities presiding over the mortar and pestle, and not the implements themselves, are addressed.

6 *O Sovran of the Forest* : (*vanaspati*) a large tree; used in this place, by metonymy, for the mortar, and in verse 8, in the dual number, for the mortar and pestle.

7 *Strength-givers* : explained by Sāyaṇa as especially givers of food. The two platters mentioned above are probably meant. When the upper platter is raised to receive the juice of the Soma stalks the aperture between the two is like a horse's mouth when he chews succulent grass.

9 This verse is addressed to the ministering priest. *What remains* : after the libation. *The filter* or sieve was used to purify the juice before it was poured into the receptacle. *Ox-hide* : laid under the mortar.

---

3 *The pair who on each other look* : 'The text is very elliptical and obscure, It is, literally : Put to sleep the two reciprocally looking: let them sleep, not being awakened. The Scholiast calls them the two female messengers of Yama (the God of the Dead).' Wilson.

5 *This ass* : our adversary, says the Scholiast, 'Therefore is he called an ass, as braying, or uttering harsh sounds intolerable to hear.'

Do thou, O Indra, give us hope of beauteous horses and of kine,
In thousands, O most wealthy One.
6 Far distant on the forest fall the tempest in a circling course!
Do thou, O Indra, give us hope of beauteous horses and of kine,
In thousands, O most wealthy One.
7 Slay each reviler, and destroy him who in secret injures us:
Do thou, O Indra, give us hope of beauteous horses and of kine
In thousands, O most wealthy One.

HYMN XXX. *Indra.*

1 We seeking strength with Soma-drops fill full your Indra like a well,
Most liberal, Lord of Hundred Powers,
2 Who lets a hundred of the pure, a thousand of the milk-blent draughts
Flow, even as down a depth, to him;
3 When for the strong, the rapturous joy he in this manner hath made room
Within his belly, like the sea.
4 This is thine own. Thou drawest near, as turns a pigeon to his mate:
Thou carest too for this our prayer.
5 O Hero, Lord of Bounties, praised in hymns, may power and joyfulness
Be his who sings the laud to thee.
6 Lord of a Hundred Powers, stand up to lend us succour in this fight:
In others too let us agree.
7 In every need, in every fray we call as friends to succour us
Indra the mightiest of all.
8 If he will hear us let him come with succour of a thousand kinds,
And all that strengthens, to our call.
9 I call him mighty to resist, the Hero of our ancient home,
Thee whom my sire invoked of old.
10 We pray to thee, O much-invoked, rich in all precious gifts, O Friend,
Kind God to those who sing thy praise.
11 O Soma-drinker, Thunder-armed, Friend of our lovely-featured dames
And of our Soma-drinking friends.
12 Thus, Soma-drinker, may it be; thus, Friend, who wieldest thunder, act
To aid each wish as we desire.
13 With Indra splendid feasts be ours, rich in all strengthening things wherewith,
Wealthy in food, we may rejoice.
14 Like thee, thyself, the singers' Friend, thou movest, as it were, besought,
Bold One, the axle of the car.
15 That, Śatakratu, thou to grace and please thy praisers, as it were,
Stirrest the axle with thy strength.
16 With champing, neighing loudly-snorting horses Indra hath ever won himself great treasures.
A car of gold hath he whose deeds are wondrous received from us, and let us too receive it.
17 Come, Aśvins, with enduring strength wealthy in horses and in kine,
And gold, O ye of wondrous deeds.
18 Your chariot yoked for both alike, immortal, ye of mighty acts,
Travels, O Aśvins, in the sea.
19 High on the forehead of the Bull one chariot wheel ye ever keep,
The other round the sky revolves.

6 *Far distant on the forest*: may the cyclone or tempest expend its fury on the wood, and not come nigh us. The word *kuṇḍṛṇācī*, which I have rendered in accordance with Sāyaṇa, means elsewhere a certain kind of animal, a lizard according to Sāyaṇa. This passage may perhaps mean, 'may the wind fall on the forest with the *kuṇḍṛṇācī*, whatever that may be.

---

1 *Lord of Hundred Powers*: Śatakratu.

3 *The strong, the rapturous joy*: the exhilarating Soma juice.

4 *This is thine own*: this Soma libation is for thee alone.

6 *In this fight*: the hymn is a prayer for aid in a coming battle.

9 *The Hero of our ancient home*: the tutelary God of our family.

11 *Friend of our lovely-featured dames*: the meaning of *śipriṇīnām* in the text is very doubtful. Wilson, following Sāyaṇa, paraphrases: (bestow upon) us, thy friends, (abundance of cows) with projecting jaws. Benfey takes the word to mean beautiful women. Ludwig suggests helmeted, from a possible form *śiprini*, agreeing with *viśām*, of men, understood. Roth considers the reading to be faulty, and suggests, *śipriṇīvan*, in the vocative case, agreeing with Soma-drinker.

14 The lines in this and the following stanza referring to the axle and the chariot or wain are somewhat obscure and have been variously interpreted. Ludwig's explanation, which I follow, appears to be the simplest and the best. The expression, movest, or stirrest, the axle, which is the firmest and strongest part of the car, is intended to signify Indra's great strength exerted at his worshippers' prayer.

16 The hymn really ends with the preceding stanza. The *car of gold* given to Indra is the hymn. The car of gold prayed for is abundant wealth.

18 *The sea*: the ocean of air.

19 *The Bull*: apparently the Sun. The car of the Aśvins stands at his head or in front of him, and the Aśvins precede him in his course round heaven. But the meaning is not very clear.

20 What mortal, O immortal Dawn, enjoyeth thee ? Where lovest thou?
To whom, O radiant, dost thou go?

21 For we have had thee in our thoughts whether anear or far away,
Red-hued and like a dappled mare.

22 Hither, O Daughter of the Sky, come thou with these thy strengthenings,
And send thou riches down to us.

HYMN XXXI. *Agni.*

1 THOU, Agni, wast the earliest Aṅgiras, a Seer; thou wast, a God thyself, the Gods' auspicious Friend.
After thy holy ordinance the Maruts, sage, active through wisdom, with their glittering spears, were born.

2 O Agni, thou, the best and earliest Aṅgiras, fulfillest as a Sage the holy law of Gods.
Sprung from two mothers, wise, through all existence spread, resting in many a place for sake of living man.

3 To Mātariśvan first thou, Agni, wast disclosed, and to Vivasvān through thy noble inward power.
Heaven and Earth, Vasu ! shook at the choosing of the Priest : the burthen thou didst bear, didst worship mighty Gods.

4 Agni thou madest heaven to thunder for mankind; thou, yet more pious, for pious Purūravas.
When thou art rapidly freed from thy parents, first eastward they bear thee round, and, after, to the west.

5 Thou, Agni, art a Bull who makes our store increase, to be invoked by him who lifts the ladle up.
Well knowing the oblation with the hallowing word, uniting all who live, thou lightenest first our folk

6 Agni, thou savest in the synod when pursued e'en him, farseeing One ! who walks in evil ways.
Thou, when the heroes fight for spoil which men rush round, slayest in war the many by the hands of few.

7 For glory, Agni, day by day, thou liftest up the mortal man to highest immortality,
Even thou who yearning for both races givest them great bliss, and to the prince grantest abundant food.

8 O Agni, highly lauded, make our singer famous that he may win us store of riches:
May we improve the rite with new performance. O Earth and Heaven, with all the Gods, protect us.

9 O blameless Agni lying in thy Parents' lap, a God among the Gods, be watchful for our good.
Former of bodies, be the singer's Providence : all good things hast thou sown for him, auspicious One !

10 Agni, thou art our Providence, our Father thou : we are thy brethren and thou art our spring of life.
In thee, rich in good heroes, guard of high decrees, meet hundred, thousand treasures, O infallible !

11 Thee, Agni, have the Gods made the first living One for living man, Lord of the house of Nahuṣa.

20 We are reminded of the old Grecian myth of Eos and Tithonus. Uṣas, Dawn, or Morning, is the daughter of personified Heaven, Dyaus, or Dyu.

This hymn, and the four following, are ascribed to Hiraṇyastūpa, son of Aṅgiras.

1 *Thou, Agni, wast the earliest Aṅgiras* : the Aṅgirases are the most important priestly family mentioned in the Veda. See I. 1. 6.

With their glittering spears : the spears of the Maruts or Storm-Gods are lightning flashes.

2 *The holy law of Gods* : sacrifice to the Gods, which Agni performs.

Sprung from two mothers : from the two pieces of wood used to produce fire.

3 *Mātariśvan* : the name of a divine being described in I.60.1 as bringing the hidden Agni to Bhṛgu, and identified by Sāyaṇa with Vāyu the God of wind.

Vivasvān : 'the brilliant'; he appears to be the God of daylight and the morning sun, the personification of all manifestations of light. He is said to be the father of Yama, and the Gods are called his offsprings.

Vasu : (good) often used as a name or epithet of Agni. The Vasus as a class of Gods, eight in number, were at first personifications of natural phenomena.

4 *Purūravas* : son of Budha. He is said to have instituted the three sacrificial fires. Agni, to reward him, sent thunder the forerunner of rain.

Freed from thy parents : produced and separated from the fire-sticks.

Eastward they bear thee : the fire is first applied to light the Āhavanīya fire and then the Gārhapatya.

5 *A Bull* : exceedingly strong.

With the hallowing word : the exclamation *Vaṣaṭ*: may he (Agni) bear it (to the Gods), used at the moment of pouring the sacrificial oil or clarified butter on the fire.

6 *Agni, thou savest in the synod* : the *vidátha*, synod or sacrificial assembly, seems to have been regarded as an inviolable asylum.

7 *Both races* : Gods and men.

The prince : the Sūri, the noble or eminent man who institutes and pays the charges of the sacrifice.

9 *Thy Parents* : here said to mean Heaven and Earth.

Former of bodies : giver of children

11 *Nahuṣa* : one of the great progenitors of the human race.

Iḷā : the personification of prayer, and the first teacher of the rules of sacrifice.

What time a Son was born : this Son is Agni himself.

Hiraṇyastūpa, the Ṛṣi of the hymn, is the son or

Ilā they made the teacher of the sons of men, what time a Son was born to the father of my race.

12 Worthy to be revered, O Agni, God, preserve our wealthy patrons with thy succours, and ourselves.

Guard of our seed art thou, aiding our cows to bear, incessantly protecting in thy holy way.

13 Agni, thou art a guard close to the pious man; kindled art thou, four-eyed ! for him who is unarmed.

With fond heart thou acceptest e'en the poor man's prayer, when he hath brought his gift to gain security.

14 Thou, Agni gainest for the loudly-praising priest the highest wealth, the object of a man's desire.

Thou art called Father, caring even for the weak, and wisest, to the simple one thou teachest lore.

15 Agni, the man who giveth guerdon to the priests, like well-sewn armour thou guardest on every side.

He who with grateful food shows kindness in his house, an offerer to the living, is the type of heaven.

16 Pardon, we pray, this sin of ours, O Agni,— the path which we have trodden, widely straying,

Dear Friend and Father, caring for the pious, who speedest nigh and who inspirest mortals.

17 As erst to Manus, to Yayāti, Aṅgiras, so Aṅgiras ! pure Agni ! come thou to our hall.

Bring hither the celestial host and seat them here upon the sacred grass, and offer what they love.

18 By this our prayer be thou, O Agni, strengthened, prayer made by us after our power and knowledge.

Lead thou us, therefore, to increasing riches; endow us with thy strength-bestowing favour.

HYMN XXXII.   Inrda.

1 I WILL declare the manly deeds of Indra, the first that he achieved, the Thunder-wielder.

He slew the Dragon, then disclosed the waters, and cleft the channels of the mountain torrents.

2 He slew the Dragon lying on the mountain : his heavenly bolt of thunder Tvaṣṭar fashioned.

Like lowing kine in rapid flow descending the waters glided downward to the ocean.

3 Impetuous as a bull, he chose the Soma, and in three sacred beakers drank the juices.

Maghavan grasped the thunder for his weapon, and smote to death this firstborn of the dragons.

4 When, Indra, thou hadst slain the dragon's firstborn, and overcome the charms of the enchanters,

Then, giving life to Sun and Dawn and Heaven, thou foundest not one foe to stand against thee.

5 Indra with his own great and deadly thunder smote into pieces Vṛtra, worst of Vṛtras.

As trunks of trees, what time the axe hath felled them, low on the earth so lies the prostrate Dragon.

6 He, like a mad weak warrior, challenged Indra, the great impetuous many-slaying Hero.

He, brooking not the clashing of the weapons, crushed—Indra's foe—the shattered forts in falling.

---

descendant of Aṅgiras, who, as one of the first introducers of the sacrificial fire and the rites of worship, is regarded as the generator or father of Agni. The meaning of the verse is that Agni was appointed priest, and *Iḷā* teacher of the rules of divine worship in the earliest time when Agni was first born on earth as sacrificial fire.

13 *Four-eyed* : illuminating the four cardinal points, or looking in all directions.

15 *An offerer to the living* : probably, one who offers food and hospitality to a human being, the *nṛyajña*, worship of man, of Manu. Or it may mean, as Ludwig suggests, one who offers a sacrifice that transports the sacrificer at once, living, to heaven.

16 *Yayāti* : a celebrated king, one of the sons of Nahuṣa.

---

1 'In this and subsequent Sūktas we have an ample elucidation of the original purport of the legend of Indra's slaying Vṛtra, converted by the Paurāṇik writers into a literal contest between Indra and an Asura, or chief o the Asuras, from what in the Vedas is merely an allegorical narrative of the production of rain. Vṛtra, sometimes also named Ahi, is nothing more than the accumulation of vapour condensed or figuratively shut up in, or obstructed by, a cloud. Indra, with his thunderbolt, or atmospheric or electrical influence, divides the agg.egated mass, and vent is given to the rain which then descends upon the earth.' Wilson.

2 *The Dragon* : Ahi, literally a serpent. *Tvaṣṭar* is the artist of the Gods.

3 *Maghavan* : the wealthy and liberal; Lord Bountiful.

In three sacred beakers : tikadrukeṣu : according to Sāyaṇa, on the Tikadrukas, the first three days of the Abhiplava ceremony.

4 *The charms of the enchanters* : magical or supernatural powers ascribed to Vṛtra and his allies.

7 Footless and handless still he challenged Indra, who smote him with his bolt between the shoulders.
Emasculate yet claiming manly vigour, thus Vṛtra lay with scattered limbs dissevered.

8 There as he lies like a bank-bursting river, the waters taking courage flow above him.
The Dragon lies beneath the feet of torrents which Vṛtra with his greatness had encompassed.

9 Then humbled was the strength of Vṛtra's mother: Indra hath cast his deadly bolt against her.
The mother was above, the son was under, and like a cow beside her calf lay Dānu.

10 Rolled in the midst of never-ceasing currents flowing without a rest for ever onward.
The waters bear off Vṛtra's nameless body: the foe of Indra sank to during darkness.

11 Guarded by Ahi stood the thralls of Dāsas, the waters stayed like kine held by the robber.
But he, when he had smitten Vṛtra, opened the cave wherein the floods had been imprisoned.

12 A horse's tail wast thou when he, O Indra, smote on thy bolt; thou, God without a second,
Thou hast won back the kine, hast won the Soma; thou hast let loose to flow the Seven Rivers.

13 Nothing availed him lightning, nothing thunder, hailstorm or mist which had spread around him:
When Indra and the Dragon strove in battle, Maghavan gained the victory for ever.

14 Whom sawest thou to avenge the Dragon, Indra, that fear possessed thy heart when thou hadst slain him;
That, like a hawk affrighted through the regions, thou crossedst nine-and-ninety flowing rivers?

15 Indra is King of all that moves and moves not, of creatures tame and horned, the Thunder-wielder.
Over all living men he rules as Sovran, containing all as spokes within the felly.

HYMN XXXIII. *Indra.*

1 COME, fain for booty let us seek to Indra: yet more shall he increase his care that guides us.
Will not the Indestructible endow us with perfect knowledge of this wealth, of cattle?

2 I fly to him invisible Wealth-giver as flies the falcon to his cherished eyrie,
With fairest hymns of praise adoring Indra, whom those who laud him must invoke in battle.

3 Mid all his host, he bindeth on the quiver: he driveth cattle from what foe he pleaseth:
Gathering up great store of riches, Indra. be thou no trafficker with us, most mighty.

4 Thou slewest with thy bolt the wealthy Dasyu, alone, yet going with thy helpers, Indra!
Far from the floor of heaven in all directions, the ancient riteless ones fled to destruction.

5 Fighting with pious worshippers, the riteless turned and fled, Indra! with averted faces.

9 *Dānu*: according to Sāyaṇa, the mother of Vṛtra.

11 *Thralls of Dāsas*: in the power of Vṛtra and his allies. Dāsa is a general name applied in the Veda to certain evil beings or demons, hostile to Indra and to men. It means, also, a savage, a barbarian, one of the non-Āryan inhabitants of India.

The robber: *paṇí* (literally, one who barters and traffics) means a miser, a niggard; an impious man who gives little or nothing to the Gods. The word is used also as the name of a class of envious demons watching over treasures, and as an epithet of the fiends who steal cows and hide them in mountain caverns.

12 *A horse's tail wast thou*: destroying thy enemies as easily as a horse sweeps away flies with his tail. Cf. I.27.1.

The Seven Rivers: according to Professor Max Müller, the Indus, the five rivers of the Panjab (Vitastā, Asiknī, Paruṣṇī, Vipāś, Śutudrī) and the Sarasvatī. Lassen and Ludwig put the Kubhā in the place of the last-named.

14 This flight of Indra is frequently alluded to. It is said that he fled thinking that he had committed a great sin in killing Vṛtra.

Nine-and-ninety: used indefinitely for a great number.

---

1 *Fain for booty*: *gavyántaḥ*, literally seeking or eager for kine, that is, booty or wealth consisting chiefly of cattle.

3 *Be thou no trafficker with us*: Do not deal illiberally with us like a petty trader: do not give sparingly, nor demand too much in return.

4 *The wealthy Dasyu*: according to Sāyaṇa, 'Vṛtra the robber,' the withholder of the fertilizing rain. The Dasyus are also a class of demons, enemies of gods and men, and sometimes the word means a savage, a barbarian.

The ancient riteless ones: the followers of Vṛtra; here apparently identified with indigenous races who had not adopted, or were hostile to, the ritual of the Veda.

5 *The Stayer*: he who stands firm in battle. The word in the text *sthātar* appears to correspond exactly with the Latin Stator (Jupiter Stator). See Benfey, *Orient und Occident*, 1. 48.

When thou, fierce Lord of the Bay Steeds, the Stayer, blewest from earth and heaven and sky the godless.

6 They met in fight the army of the blameless : then the Navagvas put forth all their power.

They, like emasculates with men contending, fled, conscious, by steep paths from Indra, scattered.

7 Whether they weep or laugh, thou hast o'erthrown them, O Indra, on the sky's extremest limit.

The Dasyu thou hast burned from heaven, and welcomed the prayer of him who pours the juice and lauds thee.

8 Adorned with their array of gold and jewels, they o'er the earth a covering veil extended.

Although they hastened, they o'ercame not Indra : their spies he compassed with the Sun of morning.

9 As thou enjoyest heaven and earth, O Indra, on every side surrounded with thy greatness,

So thou with priests hast blown away the Dasyu, and those who worship not with those who worship.

10 They who pervaded earth's extremest limit subdued not with their charms the Wealth-bestower :

Indra, the Bull, made his ally the thunder, and with its light milked cows from out the darkness.

11 The waters flowed according to their nature; he mid the navigable streams waxed mighty.

Then Indra, with his spirit concentrated, smote him for ever with his strongest weapon.

12 Indra broke through Ilībiśa's strong castles, and Śuṣṇa with his horn he cut to pieces :

Thou, Maghavan, for all his might and swiftness, slewest thy fighting foeman with thy thunder.

13 Fierce on his enemies fell Indra's weapon : with his sharp bull he rent their forts in pieces.

He with his thunderbolt dealt blows on Vṛtra; and conquered, executing all his purpose.

14 Indra, thou helpest Kutsa whom thou lovedst, and guardedst brave Daśadyu when he battled.

The dust of trampling horses rose to heaven, and Śvitrā's son stood up again for conquest.

15 Śvitrā's mild steer, O Maghavan thou helpest in combat for the land, mid Tugra's houses.

Long stood they there before the task was ended : thou wast the master of the foemen's treasure.

6 *The Navagvas* : the name of a mythological family often associated with that of Aṅgiras, and described as sharing in Indra's battles, regulating the worship of the Gods, etc.

8 *With the Sun of morning* : 'We revert here to the allegory. The followers of Vṛtra are here said to be the shades of night which are dispersed by the rising of the sun : according to the Brāhmaṇa "Verily the sun, when he rises in the east, drives away the Rākṣasas." Wilson.

10 *Milked cows* : struck the cloud with his lightning, and made the milky streams of fertilizing rain flow forth.

12 *Ilībiśa's strong castles* : Ilībiśa is said by Sāyaṇa to be Vṛtra 'who sleeps in caverns of the earth.' Probably one of the confederate demons is intended.

Śuṣṇa with his horn : the demon of drought, 'furnished', says the Scholiast, 'with weapons like the horns of bulls and buffaloes.' The meaning of 'horned' or 'with his horn' is simply 'mighty', the horn being used, as in Hebrew potery, as the emblem of strength.

13 *With his sharp bull* : the rushing thunderbolt.

14 *Kutsa* said to have been a Ṛṣi or seer, founder of a religious family or school, and elsewhere spoken of as the particular friend of Indra.

Daśadyu, is also said to have been a Ṛṣi, but nothing is known of him. The same may be said of Śvaitreya or Śvitrya, the son of a woman named Śvitrā.

15 The meaning of *tugryāsu* in the text is not clear. Sāyaṇa explains it by 'in the waters;' Benfey translates 'among Tugra's daughters,' and the Petersburg Lexicon takes it to mean 'among the families of the Tugryans.' *Mild steer* : strong but gentle son.

HYMN XXXIV. *Aśvins.*

1 Ye who observe this day be with us even thrice : far-stretching is you bounty, Aśvins and your course.

To you, as to a cloak in winter, we cleave close : you are to be drawn nigh unto us by the wise.

2 Three are the fellies in your honey-bearing car, that travels after Soma's loved one, as all know.

Three are the pillars set upon it for support: thrice journey ye by night, O Aśvins, thrice by day.

3 Thrice in the self-same day, ye Gods who banish want, sprinkle ye thrice to-day our sacrifice with meath ;

---

1 *Be present with us even thrice* ; that is, at all the three daily sacrifices.

2 *Soma* : is here the Moon. His darling is Jyotsnā or Kaumudi Moonlight, identified with Sūryā, the light borrowed from the Sun.

And thrice vouchsafe us store of food with plenteous strength, at evening, O ye Aśvins, and at break of day.

4 Thrice come ye to our home, thrice to the righteous folk, thrice triply aid the man who well deserves your help.

Thrice, O ye Aśvins, bring us what shall make us glad ; thrice send us store of food as nevermore to fail.

5 Thrice, O ye Aśvins, bring to us abundant wealth : thrice in the Gods' assembly, thrice assist our thoughts.

Thrice, grant ye us prosperity, thrice grant us fame ; for the Sun's daughter hath mounted your three-wheeled car.

6 Thrice, Aśvins, grant to us the heavenly medicines, thrice those of earth and thrice those that the waters hold.

Favour and health and strength bestow upon my son ; triple protection, Lords of Splendour, grant to him.

7 Thrice are ye to be worshipped day by day by us : thrice, O ye Aśvins, ye travel around the earth.

Car-borne from far away, O ye Nāsatyas, come, like vital air to bodies, come ye to the three.

8 Thrice, O ye Aśvins, with the Seven Mother Streams; three are the jars, the triple offering is prepared.

Three are the worlds, and moving on above the sky ye guard the firm-set vault of heaven through days and nights.

9 Where are the three wheels of your triple chariot, where are the three seats thereto firmly fastened ?

When will ye yoke the mighty ass that draws it, to bring you to our sacrifice. Nāsatyas ?

10 Nāsatyas, come : the sacred gift is offered up; drink the sweet juice with lips that know the sweetness well.

Savitar sends, before the dawn of day, your car, fraught with oil, various-coloured, to our sacrifice.

11 Come, O Nāsatyas, with the thrice-eleven Gods; come, O ye Aśvins, to the drinking of the meath.

Make long our days of life, and wipe out all our sins : ward off our enemies; be with us evermore.

12 Borne in your triple car, O Aśvins, bring us present prosperity with noble offspring.

I cry to you who hear me for protection : be ye our helpers where men win the booty.

HYMN XXXV. *Savitar.*

1 Agni I first invoke for our prosperity; I call on Mitra, Varuṇa, to aid us here.

I call on Night who gives rest to all moving life; I call on Savitar the God to lend us help.

2 Throughout the dusky firmament advancing, laying to rest the immortal and the mortal,

Borne in his golden chariot he cometh, Savitar, God who looks on every creature.

3 The God moves by the upward path, the downward; with two bright Bays, adorable, he journeys.

Savitar comes, the God from the far distance, and chases from us all distress and sorrow.

4 His chariot decked with pearl, of various colours, lofty, with golden pole, the God hath mounted,

The many-rayed One, Savitar the holy, bound, bearing power and might, for darksome regions.

5 Drawing the gold-yoked car his Bays, white-footed, have manifested light to all the peoples.

Held in the lap of Savitar, divine One, all men, all beings have their place for ever.

6 Three heavens there are ; two Savitar's, adjacent : in Yama's world is one, the home of heroes.

5 *For the Sun's daughter.* Sūryā who is called the consort of the Aśvins.

7 *Nāsatyas* ; a common appellation of the Aśvins See I. 3. 3.

To the three : to the three daily sacrifices.

8 *The Seven Mother Streams* : see I. 32. 12

Three are the jars : three sorts of pitchers, used to contain and pour out the Soma juice at the three daily sacrifices.

Three worlds : earth, middle air, and heaven.

9 *The mighty ass* : according to the *Nighaṇṭu* 'two asses are the steeds of the Aśvins.'

10 *Savitar* : implying that the Aśvins are to be worshipped with this hymn at dawn. Savitar is the Sun.

11 *The thrice-eleven Gods* : 'This is authority for the usual Paurāṇik enumeration of thirty-three deities, avowedly resting on Vedic texts. The list is, there, made up of the eight Vasus; eleven Rudras; twelve Ādityas, Prajāpati, and Vaṣaṭkāra.' Wilson.

6 *Two Savitar's* : heaven and earth, or the heaven of day and the heaven of night. *As on a linch-pin*; the linch-pin is the emblem of stability, retaining its position unchanged by the revolution of the wheels. So the Gods remain unmoved, unaffected by death or change, unlike the mortals who depart to the realm of Yama. See J. Ehni, Der Mythus des Yama, p. 115.

As on a linch-pin, firm, rest things immortal : he who hath known it let him here declare it.

7 He, strong of wing, hath lightened up the regions, deep-quivering Asura, the gentle Leader.
Where now is Sūrya, where is one to tell us to what celestial sphere his ray hath wandered ?

8 The earth's eight points his brightness hath illumined, three desert regions and the Seven Rivers.
God Savitar the gold-eyed hath come hither, giving choice treasures unto him who worships.

9 The golden-handed Savitar, far-seeing, goes on his way between the earth and heaven,
Drives away sickness, bids the Sun approach us, and spreads the bright sky through the darksome region.

10 May he, gold-handed Asura, kind Leader, come hither to us with his help and favour.
Driving off Rākṣasas and Yātudhānas, the God is present, praised in hymns at evening.

11 O Savitar, thine ancient dustless pathways are well established in the air's mid-region :
O God, come by those paths so fair to travel, preserve thou us from harm this day, and bless us.

HYMN XXXVI. *Agni.*

1 WITH words sent forth in holy hymns, Agni we supplicate, the Lord
Of many families who duly serve the Gods, yea, him whom others also praise.

2 Men have won Agni, him who makes their strength abound : we, with oblations, worship thee.
Our gracious-minded Helper in our deeds of might, be thou, O Excellent, this day.

3 Thee for our messenger we choose, thee, the Omniscient, for our Priest.
The flames of thee the mighty are spread wide around : thy splendour reaches to the sky.

4 The Gods enkindle thee their ancient messenger,—Varuṇa, Mitra, Aryaman.
That mortal man, O Agni, gains through thee all wealth, who hath poured offerings unto thee.

5 Thou, Agni, art a cheering Priest, Lord of the House, men's messenger :
All constant high decrees established by the Gods, gathered together, meet in thee.

6 In thee, the auspicious One, O Agni, youthfullest, each sacred gift is offered up :
This day, and after, gracious, worship thou our Gods, that we may have heroic sons.

7 To him in his own splendour bright draw near in worship the devout.
Men kindle Agni with their sacrificial gifts, victorious o'er the enemies.

8 Vṛtra they smote and slew, and made the earth and heaven and firmament a wide abode.
The glorious Bull, invoked, hath stood at Kaṇva's side : loud neighed the Steed in frays for kine.

9 Seat thee, for thou art mighty ; shine, best entertainer of the Gods.
Worthy of sacred food, praised Agni ! loose the smoke, ruddy and beautiful to see.

10 Bearer of offerings, whom, best sacrificing Priest, the Gods for Manu's sake ordained ;
Whom Kaṇva, whom Medhyātithi made the source of wealth, and Vṛṣan and Upastuta.

11 Him, Agni, whom Medhyātithi, whom Kaṇva kindled for his rite,
Him these our songs of praise, him, Agni, we extol : his powers shine out preëminent.

7 *He, strong of wing* : (*suparṇáḥ*) an epithet or a name of the Sun, *Asura* : the immortal and divine One.

9 *Bids the Sun approach us* : Sāyaṇa says 'approaches the Sun', and observes that although Savitar and the Sun are the same as regards their divinity, yet they are two different forms, and therefore one may be said to go to the other.

10 *Yātudhānas* : a class of demons or evil spirits, much like Rākṣasas, but more particularly practisers of sorcery.

This Hymn and the twelve following are ascribed to Kaṇva, a very celebrated Ṛṣi who is called the son of Ghora and is said to belong to the family of Aṅgiras.

5 The preservation of the whole world rests, according to the Vedic view, on the sacrifices offered by men, as these give the Gods strength and enable them to perform their duties.

8 *The glorious Bull* : the mighty Agni, strong as a bull and impetuous as a war horse, has aided his favourite Kaṇva in battle.

10 *Medhyātithi* : Sāyaṇa takes this word to be an epithet of Kaṇva, 'entertainer of guests who are worthy of sacrificial food,' But it appears to be the name of a Ṛṣi of Kaṇva's family, the seer of twenty-eight hymns of Book VIII. and IX.

Vṛṣan and Upastuta : rendered by Wilson, after Sāyaṇa, 'Indra and some other worshipper,' are also apparently the names of two other Ṛṣis.

12 Make our wealth perfect thou, O Agni, Lord divine : for thou hast kinship with the Gods.
Thou rulest as a King o'er widely-famous strength : be good to us, for thou art great.

13 Stand up erect to lend us aid, stand up like Savitar the God :
Erect as strength-bestower we call aloud, with unguents and with priests, on thee.

14 Erect, preserve us from sore trouble; with thy flame burn thou each ravening demon dead.
Raise thou us up that we may walk and live : so thou shalt find our worship mid the Gods.

15 Preserve us, Agni, from the fiend, preserve us from malicious wrong.
Save us from him who fain would injure us or slay, Most Youthful, thou with lofty light.

16 Smite down as with a club, thou who hast fire for teeth, smite thou the wicked, right and left.
Let not the man who plots against us in the night, nor any foe prevail o'er us.

17 Agni hath given heroic might to Kaṇva, and felicity :
Agni hath helped our friends, hath helped Medhyātithi, hath helped Upastuta to win.

18 We call on Ugradeva, Yadu, Turvaśa, by means of Agni, from afar;
Agni, bring Navavāstva and Bṛhadratha, Turvīti, to subdue the foe.

19 Manu hath stablished thee a light, Agni, for all the race of men :
Sprung from the Law, oil-fed, for Kaṇva hast thou blazed, thou whom the people reverence.

20 The flames of Agni full of splendour and of might are fearful, not to be approached.
Consume for ever all demons and sorcerers, consume thou each devouring fiend.

HYMN XXXVII. *Maruts.*

1 Sing forth, O Kaṇvas, to your band of Maruts unassailable,
Sporting, resplendent on their car :

2 They who, self-luminous, were born together, with the spotted deer,
Spears, swords, and glittering ornaments.

3 One hears, as though 'twere close at hand, the cracking of the whips they hold ;
They gather glory on their way.

4 Now sing ye forth the God-given hymn to your exultant Marut host,
The fiercely-vigorous, the strong.

5 Praise ye the Bull among the cows ; for 'tis the Maruts' sportive band :
It strengthened as it drank the rain.

6 Who is your mightiest, Heroes, when, O shakers of the earth and heaven,
Ye shake them like a garment's hem ?

7 At your approach man holds him down before the fury of your wrath :
The rugged-jointed mountain yields.

8 They at whose racings forth the earth, like an age-weakened lord of men,
Trembles in terror on their ways.

9 Strong is their birth : vigour have they to issue from their Mother ; strength,
Yea, even twice enough, is theirs.

10 And these, the Sons, the Singers, in their racings have enlarged the bounds,
So that the kine must walk knee-deep.

11 Before them, on the ways they go, they drop this offspring of the cloud,
Long, broad, and inexhaustible.

13 *Stand up erect* : Agni, as erect, is identified by Sāyaṇa with the *yūpa* or sacrificial post to which the victims, at an animal sacrifice, were bound. Accordingly he takes *añjibhiḥ* to mean 'with unguents' wherewith the post was anointed. This word may however refer to the ornaments—another signification of the word—worn by the ministering priests.

17 *Agni hath helped our friends* : Sāyaṇa takes *mitrā* in the text as *mitrāṇi*, friends. Benfey and Ludwig consider it to mean, the former Mitra, and the latter the two Mitras i.e. Mitra and Varuṇa; and they translate respectively 'Agni and Mitra protected.' and 'Agni, as Mitra (and Varuṇa) hath favoured.'

18 Turvaśa and Yadu are frequently mentioned together as eponymi of tribes of those names. The poet appears to pray for the return of Navavāstva, whoever he may have been, to protect the home attacked by the Dasyus or robbers, and perhaps also to strengthen his prayer by an appeal to the spirits of departed heroes.

20 *Demons and sorcerers* : Rākṣasas and evil spirits who practise sorcery.

For an exhaustive explanation of this and other Hymns to the Maruts, see M. Müller's Vedic Hymns, Part I. (Sacred Books of the East, XXXII).

5 *The Bull among the cows* : the band of Storm-Gods preeminent among the clouds as a bull is among cows.

6 That is, where all are so mighty it would be superfluous to ask who is mightiest.

Like a garment's hem : or, according to Sāyaṇa 'like a tree's high top.

10 *The Singers* : the loud-voiced Maruts.

The Maruts have spread themselves over the sky and caused so much rain to fall that the cows in the pastures are up to their knees in water. But see Ludwig, Ueber die neuesten Arbeiten auf dem Gebiete der Ṛgvedaforschung. Prag. 1893.

12 O Maruts, as your strength is great, so have ye cast men down on earth,
So have ye made the mountains fall.

13 The while the Maruts pass along, they talk together on the way :
Doth any hear them as they speak ?

14 Come quick with swift steeds, for ye have worshippers among Kaṇva's sons :
May you rejoice among them well.

15 All is prepared for your delight. We are their servants evermore,
To live as long as life may last.

HYMN XXXVIII. *Maruts.*

1 WHAT now ? When will ye take us by both hands, as a dear sire his son,
Gods, for whom sacred grass is clipped ?

2 Now whither ? To what goal of yours go ye in heaven, and not on earth ?
Where do your cows disport themselves ?

3 Where are your newest favours shown ? Where, Maruts, your prosperity ?
Where all your high felicities ?

4 If, O ye Maruts, ye the Sons whom Pṛśni bore, were mortal, and
Immortal he who sings your praise.

5 Then never were your praiser loathed like a wild beast in pasture-land,
Nor should he go on Yama's path.

6 Let not destructive plague on plague hard to be conquered, strike us down :
Let each, with drought, depart from us.

7 Truly, they the fierce and mighty Sons of Rudra send their windless
Rain e'en on the desert places.

8 Like a cow the lightning lows and follows, motherlike, her youngling,
When their rain-flood hath been loosened.

9 When they inundate the earth they spread forth darkness e'en in day time,
With the water-laden rain-cloud.

10 O Maruts, at your voice's sound this earthly habitation shakes,
And each man reels who dwells therein.

11 O Maruts, with your strong-hoofed steeds, unhindered in their courses, haste
Along the bright embanked streams.

12 Firm be the fellies of your wheels, steady your horses and your cars,
And may your reins be fashioned well.

13 Invite thou hither with this song, for praise, Agni the Lord of Prayer,
Him who is fair as Mitra is.

14 Form in thy mouth the hymn of praise : expand thee like a rainy cloud :
Sing forth the measured eulogy.

15 Sing glory to the Marut host, praiseworthy, tuneful, vigorous :
Here let the Strong Ones dwell with us.

HYMN XXXIX. *Maruts.*

1 WHEN thus, like flame, from far away, Maruts, ye cast your measure forth,
To whom go ye, to whom, O shakers of the earth, moved by whose wisdom, whose design ?

2 Strong let your weapons be to drive away your foes, firm for resistance let them be.
Yea, passing glorious must be your warrior might, not as a guileful mortal's strength.

3 When what is strong ye overthrow, and whirl about each ponderous thing,
Heroes, your course is through the forest trees of earth, and through the fissures of the rocks.

2 *Where do your cows disport themselves* ? : perhaps, as M. Müller suggests where tarry your herds ?' *viz.* the clouds. Why do you remain in the sky, and not come down to earth ? Or, according to Ludwig : 'Where do the cows feed that are to supply milk and butter for sacrifice to you ? Where is the place in which sacrifice is to be offered to you ?'

5 *Like a wild beast* : or, unwelcome like a deer in the home-pasture or meadow reserved for the cows.

Yama's path : the path that leads to Yama the God of the Departed.

6 *Destructive plague* : *nirṛtiḥ*; sin. M. Müller. *Drought* : greed. M. Müller.

7 *Sons of Rudra* : or 'dear to Rudra,' who is the father of the Maruts.

Windless rain : steady rain, not blown away ; that sinks into the ground; the wind generally ceasing as soon as heavy rain begins to fall.

8 The thunder follows the lightning as a cow lowing **follows her calf.**

13 *Agni, the Lord of Prayer* : 'Agni is frequently invoked together with the Maruts, and is even called marut-sakhā, the friend of the Maruts, viii. 92.

14. It seems better, therefore, to refer brahmaṇaspatim to Agni, than, with Sāyaṇa, to the host of the Maruts. Brahmaṇaspati and Bṛhaspati are both varieties of Agni, the priest and purohita of Gods and men, and as such he is invoked together with the Maruts in other passages, i. 40, 1. M. Müller.

14 *Expand thee* : addressed to the poet of the hymn.

15 *Tuneful* : so in I. 37. 10 'And these the Sons, the Singers.' The song of the Maruts is the music or singing of the winds.

1 *Maruts, ye cast your measure forth* : 'In this passage we must take measure, not in the abstract sense, but as a measuring line, which is cast forward to measure the distance of an object, an image perfectly applicable to the Maruts, who seem with their weapons to strike the trees and mountains when they themselves are still far off.' M. Müller.

4 Consumers of your foes, no enemy of yours is found in heaven or on the earth :
Ye Rudras, may the strength, held in this bond, be yours, to bid defiance even now.

5 They make the mountains rock and reel, they rend the forest-kings apart.
Onward, ye Maruts, drive, like creatures drunk with wine, ye Gods with all your company.

6 Ye to your chariot have yoked the spotted deer : a red deer, as a leader, draws.
Even the Earth herself listened as ye came near, and men were sorely terrified.

7 O Rudras, quickly we desire your succour for this work of ours.
Come to us with your aid as in the days of old, so now for frightened Kaṇva's sake.

8 Should any monstrous foe, O Maruts, sent by you or sent by mortals threaten us,
Tear ye him from us with your power and with your might, and with the succours that are yours.

9 For ye, the worshipful and wise, have guarded Kaṇva perfectly.
O Maruts, come to us with full protecting help, as lightning flashes seek the rain.

10 Whole strength have ye, O Bounteous Ones; perfect, earth-shakers, is your might.
Maruts, against the poet's wrathful enemy send ye an enemy like a dart.

HYMN XL. *Brahmaṇaspati*

1 O BRAHMAṆASPATI, stand up : God-serving men, we pray to thee.
May they who give good gifts, the Maruts, come to us. Indra, most swift, be thou with them.

2 O Son of Strength, each mortal calls to thee for aid when spoil of battle waits for him.
O Maruts, may this man who loves you well obtain wealth of good steeds and hero might.

3 May Brahmaṇaspati draw nigh, may Sūnṛtā the Goddess come,
And Gods bring to this rite which gives the five-fold gift the Hero, lover of mankind.

4 He who bestows a noble guerdon on the priest wins fame that never shall decay.
For him we offer sacred hero-giving food, peerless and conquering easily.

5 Now Brahmaṇaspati speaks forth aloud the solemn hymn of praise,
Wherein Indra and Varuṇa, Mitra, Aryaman, the Gods, have made their dwelling place.

6 May we in holy synods, Gods ! recite that hymn, peerless, that brings felicity.
If you, O Heroes, graciously accept this word, may it obtain all bliss from you.

7 Who shall approach the pious ? who the man whose sacred grass is trimmed ?
The offerer with his folk advances more and more : he fills his house with precious things.

8 He amplifies his lordly might, with kings he slays : e'en mid alarms he dwells secure
In great or lesser fight none checks him, none subdues,—the wielder of the thunderbolt.

HYMN XLI.

Varuṇa, Mitra, Aryaman.

1 NE'ER is he injured whom the Gods Varuṇa, Mitra, Aryaman,
The excellently wise, protect.

2 He prospers ever, free from scathe, whom they, as with full hands, enrich,
Whom they preserve from every foe.

4 *Held in this bond* : together with your race. M. Müller.

9 *As lightning-flashes seek the rain* : 'Lightning precedes the rain, and may therefore be represented as looking about for the rain.' M. Müller.

---

1 *O Brahmaṇaspati* : Agni is sometimes called Brahmaṇaspati, or Lord of Prayer. See 1. 38. 13.

3 *May Sūnṛtā the Goddess come* : Sūnṛtā (Pleasantness) is, according to Sāyaṇa the Goddess of Speech (Vāgdevatā) in the form of lover of truth.

The fivefold gift : an offering of grain, gruel, curdled milk, rice-cake, and curds.

4 *Sacred food* : *íḷā* or *íḍā*, sacrificial food, or a libation, especially a holy libation coming between the Prayāja and the Anuyāja the fore-sacrifice and the after-sacrifice; the preliminary and the final offering.

5 *Now Brahmaṇaspati speaks forth* : 'Professor Roth remarks : The thunder is his (Brahmaṇaspati's) voice. The voice of thunder, again, as the voice of the superintendent of prayer, is by a beautiful transference brought into connection with the prayer which, spoken on earth, finds, as it were, its echo in the heights of heaven.' Muir *O. S. Texts*, V. p. 279. note.

8 *The wielder of the thunderbolt* : meaning, Sāyaṇa says, Brahmaṇaspati, and so far identifying him with Indra. Ludwig refers the expression to the pious sacrificer who is said to be armed, as it were, with Brahmaṇaspati's thunderbolt.

3 The Kings drive far away from him his troubles and his enemies,
And lead him safely o'er distress.
4 Thornless, Ādityas, is the path, easy for him who seeks the Law:
With him is naught to anger you.
5 What sacrifice, Ādityas, ye Heroes guide by the path direct,—
May that come nigh unto your thought.
6 That mortal, ever unsubdued, gains wealth and every precious thing,
And children also of his own.
7 How, my friends, shall we prepare Aryaman's and Mitra's laud,
Glorious food of Varuṇa?
8 I point not out to you a man who strikes the pious, or reviles:
Only with hymns I call you nigh.
9 Let him not love to speak ill words: but fear the One who holds all four
Within his hand, until they fall.

HYMN XLII. *Pūṣan.*

1 SHORTEN our ways, O Pūṣan, move aside obstruction in the path:
Go close before us, cloud-born God.
2 Drive, Pūṣan, from our road the wolf, the wicked inauspicious wolf,
Who lies in wait to injure us.
3 Who lurks about the path we take, the robber with a guileful heart:
Far from the road chase him away.
4 Tread with thy foot and trample out the firebrand of the wicked one,
The double-tongued, whoe'er he be.
5 Wise Pūṣan, Wonder-Worker, we claim of thee now the aid wherewith
Thou furtheredst our sires of old.
6 So, Lord of all prosperity, best wielder of the golden sword,
Make riches easy to be won.
7 Past all pursuers lead us, make pleasant our path and fair to tread:
O Pūṣan, find thou power for this.
8 Lead us to meadows rich in grass: send on our way no early heat:
O Pūṣan, find thou power for this.
9 Be gracious to us, fill us full, give, feed us, and invigorate:
O Pūṣan, find thou power for this.
10 No blame have we for Pūṣan; him we magnify with songs of praise:
We seek the Mighty One for wealth.

HYMN XLIII. *Rudra.*

1 WHAT shall we sing to Rudra, strong, most bounteous, excellently wise,
That shall be dearest to his heart?
2 That Aditi may grant the grace of Rudra to our folk, our kine,
Our cattle and our progeny;
3 That Mitra and that Varuṇa, that Rudra may remember us,
Yea, all the Gods with one accord.
4 To Rudra Lord of sacrifice, of hymns and balmy medicines,
We pray for joy and health and strength.
5 He shines in splendour like the Sun, refulgent as bright gold is he,
The good, the best among the Gods.
6 May he grant health into our steeds, well-being to our rams and ewes,
To men, to women, and to kine.
7 O Soma, set thou upon us the glory of a hundred men,
The great renown of mighty chiefs.

3 *The Kings*: Varuṇa, Mitra, and Aryaman.

4 *Ādityas*: the three Gods named above, with others See I. 14. 3.

9 *But fear the One who holds all four*: Wilson remarks: 'The text has *caturaś cid dadamānād vibhīyād ā nidhātoḥ*, he may fear from one holding four until the fall. The meaning is supplied by the Scholiast with the assistance of Yāska, *caturokṣān dhārayataḥ...kitavāt*, from a gambler holding four dice...That is, where two men are playing together, the man who has not the throw of the dice is in anxious apprehension lest it should be against him.' Benfey thinks that 'the holder of the four (dice)' is God who holds in his hands and decides the destinies of man. Ludwig maintains that there is no reference to dice, either of gambling or destiny, and that 'the four' are Varuṇa, Mitra, Bhaga, and Aryaman. The pious man when he possesses these four as friends should fear to let them go. Bergaigne (La Religion Védique, III. 158) is of opinion that the cords or nooses of Varuṇa, with which he catches and punishes the wicked, are intended.

1 *Shorten our ways, O Pūṣan*: Pūṣan is usually a synonym of the Sun; that is, he is one of the twelve Ādityas. According to the tenour of this hymn, he is the deity presiding especially over roads and journeyings. *Cloud-born*: with reference, perhaps, to the close connexion between nourishing the earth, which is one of Puṣan's especial duties, and the cloud that gives the necessary rain. But in Ṛgveda. VIII. 4. 15, 16, Pūṣan is called *vimocana*, the deliverer, (from sin, according to Sāyaṇa), and perhaps *vimuco napāt* may mean the same thing. See Muir *O. S. Texts*, V. 175, where the whole hymn is translated.

2 *The wolf*: *vṛka*=Swedish and Norwegian *varg*, which signifies not only wolf, but also a wicked godless man.

1 Rudra appears in this hymn as a gentle and beneficent deity, presiding especially over medicinal plants.

2 *That Aditi may grant the grace*: Aditi is said by Sāyaṇa to mean here the earth, and is accordingly so translated by Wilson. Benfey explains the word by 'Sinlessness,' and Ludwig takes it as a masculine deity meaning Rudra himself.

6 *May he grant health*: here Rudra appears as *paśupáti*, Lord and guardian of cattle.

8 Let not malignities, nor those who trouble Soma, hinder us.
Indu, give us a share of strength.
9 Soma ! head, central point, love these ; Soma ! know these as serving thee,
Children of thee Immortal, at the highest place of holy law.

HYMN XLIV. *Agni.*

1 IMMORTAL Jātavedas, thou many-hued fulgent gift of Dawn,
Agni, this day to him who pays oblations bring the Gods who waken with the morn.
2 For thou art offering-bearer and loved messenger, the charioteer of sacrifice :
Accordant with the Aśvins and with Dawn grant us heroic strength and lofty fame.
3 As messenger we choose to-day Agni the good whom many love,
Smoke-bannered spreader of the light, at break of day glory of sacrificial rites.
4 Him noblest and most youthful, richly-worshipped guest, dear to the men who offer gifts,
Him, Agni Jātavedas, I beseech at dawn that he may bring the Gods to us.
5 Thee, Agni, will I glorify, deathless nourisher of the world,
Immortal, offering-bearer, meet for sacred food, preserver, best at sacrifice.
6 Tell good things to thy praiser, O most youthful God, as richly worshipped, honey-tongued,
And, granting to Praskaṇva lengthened days of life, show honour to the Heavenly Host.
7 For the men, Agni, kindle thee as all-possessor and as Priest;
So Agni, much-invoked, bring hither with all speed the Gods, the excellently wise,
8 At dawn of day, at night, Uṣas and Savitar, the Aśvins, Bhaga, Agni's self:
Skilled in fair rites, with Soma poured, the Kaṇvas light thee, the oblation-wafting God.
9 For, Agni, Lord of sacrifice and messenger of men art thou :
Bring thou the Gods who wake at dawn, who see the light, this day to drink the Soma juice.
10 Thou shonest forth, O Agni, after former dawns, all visible, O rich in light.
Thou art our help in battle-strife, the Friend of man, the great high priest in sacrifice.
11 Like Manu, we will stablish thee, Agni, performer of the rite,
Invoker, ministering Priest, exceeding wise, the swift immortal messenger.
12 When as the Gods' High Priest, by many loved, thou dost their mission as their nearest Friend,
Then, like the far-resounding billows of the flood, thy flames, O Agni, roar aloud.
13 Hear, Agni, who hast ears to hear, with all thy train of escort Gods;
Let Mitra, Aryaman, seeking betimes our rite, seat them upon the sacred grass.
14 Let those who strengthen Law, who bountifully give, the fire-tongued Maruts, hear our praise.
May Law-supporting Varuṇa with the Aśvins twain and Uṣas, drink the Soma juice.

HYMN XLV *Agni.*

1 WORSHIP the Vasus, Agni ! here, the Rudras, the Ādityas, all
Who spring from Manu, those who know fair rites, who pour their blessings down.

8 *Those who trouble Soma* : probably the people of the hills who interfere with the gathering of the Soma plant which has to be sought there.

Indu : literally 'drop;' from the same root as Indra, the Rainer; a name of the Moon as rain-giver, and of Soma which is identified with it.

9 *At the highest place of holy law* : at the place where sacrifice is duly performed. 'The whole verse is difficult, possibly a later addition.' Max M ller.

This Hymn and the six following are ascribed to the Ṛ i Praskaṇva, the son of Kaṇva who is the seer of the preceding group.

1 *Immortal Jātavedas* : Jātavedas is a common epithet of Agni, the meaning of which is explained in five ways; 1. 'knowing all created beings; 2. possessing all creatures; 3. known by created beings; 4. possessing riches; 5. possessing wisdom.'

2 *The Aśvins* : see I.3.1.
Dawn : *the Goddess Uṣas* ; Morning personified.

11 *Like Manu* : the representative man and father of the human race and the first institutor of religious ceremonies.

12 *Of the flood* : or of Sindhu; the word meaning either that river (the Indus) in particular, or any river or gathering of waters in general.

13 *Let Mitra, Aryaman* : and Varuṇa, understood.

14 *The fire-tongued Maruts* : who consume the sacrifice by means of the tongue-like flames of Agni.

---

1 *Vasus, Rudras, Ādityas* : three classes of Gods who make up almost the whole number of the thirty-three deities spoken of in the next stanza.

Who spring from Manu : Manu appears here as Prajāpati, the progenitor of Gods as well as of men.

2 Agni, the Gods who understand give ear unto the worshipper :
Lord of Red Steeds, who lovest song, bring thou those Three-and-Thirty Gods.
3 O Jātavedas, great in act, hearken thou to Praskaṇva's call,
As Priyamedha erst was heard, Atri, Virūpa, Aṅgiras.
4 The sons of Priyamedha skilled in lofty praise have called for help
On Agni who with fulgent flame is Ruler of all holy rites.
5 Hear thou, invoked with holy oil, bountiful giver of rewards,
These eulogies, whereby the sons of Kaṇva call thee to their aid.
6 O Agni, loved by many, thou of fame most wondrous, in their homes
Men call on thee whose hair is flame, to be the bearer of their gifts.
7 Thee, Agni, best to find out wealth, most widely famous, quick to hear,
Singers have stablished in their rites Herald and ministering Priest.
8 Singers with Soma pressed have made thee, Agni, hasten to the feast,
Great light to mortal worshipper, what time they bring the sacred gift.
9 Good, bounteous, Son of Strength, this day seat here on sacred grass the Gods
Who come at early morn, the host of heaven, to drink the Soma juice.
10 Bring with joint invocations thou, O Agni, the celestial host :
Here stands the Soma, bounteous Gods : drink this expressed ere yesterday.

HYMN XLVI. *Aśvins.*

1 Now Morning with her earliest light shines forth, dear Daughter of the Sky :
High, Aśvins, I extol your praise,
2 Sons of the Sea, mighty to save discoverers of riches, ye
Gods with deep thought who find out wealth.
3 Your giant coursers hasten on over the region all in flames,
When your car flies with winged steeds.
4 He, liberal, lover of the flood, Lord of the House, the vigilant,
Chiefs ! with oblations feeds you full.
5 Ye have regard unto our hymns, Nāsatyas, thinking of our words :
Drink boldly of the Soma juice.
6 Vouchsafe to us, O Aśvin Pair, such strength as, with attendant light,
May through the darkness carry us.
7 Come in the ship of these our hymns to bear you to the hither shore :
O Aśvins, harness ye the car.
8 The heaven's wide vessel is your own : on the flood's shore your chariot waits :
Drops, with the hymn, have been prepared.
9 Kaṇvas, the drops are in the heaven; the wealth is at the waters' place :
Where will ye manifest your form ?
10 Light came to lighten up the branch, the Sun appeared as it were gold :
And with its tongue shone forth the dark.
11 The path of sacrifice was made to travel to the farther goal :

2 *Lord of Red Steeds* : Agni, whose horses are flames of fire.

Three-and-Thirty Gods : see I. 34. 11.

3 Priyamedha, Atri, and Virūpa are famous Ṛṣis, the seers of many hymns of the Ṛgveda. Aṅgiras has already been mentioned. See I. 1. 6.

9 *Son of Strength* : made or generated by strong friction; 'kindled through agitation to a flame'.

10 *Expressed ere yesterday* : preparad two days before in order that the juice might ferment before it was used.

---

1 *Morning* : Uṣas or Dawn, personified as a Goddess.

Aśvins : see I. 3. 1.

2 *Sons of the Sea* : offspring of the celestial ocean, the atmosphere.

4 *He, liberal, lover of the flood* : evidently Agni and not the Sun. Agni's connexion with water is frequently alluded to, and he is often called the Lord and Guardian of the house or family.

6 *The darkness* : in the shape of poverty or want according to the Scholiast.

7 The poet appears to invite the Aśvins to yoke their chariot for part of the journey and come to meet his hymn which shall bear them as in a ship through the sky. The middle air or atmosphere is the sea between heaven and earth, and the earth is *the hither shore*.

8 *Vessel* : (*aritram*). a vehicle in the shape of a ship, says Sāyaṇa. You have already the ship of our songs to bear you through the sky, and now your chariot has reached the earth and the place where, together with this hymn, the Soma juice has been prepared for a libation to you.

9 The drops, or Soma libation, and the wealth or treasure, and the sky and the place of rivers appear here to be parallelisms, both pairs of expressions signifying the same thing. The oblation is said to have already reached the heaven where the Aśvins will receive it. Sāyaṇa's paraphrase which Wilson has followed, seems forced and unnatural. 'Kaṇvas, (ask this of the Aśvins): (How) do the rays (of the sun proceed) from the sky ? : (How) does the dawn (rise) in the region of the waters ?

10 *Light came to lighten up the branch* : the branch is probably the sacrificial fire. Cf. 'The other fires are verily thy branches' (I. 59. 1). The epithet 'dark' may refer to the darkening of the fire by the sunlight or by the smoke.

11 Sacrifice is the path which leads the Gods from heaven to earth, and the way through heaven is made visible by the sacrificial fire or by the daylight.

The road of heaven was manifest.
12 The singer of their praise awaits whatever grace the Aśvins give,
Who save when Soma gladdens them.
13 Ye dwellers with Vivasvān come, auspicious, as to Manu erst;
Come to the Soma and our praise.
14 O circumambient Aśvins, Dawn follows the brightness of your way:
Approve with beams our solemn rites.
15 Drink ye of our libations, grant protection, O ye Aśvins Twain,
With aids which none may interrupt.

HYMN XLVII. *Aśvins.*

1 Aśvins, for you who strengthen Law this sweetest Soma hath been shed.
Drink this expressed ere yesterday and give riches to him who offers it.
2 Come, O ye Aśvins, mounted on your triple car three-seated, beautiful of form
To you at sacrifice the Kaṇvas send the prayer: graciously listen to their call.
3 O Aśvins, ye who strengthen Law, drink ye this sweetest Soma juice.
Borne on your wealth-fraught car come ye this day to him who offers, ye of wondrous deeds.
4 Omniscient Aśvins, on the thrice-heaped grass bedew with the sweet juice the sacrifice.
The sons of Kaṇva, striving heavenward, call on you with draughts of Soma juice out-poured.
5 O Aśvins, with those aids wherewith ye guarded Kaṇva carefully,
Keep us, O Lords of Splendour: drink the Soma juice, ye strengtheners of holy law.
6 O Mighty Ones, ye gave Sudās abundant food, brought on your treasure-laden car;
So now vouchsafe to us the wealth which many crave, either from heaven or from the sea.
7 Nāsatyas, whether ye be far away or close to Turvaśa,
Borne on your lightly-rolling chariot come to us, together with the sunbeams come.
8 So let your coursers, ornaments of sacrifice, bring you to our libations here.
Bestowing food on him who acts and gives aright, sit, Chiefs, upon the sacred grass.
9 Come, O Nāsatyas, on your car decked with a sunbright canopy,
Whereon ye ever bring wealth to the worshipper, to drink the Soma's pleasant juice.
10 With lauds and songs of praise we call them down to us, that they, most rich, may succour us;
For ye have ever in the Kaṇvas' well-loved house, O Aśvins, drunk the Soma juice.

HYMN XLVIII. *Dawn.*

1 Dawn on us with prosperity, O Uṣas, Daughter of the Sky,
Dawn with great glory, Goddess, Lady of the Light, dawn thou with riches, Bounteous One.
2 They, bringing steeds and kine, boon-givers of all wealth, have oft sped forth to lighten us.
O Uṣas, waken up for me the sounds of joy: send us the riches of the great.
3 Uṣas hath dawned, and now shall dawn, the Goddess, driver forth of cars
Which, as she cometh nigh, have fixed their thought on her, like glory-seekers on the flood.
4 Here Kaṇva, chief of Kaṇva's race, sings forth aloud the glories of the heroes' names,—
The princes who, O Uṣas, as thou comest near, direct their thoughts to liberal gifts.
5 Like a good matron Uṣas comes carefully tending everything:
Rousing all life she stirs all creatures that have feet, and makes the birds of air fly up.
6 She sends the busy forth, each man to his

13 *Vivasvān*: the 'Brilliant,' a name of the morning heaven personified. He is regarded as the father of Yama, Manu, and the Aśvins. See X. 17. 2 note.

6 *Sudās*: a king, the son of Pijavana. See VII. 18. 5-25.

7 *Nāsatyas*: Aśvins. See I. 3. 3.
Turvaśa: the tribe or family called after the chief of this name, frequently mentioned in the Ṛgveda. See I. 36. 18.

10 *With lauds*: *ukthébhiḥ*, answering, according to Sāyaṇa, to what in the Brāhmaṇa is called Śastram (to be recited by the Hotar) while the Stoma (stotram) song, is sung by the Sāma-priests.

1 *Uṣas*: Morning, Dawn, personified.

2 *They*: the Dawns of preceding days.

3 The approach of Dawn sets cars or wains in motion in the same way as it causes ships or boats that have anchored during the night to move out to the open water.

4. *The princes* are the wealthy patrons or institutors of sacrifice, who bear all expenses and remunerate the priests.

pursuit : delay she knows not as she springs.
O rich in opulence, after thy dawning birds that have flown forth no longer rest.

7 This Dawn hath yoked her steeds afar, beyond the rising of the Sun :
Borne on a hundred chariots she, auspicious Dawn, advances on her way to men.

8 To meet her glance all living creatures bend them down : Excellent One, she makes the light.
Uṣas, the Daughter of the Sky, the opulent, shines foes and enmities away.

9 Shine on us with thy radiant light, O Uṣas, Daughter of the Sky,
Bringing to us great store of high felicity, and beaming on our solemn rites.

10 For in thee is each living creature's breath and life, when, Excellent ! thou dawnest forth.
Borne on thy lofty car, O Lady of the Light, hear, thou of wondrous wealth, our call.

11 O Uṣas, win thyself the strength which among men is wonderful.
Bring thou thereby the pious unto holy rites, those who as priests sing praise to thee.

12 Bring from the firmament, O Uṣas, all the Gods, that they may drink our Soma juice,
And, being what thou art, vouchsafe us kine and steeds, strength meet for praise and hero might.

13 May Uṣas whose auspicious rays are seen resplendent round about,
Grant us great riches, fair in form, of all good things, wealth which light labour may attain.

14 Mighty One, whom the Ṛṣis of old time invoked for their protection and their help,
O Uṣas, graciously answer our songs of praise with bounty and with brilliant light.

15 Uṣas, as thou with light to-day hast opened the twin doors of heaven,
So grant thou us a dwelling wide and free from foes. O Goddess, give us food with kine.

16 Bring us to wealth abundant, sent in every shape, to plentiful refreshing food,
To all-subduing splendour, Uṣas, Mighty One, to strength, thou rich in spoil and wealth.

HYMN XLIX. *Dawn.*

1 E'EN from above the sky's bright realm come, Uṣas, by auspicious ways :
Let red steeds bear thee to the house of him who pours the Soma juice.

2 The chariot which thou mountest, fair of shape, O Uṣas light to move,—
Therewith, O Daughter of the Sky, aid men of noble fame today.

3 Bright Uṣas, when thy times return, all quadrupeds and bipeds stir,
And round about flock winged birds from all the boundaries of heaven.

4 Thou dawning with thy beams of light illumest all the radiant realm.
Thee, as thou art, the Kaṇvas, fain for wealth, have called with sacred songs.

HYMN L. *Sūrya.*

1 HIS bright rays bear him up aloft, the God who knoweth all that lives,
Sūrya, that all may look on him.

2 The constellations pass away, like thieves, together with their beams,
Before the all-beholding Sun.

3 His herald rays are seen afar refulgent o'er the world of men,
Like flames of fire that burn and blaze.

4 Swift and all beautiful art thou, O Sūrya, maker of the light,
Illuming all the radiant realm.

5 Thou goest to the hosts of Gods, thou comest hither to mankind,
Hither all light to be beheld.

6 With that same eye of thine wherewith thou lookest, brilliant Varuṇa,
Upon the busy race of men,

7 Traversing sky and wide mid-air, thou metest with thy beams our days,
Sun, seeing all things that have birth.

8 Seven Bay Steeds harnessed to thy car bear thee, O thou farseeing One,
God, Sūrya, with the radiant hair.

9 Sūrya hath yoked the pure bright Seven, the daughters of the car ; with these,
His own dear team, he goeth forth.

1 *Let red steeds bear thee* : the Scholiast explains *aruṇápsavaḥ* as the purple cows, the vehicles of morning, that is, the dark red clouds that accompany the dawn.

---

1 *The God who knoweth all that live* : *jātavedasam*, here an epithet of Sūrya the Sun-God.

6 *Varuṇa* : the word is, as Sāyaṇa points out, used here as an appellative (the encompasser) and applied to Sūrya. Sāyaṇa explains it as *aniṣṭan vāraka*, averter of evil.

9 *Sūrya hath yoked the pure bright Seven* : the seven steeds that draw his car, and which, as intimately connected therewith, are called the daughters of the chariot. The number seven has reference to the seven days of the week.

10 Looking upon the loftier light above the darkness we have come
To Sūrya, God among the Gods, the light that is most excellent.

11 Rising this day, O rich in friends, ascending to the loftier heaven,
Sūrya, remove my heart's disease, take from me this my yellow hue.

12 To parrots and to starlings let us give away my yellowness,
Or this my yellowness let us transfer to Haritāla trees.

13 With all his conquering vigour this Āditya hath gone up on high,
Giving my foe into mine hand : let me not be my foeman's prey.

HYMN LI. *Indra.*

1 Make glad with songs that Ram whom many men invoke, worthy of songs of praise, Indra, the sea of wealth;
Whose gracious deeds for men spread like the heavens abroad : sing praise to him the Sage, most liberal for our good.

2 As aids the skilful Ṛbhus yearned to Indra strong to save, who fills mid-air, encompassed round with might,
Rushing in rapture; and o'er Śatakratu came the gladdening shout that urged him on to victory.

3 Thou hast disclosed the kine's stall for the Aṅgirases, and made a way for Atri by a hundred doors.
On Vimada thou hast bestowed both food and wealth, making thy bolt dance in the sacrificer's fight.

4 Thou hast unclosed the prisons of the waters; thou hast in the mountain seized the treasure rich in gifts.
When thou hadst slain with might the dragon Vṛtra, thou, Indra, didst raise the Sun in heaven for all to see.

5 With wondrous might thou blewest enchanter fiends away, with powers celestial those who called on thee in jest.
Thou, hero-hearted, hast broken down Pipru's forts, and helped Ṛjiśvan when the Dasyus were struck dead.

6 Thou savedst Kutsa when Śuṣṇa was smitten down; to Atithigva gavest Śambara for a prey.
E'en mighty Arbuda thou troddest under foot : thou from of old wast born to strike the Dasyus dead.

7 All power and might is closely gathered up in thee; thy bounteous spirit joys in drinking Soma juice.

11 'This verse and the two following constitute a *tṛca* or triplet, the repetition of which, with due formalities, is considered to be curative of disease,' Wilson.

12 The yellowness here spoken of is probably the colour of the skin in jaundice. The *hāridravá* of the text is said by Sāyaṇa to mean *haritāladruma*, a haritāla tree ; but there seems to be no tree of that name. *Haritāla*, means, usually, yellow orpiment, and *haridrava* a yellow vegetable powder. The word *hāridrava* is explained in the Petersburg Lexicon as a certain yellow bird.

To parrots and to starlings : similarly among the Romans, People with the jaundice were called 'icterici' according to Pliny (H.N. xxx. II), from the fanciful notion that the disease was cured by looking at the icterus, one of the many varieties of the sturnidae or starling family. The bird was said to die instead of the patient.

This hymn and the six following are attributed to the Ṛṣi Savya, who is called the son of Aṅgiras.

1 *That Ram* : that famous ram, Indra. See I. 10. 2. Here the reference is to a fighting-ram; or, according to Sāyaṇa, to a legend which says that Indra came in the form of a ram to Medhātithi's sacrifice, and drank the Soma juice.

2 *The skilful Ṛbhus* : see I. 20. 1. Sāyaṇa says that the Maruts are here intended, who encouraged Indra when all the Gods had deserted him.

Rushing in rapture : when exhilarated by draughts of Soma.

'Here again,' says Professor Max Müller, 'the difficulty of rendering Vedic thought in English, or any other modern language, becomes apparent, for we have no poetical word to express a high state of mental excitement produced by drinking the intoxicating juice of the Soma or other plants, which has not something opprobrious mixed up with it, while in ancient times that state of excitement was celebrated as a blessing of the gods, as not unworthy of the gods themselves, nay, as a state in which both the warrior and the poet would perform their highest achievements. The German *Rausch* is the nearest approach to the Sanskrit mada.'

In this version *mada* has generally been rendered by rapture, delight, transport, or wild joy.

Śatakratu : Indra. See I. 4. 8.

The kine's stall : the dark cloud that holds the waters imprisoned.

The Aṅgirases : an ancient priestly family. See I. 1. 6.

Atri : a Ṛṣi usually enumerated with the Aṅgirases among the *prajāpatis* or progenitors of men. Indra freed him from captivity, showing him a hundred ways of escape. *Vimada* was also a Ṛṣi of ancient times.

4. *The mountain* : the cloud. *The treasure* is the fertilizing rain.

Didst raise the Sun : according to Sāyaṇa, didst free the Sun which had been hidden by Vṛtra.

5. *Those who called on thee in jest* : literally, called on thee or offered to thee above or over the shoulder, apparently an ancient proverbial expression applied to those who instead of sacrificing to the Gods put the intended oblation into their own mouths.

Pipru is one of the demons of the air; his *forts* are the clouds that withhold the rain; *Ṛjiśván* is a pious worshipper oppressed by the Dasyus, robbers or barbarians.

6. *Śuṣṇa*, 'the Drier-up,' is the personification of the excessive heat before the rains ; a demon of drought. *Śambara* and *Arbuda* are similar demons of the atmosphere. *Atithigva* is another name of the liberal prince Divodāsa.

Known is the thunderbolt that lies within thine arms : rend off therewith all manly prowess of our foe.

8 Discern thou well Āryas and Dasyus; punishing the lawless give them up to him whose grass is strewn.
Be thou the sacrificer's strong encourager : all these thy deeds are my delight at festivals.

9 Indra gives up the lawless to the pious man, destroying by the Strong Ones those who have no strength.
Vamra when glorified destroyed the gathered piles of the still waxing great one who would reach the heaven.

10 The might which Uśanā hath formed for thee with might rends in its greatness and with strength both worlds apart.
O Hero-souled, the steeds of Vāta, yoked by thought, have carried thee to fame while thou art filled with power.

11 When Indra hath rejoiced with Kāvya Uśanā, he mounts his steeds who swerve wider and wider yet.
The Strong hath loosed his bolt with the swift rush of rain, and he hath rent in pieces Śuṣṇa's firm-built forts.

12 Thou mountest on thy car amid strong Soma draughts : Śāryāta brought thee those in which thou hast delight.
Indra, when thou art pleased with men whose Soma flows thou risest to unchallenged glory in the sky.

13 To old Kakṣivān, Soma-presser, skilled in song, O Indra, thou didst give the youthful Vṛcayā.
Thou, very wise, wast Menā, Vṛṣaṇaśva's child : those deeds of thine must all be told at Soma feasts.

14 The good man's refuge in his need is Indra, firm as a doorpost, praised among the Pajras.
Indra alone is Lord of wealth, the Giver, lover of riches, chariots, kine, and horses.

15 To him the Mighty One, the self-resplendent, verily strong and great, this praise is uttered.
May we and all the heroes, with the princes, be, in this fray, O Indra, in thy keeping.

HYMN LII. *Indra.*

1 I GLORIFY that Ram who finds the light of heaven, whose hundred nobly-natured ones go forth with him.
With hymns may I turn hither Indra to mine aid,—the Car which like a strong steed hasteth to the call.

2 Like as a mountain on firm basis, unremoved, he, thousandfold protector, waxed in mighty strength,
When Indra, joying in the draughts of Soma juice, forced the clouds, slaying Vṛtra stayer of their flow.

3 For he stays e'en the stayers, spread o'er laden cloud, rooted in light, strengthened in rapture by the wise.

8 The Āryas are, first, the people who speak the language of the Veda, and the Dasyus are the original and hostile peoples of India. Later, the former and the true and loyal people, faithful to Indra and the Gods, and the latter are the wicked and godless.

Whose grass is strewn : the faithful worshipper, the priest who has trimmed and strewn the sacred grass for the Gods.

9 *Vamra* : the second half of the stanza is unintelligible. Wilson remarks : 'The text is obscure, *Vamro vi jaghāna sandihaḥ*; Vamra destroyed the collection. The Scholiast says that a Ṛṣi named Vamra took advantage of Indra's absence from sacrifice, to carry away the accumulated heap of offerings.

10 The Ṛṣi Uśanā, called also Kāvya or Kavi's son, appears in the Veda as the especial friend of Indra. In I. 121, 12. he is said to have given Indra, his thunderbolt : 'The bolt which Kāvya Uśanā erst gave thee.' Here, also, 'the might' means the conquering thunderbolt, although in other places its fabrication is attributed to Tvaṣṭar.

The steeds of Vāta : horses of the Wind-God, horses swift as wind.

11 *When Indra hath rejoiced*: drunk the exhilarating Soma.

12 *Śāryāta* : a Rājarṣi or royal Ṛṣi of the family of Bhṛgu.

Brought thee those : draughts of Soma juice.

Thou risest to unchallenged glory : when thou hast exhilarated thyself with the Soma offered by thy worshippers thou performest thy most glorious deeds.

13 *Kakṣivān* : a Ṛṣi, son of Uśij. See I. 18. I. I. Vṛcayā, the damsel who was given to him, is not mentioned elsewhere.

Menā : according to a later legend, Indra became, himself, the daughter of Vṛṣaṇaśva.

14 *Among the Pajras* : an ancient priestly family said to be identical with the Aṅgirases.

15 *In this fray* : the hymn appears to have been addressed to Indra for aid in a coming battle.

I *That Ram* : that famous warrior. See I. 51. I.
Whose hundred nobly-natured ones : see verse 4.

3 *For he stays e'en the stayers* : the words of the text *sá hi dvaro dvariṣu vavrá ūdhani*, are very difficult. Sāyaṇa's paraphrase, adopted by Wilson, is loose but seems to give the general sense of the passage. 'He who is victorious over his enemies, who is spread through the dewy (firmament)' 'The stayer among the stayers,' is probably the conqueror who checks the demons who obstruct the rain, and *ūdhan*, the udder (of the sky) means the rain-giving clouds, over which Indra, as God of the firmament, is extended as a covering.

Indra with thought, with skilled activity, I call, most liberal giver, for he sates him with the juice.

4 Whom those that flow in heaven on sacred grass, his own assistants, nobly-natured, fill full like the sea,—
Beside that Indra when he smote down Vṛtra stood his helpers, straight in form, mighty, invincible.

5 To him, as in wild joy he fought with him who stayed the rain, his helpers sped like swift streams down a slope,
When Indra, thunder-armed, made bold by Soma draughts, as Tṛta cleaveth Vala's fences, cleft him through.

6 Splendour encompassed thee, forth shone thy warrior might: the rain-obstructer lay in mid-air's lowest deep,
What time, O Indra, thou didst cast thy thunder down upon the jaws of Vṛitra hard to be restrained.

7 The hymns which magnify thee, Indra, reach to thee even as water-brooks flow down and fill the lake.
Tvaṣṭar gave yet more force to thine appropriate strength, and forged thy thunderbolt of overpowering might.

8 When, Indra, thou whose power is linked with thy Bay Steeds hadst smitten Vṛtra, causing floods to flow for man,
Thou heldst in thine arms the metal thunderbolt, and settest in the heaven the Sun for all to see.

9 In fear they raised the lofty self-resplendent hymn, praisegiving and effectual, leading up to heaven,
When Indra's helpers fighting for the good of men, the Maruts, faithful to mankind, joyed in the light.

10 Then Heaven himself, the mighty, at that Dragon's roar reeled back in terror when, Indra, thy thunderbolt
In the wild joy of Soma had struck off with might the head of Vṛtra, tyrant of the earth and heaven.

11 O Indra, were this earth extended forth tenfold, and men who dwell therein multiplied day by day,
Still here thy conquering might, Maghavan, would be famed: it hath waxed vast as heaven in majesty and power.

12 Thou, bold of heart, in thine own native might, for help, upon the limit of this mid-air and of heaven,
Hast made the earth to be the pattern of thy strength: embracing flood and light thou reachest to the sky.

13 Thou art the counterpart of earth, the Master of lofty heaven with all its mighty Heroes:
Thou hast filled all the region with thy greatness: yea, of a truth there is none other like thee.

14 Whose amplitude the heaven and earth have not attained, whose bounds the waters of mid-air have never reached,—
Not, when in joy he fights the stayer of the rain: thou, and none else, hast made all things in order due.

15 The Maruts sang thy praise in this encounter, and in thee all the Deities delighted,
What time thou, Indra, with thy spiky weapon, thy deadly bolt, smotest the face of Vṛtra.

4 *His own assistants*: the inspiring Soma draughts.

5 *His helpers*: his constant allies, the Maruts.

As Tṛta cleaveth: Sāyaṇa refers to a legend which says that Tṛta fell into a well, and the Asuras heaped coverings over its mouth; but he broke through them with ease. So Indra broke down the defences of the demon Vala. See Wilson's note on the passage.

But Tṛta appears to be Indra's associate Agni. See Macdonell, J.R.A.S. July, 1893.

6 *The rain-obstructer*: the demon Vṛtra.

7 *Tvaṣṭar*: the Vulcan or Hephaestus of the Indian Gods.

8 *The metal thunderbolt*: *vájram āyasám*, usually translated 'iron thunderbolt'; but we do not know for certain what metal *áyas* (Latin aes) was.

9 *In fear they raised*: that is, Indra's worshippers in fear of Vṛtra.

11 If the earth were ten times as large and populous as it is, thy fame would extend over the whole of it.

14 *The waters of mid-air*: the aerial ocean the firmament.

He fights: said of Indra. We should expect 'thou fightest;' but this and similar sudden changes of person are common in the Veda.

HYMN LIII. *Indra.*

1 WE will present fair praise unto the Mighty One, our hymns to Indra in Vivasvān's dwelling-place;
For he hath ne'er found wealth in those who seem to sleep: those who give wealth to men accept no paltry praise.

2 Giver of horses, Indra, giver, thou, of kine, giver of barley, thou art Lord and guard of wealth:
Man's helper from of old, not disappointing hope, Friend of our friends, to thee as such we sing this praise.

1 *Vivasvān's dwelling-place*: the seat of the sacrificer, the representative of the celestial Vivasvān.

Those who seem to sleep: Indra derives no advantage from those who are remiss in their religious duties.

3 Indra most splendid, powerful, rich in mighty deeds, this treasure spread around is known to be thine own.
Gather therefrom, O Conqueror, and bring to us : fail not the hope of him who loves and sings to thee.

4 Well pleased with these bright flames and with these Soma drops, take thou away our poverty with seeds and kine.
With Indra scattering the Dasyu through these drops, freed from their hate may we obtain abundant food.

5 Let us obtain, O Indra, plenteous wealth and food, with strength exceeding glorious, shining to the sky :
May we obtain the Goddess Providence, the strength of heroes, special source of cattle, rich in steeds.

6 These our libations strength-inspiring, Soma draughts, gladdened thee in the fight with Vṛtra, Hero Lord,
What time thou slewest for the singer with trimmed grass ten thousand Vṛtras, thou resistless in thy might.

7 Thou goest on from fight to fight intrepidly, destroying castle after castle here with strength.
Thou, Indra, with thy friend who makes the foe bow down, slewest from far away the guileful Namuci.

8 Thou hast struck down in death Karañja, Parṇaya, in Atithigva's very glorious going forth.
Unyielding, when Ṛjiśvan compassed them with siege, thou hast destroyed the hundred forts of Vaṅgṛida.

9 With all-outstripping chariot-wheel, O Indra, thou far-famed, hast overthrown the twice ten Kings of men,
With sixty thousand nine-and-ninety followers, who came in arms to fight with friendless Suśravas.

10 Thou hast protected Suśravas with succour, and Tūrvayāṇa with thine aid, O Indra.
Thou madest Kutsa, Atithigva, Āyu, subject unto this King, the young, the mighty.

11 May we protected by the Gods hereafter remain thy very prosperous friends, O Indra.
Thee we extol, enjoying through thy favour life long and joyful and with store of heroes.

HYMN LIV. *Indra.*

1 URGE us not, Maghavan, to this distressful fight, for none may comprehend the limit of thy strength.
Thou with fierce shout hast made the woods and rivers roar : did not men run in crowds together in their fear?

2 Sing hymns of praise to Śakra, Lord of power and might ; laud thou and magnify Indra who heareth thee,
Who with his daring might, a Bull exceeding strong in strength, maketh him master of the heaven and earth.

3 Sing forth to lofty Dyaus a strength-bestowing song, the Bold, whose resolute mind hath independent sway.
High glory hath the Asura, compact of strength, drawn on by two Bay Steeds : a Bull, a Car is he.

4 The ridges of the lofty heaven thou madest shake ; thou, daring, of thyself smotest through Śambara,
When bold with gladdening juice, thou warredst with thy bolt, sharp and two-edged, against the banded sorcerers.

6 *Ten thousand Vṛtras* : countless demons like Vṛtra.

7 *With thy friend* : the thunderbolt. Or *námyā* may mean 'with Nami' as thy confederate.

Namuci : 'non-looser (of the heavenly waters)' another demon of drought.

8 *Karañja*, *Parṇaya* and *Vaṅgṛda* are Asuras or demons; *Atithigva* has been mentioned before, I. 51. 6, and Ṛjiśvan in verse 5 of the same hymn.

9. *Suśravas*, and *Tūrvayāṇa* in the next verse, are said to be kings.

10 *Kutsa* has been mentioned (I. 33. 14.) as a favourite of Indra, but is here represented, together with Atithigva and Āyu, as chastised by him.

This King : Suśravas, or Turvayāṇa these names perhaps denote the same individual.

—

1 *Urge us not, Maghavan* : the verb, urge, which is not in the text, is supplied by Sāyaṇa. The meaning appears to be, Do not, O Indra, force us into any conflict in which we may have thee for our opponent.

2 *Śakra* : 'the Mighty,' a name of Indra.

3 *Sing forth to lofty Dyaus* : Heaven. The God who is represented in the Veda as the consort of Earth and the progenitor of the Gods is called Dyaus or Dyauṣpitar, names identical in origin with Zeus, or Zeus, pater, and Jupiter, or Diespiter, the appellations given to the supreme God of the Greeks and Romans. In this place Sāyaṇa identifies Dyaus with Indra, who seems, in later times, to have succeeded to the functions assigned to the former God. See Muir, *Original Sanskrit Texts*, v. 33.

The Asura : the divine One, Indra as the supreme Dyaus.

4 *Śambara* : a demon. See I. 51. 6.

The banded sorcerers : the fiends of the atmosphere who use enchantments or supernatural powers in their conflicts with Indra.

5 When with a roar that fills the woods, thou forcest down on wind's head the stores which Śuṣṇa kept confined,
Who shall have power to stay thee firm and eager-souled from doing still this day what thou of old hast done?

6 Thou helpest Narya, Turvaśa, and Yadu, and Vayya's son Turvīti, Śatakratu !
Thou helpest horse and car in final battle ; thou breakest down the nine-and-ninety castles.

7 A hero-lord is he, King of a mighty folk, who offers free oblations and promotes the Law,
Who with a bounteous guerdon welcomes hymns of praise : for him flows down the abundant stream below the sky.

8 His power is matchless, matchless is his wisdom; chief, through their work, be some who drink the Soma,
Those, Indra, who increase the lordly power, the firm heroic strength of thee the Giver.

9 Therefore for thee are these abundant beakers Indra's drink, stone-pressed juices held in ladles.
Quaff them and satisfy therewith thy longing; then fix thy mind upon bestowing treasure.

10 There darkness stood, the vault that stayed the waters' flow: in Vṛtra's hollow side the rain-cloud lay concealed.
But Indra smote the rivers which the obstructer stayed, flood following after flood, down steep declivities.

11 So give us, Indra, bliss-increasing glory ; give us great sway and strength that conquers people.
Preserve our wealthy patrons, save our princes ; vouchsafe us wealth and food with noble offspring.

HYMN LV. *Indra.*

1 THOUGH e'en this heaven's wide space and earth have spread them out, nor heaven nor earth may be in greatness Indra's match.
Awful and very mighty, causing woe to men, he whets his thunderbolt for sharpness, as a bull.

2 Like as the watery ocean, so doth he receive the rivers spread on all sides in their ample width.
He bears him like a bull to drink of Soma juice, and will, as Warrior from of old, be praised for might.

3 Thou swayest, Indra, all kinds of great manly power, so as to bend, as't were, even that famed mountain down.
Foremost among the Gods is he through hero might, set in the van, the Strong One, for each arduous deed.

4 He only in the wood is praised by worshippers, when he shows forth to men his own fair Indra-power.
A friendly Bull is he, a Bull to be desired when Maghavan auspiciously sends forth his voice.

5 Yet verily the Warrior in his vigorous strength stirreth up with his might great battles for mankind ;
And men have faith in Indra, the resplendent One, what time he hurleth down his bolt, his dart of death.

6 Though, fain for glory, and with strength increased on earth, he with great might destroys the dwellings made with art,
He makes the lights of heaven shine forth secure, he bids, exceeding wise, the floods flow for his worshipper.

7 Drinker of Soma, let thy heart incline to give ; bring thy Bays hitherward, O thou who hearest praise.
Those charioteers of thine, best skilled to draw the rein, the rapid sunbeams, Indra, lead thee not astray.

8 Thou bearest in both hands treasure that never fails ; the famed One in his body holds unvanquished might.

5 *Śuṣṇa* : a demon of drought.

6 *Thou helpest Narya* : some chief or Ṛṣi so named or the word may be an adjective, manly, qualifying Turvaśa.

Turvaśa, Yadu, Turvīti have been mentioned before. See I. 36. 18.

—

1 *As a bull* : as a bull sharpens his horns.
Causing woe to men : as the punisher of the wicked.

4 *A friendly Bull is he* : Maghavan, the mighty Indra, is here represented in his gracious mood, strong yet gentle. But *vṛśā*, the male, the bull, the strong, may also mean the strong Soma; *maghávā* means also the rich institutor of a sacrifice, a worshipper; and *dhenā* means cow as well as voice. Accordingly Professor Max Müller translates the passage : 'The strong Soma is pleasing, the strong Soma is delicious, when the sacrificer safely brings the cow', in order that the Soma may be mixed with milk. See *Vedic Hymns*, Part I., p. 148.

In the wood, in the first line of the verse seems to be an allusion to the forest life of Brāhmans.

5 In this verse Indra is represented as a terrible God, and in the following verse as sometimes sending affliction' but generally blessing men with light and with kindly rain.

O Indra, in thy members many powers abide, like wells surrounded by the ministering priests.

HYMN LVI. *Indra.*

1 For this man's full libations held in ladles, he hath roused him, eager, as a horse to meet the mare.
He stays his golden car, yoked with Bay Horses, swift, and drinks the Soma juice which strengthens for great deeds.

2 To him the guidance-following songs of praise flow full, as those who seek gain go in company to the flood.
To him the Lord of power, the holy synod's might, as to a hill, with speed, ascend the loving ones.

3 Victorious, great is he ; in manly battle shines, unstained with dust, his might, as shines a mountain peak ;
Wherewith the iron one, fierce e'en against the strong, in rapture, fettered wily Śushṇa fast in bonds.

4 When Strength the Goddess, made more strong for help by thee, waits upon Indra as the Sun attends the Dawn,
Then he who with his might unflinching kills the gloom stirs up the dust aloft, with joy and triumphing.

5 When thou with might, upon the framework of the heaven, didst fix, across, air's region firmly, unremoved,
In the light-winning war, Indra, in rapturous joy, thou smotest Vṛtra dead and broughtest floods of rain.

6 Thou with thy might didst grasp the holder-up of heaven, thou who art mighty also in the seats of earth.
Thou, gladdened by the juice, hast set the waters free, and broken Vṛtra's stony fences through and through.

1. *This man* : the institutor of the sacrifice. *He* : Indra.

2. *The flood* : (*samudrá*) any large gathering of waters not necessarily the sea or ocean.

The holy synod : an assembly for worship of the Gods.

The loving ones : the songs of loving praise. I find the stanza unintelligible; and the version (based chiefly on Grassmann's) which I offer is merely a temporary makeshift.

3. *The iron one* : the thunderbolt, made o *áyas*, iron or other metal.

4. *By thee* : by Soma.

5. *In the light-winning war* : waged with the demons of the air for rain and the light which follows the dispersion of the clouds.

6. *The holder-up of heaven* : perhaps the thunderbolt, with which Indra maintains order.

HYMN LVII. *Indra.*

1 To him most liberal, lofty Lord of lofty wealth, verily powerful and strong, I bring my hymn,—
Whose checkless bounty, as of waters down a slope, is spread abroad for all that live, to give them strength.

2 Now all this world, for worship, shall come after thee—the offerer's libations like floods to the depth,
When the well-loved one seems to rest upon the hill, the thunderbolt of Indra, shatterer wrought of gold.

3 To him the terrible, most meet for lofty praise, like bright Dawn, now bring gifts with reverence in this rite,
Whose being, for renown, yea, Indra-power and light, have been created, like bay steeds, to move with speed.

4 Thine, Indra, praised by many, excellently rich ! are we who trusting in thy help draw near to thee.
Lover of praise, none else but thou receives our laud : as earth loves all her creatures, love thou this our hymn.

5 Great is thy power, O Indra, we are thine. Fulfil, O Maghavan, the wish of this thy worshipper.
After thee lofty heaven hath measured out its strength : to thee and to thy power this earth hath bowed itself.

6 Thou, who hast thunder for thy weapon, with thy bolt hast shattered into pieces this broad massive cloud.
Thou hast sent down the obstructed floods that they may flow : thou hast, thine own for ever, all victorious might.

HYMN LVIII. *Agni.*

1 Ne'er waxeth faint the Immortal, Son of Strength, since he, the Herald, hath become Vivasvān's messenger.
On paths most excellent he measured out

2. *When the well-loved one* : when the lightning-laden cloud is resting on the mountain, men pray to Indra in order that he may discharge his celestial artillery and bring down the rain.

5. *After thee* : the heaven has taken thy might as a pattern for its own might.

This Hymn and the five following are ascribed to Nodhas, the son of Gotama.

1. *Vivasvān's messenger* : Vivasvān is the morning heaven and personification of the sacrificer of the Gods.

He measured out mid-air : this act is ascribed to Indra in I. 56. 5.

mid-air: he with oblation calls to service of the Gods.

2 Never decaying, seizing his appropriate food, rapidly, eagerly through the dry wood he spreads.

His back, as he is sprinkled, glistens like a horse : loud hath he roared and shouted like the heights of heaven?

3 Set high in place o'er all that Vasus, Rudras do, immortal, Lord of riches, seated as High Priest;

Hastening like a car to men, to those who live, the God without delay gives boons to be desired.

4 Urged by the wind he spreads through dry wood as he lists, armed with his tongues for sickles, with a mighty roar.

Black is thy path, Agni, changeless, with glittering waves! when like a bull thou rushest eager to the trees.

5 With teeth of flame, wind-driven, through the wood he speeds, triumphant like a bull among the herd of cows,

With bright strength roaming to the everlasting air: things fixed, things moving quake before him as he flies.

6 The Bhṛgus established thee among mankind for men, like as a treasure, beauteous, easy to invoke;

Thee, Agni, as a herald and choice-worthy guest, as an auspicious Friend to the Celestial Race.

7 Agni, the seven tongues' deftest Sacrificer, him whom the priests elect at solemn worship,

The Herald, messenger of all the Vasus, I serve with dainty food, I ask for riches.

8 Grant, Son of Strength, thou rich in friends, a refuge without a flaw this day to us thy praisers.

O Agni, Son of Strength, with forts of iron preserve thou from distress the man who lauds thee.

9 Be thou a refuge, Bright One, to the singer, a shelter, Bounteous Lord, to those who worship.

Preserve the singer from distress, O Agni. May he, enriched with prayer, come soon and early.

2 *As he is sprinkled* : with clarified butter.

3 *Vasus, Rudras* : two classes of Gods. See I. 34. 11.

4 The description of Agni in this verse and the next applies, not to the sacrificial fire, but to the fire that clears the jungle as the new settlers advance into the country.

6 *The Bhṛgus* : one of the most eminent priestly families of more ancient times.

Friend to the Celestial Race : as bearing to the Gods the oblations of their worshippers.

7 *Agni, the seven tongues' deftest Sacrificer* : the seven tongues appear to be the tongue-like flames which Agni employs to consume the oblations.

HYMN LIX. *Agni.*

1 The other fires are, verily, thy branches; the Immortals all rejoice in thee, O Agni.

Centre art thou, Vaiśvānara, of the people, sustaining men like a deep-founded pillar.

2 The forehead of the sky, earth's centre, Agni became the messenger of earth and heaven.

Vaiśvānara, the Deities produced thee, a God, to be a light unto the Ārya.

3 As in the Sun firm rays are set for ever, treasures are in Vaiśvānara, in Agni.

Of all the riches in the hills, the waters, the herbs, among mankind, thou art the Sovran.

4 As the great World-halves, so are their Son's praises; skilled, as a man, to act, is he the Herald.

Vaiśvānara, celestial, truly mighty, most manly One, hath many a youthful consort.

5 Even the lofty heaven, O Jātavedas Vaiśvānara, hath not attained thy greatness.

Thou art the King of lands where men are settled, thou hast brought comfort to the Gods in battle.

6 Now will I tell the greatness of the Hero whom Pūru's sons follow as Vṛtra's slayer:

Agni Vaiśvānara struck down the Dasyu, cleave Śambara through and shattered down his fences.

1 *Thy branches* : merely offshoots of thee.

Vaiśvānara : a name of Agni; common to, dwelling with, and benefiting all Ārya men.

4 Vast as heaven and earth, which constitute the world, are the praises offered to Agni their son.

Skilled, as a man, to act : duties of the heavenly Hotar, invoking priest, or herald, being regarded as similar to those of the earthly functionary.

Many a youthful consort : the flames.

6 *Pūru's sons* : men in general; Pūru being regarded as their progenitor.

Struck down the Dasyu : the demon who stayed the rain. The deeds usually ascribed to Indra are here attributed to Agni, that is, Agni is identified with Indra.

7 Vaiśvānara, dwelling by his might with all men, far-shining, holy mid the Bharadvājas,
Is lauded, excellent, with hundred praises by Purūṇītha, son of Śatavani.

HYMN LX. *Agni.*

1 As 'twere some goodly treasure Mātariśvan brought, as a gift, the glorious Priest to Bhṛgu,
Banner of sacrifice, the good Protector, child of two births, the swiftly moving envoy.

2 Both Gods and men obey this Ruler's order, Gods who are worshipped, men who yearn and worship.
As Priest he takes his seat ere break of morning, House-Lord, adorable with men, Ordainer.

3 May our fair praise, heart-born, most recent, reach him whose tongue, e'en at his birth, is sweet as honey;
Whom mortal priests, men, with their strong endeavour, supplied with dainty viands, have created.

4 Good to mankind, the yearning Purifier hath among men been placed as Priest choice-worthy.
May Agni be our Friend, Lord of the Household, protector of the riches in the dwelling.

5 As such we Gotamas with hymns extol thee, O Agni, as the guardian Lord of riches,
Decking thee like a horse, the swift prize-winner. May he, enriched with prayer, come soon and early.

7 *The Bharadvājas* : the descendants of the Ṛṣi Bharadvāja.

Purūṇītha : a king of that name, says Sāyaṇa; probably the institutor of the sacrifice. The name does not occur again, and nothing is known regarding him.

---

1 *Mātariśvan* : a divine or semi-divine being, who as the messenger of Vivasvān brings down from heaven Agni who had hitherto been concealed. The explanation of Mātariśvan as Vāyu, the God of wind, does not appear to be justified by Ṛgveda texts. See Muir, *O. S. Texts*, v. 204.

The glorious Priest : Agni. *Bhṛgu* : the chief of the ancient priestly family who bear that name. *Banner of sacrifice* : announcer of sacrifice by his crackling flames. *Child of two births* : born of heaven and earth and again from the two fire-sticks, when he is consecrated.

Swiftly moving envoy : messenger between Gods and men. See I.1. 1. note.

3 *Sweet as honey* : with tasting the sweet libations. *Have created* : by rapid agitation of the fire-stick.

5 *We Gotamas* : descendants of Gotama, men of the family to which the Ṛṣi of the hymn belongs.

Decking thee : trimming thee, to make thee shine as men groom a race-horse in the morning.

HYMN LXI *Indra.*

1 Even to him, swift, strong, and high-exalted, I bring my song of praise as dainty viands,
My thought to him resistless, praise-deserving, prayers offered most especially to Indra.

2 Praise, like oblation, I present, and utter aloud my song, my fair hymn to the Victor.
For Indra, who is Lord of old, the singers have decked their lauds with heart and mind and spirit.

3 To him then with my lips mine adoration, winning heaven's light, most excellent, I offer,
To magnify with songs of invocation and with fair hymns the Lord, most bounteous Giver.

4 Even for him I frame a laud, as fashions the wright a chariot for the man who needs it,—
Praises to him who gladly hears our praises, a hymn well-formed, all-moving, to wise Indra.

5 So with my tongue I deck, to please that Indra, my hymn, as 'twere a horse, through love of glory,
To reverence the Hero, bounteous Giver, famed far and wide, destroyer of the castles.

6 Even for him hath Tvaṣṭar forged the thunder, most deftly wrought, celestial, for the battle,
Wherewith he reached the vital parts of Vṛtra, striking—the vast, the mighty—with the striker.

7 As soon as, at libations of his mother, great Viṣṇu had drunk up the draught, he plundered.
The dainty cates, the cooked mess; but

4 *For the man who needs it* : and orders it to be made. *Tátsināya* is a difficult word. Wilson renders it, after Sāyaṇa, (that the driver) may, thence, (obtain) food.

5 *The castles* : the strongholds of the atmospheric demons of drought, the castles of rain-imprisoning cloud.

6 *The striker* : the thunderbolt or lightning.

7 *His mother* Indra's mother Aditi who gave him Soma to drink as soon as he was born. See III. 32. 9, 10; 48. 2. 3; VII. 98. 3. *Dainty cates* : the demon's store of rain. *One stronger* : the mightier Indra. *The wild boar* : the fierce demon Vṛtra. Cf. VIII. 66. 10. *The mountain* : the massive cloud in which Vṛtra was enveloped. For my corrected version of this stanza I am indebted to Prof. A.A. Macdonell's article on Mythological Studies in the Ṛgveda, Royal Asiatic Society Journal, January, 1895.

One stronger transfixed the wild boar, shooting through the mountain.

8 To him, to Indra, when he slew the Dragon, the Dames, too, Consorts of the Gods, wove praises.
The mighty heaven and earth hath he encompassed : thy greatness heaven and earth, combined, exceed not.

9 Yea, of a truth, his magnitude surpasseth the magnitude of earth, mid-air, and heaven.
Indra, approved by all men, self-resplendent, waxed in his home, loud-voiced and strong for battle.

10 Through his own strength Indra with bolt of thunder cut piece-meal Vṛtra, drier up of waters.
He let the floods go free, like cows imprisoned, for glory, with a heart inclined to bounty.

11 The rivers played, through his impetuous splendour, since with his bolt he compassed them on all sides.
Using his might and favouring him who worshipped, he made a ford, victorious, for Turvīti.

12 Vast, with thine ample power, with eager movement, against this Vṛtra cast thy bolt of thunder.
Rend thou his joints, as of an ox, dissevered, with bolt oblique, that floods of rain may follow.

13 Sing with new lauds his exploits wrought aforetime, the deeds of him, yea, him who moveth swiftly,
When, hurling forth his weapons in the battle, he with impetuous wrath lays low the foemen.

14 When he, yea, he, comes forth the firm-set mountains and the whole heaven and earth, tremble for terror.
May Nodhas, ever praising the protection of that dear Friend, gain quickly strength heroic.

15 Now unto him of these things hath been given what he who rules alone o'er much, electeth.
Indra hath helped Etaśa, Soma-presser, contending in the race of steeds with Sūrya.

16 Thus to thee, Indra, yoker of Bay Coursers, the Gotamas have brought their prayers to please thee.
Bestow upon them thought, decked with all beauty. May he, enriched with prayer, come soon and early.

8 *The Dames, the Consorts of the Gods* : according to Sāyaṇa these are the personified Gāyatrī and other metres of the Veda. The Celestial Waters are probably intended.

11. *Turvīti* : Sāyaṇa says that this Ṛṣi had been immersed in water, and that Indra brought him to dry land.

14 *Nodhas* : the Ṛṣi or seer of the hymn.

15 Praises and sacrifice have been offered to Indra. He himself possesses everything else. Such praises and sacrifice led Indra to help Etaśa, his worshipper, in his rivalry of Sūrya and his horses. See II. 19. 5, note.

16 The hymn ends with the refrain that concludes also Hymns I. 58 and 60.

HYMN LXII. *Indra.*

1. LIKE Aṅgiras a gladdening laud we ponder to him who loveth song, exceeding mighty.
Let us sing glory to the far-famed Hero who must be praised with fair hymns by the singer.

2 Unto the great bring ye great adoration, a chant with praise to him exceeding mighty,
Through whom our sires, Aṅgirases, singing praises and knowing well the places, found the cattle.

3 When Indra and the Aṅgirases desired it, Saramā found provision for her offspring.
Bṛhaspati cleft the mountain, found the cattle : the heroes shouted with the kine in triumph.

4 Mid shout, loud shout, and roar, with the

1 *Like Aṅgiras* : after the manner of Aṅgiras, one of the first institutors of religious ceremonies.

2 *Found the cattle* : the rain-clouds, or the rays of light which follow the effusion of rain.

3 *Saramā found provision for her offspring* : Saramā, the hound of Indra and mother of the two dogs called after their mother Sārameyas who are the watchdogs of Yama the God of the Dead, is said to have pursued and recovered the cows stolen by the Paṇis; which has been supposed to mean that Saramā is the Dawn who recovers the rays of the Sun that have been carried away by night. The legend says that Saramā agreed to go in search of the stolen cattle on condition that the milk of the cows should be given to her young ones. Ludwig is of opinion that the word 'offspring' in the text refers not to Saramā's young ones, but to the decendants of the Aṅgirases Cf. I. 72. 8.

Bṛhaspati cleft the mountain : Bṛhaspati or Brahamaṇaspati is the Lord of prayer. 'It is, therefore,' as Professor Roth observes, 'brahma, prayer, with which the God breaks open the hiding-place of the enemy. Prayer pierces through to the object of its desire, and attains it.'

4 The *seven singers* are probably the Aṅgirases themselves : the *Navagvas* and *Daśagvas* are also the Aṅgirases or their priestly allies. They are called *speeder* as hastily following the track of the stolen cows. *Vala* is the fiend who keeps the cows imprisoned.

Navagvas, seven singers, hast thou, heavenly, rent the mountain;
Thou hast, with speeders, with Daśagvas, Indra, Śakra, with thunder rent obstructive Vala.

5 Praised by Aṅgirases, thou, foe-destroyer, hast, with the Dawn, Sun, rays, dispelled the darkness.
Thou Indra, hast spread out the earth's high ridges, and firmly fixed the region under heaven.

6 This is the deed most worthy of all honour, the fairest marvel of the Wonder-Worker,
That, nigh where heaven bends down, he made four rivers flow full with waves that carry down sweet water.

7 Unwearied, won with lauding hymns, he parted of old the ancient Pair, united ever.
In highest sky, like Bhaga, he the doer of marvels set both Dames and earth and heaven.

8 Still born afresh, young Dames, each in her manner, unlike in hue, the Pair in alternation
Round heaven and earth from ancient time have travelled, Night with her dark limbs, Dawn with limbs of splendour.

9 Rich in good actions, skilled in operation, the Son with might maintains his perfect friendship.
Thou in the raw cows, black of hue or ruddy, storest the ripe milk glossy white in colour.

10 Their paths, of old connected, rest uninjured; they with great might preserve the immortal statutes.
For many thousand holy works the Sisters wait on the haughty Lord like wives and matrons.

11 Thoughts ancient, seeking wealth, with adoration, with newest lauds have sped to thee, O Mighty.
As yearning wives cleave to their yearning husband, so cleave our hymns to thee, O Lord most potent.

12 Strong God, the riches which thy hands have holden from days of old have perished not nor wasted.
Splendid art thou, O Indra, wise, unbending : strengthen us with might, O Lord of Power.

13 O mighty Indra, Gotama's son Nodhas hath fashioned this new prayer to thee Eternal,
Sure leader, yoker of the Tawny Coursers. May he, enriched with prayer, come soon and early.

6 *Nigh where heaven bends down* : flowing away to the distant horizon. The *four rivers* are not specified by Sāyaṇa, who merely says they are the Ganges and others.

7 *The ancient Pair* : Heaven and Earth. *Bhaga* is here the Supreme God. *Both Dames* : Night and Morning.

9 *The Son with might* : Sāyaṇa takes *śávasā*, 'with might,' in the sense of the genitive *śávasaḥ*, and explains : the Son of Might, that is the exceedingly strong one. But this seems forced. *The son* is Indra.

Thou in the raw cows : the cows are called raw, as contrasted with the warm milk matured or cooked in their udders. The colour of the milk is also contrasted with that of the cows, as in the German child's ditty quoted by Zimmer: 'O sage mir, wie geht es zu, gibt weisse Milch die rothe Kuh.'

10 *Their paths* : the courses of Night and Morning.

The Sisters : a frequently occurring appellation of the fingers as employed in acts of worship. *The haughty Lord* : Indra.

HYMN LXIII. *Indra.*

1. THOU art the Mighty One ; when born, O Indra, with power thou terrifiedst earth and heaven;
When, in their fear of thee, all firm-set mountains and monstrous creatures shook like dust before thee.

2 When thy two wandering Bays thou dravest hither, thy praiser laid within thine arms the thunder,
Wherewith, O Much-invoked, in will resistless, thou smitest foemen down and many a castle.

3 Faithful art thou, these thou defiest, Indra; thou art the Ṛbhus' Lord, heroic, victor.
Thou, by his side, for young and glorious Kutsa, with steed and car in battle slewest Śuṣṇa,

4 That, as a friend, thou furtheredst, O Indra, when, Thunderer, strong in act, thou crushedst Vṛtra ;
When, Hero, thou, great-souled, with easy conquest didst rend the Dasyus in their distant dwelling.

2 *Thy praiser* : the praises of the worshipper strengthen Indra, and urge him to the performance of glorious exploits.

3 *The Ṛbhus' Lord* : Chief over the three semi-divine beings who by their good works raised themselves to immortality and godhead. See I. 20. *Kutsa* : has been mentioned before as protected by Indra. See I. 33. 14; 51. 6.

4 *Dasyus* : hostile demons, or perhaps savage tribes.

5 This doest thou, and art not harmed, O Indra, e'en in the anger of the strongest mortal.
Lay thou the race-course open for our horses : as with a club, slay, Thunder-armed ! our foemen.

6 Hence men invoke thee, Indra, in the tumult of battle, in the light-bestowing conflict.
This aid of thine, O Godlike One, was ever to be implored in deeds of might in combat.

7 Warring for Purukutsa thou, O Indra, Thunder-armed ! breakest down the seven castles ;
Easily, for Sudās, like grass didst rend them, and out of need, King, broughtest gain to Pūru.

8 O Indra, God who movest round about us, feed us with varied food plenteous as water—
Food wherewithal, O Hero, thou bestowest vigour itself to flow to us for ever.

9 Prayers have been made by Gotamas, O Indra, addressed to thee, with laud for thy Bay Horses.
Bring us in noble shape abundant riches. May he, enriched with prayer, come soon and early.

HYMN LXIV. *Maruts.*

1. Bring for the manly host, wise and majestical, O Nodhas, for the Maruts bring thou a pure gift.
I deck my songs as one deft-handed, wise in mind prepares the water that hath power in solemn rites.

2 They spring to birth, the lofty Ones, the Bulls of Heaven, divine, the youths of Rudra, free from spot and stain;
The purifiers, shining brightly even as suns, awful of form like giants, scattering rain-drops down.

3 Young Rudras, demon-slayers, never growing old, they have waxed, even as mountains, irresistible.
They make all beings tremble with their mighty strength, even the very strongest, both of earth and heaven.

4 With glittering ornaments they deck them forth for show ; for beauty on their breasts they bind their chains of gold.
The lances on their shoulders pound to pieces ; they were born together, of themselves, the Men of Heaven.

5 Loud roarers, giving strength, devourers of the foe, they make the winds, they make the lightnings with their powers.
The restless shakers drain the udders of the sky, and ever wandering round fill the earth full with milk.

6 The bounteous Maruts with the fatness-dropping milk fill full the waters which avail in solemn rites.
They lead, as 'twere, the Strong Horse forth, that it may rain: they milk the thundering, the never-failing spring.

7 Mighty, with wondrous power and marvellously bright, selfstrong like mountains, ye glide swiftly on your way.
Like the wild elephants ye eat the forests up when ye assume your strength among the bright red flames.

8 Exceeding wise they roar like lions mightily, they, all-possessing, are beauteous as antelopes ;
Stirring the darkness with lances and spotted deer, combined as priests, with serpents' fury through their might.

9 Heroes who march in companies, befriending man, with serpents' ire through strength, ye greet the earth and heaven.
Upon the seats, O Maruts, of your chariots, upon the cars stands lightning visible as light.

7 *Purukutsa* : a favourite of Indra and of the Aśvins. See I. 112. 7; 174. 2; IV. 42. 8, note. *Sudās* (See I. 47. 6) and *Pūru* are kings or chiefs of clans.

8 *Who movest round about us*; *parijman*, circumambient, is an epithet applied to the Sun also and to the chariot of the Aśvins.

9 *With laud for thy Bay Horses* : this is clearly the sense of the words as they stand. Sāyaṇa explains 'with reverence to thee connected with thy bay horses.'

---

1 *O Nodhas* : the Ṛṣi or seer of the hymn addresses this line to Nodhas.

2 *The Bulls of Heaven* : or of Dyu or Dyaus.

3 *Young Rudras* : the Maruts, or Storm-Gods, are the sons of Rudra.

Demon-slayers : slayers of the clouds that give no rain.

4 *The lances*, as well as their other bright ornaments, are the lightning flashes.

5 *The udders of the sky* : the full clouds. *The milk*, is the sweet fertilizing rain.

6 *The Strong Horse* : is the rain cloud, which in the same line is called a spring or well.

8 *Combined as priests* : the music of wind and storm being regarded as the Maruts' song of praise. But the meaning of the words thus rendered is not clear. Sāyaṇa, Benfey, and Max Müller give other interpretations.

10 Lords of all riches, dwelling in the home of wealth, endowed with mighty vigour, singers loud of voice,
Heroes, of powers infinite, armed with strong men's rings, the archers, they have laid the arrow on their arms.

11 They who with golden fellies make the rain increase drive forward the big clouds like wanderers on the way.
Self-moving, brisk, unwearied, they o'er-throw the firm ; the Maruts with bright lances make all things to reel.

12 The progeny of Rudra we invoke with prayer, the brisk, the bright, the worshipful, the active Ones
To the strong band of Maruts cleave for happiness, the chasers of the sky, impetuous, vigorous.

13 Maruts, the man whom ye have guarded with your help, he verily in strength surpasseth all mankind.
Spoil with his steeds he gaineth, treasure with his men ; he winneth honourable strength and prospereth.

14 O Maruts, to the worshippers give glorious strength invincible in battle, brilliant, bringing wealth,
Praiseworthy, known to all men. May we foster well, during a hundred winters, son and progeny.

15 Will ye then, O ye Maruts, grant us riches, durable, rich in men, defying onslaught.
A hundred, thousandfold, ever increasing ? May he, enriched with prayer, come soon and early.

HYMN LXV.* *Agni.*

1. ONE-MINDED, wise, they tracked thee like a thief lurking in dark cave with a stolen cow ;
Thee claiming worship, bearing it to Gods : there nigh to thee sate all the Holy Ones.

2 The Gods approached the ways of holy Law ; there was a gathering vast as heaven itself.
The waters feed with praise the growing Babe, born nobly in the womb, the seat of Law.

3 Like grateful food, like some wide dwelling-place, like a fruit-bearing hill, a whole-some stream.
Like a steed urged to run in swift career, rushing like Sindhu, who may check his course ?

4 Kin as a brother to his sister floods, he eats the woods as a King eats the rich.
When through the forest, urged by wind, he spreads, verily Agni shears the hair of earth.

5 Like a swan sitting in the floods he pants ; wisest in mind mid men he wakes at morn.
A Sage like Soma, sprung from Law, he grew like some young creature, mighty, shining far.

HYMN LXVI. *Agni.*

1. LIKE the Sun's glance, like wealth of varied sort, like breath which is the life, like one's own son,
Like a swift bird, a cow who yields her milk, pure and refulgent to the wood he speeds.

2 He offers safety like a pleasant home, like ripened corn, the Conqueror of men.

10 *Armed with strong men's rings* : the meaning of *vṛṣakhādayaḥ* is uncertain; but the *khādi* seems to have been a ring worn on the arm and foot. It may also have been used as a weapon, as the sharp-edged quoits are used by the Sikhs. *Vṛṣan*, as Professor Max Müller observes, 'conveys the meaning of strong, though possibly with the implied idea of rain-producing, ferti-lizing'.

12 *The worshipful* : the meaning of *vaninam* is uncertain. Wilson, after Sāyaṇa, translates it by 'water shedding,' *vana* being said to mean water. Ludwig suggests 'dwelling in the woods,' instead of 'fighting' which he gives in his translation. 'Worshipful' is Professor Max Müller's suggestion, and I adopt it for the present.

15 *Enriched with prayer* : either,generally, invoked by many worshippers, or rich through the hymn just recited. This last hemistich is the usual refrain of the hymns ascribed to Nodhas.

I have generally followed Professor Max Müller in his translation of this hymn. See his *Vedic Hymns*, Part I.

*This and the eight following hymns are ascribed to the Ṛṣi Parāśara, son of Śakti the son of Vasiṣṣha. They are generally difficult, and not seldom unintelligible.

1 *They tracked thee* : the Gods followed Agni who had fled away, carrying with him the sacrifice as a thief carries off a cow. The *dark cave* is the depth of the waters in which Agni hid himself.

2 *The seat of Law* : the place of sacrifice, the law ordained for ever.

3 *Sindhu* : the Indus, or any great river.

4 *As a King eats the rich* supports his state by levy-ing contributions from the wealthy.

The hair of earth : grass and shrubs, which forest-fires destroy.

5 *He pants* : after his rapid flight to the waters in which he hid himself.

He wakes at morn : at the time of the early morn-ing sacrifice.

A Sage like Soma : like the deified Soma. 'As Soma creates or causes useful plants to grow, so Agni creates, or extracts from them, their nutritive faculty,—Wilson (from Sāyaṇa).

---

2 *Like a steed* : like a war-horse who helps to win spoil in battle.

Like a Seer lauding, famed among the folk ; like a steed friendly he vouchsafes us power.

3 With flame insatiate, like eternal might; caring for each one like a dame at home ;
Bright when he shines forth, whitish mid the folk, like a car, gold-decked, thundering to the fight.

4 He strikes with terror like a dart shot forth, e'en like an archer's arrow tipped with flame;
Master of present and of future life, the maidens' lover and the matrons' Lord.

5 To him lead all your ways : may we attain the kindled God as cows their home at eve.
He drives the flames below as floods their swell : the rays rise up to the fair place of heaven.

HYMN LXVII. *Agni.*

1. VICTORIOUS in the wood, Friend among men, ever he claims obedience as a King.
Gracious like peace, blessing like mental power, Priest was he, offering-bearer, full of thought.

2 He, bearing in his hand all manly might, crouched in the cavern, struck the Gods with fear.
Men filled with understanding find him there, when they have sung prayers formed within their heart.

3 He, like the Unborn, holds the broad earth up; and with effective utterance fixed the sky.
O Agni, guard the spots which cattle love: thou, life of all, hast gone from lair to lair.

4 Whoso hath known him dwelling in his lair, and hath approached the stream of holy Law,—
They who release him, paying sacred rites, —truly to such doth he announce great wealth.

5 He who grows mightily in herbs, within each fruitful mother and each babe she bears,
Wise, life of all men, in the waters' home,—for him have sages built as 'twere a seat.

HYMN LXVIII. *Agni.*

1. COMMINGLING, restless, he ascends the sky, unveiling nights and all that stands or moves,
As he the sole God is preëminent in greatness among all these other Gods.

2 All men are joyful in thy power, O God, that living from the dry wood thou art born.
All truly share thy Godhead while they keep, in their accustomed ways, eternal Law.

3 Strong is the thought of Law, the Law's behest; all works have they performed; he quickens all.
Whoso will bring oblation, gifts to thee, to him, bethinking thee, vouchsafe thou wealth.

4 Seated as Priest with Manu's progeny, of all these treasures he alone is Lord.
Men yearn for children to prolong their line, and are not disappointed in their hope.

5 Eagerly they who hear his word fulfil his wish as sons obey their sire's behest.

4 *The maidens' lover* : the offering to Agni being an essential part of the marriage-service.

The matrons' Lord : children being especially the gift of Agni, in whose worship the wife of the sacrificer bears an important part. I have not attempted to imitate the rhythm of the original, and have contented myself with preserving the same number of syllables in each line.

---

1 *Victorious in the wood* : subduing the fuel and burning it to ashes.

2 *Couched in the cavern* : concealed in the dark depth of the waters. See I. 65. 1.

3 *The Unborn* : the Sun ; regarded as the Supreme God.

The spots which cattle love : as thou knowest by experience how pleasant it is to find a safe place of refuge, do not burn up the places where the cattle find refuge and food.

4 *The stream of holy Law* : or as Sāyaṇa explains, the supporter of the truth or of sacrifice, that is, Agni.

They who release him : free him, by attrition, from the fire-sticks.

---

1 *Commingling* : Agni, devouring and fusing together with his flames and smoke the elements of the oblations which he bears to the Gods.

3 I can make nothing of the first hemistich. Wilson, after Sāyaṇa, paraphrases : 'Praises are addressed to him who has repaired (to the solemnity) ; oblations are offered to him who has gone (to the sacrifice); in him is all sustenance; (and to him) have all (devout persons) performed (the customary) rites'.

4 *Manu's progeny* : all Āryan men.

Men yearn for children : men have children at their desire, as the reward of their faithful worship of Agni.

5 *He, the House-Friend* : he Agni, who is the friend and guardian of every house in his character of the household fire, as the Sun, the Creator, the Supreme God, made the heaven and adorned it with stars.

He, rich in food, unbars his wealth like doors : he, the House-Friend, hath decked heaven's vault with stars.

HYMN LXIX. *Agni.*

1. BRIGHT, splendid, like Dawn's lover, he hath filled the two joined worlds as with the light of heaven.
When born, with might thou hast encompassed them : Father of Gods, and yet their Son wast thou.

2 Agni, the Sage, the humble, who discerns like the cow's udder, the sweet taste of food,
Like a bliss-giver to be drawn to men, sits gracious in the middle of the house.

3 Born in the dwelling like a lovely son, pleased, like a strong steed, he bears on the folk.
What time the men and I, with heroes, call, may Agni then gain all through Godlike power.

4 None breaks these holy laws of thine when thou hast granted audience to these chieftains here.
This is thy boast, thou smotest with thy peers, and joined with heroes dravest off disgrace.

Like the Dawn's lover, spreading light, well-known as hued like morn, may he remember me.
They, bearing of themselves, unbar the doors : they all ascend to the fair place of heaven.

HYMN LXX. *Agni.*

1. MAY we, the pious, win much food by prayer, may Agni with fair light pervade each act,—
He the observer of the heavenly laws of Gods, and of the race of mortal man.

2 He who is germ of waters, germ of woods, germ of all things that move not and that move,—
To him even in the rock and in the house: Immortal One, he cares for all mankind.

3 Agni is Lord of riches for the man who serves him readily with sacred songs.
Protect these beings thou with careful thought, knowing the races both of Gods and men.

4 Whom many dawns and nights, unlike, make strong, whom, born in Law, all things that move and stand,—
He hath been won, Herald who sits in light, making effectual all our holy works.

5 Thou settest value on our cows and woods: all shall bring tribute to us to the light.
Men have served thee in many and sundry spots, parting, as 'twere, an aged father's wealth.

6 Like a brave archer, like one skilled and bold, a fierce avenger, so he shines in fight.

HYMN LXXI. *Agni.*

1. LOVING the loving One, as wives their husband, the sisters of one home have urged him forward,
Bright-coloured, even as the cows love morning, dark, breaking forth to view, and redly beaming.

2 Our sires with lauds burst e'en the firmset fortress, yea, the Aṅgirases, with roar, the mountain.
They made for us a way to reach high heaven, they found us day, light, day's sign, beams of morning.

3 They stablished order, made his service fruitful ; then parting them among the longing faithful,

1 *Like Dawn's lover* : both the Sun and Agni are called the lovers of Uṣas or Dawn. Agni is so called from his making his appearance as sacrificial fire at the earliest break of day.

The two joined worlds : earth and heaven coupled into a single dual conception.

2 *Like the cow's udder* ; Agni discerns and selects the sweet savours of oblations in the same manner as the udder of a cow selects and assimilates the sweet juices of grass and herbs for the production of milk.

3 The meaning of the second hemistich is not clear. Wilson, after Sāyaṇa, renders it : 'Whatever (divine) beings I may, along with other men, invoke (to the ceremony) thou, Agni, assumest all (their) celestial natures.'

5 *They, bearing of themselves* ; either, his rays bearing up the oblation of their own accord, or the steeds who freely draw the chariot of Dawn.

---

1 *Pervade each act* ; be present and regulate all our acts of worship; or the meaning may be 'attain each gift,' receive every oblation that we offer.

2 *To him even in the rock* ; I can make nothing out of this. Wilson, after Sāyaṇa, paraphrases : '(They offer oblations) on the mountain, or in the mansion, to that Agni ;' but this cannot be the meaning. Ludwig suggests an alteration of the text, so that the meaning would be, 'even within the stone is his dwelling.'

5 'Agni, confer excellence upon our valued cattle; and may all men bring us acceptable tribute.'—Wilson.

---

1 *The loving One*, : Agni. *The sisters of one home* ; the fingers that serve him by kindling the fire, etc. *The cows* : the clouds brightened by the approach of Dawn.

2 The priestly Aṅgirases, the earliest institutors of religious worship, caused by prayer and praise the mountain-like cloud, that held the rain imprisoned, to be opened.

3 *His service* ; the worship of Agni.

Not thirsting after aught, they come, most active, while with sweet food the race of Gods they strengthen.

4 Since Mātariśvan, far-diffused, hath stirred him, and he in every house grown bright and noble,
He, Bhṛgu-like, hath gone as his companion, as on commission to a greater Sovran.

5 When man poured juice to Heaven, the mighty Father, he knew and freed himself from close embracement.
The archer boldly shot at him his arrow, and the God threw his splendour on his Daughter.

6 Whoso hath flames for thee within his dwelling, or brings the worship which thou lovest daily,
Do thou of double might increase his substance: may he whom thou incitest meet with riches.

7 All sacrificial viands wait on Agni as the Seven mighty Rivers seek the ocean.
Not by our brethren was our food discovered: find with the Gods care for us, thou who knowest.

8 When light hath filled the Lord of men for increase, straight from the heaven descends the limpid moisture.
Agni hath brought to light and filled with spirit the youthful host blameless and well providing.

9 He who like thought goes swiftly on his journey, the Sun, alone is ever Lord of riches.
The Kings with fair hands, Varuṇa and Mitra, protect the precious nectar in our cattle.

10 O Agni, break not our ancestral friendship, Sage as thou art, endowed with deepest knowledge.
Old age, like gathering cloud, impairs the body: before that evil be come nigh protect me.

4 *Mātariśvan* : the divine or semi-divine being who brought Agni to Bhṛgu.

5 This verse is very obscure. The meaning of the first hemistich seems to be that when oblations were offered to Dyaus or Heaven Agni shone forth freed from encompassing night. Who the archer is, whether Mātariśvan or Agni, is uncertain, nor is it clear at whom the arrow was shot. *The God* may be Dyaus, and *his Daughter* may be Uṣas or Dawn.

7 *The Seven mighty Rivers* : see I. 32 12.

Not by our brethren ; we do not look to our kinsmen for food, but depend upon Agni and the other Gods.

8 *The Lord of men* : according to Sāyaṇa, the sacrificer. Perhaps Indra is meant who comes attended by *the youthful host* of Maruts.

HYMN LXXII. *Agni.*

1. THOUGH holding many gifts for men, he humbleth the higher powers of each wise ordainer.
Agni is now the treasure-lord of treasures, for ever granting all immortal bounties.

2 The Gods infallible all searching found not him, the dear Babe who still is round about us.
Worn weary, following his track, devoted, they reached the lovely highest home of Agni.

3 Because with holy oil the pure Ones, Agni, served thee the very pure three autumn seasons,
Therefore they won them holy names for worship, and nobly born they dignified their bodies.

4 Making them known to spacious earth and heaven, the holy Ones revealed the powers of Rudra.
The mortal band, discerning in the distance, found Agni standing in the loftiest station.

5 Nigh they approached, one-minded, with their spouses, kneeling to him adorable paid worship.
Friend finding in his own friend's eye protection, they made their own the bodies which they chastened.

1 Wilson, after Sāyaṇa, translates : 'Agni...... appropriates the prayers addressed to the eternal creator.' The meaning appears to be that although Agni bestows many good gifts on men, his flames are at times terribly destructive.

2 The flight of Agni and his pursuit by the Gods have been mentioned before (I. 65. 1). The idea here is as Ludwig observes, that the Gods did not really find Agni—visible though he be in his earthly form—until they attained to the true philosophical knowledge of the Deity as he is.

3 *The pure Ones*: 'The text has on *śucáyaḥ*, the pure : the Scholiast supplies *Maruts*, for whom, it is said, seven platters are placed at the Agnicayana ceremony ; and they are severally invoked by the appellations Idṛś, Anyādṛś, Tādṛś, Pratidṛś, Mitaḥ, Saṃmitaḥ, and others. In consequence of this participation, with Agni, of sacrificial offerings, they exchanged their perishable, for immortal, bodies, and obtained heaven. The Maruts are, therefore, like the Ṛbhus, deified mortals.' Wilson.

Three autumn seasons : during three years. Ludwig observes that the period of three years in connexion with religious vows or ceremonies is mentioned elsewhere also.

4 *The powers of Rudra* : Rudra here is a name of Agni.

The mortal band: the Maruts, so called as not having been originally immortal.

6 Soon as the holy beings had discovered the thrice-seven mystic things contained within thee,
With these, one-minded, they preserve the Amṛta : guard thou the life of all their plants and cattle.

7 Thou, Agni, knower of men's works, hast sent us good food in constant course for our subsistence :
Thou deeply skilled in paths of Gods becamest an envoy never wearied, offering-bearer.

8 Knowing the Law, the seven strong floods from heaven, full of good thought, discerned the doors of riches.
Saramā found the cattle's firm-built prison whereby the race of man is still supported.

9 They who approached all noble operations making a path that leads to life immortal,
To be the Bird's support, the spacious mother, Aditi, and her great Sons stood in power.

10 When Gods immortal made both eyes of heaven, they gave to him the gift of beauteous glory.
Now they flow forth like rivers set in motion : they knew the Red Steeds coming down, O Agni.

HYMN LXXIII. *Agni.*

1. HE who gives food, like patrimonial riches and guides aright like some wise man's instruction,
Loved like a guest who lies in pleasant lodging,—may he, as Priest, prosper his servant's dwelling.

2 He who like Savitar the God, true-minded, protecteth with his power all acts of vigour,
Truthful, like splendour, glorified by many, like breath joy-giving,—all must strive to win him.

3 He who on earth dwells like a king surrounded by faithful friends, like a God all-sustaining,
Like heroes who preside, who sit in safety : like as a blameless dame dear to her husband.

4 Thee, such, in settlements secure, O Agni, our men serve ever kindled in each dwelling.
On him have they laid splendour in abundance : dear to all men, bearer be he of riches.

5 May thy rich worshippers win food, O Agni, and princes gain long life who bring oblation.
May we get booty from our foe in battle, presenting to the Gods their share for glory.

6 The cows of holy law, sent us by Heaven, have swelled with laden udders, loudly lowing;
Soliciting his favour, from a distance the rivers to the rock have flowed together.

7 Agni, with thee, soliciting thy favour, the holy Ones have gained glory in heaven.
They made the Night and Dawn of different colours, and set the black and purple hues together.

8 May we and those who worship be the mortals whom thou, O Agni, leadest on to riches.
Thou hast filled earth and heaven and air's mid-region, and followest the whole world like a shadow.

9 Aided by thee, O Agni, may we conquer steeds with steeds, men with men, heroes with heroes,
Lords of the wealth transmitted by our fathers : and may our princes live a hundred winters.

6 *The thrice-seven mystic things* the secret or mysterious rites by which heaven is to be obtained; offerings of various kinds, food, clarified butter, Soma juice etc., arranged in three classes of seven. All these offerings require fire, and so are contained in Agni.

They preserve the Amṛta : the nectar or drink of the Gods; by the performance of these sacrifices they secure the fall of rain in due season.

8 *Saramā found the cattle's firm-built prison* : see I. 62. 3.

9 *To be the Bird's support* : the Bird is the Sun. *Aditi* is infinite Nature, and *her great Sons* are the Ādityas.

10 *Both eyes of heaven* : the Sun and Moon. *The deR Steeds* : the Sun's rays.

6 *The cows of holy law* : the cows whose milk is used in the various sacrifices offered in accordance with the eternal ordinance.

The rivers : the water used in sacrifice which flows or is brought to *the rock* or stone with which the Soma juice is expressed.

7 Through Agni's favour *the holy Ones*, the immortal Gods, receive the oblations which strengthen them for the performance of the great deeds which bring them glory.

8 *Like a shadow* : averting distress, as the shade of a great rock or tree wards off the oppressive heat of the sun.

9 *May our princes* : may the wealthy men who institute our sacrifices live to the greatest age usually allotted to man.

10 May these our hymns of praise, Agni, Ordainer, be pleasant to thee in thy heart and spirit.
May we have power to hold thy steeds of riches, laying on thee the God-sent gift of glory.

HYMN LXXIV. *Agni.*

1. As forth to sacrifice we go, a hymn to Agni let us say,
Who hears us even when afar ;
2 Who, from of old, in carnage, when the people gathered, hath preserved
His household for the worshipper.
3 And let men say, Agni is born, e'en he who slayeth Vṛtra, he
Who winneth wealth in every fight.
4 Him in whose house an envoy thou lovest to taste his offered gifts,
And strengthenest his sacrifice,
5 Him, Aṅgiras, thou Son of Strength, all men call happy in his God,
His offerings, and his sacred grass.
6 Hitherward shalt thou bring these Gods to our laudation and to taste.
These offered gifts, fair-shining One.
7 When, Agni, on thine embassage thou goest not a sound is heard of steed or straining of thy car.
8 Aided by thee uninjured, strong, one after other, goes he forth :
Agni, the offerer forward steps.
9 And splendid strength, heroic, high, Agni, thou grantest from the Gods,
Thou God, to him who offers gifts.

HYMN LXXV. *Agni.*

1. ACCEPT our loudest-sounding hymn, food most delightful to the Gods,
Pouring our offerings in thy mouth.
2 Now, Agni, will we say to thee, O wisest and best Aṅgiras,
Our precious, much-availing prayer.
3 Who, Agni, is thy kin, of men? who is thy worthy worshipper ?
On whom dependent ? who art thou ?
4 The kinsman, Agni, of mankind, their well beloved Friend art thou,
A Friend whom friends may supplicate.
5 Bring to us Mitra, Varuṇa, bring the Gods to mighty sacrifice.
Bring them, O Agni, to thine home.

HYMN LXXVI. *Agni.*

1. How may the mind draw nigh to please thee, Agni? What hymn of praise shall bring us greatest blessing?
Or who hath gained thy power by sacrifices ? or with what mind shall we bring thee oblations?
2 Come hither, Agni ; sit thee down as Hotar ; be thou who never wast deceived our leader.
'May Heaven and Earth, the all-pervading, love thee : worship the Gods to win for us their favour.
3 Burn thou up all the Rākṣasas, O Agni; ward thou off curses from our sacrifices.
Bring hither with his Bays the Lord of Soma : here is glad welcome for the Bounteous Giver.
4 Thou Priest with lip and voice that bring us children hast been invoked. Here with the Gods be seated.
Thine is the task of Cleanser and Presenter : waken us, Wealth-bestower and Producer.
5 As with oblations of the priestly Manus thou worshippedst the Gods, a Sage with sages,
So now, O truthfullest Invoker, Agni, worship this day with joy-bestowing ladle.

HYMN LXXVII. *Agni.*

1. How shall we pay oblation unto Agni? What hymn, Godloved, is said to him refulgent ?
Who, deathless, true to Law, mid men a herald, bringeth the Gods as best of sacrificers ?
2 Bring him with reverence hither, most propitious in sacrifices, true to Law, the herald ;

10 *To hold thy steeds of riches* : to retain by us thy horses which bring wealth, that is, coutinue to receive and keep the riches which thou sendest.

This Hymn and the nineteen following are ascribed to the Ṛṣi Gotama, son of Rahūgaṇa.

3 *Who slayeth Vṛtra* : Agni may here be identified with Indra.

5 *Aṅgiras* ; a name of Agni. See I. I. 6,

---

3 *The Lord of Soma* : Indra.

4 Agni, the priest or bearer of oblations, has been invoked with a hymn which will bring the blessing of children.

The cleanser (Potar) and *the Presenter* or Invoker (Hotar) are two of the sixteen officiating priests.

5 *Manus* : another form of the word Manu, Man, the great fore-father of men.

With joy-bestowing ladle : with the sacrificial ladle used in pouring the holy oil or clarified butter into the fire, an offering especially pleasing to the Gods.

For Agni, when he seeks the Gods for mortals, knows them full well and worships them in spirit.

3 For he is mental power, a man, and perfect; he is the bringer, friend-like, of the wondrous.
The pious Āryan tribes at sacrifices address them first to him who doeth marvels.

4 May Agni, foe-destroyer, manliest Hero, accept with love our hymns and our devotion.
So may the liberal lords whose strength is strongest, urged by their riches, stir our thoughts with vigour.

5 Thus Agni Jātavedas, true to Order, hath by the priestly Gotamas been lauded.
May he augment in them splendour and vigour : observant, as he lists, he gathers increase.

HYMN LXXVIII. *Agni.*

1. O JĀTAVEDAS, keen and swift, we Gotamas with sacred song exalt thee for thy glories' sake.

2 Thee, as thou art, desiring wealth Gotama worships with his song :
We laud thee for thy glories' sake.

3 As such, like Aṅgiras we call on thee best winner of the spoil :
We laud thee for thy glories' sake.

4 Thee, best of Vṛtra-slayers, thee who shakest off our Dasyu foes :
We laud thee for thy glories' sake.

5 A pleasant song to Agni we, sons of Rahūgaṇa, have sung :
We laud thee for thy glories' sake.

HYMN LXXIX. *Agni.*

1. HE in mid-air's expanse hath golden tresses ; a raging serpent, like the rushing tempest :
Purely refulgent, knowing well the morning ; like honourable dames, true, active workers.

2 Thy well-winged flashes strengthen in their manner, when the black Bull hath bellowed round about us.
With drops that bless and seem to smile he cometh : the waters fall, the clouds utter their thunder.

3 When he comes streaming with the milk of worship, conducting by directest paths of Order,
Aryaman, Mitra, Varuṇa, Parijman fill the hide full where lies the nether press-stone.

4 O Agni, thou who art the Lord of wealth in kine, thou Son of Strength,
Vouchsafe to us, O Jātavedas, high renown.

5 He, Agni, kindled, good and wise, must be exalted in our song :
Shine, thou of many forms, shine radiantly on us.

6 O Agni, shining of thyself by night and when the morning breaks,
Burn, thou whose teeth are sharp, against the Rākṣasas.

7 Adorable in all our rites, favour us, Agni, with thine aid,
When the great hymn is chanted forth.

8 Bring to us ever-conquering wealth, wealth, Agni, worthy of our choice,
In all our frays invincible.

9 Give us, O Agni, through thy grace wealth that supporteth all our life,
Thy favour so that we may live.

10 O Gotama, desiring bliss present thy songs composed with care
To Agni of the pointed flames.

11 May the man fall, O Agni, who near or afar assaileth us :
Do thou increase and prosper us.

12 Keen and swift Agni, thousand-eyed, chaseth the Rākṣasas afar :
He singeth, herald meet for lauds.

HYMN LXXX. *Indra.*

1. THUS in the Soma, in wild joy the Brahman hath exalted thee :

3 *The wondrous* : extraordinary wealth.
4 *Liberal lords* : wealthy patrons whose gifts will encourage and strengthen the devotions of the priests :

---

3 *Like Aṅgiras* : after the manner of Aṅgiras, one of the earliest performers of sacrifice.
4 *Best of Vṛtra-slayers* : here again Agni is identified with Indra.

---

1 Agni is here spoken of in his three forms, the golden-haired Sun, the serpentine lightning, and the household fire for religious purposes and ordinary use. He is said to know the morning as being re-kindled for sacrifice at day-break, and is compared to an active matron on account of his employment to domestic purposes.

2 *The black Bull hath bellowed* : the dark rain-clouds have thundered.
3 *When he comes* to the Gods with *the milk of worship*, the rich sacrificial offering, the Gods send copious rain. *Parijman*, the Wanderer, the circumambient, is in this place the stormy Wind. *The nether press-stone* (which rests upon an ox-hide) is here the earth, the heaven being the upper stone. Wilson, following Sāyaṇa, translates : 'pierce through the (investing) membrane into the womb of the cloud.'

---

1 *The Dragon* : the great serpent Ahi, one of the demons of drought.

Thou, mightiest, thunder-armed, hast driven by force the Dragon from the earth, lauding thine own imperial sway.

2 The mighty flowing Soma-draught, brought by the Hawk, hath gladdened thee,
That in thy strength, O Thunderer, thou hast struck down Vṛtra from the floods, lauding thine own imperial sway.

3 Go forward, meet the foe, be bold; thy bolt of thunder is not checked.
Manliness, Indra, is thy might : slay Vṛtra, make the waters thine, lauding thine own imperial sway.

4 Thou smotest Vṛtra from the earth, smotest him, Indra, from the sky.
Let these life-fostering waters flow attended by the Marut host, lauding thine own imperial sway.

5 The wrathful Indra with his bolt of thunder rushing on the foe,
Smote fierce on trembling Vṛtra's back, and loosed the waters free to run, lauding his own imperial sway.

6 With hundred-jointed thunderbolt Indra hath struck him on the back,
And, while rejoicing in the juice, seeketh prosperity for friends, lauding his own imperial sway.

7 Indra, unconquered might is thine, Thunderer, Caster of the Stone;
For thou with thy surpassing power smotest to death the guileful beast, lauding thine own imperial sway.

8 Far over ninety spacious floods thy thunderbolts were cast abroad :
Great, Indra, is thy hero might, and strength is seated in thine arms, lauding thine own imperial sway.

9 Laud him a thousand all at once, shout twenty forth the hymn of praise.
Hundreds have sung aloud to him, to Indra hath the prayer been raised, lauding his own imperial sway.

10 Indra hath smitten down the power of Vṛtra,—might with stronger might.
This was his manly exploit, he slew Vṛtra and let loose the floods, lauding his own imperial sway.

11 Yea, even this great Pair of Worlds trembled in terror at thy wrath,
When, Indra, Thunderer, Marut-girt, thou slewest Vṛtra in thy strength, lauding thine own imperial sway.

12 But Vṛtra scared not Indra with his shaking or his thunder roar.
On him that iron thunderbolt fell fiercely with its thousand points, lauding his own imperial sway.

13 When with the thunder thou didst make thy dart and Vṛtra meet in war,
Thy might, O Indra, fain to slay the Dragon, was set firm in heaven, lauding thine own imperial sway.

14 When at thy shout, O Thunder-armed, each thing both fixed and moving shook,
E'en Tvaṣṭar trembled at thy wrath and quaked with fear because of thee, lauding thine own imperial sway.

15 There is not, in our knowledge, one who passeth Indra in his strength :
In him the Deities have stored manliness, insight, power and might, lauding his own imperial sway.

16 Still as of old, whatever rite Atharvan, Manus sire of all,
Dadhyach performed, their prayer and praise united in that Indra meet, lauding his own imperial sway.

HYMN LXXXI. *Indra.*

1. THE men have lifted Indra up, the Vṛtra-slayer, to joy and strength :
Him, verily, we invocate in battles whether great or small : be he our aid in deeds of might.

2 Thou, Hero, art a warrior, thou art giver of abundant spoil.
Strengthening e'en the feeble, thou aidest the sacrificer, thou givest the offerer ample wealth.

3 When war and battles are on foot, booty is laid before the bold.
Yoke thou thy wildly-rushing Bays. Whom wilt thou slay and whom enrich ? Do thou, O Indra, make us rich.

4 Mighty through wisdom, as he lists, terrible, he hath waxed in strength.

2 *Brought by the Hawk* : the Soma is said to have been brought from heaven by a hawk or falcon. Cf. I. 93. 6.

7 *The guileful beast* : the demon Vṛtra.

8 *Ninety spacious floods* : the many waters obstructed by Vṛtra.

16 Atharvan is the priest who first obtained fire and offered Soma and prayers to the Gods. Dadhyac is his son. Manus or Manu is the progenitor of mankind.

The refrain, 'lauding his own imperial sway,' is not always in syntactical connexion with the verse of which it forms the conclusion.

1 *The men* : the ministering priests who exalt and strengthen with oblations.

Lord of Bay Steeds, strong-jawed, sublime, he in joined hands for glory's sake hath grasped his iron thunderbolt.

5 He filled the earthly atmosphere and pressed against the lights in heaven.
None like thee ever hath been born, none, Indra, will be born like thee. Thou hast waxed mighty over all.

6 May he who to the offerer gives the foeman's man-sustaining food,
May Indra lend his aid to us. Deal forth —abundant is thy wealth—that in thy bounty I may share.

7 He, righteous-hearted, at each time of rapture gives us herds of kine.
Gather in both thy hands for us treasures of many hundred sorts. Sharpen thou us, and bring us wealth.

8 Refresh thee, Hero, with the juice outpoured for bounty and for strength.
We know thee Lord of ample store, to thee have sent our hearts' desires : be therefore our Protector thou.

9 These people, Indra, keep for thee all that is worthy of thy choice.
Discover thou, as Lord, the wealth of men who offer up no gifts : bring thou to us this wealth of theirs.

HYMN LXXXII. *Indra.*

1. Graciously listen to our songs, Maghavan, be not negligent.
As thou hast made us full of joy and lettest us solicit thee, now, Indra, yoke thy two Bay Steeds.

2 Well have they eaten and rejoiced ; the friends have risen and passed away.
The sages luminous in themselves have praised thee with their latest hymn. Now, Indra, yoke thy two Bay Steeds.

3 Maghavan, we will reverence thee who art so fair to look upon.
Thus praised, according to our wish come now with richly laden car. Now, Indra, yoke thy two Bay Steeds.

4 He will in very truth ascend the powerful car that finds the kine,
Who thinks upon the well-filled bowl, the Tawny Coursers' harnesser. Now, Indra, yoke thy two Bay Steeds.

9 *These people* : thy worshippers here.

---

1 *Maghavan* : Indra, the rich and liberal.
2 *Well have they eaten* : they, meaning the worshippers.

5 Let, Lord of Hundred Powers, thy Steeds be harnessed on the right and left.
Therewith in rapture of the juice, draw near to thy beloved Spouse. Now, Indra, yoke thy two Bay Steeds.

6 With holy prayer I yoke thy long-maned pair of Bays : come hitherward; thou holdest them in both thy hands.
The stirring draughts of juice outpoured have made thee glad : thou, Thunderer, hast rejoiced with Pūṣan and thy Spouse.

HYMN LXXXIII. *Indra.*

1. Indra, the mortal man well guarded by thine aid goes foremost in the wealth of horses and of kine.
With amplest wealth thou fillest him, as round about the waters clearly seen afar fill Sindhu full.

2 The heavenly Waters come not nigh the priestly bowl : they but look down and see how far mid-air is spread :
The Deities conduct the pious man to them : like suitors they delight in him who loveth prayer.

3 Praiseworthy blessing hast thou laid upon the pair who with uplifted ladle serve thee, man and wife.
Unchecked he dwells and prospers in thy law : thy power brings blessing to the sacrificer pouring gifts.

4 First the Aṅgirases won themselves vital power, whose fires were kindled through good deeds and sacrifice.
The men together found the Paṇi's hoarded wealth, the cattle, and the wealth in horses and in kine.

5 Atharvan first by sacrifices laid the paths ; then, guardian of the Law, sprang up the loving Sun.
Uśanā Kāvya straightway hither drove the kine. Let us with offerings honour Yama's deathless birth.

5 *Thy Spouse* : Indrāṇī. See I. 22. 12.

---

3 *Man and wife* : the text has only *mithunā*, a couple. The word apparently means here the offerer of the sacrifice and his wife, who took part in the ceremony. Sāyaṇa explains it as the grain and the butter of oblation.

4 *The Paṇi* : is the illiberal demon who withholds the rain.

5 *The paths* : for the rising Śun to travel. *Uśanā Kāvya* is the name of a celebrased ancient Ṛṣi. See I. 51. 10. The meaning of the latter half of the second verse is obscure. Ludwig renders it 'Seek we to win by sacrifice the immortality which has sprung from Yama.' Yama seems here to represent the rising Sun. See Ehni, Der Mythus des Yama, p. 62.

6 When sacred grass is trimmed to aid the auspicious work, or the hymn makes its voice of praise sound to the sky.
Where the stone rings as 'twere a singer skilled in laud,—Indra in truth delights when these come near to him.

HYMN LXXXIV. *Indra.*

1. THE Soma hath been pressed for thee, O Indra ; mightiest, bold One, come.
May Indra-vigour fill thee full, as the Sun fills mid-air with rays.

2 His pair of Tawny Coursers bring Indra of unresisted might
Hither to Ṛṣis' songs of praise and sacrifice performed by men.

3 Slayer of Vṛtra, mount thy car ; thy Bay Steeds have been yoked by prayer.
May, with its voice, the pressing-stone draw thine attention hitherward.

4 This poured libation, Indra, drink, immortal, gladdening, excellent.
Streams of the bright have flowed to thee here at the seat of holy Law.

5 Sing glory now to Indra, say to him your solemn eulogies.
The drops poured forth have made him glad : pay reverence to his might supreme.

6 When, Indra, thou dost yoke thy Steeds, there is no better charioteer :
None hath surpassed thee in thy might, none with good steeds o'ertaken thee.

7 He who alone bestoweth on mortal man who offereth gifts,
The ruler of resistless power, is Indra, sure.

8 When will he trample, like a weed, the man who hath no gift for him?
When, verily, will Indra hear our songs of praise?

9 He who with Soma juice prepared amid the many honours thee,—
Verily Indra gains thereby tremendous might.

10 The juice of Soma thus diffused, sweet to the taste, the bright cows drink,
Who for the sake of splendour close to mighty Indra's side rejoice, good in their own supremacy.

11 Craving his touch the dappled kine mingle the Soma with their milk.
The milch-kine dear to Indra send forth his death-dealing thunderbolt, good in their own supremacy.

12 With veneration, passing wise, honouring his victorious might,
They follow close his many laws to win them due preëminence, good in their own supremacy.

13 With bones of Dadhyac for his arms, Indra, resistless in attack,
Struck nine-and-ninety Vṛtras dead.

14 He, searching for the horse's head, removed among the mountains, found
At Śaryaṇāvān what he sought.

15 Then verily they recognized the essential form of Tvaṣṭar's Bull,
Here in the mansion of the Moon.

16 Who yokes to-day unto the pole of Order the strong and passionate steers of checkless spirit,
With shaft-armed mouths, heart-piercing, health-bestowing?
Long shall he live who richly pays their service.

4 *The bright* : Soma juice. *The seat of holy Law* : the place where sacrifice, ordained by *ṛtá*, or eternal Law, is performed.

10 *The bright cows* : the pure and glossy milk which absorbs or drinks the Soma juice with which it is mixed, and which is close to, or united with, Indra when offered to and accepted by him in libation.

11 *Send forth* : the cows, that is, their milk, exalt and strengthen Indra, and incite him to battle with the demons. The meaning of the refrain of this triad (verses 10, 11, 12) is not very clear. Wilson, following Sāyaṇa, translates it : 'abiding (in their stalls) expectant of his sovereignty.'

13 *Dadhyac*, or in a later form, Dadhīca, was a Ṛṣi, son of Atharvan, he and his father being regarded as the first founders of sacrifice. He is described as having the head of a horse given to him by the Aśvins which was afterwards cut off by Indra. With his bones or, as the legend says, the bones of this horse's head, converted into a thunderbolt, Indra slew the Vṛtras or demons who withheld the rain. The Vedic legend, which was modified and amplified in later times, appears to have been connected in its origin with that of Dadhikrās, often mentioned in the Veda and described as a kind of divine horse, probably a personification of the morning Sun in his rapid course. Dadhyac may be the old Moon whose bones, when he dies, become the stars with which Indra slays the fiends of darkness.

14 *Mountains* : the morning clouds. *Śaryaṇāvān* : said to be a lake and district in Kurukṣetra, near the modern Delhi.

15 *Tvaṣṭar's Bull* : an obscure expression for the Sun. The purport of the verse may be that when, after the rains, the bright moonlight nights came, men recognized the fact that the light was borrowed from the Sun. Wilson, following Sāyaṇa, translates the verse : 'The (solar rays) found, on this occasion the light of Tvaṣṭṛ, verily, concealed in the mansion of the moving moon.' See Hymns of the Atharva-veda, XX. 41.

16 *The strong and passionate steers* : the zealous and indefatigable priests, who are yoked to the chariot-pole of Order or employed in the performance of sacrifice ordained by eternal Law. The words of the priests are the arrows with which their mouths are armed.

17 Who fleeth forth? who suffereth? who feareth? Who knoweth Indra present, Indra near us ?
Who sendeth benediction on his offspring, his household, wealth and person, and the people ?

18 Who with poured oil and offering honours Agni, with ladle worships at appointed seasons ?
To whom to the Gods bring oblation quickly? What offerer, God-favoured, knows him thoroughly ?

19 Thou as a God, O Mightiest, verily blessest mortal man.
O Maghavan, there is no comforter but thou : Indra, I speak my words to thee.

20 Let not thy bounteous gifts, let not thy saving help fail us, good Lord, at any time ;
And measure out to us, thou lover of mankind, all riches hitherward from men.

HYMN LXXXV. *Maruts.*

1. THEY who are glancing forth, like women, on their way, doers of mighty deeds, swift racers, Rudra's Sons,
The Maruts have made heaven and earth increase and grow : in sacrifices they delight, the strong and wild.

2 Grown to their perfect strength greatness have they attained ; the Rudras have established their abode in heaven.
Singing their song of praise and generating might, they have put glory on, the Sons whom Pṛśni bare.

3 When, Children of the Cow, they shine in bright attire, and on their fair limbs lay their golden ornaments,
They drive away each adversary from their path, and, following their traces, fatness floweth down,

4 When, mighty Warriors, ye who glitter with your spears, o'erthrowing with your strength e'en what is ne'er o'erthrown,
When, O ye Maruts, ye the host that send the rain, had harnessed to your cars the thought-fleet spotted deer.

5 When ye have harnessed to your cars the spotted deer, urging the thunderbolt, O Maruts, to the fray,
Forth rush the torrents of the dark-red stormy cloud, and moisten, like a skin, the earth with water-floods.

6 Let your swift-gliding coursers bear you hitherward with their fleet pinions. Come ye forward with your arms.
Sit on the grass; a wide seat hath been made for you : delight yourselves, O Maruts, in the pleasant food.

7 Strong in their native strength to greatness have they grown, stepped to the firmament and made their dwelling wide.
When Viṣṇu saved the Soma bringing wild delight, the Maruts sate like birds on their dear holy grass.

8 In sooth like heroes fain for fight they rush about, like combatants fame-seeking have they striven in war.
Before the Maruts every creature is afraid: the men are like to Kings, terrible to behold.

9 When Tvaṣṭar deft of hand had turned the thunderbolt, golden, with thousand edges, fashioned more skilfully,
Indra received it to perform heroic deeds. Vṛtra he slew, and forced the flood of water forth.

10 They with their vigorous strength pushed the well up on high, and clove the cloud in twain though it was passing strong.
The Maruts, bounteous Givers, sending forth their voice, in the wild joy of Soma wrought their glorious deeds.

11 They drave the cloud transverse directed hitherward, and poured the fountain forth for thirsting Gotama.

17 The answer to these questions is, the priests, who represent the feelings of the man who institutes the sacrifice.

18 The second line of this verse is rendered by Wilson, following Sāyaṇa : 'To whom do the gods, quickly bring (the wealth) that has been called for ?' This would be intelligible enough ; but *homa* (oblation) can hardly bear the interpretation thus forced upon it.

---

1 *Rudra's Sons* : the Maruts, or Storm-Gods, are the sons of Rudra and of Pṛśni, the earth or the speckled cloud.

2 *The Rudras* : the sons of Rudra.

3 *Children of the Cow* : that is, of Pṛśni or the cloud under that type.

Fatness floweth down : the clouds drop fatness ; the fertilizing rain descends.

4 The glittering spears are the flashes of lightning. The chariot of the Maruts is said to be drawn by spotted deer or antelopes.

6 *Sit on the grass* : on the sacred grass trimmed and strewn for the Gods.

7 *When Viṣṇu saved the Soma* : Viṣṇu prepared the Soma and brought it to Indra, and the Maruts, Indra's companions, sat down with him to enjoy it.

8 *The men* : the Maruts. *Kings* : that is, warriors.

10 *The well* : here the cloud, as a reservoir of water.

11 *Gotama* : the Ṛṣi to whom the hymn was revealed.

Shining with varied light they come to him with help : they with their might fulfilled the longing of the sage.

12 The shelters which ye have for him who lauds you, bestow them threefold on the man who offers.
Extend the same boons unto us, ye Maruts. Give us, O Heroes, wealth with noble offspring.

HYMN LXXXVI. *Maruts.*

1. The best of guardians hath that man within whose dwelling place ye drink,
O Maruts, giants of the sky.

2 Honoured with sacrifice or with the worship of the sages' hymns,
O Maruts, listen to the call.

3 Yea, the strong man to whom ye have vouchsafed to give a sage, shall move
Into a stable rich in kine.

4 Upon this hero's sacred grass Soma is poured in daily rites :
Praise and delight are sung aloud.

5 Let the strong Maruts hear him, him surpassing all men : strength be his
That reaches even to the Sun.

6 For, through the swift Gods' loving help, in many an autumn, Maruts, we
Have offered up our sacrifice.

7 Fortunate shall that mortal be, O Maruts most adorable,
Whose offerings ye bear away.

8 O Heroes truly strong, ye know the toil of him who sings your praise,
The heart's desire of him who loves.

9 O ye of true strength, make this thing manifest by your greatness : strike
The demon with your thunderbolt.

10 Conceal the horrid darkness, drive far from us each devouring fiend.
Create the light for which we long.

3 *Shall move into a stable rich in kine* : shall become the wealthy possessor of many cows.

8 *Of him who loves* : of the suppliant who loves and prays to you.

10 *Devouring fiend* : 'Atrin, which stands for attrin, is one of the many names assigned to the powers of darkness and mischief. It is derived from atra, which means, tooth or jaw, and therefore meant originally an ogre with large teeth or jaws, a devourer.'—Max Müller See Vedic Hymns, Part I. (Sacred Books of the East, XXXII.) for a translation and full explanation of this and other Hymns to the Maruts.

HYMN LXXXVII. *Maruts.*

1. Loud Singers, never humbled, active, full of strength, immovable, impetuous, manliest, best-beloved,
They have displayed themselves with glittering ornaments, a few in number only, like the heavens with stars.

2 When, Maruts, on the steeps ye pile the moving cloud, ye are like birds on whatsoever path it be.
Clouds everywhere shed forth the rain upon your cars. Drop fatness, honey-hued, for him who sings your praise.

3 Earth at their racings trembles as if weak and worn, when on their ways they yoke their cars for victory.
They, sportive, loudly roaring, armed with glittering spears, shakers of all, themselves admire their mightiness.

4 Self-moving is that youthful band, with spotted steeds; thus it hath lordly sway, endued with power and might.
Truthful art thou, and blameless, searcher-out of sin : so thou, Strong Host, wilt be protector of this prayer.

5 We speak by our descent from our primeval Sire ; our tongue, when we behold the Soma, stirs itself.
When, shouting, they had joined Indra in toil of fight, then only they obtained their sacrificial names.

6 Splendours they gained for glory, they who wear bright rings; rays they obtained, and men to celebrate their praise.
Armed with their swords, impetuous and fearing naught, they have possessed the Maruts' own beloved home.

HYMN LXXXVIII. *Maruts.*

1. Come hither, Maruts, on your lightning-laden cars, sounding with sweet songs, armed with lances, winged with steeds.
Fly unto us with noblest food, like birds, O ye of mighty power.

1 *A few in number only* : 'refers to the Maruts, who are represented as gradually rising or just showing themselves, as yet only a few in number, like the first stars in the sky.—' Max Müller.

5 The Soma juice inspires us, and we are guided by the tradition received from our ancestors.

The Maruts obtained divine honours only as a reward for assisting Indra in his battle with the demon Vṛtra.

6 *They have possessed the Maruts' own beloved home* : 'have established themselves in what became afterwards known as their own abode, their own place among the gods invoked at the sacrifice.'—Max Müller.

2 With their red-hued or, haply, tawny coursers which speed their chariots on, they come for glory.
Brilliant like gold is he who holds the thunder. Earth have they smitten with the chariot's felly.

3 For beauty ye have swords upon your bodies. As they stir woods so may they stir our spirits.
For your sake, O ye Maruts very mighty and well-born, have they set the stone, in motion.

4 The days went round you and came back O yearners, back, to this prayer and to this solemn worship.
The Gotamas making their prayer with singing have pushed the well's lid up to drink the water.

5 No hymn was ever known like this aforetime which Gotama sang forth for you, O Maruts,
What time upon your golden wheels he saw you, wild boars rushing about with tusks of iron.

6 To you this freshening draught of Soma rusheth, O Maruts, like the voice of one who prayeth.
It rusheth freely from our hands as these libations wont to flow.

HYMN LXXXIX. *Viśvedevas.*

1. MAY powers auspicious come to us from every side, never deceived, unhindered, and victorious,
That the Gods ever may be with us for our gain, our guardians day by day unceasing in their care.

2 May the auspicious favour of the Gods be ours, on us descend the bounty of the righteous Gods.
The friendship of the Gods have we devoutly sought : so may the Gods extend our life that we may live.

3 We call them hither with a hymn of olden time, Bhaga, the friendly Dakṣa, Mitra, Aditi,
Aryaman, Varuṇa, Soma, the Aśvins. May Sarasvatī, auspicious, grant felicity.

4 May the Wind waft to us that pleasant medicine, may Earth our Mother give it, and our Father Heaven,
And the joy-giving stones that press the Soma's juice. Aśvins, may ye, for whom our spirits long, hear this.

5 Him we invoke for aid who reigns supreme, the Lord of all that stands or moves, inspirer of the soul,
That Pūṣan may promote the increase of our wealth, our keeper and our guard infallible for our good.

6 Illustrious far and wide, may Indra prosper us : may Pūṣan prosper us, the Master of all wealth.
May Tārkṣya with uninjured fellies prosper us: Bṛhaspati vouchsafe to us prosperity.

7 The Maruts, Sons of Pṛśni, borne by spotted steeds, moving in glory, oft visiting holy rites,
Sages whose tongue is Agni, brilliant as the Sun,—hither let all the Gods for our protection come.

8 Gods, may we with our ears listen to what is good, and with our eyes see what is good, ye Holy Ones.
With limbs and bodies firm may we extolling you attain the term of life appointed by the Gods.

9 A hundred autumns stand before us, O ye Gods, within whose space ye bring our bodies to decay;
Within whose space our sons become fathers in turn. Break ye not in the midst our course of fleeting life.

2 *He who holds the thunder* : the holder of the thunder or thunderbolt is Indra.

3 *Have they set the stone in motion* : men have pressed out the Some juice and offered libations to you.

4 *And to this solemn worship* : (*vārkāryāṁ ca devīm*) 'The most likely supposition is that vārkāryā was the name given to some famous hymn, some paean or song of triumph belonging to the Gotamas. The purport of the whole line then would be that many days have gone for the Maruts as well as for the famous hymn addressed to them, or, in other words, that the Gotamas have long been devoted to the Maruts....The pushing up of the lid of the well for to drink, means that they obtained rain from the cloud, which is here, as before, represented as a covered well.'—Max Müller.

6 This verse is very obscure. I follow M.M.'s translation which 'is to a great extent conjectural.'

3 *Bhaga*, enumerated by Yāska among the deities of the highest sphere, is an Āditya regarded in the Veda as bestowing wealth and instituting or presiding over love and marriage. *Dakṣa* is a creative power associated with Aditi, and therefore sometimes identified with Prajāpati.

4 *Our Father Heaven*: pitā Dyaús=Pater Ζeús, Jupiter.

6 *Tārkṣya* : usually described as a divine horse and probably a personification of the Sun, *Bṛhaspati* : Lord of Prayer.

7 *Whose tongue is Agni* : who receive oblations through Agni or fire.

9 *A hundred autumns* : regarded as the natural length of human life. Cf. Isaiah, LXV. 20 'There shall be no more thence an infant of days, nor an old man that hath not filled his days : for the child shall die an hundred years old.'

10 Aditi is the heaven, Aditi is mid-air, Aditi is the Mother and the Sire and Son.
Aditi is all Gods, Aditi five-classed men, Aditi all that hath been born and shall be born.

HYMN XC. *Viśvedevas.*

1. May Varuṇa with guidance straight, and Mitra lead us, he who knows,
And Aryaman in accord with Gods.

2 For they are dealers forth of wealth, and, not deluded, with their might
Guard evermore the holy laws.

3 Shelter may they vouchsafe to us, Immortal Gods to mortal men,
Chasing our enemies away.

4 May they mark out our paths to bliss, Indra, the Maruts, Pūṣan, and
Bhaga, the Gods to be adored.

5 Yea, Pūṣan, Viṣṇu, ye who run your course, enrich our hymns with kine;
Bless us with all prosperity.

6 The winds waft sweets, the rivers pour sweets for the man who keeps the Law:
So may the plants be sweet for us.

7 Sweet be the night and sweet the dawns, sweet the terrestrial atmosphere;
Sweet be our Father Heaven to us.

8 May the tall tree be full of sweets for us, and full of sweets the Sun:
May our milch-kine be sweet for us.

9 Be Mitra gracious unto us, and Varuṇa and Aryaman:
Indra, Bṛhaspati be kind, and Viṣṇu of the mighty stride.

HYMN XCI. *Soma.*

1. Thou, Soma, art preëminent for wisdom; along the straightest path thou art our leader.
Our wise forefathers by thy guidance, Indu, dealt out among the Gods their share of treasure.

2 Thou by thine insight art most wise, O Soma, strong by thine energies and all-possessing,
Mighty art thou by all thy powers and greatness, by glories art thou glorious, guide of mortals.

3 Thine are King Varuṇa's eternal statutes, lofty and deep, O Soma, is thy glory.
All-pure art thou like Mitra the beloved, adorable, like Aryaman, O Soma.

4 With all thy glories on the earth, in heaven, on mountains, in the plants, and in the waters,—
With all of these, well-pleased and not in anger, accept, O royal Soma, our oblations.

5 Thou, Soma, art the Lord of heroes, King, yea, Vṛtra-slayer thou:
Thou art auspicious energy.

6 And, Soma, let it be thy wish that we may live and may not die:
Praise-loving Lord of plants art thou.

7 To him who keeps the law, both old and young, thou givest happiness,
And energy that he may live.

8 Guard us, King Soma, on all sides from him who threatens us: never let
The friend of one like thee be harmed.

9 With those delightful aids which thou hast, Soma, for the worshipper,—
Even with those protect thou us.

10 Accepting this our sacrifice and this our praise, O Soma, come,
And be thou nigh to prosper us.

11 Well-skilled in speech we magnify thee, Soma, with our sacred songs:
Come thou to us, most gracious One.

12 Enricher, healer of disease, wealth-finder, prospering our store,
Be, Soma, a good Friend to us.

13 Soma, be happy in our heart, as milch-kine in the grassy meads,
As a young man in his own house.

14 O Soma, God, the mortal man who in thy friendship hath delight,
Him doth the mighty Sage befriend.

15 Save us from slanderous reproach, keep us, O Soma, from distress:
Be unto us a gracious Friend.

16 Soma, wax great. From every side may vigorous powers unite in thee:
Be in the gathering-place of strength.

17 Wax, O most gladdening Soma, great through all thy rays of light, and be

10 *Aditi*: the Infinite, infinite Nature.

9 *Viṣṇu of the mighty stride*: as the Sun, striding over or traversing the three worlds.

1 *Indu*: another name of Soma, here identified with the Moon who teaches men the proper seasons at which to worship the Manes or deified Fathers. See 1. 43. 8, note.

3 *Thine are King Varuṇa's eternal statutes*: thy laws are the same as Varuṇa's laws have their origin in thee.

14 *The mighty Sage*: Soma himself.

16 *Be in the gathering place of strength*: be thou the central point and source of all power.

17 *Through all thy rays of light*: through all thy stalks, according to Ludwig who takes Soma to be the plant. Wilson, following Sāyaṇa, translates: 'Increase with all twining plants.'

A Friend of most illustrious fame to prosper us.

18 In thee be juicy nutriments united, and powers and mighty foe-subduing vigour,
Waxing to immortality, O Soma: win highest glories for thyself in heaven.

19 Such of thy glories as with poured oblations men honour, may they all invest our worship.
Wealth-giver, furtherer with troops of heroes, sparing the brave, come, Soma, to our houses.

20 To him who worships Soma gives the milch-cow, a fleet steed and a man of active knowledge,
Skilled in home duties, meet for holy synod, for council meet, a glory to his father.

21 Invincible in fight, saver in battles, guard of our camp, winner of light and water,
Born amid hymns, well-housed, exceeding famous, victor, in thee will we rejoice, O Soma.

22 These herbs, these milch-kine, and these running waters, all these, O Soma thou hast generated.
The spacious firmament hast thou expanded, and with the light thou hast dispelled the darkness.

23 Do thou, God Soma, with thy Godlike spirit, victorious, win for us a share of riches.
Let none prevent thee: thou art Lord of valour. Provide for both sides in the fray for booty.

HYMN XCII. *Dawn.*

1. THESE Dawns have raised their banner; in the eastern half of the mid-air they spread abroad their shining light.
Like heroes who prepare their weapons for the war, onward they come bright red in hue, the Mother Cows.

2 Readily have the purple beams of light shot up; the Red Cows have they harnessed, easy to be yoked.
The Dawns have brought distinct perception as before: red-hued, they have attained their fulgent brilliancy.

3 They sing their song like women active in their tasks, along their common path hither from far away,
Bringing refreshment to the liberal devotee, yea, all things to the worshipper who pours the juice.

4 She, like a dancer, puts her broidered garments on: as a cow yields her udder so she bares her breast.
Creating light for all the world of life, the Dawn hath laid the darkness open as the cows their stall.

5 We have beheld the brightness of her shining; it spreads and drives away the darksome monster.
Like tints that deck the Post at sacrifices, Heaven's Daughter hath attained her wondrous splendour.

6 We have o'erpast the limit of this darkness; Dawn breaking forth again brings clear perception.
She like a flatterer smiles in light for glory, and fair of face hath wakened to rejoice us.

7 The Gotamas have praised Heaven's radiant Daughter, the leader of the charm of pleasant voices.
Dawn, thou conferrest on us strength with offspring and men, conspicuous with kine and horses.

8 O thou who shinest forth in wondrous glory, urged onward by thy strength, auspicious Lady,
Dawn, may I gain that wealth, renowned and ample, in brave sons, troops of slaves, far-famed for horses.

9 Bending her looks on all the world, the Goddess shines, widely spreading with her bright eye westward.
Waking to motion every living creature, she understands the voice of each adorer.

22 *These milch-kine*: the milk which is to be mixed with the Soma juice.

---

1 *These Dawns*: 'We have the term *Uṣasaḥ*, in the plural, intending, according to the Commentator, the divinities that preside over the morning: but, according to Yāska, the plural is used honorifically only, for the singular personification.'—Wilson.

The Mother Cows: the Dawns, with their red clouds, who have just given birth to the day.

2 *The Red Cows*: the red clouds of morning.

3 *Who pours the juice*: presses out and offers libations of Soma juice.

4 *Hath laid the darkness open*: the meaning, rather obscurely expressed with a harsh zeugma or ellipsis, is, Dawn, with her bright clouds, has opened and emerged from the darkness which surrounded her, in the same manner as cows leave the dark pen or stable in which they have been shut up, as soon as it is opened in the early morning.

5 *Like tints that deck the Post*: the sacrificial post or pillar, to which the victims were tied, was anointed by the priests.

7 *Pleasant voices*: of the newly-awakened birds, other animals, and human beings.

10 Ancient of days, again again born newly, decking her beauty with the self-same raiment.
The Goddess wastes away the life of mortals, like a skilled hunter cutting birds in pieces.

11 She hath appeared discovering heaven's borders: to the far distance she drives off her Sister.
Diminishing the days of human creatures, the Lady shines with all her lover's splendour.

12 The bright, the blessed One shines forth extending her rays like kine, as a flood rolls his waters.
Never transgressing the divine commandments, she is beheld visible with the sunbeams.

13 O Dawn enriched with ample wealth, bestow on us the wondrous gift
Wherewith we may support children and children's sons.

14 Thou radiant mover of sweet sounds, with wealth of horses and of kine
Shine thou on us this day, O Dawn auspiciously.

15 O Dawn enriched with holy rites, yoke to thy car thy purple steeds,
And then bring thou unto us all felicities.

16 O Aśvins wonderful in act, do ye unanimous direct
Your chariot to our home wealthy in kine and gold.

17 Ye who brought down the hymn from heaven, a light that giveth light to man,
Do ye, O Aśvins, bring strength hither unto us.

18 Hither may they who wake at dawn bring, to drink Soma, both the Gods,
Health-givers, Wonder-Workers, borne on paths of gold.

10 *Like a skilled hunter cutting birds in pieces* : Sāyaṇa takes *śvaghnī* for a fowler's wife', and *vijaḥ* for 'birds.' Benfey takes *vijaḥ* for 'dice,' and explains the clause as denoting a cunning gambler who tampers with the dice by shaving them down...The phrase *vijaḥ iva ā mināti* occurs again in RV,II. 12. 5, where Sāyaṇa takes *vijaḥ* for *udvejakaḥ* 'a vexer.' So uncertain are his explanations '—J. Muir, *O.S. Texts*, V. 186.

11 *Her sister* : Night. *Her lover* : the Sun.

12 *Never transgressing* : always obedient to the eternal Law or divine order of the universe.

18 *They who wake at dawn* : according to Sāyaṇa, the horses of the Aśvins. The expression may apply, with at least equal propriety, to the priests who rise at day-break to perform the morning sacrifices.

HYMN XCIII. *Agni-Soma.*

1 Agni and Soma, mighty Pair, graciously hearken to my call,
Accept in friendly wise my hymn, and prosper him who offers gifts.

2 The man who honours you to-day, Agni and Soma, with this hymn,
Bestow on him heroic strength, increase of kine, and noble steeds.

3 The man who offers holy oil and burnt oblations unto you,
Agni and Soma, shall enjoy great strength, with offspring, all his life.

4 Agni and Soma, famed is that your prowess wherewith ye stole the kine, his food, from Paṇi.
Ye caused the brood of Bṛsaya to perish; ye found the light, the single light for many.

5 Agni and Soma, joined in operation ye have set up the shining lights in heaven.
From curse and from reproach, Agni and Soma, ye freed the rivers that were bound in fetters.

6 One of you Mātariśvan brought from heaven, the Falcon rent the other from the mountain.
Strengthened by holy prayer Agni and Soma have made us ample room for sacrificing.

7 Taste, Agni, Soma, this prepared oblation; accept it, Mighty Ones, and let it please you.
Vouchsafe us good protection and kind favour: grant to the sacrificer health and riches.

8 Whoso with oil and poured oblation honours, with God-devoted heart, Agni and Soma,—
Protect his sacrifice, preserve him from distress, grant to the sacrificer great felicity.

1 *Agni and Soma* : or, O Agni-Soma, the two Gods forming a dual deity *ágnīṣomau*.

4 *Ye stole the kine* : recovered the cows (the rainclouds, or rays of light) which the niggard demon had carried off and concealed. *Bṛsaya* : the name of a demon or savage enemy.

5 *From curse and from reproach* : according to Sāyaṇa, 'the rivers were defiled by the dead body of Vṛtra, which had fallen into them ; their waters were, consequently, unfit to bear any part in sacred rites, until they were purified by Agni and Soma, that is, by oblations to fire and libations of Soma Juice.'—Wilson.

6 *Mātariśvan*, or in the nominative case, Mātariśvā, brought Agni or fire from heaven, and the Falcon brought Soma from the mountain or cloud, that is, says Sāyaṇa, from Svarga on the top of Mount Meru.

9 Invoked together, mates in wealth, Agni-Soma, accept our hymns:
Together be among the Gods.

10 Agni and Soma, unto him who worships you with holy oil
Shine forth an ample recompense.

11 Agni and Soma, be ye pleased with these oblations brought to you,
And come, together, nigh to us.

12 Agni and Soma, cherish well our horses, and let our cows be fat who yield oblations.
Grant power to us and to our wealthy patrons, and cause our holy rites to be successful.

HYMN XCIV. *Agni*

1 For Jātavedas worthy of our praise will we frame with our mind this eulogy as 'twere a car.
For good, in his assembly, is this care of ours. Let us not, in thy friendship, Agni, suffer harm.

2 The man for whom thou sacrificest prospereth, dwelleth without a foe, gaineth heroic might.
He waxeth strong, distress never approacheth him. Let us not, in thy friendship, Agni, suffer harm.

3 May we have power to kindle thee. Fulfil our thoughts. In thee the Gods eat the presented offering,
Bring hither the Ādityas, for we long for them. Let us not in thy friendship, Agni, suffer harm.

4 We will bring fuel and prepare burnt offerings, reminding thee at each successive festival.
Fulfil our thought that so we may prolong our lives. Let us not in thy friendship, Agni, suffer harm.

5 His ministers move forth, the guardians of the folk, protecting quadruped and biped with their rays.
Mighty art thou, the wondrous herald of the Dawn. Let us not in thy friendship, Agni, suffer harm.

6 Thou art Presenter and the chief Invoker, thou Director, Purifier, great High Priest by birth.
Knowing all priestly work thou perfectest it, Sage. Let us not in thy friendship, Agni, suffer harm.

7 Lovely of form art thou, alike on every side; though far, thou shinest brightly as if close at hand.
O God, thou seest through even the dark of night. Let us not in thy friendship, Agni, suffer harm.

8 Gods, foremost be his car who pours libations out, and let our hymn prevail o'er evil-hearted men.
Attend to this our speech and make it prosper well. Let us not in thy friendship, Agni, suffer harm.

9 Smite with thy weapons those of evil speech and thought, devouring demons, whether near or far away.
Then to the singer give free way for sacrifice. Let us not in thy friendship, Agni, suffer harm.

10 When to thy chariot thou hadst yoked two red steeds and two ruddy steeds, wind-sped, thy roar was like a bull's.
Thou with smoke-bannered flame attackest forest trees. Let us not in thy friendship, Agni, suffer harm.

11 Then at thy roar the very birds are terrified, when, eating-up the grass, thy sparks fly forth abroad.
Then is it easy for thee and thy car to pass. Let us not in thy friendship, Agni, suffer harm.

12 He hath the power to soothe Mitra and Varuṇa: wonderful is tht Maruts' wrath when they descend.
Be gracious: let their hearts be turned to us again. Let us not in thy friendship, Agni, suffer harm.

12 *Who yield oblations* : who supply milk to be mixed with Soma juice.

Our wealthy patrons : the rich house-holders who institute the sacrifices.

This Hymn and the four following are attributed to the Ṛṣi Kutsa, the son of Aṅgiras.

1 *Jātavedas* : Agni. See I. 44. 1.

As 'twere a car : as a carpenter constructs a car or wain.

In his assembly : among those who have met together to worship him. The meaning might also be : good, or auspicious, is his providence or loving care of us.

3 *Bring hither the Ādityas* : the sons of Aditi ; all the Gods, according to Sāyaṇa.

5 *His ministers* : his beams of light.

6 'Agni is here identified with the chief of the sixteen priests engaged at solemn sacrifices. He is *Adhvaryu* usually called the reciter of the *Yajuṣ*—here defined, by the scholiast, as the presenter of the offerings : he is the *Hotṛ*, or invoking priest : he is the *Praśāstṛ* or the *Maitrāvaruṇa*, whose duty it is to direct the other priests what to do, and when to perform their functions : he is the *potṛ*, or priest so termed and the family or hereditary *purohita* : or *purohita* may be the same as the *Brahma* of a ceremony'—being, to men, what *Bṛhaspati* is to the gods'.—Wilson.

12 *He hath the power* : Agni persuades Mitra and Varuṇa to send the rain and protects men from the fury of the Storm-Gods.

13 Thou art a God, thou art the wondrous Friend of Gods, the Vasu of the Vasus, fair in sacrifice.
Under, thine own most wide protection may we dwell. Let us not in thy friendship, Agni, suffer harm.

14 This is thy grace that, kindled in thine own abode, invoked with Soma thou soundest forth most benign,
Thou givest wealth and treasure to the worshipper. Let us not in thy friendship, Agni, suffer harm.

15 To whom thou, Lord of goodly riches, grantest freedom from every sin with perfect wholeness,
Whom with good strength thou quikenest, with children and wealth—may we be they, Eternal Being.

16 Such, Agni, thou who knowest all good fortune, God, lengthen here the days of our existence.
This prayer of ours may Varuṇa grant, and Mitra, and Aditi and Sindhu, Earth and Heaven.

HYMN XCV. *Agni*

1. To fair goals travel Two unlike in semblance: each in succession nourishes an infant.
One bears a Godlike Babe of golden colour; bright and fair-shining is he with the other.

2 Tvaṣṭar's ten daughters, vigilant and youthful, produced this Infant borne to sundry quarters.
They bear around him whose long flames are pointed, fulgent among mankind with native splendour.

3. Three several places of his birth they honour, in mid-air, in the heaven, and in the waters.
Governing in the east of earthly regions, the seasons hath he stablished in their order.

4 Who of you knows this secret One? The Infant by his own nature hath brought forth his Mothers.
The germ of many, from the waters' bosom he goes forth, wise and great, of Godlike nature.

5 Visible, fair, he grows in native brightness uplifted in the lap of waving waters.
When he was born both Tvaṣṭar's worlds were frightened: they turn to him and reverence the Lion.

6 The Two auspicious Ones, like women, tend him: like lowing cows they seek him in their manner.
He is the Lord of Might among the mighty; him, on the right, they balm with their oblations.

7 Like Savitar his arms with might he stretches; awful, he strives grasping the world's two borders.
He forces out from all a brilliant vesture, yea, from his Mothers draws he forth new raiment.

8 He makes him a most noble form of splendour, decking him in his home with milk and waters.
The Sage adorns the depths of air with wisdom: this is the meeting where the Gods are worshipped.

9 Wide through the firmament spreads forth triumphant the far-resplendent strength of thee the Mighty.

13 *The Vasu of the Vasus* best of the class of Gods called Vasus; or 'the good among the good.'

16 The second line of this verse terminates the following hymns, with two exceptions, as far as the hundred and first *Sūkta*. Mitra, Varuṇa, and Aditi have been before noticed. By *Sindhu* is to be understood the divinity presiding over, or identified with, flowing water; and it may mean either the sea or flowing streams collectively, or the river Indus. *Pṛthivī* and *Div* are the personified earth and heaven. These are requested to *honour*, meaning, to preserve, or perpetuate, whatever blessing has been asked for (*tat...māmahantām*); from *mah*, to venerate or worship.'-Wilson.

---

1 The *Two* are Day and Night, and the infant that each suckles in turn is Agni, as the Sun by day and Fire, or the Moon, by night.

2 *Tvaṣṭar's ten daughters*: the fingers, called daughters of the artist of the Gods on account of the skill and speed with which they perform their work, generate Agni by the attrition of the fire-sticks, and then the newly-born babe is carried about hither and thither to light the various sacrificial fires.

3 In his character of the Sun he rules especially in the east, and has established and regulates the seasons of the year.

4 *This secret One*: Agni latent in the waters, in the woods etc. '*Agni*, in the form of lightning, may be considered as the son of waters collected in the clouds; and those waters he is said to generate by the oblations he conveys.'—Wilson.

5 *Both Tvaṣṭar's worlds*: heaven and earth, formed by the divine artist represented as the Creator. Sāyaṇa takes *tvaṣṭuḥ* as an epithet of Agni, and accordingly Wilson translates: 'Both (heaven and earth) are alarmed, as the radiant Agni is born.'

6 *The Two auspicious Ones*: Heaven and Earth.

On the right: standing on the right side of the altar, the priests anoint him with offerings of clarified butter.

7 *Savitar*: the Sun. According to Sāyaṇa the Sun is called Savitar before rising, and Sūrya from his rising till his setting. *His Mothers*: are the Waters.

8 *The Sage*: Agni. *This is the meeting*: all this is the reason why men assemble to worship the Gods.

Kindled by us do thou preserve us, Agni, with all thy self-bright undiminished succours.

10 In dry spots he makes stream, and course, and torrent, and inundates the earth with floods that glisten.
All ancient things within his maw he gathers, and moves among the new fresh-sprouting grasses.

11 Fed with our fuel, purifying Agni, so blaze to us auspiciously for glory.
This prayer of ours may Varuṇa grant, and Mitra, and Aditi and Sindhu, Earth and Heaven.

HYMN XCVI. *Agni.*

1. He in the ancient way by strength engendered, lo ! straight hath taken to himself all wisdom.
The waters and the bowl have made him friendly. The Gods possessed the wealth-bestowing Agni.

2 At Āyu's ancient call he by his wisdom gave all this progeny of men their being,
And, by refulgent light, heaven and the waters. The Gods possessed the wealth-bestowing Agni.

3 Praise him, ye Āryan folk, as chief performer of sacrifice adored and ever toiling,
Well-tended, Son of Strength, the constant Giver. The Gods possessed the wealth-bestowing Agni.

4 That Mātariśvan rich in wealth and treasure, light-winner, finds a pathway for his offspring,
Guard of our folk, Father of earth and heaven. The Gods possessed the wealth-bestowing Agni.

5 Night and Dawn, changing each the other's colour, meeting together suckle one same Infant :
Golden between the heaven and earth he shineth. The Gods possessed the wealth-bestowing Agni.

6 Root of wealth, gathering-place of treasures, banner of sacrifice, who grants the suppliant's wishes :
Preserving him as their own life immortal, the Gods possessed the wealth-bestowing Agni.

7 Now and of old the home of wealth, the mansion of what is born and what was born aforetime,
Guard of what is and what will be hereafter,—the Gods possessed the wealth-bestowing Agni.

8 May the Wealth-Giver grant us conquering riches; may the Wealth-Giver grant us wealth with heroes.
May the Wealth-Giver grant us food with offspring, and length of days may the Wealth-Giver send us.

9 Fed with our fuel, purifying Agni, so blaze to us auspiciously for glory.
This prayer of ours may Varuṇa grant, and Mitra, and Aditi and Sindhu, Earth and Heaven.

1 *By strength engendered* : produced by violent agitation of the fire-sticks.

Possessed : before he was visible to men.

The bowl : the Soma juice contained in the *dhiṣáṇā*, or bowl. *Dhiṣáṇā* may be otherwise explained. Sāyaṇa, who is followed by Wilson, takes it to mean *vāk*, speech. Ludwig renders it by 'wish, or Wish-Goddess Dhiṣaṇā;' Grassmann by 'sacrificial offerings.'

2 *At Āyu's ancient call* : at the invitation of Āyu (living man) said by Sāyaṇa to be another name of Manu, the progenitor of mankind.

4 *Mātariśvan* : usually the name of the divine being who brought Agni from heaven (see I. 31.8), said by Sāyaṇa to mean in this place Agni himself.

5 *One same Infant* : Agni (see I.95.1.) whom they nourish with the oblation offered by men.

Golden : as the Sun.

HYMN XCVII. *Agni.*

1. Chasing with light our sin away, O Agni, shine thou wealth on us.
May his light chase our sin away.

2 For goodly fields, for pleasant homes, for wealth we sacrifice to thee.
May his light chase our sin away.

3 Best praiser of all these be he ; foremost, our chiefs who sacrifice.
May his light chase our sin away.

4 So that thy worshippers and we, thine, Agni, in our sons may live.
May his light chase our sin away.

5 As ever-conquering Agni's beams of splendour go to every side,
May his light chase our sin away.

6 To every side thy face is turned, thou art triumphant everywhere.
May his light chase our sin away.

7 O thou whose face looks every way, bear us past foes as in a ship.
May his light chase our sin away.

8 As in a ship, convey thou us for our advantage o'er the flood.
May his light chase our sin away.

3 May he, that is Kutsa, the Ṛṣi of the hymn, be preëminent among these who celebrate thy praises, and may the householders who have instituted this sacrifice be similarly distinguished.

HYMN XCVIII. *Agni.*

1. Still in Vaiśvānara's grace may we continue : yea, he is King supreme o'er all things living.
Sprung hence to life upon this All he looketh. Vaiśvānara hath rivalry with Sūrya.

2 Present in heaven, in earth, all-present Agni,—all plants that grow on ground hath he pervaded.
May Agni, may Vaiśvānara with vigour, present, preserve us day and night from foemen.

3 Be this thy truth, Vaiśvānara, to us-ward: let wealth in rich abundance gather round us.
This prayer of ours may Varuṇa grant, and Mitra, and Aditi and Sindhu, Earth and Heaven.

HYMN XCIX. *Agni.*

1. For Jātavedas let us press the Soma : may he consume the wealth of the malignant.
May Agni carry us through all our troubles, through grief as in a boat across the river.

HYMN C. *Indra.*

1. May he who hath his home with strength, the Mighty, the King supreme of earth and spacious heaven,
Lord of true power, to be invoked in battles,—may Indra, girt by Maruts, be our succour.

2 Whose way is unattainable like Sūrya's : he in each fight is the strong Vṛtra-slayer,
Mightiest with his Friends in his own courses. May Indra, girt by Maruts, be our succour.

3 Whose paths go forth in their great might resistless, forthmilking, as it were, heaven's genial moisture.
With manly strength triumphant, foe-subduer,—may Indra, girt by Maruts, be our succour.

4 Among Aṅgirases he was the chiefest, a Friend with friends, mighty amid the mighty.
Praiser mid praisers, honoured most of singers. May Indra, girt by Maruts, be our succour.

5 Strong with the Rudras as with his own children, in manly battle conquering his foemen,
With his close comrades doing deeds of glory,—may Indra, girt by Maruts, be our succour.

6 Humbler of pride, exciter of the conflict, the Lord of heroes, God invoked of many,
May he this day gain with our men the sunlight. May Indra, girt by Maruts, be our succour.

7 His help hath made him cheerer in the battle, the folk have made him guardian of their comfort.
Sole Lord is he of every holy service. May Indra, girt by Maruts, be our succour.

8 To him the Hero, on high days of prowess, heroes for help and booty shall betake them.
He hath found light even in the blinding darkness. May Indra, girt by Maruts, be our succour.

9 He with his left hand checketh even the mighty, and with his right hand gathereth up the booty.
Even with the humble he acquireth riches. May Indra, girt by Maruts, be our succour.

10 With hosts on foot and cars he winneth treasures : well is he known this day by all the people.
With manly might he conquereth those who hate him. May Indra, girt by Maruts, be our succour.

11 When in his ways with kinsmen or with strangers he speedeth to the fight, invoked of many,

1 *Vaiśvānara,* is an epithet of Agni or Fire as present with, common to, or benefiting, all men.
Sprung hence to life : produced from these two *araṇis* or fire-sticks.

This Hymn, consisting of a single stanza, is ascribed to the Ṛṣi Kaśyapa, the son of Marīci.

This Hymn is ascribed to the regal Ṛṣis the Vārṣāgiras, the five sons of the Rājā Vṛṣāgir, whose names are mentioned in the seventeenth stanza.

3 *Whose paths* : *pānthāsaḥ*, paths, is explained as 'rays' by Sāyaṇa. Indra is here represented as the God of light and of rain.

5 *Rudras* : the Maruts, sons of Rudra the chief Storm-God. They are the *close comrades* or faithful companions of Indra, who regards them not as his equals but as his children.

6 *The sunlight* : the hymn is addressed to Indra for aid in approaching battle. Sāyaṇa says that the Vārṣāgiras pray that they may have daylight and that their enemies may fight in the dark.

7 Indra is regarded as their helper and inspiriter in battle and their protector in peace. He also presides over all acts of worship, and as such rewards those who serve him.

9 *Even the humble* : not the strong only, but the feeble man also acquires riches with his help.

For gain of waters, and of sons and grandsons, may Indra, girt by Maruts, be our succour.

12 Awful and fierce, fiend-slayer, thunder-wielder, with boundless knowledge, hymned by hundreds, mighty,
In strength like Soma, guard of the Five Peoples, may Indra, girt by Maruts, be our succour.

13 Winning the light, hitherward roars his thunder like the terrific mighty voice of Heaven.
Rich gifts and treasures evermore attend him. May Indra, girt by Maruts, be our succour.

14 Whose home eternal through his strength surrounds him on every side, his laud, the earth and heaven,
May he, delighted with our service, save us. May Indra, girt by Maruts, be our succour.

15 The limit of whose power not Gods by Godhead, nor mortal men have reached, nor yet the Waters.
Both Earth and Heaven in vigour he surpasseth. May Indra, girt by Maruts, be our succour.

16 The red and tawny mare, blaze-marked, high standing, celestial who, to bring Ṛjrāśva riches,
Drew at the pole the chariot yoked with stallions, joyous, among the hosts of men was noted.

17 The Vārṣāgiras unto thee, O Indra, the Mighty One, sing forth this laud to please thee,
Ṛjrāśva with his fellows, Ambarīṣa, Surādhas, Sahadeva, Bhayamāna.

18 He, much invoked, hath slain Dasyus and Śimyus, after his wont, and laid them low with arrows.
The mighty Thunderer with his fair-complexioned friends won the land, the sunlight, and the waters.

19 May Indra evermore be our protector, and unimperilled may we win the booty.
This prayer of ours may Varuṇa grant, and Mitra, and Aditi and Sindhu, Earth and Heaven.

12 *Guard of the Five Peoples* : of the five classes of beings, according to Sāyaṇa, that is, Gods, Gandharvas, Apsarases, Asuras and Rākṣasas. Probably the five Ārya tribes are intended See I, 7.9.

14 *The Earth and Heaven*, his dwelling-place, are his everlasting song of praise because they have been established and regulated by him. This is Ludwig's explanation of this obscure verse.

16 The epithets in this stanza are taken by Ludwig as names of the six horses with which Ṛjrāśva drove to battle and conquered. The last four verses of the hymn appear to have been added after the victory.

18 *Dasyus and Śimyus* : men of indigenous hostile races.

His fair-complexioned friends : explained by Sāyaṇa as the glittering Maruts, means probably the Āryan invaders as opposed to the dark-skinned races of the country.

HYMN CI. *Indra.*

1. SING, with oblation, praise to him who maketh glad, who with Ṛjiśvan drove the dusky brood away.
Fain for help, him the strong whose right hand wields the bolt, him girt by Maruts we invoke to be our Friend.

2 Indra, who with triumphant wrath smote Vyaṁsa down, and Śambara, and Pipru the unrighteous one;
Who extirpated Śuṣṇa the insatiate,—him girt by Maruts we invoke to be our Friend.

3 He whose great work of manly might is heaven and earth, and Varuṇa and Sūrya keep his holy law ;
Indra, whose law the rivers follow as they flow,—him girt by Maruts we invoke to be our Friend.

4 He who is Lord and Master of the steeds and kine, honoured—the firm and sure—at every holy act;
Slayer even of the strong who pours no offering out,—him girt by Maruts we invoke to be our Friend.

5 He who is Lord of all the world that moves and breathes, who for the Brāhman first before all found the Cows;
Indra who cast the Dasyus down beneath his feet,—him girt by Maruts we invoke to be our Friend.

6 Whom cowards must invoke and valiant men of war, invoked by those who conquer and by those who flee;
Indra, to whom all beings turn their constant thought,—him girt by Maruts we invoke to be our Friend.

This Hymn and the following thirteen are ascribed to the Ṛṣi Kutsa.

1 *Ṛjiśvan* : a king, favoured and protected by Indra. See I. 51.5 ; 53.8.

The dusky brood : the dark aborigines who opposed the Āryans.

2 *Vyaṁsa, Śambara,* and *Śuṣṇa* are names of fiends of drought.

5 *Who for the Brāhman* : according to Sāyaṇa, who recovered for the Aṅgirases the cows that had been carried off by the Paṇis. See I. 32. 11.

7 Refulgent in the Rudras' region he proceeds, and with the Rudras through the wide space speeds the Dame.
The hymn of praise extols Indra the far-renowned : him girt by Maruts we invoke to be our Friend.

8 O girt by Maruts, whether thou delight thee in loftiest gathering-place or lowly dwelling,
Come thence unto our rite, true boon-bestower : through love of thee have we prepared oblations.

9 We, fain for thee, strong Indra, have pressed Soma, and, O thou sought with prayer, have made oblations.
Now at this sacrifice, with all thy Maruts, on sacred grass, O team-borne God, rejoice thee.

10 Rejoice thee with thine own Bay Steeds, O Indra, unclose thy jaws and let thy lips be open.
Thou with the fair cheek, let thy Bay Steeds bring thee : gracious to us, be pleased with our oblation.

11 Guards of the camp whose praisers are the Maruts, may we through Indra, get ourselves the booty.
This prayer of ours may Varuṇa grant, and Mitra, and Aditi and Sindhu, Earth and Heaven.

HYMN CII. *Indra.*

1. To thee the Mighty One I bring this mighty hymn, for thy desire hath been gratified by my laud.
In Indra, yea in him victorious through his strength, the Gods have joyed at feast and when the Soma flowed.

2 The Seven Rivers bear his glory far and wide, and heaven and sky and earth display his comely form.
The Sun and Moon in change alternate run their course, that we, O Indra, may behold and may have faith.

3 Maghavan, grant us that same car to bring us spoil, thy conquering car in which we joy in shock of fight.
Thou, Indra, whom our hearts praise highly in the war, grant shelter, Maghavan, to us who love thee well.

4 Encourage thou our side in every fight: may we, with thee for our ally, conquer the foeman's host.
Indra, bestow on us joy and felicity: break down, O Maghavan, the vigour of our foes.

5 For here in divers ways these men invoking thee, holder of treasures, sing thee hymns to win thine aid.
Ascend the car that thou mayest bring spoil to us, for, Indra, thy fixt mind winneth the victory.

6 His arms win kine, his power is boundless, in each act best, with a hundred helps, waker of battle's din
Is Indra : none may rival him in mighty strength. Hence, eager for the spoil, the people call on him.

7 Thy glory, Maghavan, exceeds a hundred, yea, more than a hundred, than a thousand mid the folk,
The great bowl hath inspirited thee boundlessly : so mayst thou slay the Vṛtras, breaker-down of forts !

8 Of thy great might there is a threefold counterpart, the three earths, Lord of men and the three realms of light.
Above this whole world, Indra, thou hast waxen great : without a foe art thou, by nature, from of old.

9 We invocate thee first among the Deities : thou hast become a mighty Conqueror in fight.
May Indra fill with spirit this our singer's heart, and make our car impetuous, foremost in attack.

10 Thou hast prevailed, and hast not kept the booty back, in trifling battles or in those of great account.
We make thee keen, the Mighty One, to succour us : inspire us, Maghavan, when we defy the foe.

11 May Indra evermore be our Protector, and unimperilled may we win the booty.

7 *The Dame* : Ludwig suggests that Rodasī, the wife of Rudra, is intended, and refers to the Old-German myth of the Wind's Bride.

11 *Guards of the camp* : may we who are the guardians of the camp or new settlement, praised and favoured by the Maruts, win the spoil. The words *marútstotrasya vṛjánasya* are somewhat obscure.

---

2 *The Seven Rivers* : the chief rivers in the neighbourhood of the earliest Āryan settlements. See I, 32, 12.

7 *The great bowel* : the vessel containing the exhilarating Soma juice, or the mighty libation itself. The *forts* are the cloud-castles of the demons of the air which Indra destroys with his lightning : 'the clouds whose moving turrets make the bastions of the storm.'-Shelley, *Witch of Atlas*.

8 *The three earths* : perhaps the earth, the atmosphere, and the heaven.

The three realms of light : or according to Sāyaṇa, the three fires or fire in three forms, as the sun in heaven, the lightning in mid-air, and terrestrial fire on earth. See also I. 105, 5.

This prayer of ours may Varuṇa grant and Mitra, and Aditi and Sindhu, Earth and Heaven.

HYMN CIII. *Indra.*

1. THAT highest Indra-power of thine is distant : that which is here sages possessed aforetime.
This one is on the earth, in heaven the other, and both unite as flag with flag in battle.

2 He spread the wide earth out and firmly fixed it, smote with his thunderbolt and loosed the waters.
Maghavan with his puissance struck down Ahi, rent Rauhiṇa to death and slaughtered Vyaṁsa.

3 Armed with his bolt and trusting in his prowess he wandered shattering the forts of Dāsas.
Cast thy dart, knowing, Thunderer, at the Dasyu ; increase the Ārya's might and glory, Indra.

4 For him who thus hath taught these human races, Maghavan, bearing a fame-worthy title,
Thunderer, drawing nigh to slay the Dasyus, hath given himself the name of Son for glory.

5 See this abundant wealth that he possesses, and put your trust in Indra's hero vigour.
He found the cattle, and he found the horses, he found the plants, the forests and the waters.

6 To him the truly strong, whose deeds are many, to him the strong Bull let us pour the Soma.
The Hero, watching like a thief in ambush, goes parting the possessions of the godless.

7 Well didst thou do that hero deed, O Indra, in waking with thy bolt the slumbering Ahi.
In thee, delighted, Dames divine rejoiced them, the flying Maruts and all Gods were joyful.

8 As thou hast smitten Śuṣṇa, Pipru, Vṛtra and Kuyava, and Śambara's forts O Indra.
This prayer of ours may Varuṇa grant, and Mitra, and Aditi and Sindhu, Earth and Heaven.

HYMN CIV. *Indra.*

1. THE altar hath been made for thee to rest on : come like a panting courser and be seated.
Loosen thy flying Steeds, set free thy Horses who bear thee swiftly nigh at eve and morning.

2 These men have come to Indra for assistance : shall he not quickly come upon these pathways?
May the Gods quell the fury of the Dāsa, and may they lead our folk to happy fortune.

3 He who hath only wish as his possession casts on himself, casts foam amid the waters.
Both wives of Kuyava in milk have bathed them: may they be drowned within the depth of Śiphā.

4 This hath his kinship checked who lives beside us : with ancient streams forth speeds and rules the Hero,

1 *That highest Indra-power* : Benfey explains this verse as meaning : Indra's might is in a certain way divided : one part of it is possessed by the sages who by their hymns, sacrifices and libations of Soma juice give him complete power to perform his great deeds. Sāyaṇa says that the Sun and fire are equally the lustre of Indra, one in heaven and the other on earth : and that by day fire is combined with the Sun, and by night the Sun is combined with fire.

2 *Rauhiṇa*, said to be a demon, is, like the other fiends of drought, a purple cloud that withholds the rain.

3 *Dāsas* : or Dasyus, the non-Āryan inhabitants of the land.

Knowing : distinguishing the Āryan from the barbarian.

4 The meaning of this verse appears to be, as Ludwig says, that Indra, in preparing to slay the Dasyus, has become, as it were, a son to the pious worshipper who has proclaimed his great deeds to men.

7 *Dames divine* : the Consorts of the Gods.

8 *Kuyava* : meaning, probably, 'causing bad harvests,' is the name of another of the demons of drought.

2 *The Dāsa* : explained by Sāyaṇa as the destroying demon. It apparently means here a chief of non-Āryan race whom the suppliants were going to attack.

3 Sāyaṇa explains : the Asura, or demon, Kuyava, who knows the wealth of others carries it away of himself, and being present in the water he carries off the water with the foam. In this water which has been carried away Kuyava's two wives bathe. Benfey takes the foamy water to mean the fertilizing rain. Ludwig's explanation is : While the poor Ārya who can only wish for the wealth which he does not possess has not even ordinary water to wash himself in, the wives of the enemy, in the insolent pride of their riches, bathe in milk.

Kuyava : perhaps a name given by the Āryans to one of the non-Āryan chieftains.

Śiphā, is said by Sāyaṇa to be the name of a river.

4 This stanza is very obscure. The meaning appears to be that the friendship of Indra, who sends down the rain as before, has put an end to the

Añjasī, Kuliśī, and Vīrapatnī, delighting him, bear milk upon their waters.

5 Soon as this Dasyu's traces were discovered, as she who knows her home, he sought the dwelling.

Now think thou of us, Maghavan, nor cast us away as doth a profligate his treasure.

6 Indra, as such, give us a share of sunlight, of waters, sinlessness, and reputation.

Do thou no harm to our yet unborn offspring: our trust is in thy mighty Indra-power.

7 Now we, I think, in thee as such have trusted: lead us on, Mighty One, to ample riches.

In no unready house give us, O Indra invoked of many, food and drink when hungry.

8 Slay us not, Indra; do not thou forsake us: steal not away the joys which we delight in.

Rend not our unborn brood, strong Lord of Bounty! our vessels with the life that is within them.

9 Come to us; they have called thee Soma-lover: here is the pressed juice. Drink thereof for rapture.

Widely-capacious, pour it down within thee, and, invocated, hear us like a Father.

HYMN CV. *Viśvedevas.*

1. WITHIN the waters runs the Moon, he with the beauteous wings in heaven.

Ye lightnings with your golden wheels, men find not your abiding-place. Mark this my woe, ye Earth and Heaven.

2 Surely men crave and gain their wish. Close to her husband clings the wife.

And, in embraces intertwined, both give and take the bliss of love. Mark this my woe, ye Earth and Heaven.

3 O never may that light, ye Gods, fall from its station in the sky.

Ne'er fail us one like Soma sweet, the spring of our felicity. Mark this my woe ye Earth and Heaven.

4 I ask the last of sacrifice. As envoy he shall tell it forth.

Where is the ancient law divine? Who is its new diffuser now? Mark this my woe, ye Earth and Heaven.

5 Ye Gods who yonder have your home in the three lucid realms of heaven,

What count ye truth and what untruth? Where is mine ancient call on you? Mark this my woe, ye Earth and Heaven.

6 What is your firm support of Law? What Varuṇa's observant eye?

How may we pass the wicked on the path of mighty Aryaman? Mark this my woe, ye Earth and Heaven.

7 I am the man who sang of old full many a laud when Soma flowed.

Yet torturing cares consume me as the wolf assails the thirsty deer. Mark this my woe, ye Earth and Heaven.

8 Like rival wives on every side enclosing ribs oppress me sore.

O Śatakratu, biting cares devour me, singer of thy praise, as rats devour the weaver's threads. Mark this my woe, ye Earth and Heaven.

insolence of Kuyaya. See Ludwig, Ueber die neuesten Arbeiten auf dem Gebiete der Ṛgveda-forschung.

The signification of the three rivers in the second line is obscure. Benfey considers the names to be feminine personifications of the clouds.

Vīrapatnī, 'the hero's wife,' occurs, as Dr. Hall has pointed out, in VI. 49. 7, as an epithet of Sarasvatī the Goddess, and it may possibly here mean the river Sarasvatī.

5 *As she who knows her dwelling*: as a cow who knows her stall.

7 *In no unready house*: that is, in a house well supplied and furnished.

8 *The joys which we delight in*: probably, our children.

Our vessels: our wives with their unborn babes. Sāyaṇa gives other explanations of the expression.

This Hymn is ascribed either to Tṛta or to Kutsa. It is addressed to the Viśvedevas on behalf of Tṛta who had been imprisoned in a well. See I. 52.5. But see Macdonell, J.R.A.S., July, 1893, pp. 422 note 2, and 460.

1 *Within the waters*: in the ocean of air. *He with the beauteous wings*: the Sun.

Mark this my woe: the text has only *vittam me asyá rodasī*, 'know of this of me, O Heaven and Earth,' which means, according to Sāyaṇa, either 'be aware of this my affliction,' or 'attend to this my hymn.'

4 *I ask the last*: the latest or youngest of the Gods, Agni, as being continually reproduced.

5 *The three lucid realms of heaven*: the world is divided into earth, sky, and heaven, and each of these, again, is sometimes spoken of as threefold.

6 *The path of mighty Aryaman*: probably the milky way, regarded as the path to heaven.—Ludwig. The general meaning of the questions in this and the two preceding verses is: Is there no longer any distinction between right and wrong? Is there no moral government of the world? If there be, why am I, a faithful worshipper, allowed to suffer this undeserved misery?

8 *Enclosing ribs*: according to Sāyaṇa, the walls of the well in which Tṛta was confined. *Weaver's threads*: the meaning of *śiśnā* thus explained by Sāyaṇa is uncertain. Ludwig is of opinion that wooden phallus-idols are intended. The line recurs in X. 33.3.

9 Where those seven rays are shining, thence my home and family extend.
This Trta Āptya knoweth well, and speaketh out for brotherhood. Mark this my woe, ye Earth and Heaven.

10 May those five Bulls which stand on high full in the midst of mighty heaven,
Having together swiftly borne my praises to the Gods, return. Mark this my woe, ye Earth and Heaven.

11 High in the mid ascent of heaven those Birds of beauteous pinion sit.
Back from his path they drive the wolf as he would cross the restless floods. Mark this my woe, ye Earth and Heaven.

12 Firm is this new-wrought hymn of praise, and meet to be told forth, O Gods.
The flowing of the floods is Law, Truth is the Sun's extended light. Mark this my woe, ye Earth and Heaven.

13 Worthy of laud, O Agni, is that kinship which thou hast with Gods.
Here seat thee like a man : most wise, bring thou the Gods for sacrifice. Mark this my woe, ye Earth and Heaven.

14 Here seated, man-like as a priest shall wisest Agni to the Gods
Speed onward our oblations, God among the Gods, intelligent. Mark this my woe, ye Earth and Heaven.

15 Varuṇa makes the holy prayer. To him who finds the path we pray.
He in the heart reveals his thought. Let sacred worship rise anew. Mark this my woe, ye Earth and Heaven.

16 That pathway of the Sun in heaven, made to be highly glorified,
Is not to be transgressed, O Gods. O mortals, ye behold it not. Mark this my woe, ye Earth and Heaven.

17 Trta, when buried in the well, calls on the Gods to succour him.
That call of his Bṛhaspati heard and released him from distress. Mark this my woe, ye Earth and Heaven.

18 A ruddy wolf beheld me once, as I was faring on my path.
He, like a carpenter whose back is aching crouched and slunk away. Mark this my woe, ye Earth and Heaven.

19 Through this our song may we, allied with Indra, with all our heroes conquer in the battle.
This prayer of ours may Varuṇa grant, and Mitra, and Aditi and Sindhu, Earth and Heaven.

9 *Those seven rays* : of the Sun, says Sāyaṇa. But probably, as Ludwig suggests, the rays are the flames of Agni. That is, Agni with his bright beams, or the worship of Agni, is the central point through which I and all the members of my family are connected and held together.

Tṛta Āptya : A mythical being who dwells in the remotest part of the heavens, and who knows the celestial origin of the human race.

10 *Those five Bulls* : the stars of some constellation. According to Sāyaṇa, Indra, Varuṇa, Agni, Aryaman, and Savitar, or Fire, Wind, Sun, Moon, and Lightning. Sāyaṇa explains *ukṣáṇaḥ*, bulls or oxen, as 'shedders of benefits.'

11 *Those Birds of beauteous pinion* : the stars.

The wolf ; darkness or eclipse of the Moon.

12 *Law* (*ṛtám.*) eternal order. 'The meaning of the word as applied to the natural world connects itself with the alternation of day and night, the regular passage of the sun through the heavens, or the unswerving motion of the rain in its fall from heaven and of the streams along their courses. This last application of the word may have determined its special sense of 'water' in the later language. Wallis, *Cosmology of the Ṛgveda*, p. 93.

16 *That pathway of the Sun* : according to Benfey, the way of truth, right, eternal order, as in verse 12. According to Ludwig the path of the Sun between the tropics is meant. The Gods, says Sāyaṇa, must not disregard the path of the Sun, because their existence depends upon him as regulator of the seasons at which sacrifices are offered to them. Still less may men disregard it, who as sinners do not behold or understand it aright.

17 *Bṛhaspati* ; the Lord of Prayer.

18 *Like a carpenter* : the comparison is not very clear. It apparently means that the wolf crept away, arching his back or contracting his limbs, like a carpenter bending over his work till his back aches. Sāyaṇa suggests also an alternative and totally different explanation of the whole passage, by interpreting *vṛka*, the wolf, as the Moon, and reading *māsakṛt*, maker of months, instead of *mā sakṛt*, me once. See Ludwig, Uber die neuesten Arbeiten auf dem Gebiete der Ṛgveda-forschung.

HYMN CVI. *Viśvedevas.*

1. CALL we for aid on Indra, Mitra, Varuṇa and Agni and the Marut host and Aditi.
Even as a chariot from a difficult ravine, bountiful Vasus, rescue us from all distress.

2 Come ye Ādityas for our full prosperity, in conquests of the foe, ye Gods, bring joy to us.
Even as a chariot from a difficult ravine, bountiful Vasus, rescue us from all distress.

1 *Vasus* : originally meaning 'the good' is sometimes used, as in this place to designate Gods in general.

3 May the most glorious Fathers aid us, and the two Goddesses, Mothers of the Gods, who strengthen Law.
Even as a chariot from a difficult ravine, bountiful Vasus, rescue us from all distress.

4 To mighty Narāśaṁsa, strengthening his might, to Pūṣan, ruler over men, we pray with hymns.
Even as a chariot from a difficult ravine, bountiful Vasus, rescue us from all distress.

5 Bṛhaspati, make us evermore an easy path: we crave what boon thou hast for men in rest and stir.
Like as a chariot from a difficult ravine, bountiful Vasus, rescue us from all distress.

6 Sunk in the pit the Ṛṣi Kutsa called, to aid, Indra the Vṛtra-slayer, Lord of power and might.
Even as a chariot from a difficult ravine, bountiful Vasus, rescue us from all distress.

7 May Aditi the Goddess guard us with the Gods: may the protecting God keep us with ceaseless care.
This prayer of ours may Varuṇa grant, and Mitra, and Aditi and Sindhu, Earth and Heaven.

HYMN CVII. *Viśvedevas.*

1. The sacrifice obtains the Gods' acceptance: be graciously inclined to us, Ādityas.
Hitherward let your favour be directed, and be our best deliverer from trouble.

2 By praise-songs of Aṅgirases exalted, may the Gods come to us with their protection.
May Indra with his powers, Maruts with Maruts, Aditi with Ādityas grant us shelter.

3 This laud of ours may Varuṇa and Indra, Aryaman, Agni, Savitar find pleasant.
This prayer of ours may Varuṇa grant, and Mitra, and Aditi and Sindhu, Earth and Heaven.

3 *The Fathers* : the Manes or spirits of departed ancestors.

The two Goddesses : Heaven and Earth.

4 *Narāśaṁsa* : a mystical name of Agni, 'the Praise of Men.'

Pūṣan : the God who nourishes men and 'flocks and herds.

6 *Sunk in the pit* : perhaps figuratively for 'in distress.' Kutsa is the Ṛṣi to whom the hymn is ascribed.

---

2 *Maruts with Maruts* : that is, all the Maruts together, or Maruts with their winds and storm.

HYMN CVIII. *Indra-Agni.*

1. On that most wondrous car of yours, O Indra and Agni, which looks round on all things living,
Take ye your stand and come to us together, and drink libations of the flowing Soma.

2 As vast as all this world is in its compass, deep as it is, with its far-stretching surface,
So let this Soma be, Indra and Agni, made for your drinking till your soul be sated.

3 For ye have won a blessed name together: yea, with one aim ye strove, O Vṛtra-slayers.
So Indra-Agni, seated here together, pour in, ye Mighty Ones, the mighty Soma.

4 Both stand adorned, when fires are duly kindled, spreading the sacred grass, with lifted ladles.
Drawn by strong Soma juice poured forth around us, come, Indra-Agni, and display your favour.

5 The brave deeds ye have done, Indra and Agni, the forms ye have displayed and mighty exploits,
The ancient and auspicious bonds of friendship,—for sake of these drink of the flowing Soma.

6 As first I said when choosing you, in battle we must contend with Asuras for this Soma.
So came ye unto this my true conviction, and drank libations of the flowing Soma.

7 If in your dwelling, or with prince or Brāhman, ye, Indra-Agni, Holy Ones, rejoice you,
Even from thence, ye mighty Lords, come hither, and drink libation of the flowing Soma.

8 If with the Yadus, Turvaśas, ye sojourn, with Druhyus, Anus, Pūrus, Indra-Agni!
Even from thence, ye mighty Lords, come hither, and drink libations of the flowing Soma.

4 'We have, merely, in the text, the epithets in the dual number : the commentator supplies the *Adhvaryu* and his assistant priest.'—Wilson. Benfey refers the dual epithets to Indra and Agni, translating them severally by 'honoured,' 'for whom sacred grass has been strewn', 'towards whom the ladles have been uplifted.'

8 This verse contains the names of the five well-known Āryan tribes or families, said to be descendants of the five similarly named sons of Yayāti. See 1.7.9.

9 Whether, O Indra-Agni, ye be dwelling in lowest earth, in central, or in highest.
Even from thence, ye mighty Lords, come hither, and drink libations of the flowing Soma.

10 Whether, O Indra-Agni, ye be dwelling in highest earth, in central, or in lowest,
Even from thence, ye mighty Lords, come hither, and drink libations of the flowing Soma.

11 Whether ye be in heaven, O Indra-Agni, on earth, on mountains, in the herbs, or waters,
Even from thence, ye mighty Lords, come hither, and drink libations of the flowing Soma.

12 If, when the Sun to the mid-heaven hath mounted, ye take delight in food, O Indra-Agni,
Even from thence, ye mighty Lords, come hither, and drink libations of the flowing Soma.

13 Thus having drunk your fill of our libation, win us all kinds of wealth, Indra and Agni.
This prayer of ours may Varuṇa grant, and Mitra, and Aditi and Sindhu, Earth and Heaven.

HYMN CIX. *Indra-Agni.*

1. Longing for weal I looked around, in spirit, for kinsmen, Indra-Agni, or for brothers.
No providence but yours alone is with me : so have I wrought for you this hymn for succour.

2 For I have heard that ye give wealth more freely than worthless son-in-law or spouse's brother.
So offering to you this draught of Soma, I make you this new hymn, Indra and Agni,

3 Let us not break the cords : with this petition we strive to gain the powers of our forefathers.
For Indra-Agni the strong drops are joyful, for here in the bowl's lap are both the press-stones.

4 For you the bowl divine, Indra and Agni, presses the Soma gladly to delight you.
With hands auspicious and fair arms, ye Aśvins, haste, sprinkle it with sweetness in the waters.

5 You, I have heard, were mightiest, Indra-Agni, when Vṛtra fell and when the spoil was parted.
Sit at this sacrifice, ye ever active, on the strewn grass, and with the juice delight you.

6 Surpassing all men where they shout for battle, ye Twain exceed the earth and heaven in greatness.
Greater are ye than rivers and than mountains, O Indra-Agni, and all things beside them.

7 Bring wealth and give it, ye whose arms wield thunder : Indra and Agni, with your powers protect us.
Now of a truth these be the very sunbeams wherewith our fathers were of old united.

8 Give, ye who shatter forts, whose hands wield thunder : Indra and Agni, save us in our battles.
This prayer of ours may Varuṇa grant, and Mitra, and Aditi and Sindhu, Earth and Heaven.

HYMN CX. *Ṛbhus.*

1. The holy work I wrought before is wrought again : my sweetest hymn is sung to celebrate your praise.

9 *In lowest earth, in central, or in highest* : in earth, mid-air, or heaven, the word earth being used loosely for sphere or world. Or the reference may be to the fanciful threefold division of the earth.

---

2 *Than worthless son-in-law or spouse's brother* : the worthless or defective son-in-law, or suitor, who has not, as Yāska explains the necessary qualifications, is obliged to win the consent of his future father-in-law by very liberal gifts. The maiden's brother gives her rich presents out of natural affection.

3 *Let us not break the cords* : let us not break or interrupt the long series of religious rites observed by our ancestors and continued to our time. Or, as Sāyaṇa explains, let us not cut or break off the long line of posterity, but ask for and obtain 'descendants endowed with the vigour of their progenitors.'

The strong drops : the exhilarating Soma.

In the bowl's lap : close to the vessel which receives the juice. But see Ludwig, Ueber die neuesten Arbeiten, etc. pp. 85-88.

4 *Ye Aśvins* : here called upon to perform the duties of the Adhvaryu and his assistant priest, to mix the sweetness, or Soma, with water to be offered to Indra and Agni.

7 *These be the very sunbeams* : The meaning of the line may be that the worship of Indra and Agni is the great bond which has kept the Ṛṣi's ancestors united. Wilson, following Sāyaṇa translates : 'May those rays of the Sun, by which our forefathers have attained, together, a heavenly region, shine also upon us.'

---

1 *This sea for all the Gods* : this vessel containing Soma juice for all the Gods, or for the particular class of Gods called Viśvedevāḥ or Viśvedevas.

The hallowing word : *Svāhā* (Ave ! Hail !) ; an exclamation used in making oblations to the Gods.

Here, O ye Ṛbhus, is this sea for all the Gods : sate you with Soma offered with the hallowing word.

2 When, seeking your enjoyment onward from afar, ye, certain of my kinsmen, wandered on your way,
Sons of Sudhanvan, after your long journeying, ye came unto the home of liberal Savitar.

3 Savitar therefore gave you immortality, because ye came proclaiming him whom naught can hide ;
And this the drinking-chalice of the Asura, which till that time was one, ye made to be fourfold.

4 When they had served with zeal at sacrifice as priests, they, mortal as they were, gained immortality.
The Ṛbhus, children of Sudhanvan, bright as suns, were in a year's course made associate with prayers.

5 The Ṛbhus, with a rod measured, as 'twere a field, the single sacrificial chalice wide of mouth,
Lauded of all who saw, praying for what is best, desiring glorious fame among Immortal Gods.

6 As oil in ladles, we through knowledge will present unto the Heroes of the firmament our hymn,—
The Ṛbhus who came near with this great Father's speed, and rose to heaven's high sphere to eat the strengthening food.

7 Ṛbhu to us is Indra freshest in his might, Ṛbhu with powers and wealth is giver of rich gifts.
Gods, through your favour may we on the happy day quell the attacks of those who pour no offerings forth.

8 Out of a skin, O Ṛbhus, once ye formed a cow, and brought the mother close unto her calf again.
Sons of Sudhanvan, Heroes, with surpassing skill ye made your aged Parents youthful as before.

9 Help us with strength where spoil is won, O Indra : joined with the Ṛbhus give us varied bounty.
This prayer of ours may Varuṇa grant, and Mitra, and Aditi and Sindhu, Earth and Heaven.

2 *Seeking your enjoyment* : desirous of enjoying libation of Soma juice.

My kinsmen : Sudhanvan, father of the Ṛbhus, was a descendant of Aṅgiras, as was also Kutsa the Ṛṣi of the hymn.

3 *Him whom naught can hide* : or, from whom nothing can be hidden, that is, Savitar as the Sun.

The drinking-chalice of the Asura : the cup that had been made by the Asura or immortal God Tvaṣṭar. See I. 20. 6. This chalice appears to be the moon which contains the Amṛta or nectar of the Gods. The legend seems to mean that Tvaṣṭar as God of the year created it uniformly bright, and that the Ṛbhus, as Gods of the seasons, made it fourfold or diversified with four phases. See Hillebrandt. Vedische Mythologie, I. p. 515.

4 *Associate with prayers* : 'connected with the ceremonies (appropriated to the different seasons) of the year.'—Wilson.

5 *Measured* : in order to divide it into four, as is said in verse 3.

6 *This great Father* : Savitar as the Sun, the source of all life. *Strengthening food* : Soma.

8 *A skin* : perhaps the dried-up earth. *A cow* : the earth refreshed by the Rains. *The mother* : the earth. *Her calf* : the autumn Sun. *Parents* : Heaven and Earth.

HYMN CXI. *Ṛbhus.*

1. WORKING with skill they wrought the lightly rolling car : they wrought the Bays who bear Indra and bring great gifts.
The Ṛbhus for their Parents made life young again ; and fashioned for the calf a mother by its side.

2 For sacrifice make for us active vital power ; for skill and wisdom food with noble progeny.
Grant to our company this power most excellent, that with a family all-heroic we may dwell.

3 Do ye, O Ṛbhus, make prosperity for us, prosperity for car, ye Heroes, and for steed.
Grant us prosperity victorious evermore, conquering foes in battle, strangers or akin.

4 Indra, the Ṛbhus' Lord, I invocate for aid, the Ṛbhus, Vājas, Maruts to the Soma draught.
Varuṇa, Mitra, both, yea, and the Aśvins Twain : let them speed us to wealth, wisdom, and victory.

5 May Ṛbhu send prosperity for battle, may Vāja conquering in the fight protect us.
This prayer of ours may Varuṇa grant, and Mitra, and Aditi and Sindhu, Earth and Heaven.

4 *Vājas* that is, Vāja and his two brothers Ṛbhu and Vibhvan, more usually called collectively the Ṛbhavaḥ or Ṛbhus. Similarly, in this line *the Ṛbhus* are Ṛbhu and his brothers.

HYMN CXII. *Aśvins.*

1 To give first thought to them, I worship Heaven and Earth, and Agni, fair bright glow, to hasten their approach.
Come hither unto us, O Aśvins, with those aids wherewith in fight ye speed the war-cry to the spoil.

2 Ample, unfailing, they have mounted as it were an eloquent car that ye may think of us and give.
Come hither unto us, O Aśvins, with those aids wherewith ye help our thoughts to further holy acts.

3 Ye by the might which heavenly nectar giveth you are in supreme dominion Lords of all these folk.
Come hither unto us, O Aśvins, with those aids wherewith ye, Heroes, made the barren cow give milk.

4 The aids wherewith the Wanderer through his offspring's might, or the Two-Mothered Son shows swiftest mid the swift ;
Wherewith the sapient one acquired his triple lore,—Come hither unto us, O Aśvins, with those aids.

5 Wherewith ye raised from waters, prisoned and fast bound, Rebha, and Vandana to look upon the light ;
Wherewith ye succoured Kaṇva as he strove to win,—Come hither unto us, O Aśvins, with those aids.

6 Wherewith ye rescued Antaka when languishing deep in the pit, and Bhujyu with unfailing help.
And comforted Karkandhu, Vayya, in their woe,—Come hither unto us, O Aśvins, with those aids.

7 Wherewith ye gave Śucanti wealth and happy home, and made the fiery pit friendly for Atri's sake ;
Wherewith ye guarded Purukutsa, Pṛśnigu, —Come hither unto us, O Aśvins, with those aids.

8 Mighty Ones, with what powers ye gave Parāvṛj aid what time ye made the blind and lame to see and walk ;
Wherewith ye set at liberty the swallowed quail,—Come hither unto us, O Aśvins, with those aids.

9 Wherewith ye quickened the most sweet exhaustless flood, and comforted Vasiṣṭha, ye who ne'er decay ;
And to Śrutarya, Kutsa, Narya gave your help,—Come hither unto us, O Aśvins, with those aids.

10 Wherewith ye helped, in battle of a thousand spoils, Viśpalā seeking booty, powerless to move.
Wherewith ye guarded friendly Vaśa, Aśva's son,—Come hither unto us, O Aśvins, with those aids.

1 *To give first thought to them* : Heaven and Earth are to be the first objects of invocation, Agni, with his signal of bright fire, is also called upon to hasten the approach of the Aśvins to the sacrifice.

2 *They* : our offerings. *An eloquent car* : the chariot of our hymns.

3 *Heavenly nectar* : the Soma. *The barren cow* : of the Ṛṣi Śayu.

4 *The Wanderer* : according to Sāyaṇa, the Wind. Agni is called his offspring as having been excited into flame by the wind. Or Mātariśvan may be intended (See I. 31.3), who brought Agni from heaven.

The Two-Mothered Son : Agni sprung from the two fire-sticks.

The sapient one : said to be the Ṛṣi Kakṣīvān. *His triple lore* : knowledge of sacrificial food, oblations of clarified butter, and libations of Soma juice. The meaning of the passage is uncertain.

5 *Rebha* and *Vandana* are said to have been thrown into wells by the Asuras or demons, Kaṇva was somewhat similarly treated. 'In these, and similar instances subsequently noticed,' says Wilson, 'we may possibly have allusions to the dangers undergone by some of the first teachers of Hinduism among the people whom they sought to civilize.'

6 *Antaka* : said to have been a Rājarṣi or regal Ṛṣi, *Bhujyu* : a Rājarṣi, son of Tugra, rescued when in danger of drowning. *Vayya* : see II. 13,12 ; IV. 19.6.

7 *Purukutsa* : see I. 63.7. Of *Śucanti* and *Pṛśnigu* nothing more is related.

Atri : see I. 45.3 ; 51.3. He is said to have been thrown by the Asuras into a fiery pit.

8 *Parāvṛj* : according to Sāyaṇa, the name of a man. Benfey explains the word as the setting Sun (sideways departing), called *blind* because his light is nearly gone, and *lame* because he no longer travels. *The swallowed quail* : swallowed, or seized, by a wolf. The quail is said by Yāska, as quoted by Sāyaṇa, to signify the Dawn seized and swallowed by the bright Sun. Benfey takes it to mean the Sun after setting.

9 As the earliest bringers of light, the Aśvins may be said to quicken and animate by their coming the streams of the ocean of air. We are not told how the famous *Vasiṣṭha* was comforted; and *Śrutarya*, *Kutsa* and *Narya* are merely said by Sāyaṇa to be three Ṛṣis. Kutsa has been mentioned before. See I. 33. 14; 51. 6; 63. 3.

10 *Viśpalā* : a lady who was wounded in battle, and made whole by the Asvins. See I. 116. 15; 117. 11; 118. 8; X. 39. 8. *Powerless to move* : pierced through with a lance, according to Ludwig. The meaning of *atharvyám* is uncertain. *Vaśa* : a celebrated Ṛṣi, the seer of Hymn VIII. 46.

11 Whereby the cloud, ye Bounteous Givers, shed sweet rain for Dīrghaśravas, for the merchant Auśija,
Wherewith ye helped Kakṣīvān, singer of your praise,—Come hither unto us, O Aśvins, with those aids.

12 Wherewith ye made Rasā swell full with water-floods, and urged to victory the car without a horse;
Wherewith Triśoka drove forth his recovered cows,—Come hither unto us, O Aśvins, with those aids.

13 Wherewith ye compass round the Sun when far away, strengthened Mandhātar in his tasks as lord of lands,
And to sage Bharadvāja gave protecting help,—Come hither unto us, O Aśvins, with those aids.

14 Wherewith, when Śambara was slain, ye guarded well great Atithigva, Divodāsa, Kaśoju,
And Trasadasyu when the forts were shattered down,—Come hither unto us, O Aśvins, with those aids.

15 Wherewith ye honoured the great drinker Vamra, and Upastuta and Kali when he gained his wife,
And lent to Vyaśva and to Pṛthi favouring help,—Come hither unto us, O Aśvins, with those aids.

16 Wherewith, O Heroes, ye vouchsafed deliverance to Śayu, Atri, and to Manu long ago;
Wherewith ye shot your shafts in Syūmaraśmi's cause,—Come hither unto us, O Aśvins, with those aids.

17 Wherewith Paṭharvā, in his majesty of form, shone in his course like to a gathered kindled fire;
Wherewith ye helped Śaryāta in the mighty fray,—Come hither unto us, O Aśvins, with those aids.

18 Wherewith, Aṅgirases! ye triumphed in your heart, and onward went to liberate the flood of milk;
Wherewith ye helped the hero Manu with new strength,—Come hither unto us, O Aśvins, with those aids.

11 *Dīrghaśravas* : said to be a Ṛṣi who traded for his livelihood. *Auśija* is a patronymic meaning son of Uśij. *Kakṣīvān* is also said to have been a son of Uśij. See I. 18. 1.

12 *Rasā* : 'The Rasā, known to the Zoroastrians as the Raṇhā, was originally the name of a real river, but when the Āryas moved away from it into the Punjāb, it assumed a mythical character, and became a kind of Okeanos, surrounding the extreme limits of the earth.'—M. Müller, *Vedic Hymns*, 1. 323. No further account is given of the events mentioned in this verse.

13 Aśvins are said to compass the Sun in order to save him from eclipse.

Mandhātar : a Rājarṣi or regal Ṛṣi. See VIII. 39. 8.

Bharadvāja : a very celebrated Ṛṣi, said to be the son of Bṛhaspati.

14 *Śambara* : one of the demons of drought slain by Indra. Sāyaṇa takes *atithigvám* and *kaśojúm* as epithets of Divodāsa the king who was aided by the Aśvins : 'the hospitable Divodāsa as he sought the water (through fear of the Asuras).' *Trasadasyu* : a prince renowned for his victories and liberality, and for the favour shown him by the Gods. See IV. 42. 9; VII. 19. 3; VIII. 9. 21; 19.36; 36. 7.

15 *Vamra* : called a Ṛṣi, son of Vikhanas, by Sāyaṇa. 'The text calls him *vipipāná*, drinking much and variously, which the Scholiast explains, drinking, especially earthly moisture or dew.'—Wilson. Benfey thinks that Indra is intended under the name Vamra.

Upastuta : taken by Sāyaṇa as an epithet of Vamra, 'praised by all around him.'

Kali : a Ṛṣi, mentioned again in X. 39. 8. The Aśvins may have restored him to youth.

Vyaśva : taken by Sāyaṇa as an epithet of Pṛthi, 'horseless, or who had lost his horse.' *Pṛthi* is said to have been a Rājarṣi.

16 *Śayu* : see note on verse 3 of this Hymn; see also I. 116. 22; 117. 20.

Atri : see note on verse 7 ; also I. 116.8.

Manu : this Manu is said by Sāyaṇa to have been a Rājarṣi whom the Aśvins taught to sow barley and other grain.

Syūmaraśmi : said to have been a Ṛṣi, seer of hymns 77, 78, Book X.

17 *Paṭharvā* : said by Sāyaṇa to have been a Rājarṣi. Benfey thinks that the word *páṭharvan*, is a dialectical form of *patrārvan*, 'having winged horses.' Ludwig considers Sāyaṇa's explanation (which I have followed) to be erroneous and impossible. He thinks that Paṭhurū was the name of some stronghold which the Aśvins saved from burning, either through the instrumentality of a man called Jaṭhara or by means of the rain-clouds. He accordingly renders : 'By means of which, at Paṭharū, through the power of Jaṭhara (violence of the rain-clouds) the fire did not flame up, though prepared and lighted on the way.' The passage is difficult, and the interpretations put upon the words by Sāyaṇa certainly appear to be forced, but on the whole I think it safer to follow his guidance. I may observe here that 'ná' which in the Veda means both 'not' and 'like' sometimes makes the meaning of a passage uncertain. In this line Sāyaṇa takes it in the latter sense, and Ludwig in the former.

Śaryāta : perhaps the same as Śaryāti, a son of Manu Vaivasvata.

18 *Aṅgirases* : the text has Aṅgiras only in the singular form, which may stand, as Ludwig remarks, for the dual. Wilson, following Sāyaṇa, translates : 'Aṅgiras, (praise the Aśvins).' Sāyaṇa supposes the Ṛṣi to address himself by this title. Benfey joins Aṅgiras with the following word, making *aṅgirománasā*, 'through affection for the Aṅgirases.'

The flood of milk : the cows shut up in the cave, that is, the rain-clouds prevented from pouring out their water.

Manu : see verse 16.

19 Wherewith ye brought a wife for Vimada to wed, wherewith ye freely gave the ruddy cows away;
Wherewith ye brought the host of kind Gods to Sudās—Come hither unto us, O Aśvins, with those aids.

20 Wherewith ye bring great bliss to him who offers gifts, wherewith ye have protected Bhujyu, Adhrigu,
And good and gracious Subharā and Ṛtastup,—Come hither unto us, O Aśvins, with those aids.

21 Wherewith ye served Kṛśānu where the shafts were shot, and helped the young man's horse to swiftness in the race;
Wherewith ye bring delicious honey to the bees,—Come hither unto us, O Aśvins, with those aids.

22 Wherewith ye speed the hero as he fights for kine in hero battle, in the strife for land and sons,
Wherewith ye safely guard his horses and his car,—Come hither unto us, O Aśvins with those aids.

23 Wherewith ye, Lords of Hundred Powers, helped Kutsa, son of Ārjuni, gave Turvīti and Dabhīti strength,
Favoured Dhvasanti and lent Puruṣanti help,—Come hither unto us, O Aśvins, with those aids.

24 Make ye our speech effectual, O ye Aśvins, and this our hymn, ye mighty Wonder-Workers.
In luckless game I call on you for succour: strengthen us also on the field of battle.

25 With undiminished blessings, O ye Aśvins, for evermore both night and day protect us.
This prayer of ours may Varuṇa grant, and Mitra, and Aditi and Sindhu, Earth and Heaven.

19 *Vimada*: a Ṛṣi, whose name occurs again in I. 116. I; 117. 20; VIII. 9. 15; X. 20. 10; and X. 23. 7. The wife is said to have been the daughter of Purumitra.

The ruddy cows: perhaps the red rain-clouds.
Sudās: son of Pijavana. See I. 47.7.

20 *Bhujyu*: see note on verse 6. *Adhrigu*, taken by Sāyaṇa as a proper name, is said to have been a sacrificer of the Gods. *Ṛtastup* is called a Ṛṣi. Sāyaṇa takes *subhārām* as an adjective, but has to supply *iṣam* food, for it to qualify.

21 *Kṛśānu*: the Kereśāni of the Avesta; one of the guardians of the celestial Soma. See IV. 27. 3.

The young man: whose horse was aided, was Purukutsa.

23 *Kutsa*: has been mentioned before as a favourite of Indra. See I. 51. 6. *Turvīti*: see I. 36. 18 *Dabhīti*: see II. 13. 9; 15. 9; IV. 30. 21; VI. 20. 13; 26. 6. *Puruṣanti*: a liberal prince. See IX. 5. 8.3.

24 *Luckless game*: a metaphor borrowed from dicing; that is, in a time of difficulty, perhaps the eve of a desperate battle. Sāyaṇa, following a different derivation of the word, explains it, in the absence of light, or in the last watch of night, when the Aśvins are especially to be worshipped.

HYMN CXIII. *Dawn.*

1. THIS light is come, amid all lights the fairest; born is the brilliant, far-extending brightness.
Night, sent away for Savitar's uprising, hath yielded up a birth-place for the Morning.

2 The Fair, the Bright is come with her white offspring; to her the Dark One hath resigned her dwelling.
Akin, immortal, following each other, changing their colours both the heavens move onward.

3 Common, unending is the Sisters' pathway; taught by the Gods, alternately they travel.
Fair-formed, of different hues and yet one-minded, Night and Dawn clash not, neither do they tarry.

4 Bright leader of glad sounds, our eyes behold her; splendid in hue she hath unclosed the portals.
She, stirring up the world, hath shown us riches: Dawn hath awakened every living creature.

5 Rich Dawn, she sets afoot the coiled-up sleeper, one for enjoyment, one for wealth or worship,
Those who saw little for extended vision. All living creatures hath the Dawn awakened.

6 One to high sway, one to exalted glory, one to pursue his gain, and one his labour:
All to regard their different vocations, all moving creatures hath the Dawn awakened.

7 We see her there, the Child of Heaven apparent, the young Maid, flushing in her shining raiment.

1. *Savitar*: the Sun.

2 *Her white offspring*: white clouds that attend her. Or the word in the text may be rendered 'bright offspring, the Sun whom she precedes.'

Both the heavens: or Day and Night.

4 *Leader of glad sounds*: awakener of 'the charm of earliest birds' and the joyful voices of other animals.

5 *Those who saw little*: during the darkness of night.

6 This verse apparently alludes to a division into four castes or classes, regal and military, priestly, mercantile, and servile. But verses 4,5,6 seem to be separated by their refrain from the rest of the hymn, and may perhaps be a later addition to it.

Thou sovran Lady of all earthly treasure, flush on us here, auspicious Dawn, this morning.

8 She, first of endless morns to come hereafter, follows the path of morns that have departed.

Dawn, at her rising, urges forth the living: him who is dead she wakes not from his slumber.

9 As thou, Dawn, hast caused Agni to be kindled, and with the Sun's eye hast revealed creation.

And hast awakened men to offer worship, thou hast performed, for Gods, a noble service.

10 How long a time, and they shall be together,—Dawns that have shone and Dawns to shine hereafter?

She yearns for former Dawns with eager longing, and goes forth gladly shining with the others.

11 Gone are the men who in the days before us looked on the rising of the earlier Morning.

We, we the living, now behold her brightness and they come nigh who shall hereafter see her.

12 Foe-chaser, born of Law, the Law's protectress, joy-giver, waker of all pleasant voices,

Auspicious, bringing food for Gods' enjoyment, shine on us here, most bright, O Dawn, this morning.

13 From days eternal hath Dawn shone, the Goddess, and shows this light to-day, endowed with riches.

So will she shine on days to come; immortal she moves on in her own strength, undecaying.

14 In the sky's borders hath she shone in splendour: the Goddess hath thrown off the veil of darkness.

Awakening the world with purple horses, on her well-harnessed chariot Dawn approaches.

15 Bringing all life-sustaining blessings with her, showing herself she sends forth brilliant lustre.

Last of the countless mornings that have vanished, first of bright morns to come hath Dawn arisen.

16 Arise! the breath, the life, again hath reached us: darkness hath passed away and light approacheth.

She for the Sun hath left a path to travel: we have arrived where men prolong existence.

17 Singing the praises of refulgent Mornings with his hymn's web the priest, the poet rises.

Shine then to-day, rich Maid, on him who lauds thee, shine down on us the gift of life and offspring.

18 Dawns giving sons all heroes, kine and horses, shining upon the man who brings oblations,—

These let the Soma-presser gain when ending his glad songs louder than the voice of Vāyu.

19 Mother of Gods, Aditi's form of glory, ensign of sacrifice, shine forth exalted.

Rise up, bestowing praise on our devotion: all-bounteous, make us chief among the people.

20 Whatever splendid wealth the Dawns bring with them to bless the man who offers praise and worship,

Even that may Mitra, Varuṇa vouchsafe us, and Aditi and Sindhu, Earth and Heaven.

HYMN CXIV. *Rudra.*

1. To the strong Rudra bring we these our songs of praise, to him the Lord of Heroes, with the braided hair,

That it be well with all our cattle and our men, that in this village all be healthy and well-fed.

9 *Caused Agni to be kindled*: daybreak being the proper time for lighting the sacrificial fires.

10 The meaning appears to be: How long have we to live? When will all our future Dawns be with those that have passed away? Wilson, following Sāyaṇa translates: 'For how long a period is it that the dawns have risen? For how long a period will they rise?'

She yearns: the Dawn that now shines as the first of Dawns to come is already eager to join those that have past.

12 Evil spirits vanish when Dawn appears. She comes in accordance with the eternal law of the universe which she observes and guards. Her coming is the signal for men to offer oblations to the Gods.

16. *Where men prolong existence*: a new life begins at the return of day-light.

17 *His hymn's web*: the words which he weaves, or carefully composes.

18 *Louder than the voice of Vāyu*: louder even than the roaring of the wind. Wilson translates: 'At the conclusion of his praises, (enunciated) like the wind, (with speed).'

1 *Rudra*: generally explained as the Roarer, from the sound of stormy winds, the God of tempests and father of the Maruts. He is called *Kapardin* as wearing hair braided and knotted like a cowry shell (*kapaṛda*). Prof. Pischel (Vedische Studien, I. 55. sqq.) derives *Rudra* (the Red, the Brilliant) from a lost root *rud*, to be red.

2 Be gracious unto us, O Rudra, bring us joy : thee, Lord of Heroes, thee with reverence will we serve.
Whatever health and strength our father Manu won by sacrifice may we, under thy guidance, gain.

3 By worship of the Gods may we, O Bounteous One, O Rudra, gain thy grace, Ruler of valiant men.
Come to our families, bringing them bliss: may we, whose heroes are uninjured, bring thee sacred gifts.

4 Hither we call for aid the wise, the wanderer, impetuous Rudra, perfecter of sacrifice.
May he repel from us the anger of the Gods : verily we desire his favourable grace.

5 Him with the braided hair we call with reverence down, the wild-boar of the sky, the red, the dazzling shape.
May he, his hand filled full of sovran medicines, grant us protection, shelter, and a home secure.

6 To him the Maruts' Father is this hymn addressed, to strengthen Rudra's might, a song more sweet than sweet.
Grant us, Immortal One, the food which mortals eat : be gracious unto me, my seed, my progeny.

7 O Rudra, harm not either great or small of us, harm not the growing boy, harm not the full-grown man.
Slay not a sire among us, slay no mother here, and to our own dear bodies, Rudra, do not harm.

8 Harm us not, Rudra, in our seed and progeny, harm us not in the living, nor in cows or steeds,
Slay not our heroes in the fury of thy wrath. Bringing oblations evermore we call to thee.

9 Even as a herdsman I have brought thee hymns of praise : O Father of the Maruts, give us happiness.
Blessed is thy most favouring benevolence, so, verily, do we desire thy saving help.

10 Far be thy dart that killeth men or cattle : thy bliss be with us, O thou Lord of Heroes.
Be gracious unto us, O God, and bless us, and then vouchsafe us doubly-strong protection.

11 We, seeking help, have spoken and adored him : may Rudra, girt by Maruts, hear our calling.
This prayer of ours may Varuṇa grant, and Mitra, and Aditi and Sindhu, Earth and Heaven.

2 *Won by sacrifice* : that is, as an institutor of earliest sacrifice, enabled us to obtain by offerings to the Gods.

9 *Even as a herdsman* : as a herdsman prays for the well-being of his cattle, so the poet prays for the prosperity of those for whom he speaks.

HYMN CXV. *Sūrya.*

1. THE brilliant presence of the Gods hath risen, the eye of Mitra, Varuṇa and Agni.
The soul of all that moveth not or moveth, the Sun hath filled the air and earth and heaven.

2 Like as a young man followeth a maiden, so doth the Sun the Dawn, refulgent Goddess :
Where pious men extend their generations, before the Auspicious One for happy fortune.

3 Auspicious are the Sun's Bay-coloured Horses, bright, changing hues, meet for our shouts of triumph.
Bearing our prayers, the sky's ridge have they mounted, and in a moment speed round earth and heaven.

4 This is the Godhead, this might of Sūrya : he hath withdrawn what spread o'er work unfinished.
When he hath loosed his Horses from their station, straight over all Night spreadeth out her garment.

5 In the sky's lap the Sun this form assumeth that Varuṇa and Mitra may behold it.
His Bay Steeds well maintain his power eternal, at one time bright and darksome at another.

2 The exact meaning of the second line is somewhat uncertain. As I have rendered it, in accordance with Ludwig, it reminds one of Shelley's 'Man, the imperial shape, then multiplied His generations under the pavilion Of the Sun's throne.' Wilson, following Sāyaṇa paraphrases, 'At which season pious men perform (the ceremonies established for) ages.' Sāyaṇa proposes an alternative rendering by taking *yugani* (generations, ages,) to mean 'yokes for ploughs'; 'for, at this season, men seeking to propitiate the gods by the profit which agriculture yields, equip their ploughs.'

4 *He hath withdrawn* : that is, says Wilson, 'the cultivator or artisan desists from his labour, although unfinished, upon the setting of the sun'; when the sun 'has withdrawn (into himself) the diffused (light which has been shed) upon the unfinished task.'

5 *His power eternal,* as maker and ruler of day and night.

6 This day, O Gods, while Sūrya is ascending, deliver us from trouble and dishonour.
This prayer of ours may Varuṇa grant, and Mitra, and Aditi and Sindhu, Earth and Heaven.

HYMN CXVI. *Aśvins.*

1. I TRIM like grass my song for the Nāsatyas and send their lauds forth as the wind drives rain-clouds,
Who, in a chariot rapid as an arrow, brought to the youthful Vimada a consort.

2 Borne on by rapid steeds of mighty pinion, or proudly trusting in the Gods' incitements.
That stallion ass of yours won, O Nāsatyas, that thousand in the race, in Yama's contest.

3 Yea, Aśvins, as a dead man leaves his riches, Tugra left Bhujyu in the cloud of waters.
Ye brought him back in animated vessels, traversing air, unwetted by the billows.

4 Bhujyu ye bore with winged things, Nāsatyas, which for three nights, three days full swiftly travelled,
To the sea's farther shore, the strand of ocean, in three cars, hundred-footed, with six horses.

5 Ye wrought that hero exploit in the ocean which giveth no support, or hold or station,
What time ye carried Bhujyu to his dwelling, borne in a ship with hundred oars, O Aśvins.

6 The white horse which of old ye gave Aghāśva, Aśvins, a gift to be his wealth for ever,—
Still to be praised is that your glorious present, still to be famed is the brave horse of Pedu.

7 O Heroes, ye gave wisdom to Kakṣīvān who sprang from Pajra's line, who sang your praises.
Ye poured forth from the hoof of your strong charger a hundred jars of wine as from a strainer.

8 Ye warded off with cold the fire's fierce burning ; food very rich in nourishment ye furnished.
Atri, cast downward in the cavern, Aśvins ye brought, with all his people, forth to comfort.

9 Ye lifted up the well, O ye Nāsatyas, and set the base on high to open downward.
Streams flowed for folk of Gotama who thirsted, like rain to bring forth thousandfold abundance.

10 Ye from the old Cyavāna, O Nāsatyas, stripped, as 'twere mail, the skin upon his body,
Lengthened his life when all had left him helpless, Dasras ! and made him lord of youthful maidens.

11 Worthy of praise and worth the winning, Heroes, is that your favouring succour O Nāsatyas,
What time ye, knowing well his case, delivered Vandana from the pit like hidden treasure.

12 That mighty deed of yours, for gain, O Heroes, as thunder heraldeth the rain, I publish,

This Hymn and the five following are ascribed to the Ṛṣi Kakṣīvān.

1 *Grass* : the sacred grass which is spread on the altar.

Nāsatyas : a common name of the Aśvins. See I. 3.3.

Vimada : the Aśvins assisted Vimada, who was attacked when returning home with newly-won bride, whom they carried to his house in their own chariot. Most of the deeds ascribed to the Aśvins in this hymn have been mentioned in I. 112.

2 *Stallion ass* : that draws the car of the Aśvins. See I. 34. 9.

Yama's contest : apparently the race instituted by the Gods when Prajāpati (here represented by Yama) gave his daughter Suryā in marriage to King Soma, the Moon, as related in Aitareya-Brāhmaṇa, IV. 2, See Ehni, Der Mythus des Yama, p. 160.

3 *Bhujyu* : see I. 112. 6.

5 'This', observes Wilson, 'is a rather unintelligible account of a sea-voyage, although the words of the text do not admit of any other rendering.'

6 *Aghāśva* : another name of Pedu ; or an epithet of Pedu 'having bad or vicious horses.' Pedu was a royal Ṛṣi who worshipped the Aśvins and was thus rewarded.

7 *Kakṣīvān* : a famous Ṛṣi, (see I. 18. 1,) a descendant of the Pajras or Aṅgirases. *Strong charger* : that is, the rushing rain-cloud, from which the Aśvins poured down copious showers. Cf. the Greek myth of the horse Pegasus and the fountain Hippocrene.

8 *Atri* : see I. 112. 7.

9 *The well* : that is the watery cloud. This deed is ascribed to the Maruts in I. 85. 11.

10 *Dasras* : a name of the Aśvins; Wonder-Workers, or Mighty Ones.

11 *Vandana* : see I. 112. 5.

12 *By the horse's head* : 'Indra, having taught the sciences called *Pravargyavidyā* and *Madhuvidyā* to Dadhyac, threatened that he would cut off his head if ever he taught them to any one else. The Aśvins prevailed upon him to teach them the prohibited knowledge, and, to evade Indra's threat, took off the head of the sage, replacing it by that of a horse.'—Wilson. See I. 84. 13.

When, by the horse's head, Atharvan's offspring Dadhyac made known to you the Soma's sweetness.

13 In the great rite the wise dame called, Nāsatyas, you, Lords of many treasures, to assist her.
Ye heard the weakling's wife, as 'twere an order, and gave to her a son Hiraṇyahasta.

14 Ye from the wolf's jaws, as ye stood together, set free the quail, O Heroes, O Nāsatyas.
Ye, Lords of many treasures, gave the poet his perfect vision as he mourned his trouble.

15 When in the time of night, in Khela's battle, a leg was severed like a wild bird's pinion,
Straight ye gave Viśpalā a leg of iron that she might move what time the conflict opened.

16 His father robbed Ṛjrāśva of his eyesight who for the she-wolf slew a hundred wethers.
Ye gave him eyes, Nāsatyas, Wonder-Workers, Physicians, that he saw with sight uninjured.

17 The Daughter of the Sun your car ascended, first reaching as it were the goal with coursers.
All Deities within their hearts assented, and ye, Nāsatyas, are close linked with glory.

18 When to his house ye came, to Divodāsa, hasting to Bharadvāja, O ye Aśvins,
The car that came with you brought splendid riches: a porpoise and a bull were yoked together.

19 Ye, bringing wealth with rule, and life with offspring, life rich in noble heroes; O Nāsatyas,
Accordant came with strength to Jahnu's children who offered you thrice every day your portion.

20 Ye bore away at night by easy pathways Jāhuṣa compassed round on every quarter,
And, with your car that cleaves the foe asunder, Nāsatyas never decaying! rent the mountains.

21 One morn ye strengthened Vaśa for the battle, to gather spoils that might be told in thousands.
With Indra joined ye drove away misfortunes, yea foes of Pṛthuśravas, O ye mighty.

22 From the deep well ye raised on high the water, so that Ṛcatka's son, Śara, should drink it;
And with your might, to help the weary Śayu, ye made the barren cow yield milk, Nāsatyas.

23 To Viśvaka, Nāsatyas! son of Kṛṣṇa, the righteous man who sought your aid and praised you,
Ye with your powers restored, like some lost creature, his son Viṣṇāpū for his eyes to look on.

24 Aśvins, ye raised, like Soma in a ladle Rebha, who for ten days and ten nights, fettered.
Had lain in cruel bonds, immersed and wounded, suffering sore affliction, in the waters.

25 I have declared your wondrous deeds, O Aśvins: may this be mine, and many kine and heroes.
May I, enjoying lengthened life, still seeing, enter old age as 'twere the house I live in.

HYMN CXVII. *Aśvins.*

1. AŚVINS, your ancient priest invites you hither to gladden you with draughts of meath of Soma.

13 *The weakling's wife*: or Vadhrimatī, which has that meaning.

14 *Set free the quail*: see I. 112. 8.

15 *Khela's battle*: the Commentator says that Khela was a Rājā, whose relative Viśpalā lost a foot in battle and received an iron leg from the Aśvins at the prayer of Agastya, Khela's family priest. See I. 112. 10.

16 *Ṛjrāśva*, mentioned in I. 101. 17, was one of the sons of Vṛṣāgir. The she-wolf for whom he slaughtered the sheep was one of the asses of the Aśvins in disguise, and the Aśvins consequently restored to him the eyesight of which his angry father had deprived him.

17 *The Daughter of the Sun*: 'Sūrya, it is related, was desirous of giving his daughter Sūryā to Soma; but all the gods desired her as a wife. They agreed that he who should first reach the sun, as a goal, should wed the damsel. The Aśvins were victorious; and Sūryā, well-pleased by their success, rushed immediately into their chariot.'—Wilson. See note on verse 2 of this hymn.

18 *Divodāsa*: see I. 112. 14. His family priest was one of the Bharadvājas. The Aśvins, it is said, yoked the porpoise and the bull together as a proof of power.

19 *Jahnu's children*: Jahnu was a Maharṣi or great Ṛṣi.

21 *Vaśa*: see I. 112. 10. *Pṛthuśravas* appears to be identical with Pṛthuśravas Kānīta, mentioned in VIII. 46. 21, whose family priest was Vaśa.

22 *Śayu*: has been mentioned in I. 112. 16. Of Śara in this verse and of Viśvaka, Kṛṣṇa, and Viṣṇāpū in the next we are only told that they were Ṛṣis.

24 *Rebha*: see I. 112. 5.

25 *May this be mine*: may I be master of this place or district, a substantive of some such signification being understood.

Our gift is on the grass, our song apportioned : with food and strength come hither, O Nāsatyas.

2 That car of yours, swifter than thought, O Aśvins, which drawn by brave steeds cometh to the people,
Whereon ye seek the dwelling of the pious,—come ye thereon to our abode, O Heroes.

3 Ye freed sage Atri, whom the Five Tribes honoured, from the strait pit, ye Heroes with his people,
Baffling the guiles of the malignant Dasyu, repelling them, ye Mighty in succession.

4 Rebha the sage, ye mighty Heroes, Aśvins ! whom, like a horse, vile men had sunk in water,—
Him, wounded, with your wondrous power ye rescued : your exploits of old time endure for ever.

5 Ye brought forth Vandana, ye Wonder-Workers, for triumph, like fair gold that hath been buried,
Like one who slumbered in destruction's bosom, or like the Sun when dwelling in the darkness.

6 Kakṣīvān, Pajra's son, must laud that exploit of yours, Nāsatyas, Heroes, ye who wander !
When from the hoof of your strong horse ye showered a hundred jars of honey for the people.

7 To Kṛṣṇa's son, to Viśvaka who praised you, O Heroes, ye restored his son Viṣṇāpū.
To Ghoṣā, living in her father's dwelling, stricken in years, ye gave a husband, Aśvins.

8 Ruṣatī, of the mighty people, Aśvins, ye gave to Śyāva of the line of Kaṇva.
This deed of yours, ye Strong Ones should be published, that ye gave glory to the son of Nṛṣad.

9 O Aśvins, wearing many forms at pleasure, on Pedu ye bestowed a fleet-foot courser,
Strong, winner of a thousand spoils, resistless the serpent slayer, glorious, triumphant.

10 These glorious things are yours, ye Bounteous Givers ; prayer, praise in both worlds are your habitation.
O Aśvins, when the sons of Pajra call you, send strength with nourishment to him who knoweth.

11 Hymned with the reverence of a son, O Aśvins ye Swift Ones giving booty to the singer,
Glorified by Agastya with devotion, established Viśpalā again, Nāsatyas.

12 Ye Sons of Heaven, ye Mighty, whither went ye, sought ye, for his fair praise the home of Kāvya.
When, like a pitcher full of gold, O Aśvins, on the tenth day ye lifted up the buried ?

13 Ye with the aid of your great powers, O Aśvins, restored to youth the ancient man Cyavāna.
The Daughter of the Sun with all her glory, O ye Nāsatyas, chose your car to bear her.

14 Ye, ever-youthful Ones, again remembered Tugra, according to your ancient manner :
With horses brown of hue that flew with swift wings ye brought back Bhujyu from the sea of billows.

15 The son of Tugra had invoked you, Aśvins ; borne on he went uninjured through the ocean.
Ye with your chariot swift as thought, well-harnessed, carried him off, O Mighty Ones, to safety.

16 The quail had invocated you, O Aśvins, when from the wolf's devouring jaws ye freed her.
With conquering car ye cleft the mountain's ridges : the offspring of Viśvāc ye killed with poison.

17 He whom for furnishing a hundred wethers to the she-wolf, his wicked father blinded,—

3 *Atri* : see I. 116. 8. *The Five Tribes* : are the confederate Āryan families named in the note to I. 7. 9.

4 *Rebha* : see I. 112. 5. *Like a horse* : sunk deep in water like a horse when he is bathed in a river.

5 *Vandana* : see I. 116. 11.

6 *Kakṣīvān*: see I. 116. 7. *Strong horse* : see I. 116.7.

7 *Ghoṣā* : Kakṣīvān's daughter, said to have been afflicted with leprosy and healed by the Aśvins, who found her a husband.

8 *Śyāva* : a Ṛṣi whom the Aśvins cured of leprosy and enabled to marry Ruṣatī. *The son of Nṛṣad* : Kaṇva or his descendant Śyāva.

9 *Pedu* : see I. 116. 6. *The serpent-slayer* : see IX. 88. 4, and Hymns of the Atharva-veda, X. 4. 47.

11 *Agastya* : the family priest of Khela. See I. 116. 15.

12 *Kāvya* : Uśanā, son of Kavi, See I. 83. 6. *The buried* : Rebha. The meaning is, 'why did ye delay so long the rescue of Rebha?'

13 *Chyavāna* : see I. 116. 10. *The Daughter of the Sun* : see I. 116. 17.

14 *Ye brought back Bhujyu* : see I. 116. 3.

16 *The quail* : see I. 116. 14. *Viśvāc* : said to be an Asura or fiend.

17 *Ṛjrāśva* : see I. 116. 16.

To him, Ṛjrāśva, gave ye eyes, O Aśvins; light to the blind ye sent for perfect vision.

18 To bring the blind man joy thus cried the she-wolf: O Aśvins, O ye Mighty Ones, O Heroes,
For me Ṛjrāśva, like a youthful lover, hath cut piecemeal one and a hundred wethers.

19 Great and weal-giving is your aid, O Aśvins, ye, objects of all thought, made whole the cripple.
Purandhi also for this cause invoked you, and ye, O mighty, came to her with succours.

20 Ye, Wonder-Workers, filled with milk for Śayu the milkless cow, emaciated, barren;
And by your powers the child of Purumitra ye brought to Vimada to be his consort.

21 Ploughing and sowing barley, O ye Aśvins, milking out food for men, ye Wonder-Workers,
Blasting away the Dasyu with your trumpet, ye gave far-spreading light unto the Ārya.

22 Ye brought the horse's head, Aśvins, and gave it unto Dadhyac the offspring of Atharvan.
True, he revealed to you, O Wonder-Workers, sweet Soma, Tvaṣṭar's secret, as your girdle.

23 O Sages, evermore I crave your favour: be gracious unto all my prayers, O Aśvins.
Grant me, Nāsatyas, riches in abundance, wealth famous and accompanied with children.

24 With liberal bounty to the weakling's consorts ye, Heroes, gave a son Hiraṇyahasta;
And Śyāva, cut into three several pieces, ye brougnt to life again, O bounteous Aśvins.

25 These your heroic exploits, O ye Aśvins, done in the days of old, have men related.
May we, addressing prayer to you, ye Mighty, speak with brave sons about us to the synod.

19 *Purandhi* : or as Sāyaṇa explains, 'the wise maid,' Ghoṣā.

20 *Śayu* : see I. 112. 16; and I. 116. 22. *Vimada* : see I. 112. 19.

22 *Dadhyac* : see I. 116. 12. *As your girdle* : to strengthen and support you.

24 *The weakling's consort* : see I. 116. 13. *Śyāva* : cut to pieces by the Asuras, was made whole by the Aśvins.

25 *The synod* : the congregation of worshippers.

HYMN CXVIII. *Aśvins.*

1. Flying, with falcons, may your chariot, Aśvins, most gracious, bringing friendly help, come hither,—
Your chariot, swifter than the mind of mortal, fleet as the wind, three-seated, O ye Mighty.

2 Come to us with your chariot triple seated, three-wheeled, of triple form, that rolleth lightly.
Fill full our cows, give mettle to our horses, and make each hero son grow strong, O Aśvins.

3 With your well-rolling car, descending swiftly, hear this the press-stone's song, ye Wonder-Workers.
How then have ancient sages said, O Aśvins, that ye most swiftly come to stay affliction?

4 O Aśvins, let your falcons bear you hither, yoked to your chariot, swift, with flying pinions,
Which, ever active, like the airy eagles, carry you, O Nāsatyas, to the banquet.

5 The youthful Daughter of the Sun, delighting in you, ascended there your chariot, Heroes.
Borne on their swift wings let your beauteous horses, your birds of ruddy hue, convey you near us.

6 Ye raised up Vandana, strong Wonder-Workers! with great might, and with power ye rescued Rebha.
From out the sea ye saved the son of Tugra, and gave his youth again unto Cyavāna.

7 To Atri, cast down to the fire that scorched him, ye gave, O Aśvins, strengthening food and favour.
Accepting his fair praises with approval, ye gave his eyes again to blinded Kaṇva.

8 For ancient Śayu in his sore affliction ye caused his cow to swell with milk, O Aśvins.
The quail from her great misery ye delivered, and a new leg for Viśpalā provided.

5 In this and the following verses most of the wonderful deeds of the Aśvins mentioned in the preceding hymn are briefly referred to.

9 A white horse, Aśvins, ye bestowed on Pedu, a serpent-slaying steed sent down by Indra,
Loud-neighing, conquering the foe, high-mettled, firm-limbed and vigorous, winning thousand treasures.

10 Such as ye are, O nobly born, O Heroes, we in our trouble call on you for succour.
Accepting these our songs, for our well-being come to us on your chariot treasure-laden.

11 Come unto us combined in love, Nāsatyas; come with the fresh swift vigour of the falcon.
Bearing oblations I invoke you, Aśvins, at the first break of everlasting morning.

HYMN CXIX. *Aśvins.*

1. Hither, that I may live, I call unto the feast your wondrous car, thought-swift, borne on by rapid steeds.
With thousand banners, hundred treasures, pouring gifts, promptly obedient, bestowing ample room.

2 Even as it moveth near my hymn is lifted up, and all the regions come together to sing praise.
I sweeten the oblations; now the helpers come. Ūrjānī hath, O Aśvins, mounted on your car.

3 When striving man with man for glory they have met, brisk, measureless, eager for victory in fight,
Then verily your car is seen upon the slope when ye, O Aśvins, bring some choice boon to the prince.

4 Ye came to Bhujyu while he struggled in the flood, with flying birds, self-yoked, ye bore him to his sires.
Ye went to the far-distant home, O Mighty Ones; and famed is your great aid to Divodāsa given.

5 Aśvins, the car which you had yoked for glorious show your own two voices urged directed to its goal.
Then she who came for friendship, Maid of noble birth, elected you as Husbands, you to be her Lords.

6 Rebha ye saved from tyranny; for Atri's sake ye quenched with cold the fiery pit that compassed him.
Ye made the cow of Śayu stream refreshing milk, and Vandana was holpen to extended life.

7 Doers of marvels, skilful workers, ye restored Vandana, like a car, worn out with length of days.
From earth ye brought the sage to life in wondrous mode; be your great deeds done here for him who honours you.

8 Ye went to him who mourned in a far distant place, him who was left forlorn by treachery of his sire.
Rich with the light of heaven was then the help ye gave, and marvellous your succour when ye stood by him.

9 To you in praise of sweetness sang the honey-bee: Auśija calleth you in Soma's rapturous joy.
Ye drew unto yourselves the spirit of Dadhyac, and then the horse's head uttered his words to you.

10 A horse did ye provide for Pedu, excellent, white, O ye Aśvins, conqueror of combatants,
Invincible in war by arrows, seeking heaven worthy of fame, like Indra, vanquisher of men.

HYMN CXX. *Aśvins.*

1. Aśvins, what praise may win your grace? Who may be pleasing to you both?
How shall the ignorant worship you?

2 Here let the ignorant ask the means of you who know—for none beside you knoweth aught—

2 *Ūrjānī*: strength, personified. According to Sāyaṇa, Ūrjānī is Sūryā the daughter of the Sun.

3 *Upon the slope*: that is, of the sky.

4 *Bhujyu*, and other persons and incidents referred to in this hymn have been mentioned in I. 116.

5 *She who came for friendship*: Sūryā. The meaning seems to be, as Ludwig says, that she came intending to avail herself of the services of the Aśvins as bridesmen, and that they became her bridegrooms instead.

8 *To him who mourned*: Bhujyu.

9 *The honey-bee*: meaning Auśija or the son of Uśij, the sage Kakṣivān.

With regard to the legends recounted in these hymns to the Aśvins, Mr. Muir remarks (*O. S. Texts*, V. 248): 'The deliverances of Rebha, Vandana, Parāvṛj, Bhujyu, Cyavāna, and others are explained by Professor Benfey (following Dr. Kuhn and Professor Müller,) as referring to certain physical phenomena with which the Aśvins are supposed by these scholars to be connected. But this allegorical method of interpretation seems unlikely to be correct, as it is difficult to suppose that the phenomena in question should have been alluded to under such a variety of names and circumstances. It appears, therefore, to be more probable that the ṛsis merely refer to certain legends which were popularly current of interventions of the Aśvins in behalf of the persons whose names are mentioned.'

Parts of this Hymn are difficult and obscure. The first nine stanzas are in nine different metres.

2 In line 2 I adopt Ludwig's emendation *akratau* for *ákrau* of the text.

Not of a spiritless mortal man.

3 Such as ye are, all-wise, we call you. Ye wise, declare to us this day accepted prayer.
Loving you well your servant lauds you.

4 Simply, ye Mighty Ones, I ask the Gods of that wondrous oblation hallowed by the mystic word.
Save us from what is stronger, fiercer than ourselves.

5 Forth go the hymn that shone in Ghoṣa Bhṛgu's like, the song wherewith the son of Pajra worships you,
Like some wise minister.

6 Hear ye the song of him who hastens speedily. O Aśvins, I am he who sang your praise.
Hither, ye Lords of Splendour, hither turn your eyes.

7 For ye were ever nigh to deal forth ample wealth, to give the wealth that ye had gathered up.
As such, ye Vasus, guard us well, and keep us safely from the wicked wolf.

8 Give us not up to any man who hateth us, nor let our milch-cows stray, whose udders give us food,
Far from our homes without their calves.

9 May they who love you gain you for their Friends. Prepare ye us for opulence with strengthening food,
Prepare us for the food that floweth from our cows.

10 I have obtained the horseless car of Aśvins rich in sacrifice,
And I am well content therewith.

11 May it convey me evermore : may the light chariot pass from men
To men unto the Soma draught.

12 It holdeth slumber in contempt. and the rich who enjoyeth not :
Both vanish quickly and are lost.

HYMN CXXI. *Indra.*

1. WHEN will men's guardians hasting hear with favour the song of Aṅgiras's pious childern ?
When to the people of the home he cometh he strideth to the sacrifice, the Holy.

2 He stablished heaven; he poured forth, skilful worker, the wealth of kine, for strength, that nurtures heroes.
The Mighty One his self-born host regarded, the horse's mate, the mother of the heifer.

3 Lord of red dawns, he came victorious, daily to the Aṅgirases' former invocation.
His bolt and team hath he prepared, and stablished the heaven for quadrupeds and men two-footed.

4 In joy of this thou didst restore, for worship, the lowing company of hidden cattle.
When the three-pointed one descends with onslaught he opens wide the doors that cause man trouble.

5 Thine is that milk which thy swift-moving Parents brought down, a strengthening genial gift for conquest;
When the pure treasure unto thee they offered, the milk shed from the cow who streameth nectar.

6 There is he born. May the Swift give us rapture, and like the Sun shine forth from yonder dawning,
Indu, even us who drank, whose toils are offerings, poured from the spoon, with praise, upon the altar.

4 *Hallowed by the mystic word* : by the exclamation *vàṣaṭ*, used in making an oblation to a God with fire. This word is of the most essential importance in sacrifice but if carelessly and inconsiderately used its effects are deadly, and against these the Ṛṣi prays for protection.

5 *Ghoṣa* : Sāyaṇa says that Suhastya, the son of Ghoṣā, is intended.

The son of Pajra : one of the descendants of the Aṅgirases ; here, according to Sāyaṇa, the Ṛṣi Kakṣīvān.

In this Hymn, as in the preceding, there are several very obscure passages which can only conjecturally be translated and explained.

2 *The Mighty One* : Indra is here said to have regarded or looked on the host born from, or produced by him, that is, perhaps, the heaven and the earth in general. Specially has he regarded the animals in which the wealth of the people chiefly consists, among which the mare and the cow naturally hold the chief place. Ludwig would read *mātaram gām* instead of *mātáram goḥ*. He thinks that the mate of the horse (Sūrya) is the earth, the motherly cow. Sāyaṇa says that Indra in sport made a mare bring forth a calf, and Wilson following him translates : 'he made the female of the horse unnaturally the mother of the cow.'

4 *In joy of this* : in the rapture arising from drinking this Soma juice.

The lowing company of hidden cattle : the rain-clouds carried off and kept concealed by the Paṇis.

The three-pointed one : apparently the thunderbolt. Sāyaṇa takes it to mean Indra (elevated as a triple crest in the three worlds). *He* : Indra.

5 *Thy swift-moving Parents* : Heaven and Earth.

6 *The Swift* : the swiftly flowing and efficacious Indu or Soma.

Whose toils are offerings : whose drops of sweat, as we labour in our sacred duties, count as oblations to the Gods we serve.

From yonder dawning : probably an indication of time only.

7 When the wood-pile, made of good logs, is ready, at the Sun's worship to bind fast the Bullock,
Then when thou shinest forth through days of action for the Car-borne, the Swift, the Cattle-seeker.

8 Eight steeds thou broughtest down from mighty heaven, when fighting for the well that giveth splendour,
That men might press with stones the gladdening yellow, strengthened with milk, fermenting, to exalt thee.

9 Thou hurledst forth from heaven the iron missile, brought by the Skilful, from the sling of leather,
When thou, O Much-invoked, assisting Kutsa with endless deadly darts didst compass Śuṣṇa.

10 Bolt-armed, ere darkness overtook the sunlight, thou castest at the veiling cloud thy weapon,
Thou rentest, out of heaven, though firmly knotted, the might of Śuṣṇa that was thrown around him.

11 The mighty Heaven and Earth, those bright expanses that have no wheels, joyed, Indra, at thine exploit.
Vṛtra, the boar who lay amid the waters, to sleep thou sentest with thy mighty thunder.

12 Mount Indra, lover of the men thou guardest, the well-yoked horses of the wind, best bearers.
The bolt which Kāvya Uśanā erst gave thee, strong, gladdening, Vṛtra-slaying, hath he fashioned.

13 The strong Bay Horses of the Sun thou stayedst: this Etaśa drew not the wheel, O Indra.
Casting them forth beyond the ninety rivers thou dravest down into the pit the godless.

14 Indra, preserve thou us from this affliction Thunder-armed, save us from the misery near us.
Vouchsafe us affluence in chariots, founded on horses, for our food and fame and gladness.

15 Never may this thy loving-kindness fail us; mighty in strength, may plenteous food surround us.
Maghavan, make us share the foeman's cattle : may we be thy most liberal feast companions.

HYMN CXXII. *Viśvedevas.*

1. SAY, bringing sacrifice to bounteous Rudra, This juice for drink to you whose wrath is fleeting!
With Dyaus the Asura's Heroes I have lauded the Maruts as with prayer to Earth and Heaven.

2 Strong to exalt the early invocation are Night and Dawn who show with varied aspect.
The Barren clothes her in wide-woven raiment, and fair Morn shines with Sūrya's golden splendour.

3 Cheer us the Roamer round, who strikes at morning, the Wind delight us, pourer forth of waters !

7 *To bind fast the Bullock* : the Bullock is the Sun himself : the sacrifice is to secure the blessings of sunlight. Sāyaṇa explains : the priest is competent for the attachment of the animal to the stake.

The Car-borne, the Swift, the Cattle-seeker : apparently appellations of Indra.

8 *The well that giveth splendour* : the cloud that sheds fertilizing rain.

The yellow : the Soma juice.

9 *The Skilful* : Tvaṣṭar.

Kāvya Uśanā : see I.51. 10.

13 The first hemistich of this stanza is most difficult, and I do not see how it can be satisfactorily translated and explained. I have followed Grassmann who translates : 'Du liessest ruhn der Sonne starke Rosse, nicht zog der Renner mehr ihr Rad, O Indra.' If this be the meaning, the reference may be, perhaps, to an eclipse of the sun.

Etaśa : appears in a double character, first as a sacrificer who offered Soma juice to Indra and was aided and favoured by that God (I. 51. 15), and secondly, Etaśa is the name of the horses or of one of the horses, or of the single horse, of Sūrya or the Sun, especially, it seems, of the horse who, during the night, draws back the chariot of the Sun from the west to the east. In this verse, according to M. Bergaigne, Etaśa himself or his substitute (the word 'ná' which I have taken to mean 'not' being understood in its alternative sense of 'like or as') is represented as drawing the wheel when Indra has stayed the course of the Harits or Bay Horses of the Sun. It is not difficult, says M. Bergaigne, to reconcile these two different conceptions of the role of Etaśa. A sacrificer especially favoured by Indra may represent either the sacrificial fire or the Soma juice that is prepared, consecrated, and offered to the God, and Soma, in the Veda, is frequently represented as a horse. See Bergaigne, *La Religion Védique*, Vol. II. 330—333.

1 The meaning of this very difficult verse appears to be, that the offering of Soma juice is presented to Rudra and to his sons the fierce but easily appeased Maruts or Storm-Gods, whom the poet has lauded as the Heroes of Dyaus, the Immortal, and has at the same time supplicated the Deities Heaven and Earth. Wilson, following Sāyaṇa, paraphrases the second hemistich : 'I praise him who with his heroic (followers) as (with shafts) from a quiver expelled (the *Asuras*) from heaven : and (I praise) the *Maruts*, (who abide) between heaven and earth.'

2 *The barren* : the unfruitful Night; in which no work is done.

3 *The Roamer round* : 'the circumambient divinity', the Wind.'

Who strikes at morning : perhaps, blows away all evil spirits of the night.

Parvata : the presiding Genius of the mountains and ruler of the clouds, frequently associated with Indra.

Sharpen our wits, O Parvata and Indra. May all the Gods vouchsafe to us this favour.

4 And Auśija shall call for me that famous Pair who enjoy and drink, who come to brighten.
Set ye the Offspring of the Floods before you; both Mothers of the Living One who beameth.

5 For you shall Auśija call him who thunders, as, to win Arjuna's assent, cried Ghoṣā.
I will invoke, that Pūṣan may be bounteous to you, the rich munificence of Agni.

6 Hear, Mitra-Varuṇa, these mine invocations, hear them from all men in the hall of worship.
Giver of famous gifts, kind hearer, Sindhu who gives fair fields, listen with all his waters !

7 Praised, Mitra, Varuṇa ! is your gift, a hundred cows to the Pṛkṣayāmas and the Pajra.
Presented by car-famous Priyaratha, supplying nourishment, they came directly.

8 Praised is the gift of him the very wealthy: may we enjoy it, men with hero children:
His who hath many gifts to give the Pajras, a chief who makes me rich in cars and horses.

9 The folk, O Mitra-Varuṇa, who hate you, who sinfully hating pour you no libations,
Lay in their hearts, themselves, a wasting sickness, whereas the righteous gaineth all by worship.

10 That man, most puissant, wondrously urged onward, famed among heroes, liberal in giving,
Moveth a warrior, evermore undaunted in all encounters even with the mighty.

11 Come to the man's, the sacrificer's calling: hear, Kings of Immortality, joy-givers!
While ye who speed through clouds decree your bounty largely, for fame, to him the chariot rider.

12 Vigour will we bestow on that adorer whose tenfold draught we come to taste, so spake they.
May all in whom rest splendour and great riches obtain refreshment in these sacrifices.

13 We will rejoice to drink the tenfold present when the twicefive come bearing sacred viands.
What can he do whose steeds and reins are choicest? These, the all-potent, urge brave men to conquest.

14 The sea and all the Deities shall give us him with the golden ear and neck bejewelled.
Dawns, hasting to the praises of the pious, be pleased with us, both offerers and singers.

15 Four youthful sons of Maśarśāra vex me, three, of the king, the conquering Āyavasa.
Now like the Sun, O Varuṇa and Mitra, your car hath shone, long-shaped and reined with splendour.

HYMN CXXIII. *Dawn.*

1. THE Dakṣiṇā's broad chariot hath been harnessed: this car the Gods Immortal have ascended.

4 *Auśija* : the son of *Uśij*, that is, Kakṣīvān himself, the Ṛṣi of the hymn.

That famous Pair : the Aśvins. *The Offspring of the Flood* : Agni.

The Living One who beameth : or praiseth. Agni appears to be meant.

5 *Him who thunders* : Indra. *Ghoṣā*, in I. 117. 5, is said to have been provided with a husband by the Aśvins. *Arjuna*, in this verse, may perhaps have been the husband's name. The meaning of the passage is uncertain. Sāyaṇa takes *arjuna* to mean white skin, or leprosy, from which Ghoṣā prayed to be made free.

6 *Sindhu* : the Indus; the Deity presiding over waters.

7 Who the *Pṛkṣayāmas*, or drivers of swift horses are, is uncertain.

The Pajra : the Ṛṣi Kakṣīvān himself, a member of the priestly family of the Pajras.

11 *Kings of Immortality* : Varuṇa and Mitra.

12 *Tenfold draught* : Soma juice offered in ten ladles, the *twice-five* of the following verse.

14. *Him with the golden ear* : perhaps the Sun; but the meaning of the hemistich is uncertain.

15 There is no verb in the first hemistich, and I follow Sāyaṇa in supplying 'vex.' But *śiśvaḥ* may mean 'young horses' as well as 'youthful sons,' and the verb to be supplied may be 'carry,' as suggested by Grassmann. The whole hymn, as Wilson observes, 'is very elliptical and obscure', and much of it is at present unintelligible.

---

1 *The Dakṣiṇā's broad chariot* : the Dakṣiṇā itself, that is the honorarium or fee presented by the institutor of a sacrifice to the priests who perform the ceremony. The meaning of the first hemistich appears to be that all preparations have been made for the morning sacrifice, and especially that the foe for its performance—a most essential element—is ready, and that the Gods are coming to the rite. The word *dākśiṇāyāḥ* is considered by Sāyaṇa to be an epithet of *uṣodevatāyāḥ*, understood, that is, 'of the Goddess Uṣas or Dawn.' Wilson accordingly, translates, 'the spacious chariot of the graceful (*Dawn*); Ludwig renders the word by 'friendly,' and Grassmann by 'wealth,' both scholars applying the epithet to Uṣas or Dawn who is not mentioned in the text. I have followed M. Bergaigne who says : 'The interpretation of the word *dakṣiṇā* in the

Fain to bring light to homes of men the noble and active Goddess hath emerged from darkness.

2 She before all the living world hath wakened, the Lofty One who wins and gathers treasure.
Revived and ever young on high she glances. Dawn hath come first unto our morning worship.

3 If, Dawn, thou Goddess nobly born, thou dealest fortune this day to all the race of mortals,
May Savitar the God, Friend of the homestead, declare before the Sun that we are sinless.

4 Showing her wonted form each day that passeth, spreading the light she visiteth each dwelling.
Eager for conquest, with bright sheen she cometh. Her portion is the best of goodly treasures.

5 Sister of Varuṇa, sister of Bhaga, first among all sing forth, O joyous Morning.
Weak be the strength of him who worketh evil: may we subdue him with our car the guerdon.

6 Let our glad hymns and holy thoughts rise upward, for the flames brightly burning have ascended.
The far-refulgent Mornings make apparent the lovely treasures which the darkness covered.

7 The one departeth and the other cometh: unlike in hue day's halves march on successive.
One hides the gloom of the surrounding Parents. Dawn on her shining chariot is resplendent.

8 The same in form to-day, the same to-morrow, they still keep Varuṇa's eternal statute.
Blameless, in turn they traverse thirty regions, and dart across the spirit in a moment.

9 She who hath knowledge of the first day's nature is born refulgent white from out the darkness.
The Maiden breaketh not the law of Order, day by day coming to the place appointed.

10 In pride of beauty like a maid thou goest, O Goddess, to the God who longs to win thee,
And smiling, youthful, as thou shinest brightly, before him thou discoverest thy bosom.

11 Fair as a bride embellished by her mother thou showest forth thy form that all may see it.
Blessed art thou, O Dawn. Shine yet more widely. No other Dawns have reached what thou attainest.

12 Rich in kine, horses, and all goodly treasures, in constant operation with the sunbeams,
The Dawns depart and come again assuming their wonted forms that promise happy fortune.

13 Obedient to the rein of Law Eternal give us each thought that more and more shall bless us.
Shine thou on us to-day, Dawn, swift to listen. With us be riches and with chiefs who worship.

HYMN CXXIV. *Dawn.*

1. THE Dawn refulgent when the fire is kindled, and the Sun rising, far diffuse their brightness.
Savitar, God, hath sent us forth to labour, each quadruped, each biped, to be active.

sense of sacrificial salary, in the first verse of our hymn as also in the fifth, is, not only *possible* but the *only possible* one, for the reason that this word has no other sense in the Ṛg-Veda than that of "salary, recompense," given either by the earthly *maghavan*, that is to say by those who pay the priest for performing the sacrifice, or by the heavenly *maghavan*, Indra, who in his turn pays for the sacrifice by favours of every kind to the man who causes it to be offered.' See *La Religion Vedique*, Vol. III, pp. 283, ff., for M. Bergaigne's translation of, and polemical commentary on, this hymn.

The noble and active Goddess: Uṣas, Aurora, or Dawn. The word Goddess is not in the text.

3 *May Savitar*: the all-seeing deity Savitar who presides over, but is sometimes distinguished from, the Sun, is appealed to as the best judge of the suppliant's innocence.

5 *Our car the guerdon*: may the liberal fee given for the performance of the sacrifice be to us as a war-chariot to enable us to overpower those who would injure us.

7 *Day's halves*: day and night. *The surrounding Parents* are the all en-compassing Heaven and Earth: the nightly darkness which envelops them is hidden or dispelled by the day.

8 *They traverse thirty regions*: I follow M. Bergaigne in understanding the thirty regions or spaces to be an indefinite expression for the whole universe. A more elaborate attempt at explanation will be found in Wilson's Translation in a Note from Bentley's *Hindu Astronomy*. *They* are the Dawns, and they may be said to pass across or through the spirit, to enlighten it. The second hemistich is very difficult and obscure, and can be translated only provisionally.

10 *The God who longs to win thee*: the Sun, the lover of Dawn.

13 *Chiefs who worship*: the wealthy institutors of sacrifices.

---

1 *The fire*: the sacrificial fire lighted for the morning rites.

2 Not interrupting heavenly ordinances, although she minisheth human generations.
The last of endless morns that have departed, the first of those that come, Dawn brightly shineth.

3 There in the eastern region she, Heaven's Daughter, arrayed in garments all of light, appeareth.
Truly she followeth the path of Order, nor faileth, knowing well, the heavenly quarters.

4 Near is she seen, as 'twere the Bright One's bosom: she showeth sweet things like a new song-singer.
She cometh like a fly awaking sleepers, of all returning dames most true and constant.

5 There in the east half of the watery region the Mother of the Cows hath shown her ensign.
Wider and wider still she spreadeth onward, and filleth full the laps of both her Parents.

6 She, verily, exceeding vast to look on debarreth from her light nor kin nor stranger.
Proud of her spotless form she, brightly shining, turneth not from the high nor from the humble.

7 She seeketh men as she who hath no brother, mounting her car, as 'twere to gather riches.
Dawn, like a loving matron for her husband, smiling and well attired, unmasks her beauty.

8 The Sister quitteth, for the elder Sister, her place, and having looked on her departeth.
She decks her beauty, shining forth with sunbeams, like women trooping to the festal meeting.

9 To all these Sisters who ere now have vanished a later one each day in course succeedeth.
So, like the past, with days of happy fortune, may the new Dawns shine forth on us with riches.

10 Rouse up, O Wealthy One, the liberal givers; let niggard traffickers sleep on unwakened:
Shine richly, Wealthy One, on those who worship, richly, glad. Dawn while wasting, on the singer.

11 This young Maid from the east hath shone upon us; she harnesseth her team of bright red oxen.
She will beam forth, the light will hasten hither, and Agni will be present in each dwelling.

12 As the birds fly forth from their resting places, so men with store of food rise at thy dawning.
Yea, to the liberal mortal who remaineth at home, O Goddess Dawn, much good thou bringest.

13 Praised through my prayer be ye who should be lauded. Ye have increased our wealth, ye Dawns who love us.
Goddesses, may we win by your good favour wealth to be told by hundreds and by thousands.

HYMN CXXV. *Svanaya.*

1. COMING at early morn he gives his treasure; the prudent one receives and entertains him.
Thereby increasing still his life and offspring, he comes with brave sons to abundant riches.

2 Rich shall he be in gold and kine and horses. Indra bestows on him great vital power,
Who stays thee, as thou comest, with his treasure, like game caught in the net, O early comer.

3 Longing, I came this morning to the pious, the son of sacrifice, with car wealth-laden.
Give him to drink juice of the stalk that gladdens; prosper with pleasant hymns the Lord of Heroes.

4 Health-bringing streams, as milch-cows,

2. *She minisheth* : by marking the lapse of man's allotted time. Cf. I. 92. 10, 11.

4 *Like a fly* : *admasán ná*; see Geldner, Vedische Studien, II. 179.

5 *The watery region* : the misty sky. *The Cows* : rays of light.

Both her Parents : Heaven and Earth.

7 *She seeketh men* : this is not very clear. Perhaps the Sun, her lover or husband, is intended.

8 *The elder Sister* : Day, for whom Night makes room.

10 *While wasting* : as in verse 2.

12 *With store of food* : we should expect 'who seek their food,' and so Sāyaṇa explains *pitubhājaḥ*. The wealthy may be meant who share their store with others and must work to replenish it.

This hymn is a dialogue between a wandering priest and a pious liberal prince. For the explanatory legend, which is cited by Sāyaṇa, see the note in Wilson's translation.

1 The priest (Kakṣīvān) speaks. *His treasure* : the wealth that will follow sacrifice. *The prudent one* : the prince.

2 The prince (Svanaya) speaks.

3 The priest speaks. *Him* : Indra.

flow to profit him who hath worshipped, him who now will worship.
To him who freely gives and fills on all sides full streams of fatness flow and make him famous.

5 On the high ridge of heaven he stands exalted, yea, to the Gods he goes, the liberal giver.
The streams, the waters flow for him with fatness : to him this guerdon ever yields abundance.

6 For those who give rich meeds are all these splendours, for those who give rich meeds suns shine in heaven.
The givers of rich meeds are made immortal ; the givers of rich fees prolong their lifetime.

7 Let not the liberal sink to sin and sorrow, never decay the pious chiefs who worship !
Let every man besides be their protection, and let affliction fall upon the niggard.

HYMN CXXVI. *Bhāvayavya.*

1. WITH wisdom I present these lively praises of Bhāvya dweller on the bank of Sindhu ;
For he, unconquered King, desiring glory, hath furnished me a thousand sacrifices.

2 A hundred necklets from the King, beseeching, a hundred gift-steeds I at once accepted ;
Of the lord's cows a thousand, I Kakṣīvān. His deathless glory hath he spread to heaven.

3 Horses of dusky colour stood beside me, ten chariots, Svanaya's gift, with mares to draw them.
Kine numbering sixty thousand followed after. Kakṣīvān gained them when the days were closing.

4 Forty bay horses of the ten cars' master before a thousand lead the long procession.
Reeling in joy Kakṣīvān's sons and Pajra's have grounded the coursers decked with pearly trappings.

5 An earlier gift for you have I accepted eight cows, good milkers, and three harnessed horses,
Pajras, who with your wains with your great kinsman, like troops of subjects, have been fain for glory.

HYMN CXXVII. *Agni.*

1. AGNI I hold as herald, the munificent, the gracious, Son of Strength, who knoweth all that live, as holy Singer, knowing all,
Lord of fair rites, a God with form erected turning to the Gods,
He, when the flame hath sprung forth from the holy oil, the offered fatness, longeth for it with his glow.

2 We, sacrificing, call on thee best worshipper, the eldest of Aṅgirases, Singer, with hymns, thee, brilliant One ! with singers' hymns ;
Thee, wandering round as 't were the sky, who art the invoking Priest of men,
Whom, Bull with hair of flame, the people must observe, the people that he speed them on.

3 He with his shining glory blazing far and wide, he verily it is who slayeth demon foes, slayeth the demons like an axe :
At whose close touch things solid shake, and what is stable yields like trees.
Subduing all, he keeps his ground and flinches not, from the skilled archer flinches not.

4 To him, as one who knows, even things solid yield : unrough fire-sticks heated hot he gives his gifts to aid. Men offer Agni gifts for aid.
He deeply piercing many a thing hews it like wood with fervent glow.
Even hard and solid food he crunches with his might, yea, hard and solid food

1 *Bhāvya* : the prince Svanaya of the preceding hymn is here again eulogized for his munificence under the name of his father Bhāvya or Bhāvayavya, who lived on the bank of Sindhu or the Indus.

3 *With mares to draw them* : or, with damsels or female slaves. Cf. VI. 27. 8.

4 *Pajra* : the founder of the priestly family from which Kak īvān was descended.

The sixth stanza of the hymn is ascribed to Svanaya, and the seventh to his wife Romaśā. They have no apparent connexion with what precedes, and are in a different metre. They seem to be a fragment of a popular song. See Appendix.

This hymn, and the twelve that follow it, are attributed to the Ṛṣi Parucchepa. They are generally very obscure and frequently unintelligible. One of their peculiarities is 'to reiterate a leading word which occurs the third or fourth from the end of the first line, and sometimes also of the third, and to repeat it as the last word of the line. Thus we have here *sānum sahaso. Jātavedasam vipram na Jātavedasam*; this is little else than a kind of verbal alliterative jingle, but the Scholiast thinks it necessary to assign to the repeated word a distinct signification.'—Wilson.

2 *Eldest of Aṅgirases* : see I. 1.6.

3 *From the skilled archer flinches not* : not even a strong man armed with his bow can turn him from his course.

4 *Fire-sticks* : the two pieces of wood which are still used to produce the sacrificial fire.

with might.

5 Here near we place the sacrificial food for him who shines forth fairer in the night than in the day, with life then stronger than by day.
His life gives sure and firm defence as that one giveth to a son.
The during fires enjoy things given and things not given, the during fires enjoy as food.

6 He, roaring very loudly like the Maruts' host, in fertile cultivated fields adorable, in desert spots adorable,
Accepts and eats our offered gifts, ensign of sacrifice by desert ;
So let all, joying, love his path when he is glad, as men pursue a path for bliss.

7 Even as they who sang forth hymns, addressed to heaven, the Bhṛgus with their prayer and praise invited him, the Bhṛgus rubbing, offering gifts.
For radiant Agni, Lord of all these treasures, is exceeding strong.
May he, the wise, accept the grateful coverings, the wise accept the coverings.

8 Thee we invoke, the Lord of all our settled homes, common to all, the household's guardian, to enjoy, bearer of true hymns, to enjoy.
Thee we invoke, the guest of men, by whose mouth, even as a sire's,
All these Immortals come to gain their food of life, oblations come to Gods as food.

9 Thou, Agni, most victorious with thy conquering strength, most Mighty One, art born for service of the Gods, like wealth for service of the Gods.
Most mighty is thine ecstasy, most splendid is thy mental power.
Therefore men wait upon thee, undecaying One, like vassals, undecaying One.

10 To him the mighty, conquering with victorious strength, to Agni walking with the dawn, who sendeth kine, be sung your laud, to Agni sung ;
As he who with oblation comes calls him aloud in every place.
Before the brands of fire he shouteth singer-like, the herald, kindler of the brands.

11 Agni, beheld by us in nearest neighbourhood, accordant with the Gods, bring us, with gracious love, great riches with thy gracious love.
Give us O Mightiest, what is great, to see and to enjoy the earth.
As one of awful power, stir up heroic might for those who praise thee, Bounteous Lord !

5 *Things given and things not given* : both sacrificial offerings and the grass brushwood of the jungle.

7 *The Bhṛgus* : descendants of Bhṛgu, the earliest cherisher of Agni, or kindler of fire. *Rubbing* : agitating the fire-sticks. *The coverings* : according to Sāyaṇa, the oblations of clarified butter, etc.

HYMN CXXVIII. *Agni.*

1. By Manu's law was born this Agni, Priest most skilled, born for the holy work of those who yearn therefore, yea, born for his own holy work.
All ear to him who seeks his love and wealth to him who strives for fame,
Priest ne'er deceived, he sits in Iḷā's holy place, girt round in Iḷā's holy place.

2 We call that perfecter of worship by the path of sacrifice; with reverence rich in offerings, with worship rich in offerings.
Through presentation of our food he grows not old in this his from ;
The God whom Mātariśvan brought from far away, for Manu brought from far away.

3 In ordered course forthwith he traverses the earth, swift-swallowing, bellowing Steer, bearing the genial seed, bearing the seed and bellowing.
Observant with a hundred eyes the God is conqueror in the wood :
Agni, who hath his seat in broad plains here below, and in the high lands far away.

4 That Agni, wise High-Priest, in every house takes thought for sacrifice and holy service, yea, takes thought, with mental power, for sacrifice.
Disposer, he with mental power shows all things unto him who strives;
Whence he was born a guest enriched with holy oil, born as Ordainer and as Priest.

5 When through his power and in his strong prevailing flames the Maruts' gladdening boons mingle with Agni's roar, boons gladdening for the active One,
Then he accelerates the gift, and by the greatness of his wealth,
Shall rescue us from overwhelming misery, from curse and overwhelming woe.

1 *Iḷā's holy place* : the altar ; Iḍā or Iḷā is personified Prayer and Worship.

2 *Mātariśvan* : see I. 31. 3.

5 *The Maruts' gladdening boons* : storm and rain.

6 Vast, universal, good he was made messenger ; the speeder with his right hand hath not loosed his hold, through love of fame not loosed his hold.
He bears oblations to the Gods for whosoever supplicates.
Agni bestows a blessing on each pious man, and opens wide the doors for him.

7 That Agni hath been set most kind in camp of men, in sacrifice like a Lord victorious, like a dear Lord in sacred rites.
His are the oblations of mankind when offered up at Iḷā's place.
He shall preserve us from Varuṇa's chastisement, yea, from the great God's chastisement.

8 Agni the Priest they supplicate to grant them wealth : him, dear, most thoughtful, have they made their messenger, him, offering-bearer have they made,
Beloved of all, who knoweth all, the Priest, the Holy one, the Sage—
Him, Friend, for help, the Gods when they are fain for wealth, him, Friend, with hymns, when fain for wealth.

HYMN CXXIX *Indra.*

1. THE car which Indra, thou, for service of the Gods, though it be far away, O swift One, bringest near, which, Blameless One, thou bringest near,
Place swiftly nigh us for our help : be it thy will that it be strong.
Blameless and active, hear this speech of orderers, this speech of us like orderers.

2 Hear, Indra, thou whom men in every fight must call to show thy strength, for cry of battle with the men, with men of war for victory.
He who with heroes wins the light, who with the singers gains the prize,
Him the rich seek to gain even as a swift strong steed, even as a courser fleet and strong.

3 Thou, Mighty, pourest forth the hide that holds the rain, thou keepest far away, Hero, the wicked man, thou shuttest out the wicked man.
Indra, to thee I sing, to Dyaus, to Rudra glorious in himself,
To Mitra, Varuṇa I sing a far-famed hymn to the kind God a far-famed hymn.

4 We wish our Indra here that he may further you, the Friend, beloved of all, the very strong ally, in wars the very strong ally
In all encounters strengthen thou our prayer to be a help to us.
No enemy—whom thou smitest down—subdueth thee, no enemy, whom thou smitest down.

5 Bow down the overweening pride of every foe with succour like to kindling-wood in fiercest flame, with mighty succour, Mighty One.
Guide us, thou Hero, as of old, so art thou counted blameless still.
Thou drivest, as a Priest, all sins of man away, as Priest, in person, seeking us.

6 This may I utter to the present Soma-drop, which, meet to be invoked, with power, awakes the prayer, awakes the demon-slaying prayer.
May he himself with darts of death drive far from us the scorner's hate.
Far let him flee away who speaketh wickedness and vanish like a mote of dust.

7 By thoughtful invocation this may we obtain, obtain great wealth, O Wealthy One, with Hero sons, wealth that is sweet with hero sons.
Him who is wroth we pacify with sacred food and eulogies,
Indra the Holy with our calls inspired and true, the Holy One with calls inspired.

8 On, for your good and ours, come Indra with the aid of his own lordliness to drive the wicked hence, to rend the evil-hearted ones !
The weapon which devouring fiends cast at us shall destroy themselves.
Struck down, it shall not reach the mark; hurled forth, the fire-brand shall not strike.

9 With riches in abundance, Indra, come to us, come by an unobstructed path, come by a path from demons free.
Be with us when we stray afar, be with us when our home is nigh.
Protect us with thy help both near and far away : protect us ever with thy help.

10 Thou art our own, O Indra, with victorious wealth : let might accompany thee, the Strong, to give us aid, like Mitra, to give mighty aid.
O strongest saviour, helper thou, Immortal ! of each warrior's car.
Hurt thou another and not us, O Thunder-armed, one who would hurt, O Thunder-armed !

11 Save us from injury, thou who art well extolled : ever the warder-off art thou of wicked ones, even as a God, of wicked ones ;
Thou slayer of the evil fiend, saviour of singer such as I.
Good Lord, the Father made thee slayer of the fiends, made thee, good Lord, to slay the fiends.

HYMN CXXX. *Indra.*

1. Come to us, Indra, from afar, conducting us even as a lord of heroes to the gatherings, home, like a King, his heroes' lord.
We come with gifts of pleasant food, with juice poured forth, invoking thee,
As sons invite a sire, that thou mayst get thee strength, thee, bounteousest, to get thee strength.

2 O Indra, drink the Soma juice pressed out with stones, poured from the reservoir, as an ox drinks the spring, a very thirsty bull the spring.
For the sweet draught that gladdens thee, for mightiest freshening of thy strength.
Let thy Bay Horses bring thee hither as the Sun, as every day they bring the Sun.

3 He found the treasure brought from heaven that lay concealed, close-hidden, like the nestling of a bird, in rock, enclosed in never-ending rock.
Best Aṅgiras, bolt-armed, he strove to win, as 'twere, the stall of kine ;
So Indra hath disclosed the food concealed, disclosed the doors, the food that lay concealed.

4 Grasping his thunderbolt with both hands, Indra made its edge most keen, for hurling, like a carving-knife for Ahi's slaughter made it keen.
Endued with majesty and strength, O Indra, and with lordly might,
Thou crashest down the trees, as when a craftsman fells, crashest them down as with an axe.

5 Thou, Indra, without effort hast let loose the floods to run their free course down, like chariots, to the sea, like chariots showing forth their strength.
They, reaching hence away, have joined their strength for one eternal end,
Even as the cows who poured forth every thing for man, yea, poured forth all things for mankind.

6 Eager for riches, men have formed for thee this song, like as a skilful craftsman fashioneth a car, so have they wrought thee to their bliss ;
Adorning thee, O Singer, like a generous steed for deeds of might,
Yea, like a steed to show his strength and win the prize, that he may bear each prize away.

7 For Pūru thou hast shattered, Indra ! ninety forts, for Divodāsa thy boon servant with thy bolt, O Dancer, for thy worshipper.
For Atithigva he, the Strong, brought Śambara from the mountain down,
Distributing the mighty treasures with his strength, parting all treasures with his strength.

8 Indra in battles help his Āryan worshipper, he who hath hundred helps at hand in every fray, in frays that win the light of heaven.
Plaguing the lawless he gave up to Manu's seed the dusky skin ;
Blazing, 'twere, he burns each covetous man away, he burns, the tyrannous away.

9 Waxed strong in might at dawn he tore the Sun's wheel off. Bright red, he steals away their speech, the Lord of Power, their speech he steals away from them,
As thou with eager speed, O Sage, hast come from far away to help,
As winning for thine own all happiness of men, winning all happiness each day.

11 *The Father* : Janitā, the Latin genitor; the Supreme God, the Maker and Father of the Universe.

3 *He found the treasure* : the Soma. *The food concealed* : according to Sāyaṇa, in the first place the rain enclosed in the clouds, and in the second place the seeds shut up in the earth which await the rain to make them germinate.

5 *For man* : or for Manu, the great progenitor of the human race.

7 *Pūru* : the name of a prince protected by Indra. *Divodāsa* : called also *Atithigva*. See I. 92, 191.

Dancer : thou who dancest in battle; dancer of the war-dance.

Śambara : a demon of the air ; or perhaps in this place some human adversary of Atithigva.

9 *He tore the Sun's wheel off* : according to Sāyaṇa, Brahmā had promised the Asuras or fiends that Indra's thunderbolt should never destroy them. Indra, accordingly, cast at them the wheel of the Sun's chariot and slew them therewith.

He steals their speech : Sāyaṇa thinks that the meaning is that Indra deprived his enemies of life.

O Sage : O Indra.

10 Lauded with our new hymns, O vigorous in deed, save us with strengthening help, thou Shatterer of the Forts !
Thou, Indra, praised by Divodāsa's clansmen, as heaven grows great with days, shalt wax in glory.

HYMN CXXXI. *Indra.*

1. To Indra Dyaus the Asura hath bowed him down, to Indra mighty Earth with wide-extending tracts, to win the light, with wide-spread tracts.
All Gods of one accord have set Indra in front preëminent.
For Indra all libations must be set apart, all man's libations set apart.

2 In all libations men with hero spirit urge the Universal One, each seeking several light, each fain to win the light apart.
Thee, furthering like a ship, will we set to the chariot-pole of strength,
As men who win with sacrifices Indra's thought, men who win Indra with their lauds.

3 Couples desirous of thine aid are storming thee, pouring their presents forth to win a stall of kine, pouring gifts, Indra, seeking thee.
When two men seeking spoil or heaven thou bringest face to face in war,
Thou showest, Indra, then the bolt thy constant friend, the Bull that ever waits on thee.

4 This thine heroic power men of old time have known, wherewith thou breakest down, Indra, autumnal forts, breakest them down with conquering might.
Thou hast chastised, O Indra, Lord of Strength, the man who worships not,
And made thine own this great earth and these water-floods ; with joyous heart these waterfloods.

5 And they have bruited far this hero-might when thou, O Strong One, in thy joy helpest thy suppliants, who sought to win thee for their Friend.
Their battle-cry thou madest sound victorious in the shocks of war.
One stream after another have they gained from thee, eager for glory have they gained.

6. Also this morn may he be well inclined to us, mark at our call our offerings and our song of praise, our call that we may win the light.
As thou, O Indra Thunder-armed, wilt, as the Strong One, slay the foe,
Listen thou to the prayer of me a later sage, hear thou a later sage's prayer.

7 O Indra, waxen strong and well-inclined to us, thou very mighty, slay the man that is our foe, slay the man, Hero ! with thy bolt.
Slay thou the man who injures us : hear thou, as readiest to hear.
Far be malignity, like mischief on the march, afar be all malignity.

HYMN CXXXII. *Indra.*

1. Helped, Indra Maghavan, by thee in war of old, may we subdue in fight the men who strive with us, conquer the men who war with us.
This day that now is close at hand bless him who pours the Soma juice.
In this our sacrifice may we divide the spoil, showing our strength, the spoil of war.

2 In war which wins the light, at the free-giver's call, at due oblation of the early-rising one, oblation of the active one,
Indra slew, even as we know—whom each bowed head must reverence.
May all thy bounteous gifts be gathered up for us, yea, the good gifts of thee the Good.

3 This food glows for thee as of old at sacrifice, wherein they made thee chooser of the place, for thou choosest the place of sacrifice.
Speak thou and make it known to us : they see within with beams of light.

10 *By Divodāsa's clansmen* : by me, Parucchepa, a member of the house or family of Divodāsa.

3 *Couples* : sacrificers and their wives who are associated with them in offering oblations.

The Bull : the fiercely rushing thunderbolt.

4 *Autumnal forts* : strongholds on high ground, occupied as places of refuge during the heavy rains, or 'the brilliant battlemented cloud-castles, which are so often visible in the Indian sky at this period of the year.'—Muir, O. S. Texts, II. 379.

Men of old time : I have followed Sāyaṇa here. But *pūrvāḥ* probably means the Pūrus, one of the five great Āryan tribes or clans.

1 *This day* : the hymn is addressed to Indra just before an expected battle.

May we divide the spoil : divide it in anticipation ; secure it by our sacrifice.

2 *The early-rising* and *active one* is the offerer of the sacrifice.

3 *They made thee chooser of the place* : the meaning appears to be that Indra is present at such sacrifices only as he chooses to favour.

Indra, indeed, is found a seeker after spoil, spoil-seeker for his own allies.

4 So now must thy great deed be lauded as of old, when for the Aṅgirases thou openedst the stall, openedst, giving aid, the stall.
In the same manner for us here fight thou and be victorious :
To him who pours the juice give up the lawless man, the lawless who is wroth with us.

5 When with wise plan the Hero leads the people forth, they conquer in the ordered battle, seeking fame, press, eager, onward seeking fame.
To him in time of need they sing for life with offspring and with strength.
Their hymns with Indra find a welcome place of rest : the hymns go forward to the Gods.

6 Indra and Parvata, our champions in the fight, drive ye away each man who fain would war with us, drive him far from us with the bolt.
Welcome to him concealed afar shall be the lair that he hath found.
So may the Render rend our foes on every side, rend them, O Hero, everywhere.

HYMN CXXXIII. *Indra.*

1. WITH sacrifice I purge both earth and heaven : I burn up great she-fiends who serve not Indra,
Where throttled by thy hand the foes were slaughtered, and in the pit of death lay pierced and mangled.

2 O thou who castest forth the stone, crushing the sorceresses' heads,
Break them with thy wide-spreading foot, with thy wide-spreading mighty foot.

3 Do thou, O Maghavan, beat off these sorceresses' daring strength.
Cast them within the narrow pit, within the deep and narrow pit.

4 Of whom thou hast ere now destroyed thrice-fifty with thy fierce attacks.
That deed they count a glorious deed, though small to thee, a glorious deed.

5 O Indra, crush and bray to bits the fearful fiery-weaponed fiend :
Strike every demon to the ground.

6 Tear down the mighty ones. O Indra, hear thou us. For heaven hath glowed like earth in fear, O Thunder-armed, as dreading fierce heat, Thunder-armed !
Most Mighty mid the Mighty Ones thou speedest with strong bolts of death.
Not slaying men, unconquered Hero ! with the brave, O Hero, with the thrice-seven brave.

7 The pourer of libations gains the home of wealth, pouring his gift conciliates hostilities, yea, the hostilities of Gods.
Pouring, he strives, unchecked and strong, to win him riches thousandfold.
Indra gives lasting wealth to him who pours forth gifts, yea, wealth he gives that long shall last.

HYMN CXXXIV. *Vāyu.*

1. VĀYU, let fleet-foot coursers bring thee speedily to this our feast, to drink first of the juice we pour, to the first draught of Soma juice.
May our glad hymn, discerning well, uplifted, gratify thy mind.
Come with thy team-drawn car, O Vāyu, to the gift, come to the sacrificer's gift.

2 May the joy-giving drops, O Vāyu gladden thee, effectual, well prepared, directed to the heavens, strong, blent with milk and seeking heaven ;
That aids, effectual to fulfil, may wait upon our skilful power.
Associate teams come hitherward to grant our prayers : they shall address the hymns we sing.

3 Two red steeds Vāyu yokes, Vāyu two purple steeds, swift-footed, to the chariot, to the pole to draw, most able, at the pole, to draw.
Wake up intelligence, as when a lover wakes his sleeping love.
Illumine heaven and earth, make thou the Dawns to shine, for glory make the Dawns to shine.

Speak thou and make it known : Wilson, following Sāyaṇa, paraphrases : 'do thou declare that (rite), that men may thence behold the intermediate (firmament bright) with the rays (of the sun).' I find the passage unintelligible.

4 The man *who pours the juice* is the worshipper of Indra, and *the lawless man* is the non-Āryan inhabitant of the country, the natural enemy of the new settlers.

6 *Parvata* : the presiding Genius of mountains and clouds, frequently associated with Indra, or, according to Sāyaṇa, another form of that God. Cf. II 122. 3.

This hymn is a prayer for the destruction of witches, goblins, and evil spirits of various sorts.

2 *Who castest forth the stone* : hurlest the thunderbolt.

6 *Not slaying men* : that is destroying evil spirits only. *The thrice-seven brave* : the Maruts, Indra's allies. These were forty-nine in number, and thrice-seven is used indefinitely for a larger multiple of seven.

1 *Vāyu* : the God of wind.

4 For thee the radiant Dawns in the far-distant sky broaden their lovely garments forth in wondrous beams, bright-coloured in their new-born beams.
For thee the nectar-yielding Cow pours all rich treasures forth as milk.
The Marut host hast thou engendered from the womb, the Maruts from the womb of heaven.

5 For thee the pure bright quickly-flowing Soma-drops, strong in their heightening power, hasten to mixthemselves, hasten to the water to be mixed.
To thee the weary coward prays for luck that he may speed away.
Thou by thy law protectest us from every world, yea, from the world of highest Gods.

6 Thou, Vāyu, who hast none before thee, first of all hast right to drink these offerings of Soma juice, hast right to drink the juice out-poured,
Yea, poured by all invoking tribes who free themselves from taint of sin,
For thee all cows are milked to yield the Soma-milk, to yield the butter and the milk.

HYMN CXXXV. *Vāyu, Indra-Vāyu.*

1. Strewn is the sacred grass ; come Vāyu, to our feast, with team of thousands, come, Lord of the harnessed team, with hundreds, Lord of harnessed steeds !
The drops divine are lifted up for thee, the God, to drink them first.
The juices rich in sweets have raised them for thy joy, have raised themselves to give thee strength.

2 Purified by the stones the Soma flows for thee, clothed with its lovely splendours, to the reservoir, flows clad in its refulgent light.
For thee the Soma is poured forth, thy portioned share mid Gods and men.
Drive thou thy horses, Vāyu, come to us with love, come well-inclined and loving us.

3 Come thou with hundreds, come with thousands in thy team to this our solemn rite, to taste the sacred food, Vāyu, to taste the offerings.
This is thy seasonable share, that comes co-radiant with the Sun.
Brought by attendant priests pure juice is offered up, Vāyu, pure juice is offered up.

4 The chariot with its team of horses bring you both, to guard us and to taste the well-appointed food, Vāyu, to taste the offerings !
Drink of the pleasant-flavoured juice : the first draught is assigned to you.
O Vāyu, with your splendid bounty come ye both, Indra, with bounty come ye both.

5 May our songs bring you hither to our solemn rites : these drops of mighty vigour have they beautified, like a swift steed of mighty strength.
Drink of them well-inclined to us, come hitherward to be our help.
Drink, Indra-Vāyu, of these juices pressed with stones, Strength-givers ! till they gladden you.

6 These Soma juices pressed for you in waters here, borne by attendant priests, are offered up to you : bright, Vāyu, are they offered up.
Swift through the strainer have they flowed, and here are shed for both of you,
Soma-drops, fain for you, over the wether's fleece, Somas over the wether's fleece.

7 O Vāyu, pass thou over all the slumberers, and where the press-stone rings enter ye both that house, yea, Indra, go ye both within.
The joyous Maiden is beheld, the butter flows. With richly laden team come to our solemn rite, yea, Indra, come ye to the rite.

8 Ride hither to the offering of the pleasant juice, the holy Fig-tree which victorious priests surround : victorious be they still for us.
At once the cows yield milk, the barley-meal is dressed. For thee,
O Vāyu, never shall the cows grow thin, never for thee shall they be dry.

9 These Bulls of thine, O Vāyu with the arm of strength, who swiftly fly within

---

4 *Nectar-yielding Cow* : Sabardughā; yielding amṛta, ambrosia, nectar, or food for the Gods.

6 *The Soma-milk* : the libation consisting of Soma juice mixed with milk.

6 *The wether's fleece* : the filter or strainer made of wool, used in purifying the Soma juice. See I. 2. 1.

7 *Where the press-stone rings* : where men are pressing out the Soma juice. *The joyous Maiden* : probably Uṣas or Dawn.

8 *The holy Fig-tree* : the vessel for holding the Soma juice, made of the wood of the Aśvattha or Ficus Religiosa; or, as Sāyaṇa explains it here, the Soma itself.
The barley-meal : forming a part of the offering.

9 *Bulls* : blasts of wind

the current of thy stream, the Bulls increasing in their might,
Horseless, yet even through the waste swift-moving, whom no shout can stay,
Hard to be checked are they, like sunbeams, in their course. hard to be checked by both the hands.

HYMN CXXXVI. *Mitra-Varuṇa.*

1. BRING adoration ample and most excellent, hymn, offerings, to the watchful Twain, the bountiful, your sweetest to the bounteous Ones.
Sovrans adored with streams of oil and praised at every sacrifice.
Their high imperial might may nowhere be assailed, ne'er may their Godhead be assailed.

2 For the broad Sun was seen a path more widely laid, the path of holy law hath been maintained with rays, the eye with Bhaga's rays of light.
Firm-set in heaven is Mitra's home, and Aryaman's and Varuṇa's.
Thence they give forth great vital strength which merits praise, high power of life that men shall praise.

3 With Aditi the luminous, the celestial, upholder of the people, come ye day by day, ye who watch sleepless, day by day.
Resplendent might have ye obtained, Ādityas, Lords of liberal gifts.
Movers of men, mild both, are Mitra, Varuṇa, mover of men is Aryaman.

4 This Soma be most sweet to Mitra, Varuṇa : he in the drinking-feasts, shall have a share thereof, sharing, a God, among the Gods.
May all the Gods of one accord accept it joyfully to-day.
Therefore do ye, O Kings, accomplish what we ask, ye Righteous Ones, whate'er we ask.

5 Whoso with worship serves Mitra and Varuṇa, him guard ye carefully, uninjured, from distress, guard from distress the liberal man.
Aryaman guards him well who acts uprightly following his law,
Who beautifies their service with his lauds, who makes it beautiful with songs of praise.

6 Worship will I profess to lofty Dyaus, to Heaven and Earth, to Mitra and to bounteous Varuṇa, the Bounteous, the Compassionate.
Praise Indra, praise thou Agni, praise Bhaga and heavenly Aryaman.
Long may we live and have attendant progeny, have progeny with Soma's help.

7 With the Gods' help, with Indra still beside us, may we be held self-splendid with the Maruts.
May Agni, Mitra, Varuṇa give us shelter : this may we gain, we and our wealthy princes.

HYMN CXXXVII. *Mitra-Varuṇa.*

1. WITH stones have we pressed out : O come ; these gladdening drops are blent with milk, these Soma-drops which gladden you.
Come to us, Kings who reach to heaven, approach us, coming hitherward.
These milky drops are yours, Mitra and Varuṇa, bright Soma juices blent with milk.

2 Here are the droppings ; come ye nigh ; the Soma-droppings blent with curd, juices expressed and blent with curd.
Now for the wakening of your Dawn together with the Sun-God's rays,
Juice waits for Mitra and for Varuṇa to drink, fair juice for drink, for sacrifice.

3 As 'twere a radiant-coloured cow, they milk with stones the stalk for you, with stones they milk the Soma-plant.
May ye come nigh us, may ye turn hither to drink the Soma juice.
The men pressed out this juice, Mitra and Varuṇa, pressed out this Soma for your drink.

HYMN CXXXVIII. *Pūṣan.*

1. STRONG Pūṣan's majesty is lauded evermore, the glory of his lordly might is never faint, his song of praise is never faint.

2 *Bhaga's rays of light* : 'the ancient god, Bhaga,' says Mr. Wallis, 'has become in the Ṛgveda little more than a source from which descriptions of the functions of other gods are obtained, or a standard of comparison by which their greatness is enhanced. His name has survived in the Slavonic languages as a general name for god, a sense which it also has in the Avesta. To judge from the Ṛgveda, Bhaga would seem to be a survival from an ancient Sun-worship.' *The Cosmology of the Ṛgveda*, p. 11. It is difficult to explain every expression in the verse; but the general meaning appears to be that the heaven has been lighted by the Sun, and that there is the home of the Gods who thence show forth the powers which men should glorify.

3 *Aditi* and *Ādityas* : see I. 14. 3.

4 *He* : Soma himself, meaning perhaps the Moon

1 *Pūṣan* : see I. 14. 3, and 42. 1.

Seeking felicity I laud him nigh to help, the source of bliss,
Who, Vigorous one, hath drawn to him the hearts of all, drawn them, the Vigorous One, the God.

2 Thee, then, O Pūṣan, like a swift one on his way, I urge with lauds that thou mayst make the foemen flee, drive, camel-like, our foes afar.
As I, a man, call thee, a God, giver of bliss, to be my Friend,
So make our loudly-chanted praises glorious, in battles make them glorious.

3 Thou, Pūṣan, in whose friendship they who sing forth praise enjoy advantage, even in wisdom, through thy grace, in wisdom even they are advanced.
So, after this most recent course, we come to thee with prayers for wealth.
Not stirred to anger, O Wide-Ruler, come to us, come thou to us in every fight.

4 Not stirred to anger, come, Free-giver, nigh to us, to take this gift of ours, thou who hast goats for steeds, Goat-borne ! their gift who long for fame.
So, Wonder-Worker ! may we turn thee hither with effectual lauds.
I slight thee not, O Pūṣan, thou Resplendent One : thy friendship may not be despised.

HYMN CXXXIX. *Viśvedevas.*

1. Heard be our prayer ! In thought I honour Agni first : now straightway we elect this heavenly company, Indra and Vāyu we elect.
For when our latest thought is raised and on Vivasvān centred well,
Then may our holy songs go forward on their way, our songs as 'twere unto the Gods.

2 As there ye, Mitra, Varuṇa, above the true have taken to yourselves the untrue with your mind, with wisdom's mental energy,
So in the seats wherein ye dwell have we beheld the Golden One,
Not with our thoughts or spirit, but with these our eyes, yea, with the eyes that Soma gives.

3 Aśvins, the pious call you with their hymns of praise, sounding their loud song forth to you, these living men, to their oblations, living men.
All glories and all nourishment, Lords of all wealth ! depend on you.
The fellies of your golden chariot scatter drops, Mighty Ones ! of your golden car.

4 Well is it known, O Mighty Ones : ye open heaven ; for you the chariot-steeds are yoked for morning rites, unswerving steeds for morning rites.
We set you on the chariot-seat, ye Mighty, on the golden car.
Ye seek mid-air as by a path that leads aright, as by a path that leads direct.

5 O Rich in Strength, through your great power vouchsafe us blessings day and night.
The offerings which we bring to you shall never fail, gifts brought by us shall never fail.

6 These Soma-drops, strong Indra ! drink for heroes, poured, pressed out by pressing-stones, are welling forth for thee, for thee the drops are welling forth.
They shall make glad thy heart to give, to give wealth great and wonderful.
Thou who acceptest praise come glorified by hymns, come thou to us benevolent.

7 Quickly, O Agni, hear us : magnified by us thou shalt speek for us to the Gods adorable, yea, to the Kings adorable :
When, O ye Deities, ye gave that Milch-cow to the Aṅgirases,
They milked her : Aryaman, joined with them, did the work : he knoweth her as well as I.

2 *Camel-like* : Sāyaṇa explains : 'as a camel carries away his load, so carry away our enemies from the battle.' The meaning is obscure.

4 *Thou who hast goats for steeds* : Pūṣan's chariot, like Thorr's in the Edda, is said to be drawn by a team of goats.

---

1 *Vivasvān* : the radiant celestial Agni.

2 This verse is exceedingly difficult. Ludwig's explanation, if I have understood him rightly, is to the following effect : The Golden One, which is in the home of Mitra and Varuṇa, is the Sun which is only the image or copy of the transcendental reality, the golden shell that covers the face of the *satyam* or verity. This apparent Sun Mitra and Varuṇa have taken to themselves in addition to their real essence. As this real essence is perceived not with the eyes of the body but by the eyes of the spirit strengthened by the elevating Soma-draught, so on the other hand the apparent Sun is not an object of spiritual perception. Consequently the poet says : 'With our bodily eyes we have seen the Sun, but enlightened by the Soma juice we have recognized it as being only an image of you.' *The untrue* is the Sun; *the true* is the transcendental essence of the God.

7 *That Milch-cow* : according to Sāyaṇa, the Cow of Plenty. M. Bergaigne (La Religion Vedique, I. 135, 310) thinks that prayer is meant, 'the ancient prayer of the Fathers.' The meaning of the latter part of the verse is uncertain.

8 Ne'er may these manly deeds of yours for us grow old, never may your bright glories fall into decay, never before our time decay.
What deed of yours, new every age, wondrous, surpassing man, rings forth,
Whatever, Maruts ! may be difficult to gain, grant us, whate'er is hard to gain.

9 Dadhyac of old, Aṅgiras, Priyamedha these, and Kaṇva, Atri, Manu knew my birth, yea, those of ancient days and Manu knew.
Their long line stretcheth to the Gods, our birth-connexions are with them.
To these, for their high station, I bow down with song, to Indra, Agni, bow with song.

10 Let the Invoker bless : let offerers bring choice gifts ; Bṛhaspati the Friend doth sacrifice with Steers, Steers that have many an excellence.
Now with our ears we catch the sound of the press-stone that rings afar.
The very Strong hath gained the waters by himself, the strong gained many a resting-place.

11 O ye Eleven Gods whose home is heaven, O ye Eleven who make earth your dwelling,
Ye who with might, Eleven, live in waters, accept this sacrifice, O Gods, with pleasure.

HYMN CXL. *Agni.*

1. To splendid Agni seated by the altar, loving well his home, I bring the food as 'twere his place of birth.
I clothe the bright One with my hymn as with a robe, him with the car of light, bright-hued, dispelling gloom.

2 Child of a double birth he grasps at triple food ; in the year's course what he hath swallowed grows anew.
He, by another's mouth and tongue a noble Bull, with other, as an elephant, consumes the trees.

3 The pair who dwell together, moving in the dark bestir themselves : both parents hasten to the babe,
Impetuous-tongued, destroying, springing swiftly forth, one to be watched and cherished, strengthener of his sire.

4 For man, thou Friend of men, these steeds of thine are yoked, impatient, lightly running, ploughing blackened lines,
Discordant-minded, fleet, gliding with easy speed, urged onward by the wind and rapid in their course.

5 Dispelling on their way the horror of black gloom, making a glorious show these flames of his fly forth,
When o'er the spacious tract he spreads himself abroad, and rushes panting on with thunder and with roar.

6 Amid brown plants he stoops as if adorning them, and rushes bellowing like a bull upon his wives.
Proving his might, he decks the glory of his form, and shakes his horns like one terrific, hard to stay.

7 Now covered, now displayed, he grasps as one who knows, having his resting-place in those who know him well.

9 *Dadhyac of old* : all these ancient sages have been mentioned in former hymns. As predecessors of Parucchepa, the Ṛṣi of this hymn, they are said to have known his ancestry.

10 *Let the Invoker bless* : let the Hotar, or invoking priest utter the *Yājyā*, words of consecration used at sacrifice.

Bṛhaspati : see I. 14. 3.

With Steers : according to Sāyaṇa, a metaphorical expression for strong and copious libations of Soma juice.

The very Strong : the Soma. The resting-places are the different receptacles into which the juice flows.

11 *O ye Eleven Gods* : on this Sāyaṇa remarks : 'Although, according to the text, 'There are only three gods', (Nirukta, vii. 5), the deities who represent the earth, etc., are but three, still through their greatness, *i. e.* their respective varied manifestations, they amount to thirty-three, according to the saying, 'other manifestations of Him exist in different places.'—J. Muir, *O. S. Texts*, v. 10.

This and the twenty-four following hymns are ascribed to the Ṛṣi Dirghatamas, the son of Ucathya.

1 *The food as 'twere his place of birth* : the oblation of clarified butter which makes the fire spring up into fresh life.

2 *Child of a double birth* : born first from the fire-sticks and then anew by consecration.

Triple food : clarified butter, fried cakes, Soma juice.

By another's mouth : according to Sāyaṇa, 'he receives the oblation by means of the ladle of the ministering priests, and in another form, that is the fire that burns forests, he consumes the trees.'

3 *The pair who dwell together* : the two fire-sticks from which Agni is produced by friction. *His sire* : said to be the institutor of the sacrifice.

4 In this and the four following stanzas Agni is described not in his sacrificial form but as the fire that destroys the jungle and prepares the way for new settlements.

6 *As adorning them* : with the glory of his flame.

7 *As one who knows* : because, coming from heaven with the waters, he makes the plants grow, and is said to live within them.

Change their Parents' form : perhaps, as Ludwig suggests the plants alter the appearance of the earth, and Agni or fire that of the sky.

A second time they wax and gather God-like power, and blending both together change their Parents' form.

8 The maidens with long tresses hold him in embrace ; dead, they rise up again to meet the Living One.

Releasing them from age with a loud roar he comes, filling them with new spirit, living, unsubdued.

9 Licking the mantle of the Mother, far and wide he wanders over fields with beasts that flee apace.

Strengthening all that walk, licking up all around, a blackened path, forsooth, he leaves where'er he goes.

10 O Agni, shine resplendent with our wealthy chiefs, like a loud-snorting bull, accustomed to the house.

Thou casting off thine infant wrappings blazest forth as though thou hadst put on a coat of mail for war.

11 May this our perfect prayer be dearer unto thee than an imperfect prayer although it please thee well.

With the pure brilliancy that radiates from thy form, mayest thou grant to us abundant store of wealth.

12 Grant to our chariot, to our house, O Agni, a boat with moving feet and constant oarage,

One that may further well our wealthy princes and all the folk, and be our certain refuge.

13 Welcome our laud with thine approval, Agni. May earth and heaven and freely-flowing rivers

Yield us long life and food and corn and cattle, and may the red Dawns choose for us their choicest.

HYMN CXLI. *Agni.*

1. YEA, verily, the fair effulgence of the God for glory was established, since he sprang from strength.

When he inclines thereto successful is the hymn : the songs of sacrifice have brought him as they flow.

2 Wonderful, rich in nourishment, he dwells in food ; next, in the seven auspicious Mothers is his home.

Thirdly, that they might drain the treasures of the Bull, the maidens brought forth him for whom the ten provide.

3 What time from out the deep, from the Steer's wondrous form, the Chiefs who had the power produced him with their strength ;

When Mātariśvan rubbed forth him who lay concealed, for mixture of the sweet drink, in the days of old.

4 When from the Highest Father he is brought to us, amid the plants he rises hungry, wondrously.

As both together join to expedite his birth, most youthful he is born resplendent in his light.

5 Then also entered he the Mothers, and in them pure and uninjured he increased in magnitude.

As to the first he rose, the vigorous from of old, so now he runs among the younger lowest ones.

6 Therefore they choose him Herald at the morning rites, pressing to him as unto Bhaga, pouring gifts,

When, much-praised, by the power and will of Gods, he goes at all times to his mortal worshipper to drink.

7 What time the Holy One, wind-urged, hath risen up, serpent-like winding through the dry grass unrestrained,

Dust lies upon the way of him who burneth all, black-winged and pure of birth who follows sundry paths.

8 Like a swift chariot made by men who know their art, he with his red limbs lifts himself aloft to heaven.

Thy worshippers become by burning black

8 *The maidens with long tresses* : the curling flames.

9 *The Mother* : the earth, whose vesture of grass and shrubs he licks and consumes.

Strengthening all that walk : giving them strength and speed to fly before him.

10 *Thine infant wrappings* : the waters that enveloped the 'Child of the Floods.'

11 *This our perfect prayer* : see Vedic Hymns, I. 225.

12 *A boat* : according to Sāyaṇa, the sacrifice, with priests for oars, and Gods, prayers and offerings, for feet.

---

1 *From strength* : from violent agitation of the fire-stick.

2 *He dwells in food* : he is the cause of the production of men's food, as sender of rain and as sacrificial fire.

The seven auspicious Mothers : according to Sāyaṇa, the rains which fertilize the seven *lokas* or worlds.

The Bull : Agni. *The maidens*, and *the ten*, are the fingers which produce the fire by attrition and tend it afterwards.

3 Agni appears here to have been partly produced by the Chiefs, the Sūris or Gods, from the depth of the atmosphere, from Parjanya the rainy cloud symbolically represented as a bull, and partly generated by Mātariśvan (see I. 31. 3) by attrition, and brought by him to the earth to receive libations of Soma juice.

4 *The Highest Father* : Dyaus. *Both together* : Heaven and Earth.

5 *The Mothers* : the waters. *The younger lowest ones* : the plants in which also he dwells.

6 *Herald* : or, Hotar. *Bhaga* : see I. 136. 2.

of hue: their strength flies as before a hero's violence.

9 By thee, O Agni, Varuṇa who guards the Law, Mitra and Aryaman, the Bounteous, are made strong;
For, as the felly holds the spokes, thou with thy might pervading hast been born encompassing them round.

10 Agni, to him who toils and pours libations, thou, Most Youthful! sendest wealth and all the host of Gods.
Thee, therefore, even as Bhaga, will we set anew, young Child of Strength, most wealthy! in our battle-song.

11 Vouchsafe us riches turned to worthy ends, good luck abiding in the house, and strong capacity,
Wealth that directs both worlds as they were guiding-reins, and, very Wise, the Gods' assent in sacrifice.

12 May he, the Priest resplendent, joyful, hear us, he with the radiant car and rapid horses.
May Agni, ever wise, with best directions to bliss and highest happiness conduct us.

13 With hymns of might hath Agni now been lauded, advanced to height of universal kingship.
Now may these wealthy chiefs and we together spread forth as spreads the Sun above the rain-clouds.

HYMN CXLII. *Āprīs.*

1. KINDLED, bring, Agni, Gods to-day for him who lifts the ladle up.
Spin out the ancient thread for him who sheds, with gifts, the Soma juice.

2 Thou dealest forth, Tanūnapāt, sweet sacrifice enriched with oil,
Brought by a singer such as I who offers gifts and toils for thee.

3 He wondrous, sanctifying, bright, sprinkles the sacrifice with mead,
Thrice, Narāśaṁsa from the heavens, a God mid Gods adorable.

4 Agni, besought, bring hitherward Indra the Friend, the Wonderful,
For this my hymn of praise, O sweet of tongue, is chanted forth to thee.

5 The ladle-holders strew trimmed grass at this well-ordered sacrifice;
A home for Indra is adorned, wide, fittest to receive the Gods.

6 Thrown open be the Doors Divine, unfailing, that assist the rite,
High, purifying, much-desired, so that the Gods may enter in.

7 May Night and Morning, hymned with lauds, united, fair to look upon,
Strong Mothers of the sacrifice, seat them together on the grass.

8 May the two Priests Divine, the sage, the sweet-voiced lovers of the hymn,
Complete this sacrifice of ours, effectual, reaching heaven to-day.

9 Let Hotrā pure, set among Gods, amid the Maruts Bhāratī, Iḷā, Sarasvatī, Mahī, rest on the grass, adorable.

10 May Tvaṣṭar send us genial dew abundant, wondrous, rich in gifts,
For increase and for growth of wealth, Tvaṣṭar our kinsman and our Friend.

11 Vanaspati, give forth, thyself, and call the Gods to sacrifice.
May Agni, God intelligent, speed our oblation to the Gods.

12 To Vāyu joined with Pūṣan, with the Maruts, and the host of Gods,
To Indra who inspires the hymn cry Glory! and present the gift.

13 Come hither to enjoy the gifts prepared with cry of Glory! Come,
O Indra, hear their calling; they invite thee to the sacrifice.

HYMN CXLIII. *Agni.*

1. To Agni I present a newer mightier hymn, I bring my words and song unto the Son of Strength,
Who, Offspring of the Waters, bearing precious things sits on the earth, in season, dear Invoking Priest.

2 Soon as he sprang to birth that Agni was shown forth to Mātariśvan in the highest firmament.
When he was kindled, through his power and majesty his fiery splendour made the heavens and earth to shine.

---

1 *The ladle*: the sacrificial ladle containing the oblation.

Spin out the ancient thread: perform the sacrifice ordained of old.

2 *Tanūnapāt*: Son of Thyself; Agni. See I. 13. 2.

3 *Narāśaṁsa*: a name of Agni. See I. 13. 2.

6 *The Doors Divine*: of the hall of sacrifice. See I. 13. 6.

8 *The two Priests Divine*: see I. 13. 8.

9 *Hotrā*: a Goddess of sacrifice, regarded as the consort of Agni.

Bhāratī: a Goddess of sacred speech.

Iḷā, Sarasvatī, Mahī: see I. 13. 9.

11 *Vanaspati*: the sacrificial post said to be a form of Agni.

12 *Cry Glory!*: Svāhā! the sacred word uttered at the end of sacrificial invocations.

---

2 *Mātariśvan*: see I. 31. 3.

3 His flames that wax not old, beams fair to look upon of him whose face is lovely, shine with beauteous sheen.
The rays of Agni, him whose active force is light, through the nights glimmer sleepless, ageless, like the floods.

4 Send thou with hymns that Agni to his own abode, who rules, one Sovran Lord of wealth, like Varuṇa,
Him, All-possessor, whom the Bhṛgus with their might brought to earth's central point, the centre of the world.

5 He whom no force can stay, even as the Maruts' roar, like to a dart sent forth, even as the bolt from heaven,
Agni with sharpened jaws chews up and eats the trees, and conquers them as when the warrior smites his foes.

6 And will not Agni find enjoyment in our praise, will not the Vasu grant our wish with gifts of wealth ?
Will not the Inspirer speed our prayers to gain their end ? Him with the radiant glance I laud with this my song.

7 The kindler of the flame wins Agni as a Friend, promoter of the Law, whose face is bright with oil.
Inflamed and keen, refulgent in our gatherings, he lifts our hymn on high clad in his radiant hues.

8 Keep us incessantly with guards that cease not, Agni, with guards auspicious, very mighty.
With guards that never slumber, never heedless, never beguiled, O Helper, keep our children.

HYMN CXLIV. *Agni.*

1. THE Priest goes forth to sacrifice, with wondrous power sending aloft the hymn of glorious brilliancy.
He moves to meet the ladles turning to the right, which are the first to kiss the place where he abides.

2 To him sang forth the flowing streams of Holy Law, encompassed in the home and birth-place of the God.
He, when he dwelt extended in the waters' lap, absorbed those Godlike powers for which he is adored.

3 Seeking in course altern to reach the selfsame end the two copartners strive to win this beauteous form.
Like Bhaga must he be duly invoked by us, as he who drives the car holds fast the horse's reins.

4 He whom the two copartners with observance tend, the pair who dwell together in the same abode,
By night as in the day the grey one was born young, passing untouched by eld through many an age of man.

5 Him the ten fingers, the devotions. animate: we mortals call on him a God to give us help.
He speeds over the sloping surface of the land : new deeds hath he performed with those who gird him round.

6 For, Agni, like a herdsman, thou by thine own might rulest o'er all that is in heaven and on the earth ;
And these two Mighty Ones, bright, golden closely joined, rolling them round are come unto thy sacred grass.

7 Agni, accept with joy, be glad in this our prayer, joy-giver, self-sustained, strong, born of Holy Law !
For fair to see art thou turning to every side, pleasant to look on as a dwelling filled with food.

HYMN CXLV. *Agni.*

1. ASK ye of him for he is come, he knoweth it ; he, full of wisdom, is implored, is now implored.
With him are admonitions and with him commands : he is the Lord of Strength, the Lord of Power and Might.

2 They ask of him : not all learn by their questioning what he, the Sage, hath grasped, as 'twere, with his own mind.
Forgetting not the former nor the later word, he goeth on, not careless, in his mental power.

3 To him these ladles go, to him these racing mares : he only will give ear to all the words I speak.

4 *Earth's central point* : the altar.
6 *The Vasu* : the God Agni.

---

1 *The place where he abides* : Agni's dwelling-place ; the altar.
2 *Of Holy Law* : flowing in accordance with the order of the universe.

3 *The two copartners* : the two priests, Hotar and Adhvaryu, according to Sāyaṇa. Perhaps Day and Night are intended, as Ludwig suggests.
4 *The grey one* : Agni. Cf. I. 164, 1.
5 *Him the ten fingers* : see I. 141. 2. *Those who gird him round* : his worshippers.
6 *These two Mighty Ones* : Heaven and Earth.

---

3 *These racing mares* : these libations that quickly reach Agni.
The Babe with flawless help : the ever-youthful Agni who protects his worshippers.

All-speeding, victor, perfecter of sacrifice, the Babe with flawless help hath mustered vigorous might.

4 Whate'er he meets he grasps and then runs farther on, and straightway, newly born, creeps forward with his kin.
He stirs the wearied man to pleasure and great joy what time the longing gifts approach him as he comes.

5 He is a wild thing of the flood and forest : he hath been laid upon the highest surface.
He hath declared the lore of works to mortals, Agni the Wise, for he knows Law, the Truthful.

HYMN CXLVI. *Agni.*

1. I LAUD the seven-rayed, the triple-headed, Agni all-perfect in his Parents' bosom,
Sunk in the lap of all that moves and moves not, him who hath filled all luminous realms of heaven.

2 As a great Steer he grew to these his Parents ; sublime he stands, untouched by eld, far-reaching.
He plants his footsteps on the lofty ridges of the broad earth : his red flames lick the udder.

3 Coming together to their common youngling both Cows, fairshaped, spread forth in all directions,
Measuring out the paths that must be travelled, entrusting all desires to him the Mighty.

4 The prudent sages lead him to his dwelling, guarding with varied skill the Ever-Youthful.
Longing, they turned their eyes unto the River : to these the Sun of men was manifested.

5 Born noble in the regions, aim of all mens' eyes to be implored for life by great and small alike,
Far as the Wealthy One hath spread himself abroad, he is the Sire all-visible of this progeny.

HYMN CXLVII. *Agni.*

1. How, Agni, have the radiant ones, aspiring, endued thee with the vigour of the living,
So that on both sides fostering seed and offspring, the Gods may joy in Holy Law's fulfilment ?

2 Mark this my speech, Divine One, thou, Most Youthful! offered to thee by him who gives most freely.
One hates thee, and another sings thy praises : I thine adorer laud thy form, O Agni.

3 Thy guardian rays, O Agni, when they saw him, preserved blind Māmateya from affliction.
Lord of all riches, he preserved the pious : the foes who fain would harm them did no mischief.

4 The sinful man who worships not, O Agni, who, offering not, harms us with double-dealing,—
Be this in turn to him a heavy sentence : may he distress himself by his revilings.

5 Yea, when a mortal knowingly, O Victor, injures with double tongue a fellow-mortal,
From him, praised Agni ! save thou him that lauds thee : bring us not into trouble and affliction.

HYMN CXLVIII. *Agni.*

1. WHAT Mātariśvan, piercing, formed by friction, Herald of all the Gods, in varied figure,
Is he whom they have set mid human houses, gay-hued as light and shining forth for beauty.

2 They shall not harm the man who brings thee praises : such as I am, Agni my help approves me.

5 *Upon the highest surface* : the meaning is not clear, but the reference appears to be to celestial Agni in the firmament rather than to the sacrificial fire upon the altar.

---

1 'The three heads may be the three daily sacrifices, or the three household fires, or the three regions, earth, heaven and mid-air. The seven rays are the seven flames of fire.'—Wilson.

His Parents' bosom : the lap of Heaven and Earth.

2 *The udder* : the clouds of the sky.

3 *Both Cows* : apparently Heaven and Earth ; according to Sāyaṇa, the institutor of the rite and the priest or the sacrificer and his wife.

4 *The River* : Agni, whose bounties flow like streams of water.

5 *The Wealthy One* : the rich and mighty Agni.

1 *The radiant ones* : thy bright rays.

On both sides : both in men and women ; or (offspring) of both sexes.

3 *Māmateya* : Dīrghatamas, the Ṛṣi of the hymn, son of Mamatā, the wife of Ucathya.

---

1 Wilson, following Sāyaṇa, translates : 'The wind, penetrating (amidst the fuel) has excited (Agni) the invoker (of the gods) the multiform, the minister of all the deities.' But then *yát*, what or when is left untranslated, and the explanation of Mātariśvan as Vāyu or wind cannot be justified by any Ṛgveda text.

All acts of mine shall they accept with pleasure, laudation from the singer who presents it.

3 Him in his constant seat men skilled in worship have taken and with praises have established.
As, harnessed to a chariot fleet-foot horses, at his command let bearers lead him forward.

4 Wondrous, full many a thing he chews and crunches : he shines amid the wood with spreading brightness.
Upon his glowing flames the wind blows daily, driving them like the keen shaft of an archer.

5 Him, whom while yet in embryo the hostile, both skilled and fain to harm, may never injure,
Men blind and sightless through his splendour hurt not : his never-failing lovers have preserved him.

HYMN CXLIX. *Agni.*

1. HITHER he hastens to give, Lord of great riches, King of the mighty, to the place of treasure.
The pressing-stones shall serve him speeding near us.

2 As Steer of men so Steer of earth and heaven by glory, he whose streams all life hath drunken,
Who hasting forward rests upon the altar.

3 He who hath lighted up the joyous castle, wise Courser like the Steed of cloudy heaven,
Bright like the Sun, with hundredfold existence.

4 He, doubly born, hath spread in his effulgence through the three luminous realms, through all the regions,
Best sacrificing Priest where waters gather.

5 Priest doubly born, he through his love of glory hath in his keeping all things worth the choosing,
The man who brings him gifts hath noble offspring.

1 *The place of treasure* : the altar, where riches are obtained by sacrifice and prayer.

2 *As Steer of men* : preëminent, like a strong bull, among men.

3 *The joyous castle* : or the castle Nārmiṇī; meaning, probably, the proud stronghold of some demon.

4 *Where waters gather* : according to Sāyaṇa, in the place of sacrifice where water is collected for ceremonial purpose. But the reference is probably to Agni's appearance in the firmament, the waters above the earth, in the form of lightning.

5 *Doubly born* : from the fire-sticks and again at consecration.

HYMN CL. *Agni.*

1. AGNI, thy faithful servant I call upon thee with many a gift,
As in the keeping of the great inciting God ;

2 Thou who ne'er movest thee to aid the indolent, the godless man,
Him who though wealthy never brings an offering.

3 Splendid, O Singer, is that man, mightiest of the great in heaven.
Agni, may we be foremost, we thy worshippers.

HYMN CLI. *Mitra and Varuṇa*

1. HEAVEN and earth trembled at the might and voice of him, whom, loved and Holy One, helper of all mankind,
The wise who longed for spoil in fight for kine brought forth with power, a Friend, mid waters, at the sacrifice.

2 As these, like friends, have done this work for you, these prompt servants of Purumīḷha Soma-offerer,
Give mental power to him who sings the sacred song, and hearken, Strong Ones, to the master of the house.

3 The folk have glorified your birth from Earth and Heaven, to be extolled, ye Strong Ones, for your mighty power.
Ye, when ye bring to singer and the rite, enjoy the sacrifice performed with holy praise and strength.

4 The people prospers, Asuras ! whom ye dearly love : ye, Righteous Ones, proclaim aloud the Holy Law.
That efficacious power that comes from lofty heaven, ye bind unto the work, as to the pole an ox.

5 On this great earth ye send your treasure down with might : unstained by dust, the crowding kine are in the stalls.

3 *That man* : who propitiates thee by sacrifice and praise.
O Singer : singer of hymns, sage, or priest.

---

1 *Of him* : Agni.

2 *As these* : the priests. *Purumīḷha* : the prince who offers the sacrifice. *Strong Ones* : ye mighty Gods, Mitra and Varuṇa.

3 *When ye bring* : him, Agni, to the sacrifice.

4 *Asuras* : immortal Gods, especially the ancient deities.

That efficacious power : as Wilson observes, the meaning is not very obvious, although it is clear that the adequacy of worship or sacrifice to effect its objects, or realize its rewards, is intended.

Here in the neighbourhood they cry unto the Sun at morning and at evening, like swift birds of prey.

6 The flames with curling tresses serve your sacrifice, whereto ye sing the song, Mitra and Varuṇa.

Send down of your free will, prosper our holy songs : ye are sole Masters of the singer's hymn of praise.

7 Whoso with sacrifices toiling brings you gifts, and worships, sage and priest, fulfilling your desire,—

To him do ye draw nigh and taste his sacrifice. Come well-inclined to us unto our songs and prayer.

8 With sacrifices and with milk they deck you first, ye Righteous Ones, as if through stirrings of the mind.

To you they bring their hymns with their collected thought, while ye with earnest soul come to us gloriously.

9 Rich strength of life is yours : ye, Heroes, have obtained through your surpassing powers rich far-extending might.

Not the past days conjoined with nights, not rivers, not the Paṇis have attained your Godhead and your wealth.

HYMN CLII. *Mitra-Varuṇa.*

1. THE robes which ye put on abound with fatness : uninterrupted courses are your counsels.

All falsehood, Mitra-Varuṇa ! ye conquer, and closely cleave unto the Law Eternal.

2 This might of theirs hath no one comprehended. True is the crushing word the sage hath uttered,

The fearful four-edged bolt smites down the three-edged, and those who hate the Gods first fall and perish.

3 The Footless Maid precedeth footed creatures. Who marketh, Mitra-Varuṇa, this your doing ?

The Babe Unborn supporteth this world's burthen, fulfilleth Law and overcometh falsehood.

4 We look on him the darling of the Maidens, always advancing, never falling downward,

Wearing inseparable, wide-spread raiment, Mitra's and Varuṇa's delightful glory.

5 Unbridled Courser, born but not of horses, neighing he flieth on with back uplifted.

The youthful love mystery thought-surpassing, praising in Mitra-Varuṇa, its glory.

6 May the milch-kine who favour Māmateya prosper in this world him who loves devotion.

May he, well skilled in rites, beg food, and calling Aditi with his lips give us assistance.

7 Gods, Mitra-Varuṇa, with love and worship, let me make you delight in this oblation.

May our prayer be victorious in battles, may we have rain from heaven to make us prosper.

HYMN CLIII. *Mitra-Varuṇa.*

1. WE worship with our reverence and oblations you, Mitra Varuṇa, accordant, mighty,

So that with us, ye Twain whose backs are sprinkled with oil, the priests with oil and hymns support you.

2 Your praise is like a mighty power, an impulse : to you, Twain Gods, a well-formed hymn is offered,

As the priest decks yon, Strong Ones, in assemblies, and the prince fain to worship you for blessings.

9 *The Paṇis* : the envious demons who carry away and conceal the cows or rays of light.

---

1 *The robes which ye put on* : the oblations of clarified butter with which the Gods may be said to be clothed.

Uninterrupted courses are your counsels : your designs are always fully carried into effect. Or the meaning may be as Wilson, following Sāyaṇa, renders it : 'your natures are to be regarded as without defect.'

2 *The fearful four-edged bolt* : Ludwig suggests an emendation of the text and then translates : 'thrice strikes the edge (of Indra's thunderbolt), four times the fearful edge.' I give the literal English of the words as they stand, the sense being, according to Sāyaṇa, that he who has more arms is stronger than he who has fewer, the arms intended being, perhaps sacrifice and prayer.

3 *The Footless Maid* : Dawn. *The Babe Unborn* : the Sun before his appearance in heaven.

4 *The darling of the Maidens* : the Sun, the lover of the Dawns.

5 *The mystery thought-surpassing* : the mystery of the Sun's motion excites wonder, and Mitra and Varuṇa are praised in connexion with it.

6 *Māmateya* : the son of Mamatā, Dīrghatamas the Ṛṣi of the hymn.

Him who loves devotion : apparently Purumīḷha the institutor of the sacrifice, mentioned in stanza 6 of the preceding hymn.

May he beg food : the food that remains after the oblations have been presented and consumed.

Aditi : I follow Ludwig in taking Aditi in the usual signification. Sāyaṇa takes it as meaning 'a perfect ceremony' which is to be completed, and Grassmann as famine, dearth, or want, which is to be averted.

The hymn is full of difficulties, and cannot at present be satisfactorily translated.

---

2 *The prince* : the wealthy man who institutes the sacrifice.

3 O Mitra-Varuṇa, Aditi the Milch-cow streams for the rite, for folk who bring oblation,
When in the assembly he who worships moves you, like to a human priest, with gifts presented.

4 So may the kine and heavenly Waters pour you sweet drink in families that make you joyful.
Of this may he, the ancient House-Lord, give us. Enjoy, drink of the milk the cow provideth.

HYMN CLIV. *Viṣṇu.*

1. I WILL declare the mighty deeds of Viṣṇu, of him who measured out the earthly regions,
Who propped the highest place of congregation, thrice setting down his footstep, widely striding.

2 For this his mighty deed is Viṣṇu lauded, like some wild beast, dread, prowling, mountain-roaming ;
He within whose three wide-extended paces all living creatures have their habitation.

3 Let the hymn lift itself as strength to Viṣṇu, the Bull far-striding, dwelling on the mountains,
Him who alone with triple step hath measured this common dwelling-place, long, far extended.

4 Him whose three places that are filled with sweetness, imperishable, joy as it may list them,
Who verily alone upholds the threefold, the earth, the heaven, and all living creatures.

5 May I attain to that his well-loved mansion where men devoted to the Gods are happy.
For there springs, close akin to the Wide-Strider, the well of meath in Viṣṇu's highest footstep.

6 Fain would we go unto your dwelling-places where there are many-horned and nimble oxen,
For mightily, there, shineth down upon us the widely-striding Bull's sublimest mansion.

HYMN CLV. *Viṣṇu-Indra.*

1. To the great Hero, him who sets his mind thereon, and Viṣṇu, praise aloud in song your draught of juice,—
Gods ne'er beguiled, who borne as 'twere by noble steed, have stood upon the lofty ridges of the hills.

2 Your Soma-drinker keeps afar your furious rush, Indra and Viṣṇu, when ye come with all your might.
That which hath been directed well at mortal man, bow-armed Kṛśānu's arrow, ye turn far aside.

3 These offerings increase his mighty manly strength : he brings both Parents down to share the genial flow.
He lowers, though a son, the Father's highest name ; the third is that which is high in the light of heaven.

4 We laud this manly power of him the Mighty One, preserver, inoffensive, bounteous and benign ;
His who strode, widely pacing, with three steppings forth over the realms of earth for freedom and for life.

5 A mortal man, when he beholds two steps of him who looks upon the light, is restless with amaze.
But his third step doth no one venture to approach, no, nor the feathered birds of air who fly with wings.

3 *Aditi, the Milch-cow* : aditi regarded as the source of rewards for the pious; or Aditi may be taken as an epithet, 'the exhaustless,' qualifying Milch-cow.

4 *The ancient House-Lord* : Agni, the guardian of the homestead.

---

1 *The highest place of congregation* : heaven, where the Gods are assembled.

Thrice setting down his footstep : see I. 22. 16.

2 *For this his mighty deed* : I have followed Sāyaṇa who takes the active verb in a passive signification. Prof. Peterson translates : 'Viṣṇu makes loud boast of this,' which is perhaps a more accurate rendering.

5 *Meath* : or nectar, or honey ; meaning celestial Soma.

6 *Your dwelling-places* : Viṣṇu's and probably Indra's.

Many-horned and nimble oxen : the stars with their ever-twinkling rays. Cf. I. 105. 10; Vālakhilya 7. 2.

---

1 *To the great Hero* : Indra. *Who sets his mind thereon* : who loves praise.

2 *Your Soma-drinker* : you gently approach your devout worshipper and do him no harm.

Kṛśānu : one of the guardians of the heavenly Soma, apparently a demon of drought who prevents men from enjoying the ambrosial rain.

3 *Both Parents* : Heaven and Earth. *The genial flow* : the sacrificial offering, the libation of Soma juice.

He lowers, though a son : the meaning appears to be that Viṣṇu takes rank in the sacrifice above his own father Dyaus, and that Agni has the third place.

5 'His (Viṣṇu's) path on earth and in the firmament is within mortal observation ; not so that in heaven.' —Wilson. *His third step* : in the highest heaven. Cf. I. 154. 5.

6 He, like a rounded wheel, hath in swift motion set his ninety racing steeds together with the four.
Developed, vast in form, with those who sing forth praise, a youth, no more a child, he cometh to our call.

HYMN CLVI. *Viṣṇu.*

1. FAR-SHINING, widely famed, going thy wonted way, fed with the oil, be helpful, Mitra-like, to us.
So, Viṣṇu, e'en the wise must swell thy song of praise, and he who hath oblations pay thee solemn rites.

2 He who brings gifts to him the Ancient and the Last, to Viṣṇu who ordains, together with his Spouse,
Who tells the lofty birth of him the Lofty One, shall verily surpass in glory e'en his peer.

3 Him have ye satisfied, singers, as well as ye know, primeval germ of Order even from his birth.
Ye, knowing e'en his name, have told it forth: may we, Viṣṇu, enjoy the grace of thee the Mighty One.

4 The Sovran Varuṇa and both the Aśvins wait on this the will of him who guides the Marut host.
Viṣṇu hath power supreme and might that finds the day, and with his Friend unbars the stable of the kine.

5 Even he the Heavenly One who came for fellowship, Viṣṇu to Indra, godly to the godlier,
Who Maker, throned in three worlds, helps the Āryan man, and gives the worshipper his share of Holy Law.

6 This verse is not very intelligible. Wilson following Sāyaṇa, gives the following explanation : 'Viṣṇu is here identified with Time, comprising ninety-four periods: the year, two solstices, five seasons, twelve months, twenty-four half months, thirty days, eight watches, and twelve zodiacal signs. Ludwig translates the first hemistich : 'and under four names (of the four seasons) he, like a round wheel, hath set in motion ninety spokes.' The steeds, or spokes, are the days of the solar year, ninety in each of the four seasons.

---

2 *Together with his Spouse* : *sumájjānaye* ; explained by Sāyaṇa to mean 'self-born', and by Ludwig 'very delightful.'

4 *With his Friend* : assists his friend Indra in releasing the rain imprisoned in the mountains of cloud, or the rays of light that have been stolen.

5 *His share of Holy Law* : his share of the blessings which follow the performance of sacrifice.

HYMN CLVII. *Aśvins.*

1. AGNI is wakened: Sūrya riseth from the earth. Mighty, refulgent Dawn hath shone with all her light.
The Aśvins have equipped their chariot for the course. God Savitar hath moved the folk in sundry ways.

2 When, Aśvins, ye equip your very mighty car, bedew, ye Twain, our power with honey and with oil.
To our devotion give victorious strength in war: may we win riches in the heroes' strife for spoil.

3 Nigh to us come the Aśvins' lauded three-wheeled car, the car laden with meath and drawn by fleet-foot steeds,
Three-seated, opulent, bestowing all delight: may it bring weal to us, to cattle and to men.

4 Bring hither nourishment for us, ye Aśvins Twain; sprinkle us with your whip that drops with honey-dew.
Prolong our days of life, wipe out our trespasses; destroy our foes, be our companions and our Friends.

5 Ye store the germ of life in female creatures, ye lay it up within all living beings.
Ye have sent forth, O Aśvins passing mighty, the fire, the sovrans of the wood, the waters,

6 Leeches are ye with medicines to heal us, and charioteers are ye with skill in driving.
Ye Strong, give sway to him who brings oblation and with his heart pours out his gift before you.

HYMN CLVIII. *Aśvins.*

1. YE Vasus Twain, ye Rudras full of counsel, grant us, Strong Strengtheners, when ye stand beside us,
What wealth Aucathya craves of you, great Helpers when ye come forward with no niggard succour.

1 *Savitar* : the Sun as the great cause of life.

3 *Three-wheeled car* : see I. 34. 5.

4 *Your whip* : see Hymns of the Atharva-veda, IX. 1. which is a glorification of the Aśvins' Honey-Whip, signifying, perhaps, the early stimulating and life-giving breeze which accompanies the first appearance of these Lords of Light and Heralds of Dawn.

5 *The sovrans of the wood* : the tall trees of the forest.

---

1 *Ye Vasus Twain, ye Rudras* : the Aśvins are addressed as identical with these two classes of Gods. See I. 31. 3. and 34. 11.

Aucathya : the son of Ucathya, Dīrghatamas the Ṛṣi of the hymn.

2 Who may give you aught, Vasus, for your favour, for what, at the Cow's place, ye grant through worship ?
Wake for us understanding full of riches, come with a heart that will fulfil our longing.

3 As erst for Tugra's son your car, sea-crossing, strong, was equipped and set amid the waters,
So may I gain your shelter and protection as with winged course a hero seeks his army.

4 May this my praise preserve Ucathya's offspring: let not these Twain who fly with wings exhaust me.
Let not the wood ten times up-piled consume me, when fixed for you it bites the ground it stands on.

5 The most maternal streams, wherein the Dāsas cast me securely bound, have not devoured me.
When Traitana would cleave my head asunder, the Dāsa wounded his own breast and shoulders.

6 Dīrghatamas the son of Mamatā hath come to length of days in the tenth age of human kind.
He is the Brahman of the waters as they strive to reach their end and aim: their charioteer is he.

HYMN CLIX.

Heaven and Earth.

1. I PRAISE with sacrifices mighty Heaven and Earth at festivals, the wise, the Strengtheners of Law.
Who, having Gods for progeny, conjoined with Gods, through wonder-working wisdom bring forth choicest boons.

2 With invocations, on the gracious Father's mind, and on the Mother's great inherent power I muse.
Prolific Parents, they have made the world of life, and for their brood all round wide immortality.

3 These Sons of yours well skilled in work, of wondrous power, brought forth to life the two great Mothers first of all.
To keep the truth of all that stands and all that moves, ye guard the station of your Son who knows no guile.

4 They with surpassing skill, most wise, have measured out the Twins united in their birth and in their home.
They, the refulgent Sages, weave within the sky, yea, in the depths of sea, a web for ever new.

5 This is to-day the goodliest gift of Savitar: this thought we have when now the God is furthering us.
On us with loving-kindness Heaven and Earth bestow riches and various wealth and treasure hundredfold!

HYMN CLX. *Heaven and Earth.*

1. THESE, Heaven and Earth, bestow prosperity on all, sustainers of the region, Holy Ones and wise,
Two Bowls of noble kind: between these Goddesses the God, the fulgent Sun, travels by fixed decree.

2 Widely-capacious Pair, mighty, that never fail, the Father and the Mother keep all creatures safe:
The two world-halves, the spirited, the beautiful, because the Father hath clothed them in goodly forms.

3 Son of these Parents, he the Priest with power to cleanse, Sage, sanctifies the worlds with his surpassing power.
Thereto for his bright milk he milked through all the days the party-coloured Cow and the prolific Bull.

2 *The Cow's place* : according to Sāyaṇa, the altar; the Cow being the earth.

3 *Tugra's son* : see I. 116. 3.

4 *Ucathya's offspring* : the poet himself *These Twain* : day and night. From this and the following verse it would appear that Dīrghatamas had been subjected to the ordeals of fire, water, and single combat with a man called Traitana, and preserved in all three by the Aśvins. See Ludwig, Der Ṛg-veda, IV. p. 44.

6 *The tenth age* : perhaps the tenth decade. The meaning of the verse, which appears to be a later addition, is obscure.

3 *These Sons of yours* : the Ṛbhus, who restored their Parents' youth. See I. 20. 4. *The two great Mothers* : the Parents of all, Heaven and Earth.

Your Son who knows no guile : Sūrya, or the Sun, who is regarded as the symbol of truth. 'Solem quis dicere falsum Audeat?'

4 *The Twins* : Heaven and Earth. *In the depths of sea* : in the aerial ocean or atmosphere.

1 *Two Bowls* : so called from their hemispherical appearance. But see Hillebrandt, Vedische Mythologie, I. p. 177, and Ludwig, Ueber die N. A. auf dem G. der Ṛgveda-forschung, p. 87.

2 *The Father* : Dyaus, or perhaps Tvaṣṭar.

3 *Son of these Parents* : the Sun, the offspring of Heaven and Earth.

For his bright milk : he has drawn the dew as milk from his mother Earth, and obtained his light from Heaven his father.

4 Among the skilful Gods most skilled is he, who made the two world-halves which bring prosperity to all;
Who with great wisdom measured both the regions out, and stablished them with pillars that shall ne'er decay.

5 Extolled in song, O Heaven and Earth, bestow on us, ye mighty Pair, great glory and high lordly sway,
Whereby we may extend ourselves ever over the folk; and send us strength that shall deserve the praise of men.

HYMN CLXI. *Ṛbhus.*

1 Why hath the Best, why hath the Youngest come to us? Upon what embassy comes he? What have we said?
We have not blamed the chalice of illustrious birth. We, Brother Agni, praised the goodness of the wood.

2 The chalice that is single make ye into four: thus have the Gods commanded; therefore am I come.
If, O Sudhanvan's Children, ye will do this thing ye shall participate in sacrifice with Gods.

3 What to the envoy Agni in reply ye spake, A courser must be made, a chariot fashioned here,
A cow must be created, and the Twain made young. When we have done these things, Brother, we turn to you.

4 When thus, O Ṛbhus, ye had done ye questioned thus, Whither went he who came to us a messenger?
Then Tvaṣṭar, when he viewed the four wrought chalices, concealed himself among the Consorts of the Gods.

5 As Tvaṣṭar thus had spoken, Let us slay these men who have reviled the chalice, drinking-cup of Gods,
They gave themselves new names when Soma juice was shed, and under these new names the Maiden welcomed them.

6 Indra hath yoked his Bays, the Aśvins' car is horsed, Bṛhaspati hath brought the Cow of every hue.
Ye went as Ṛbhu, Vibhvan, Vāja to the Gods, and skilled in war, obtained your share in sacrifice.

7 Ye by your wisdom brought a cow from out a hide; unto that ancient Pair ye gave again their youth.
Out of a horse, Sudhanvan's Sons, ye formed a horse: a chariot ye equipped, and went unto the Gods.

8 Drink ye this water, were the words ye spake to them; or drink ye this, the rinsing of the Muñja-grass.
If ye approve not even this, Sudhanvan's Sons, then at the third libation gladden ye yourselves.

9 Most excellent are waters, thus said one of you; most excellent is Agni, thus another said.
Another praised to many a one the lightning cloud. Then did ye shape the cups, speaking the words of truth.

10 One downward to the water drives the crippled cow, another trims the flesh brought on the carving-board.
One carries off the refuse at the set of sun. How did the Parents aid their children in their task!

11 On the high places ye have made the grass for man, and water in the valleys, by your skill, O Men.
Ṛbhus, ye iterate not to-day that act of yours, your sleeping in the house of him whom naught can hide.

4 *Most skilled is he*: Sāyaṇa observes that having magnified Heavan and Earth by praising their son, the poet now magnifies them by lauding their maker. See Muir, *O. S. Texts*, v. 30.

The Ṛbhus ask Agni why he comes to them. *The chalice*: see I. 20. 6.

3 *A courser must be made, etc.*: See I. 20. 2, 3, 4, and I. 110 and 111.

4. *Then Tvaṣṭar*: represented as hiding himself for shame among the Goddesses—probably the Celestial Waters—when he saw this alteration of his work, and in anger proposing to slay the Ṛbhus who had thus disgraced him.

5 *New names*: probably Ṛtus, Seasons, in place of Ṛbhus.—Ludwig. *The Maiden*: apparently the daughter of Tvaṣṭar, meaning, perhaps, as Ludwig suggests, the first Dawn of the year, of which Tvaṣṭar is the God.

6 *The Cow of every hue*: the fruitful earth restored to youth by the Gods of the Seasons.

8 *The rinsing of the Muñja-grass*: or Soma juice which has been filtered through a strainer made of that grass. 'The two first alternatives intimate that the Ṛbhus may be participant of the libations offered at dawn or at noon; the third applies to the evening sacrifice; the right of the Ṛbhus to share in this being elsewhere acknowledged.' —Wilson.

9 The meaning of these sayings in this place is not clear.

10 The restoration to youth of the aged Parents, Heaven and Earth, appears to be symbolically described under the figure of a sacrifice.

How did the Parents aid?: weak and exhausted with age they were unable to give any assistance.

11 *In the house of him whom naught can hide*: in the mansion of the Sun, to whom the Ṛbhus went to obtain immortality. In this and the remaining stanza, according to Sāyaṇa, the Ṛbhus are identified with the rays of the sun.

12 As, compassing them round, ye glided through the worlds, where had the venerable Parents their abode ?
Ye laid a curse on him who raised his arm at you : to him who spake aloud to you ye spake again.

13 When ye had slept your fill, ye Ṛbhus, thus ye asked, O thou whom naught may hide, who now hath wakened us ? The goat declared the hound to be your wakener. That day, in a full year, ye first unclosed your eyes.

14 The Maruts move in heaven, on earth this Agni ; through the mid-firmament the Wind approaches.
Varuṇa comes in the sea's gathered waters, O Sons of Strength, desirous of your presence.

HYMN CLXII. *The Horse.*

1. SLIGHT us not Varuṇa, Aryaman, or Mitra, Ṛbhukṣan, Indra, Āyu, or the Maruts,
When we declare amid the congregation the virtues of the strong Steed, God-descended.

2 What time they bear before the Courser, covered with trappings and with wealth, the grasped oblation,
The dappled goat goeth straightforward, bleating, to the place dear to Indra and to Pūṣan.

3 Dear to all Gods, this goat, the share of Pūṣan, is first led forward with the vigorous Courser,
While Tvaṣṭar sends him forward with the Charger, acceptable for sacrifice, to glory.

4 When thrice the men lead round the Steed, in order, who goeth to the Gods as meet oblation,
The goat precedeth him, the share of Pūṣan, and to the Gods the sacrifice announceth.

5 Invoker, ministering priest, atoner, fire-kindler, Soma-presser, sage, reciter,
With this well ordered sacrifice, well finished, do ye fill full the channels of the rivers.

6 The hewers of the post and those who carry it, and those who carve the knob to deck the Horse's stake ;
Those who prepare the cooking-vessels for the Steed,—may the approving help of these promote our work.

7 Forth, for the regions of the Gods, the Charger with his smooth back is come ; my prayer attends him.
In him rejoice the singers and the sages. A good friend have we won for the Gods' banquet.

8 May the fleet Courser's halter and his heel-ropes, the head-stall and the girths and cords about him.
And the grass put within his mouth to bait him,—among the Gods, too, let all these be with thee.

9 What part of the Steed's flesh the fly hath eaten, or is left sticking to the post or hatchet,
Or to the slayer's hands and nails adhereth,—among the Gods, too, may all this be with thee.

10 Food undigested steaming from his belly, and any odour of raw flesh remaining,
This let the immolators set in order and dress the sacrifice with perfect cooking.

11 What from thy body which with fire is roasted, when thou art set upon the spit, distilleth,—
Let not that lie on earth or grass neglected, but to the longing Gods let all be offered.

12 They who observing that the Horse is

13 *When ye had slept* : in the mansion of the Sun.

The goat declared the hound to be your wakener : the meaning is obscure. Sāyaṇa's rendering is, 'the Sun replied that the awakener was the wind.'

That day : Wilson, following Sāyaṇa, explains : 'you have made this world to-day luminous, after the year has expired ; that is, the rainy season being past, the rays of the sun and moon are again visible.'

14 *Sons of Strength* : ye powerful Ṛbhus.

---

1 *Ṛbhukṣan* : a name of Indra, as lord of the Ṛbhus.

Āyu : said by both commentators, Sāyaṇa and Mahīdhara, to be used in this place for Vāyu, the God of Wind. Āyu is probably Agni.

Amid the congregation : at sacrifice.

God-descended : sprung from the Gods, or, according to Sāyaṇa, born as the type of various deities.

2 *Grasped oblation* : the offering that is to be made for the horse, and which has been taken from the remains of the burnt-offering made the night before.

The dappled goat : this goat is to be tied to the horse at the sacrificial post. *Pūṣan* here is said by Sāyaṇa to stand for Agni.

4 *Who goeth to the Gods* : the object of the sacrifice is to send the horse to the Gods that he may obtain wealth and other blessings for his sacrificers.

5 *Invoker, etc* : these are the designations of eight of the sixteen priests employed at solemn rites. The *sage* (*suvípraḥ*, a priest of profound knowledge) is the superintendent of the whole ceremony.

Fill full the channels : obtain abundance of rain; or perhaps offer oblations in abundance.

ready call out and say, the smell is good ; remove it ;
And, craving meat, await the distribution, —may their approving help promote our labour.

13 The trial-fork of the flesh-cooking caldron, the vessels out of which the broth is sprinkled,
The warming-pots, the covers of the dishes, hooks, carving-boards,—all these attend the Charger.

14 The starting-place, his place of rest and rolling, the ropes wherewith the Charger's feet were fastened,
The water that he drank, the food he tasted,—among the Gods, too, may all these attend thee.

15 Let not the fire, smoke-scented, make thee crackle, nor glowing caldron smell and break to pieces.
Offered, beloved, approved, and consecrated,—such Charger do the Gods accept with favour.

16 The robe they spread upon the Horse to clothe him, the upper covering and the golden trappings,
The halters which restrain the Steed, the heel-ropes,—all these, as grateful to the Gods, they offer.

17 If one, when seated, with excessive urging hath with his heel or with his whip distressed thee,
All these thy woes, as with the oblations' ladle at sacrifices, with my prayer I banish.

18 The four-and-thirty ribs of the swift Charger, kin to the Gods, the slayer's hatchet pierces.
Cut ye with skill, so that the parts be flawless, and piece by piece declaring them dissect them.

19 Of Tvaṣṭar's Charger there is one dissector,—this is the custom—two there are who guide him.
Such of his limbs as I divide in order, all these, amid the balls, in fire I offer.

20 Let not thy dear soul burn thee as thou comest, let not the hatchet linger in thy body.
Let not a greedy clumsy immolator, missing the joints, mangle thy limbs unduly.

21 No, here thou diest not, thou art not injured : by easy paths unto the Gods thou goest.
Both Bays, both spotted mares are now thy fellows, and to the ass's pole is yoked the Charger.

22 May this Steed bring us all-sustaining riches, wealth in good kine, good horses, manly offspring.
Freedom from sin may Aditi vouchsafe us : the Steed with our oblations gain us lordship !

18 *Four-and-thirty* : so many out of the thirty-six. As the Sacrificial Horse is the symbol of the heavens, the thirty-four ribs represent the sun, the moon, the five planets, and the twenty-seven *nakṣatras* or lunar asterisms. See Ludwig, Der Ṛgveda, III. p. 186. *Piece by piece declaring them* : the dissectors are to name the several parts as they divide them, each part being sacred to a separate divinity.

19 *Amid the balls* : the meat made up into balls.

20 *Burn thee* : make thee sad.

21 *Both Bays* : thou art now associated in heaven with the two bay horses of Indra, the two spotted mares of the Maruts, and the ass that draws the chariot of the Aśvins.

A full description of an Aśvamedha or Horse-sacrifice in later times may be found in the Rāmāyaṇa, Book I., Cantos 10-13.

HYMN CLXIII. *The Horse.*

1. WHAT time, first springing into life, thou neighedst, proceeding from the sea or upper waters,
Limbs of the deer hadst thou, and eagle pinions. O Steed, thy birth is high and must be lauded.

2 This Steed which Yama gave hath Trita harnessed, and him, the first of all, hath Indra mounted.
His bridle the Gandharva grasped. O Vasus, from out the Sun ye fashioned forth the Courser.

3 Yama art thou, O Horse ; thou art Āditya ; Trita art thou by secret operation.
Thou art divided thoroughly from Soma. They say thou hast three bonds in heaven that hold thee.

4 Three bonds, they say, thou hast in heaven that bind thee, three in the waters, three within the ocean.

---

1 *From the sea* : the Sacrificial Horse is here identified with the Sun in the ocean of air.

2 *Yama* : here said to mean Agni, as a solar deity. *Trita* : as God of the remote birth-place of the Sun. See I. 187, note.

The Gandharva : Viśvāvasu, a heavenly being who dwells in the region of the air and guards the celestial Soma.

3 *Āditya* : the Sun.

By secret operation : by the mysterious effect of the sacrifice.

Soma : here, perhaps, the Moon; but the meaning is uncertain.

4 The *three bonds* in heaven are said by Sāyaṇa to be his 'media of origin; that is the Vasus, Āditya, and Heaven.' By the waters, it is said that the habitable world is intended, and that the three *bonds* therein are tillage, rain, and seed. In *the ocean*, that is the firmament, they are cloud, lightning, and thunder. *Varuṇa* : on account of the three bonds (see I.24. 15).

To me thou seemest Varuṇa, O Courser, there where they say is thy sublimest birth-place.

5 Here, Courser, are the places where they groomed thee, here are the traces of thy hoofs as winner.
Here have I seen the auspicious reins that guide thee, which those who guard the holy Law keep safely.

6 Thyself from far I recognized in spirit,—a Bird that from below flew through the heaven.
I saw thy head still soaring, striving upward by paths unsoiled by dust, pleasant to travel.

7 Here I beheld thy form, matchless in glory, eager to win thee food at the Cow's station.
Whene'er a man brings thee to thine enjoyment, thou swallowest the plants most greedy eater.

8 After thee, Courser, come the car, the bridegroom, the kine come after, and the charm of maidens.
Full companies have followed for thy friendship : the pattern of thy vigour Gods have copied.

9 Horns made of gold hath he : his feet are iron : less fleet than he, though swift as thought, is Indra.
The Gods have come that they may taste the oblation of him who mounted, first of all, the Courser.

10 Symmetrical in flank, with rounded haunches, mettled like heroes, the Celestial Coursers
Put forth their strength, like swans in lengthened order, when they, the Steeds, have reached the heavenly causeway.

11 A body formed for flight hast thou, O Charger ; swift as the wind in motion is thy spirit.
Thy horns are spread abroad in all directions : they move with restless beat in wildernesses.

12 The strong Steed hath come forward to the slaughter, pondering with a mind directed God-ward.
The goat who is his kin is led before him : the sages and the singers follow after.

13 The Steed is come unto the noblest mansion, is come unto his Father and his Mother.
This day shall he approach the Gods, most welcome : then he declares good gifts to him who offers.

HYMN CLXIV. *Viśvedevas.*

1. Of this benignant Priest, with eld grey-coloured, the brother midmost of the three is lightning.
The third is he whose back with oil is sprinkled. Here I behold the Chief with seven male children.

2 Seven to the one-wheeled chariot yoke the Courser; bearing seven names the single Courser draws it.
Three-naved the wheel is, sound and undecaying, whereon are resting all these worlds of being.

3 The seven who on the seven-wheeled car are mounted have horses, seven in tale, who draw them onward.
Seven Sisters utter songs of praise together, in whom the names of the seven Cows are treasured.

6 In this and the following stanza the horse is regarded as identical with the Sun in his course through heaven, and as accepting the oblations offered by the worshipper. *The Cow's station* : the chief place of earth, the Cow, is the altar.

7 *Most greedy eater* : regarded as a mere earthly horse.

9 *Horns made of gold* : according to Sāyaṇa, the word *horns* is used figuratively for mane. The Sun's rays are probably intended.

Who mounted, first of all, the Courser : Indra, as is said in verse 2.

10 The horses of the Sun are said to be spoken of. The exact meaning of the words is uncertain.

11 *Thy horns* : meaning, here, perhaps hoofs.

13 *His Father and his Mother* : Heaven and Earth.

Wilson remarks : 'Although more mystical than the preceding hymn, especially in regard to the intimations of the identity of the horse with the sun, there is nothing in it incompatible with the more explicit description in the former *Sūkta* of the actual sacrifice of a horse.'

1 The *priest* is Āditya, the Sun. His next brother is lightning, another form of fire, and the third brother is *Agni Gārhapatya*, the western sacred fire maintained by each householder, and fed with oblations of clarified butter.

The *seven male children* are probably the priests.

2 *Seven* : priests. *The one-wheeled chariot* : the Sun. *Seven names* : perhaps the seven solar rays. *Three-naved* : with reference, probably, to the three seasons, the hot weather, the rains, and the cold weather. On this wheel of the Sun all existing things depend.

3 *The seven* : according to Sāyaṇa, the seven solar rays, or the seven divisions of the year, solstice, season, month, fortnight, day, night, hour. The seven wheels of the chariot and the seven horses may also, according to Sāyaṇa, be the solar rays.

Seven Sisters: probably the seven celestial rivers, which, as emblems of fertility may bear the name of cows. Sāyaṇa explains the *seven Sisters* as the solar rays, or the six seasons and the year, or the six pairs of months with the intercalary month, and *the seven Cows* as the seven notes of music as employed in chanting the praises of the Sun.

4 Who hath beheld him as he sprang to being, seen how the boneless One supports the bony?
Where is the blood of earth, the life, the spirit? Who may approach the man who knows, to ask it ?

5 Unripe in mind, in spirit undiscerning, I ask of these the Gods' established places;
For up above the yearling Calf the sages, to form a web, their own seven threads have woven.

6 I ask, unknowing, those who know, the sages, as one all ignorant for sake of knowledge,
What was that ONE who in the Unborn's image hath stablished and fixed firm these worlds' six regions.

7 Let him who knoweth presently declare it, this lovely Bird's securely founded station.
Forth from his head the Cows draw milk, and, wearing his vesture, with their foot have drunk the water.

8 The Mother gave the Sire his share of Order : with thought, at first, she wedded him in spirit.
She, the coy Dame, was filled with dew prolific : with adoration men approached to praise her.

9 Yoked was the Mother to the boon Cow's car-pole : in the dank rows of cloud the Infant rested.
Then the Calf lowed, and looked upon the Mother, the Cow who wears all shapes in three directions.

10 Bearing three Mothers and three Fathers, single he stood erect : they never make him weary.
There on the pitch of heaven they speak together in speech all-knowing but not all-impelling.

11 Formed with twelve spokes, by length of time, unweakened, rolls round the heaven this wheel of during Order.
Herein established, joined in pairs together, seven hundred Sons and twenty stand, O Agni.

12 They call him in the farther half of heaven the Sire five-footed, of twelve forms, wealthy in watery store.
These others say that he, God with far-seeing eyes, is mounted on the lower seven-wheeled, six-spoked car.

13 Upon this five-spoked wheel revolving ever all living creatures rest and are dependent.
Its axle, heavy-laden, is not heated : the nave from ancient time remains unbroken.

14 The wheel revolves, unwasting, with its felly : ten draw it, yoked to the far-stretching car-pole.
The Sun's eye moves encompassed by the region : on him dependent rest all living creatures.

15 Of the co-born they call the seventh single-born ; the six twin pairs are called Ṛṣis, Children of Gods.

4 *How the boneless One supports the bony* : or in more conventional and less literal words, how the unsubstantial one (feminine) supports that (masculine) which is endowed with substance.

The *boneless* or unsubstantial is Prakṛti, Nature, the original source of the substantial, that is the material and visible world. According to Hillebrandt, Vedische Mythologie, I. p. 338, the *boneless One* is the Sun and the *bony* the Moon. See M. Müller, India, What can it Teach us ? pp. 245, 246.

5 *The yearling Calf* : probably the Sun, in reference to his yearly course. What the *seven threads* are is uncertain. Sāyaṇa says they are the seven forms of the Soma sacrifice, or the seven metres of the Vedas. Ludwig thinks that the general meaning of the stanza is : I (the poet) content myself with asking for information about the places or traces of the Gods in our world; but the sages talk about things which are beyond my power of comprehension.

6 *In the Unborn's image* : in the form of Aja or the Unborn Creator, represented by the Sun. Cf. VIII. 41. 10.

7 *This lovely Bird's...station* : the place of the Sun.

The Cows draw milk: 'The solar rays, although especial agents in sending down rain, are equally active in its re-absorption.'—Wilson.

8 The mother Earth gave the father Heaven his share in the great work of cosmical production.

Dew prolific : the fertilizing rain.

9 *Yoked was the Mother* : Earth undertook the functions of the cow who supplies milk for sacrifices.

The Infant : the young Sun.

The Calf lowed : the cloud thundered. *In three directions* : heaven, mid-air, and earth.

10 *Three Mothers and three Fathers* : the three earths and the three heavens. This fanciful threefold division has occurred before. See I. 105. 5.

They speak : the Gods converse together about the Sun, says Sāyaṇa, in speech that knows all but does not extend to or impress all.

11 The wheel formed with twelve spokes is the year with its twelve months. The seven hundred and twenty sons, joined in pairs, are the days and nights of the year, three hundred and sixty of each.

12 *Five-footed* : the five feet are, Sāyaṇa says, the five seasons, the dewy and cold seasons being counted as one. The twelve forms are the months of the year. The seven wheels of the car are said to be the seven solar rays, and the six spokes of each wheel are the six seasons. I find the stanza unintelligible.

13 *The five-spoked wheel* : in reference, perhaps, to the five seasons, as in verse 12.

14 *Ten draw it* : probably the ten regions of space.

The region : the firmament, mid-air.

15 *The co-born* : the six pairs of months, or six seasons of two months each. The *single-born* is the thirteenth and intercalary month. Sāyaṇa explains *ṛṣayaḥ*, Ṛṣis, in this stanza as *gantāraḥ*, goers; but in what sense is uncertain.

Their good gifts sought of men are ranged in order due, and various in their form move for the Lord who guides.

16 They told me these were males, though truly females : he who hath eyes sees this, the blind discerns not.
The son who is a sage hath comprehended : who knows this rightly is his father's father.

17 Beneath the upper realm, above this lower, bearing her calf at foot the Cow hath risen.
Witherward, to what place hath she departed ? Where calves she ? Not amid this herd of cattle.

18 Who, that the father of this Calf discerneth beneath the upper realm, above the lower,
Showing himself a sage, may here declare it ? Whence hath the Godlike spirit had its rising ?

19 Those that come hitherward they call departing, those that depart they call directed hither.
And what so ye have made, Indra and Soma, steeds bear as 'twere yoked to the region's car-pole.

20 Two Birds with fair wings, knit with bonds of friendship, in the same sheltering tree have found a refuge.
One of the twain eats the sweet Fig-tree's fruitage ; the other eating not regardeth only.

21 Where those fine Birds hymn ceaselessly their portion of life eternal, and the sacred synods,
There is the Universe's mighty Keeper, who, wise, hath entered into me the simple.

22 The tree whereon the fine Birds eat the sweetness, where they all rest and procreate their offspring,—
Upon its top they say the fig is luscious : none gaineth it who knoweth not the Father.

23 How on the Gāyatrī the Gāyatrī was based, how from the Triṣṭup they fashioned the Triṣṭup forth,
How on the Jagatī was based the Jagatī,- they who know this have won themselves immortal life.

24 With Gāyatri he measures out the praise-song, Sāma with praise-song, triplet with the Triṣṭup.
The triplet with the two or four-foot measure, and with the syllable they form seven metres.

16 *They told me these were males* : Wilson observes : 'This is a piece of grammatical mysticism ; *raśmi*, a ray of the sun, here personified as a female, is properly a noun masculine.' But this is just the reverse of the explanation required. The meaning is obscure.

Grassmann suggests that the meaning is that Night and Morning, both feminine, have received the masculine name of Day.

The son who is a sage : 'According to the Scholiast, the Sun is to be considered as the father of the rays of light, which again, in their collective capacity, being the cause of rain, are the fosterers or parents of the earth : the Sun is therefore father of the father, and he who knows this is identical with the Sun.'—Wilson. The meaning of the last semi-hemistich is probably that an intelligent son may be called the parent of an ignorant father as being his superior in knowledge.

17 Uṣas or Dawn hath risen between heaven and earth, carrying with her the young Sun her offspring. *This herd of cattle* : the visible world.

18 Uṣas is the mother, but who is able to say who the father of the Sun is ?

19 This stanza may refer to the planets which change their relative position as they revolve. Indra is here the Sun, and Soma the Moon.

20 Sāyaṇa says that the *two Birds* are the vital and the Supreme Spirit, dwelling in one body. The vital spirit enjoys the fruit or rewards of actions while the Supreme Spirit is merely a passive spectator.

21 The *fine Birds* here are perhaps the priests, and the Keeper of the Universe may be Soma.

22 Sāyaṇa explains *suparṇā*, well-winged, in this and the preceding stanza as smooth-gliding (*rays*). *Their offspring* is, he says, the light, and *the Father* is the cherishing and protecting Sun. All explanations of these three stanzas can be only conjectural. Ludwig is of opinion that they are originally unconnected fragments and that they have been inserted together in this hymn merely because the word *suparṇā* (used apparently in various senses) has a prominent place in each stanza.

Suparṇā (dual) has been explained by different scholars as two species of souls; day and night, Sun and Moon; (plural) as rays of light ; stars; metres, spirits of the dead; pri ests; and *the tree* on which they rest as the body; the orb or region of the Sun ; the sacrificial post ; the world: and the mythical World-Tree. A generally satisfactory explanation is scarcely to be hoped for.

23 Wilson, following Sāyaṇa, paraphrases this stanza as follows : 'They who know the station of Agni upon the earth; the station of Vāyu that was fabricated from the firmament, and that station of the Sun which is placed in heaven, obtain immortality.' He observes that the purport of the phraseology, borrowed from the several metres Gāyatrī, Tri ṭubh, and Jagatī, is not very clear, and that it may be merely an obscure and mystic reference to the text of the Veda, a knowledge of which is essential to final felicity. The meaning seems to be that those who are thoroughly acquainted with the appropriate rewards which follow the employment of each of the sacred metres named are on the right road to immortal life.

24 *Triplet* : the word in the text *vākā* is said to mean either two or three connected stanzas.

Two or four-foot measure : consisting of two or four *pādas* or semi-hemistichs.

And with the syllable : they form the seven generic metres of the Veda with the syllable, which is the chief element of metre, the Gāyatrī consisting of eight syllables, the Triṣṭup of eleven, and the Jagati of twelve. See Wilson's note.

25 With Jagatī the flood in heaven he stablished, and saw the Sun in the Rathantara Sāman.
Gāyatrī hath, they say, three brands for kindling : hence it excels in majesty and vigour.

26 I invocate the milch-cow good for milking so that the milker, deft of hand, may drain her.
May Savitar give goodliest stimulation. The caldron is made hot ; I will proclaim it.

27 She, lady of all treasure, is come hither yearning in spirit for her calf and lowing.
May this cow yield her milk for both the Aśvins, and may she prosper to our high advantage.

28 The cow hath lowed after her blinking youngling ; she licks his forehead, as she lows, to form it.
His mouth she fondly calls to her warm udder, and suckles him with milk while gently lowing.

29 He also snorts, by whom encompassed round the Cow lows as she clings unto the shedder of the rain.
She with her shrilling cries hath humbled mortal man, and, turned to lightning, hath stripped off her covering robe.

30 That which hath breath and speed and life and motion lies firmly stablished in the midst of houses.
Living, by offerings to the Dead he moveth, Immortal One, the brother of the mortal.

31 I saw the Herdsman, him who never stumbles, approaching by his pathways and departing.
He, clothed with gathered and diffusive splendour, within the worlds continually travels.

32 He who hath made him doth not comprehend him : from him who saw him surely is he hidden.
He, yet enveloped in his Mother's bosom, source of much life, hath sunk into destruction.

33 Dyaus is my Father, my begetter : kinship is here. This great earth is my kin and Mother.
Between the wide-spread world-halves is the birth-place : the Father laid the Daughter's germ within it.

34 I ask thee of the earth's extremest limit, where is the centre of the world, I ask thee.
I ask thee of the Stallion's seed prolific, I ask of highest heaven where Speech abideth.

35 This altar is the earth's extremest limit ; this sacrifice of ours is the world's centre.
The Stallion's seed prolific is the Soma ; this Brahman highest heaven where Speech abideth.

36 Seven germs unripened yet are heaven's prolific seed : their functions they maintain by Viṣṇu's ordinance.
Endued with wisdom through intelligence and thought, they compass us about present on every side.

37 What thing I truly am I know not clearly : mysterious, fettered in my mind I wander.
When the first-born of holy Law approached me, then of this speech I first obtain a portion.

38 Back, forward goes he, grasped by strength inherent, the Immortal born the brother of the mortal.

25 *He* : Brahmā, according to Sāyaṇa.

Rathantara : one of the most important Sāma-hymns; Sāmaveda II. i. i. 11 = Ṛgveda VII. 32. 22, 23.

Three brands : the three *pādas*, divisions, or lines of the verse being fancifully likened to the sticks with which the sacrificial fire is kindled.

26 The milch-cow in this and the two following stanzas may be the cow who supplies milk for the sacrifice. But Sāyaṇa says that the cow may be the rain-cloud, the milk being the rain and the milker Vāyu the God of Wind who causes it to flow. The calf, Sāyaṇa says, is the world longing for the rain to fall.

29 *He also* : probably Parjanya, the personified Storm-Cloud. The Cow here is undoubtedly a cloud.

30 The subject of the first hemistich is apparently Agni. The Moon, sustained by sacrificial offerings to the Departed, appears to be the subject of the second. But see Hymns of the Atharva-veda IX. 10. 8.

31 *The Herdsman* : the Sun, the guardian of the world.

32 Lightning, the immediate cause of rain, with his countless offspring the fertilizing rain-drops, appears to be alluded to.

33 *World-halves* : literally bowls or vessels into which the Soma is poured, a figurative expression for heaven and earth. The firmament or space between these two is, as the region of the rain, the womb of all beings. The Father is Dyaus and the daughter is Earth whose fertility depends upon the germ of rain laid in the firmament.

35 *The earth's extremest limit* : the altar, as the place nearest to heaven, the place where the Gods visit men.

The Stallion : Dyaus, or Father Heaven.

This Brahman : The priest so named who recites the texts of the Veda.

36 This stanza, as Ludwig remarks, is one of the most unintelligible in the whole Veda. *The seven*, according to Sāyaṇa, are the solar rays, and Viṣṇu is said to be the Sun.

37 *The first-born of holy Law* : according to Sāyaṇa, the first-born (perceptions) of the truth. Soma may be intended, as suggested by Bergaine, Religion Védique, I. 150.

38 This stanza appears to refer to the Sun in his daily course from east to west and his nightly return to the

Ceaseless they move in opposite directions : men mark the one and fail to mark the other.

39 Upon what syllable of holy praise-song, as 'twere their highest heaven, the Gods repose them,—
Who knows not this, what will he do with praise-song? But they who know it well sit here assembled.

40 Forunate mayst thou be with goodly pasture, and may we also be exceeding wealthy.
Feed on the grass, O Cow, at every season, and coming hitherward drink limpid water.

41 Forming the water-floods, the buffalo hath lowed, one-footed or two-footed or four-footed, she,
Who hath become eight-footed or hath got nine feet, the thousand-syllabled in the sublimest heaven.

42 From her descend in streams the seas of water ; thereby the world's four regions have their being.
Thence flows the imperishable flood and thence the universe hath life.

43 I saw from far away the smoke of fuel with spires that rose on high o'er that beneath it.
The Mighty Men have dressed the spotted bullock. These were the customs in the days aforetime.

44 Three with long tresses show in ordered season. One of them sheareth when the year is ended.
One with his powers the universe regardeth: of one the sweep is seen, but figure.

45 Speech hath been measured out in four divisions, the Brāhmans who have understanding know them.
Three kept in close concealment cause no motion ; of speech, men speak only the fourth division.

46 They call him Indra, Mitra, Varuṇa, Agni, and he is heavenly nobly-winged Garutmān.
To what is One, sages give many a title : they call it Agni, Yama, Mātariśvan.

47 Dark the descent : the birds are golden-coloured ; up to the heaven they fly robed in the waters.
Again descend they from the seat of Order, and all the earth is moistened with their fatness.

48 Twelve are the fellies, and the wheel is single ; three are the naves. What man hath understood it ?
Therein are set together spokes three hundred and sixty, which in nowise can be loosened.

49 That breast of thine exhaustless, spring of pleasure, wherewith thou feedest all things that are choicest,
Wealth-giver, treasure-finder, free bestower,—bring that, Sarasvatī, that we may drain it.

50 By means of sacrifice the Gods accomplished their sacrifice : these were the earliest ordinances.
These Mighty Ones attained the height of heaven, there where the Sādhyas, Gods of old, are dwelling.

east, the former visible to men and the latter invisible. *They*, in this case, would mean the Sun by day and the Sun by night.

39 The syllable is the *Praṇava*, the mystical sacred syllable Om. This syllable is set forth in the Upaniṣads as the object of profound religious meditation, and the highest spiritual efficacy is attributed to it.

40 This stanza is addressed to the cow who supplies the milk for libations.

41 *The buffalo hath lowed* : the great rain-cloud has thundered. Sāyaṇa explains *one-footed*, as sounding from the cloud; *two-footed*, from cloud and sky; *four-footed*, from the four cardinal points; *eight-footed*, from the four points and the four-intermediate points ; *nine-footed*, from these points and the zenith. *Gaurī*, the buffalo, is, according to Sāyaṇa, *Vāk*, Speech, the voice of heaven.

42 *From her* : from the buffalo, or cloud, *The world's four regions* : the whole world.

43 *The smoke of fuel* : arising from burning cow-dung. *The Mighty Men* : the Heroes, the Gods. *The spotted bullock* : the Soma. The whole may, perhaps, be a figurative description of the gathering of the rain-clouds.

44 The three are Agni who burns up the vegetation, the all-seeing Sun, and the invisible Vāyu or Wind.

45 *Three kept in close concealment* : the *three* might mean the three Vedas; but this interpretation does not suit the rest of the half-line. *The fourth division* : ordinary language. See Wilson for Sāyaṇa's elaborate explanation of this stanza, and Muir, O. S. Texts, II. 155.

46 *Garutmān* : the Celestial Bird, the Sun. All these names says the poet, are names of one and the same Divine Being, the One Supreme Spirit under various manifestations.

47 *Dark the descent* : the rays of light descend into the darkness of the earth when wrapped in night, and rise again to heaven with the moisture which they have absorbed to descend again in the form of fertilizing rain.

48 The single wheel is the year ; the twelve spokes are the months; the three naves are the three seasons of four months each; and the spokes are the days of the luni-solar year. The stanza is out of place here.

49 *Sarasvatī* : See I. 3. 10.

50 *The Sādhyas* : said by Yāska to be 'the Gods whose dwelling-place is the sky.' They are named among the minor divinities in the *Amarakośa*, and, as Wilson observes, 'it would seem that in Sāyaṇa's day the purport of the designation had become uncertain.'

51 Uniform, with the passing days, this water mounts and falls again.
The tempest-clouds give life to earth, and fires re-animate the heaven.

52 The Bird Celestial, vast with noble pinion, the lovely germ of plants, the germ of waters,
Him who delighteth us with rain in season, Sarasvān I invoke that he may help us.

HYMN CLXV. *Indra. Maruts.*

1. WITH what bright beauty are the Maruts jointly invested, peers in age, who dwell together?
From what place have they come? With what intention? Sing they their strength through love of wealth, these Heroes?

2 Whose prayers have they, the Youthful Ones, accepted? Who to his sacrifice hath turned the Maruts?
We will delay them on their journey sweeping—with what high spirit!—through the air like eagles.

3 Whence comest thou alone, thou who art mighty, Indra, Lord of the Brave? What is thy purpose?
Thou greetest us when meeting us the Bright Ones. Lord of Bay Steeds, say what thou hast against us.

4 Mine are devotions, hymns; sweet are libations. Strength stirs, and hurled forth is my bolt of thunder.
They call for me, their lauds are longing for me. These my Bay Steeds bear me to these oblations.

5 Therefore together with our strong companions, having adorned our bodies, now we harness,
Our spotted deer with might, for thou, O Indra, hast learnt and understood our Godlike nature.

6 Where was that nature then of yours, O Maruts, that ye charged me alone to slay the Dragon?
For I in truth am fierce and strong and mighty. I bent away from every foeman's weapons.

7 Yea, much hast thou achieved with us for comrades, with manly valour like thine own, thou Hero.
Much may we too achieve, O mightiest Indra, with our great power, we Maruts, when we will it.

8 Vṛtra I slew by mine own strength, O Maruts, having waxed mighty in mine indignation.
I with the thunder in my hand created for man these lucid softly flowing waters.

9 Nothing, O Maghavan, stands firm before thee; among the Gods not one is found thine equal.
None born or springing into life comes nigh thee. Do what thou hast to do, exceeding mighty?

10 Mine only be transcendent power, whatever I, daring in my spirit, may accomplish.
For I am known as terrible, O Maruts: I, Indra, am the Lord of what I ruined.

11 Now, O ye Maruts, hath your praise rejoiced me, the glorious hymn which ye have made me, Heroes!
For me, for Indra, champion strong in battle, for me, yourselves, as lovers for a lover.

12 Here, truly, they send forth their sheen to meet me, wearing their blameless glory and their vigour.
When I have seen you, Maruts, in gay splendour, ye have delighted me, so now delight me.

13 Who here hath magnified you, O ye Maruts? speed forward, O ye lovers, to your lovers.
Ye Radiant Ones, assisting their devotions, of these my holy rites be ye regardful.

51 *Fires re-animate the heaven*: the oblations offered in sacrificial fires delight and strengthen the gods.

52 *Sarasvān*: or Sarasvat, is the name of a River-God usually assigned as a consort to Sarasvatī. In this place the Sun is meant, and *sārasvantam* may be taken as a mere epithet, 'rich in water' which he absorbs.

Indra, the Maruts, and the great sage Agastya are regarded as the Ṛṣis of this hymn, which appears to be, as Wilson observes, a vindication of 'the separate, or at least preferential, worship of Indra, without comprehending, at the same time, as a matter of course, the adoration of the Maruts. The hymn is translated and fully explained in Prof. Max Müller's *Vedic Hymns*, Part I.

1 Indra speaks.

3 Here the Maruts address Indra whom they meet alone, unattended by them as was usual.

4 Indra replies.

5 The Maruts again speak.

6 Indra claims for himself the glory of the victory over Vṛtra.

11 'In this verse Indra, after having declined with no uncertain sound the friendship of the Maruts, repents himself of his unkindness towards his old friends. The words of praise which they addressed to him in verse 9, in spite of the rebuff which they had received from Indra, have touched his heart, and we may suppose that, after this, their reconciliation was complete.'—Max Müller.

14 To this hath Mānya's wisdom brought us, so as to aid, as aids the poet him who worships.
Bring hither quick ! On to the sage, ye Maruts ! These prayers for you the singer hath recited.

15 May this your praise, may this your song, O Maruts, sung by the poet, Māna's son, Māndārya,
Bring offspring for ourselves with food to feed us. May we find strengthening food in full abundance !

HYMN CLXVI. *Maruts.*

1. Now let us publish, for the vigorous company the herald of the Strong One, their primeval might.
With fire upon your way, O Maruts loud of voice, with battle, Mighty Ones, achieve your deeds of strength.

2 Bringing the pleasant meath as 'twere their own dear son, they sport in sportive wise gay at their gatherings.
The Rudras come with succour to the worshipper ; self-strong they fail not him who offers sacrifice.

3 To whomsoever, bringer of oblations, they immortal guardians, have given plenteous wealth,
For him, like loving friends, the Maruts bringing bliss bedew the regions round with milk abundantly.

4 Ye who with mighty powers have stirred the regions up, your coursers have sped forth directed by themselves.
All creatures of the earth, all dwellings are afraid, for brilliant is your coming with your spears advanced.

5 When they in dazzling rush have made the mountains roar, and shaken heaven's high back in their heroic strength,
Each sovran of the forest fears as ye drive near, and the shrubs fly before you swift as whirling wheels.

6 Terrible Maruts, ye with ne'er-diminished host, with great benevolence fulfil our heart's desire.
Where'er your lightning bites armed with its gory teeth it crunches up the cattle like a well-aimed dart.

7 Givers of during gifts whose bounties never fail, free from ill-will, at sacrifices glorified,
They sing their song aloud that they may drink sweet juice : well do they know the Hero's first heroic deeds.

8 With castles hundredfold, O Maruts, guard ye well the man whom ye have loved from ruin and from sin,—
The man whom ye the fierce, the Mighty Ones who roar, preserve from calumny by cherishing his seed.

9 O Maruts, in your cars are all things that are good : great powers are set as 'twere in rivalry therein.
Rings are upon your shoulders when ye journey forth : your axle turns together both the chariot wheels.

10 Held in your manly arms are many goodly things, gold chains are on your chests, and glistering ornaments,
Deer-skins are on their shoulders, on their fellies knives : they spread their glory out as birds spread out their wings.

11 Mighty in mightiness, pervading, passing strong, visible from afar as 'twere with stars of heaven,
Lovely with pleasant tongues, sweet singers with their mouths, the Maruts, joined with Indra, shout forth all around.

12 This is your majesty, ye Maruts nobly born, far as the sway of Aditi your bounty spreads.

---

14 This verse is exceedingly difficult, and its translation at present can be only conjectural.

Mānya, apparently, means the son of Māna.

15 *Māndārya,* probably the name of the poet, but explained differently by Sāyaṇa and Mahīdhara.

I borrow three-fourths of this verse from Prof. M. Müller.

This hymn and the twenty-five following are ascribed to the Ṛṣi Agastya, who appears in the Rāmāyaṇa as the friend and counsellor of Rāma. He is one of those indefinable mythic personages who are found in the ancient traditions of many nations, and in whom cosmogonical or astronomical notions are generally figured. Thus it is related of Agastya that the Vindhyan mountains prostrated themselves before him; and yet the same Agastya is believed to be the regent of the star Canopus.

1 *The Strong One* : Indra, who is preceded by the Maruts.

2 *The Rudras* : the Maruts, sons of the Strong-God Rudra.

3 *Milk* : fertilizing rain.

5 *As ye drive near* : similar abrupt changes of person are common in the Veda.

10 *On their fellies knives* : their war-chariots have sharp scythe-like blades attached to their wheels, or sharp edges to their fellies.

11 *Sweet singers* : the Maruts' song in the music of the winds.

12 *The sway of Aditi* : What the poet says is simply this, that the bounty of the Maruts extends as far as the realm of Aditi, i. e. is endless, or extends everywhere, Aditi being in its original conception the deity of the unbounded world beyond, the earliest attempt at expressing the Infinite.'—Max Müller.

This also is one of the hymns translated and fully explained by Prof. Max Müller in *Vedic Hymns,* Part I.

Even Indra by desertion never disannuls the boon bestowed by you upon the pious man.

13 This is your kinship, Maruts, that, Immortals, ye were oft in olden time regardful of our call,
Having vouchsafed to man a hearing through this prayer, by wondrous deeds the Heroes have displayed their might.

14 That, O ye Maruts, we may long time flourish through your abundant riches, O swift movers,
And that our men may spread in the encampment, let me complete the rite with these oblations.

15 May this your laud, may this your song, O Maruts, sung by the poet, Māna's son, Māndārya,
Bring offspring for ourselves with food to feed us. May we find strengthening food in full abundance.

HYMN CLXVII. *Indra. Maruts.*

1. A THOUSAND are thy helps for us, O Indra : a thousand, Lord of Bays, thy choice refreshments.
Wealth of a thousand sorts hast thou to cheer us : may precious goods come nigh to us in thousands.

2 May the most sapient Maruts, with protection, with best boons brought from lofty heaven, approach us,
Now when their team of the most noble horses speeds even on the sea's extremest limit.

3 Close to them clings one moving in seclusion, like a man's wife, like a spear carried rearward,
Well grasped, bright, decked with gold ; there is Vāk also, like to a courtly, eloquent dame, among them.

4 Far off the brilliant, never-weary Maruts cling to the young Maid as a joint possession.
The fierce Gods drave not Rodasī before them, but wished for her to grow their friend and fellow.

5 When chose immortal Rodasī to follow—she with loose tresses and heroic spirit—
She climbed her servant's chariot, she like Sūryā with cloud-like motion and refulgent aspect.

6 Upon their car the young men set the Maiden wedded to glory, mighty in assemblies,
When your song, Maruts, rose, and, with oblation, the Soma-pourer sang his hymn in worship.

7 I will declare the greatness of these Maruts, their real greatness, worthy to be lauded,
How, with them, she though firm, strong-minded, haughty, travels to women happy in their fortune.

8 Mitra and Varuṇa they guard from censure: Aryaman too, discovers worthless sinners
Firm things are overthrown that ne'er were shaken : he prospers, Maruts, who gives choice oblations.

9 None of us, Maruts, near or at a distance, hath ever reached the limit of your vigour.
They in courageous might still waxing boldly have compassed round their foemen like an ocean.

10 May we this day be dearest friends of Indra, and let us call on him in fight to-morrow.
So were we erst. New might attend us daily ! So be with us Ṛbhukṣan of the Heroes !

11 May this your laud, may this your song, O Maruts, sung by the poet, Māna's son, Māndārya,
Bring offspring for ourselves with food to feed us. May we find strengthening food in full abundance.

HYMN CLXVIII. *Maruts.*

1. SWIFT gain is his who hath you near at every rite : ye welcome every song of him who serves the Gods.

2 *The sea's extremest limit* : the skirts of the sea of air, the firmament.

3 Sāyaṇa says that the lightning is spoken of, moving in the clouds, as if in secret, like the well-attired wife who remains in the women's apartment, but sometimes showing itself, like the hymn or prayer recited at religious ceremonies. The comparisons are scarcely intelligible. Vāk here is the voice of Heaven, the thunder. See Max Müller, *Vedic Hymns*, Part I.

5 *Rodasī* : usually regarded as the consort of Rudra, said by Sāyaṇa to mean here the lightning, the bride of the Maruts.

Sūryā : the daughter of the Sun, who mounted the chariot of the Aśvins. See I. 116. 17.

7 *She* : Rodasī. In the second hemistich there is no substantive, only adjectives in the feminine gender. Wilson, following Sāyaṇa, renders the last half-line by 'supports a flourishing progeny.' Ludwig thinks that Rodasī appears as Eileithuia of the Greek pantheon, the Goddess who presides over childbirth.

10 The hymn appears to have been recited on the eve of an expected battle.

Ṛbhukṣan : a name of Indra, as lord of the Ṛbhus.

1 The text of the first line is manifestly corrupt and translation is conjectural. See Max Müller, Sacred Books of the East, XXXII, p. 281.

So may I turn you hither with fair hymns of praise to give great succour for the weal of both the worlds.

2 Surrounding, as it were, self-born, self-powerful, they spring to life the shakers-down of food and light ;
Like as the countless undulations of the floods, worthy of praise when near, like bullocks and like kine.

3 They who, like Somas with their well-grown stalks pressed out, imbibed within the heart, dwell there in friendly wise.
Upon their shoulders rests as 'twere a warrior's spear, and in their hand they hold a dagger and a ring.

4 Self-yoked they have descended lightly from the sky. With your own lash, Immortals, urge yourselves to speed.
Unstained by dust the Maruts, mighty in their strength, have cast down e'en firm things, armed with their shining spears.

5 Who among you, O Maruts armed with lightning-spears, moveth you by himself, as with the tongue his jaws ?
Ye rush from heaven's floor as though ye sought for food, on many errands like the Sun's diurnal Steed.

6 Say where, then, is this mighty region's farthest bound, where, Maruts, is the lowest depth that ye have reached,
When ye cast down like chaff the firmly stablished pile, and from the mountain send the glittering water-flood ?

7 Your winning is with strength, dazzling, with heavenly light, with fruit mature, O Maruts, full of plenteousness.
Auspicious is your gift like a free giver's meed, victorious, spreading far, as of immortal Gods.

8 The rivers roar before your chariot fellies when they are uttering the voice of rain-clouds.
The lightnings laugh upon the earth beneath them, what time the Maruts scatter forth their fatness.

9 Pṛśni brought forth, to fight the mighty battle, the glittering army of the restless Maruts.
Nurtured together they begat the monster, and then looked round them for the food that strengthens.

10 May this your laud, may this your song O Maruts, sung by the poet Māna's son, Māndārya,
Bring offspring for ourselves with food to feed us. May we find strengthening food in full abundance.

2 *The shakers-down* : violently sending down the rain which is followed by sunlight and fertility.

When near : terrific in appearance at a distance, but gentle when propitiated with worship.

3 The first hemistich is obscure. Perhaps the meaning is that the beneficial effects of the storm are lasting like the inspiring influence of Soma juice.

Warrior's spear : 'Rambhiṇī I now take with Sāyaṇa in the sense of a wife clinging to the shoulders of her husband, though what is meant is the spear, or some other weapon, slung over the shoulders. See I. 167, 3. —M. Müller, *Vedic Hymns*, I. 283.

5 What, asks the poet, is the moving principle of the Maruts ? Who gives them their first impulse, as a man when he wishes moves his tongue and jaws? 'This stanza,' remarks Wilson, 'is exceedingly elliptical and obscure: Sāyaṇa's completion of the text is entirely conjectural.'

9 *Pṛśni* : the mother of the Maruts. See I. 24. 3. *The monster* : the mass of dark storm-clouds.

HYMN CLXIX. *Indra.*

1. As, Indra, from great treason thou protectest, yea, from great treachery these who approach us,
So, marking well, Controller of the Maruts grant us their blessings, for they are thy dearest.

2 The various doings of all mortal people by thee are ordered, in thy wisdom, Indra.
The host of Maruts goeth forth exulting to win the light-bestowing spoil of battle.

3 That spear of thine sat firm for us, O Indra : the Maruts set their whole dread power in motion.
E'en Agni shines resplendent in the brushwood : the viands hold him as floods hold an island.

4 Vouchsafe us now that opulence, O Indra, as guerdon won by mightiest donation.
May hymns that please thee cause the breast of Vāyu to swell as with the mead's refreshing sweetness.

5 With thee, O Indra, are most bounteous riches that further every one who lives uprightly.
Now may these Maruts show us loving-kindness, Gods who of old were ever prompt to help us.

6 Bring forth the Men who rain down boons, O Indra : exert thee in the great terrestrial region;

1 *These who approach us* : the Maruts.

3 *Sat firm* : was firmly and properly held by the Warrior-God.

6 *The Men* : the Maruts. Their chariot is drawn by spotted deer.

For their broad-chested speckled deer are standing like a King's armies on the field of battle.

7 Heard is the roar of the advancing Maruts, terrific, glittering, and swiftly moving,
Who with their rush o'erthrow as 'twere a sinner the mortal who would fight with those who love him.

8 Give to the Mānas, Indra with Maruts, gifts universal, gifts of cattle foremost.
Thou, God, art praised with Gods who must be lauded. May we find strengthening food in full abundance.

HYMN CLXX. *Indra. Maruts.*

1. Naught is to-day, to-morrow naught. Who comprehends the mystery?
We must address ourselves unto another's thought, and lost is then the hope we formed.

2 The Maruts are thy brothers. Why, O Indra, wouldst thou take our lives?
Agree with them in friendly wise, and do not slay us in the fight.

3 Agastya, brother, why dost thou neglect us, thou who art our friend?
We know the nature of thy mind. Verily thou wilt give us naught.

4 Let them prepare the altar, let them kindle fire in front : we two
Here will spread sacrifice for thee, that the Immortal may observe.

5 Thou, Lord of Wealth, art Master of all treasures, thou, Lord of friends, art thy friends' best supporter.
O Indra, speak thou kindly with the Maruts, and taste oblations in their proper season.

HYMN CLXXI. *Maruts.*

1. To you I come with this mine adoration, and with a hymn I crave the Strong Ones' favour,
A hymn that truly makes you joyful, Maruts. Suppress your anger and unyoke your horses.

2 Maruts, to you this laud with prayer and worship, formed in the mind and heart, ye Gods, is offered.
Come ye to us, rejoicing in your spirit, fo ye are they who make our prayer effecr tive.

3 The Maruts, praised by us, shall show us favour; Maghavan, lauded, shall be most propitious.
Maruts, may all our days that are to follow be very pleasant, lovely and triumphant.

4 I fled in terrror from this mighty Indra, my body trembling in alarm, O Maruts.
Oblations meant for you had been made ready; these have we set aside : for this forgive us.

5 By whom the Mānas recognize the dayssprings, by whose strength at the dawn of endless mornings,
Give us, thou Mighty, glory with Maruts. fierce with the fierce, the Strong who givest triumph.

6 Do thou, O Indra, guard the conquering Heroes, and rid thee of thy wrath against the Maruts,
With them, the wise, victorious and bestowing. May we find strengthening food in full abundance.

HYMN CLXXII. *Maruts.*

1. Wonderful let your coming be, wondrous with help, ye Bounteous Ones,
Maruts, who gleam as serpents gleam.

2 Far be from us, O Maruts, ye free givers, your impetuous shaft;
Far from us be the stone ye hurl.

3 O Bounteous Givers, touch ye not, O Maruts, Tṛṇaskanda's folk;
Lift ye us up that we may live.

8 *The Mānas* : men of the family of the poet Māna.

---

1 *Lost is then the hope we formed* : Indra appears to have appropriated to himself the sacrifice intended for the Maruts, who complain, accordingly, of their dependence on another's will and of their disappointed hopes.

2 This is spoken by Agastya, who offered the sacrifice.

3 The Maruts complain that Agastya does not support their claim.

4 Spoken by Agastya to Indra. *We* : Agni and I. *The Immortal* : Agni.

5 Agastya continues his conciliatory speech.

---

1 *Unyoke your horses* : stay with us and enjoy the sacrifice. 'This hymn, again,' as Wilson remarks, 'indicates a sort of trimming between the worship of Indra and the Maruts.'

3 Unable to translate the second hemistich satisfactorily, I have followed Sāyaṇa who takes *vánāni* as an adjective, lovely. Grassmann translates : 'May all our days stand upright like beautiful trees,' and Ludwig suggests 'battling ? spears ? for *komyā vánāni*. 'May our trees (our lances) through our valour stand always erect.' —Max Müller.

4 Agastya apologizes for having allowed Indra to enjoy the offerings intended for the Maruts.

5 *By whom* : thou, Indra, by whom, etc.

---

1 *Who gleam as serpents gleam* : referring to the flashes of lightning that accompany the Gods of storm.

2 *The stone* : the thunderbolt.

3 *Tṛṇaskanda's folk* : Tṛṇaskanda appears to be the name of some chief not elsewhere mentioned. Wilson, following Sāyaṇa, translates : 'protect my people (although I be) as insignificant as grass.'

HYMN CLXXIII. *Indra.*

1. THE praise-song let him sing forth bursting bird-like: sing we that hymn which like heaven's light expandeth,
That the milk-giving cows may, unimpeded call to the sacred grass the Gods' assembly.

2 Let the Bull sing with Bulls whose toil is worship, with a loud roar like some wild beast that hungers.
Praised God ! the glad priest brings his heart's devotion; the holy youth presents twofold oblation.

3 May the Priest come circling the measured stations, and with him bring the earth's autumnal fruitage.
Let the Horse neigh led near, let the Steer bellow : let the Voice go between both worlds as herald,

4 To him we offer welcomest oblations, the pious bring their strength-inspiring praises.
May Indra, wondrous in his might, accept them, car-borne and swift to move like the Nāsatyas.

5 Praise thou that Indra who is truly mighty, the car-borne Warrior, Maghavan the Hero;
Stronger in war than those who fight against him, borne by strong steeds, who kills enclosing darkness;

6 Him who surpasses heroes in his greatness: the earth and heavens suffice not for his girdles.
Indra endues the earth to be his garment, and, God-like, wears the heaven as 'twere a frontlet,

7 Thee, Hero, guardian of the brave in battles, who roamest in the van,—to draw thee hither,
Indra, the hosts agree beside the Soma, and joy, for his great actions, in the Chieftain.

8 Libations in the sea to thee are pleasant, when thy divine Floods come to cheer these people.
To thee the Cow is sum of all things grateful when with the wish thou seekest men and princes.

9 So may we in this One be well befriended, well aided as it were through praise of chieftains,
That Indra still may linger at our worship, as one led swift to work, to hear our praises.

10 Like men in rivalry extolling princes, our Friend be Indra, wielder of the thunder.
Like true friends of some city's lord within them held in good rule with sacrifice they help him.

11 For every sacrifice makes Indra stronger, yea, when he goes around angry in spirit ;
As pleasure at the ford invites the thirsty, as the long way brings him who gains his object.

12 Let us not here contend with Gods, O Indra, for here, O Mighty One, is thine own portion,
The Great, whose Friends the bounteous Maruts honour, as with a stream, his song who pours oblations.

13 Addressed to thee is this our praise, O Indra : Lord of Bay Steeds, find us hereby advancement.
So mayst thou lead us on, O God, to comfort. May we find strengthening food in full abundance.

1 *Let him sing* : let the Udgātar priest sing the Sāman or metrical hymn of praise, which spreads and blesses like the light of heaven.

2 *The Bull* : perhaps the institutor of the sacrifice; or Indra himself may be intended. Sāyaṇa offers both explanations.

The *Bulls* : the officiating priests.

Praised God ! : addressed to Indra. The meaning of the hemistich is obscure. The word *mithunā* (literally, pairs) which I have rendered in accordance with Sāyaṇa and Wilson, means according to Grassmann, 'both the worlds,' and according to Ludwig, 'the couples consisting of the sacrificers and the respective wives.'

3 *The Priest* : Agni, who is also the *Horse* and the *Steer. The measured stations* : the different fire-altars. *Fruitage* : grain for the oblation. *The Voice* : thunder.

4 *The Nāsatyas* : the Aśvins, whose chariot is famed for swiftness.

8 *In the sea* : reaching thee in the sea of air; or 'the sea' may mean the large reservoir of Soma juice. *The wish* : granting all their desires.

9 *In this One* : this one true friend Indra.

10 The stanza is difficult. Wilson, following Sāyaṇa, translates: 'Emulous in commendation like (those contending for the favour) of men, may Indra, the wielder of the thunderbolt, be equally (a friend) to us : like those who, desirous of his friendship (conciliate) the lord of a city (ruling) with good government, so do our intermediate (representatives) propitiate (Indra) with sacrifices.

11 Indra will come at last although he tarries now. We must wait patiently. The thirsty traveller comes to the stream and reaches his journey's end at last.

Wilson observes with truth that 'this hymn is in general elliptical and obscure.' A translator has to endeavour to give the probable meaning of the words as they stand, without venturing on conjectural completion of fancied ellipses and the insertion of words at pleasure after the manner of Sāyaṇa.

HYMN CLXXIV. *Indra.*

1. THOU art the King of all the Gods, O Indra: protect the men, O Asura, preserve us.
Thou Lord of Heroes, Maghavan, our saver, art faithful, very rich, the victory-giver.

2 Indra, thou humbledst tribes that spake with insult by breaking down seven autumn forts, their refuge.
Thou stirredst, Blameless! billowy floods, and gavest his foe a prey to youthful Purukutsa.

3 With whom thou drivest troops whose lords are heroes, and bringest daylight now, much worshipped Indra,
With them guard lion-like wasting active Agni to dwell in our tilled fields and in our homestead.

4 They through the greatness of thy spear, O Indra, shall, to thy praise, rest in this earthly station.
To loose the floods, to seek, for kine, the battle, his Bays he mounted boldly seized the booty.

5 Indra, bear Kutsa, him in whom thou joyest: the dark-red horses of the Wind are docile.
Let the Sun roll his chariot wheel anear us, and let the Thunderer go to meet the foemen.

6 Thou Indra, Lord of Bays, made strong by impulse, hast slain the vexers of thy friends, who give not.
They who beheld the Friend beside the living were cast aside by thee as they rode onward.

7 Indra, the bard sang forth in inspiration: thou madest earth a covering for the Dāsa.
Maghavan made the three that gleam with moisture, and to his home brought Kuyavāc to slay him.

8 These thine old deeds new bards have sung, O Indra. Thou conqueredst, boundest many tribes for ever.
Like castles thou hast crushed the godless races, and bowed the godless scorner's deadly weapon.

9 A Stormer thou hast made the stormy waters flow down, O Indra, like the running rivers.
When o'er the flood thou broughtest them, O Hero, thou keptest Turvaśa and Yadu safely.

10 Indra, mayst thou be ours in all occasions, protector of the men, most gentle-hearted,
Giving us victory over all our rivals. May we find strengthening food in full abundance.

1 *The men*: the priests. *Us*: thy worshippers. *Asura*: immortal and divine.

2 *Autumn forts*: probably strongholds on high ground occupied in the rainy season. *Purukutsa*: has been mentioned before. See I. 63. 7.

3 *With whom*: the Maruts.

4 *They*: the enemy, *He*: Indra.

5 *Kutsa*: the Ṛṣi of that name. Wilson paraphrases after Sāyaṇa: 'Bear (the sage) Kutsa to that ceremony (to which) thou desirest (to convey him).'

6 *Who give not*: who offer no oblations; barbarians who do not worship the Gods of the Āryans. *The Friend*: Indra. *Beside the living*: Āyu, the living, may perhaps be a proper name here.

7 *The three that gleam with moisture*: what *the three* are is not clear. Wilson translates: 'has made the three (regions) marvellous by his gifts.' Some reference to three mornings appears to be intended. *Kuyavāc*: probably the name of a demon, or barbarian.

9 *Turvaśa* and *Yadu*: eponymi of Āryan tribes. See I. 36. 8.

HYMN CLXXV. *Indra.*

1. GLAD thee: thy glory hath been quaffed, Lord of Bay Steeds, as 'twere the bowl's enlivening mead.
For thee the Strong there is strong drink, mighty, omnipotent to win.

2 Let our strong drink, most excellent, exhilarating, come to thee,
Victorious, Indra! bringing gain, immortal conquering in fight,

3 Thou, Hero, winner of the spoil, urgest to speed the car of man.
Burn, like a vessel with the flame, the lawless Dasyu, Conqueror!

4 Empowered by thine own might, O Sage, thou stolest Sūrya's chariot wheel.
Thou barest Kutsa with the steeds of Wind to Śuṣṇa as his death.

5 Most mighty is thy rapturous joy, most splendid is thine active power,
Wherewith, foe-slaying, sending bliss, thou art supreme in gaining steeds.

1 *Thy glory hath been quaffed*: thou hast drunk what incites thee to glorious deeds, namely the Soma juice contained in the bowl.

4 *Thou stolest Sūrya's chariot wheel*: Indra is said to have taken the wheel of the chariot of the Sun and to have cast it like a quoit against the demon of drought.

Kutsa: the Ṛṣi mentioned in the preceding hymn. Indra defended him against Śuṣṇa, or protected mankind from drought. See I. 51. 6.

5 *Most mighty is thy rapturous joy*: Wilson translates; 'Thy inebriety is most intense.' See I. 51. 2.

6 As thou, O Indra, to the ancient singers wast ever joy, as water to the thirsty,
So unto thee I sing this invocation. May we find strengthening food in full abundance.

HYMN CLXXVI. *Indra.*

1. Cheer thee with draughts to win us bliss : Soma, pierce Indra in thy strength. Thou stormest trembling in thy rage, and findest not a foeman nigh.

2 Make our songs penetrate to him who is the Only One of men;
For whom the sacred food is spread, as the steer ploughs the barley in.

3 Within whose hands deposited all the Five Peoples' treasures rest.
Mark thou the man who injures us and kill him like the heavenly bolt.

4 Slay everyone who pours no gift, who, hard to reach, delights thee not.
Bestow on us what wealth he hath : this even the worshipper awaits.

5 Thou helpest him the doubly strong whose hymns were sung unceasingly.
When Indra fought, O Soma, thou helpest the mighty in the fray.

6 As thou, O Indra, to the ancient singers wast ever joy, like water to the thirsty,
So unto thee I sing this invocation. May we find strengthening food in full abundance.

HYMN CLXXVII. *Indra.*

1. The Bull of men, who cherishes all people, King of the Races, Indra, called of many,
Fame-loving, praised, hither to me with succour turn having yoked both vigorous Bay Horses !

2 Thy mighty Stallions, yoked by prayer, O Indra, thy Coursers to thy mighty chariot harnessed,—
Ascend thou these, and borne by them come hither : with Soma juice outpoured, Indra, we call thee.

3 Ascend thy mighty car : the mighty Soma is poured for thee and sweets are sprinkled round us.
Come down to us-ward, Bull of human races, come, having harnessed them, with strong Bay Horses.

4 Here is God-reaching sacrifice, here the victim; here, Indra, are the prayers, here is the Soma.
Strewn is the sacred grass : come hither, Śakra; seat thee and drink : unyoke thy two Bay Coursers.

5 Come to us, Indra, come thou highly lauded to the devotions of the singer Māna.
Singing, may we find early through thy succour, may we find strengthening food in full abundance.

HYMN CLXXVIII. *Indra.*

1. If, Indra, thou hast given that gracious hearing wherewith thou helpest those who sang thy praises.
Blast not the wish that would exalt us : may I gain all from thee, and pay all man's devotions.

2 Let not the Sovran Indra disappoint us in what shall bring both Sisters to our dwelling.
To him have run the quickly flowing waters. May Indra come to us with life and friendship.

3 Victorious with the men, Hero in battles, Indra, who hears the singer's supplication,
Will bring his car nigh to the man who offers, if he himself upholds the songs that praise him.

4 Yea, Indra, with the men, through love of glory consumes the sacred food which friends have offered.
The ever-strengthening song of him who worships is sung in fight amid the clash of voices.

5 Aided by thee, O Maghavan, O Indra, may we subdue our foes who count them mighty.
Be our protector, strengthen and increase us. May we find strengthening food in full abundance.

HYMN CLXXX. *Aśvins.*

1. Lightly your coursers travel through the regions when round the sea of air your car is flying.

3. *The Five Peoples' treasures* : the wealth of all the Āryans. See I. 7. 9.

1 *The Bull* : the hero, or chief distinguished by superior strength.

2—3 The word here rendered by 'mighty' (*vṛṣan*) is commonly applied in the Veda to living beings and things preëminent for strength, and the Vedic poets delight in repeating it and its compounds and derivatives. 'But this is nothing yet,' observes Prof. Max Müller. 'compared to other passages, when the poet cannot get enough of vṛṣan and vṛṣabhá.' Cf. II. 16. 6; V. 36. 5; V. 40 2, 3; VIII. 13. 31—33.

2 *Both Sisters* : Night and Morning. *The quickly flowing waters* : for the libations.

For Hymn CLXXIX. See Appendix.

Your golden fellies scatter drops of moisture : drinking the sweetness ye atend the Mornings.

2 Ye as ye travel overtake the Courser who flies apart, the Friend of man, most holy.
The prayer is that the Sister may convey you, all praised, meath-drinkers ! to support and strengthen.

3 Ye have deposited, matured within her, in the raw cow the first milk of the milch-cow,
Which the bright offerer, shining like a serpent mid trees, presents to you whose form is perfect.

4 Ye made the fierce heat to be full of sweetness for Atri at his wish, like streaming water.
Fire-offering thence is yours, O Aśvins, Heroes : your car-wheels speed to us like springs of honey.

5 Like Tugra's ancient son may I, ye Mighty, bring you to give your gifts with milk-oblations.
Your greatness compasseth Earth, Heaven, and Waters : decayed for you is sorrow's net, ye Holy.

6 When, Bounteous Ones, ye drive your yoked team downward, ye send, by your own natures, understanding.
Swift as the wind let the prince please and feast you : he, like a pious man, gains strength for increase.

7 For verily we truthful singers praise you : the niggard trafficker is here excluded.
Now, even now do ye O blameless Aśvins, ye Mighty, guard the man whose God is near him.

8 You of a truth day after day, O Aśvins, that he might win the very plenteous torrent,
Agastya, famous among mortal heroes, roused with a thousand lauds like sounds of music.

9 When with the glory of your car ye travel, when we go speeding like the priest of mortals,
And give good horses to sacrificers, may we, Nāsatyas ! gain our share of riches.

10 With songs of praise we call to-day, O Aśvins, that your new chariot, for our own well-being,
That circles heaven with never-injured fellies. May we find strengthening food in full abundance.

2 *The Courser* : the Sun. *The Sister* : Uṣas, Dawn.

3 *The first milk* : ye deposited the milk within the Cosmic Cow, and this is found unaltered in the cows of earth.

The bright offerer : I follow Roth in taking this to be the fire, creeping through the fuel as a snake that creeps and gleams through the bushes. But the hemistich is very difficult and the meaning is doubtful. Wilson, after Sāyaṇa, paraphrases : '(as vigilant in the midst of the ceremony) as a thief (in the midst) of a thicket.' Ludwig says that *hvārā* means neither snake nor thief, but a tub or wooden vessel.

4 *Atri* : See I. 112. 7.

5 *Tugra's ancient son* : See I. 117. 4. *Greatness* : I adopt Ludwig's conjecture *māhimā* for *māhinā*.

6 *The prince* : the institutor of the sacrifice.

8 *The very plenteous torrent* : to obtain abundance of rain. *Agastya* : the Ṛṣi of the hymn.

9 When you assist the pious chiefs in battle, and they win the spoil, let the priests who officiated at the sacrifices which won that aid receive their due share of the booty as their reward.

HYMN CLXXXI. *Aśvins*

1. WHAT, dearest Pair, is this in strength and riches that ye as Priests are bringing from the waters ?
This sacrifice is your glorification, ye who protect mankind and give them treasures.

2 May your pure steeds, rain-drinkers, bring you hither, swift as the tempest, your celestial coursers,
Rapid as thought, with fair backs, full of vigour, resplendent in their native light, O Aśvins.

3 Your car is like a torrent rushing downward : may it come nigh, broad-seated, for our welfare,—
Car holy, strong, that ever would be foremost, thought-swift, which ye, for whom we long, have mounted.

4 Here sprung to life, they both have sung together, with bodies free from stain, with signs that mark them ;
One of you Prince of Sacrifice, the Victor, the other counts as Heaven's auspicious offspring.

5 May your car-seat, down-gliding, golden-coloured, according to your wish approach our dwellings.
Men shall feed full the bay steeds of the other, and, Aśvins they with roars shall stir the regions.

6 Forth comes your strong Bull like a cloud of autumn, sending abundant food of liquid sweetness.

---

1 *From the waters* : from the firmament

6 *Your strong Bull* : your swift chariot Wilson remarks : 'This and the preceding stanza are not very explicit in the comparison which is intimated between the functions of the two Aśvins, for the use of *anyasya*, of the other, in the second half of the verse, is all that intimates that *ekasya*, of the one, is understood in the first half.'

Let them feed with the other's ways and vigour : the upper streams have come and do us service.

7 Your constant song hath been sent forth, Disposers ! that flows threefold in mighty strength, O Aśvins.

Thus lauded, give the suppliant protection : moving or resting hear mine invocation.

8 This song of bright contents for you is swelling in the men's hall where threefold grass is ready.

Your strong rain-cloud, ye Mighty Ones, hath swollen, honouring men as 'twere with milk's outpouring.

9 The prudent worshipper, like Pūṣan, Aśvins ! praises you as he praises Dawn and Agni,

When, singing with devotion, he invokes you. May we find strengthening food in full abundance.

HYMN CLXXXII. *Aśvins.*

1. This was the task. Appear promptly, ye prudent Ones. Here is the chariot drawn by strong steeds : be ye glad.

Heart-stirring, longed for, succourers of Viśpalā, here are Heaven's Sons whose sway blesses the pious man.

2 Longed for, most Indra-like, mighty, most Marut-like, most wonderful in deed, carborne, best charioteers,

Bring your full chariot hither heaped with liquid sweet : thereon, ye Aśvins, come to him who offers gifts.

3 What make ye there, ye Mighty? Wherefore linger ye with folk who, offering not, are held in high esteem ?

Pass over them ; make ye the niggard's life decay : give light unto the singer eloquent in praise.

4 Crunch up on every side the dogs who bark at us : slay ye our foes, O Aśvins ; this ye understand.

Make wealthy every word of him who praises you : accept with favour, both Nāsatyas, this my laud.

5 Ye made for Tugra's son amid the waterfloods that animated ship with wings to fly withal,

Whereon with God-devoted mind ye brought him forth, and fled with easy flight from out the mighty surge.

6 Four ships most welcome in the midst of ocean, urged by the Aśvins, save the son of Tugra,

Him who was cast down headlong in the waters, plunged in the thick inevitable darkness.

7 What tree was that which stood fixed in surrounding sea to which the son of Tugra supplicating clung?

Like twigs, of which some winged creature may take hold, ye, Aśvins, bore him off safely to your renown.

8 Welcome to you be this the hymn of praises uttered by Mānas, O Nāsatyas, Heroes,

From this our gathering where we offer Soma. May we find strengthening food in full abundance.

HYMN CLXXXIII. *Aśvins.*

1. Make ready that which passes thought in swiftness, that hath three wheels and triple seat, ye Mighty,

Whereon ye seek the dwelling of the pious, whereon, threefold, ye fly like birds with pinions.

2 Light rolls your easy chariot faring earthward, what time, for food, ye, full of wisdom, mount it.

May this song, wondrous fair, attend your glory : ye, as ye travel, wait on Dawn Heaven's Daughter.

3 Ascend your lightly rolling car, approaching the worshipper who turns him to his duties,—

Whereon ye come unto the house to quicken man and his offspring, O Nāsatyas, Heroes.

4 Let not the wolf, let not the she-wolf harm you. Forsake me not, nor pass me by for others.

7 *That flows threefold* : from three priests.

8 *Threefold grass* : sacred grass arranged to form three layers or seats.

9 *As he praises Dawn and Agni* : that is, at the morning sacrifice.

1 *This was the task* : this sacrifice is the work at which you have to preside.

Be ye glad : delight yourselves with the Soma juice.

Succourers of Viśpalā : by giving her an iron leg. See I. 116. 15. Or the word in the text may mean, as explained by Sāyaṇa, 'rich in benevolence to men.'

5 *Tugra's son* : see I. 116. 3, 4.

6 *In the midst of ocean* : I can make nothing of the *jaṭhalasya* of the text, and insert these words as substitute for translation.

7 *What tree was that* : figuratively of the Aśvins who saved him, as, in a sudden inundation, a tree saves the man who climbs it. An ingenious interpretation of the legend will be found in M. Bergaigne's *La Religion Védique*, III. 10. 17.

1 The three-wheeled chariot of the Aśvins has been mentioned before, See I. 34. 1.

4 *Let not the wolf* : let no enemy prevent your coming. Ludwig thinks that there is an ironical reference to the

Here stands your share, here is your hymn, ye Mighty : yours are these vessels, full of pleasant juices.

5 Gotama, Purumīḷha, Atri bringing oblations all invoke you for protection.
Like one who goes straight to the point directed, come, ye Nāsatyas, to mine invocation.

6 We have passed o'er the limit of this darkness : our praise hath been bestowed on you, O Aśvins.
Come hitherward by paths which Gods have travelled. May we find strengthening food in full abundance.

HYMN CLXXXIV *Aśvins.*

1. Let us invoke you both this day and after the priest is here with lauds when morn is breaking :
Nāsatyas, wheresoe'er ye be, Heaven's Children, for him who is more liberal than the godless.

2 With us, ye Mighty, let yourselves be joyful, glad in our stream of Soma slay the niggards.
Graciously hear my hymns and invitations, marking, O Heroes, with your ears my longing.

3 Nāsatyas, Pūṣans, ye as Gods for glory arranged and set in order Sūryā's bridal.
Your giant steeds move on, sprung from the waters, like ancient times of Varuṇa the Mighty.

4 Your grace be with us, ye who love sweet juices : further the hymn sung by the poet Māna,
When men are joyful in your glorious actions, to win heroic strength, ye Bounteous Givers.

5 This praise was made, O liberal Lords, O Aśvins, for you with fair adornment by the Mānas.
Come to our house for us and for our children, rejoicing, O Nāsatyas, in Agastya.

6 We have passed o'er the limit of this darkness : our praise hath been bestowed on you, O Aśvins.
Come hitherward by paths which Gods have travelled. May we find strengthening food in full abundance.

HYMN CLXXXV. *Heaven and Earth.*

1. Whether of these is elder, whether later? How were they born? Who knoweth it, ye sages?
These of themselves support all things existing : as on a car the Day and Night roll onward.

2 The Twain uphold, though motionless and footless, a widespread offspring having feet and moving.
Like your own son upon his parents' bosom, protect us, Heaven and earth, from fearful danger.

3 I call for Aditi's unrivalled bounty, perfect, celestial, deathless, meet for worship.
Produce this, ye Twain Worlds, for him who lauds you. Protect us, Heaven and Earth, from fearful danger.

4 May we be close to both the Worlds who suffer no pain, Parents of Gods, who aid with favour,
Both mid the Gods, with Day and Night alternate. Protect us, Heaven and Earth, from fearful danger.

5 Faring together, young, with meeting limits, Twin Sisters lying in their Parents' bosom,
Kissing the centre of the world together. Protect us, Heaven and Earth, from fearful danger.

6 Duly I call the two wide seats, the mighty, the general Parents, with the God's protection.
Who, beautiful to look on, make the nectar. Protect us, Heaven and Earth, from fearful danger.

7 Wide, vast, and manifold, whose bounds are distant,—these, reverent, I address at this our worship,
The blessed Pair, victorious, all-sustaining. Protect us, Heaven and Earth, from fearful danger.

wolf from whose jaws the Aśvins rescued the quail. See I. 117. 16.

5 *Gotama, Purumīḷha, Atri* : sages favoured by the Aśvins.

---

3 *Pūṣans* : ye who cherish men like Pūṣan himself.

Sūryā : the daughter of the Sun and the consort of the Aśvins. See I. 116. 17. *Giant steeds* : cf. I. 46. 3.

What the times or ages of Varuṇa are is uncertain.

---

3 *Aditi's gift* : all the blessings of infinite Nature. According to Sāyaṇa, Aditi means here the firmament, in which case her gift would be seasonable rain and consequent wealth.

4 *Parents of Gods* : as with the Greeks, Heaven and Earth are regarded as the father and mother of the Gods.

5 The meaning is obscure. Ludwig suggests Dakṣa and Aditi as the parents. *The centre of the world* means usually the altar.

6 *With the God's protection* : to come to us with the favouring help of the Gods. *The nectar* : the rain.

8 What sin we have at any time committed against the Gods, our friend, our house's chieftain,
Thereof may this our hymn be expiation. Protect us, Heaven and Earth, from fearful danger.

9 May both these Friends of man, who bless, preserve me, may they attend me with their help and favour.
Enrich the man more liberal than the godless. May we, ye Gods, be strong with food rejoicing.

10 Endowed with understanding, I have uttered this truth, for all to hear, to Earth and Heaven.
Be near us, keep us from reproach and trouble. Father and Mother, with your help preserve us.

11 Be this my prayer fulfilled, O Earth and Heaven, wherewith, Father and Mother, I address you.
Nearest of Gods be ye with your protection. May we find strengthening food in full abundance.

HYMN CLXXXVI. *Viśvedevas.*

1. LOVED of all men, may Savitar, through praises offered as sacred food, come to our synod,
That you too, through our hymn, ye ever-youthful, may gladden, at your visit, all our people.

2 To us may all the Gods come trooped together, Aryaman, Mitra, Varuṇa concordant,
That all may be promoters of our welfare, and with great might preserve our strength from slackness.

3 Agni I sing, the guest you love most dearly : the Conqueror through our lauds is friendly-minded :
That he may be our Varuṇa rich in glory and send food like a prince praised by the godly.

4 To you I seek with reverence, Night and Morning, like a cow good to milk, with hope to conquer,
Preparing on a common day the praise-song with milk of various hues within this udder.

5 May the great Dragon of the Deep rejoice us : as one who nourishes her young comes Sindhu,
With whom we will incite the Child of Waters whom vigorous course swift as thought bring hither.

6 Moreover Tvaṣṭar also shall approach us, one-minded with the princes at his visit.
Hither shall come the Vṛtra-slayer Indra, Ruler of men, as strongest of the Heroes.

7 Him too our hymns delight, that yoke swift horses, like mother cows who lick their tender youngling.
To him our songs shall yield themselves like spouses, to him the most delightful of the Heroes.

8 So may the Maruts, armed with mighty weapons, rest here on heaven and earth with hearts in concord,
As Gods whose cars have dappled steeds like torrents, destroyers of the foe allies of Mitra.

9 They hasten on to happy termination their orders when they are made known by glory.
As on a fair bright day the arrow flieth, o'er all the barren soil their missiles sparkle.

10 Incline the Aśvins to show grace, and Pūṣan, for power and might have they, their own possession.
Friendly are Viṣṇu, Vāta, and Ṛbhukṣan : so may I bring the Gods to make us happy.

11 This is my reverent thought of you, ye Holy ; may it inspire you, make you dwell among us,—
Thought, toiling for the Gods and seeking treasure. May we find strengthening food in full abundance.

1 *Savitar* : the Sun, especially regarded as the vivifier and generator. *Ye ever youthful* : Viśvedevas, or All-Gods.

3 *Our Varuṇa* : our lord and protector.

4 *Like a cow* : the singer is the cow and his hymn the milk.

With hope to conquer : to overcome sins, according to Sāyaṇa.

A common day : belonging to the past night and the present morning.

Milk of various hues : the libations of milk mixed with the yellow or brown Soma juice.

This udder : apparently a figurative expression for the place of sacrifice whence the milky libations flow.

5 *Dragon of the Deep* : Ahibudhnya, a divine being that dwells in, and presides over the firmament. *Sindhu* : the Indus.

The Child of Waters : Agni.

6 *Tvaṣṭar* : the heavenly artist. *The princes* : institutors of the sacrifice.

7 *That yoke swift horses* : that quickly bring the Gods to the sacrifice.

Their tender youngling : Sāyaṇa takes the epithet *táruṇam* as applying to Indra 'the ever-youthful.'

10 *Ṛbhukṣan* : a name of Indra as Lord of the Ṛbhus. See I. 162. 1.

HYMN CLXXXVII. *Praise of Food.*

1. Now will I glorify Food that upholds great strength,
By whose invigorating power Trita rent Vṛtra limb from limb.

2 O pleasant Food, O Food of meath, thee have we chosen for our own,
So be our kind protector thou.

3 Come hitherward to us, O Food, auspicious with auspicious help,
Health-bringing, not unkind, a dear and guileless friend.

4 These juices which, O Food, are thine throughout the regions are diffused.
Like winds they have their place in heaven.

5 These gifts of thine, O Food, O Food most sweet to taste,
These savours of thy juices work like creatures that have mighty necks.

6 In thee, O Food, is set the spirit of great Gods.
Under thy flag brave deeds were done: he slew the Dragon with thy help.

7 If thou be gone unto the splendour of the clouds,
Even from thence, O Food of meath, prepared for our enjoyment, come.

8 Whatever morsel we consume from waters or from plants of earth, O Soma, wax thou fat thereby.

9 What, Soma, we enjoy from thee in milky food or barley-brew, Vātāpi, grow thou fat thereby.

10 O Vegetable, Cake of meal, be wholesome, firm, and strengthening:
Vātāpi, grow thou fat thereby.

11 O Food, from thee as such have we drawn forth with lauds, like cows, our sacrificial gifts,
From thee who banquetest with Gods, from thee who banquetest with us.

1 *Trita* : a mysterious ancient deity frequently mentioned in the Ṛgveda, principally in connexion with Indra, Vāyu, and the Maruts. His home is in the remotest part of heaven, and he is called Āptya, the Watery, that is, sprung from, or dwelling in the sea of cloud and vapour. By Sāyaṇa he is identified sometimes with Vāyu, sometimes with Indra as the pervader of the three worlds, and sometimes with Agni stationed in the three fire-receptacles.

2 The God addressed is the Soma.

5 *Like creatures that have mighty necks* : like strong bullocks.

6 *The spirit of great Gods* : thou incitest Indra and the Gods to perform glorious and benevolent acts.

9 *Vātāpi* : the fermenting Soma. According to Sāyaṇa, the body.

HYMN CLXXXVIII. *Āprīs*

1. WINNER of thousands, kindled, thou shinest a God with Gods to-day.
Bear out oblations, envoy, Sage.

2 Child of Thyself the sacrifice is for the righteous blent with meath,
Presenting viands thousandfold.

3 Invoked and worthy of our praise bring Gods whose due is sacrifice:
Thou, Agni, givest countless gifts.

4 To seat a thousand Heroes they eastward have strewn the grass with might,
Whereon, Ādityas, ye shine forth.

5 The sovran all-imperial Doors, wide, good, many and manifold,
Have poured their streams of holy oil.

6 With gay adornment, fair to see, in glorious beauty shine they forth:
Let Night and Morning rest them here.

7 Let these two Sages first of all, heralds divine and eloquent,
Perform for us this sacrifice.

8 You I address, Sarasvatī, and Bhāratī, and Iḷā, all:
Urge ye us on to glorious fame.

9 Tvaṣṭar the Lord hath made all forms and all the cattle of the field:
Cause them to multiply for us.

10 Send to the Gods, Vanaspati, thyself, the sacrificial draught:
Let Agni make the oblations sweet.

11 Agni, preceder of the Gods, is honoured with the sacred song:
He glows at offerings blest with Hail!

HYMN CLXXXIX. *Agni.*

1. BY goodly paths lead us to riches, Agni, God who knowest every sacred duty.
Remove the sin that makes us stray and wander: most ample adoration will we bring thee.

The Āprīs are the various forms of Agni, according to Sāyaṇa, which are invoked in the hymn.

1 *Thou* : Agni.

2 *Child of Thyself* : Agni. See I. 13.2.

4 *Ādityas* : See I. 14. 3.

5 *The sovran all-imperial Doors* : of the sacrificial hall through which Gods enter. They are types of the portals of the East through which light comes into the world. See Wallis, *Cosmology of the Ṛgveda*, p. 19.

7 *These two Sages* : heralds or invokers, because they call the Gods. See I. 13. 8.

8 *Sarasvatī and Bhāratī and Iḷā* : See I. 13. 9.

10 *Vanaspati* : see I. 13. 11.

11 *Blest with Hail* : See I. 13. 12.

This hymn, as Ludwig observes, appears to have been composed at a time of pestilence.

2 Lead us anew to happiness, O Agni; lead us beyond all danger and affliction.
Be unto us a wide broad ample castle : bless, prosper on their way our sons and offspring.

3 Far from us, Agni, put thou all diseases : let them strike lauds that have no saving Agni.
God, make our home again to be a blessing, with all the Immortal Deities, O Holy.

4 Preserve us, Agni, with perpetual succour, refulgent in the dwelling which thou lovest.
O Conqueror, most youthful, let no danger touch him who praises thee to-day or after.

5 Give not us up a prey to sin, O Agni, the greedy enemy that brings us trouble ;
Not to the fanged that bites, not to the toothless : give not us up, thou Conqueror, to the spoiler.

6 Such as thou art, born after Law, O Agni when lauded give protection to our bodies,
From whosoever would reproach or injure: for thou, God, rescuest from all oppression.

7 Thou, well discerning both these classes, comest to men at early morn, O holy Agni.
Be thou obedient unto man at evening, to be adorned, as keen, by eager suitors.

8 To him have we addressed our pious speeches, I, Māna's son, to him victorious Agni.
May we gain countless riches with the sages. May we find strengthening food in full abundance.

HYMN CXC. *Bṛhaspati.*

1. GLORIFY thou Bṛhaspati, the scatheless, who must be praised with hymns, sweet-tongued and mighty,
To whom as leader of the song, resplendent, worthy of lauds, both Gods and mortals listen.

2 On him wait songs according to the season even as a stream of pious men set moving.
Bṛhaspati—for he laid out the expanses—was, at the sacrifice, vast Mātariśvan.

3 The praise, the verse that offers adoration, may he bring forth, as the Sun sends his arms out,
He who gives daily light through this God's wisdom, strong as a dread wild beast, and inoffensive.

4 His song of praise pervades the earth and heaven : let the wise worshipper draw it, like a courser.
These of Bṛhaspati, like hunters' arrows, go to the skies that change their hue like serpents.

5 Those, God, who count thee as a worthless bullock, and, wealthy sinners, live on thee the Bounteous,—
On fools like these no blessing thou bestowest : Bṛhaspati, thou punishest the spiteful.

6 Like a fair path is he, where grass is pleasant, though hard to win, a Friend beloved most dearly.
Those who unharmed by enemies behold us, while they would make them bare, stood closely compassed.

3 *That have no saving Agni* : or, which do not maintain the sacred fire ; whose inhabitants do not worship Agni.

5 *The fanged* : venomous serpents. *The toothless* : wild animals that do not bite, but injure with their horns, etc.

7 *Both these classes* : worshippers and non-worshippers.

Be thou obedient : be a useful servant in the house.

As keen : *akrāḥ*, applied to Agni in all the places where it occurs in the Ṛgveda, appears to mean hasty, violent, eager, or keen. Ludwig thinks that it means here a sacrificial post, and Grassmann, a banner. Wilson, following Sāyaṇa, paraphrases : 'be compliant (with his wishes); like an institutor of the rite, (who is directed) by the desires (of the priests).

1 *Bṛhaspati* : Lord of Prayer. See I. 14. 3.

2 *For he laid out the expanses* : spread out and revealed to the eyes of men the broad regions of heaven and earth. The meaning of the second hemistich is not clear. Wilson paraphrases : 'for that Bṛhaspati is the manifestor (of all), the expansive wind that (diffusing) blessings has been produced for (the diffusion of) water.' There seems to be nothing in the Ṛgveda to justify the identification of Mātariśvan with the wind, and only in the later language has *ṛtá* the sense of water. See I.31.3.

3 *He* : Bṛhaspati. *He who gives daily light* : the regular appearance of the Sun depends upon Bṛhaspati's wisdom.

Inoffensive : *arakṣásaḥ*, according to Sāyaṇa, 'free from the opposition of Rākṣasas.'

4 *These of Bṛhaspati* : these sacred songs, compared to arrows.

That change their hue like serpents : *áhimāyān*. See I. 3. 9.

6 This stanza is unintelligible to me. Wilson renders it : 'Be a (pleasant) way to him who goes well and makes good offerings, like the affectionate friend of (a ruler who) restrains the bad; and may those sinless men who instruct us, although yet enveloped (by ignorance) stand extricated from their covering'; and remarks : 'it is not clear how those who are enveloped by ignorance should be competent to teach : another explanation is, let those who revile us, and are being protected, be deprived of that protection.'

7 He to whom songs of praise go forth like torrents, as rivers eddying under banks flow sea-ward—
Bṛhaspati the wise, the eager, closely looks upon both, the waters and the vessel.

8 So hath Bṛhaspati, great, strong and mighty, the God exceeding powerful, been brought hither.
May he thus lauded give us kine and horses. May we find strengthening food in full abundance.

HYMN CXCI *Water. Grass. Sun.*

1. VENOMOUS, slightly venomous, or venomous aquatic worm,—
Both creatures, stinging, unobserved, with poison have infected me.

2 Coming, it kills the unobserved; it kills them as it goes away,
It kills them as it drives them off, and bruising bruises them to death.

3 Śara grass, Darbha, Kuśara, and Sairya, Muñja, Vīraṇa,
Where all these creatures dwell unseen, with poison have infected me.

4 The cows had settled in their stalls, the beasts of prey had sought their lairs,
Extinguished were the lights of men, when things unseen infected me.

5 Or these, these reptiles, are observed, like lurking thieves at evening time.
Seers of all, themselves unseen : be therefore very vigilant.

6 Heaven is your Sire, your Mother Earth, Soma your Brother, Aditi
Your Sister : seeing all, unseen, keep still and dwell ye happily.

7 Biters of shoulder or of limb, with needle-stings, most venomous,
Unseen, whatever ye may be, vanish together and be gone.

8 Slayer of things unseen, the Sun, beheld of all, mounts, eastward, up,
Consuming all that are not seen, and evil spirits of the night.

9 There hath the Sun-God mounted up, who scorches much and everything.
Even the Āditya from the hills, all-seen, destroying things unseen.

10 I hang the poison in the Sun, a wine-skin in a vintner's house,
He will not die, nor shall we die : his path is far : he whom Bay Horses bear hath turned thee to sweet meath.

11 This little bird, so very small, hath swallowed all thy poison up.
She will not die, nor shall we die : his path is far : he whom Bay Horses bear hath turned thee to sweet meath.

2 The three-times-seven bright sparks of fire have swallowed up the poison's strength.
They will not die, nor shall we die : his path is far : he whom Bay Horses bear hath turned thee to sweet meath.

13 Of ninety rivers and of nine with power to stay the venom's course,—
The names of all I have secured : his path is far : he whom Bay Horses bear hath turned thee to sweet meath.

7 This stanza also is very obscure. Bṛhaspati is said to look upon the waters and the vessel, that is the river to be crossed and the boat which is to be used, meaning perhaps the sacrifice and all that is used in performing it. Ludwig thinks that a play upon the words is intended, *āpaḥ* meaning both water and a religious ceremony and *táraḥ* both ferry-boat and prompt energy.

This so-called hymn is a spell or charm said to have been recited by Agastya when he suspected that he had been poisoned. Its silent repetition is said to be an effectual antidote against 'all venom in reptiles, insects, scorpions, roots, and artificial poisons.' I generally follow Sāyaṇa; but his explanations are not always satisfactory, and several passages must be left in their original obscurity.

1 The exact meaning of the words in the first line is uncertain.

Both creatures : both classes, either the venomous and the slightly venomous, or land-reptiles and water-snakes.

2 *Coming, it kills the unobserved* : the herb, used as an antidote, coming to the man who has been bitten kills the venomous creatures who secretly attacked him.

3 *Śara grass, etc.* : these are different sorts of grass in which snakes and other venomous reptiles lurk.

6 *Heaven*, or Dyaus, is here said to be the father of the snakes.

Soma : the Moon.

10 *I hang the poison in the Sun* : 'I deposit the poison in the solar orb, like a leather bottle in the house of a vendor of spirits'—Wilson. See Wilson's note in which he says that by the Sun or as Sāyaṇa paraphrases it, the orb of the Sun, 'is probably to be understood a mystical diagram, or figure wholly or partly typical of the solar orb : the Sun being considered as especially instrumental in counteracting the operation of poison.

He will not die : the Sun will not die from the effects of the poison thus applied, and we also who have been bitten shall through his favour recover.

11 *This little bird* : according to Sāyaṇa the bird which we call the francoline partridge, said to be a 'remover of poison.'

12 *Bright sparks of fire* : either, says Sāyaṇa, the seven flames of fire multiplied, or the twenty-one varieties of another kind of bird unaffected by eating poison.

13 *Of ninety rivers and of nine* : the numbers are used indefinitely for all the rivers of the country.

14 So have the peahens three-times-seven, so have the maiden Sisters Seven
Carried thy venom far away, as girls bear water in their jars.
15 The poison-insect is so small ; I crush the creature with a stone.
I turn the poison hence away, departed unto distant lands.
16 Forth issuing from the mountain's side the poison-insect spake and said :
The scorpion's venom hath no strength ; Scorpion, thy venom is but weak.

14 *The peahens three-times-seven* : peafowls are regarded as the great enemies of snakes. The number appears to be merely fanciful and borrowed from verse 12.

The maiden Sisters Seven : the seven chief rivers of the land.

15 As *kuṣúmbha* means poison-bag, *kuṣumbhakáḥ* in the text is taken by Ludwig and Grassmann to mean venomous insect.

Sāyaṇa explains it as the *nakula*, nëul or mungoose whose hostility to the snake is proverbial. Wilson paraphrases : 'May the insignificant mungoose carry off thy venom, (Poison) : if not, I will crush the vile (creature) with a stone.'

BOOK THE SECOND.

HYMN I. *Agni.*

1. THOU, Agni, shining in thy glory through the days, art brought to life from out the waters, from the stone:
From out the forest trees and herbs that grow on ground, thou, Sovran Lord of men art generatad pure.

2 Thine is the Herald's task and Cleanser's duly timed; Leader art thou, and Kindler for the pious man.
Thou art Director, thou the ministering Priest: thou art the Brahman, Lord and Master in our home.

3 Hero of Heroes, Agni! thou art Indra, thou art Viṣṇu of the Mighty Stride, adorable:
Thou, Brahmaṇaspati, the Brahman finding wealth: thou, O Sustainer, with thy wisdom tendest us.

4 Agni, thou art King Varuṇa whose laws stand fast; as Mitra, Wonder-Worker, thou must be implored.
Aryaman, heroes' Lord, art thou, enriching all, and liberal Aṁśa in the synod, O thou God.

5 Thou givest strength, as Tvaṣṭar, to the worshipper: thou wielding Mitra's power hast kinship with the Dames.
Thou, urging thy fleet coursers, givest noble steeds: a host of heroes art thou with great store of wealth.

6 Rudra art thou, the Asura of mighty heaven: thou art the Maruts' host, thou art the Lord of food,
Thou goest with red winds: bliss hast thou in thine home. As Pūṣan thou thyself protectest worshippers.

7 Giver of wealth art thou to him who honours thee; thou art God Savitar, granter of precious things.
As Bhaga, Lord of men! thou rulest over wealth, and guardest in his house him who hath served thee well.

8 To thee, the people's Lord within the house, the folk press forward to their King most graciously inclined.
Lord of the lovely look, all things belong to thee: ten, hundred, yea, a thousand are outweighed by thee.

9 Agni, men seek thee as a Father with their prayers, win thee, bright-formed, to brotherhood with holy act.
Thou art a Son to him who duly worships thee, and as a trusty Friend thou guardest from attack.

10 A Ṛbhu art thou, Agni, near to be adored; thou art the Sovran Lord of foodful spoil and wealth.
Thou shinest brightly forth, thou burnest to bestow: pervading sacrifice, thou lendest us thine help.

11 Thou, God, art Aditi to him who offers gifts: thou, Hotrā, Bhāratī, art strengthened by the song.
Thou art the hundred-wintered Iḷā to give strength, Lord of Wealth! Vṛtra-slayer and Sarasvatī.

12 Thou, Agni, cherished well, art highest vital power; in thy delightful hue are glories visible.
Thou art the lofty might that furthers each design: thou art wealth manifold, diffused on every side.

The hymns of this Book, with the few exceptions that will be noted, are ascribed to the Ṛṣi Gṛtsamada. As Book I. is called the Book of the Śatarcins, that is of the seers of a hundred or large indefinite number of Ṛcas or verses, so this Book is commonly called the Gārtsamada Maṇḍala or Book of Gṛtsamada.

1 *Through the days*: for the days of sacrifice, according to Sāyaṇa.

The waters: from the waters of the firmament, as lightning.

From out the forest trees: in the frequently occurring conflagrations caused by the friction of dry branches. Agni is also said to have his home in plants, perhaps originally on account of a phosphorescent light which some plants emit.

2 Agni concentrates in himself the various functions of different classes of human priests, the most important of which are mentioned in the verse. The classification of the priests and the description of their duties are given with variations by different authorities. The Hotar or Herald invokes the Gods; the Potar, Purifier, or Cleanser, is the assistant of the Brahman or praying priest who remedies any defect in the ritual; the Neṣṭar or Leader leads forward the wife of the sacrificer; the Agnīdh or Kindler lights the sacrificial fire; the Praśāstar or Director is the assistant of the Hotar; and the Adhvaryu or ministering priest is the deacon who measures the ground, builds the altar, and makes all the preparations necessary for the sacrifice. The duties of the priests, however, varied at different times and according to the nature of the ceremony which they were engaged to perform.

3 *Viṣṇu of the Mighty Stride*: See I. 32. 16.

4 *Aṁśa*: the Distributor; one of the Ādityas.

5 *The Dames*: the Consorts of the Gods.

11 *Hotrā, Bhāratī, Iḷā* are personifications of parts of religious worship. The epithet 'hundred-wintered' appears to refer to the natural duration of human life. *Sarasvatī*: See I. 3. 10.

13 Thee, Agni, have the Ādityas taken as their mouth; the Bright Ones have made thee, O Sage, to be their tongue.
They who love offerings cling to thee at solemn rites : by thee the Gods devour the duly offered food.

14 By thee, O Agni, all the Immortal guileless Gods eat with thy mouth the oblation that is offered them.
By thee do mortal men give sweetness to their drink. Bright art thou born, the embryo of the plants of earth.

15 With these thou art united, Agni; yea thou, God of noble birth, surpassest them in majesty,
Which, through the power of good, here spreads abroad from thee, diffused through both the worlds, throughout the earth and heaven.

16 The princely worshippers who send to those who sing thy praise, O Agni, guerdon graced with kine and steeds,—
Lead thou both these and us forward to higher bliss. With brave men in the assembly may we speak aloud.

HYMN II. *Agni.*

1. WITH sacrifice exalt Agni who knows all life ; worship him with oblation and the song of praise,
Well kindled, nobly fed, heaven's Lord, Celestial Priest, who labours at the pole where deeds of might are done.

2 At night and morning, Agni, have they called to thee, like milch-kine in their stalls lowing to meet their young.
As messenger of heaven thou lightest all night long the families of men, thou Lord of precious boons.

3 Him have the Gods established at the region's base, doer of wondrous deeds, Herald of heaven and earth;
Like a most famous car, Agni the purely bright, like Mitra to be glorified among the folk.

4 Him have they set in his own dwelling, in the vault, like the Moon waxing, fulgent, in the realm of air.
Bird of the firmament, observant with his eyes, guard of the place as 'twere, looking to Gods and men.

5 May he as Priest encompass all the sacrifice : men throng to him with offerings and with hymns of praise.
Raging with jaws of gold among the growing plants, like heaven with all the stars, he quickens earth and sky.

6 Such as thou art, brilliantly kindled for our weal, a liberal giver, send us riches in thy shine,
For our advantage, Agni, God, bring Heaven and Earth hither that they may taste oblation brought by man.

7 Agni, give us great wealth, give riches thousandfold : unclose to us, like doors, strength that shall bring renown.
Make Heaven and Earth propitious through the power of prayer, and like the sky's bright sheen let mornings beam on us.

8 Enkindled night by night at every morning's dawn, may he shine forth with red flame like the realm of light,—
Agni adored in beauteous rites with lauds of men, fair guest of living man and King of all our folk.

9 Song chanted by us men, O Agni, Ancient One, has swelled unto the deathless Gods in lofty heaven—
A milch-cow yielding to the singer in the rites wealth manifold, in hundreds, even as he wills.

10 Agni, may we show forth our valour with the steed or with the power of prayer beyond all other men;
And over the Five Races let our glory shine high like the realm of light and unsurpassable.

11 Such, Conqueror ! be to us, be worthy of our praise, thou for whom princes nobly born exert themselves;
Whose sacrifice the strong seek, Agni, when it shines for never-failing offspring in thine own abode.

16 *With brave men* : attended by brave sons, who will support and strengthen us.

---

1 *Who labours at the pole* : who takes the chief part in the performance of all-important sacrifice. A metaphor from oxen drawing a car or wain.

2 *Have they called* : the priests.

3 *At the region's base* : at the altar, according to Sāyaṇa.

4 The word *hvārē*, here rendered 'in the vault' is difficult. Sāyaṇa explains it as 'solitary'. Roth would alter the text.

Guard of the place : of the most sacred place, the altar.

8 *May he* : Agni.

9 *A milch-cow* : the hymn of praise brings riches to the worshipper.

10 *With the steed* : with the war-car in battle as well as with prayers in sacrifices.

The Five Races : the five great Āryan tribes. See I. 7. 9.

11 *The strong* : the wealthy worshippers.

Never-failing offspring : one of the chief rewards of the worship of Agni.

12 Knower of all that lives, O Agni may we both, singers of praise and chiefs, be in thy keeping still.
Help us to wealth exceeding good and glorious, abundant, rich in children and their progeny.

13 The princely worshippers who send to those who sing thy praise, O Agni, guerdon, graced with kine and steeds,—
Lead thou both these and us forward to higher bliss. With brave men in the assembly may we speak aloud.

HYMN III. *Āprīs.*

1. AGNI is set upon the earth well kindled; he standeth in the presence of all beings.
Wise, ancient, God, the Priest and Purifier, let Agni serve the Gods for he is worthy.

2 May Narāśaṁsa lighting up the chambers, bright in his majesty through threefold heaven,
Steeping the gift with oil diffusing purpose, bedew the Gods at chiefest time of worship.

3 Adored in heart, as is thy right, O Agni, serve the Gods first to-day before the mortal.
Bring thou the Marut host. Ye men, do worship to Indra seated on the grass, eternal.

4 O Grass divine, increasing, rich in heroes, strewn for wealth' sake, well laid upon this altar,—
On this bedewed with oil sit ye, O Vasus, sit all ye Gods, ye Holy, ye Ādityas.

5 Wide be the Doors, the Goddesses, thrown open, easy to pass, invoked, through adorations.
Let them unfold, expansive, everlasting, that sanctify the class famed, rich in heroes.

6 Good work for us, the glorious Night and Morning, like female weavers, waxen from aforetime,
Yielders of rich milk, interweave in concert the long-extended thread, the web of worship.

7 Let the two heavenly Heralds, first, most wise, most fair, present oblation duly with the sacred verse,
Worshipping God at ordered seasons decking them at three high places at the centre of the earth.

8 Sarasvatī who perfects our devotion, Iḷā divine, Bhāratī all surpassing,—
Three Goddesses, with power inherent, seated, protect this holy Grass, our flawless refuge!

9 Born is the pious hero swift of hearing, like gold in hue, well formed, and full of vigour.
May Tvaṣṭar lengthen our line and kindred, and may they reach the place which Gods inhabit.

10 Vanaspati shall stand anear and start us, and Agni with his arts prepare oblation.
Let the skilled heavenly Immolator forward unto the Gods the offering thrice anointed.

11 Oil has been mixt: oil is his habitation. In oil he rests: oil is his proper province.
Come as thy wont is: O thou Steer, rejoice thee; bear off the oblation duly consecrated.

HYMN IV *Agni.*

1. FOR you I call the glorious refulgent Agni, the guest of men, rich in oblations
Whom all must strive to win even as a lover, God among godly people, Jātavedas.

2 *Narāśaṁsa*: 'the Praise of Men,' Agni. *The chambers*: the receptacles of the offerings, according to Sāyaṇa. *At chiefest time of worship*: when the oblation of clarified butter is cast into the fire.

3 *Before the mortal*: before the mortal priest.

4 *O Grass divine*: the sacred grass, strewn on the floor of the hall of sacrifice as a seat for the Gods, is one of the Āprīs or deified objects which are to be propitiated in this hymn. All these are regarded as forms of Agni.

5 *The Doors*: of the hall of sacrifice. These appear to have been regarded as types of, and even fancifully identified with, the doors of the cosmic house, the portals of the East through which the morning light enters into the world. See *Cosmology of the Ṛgveda*. p. 19.

The class: the *maghavans*, the eminent and wealthy men who institute sacrifices.

6 *Yielders of rich milk*: cheerful givers of rewards.

7 *Two heavenly Heralds*: invokers or priests. According to Sāyaṇa, the personified fire of earth and of the firmament. See I. 13. 8.

The centre of the earth: the altar. *The three high places* of the three fires.

8 *Three Goddesses*: presiding over different departments of worship.

9 *The pious hero*: a son devoted to the Gods.

10 *Vanaspati*: the sacrificial post, or Agni in that form. See I. 13. 11.

The heavenly Immolator: Agni, typically so called.

11 *Oil*: the clarified butter oblation. *Thou Steer*: mighty Agni.

Duly consecrated: offered with the holy word Svāhā. See I. 13. 12.

This hymn and the three that follow are ascribed to the Ṛṣi Somāhuti of the ancient priestly family of Bhṛgu, one of the first institutors of sacrifice.

1 *Jātavedas*: Agni who knows all life. See I. 44. 1.

2 Bhṛgus who served him in the home of waters set him of old in houses of the living.
Over all worlds let Agni be the Sovran, the messenger of Gods with rapid coursers.

3 Among the tribes of men the Gods placed Agni as a dear Friend when they would dwell among them.
Against the longing nights may he shine brightly, and show the offerer in the house his vigour.

4 Sweet is his growth as of one's own possessions; his look when rushing fain to burn is lovely.
He darts his tongue forth, like a harnessed courser who shakes his flowing tail, among the bushes.

5 Since they who honour me have praised my greatness,—he gave, as 'twere, his hue to those who love him.
Known is he by his bright delightful splendour, and waxing old renews his youth for ever.

6 Like one athirst, he lighteth up the forests; like water down the chariot ways he roareth.
On his black path he shines in burning beauty, marked as it were the heaven that smiles through vapour.

7 Around, consuming the broad earth, he wanders, free roaming like an ox without a herdsman,—
Agni refulgent, burning up the bushes, with blackened lines, as though the earth he seasoned.

8 I, in remembrance of thine ancient favour have sung my hymn in this our third assembly.
O Agni, give us wealth with store of heroes and mighty strength in food and noble offspring.

9 May the Gṛtsamadas, serving in secret, through thee, O Agni, overcome their neighbours,
Rich in good heroes and subduing foemen. That vital power give thou to chiefs and singers.

2 *Who served him in the home of waters* : existing in the form of lightning in the firmament before he was brought down to earth.

5 *Since they who honour me* : Agni appears to be the speaker of these words.

7 *As though the earth he seasoned* : as though, by burning the weeds and bushes, he dressed and prepared the ground for tillage.

8 *Third assembly* : at the third of the three daily sacrifices.

9 *Serving in secret* : by the peaceful discharge of priestly duties, not by warfare like the chiefs who institute the sacrifice.

HYMN V. *Agni.*

1. HERALD and teacher was he born, a guardian for our patrons' help,
Earner by rites of noble wealth. That Strong One may we grasp and guide;

2 In whom, Leader of sacrifice, the seven reins, far extended, meet;
Who furthers, man-like, eighth in place, as Cleanser, all the work divine.

3 When swift he follows this behest, bird-like he chants the holy prayers.
He holds all knowledge in his grasp even as the felly rounds the wheel.

4 Together with pure mental power, pure, as Director, was he born.
Skilled in his own unchanging laws he waxes like the growing boughs.

5 Clothing them in his hues, the kine of him the Leader wait on him.
Is he not better than the Three, the Sisters who have come to us ?

6 When, laden with the holy oil, the Sitster by the Mother stands,
The Priest delights in their approach, as corn at coming of the rain.

7 For his support let him perform as ministrant his priestly task;
Yea, song of praise and sacrifice : we have bestowed, let us obtain.

8 That so this man well skilled, may pay worship to all the Holy Ones.
And, Agni, this our sacrifice which we have here prepared, to thee.

1 *Our patrons* : the wealthy institutors of the sacrifice. *That Strong One*: Agni.

2 *The seven reins* : the seven priests engaged in their several duties.

Cleanser : Potar, one of the sixteen priests. See II. 1.2.

3 The first hemistich, as it stands, is unintelligible to me. Wilson, after Sāyaṇa, paraphrases : 'Whatever (offerings the priests) presents, whatever prayers he recites.'

4 *Director* : Praśāstar, one of the priests. See II. 1. 2.

5 The stanza is obscure. Ludwig thinks that Agni is here called the Leader because he leads the sister Dawns to the sacrifice, and that they are said to be three in number to correspond with the number of the cows.

6 *The Sister* : Uṣas or Dawn. *The Mother* : the northern altar, representing Earth.

7 *Let him* : Agni as priest.

8 *This man* : the worshipper.

HYMN VI. *Agni.*

1. AGNI, accept this flaming brand, this waiting with my prayer on thee :
Hear graciously these songs of praise.
2 With this hymn let us honour thee, seeker of horses, Son of Strength,
With this fair hymn, thou nobly born.
3 As such, lover of song, with songs, wealth-lover, giver of our wealth !
With reverence let us worship thee.
4 Be thou for us a liberal Prince, giver and Lord of precious things.
Drive those who hate us far away.
5 Such as thou art, give rain from heaven, give strength which no man may resist:
Give food exceeding plentiful.
6 To him who lauds thee, craving help, most youthful envoy ! through our song,
Most holy Herald ! come thou nigh.
7 Between both races, Agni, Sage, well skilled thou passest to and fro,
As envoy friendly to mankind.
8 Befriend us thou as knowing all. Sage, duly worship thou the Gods,
And seat thee on this sacred grass.

HYMN VII. *Agni.*

1. VASU, thou most youthful God, Bhārata, Agni, bring us wealth,
Excellent, splendid, much-desired.
2 Let no malignity prevail against us, either God's or man's :
Save us from this and enmity.
3 So through thy favour may we force through all our enemies a way,
As 'twere through streaming water-floods.
4 Thou, Purifier Agni, high shinest forth, bright, adorable,
When worshipped with the sacred oil.
5 Ours art thou, Agni, Bhārata, honoured by us with barren cows,
With bullocks and with kine in calf :
6 Wood-fed, bedewed with sacred oil, ancient, Invoker, excellent,
The Son of Strength, the Wonderful.

HYMN VIII. *Agni.*

1. Now praise, as one who strives for strength, the harnessing of Agni's car,
The liberal, the most splendid One;
2 Who, guiding worshippers aright, withers, untouched by age, the foe :
When worshipped fair to look upon;
3 Who for his glory is extolled at eve and morning in our homes,
Whose statute is inviolate;
4 Who shines refulgent like the Sun, with brilliance and with fiery flame,
Decked with imperishable sheen.
5 Him Atri, Agni, have our songs strengthened according to his sway :
All glories hath he made his own.
6 May we with Agni's, Indra's help, with Soma's, yea, of all the Gods,
Uninjured dwell together still, and conquer those who fight with us.

HYMN IX. *Agni.*

1. ACCUSTOMED to the Herald's place, the Herald hath seated him, bright, splendid, passing mighty,
Whose foresight keeps the Law from violation, excellent, pure-tongued, bringing thousands, Agni.
2 Envoy art thou, protector from the foeman; strong God, thou leadest us to higher blessings.
Refulgent, be an ever-heedful keeper, Agni, for us and for our seed offspring.
3 May we adore thee in thy loftiest birth-place, and, with our praises, in thy lower station.
The place whence thou issued forth I worship : to thee well kindled have they paid oblations.
4 Agni, best Priest, pay worship with oblation; quickly commend the gift to be presented ;

1 *This waiting with my prayer on thee* : this 'beseeching and besieging' as Milton says. Or *upasádam* taken in a special sense may mean the ceremony called Upasad which formed part of the Jyotiṣṭoma, a very important Soma ceremony.

2 *Seeker of horses* : in order to bestow them on the worshipper.

7 *Both races* : Gods and men. *Well skilled* : acquainted with both.

1 *Vasu* : one of the class of Gods so named. *Bhārata*: Agni is so called according to Sāyaṇa, either as having been produced by attrition by the priests, or as being the bearer of oblations. The meaning is, probably, specially connected with the Bharatas or Warriors.'

5 *With kine in calf* : *aṣṭāpadībhiḥ* is thus explained by Sāyaṇa, and is used in the language of the ritual for animals with young. Roth and Grassmann understood 'verses' consisting of eight feet, divisions, or syllables, According to Bergaigne, these cows represent prayers.

5 *Him Atri* : Agni appears here to be called by the name of the ancient sage Atri. Or *átrim* may be an epithet of Agni, signifying the devourer of the food with which he is supplied, as Sāyaṇa explains it.

1 *The Herald* : or Hotar; Agni, the Invoker of the Gods. The name comes, with more emphasis, at the end of the verse. *The Law* : especially sacrifice.

3 *In thy loftiest birth-place* : as the fire of the Sun in heaven. *Thy lower station* : the firmament, where Agni is born as lightning. *The place whence thou hast issued forth* : the altar where the sacrificial fire burns.

For thou art Lord of gathered wealth and treasure: of the bright song of praise thou art inventor.

5 The twofold opulence, O Wonder-Worker, of thee new-born each day never decreases.

Enrich with food the man who lauds thee, Agni : make him the lord of wealth with noble offspring.

6 May he, benevolent with this fair aspect, best sacrificer, bring the Gods to bless us.

Sure guardian, our protector from the foemen, shine, Agni, with thine affluence and splendour.

HYMN X. *Agni.*

1. Agni, first, loudly calling, like a Father, kindled by man upon the seat of worship.

Clothed in his glory, deathless, keen of insight, must be adorned by all, the Strong, the Famous.

2 May Agni the resplendent hear my calling through all my songs, Immortal, keen of insight.

Dark steeds or ruddy draw his car, or carried in sundry ways he makes them red of colour.

3 On wood supine they got the well-formed Infant : a germ in various-fashioned plants was Agni ;

And in the night, not compassed round by darkness, he dwells exceeding wise, with rays of splendour.

4 With oil and sacred gifts I sprinkle Agni who makes his home in front of all things living,

Broad, vast, through vital power o'er all expanded, conspicuous, strong with all the food that feeds him.

5 I pour to him who looks in all directions: may he accept it with a friendly spirit.

Agni with bridegroom's grace and lovely colour may not be touched when all his form is fury.

6 By choice victorious, recognize thy portion: with thee for envoy may we speak like Manu.

Obtaining wealth, I call on perfect Agni who with an eloquent tongue dispenses sweetness.

HYMN XI. *Indra.*

1. Hear thou my call, O Indra; be not heedless : thine may we be for thee to give us treasures ;

For these presented viands, seeking riches, increase thy strength like streams of water flowing.

2 Floods great and many, compassed by the Dragon, thou badest swell and settest free, O Hero.

Strengthened by songs of praise thou rentest piecemeal the Dāsa, him who deemed himself immortal.

3 For, Hero, in the lauds wherein thou joyedst, in hymns of praise, O Indra, songs of Rudras,

These streams in which is thy delight approach thee, even as the brilliant ones draw near to Vāyu.

4 We who add strength to thine own splendid vigour, laying within thine arms the splendid thunder—

With us mayst thou, O Indra, waxen splendid, with Sūrya overcome the Dāsa races.

5 Hero, thou slewest in thy valour Ahi concealed in depths, mysterious, great enchanter,

Dwelling enveloped deep within the waters, him who checked heaven and stayed the floods from flowing.

6 Indra, we laud thy great deeds wrought aforetime, we laud thine exploits later of achievement ;

5 *The twofold opulence* : enriching Gods with sacrifice and men with earthly blessings.

New-born each day : rekindled at the morning sacrifice.

1 *First* : chief of the Gods. *Loudly calling* : roaring as fire, or, to be invoked by all, according to Sāyaṇa. *Like a Father* : supporting the Gods by conveying oblations to them.

2 *Carried in sundry ways* : to one fire-receptable after another.

3 *On wood supine* : the lower piece of wood in which fire is produced.

A germ : latent in plants, with reference to the luminosity of some plants, See II. 1. 1.

6 *By choice* : according to Sāyaṇa, 'with lustre.' *Recognize thy portion* : acknowledge the sacrificial offering to be suitable.

Like Manu : with the wisdom and authority of Manu who was instructed directly by the Gods.

2 *Compassed by the Dragon* : obstructed by the great serpent Ahi.

The Dāsa : 'the savage or demon Ahi. See I. 32. 11.

3 *Songs of Rudras* : like those sung by the Rudras or Maruts, Indra's allies.

These streams : sacrificial waters or libations. *Vāyu*, the God of wind, was entitled to the first draught of the Soma juice. See verse 14 of this hymn.

4 *Splendid* : the word *śubhrā*, splendid, occurs in all three places in the text.

5 *Concealed in depths* : of the atmosphere.

6 *Heralds of Sūrya* : announcing the coming of the sunlight after the heavy rain which Indra has sent.

We laud the bolt that in thine arms lies eager ; we laud thy two Bay Steeds, heralds of Sūrya.

7 Indra, thy Bay Steeds showing forth their vigour have sent a loud cry out that droppeth fatness.

The earth hath spread herself in all her fulness : the cloud that was about to move hath rested.

8 Down, never ceasing, hath the rain-cloud settled : bellowing, it hath wandered with the Mothers.

Swelling the roar in the far distant limits, they have spread wide the blast sent forth by Indra.

9 Indra hath hurled down the magician Vṛtra who lay beleaguering the mighty river.

Then both the heaven and earth trembled in terror at the strong Hero's thunder when he bellowed.

10 Loud roared the mighty Hero's bolt of thunder, when he, the Friend of man, burnt up the monster,

And, having drunk his fill of flowing Soma, baffled the guileful Dānava's devices.

11 Drink thou, O Hero Indra, drink the Soma; let the joy-giving juices make thee joyful.

They, filling both thy flanks, shall swell thy vigour. The juice that satisfies hath helped Indra.

12 Singers have we become with thee, O Indra : may we serve duly and prepare devotion.

Seeking thy help we meditate thy praises: may we at once enjoy thy gift of riches.

13 May we be thine, such by thy help, O Indra, as swell thy vigour while they seek thy favour.

Give us, thou God, the riches that we long for, most powerful, with store of noble children.

14 Give us a friend, give us an habitation; Indra, give us the company of Maruts,

And those whose minds accord with theirs, the Vāyus, who drink the first libation of the Soma.

15 Let those enjoy in whom thou art delighted. Indra, drink Soma for thy strength and gladness.

Thou hast exalted us to heaven, Preserver, in battles, through the lofty hymns that praise thee.

16 Great, verily, are they, O thou Protector, who by their songs of praise have won the blessing.

They who strew sacred grass to be thy dwelling, helped by thee have got them strength, O Indra.

17 Upon the great Trikadruka days, Hero, rejoicing thee, O Indra, drink the Soma.

Come with Bay Steeds to drink of libation, shaking the drops from out thy beard, contented.

18 Hero, assume the might wherewith thou clavest Vṛtra piecemeal, the Dānava Aurṇavābha.

Thou hast disclosed the light to light the Ārya : on thy left hand, O Indra, sank the Dasyu.

19 May we gain wealth, subduing with thy succour and with the Ārya, all our foes, the Dasyus.

Our gain was that to Tṛta of our party thou gavest up Tvaṣṭar's son Viśvarūpa.

20 He cast down Arbuda what time his vigour was strengthened by libations poured by Tṛta.

Indra sent forth his whirling wheel like Sūrya, and aided by the Aṅgirases rent Vala.

7 *The loud cry that droppeth fatness* : is the thunder that precedes the fertilizing rain. *The earth hath spread herself* : to receive the rain.

8 *The Mothers* : the original waters above the firmament.

They : Indra's attendants, the Maruts or Storm-Gods.

9 *The mighty river* : the great cloud that holds the rain.

10 *The guileful Dānava's devices* : the magic arts of the demon Vṛtra.

14 *The Vāyus* : the plural is used honorifically for the singular.

17 *Trikadruka days* : the first three days of the Abhiplava festival.

18 *Aurṇavābha* : son of Urṇavābha, a demon *The Dasyu* : the barbarian, the original inhabitant of the land. According to Sāyaṇa the demon Vṛtra is meant.

19 It is difficult to make anything intelligible of this stanza. *Trita* is said by Sāyaṇa to be a *Maharṣi* or great *Ṛṣi*, and Viśvarūpa is said to be a three-headed monster slain by Indra. See Sacred Books of the East, XII. 164. Prof. Macdonell's interpretation of the stanza has much to recommend it : 'That we, overcoming all our foes by thy aids, (and) the barbarian by Āryan prowess, might prosper, therefore for our benefit thou didst deliver over Viśvarūpa, the son of Tvaṣṭṛ, to the Tṛta of (thy) frindship', i.e. to thy ally, the God Trita. See J.R.A.S., July, 1893 pp. 432, 433.

20 *Arbuda* : a demon of the atmosphere. See I. 51 6.

Sent forth his whirling wheel : Indra is said to have used a wheel of the Sun's chariot as a missile.

Vala : the brother of Vṛtra or Vṛtra himself. See I. 11. 5.

21 Now let that wealthy Cow of thine, O Indra, yield in return a boon to him who lauds thee.
Give to thy praisers : let not fortune fail us. Loud may we speak, with brave men, in the assembly.

HYMN XII. *Indra.*

1. HE who, just born, chief God of lofty spirit by power and might became the Gods' protector,
Before whose breath through greatness of his valour the two worlds trembled, He, O men, is Indra.

2 He who fixed fast and firm the earth that staggered, and set at rest the agitated mountains,
Who measured out the air's wide middle region and gave the heaven support, He, men, is Indra.

3 Who slew the Dragon, freed the Seven Rivers, and drove the kine forth from the cave of Vala,
Begat the fire between two stones, the spoiler in warriors' battle, He, O men, is Indra.

4 By whom this universe was made to tremble, who chased away the humbled brood of demons,
Who, like a gambler gathering his winnings seized the foe's riches, He, O men, is Indra.

5 Of whom, the Terrible, they ask, Where is He ? or verily they say of him, He is not.
He sweeps away, like birds, the foe's possessions. Have faith in him, for He, O men, is Indra.

6 Stirrer to action of the poor and lowly, of priest, of suppliant who sings his praises;
Who, fair-faced, favours him who presses Soma with stones made ready, He, O men, is Indra.

7 He under whose supreme control are horses, all chariots, and the villages, and cattle ;
He who gave being to the Sun and Morning, who leads the waters, He, O men, is Indra.

8 To whom two armies cry in close encounter, both enemies, the stronger and the weaker ;
Whom two invoke upon one chariot mounted, each for himself, He, O ye men, is Indra.

9 Without whose help our people never conquer ; whom, battling, they invoke to give them succour ;
He of whom all this world is but the copy, who shakes things moveless, He, O men, is Indra.

10 He who hath smitten, ere they knew their danger, with his hurled weapon many grievous sinners ;
Who pardons not his boldness who provokes him, who slays the Dasyu, He, O men, is Indra.

11 He who discovered in the fortieth autumn Śambara as he dwelt among the mountains;
Who slew the Dragon putting forth his vigour, the demon lying there, He, men, is Indra.

12 Who with seven guiding reins, the Bull, the Mighty, set free the Seven great Floods to flow at pleasure;
Who, thunder-armed, rent Rauhiṇa in pieces when scaling heaven, He, O ye men, is Indra.

13 Even the Heaven and Earth bow down before him, before his very breath the mountains tremble.
Known as the Soma-drinker, armed with thunder, who wields the bolt, He, O ye men, is Indra.

14 Who aids with favour him who pours the Soma and him who brews it, sacrificer, singer.
Whom prayer exalts, and pouring forth of Soma, and this our gift, He, O ye men, is Indra.

15 Thou verily art fierce and true who sendest strength to the man who brews and pours libation.
So may we evermore, thy friends, O Indra, speak loudly to the synod with our heroes.

21 *That wealthy Cow of thine* : meaning, probably, Uṣas or Dawn, who brings good gifts to man. Or *sā dakṣiṇā maghoni* may be translated 'that liberal meed' of thine, that is the rich reward which Indra bestows upon his worshippers, regarded as the counterpart of the *dakṣiṇā* or honorarium given by the institutors of sacrifices to the priests who perform the ceremonies.

3 *Begat the fire between two stones* : generated lightning between heaven and earth.

5 *Like birds* : as birds are captured by the fowler. According to others 'like stakes of gamblers,' the meaning of *vijaḥ* being uncertain. See I. 92. 10, note.

7 *Who leads the waters* : brings the periodical rains.

8 *Whom two invoke* : the warrior and the charioteer.

12 *Seven guiding reins* : or, according to Ludwig, seven bright rays, said to mean seven forms of Indra. *Rauhiṇa*: the name of a demon of drought.

15 *With our heroes*: with our brave sons around us.

HYMN XIII. *Indra.*

1. The Season was the parent, and when born therefrom it entered rapidly the floods wherein it grows.
Thence was it full of sap, streaming with milky juice : the milk of the plant's stalk is chief and meet for lauds.

2 They come trooping together bearing milk to him, and bring him sustenance who gives support to all.
The way is common for the downward streams to flow. Thou who didst these things first art worthy of our lauds.

3 One priest announces what the institutor gives : one, altering the forms, zealously plies his task,
The third corrects the imperfections left by each. Thou who didst these things first art worthy of our lauds.

4 Dealing out food unto their people there they sit, like wealth to him who comes, more than the back can bear.
Greedily with his teeth he eats the master's food. Thou who didst these things first art worthy of our lauds.

5 Thou hast created earth to look upon the sky : thou, slaying Ahi, settest free the river's paths.
Thee, such, a God, the Gods have quickened with their lauds, even as a steed with waters : meet for praise art thou.

6 Thou givest increase, thou dealest to us our food : thou milkest from the moist the dry, the rich in sweets.
Thou by the worshipper layest thy precious store : thou art sole Lord of all. Meet for our praise art thou.

7 Thou who hast spread abroad the streams by stablished law, and in the field the plants that blossom and bear seed ;
Thou who hast made the matchless lightnings of the sky,—vast, compassing vast realms, meet for our praise art thou.

8 Who broughtest Nārmara with all his wealth, for sake of food, to slay him that the fiends might be destroyed,
Broughtest the face unclouded of the strengthening one, performing much even now, worthy art thou of praise.

9 Thou boundest up the Dāsa's hundred friends and ten, when, at one's hearing, thou helpest thy worshipper.
Thou for Dabhīti boundest Dasyus not with cords ; thou wast a mighty help. Worthy of lauds art thou.

10 All banks of rivers yielded to his manly might ; to him they gave, to him, the Strong, gave up their wealth.
The six directions hast thou fixed, a fivefold view : thy victories reached afar. Worthy of lauds art thou.

11 Meet for high praise, O Hero, is thy power, that with thy single wisdom thou obtainest wealth,
The life-support of conquering Jātūṣṭhira. Indra, for all thy deeds, worthy of lauds art thou.

1 *The Season* : the Rains, the most important of the season. So monsoon, a corruption of *mousim*, any season, means the Rains especially. *It* : the Soma-plant.

2 *They come* : probably the cows whose milk is to be used in sacrifice.

The way is common : referring to the water used in the Soma ceremony. Sāyaṇa explains the stanza differently, and Wilson paraphrases it thus : 'The aggregated (streams) come, bearing everywhere the water, and conveying it as sustenance for the asylum of all rivers, (the ocean) : the same path is assigned to all the descending (currents) to follow; and as he who has (assigned) them (their course), thou, (Indra), art especially to be praised.'

3 According to Sāyaṇa three priests are here indicated, the Hotar who announces the sacrifice, the Adhvaryu who apportions the several pieces of the victim, and the Brahman who corrects mistakes and remedies defects in the ritual.

The first four stanzas are full of difficulties and in places absolutely unintelligible. My version of stanza 3, which generally follows Sāyaṇa, will not bear critical examination, but at present I have nothing better to propose.

4 *There they sit* : according to Sāyaṇa, 'the householders abide in their homes.' *To him who comes* : to a guest. *He eats the master's food* : probably, Agni consumes the oblations of the householder.

6 *Thou milkest from the moist* : producest the dry nutritious grain from the moist stalk.

8 This stanza is unintelligible. *Nārmara* : said to be a fiend slain by Indra.

The strengthening one : according to Sāyaṇa, Ūrjayantī is the name of a female demon or Piśācī. Grassmann takes it to mean the Sun. Ludwig thinks it is the name of a stronghold used as a store-house of provisions.

9 The meaning of the first half-verse is uncertain, the text being evidently corrupt. I adopt Ludwig's emendation, *dāsasya*, in place of the unintelligible *vā yāsya*.

Dabhīti : a Ṛṣi named in I. 112.23. *Not with cords*: in a prison without cords, the grave.

10 *All banks of rivers* : the dams that prevented the rivers of the clouds from flowing. *The six directions* : above, below, before, behind, right, left. *The fivefold view* : inasmuch as we cannot see what is below the ground. Sāyaṇa explains the *ṣaḍ viṣṭiraḥ* as heaven, earth, day, night, water, and plants, and the *Pañca sandṛśaḥ* as the five races of men.

11 *Jātūṣṭhira* : a certain man of that name, says Sāyaṇa; perhaps the institutor of the sacrifice.

12 Thou for Turvīti heldest still the flowing floods, the river-stream for Vayya easily to pass,
Didst raise the outcast from the depths, and gavest fame unto the halt and blind. Worthy of lauds art thou.

13 Prepare thyself to grant us that great bounty, O Vasu, for abundant is thy treasure.
Snatch up the wonderful, O Indra, daily. Loud may we speak, with heroes, in assembly.

HYMN XIV. *Indra.*

1. MINISTERS, bring the Soma juice for Indra, pour forth the gladdening liquor with the beakers.
To drink of this the Hero longeth ever; offer it to the Bull, for this he willeth.

2 Ye ministers, to him who with the lightning smote, like a tree, the rain-withholding Vṛtra—
Bring it to him, him who is fain to taste it, a draught of this which Indra here deserveth.

3 Ye ministers, to him who smote Dṛbhīka, who drove the kine forth, and discovered Vala,
Offer this draught, like Vāta in the region: clothe him with Soma even as steeds with trappings.

4 Him who did Uraṇa to death, Adhvaryus! though showing arms ninety-and-nine in number;
Who cast down headlong Arbuda and slew him,—speed ye that Indra to our offered Soma.

5 Ye ministers, to him who struck down Svaśna, and did to death Vyaṁsa and greedy Śuṣṇa,
And Rudhikrās and Namuci and Pipru,—to him, to Indra, pour ye forth libation.

6 Ye ministers, to him who, as with thunder demolished Śambara's hundred ancient castles;
Who cast down Varcin's sons, a hundred thousand,—to him, to Indra, offer ye the Soma.

7 Ye ministers, to him who slew a hundred thousand, and cast them down upon earth's bosom;
Who quelled the valiant men of Atithigva, Kutsa, and Āyu,—bring to him the Soma.

8 Ministers, men, whatever thing ye long for obtain ye quickly bringing gifts to Indra.
Bring to the Glorious One what hands have cleansed; to Indra bring, ye pious ones, the Soma.

9 Do ye, O ministers, obey his order: that purified in wood, in wood uplift ye.
Well pleased he longs for what your hands have tended: offer the gladdening Soma juice to Indra.

10 As the cow's udder teems with milk, Adhvaryus, so fill with Soma Indra, liberal giver.
I know him: I am sure of this, the Holy knows that I fain would give to him more largely.

11 Him, ministers, the Lord of heavenly treasure and all terrestrial wealth that earth possesses,
Him, Indra, fill with Soma as a garner is filled with barley full: be this your labour.

12 Prepare thyself to grant us that great booty, O Vasu, for abundant is thy treasure.
Gather up wondrous wealth, O Indra, daily. Loud may we speak, with heroes, in assembly.

12 *Turvīti* and *Vayya* appear to have been enabled to ford a great river by the aid of Indra. See I. 61 11. Turvīti was the son of Vayya. See I. 54. 6.

The outcast: or Parāvṛj as a proper name. See I. 112. 8, where the miracle is ascribed to the Aśvins.

13 *Snatch up the wonderful*: that is, gain quickly wondrous wealth. This appears to be the literal meaning of the words which Wilson paraphrases, after Sāyaṇa: 'mayest thou be disposed to grant us exceeding abundance.

---

1 *Ministers*: Adhvaryus, or priests, whose duty was to make the preparations for sacrifice.

3 *Dṛbhīka*: one of the numerous demons slain by Indra.

Like Vāta in the region: bringing rain, as the Wind-God does.

As steeds with trappings: the meaning of *jūḥ* is uncertain. Sāyaṇa explains it, 'as an old man (is covered) with garments.'

4 *Uraṇa*: another demon. *Arbuda*: a demon mentioned in I. 51. 6.

5 *Śuṣṇa*, *Vyaṁsa*, and the rest, are demons, some of whom have been previously mentioned.

6 *Śambara*: a fiend mentioned several times in Book. I. *Varcin*: a demon who reviled Indra, and was slain with all his sons and followers.

7 *The valiant men*: *virān*; heroes. Sāyaṇa supplies 'assailants,' as Atithigva, Kutsa, and Āyu appear in Book I, as favoured by Indra. Here their battle with Tūrvayāṇa (I. 53. 10) is referred to.

9 *In wood*: in the wooden receptacle.

HYMN XV. *Indra*

1. Now, verily, will I declare the exploits, mighty and true, of him the True and Mighty.
In the Trikadrukas he drank the Soma: then in its rapture Indra slew the Dragon.

2 High heaven unsupported in space he stablished: he filled the two worlds and the air's mid-region.
Earth he upheld, and gave it wide expansion. These things did Indra in the Soma's rapture.

3 From front, as 'twere a house, he ruled and measured; pierced with his bolt the fountains of the rivers,
And made them flow at ease by paths far-reaching, These things did Indra in the Soma's rapture.

4 Compassing those who bore away Dabhīti, in kindled fire he burnt up all their weapons.
And made him rich with kine and cars and horses. These things did Indra in the Soma's rapture.

5 The mighty roaring flood he stayed from flowing, and carried those who swam not safely over.
They having crossed the stream attained to riches. These things did Indra in the Soma's rapture.

6 With mighty power he made the stream flow upward, crushed with his thunderbolt the car of Uṣas,
Rending her slow steeds with his rapid coursers. These things did Indra in the Soma's rapture.

7 Knowing the place wherein the maids were hiding, the outcast showed himself and stood before them.
The cripple stood erect, the blind beheld them. These things did Indra in the Soma's rapture.

8 Praised by the Aṅgirases he slaughtered Vala, and burst apart the bulwarks of the mountain.
He tore away their deftly-built defences. These things did Indra in the Soma's rapture.

9 Thou, with sleep whelming Cumuri and Dhuni, slewest the Dasyu, keptest safe Dabhīti.
There the staff-bearer found the golden treasure. These things did Indra in the Soma's rapture.

10 Now let that wealthy Cow of thine, O Indra, yield in return a boon to him who lauds thee.
Give to thy praisers: let not fortune fail us. Loud may we speak, with brave men, in assembly.

1 *In The Trikadrukas*: See II. 11. 17. *In its rapture*: in the exhilaration produced by drinking the fermented juice. See I. 51. 2 and note.

3 *From front, as 'twere a house*: the formation of the world is compared to the building of a house. Wilson renders: '(He it is) who has measured the eastern (quarters) with measures like a chamber.'

4 *Dabhīti*: See II. 13. 9.

5 Cf. I. 13. 12.

6 *The car of Uṣas*: the destruction of the chariot of Uṣas or Dawn by Indra is described more fully in IV. 30. 8.

7 Parāvṛj, here rendered 'the outcast,' is taken by Sāyaṇa as the name of a Ṛṣi who was lame and blind. When some girls made sport of him he prayed to Indra and was made sound.

9 *Cumuri and Dhuni*: Asuras or demons.

The staff-bearer: the door-keeper, or chamberlain, of Dabhīti. '*The golden treasure*: of Cumuri and Dhuni.

HYMN XVI *Indra.*

1. To him, your own, the best among the good, I bring eulogy, like oblation in the kindled fire.
We invocate for help Indra untouched by eld, who maketh all decay, strengthened, for ever young.

2 Without whom naught exists, Indra the Lofty One; in whom alone all powers heroic are combined.
The Soma is within him, in his frame vast strength, the thunder in his hand and wisdom in his head.

3 Not by both worlds is thine own power to be surpassed, nor may thy car be stayed by mountains or by seas.
None cometh near, O Indra, to thy thunderbolt, when with swift steeds thou fliest over many a league.

4 For all men bring their will to him the Resolute, to him the Holy One, to him the Strong they cleave.
Pay worship with oblation, strong and passing wise. Drink thou the Soma, Indra, through the mighty blaze.

1 *Like oblation*: praise that magnifies and strengthens Indra as oblations of clarified butter cast into the fire increase the flame.

5 The vessel of the strong flows forth, the flood of meath, unto the Strong who feeds upon the strong, for drink,
Strong are the two Adhvaryus, strong are both the stones. They press the Soma that is strong for him the Strong.

6 Strong is thy thunderbolt, yea, and thy car is strong; strong are thy Bay Steeds and thy weapons powerful.
Thou, Indra, Bull, art Lord of the strong gladdening drink: with the strong Soma, Indra, satisfy thyself.

7 I, bold by prayer, come near thee in thy sacred rites, thee like a saving ship, thee shouting in the war.
Verily he will hear and mark this word of ours: we will pour Indra forth as 'twere a spring of wealth.

8 Turn thee unto us ere calamity come nigh, as a cow full of pasture turns her to her calf.
Lord of a Hundred Powers, may we once firmly cling to thy fair favours even as husbands to their wives.

9 Now let that wealthy Cow of thine, O Indra, yield in return a boon to him who lauds thee.
Give to thy praisers: let not fortune fail us. Loud may we speak, with heroes, in assembly.

HYMN XVII. *Indra.*

1. LIKE the Aṅgirases, sing this new song forth to him, for, as in ancient days, his mighty powers are shown,
When in the rapture of the Soma he unclosed with strength the solid firm-shut stables of the kine.

2 Let him be even that God who, for the earliest draught measuring out his power, increased his majesty;
Hero who fortified his body in the wars, and through his greatness set the heaven upon his head.

3 Thou didst perform thy first great deed of hero might what time thou showedst power, through prayer, before this folk.
Hurled down by thee the car-borne Lord of Tawny Steeds, the congregated swift ones fled in sundry ways.

4 He made himself by might Lord of all living things, and strong in vital power waxed great above them all.
He, borne on high, o'erspread with light the heaven and earth, and, sewing up the turbid darkness, closed it in.

5 He with his might made firm the forward-bending hills, the downward rushing of the waters he ordained.
Fast he upheld the earth that nourisheth all life, and stayed the heaven from falling by his wondrous skill.

6 Fit for the grasping of his arms is what the Sire hath fabricated from all kind of precious wealth.
The thunderbolt, wherewith, loud-roaring, he smote down, and striking him to death laid Krivi on the earth.

7 As she who in her parents' house is growing old, I pray to thee as Bhaga from the seat of all.
Grant knowledge, mete it out and bring it to us here: give us the share wherewith thou makest people glad.

8 May we invoke thee as a liberal giver: thou givest us, O Indra, strength and labours.
Help us with manifold assistance, Indra: Migthy One, Indra, make us yet more wealthy.

9 Now may that wealthy Cow of thine, O Indra, give in return a boon to him who lauds thee.
Give to thy praisers: let not fortune fail us. Loud may we speak, with heroes, in assembly.

HYMN XVIII *Indra*

1. THE rich new car hath been equipped at morning; four yokes it hath, three whips, seven reins to guide it:

5 *The vessel of the strong*: the reservoir containing the strong Soma. In reference to the repetition of the word 'strong' in this and the following stanza see I. 177. 2, 3.

Both the stones: for pressing out the Soma juice.

1 Praise Indra after the manner of the ancient Aṅgirases with a new song, because his ancient deeds are continually renewed for our advantage.

2 *Fortified his body*: protected it with a coat of mail.

3 *The congregated swift ones*: according to Sāyaṇa, the Asuras or enemies of the Gods. According to Roth the waters of the heaven.

4 *Borne on high*: or perhaps 'luminous,' as Prof. Max Müller renders it.

5 *Forward-bending*: ready to fall until Indra fixed them.

6 *Krivi*: *originally* 'a leather bag' and metaphorically 'a cloud', said by Sāyaṇa to be an Asura or demon.

7 *As Bhaga*: as the God who distributes wealth, and also presides over love and marriage. *From the seat of all*: from the hall of sacrifice where seats of sacred grass are provided for all the Gods.

1 *The rich new car* is the morning sacrifice which travels to the Gods and obtains wealth for the worshipper. The *four yokes* are the four pair of stones for pressing out the Soma juice; the *three whips* are the three tones of

Ten-sided, friendly to mankind, light-winner, that must be urged to speed with prayers and wishes.

2 This is prepared for him the first, the second, and the third time : he is man's Priest and Herald.

Others get offspring of another parent : he goeth, as a noble Bull, with others.

3 To Indra's car the Bay Steeds have I harnessed, that new well-spoken words may bring him hither.

Here let not other worshippers detain thee, for among us are many holy singers.

4 Indra, come hitherward with two Bay Coursers, come thou with four, with six when invocated.

Come thou with eight, with ten, to drink the Soma. Here is the juice, brave Warrior : do not scorn it.

5 O Indra, come thou hither having harnessed thy car with twenty, thirty, forty horses.

Come thou with fifty well trained coursers, Indra, sixty or seventy, to drink the Soma.

6 Come to us hitherward, O Indra, carried by eighty, ninety, or an hundred horses.

This Soma juice among the Śunahotras hath been poured out, in love, to glad thee, Indra.

7 To this my prayer, O Indra, come thou hither : bind to thy car's pole all thy two Bay Coursers.

Thou art to be invoked in many places : Hero, rejoice thyself in this libation.

8 Ne'er be my love from Indra disunited : still may his liberal Milch-cow yield us treasure.

So may we under his supreme protection, safe in his arms, succeed in each forthgoing.

9 Now may that wealthy Cow of thine, O Indra, give in return a boon to him who lauds thee.

Give to thy praisers : let not fortune fail us. Loud may we speak, with heroes, in assembly.

HYMN XIX *Indra.*

1. DRAUGHTS of this sweet juice have been drunk for rapture, of the wise Soma-presser's offered dainty,

Wherein, grown mighty in the days aforetime, Indra hath found delight, and men who worship.

2 Cheered by this meath Indra, whose hand wields thunder, rent piecemeal Ahi who barred up the waters,

So that the quickening currents of the rivers flowed forth like birds unto their resting-places.

3 Indra, this Mighty One, the Dragon's slayer, sent forth the flood of waters to the ocean.

He gave the Sun his life, he found the cattle, and with the night the works of days completed.

4 To him who worshippeth hath Indra given many and matchless gifts. He slayeth Vṛtra.

Straight was he to be sought with supplications by men who struggled to obtain the sunlight.

5 To him who poured him gifts he gave up Sūrya,—Indra, the God, the Mighty, to the mortal;

prayer; the *seven reins* are the seven metres. The meaning of *dáśāritrah*, 'ten-sided,' is not clear. Sāyaṇa explains *aritrāḥ* as 'preservers from enemies, *i. e.* sins,' the planets. Grassman thinks that wheels are meant.

2 *The first, the second, and the third time* : the three daily sacrifices are referred to. *He is man's Priest* : Agni must be meant.

The second hemistich is obscure. Wilson, after Sāyaṇa, paraphrases: 'Other (priests) engender the embryo of a different (rite), but this victorious (sacrifice), the showerer (of benefits) combines with other (ceremonies).'

4 *With two Bay Coursers* : this is the usual number. The progressive multiplication in this and the following stanzas is perhaps intended to indicate the ever increasing rapidity with which the eager worshipper prays Indra to approach. The Scholiast says that by their supernatural power the two horses of Indra multiply themselves indefinitely.

6 *The Śunahotras* : apparently a family so called; etymologically 'those who sacrifice with happy result.' According to Sāyaṇa, *śunahotrāḥ* means certain vessels into which the Soma juice was poured.

1 *Have been drunk* : by Indra.

3 *And with the night* : perhaps, by giving the night for rest enabled men to perform the labours of the day. Or, as *aktúnā* may mean 'by light.' 'effected the manifestation of the days by light, as Wilson renders it after Sāyaṇa.

5 See I. 61. 15. The legend says that a certain King who wished for son worshipped Sūrya who, to grant his prayer, was born himself as the King's son. Afterwards when some dispute arose between this King's son who was named Sūrya and the Ṛṣi Etaśa, Indra sided with the latter. In I. 61. 15, a chariot race appears to be referred to, and I have translated the passage accordingly, following Sāyaṇa in taking Sūrya to be the name of a man. If, however, as is very possible, Sūrya there is the Sun-God the meaning is that Indra, in order to favour his faithful worshipper Etaṣa, compelled Sūrya or the Sun to bring back his chariot and horses to the east; that is the return of day on some particular occasion is attributed to Indra's intervention on behalf of his favourite. This appears to be the meaning of this verse also. See also I. 121. 13.

For Etaśa with worship brought him riches that keep distress afar, as 'twere his portion.

6 Once to the driver of his chariot, Kutsa, he gave up greedy Śuṣṇa, plague of harvest;
And Indra, for the sake of Divodāsa demolished Śambara's nine-and-ninety castles.

7 So have we brought our hymn to thee, O Indra, strengthening thee and fain ourselves for glory.
May we with best endeavours gain this friendship, and mayst thou bend the godless scorner's weapons.

8 Thus the Gṛtsamadas for thee, O Hero, have wrought their hymn and task as seeking favour.
May they who worship thee afresh, O Indra, gain food and strength, bliss, and a happy dwelling.

9 Now may that wealthy Cow of thine, O Indra, give in return a boon to him who lauds thee,
Give to thy praisers : let not fortune fail us. Loud may we speak, with heroes, in assembly.

HYMN XX *Indra.*

1. As one brings forth his car when fain for combat, so bring we power to thee—regard us, Indra—
Well skilled in song, thoughtful in spirit, seeking great bliss from one like thee amid the Heroes.

2 Indra, thou art our own with thy protection, a guardian near to men who love thee truly,
Active art thou, the liberal man's defender, his who draws near to thee with right devotion.

3 May Indra, called with solemn invocations, the young, the Friend, be men's auspicious keeper,
One who will further with his aid the singer, the toiler, praiser, dresser of oblations.

4 With laud and song let me extol that Indra in whom of old men prospered and were mighty.
May he, implored, fulfil the prayer for plenty of him who worships, of the living mortal.

5 He, Indra whom the Aṅgirases' praise delighted, strengthened their prayer and made their goings prosper.
Stealing away the mornings with the sunlight, he, lauded, crushed even Aśna's ancient powers.

6 He verily, the God, the glorious Indra, hath raised him up for man, best Wonder-Worker.
He, self-reliant, mighty and triumphant, brought low the dear head of the wicked Dāsa.

7 Indra the Vṛtra-slayer, Fort-destroyer, scattered the Dāsa hosts who dwelt in darkness.
For men hath he created earth and waters, and ever helped the prayer of him who worships.

8 To him in might the Gods have ever yielded, to Indra in the tumult of the battle.
When in his arms they laid the bolt, he slaughtered the Dasyus and cast down their forts of iron.

9 Now may that wealthy Cow of thine, O Indra, give in return a boon to him who lauds thee.
Give to thy praisers : let not fortune fail us. Loud may we speak, with heroes, in assembly.

As 'twere his portion : as (a father gives) his portion (to a son), according to Sāyaṇa.

6 *Kutsa* and *Divodāsa*, favourites of Indra, and *Śuṣṇa* and *Śambara*, demons of drought, have occurred frequently in Book I.

---

1 *For combat* : or, perhaps, for the race.

3 *The toiler* : the man who labours in the discharge of religious duties.

4 *The living mortal* : the present worshipper, as distinguished from the men of old.

5 *Made their goings prosper* : by recovering for them the stolen cows, frequently mentioned in Book I. *Aśna*, 'the voracious,' said to be the name of a demon, one of the many foes overthrown by Indra.

6 *Dāsa* : said by Sāyaṇa to be an Asura, or demon of that name. The word is frequently applied to the foes of the Āryas, to the malignant demons of the air as well as to the barbarous and hostile inhabitants of the land, and it is not always clear whether human or superhuman enemies are intended.

The dear head : the Dāsa's own head.

7 *The Dāsa hosts who dwelt in darkness* : the words thus rendered are variously explained. It is uncertain whether the aborigines of the country are meant, or the demons of air who dwell in the dark clouds.

8 *The Dasyus* : the Asuras or demons, according to Sāyaṇa.

HYMN XXI

1. To him the Lord of all, the Lord of wealth, of light; him who is Lord for ever, Lord of men and tilth,
Him who is Lord of horses, Lord of kine, of floods, to Indra, to the Holy bring sweet Soma juice.

2 To him the potent One, who conquers and breaks down, the Victor never vanquished who disposes all,
The mighty-voiced, the rider, unassailable, to Indra everconquering speak your reverent prayer.

3 Still Victor, loved by mortals, ruler over men, o'erthrower, warrior, he hath waxen as he would;
Host-gatherer, triumphant, honoured mid the folk. Indra's heroic deeds will I tell forth to all.

4 The strong who never yields, who slew the furious fiend, the deep, the vast, of wisdom unattainable;
Who speeds the good, the breaker-down, the firm, the vast,—Indra whose rites bring joy hath made the light of Dawn.

5 By sacrifice the yearning sages sending forth their songs found furtherance from him who speeds the flood.
In Indra seeking help with worship and with hymn, they drew him to themselves and won them kine and wealth.

6 Indra, bestow on us the best of treasures, the spirit of ability and fortune;
Increase of riches, safety of our bodies, charm of sweet speech, and days of pleasant weather.

HYMN XXII. *Indra.*

1. At the Trikadrukas the Great and Strong hath drunk drink blent with meal. With Viṣṇu hath he quaffed the poured out Soma juice, all that he would.
That hath so heightened him the Great, the Wide, to do his mighty work.
So may the God attain the God, true Indu Indra who is true.

2 So he resplendent in the battle overcame Krivi by might. He with his majesty hath filled the earth and heaven, and waxen strong.
One share of the libation hath he swallowed down : one share he left.
So may the God attend the God, true Indu Indra who is true.

3 Brought forth together with wisdom and mighty power thou grewest great; with hero deeds subduing the malevolent, most swift in act;
Giving prosperity, and lovely wealth to him who praiseth thee. So may the God attend the God, true Indu Indra who is true.

4 This, Indra, was thy hero deed, Dancer, thy first and ancient work, worthy to be told forth in heaven,
What time thou sentest down life with a God's own power, freeing the floods.
All that is godless may he conquer with his might, and, Lord of Hundred Powers, find for us strength and food.

HYMN XXIII. *Brahmaṇaspati.*

1. We call thee, Lord and Leader of the heavenly hosts, the wise among the wise, the famousest of all,
The King supreme of prayers, O Brahmaṇaspati : hear us with help ; sit down in place of sacrifice.

2 Bṛhaspati, God immortal ! verily the Gods have gained from thee, the wise, a share in holy rites.
As with great light the Sun brings forth the rays of morn, so thou alone art Father of all sacred prayer.

3 When thou hast chased away revilers and the gloom, thou mountest the refulgent car of sacrifice ;
The awful car, Bṛhaspati, that quells the foe, slays demons, cleaves the stall of kine, and finds the light.

1 *The Lord* : literally, conqueror of all, of wealth, etc.
2 *Mighty-voiced* : Sāyaṇa gives two explanations, 'having a full throat,' or 'praised by many.' *Rider* : borne through the sky.
4 *The furious fiend* : Vṛtra.
6 *Ability* : to perform sacred ceremonies, according to Sāyaṇa.

1 *The Trikadrukas* : the first three days of the Abhiplava ceremony.
Indu : a drop, especially of Soma juice, another name of the deified Soma.
2 *Krivi* : a demon, See II. 17. 6.
4 Dancer : active in battle, dancer of the war-dance.

1 *Brahmaṇaspati* : alternating with Bṛhaspati, the Deity in whom the action of the worshipper upon the Gods is personified. See I. 14. 3. A comparatively recent God, as the representative of the hierarchy, he is gradually encroaching on the jurisdiction of Indra the Worrior God of the Kṣatriyas, claiming his achievements as his own and assuming his attributes. See Weber, Uber den Vājapeya, Sitzungsberichte der K. P. Academie der Wissenschaften, 1892, XXXIX, p. 15.
3 *Revilers* : blaspheming demons of darkness. *Cleaves the stall of kine* : opens the prison where the cows or rays of light have been shut up.

4 Thou leadest with good guidance and preservest men ; distress o'ertakes not him who offers gifts to thee.
Him who hates prayer thou punishest, Bṛhaspati, quelling his wrath : herein is thy great mightiness.

5 No sorrow, no distress from any side, no foes, no creatures double-tongued have overcome the man,—
Thou drivest all seductive fiends away from him whom, careful guard, thou keepest Brahmaṇaspati.

6 Thou art our keeper, wise, preparer of our paths : we, for thy service, sing to thee with hymns of praise.
Bṛhaspati, whoever lays a snare for us, him may his evil fate, precipitate, destroy.

7 Him, too, who threatens us without offence of ours, the evilminded, arrogant, rapacious man,—
Him turn thou from our path away, Bṛhaspati : give us fair access to this banquet of the Gods.

8 Thee as protector of our bodies we invoke, thee, saviour, as the comforter who loveth us.
Strike, O Bṛhaspati, the Gods' revilers down, and let not the unrighteous come to highest bliss.

9 Through thee, kind prosperer, O Brahmaṇaspati, may we obtain the wealth of men which all desire :
And all our enemies, who near or far away prevail against us, crush, and leave them destitute.

10 With thee as our own rich and liberal ally may we, Bṛhaspati, gain highest power of life.
Let not the guileful wicked man be lord of us : still may we prosper, singing goodly hymns of praise.

11 Strong, never yielding, hastening to the battle-cry, consumer of the foe, victorious in the strife,
Thou art sin's true avenger, Brahmaṇspati, who tamest e'en the fierce, the wildly passionate.

12 Whoso with mind ungodly seeks to do us harm, who, deeming him a man of might mid lords, would slay,—
Let not his deadly blow reach us, Bṛhaspati ; may we humiliate the strong ill-doer's wrath.

13 The mover mid the spoil, the winner of all wealth, to be invoked in fight and reverently adored,
Bṛhaspati hath overthrown like cars of war all wicked enemies who fain would injure us.

14 Burn up the demons with thy fiercest flaming brand, those who have scorned thee in thy manifested might.
Show forth that power that shall deserve the hymn of praise : destroy the evil speakers, O Bṛhaspati.

15 Bṛhaspati, that which the foe deserves not which shines among the folk effectual, splendid,
That, Son of Law ! which is with might refulgent—that treasure wonderful bestow thou on us.

16 Give us not up to those who, foes in ambuscade, are greedy for the wealth of him who sits at ease,
Who cherish in their heart abandonment of Gods. Bṛhaspati, no further rest shall they obtain.

17 For Tvaṣṭar, he who knows each sacred song, brought thee to life, preëminent o'er all the things that be.
Guilt-scourger, guilt-avenger is Bṛhaspati, who slays the spoiler and upholds the mighty Law.

18 The mountain, for thy glory, cleft itself apart when, Aṅgiras ! thou openedst the stall of kine.
Thou, O Bṛhaspati, with Indra for ally didst hurl down water-floods which gloom had compassed round.

19 O Brahmaṇaspati, be thou controller of this our hymn and prosper thou our children.
All that the Gods regard with love is blessed. Loud may we speak, with heroes, in assembly.

HYMN XXIV. *Brahmaṇaspati.*

1. Be pleased with this our offering, thou who art the Lord ; we will adore thee with this new and mighty song.

7 *This banquet of the Gods* : sacrifice in general, and especially the sacrifice which he is performing.

15 *Son of Law* : who hast thy being in accordance with *ṛtá*, truth or eternal Law and Order.

16 This stanza is difficult, and the translation is conjectural. Wilson observes that Sāyaṇa's explanation is not very intelligible.

18 *Aṅgiras* : Bṛhaspati is here called by the name of the ancient patriarch as Agni is in I. 1. 6 According to the *Bhāgavata Purāṇa* Brhaspati is the son of Aṅgiras.

Thou......didst hurl down : the deed usually ascribed to Indra is here attributed to Bṛhaspati as the Lord of effectual prayer. See I. 14. 3, and 62 3.

1 *Thy friend, our liberal patron* : the institutor of the sacrifice, the faithful worshipper of the God and the rewarder of the priests.

As this thy friend, our liberal patron, praises thee, do thou, Bṛhaspati, fulfil our hearts' desire.

2 He who with might bowed down the things that should be bowed, and in his fury rent the holds of Śambara :
Who overthrew what shook not, Brahmaṇaspati,—he made his way within the mountain stored with wealth.

3 That was a great deed for the Godliest of the Gods : strong things were loosened and the firmly fixed gave way.
He drave the kine forth and cleft Vala through by prayer, dispelled the darkness and displayed the light of heaven.

4 The well with mouth of stone that poured a flood of meath, which Brahmaṇaspati hath opened with his might—
All they who see the light have drunk their fill thereat : together they have made the watery fount flow forth.

5 Ancient will be those creatures, whatsoe'er they be ; with moons, with autumns, doors unclose themselves to you.
Effortless they pass on to perfect this and that, appointed works which Brahmaṇaspati ordained.

6 They who with much endeavour searching round obtained the Paṇis' noblest treasure hidden in the cave,—
Those sages, having marked the falsehoods, turned them back whence they had come, and sought again to enter in.

7 The pious ones when they had seen the falsehoods turned them back, the sages stood again upon the lofty ways.
Cast down with both their arms upon the rock they left the kindled fire, and said, No enemy is he.

8 With his swift bow, strung truly, Brahmaṇaspati reaches the mark whate'er it be that he desires.
Excellent are the arrows wherewithal he shoots, keen-eyed to look on men and springing from his ear.

9 He brings together and he parts, the great High Priest ; extolled is he, in battle Brahmaṇaspati.
When, gracious, for the hymn he brings forth food and wealth, the glowing Sun untroubled sends forth fervent heat.

10 First and preëminent, excelling all besides are the kind gifts of liberal Bṛhaspati.
These are the boons of him the Strong who should be loved, whereby both classes and the people have delight.

11 Thou who in every way supreme in earthly power, rejoicing, by thy mighty strength hast waxen great,—
He is the God spread forth in breadth against the Gods : he, Brahmaṇaspati, encompasseth this All.

12 From you, twain Maghavans, all truth proceedeth : even the waters break not your commandment.
Come to us, Brahmaṇaspati and Indra, to our oblation like yoked steeds to fodder.

13 The sacrificial flames most swiftly hear the call : the priest of the assembly gaineth wealth for hymns.
Hating the stern, remitting at his will the debt, strong in the shock of fight is Brahmaṇaspati.

14 The wrath of Brahmaṇaspati according to his will had full effect when he would do a mighty deed.
The kine he drave forth and distributed to heaven, even as a copious flood with strength flows sundry ways.

15 O Brahmaṇaspati, may we be evermore masters of wealth well-guided, full of vital strength.

2 *The holds of Śambara* : great black clouds before they pour their rain.

The mountain stored with wealth : the cloud full of precious rain.

5 This stanza is difficult. Ludwig takes *tā bhúvanā*, 'those creatures,' whose nature is imperfectly known, to be the sun and moon, the parents of months and years, which without any effort on their part bring to pass whatever Brahmaṇaspati decrees.

6 The Paṇis are the robber-fiends who carry off and hide the cows or rays of light. *Those sages* : the Aṅgirases, to whom the stolen cows are said to have belonged. *Having marked the falsehoods* : having seen through the guiles of the fiends who sought to mislead them.

7 *They left the kindled fire* : the cows, or waters and the light which follows their effusion, were set free by fire-oblations of which the Aṅgirases are regarded as the earliest institutors. *No enemy* : that is, man's greatest friend. The stanza is obscure, and Sāyaṇa's explanation is unsatisfactory.

8 *Springing from his ear* : the bow-string being drawn to the right ear. The word may, perhaps mean also, 'finding their home in, *i. e.* reaching the ears of men, and might be translated 'levelled to the ear.'

9 *He brings together and he parts* : brings friends together in worship, and disperses enemies in battle.

10 *Both classes* : according to Sāyaṇa, the institutors of the sacrifice and the priests, or Gods and men.

11 *In breadth against the Gods* : in his mightiness the representative of all the Gods.

12 *Even the waters* : all nature, even the strong and rapid water floods.

Heroes on heroes send abundantly to us, when thou omnipotent through prayer seekest my call.

16 O Brahmaṇaspati, be thou controller of this our hymn, and prosper thou our children.
All that the Gods regard with love is blessed. Loud may we speak, with heroes, in assembly.

HYMN XXV. *Brahmaṇaspati.*

1. HE lighting up the flame shall conquer enemies : strong shall he be who offers prayer and brings his gift.
He with his seed spreads forth beyond another's seed, whomever Brahmaṇaspati takes for his friend.

2 With heroes he shall overcome his hero foes, and spread his wealth by kine : wise by himself is he.
His children and his children's children grow in strength, whomever Brahmaṇaspati takes for his friend.

3 He, mighty like a raving river's billowy flood, as a bull conquers oxen, overcomes with strength.
Like Agni's blazing rush he may not be restrained, whomever Brahmaṇaspati takes for his friend.

4 For him the floods of heaven flow never failing down : first with the heroes he goes forth to war for kine.
He slays in unabated vigour with great might, whomever Brahmaṇaspati takes for his friend.

5 All roaring rivers pour their waters down for him, and many a flawless shelter hath been granted him.
Blest with the happiness of Gods he prospers well, whomever Brahmaṇaspati takes for his friend.

HYMN XXVI. *Brahmaṇaspati.*

1. THE righteous singer shall o'ercome his enemies, and he who serves the Gods subdue the godless man.
The zealous man shall vanquish the invincible, the worshipper share the food of him who worships not.

2 Worship, thou hero, chase the arrogant afar : put on auspicious courage for the fight with foes.
Prepare oblation so that thou mayst have success : we crave the favouring help of Brahmaṇaspati.

3 He with his folk, his house, his family, his sons, gains booty for himself, and, with the heroes, wealth,
Who with oblation and a true believing heart serves Brahmaṇaspati the Father of the Gods.

4 Whoso hath honoured him with offerings rich in oil, him Brahmaṇaspati leads forward on his way,
Saves him from sorrow, frees him from his enemy, and is his wonderful deliverer from woe.

2 *Worship, thou hero* : the Ṛṣi addresses the exhortation to himself.

3 *The Father of the Gods* : Sāyaṇa explains *pitáram*, father, by *pālayitāram*, protector.

HYMN XXVII. *Ādityas.*

1. THESE hymns that drop down fatness, with the ladle I ever offer to the Kings Ādityas.
May Mitra, Aryaman, and Bhaga hear us, the mighty Varuṇa Dakṣa, and Aṁśa.

2 With one accord may Aryaman and Mitra and Varuṇa this day accept this praise-song—
Ādityas bright and pure as streams of water, free from all guile and falsehood, blameless, perfect.

3 These Gods, Ādityas, vast, profound, and faithful, with many eyes, fain to deceive the wicked,
Looking within behold the good and evil : near to the Kings is even the thing most distant.

4 Upholding that which moves and that which moves not, Ādityas, Gods, protectors of all being,
Provident, guarding well the world of spirits, true to eternal Law, the debt-exactors.

5 May I, Ādityas, share in this your favour which, Aryaman, brings profit e'en in danger.
Under your guidance, Varuṇa and Mitra, round troubles may I pass, like rugged places.

1 *With the ladle* : that is, with my tongue that utters praises as the sacrificial ladle pours out the oblations of clarified butter.

Ādityas : See I. 14. 3.

Bhaga : the name of this ancient God still survives in the Slavonic languages as a general name for God. He is frequently invoked together with Pūṣan and the Ādityas. See I. 14. 3.

Dakṣa : active energy, spiritual power personified, and called an Āditya or son of Aditi. Sāyaṇa takes the word as an epithet of Aṁśa, powerful.

Aṁśa : another of the Ādityas, the Distributor. See II. 1. 4.

3 *Looking within* : into the hearts of men.

4 *The debt-exactors* : the punishers of sin.

6 Smooth is your path, O Aryaman and Mitra ; excellent is it, Varuṇa, and thornless.
Thereon, Ādityas, send us down your blessing : grant us a shelter hard to be demolished.

7 Mother of Kings, may Aditi transport us, by fair paths Aryaman, beyond all hatred.
May we uninjured, girt by many heroes, win Varuṇa's and Mitra's high protection.

8 With their support they stay three earths, three heavens ; three are their functions in the Gods' assembly.
Mighty through Law, Ādityas, is your greatness ; fair is it, Aryaman, Varuṇa, and Mitra.

9 Golden and splendid, pure like streams of water, they hold aloft the three bright heavenly regions.
Ne'er do they slumber, never close their eyelids, faithful, far-ruling for the righteous mortal.

10 Thou over all, O Varuṇa, art Sovran, be they Gods, Asura ! or be they mortals.
Grant unto us to see a hundred autumns : ours be the blest long lives of our forefathers.

11 Neither the right nor left do I distinguish, neither the east nor yet the west, Ādityas.
Simple and guided by your wisdom, Vasus ! may I attain the light that brings no danger.

12 He who bears gifts unto the Kings, true Leaders, he whom their everlasting blessings prosper,
Moves with his chariot first in rank and wealthy, munificent and lauded in assemblies.

13 Pure, faithful, very strong, with heroes round him, he dwells beside the waters rich with pasture.
None slays, from near at hand or from a distance, him who is under the Ādityas' guidance.

14 Aditi, Mitra, Varuṇa, forgive us however we have erred and sinned against you.
May I obtain the broad light free from peril : O Indra, let not during darkness seize us.

15 For him the Twain united pour their fulness, the rain from heaven : he thrives most highly favoured.
He goes to war mastering both the mansions : to him both portions of the world are gracious.

16 Your guiles, ye Holy Ones, to quell oppressors, your snares spread out against the foe, Ādityas,
May I car-borne pass like a skilful horseman : uninjured may we dwell in spacious shelter.

17 May I not live, O Varuṇa, to witness my wealthy, liberal, dear friend's destitution.
King, may I never lack well-ordered riches. Loud may we speak, with heroes, in assembly.

HYMN XXVIII. *Varuṇa*

1. THIS laud of the self-radiant wise Āditya shall be supreme o'er all that is in greatness.
I beg renown of Varuṇa the Mighty, the God exceeding kind to him who worships.

2. Having extolled thee, Varuṇa, with thoughtful care may we have high fortune in thy service,
Singing thy praises like the fires at coming, day after day, of mornings rich in cattle.

3 May we be in thy keeping, O thou Leader wide-ruling Varuṇa, Lord of many heroes.
O sons of Aditi, for ever faithful, pardon us, Gods, admit us to your friendship.

4 He made them flow, the Āditya, the Sustainer : the rivers run by Varuṇa's commandment.

7 *Mother of Kings* : Aditi, the Infinite, mother of the Ādityas.

8 *Three are their functions* : perhaps the absorption, retention, and effusion of rain.

10 *Asura* : a divine and immortal being; apparently a higher title than *devāḥ*, Gods or Bright Ones.

11 I know nothing of myself and cannot attain to the light of day, or the light of true knowledge, without your assistance.

14 *During darkness*; death, night, darkness are to be dreaded : daylight is comparatively free from danger.

15 *The Twain united* : heaven and earth which together make up the world.

Both the mansions : that is, he retains possession of his own dwelling and gains possession of that of his enemy.

Both portions of the world : heaven and earth.

17 May I never see my wealthy patron, the institutor of the ceremony reduced to poverty.

---

1 *This laud* : the poet magnifies the importance of the worship which he offers to the Āditya Varuṇa, the great King over all, the God of natural, peaceful, moral order as contrasted with Indra, the God of battles.

These feel no weariness, nor cease from flowing: swift have they flown like birds in air around us.

5 Loose me from sin as from a bond that binds me: may we swell, Varuṇa, thy spring of Order.
Let not my thread, while I weave song, be severed, nor my work's sum, before the time, be shattered.

6 Far from me, Varuṇa, remove all danger: accept me graciously, thou Holy Sovran.
Cast off, like cords that hold a calf, my troubles: I am not even mine eyelid's lord without thee.

7 Strike us not, Varuṇa, with those dread weapons which, Asura, at thy bidding wound the sinner.
Let us not pass away from light to exile. Scatter, that we may live, the men who hate us

8 O mighty Varuṇa, now and hereafter, even as of old, will we speak forth our worship.
For in thyself, invincible God, thy statutes ne'er to be moved are fixed as on a mountain.

9 Move far from me what sins I have committed: let me not suffer, King, for guilt of others.
Full many a morn remains to dawn upon us: in these, O Varuṇa, while we live direct us.

10 O King, whoever, be he friend or kinsman, hath threatened me affrighted in my slumber—
If any wolf or robber fain would harm us, therefrom, O Varuṇa, give thou us protection.

11 May I not live O Varuṇa, to witness my wealthy, liberal dear friend's destitution.
King, may I never lack well-ordered riches. Loud may we speak, with heroes, in assembly.

HYMN XXIX. *Viśvedevas.*

1. UPHOLDERS of the Law, ye strong Ādityas, remove my sin like her who bears in secret.
You, Varuṇa, Mitra and all Gods who listen, I call to help me, I who know your goodness.

2 Ye, Gods, are providence and ye are power: remove ye utterly all those who hate us.
As givers of good things deal with us kindly: this day be gracious to us and hereafter.

3 What service may we do you with our future, what service, Vasus, with our ancient friendship?
O Aditi, and Varuṇa and Mitra, Indra and Maruts, make us well and happy.

4 Ye, O ye Gods, are verily our kinsmen; as such be kind to me who now implore you.
Let not your car come slowly to our worship: of kinsmen such as you ne'er let us weary.

5 I singly have sinned many a sin against you, and ye chastised me as a sire the gambler.
Far be your nets, far, Gods, be mine offences: seize me not like a bird upon her offspring.

6 Turn yourselves hitherward this day, ye Holy, that fearing in my heart I may approach you.
Protect us, God; let not the wolf destroy us. Save us, ye Holy, from the pit and falling.

7 May I not live, O Varuṇa, to witness my wealthy, liberal, dear friend's destitution.
King, may I never lack well-ordered riches. Loud may we speak, with heroes, in assembly.

HYMN XXX. *Indra and Others.*

1. THE streams unceasing flow to Indra, slayer of Ahi, Savitar, God, Law's fulfiller,
Day after day goes on the sheen of waters. What time hath past since they were first set flowing?

2 His Mother—for she knew—spake and proclaimed him who was about to cast his bolt at Vṛtra.
Cutting their paths according to his pleasure day after day flow to their goal the rivers.

---

5 *Swell......thy spring of Order*: observe and strengthen thy statutes and ordinances from which life and all blessings flow.

1 *Like her who bears in secret*: as an unwedded mother abandons her secretly born child in some distant place.

5 *As a sire the gambler*: as a father punishes his son for gambling.

Your nets: the nooses or snares which ye spread for the wicked.

1 *Savitar*: the Sun, as identical with Indra. The Scholiast explains the word here as the instigator or impeller of all.

What time hath past?: meaning that the waters are eternal.

3 Aloft he stood above the airy region, and against Vṛtra shot his deadly missile.
Enveloped in a cloud he rushed upon him. Indra subdued the foe with sharpened weapons.

4 As with a bolt, Bṛhaspati, fiercely flaming, pierce thou Vṛkadvaras', the Asura's, heroes.
Even as in time of old with might thou slewest, so slay even now our enemy, O Indra.

5 Cast down from heaven on high thy bolt of thunder wherewith in joy thou smitest dead the foeman.
For gain of children make us thine, O Indra, of many children's children and of cattle.

6 Whomso ye love, his power ye aid and strengthen ; ye Twain are the rich worshipper's advancers.
Graciously favour us, Indra and Soma ; give us firm standing in this time of danger.

7 Let it not vex me, tire me, make me slothful, and never let us say, Press not the Soma ;
For him who cares for me, gives gifts, supports me, who comes with kine to me who pour libations.

8 Sarasvatī, protect us : with the Maruts allied thou boldly conquerest our foemen,
While Indra does to death the daring chieftain of Śaṇḍikas exulting in his prowess.

9 Him who waylays, yea, him who would destroy us,—aim at him, pierce him with thy sharpened weapon.
Bṛhaspati, with arms thou slayest foemen : O King, give up the spoiler to destruction.

10 Perform, O Hero, with our valiant heroes the deeds heroic which thou hast to finish.
Long have they been inflated with presumption : slay them, and bring us hither their possessions.

2 The first hemistich is obscure. I follow Ludwig's conjectural interpretation (Der Ṛgveda, V. 63), who reads *viduṣī* for *viduṣe*, and refers to the legend related in IV. 18. *His Mother* : Aditi, the mother of Indra.

3 *Aloft he stood* : Indra. See I.32. *Enveloped in a cloud*: referring to Vṛtra.

4 *Vṛkadvaras* : supposed by Ludwig to be the King of the Śaṇḍikas, the hymn being a prayer for victory in an approaching battle with him. *The Asura* would then mean King.

7 *Comes with kine* : referring to Indra who rewards his worshippers with gifts of cattle.

11 I craving joy address with hymn and homage your heavenly host, the company of Maruts,
That we may gain wealth with full store of heroes, each day more famous, and with troops of children.

HYMN XXXI. *Viśvedevas.*

1. Help, Varuṇa and Mitra, O ye Twain allied with Vasus, Rudras, and Ādityas, help our car,
That, as the wild birds of the forest from their home, our horses may fly forth, glad, eager for renown.

2 Yea, now ye Gods of one accord speed on our car what time among the folk it seeks an act of might ;
When, hasting through the region with the stamp of hoofs, our swift steeds trample on the ridges of the earth.

3 Or may our Indra here, the Friend of all mankind, coming from heaven, most wise, girt by the Marut host,
Accompany, with aid untroubled by a foe, our car to mighty gain, to win the meed of strength.

4 Or may this Tvaṣṭar, God who rules the world with power, one-minded with the Goddesses speed forth our car ;
Iḷā and Bhaga the celestial, Earth and Heaven, Pūṣan, Purandhi, and the Aśvins, ruling Lords.

5 Or, seen alternate, those two blessed Goddesses, Morning and Night who stir all living things to act :
While with my newest song I praise you both, O Earth, that from what moves not ye may spread forth threefold food.

6 Your blessing as a boon for suppliants we desire : the Dragon of the Deep, and Aja-Ekapād,

1 *Help our car* : in the chariot-race. According to Prof. Windisch, 'car' is a figurative expression for 'hymn of praise.' See that scholar's exhaustive discussion of this hymn in Festgruss an Rudolf von Roth, 1893 pp. 139—144.

4 *Purandhi* : meaning the bold, or the intelligent, may be either an epithet of Pūṣan or the name of a separate deity.

5 *I praise you both, O Earth*: *i.e.* O Heaven and Earth; the pair being always regarded as closely connected, the mention of one is sufficient.

From what moves not : from plants as distinguished from animals.

6 *The Dragon of the Deep* : Ahibudhnya, who dwells in the depth of air. See I. 186. 5. *Aja-Ekapād* : 'the unborn one-footed,' the Sun. See VI. 50. 14, note. *Trita* : a Vedic God, appearing in connexion with Indra. *The Floods' swift Child* : Agni. For the other names see Index.

Trita, Ṛbhukṣan, Savitar shall joy in us, and the Floods' swift Child in our worship and our prayer.

7 These earnest prayers I pray to you, ye Holy : to pay you honour, living men have formed them,
Men fain to win the prize and glory. May they win, as a car-horse might the goal, your notice.

HYMN XXXII. *Various Deities.*

1. GRACIOUSLY further, O ye Heaven and Earth, this speech striving to win reward, of me your worshipper.
First rank I give to you, Immortal, high extolled ! I, fain to win me wealth, to you the mighty Pair.

2 Let not man's guile annoy us, secret or by day : give not us up a prey to these calamities.
Sever not thou our friendship : think thereon for us. This, with a heart that longs for bliss, we seek from thee.

3 Bring hither with benignant mind the willing Cow teeming with plenteous milk, full, inexhaustible.
O thou invoked by many, day by day I urge thee with my word, a charger rapid in his tread.

4 With eulogy I call on Rākā swift to hear : may she, auspicious, hear us, and herself observe.
With never-breaking needle may she sew her work, and give a hero son most wealthy, meet for praise.

5 All thy kind thoughts, O Rākā, lovely in their form, wherewith thou grantest wealth to him who offers gifts—
With these come thou to us this day benevolent, O Blessed One, bestowing food of thousand sorts.

6 O broad-tressed Sinīvālī, thou who art the Sister of the Gods,
Accept the offered sacrifice, and, Goddess, grant us progeny.

7 With lovely fingers, lovely arms, prolific Mother of many sons—
Present the sacred gifts to her, to Sinīvālī Queen of men.

8 Her, Sinīvālī, her, Gungū, her, Rākā, her, Sarasvatī, Indrāṇī to mine aid I call, and Varuṇānī for my weal.

HYMN XXXIII. *Rudra.*

1. FATHER of Maruts, let thy bliss approach us : exclude us not from looking on the sunlight.
Gracious to our fleet courser be the Hero : may we transplant us, Rudra, in our children.

2 With the most saving medicines which thou givest, Rudra, may I attain a hundred winters.
Far from us banish enmity and hatred, and to all quarters maladies and trouble.

3 Chief of all born art thou in glory, Rudra, armed with the thunder, mightiest of the mighty.
Transport us over trouble to well-being : repel thou from us all assaults of mischief.

4 Let us not anger thee with worship, Rudra, ill praise, Strong God ! or mingled invocation.
Do thou with strengthening balms incite our heroes : I hear thee famed as best of all physicians.

5 May I with praise-songs win that Rudra's favour who is adored with gifts and invocations.
Ne'er may the tawny God, fair-cheeked, and gracious, swifthearing, yield us to this evil purpose.

6 The Strong, begirt by Maruts, hath refreshed me, with most invigorating food, imploring.
As he who finds a shade in fervent sunlight may I, uninjured, win the bliss of Rudra.

7 Where is that gracious hand of thine, O Rudra, the hand that giveth health and bringeth comfort,

2 *These calamities* : some pressing troubles or imminent dangers not further specified. *From thee* : probably Indra.

4 *Rākā* : the Goddess presiding over the actual day of full moon, and apparently associated with childbirth.

6 *Sinīvālī* : a similar lunar Goddess, who aids the birth of children.

8 *Gungū* : identified by Sāyaṇa with Kuhū, another lunar Goddess, or the day of conjunction when the moon rises invisible. *Indrāṇī* and *Varuṇānī* are the consorts respectively of Indra and Varuṇa.

---

1 *The Hero* : Rudra. According to Ludwig : Let our brave son be mighty with the charger.

4 *With worship* : with imperfect worship. *mingled invocation* : in which other Gods also, who have no claim to the particular oblation, are addressed.

5 *Yield us to this evil purpose* : give us up to the malice of our enemy.

6 *The Strong* : or the Bull, Rudra, accompanied by his sons the Maruts.

Remover of the woe that Gods have sent us ? O Strong One, look thou on me with compassion.

8 To him the strong, great, tawny, fair-complexioned, I utter forth a mighty hymn of praises.
We serve the brilliant God with adorations, we glorify the splendid name of Rudra.

9 With firm limbs, multiform, the strong, the tawny adorns himself with bright gold decorations :
The strength of Godhead ne'er departs from Rudra, him who is Sovran of this world, the mighty.

10 Worthy, thou carriest thy bow and arrows, worthy, thy manyhued and honoured necklace.
Worthy, thou cuttest here each fiend to pieces : a mightier than thou there is not, Rudra.

11 Praise him the chariot-borne, the young, the famous, fierce, slaying like a dread beast of the forest.
O Rudra, praised, be gracious to the singer : let thy hosts spare us and smite down another.

12 I bend to thee as thou approachest, Rudra, even as a boy before the sire who greets him.
I praise thee Bounteous Giver, Lord of heroes : give medicines to us as thou art lauded.

13 Of your pure medicines, O potent Maruts, those that are wholesomest and health-bestowing,
Those which our father Manu hath selected, I crave from Rudra for our gain and welfare.

14 May Rudra's missile turn aside and spare us, the great wrath of the impetuous One avoid us.
Turn, Bounteous God, thy strong bow from our princes, and be thou gracious to our seed and offspring.

15 O tawny Bull, thus showing forth thy nature, as neither to be wroth, O God, nor slay us.
Here, Rudra, listen to our invocation. Loud may we speak, with heroes, in assembly.

8 *Fair-complexioned* : the white complexion of Śiva, the later representative of Rudra, has, therefore, as Wilson observes, its origin in the Ṛgveda.

13 *Those which our father Manu hath selected* : Wilson observes that 'this alludes to the vegetable seeds which Manu, according to the *Mahābhārata*, was directed to take with him into the vessel in which he was preserved at the time of the deluge.'

14 *Our princes* : our wealthy patrons, the institutors of our sacrifices.

HYMN XXXIV. *Maruts*

1. THE Maruts of resistless might who love the rain, resplendent, terrible like wild beasts in their strength,
Glowing like flames of fire, impetuous in career, blowing the wandering rain-cloud, have disclosed the kine.

2 They gleam with armlets as the heavens are decked with stars, like cloud-born lightnings shine the torrents of their rain.
Since the strong Rudra, O Maruts with brilliant chests, sprang into life for you in Pṛṣni's radiant lap.

3 They drip like horses in the racings of swift steeds; with the stream's rapid ears they hasten on their way.
Maruts with helms of gold, ye who make all things shake, come with your spotted deer, one-minded, to our food.

4 They have bestowed on Mitra all that live, to feed, they who for evermore cause their swift drops to flow;
Whose steeds are spotted deer, whose riches never fail, like horses in full speed, bound to the pole in works.

5 With brightly-flaming kine whose udders swell with milk, with glittering lances on your unobstructed paths,
O Maruts, of one mind, like swans who seek their nests, come to the rapturous enjoyment of the meath.

6 To these our prayers, O Maruts, come unanimous, come ye to our libations like the praise of men.

1 *Have disclosed the kine* : 'give vent to its (collected) rain.'—Wilson.

2 *Pṛṣni's radiant lap* : Pṛṣni the mother of the Maruts, probably 'the speckled cloud,' is, according to Sāyaṇa, the Earth who in the form of a brindled cow was impregnated by Rudra.

3 *With the stream's rapid ears* : 'The waves raised by the storm may be regarded as the ears with which the stream listens to the roaring of the tempest.'—Ludwig. Wilson, after Sāyaṇa, paraphrases : 'and they rush along with swift (horses) on the skirts of the sounding (cloud).'

4 The meaning of the first line is not clear. Wilson renders it; 'The prompt-giving Maruts ever confer upon the (offerer of sacrificial) food, as upon a friend, all these (world-supporting) waters.'

Bound to the pole in works : carrying on their appointed duties as horses draw the chariot to whose pole they are harnessed.

5 *With brightly-flaming kine* : clouds that emit flashes of lightning before they pour down their stores of fertilizing rain

6 *Like the praise of men* : which attends pious worshippers.

Make it swell like a mare, in udder like a cow, and for the singer grace the song with plenteous strength.

7 Give us a steed, O Maruts mighty in the car; prevailing prayer that brings remembrance day by day;

Food to your praisers, to your bard in deeds of might give winning wisdom, power uninjured, unsurpassed.

8 When the bright-chested Maruts, lavish of their gifts, bind at the time of bliss their horses to the cars,

Then, as the milch-cow feeds her calf within the stalls, they pour forth food for all oblation-bringing men.

9 Save us, O Maruts, Vasus, from the injurer, the mortal foe who makes us looked upon as wolves.

With chariot all aflame compass him round about: O Rudras, cast away the foeman's deadly bolt.

10 Well-known, ye Maruts, is that wondrous course of yours, when they milked Pṛśni's udder, close akin to her.

Or when to shame the bard who lauded, Rudra's Sons, ye O infallible brought Trita to decay.

11 We call you, such, great Maruts, following wonted ways, to the oblation paid to Viṣṇu Speeder-on.

With ladles lifted up, with prayer, we seek of them preëminent, golden-hued, the wealth which all extol.

12 They, the Daśagvas, first of all brought sacrifice : they at the break of mornings shall inspirit us.

Dawn with her purple beams uncovereth the nights, with great light glowing like a billowy sea of milk.

13 The Rudras have rejoiced them in the gathered bands at seats of worship as in purple ornaments.

They with impetuous vigour sending down the rain have taken to themselves a bright and lovely hue.

14 Soliciting their high protection for our help, with this our adoration we sing praise to them,

Whom, for assistance, like the five terrestrial priests. Trita hath brought to aid us hither on his car.

15 So may your favouring help be turned to us-ward, your kindness like a lowing cow approach us,

Wherewith ye bear your servant over trouble, and free your worshipper from scoff and scorning.

HYMN XXXV. *Son of Waters.*

1. EAGER for spoil my flow of speech I utter: may the Floods' Child accept my songs with favour.

Will not the rapid Son of Waters make them lovely, for he it is who shall enjoy them?

2 To him let us address the song well-fashioned, forth from the heart. Shall he not understand it?

The friendly Son of Waters by the greatness of Godhead hath produced all things existing.

3 Some floods unite themselves and others join them : the sounding rivers fill one common storehouse.

On every side the bright Floods have encompassed the bright resplendent Offspring of the Waters.

4 The never-sullen waters, youthful Maidens, carefully decking, wait on him the youthful.

He with bright rays shines forth in splendid beauty, unfed with wood. in waters, oil-enveloped.

5 To him three Dames are offering food to feed him, Goddesses to the God whom none may injure.

Make it swell : make our sacred song effectual, metaphorically full of milk. Prof. M. Müller would read *asvām* instead of *áśvām* : 'Fulfil (our prayer) like the udder of a barren cow.'

7 *Brings remembrance* : makes the Gods remember us.

10 Pṛśni here is the firmament, and her udder is the cloud from which the Maruts drew the rain. There is a very abrupt change from the second person to the third, from 'ye' to 'they.'

I can make nothing of the second hemistich. Wilson paraphrases it : 'You (destroyed) the reviler of your worshipper, and (came), irresistible sons of Rudra, to Trita for the destruction of his enemies.' Trita is said by Sāyaṇa to be a Ṛṣi. Ludwig in his note on the passage takes Trita to be a name of the Soma.

11 *Viṣṇu Speeder-on* : who runs his rapid course round heaven. Sāyaṇa explains Viṣṇu to mean 'the diffusive and desirable Soma.' Perhaps, as Ludwig thinks, sacrifice in general is intended, of which Viṣṇu is the representative.

12 *The Daśagvas* : the Maruts are here said to have been the first performers of sacrifice, the true Daśagvas. The priests so called belonged originally to the race or school of Aṅgiras.

14 The second hemistich is very obscure. Sāyaṇa's explanation (see Wilson) is altogether unsatisfactory.

1 *The Floods' Child* : or Son of the Waters, Apāṁnapāt, a name of Agni as born in the form of lightning from the waters of the aerial ocean or firmament. *Make them lovely* : grace them with acceptance.

Within the waters hath he pressed, as hollows, and drinks their milk who now are first made mothers.

6 Here was the horse's birth; his was the sunlight. Save thou our princes from the oppressor's onslaught.
Him, indestructible, dwelling at a distance in forts unwrought lies and ill spirits reach not.

7 He, in whose mansion is the teeming Milch-cow, swells the Gods' nectar and eats noble viands.
The Son of Waters, gathering strength in waters, shines for his worshipper to give him treasures.

8 He who in waters with his own pure Godhead shines widely, law-abiding, everlasting—
The other worlds are verily his branches, and plants are born of him with all their offspring.

9 The Waters' Son hath risen, and clothed in lightning ascended up unto the curled cloud's bosom;
And bearing with them his supremest glory the Youthful Ones, gold-coloured, move around him.

10 Golden in form is he, like gold to look on, his colour is like gold, the Son of Waters.
When he is seated fresh from golden birthplace those who present their gold give food to feed him.

11 This the fair name and this the lovely aspect of him the Waters' Son increase in secret.
Whom here the youthful Maids together kindle, his food is sacred oil of golden colour.

12 Him, nearest Friend of many, will we worship with sacrifice and reverence and oblation.
I make his back to shine, with chips provide him; I offer food and with my songs exalt him.

13 The Bull hath laid his own life-germ within them. He sucks them as an infant, and they kiss him.
He, Son of Waters, of unfading colour, hath entered here as in another's body.

14 While here he dwelleth in sublimest station, resplendent with the rays that never perish,
The Waters, bearing oil to feed their offspring, flow, Youthful Ones, in wanderings about him.

15 Agni, I gave good shelter to the people, and to the princes goodly preparation.
Blessed is all that Gods regard with favour. Loud may we speak, with heroes, in assembly.

HYMN XXXVI *Various Gods.*

1. WATER and milk hath he endued, sent forth to thee : the men have drained him with the filters and the stones.
Drink, Indra, from the Hotar's bowl—first right is thine—Soma hallowed and poured with Vaṣaṭ and Svāhā.

2 Busied with sacrifice, with spotted deer and spears, gleaming upon your way with ornaments, yea, our Friends,
Sitting on sacred grass, ye Sons of Bharata, drink Soma from the Potar's bowl, O Men of heaven.

5 *Three Dames* : Iḷā, Sarasvatī, and Bhāratī, the personifications of sacred prayer and worship. *Within the waters* : Agni dwelt within the waters as their unborn babe.

6 *Here was the horse's birth* : the production of the rapid lightning, or perhaps of the Sun ; but the meaning is doubtful. The expression may, as Ludwig suggests, refer to the creation of the natural horse as a descendant of the original heavenly horse. *His was the sunlight* : Apāṁnapāt's or Agni's. *In forts unwrought* : in the castles of the clouds as opposed to the stone strongholds of men.

9 *The Youthful Ones* : the rivers or waters of the aerial ocean.

10 *Golden in form* : when wearing the shape of lightning. *Those who present their gold* : the institutors of sacrifice who reward tte priests.

11 *In secret* : Apāṁnapāt, the celestial Agni, increases and grows strong without men seeing the process. The terrestrial Agni is kindled and tended by the sister fingers and fed with oil or clarified butter.

12 *Nearest Friend of many* : lowest down, and so nearest to men, of all the Gods. *Make his back to shine* : with butter offered in sacrifice.

13 *Within them* : within the waters. *The Bull* : apparently Agni himself.

As in another's body : that is, fire originally celestial as Apāṁnapāt, has come to men as terrestrial and sacrificial fire, contained in the wooden drill from which it is produced by friction.

15 As the result of my hymns to Agni our people have dwelt safely, and our wealthy men have been enabled to offer well-conducted sacrifices.

---

1 The Soma juice has been pressed out with the stones, strained through the filters, and then mixed with water and milk before it is offered to Indra, The *Hotar's bowl* : the sacred vessel held by the Hotar or Hotṛ, one of the chief officiating priests.

Vaṣaṭ and *Svāhā*, meaning respectively 'may he (Agni) bear it (to the Gods)' and Ave ! or Hail ! are words of consecration and blessing used when oblations are offered.

2 *Sons of Bharata* : the Maruts, sons of Rudra the Warrior. *Potar* : etymologically Cleanser, the title of another of the priests.

3 Come unto us, ye swift to listen: as at home upon the sacred grass sit and enjoy yourselves.
And, Tvaṣṭar, well-content be joyful in the juice with Gods and Goddesses in gladsome company.

4 Bring the Gods hither, Sage, and offer sacrifice: at the three altars seat thee willingly, O Priest.
Accept for thy delight the proffered Soma meath: drink from the Kindler's bowl and fill thee with thy share.

5 This is the strengthener of thy body's manly might: strength, victory for all time are placed within thine arms.
Pressed for thee, Maghavan, it is offered unto thee: drink from the chalice of this Brahman, drink thy fill.

6 Accept the sacrifice; mark both of you, my call: the Priest hath seated him after the ancient texts.
My prayer that bids them come goes forth to both the Kings: drink ye the Soma meath from the Director's bowl.

HYMN XXXVII. *Various Gods.*

1. ENJOY thy fill of meath out of the Hotar's cup: Adhvaryus, he desires a full draught poured for him.
Bring it him: seeking this he gives. Granter of Wealth, drink Soma with the Ṛtus from the Hotar's cup.

2 He whom of old I called on, him I call on now. He is to be invoked; his name is He who Gives.
Here brought by priests is Soma meath. Granter of Wealth, drink Soma with the Ṛtus from the Potar's cup.

3 Fat may the horses be wherewith thou speedest on: Lord of the Wood, unharming, strengthen thou thyself.
Drawing and seizing, Bold One, thou who grantest wealth, drink Soma with the Ṛtus from the Neṣṭar's cup.

4 From Hotar's cup and Potar's he hath drunk and joyed: the proffered food hath pleased him from the Neṣṭar's bowl.
The fourth cup undisturbed, immortal, let him drink who giveth wealth, the cup of the wealth-giving God.

5 Yoke, O ye Twain, to-day your hero-bearing car, swift-moving hitherward: your loosing-place is here.
Mix the oblations, then come hither with the meath, and drink the Soma, ye rich in abundant strength.

6 Agni, accept the fuel and our offered gift: accept the prayer of man, accept our eulogy.
Do thou with all, with Ṛtu, O thou Excellent, fain, make the great Gods all fain taste the gift we bring.

HYMN XXXVIII. *Savitar.*

1. UPRISEN is Savitar, this God, to quicken, Priest who neglects not this most constant duty.
To the Gods, verily, he gives rich treasure, and blesses him who calls them to the banquet.

2 Having gone up on high, the God broad-handed spreads his arms widely forth that all may mark him.
Even the waters bend them to his service: even this wind rests in the circling region.

3 Though borne by swift steeds he will yet unyoke them: e'en the fleet chariot hath he stayed from going.
He hath checked e'en their haste who glide like serpents. Night closely followed Savitar's dominion.

4 What was spread out she weaves afresh, re-weaving: the skilful leaves his labour half-completed.

4 *Sage*: Agni. *The Kindler*: the Agnīdh, the priest who lights the fire. *The three altars*: of the Gārhapatya, Āhavanīya, and Dakṣiṇa fires.

6 *Both the Kings*: Mitra and Varuṇa. *The Director*: Praśāstar, another priest, first assistant of the Hotar.

---

1 Agni is addressed as Draviṇodās or Wealth-giver. *Adhvaryus*: ministering priests. *The Ṛtus*: the Seasons or the deities presiding over the Seasons. See I. 15.

3 *Lord of the Wood*: Agni, regarded as the King of plants. *The Neṣṭar's cup*: the Neṣṭar is the priest who leads forward the wife of the sacrificer.

5 *O ye Twain*: Aśvins.

6. *With all, with Ṛtu*: the meaning is, apparently, with all the Ṛtus; but Ṛtu in the text is in the singular number.

---

1 *To quicken*: the meaning of Savitar, as a náme of the Sun, being the great generator or vivifier. *Priest*: *váhniḥ*; or, perhaps, the supporter, or, the luminous.

3 *Their haste who glide like serpents*: the speed of the fleet-footed horses who draw the chariot of the Sun.

4 The meaning of this stanza is obscure. I have given what appears to be the sense of the words as they stand, but the verse, as a whole, is scarcely intelligible. Wilson, following Sāyaṇa, paraphrases it thus: 'She (Night), enwraps the extended (world) like (a woman) weaving (a garment): the prudent man lays aside the work he is able (to execute) in the midst (of his labour): but all spring up (from repose) when the divine, unwearied Sun, who has divided the seasons, again appears.' Roth takes *arámatiḥ*, which I have

He hath arisen from rest, and parted seasons : Savitar hath approached, God, holy-minded.

5 Through various dwellings, through entire existence, spreads, manifest, the household light of Agni.
The Mother gives her Son the goodliest portion, and Savitar hath sped to meet his summons.

6 He comes again, unfolded, fain for conquest: at home was he, the love of all things moving.
Each man hath come leaving his evil doings, after the Godlike Savitar's commandment.

7 The wild beasts spread through desert places seeking their watery share which thou hast set in waters.
The woods are given to the birds. These statutes of the God Savitar none disobeyeth.

8 With utmost speed, in restless haste at sunset Varuṇa seeks his watery habitation.
Then seeks each bird his nest, each beast his lodging. In due place Savitar hath set each creature.

9 Him whose high law not Varuṇa nor Indra, not Mitra, Aryaman, nor Rudra breaketh,
Nor evil-hearted fiends, here for my welfare him I invoke, God Savitar, with worship.

10 May they who strengthen bliss, and thought and wisdom, and the Dames' Lord and Narāśaṁsa aid us.
That good may come to us and wealth be gathered, may we be Savitar the God's beloved.

11 So come to us our hearts' desire, the bounty bestowed by thee, from heaven and earth and waters,
That it be well with friends and those who praise thee, and, Savitar, with the loud-lauding singer.

HYMN XXXIX. *Aśvins.*

1. SING like the two press-stones for this same purpose; come like two misers to the tree of treasure;
Like two laud-singing Brahmans in the assembly, like the folk's envoys called in many places.

2 Moving at morning like two car-borne heroes, like to a pair of goats ye come electing ;
Like two fair dames embellishing their bodies, like a wise married pair among the people.

3 Like to a pair of horns come first to usward, like to a pair of hoofs with rapid motion ;
Come like two Cakavās in the grey of morning, come like two chariot wheels at dawn, ye Mighty.

4 Bear us across the rivers like two vessels, save us as ye were yokes, naves, spokes and fellies.
Be like two dogs that injure not our bodies ; preserve us, like two crutches, that we fall not.

5 Like two winds ageing not, two confluent rivers, come with quick vision like two eyes before us.

rendered by holy-minded, as a substantive, the Genius of Devotion, and translates : 'Again had the Weaver (Aramati) drawn in what she had spun out (the web or tissue of devotion and sacrifice), the devout man had left off in the midst of his task (at the approach of night); then Aramati arises anew and arranges the seasons : the divine Savitar is present (i. e. morning returns).'

5 *The Mother* : Uṣas or Dawn assigns to *her Son* Agni the Agnihotra rite which is performed at day-break, and Savitar, or the rising Sun, is present at the ceremony after the lighting of the sacrificial fire. Thus Agni is honoured by deities in heaven as well as by men on earth.

6 *He comes again* : Agni, re-kindled in the morning, resumes his full power, He whom all living beings love, was present, but latent, during the night.

7 Savitar provides for the wild beasts of the desert and for the birds of the air.

8 Though not generally regarded in the Veda as the God of the ocean, Varuṇa is yet frequently connected with the waters, either of the firmament or of earth.

10 *They who strengthen bliss* : the Gods in general. *The Dames' Lord* : the guardian of the consorts of the Gods, Tvaṣṭar, who is generally represented as attending or attended by them.

Narāśaṁsa : 'the Praise of Men,' a name of Agni.

1 In this hymn the Aśvins are compared to a number of objects animate and inanimate, in many of which the only point of resemblance is duality.

Sing like the two press-stones : may your auspicious brightness as you approach be as clear as the ringing-sound of the press-stones, and may similar blessings reward the worshippers.

Like two misers to the tree of treasure : as misers come to dig up the gold they have buried at the foot of a tree, so come ye to the libation made of the juice of the precious Soma plant. *The folk's envoys*: the messengers whom the institutors of sacrifices send to the priests when they wish to secure their services.

2 *Ye come electing* : to choose and accept the offerings made.

3 *Cakavās* : the Cakravāka, or as it is now called in Hindi, the Cakavā, is a bird frequently mentioned in later poetry as a type of love and constancy. The male bird and his mate are condemned to spend their nights on opposite banks of a river, and are allowed to meet again in the early morning. The English name of the bird is Brahmany duck. Cakavā is properly the male bird, and Cakavī the female.

Come like two hands most helpful to the body, and guide us like two feet to what is precious.

6 Even as two lips that with the mouth speak honey, even as two breasts that nourish our existence,

Like the two nostrils that protect our being, be to us as our ears that hear distinctly.

7 Like two hands give ye us increasing vigour ; like heaven and earth constrain the airy regions.

Aśvins, these hymns that struggle to approach you, sharpen ye like an axe upon a whetstone.

8 These prayers of ours exalting you, O Aśvins, have the Gṛtsamadas, for a laud, made ready.

Welcome them, O ye Heroes, and come hither. Loud may we speak with brave men, in assembly.

HYMN XL.　　*Soma and Pūṣan.*

1 SOMA and Pūṣan, Parents of all riches, Parents of earth and Parents of high heaven,

You Twain, brought forth as the whole world's protectors, the Gods have made centre of life eternal.

2 At birth of these two Gods all Gods are joyful : they have caused darkness, which we hate, to vanish.

With these, with Soma and with Pūṣan, Indra generates ripe warm milk in the raw milch-cows.

3 Soma and Pūṣan, urge your chariot hither, the seven-wheeled car that measures out the region,

That stirs not all, that moves to every quarter, five-reined and harnessed by the thought, ye Mighty.

4 One in the heaven on high hath made his dwelling, on earth and in the firmament the other.

May they disclose to us great store of treasure, much-longed for, rich in food, source of enjoyment.

5 One of you Twain is Parent of all creatures, the other journeys onward all-beholding.

Soma and Pūṣan, aid my thought with favour : with you may we o'ercome in all encounters.

6 May Pūṣan stir our thought, the all-impelling, may Soma Lord of riches grant us riches.

May Aditi the perfect Goddess aid us. Loud may we speak, with heroes, in assembly.

HYMN XLI.　　*Various Deities.*

1. O VĀYU, come to us with all the thousand chariots that are thine,

Team-borne, to drink the Soma juice.

2 Drawn by thy team, O Vāyu, come ; to thee is offered this, the pure.

Thou visitest the presser's house.

3 Indra and Vāyu, drawn by teams, ye Heroes, come today and drink.

Of the bright juice when blent with milk.

4 This Soma hath been shed for you, Law-strengtheners, Mitra-Varuṇa !

Listen ye here to this my call.

5 Both Kings who never injure aught seat them in their supremest home,

The thousand-pillared, firmly-based.

6 Fed with oblation, Sovran Kings, Ādityas, Lords of liberal gifts.

They wait on him whose life is true.

7 With kine, Nāsatyas, and with steeds, come, Aśvins, Rudras, to the house

That will protect its heroes well ;

8 Such, wealthy Gods ! as none afar nor standing nigh to us may harm,

Yea, no malicious mortal foe.

9 As such, O longed-far Aśvins, lead us on to wealth of varied sort,

Wealth that shall bring us room and rest.

10 Verily Indra, conquering all, driveth e'en mighty fear away,

For firm is he and swift to act.

11 Indra be gracious unto us : sin shall not reach us afterward,

And good shall be before us still.

---

1 *Soma* : addressed in this hymn is the God who represents and animates the juice of the Soma plant. See I. 18. 4.

Pūṣan : a solar deity who protects and multiplies cattle and other property. See I. 42.

2 *Ripe warm milk* : see I. 62. 9.

3 *That stirs not all* : that moves and influences the highest beings only.

4 *One in the heaven on high* : Pūṣan, as a celestial God. *The other* : Soma, who dwells on earth in plants, and in the firmament as the Moon.

---

5 *One of you* : Soma. With allusion, perhaps, to the libations of Soma juice which produce the rain upon which the production and growth of all creatures depend. *All-beholding* : as a solar deity, or the Sun.

1 *Vāyu*, the God of wind, is addressed in the first two stanzas. In those that follow the poet invokes Indra and Vāyu, Mitra and Varuṇa, the Aśvins, Indra, the Viśvedevas, Sarasvatī, and Heaven and Earth.

12 From all the regions of the world let Indra send security,
The foe-subduer, swift to act.

13 O all ye Gods, come hitherward : hear this mine invocation, seat
Yourselves upon this sacred grass.

14 Among the Śunahotras strong for you is this sweet gladdening draught.
Drink ye of this delightsome juice.

15 Ye Martus led by Indra, Gods with Pūṣan for your bounteousest,
Hear all of you this call of mine.

16 Best Mother, best of Rivers, best of Goddesses, Sarasvatī, We are, as 'twere, of no repute and dear Mother, give thou us renown.

17 In thee, Sarasvatī, divine, all generations have their stay.
Be, glad with Śunahotra's sons : O Goddess grant us progeny.

18 Enriched with sacrifice, accept Sarasvatī, these prayers of ours,
Thoughts which Gṛtsamadas beloved of Gods bring, Holy One,to thee.

19 Ye who bless sacrifice, go forth, for verily we choose you both,
And Agni who conveys our gifts.

20 This our effectual sacrifice, reaching the sky, shall Heaven and Earth
Present unto the Gods to-day.

21 In both your laps, ye guileless Ones, the Holy Gods shall sit them down
To-day to drink the Soma here.

HYMN XLII *Kapiñjala.*

1. TELLING his race aloud with cries repeated, he sends his voice out as his boat a steersman.
O Bird, be ominous of happy fortune : from no side may calamity befall thee.

2 Let not the falcon kill thee, nor the eagle : let not the arrow-bearing archer reach thee.
Still crying in the region of the Fathers, speak here auspicious, bearing joyful tidings.

3 Bringing good tidings, Bird of happy omen, call thou out loudly southward of our dwellings,
So that no thief, no sinner may oppress us. Loud may we speak, with heroes, in assembly.

HYMN XLIII. *Kapiñjala.*

1. HERE on the right sing forth chanters of hymns of praise, even the winged birds that in due season speak.
He, like a Sāma-chanter utters both the notes, skilled in the mode of Triṣṭup and of Gāyatrī.

2 Thou like the chanter-priest chantest the Sāma, Bird ; thou singest at libations like a Brahman's son.
Even as a vigorous horse when he comes near the mare, announce to us good fortune, Bird, on every side, proclaim in all directions happy luck, O Bird.

3 When singing here, O Bird. announce good luck to us, and when thou sittest still think on us with kind thoughts.
When flying off thou singest thou art like a lute. With brave sons in assembly may we speak aloud.

14 *Among the Śunahotras* : the family of which Gṛtsamada, the Ṛṣi of the hymn, was a member. Cf. II. 18. 6, note.

15 *With Pūṣan for your bounteousest* : that is, among whom Pūṣan is the most liberal giver of good gifts; or the meaning may be, whose benefactor is Pūṣan.

16 *Sarasvatī* : see I. 3. 10.

19 *Ye who bless sacrifice* : according to Sāyaṇa, the two *havirdhānas* or vehicles on which the Soma and other offerings are put, and which are supposed to represent Heaven and Earth, are addressed. It is more likely, as Ludwig suggests, that Agni and the human priest are intended. 'We choose you both, thee, the human priest, and Agni the God.'

This Hymn is said to be addressed to Indra in the form of a kapiñjala, the bird which we call the Francoline partridge.

1 *He* : the kapiñjala.

2 *In the region of the Fathers* : towards the quarter where the Fathers Pitaras, or spirits of deceased ancestors dwell, that is, the south the cry of birds from that quarter being regarded as auspicious.

This Hymn is said to be addressed, like the preceding, to Indra in the form of a kapiñjala or Francoline partridge.

1 *Sāma-chanter* : the Udgātar, one of the four chief priests whose duty is to chant the hymns of the Sāmaveda *Both the notes* : a high and a middle. *Triṣṭup* : the measure consisting of forty-four syllables in a verse or stanza; four Pādas or demi-hemistichs of eleven syllables each. *Gāyatrī* : the measure consisting of twenty-four syllables in a stanza, three lines of eight syllables each, or one line of sixteen and one of eight.

2 *A Brahman's son* : the Brahmaputra, or Brahman-priest's son, is said to be the same as the Brāhmaṇācchaṁsī, one of the sixteen priests who recites the *mantra* that is not to be sung or chanted.

BOOK THE THIRD

HYMN I. *Agni.*

1. THOU, Agni, who wilt have the strong, hast made me the Soma's priest, to worship in assembly.
Thou shinest to the Gods, I set the press-stones. I toil ; be joyful in thyself, O Agni.

2 East have we turned the rite ; may the hymn aid it. With wood and worship shall they honour Agni.
From heaven the synods of the wise have learnt it : e'en for the quick and strong they seek advancement.

3 The Prudent, he whose will is pure, brought welfare, allied by birth to Heaven and Earth in kinship.
The Gods discovered in the midst of waters beautiful Agni with the Sisters' labour.

4 Him, Blessed One, the Seven strong Floods augmented, him white at birth and red when waxen mighty.
As mother mares run to their new-born youngling, so at his birth the Gods wondered at Agni.

5 Spreading with radiant limbs throughout the region, purging his power with wise purifications,
Robing himself in light, the life of waters, he spreads abroad his high and perfect glories.

6 He sought heaven's Mighty Ones, the unconsuming, the unimpaired, not clothed and yet not naked.
Then they, ancient and young, who dwell together, Seven sounding Rivers, as one germ received him.

7 His piles, assuming every form, are scattered where flow sweet waters, at the spring of fatness ;
There stood the milch-kine with full-laden udders, and both paired Mighty Mothers of the Wondrous.

8 Carefully cherished, Son of Strength, thou shonest assuming lasting and refulgent beauties.
Full streams of fatness and sweet juice descended, there where the Mighty One grew strong by wisdom.

9 From birth he knew even his Father's bosom, he set his voices and his streams in motion ;
Knew him who moved with blessed Friends in secret, with the young Dames of heaven. He stayed not hidden.

10 He nursed the Infant of the Sire and Maker : alone the Babe sucked many a teeming bosom.
Guard, for the Bright and Strong, the fellow-spouses friendly to men and bound to him in kinship.

11 The Mighty One increased in space unbounded ; full many a glorious flood gave strength to Agni.

The Hymns of Book III. are ascribed to the Ṛṣi Viśvāmitra or to members of his family. Viśvāmitra holds an important place in Indian tradition, according to which he was born a Kṣatriya, but by the virtue of his intense austerities raised himself to the Brāhman caste. The rivalry between Viśvāmitra and the Ṛṣi Vasiṣṭha is alluded to in many passages of the Ṛgveda, and, it is thought that as caste distinctions had not at that time become fixed, the later stories on the subject of this rivalry may have rested on a Vedic legend which says that King Sudās, having employed Vasiṣṭha as his domestic priest, allowed on various occasions Viśvāmitra also to officiate, which led to jealousies and quarrel between these two functionaries. The story of Viśvāmitra is told at full length in the *Rāmāyaṇa*, I. 51—55, (Schlegel's edition, and Griffith's translation).

The first and eleven following hymns are ascribed to Viśvāmitra himself.

1 *East have we turned the rite* : towards the region of the Gods; 'we have performed a successful sacrifice.' —Wilson.

2 *The quick and strong* : Agni, according to Sāyaṇa. Ludwig suggests that 'the quick, or clever' may mean the priest, and 'the strong' the warrior, the Maghavan or institutor of the sacrifice.

3 *The Prudent* : all-knowing Agni, son of Heaven and Earth.

With the Sisters' labour : the meaning is not clear. Ludwig suggests *upasi* instead of *apási* ; 'in the sisters' 'bosom,' in the depth of the sister rivers.

6 *Heaven's mighty Ones* : the waters above the firmament, the seven rivers of the next hemistich. *Not clothed and yet not naked* : having only the lucid waters for robes.

7 *His piles* : the heaped clouds. *Spring of fatness* : the place whence the fertilizing rain flows. *The milch kine* also are the laden clouds, and the *paired Mighty Mothers* are Heaven and Earth, the parents of *the Wondrous* Agni.

9 *His Father's bosom*: his father, according to Sāyaṇa, is the firmament ; but as the firmament is not represented in the Veda as a God, Dyaus, or Tvaṣṭar, is probably intended, as Ludwig suggests.

The *blessed Friends* must be the Ṛbhus, and *the young Dames* the Gnās or consorts of the Gods. *He stayed not hidden* : refers not to Agni but to his father, Tvaṣṭar.

10 *He* : the father, *Many a swelling bosom* : of the celestial Waters.

The Bright and Strong : Agni. *The fellow-spouses* : Heaven and Earth, or Night and Morning.

11 *In the Sister Rivers' service* : or in their bosom, if *upasi* may be read for *apási*.

Friend of the house, within the lap of Order lay Agni, in the Sister Rivers' service.

12 As keen supporter where great waters gather, light-shedder whom the brood rejoice to look on ;
He who begat, and will beget, the dawn-lights, most manly, Child of Floods, is youthful Agni.

13 Him, varied in his form, the lovely Infant of floods and plants the blessed wood hath gendered.
Gods even, moved in spirit, came around him, and served him at his birth, the Strong, the Wondrous.

14 Like brilliant lightnings, mighty luminaries accompany the light-diffusing Agni,
Waxen, as 'twere in secret, in his dwelling, while in the boundless stall they milk out Amṛta.

15 I sacrificing serve thee with oblations and crave with longing thy good-will and friendship.
Grant, with the Gods, thy grace to him who lauds thee, protect us with thy rays that guard the homestead.

16 May we, O Agni, thou who leadest wisely, thy followers and masters of all treasures,
Strong in the glory of our noble offspring, subdue the godless when they seek the battle.

17 Ensign of Gods hast thou become, O Agni, joy-giver, knower of all secret wisdom.
Friend of the homestead, thou hast lightened mortals : carborne thou goest to the Gods, fulfilling.

18 Within the house hath sate the King immortal of mortals, filling full their sacred synods.
Bedewed with holy oil he shineth widely, Agni, the knower of all secret wisdom.

19 Come unto us with thine auspicious friendship, come speeding, Mighty, with thy mighty succours.
Grant us abundant wealth that saves from danger, that brings a good repute, a glorious portion.

20 To thee who art of old these songs, O Agni, have I declared, the ancient and the later.
These great libations to the Strong are offered : in every birth is Jātavedas stablished.

21 Stablished in every birth is Jātavedas, kindled perpetual by the Viśvāmitras.
May we rest ever in the loving-kindness, in the auspicious grace of him the Holy.

22 This sacrifice of ours do thou, O Mighty, O truly Wise, bear to the Gods rejoicing.
Grant us abundant food, thou priestly Herald, vouchsafe to give us ample wealth, O Agni.

23 As holy food, Agni, to thine invoker give wealth in cattle, lasting, rich in marvels.
To us be born a son, and spreading offspring. Agni, be this thy gracious will to us-ward.

HYMN II. *Agni.*

1. To him, Vaiśvānara, who strengthens Holy Law, to Agni we present our praise like oil made pure.
With thoughtful insight human priests bring him anear, our Herald from of old, as an axe forms a car.

2 He made the heaven and earth resplendent by his birth : Child of two Mothers he was meet to be implored,
Agni, oblation-bearer, gracious, ever-young, infallible, rich in radiant light, the guest of men.

3 Within the range of their surpassing power, by might, the Gods created Agni with inventive thought.
I, eager to win strength, address him, like a steed, resplendent with his brilliance, with his ample light.

4 Eager to gain, we crave from him the friendly God strength confident, choice-worthy, meet to be extolled :

12 *The brood* : *par excellence*, the host of Maruts.

13 *The blessed wood* : one of the fire-sticks by which Agni is kindled.

14 *The boundless stall* : limitless aerial space. *Amṛta* : water, according to Sāyaṇa.

17 *Thou goest to the Gods, fulfilling* : completing our sacrifices and making them effectual.

20 *Songs* : literally, births; that is, productions. *In every birth is Jātavedas stablished* : Agni who knows all life is appointed in every generation as the great high priest who mediates between Gods and men.

1 *Vaiśvānara* : Agni who belongs to all men ; the God of all Āryan families.

Our praise : literally 'the wish,' explained by Sāyaṇa as *stutim*, that is the praise which thou wishest for and which we now offer.

2 *Child of two Mothers* : of Heaven and Earth, or of the two fire-sticks.

4 *The Bhṛgus' bounty* : Agni, the treasure which the Bhṛgus received from Mātariśvan and bestowed on other men.

The Bhṛgus' bounty, willing, strong with sages' lore, even Agni shining forth with light that comes from heaven.

5 For happiness, men, having trimmed the sacred grass, set Agni glorious for his strength before them here ;
Yea, with raised ladles, him bright, dear to all the Gods, perfecting aims of works, Rudra of solemn rites.

6 Around thy dwelling-place, O brightly-shining Priest, are men at sacrifice whose sacred grass is trimmed.
Wishing to do thee service, Agni, they are there, desirous of thy friendship : grant them store of wealth.

7 He hath filled heaven and earth and the great realm of light, when at his birth the skilful held him in their hold.
He like a horse is led forth to the sacrifice Sage, graciously inclined, that he may win us strength.

8 Honour the oblation-bearer, him who knows fair rites, serve ye the Household Friend who knows all things that be.
He drives the chariot of the lofty ordinance : Agni most active, is the great High Priest of Gods.

9 They who are free from death, fain for him, purified three splendours of the mighty Agni, circling all.
To man, for his enjoyment, one of these they gave : the other two have passed into the sister sphere.

10 Man's sacrificial food hath sharpened like an axe, for brightness, him the Sage of men, the people's Lord,
Busied with sacred rites he mounts and he descends. He hath laid down his vital germ within these worlds.

11 He stirs with life in wombs dissimilar in kind, born as a Lion or a loudly-bellowing Bull :
Vaiśvānara immortal with wide-reaching might, bestowing goods and wealth on him who offers gifts.

12 Vaiśvānara, as of old, mounted the cope of heaven, heaven's ridge, well greeted, by those skilled in noble songs.
He, as of old, producing riches for the folk, still watchful, traverses the common way again.

13 For new prosperity we seek to Agni, him whose course is splendid, gold-haired, excellently bright,
Whom Mātariśvan stablished, dweller in the heaven, meet for high praise and holy, sage and true to Law.

14 As pure and swift of course, beholder of the light, who stands in heaven's bright sphere a sign, who wakes at dawn,
Agni, the head of heaven, whom none may turn aside—to him the Powerful with mighty prayer we seek.

15 The cheerful Priest, the pure, in whom no guile is found, Friend of the House, praise-worthy, dear to all mankind,
Fair to behold for beauty like a splendid car,—Agni the Friend of men we ever seek for wealth.

HYMN III. *Agni.*

1. To him who shines afar, Vaiśvānara, shall bards give precious things that he may go on certain paths :
For Agni the Immortal serves the Deities, and therefore never breaks their everlasting laws.

2 He, wondrous envoy, goes between the earth and heaven, firm seated as the Herald, great High Priest of men.
He compasseth with rays the lofty dwelling-place, Agni, sent forward by the Gods, enriched with prayer.

3 Sages shall glorify Agni with earnest thoughts, ensign of sacrifice, who fills the synod full :
In whom the singers have stored up their holy acts to him the worshipper looks for joy and happiness.

4 The Sire of sacrifice, great God of holy bards, Agni, the measure and the symbol of the priests,

5 *Rudra* : here a synonym of Agni. See I. 27. 10.
7 *He* : Agni. *The skilful* : the priests.
8 *He drives the chariot* : he is the leader of sacrifice ordained by holy law.
9 *They who are free from death* : the immortal Gods. *Three splerdours* : with reference to his appearance as the Sun, the lightning, and domestic fire, the last of which is given to man as his own special possession.
10 *Within these worlds* : the germ of fire is always latent in the fire-sticks or two pieces of wood which are employed to produce the flame.
11 *Born as a Lion* : destructive and voracious, and as *a loudly-bellowing Bull,* with reference to his strength and the roar of his flames.

12 *The common way* : the path of the Gods, which as the Sun he travels.
14 *Who wakes at dawn* : when re-kindled for the morning sacrifice.

1 *That he may go on certain paths* : may constantly visit men.
2 *The lofty dwelling-place* : the hall or chamber in which sacrifice is celebrated.

Hath entered heaven and earth that show in varied form : the Sage whom many love rejoiceth in his might.

5 Bright Agni with the bright car, Lord of green domains, Vaiśvānara dweller in the floods, who finds the light,
Pervading, swift and wild, encompassed round with powers, him very glorious have the Gods established here.

6 Agni, together with the Gods and Manu's folk by thought extending sacrifice in varied form,
Goes, car-borne, to and fro with those who crown each rite, the fleet, the Household Friend, who turns the curse aside.

7 Sing, Agni, for long life to us and noble sons : teem thou with plenty, shine upon us store of food.
Increase the great man's strength, thou ever-vigilant : thou, longing for the Gods, knowest their hymns full well.

8 The Mighty One, Lord of the people and their guest, the leader of their thoughts, devoted Friend of priests,
Our solemn rites' announcer, Jātavedas, men with worship ever praise, with urgings for their weal.

9 Agni the God resplendent, giver of great joy, hath on his lovely car compassed the lands with might.
Let us with pure laudations in his house approach the high laws of the nourisher of multitudes.

10 I celebrate thy glories, O Vaiśvānara, wherewith thou, O farsighted God, has found the light.
Thou filledst at thy birth both worlds, the earth and heaven : all this, O Agni, hast thou compassed of thyself.

11 By his great skill the Sage alone hath brought to pass a great deed, mightier than Vaiśvānara's wondrous acts.
Agni sprang into being, magnifying both his Parents, Heaven and Earth, rich in prolific seed.

5 *Lord of green domains* : who has dominion over bushes and trees.

6 *To and fro* : between heaven and earth. *Those who crown each rite* : the Gods who make sacrifice effectual.

7 *The great man's strength* : the strength of the eminent man who is the institutor of the sacrifice.

9 *Approach the high laws* : perform the sacrifices——M. Müller.

11 The first hemistich of this stanza is somewhat obscure. Sāyaṇa's paraphrase as given by Wilson is : 'From acts that are acceptable to Vaiśvānara comes great (wealth) ; for he, the sage (Agni) alone, bestows (the reward) of zeal in (the performance of) his worship.

HYMN IV *Āprīs.*

1. Be friendly with each kindled log of fuel, with every flash bestow the boon of riches.
Bring thou the Gods, O God, unto our worship : serve, well-inclined, as Friend thy friends, O Agni.

2 Agni whom daily Varuṇa and Mitra the Gods bring thrice a day to this our worship,
Tanūnapāt, enrich with meath our service that dwells with holy oil, that offers honour.

3 The thought that bringeth every boon proceedeth to worship first the Priest of the libation,
That we may greet the Strong One with our homage. Urged, may he bring the Gods, best Sacrificer.

4 On high your way to sacrifice was made ready ; the radiant flames went upward to the regions.
Full in the midst of heaven the Priest is seated : strew we the sacred grass where Gods may rest them.

5 Claiming in mind the seven priests' burnt-oblations, inciting all, they came in settled order.
To this our sacrifice approach the many who show in hero beauty at assemblies.

6 Night and Dawn, lauded, hither come together, both smiling, different are their forms in colour,
That Varuṇa and Mitra may accept us, and Indra, girt by Maruts, with his glories.

7 I crave the grace of heaven's two chief Invokers : the seven swift steeds joy in their wonted manner.

The Āprīs who are said to be the deities of this hymn are the divine or deified beings and objects to which the propitiatory verses are addressed. The hymn, as Wilson remarks, 'is more complicated and obscure than any of the preceding addressed to the Āprīs, except Sūkta III, of the Second Maṇḍala (II. 3), to which it bears the nearest analogy : they are both perhaps of somewhat later date than the others.'

2 *Tanūnapāt* : a name of Agni 'Child of Thyself.' See I. 12. 2

4 *Your way* : a path for Agni and the *Barhis* or sacred grass, the God and the deified object addressed in the stanza.

In the midst of heaven : in the centre of the radiant hall of sacrifice, as Sāyaṇa explains it.

5 This stanza refers to the deified doors of the hall of sacrifice, and to the deities who preside over them.

7 *Heaven's two chief Invokers* : Agni and perhaps Varuṇa. See I. 13. 8.

These speak of truth, praising the truth eternal, thinking on Order as the guards of Order.

8 May Bhāratī with all her Sisters, Iḷā accordant with the Gods, with mortals Agni,
Sarasvatī with all her kindred Rivers, come to this grass, Three Goddesses, and seat them.

9 Well pleased with us do thou O God, O Tvaṣṭar, give ready issue to our procreant vigour,
Whence springs the hero, powerful, skilled in action, lover of Gods, adjuster of the press-stones.

10 Send to the Gods the oblation, Lord of Forests; and let the Immolator, Agni, dress it.
He as the truer Priest shall offer worship, for the Gods' generations well he knoweth.

11 Come thou to us, O Agni, duly kindled, together with the potent Gods and Indra.
On this our grass sit Aditi, happy Mother, and let our Hail delight the Gods Immortal.

HYMN V. *Agni.*

1. AGNI who shines against the Dawns is wakened. The holy Singer who precedes the sages.
With far-spread lustre, kindled by the pious, the Priest hath thrown both gates of darkness open.

2 Agni hath waxen mighty by laudations, to be adored with hymns of those who praise him.
Loving the varied shows of holy Order at the first flush of dawn he shines as envoy.

3 Amid men's homes hath Agni been established, fulfilling with the Law, Friend, germ of waters.
Loved and adored, the height he hath ascended, the Singer, object of our invocations.

4 Agni is Mitra when enkindled duly, Mitra as Priest, Varuṇa, Jātavedas;
Mitra as active minister, and House-Friend, Mitra of flowing rivers and of mountains.

5 The Earth's, the Bird's dear lofty place he guardeth, he guardeth in his might the course of Sūrya,
Guardeth the Seven-headed in the centre, guardeth sublime the Deities enjoyment.

6 The skilful God who knows all forms of knowledge made for himself a fair form, meet for worship.
This Agni guards with care that never ceases the Soma's skin, the Bird's place rich in fatness.

7 Agni hath entered longingly the longing shrine rich with fatness, giving easy access.
Resplendent, pure, sublime and purifying, again, again he renovates his Mothers.

8 Born suddenly, by plants he grew to greatness, when tender shoots with holy oil increased him,
Like waters lovely when they hasten downward may Agni in his Parents' lap protect us.

9 Extolled, the Strong shone forth with kindled fuel to the earth's centre, to the height of heaven.
May Agni, Friend, adorable Mātariśvan, as envoy bring the Gods unto our worship.

The seven swift steeds: seven ministering priests.

8 *Bhāratī*, *Iḷā*, and *Sarasvatī* are Goddesses presiding over different departments of religious worship. See I. 13. 9. The name of Agni is inserted somewhat unconnectedly.

10 *Lord of Forests*: Vanaspati, a large tree; here the sacrificial post which is said to be a form of Agni.

Truer Priest as compared with human priests.

11 *Happy Mother*: literally, having excellent sons, the Ādityas.

---

1 *Who shines against the Dawns*: rekindled for the morning sacrifices.

Who precedes the sages: as their guide and teacher. *The Priest*: Agni.

3 *The height*: the place called the north altar, says Sāyaṇa. Perhaps the height of heaven may be intended.

4 Agni is here identified with Mitra, the Sun, and both these Gods are identified with Varuṇa.

5 *The dear lofty place* of the earth may be the altar, or the eastern point. *The Bird* is the Sun who flies through heaven. *The Seven-headed*, said by Sāyaṇa to be the host of Maruts, is more probably the Sun drawn by his seven horses.

6 *The Soma's skin*: the meaning of the words *sasásya cárma* is not clear. An envelope or a covering, which in some mystical way is supposed to conceal the Soma-plant, appears to be intended. *The Bird's place*: the station of the Sun, who is adored with oblations of clarified butter.

7 *His Mothers*: or his parents, Heaven and Earth, who are strengthened and restored to their youth by sacrifice.

The *plants* are the twigs used as fuel, and the *tender shoots* are the bunch of grass used in sprinkling the clarified butter over the fire.

9 *The earth's centre*: earth's most important place, the altar.

In the second hemistich Agni is identified with Mātariśvan the divine or semi-divine being who brought him from heaven.

10 Best of all luminaries lofty Agni supported with his flame the height of heaven,
When, far from Bhṛgus, Mātariśvan kindled the oblation-bearer where he lay in secret.

11 As holy food, Agni to thine invoker give wealth in cattle, lasting, rich in marvels.
To us be born a son and spreading offspring. Agni, be this thy gracious will to us-word.

HYMN VI. *Agni.*

1. Urged on by deep devotion, O ye singers, bring, pious ones, the God-approaching ladle.
Borne onward to the right it travels eastward, and, filled with oil, to Agni bears oblation.

2 Thou at thy birth didst fill both earth and heaven, yea, Most Adorable, thou didst exceed them.
Even through the heaven's and through the earth's expanses let thy swift seven-tongued flames roll on, O Agni.

3 Both Heaven and Earth and Gods who should be worshipped establish thee as Priest for every dwelling,
Whenever human families, God-devoted, bringing oblations; laud thy splendid lustre.

4 Firm in the Gods' home is the Mighty seated, between vast Heaven and Earth the well-beloved—
Those Cows who yield, unharmed, their nectar, Spouses of the Far-Strider, ever-young, united.

5 Great are the deeds of thee, the Great, O Agni : thou by thy power hast spread out earth and heaven.
As soon as thou wast born thou wast an envoy, thou, Mighty One, was Leader of the people.

6 Bind to the pole with cords of holy Order the long-maned ruddy steeds who sprinkle fatness.
Bring hither, O thou God, all Gods together : provide them noble worship, Jātavedas.

7 Even from the sky thy brilliant lights shone hither : still hast thou beamed through many a radiant morning,
That the Gods praised their joyous Herald's labour eagerly burning, Agni, in the forests.

8 The Gods who take delight in air's wide region, or those the dwellers in heaven's realm of brightness,
Or those, the Holy, prompt to hear, our helpers, who, carborne, turn their horses hither, Agni—

9 With these, borne on one ear, Agni, approach us, or borne on many, for thy steeds are able.
Bring, with their Dames, the Gods, the Three and-Thirty, after thy Godlike nature, and be joyful.

10 He is the Priest at whose repeated worship even wide Heaven and Earth sing out for increase.
They fair and true and holy coming forward stand at his sacrifice who springs from Order.

11 As holy food, Agni, to thine invoker give wealth in cattle, lasting, rich in marvels.
To us be born a son and spreading offspring. Agni, be this thy gracious will to usward.

HYMN VII.

1. The seven tones risen from the white-backed viand have made their way between the pair of Mothers.
Both circumjacent Parents come together : to yield us length of days they hasten forward.

10 *Far from Bhṛgus* : the words in the text would seem to mean that Mātariśvan took the fire from the Bhṛgus ; but as Ludwig suggests, *pári* perhaps implies separation. Sāyaṇa explains *Bhṛgus* in this place by rays of the Sun.

---

1 *The God-approaching ladle* : the sacrificial ladle with which the oblation of clarified butter or oil is offered to the Gods.

Borne onward to the right : or to the south of the fire-altar. According to Ludwig, bearing the sacrificial gift.

4 *The Mighty* : Agni. *Those Cows* : Heaven and Earth who yield all blessings, here called also the spouses of Viṣṇu, the God of the mighty stride, that is, the Sun, or as Sāyaṇa says, of the far-extending Agni.

9 *The Three-and-Thirty* : See I. 34. 11.

This hymn and the five following are ascribed to the Ṛṣi Viśvāmitra.

---

1 *The seven tones* are the hymns sung in seven tones, or metres. *The white-backed wand* is the Soma mingled with milk, and *the pair of Mothers* or Mother and Father are heaven and Earth whose intermediate space the hymns have reached. The *circumjacent Parents* are heaven and Earth. The construction in the first half of the stanza is difficult, the masculine form *ye* being apparently used for the feminine. Sāyaṇa inserts *raśmayaḥ*, rays, which he makes the subject of the first sentence, and explains *dhā́si*, viand, by 'the all-sustaining Agni,' and *saptá vā́ṇīḥ*, seven voices or tones, by 'the flowing rivers.' The hymn is full of difficulties ; 'an intentionally obscure hymn, says Professor Grassmann, 'whose partially corrupt text cannot, on account of this obscurity, be satisfactorily re-established.'

2 The Male who dwells in heaven hath Mares and Milchkine : he came to Goddesses who bring sweet treasure.
To thee safe resting in the seat of Order the Cow alone upon her way proceedeth.

3 Wise Master, wealthy finder-out of riches, he mounted those who may with ease be guided.
He, dark-backed, manifold with varied aspect, hath made them burst forth from their food the brush-wood.

4 Strength-giving streams bear hither him eternal, fain to support the mighty work of Tvaṣṭar.
He, flashing in his home with all his members, hath entered both the worlds as they were single.

5 They know the red Bull's blessing, and are joyful under the flaming-coloured Lord's dominion :
They who give shine from heaven with fair effulgence, whose lofty song like Iḷā must be honoured.

6 Yea, by tradition from the ancient sages they brought great strength from the two mighty Parents,
To where the singer's Bull, the night's dispeller, after his proper law hath waxen stronger.

7 Seven holy singers guard with five Adhvaryus the Bird's beloved firmly-settled station.
The willing Bulls, untouched by old, rejoice them : as Gods themselves the ways of Gods they follow.

8 I crave the grace of heaven's two chief Invokers : the seven swift steeds joy in their wonted manner.
These speak of truth, praising the Truth Eternal, thinking on Order as the guards of Order.

9 The many seek the great Steed as a stallion : the reins obey the Lord of varied colour.
O heavenly Priest, most pleasant, full of wisdom, bring the great Gods to us, and Earth and Heaven.

10 Rich Lord, the Mornings have gleamed forth in splendour, fair-rayed, fair-speaking, worshipped with all viands,
Yea, with the glory of the earth, O Agni. Forgive us, for our weal, e'en sin committed.

11 As holy food, Agni, to thine invoker, give wealth in cattle, lasting, rich in marvels.
To us be born a son, and spreading offspring Agni, be this thy gracious will to usward.

HYMN VIII *Sacrificial Post.*

1. GOD-SERVING men, O Sovran of the Forest, with heavenly meath at sacrifice anoint thee.
Grant wealth to us when thou art standing upright as when reposing on this Mother's bosom.

2 Set up to eastward of the fire enkindled, accepting prayer that wastes not, rich in hero.
Driving far from us poverty and famine, lift thyself up to bring us great good fortune.

3 Lord of the Forest, raise thyself up on the loftiest spot of earth.

2 *The Male who dwells in heaven* : celestial Agni. The *Mares and Milch-kine* are the Goddesses of the air : *To thee* : to Agni.

The Cow : Vāk the Goddess of Speech, i.e., speech itself, prayer.

3 *Wise Master* : Agni. *Those* : his mares, the rapidly advancing flames that bear him onward. *Dark-backed* : with smoke.

4 *Strength-giving streams* : the waters of the air which bring down the embryo Agni in rain. *The mighty work of Tvaṣṭar* : the whole creation, or, as there is no substantive expressed, the sun of Tvaṣṭar, the Sun, may be intended. *As they were single* : hath pervaded and illumined heaven and earth simultaneously, as though they were one world.

5 *The red Bull* : Agni. *They* : perhaps the Gods. *Iḷā* : Prayer or Praise.

6 *They* : the men who first honoured Agni, who is called *the singer's Bull*, the strong God who protects his worshipper.

7 *Adhvaryus* : ministering priests. *The Bird* : the rapidly-flying Agni. *The willing Bulls* : the zealous priests, who in this stanza are boldly called Gods. Cf. 'Is it not written in your law, I said, Ye are Gods ?' (St. John, x. 11).

8 *Heaven's two chief Invokers* : or Hotars ; according to Sāyaṇa, the celestial and the terrestrial Agni. This stanza is repeated from III. 4. 7.

9 *The many* : the adjective is feminine and has no substantive expressed. The Dawns may be intended, or perhaps libations.

10 This concluding stanza is the burden of several hymns of this Book, and there is considerable variation in Sāyaṇa's interpretation of it in the different places in which it occurs.

---

1 *O Sovran of the Forest* : the tall tree (*vánaspáti*) out of which is made the sacrificial post to which the victim is tied. The post when consecrated is a deified object and is regarded as a form of Agni.

With heavenly meath : or balm ; sacred oil or clarified butter. For a full account of the ceremony of anointing the Sacrificial Post, see Haug's Aitareya Brāhmaṇa. Vol. II. pp. 74-78.

3 *The loftiest spot of earth* : the altar.

Give splendour, fixt and measured well, to him who brings the sacrifice.

4 Well-robed, enveloped he is come, the youthful : springing to life his glory waxeth greater.
Contemplative in mind and God-adoring, sages of high intelligence upraise him.

5 Sprung up he rises in the days' fair weather, increasing in the men-frequented synod.
With song the wise and skilful consecrate him : his voice the God-adoring singer utters.

6 Ye whom religious men have firmly planted; thou Forest Sovran whom the axe hath fashioned,—
Let those the Stakes divine which here are standing be fain to grant us wealth with store of children.

7 O men who lift the ladles up, these hewn and planted in the ground,
Bringing a blessing to the field, shall bear our precious gift to Gods.

8 Ādityas, Rudras, Vasus, careful leaders, Earth, Heaven, and Pṛthivi and Air's mid-region,
Accordant Deities, shall bless our worship and make our sacrifice's ensign lofty.

9 Like swan's that flee in lengthened line, the Pillars have come to us arrayed in brilliant colour.
They, lifted up on high, by sages, eastward, go forth as Gods to the God's dwelling-places.

10 Those Stakes upon the earth with rings that deck them seem to the eye like horns of horned creatures;
Or, as upraised by priests in invocation, let them assist us in the rush to battle.

11 Lord of the Wood, rise with a hundred branches : with thousand branches may we rise to greatness,
Thou whom this hatchet, with an edge well whetted for great felicity, hath brought before us.

4 *Well-robed, enveloped* : with a cord or garland.

5 *In the days' fair weather* : when the periodical Rains are over.

7 *These hewn and planted* : apparently splinters cut from the tree.

8 *Pṛthivī* : Earth regarded as single, and not as one of the constantly connected pair Heaven and Earth.

9 *Pillars* : apparently chips or splinters (cf. stanza 7) which fall from the tree, as it is cut to form the Sacrificial Stake, like white or grey birds alighting on the ground.

HYMN IX.

1. We as thy friends have chosen thee, mortals a God, to be our help,
The Waters' Child, the blessed, the resplendent One, victorious and beyond compare.

2 Since thou delighting in the woods hast gone unto thy mother streams,
Not to be scorned, Agni, is that return of thine when from afar thou now art here.

3 O'er pungent smoke host thou prevailed, and thus art thou benevolent.
Some go before, and others round about thee sit, they in whose friendship thou hast place.

4 Him who had passed beyond his foes, beyond continual pursuits, Him the unerring Ones, observant, found in floods, couched like a lion in his lair.

5 Him wandering at his own free will, Agni here hidden from our view,
Him Mātariśvan brought to us from far away produced by friction, from the Gods.

6 O Bearer of Oblations, thus mortals received thee from the Gods,
Whilst thou, the Friend of man, guardest each sacrifice with thine own power, Most Youthful One.

7 Amid thy wonders this is good, yea, to the simple is it clear,
When gathered round about thee, Agni, lie the herds where thou art kindled in the morn.

8 Offer to him who knows fair rites, who burns with purifying glow,
Swift envoy, active, ancient, and adorable: serve ye the God attentively.

9 Three times a hundred Gods and thrice a thousand, and three times ten and nine have worshipped Agni,

2 *That return of thine* : thy descent from the celestial waters in which thou art born as lightning.

3 *Some* : according to Sāyaṇa, the Adhvaryus ; *others* : the Sāma-priests who sit and recite the prayers and hymns.

4 *The unerring Ones* : The Gods, who followed and found the fugitive Agni.

5 *Mātariśvan* : the divine or semi-divine being who brought Agni to men. See Index.

7 *In the morn* : before the cattle are sent out to graze. *The herds*, according to the Scholiast, include men as well as quadrupeds.

9 In the Vaiśvadeva Nivid or Hymn of Invitation to the Viśvedevas, the number of the Gods is said to be 3 times 11, then 33, then 303, then 3003. By adding together 33 + 303 + 3003 the number 3339 is obtained. See Haug's Aitareya Brāhmaṇa, II. p. 212, note.

For him spread sacred grass, with oil bedewed him, and stablished him as Priest and Sacrificer.

HYMN X. *Agni.*

1. Thee Agni, God, Imperial Lord of all mankind, do mortal men
With understanding kindle at the sacrifice.
2 They laud thee in their solemn rites, Agni, as Minister and Priest,
Shine forth in thine own home as guardian of the Law.
3 He, verily, who honours thee with fuel, Knower of all life,
He, Agni! wins heroic might, he prospers well.
4 Ensign of sacrifices, he, Agni, with Gods is come to us,
Decked by the seven priests, to him who bringeth gifts.
5 To Agni, the Invoking Priest, offer your best, your lofty speech,
To him Ordainer-like who brings the light of songs.
6 Let these our hymns make Agni grow, whence, meet for laud, he springs to life,
To mighty strength and great possession, fair to see.
7 Best Sacrificer, bring the Gods, O Agni, to the pious man :
A joyful Priest, thy splendour drive our foes afar !
8 As such, O Purifier, shine on us heroic glorious might :
Be nearest Friend to those who laud thee, for their weal.
9 So, wakeful, versed in sacred hymns, the holy singers kindly thee.
Oblation-bearer, deathless, cherisher of strength.

HYMN XI. *Agni.*

1. Agni is Priest, the great High Priest of sacrifice, most swift in act :
He knows the rite in constant course.
2 Oblation-bearer, deathless, well inclined, an eager messenger,
Agni comes nigh us with the thought.
3 Ensign of sacrifice from of old, Agni well knoweth with his thought
To prosper this man's aim and hope.
4 Agni, illustrious from old time, the Son of Strength who knows all life,
The Gods have made to their Priest.
5 Infallible is Agni, he who goes before the tribes of men,
A chariot swift and ever new.
6 Strength of the Gods which none may harm, subduing all his enemies,
Agni is mightiest in fame.
7 By offering sacred food to him the mortal worshipper obtains.
A home from him whose light makes pure.
8 From Agni, by our hymns, may we gain all things that bring happiness,
Singers of him who knows all life.
9 O Agni, in our deeds of might may we obtain all precious things :
The Gods are centred all in thee.

HYMN XII. *Indra-Agni.*

1. Moved, Indra-Agni, by our hymn, come to the juice, the precious dew:
Drink ye thereof, impelled by song.
2 O Indra-Agni, with the man who lauds you comes the wakening rite :
So drink ye both this juice assured.
3 Through force of sacrifice I choose Indra-Agni who love the wise :
With Soma let these sate them here.
4 Indra and Agni I invoke, joint-victors, bounteous, unsubdued,
Foe-slayers, best to win the spoil.
5 Indra and Agni, singers skilled in melody hymn you, bringing lauds :
I choose you for the sacred food.
6 Indra and Agni, ye cast down the ninety forts which Dāsas held,
Together, with one mighty deed.
7 To Indra-Agni reverent thoughts go forward from the holy task
Along the path of sacred Law.
8 O Indra-Agni, powers are yours, and dwellings and delightful food :
Good is your readiness to act.
9 Indra and Agni, in your deeds of might ye deck heaven's lucid realms :
Famed is that hero strength of yours.

5 *Who brings the light of songs* : Who brightens and inspires our hymns.

2 *With the thought* : or, through our prayer.

3 *This man's* : who institutes the sacrifice.

6 *The ninety forts* : ninety is used indefinitely for a large number. The forts are the strongholds of the non-Āryan inhabitants of the country.

7 *The holy task* : sacrifice.

HYMN XIII. *Agni.*

1. To Agni, to this God of yours I sing aloud with utmost power.
May he come to us with the Gods, and sit, best Offerer, on the grass.

2 The Holy, whose are earth and heaven, and succour waits upon his strength;
Him men who bring oblations laud, and they who wish to gain, for grace.

3 He is the Sage who guides these men, Leader of sacred rites is he.
Him your own Agni, serve ye well, who winneth and bestoweth wealth.

4 So may the gracious Agni grant most goodly shelter for our use;
Whence in the heavens or in the floods he shall pour wealth upon our lands.

5 The singers kindle him, the Priest, Agni the Lord of tribes of men,
Resplendent and without a peer through his own excellent designs.

6 Help us, thou Brahman, best of all invokers of the Gods in song.
Beam, Friend of Maruts, bliss on us, O Agni, a most liberal God.

7 Yea, grant us treasure thousandfold with children and with nourishment,
And, Agni, splendid hero strength, exalted, wasting not away.

HYMN XIV. *Agni.*

1 The pleasant Priest is come into the synod, true, skilled in sacrifice, most wise, Ordainer.
Agni, the Son of Strength, whose car is lightning, whose hair is flame, hath shown on earth his lustre.

2 To thee I offer reverent speech: accept it: to thee who markest it, victorious, faithful!
Bring, thou who knowest, those who know, and seat thee amid the sacred grass, for help, O Holy.

3 The Two who show their vigour, Night and Morning, by the wind's paths shall haste to thee, O Agni.
When men adorn the Ancient with oblations, these seek, as on two chariot-seats, the dwelling.

4 To thee, strong Agni! Varuṇa and Mitra and all the Maruts sang a song of triumph,
What time unto the people's lands thou camest, spreading them as the Sun of men, with lustre.

5 Approaching with raised hands and adoration, we have this day fulfilled for thee thy longing.
Worship the Gods with most devoted spirit, a Priest with no unfriendly thought, O Agni.

6 For, Son of Strength, from thee come many succours, and powers abundant that a God possesses.
Agni, to us with speech that hath no falsehood grant riches, real, to be told in thousands.

7 Whatever, God, in sacrifice we mortals have wrought is all for thee, strong, wise of purpose!
Be thou the Friend of each good chariot's master. All this enjoy thou here, immortal Agni.

HYMN XV. *Agni.*

1. Resplendent with thy wide-extending lustre, dispel the terrors of the fiends who hate us
May lofty Agni be my guide and shelter, the easily-invoked, the good Protector.

2 Be thou to us, while now the morn is breaking, be thou a guardian when the Sun hath mounted.
Accept, as men accept a true-born infant, my laud, O Agni nobly born in body.

3 Bull, who beholdest men, through many mornings, among the dark ones shine forth red, O Agni.
Lead us, good Lord, and bear us over trouble: Help us who long, Most Youthful God, to riches.

4 Shine forth, a Bull invincible, O Agni, winning by conquest all the forts and treasures,
Thou Jātavedas who art skilled in guiding, the chief high saving sacrifice's Leader.

The hymn and that which follows are ascribed to the Ṛṣi Ṛṣabha, a son of Viśvāmitra.

6 *Thou Brahman*: Agni is here addressed as the Brahman or praying priest.

---

2 *Those who know*: the Gods.

3 *The Ancient*: Agni.

4 *Spreading them*: causing Āryan men to spread as the sun spreads his rays.

5 *Thy longing*: for oblations.

7 *All this*: all our sacrificial offerings.

---

3 *Among the dark ones*: in the darkness of the nights.

5 Lighting Gods hither, Agni, wisest Singer, bring thou to us many and flawless shelters.
Bring vigour, like a car that gathers booty : bring us, O Agni, beauteous Earth and Heaven.
6 Swell, O thou Bull and give those powers an impulse, e'en Earth and Heaven who yield their milk in plenty,
Shining, O God, with Gods in clear effulgence. Let not a mortal's evil will obstruct us.
7 Agni, as holy food to thine invoker, give wealth in cattle, lasting, rich in marvels.
To us be born a son and spreading offspring. Agni, be this thy gracious will to us-ward.

HYMN XVI. *Agni.*

1. THIS Agni is the Lord of great felicity and hero strength ; Lord of wealth in herds of kine ; Lord of the battles with the foe.
2 Wait, Maruts, Heroes, upon him the Prosperer in whom is bliss-increasing wealth ;
Who in fights ever conquer evil-hearted men, who overcome the enemy.
3 As such, O Agni, deal us wealth and hero might, O Bounteous One !
Most lofty, very glorious, rich in progeny, free from disease and full of power.
4 He who made all that lives, who passes all in might, who orders service to the Gods,
He works among the Gods, he works in hero strength, yea, also in the praise of men.
5 Give us not up to indigence, Agni, nor want of hero sons,
Nor, Son of Strength, to lack of cattle, nor to blame. Drive thou our enemies away.
6 Help us to strength, blest Agni ! rich in progeny, abundant, in our sacrifice.
Flood us with riches yet more plenteous, bringing weal, with high renown, most Glorious One !

HYMN XVII. *Agni.*

1. DULY enkindled after ancient customs, bringing all treasures, he is balmed with unguents,—
Flame-haired, oil-clad, the purifying Agni, skilled in fair rites, to bring the Gods for worship.
2 As thou, O Agni, skilful Jātavedas, hast sacrificed as Priest of Earth, of Heaven,
So with this offering bring the Gods, and prosper this sacrifice today as erst for Manu.
3 Three are thy times of life, O Jātavedas, and the three mornings are thy births, O Agni.
With these, well-knowing, grant the Gods' kind favour, and help in stir and stress the man who worships.
4 Agni most bright and fair with song we honour, yea, the adorable, O Jātavedas.
Thee, envoy, messenger, oblation-bearer, the Gods have made centre of life eternal.
5 That Priest before thee, yet more skilled in worship, stablished of old, health-giver by his nature,—
After his custom offer, thou who knowest, and lay our sacrifice where Gods may taste it.

HYMN XVIII. *Agni.*

1. AGNI, be kind to us when we approach thee, good as a friend to friend, as sire and mother.
The races of mankind are great oppressors : burn up malignity that strives against us.
2 Agni, burn up the unfriendly who are near us, burn thou the foeman's curse who pays no worship.
Burn, Vasu, thou who markest well, the foolish : let thine eternal nimble beams surround thee.
3 With fuel, Agni, and with oil, desirous, mine offering I present for strength and conquest,
With prayer, so far as I have power, adoring—this hymn divine to gain a hundred treasures.

---

6 *Their milk* : rain and all fertilizing influence.

2 *Who* : referring to the Maruts : the verbs being in the third person.

3 *Most lofty etc.* : these epithets qualify wealth and hero might.

3 *Three are thy times of life* : the existence of Agni upon earth is said to be threefold as dependent on the supply of fuel, clarified butter, and Soma. *The three mornings* : Agni is re-born every morning, and the number three appears to be used merely for the sake of accordance with the three times of life previously mentioned.

5 *That Priest before thee* : Agni's more skilful predecessor is probably the celestial Agni, the high priest who sacrifices for the Gods. The terrestrial Agni is to take him for his model.

4 Give with thy glow, thou Son of Strength, when lauded, great vital power to those who toil to serve thee.
Give richly, Agni, to the Viśvāmitras in rest and stir. Oft have we decked thy body.

5 Give us, O liberal Lord, great store of riches, for, Agni, such art thou when duly kindled.
Thou in the happy singer's home bestowest, amply with arms extended, things of beauty.

HYMN XIX. *Agni.*

1. **Agni,** quick, sage, infallible, all-knowing, I choose to be our Priest at this oblation.
In our Gods' service he, best skilled, shall worship : may he obtain us boons for strength and riches.

2 Agni, to thee I lift the oil-fed ladle, bright, with an offering, bearing our oblation.
From the right hand, choosing the Gods' attendance, he with rich presents hath arranged the worship.

3 Of keenest spirit is the man thou aidest : give us good offspring, thou who givest freely.
In power of wealth most rich in men. O Agni, of thee, the Good, may we sing forth fair praises.

4 Men as they worship thee the God, O Agni, have set on thee full many a brilliant aspect.
So bring, Most Youthful One, the Gods' assembly, the Heavenly Host which thou to-day shalt honour.

5 When Gods anoint thee Priest at their oblation, and seat thee for thy task as Sacrificer,
O Agni, be thou here our kind defender, and to ourselves vouchsafe the gift of glory.

HYMN XX *Agni.*

1. **With** lauds at break of morn the priest invoketh Agni, Dawn, Dadhikrās, and both the Aśvins.
With one consent the Gods whose light is splendid, longing to taste our sacrifice, shall hear us.

2 Three are thy powers, O Agni, three thy stations, three are thy tongues, yea, many, Child of Order !
Three bodies hast thou which the Gods delight in : with these protect our hymns with care unceasing.

3 O Agni, many are the names thou bearest, Immortal, God, Divine, and Jātavedas :
And many charms of charmers, All-Inspirer ! have they laid in thee, Lord of true attendants !

4 Agni, like Bhaga, leads the godly people, he who is true to Law and guards the seasons.
Ancient, all-knowing, he the Vṛtra-slayer shall bear the singer safe through every trouble.

5 I call on Savitar the God, on Morning, Bṛhaspati, and Dadhikrās, and Agni,
On Varuṇa and Mitra, on the Aśvins, Bhaga, the Vasus, Rudras and Ādityas.

HYMN XXI. *Agni.*

1. **Set** this our sacrifice among the Immortals : be pleased with these our presents, Jātavedas.
O Priest, O Agni, sit thee down before us, and first enjoy the drops of oil and fatness.

2 For thee, O Purifier, flow the drops of fatness rich in oil.
After thy wont vouchsafe to us the choicest boon that Gods may feast.

3 Agni, Most Excellent ! for thee the Sage are drops that drip with oil.
Thou art enkindled as the best of Seers. Help thou the sacrifice.

4 To thee, O Agni, mighty and resistless, to thee stream forth the drops of oil and fatness.
With great light art thou come, O praised by poets ! Accept our offering, O thou Sage.

---

4 *Full many a brilliant aspect* : bright appearance, or splendid presence.

1 *Dadhikrās* : or Dadhikrā, is a mythical being described as a kind of divine horse, and probably a personification of the morning Sun. He is invoked in the morning together with Agni, Uṣas and the Aśvins.

2 *Three are thy powers* : or three kinds of strengthening food, clarified butter, fuel, and Soma. *Three thy stations* : Three altars, or the three worlds. *Three are thy tongues* : the three fires, Gārhapatya, Āhavanīya and Dakṣiṇā, *Three bodies* : or forms as Pāvaka, Pavamāna, and Śuci.

3 *The names thou bearest* : or the natures thou possessest. *Many charms* : or supernatural powers.

5 Fatness exceeding rich, extracted from the midst,—this as our gift we offer thee.
Excellent God, the drops run down upon thy skin. Deal them to each among the Gods.

HYMN XXII. *Agni.*

1. THIS is that Agni whence the longing Indra took the pressed Soma deep within his body.
Winner of spoils in thousands, like a courser, with praise art thou exalted, Jātavedas.

2 That light of thine in heaven and earth, O Agni, in plants, O Holy One, and in the waters,
Wherewith thou hast spread wide the air's mid-region—bright is that splendour, wavy, man-beholding.

3 O Agni, to the sea of heaven thou goest: thou hast called hither Gods beheld in spirit.
The waters, too, come hither, those up yonder in the Sun's realm of light, and those beneath it.

4 Let fires that dwell in mist, combined with those that have their home in floods,
Guileless accept our sacrifice, great viands free from all disease.

5 Agni, as holy food to thine invoker give wealth in cattle, lasting, rich in marvels.
To us be born a son and spreading offspring. Agni, be this thy gracious will to us-ward.

HYMN XXIII. *Agni.*

1. RUBBED into life, well stablished in the dwelling, Leader of sacrifice, the Sage, the youthful,
Here in the wasting fuel Jātavedas, eternal, hath assumed immortal being.

2 Both Bhāratas, Devaśravas, Devavāta, have strongly rubbed to life effectual Agni.
O Agni, look thou forth with ample riches : be, every day, bearer of food to feed us.

3 Him nobly born of old the fingers ten produced, him whom his Mothers counted dear.
Praise Devavāta's Agni, thou Devaśravas, him who shall be the people's Lord.

4 He set thee in the earth's most lovely station, in Iḷā's place, in days of fair bright weather.
On man, on Āpayā, Agni ! on the rivers Dṛṣadvatī, Sarasvatī, shine richly.

5 Agni, as holy food to thine invoker give wealth in cattle, lasting, rich in marvels.
To us be born a son and spreading offspring Agni, be this thy gracious will to us-ward

HYMN XXIV. *Agni.*

1. AGNI, subdue opposing bands, and drive our enemies away.
Invincible, slay godless foes : give splendour to the worshipper.

2 Lit with libation, Agni, thou, deathless, who callest Gods to feast,
Accept our sacrifice with joy.

3 With splendour, Agni, Son of Strength, thou who art worshipped, wakeful One.
Seat thee on this my sacred grass.

4 With all thy fires, with all the Gods, Agni, exalt the songs we sing.
And living men in holy rites.

5 Grant, Agni, to the worshipper wealth rich in heroes, plenteous store,
Make thou us rich with many sons.

HYMN XXV. *Agni.*

1. THOU art the sapient Son of Dyaus, O Agni, yes and the Child of Earth, who knowest all things.
Bring the Gods specially, thou Sage, for worship.

5 *Fatness exceeding rich, extracted from the midst* : this hymn, Sāyaṇa says, is suitable for animal sacrifices. The fatness here spoken of is, as Professor Wilson remarks, the same that is described in Leviticus, IV, 9, as 'the fat that covereth the inwards, and all the fat that is upon the inwards.'

1 *Whence* : literally, wherein: that is poured out on whom or which.

2 *Both Bhāratas* : sons of Bharata, the two Ṛṣis of the hymn.

3 *His Mothers* : the two fire-sticks from which Agni springs to life.

4 *He* : the worshipper. *Earth's most lovely station* : according to Sāyaṇa, on the northern altar. *Iḷā's place* : the place of prayer and praise.

Dṛṣadvatī and *Sarasvatī* (see Book I 3 10) are well known streams : *Āpayā* which is not mentioned elsewhere, appears to have been a little stream in the same neighbourhood, near the earlier settlements of the Aryan immigrants.

This hymn and the eight following are ascribed to the Ṛṣi Viśvāmitra.

2. Agni the wise bestows the might of heroes grants strengthening food, preparing it for nectar.
Thou who art rich in food bring the Gods hither.
3 Agni, infallible, lights Earth and Heaven, immortal Goddesses gracious to all men,-
Lord through his strength, splendid through adorations.
4 Come to the sacrifice, Agni and Indra : come to the offerer's house who hath the Soma.
Come, friendly-minded, Gods, to drink the Soma.
5 In the floods' home art thou enkindled, Agni, O Jātavedas, Son of Strength, eternal,
Exalting with thine help the gathering-places.

HYMN XXVI. *Agni.*

1. Revering in our heart Agni Vaiśvānara, the finder of the light, whose promises are true,
The liberal, gladsome, car-borne God, we Kuśikas invoke him with oblation, seeking wealth with songs.
2 That Agni, bright, Vaiśvānara, we invoke for help, and Mātariśvan worthy of the song of praise;
Bṛhaspati for man's observance of the Gods, the Singer prompt to hear, the swiftly-moving guest.
3 Age after age Vaiśvānara, neighing like a horse, is kindled with the women by the Kuśikas.
May Agni, he who wakes among Immortal Gods, grant us heroic strength and wealth in noble steeds.
4 Let them go forth, the strong, as flames of fire with might. Gathered for victory they have yoked their spotted deer.
Pourers of floods, the Maruts, Masters of all wealth, they who can ne'er be conquered, make the mountains shake.
5 The Maruts, Friends of men, are glorious as the fire : their mighty and resplendent succour we implore.
Those storming Sons of Rudra clothed in robes of rain, boon-givers of good gifts, roar as the lions roar.
6 We, band on band and troop following troop, entreat with fair lauds Agni's splendour and the Maruts' might,
With spotted deer for steeds, with wealth that never fails, they, wise Ones, come to sacrifice at our gatherings.
7 Agni am I who know, by birth, all creatures. Mine eye is butter, in my mouth is nectar.
I am light threefold, measurer of the region exhaustless heat am I, named burnt-oblation.
8 Bearing in mind a thought with light accordant, he purified the Sun with three refinings;
By his own nature gained the highest treasure, and looked abroad over the earth and heaven.
9 The Spring that fails not with a hundred streamlets, Father inspired of prayers that men should utter,
The Sparkler, joyous in his Parents' bosom,—him, the Truth-speaker, sate ye, Earth and Heaven.

HYMN XXVII. *Agni.*

1. In ladle dropping oil your food goes in oblation up to heaven,
Goes to the Gods in search of bliss.
2 Agni I laud, the Sage inspired, crowner of sacrifice through song,
Who listens and gives bounteous gifts.
3 O Agni, if we might obtain control of thee the potent God,
Then should we overcome our foes.

5 *In the floods' home* : in the firmament, the home of the aerial waters.

The gathering places: the worlds or regions inhabited by living beings, according to Sāyaṇa.

1 *Vaiśvānara* : common to, dear to, or dwelling with, all Āryan men.

Kuśikas : men of the family of the Ṛṣi Kuśika.

2 *Mātariśvan* : said here by Sāyaṇa to mean Agni as God of the lightning; but the usual sense of the word is appropriate enough.

3 *With the women* : the fingers, elsewhere called the damsels, and the sisters, which agitate the fire-stick.

4 *Let them go forth* : the Maruts, or Storm-Gods.

7 Here Agni speaks and declares his universality as the Soul of all. He knows all living creatures. His eye, or in his eye, is the light which is fed with offerings of sacred oil. The amṛta, nectar, or ambrosia, which is the reward of piety, is obtained by burnt-offerings or through the mouth of Agni. He traverses or measures out the firmament, and as light he shines as the sun in heaven, the lightning in mid-air, and fire on earth. See note on the passage in Wilson's Translation.

8 *With three refinings* : according to Sāyaṇa, with his three purifying forms as Agni, Vāyu, and Sūrya, or fire, wind, and sun. But *Pavitraiḥ* may mean 'with mental divisions, and the sense would be that Agni divided light into three, sun, lightning and fire.

9 *His Parents' bosom* : in close connexion with Heaven and Earth.

4 Kindled at sacrifices he is Agni, hallower, meet for praise,
With flame for hair : to him we seek.
5 Immortal Agni, shining far, enrobed with oil, well worshipped, bears
The gifts of sacrifice away.
6 The priests with ladles lifted up, worshipping here with holy thought,
Have brought this Agni for our aid.
7 Immortal, Sacrificer, God, with wondrous power he leads the way,
Urging the great assembly on.
8 Strong, he is set on deeds of strength. In sacrifices led in front,
As Singer he completes the rite.
9 Excellent, he was made by thought. The Germ of beings have I gained,
Yea, and the Sire of active strength.
10 Thee have I stablished, Excellent, O strengthened by the sage's prayer,
Thee, Agni, longing, nobly bright.
11 Agni, the swift and active One, singers, at time of sacrifice,
Eagerly kindle with their food.
12 Agni the Son of Strength who shines up to the heaven in solemn rites,
The wise of heart, I glorify.
13 Meet to be lauded and adored, showing in beauty through the dark,
Agni, the Strong, is kindled well.
14 Agni is kindled as a bull, like a horse-bearer of the Gods:
Men with oblations worship him.
15 Thee will we kindle as a bull, we who are Bulls ourselves, O Bull.
Thee, Agni, shining mightily.

HYMN XXVIII. *Agni.*

1. AGNI who knowest all, accept our offering and the cake of meal,
At dawn's libation, rich in prayer !
2 Agni, the sacrificial cake hath been prepared and dressed for thee :
Accept it, O Most Youthful God.
3 Agni, enjoy the cake of meal and our oblation three days old:
Thou, Son of Strength, art stablished at our sacrifice.

9 *He was made by thought* : by holy thought, or devotion.

15 *We who are Bulls ourselves* : Priests are frequently called bulls, on account of their great power. Cf. III. 7. 7.

---

3 *Our oblation three days old* : the Soma juice prepared the day before yesterday and left to ferment.

4 Here at the midday sacrifice enjoy thou the sacrificial cake, wise, Jātavedas!
Agni, the sages in assemblies never minish the portion due to thee the Mighty.
5 O Agni, at the third libation take with joy the offered cake of sacrifice, thou, Son of Strength.
Through skill in song bear to the Gods our sacrifice, watchful and fraught with riches, to Immortal God.
6 O waxing Agni, knower, thou, of all, accept our gifts, the cake,
And that prepared ere yesterday.

HYMN XXIX. *Agni.*

1. HERE is the gear for friction, here tinder made ready for the spark.
Bring thou the Matron : we will rub Agni in ancient fashion forth.
2 In the two fire-sticks Jātavedas lieth, even as the well-set germ in pregnant women,
Agni who day by day must be exalted by men who watch and worship with oblations.
3 Lay this with care on that which lies extended : straight hath she borne the Steer when made prolific.
With his red pillar—radiant is his splendour—in our skilled task is born the Son of Iḷā.
4 In Iḷā's place we set thee down, upon the central point of earth,
That, Agni Jātavedas, thou mayst bear our offerings to the Gods.
5 Rub into life, ye men, the Sage, the guileless, Immortal, very wise and fair to look on.
O men, bring forth the most propitious Agni, first ensign of the sacrifice to eastward.
6 When with their arms they rub him straight he shineth forth like a strong courser, red in colour, in the wood.

1 *Here is the gear for friction* : the word *adhimánthanam* means the upper fire stick and the string used in agitating it. The tinder is a tuft of dry Kuśa grass placed so as to catch the flame produced by attrition.

The Matron : the lower piece of wood in which the spark is generated. Sāyaṇa explains the word *viśpátnīm*, feminine of *viśpáti*, lord of the people, as protectress of men by means of the sacrifices which are performed with the help of the fire which she produces.

3 *Lay this with care* : place the upper fire-stick, which is to be turned rapidly round, upon the lower piece of wood which is prepared to receive it. *The Son of Iḷā* : Agni.

4 *In Iḷā's place* : on the northern altar, the place of worship and libation, or prayer and praise.

Bright, checkless, as it were upon the Aśvins' path, he passeth by the stones and burneth up the grass.

7 Agni shines forth when born, observant, mighty, the bountiful, the Singer praised by sages;
Whom, as adorable and knowing all things, Gods set at solemn rites as offering-bearer.

8 Set thee, O Priest, in thine own place, observant : lay down the sacrifice in the home of worship.
Thou, dear to Gods, shalt serve them with oblation: Agni, give long life to the sacrificer.

9 Raise ye a mighty smoke, my fellow-workers ! Ye shall attain to wealth without obstruction.
This Agni is the battle-winning Hero by whom the Gods have overcome the Dasyus.

10 This is thine ordered place of birth whence sprung to life thou shonest forth.
Knowing this, Agni, sit thee down, and prosper thou the songs we sing.

11 As Germ Celestial he is called Tanūnapāt, and Narāśaṁsa born diffused in varied shape.
Formed in his Mother he is Mātariśvan; he hath, in his course, become the rapid flight of wind.

12 With strong attrition rubbed to life, laid down with careful hand, a Sage,
Agni, make sacrifices good, and for the pious bring the Gods.

13 Mortals have brought to life the God Immortal, the Conqueror with mighty jaws, unfailing.
The sisters ten, unwedded and united, together grasp the Babe, the new-born Infant.

14 Served by the seven priests, he shone forth from ancient time, when in his Mother's bosom, in her lap, he glowed.
Giving delight each day he closeth not his eye, since from the Asura's body he was brought to life.

6 *As it were upon the Aśvins' path* : with the speed of the Aśvins' chariot.

8 *In thine own place* : the centre of the north altar.

11 *As Germ Celestial* : or child of the Asura Dyaus, that is, in the form of lightning. *In his Mother* : according to Sāyaṇa, in the maternal atmosphere.

13 *The sisters ten* : the fingers used in producing fire.

14 *The Asura's body* : the Asura is, apparently, Dyaus. Professor Wilson, following Sāyaṇa translates, 'from the interior of the (spark) emitting wood.

15 Even as the Maruts' onslaughts who attack the foe, those born the first of all knew the full power of prayer.
The Kuśikas have made the glorious hymn ascend, and, each one singly in his home, have kindled fire.

16 As we, O Priest observant, have elected thee this day, what time the solemn sacrifice began,
So surely hast thou worshipped, surely hast thou toiled : come thou unto the Soma, wise and knowing all.

HYMN XXX. *Indra.*

1. THE friends who offer Soma long to find thee : they pour forth Soma and present their viands.
They bear unmoved the cursing of the people, for all our wisdom comes from thee, O Indra.

2 Not far for thee are mid-air's loftiest regions : start hither, Lord of Bays, with thy Bay Horses.
Made for the Firm and Strong are these libations. The pressing-stones are set and fire is kindled.

3 Fair cheeks hath Indra, Maghavan, the Victor, Lord of a great host, Stormer, strong in action.
What once thou didst in might when mortals vexed thee,—where now, O Bull, are those thy hero exploits ?

4 For, overthrowing what hath ne'er been shaken, thou goest forth alone destroying Vṛtras.
For him who followeth thy Law the mountains and heaven and earth stand as if firmly stablished.

5 Yea, Much-invoked ! in safety through thy glories alone thou speakest truth as Vṛtra's slayer.
E'en these two boundless worlds to thee, O Indra, what time thou graspest them, are but a handful.

6 Forthwith thy Bay steeds down the steep, O Indra, forth, crushing foemen, go thy bolt of thunder !
Slay those who meet thee, those who flee, who follow : make all thy promise true; be all completed.

7 The man to whom thou givest as Provider enjoys domestic plenty undivided.

15 *Those born the first of all* : the most ancient Ṛṣis such as Kuśika and his sons.

Blest, Indra, is thy favour dropping fatness: thy worship, Much-invoked ! brings gifts in thousands.

8 Thou, Indra, Much-invoked ! didst crush to pieces Kuṇāru handless fiend who dwelt with Dānu.

Thou with might, Indra, smotest dead the scorner, the footless Vṛtra as he waxed in vigour.

9 Thou hast established in her seat, O Indra, the level earth, vast, vigorous, unbounded.

The Bull hath propped the heaven and air's mid-region. By thee sent onward let the floods flow hither.

10 He who withheld the kine, in silence yielded in fear before thy blow, O Indra.

He made paths easy to drive forth the cattle. Loud-breathing praises helped the Much-invoked One.

11 Indra alone filled full the earth and heaven, the Pair who meet together, rich in treasures.

Yea, bring thou near us from the air's mid-region strength, on thy car, and wholesome food, O Hero.

12 Sūrya transgresses not the ordered limits set daily by the Lord of Tawny Coursers.

When to the goal he comes, his journey ended, his Steeds he looses: this is Indra's doing.

13 Men gladly in the course of night would look on the broad bright front of the refulgent Morning;

And all acknowledge, when she comes in glory, the manifold and goodly works of Indra.

14 A mighty splendour rests upon her bosom: bearing ripe milk the Cow, unripe, advances.

All sweetness is collected in the Heifer, sweetness which Indra made for our enjoyment.

15 Barring the way they come. Be firm, O Indra; aid friends to sacrifice and him who singeth.

These must be slain by thee, malignant mortals, armed with ill arts, our quiver-bearing foemen.

16 A cry is heard from enemies most near us : against them send thy fiercest-flaming weapon.

Rend them from under, crush them and subdue them. Slay, Maghavan, and make the fiends our booty.

17 Root up the race of Rākṣasas, O Indra ; rend it in front and crush it in the middle.

How long hast thou behaved as one who wavers ? Cast thy hot dart at him who hates devotion :

18 When borne by strong Steeds for our weal, O Leader, thou seatest thee at many noble viands.

May we be winners of abundant riches. May Indra be our wealth with store of children.

19 Bestow on us resplendent wealth. O Indra ; let us enjoy thine overflow of bounty.

Wide as a sea our longing hath expanded, fulfil it, O thou Treasure-Lord of treasures.

20 With kine and horses satisfy this longing ; with very splendid bounty skill extend it.

Seeking the light, with hymns to thee, O Indra, Kuśikas have brought their gift, the singers.

21 Lord of the kine, burst the kine's stable open : cows shall be ours, and strength that wins the booty.

Hero, whose might is true, thy home is heaven : to us, O Maghavan, grant gifts of cattle.

22 Call we on Maghavan, auspicious Indra, best Hero in this fight where spoil is gathered,

The Strong who listens, who gives aid in battles, who slays the Vṛtras, wins and gathers riches.

HYMN XXXI. *Indra.*

1. WISE, teaching, following the thought of Order, the sonless gained a grandson from his daughter.

8 *Kuṇāru* : the name of a demon. *Dānu* : mother of Vṛtra. See I. 32. 9.

9 *The Bull* : the mighty Indra.

10 *In silence* : I adopt Prof. M. Müller's interpretation (Vedic Hymns, I. pp. 227 228) of the difficult word *alātṛṇaḥ*, 'which had evidently become unintelligible even at the time of Yāska.'

12 *Set daily* : with reference, perhaps, as Professor Ludwig remarks, to the apparent change in the sun's place of rising.

14 *The Cow*, and *the Heifer* : beneficent Uṣas or Morning.

15 *They come* : those who revile and hinder the worship of Indra.

1 I am unable to give a satisfactory or even an intelligible version or explanation of the first two stanzas which appear to attribute, in a very obscure manner, to Agni and the Gods in heaven the customs or laws of succession to property among men. In the first stanza *vāhniḥ*, which usually means an oblation-bearer, a sacrificer, a priest, or one who is borne along as a God in a celestial car, is said by Sāyaṇa to mean sonless, the father of a daughter only, because he transfers his property through his married daughter into another family. The sonless father, according to Sāyaṇa, 'stipulates that his daughter's son, his grandson, shall be his son, a mode of affiliation recognized by law; and, relying on an

Fain, as a sire, to see his child prolific, he sped to meet her with an eager spirit.

2 The Son left not his portion to the brother, he made a home to hold him who should gain it.
What time his Parents gave the Priest his being, of the good pair one acted, one promoted.

3 Agni was born trembling with tongue that flickered, so that the Red's great children should be honoured.
Great is their germ, that born of them is mighty, great the Bays' Lord's approach through sacrifices.

4 Conquering bands upon the Warrior waited: they recognized great light from out the darkness.
The conscious Dawns went forth to meet his coming, and the sole Master of the kine was Indra.

5 The sages freed them from their firm-built prison: the seven priests drove them forward with their spirit.
All holy Order's pathway they discovered; he, full of knowledge, shared these deeds through worship.

6 When Saramā had found the mountain's fissure, that vast and ancient place she plundered thoroughly.
In the floods' van she led them forth, light-footed: she who well knew came first unto their lowing.

7 Longing for friendship came the noblest singer: the hill poured forth its treasure for the pious.
The Hero with young followers fought and conquered, and straightway Aṅgiras was singing praises,

8 Peer of each noble thing, yea, all excelling, all creatures doth he know, he slayeth Śuṣṇa.
Our leader, fain for war, singing from heaven, as Friend he saved his lovers from dishonour.

9 They sate them down with spirit fain for booty, making with hymns a way to life eternal.
And this is still their place of frequent session, whereby they sought to gain the months through Order.

10 Drawing the milk of ancient seed prolific, they joyed as they beheld their own possession.
Their shout of triumph heated earth and heaven. When the kine showed, they bade the heroes rouse them.

11 Indra drove forth the kine, that Vṛtra-slayer, while hymns of praise rose up and gifts were offered.
For him the Cow, noble and far-extending, poured pleasant juices, bringing oil and sweetness.

heir thus obtained, and one who can perform his funeral rites, he is satisfied.' This may be intelligible, but what it has to do with Agni or with the rest of the the hymn is not clear. Grassmann takes *váhniḥ* to mean the upper fire-stick, and the daughter to mean the lower piece of wood.

2 *The Son left not his portion to the brother*: Wilson, following Sāyaṇa translates: '(a son) born of the body does not transfer (paternal) wealth to a sister.' Ludwig takes the meaning to be: the bodily son (of Dyaus, or of the heavenly waters) did not transmit his inheritance (that is, sacrifice) to a brother. *A home*: the plants which receive and hold Agni, who obtains the inheritance of sacrifice. *His Parents*: perhaps the fire-sticks, one of which by agitation produces the flame in the other. *The good pair*: the terrestrial offerer who performs the sacrifice, and the celestial offerer who makes it effectual. See Bergaigne, *La Religion Védique*, I. 284.

Ludwig allows that the meaning of the first two stanzas is problematical, and Wilson says of his own translation: 'these two verses, if rightly interpreted, are wholly unconnected with the subject of the *Sūkta*, and come in without any apparent object: they are very obscure, and are only made somewhat intelligible by interpretations which seem to be arbitrary, and are very unusual, although not peculiar to Sāyaṇa, his explanations being based on those of Yāska.

3 *The Red's great children*: the hot rays of the glowing fire. *That born of them*: Indra's coming, which is caused by the kindling of sacrificial fire.

4 *Conquering lands*: the ever-victorious Maruts. *The Warrior*: Indra, their leader. *Master of the kine*: recoverer of the vanished rays of light.

5 *The sages* and *the seven priests*: are the Aṅgirases.

6 *Saramā*: the hound of Indra. See I. 62. 3. *In the floods' van*: hastening out of the mountain cavern in advance of the liberated waters. *Them*: the cows, the waters and the rays of light.

7 *The noblest singer*: as a noun of multitude, all the Aṅgirases.

The Hero: Indra with his allies the Maruts.

9 *They*: the Aṅgirases, who had been eager to recover the cows. *To gain the months*: to acquire the power of keeping the monthly festivals.

10 Or, 'They joyed to see them, as their own possession, yielding the milk of ancient seed prolific.' The Aṅgirases rejoiced as they again beheld the rays of light, shedding what originates and supports all life' Sāyaṇa's rendering of this difficult stanza is thus given by Wilson: 'Contemplating their own (cattle) giving milk to their former progeny (the *Aṅgirasas*) were delighted; their shouts spread through heaven and earth; they replaced the recovered kine in their places, and stationed guards over the cows.'

12 They made a mansion for their Father, deftly provided him a great and glorious dwelling ;
With firm support parted and stayed the Parents, and, sitting, fixed him there erected, mighty.

13 What time the ample chalice had impelled him, swift waxing, vast, to pierce the earth and heaven,—
Him in whom blameless songs are all united : all powers invincible belong to Indra.

14 I crave thy powers, I crave thy mighty friendship : full many a team goes to the Vṛtra-slayer.
Great is the laud, we seek the Princes' favour. Be thou, O Maghavan, our guard and keeper.

15 He, having found great, splendid, rich dominion, sent life and motion to his friends and lovers.
Indra who shone together with the Heroes begot the song, the fire, and Sun and Morning.

16 Vast, the House-Friend, he set the waters flowing, all-lucid, widely spread, that move together.
By the wise cleansings of the meath made holy, through days and nights they speed the swift streams onward.

17 To thee proceed the dark, the treasure-holders, both of them sanctified by Sūrya's bounty.
The while thy lovely storming Friends, O Indra, fail to attain the measure of thy greatness.

18 Be Lord of joyous songs, O Vṛtra-slayer, Bull dear to all, who gives the power of living.
Come unto us with thine auspicious friendship, hastening, Mighty One, with mighty succours.

19 Like Aṅgiras I honour him with worship, and renovate old song for him the Ancient.
Chase thou the many godless evil creatures, and give us, Maghavan, heaven's light to help us.

20 Far forth are spread the purifying waters : convey thou us across them unto safety.
Save us, our Charioteer, from harm, O Indra, soon, very soon, make us win spoil of cattle.

21 His kine their Lord hath shown, e'en Vṛtra's slayer, through the black hosts he passed with red attendants.
Teaching us pleasant things by holy Order, to us hath he thrown open all his portals.

22 Call we on Maghavan, auspicious Indra, best Hero in this fight where spoil is gathered.
The Strong who listens, who gives aid in battles, who slays the Vṛtras, wins and gathers riches.

HYMN XXXII. *Indra*

1. DRINK thou this Soma, Indra, Lord of Soma ; drink thou the draught of noonday which thou lovest.
Puffing thy cheeks, impetuous, liberal Giver, here loose thy two Bay Horses and rejoice thee.

2 Quaff it pure, meal-blent, mixt with milk, O Indra ; we have poured forth the Soma for thy rapture.
Knit with the prayer-fulfilling band of Maruts, yea, with the Rudras, drink till thou art sated ;

12 *For their Father* : according to Sāyaṇa, for their protector Indra. But Agni may be meant, the mansion being the place of sacrifice. *The Parents* : Heaven and Earth, parents of all things.

13 *The ample chalice* : the bowl of Soma juice. But according to Ludwig, *dhiṣaṇā* here and elsewhere, means earnest wish, longing.

14 *Full many a team* : hymns sent forth like teams of horses.

16 *By the wise cleansings* : or according to Sāyaṇa, the wise purifiers, that is, Agni, Vāyu, and Sūrya, who act as purifiers of the libation of Soma juice.

17 *The dark, the treasure-holders* : or, the dark one and the treasure-holder; Night and Day. *Storming Friends* : the Maruts.

20 *The purifying waters* : the epithet *pāvakāḥ*, purifying, is entirely out of place here Ludwig suggests *pāpakāḥ*, wicked, which would be more suitable.

21 *Kine* : rays of light. *Red attendants* : the Maruts. 'Many of the verses in this hymn,' Prof. Wilson observes, 'are of more than usual obscurity.' Prof. Grassmann places the hymn in his Appendix.

1 *Puffing thy cheeks* : meaning, apparently, smacking thy lips in anticipation of the Soma-draught. Sāyaṇa explains it as, 'filling their (Indra's horses) jaws with fodder.' *Impetuous* : this appears to be the meaning of the epithet *ṛjīṣin* as derived from the root *ṛj*, rather than, as Sāyaṇa explains it, 'drinker of the spiritless residue of the Soma.' The latter meaning, however, is admissible, and is supported by good authority.

3 Those who gave increase to thy strength and vigour ; the Maruts singing forth thy might, O Indra.
Drink thou, O fair of cheek, whose hand wields thunder, with Rudras banded, at our noon libation.

4 They, even the Maruts who were there, excited with song the meath-created strength of Indra.
By them impelled to act he reached the vitals of Vṛtra, though he deemed that none might wound him.

5 Pleased, like a man, with our libation, Indra, drink, for enduring hero might, the Soma.
Lord of Bays, moved by sacrifice come hither : thou with the Swift Ones stirrest floods and waters.

6 When thou didst loose the streams to run like racers in the swift contest, having smitten Vṛtra
With flying weapon where he lay, O Indra, and, godless, kept the Goddesses encompassed.

7 With reverence let us worship mighty Indra, great and sublime, eternal, ever-youthful,
Whose greatness the dear world-halves have not measured, no, nor conceived the might of him the Holy.

8 Many are Indra's nobly wrought achievements, and none of all the Gods transgress his statutes.
He beareth up this earth and heaven, and, doer of marvels, he begot the Sun and Morning.

9 Herein, O Guileless One, is thy true greatness, that soon as born thou drankest up the Soma.
Days may not check the power of thee the Mighty, nor the nights, Indra, nor the months, nor autumns.

10 As soon as thou wast born in highest heaven thou drankest Soma to delight thee, Indra ;
And when thou hadst pervaded earth and heaven thou wast the first supporter of the singer.

11 Thou, puissant God, more mighty, slewest. Ahi showing his strength when couched around the waters.
The heaven itself attained not to thy greatness when with one hip of thine the earth was shadowed.

12 Sacrifice, Indra, made thee wax so mighty, the dear oblation with the flowing Soma.
O Worshipful, with worship help our worship, for worship helped thy bolt when slaying Ahi.

13 With sacrifice and wish have I brought Indra ; still for new blessings may I turn him hither,
Him magnified by ancient songs and praises, by lauds of later time and days yet recent.

14 I have brought forth a song when longing seized me : ere the decisive day will I laud Indra ;
Then may he safely bear us over trouble, as in a ship, when both sides invocate him.

15 Full is his chalice : Glory ! Like a pourer I have filled up the vessel for his drinking.
Presented on the right, dear Soma juices have brought us Indra, to rejoice him, hither.

16 Not the deep-flowing flood, O Much-invoked One ! not hills that compass thee about restrain thee,
Since here incited, for thy friends, O Indra, thou breakest e'en the firm built stall of cattle.

17 Call we on Maghavan, auspicious Indra, best Hero in this fight where spoil is gathered,
The Strong who listens, who gives aid in battles, who slays the Vṛtras, wins and gathers riches.

3 *The Maruts singing forth thy might* : the song of the Maruts is the music of 'The winged storms, chanting their thunder-psalm.'—Shelley.

5 *Like a man* : or, as thou wast pleased with the libation of Manu.

The Swift Ones : the Maruts.

6 *The Goddesses* : the heavenly waters.

7 *The dear world-halves* : heaven and earth.

11 *When with one hip of thine the earth was shadowed* : Prof. Wilson, following Sāyaṇa, translates : as thou remainedst concealing the earth by one of (the) flames,' and observes that meaning is not very clear. But *sphigt* means a hip and not a flame, and the poet appears to mean that a portion of Indra's body shadowed or covered the earth while the rest was in the heavens. So, in Book X. 119. 11, Indra is represented as saying when exhilarated by Soma : *diví me anyáḥ pakṣo 'dhó anyám acīkṛṣam*, one side of me is in the sky, and I have drawn the other down.

14 *Ere the decisive day* : on the eve of an important battle.

HYMN XXXIII. *Indra.*

1. FORTH from the bosom of the mountains, eager as two swift mares with loosened rein contending,
Like two bright mother cows who lick their youngling, Vipāś and Śutudrī speed down their waters.

2 Impelled by Indra whom ye pray to urge you, ye move as 'twere on chariots to the ocean.
Flowing together, swelling with your billows, O lucid Streams, each of you seeks the other.

3 I have attained the most maternal River, we have approached Vipāś, the broad, the blessed.
Licking as 'twere their calf the pair of Mothers flow onward to their common home together.

4 We two who rise and swell with billowy waters move forward to the home which Gods have made us.
Our flood may not be stayed when urged to motion. What would the singer, calling to the Rivers ?

5 Linger a little at my friendly bidding ; rest, Holy Ones, a moment in your journey.
With hymn sublime soliciting your favour Kuśika's son hath called unto the River.

6 Indra who wields the thunder dug our channels : he smote down Vṛtra, him who stayed our currents.
Savitar, God, the lovely-handed, led us, and at his sending forth we flow expanded.

7 That hero deed of Indra must be lauded for ever that he rent Ahi in pieces.
He smote away the obstructors with his thunder, and eager for their course forth flowed the waters.

8 Never forget this word of thine, O singer, which future generations shall reëcho.
In hymns, O bard, show us thy loving kindness. Humble us not mid men. To thee be honour !

9 List quickly, Sisters, to the bard who cometh to you from far away with car and wagon.
Bow lowly down ; be easy to be traversed : stay, Rivers, with your floods below our axles.

10 Yea, we will listen to thy words, O singer. With wain and car from far away thou comest.
Low, like a nursing mother, will I bend me, and yield me as a maiden to her lover.

11 Soon as the Bharatas have fared across thee, the warrior band, urged on and sped by Indra,
Then let your streams flow on in rapid motion. I crave your favour who deserve our worship.

12 The warrior host, the Bharatas, fared over : the singer won the favour of the Rivers.
Swell with your billows, hasting, pouring riches. Fill full your channels, and roll swiftly onward.

13 So let your wave bear up the pins, and ye, O Waters, spare the thongs ;
And never may the pair of Bulls, harmless and sinless, waste away.

The hymn is a dialogue between Viśvāmitra and the rivers Vipāś and Śutudrī who are regarded severally as the Ṛṣis or seers of the verses ascribed to them. The legend cited by Sāyaṇa says that Viśvāmitra, the Purohita or family priest of King Sudās, having obtained wealth by means of his office, took the whole of it and came to the confluence of the Vipāś and the Śutudrī. Others followed. In order to make the rivers fordable he lauded them with the first three verses of the hymn. The hymn has some poetical beauty, and is interesting as a relic of the traditions of the Āryans regarding their progress eastward in the Land of the Five Rivers.

1 *Vipāś* : considered to be identical with the Hyphasis of Arrian, is the modern Beās which rises in the Himālayas and falls into the Sutlej, the *Śatudrī* of the text, a little to the south-east of Amritsar.

4 The rivers speak in reply to Viśvāmitra's address.

5 Viśvāmitra speaks again. *At my friendly bidding* : according to the Scholiasts, Yāska and Sāyaṇa, the meaning of *me vácase somyāya* is, 'to my speech importing the Soma;' that is, the object of my address is that I may cross over and gather the Soma-plant. The word *somya*, consisting of, connected with, or inspired by, Soma, appears to have here its more general meaning of lovely, pleasant, or friendly. *Kuśika's son* : Viśvāmitra.

6 The rivers speak. *Savitar* : said by Sāyaṇa to be used here as an epithet of Indra, 'the impeller of the whole world.'

7 Viśvāmitra speaks.

8 The rivers speak.

9 Viśvāmitra speaks.

10 The rivers speak.

11 Viśvāmitra speaks. *The Bharatas* : the family of Viśvāmitra.

13 This verse, in a different metre, is manifestly a later addition. *The pins* : of the yokes. *The pair of Bulls* : the two strong rushing rivers. Cf Horace's *tauriformis Aufidus*. Prof. Wilson, following Sāyaṇa, gives a somewhat different version of the stanza : 'Let your waves (rivers) so flow that the pin of the yoke may be above (their) waters : leave the trace full, and may (the two streams) exempt from misfortune or defect, and uncensured, exhibit no (present) increase.'

HYMN XXXIV.   Indra.

1. FORT-RENDER, Lord of Wealth, dispelling foemen, Indra with lightnings hath o'ercome the Dāsa.
  Impelled by prayer and waxen great in body, he hath filled earth and heaven, the Bounteous Giver.

2 I stimulate thy zeal, the Strong, the Hero, decking my song of praise for thee Immortal.
  O Indra, thou art equally the Leader of heavenly hosts and human generations.

3 Leading his band Indra encompassed Vṛtra ; weak grew the wily leader of enchanters.
  He who burns fierce in forests slaughtered Vyaṁsa, and made the Milch-kine of the nights apparent.

4 Indra, light-winner, days' Creator, conquered, victorious, hostile bands with those who loved him.
  For man the days' bright ensign he illumined, and found the light for his joy and gladness.

5 Forward to fiercely falling blows pressed Indra, herolike doing many hero exploits.
  These holy songs he taught the bard who praised him, and widely spread these Dawns' resplendent colour.

6 They laud the mighty acts of him the Mighty, the many glorious deeds performed by Indra.
  He in his strength, with all-surpassing prowess, through wondrous arts crushed the malignant Dasyus.

7 Lord of the brave, Indra who rules the people gave freedom to the Gods by might and battle.
  Wise singers glorify with chanted praises these his achievements in Vivasvān's dwelling.

8 Excellent, Conqueror, the victory-giver, the winner of the light and Godlike Waters,

He who hath won this broad earth and this heaven,—in Indra they rejoice who love devotions.

9 He gained possession of the Sun and Horses, Indra obtained the Cow who feedeth many.
  Treasure of gold he won ; he smote the Dasyús, and gave protection to the Āryan colour.

10 He took the plants and days for his possession ; he gained the forest trees and air's mid-region.
  Vala he cleft, and chased away opponents : thus was he tamer of the overweening.

11 Call we on Maghavan, auspicious Indra, best Hero in the fight where spoil is gathered,
  The Strong, who listens, who gives aid in battles, who slays the Vṛtras, wins and gathers treasures.

HYMN XXXV   Indra.

1. MOUNT the Bay Horses to thy chariot harnessed, and come to us like Vāyu with his coursers.
  Thou, hastening to us, shalt drink the Soma. Hail, Indra. We have poured it for thy rapture.

2 For him, the God who is invoked by many, the two swift Bay Steeds to the pole I harness,
  That they in fleet course may bring Indra hither, e'en to this sacrifice arranged completely.

3 Bring the strong Steeds who drink the warm libation, and, Bull of Godlike nature, be thou gracious.
  Let thy Steeds eat ; set free thy Tawny Horses, and roasted grain like this consume thou daily.

4 Those who are yoked by prayer I harness, fleet friendly Bays who take their joy together.
  Mounting thy firm and easy car, O Indra, wise and all-knowing come thou to the Soma.

---

1 *Fort-render* : breaker-down of the cloud-castles of the demons who withhold the rain as well as of the hostile non-Āryan tribes.

3 *He who burns fierce in forests* : perhaps the thunderbolt. *Vyaṁsa* : the name of one of the demons of drought. See I. 101. 2, and 103 . 2.

Mad. the Milch-kine of the nights apparent : according to Sāyaṇa, made manifest the (stolen) cows (that had been hidden) in the night ; that is, recovered the rays of light.

7 *In Vivasvān's dwelling* : in the sacrifiical chamber, in the home of the worshipper who represents Vivasvān, the Radiant God, regarded as the Celestial Sacrificer.

9 *The Āryan colour* : or, race of Āryas ; according to S yaṇa, the noblest tribe or order, meaning the first three classes or castes.

---

2 *I harness* : my prayer causes Indra to harness.

3 *Who drink the warm libation* : or, according to Sāyaṇa, 'who protect us from our enemies. *Roasted grain* : fried barley, according to Sāyaṇa. The grain would appear to be intended for Indra's horses. **See stanza 7.**

5 No other worshippers must stay beside them thy Bays, thy vigorous and smooth-backed Coursers.
Pass by them all and hasten onward hither : with Soma pressed we will prepare to feast thee.

6 Thine is this Soma : hasten to approach it. Drink thou thereof, benevolent, and cease not.
Sit on the sacred grass at this our worship, and take these drops into thy belly, Indra.

7 The grass is strewn for thee, pressed is the Soma ; the grain is ready for thy Bays to feed on.
To thee who lovest them, the very mighty, strong, girt by Maruts, are these gifts presented.

8 This the sweet draught, with cows, the men, the mountains, the waters, Indra, have for thee made ready.
Come, drink thereof, Sublime One, friendly-minded, foreseeing, knowing well the ways thou goest.

9 The Maruts, they with whom thou sharedst Soma, Indra, who made thee strong and were thine army,—
With these accordant, eagerly desirous drink thou this Soma with the tongue of Agni.

10 Drink, Indra, of the juice by thine own nature, or by the tongue of Agni, O thou Holy.
Accept the sacrificial gift, O Śakra, from the Adhvaryu's hand or from the Hotar's.

11 Call we on Maghavan, auspicious Indra, best Hero in the fight where spoil is gathered,
The Strong, who listens, who gives aid in battles, who slays the Vṛtras, wins and gathers riches.

HYMN XXXVI. *Indra.*

1. WITH constant succours, fain thyself to share it, make this oblation which we bring effective.
Grown great through strengthening gifts at each libation, he hath become renowned by mighty exploits.

2 For Indra were the Somas erst-discovered, whereby he grew strong-jointed, vast, and skilful.
Indra, take quickly these presented juices : drink of the strong, that which the strong have shaken.

3 Drink and wax great. Thine are the juices, Indra, both Somas of old time and these we bring thee.
Even as thou drankest, Indra, earlier Somas, so drink to-day, a new guest, meet for praises.

4 Great and impetuous, mighty-voiced in battle, surpassing power is his, and strength resistless.
Him the broad earth hath never comprehended when Somas cheered the Lord of Tawny Coursers.

5 Mighty and strong he waxed for hero exploit : the Bull was furnished a Sage's wisdom.
Indra is our kind Lord ; his steers have vigour ; his cows are many with abundant offspring.

6 As floods according to their stream flow onward, so to the sea, as borne on cars, the waters.
Vaster is Indra even than his dwelling, what time the stalk milked out, the Soma, fills him.

7 Eager to mingle with the sea, the rivers carry the well-pressed Soma juice to Indra.
They drain the stalk out with their arms, quick-handed, and cleanse it with a stream of mead and filters.

8 Like lakes appear his flanks filled full with Soma : yea, he contains libations in abundance.
When Indra had consumed the first sweet viands, he, after slaying Vṛtra, claimed the Soma.

8 *With cows* : that is, with the milk which is mixed with Soma. *The men* : who make all preparations for the sacrifice. *The mountains* : on which the Soma grows ; or perhaps the pressing-stones brought from the hill-side. *The waters* : used to purify the Soma.

10 *By thine own nature* : by thine own strength, or effort ; spontaneously. *Śakra* : Mighty One ; a common name of Indra.

2 *Drink of the strong* : that is, of the strong Soma juice, which has been *shaken*, i. e. violently pressed out, by *the strong* pressing-stones.

4 *Mighty-voiced* : the exact meaning of *virapśin* is uncertain. Prof. Wilson renders it, after Sāyaṇa, by 'defier of foes.'

5 *His cows* : I follow Sāyaṇa, Roth, Ludwig, and Grassmann in giving this meaning to *dákṣiṇāḥ*, as the meaning 'guerdons,' 'donations,' does not suit the passage.

6 As rivers increase the size of the ocean, so libations of Soma juice augment the greatness of Indra until he is too vast for his home the heaven to contain him.

7 *The sea* : perhaps the sacrificial reservoir. *The rivers* : waters used in the Soma ceremonies.
They drain : that is the officiating priests.

9 Then bring thou hither, and let none prevent it: we know thee well, the Lord of wealth and treasure.
That splendid gift which is thine own, O Indra, vouchsafe to us, Lord of the Tawny Coursers.
10 O Indra, Maghavan, impetuous mover, grant us abundant wealth that brings all blessings.
Give us a hundred autumns for our life-time: give us, O fair-cheeked Indra, store of heroes.
11 Call we on Indra, Maghavan, auspicious, best Hero in the fight where spoil is gathered,
The Strong, who listens, who gives aid in battles, who slays the Vṛtras, wins and gathers riches.

HYMN XXXVII. *Indra.*

1. O INDRA, for the strength that slays Vṛtra and conquers in the fight,
We turn thee hitherward to us.
2 O Indra, Lord of Hundred Powers, may those who praise thee hitherward.
Direct thy spirit and thine eye.
3 O Indra, Lord of Hundred Powers, with all our songs we invocate
Thy names for triumph over foes.
4 We strive for glory through the powers immense of him whom many praise,
Of Indra who supports mankind.
5 For Vṛtra's slaughter I address Indra whom many invocate,
To win us booty in the wars.
6 In battles be victorious. We seek thee, Lord of Hundred Powers,
Indra, that Vṛtra may be slain.
7 In splendid combats of the hosts, in glories where the fight is won,
Indra, be victor over foes.
8 Drink thou the Soma for our help, bright, vigilant, exceeding strong,
O Indra, Lord of Hundred Powers.
9 O Śatakratu, powers which thou mid the Five Races hast displayed—
These, Indra, do I claim of thee.
10 Indra, great glory hast thou gained. Win splendid fame which none may mar:
We make thy might perpetual.
11 Come to us either from anear, or, Śakra, come from far away.
Indra, wherever be thy home, come to us thence, O Thunder-armed.

HYMN XXXVIII. *Indra.*

1. HASTING like some strong courser good at drawing, a thought have I imagined like a workman.
Pondering what is dearest and most noble, I long to see the sages full of wisdom.
2 Ask of the sages' mighty generations: firm-minded and devout they framed the heaven.
These are thy heart-sought strengthening directions, and they have come to be sky's upholders.
3 Assuming in this world mysterious natures, they decked the heaven and earth for high dominion,
Measured with measures, fixed their broad expanses, set the great worlds apart held firm for safety.
4 Even as he mounted up they all adorned him: self-luminous he travels clothed in splendour.
That is the Bull's, the Asura's mighty figure: he, omniform, hath reached the eternal waters.
5 First the more ancient Bull engendered offspring: these are his many draughts that lent him vigour.
From days of old ye Kings, two Sons of Heaven, by hymns of sacrifice have won dominion.
6 Three seats ye Sovrans, in the Holy synod, many, yea, all, ye honour with your presence.

---

9 *Bring thou hither*: bring the wealth for which we pray.
10 *A hundred autumns*: See I. 89. 9.

---

2 *Those who praise thee*: the institutors of the sacrifice.
8 *Vigilant*: according to Sāyaṇa, Soma prevents sleep.
9 *Śatakratu*: Lord of a hundred, or countless, powers.
The Five Races: Indra is the special protector of the five Āryan tribes.

This hymn is ascribed to the Ṛṣi Prajāpati, of the family of Viśvāmitra, or Prajāpati, son of Vāk, or both together, or Viśvāmitra himself. The deity is said to be Indra, although he is mentioned only in the concluding verse. The hymn is intentionally obscure, and in parts unintelligible.
1 *Like a workman*: as a carpenter prepares his wood.
I long to see the sages: that I may learn from them what I wish to know.
3 *For high dominion*: that Indra might rule over them.
4 *Even as he mounted up*: that is, Indra as the Sun.
The eternal waters: or, according to Prof. Roth, 'the forces of eternity.'
5 *The more ancient Bull*: Indra as the Sun.
Two Sons of Heaven: or of Dyaus; Varuṇa and perhaps Mitra.
6 *The three seats* are heaven, the firmament or mid-air, and the earth. The poet appears to mean, by the

There saw I, going thither in the spirit, Gandharvas in their course with wind-blown tresses.

7 That same companionship of her, the Milch-cow, here with the strong Bull's divers forms they stablished.
Enduring still some new celestial figure, the skilful workers shaped a form around him.

8 Let no one here debar me from enjoying the golden light which Savitar diffuses.
He covers both all-fostering worlds with praises even as a woman cherishes her children.

9 Fulfil, ye twain, his work, the Great, the Ancient: as heavenly blessing keep your guard around us.
All the wise Gods behold his varied actions who stands erect, whose voice is like a herdsman's.

10 Call we on Indra, Maghavan, auspicious, best Hero in the fight where spoil is gathered,
The Strong, who listens, who gives aid in battles, who slays the Vṛtras, wins and gathers riches.

HYMN XXXIX. *Indra.*

1. To Indra from the heart the hymn proceedeth, to him the Lord, recited, built with praises ;
The wakening song sung forth in holy synod : that which is born for thee, O Indra, notice.

2 Born from the heaven e'en in the days aforetime, wakening, sung aloud in holy synod,
Auspicious, clad in white and shining raiment, this is the ancient hymn of our forefathers.

3 The Mother of the Twins hath borne Twin Children : my tongue's tip raised itself and rested silent.
Killing the darkness at the light's foundation, the Couple newly born attain their beauty.

4 Not one is found among them, none of mortals, to blame our sires who fought to win the cattle.
Their strengthener was Indra the Majestic : he spread their stalls of kine the Wonder-Worker.

5 Where as a Friend with friendly men, Navagvas, with heroes, on his knees he sought the cattle.
There, verily with ten Daśagvas Indra found the Sun lying hidden in the darkness.

6 Indra found meath collected in the milch-cow, by foot and hoof, in the cow's place of pasture.
That which lay secret, hidden in the waters, he held in his right hand, the rich rewarder.

7 He took the light, discerning it from darkness : may we be far removed from all misfortune.
These songs, O Soma-drinker, cheered by Soma, Indra, accept from thy most zealous poet.

8 Let there be light through both the worlds for worship : may we be far from most overwhelming evil.
Great woe comes even from the hostile mortal, piled up ; but good at rescue are the Vasus.

9 Call we on Maghavan, auspicious Indra, best Hero in the fight where spoil is gathered,
The Strong, who listens, who gives aid in battles, who slays the Vṛtras, wins and gathers riches.

---

words that follow, that no place of sacrifice is duly consecrated unless these Gods are present.

The *Gandharvas*, according to the Scholiast, are the guardians of the Soma. Here, probably, they are merely sunbeams.

7 The *Milch-cow* is Dawn, and *the strong Bull* is apparently Indra as the Sun. 'This stanza,' Professor Wilson remarks, 'is singularly obscure, and is very imperfectly explained by the commentators.'

8 This stanza also is hardly intelligible.

9 *Ye Twain* : apparently Mitra and Varuṇa. *The Great, the Ancient* : Dyaus.

Whose voice is like a herdsman's : Professor Wilson renders this, 'blandly-speaking.' The meaning appears to be, using his voice for the protection of man, like a herdsman who calls out to his cattle.

This hymn and the following thirteen are ascribed to the Ṛṣi Viśvāmitra.

2 *Clad in white and shining raiment* : clothed with energy and splendour.

3 *The Mother of the Twins* : according to Sāyaṇa, Uṣas or Dawn. *Twin Children* : the Aśvins. *My tongue's tip raised itself* : I prepared to praise the Aśvins, but was unequal to the task.

4 See M. Müller, Chips, IV. 29 (Edition of 1895).

5 *Navagvas* : a mythological family often associated with the Aṅgirases and described as sharing in Indra's battles. See I. 33. 6, and 62. 4.

Daśagvas : members of, or priestly allies connected with, the family of Aṅgiras. See I. 62. 4.

6 *Indra found meath* : sweet rain. *By foot and hoof* : tracking the cows by their foot-marks. *That which lay secret* : the rain which was imprisoned in the clouds.

HYMN XL. *Indra.*

1. THEE, Indra, we invoke, the Bull, what time the Soma is expressed.
So drink thou of the savoury juice.

2 Indra, whom many laud, accept the strength-conferring Soma juice :
Quaff, pour down drink that satisfies.

3 Indra, with all the Gods promote our wealth-bestowing sacrifice,
Thou highly-lauded Lord of men.

4 Lord of the brave, to thee proceed these drops of Soma juice expressed,
The bright drops to thy dwelling-place.

5 Within thy belly, Indra, take juice, Soma the most excellent : Thine are the drops celestial.

6 Drink our libation, Lord of hymns : with streams of meath thou art bedewed :
Our glory, Indra, is thy gift.

7 To Indra go the treasures of the worshipper, which never fail :
He drinks the Soma and is strong

8 From far away, from near at hand, O Vṛtra-slayer, come to us :
Accept the songs we sing to thee.

9 When from the space between the near and far thou art invoked by us,
Thence, Indra, come thou hitherward.

HYMN XLI. *Indra.*

1. INVOKED to drink the Soma juice, come with thy Bay Steeds, Thunder-armed !
Come, Indra, hitherward to me.

2 Our priest is seated, true to time ; the grass is regularly strewn ;
The pressing-stones were set at morn.

3 These prayers, O thou who hearest prayer are offered : seat thee on the grass.
Hero, enjoy the offered cake.

4 O Vṛtra-slayer, be thou pleased with these libations, with these hymns,
Song-loving Indra, with our lauds.

5 Our hymns caress the Lord of Strength, vast, drinker of the Soma's juice,
Indra, as mother-cows their calf.

6 Delight thee with the juice we pour for thine own great munificence :
Yield not thy singer to reproach.

7 We, Indra, dearly loving thee, bearing oblation, sing thee hymns :
Thou, Vasu, dearly lovest us.

8 O thou to whom thy Bays are dear, loose not thy Horses far from us :
Here glad thee, Indra, Lord divine.

9 May long-maned Coursers, dropping oil, bring thee on swift car hitherward,
Indra, to seat thee on the grass.

HYMN XLII. *Indra.*

1. COME to the juice that we have pressed, to Soma, Indra, blent with milk :
Come, favouring us, thy Bay-drawn car !

2 Come, Indra, to this gladdening drink, placed on the grass, pressed out with stones :
Wilt thou not drink thy fill thereof ?

3 To Indra have my songs of praise gone forth, thus rapidly sent hence,
To turn him to the Soma-draught.

4 Hither with songs of praise we call Indra to drink the Soma juice :
Will he not come to us by lauds ?

5 Indra, these Somas are expressed. Take them within thy belly, Lord
Of Hundred Powers, thou Prince of Wealth.

6 We know thee winner of the spoil, and resolute in battles, Sage !
Therefore thy blessing we implore.

7 Borne hither by thy Stallions, drink, Indra, this juice which we have pressed,
Mingled with barley and with milk.

8 Indra, for thee, in thine own place, I urge the Soma for thy draught :
Deep in thy heart let it remain,

9 We call on thee, the Ancient One, Indra, to drink the Soma juice,
We Kuśikas who seek thine aid.

HYMN XLIII. *Indra.*

1. MOUNTED upon thy chariot-seat approach us : thine is the Soma-draught from days aforetime.
Loose for the sacred grass thy dear companions. These men who bring oblation call thee hither.

2 Come our true Friend, passing by many people ; come with thy two Bay Steeds to our devotions ;
For these our hymns are calling thee, O Indra, hymns formed for praise, soliciting thy friendship.

---

9 *The space between the near and far*: the firmament or mid-air, between the earth and the distant sky.

9 *We Kuśikas* : members of the family of Kuśika who was the father or the grandfather of Viśvāmitra, the Ṛṣi of the hymn.

1 *Thy dear companions* : thy horses.

3 Pleased, with thy Bay Steeds, Indra, God, come quickly to this our sacrifice that heightens worship ;
For with my thoughts, presenting oil to feed thee, I call thee to the feast of sweet libations.

4 Yea, let thy two Bay Stallions bear thee hither, well limbed and good to draw, thy dear companions.
Pleased with the corn-blent offering which we bring thee, may Indra, Friend, hear his friend's adoration.

5 Wilt thou not make me guardian of the people, make me, impetuous Maghavan, their ruler ?
Make me a Ṛṣi having drunk of Soma ? Wilt thou not give me wealth that lasts for ever ?

6 Yoked to thy chariot, led thy tall Bays, Indra, companions of thy banquet, bear thee hither,
Who from of old press to heaven's farthest limits, the Bull's impetuous and well-groomed Horses.

7 Drink of the strong pressed out by strong ones, Indra, that which the Falcon brought thee when thou longedst ;
In whose wild joy thou stirrest up the people, in whose wild joy thou didst unbar the cow-stalls.

8 Call we on Indra, Maghavan, auspicious, best Hero in the fight where spoil is gathered ;
The Strong, who listens, who gives aid in battles, who slays the Vṛtras, wins and gathers riches.

HYMN XLIV. *Indra.*

1. May this delightsome Soma be expressed for thee by tawny stones.
Joying thereat, O Indra, with thy Bay Steeds come : ascend thy golden-coloured car.

2 In love thou madest Uṣas glow, in love thou madest Sūrya shine.
Thou, Indra, knowing, thinking, Lord of Tawny Steeds, above all glories waxest great.

3 The heaven with streams of golden hue, earth with her tints of green and gold—
The golden Pair yield Indra plenteous nourishment : between them moves the golden One.

4 When born to life the golden Bull illumines all the realm of light.
He takes his golden weapon, Lord of Tawny Steeds, the golden thunder in his arms.

5 The bright, the well-loved thunderbolt, girt with the bright, Indra disclosed,
Disclosed the Soma juice pressed out by tawny stones, with tawny steeds drave forth the kine.

HYMN XLV. *Indra.*

1. Come hither, Indra, with Bay Steeds, joyous, with tails like peacocks' plumes.
Let no men check thy course as fowlers stay the bird : pass o'er them as o'er desert lands.

2 He who slew Vṛtra, burst the cloud, brake the strongholds and drave the floods,
Indra who mounts his chariot at his Bay Steeds' cry, shatters e'en things that stand most firm.

3 Like pools of water deep and full, like kine thou cherishest thy might ;
Like the milch-cows that go well-guarded to the mead, like water-brooks that reach the lake.

4 Bring thou us wealth with power to strike, our share, 'gainst him who calls it his.

---

7 *The strong* : the Soma juice. *The strong ones* : the press-stones.

That which the Falcon brought thee : the Soma is said to have been brought from heaven by a falcon. See I. 80. 2, and 93. 6.

Throughout the hymn the poet rings the changes on words said to be derivatives of the root *h i* to take, as *haryatá*, delightsome, *haryán*, loving, *hári*, bay or tawny, *hárit*, green, yellow, or gold-coloured.

3 *The golden One* : the Sun.

4 *The golden Bull* : Indra as the Sun.

5 *Girt with the bright* : surrounded by flashes of light. *With tawny steeds* : or by means of the tawny pressing-stones, *i. e.*, inspirited by draughts of the expressed Soma juice.

1 *Tails like peacock's plumes* : trailing clouds with fringes of purple and gold.

3 *Like pools of water* : the meaning appears to be, as Prof. Ludwig suggests : thy mental power is as inexhaustible as the water in deep springs, as safe from harm as carefully guarded cows that go without straying to their pasture, and ever full like streams that pour water into a lake. Professor Wilson, following Sāyaṇa, paraphrases thus : 'Thou cherishest the celebrator of the pious rite as (thou fillest) the deep seas (with water) or as a careful herdsman (cherishes) the cows : thou imbibest the Soma) as cows (obtain) fodder, and the juices flow into thee) as rivulets flow into a lake.' *Kratu*, which I have, rendered by 'might,' means power, either mental or bodily and sometimes also, especially in later works, a sacrificial ceremony. Sāyaṇa has filled up supposed ellipses in the most arbitrary way.

Shake, Indra, as with hooks, the tree for ripened fruit, for wealth to satisfy our wish.

5 Indra, self-ruling Lord art thou, good Leader, of most glorious fame.
So, waxen in thy strength, O thou whom many praise, be thou most swift to hear our call.

HYMN XLVI. *Indra.*

1. Of thee, the Bull, the Warrior, Sovran Ruler, joyous and fierce, ancient and ever youthful,
The undecaying One who wields the thunder, renowned and great, great are the exploits, Indra.

2 Great art thou, Mighty Lord, through manly vigour, O fierce One, gathering spoil, subduing others,
Thyself alone the universe's Sovran : so send forth men to combat and to rest them.

3 He hath surpassed all measure in his brightness, yea, and the Gods, for none may be his equal.
Impetuous Indra in his might exceedeth wide vast mid-air and heaven and earth together.

4 To Indra, even as rivers to the ocean, flow forth from days of old the Soma juices ;
To him wide deep and mighty from his birth-time, the well of holy thoughts, all-comprehending.

5 The Soma, Indra, which the earth and heaven bear for thee as a mother bears her infant,
This they send forth to thee, this, vigorous Hero ! Adhvaryus purify for thee to drink of.

HYMN XLVII. *Indra.*

1. Drink, Indra, Marut-girt, as Bull, the Soma, for joy, for rapture even as thou listest.
Pour down the flood of meath within thy belly : thou from of old art King of Soma juices.

2 Indra, accordant, with the banded Maruts, drink Soma, Hero, as wise Vṛtra-slayer.
Slay thou our foemen, drive away assailants and make us safe on every side from danger.

3 And, drinker at due seasons, drink in season, Indra, with friendly Gods, our pressed-out Soma.
The Maruts following, whom thou madest sharers, gave thee the victory, and thou slewest Vṛtra.

4 Drink Soma, Indra, banded with the Maruts who, Maghavan, strengthened thee at Ahi's slaughter,
'Gainst Śambara, Lord of Bays ! in winning cattle, and now rejoice in thee, the holy Singers.

5 The Bull whose strength hath waxed, whom Maruts follow, free-giving Indra, the celestial Ruler,
Mighty, all-conquering, the victory-giver, him let us call to grant us new protection.

HYMN XLVIII. *Indra.*

1. Soon as the young Bull sprang into existence he longed to taste the pressed-out Soma's liquor.
Drink thou thy fill, according to thy longing, first, of the goodly mixture blent with Soma.

2 That day when thou wast born thou, fain to taste it, drankest the plant's milk which the mountains nourish.
That milk thy Mother first, the Dame who bare thee, poured for thee in thy mighty Father's dwelling.

3 Desiring food he came unto his Mother, and on her breast beheld the pungent Soma.
Wise, he moved on, keeping aloof the others, and wrought great exploits in his varied aspects.

---

3 *Impetuous* : or, according to Sāyaṇa, whom Professors Wilson and Ludwig follow, 'drinker of the spiritless Soma juice, 'er des auch dis somatrester.'

---

4 *In winning cattle* : in recovering the stolen kine, the vanished rays of light, or, generally, in battle with the demons of drought.

5 This stanza recurs in VI. 19. 11.

---

1 *The young Bull* : Indra.

2 *Which the mountains nourish* : the Soma plant is said to have grown on the hills. *Thy Mother* : Aditi. *Thy mighty Father* : according to the later mythology Kaśyapa was the husband of Aditi and father of Indra and the other deities, and Sāyaṇa says that in this passage Kaśyapa is intended. But it seems almost certain that Tvaṣṭar, whom Indra conquered at his birth, is here referred to as his mighty Father. See Bergaigne, *La Religion Védique*, III. 58 ff.

4 Fierce, quickly conquering, of surpassing vigour, he framed his body even as he listed.
E'en from his birth-time Indra conquered Tvaṣṭar, bore off the Soma and in beakers drank it.

5 Call we on Maghavan, auspicious Indra, best Hero in the fight where spoil is gathered ;
The Strong, who listens, who gives aid in battles, who slays the Vṛtras, wins and gathers riches.

HYMN XLIX. *Indra.*

1. GREAT Indra will I laud, in whom all people who drink the Soma have attained their longing ;
Whom, passing wise, Gods, Heaven and Earth, engendered, formed by a Master's hand, to crush the Vṛtras.

2 Whom, most heroic, borne by Tawny Coursers, verily none subdueth in the battle ;
Who, reaching far, most vigorous, hath shortened the Dasyu's life with Warriors bold of spirit.

3 Victor in fight, swift mover like a war-horse, pervading both worlds, rainer down of blessings,
To be invoked in war like Bhaga, Father, as 'twere, of hymns, fair, prompt to hear, strength-giver.

4 Supporting heaven, the high back of the region, his car is Vāyu with his team of Vasus.
Illumining the nights, the Sun's creator, like Dhiṣaṇā he deals forth strength and riches.

5 Call we on Maghavan, auspicious Indra, best Hero in the fight where spoil is gathered ;
The Strong, who listens, who gives aid in battles, who slays the Vṛtras, wins and gathers treasure.

1 *Formed by a Master's hand* : or fashioned by Vibhvan one of the Ṛbhus. According to Sāyaṇa, appointed by Brahmā for the government of the world. *The Vṛtras* : Vṛtra and similar fiends, or, generally, the enemies of the Gods and Āryans.

2 *With Warriors bold of spirit* : his allies the Maruts.

4 *His car is Vāyu* : the construction of the first hemistich is difficult and the sense is doubtful. The meaning may be, as Vāyu the God of wind moves like a chariot on high drawn by the coursers of the air, so Indra moves accompanied by the Vasus or Maruts.

Like Dhiṣaṇā : the Wish-Goddess, a deity presiding over prosperity. See I. 96. 1, note ; IV. 34. 1; V. 41. 8.

HYMN L. *Indra.*

1. LET Indra drink, All-hail ! for his is Soma,—the mighty Bull come, girt by Maruts, hither.
Far-reaching, let him fill him with these viands, and let our offering sate his body's longing.

2 I yoke thy pair of trusty Steeds for swiftness, whose faithful service from of old thou lovest.
Here, fair of cheek ! let thy Bay Coursers place thee : drink of this lovely well-effused libation.

3 With milk they made Indra their good Preserver, lauding for help and rule the bounteous rainer.
Impetuous God, when thou hast drunk the Soma, enraptured send us cattle in abundance.

4 With kine and horses satisfy this longing ; with very splendid bounty still extend it.
Seeking the light, with hymns to thee, O Indra, the Kuśikas have brought their gift, the singers.

5 Call we on Maghavan, auspicious Indra, best Hero in the fight where spoil is gathered ;
The Strong, who listens, who gives aid in battles, who slays the Vṛtras, wins and gathers riches.

HYMN LI. *Indra.*

1. HIGH hymns have sounded forth the praise of Maghavan, supporter of mankind, of Indra meet for lauds ;
Him who hath waxen great, invoked with beauteous songs, Immortal One, whose praise each day is sung aloud.

2 To Indra from all sides go forth my songs of praise, the Lord of Hundred Powers, strong, Hero, like the sea,
Swift, winner of the booty, breaker-down of forts, faithful and ever-glorious, finder of the light.

1 *All-hail* : I take *svāhā* here as an exclamation addressed to Indra. Sāyaṇa explains the word by *svāhākṛtamimam somam*, (let Indra drink) this Soma offered with Svāhā.

3 *With milk* : with libations of Soma juice mingled with milk.

4 This stanza is found also in Hymn XXX. 20 of this Book.

3 Where battle's spoil is piled the singer winneth praise, for Indra taketh care of matchless worshippers.
He in Vivasvān's dwelling findeth his delight : praise thou the ever-conquering slayer of the foe.

4 Thee, valorous, most heroic of the heroes, shall the priests glorify with songs and praises.
Full of all wondrous power he goes to conquest : worship is his, sole Lord from days aforetime.

5 Abundant are the gifts he gives to mortals : for him the earth bears a rich store of treasures.
The heavens, the growing plants, the living waters, the forest trees preserve their wealth for Indra.

6 To thee, O Indra, Lord of Bays, for ever are offered prayers and songs : accept them gladly.
As Kinsman think thou of some fresh assistance ; good Friend, give strength and life to those who praise thee.

7 Here, Indra, drink thou Soma with the Maruts, as thou didst drink the juice beside Śāryāta.
Under thy guidance, in thy keeping, Hero, the singers serve, skilled in fair sacrifices.

8 So eagerly desirous drink the Soma, our juice, O Indra, with thy friends the Maruts,
Since at thy birth all Deities adorned thee for the great fight, O thou invoked of many.

9 He was your comrade in your zeal, O Maruts : they, rich in noble gifts, rejoiced in Indra.
With them together let the Vṛtra-slayer drink in his home the worshipper's libation.

10 So, Lord of affluent gifts, this juice hath been expressed for thee with strength :
Drink of it, thou who lovest song.

11 Incline thy body to this juice which suits thy Godlike nature well :
May it cheer thee who lovest it.

12 Brave Indra, let it work through both thy flanks, and through thy head by prayer,
And through thine arms, to prosper us.

HYMN LII. *Indra.*

1. Indra, accept at break of day our Soma mixt with roasted corn,
With groats with cake, with eulogies.

2 Accept, O Indra, and enjoy the well-dressed sacrificial cake : Oblations are poured forth to thee.

3 Consume our sacrificial cake, accept the songs of praise we sing,
As he who woos accepts his bride.

4 Famed from of old, accept the cake at our libation poured at dawn,
For great, O Indra, is thy power.

5 Let roasted corn of our midday libation, and sacrificial cake here please thee, Indra,
What time the lauding singer, keen of purpose and eager as a bull, with hymns implores thee.

6 At the third sacrifice, O thou whom many praise, give glory to the roasted corn and holy cake.
With offered viands and with songs may we assist thee, Sage, whom Vāja and the Ṛbhus wait upon.

7 The groats have we prepared for thee with Pūṣan, corn for thee, Lord of Bay Steeds, with thy horses.
Eat thou the meal-cake, banded with the Maruts, wise Hero, Vṛtra-slayer, drink the Soma.

8 Bring forth the roasted corn to meet him quickly, cake for the bravest Hero mid the heroes.
Indra, may hymns accordant with thee daily strengthen thee, Bold One, for the draught of Soma.

3 *In Vivasvān's dwelling* : in the sacrificial chamber of the worshipper. See III. 34. 7.

Śāryāta : said by Sāyaṇa to have been a Rājā son of Śaryāta who was perhaps the same as Śaryāti, a son of Manu Vaivasvata. See I. 51. 12; 112. 17

8 *For the great fight* : the battle with Vṛtra and the demons of drought.

1 *With groats, with cake* : *karambhiṇam apūpávantam* ; *karambhá* is coarsely ground corn, or meal mixed with curds, a kind of gruel : *apūpá* is a cake made of flour.

Stanzas 1—4, in Gāyatrī metre, accompany the morning offering; stanza 5, in Triṣṭup, the offering of noon; and 6, in Jagatī, the evening libation.

6 *Give glory* : honour by accepting. *Vāja and the Ṛbhus* : the three Ṛbhus.

7 *With Pūṣan* : because *karambhá*, groats or gruel, is the usual offering to that God. *Corn* : for Indra's horses.

HYMN LIII. *Indra, Parvata, Etc.*

1. On a high car, O Parvata and Indra, bring pleasant viands, with brave heroes, hither.
Enjoy the gifts, Gods, at our sacrifices : wax strong by hymns, rejoice in our oblation.

2 Stay still, O Maghavan, advance no farther: a draught of well pressed Soma will I give thee.
With sweetest song I grasp, O Mighty Indra, thy garment's hem as a child grasps his father's.

3 Adhvaryu, sing we both ; sing thou in answer : make we a laud acceptable to Indra.
Upon this sacrificer's grass be seated : to Indra shall our eulogy be uttered.

4 A wife, O Maghavan is home and dwelling : so let thy Bay Steeds yoked convey thee hither.
Whenever we press out for thee the Soma, let Agni as our Herald speed to call thee.

5 Depart, O Maghavan ; again come hither : both there and here thy goal is Indra, Brother,
Where thy tall chariot hath a place to rest in, and where thou loosest thy loud-neighing Courser.

6 Thou hast drunk Soma, Indra, turn thee homeward ; thy joy is in thy home, thy gracious Consort ;
Where thy tall chariot hath a place to rest in, and thy strong Courser is set free with guerdon.

7 Bounteous are these, Angirases, Virūpas : the Asura's Heroes and the Sons of Heaven.
They, giving store of wealth to Viśvāmitra, prolong his life through countless Soma-pressings.

8 Maghavan weareth every shape at pleasure, effecting magic changes in his body,
Holy One, drinker out of season, coming thrice, in a moment, through fit prayers, from heaven.

9 The mighty sage, God-born and God-incited, who looks on men, restrained the billowy river.
When Viśvāmitra was Sudās's escort, then Indra through the Kuśikas grew friendly.

10 Like swans, prepare a song of praise with pressing-stones, glad in your hymns with juice poured forth in sacrifice.
Ye singers, with the Gods, sages who look on men, ye Kuśikas drink up the Soma's savoury meath.

11 Come forward, Kuśikas, and be attentive ; let loose Sudās's horse to win him riches.
East, west, and north, let the King slay the foeman, then at earth's choicest place perform his worship.

12 Praises to Indra have I sung, sustainer of this earth and heaven. This prayer of Viśvāmitra keeps secure the race of Bharatas.

13 The Viśvāmitras have sung forth this prayer to Indra Thunder-armed :
So let him make us prosperous.

14 Among the Kīkaṭas what do thy cattle ? They pour no milky draught, they heat no caldron.

In addition to Indra and his frequent associate Parvata, the Genius of the mountains and clouds, the Goddess Vāk or Speech (stanzas 15, 16), and the several parts of the chariot or wain (17—20) are regarded as the deities or objects reverently mentioned or addressed in this hymn.

1 *With brave heroes* : accompanied, or followed by heroic sons.

3 *Adhvaryu, sing we both* : the Hotar calls on the Adhvaryu to join him in the performance of the ceremony.

4 *A wife ......is home and dwelling* : or, perhaps, 'Wife, Maghavan, is home, so is this chamber; that is, Indra is to regard the sacrificial chamber as his home for the present, until he returns to his consort and his other home in heaven.

6 *Thy gracious Consort* : Indrāṇī. *With guerdon* : with corn and water.

7 Professor Wilson, following Sāyaṇa, paraphrases : 'These sacrificers are (*Bhojas*), of whom the diversified *Angirases* (are the priests): and the heroic sons of the expeller (of the foes of the Gods) from heaven, bestowing riches upon Viśvāmitra at the sacrifice of a thousand (victims), prolong his life.' The Bhojas (bounteous ones) are said to be the Kṣatriya descendants of Sudās, and the diversified Angirases Medhātithi and the rest of the race of Angiras. 'The Asura,' explained by Sāyaṇa as the expeller of the foes of the Gods from heaven, is said to be Rudra, and his sons are the Maruts. The Virūpas are connected with Angiras in X 62. 5., and a Virūpa is mentioned in I. 45. 3. and VIII. 64. 6.

8 *Drinker out of season* : drinking the celestial Soma whenever he wishes, irrespectively of the appointed times for libations on earth. *Thrice* : to the three daily libations.

9 *The mighty sage* : Viśvāmitra. See III. 33, note.

11 In this and the two following stanzas the priests implore the aid of Indra for King Sudās who is going forth to battle.

Earth's choicest place : the altar.

12 *The race of Bharatas* : the descendants of Viśvāmitra, Bharata being the son of the celebrated Śakuntalā who was Viśvāmitra's daughter by the Apsaras Menā.

See Vedic India (Story of the Nations series), pp. 319 ff.

14 *The Kīkaṭas* : the non-Āryan inhabitants of a country (probably Kośala or Oudh) usually identified with South Bihār. The meaning is that the cows bestowed by Indra are unprofitable when in the possession of men who do not worship the Āryan Gods. *Pramaganda* the prince of the Kīkaṭas ; according to Sāyaṇa the word means 'the son of the usurer.

Bring thou to us the wealth of Pramaganda ; give up to us, O Maghavan, the low-born.

15 Sasarparī, the gift of Jamadagnis, hath lowed with mighty voice dispelling famine.
The Daughter of the Sun hath spread our glory among the Gods, imperishable, deathless.

16 Sasarparī brought glory speedily to these, over the generations of the Fivefold Race ;
Daughter of Pakṣa, she bestows new vital power, she whom the ancient Jamadagnis gave to me.

17 Strong be the pair of oxen, firm the axles, let not the pole slip nor the yoke be broken.
May Indra keep the yoke-pins from decaying : attend us, thou whose fellies are uninjured.

18 O Indra, give our bodies strength, strength to the bulls who draw the wains,
Strength to our seed and progeny that they may live, for thou art he who giveth strength.

19 Enclose thee in the heart of Khayar timber, in the car wrought of Śinśapā put firmness.
Show thyself strong, O Axle, fixed and strengthened : throw us not from the car whereon we travel.

20 Let not this sovran of the wood leave us forlorn or injure us.
Safe may we be until we reach our homes and rest us and unyoke.

21 With various aids this day come to us, Indra, with best aids speed us, Maghavan, thou Hero.
Let him who hateth us fall headlong downward : him whom we hate let vital breath abandon.

22 He heats his very axe, and then cuts a mere Semal blossom off.
O Indra, like a caldron cracked and seething, so he pours out foam.

15 *Sasarparī, the gift of Jamadagnis* : according to Sāyaṇa, Sasarparī (swiftly moving or gliding everywhere), is a name or an epithet of Vāk, Voice or Speech, the daughter of Sūrya or the Sun. The following is Dr. Muir's translation of Sāyaṇa's quotation from Ṣaḍguruśiṣya's Commentary on the Anukramaṇikā, as given with an addition in Weber's *Indische Studien* : 'Regarding the two verses beginning "Sasarparīḥ" those acquainted with antiquity tell a story. At a sacrifice of king Saudāsa the power and speech of Viśvāmitra were completely vanquished by Sakti, son of Vasiṣṭha ; and the son of Gādhi (Viśvāmitra) being so overcome, became dejected. The Jamadagnis drew from the abode of the sun a voice called "Sasarparī," the daughter of Brahmā, or of the sun, and gave her to him. Then that Voice somewhat dispelled the disquiet of the Jamadagnis (or, according to the reading of the line given by Sāyaṇa, "that Voice, being intelligence, dispelled the unintelligence of the Kuśikas"). Viśvāmitra then incited the Kuśikas with the words *upapreta* 'approach' (see verse 11). And being gladdened by receiving the Voice, he paid homage to the Jamadagnis praising them with the two verses beginning 'Sasarparīḥ'.—*O. S. Texts*, I. 343. Prof Ludwig is inclined to agree with Prof. Roth who thinks that sasarparī may mean a war-trumpet, which inspirits the combatants and dispels their fear of the enemy. Prof. Grassmann argues that *mimāya*, hath lowed, is applicable only to a cow or bull, and thinks that sasarparī means the mystic cow Sabardughā, the cow who lets her milk flow abundantly. I am inclined to prefer the explanation of the Indian commentator, although it cannot be regarded as entirely satisfactory.

The *Jamadagnis*, according to Sāyaṇa are Ṛṣis who maintain a blazing fire.

16 *The Fivefold Race* : the five tribes of Āryan men ; according to Sāyaṇa, the four castes, and barbarians or non-Āryans.

Daughter of Pakṣa : that is, of the Sun who causes the light and dark periods of the moon.

17 In this and the three following stanzas Viśvāmitra being about to depart from King Sudās's sacrificial hall blesses, or invokes good luck for, the several parts of the chariot or wain on which he is going to travel.

Attend us : the chariot is here addressed.

19 *Khayar timber* : the hard wood of the Khadira, or Acacia Catechu, of which the pin of the axle was made. *Śinśapā* : Dalbergia Sisu, also a common timber-tree.

20 *This sovran of the wood* : the timber of which the body of the car is made.

21 Prof. Roth is of opinion that this hymn consists of fragments composed by Viśvāmitra or his descendants at different dates, and that the verses (9—13), in which that Ṛṣi represents himself and the Kuśikas as being the priests of Sudās are earlier than the concluding verses (21—24), which consist of imprecations directed against Vasiṣṭha. These last verses, he remarks, contain an expression of wounded pride, and threaten vengeance against an enemy who had come into possession of some power or dignity which Viśvāmitra himself had previously enjoyed. With regard to the relations between Viśvāmitra and Vasiṣṭha as priests of Sudās, see Muir's *Original Sanskrit Texts*, I. pp. 371 ff.

22 Professor Wilson remarks : 'The construction is elliptical: the ellipse is supplied by the scholiast, as the tree is cut down by the axe so may the enemy be cut down : as one cuts off without difficulty the flower of the *Simbala*, so may he be destroyed : as the cauldron when struck, and thence leaking, scatters foam or breath from its mouth, so may that hater, struck by the flower of my prayer, vomit foam from his mouth.' The phrases are probably, as Ludwig explains merely proverbial expressions for threats full of sound and fury followed by insignificant results.

The *Semal* (Śimbala) is the Silk-cotton tree.

23 Men notice not the arrow, O ye people; they bring the red beast deeming it a bullock.
A sluggish steed men run not with the courser, nor ever lead an ass before a charger.

24 These men, the sons of Bharata, O Indra, regard not severance or close connexion.
They urge their own steed as it were another's, and take him, swift as the bow's string, to battle.

HYMN LIV. *Viśvedevas.*

1. To him adorable, mighty, meet for synods, this strengthening hymn, unceasing, have they offered.
May Agni hear us with his homely splendours, hear us, Eternal One, with heavenly lustre.

2 To mighty Heaven and Earth I sing forth loudly: my wish goes out desirous and well knowing
Both, at whose laud in synods, showing favour, the Gods rejoice them with the living mortal.

3 O Heaven and Earth, may your great law be faithful: be ye our leaders for our high advantage.
To Heaven and Earth I offer this my homage, with food, O Agni, as I pray for riches.

4 Yea, holy Heaven and Earth, the ancient sages whose word was ever true had power to find you;
And brave men in the fight where heroes conquer, O Earth, have known you well and paid you honour.

5 What pathway leadeth to the Gods? Who knoweth this of a truth, and who will now declare it?
Seen are their lowest dwelling-places only, but they are in remote and secret regions.

6 The Sage who looketh on mankind hath viewed them bedewed, rejoicing in the seat of Order.
They make a home as for a bird, though parted, with one same will finding themselves together.

7 Partners though parted, with far-distant limits, on one firm place both stand for ever watchful,
And, being young for evermore, as sisters, speak to each other names that are united.

8 All living things they part and keep asunder; though bearing up the mighty Gods they reel not.

23 *Men notice not the arrow*: or, according to Sāyaṇa, men heed not the destroyer', i.e. the power of Viśvāmitra who will destroy his enemies is not known to, or regarded by, his opponents.

They bring the red beast: the meaning of *lodhám* is uncertain. Sāyaṇa explains it as *lubdham*, desirous (that) his penance might not be frustrated). Prof. Roth suggests that *lodhám* means red, and denotes an animal of some kind contrasted with *paśu* (a tame or sacrificial animal, a bullock), so that the clause would have somewhat the same meaning as 'they look on the wolf as if it were a hare.' Durga, the commentator on the Nirukta, says: 'The text in which this word (*lodhá*) occurs is a verse expressing hatred of Vasiṣṭha. But I am a Kāpiṣṭhala of the family of Vasiṣṭha; and therefore do not interpret it.' See Muir's *O.S. Texts*, I. pp. 344, 372.

Deeming it a bullock: according to Sāyaṇa, thinking the sage, Viśvāmitra, who kept silence of his own accord to be merely stupid like some inferior animal. In the second line the rivalry of Vasiṣṭha with himself appears to be ridiculed.

24 *The son of Bharata*: descendants and adherents of Viśvāmitra. Prof. Wilson, following Sāyaṇa, paraphrases the the stanza: 'These sons of Bharata, Indra, understand severance (from the Vasiṣthas), not association (with them); they urge their steeds (against them) as against a constant foe: they bear a stout bow (for their destruction) in battle.' The word *áraṇam*, strange, foreign, another's, gives no intelligible sense. Prof. Ludwig suggests in its place *karaṇam*, an ever-ready helper. Dr. Muir suggests that the word may mean 'as if to a distance.'

---

1 *To him*: Agni. *Meet for synods*: to be worshipped in sacrificial assemblies. *May Agni hear us*: both as terrestrial fire used for sacrifice and domestic purposes and as celestial fire in the form of the Sun. *They*: the priestly singers.

2 *Knowing both*: recognizing the greatness of Heaven and Earth. *The living mortal*: men as worshippers.

5 *Seen are their lowest dwelling-places*: the constellations; but the Gods are also in mysterious and higher realms beyond, and who knows the path that leads thither?

6 *The Sage who looketh on mankind*: the all-seeing and omniscient Sun. *Them*: Heaven and Earth. *Bedewed*: with the water above the firmament and rain respectively. *In the seat of Order*: in the place which the eternal Order of the Universe has assigned to them. *They make a home*: though meeting together, they leave a space, like a bird's nest, between them.

7 *Speak to each other names that are united*: address each other or perhaps, are addressed, by dual appellations, such as *urvī*, the Two Spacious Ones, *dyāvāpṛthivī*, Heaven-Earth, etc.

8 *One All*: 'We find mention in one hymn of a primordial substance or unit out of which the universe was developed. This is 'the one thing' (*ekam*) which we have met with in connection with Aja, the Unborn (Book I. 164, 6, 46.), and which is also used synonymously with the universe in accordance with the principle which is the key to much of the later mysticism that cause and effect are identical. The poet endeavours, in a strain which preludes the philosophy of the Upaniṣads, to picture to himself the first state of the world, and the first signs of life and growth in it.'—Wallis, *Cosmology of the Ṛgveda*, p. 58.

One All is Lord of what is fixed and moving, that walks, that flies, this multiform creation.

9 Afar the Ancient from of old I ponder, our kinship with our mighty Sire and Father,—
Singing the praise whereof the Gods by custom stand on the spacious far-extended pathway.

10 This laud, O Heaven and Earth, to you I utter: let the kind-hearted hear, whose tongue is Agni,
Young, Sovran Rulers, Varuṇa and Mitra, the wise and very glorious Ādityas.

11 The fair-tongued Savitar, the golden-handed, comes thrice from heaven as Lord in our assembly.
Bear to the Gods this song of praise, and send us, then, Savitar, complete and perfect safety.

12 Deft worker, skiful-handed, helpful, holy, may Tvaṣṭar, God, give us these things to aid us.
Take your delight, ye Ṛbhus joined with Pūṣan: ye have prepared the rite with stones adjusted.

13 Borne on their flashing car, the spear-armed Maruts, the nimble Youths of Heaven, the Sons of Order,
The Holy, and Sarasvatī, shall hear us: ye Mighty, give us wealth with noble offspring.

14 To Viṣṇu rich in marvels, songs and praises shall go as singers on the road of Bhaga,—
The Chieftain of the Mighty Stride, whose Mothers, the many young Dames, never disregard him.

15 Indra, who rules through all his powers heroic, hath with his majesty filled earth and heaven.
Lord of brave hosts, Fort-crusher, Vṛtra-slayer, gather thou up and bring us store of cattle.

16 My Sires are the Nāsatyas, kind to kinsmen : the Aśvins' kinship is a glorious title.
For ye are they who give us store of riches: ye guard your gift uncheated by the bounteous.

17 This is, ye Wise, your great and glorious title, that all ye Deities abide in Indra.
Friend, Much-invoked ! art thou with thy dear Ṛbhus : fashion ye this our hymn for our advantage.

18 Aryaman, Aditi deserve our worship: the laws of Varuṇa remain unbroken.
The lot of childlessness remove ye from us, and let our course be rich in kine and offspring.

19 May the Gods' envoy, sent to many a quarter, proclaim us sinless for our perfect safety.
May Earth and Heaven, the Sun, the waters, hear us, and the wide firmament and constellations.

20 Hear us the mountains which distil the rain-drops, and, resting firm, rejoice in freshening moisture.
May Aditi with the Ādityaś hear us, and Maruts grant us their auspicious shelter.

21 Soft be our path for ever, well-provisioned: with pleasant meath, O Gods, the herbs besprinkle.
Safe be my bliss, O Agni, in thy friendship : may I attain the seat of foodful riches,

22 Enjoy the offering : beam thou strength upon us; combine thou for our good all kinds of glory.
Conquer in battle, Agni, all those foemen, and light us every day with loving-kindness.

HYMN LV. *Viśvedevas.*

1. At the first shining of the earliest Mornings, in the Cow's home was born the Great Eternal.

9 *Singing the praise whereof* : that is, with reference to which kinship with our father Dyaus or Heaven the Gods themselves bear witness to its existence.

11 *Comes thrice* : at the three daily sacrifices.

12 *These things* : for which we pray.

14 *On the road of Bhaga* : or on the path of good fortune or felicity.

The Chieftain of the Mighty Stride : Viṣṇu as the Sun. The *Mothers*, according to Sāyaṇa, are the regions of space which generate all beings. Sāyaṇa supplies *ājñām*, command, after *yásya*, whose, and Prof. Wilson, renders the passage accordingly, 'whose commands the many-blending regions of space, the generators (of all being) do not disobey.'

16 *My Sires are the Nāsatyas* : the Aśvins regard me with fatherly affection, *Ye* : the Aśvins. *Uncheated by the bounteous* ; never deceived by liberal men like us.

17 *Abide in Indra* : not as Sāyaṇa explains. in the sphere or world of Indra. The meaning is, as Professor Ludwig points out, that the glory of the Gods consists in their recognition as forming a part of the true, supreme and all-embracing divine principle, in which, as the Absolute God, all their individual attributes are absorbed and vanish.

Fashion ye : perhaps merely, give a favourable issue to.

19 *The Gods' envoy* : Agni.

21 *With pleasant meath* : with refreshing rain.

1 *In the Cow's home* : in the firmament or heaven, the place of the mystical Cosmic Cow. *The Great Eternal* : the two adjectives are in the neuter gender

Now shall the statutes of the Gods be valid. Great is the Gods' supreme and sole dominion.

2 Let not the Gods here injure us, O Agni, nor Fathers of old time who know the region,
Nor the sign set between two ancient dwellings. Great is the Gods' supreme and sole dominion.

3 My wishes fly abroad to many places : I glance back to the ancient sacrifices.
Let us declare the truth when fire is kindled. Great is the Gods' supreme and sole dominion.

4 King Universal, born to sundry quarters, extended through the wood he lies on couches.
One Mother rests: another feeds the Infant. Great is the Gods' supreme and sole dominion.

5 Lodged in old plants, he grows again in younger, swiftly within the newly-born and tender.
Though they are unimpregned, he makes them fruitful. Great is the Gods' supreme and sole dominion.

6 Now lying far away, Child of two Mothers, he wanders unrestrained, the single youngling.
These are the laws of Varuṇa and Mitra. Great is the Gods' supreme and sole dominion.

7 Child of two Mothers, Priest, sole Lord in synods, he still precedes while resting as foundation.
They who speak sweetly bring him sweet addresses. Great is the Gods' supreme and sole dominion.

8 As to a friendly warrior when he battles, each thing that comes anear is seen to meet him.
The hymn commingles with the cow's oblation. Great is the Gods' supreme and sole dominion.

9 Deep within these the hoary envoy pierceth; mighty, he goeth to the realm of splendour,
And looketh on us, clad in wondrous beauty. Great is the Gods' supreme and sole dominion.

10 Viṣṇu, the guardian, keeps the loftiest station, upholding dear, immortal dwelling-places.
Agni knows well all these created beings. Great is the Gods' supreme and sole dominion.

11 Ye, variant Pair, have made yourselves twin beauties: one of the Twain is dark, bright shines the other;
And yet these two, the dark, the red, are Sisters. Great is the Gods' supreme and sole dominion.

12 Where the two Cows, the Mother and the Daughter, meet and give suck yielding their lordly nectar,
I praise them at the seat of law eternal. Great is the Gods' supreme and sole dominion.

13 Loud hath she lowed, licking the other's youngling. On what world hath the Milch-cow laid her udder?

without a substantive. Sāyaṇa supplies *jyotiḥ*, light, in the form of the Sun. *Great is*, etc. 'Great and incomparable is the divine nature of the gods.'—Muir.

2 The meaning of the stanza is, as Professor Ludwig says : May we be able to calculate correctly the time of the Sun's approach, that is, the moment of his rising, when we should begin our sacred ceremonies. Let not the Gods lead us astray, or allow us to err, in this matter; let not the Fathers, or spirits of the departed, who are acquainted with the region in which the Sun first appears, and who have transmitted their knowledge to their descendants, nor the Sun himself (or, perhaps, Agni) deceive us. *Two ancient dwellings* : heaven and earth, the homes respectively of Gods and men.

3 *I glance back* : so Prof. M. Müller translates the passage.

4 *King Universal* : Agni, the God of all Āryan men. *To sundry quarters* : to various altars, for sacrificial purposes.

One Mother : the earth. *Another* : the heaven. Or, as Prof. Ludwig suggests, the lower of the two fire-sticks remains still while the upper stick, which is agitated, gives him life and strength.

5 Agni is latent in all plants, and from those that are old decaying he passes into the young and tender ones.

6 *Far away* : or, in the west, as Sūrya or the Sun when he has set.

He wanders : when he has risen again.

7 *Priest* : Agni, the herald who calls the Gods, the *hotar* or invoker.

As foundation : as the root and basis of every religious act.

8 Agni is here represented as a champion who draws men to meet him as a friend. *The hymn commingles* : penetrates, as it were, and accompanies the libation of milk and Soma juice.

9 *Within these* : plants in general. *The hoary envoy* : Agni, the ancient messenger between Gods and man. *To the realm of splendour* : to heaven as the Sun.

10 *Loftiest station* : in the zenith. Cf. I. 154. 5, 6.

11 *Ye, variant Pair* : Day and Night.

12 *The two Cows* : Earth and Heaven, according to Sāyaṇa ; more probably Night and Morning are intended. *The seat of law eternal* : the altar, the place of sacrifice appointed by everlasting law or *ṛtá*.

13 *Loud hath she lowed* : Heaven, as the rain pours down. *The other's youngling*, or calf, is Agni. *On what world* : no one knows where the rain comes from. *This Iḷā* : a name of the earth ; or *Iḷā* may mean, with the freshening draught (of rain).

This Iḷā streameth with the milk of Order. Great is the Gods' supreme and sole dominion.

14 Earth weareth beauties manifold: uplifted, licking her Calf of eighteen months, she standeth.
Well-skilled I seek the seat of law eternal. Great is the Gods' supreme and sole dominion.

15 Within a wondrous place the Twain are treasured : the one is manifest, the other hidden.
One common pathway leads in two directions. Great is the Gods' supreme and sole dominion.

16 Let the milch-kine that have no calves storm downward, yielding rich nectar, streaming, unexhausted,
These who are ever new and fresh and youthful. Great is the Gods' supreme and sole dominion.

17 What time the Bull bellows in other regions, another herd receives the genial moisture;
For he is Bhaga, King, the earth's Protector. Great is the Gods' supreme and sole dominion.

18 Let us declare the Hero's wealth in horses, O all ye folk: of this the Gods have knowledge.
Sixfold they bear him, or by fives are harnessed. Great is the Gods' supreme and sole dominion.

19 Tvaṣṭar the God, the omniform Creator, begets and feeds mankind in various manner.
His, verily, are all these living creatures. Great is the Gods' supreme and sole dominion.

20 The two great meeting Bowls hath he united: each of the Pair is laden with his treasure.
The Hero is renowned for gathering riches. Great is the Gods' supreme and sole dominion.

21 Yea, and on this our earth the All-Sustainer dwells like a King with noble friends about him.
In his protection heroes rest in safety. Great is the Gods' supreme and sole dominion.

22 Rich in their gifts for thee are herbs and waters, and earth brings all her wealth for thee, O Indra.
May we as friends of thine share goodly treasures. Great is the Gods' supreme and sole dominion.

HYMN LVI. *Viśvedevas.*

1. NOT men of magic skill, not men of wisdom impair the Gods' first steadfast ordinances.
Ne'er may the earth and heaven which know not malice, nor the fixed hills, be bowed by sage devices.

2 One, moving not away, supports six burthens : the Cows proceed to him the true, the Highest.
Near stand three Mighty Ones who travel swiftly: two are concealed from sight, one is apparent.

14 *Earth* : *pádyā*, according to Sāyaṇa, has this meaning. *Uplifted.........she standeth* : apparently, Heaven, but according to Sāyaṇa, the Earth elevated in the northern altar.

Her calf of eighteen months : or according to Sāyana's alternative explanation, her calf who protects the three worlds.' The calf is the Sun.

15 *Within a wondrous place* : when Morning comes, Night is concealed in some mysterious place to which Morning or Day also retires in turn when Night succeeds. From this mysterious prison Morning and Night come to us by the same path, one departing as the other approaches.

16 *The milch-kine that have no calves* : the heavy clouds which pour out their fertilizing rain as cows yield their refreshing milk, but which are unlike cows inasmuch as they have no calves.

17 *The Bull* : Indra as Parjanya the God of the rain cloud.

Another herd : the fertilizing shower falls in other regions.

18 The number of Indra's horses is variously stated. Here he is said to be drawn by six horses, the six seasons of the year, or by five at a time, or the seasons regarded as five by the combination of *hemanta* and *śiśira* the cold and the dewy seasons.

20 *The two great meeting Bowls* : the heaven and earth, hemispherical in appearance, which meet at the horizon. So the author of *The Witness of the Sun* speaks of 'the great bowl of the earth, which hollowed to the horizon.'

22 *The All-Sustainer* : Indra.

1 The statutes of the Gods are unalterable ; they stand fixed for ever like the benignant heaven and earth and like the mountains that never can be moved.

2 The meaning of the stanza is uncertain. According to Sāyaṇa, the *one, moving not away*, is the stationary year which sustains the load of the six seasons, and *the Cows* are the solar rays which pervade the year, or the Sun as its representative Professor Ludwig thinks that Tvaṣṭar may be intended, and that the cows may be the consorts of the Gods who are generally represented as bearing him company. *Three Mighty Ones* : according to Sāyaṇa, heaven, the firmament, and the earth, of which the earth is fully visible and the first two are only seen imperfectly. *Who travel swiftly* : this is Sāyaṇa's explanation of *átyāḥ* coursers ; but the meaning is not clear.

3 The Bull who wears all shapes, the triple-breasted, three-uddered, with a brood in many places,
Ruleth majestic with his triple aspect, the Bull, the Everlasting Ones' impregner.

4 When nigh them, as their tracer he observed them : he called aloud the dear name of Ādityas.
The Goddesses, the Waters, stayed to meet him : they who were wandering separate enclosed him.

5 Streams ! the wise Gods have thrice three habitations. Child of three Mothers, he is Lord in synods.
Three are the holy Ladies of the Waters, thrice here from heaven supreme in our assembly.

6 Do thou, O Savitar, from heaven thrice hither, three times a day, send down thy blessings daily.
Send us, O Bhaga, triple wealth and treasure; cause the two worlds to prosper us, Preserver !

7 Savitar thrice from heaven pours down abundance, and the fair-handed Kings Varuṇa, Mitra;
And spacious Heaven and Earth, yea, and the Waters, solicit wealth that Savitar may send us.

8 Three are the bright realms, best, beyond attainment, and three, the Asura's Heroes, rule as Sovrans,
Holy and vigorous, never to be injured. Thrice may the Gods from heaven attend our synod.

3 *The Bull* : the God who presides over the year. The three breasts and the three udders are probably heaven, the firmament, and the earth. *His triple aspect*: the six seasons, reduced by combination to three, the hot season, the rains, and the cold season. *The Everlasting Ones*, according to Sāyaṇa are the plants : but the *three Mighty Ones*, or the Waters, may be intended.

4 *He* : probably, as Professor Ludwig says, Agni as Savitar, the God presiding over the year. *The Ādityas* here appear to be the months.

5 *Thrice three habitations* : each of the three worlds having three subdivisions. *Child of three Mothers* : Agni as Savitar appears to be meant, the three mothers being, perhaps, the three seasons. According to Sāyaṇa, *trimītā* here means 'the measurer of the three (worlds), the Sun. *Ladies of the Waters* : Iḷā, Sarasvatī, and Bhāratī. *Thrice* : at the three daily sacrifices.

6 *Cause the two worlds* : I follow Prof. Ludwig in taking *dhiṣaṇe* as an accusative.

8 *The bright realms* : heaven, divided into three. *The Asura's Heroes* : according to Sāyaṇa, Agni, Vāyu, and Sūrya.

HYMN LVII. *Viśvedevas.*

1. My thought with fine discernment hath discovered the Cow who wanders free without a herdsman,
Her who hath straightway poured me food in plenty: Indra and Agni therefore are her praisers.

2 Indra and Pūṣan, deft of hand and mighty, well-pleased have drained the heaven's exhaustless udder.
As in this praise the Gods have all delighted, may I win blessing here from you, O Vasus.

3 Fain to lend vigour to the Bull, the sisters with reverence recognize the germ within him.
The Cows come lowing hither to the Youngling, to him endued with great and wondrous beauties.

4 Fixing with thought, at sacrifice, the press-stones, I bid the well-formed Heaven and Earth come hither ;
For these thy flames, which give men boons in plenty, rise up on high, the beautiful, the holy.

5 Agni, thy meath-sweet tongue that tastes fair viands, which among Gods is called the far-extended,—
Therewith make all the Holy Ones be seated here for our help, and feed them with sweet juices.

6 Let thy stream give us drink, O God, O Agni, wonderful and exhaustless like the rain-clouds.

This hymn and the five following are attributed to the Ṛṣi Viśvāmitra.

1 *With fine discernment* : the participle *vivikvān* in the masculine form appears to be used instead of the feminine form with *maniṣā*, thought. Sāyaṇa reads *maniṣām* in the accusative case and following him, Professor Wilson translates : 'May the discriminating Indra apprehend my glorification (of the Gods), which is free as a milch-cow grazing alone, without a cowherd.' *The Cow* : *Vāk*, Voice or Speech, the voice of prayer and praise which the poet proceeds to appropriate and employ, and which Indra and Agni are said to approve and praise by their acceptance.

2 *As in this praise* : there is no substantive in the text. Sāyaṇa supplies *vedyām*, altar.

3 *The Bull* : Agni. *The sisters* : the fingers which produce the fire by friction. *The germ within him* : Agni's fructifying power. *The Youngling* : Agni. According to Sāyaṇa *the Cows* are the plants which spring up in the vegetable world, adorned with its various products, as cows go eagerly to their calves.

4 *Thy flames* : O Agni.

6 *Jātavedas* : knowing all things that live or exist.

Thus care for us, O Vasu Jātavedas, show us thy loving-kindness, reaching all men.

HYMN LVIII. *Aśvins.*

1. THE Ancient's Milch-cow yields the things we long for : the Son of Dakṣiṇā travels between them.
She with the splendid chariot brings refulgence. The praise of Uṣas hath awoke the Aśvins.

2 They bear you hither by well-orderd statute : our sacred offerings rise as if to parents.
Destroy in us the counsel of the niggard : come hitherward, for we have shown you favour.

3 With lightly-rolling car and well-yoked horses hear this, the press-stone's song, ye Wonder-Workers.
Have not the sages of old time, ye Aśvins, called you most prompt to come and stay misfortune ?

4 Remember us, and come to us, for ever men, as their wont is, invocate the Aśvins.
Friends as it were have offered you these juices, sweet, blent with milk at the first break of morning.

5 Even through many regions, O ye Aśvins—high praise is yours among mankind, ye Mighty—
Come, helpers, on the paths which Gods have travelled : here your libations of sweet meath are ready.

6 Ancient your home, auspicious is your friendship : Heroes, your wealth is with the house of Jahnu.
Forming again with you auspicious friendship, let us rejoice with draughts of meath together.

7 O Aśvins, Very Mighty ones, with Vāyu and with his steeds, one-minded, ever-youthful,
Nāsatyas, joying in the third day's Soma, drink it, not hostile, Very Bounteous Givers.

8 Aśvins, to you are brought abundant viands in rivalry with sacred songs, unceasing.
Sprung from high Law your car, urged on by press-stones, goes round the earth and heaven in one brief moment.

9 Aśvins, your Soma sheds delicious sweetness : drink ye thereof and come unto our dwelling.
Your car, assuming many a shape, most often goes to the Soma-presser's place of meeting.

1 *The Ancient's Milch-cow* : bounteous Uṣas or Dawn, daughter of ancient Dyaus or Heaven. *Dakṣiṇā* : the sacrificial guerdon, personified. Her son is Agni, the Sun who travels between heaven and earth.

2 *They* : our offerings of prayer and praise. *Destroy in us* : remove from us all illiberal thoughts, and let us be bounteous in our worship of the Gods.

5 *Even through many regions* : come to us even from far away, although many other worshippers also will try to detain you.

6 *The house of Jahnu* : the family of the Kuśikas, of whom Jahnu was the ancestor. 'Jahnu's children' are mentioned as having been favoured worshippers of the Aśvins in Book I. 116. 19.

7 *The third day's Soma* : pressed out the day before yesterday, and in the meantime left to ferment.

HYMN LIX. *Mitra.*

1. MITRA, when speaking, stirreth men to labour : Mitra sustaineth both the earth and heaven.
Mitra beholdeth men with eyes that close not. To Mitra bring, with holy oil, oblation.

2 Foremost be he who brings thee food, O Mitra, who strives to keep thy sacred Law, Āditya.
He whom thou helpest ne'er is slain or conquered, on him, from near or far, falls no affliction.

3 Joying in sacred food and free from sickness, with knees bent lowly on the earth's broad surface,
Following closely the Āditya's statute, may we remain in Mitra's gracious favour.

4 Auspicious and adorable, this Mitra was born with fair dominion, King, Disposer.
May we enjoy the grace of him the Holy, yea, rest in his propitious loving-kindness.

5 The great Āditya, to be served with wor ship, who stirreth men, is gracious to the singer.
To Mitra, him most highly to be lauded, offer in fire oblation that he loveth.

6 The gainful grace of Mitra, God, supporter of the race of man,
Gives splendour of most glorious fame.

7 Mitra whose glory spreads afar, he who in might surpasses heaven,
Surpasses earth in his renown.

8 All the Five Races have repaired to Mitra, ever strong to aid,
For he sustaineth all the Gods.

1 *Stirreth men to labour* : Mitra being the God of Day. Cf. VII. 362.

8 *All the Five Races* : all Āryan men.

9 Mitra to Gods, to living men, to him who strews the holy grass,
Gives food fulfilling sacred Law.

HYMN LX. *Ṛbhus.*

1. HERE is your ghostly kinship, here, O Men : they came desirous to these holy rites with store of wealth,
With wondrous arts, whereby, with schemes to meet each need,
Ye gained, Sudhanvan's Sons ! your share in sacrifice.

2 The mighty powers wherewith ye formed the chalices, the thought by which ye drew the cow from out the hide,
The intellect wherewith ye wrought the two Bay Steeds,—through these, O Ṛbhus, ye attained divinity.

3 Friendship with Indra have the Ṛbhus, fully gained : grandsons of Manu, they skilfully urged the work.
Sudhanvan's Children won them everlasting life, serving with holy rites, pious with noble acts.

4 In company with Indra come ye to the juice, then gloriously shall your wishes be fulfilled.
Not to be paragoned, ye Priests, are your good deeds, nor your heroic acts, Ṛbhus, Sudhanvan's Sons.

5 O Indra, with the Ṛbhus, Mighty Ones, pour down the Soma juice effused, wellblent, from both thy hands.
Maghavan, urged by song, in the drinkofferer's house rejoice thee with the Heroes, with Sudhanvan's Sons.

6 With Ṛbhu near, and Vāja, Indra, here exult, with Śacī, praised of many, in the juice we pour.
These homes wherein we dwell have turned themselves to thee,—devotions to the Gods, as laws of men ordain.

7 Come with the mighty Ṛbhus, Indra, come to us, strengthening with thy help the singer's holy praise ;
At hundred eager calls come to the living man, with thousand arts attend the act of sacrifice.

9 *Gives food fulfilling sacred Law* : the food which enables men to offer the appointed sacrifices.

---

1 *Here is your ghostly kinship* : here, in the sacrificial chamber where the deities are worshipped, ye, Ṛbhus, originally men, are spiritually connected with the Gods as partakers of sacrificial efferings. *They* : the Ṛbhus. *With store of wealth* : their great skill; the 'wondrous arts' of the following line.

2 See I. 20, 2, 3, 6,

6 *Śacī* : Might, personified, the Consort of Indra.

7 *The living man* : the worshipper.

HYMN LXI. *Uṣas.*

1. O Uṣas, strong with strength, endowed with knowledge, accept the singer's praise, O wealthy Lady.
Thou, Goddess, ancient, young, and full of wisdom, movest, all-bounteous ! as the Law ordaineth.

2 Shine forth, O Morning, thou auspicious Goddess, on thy bright car awaking pleasant voices.
Let docile horses of far-reaching splendour convey thee hitherward, the goldencoloured.

3 Thou, Morning, turning thee to every creature, standest on high as ensign of the Immortal,
To one same goal ever and ever wending : now, like a wheel, O newly-born, roll hither.

4 Letting her reins drop downward, Morning cometh, the wealthy Dame, the Lady of the dwelling ;
Bringing forth light, the Wonderful, the Blessed hath spread her from the bounds of earth and heaven.

5 Hither invoke the radiant Goddess Morning, and bring with reverence your hymn to praise her.
She, dropping sweets, hath set in heaven her brightness, and, fair to look on, hath beamed forth her splendour.

6 From heaven, with hymns, the Holy One was wakened : brightly to both worlds came the wealthy Lady.
To Morning, Agni, when she comes refulgent, thou goest forth soliciting fair riches.

7 On Law's firm base the speeder of the Mornings, the Bull, hath entered mighty earth and heaven.
Great is the power of Varuṇa and Mitra, which, bright, hath spread in every place its splendour.

3 *The Immortal* : the Sun.

4 *Letting her reins drop* : perhaps, sending down rays of light.

7 *The Bull* : the Sun, who, as following the Dawns, may be said to urge them onward.

HYMN LXII. *Indra and Others.*

1. YOUR well-known prompt activities aforetime needed no impulse from your faithful servant.
Where, Indra-Varuṇa, is now that glory wherewith ye brought support to those who loved you ?

2 This man, most diligent, seeking after riches, incessantly invokes you for your favour.
Accordant, Indra-Varuṇa, with Maruts, with Heaven and Earth, hear ye mine invocation.

3 O Indra-Varuṇa, ours be this treasure, ours be wealth, Maruts, with full store of heroes.
May the Varūtrīs with their shelter aid us, and Bhāratī and Hotrā with the Mornings.

4 Be pleased ! with our oblations, thou loved of all Gods, Bṛhaspati :
Give wealth to him who brings thee gifts.

5 At sacrifices, with your hymns worship the pure Bṛhaspati—
I pray for power which none may bend—

6 The Bull of men, whom none deceive, the wearer of each shape at will,
Bṛhaspati Most Excellent.

7 Divine, resplendent Pūṣan, this our newest hymn of eulogy,
By us is chanted forth to thee.

8 Accept with favour this my song, be gracious to the earnest thought,
Even as a bridegroom to his bride.

9 May he who sees all living things, sees them together at a glance,—
May he, may Pūṣan be our help.

10 May we attain that excellent glory of Savitar the God :
So May he stimulate our prayers.

11 With understanding, earnestly, of Savitar the God we crave
Our portion of prosperity.

12 Men, singers worship Savitar the God with hymn and holy rites,
Urged by the impulse of their thoughts.

13 Soma who gives success goes forth, goes to the gathering place of Gods,
To seat him at the seat of Law.

14 To us and to our cattle may Soma give salutary food,
To biped and to quadruped.

15 May Soma, strengthening our power of life, and conquering our foes,
In our assembly take his seat.

16 May Mitra-Varuṇa, sapient Pair, bedew our pasturage with oil,
With meath the regions of the air.

17 Far-ruling, joyful when adored, ye reign through majesty of might,
With pure laws everlastingly.

18 Lauded by Jamadagni's song, sit in the place of holy Law :
Drink Soma, ye who strengthen Law.

The hymn consists of six *tṛcas* or triplets, the deities of which are severally (1) Indra and Varuṇa, (2) Bṛhaspati, (3) Pūṣan, (4) Savitar, (5) Soma, (6) Mitra and Varuṇa.

1 This stanza is difficult on account of the uncertainty of the meaning of *bhṛmáyaḥ* in the first line and of *sinam* in the second. Professor Wilson renders it : Indra and Varuṇa, may these people who are relying upon you, and wandering about (in alarm), sustain no injury from a youthful (adversary); for where is that reputation (you enjoy) on account that you bestow sustenance on your friends ?' Professor Ludwig's translation is to the following effect : 'These that are counted yours, these whirling weapons, were made not to be hurled at your dependent. Varuṇa, Mitra, Where is this your glory, wherewith against your friends end your missile?' My version follows Professor Roth's interpretation in the St. Petersburg Lexicon.

2 *This man* : the worshipper.

3 *The Varūtrīs* : guardian Goddesses; the Consorts of the Gods, according to the Commentator. *Bhāratī and Hotrā* : Goddesses presiding over different departments of religious worship.

4 *Bṛhaspati* : Lord of Prayer.

10 This stanza is the Sāvitrī, the Gāyatrī *par excellence*, 'the celebrated verse of the Vedas which forms part of the daily devotions of the Brahmans, and was first made known to English readers by Sir W. Jones's translation of a paraphrastic interpretation; he renders it, Let us adore the supremacy of that divine sun, the godhead, who illuminates all, from whom all proceed, to whom all must return, whom we invoke to direct our understandings aright in our progress towards his holy seat—Wilson. See *Ṛgveda Sanhitā*, Vol. III. p. 111.

13 *The gathering-place of Gods* : the sacrificial chamber. *The seat of Law* : the place where sacrifice ordained by eternal Law is performed.

16 *With oil* : with clarified butter, with fatness, that is, with fertilizing rain. *With meath* : or with honey, that is with sweet refreshing dew.

18 *Jamadagni*, may, according to Sāyaṇa, be in this place an epithet of Viśvāmitra, and mean 'by whom the fire has been kindled; or *Jamadagni* may be another Ṛṣi and the seer of the hymn.

BOOK THE FOURTH

HYMN I. *Agni.*

1. Thee Agni, have the Gods, ever of one accord, sent hither down, a God, appointed messenger, yea, with their wisdom sent thee down.
The Immortal, O thou Holy One, mid mortal men, the God-devoted God, the wise, have they brought forth, brought forth the omnipresent God-devoted Sage.

2 As such, O Agni, bring with favour to the Gods thy Brother Varuṇa who loveth sacrifice,
True to the Law, the Āditya who supporteth men, the King, supporter of mankind.

3 Do thou, O Friend, turn hither him who is our Friend, swift as a wheel, like two car-steeds in rapid course, Wondrous! to us in rapid course.
O Agni, find thou grace for us with Varuṇa, with Maruts who illumine all.
Bless us, thou Radiant One, for seed and progeny, yea, bless us, O thou Wondrous God.

4 Do thou who knowest Varuṇa, O Agni, put far away from us the God's displeasure.
Best Sacrificer, brightest One, refulgent remove thou far from us all those who hate us.

5 Be thou, O Agni, nearest us with succour, our closest Friend while now this Morn is breaking.
Reconcile to us Varuṇa, be bounteous : enjoy the gracious juice; be swift to hear us.

6 Excellent is the glance, of brightest splendour, which the auspicious God bestows on mortals,—
The God's glance, longed-for even as the butter, pure, heated, of the cow, the milch-cow's bounty.

7 Three are those births, the true, the most exalted, eagerly longed-for, of the God, of Agni.
He came invested in the boundless region, pure, radiant, friendly, mightily resplendent.

8 This envoy joyeth in all seats of worship, borne on his golden car, sweet-tongued Invoker:
Lovely to look on, with red steeds, effulgent, like a feast rich in food, joyous for ever.

9 Allied by worship, let him give man knowledge : by an extended cord they lead him onward.
He stays, effectual in this mortal's dwelling, and the God wins a share in his possessions.

10 Let Agni—for he knows the way—conduct us to all that he enjoys of God-sent riches,
What all the Immortals have prepared with wisdom, Dyaus, Sire, Begetter, raining down true blessings.

11 In houses first he sprang into existence, at great heaven's base, and in this region's bosom;
Footless and headless, both his ends concealing, in his Bull's lair drawing himself together.

12 Wondrously first he rose aloft, defiant, in the Bull's lair, the home of holy Order,
Longed-for, young, beautiful, and far-resplendent: and seven dear friends sprang up unto the Mighty.

13 Here did our human fathers take their places, fain to fulfil the sacred Law of worship.

This hymn, and the following forty, are ascribed to the Ṛṣi Vāmadeva, son of Gotama.

7 *Three are those births* : the manifestations of Agni in heaven as the Sun in the firmament as lightning, and on earth as sacrificial and domestic fire.

8 *Sweet-tongued* : with tasting the oblations; or, perhaps, pleasant-voiced.

9 *By an extended cord* : by virtue of the endless chain or series of regularly performed sacrifices. *Effectual*: perfecting the sacrifices, or fulfilling all the desires of the worshipper.

A share in his possessions : because the wealth of the worshipper depends upon the favour of Agni.

11 *Footless and headeless* : without distinguishable head or feet.

His Bull's lair : apparently the fuel in which he grows strong; according to Sāyaṇa, 'in the nest of the rain cloud.'

12 *The home of holy Order* : the altar, the place of law-appointed sacrifices. *Seven dear friends* : seven minor priests; or the frequently mentioned seven tongues or rays of fire.

13 *Our human fathers* : the Angirases. *Teeming Milch-kine* : the rays of light.

Forth drave they, with loud call, Dawn's teeming Milch-kine hid in the mountain-stable, in the cavern.

14 Splendid were they when they had rent the mountain: others, around, shall tell forth this their exploit.
They sang their song, prepared to free the cattle: they found the light; with holy hymns they worshipped.

15 Eager, with thought intent upon the booty, the men with their celestial speech threw open,
The solid mountain firm, compact, enclosing, confining Cows, the stable full of cattle.

16 The Milch-cow's earliest name they comprehended: they found the Mother's thrice-seven noblest titles.
This the bands knew, and sent forth acclamation: with the Bull's sheen the Red One was apparent.

17 The turbid darkness fled, the heaven was splendid: up rose the bright beam of celestial Morning.
Sūrya ascended to the wide expanses, beholding deeds of men both good and evil.

18 Then, afterwards they looked around, awakened, when first they held that Heaven allotted treasure.
Now all the Gods abide in all their dwellings. Varuṇa, Mitra, be the prayer effective.

19 I will call hither brightly-beaming Agni, the Herald, all-supporting, best at worship.
He hath disclosed, like the milch cows' pure udder, the Soma's juice when cleansed and poured from beakers.

20 The freest God of all who should be worshipped, the guest who is received in all men's houses,
Agni who hath secured the Gods' high favour,—may he be gracious, to us Jātavedas.

14 *Splendid*: illumined by the recovered rays of light.

15 *The booty*: the Cows, the rays of light. *Their celestial speech*: prayer.

16 *The Milch-cow's*: here, according to Sāyaṇa, Vāk or Voice, Speech, or especially prayer. It is uncertain what is meant by *the Mother's thrice-seven noblest* (titles, names, forms, or some similar word being necessarily understood). Professor Wilson, following Sāyaṇa, renders the passage: 'knowing the thrice-seven excellent (forms) of the maternal (rhythm), 'that is, the twenty-one metres of the Vedas; or, he adds, the passage may refer 'to the ancient nomenclature of cattle, as uttered by the *Angirases as Ehi, surabhi, guggulu, gandhinī*, etc.'

With the Bull's sheen: with the splendour of the Sun. *The Red One*: Uṣas or Dawn.

18 *That Heaven-allotted treasure*: the recovered rays of light.

19 Sāyaṇa's explanation of the second line of this stanza is different, and Professor Wilson, following him translates: 'without milking the pure udder (of the cow), without purified food of the *Soma* offered in libation,' implying according to the Scholiast, 'that no offering is made to Agni on the occasion; praise alone is addressed to him.' *Nā*, in the Veda, it may be remembered, means both *not* and *like*, and in some passages it is difficult to determine in which of its senses the word is to be taken.

HYMN II. *Agni.*

1. THE Faithful One, Immortal among mortals, a God among the Gods, appointed envoy,
Priest, best at worship, must shine forth in glory: Agni shall be raised high with man's oblations.

2 Born for us here this day, O Son of Vigour, between both races of born beings, Agni,
Thou farest as an envoy, having harnessed, Sublime One! thy strong-muscled radiant stallions.

3 I laud the ruddy steeds who pour down blessing, dropping oil, fleetest through the thought of Order.
Yoking red horses to and fro thou goest between you Deities and mortal races.

4 Aryaman, Mitra, Varuṇa, and Indra with Viṣṇu, of the Gods, Maruts and Aśvins—
These, Agni, with good car and steeds, bring hither, most bountiful, to folk with fair oblations.

5 Agni, be this our sacrifice eternal, with brave friends, rich in kine and sheep and horses,
Rich, Asura! in sacred food and children, in full assembly, wealth broad-based and during.

6 The man who, sweating, brings for thee the fuel, and makes his head to ache, thy faithful servant,—
Agni, to him be a self-strong Protector: guard him from all who seek to do him mischief.

2 *Between both races of born beings*: between Gods and men, the Gods also being called *jātāḥ* or born, as sons of Heaven and Earth.

3 *The thought of Order*: the thought of Law-appointed sacrifice.

You Deities: the Gods of whom thou, Agni, art one.

6 *Makes his head to ache*: with the load of wood which he carries on it.

7 Who brings thee food, though thou hast food in plenty, welcomes his cheerful guest and speeds him onward,
Who kindles thee devoutly in his dwelling,—to him be wealth secure and freely giving.

8 Whoso sings praise to thee at eve or morning, and, with oblation, doth the thing thou lovest,—
In his own home, even as a gold-girt courser, rescue him from distress, the bounteous giver.

9 Whoso brings gifts to thee Immortal, Agni, and doth thee service with uplifted ladle,—
Let him not, sorely toiling, lose his riches; let not the sinner's wickedness enclose him.

10 Whose well-wrought worship thou acceptest, Agni, thou God a mortal's gift, thou liberal Giver,—
Dear be his sacrifice to thee, Most Youthful ! and may we strengthen him when he adores thee.

11 May he who knows distinguish sense and folly of men, like straight and crooked backs of horses.
Lead us, O God, to wealth and noble offspring : keep penury afar and grant us plenty.

12 This Sage the Sages, ne'er deceived, commanded, setting him down in dwellings of the living.
Hence mayst thou, friendly God, with rapid footsteps behold the Gods, wonderful, fair to look on.

13 Good guidance hast thou for the priest, O Agni, who, Youngest God ! with outpoured Soma serves thee.
Ruler of men, thou joyous God, bring treasure splendid and plentiful to aid the toiler.

14 Now all that we, thy faithful servants, Agni, have done with feet, with hands, and with our bodies,
The wise, with toil, the holy rite have guided, as those who frame a car with manual cunning.

15 May we, seven sages first in rank, engender, from Dawn the Mother, men to be ordainers.
May we, Angirases, be sons of Heaven, and, radiant, burst the wealth-containing mountain.

16 As in the days of old our ancient Fathers, speeding the work of holy worship, Agni,
Sought pure light and devotion, singing praises; they cleft the ground and made red Dawns apparent.

17 Gods, doing holy acts, devout, resplendent, smelting like ore their human generations.
Enkindling Agni and exalting Indra, they came encompassing the stall of cattle.

18 Strong One ! he marked them—and the Gods before them—like herds of cattle in a foodful pasture.
There they moaned forth their strong desire for mortals, to aid the True, the nearest One, the Living.

19 We have worked for thee, we have laboured nobly—bright Dawns have shed their light upon our worship—
Adding a beauty to the perfect Agni, and the God's beauteous eye that shines for ever.

20 Agni, Disposer, we have sung these praises to thee the Wise: do thou accept them gladly.
Blaze up on high and ever make us richer. Give us great wealth, O thou whose boons are many.

7 *Freely giving* : enabling the possessor to be bountiful in turn.

11 *He who knows* : the wise Agni. *Like straight and crooked backs* : *aśvānām*, of horses, is supplied by Sāyaṇa; as a horse-keeper or groom distinguishes between well-shaped and ill-shaped backs. *Keep penury afar* : I follow Professor Roth in his interpretation of *ditim* and *áditim* in this passage. Professor Wilson, following Sāyaṇa, translates : 'be bountiful to the liberal giver ; shun him who gives not.' 'Give us this life on earth, keep off the life to come.'—Max Müller.

12 *This Sage* : Agni. *The Sages* : the other Gods. *Commanded* : ordered to become a priestly herald or invoker. *With rapid footsteps* : I follow Sāyaṇa ; but the correctness of his explanation is doubtful. According to Pischel, *paḍbhiḥ* here means 'with (thine) eyes.'

15 'Again, through the identification of the fathers with the light they are brought into connection with the metaphor of generation......The fathers are united with the Dawn, and desire with her to beget male children. In a hymn to Soma they are mentioned along with the morning Sun as having placed the germ in the earth ; and the fruitfulness of heaven and earth, which give birth to gods and men, is described as produced by the fathers.'—Wallis, *Cosmology of the Ṛgveda*, p. 72.

The wealth-containing mountain : the cloud with its store of rain, or the cave in which the cows or rays of light were imprisoned.

17 *Gods* : the godlike Angirases. *Smelting like ore* : purifying their humanity, as ore is purified by smelting.

18 *Strong One* : O mighty Agni. *He marked them* : Indra saw the kine of the Angirases, the stolen rays of light. *The True, the Nearest One, the Living* : Agni appears to be meant.

HYMN III. *Agni.*

1. Win, to assist you, Rudra, Lord of worship, Priest of both worlds, effectual Sacrificer,
Agni, invested with his golden colours, before the thunder strike and lay you senseless.

2 This shrine have we made ready for thy coming, as the fond dame attires her for her husband.
Performer of good work, sit down before us, invested while these flames incline to meet thee.

3 A hymn, O Priest, to him who hears, the gentle, to him who looks on men, exceeding gracious,
A song of praise sing to the God Immortal, whom the stone, presser of the sweet juice, worships.

4 Even as true knower of the Law, O Agni, to this our solemn rite be thou attentive.
When shall thy songs of festival be sung thee? When is thy friendship shown within our dwelling?

5 Why this complaint to Varuṇa, O Agni? And why to Heaven? for what is our transgression?
How wilt thou speak to Earth and bounteous Mitra? What wilt thou say to Aryaman and Bhaga?

6 What, when thou blazest on the lesser altars, what to the mighty Wind who comes to bless us,
True, circumambient? what to Earth, O Agni, what wilt thou say to man-destroying Rudra?

7 How to great Pūṣan who promotes our welfare,—to honoured Rudra what, who gives oblations?
What sin of ours to the far-striding Viṣṇu, what, Agni, wilt thou tell the Lofty Arrow.

8 What wilt thou tell the truthful band of Maruts, how answer the great Sun when thou art questioned?
Before the Free, before the Swift, defend us: fulfil heaven's work, all-knowing Jātavedas.

9 I crave the cow's true gift arranged by Order: though raw, she hath the sweet ripe juice, O Agni.
Though she is black of hue with milk she teemeth, nutritious, brightly shining, all-sustaining.

10 Agni the Bull, the manly, hath been sprinkled with oil upon his back, by Law eternal.
He who gives vital power goes on unswerving. Pṛṣni the Bull hath milked the pure white udder.

11 By Law the Angirases cleft the rock asunder, and sang their hymns together with the cattle.
Bringing great bliss the men encompassed Morning: light was apparent at the birth of Agni.

12 By Law the Immortal Goddesses the Waters, with meath-rich waves, O Agni, and uninjured,
Like a strong courser lauded in his running, sped to flow onward swiftly and for ever.

13 Go never to the feast of one who harms us, the treacherous neighbour or unworthy kinsman.
Punish us not for a false brother's trespass. Let us not feel the might of friend or foeman.

14 O Agni, keep us safe with thy protection, loving us, honoured God! and ever guarding.
Beat thou away, destory severe affliction: slay e'en the demon when he waxes mighty.

1 *Rudra*: here meaning Agni. *Before the thunder strike*: before death overtakes you. Professor Ludwig refers to the Atharvaveda, XII. 2. 9, where Agni Kravyād, or Agni in his most terrific form, is spoken of as the God of Death who stupefies men with his thunderbolt.

2 *The flames*: there is no substantive in the text. Sāyaṇa supplies 'flames or songs of praise,' or 'ladles' may be the word understood. Professor Ludwig supplies *viśaḥ* or *prajāḥ* 'families or people,' and Professor Grassmann 'libations'.

5 *Why this complaint*: why dost thou accuse us of sin?

6 *On the lesser altars*: on the *dhiṣṇyás*, side-altars, or heaps of earth covered with sand on which the fire is placed. *Man-destroying*: the destroyer of wicked men, says the Scholiast. Rudra is generally represented as a benevolent God.

7 *The Lofty Arrow*: the lightning.

8 *How answer the great Sun*: the sense of stanzas 5—8 appears to be, as Professor Ludwig observes: thou hast no grounds for complaining of us to any one of the Gods: be, rather, our advocate if Sūrya comes forward as our accuser.

Before the Free, before the Swift: the Sun.

9 The first line is difficult. 'I solicit the milk of the cow essential for the sacrifice.'—Wilson. *Through raw*: this opposition of the uncooked cow and the milk cooked or ripened in her udder has been noticed before. See I. 62. 9.

10 *Pṛṣni*: here said to be Sūrya or the Sun, who draws his light from the sky. But see Benfey, Vedica und Verwandtes, pp. 74, 75.

15 Through these our songs of praise be gracious, Agni; moved by our prayers, O Hero, touch our viands.
Accept, O Angiras, these our devotions, and let the praise which Gods desire address thee.

16 To thee who knowest, Agni, thou Disposer, all these wise secret speeches have I uttered,
Sung to thee, Sage, the charming words of wisdom, to thee, O Singer, with my thoughts and Praises.

HYMN IV. *Agni.*

1. PUT forth like a wide-spreading net thy vigour; go like a mighty King with his attendants.
Thou, following thy swift net, shootest arrows : transfix the fiends with darts that burn most fiercely.

2 Forth go in rapid flight thy whirling weapons : follow them closely, glowing in thy fury.
Spread with thy tongue the winged flames, O Agni; unfettered, cast thy firebrands all around thee.

3 Send thy spies forward, fleetest in thy motion ; be, ne'er deceived, the guardian of this people
From him who, near or far, is bent on evil, and let no trouble sent from thee o'ercome us.

4 Rise up, O Agni, spread thee out before us : burn down our foes, thou who hast sharpened arrows.
Him, blazing Agni ! who hath worked us mischief, consume thou utterly like dried-up stubble.

5 Rise, Agni, drive off those who fight against us : make manifest thine own celestial vigour.
Slacken the strong bows of the demon-driven : destroy our foemen whether kin or stranger.

6 Most Youthful God, he knoweth well thy favour who gave an impulse to this high devotion.
All fair days and magnificence of riches hast thou beamed forth upon the good man's portals.

7 Blest, Agni, be the man, the liberal giver, who with his lauds and regular oblation
Is fain to please thee for his life and dwelling. May all his days be bright : be this his longing.

8 I praise thy gracious favour : sing in answer. May this my song sing like a loved one with thee.
Lords of good steeds and cars may we adorn thee, and day by day vouchsafe thou us dominion.

9 Here of free choice let each one serve thee richly, resplendent day by day at eve and morning.
So may we honour thee, content and joyous, passing beyond the glories of the people.

10 Whoso with good steeds and fine gold, O Agni, comes nigh thee on a car laden with treasure,
His Friend art thou, yea, thou art his Protector whose joy it is to entertain thee duly.

11 Through words and kinship I destroy the mighty : this power I have from Gotama my father.
Mark thou this speech of ours, O thou Most Youthful, Friend of the House, exceeding wise, Invoker.

12 Knowing no slumber, speedy and propitious, alert and ever friendly, most unwearied,
May thy protecting powers, unerring Agni, taking their places here, combined, preserve us.

13 Thy guardian rays, O Agni, when they saw him, preserved blind Māmateya from affliction.
Lord of all riches, he preserved the pious: the foes who fain would harm them did no mischief.

This hymn is said by Sāyaṇa to be addressed to Agni as slayer of the R kṣasas, that is, as God of the fire with which the immigrant Āryans burnt the jungle, drove back the hostile aborigines, and cleared the ground for encampment or permanent settlement.

3 *Thy spies* : thy first flames, sent forward as if to reconnoitre.

5 *The demon-driven* : those whom evil spirits incite to attack us.

8 *Sing in answer* : with the auspicious sound of thy crackling flames.

11 *Through words and kinship* : that is, through my close alliance with Agni, effected by the prayers with which my fathers and I have worshipped him.

The mighty : the Rākṣasas or demons, according to Sāyaṇa.

13 This stanza has occurred before, I. 147. 3. *Blind Māmateya* : the Ṛṣi Dīrghatamas. *Lord of all riches* : Agni.

14 Aided by thee with thee may we be wealthy, may we gain strength with thee to guide us onward.
Fulfil the words of both, O Ever Truthful: straightway do this, thou God whom power emboldens.

15 O Agni, with this fuel will we serve thee; accept the laud we sing to thee with favour.
Destroy the cursing Rākṣasas: preserve us, O rich in friends, from guile and scorn and slander.

HYMN V. *Agni.*

1. How shall we give with one accord oblation to Agni, to Vaiśvānara the Bounteous?
Great light, with full high growth hath he uplifted, and, as a pillar bears the roof, sustains it.

2 Reproach not him who, God and self-reliant, vouchsafed this bounty unto me a mortal,—
Deathless, discerner, wise, to me the simple, Vaiśvānara most manly, youthful Agni.

3 Sharp-pointed, powerful, strong, of boundless vigour, Agni who knows the lofty hymn, kept secret
As the lost milch-cow's track, the doubly Mighty,—he hath declared to me this hidden knowledge.

4 May he with sharpened teeth, the Bounteous Giver, Agni, consume with flame most fiercely glowing.
Those who regard not Varuṇa's commandments and the dear stedfast laws of sapient Mitra.

5 Like youthful women without brothers, straying, like dames who hate their lords, of evil conduct,
They who are full of sin, untrue, unfaithful, they have engendered this abysmal station.

6 To me, weak, innocent, thou, luminous Agni, hast boldly given as 'twere a heavy burthen,
This Pṛṣṭha hymn, profound and strong and mighty, of seven elements, and with offered dainties.

7 So may our song that purifies, through wisdom reach in a moment him the Universal,
Established on the height, on earth's best station, above the beauteous grassy skin of Pṛṣni.

8 Of this my speech what shall I utter further? They indicate the milk stored up in secret
When they have thrown as 'twere the cows' stalls open. The Bird protects earths' best and well-loved station.

9 This is the Great Ones' mighty apparition which from of old the radiant Cow hath followed.
This, shining brightly in the place of Order, swift, hasting on in secret, she discovered.

10 He then who shone together with his Parents remembered Pṛṣṇi's fair and secret treasure,
Which, in the Mother Cow's most lofty station, the Bull's tongue, of the flame bent forward, tasted.

11 With reverence I declare the Law, O Agni; what is, comes by thine order, Jātavedas.
Of this, whate'er it be, thou art the Sovran, yea, all the wealth that is in earth or heaven.

12 What is our wealth therefrom, and what our treasure? Tell us O Jātavedas, for thou knowest,
What is our best course in this secret passage: we, unreproached, have reached a place far distant.

14 *The words of both* : the wishes of Gods and men. Sāyaṇa gives a different explanation, and Professor Wilson translates accordingly : 'destroy both (sorts of calumniators.)'

The Ṛṣi Vāmadeva, as Professor Roth observes, 'professes to make known a mysterious and recondite wisdom, which had been revealed to him by Agni,' and the language of the hymn is correspondingly difficult and obscure.

1 *Vaiśvānara* : common God of all Āryan men.

2 *This bounty* : the gift of this mysterious knowledge.

5 *This abysmal station* : that is, says Sāyaṇa, *narakasthānam* or hell The wicked are the cause of the existence of the place of punishment prepared for them.

6 *This Pṛṣṭha hymn* : Pṛṣṭha is the name of a particular arrangement of Sāmans employed at the mid-day oblation.

7 *The Universal* : Vaiśvānara Agni. *Established on the height* : according to this conjectural translation, which follows a suggestion of Professor Ludwig, the reference is to Agni placed on the altar, above the surface of the earth (Pṛṣni). But the meaning of *jābāru* (on the height) is uncertain. Professor Wilson translates : 'whose swift-ascending brilliant (orb) is stationed on the east of the earth, to mount, like the sun, above the immoveable heaven.'

8 This stanza appears to allude to the Angirases recovering the lost rays of light, *the milk stored up in secret. The Bird* : the Sun who flies through heaven.

9 *The Great Ones' mighty apparition* : the solar orb; *the Great Ones* being the Sun's rays. *The radiant Cow* : Uṣas or Dawn who discovers the Sun as he travels in secret, or by night, from west to east, and follows him till he is about to rise.

10 *He* : Agni. *His Parents* : Heaven and Earth. *Pṛṣni* is the Cow whose milk is used in the oblation which Agni, the Bull, devours.

13 What is the limit, what the rules, the guerdon? Like fleet-foot coursers speed we to the contest.
When will the Goddesses, the Immortal's Spouses, the Dawns, spread over us the Sun-God's splendour?

14 Unsatisfied, with speech devoid of vigour, scanty and frivolous and inconclusive,
Wherefore do they address thee here, O Agni? Let these who have no weapons suffer sorrow.

15 The majesty of him the Good, the Mighty, aflame, hath shone for glory in the dwelling.
He, clothed in light, hath shone most fair to look on, wealthy in boons, as a home shines with riches.

HYMN VI. *Agni.*

1. PRIEST of our rite, stand up erect, O Agni, in the Gods' service best of sacrificers,
For over every thought thou art the Ruler: thou furtherest e'en the wisdom of the pious.

2 He was set down mid men as Priest unerring, Agni, wise, welcome in our holy synods.
Like Savitar he hath lifted up his splendour, and like a builder raised his smoke to heaven.

3 The glowing ladle, filled with oil, is lifted; choosing Gods' service to the right he circles.
Eager he rises like the new-wrought pillar which, firmly set and fixed, anoints the victims.

4 When sacred grass is strewn and Agni kindled, the Adhvaryu rises to his task rejoicing.
Agni the Priest, like one who tends the cattle, goes three times round, as from of old he wills it.

5 Agni himself, the Priest, with measured motion, goes round, with sweet speech, cheerful, true to Order.
His fulgent flames run forth like vigorous horses; all creatures are affrighted when he blazes.

6 Beautiful and auspicious is thine aspect, O lovely Agni, terrible when spreading.
Thy splendours are not covered by the darkness: detraction leaves no stain upon thy body.

7 Naught hindered his production, Bounteous Giver: his Mother and his Sire were free to send him.
Then as Friend benevolent, refulgent, Agni shone forth in human habitations.

8 He, Agni, whom the twice-five sisters, dwelling together, in the homes of men engendered,
Bright like a spear's tooth, wakened in the morning, with powerful mouth and like an axe well-sharpened.

9 These thy Bay Coursers, Agni, dropping fatness, ruddy vigorous, speeding straightly forward,
And red steeds, wonderful, of mighty muscle, are to this service of the Gods invited:

10 These brightly-shining flames of thine, O Agni, that move for ever restless, all-subduing,
Like falcons hasting eagerly to the quarry, roar loudly like the army of the Maruts.

11 To thee, O flaming God, hath prayer been offered. Let the priest laud thee: give to him who worships.
Men have established Agni as Invoker, fain to adore the glory of the living.

HYMN VII. *Agni.*

1. HERE by ordainers was this God appointed first Invoker, best at worship, to be praised at rites:
Whom Apnavāna, and the Bhṛgus caused to shine bright-coloured in the wood, spreading from home to home.

2 When shall thy glory as a God, Agni, be suddenly shown forth.

---

14 *These who have no weapons*: who are unprovided with the necessary elements of sacrifice, and therefore unable to please Agni.

2 *Like a builder*: as the builder of a house raises a pillar.

3 *To the right he circles*: is carried round to the altars. *Anoints the victims*: smears them with the clarified butter with which it (the sacrificial post) has been previously anointed.

7 *His Mother and his Sire*: Earth and Heaven. *To send him*: to be messenger between men and Gods.

8 *The twice-five sisters*: the priest's fingers which produce the sacrificial fire.

9 *Bay Coursers*: *haritaḥ*; Harits; the prototype (the word being feminine) of the Greek 'Charites.' See M. Müller, Chips from a German Workshop, IV. 141 (new edition).

11 *The glory of the living*: Agni as Narāśansa, the Praise or Glory of Men.

1 *Here*: at this ceremony. *Ordainers*: the regulators of the sacrifice. *Apnavāna*: a Ṛṣi of the family of Bhṛgu.

For mortal men have held thee fast, adorable in all their homes,

3 Seeing thee faithful to the Law, most sapient, like the starry heaven,
Illumining with cheerful ray each solemn rite in every house.

4 Vivasvān's envoy living men have taken as their ensign, swift,
The ruler over all mankind, moving like Bhṛgu in each home.

5 Him the intelligent have they placed duly as Invoking Priest,
Welcome, with sanctifying flame, best worshipper, with sevenfold might;

6 In his Eternal Mothers, in the wood, concealed and unapproached,
Kept secret though his flames are bright seeking on all sides, quickly found.

7 That as food spreads forth in this earthly udder, Gods may rejoice them in the home of Order,
Great Agni, served with reverence and oblation, flies ever to the sacrifice, the Faithful.

8 Bird of each rite, skilled in an envoy's duties, knowing both worlds and that which lies between them,
Thou goest from of old a willing Herald, knowing full well heaven's innermost recesses.

9 Bright God, thy path is black: light is before thee: thy moving splendour is the chief of wonders.
When she, yet unimpregnate, hath conceived thee, even when newly born thou art an envoy.

10 Yet newly born, his vigour is apparent when the wind blows upon his fiery splendour,
His sharpened tongue he layeth on the brushwood, and with his teeth e'en solid food consumeth.

11 When he hath borne off food with swift flame swiftly, strong Agni makes himself a speedy envoy,
Follows the rustling of the wind, consuming, and courser-like, speeds, drives the swift horse onward.

HYMN VIII. *Agni.*

1. YOUR envoy who possesses all, Immortal, bearer of your gifts,
Best worshipper, I woo with song.

2 He, Mighty, knows the gift of wealth, he knows the deep recess of heaven :
He shall bring hitherward the Gods.

3 He knows, a God himself, to guide Gods to the righteous in his home :
He gives e'en treasures that we love.

4 He is the Herald : well-informed, he doth his errand to and fro,
Knowing the deep recess of heaven.

5 May we be they who gratify Agni with sacrificial gifts,
Who cherish and enkindle him.

6 Illustrious for wealth are they, and hero deeds, victorious,
Who have served Agni reverently.

7 So unto us, day after day, may riches craved by many come,
And power and might spring up for us.

8 That holy Singer in his strength shoots forth his arrows swifter than
The swift shafts of the tribes of men.

HYMN IX. *Agni.*

1. AGNI, show favour : great art thou who to this pious man art come,
To seat thee on the sacred grass.

2 May he the Immortal, Helper, hard to be deceived among mankind,
Become the messenger of all.

4 *Vivasvān's envoy* : according to Sāyaṇa, the messenger of the worshipper. *Moving like Bhṛgu* : or shining; Bhṛgu being originally a personification of lightning.

5 *Sevenfold might* : Agni's seven flames.

6 *Eternal Mothers* : the Celestial Waters. *Seeking on all sides* : roaming at will in search of food.

7 *In this earthly udder* : here on earth, and especially at the altar from which oblations come. Only when the elements of sacrifice are forthcoming can Agni invite and bring the Gods. *The home of Order* : the place of law-ordained sacrifice.

8 *Bird of each rite* : attending all sacrifices. *That which lies between them*: the firmament or mid-air between heaven and earth.

9 *She, yet unimpregnate* : the piece of wood in which fire is produced.

11 *When he hath borne off food* : I follow Sāyaṇa, but am not satisfied with his explanation. *Courser-like* : Agni, himself a courser, drives on the wind as it were a courser. Professor Ludwig suggests that *árvā* here may mean a rider, not a courser.

2 *Knows the gift of wealth* : how to enrich his worshippers.

4 *Doth his errand to and fro* : bears to the Gods the prayers, praises, and oblations of their worshippers, and brings them down to the sacrifice.

8 *That holy Singer* : Agni the Priest. The stanza is difficult. Professor Wilson, following Sāyaṇa, translates : 'May the wise Agni entirely obviate by his power the removeable (ills) of men the descendants of Manu'. I have adopted Professor Ludwig's interpretation.

3 Around the altar is he led, welcome Chief Priest at solemn rites,
Or as the Potar sits him down.
4 Agni in fire at sacrifice, and in the house as Lord thereof,
And as a Brahman takes his seat.
5 Thou comest as the guide of folk who celebrate a sacrifice,
And to oblations brought by men.
6 Thou servest as his messenger whose sacrifice thou lovest well,
To bear the mortal's gifts to heaven.
7 Accept our solemn rite ; be pleased, Angiras, with our sacrifice :
Give ear and listen to our call.
8 May thine inviolable car, wherewith thou guardest those who give,
Come near to us from every side.

HYMN X. *Agni.*

1. THIS day with praises, Agni, we bring thee that which thou lovest.
Right judgment, like a horse, with our devotions.
2 For thou hast ever been the Car-driver, Agni, of noble
Strength, lofty sacrifice, and rightful judgment.
3 Through these our praises come thou to meet us, bright as the sunlight,
O Agni, well disposed, with all thine aspects.
4 Now may we serve thee singing these lauds this day to thee, Agni.
Loud as the voice of Heaven thy blasts are roaring.
5 Just at this time of the day and the night thy look is the sweetest :
It shineth near us even as gold for glory.
6 Spotless thy body, brilliant as gold, like clarified butter :
This gleams like gold on thee, O Self-dependent.
7 All hate and mischief, yea, if committed, Agni, thou turnest,
Holy One, from the man who rightly worships.
8 Agni, with you Gods, prosperous be our friendships and kinships.
Be this our bond here by this place, thine altar.

3 *Chief Priest* : Hotar, the presenter of the oblation. *The Potar* : literally, Cleanser or Purifier, another of the sixteen priests usually employed.

4 I read *utāgnī* as proposed by Prof. Max Müller and Prof. Ludwig in place of the almost impossible *utá gnā́ḥ* of the text.

———

2 *Car-driver* : promoter.

6 *This* : thy splendour.

8 *This altar* : literally, this udder ; that is, the place whence oblations proceed.

HYMN XI. *Agni.*

1. THY blessed majesty, victorious Agni, shines brightly in the neighbourhood of Sūrya.
Splendid to see, it shows even at night-time, and food is fair to look on in thy beauty.
2 Agni, disclose his thought for him who singeth, the well, Strong God ! while thou art praised with fervour.
Vouchsafe to us that powerful hymn, O Mighty, which, Radiant One ! with all the Gods thou lovest.
3 From thee, O Agni, springs poetic wisdom, from thee come thoughts and hymns of praise that prosper ;
From thee flows wealth, with heroes to adorn it, to the true-hearted man who gives oblation.
4 From thee the hero springs who wins the booty, bringer of help, mighty, of real courage.
From thee comes wealth, sent by the Gods, bliss-giving ; Agni, from thee the fleet impetuous charger.
5 Immortal Agni, thee whose voice is pleasant, as first in rank, as God, religious mortals
Invite with hymns ; thee who removest hatred, Friend of the Home, the household's Lord, unerring.
6 Far from us thou removest want and sorrow, far from us all ill-will when thou protectest.
Son of Strength, Agni, blest is he at evening, whom thou as God attendest for his welfare.

HYMN XII. *Agni.*

1. WHOSO enkindles thee, with lifted ladle, and thrice this day offers thee food, O Agni,
May he excel, triumphant through thy splendours, wise through thy mental power, O Jātavedas.
2 Whoso with toil and trouble brings thee fuel, serving the majesty of mighty Agni,

1 *In the neighbourhood of Sūrya* : by day, in the sunshine.

2 *The well* : the source of sacred song.

4 *The hero* : or the strong horse.

He, kindling thee at evening and at morning, prospers, and comes to wealth, and slays his foemen.

3 Agni is Master of sublime dominion, Agni is Lord of strength and lofty riches.
Straightway the self-reliant God, Most Youthful, gives treasures to the mortal who adores him.

4 Most Youthful God, whatever sin, through folly, we here, as human beings, have committed,
In sight of Aditi make thou us sinless : remit, entirely, Agni, our offences.

5 Even in the presence of great sin, O Agni, free us from prison of the Gods or mortals.
Never may we who are thy friends be injured : grant health and strength unto our seed and offspring.

6 Even as ye here, Gods Excellent and Holy, have loosed the cow that by the foot was tethered,
So also set us free from this affliction : long let our life, O Agni, be extended.

HYMN XIII. *Agni.*

1. AGNI hath looked, benevolently-minded, on the wealth-giving spring of radiant Mornings.
Come, Aśvins, to the dwelling of the pious : Sūrya the God is rising with his splendour.

2 Savitar, God, hath spread on high his lustre, waving his flag like a spoil-seeking hero.
Their stablished way go Varuṇa and Mitra, what time they make the Sun ascend the heaven.

3 Him whom they made to drive away the darkness, Lords of sure mansions, constant to their object,
Him who beholds the universe, the Sun-God, seven strong and youthful Coursers carry onward.

4 Spreading thy web with mightiest Steeds thou comest, rending apart, thou God, the black-hued mantle.
The rays of Sūrya tremulously shining sink, like a hide, the darkness in the waters.

5 How is it that, unbound and not supported, he falleth not although directed downward ?
By what self-power moves he ? Who hath seen it ? He guards the vault of heaven, a close-set pillar.

HYMN XIV. *Agni.*

1. THE God hath looked, even Agni Jātavedas, to meet the Dawns refulgent in their glories.
Come on your chariot, ye who travel widely, come to this sacrifice of ours, Nāsatyas.

2 Producing light for all the world of creatures, God Savitar hath raised aloft his banner.
Making his presence known by sunbeams, Sūrya hath filled the firmament and earth and heaven.

3 Red Dawn is come, riding with brightness onward, distinguished by her beams, gay-hued and mighty.
Dawn on her nobly-harnessed car, the Goddess, awaking men to happiness, approacheth.

4 May those most powerful steeds and chariot bring you, O Aśvins, hither at the break of morning.
Here for your draught of meath are Soma juices : at this our sacrifice rejoice, ye Mighty.

5 How is it that, unbound and unsupported, he falleth not although directed downward ?
By what self-power moves he ? Who hath seen it ? He guards the vault of heaven, a close-set pillar ?

HYMN XV. *Agni.*

1. AGNI the Herald, like a horse, is led forth at our solemn rite,

4 *Aditi* : apparently the great omnipresent Power which controls the forces of the universe, and from which no sins are hidden.

5 *Prison of the Gods or mortals* : actual imprisonment by men and corresponding chastisement by the Gods.

6 *The cow* : the cow-buffalo, tied to a post, representing symbolically the man who is in the bonds of sin. Cf. X. 126. 6.

2 *Waving his flag* : according to Sāyaṇa, 'scattering the dew.' But there can be no doubt that *drapsá*, the Zend *drafsha*, means a banner in this place. Sāyaṇa explains *sátvā*, a hero, as 'a bull,' but this interpretation cannot be accepted.

Their stablished way : the course appointed for them in the eternal order of the universe.

3 *Coursers* : *haritaḥ*; Harits. Cf. IV. 6.9.

This hymn is an imitation of the preceding. The last stanza is adopted word for word.

5 *He* : in the text *ayam*, this, that is Sūrya, the Sun, mentioned in stanza 2.

1 *Is led forth* : implying the formal bringing of fire from the household fire to light the sacrificial fire.

God among Gods adorable.
2 Three times unto our solemn rite comes Agni like a charioteer,
Bearing the viands to the Gods.
3 Round the oblations hath he paced, Agni the Wise, the Lord of Strength,
Giving the offerer precious boons.
4 He who is kindled eastward for Sṛñjaya, Devavāta's son,
Resplendent, tamer of the foe.
5 So mighty be the Agni whom the mortal hero shall command,
With sharpened teeth and bountiful.
6 Day after day they dress him, as they clean a horse who wins the prize,
Dress the red Scion of the Sky.
7 When Sahadeva's princely son with two bay horses thought of me,
Summoned by him I drew not back.
8 And truly those two noble bays I straightway took when offered me,
From Sahadeva's princely son.
9 Long, O ye Aśvins, may he live, your care, ye Gods, the princely son.
Of Sahadeva, Somaka.
10 Cause him the youthful prince, the son of Sahadeva, to enjoy
Long life, O Aśvins, O ye Gods.

HYMN XVI. *Indra.*

1. IMPETUOUS, true, let Maghavan come hither, and let his Tawny Coursers speed to reach us.
For him have we pressed juice exceeding potent: here, praised with song, let him effect his visit.

2 Unyoke, as at thy journey's end, O Hero, to gladden thee today at this libation.
Like Uśanā, the priest a laud shall utter, a hymn to thee, the Lord Divine, who markest.

3 When the Bull, quaffing, praises our libation, as a sage paying holy rites in secret,
Seven singers here from heaven hath he begotten, who e'en by day have wrought their works while singing.

4 When heaven's fair light by hymns was made apparent (they made great splendour shine at break of morning),
He with his succour, best of Heroes, scattered the blinding darkness so that men saw clearly.

5 Indra, Impetuous One, hath waxed immensely : he with his vastness hath filled earth and heaven.
E'en beyond this his majesty extendeth who hath exceeded all the worlds in greatness.

6 Śakra who knoweth well all human actions hath with his eager Friends let loose the waters.
They with their songs cleft e'en the mountain open and willingly disclosed the stall of cattle.

7 He smote away the floods' obstructer, Vṛtra ; Earth, conscious, lent her aid to speed thy thunder.
Thou sentest forth the waters of the ocean, as Lord through power and might, O daring Hero.

8 When, Much-invoked ! the water's rock thou cleftest, Saramā showed herself and went before thee.
Hymned by Aṅgirases, bursting the cowstalls, much strength thou foundest for us as our leader.

9 Come, Maghavan, Friend of Man, to aid the singer imploring thee in battle for the sunlight.
Speed him with help in his inspired invokings : down sink the sorcerer, the prayerless Dasyu.

2 *Three times* : with reference to the three sacrifices.

4 *Eastward* : on the *uttaravedī* or north altar. *Sṛñjaya* : a certain Soma-sacrificer *kaścit somayāji*, says Sāyaṇa. Professor Wilson observes : 'We have several princes of the name in the Purāṇas, but none distinguished by this patronymic : the *Sṛñjayas* are also a people in the west of India.'

6 *The red Scion of the Sky* : or, Aruṣa, the Child of Heaven, i.e. the Sun.

7 *Sahadeva's princely son* : Somaka, the institutor of the sacrifice, son of a Rājā named Sahadeva. *With two bay horses* : which were to be the priest's honorarium.

9 *Your care* : there is no substantive in the text. Sāyaṇa supplies *tarpakaḥ* satisfier, i.e. worshipper. Professor Ludwig regards *vām* as a dativus ethicus.

---

1 *Impetuous* : according to Sāyaṇa, *ṛjīṣī*, the word in the text, means accepter, or drinker, of the spiritless Soma, of the Soma when its essence or strength has passed away. Professor Ludwig follows Sāyaṇa.

2 *Like Uśanā* : the Ṛṣi Uśanā, or Uśanas, called also Kāvya or Kavi's son, appears in the Veda as the especial friend of Indra. See I. 51. 10 ; 33, 5 ; 117, 12.

3 *The Bull* : the mighty Indra. *Seven singers* : the meaning of this line is not clear. Professor Wilson, following Sāyaṇa, translates : 'and this generates the seven efficient (rays) from heaven, which, being glorified, have made (manifest) the objects of (human) perception.'

4 *Scattered, etc.* : or, fashioned blind turbid darkness so that men saw clearly.

6 *Śakra*: Indra, the powerful. *His eager Friends* : the Maruts.

8 *Saramā* : the hound of Indra, who tracked the stolen cows. See I. 62. 3, and 72. 8.

10 Come to our home resolved to slay the Dasyu : Kutsa longed eagerly to win thy friendship.
Alike in form ye both sate in his dwelling : the faithful Lady was in doubt between you.

11 Thou comest, fain to succour him, with Kutsa,—a goad that masters both the Wind-God's horses,
That, holding the brown steeds like spoil for capture, the sage may on the final day be present.

12 For Kutsa, with thy thousand, thou at day-break didst hurl down greedy Śuṣṇa, foe of harvest.
Quickly with Kutsa's friend destroy the Dasyus, and roll the chariot-wheel of Sūrya near us.

13 Thou to the son of Vidathin, Ṛjiśvan, gavest up mighty Mṛgaya and Pipru.
Thou smotest down the swarthy fifty thousand, and rentest forts as age consumes a garment.

14 What time thou settest near the Sun thy body, thy form, Immortal One, is seen expanding :
Thou a wild elephant with might invested, like a dread lion as thou wieldest weapons.

15 Wishes for wealth have gone to Indra, longing for him in war for light and at libation,
Eager for glory, labouring with praise-songs : he is like home, like sweet and fair nutrition.

16 Call we for you that Indra, prompt to listen, him who hath done so much for men's advantage ;
Who, Lord of envied bounty, to a singer like me brings quickly booty worth the capture.

17 When the sharp-pointed arrow, O thou Hero, flieth mid any conflict of the people,
When, Faithful One, the dread encounter cometh, then be thou the Protector of our body.

18 Further the holy thoughts of Vāmadeva ; be thou a guileless Friend in fight for booty.
We come to thee whose providence protects us : wide be thy sway for ever for thy singer.

19 O Indra, with these men who love thee truly, free givers, Maghavan, in every battle,
May we rejoice through many autumns, quelling our foes, as days subdue the nights with splendour.

20 Now, as the Bhṛgus wrought a car, for Indra the Strong, the Mighty, we our prayer have fashioned,
That he may, ne'er withdraw from us his friendship, but be our bodies' guard and strong defender.

21 Now, Indra ! lauded, glorified with praises, let power swell high like rivers for the singer.
For thee a new hymn, Lord of Bays, is fashioned. May we, car-borne, through song be victors ever.

10 *Kutsa* : a Rājarṣi or royal Ṛṣi, frequently mentioned as the favoured friend of Indra.

The faithful Lady : even Kutsa's wife could hardly distinguish one from the other; or, as Sāyaṇa explains, Indra took Kutsa to his own home where Śacī his consort was uncertain which of the two was Indra.

11 *The sage* : Kutsa. *The final day* : the decisive day of battle.

12 *With thy thousand* : thy many followers. *Foe of harvest* : or Kuyava may be the name of another fiend or barbarous enemy. See I. 104. 3. *Kutsa's friend* : the thunderbolt, according to Sāyaṇa. *Roll the chariot-wheel of Sūrya near us* : bring back the daylight.

13 *Ṛjiśvan* : a prince mentioned before as protected by Indra. See I. 51. 5. *Mṛgaya and Pipru* : demons of the air. *The swarthy fifty thousand* : black Rakṣasas, fiends, or hostile aborigines.

14 *What time thou settest near the Sun thy body* : perhaps, as Professor Ludwig suggests, a poetical explanation of an eclipse of the sun.

15 *Eager for glory* : a transition from 'wishes' to 'wishers' implied therein. *Nutrition* : according to Sāyaṇa, like Lakṣmī the Goddess of prosperity.

19 *Free givers* : liberal institutors of sacrifice.

20 *As the Bhṛgus* : according to Sāyaṇa=splendid carpenters ; but the reference must be to the celebrated priestly family, and 'car' may be used metaphorically for the hymn which rapidly reaches the Gods.

HYMN XVII. *Indra.*

1. GREAT art thou, Indra ; yea, the earth, with gladness, and heaven confess to thee thine high dominion.
Thou in thy vigour having slaughtered Vṛtra didst free the floods arrested by the Dragon.

2 Heaven trembled at the birth of thine effulgence ; Earth trembled at the fear of thy displeasure.

1 *The Dragon* : Ahi, the serpent-demon who stays the rain from falling.

The stedfast mountains shook in agitation : the waters flowed, and desert spots were flooded.

3 Hurling his bolt with might he cleft the mountain, while, putting forth his strength, he showed his vigour.
He slaughtered Vṛtra with his bolt, exulting, and, their lord slain, forth flowed the waters swiftly.

4 Thy Father Dyaus esteemed himself a hero : most noble was the work of Indra's Maker,
His who begat the strong bolt's Lord who roareth, immovable like earth from her foundation.

5 He who alone o'erthrows the world of creatures, Indra the peoples' King, invoked of many—
Verily all rejoice in him, extolling the boons which Maghavan the God hath sent them.

6 All Soma juices are his own for ever, most gladdening draughts are ever his, the Mighty,
Thou ever wast the Treasure-Lord of treasures : Indra, thou lettest all folk share thy bounty.

7 Moreover, when thou first wast born, O Indra, thou struckest terror into all the people.
Thou, Maghavan, rentest with thy bolt the Dragon who lay against the water-floods of heaven.

8 The ever-slaying, bold and furious Indra, the bright bolt's Lord, infinite, strong and mighty,
Who slayeth Vṛtra and acquireth booty, giver of blessings, Maghavan the bounteous:

9 Alone renowned as Maghavan in battles, he frighteneth away assembled armies.
He bringeth us the booty that he winneth : may we, well-loved, continue in his friendship.

10 Renowned is he when conquering and when slaying : 'tis he who winneth cattle in the combat.
When Indra hardeneth his indignation all that is fixed and all that moveth fear him.

11 Indra hath won all kine, all gold, all horses,—Maghavan, he who breaketh forts in pieces ;
Most manly with these men of his who help him, dealing out wealth and gathering the treasure.

12 What is the care of Indra for his Mother, what cares he for the Father who begat him ?
His care is that which speeds his might in conflicts, like wind borne onward by the clouds that thunder.

13 Maghavan makes the settled man unsettled : he scatters dust that he hath swept together,
Breaking in pieces like Heaven armed with lightning : Maghavan shall enrich the man who lauds him.

14 He urged the chariot-wheel of Sūrya forward : Etaśa, speeding on his way, he rested.
Him the black undulating cloud bedeweth, in this mid-air's depth, at the base of darkness,

15 As in the night the sacrificing priest.

16 Eager for booty, craving strength and horses, we-singers stir Indra, the strong, for friendship,
Who gives the wives we seek, whose succour fails not, to hasten, like a pitcher to the fountain.

4 *Esteemed himself a hero* : as being the father of such a son.

5 *Extolling* : I follow Professor Wilson in taking *gṛṇatáḥ* as a nominative plural, a lightened form for *gṛṇántáḥ*. Otherwise it is difficult to make sense out of the second line.

8 *Indra* : in this stanza is in the accusative case without a subject or a governing verb. Sāyaṇa supplies *vayam stotāraḥ stumeti*, 'we singers praise.'

11 *Who breaketh forts in pieces* : as it seems impossible to make any sense out of *pūrvīḥ*, I have adopted Professor Grassmann's conjecture, which is somewhat reluctantly accepted by Professor Ludwig and read *pūrbhíd* instead of the word in the text. Sāyaṇa supplies *śatrusenāḥ*, 'armies of enemies.' *These men* : who sing his praises and so increase his strength.

12 *His care is*: there are no corresponding words in the text, but it is necessary to supply something of the kind. The meaning is, Indra is independent of, and cares nothing about, his parents, but he does care for his dear ally the thunderbolt.

13 *Scatters dust* : causes commotion and keeps the world in a state of unrest.

14 This difficult stanza appears to refer to an eclipse of the Sun. Indra was urging on the Sun's chariot when suddenly he rested or stopped Etaśa the horse that drew it, and threw him back into the black moist cloud of the darkness of night. See I. 121. 13, and A. Kuhn, Mythologische Studien, I. pp. 58—60.

15 *The sacrificing priest* : lets the fire shine, understood. Sāyaṇa explains, 'as the sacrificer sprinkles Soma upon the invoking priest Agni,' taking *hótā*, a nominative case, as *hótāram*, an accusative. Professor Grassmann thinks that the single Pāda was originally a gloss on the preceding stanza.

16 *Who gives the wives we seek* : perhaps referring as, Professor Ludwig observes, to the forcible abduction of women after a victory.

17 Be thou our guardian, show thyself our kinsman, watching and blessing those who pour the Soma ;
As Friend, as Sire, most fatherly of fathers, giving the suppliant vital strength and freedom.

18 Be helping Friend of those who seek thy friendship : give life, when lauded, Indra, to the singer.
For, Indra, we the priests have paid thee worship, exalting thee with these our sacrifices.

19 Alone, when Indra Maghavan is lauded, he slayeth many ne'er-resisted Vṛtras.
Him in whose keeping is the well-loved singer never do Gods or mortals stay or hinder.

20 E'en so let Maghavan, the loud-voiced Indra, give us true blessings, foeless, men's upholder.
King of all creatures, give us glory amply, exalted glory due to him who lauds thee.

21 Now, Indra ! lauded, glorified with praises, let power swell high like rivers for the singer.
For thee a new hymn, Lord of Bays ! is fashioned. May we, car-borne, through song be victors ever.

HYMN XVIII. *Indra and Others.*

1. THIS is the ancient and accepted pathway by which all Gods have come into existence.
Hereby could one be born though waxen mighty. Let him not, otherwise, destroy his Mother.

2 Not this way go I forth : hard is the passage. Forth from the side obliquely will I issue.
Much that is yet undone must I accomplish ; one must I combat and the other question.

3 He bent his eye upon the dying Mother : My word I now withdraw. That way I follow.
In Tvaṣṭar's dwelling Indra drank the Soma, a hundredworth of juice pressed from the mortar.

4 What strange act shall he do, he whom his Mother bore for a thousand months and many autumns ?
No peer hath he among those born already, nor among those who shall be born hereafter.

5 Deeming him a reproach, his mother hid him, Indra, endowed with all heroic valour.
Then up he sprang himself, assumed his vesture, and filled, as soon as born, the earth and heaven.

6 With lively motion onward flow these waters, the Holy Ones, shouting, as 'twere, together.
Ask them to tell thee what the floods are saying, what girdling rock the waters burst asunder.

7 Are they addressing him with words of welcome ? Will the floods take on them the shame of Indra ?
With his great thunderbolt my Son hath slaughtered Vṛtra, and set these rivers free to wander.

8 I cast thee from me, mine,—thy youthful mother: thee, mine own offspring, Kuśavā hath swallowed.

Indra, Aditi, and Vāmadeva are said to be the Ṛṣis or seers as well as the deities of the hymn, as it consists of conversation in which all bear part. The hymn appears to be made up of somewhat incoherent fragments, and the Commentators do not seem to have been successful in their apportionment of the stanzas to the several speakers. See Prof. Pischel's Excursus (Vedische Studien, II pp. 42—54), and Prof. Ludwig's criticism thereon, Ueber die neuesten Arbeiten auf dem Gebiete der Ṛgveda-forschung, pp. 142 sqq.

1 The main subject is the birth and infancy of Indra. He refuses to be born in the usual manner and insists on coming into the world in another way. The speaker—Vyaṁsa his father, Aditi his mother, or some other—dissuades him, eventually, it seems, (stanza 3) with success. The Commentators erroneously take the stanza as referring to the birth of Vāmadeva.

2 Indra, as yet unborn, is the speaker. *One* : perhaps Vṛtra. *The other* : perhaps Viṣṇu, whom he addresses in stanza 11.

3 Indra, who has changed his mind, speaks the second half of the first line.

4 It is not clear who the speaker is. Professor Wilson observes : '*Aditi* defends her son upon the plea that, as his period of gestation was marvellous, his actions are not to be compared with those of any others.'

5 *Deeming him a reproach* : either because he appeared to be weak, or because, as Sāyaṇa says, he was born in a chamber in privacy unworthy of so great a God.

6 *What girdling rock* : an allusion to the prison of thick cloud from which Indra freed the waters.

7 *Words of welcome* : *nivids*, sentences or short formularies inserted in a liturgy and containing epithets or short invocations of the Gods.

The shame of Indra : his fancied guilt incurred in slaying Vṛtra. See I. 32. 14.

8 *Mine* : Sāyaṇa explains *mámat* as 'exulting.' Professor Roth, whom Professor Grassmann and the translators of the *Siebenzig Lieder* follow, renders it by now—now. I have preferred Professor Ludwig's interpretation, originally due to Benfey, and taken the word as another form of *máma*. The word is important as expressing Aditi's acknowledgment of Indra as her son. *Kuśavā* : according to Sāyaṇa, a Rākṣasī or female demon who swallowed Indra at his birth ; according to von Roth, the name of a river.

To him, mine infant, were the waters gracious. Indra, my Son, rose up in conquering vigour.

9 Thou art mine own, O Maghavan, whom Vyaṁsa struck to the ground and smote thy jaws in pieces.
But, smitten through, the mastery thou wonnest, and with thy bolt the Dāsa's head thou crushedst.

10 The Heifer hath brought forth the Strong, the Mighty, the unconquerable Bull, the furious Indra.
The Mother left her unlicked Calf to wander, seeking himself, the path that he would follow.

11 Then to her mighty Child the Mother turned her, saying, My son, these Deities forsake thee.
Then Indra said, about to slaughter Vṛtra, O my friend Viṣṇu, stride full boldly forward.

12 Who was he then who made thy Mother widow ? Who sought to slay thee lying still or moving ?
What God, when by the foot thy Sire thou tookest and slewest, was at hand to give thee comfort ?

13 In deep distress I cooked a dog's intestines. Among the Gods I found not one to comfort.
My consort I beheld in degradation. The Falcon then brought me the pleasant Soma.

10 *The Heifer* ; Aditi, the young mother of Indra.

11 *Stride full boldly forward* : that is, assist me in my battle with Vṛtra. Professor Grassmann and the translators of the *Siebenzig Lieder* render the passage differently 'O Vischnu, Freund, geh etwas doch zur Seite,' and, 'Viṣṇu mein Freund geh etwas aus dem Wege ; that is, 'step aside,' or 'out of the way,' and let me conquer Vṛtra without thy aid.

12 This appears to be Viṣṇu's answer. Why dost thou ask me to help thee now ? Didst thou not slay thine own father, thy father who sought to kill thee when yet unborn and when coming to the birth ? Vyaṁsa appears to be the father whom Indra slew (stanza 9). Sāyaṇa merely says that the allusions are variously explained by the followers of the Taittirīya school of the Yajurveda.

13 This appears to be Vāmadeva's excuse for having in his utmost need cooked and eaten, or desired to eat, impure flesh. 'So *Manu* has, Vāmadeva who well knew right and wrong, was by no means rendered impure, though desirous, when oppressed with hunger, of eating the flesh of dogs for the preservation of his life, X. 106.'—Wilson. According to Ludwig, Bergaigne, and Hillebrandt, the stanza is spoken by Indra. *The Falcon* : alluding to the way in which the Soma was first brought from heaven. Sāyaṇa explains it as 'Indra coming swiftly as a falcon.'

HYMN XIX. *Indra.*

1. THEE, verily, O Thunder-wielding Indra, all the Gods here, the Helpers swift to listen,
And both the worlds elected, thee the Mighty, High, waxen strong, alone to slaughter Vṛtra.

2 The Gods, as worn witheld, relaxed their efforts : thou, Indra, born of truth, wast Sovran Ruler.
Thou slewest Ahi who besieged the waters, and duggest out their all-supporting channels.

3 The insatiate one, extended, hard to waken, who slumbered in perpetual sleep, O Indra,—
The Dragon stretched against the seven prone rivers, where no joint was, thou rentest with thy thunder.

4 Indra with might shook earth and her foundation as the wind stirs the water with its fury.
Striving, with strength he burst the firm asunder, and tore away the summits of the mountains.

5 They ran to thee as mothers to their offspring : the clouds, like chariots, hastened forth together.
Thou didst refresh the streams and force the billows : thou, Indra, settest free obstructed rivers.

6 Thou for the sake of Vayya and Turvīti didst stay the great stream, flowing, all-sustaining :
Yea, at their prayer didst check the rushing river and make the floods easy to cross, O Indra.

7 He let the young Maids skilled in Law, unwedded, like fountains, bubbling, flow forth streaming onward.
He inundated thirsty plains and deserts, and milked the dry Cows of the mighty master.

2 *Relaxed their efforts* : or abdicated their functions as protectors and made over to Indra the duty of slaying the oppressor Vṛtra.

3 *Where no joint was* : that would have facilitated his dismemberment.

5 *The clouds* : according to Sāyaṇa *ádrayaḥ*, mountains or clouds, here means the Maruts.

6 *Vayya and Turvīti* : Turvīti has been mentioned frequently in Book I. as having been protected by Indra, and Vayya is said to have been his father and companion. See I. 54. 6 ; II. 13. 12.

7 *The young Maids skilled in Law* : the rivers that know and follow the law of their being, the Order of the universe.

He milked the dry Cows : he drew rain from the clouds which had hitherto been prevented by their mighty master Vṛtra from yielding their stores.

8 Through many a morn and many a lovely autumn, having slain Vṛtra, he set free the rivers.
Indra hath set at liberty to wander on earth the streams encompassed pressed together.

9 Lord of Bay Steeds, thou broughtest from the ant-hill the unwedded damsel's son whom ants were eating.
The blind saw clearly, as he grasped the serpent, rose, brake the jar: his joints again united.

10 To the wise man, O Sage and Sovran Ruler, the man who knoweth all thine ancient exploits.
Hath told these deeds of might as thou hast wrought them, great acts, spontaneous, and to man's advantage.

11 Now, Indra! lauded, glorified with praises, let powers swell high, like rivers, for the singer.
For thee a new hymn, Lord of Bays! is fashioned. May we, car-borne, through song be victors ever.

HYMN XX. *Indra.*

1. FROM near or far away may mighty Indra, giver of succour, come for our protection,
Lord of men, armed with thunder, with the Strongest, slaying his foes in conflict, in the battles.

2 May Indra come to us with Tawny Coursers, inclined to us, to favour and enrich us.
May Maghavan, loud-voiced and wielding thunder, stand by us at this sacrifice, in combat.

3 Thou, honouring this our sacrifice, O Indra, shalt give us strength and fill us full of courage.
To win the booty, Thunder-armed! like hunters may we with thee subdue in fight our foemen.

4 Loving us well, benevolent, close beside us, drink, Godlike Indra, of the well-pressed Soma.
Drink of the meath we offer, and delight thee with food that cometh from the mountain ridges.

5 Him who is sung aloud by recent sages, like a ripe-fruited tree, a scythe-armed victor,—
I, like a bridegroom thinking of his consort, call hither Indra, him invoked of many;

6 Him who in native strength is like a mountain, the lofty Indra born of old for conquest,
Terrific wielder of the ancient thunder. filled full with splendour as a jar with water.

7 Whom from of old there is not one to hinder, none to curtail the riches of his bounty.
Pouring forth freely, O thou Strong and Mighty, vouchsafe us riches, God invoked of many!

8 Of wealth and homes of men thou art the ruler, and opener of the stable of the cattle.
Helper of men, winner of spoil in combats, thou leadest to an ample heap of riches.

9 By what great might is he renowned as strongest, wherewith the Lofty One stirs up wild battles?
Best soother of the worshipper's great sorrow, he gives possessions to the man who lauds him.

10 Slay us not; bring, bestow on us the ample gift which thou hast to give to him who offers.
At this new gift, with this laud sung before thee, extolling thee, we, Indra, will declare it.

11 Now, Indra! lauded, glorified with praises, let power swell high, like rivers, for the singer.

9 Sāyaṇa says that Agrū (unwedded) was a woman of that name, whose son was hidden in an ant-hill, whence Indra rescued him, restored his sight, and reunited his broken joints.

Brake the jar: broke through the ant-hill in which he was confined. Professor Ludwig thinks that the son of the unwedded damsel is the lightning which burst forth from the parent cloud. The passage is obscure.

---

1 *With the Strongest*: the most powerful Maruts.

4 *That cometh from the mountain ridges*: where the Soma was said especially to grow. According to Sāyaṇa's interpretation, the translation would be, 'with the food brought thee with the hymn of noonday.' *Pṛṣṭha* means both 'back, or high ridge,' and 'a hymn employed at the midday oblation,' and the meaning of the adjective *pṛṣṭhya* is similarly ambiguous.

5 *A scythe-armed victor*: the meaning is uncertain. Sāyaṇa explains *sṛṇyaḥ* as 'armed with a hook or sickle,' 'skilled in the use of arms'. Professor Ludwig translates, 'wie ein fassender haken,' 'like a grasping hook'. Professor Aufrecht thinks that *sṛṇyo ná jetā* may perhaps mean, 'like a winner of sickles (as a prize).' Professor Grassmann thinks that a reaper, cutting down corn with his sickle, is intended.

6 *Wielder of the ancient thunder*: I follow Sāyaṇa, but am not satisfied with his explanation. Professor Grassmann follows Bollensen in reading *vrajám*, cowpen, instead of *vájram*, thunderbolt, and this is the reading given also in the St. Petersburg Lexicon. If this alteration were adopted the translation would be, 'the fierce discloser of the firm-built cow-stall.'

A new hymn, Lord of Bays ! for thee is fashioned. May we, car-born, through song be victors ever.

HYMN XXI. *Indra.*

1. MAY Indra come to us for our protection; here be the Hero, praised, our feast-companion.
May he whose powers are many, waxen mighty, cherish, like Dyaus, his own supreme dominion.

2 Here magnify his great heroic exploits, most glorious One, enriching men with bounties,
Whose will is like a Sovran in assembly, who rules the people, Conqueror, all-surpassing.

3 Hither let Indra come from earth or heaven, hither with speech from firmament or ocean;
With Maruts, from the realm of light to aid us, or from a distance, from the seat of Order.

4 That Indra will we laud in our assemblies, him who is Lord of great and lasting riches,
Victor with Vāyu where the herds are gathered, who leads with boldness on to higher fortune.

5 May the Priest, Lord of many blessings, striving,—who fixing reverence on reverence, giving
Vent to his voice, inciteth men to worship—with lauds bring Indra hither to our dwellings.

6 When sitting pondering in deep devotion in Auśija's abode they ply the press-stone,
May he whose wrath is fierce, the mighty bearer, come as the house-lord's priest within our chambers.

7 Surely the power of Bhārvara the mighty for ever helpeth to support the singer;
That which in Auśija's abode lies hidden, to come forth for delight and for devotion.

8 When he unbars the spaces of the mountains, and quickens with his floods the water-torrents,
He finds in lair the buffalo and wild-ox when the wise lead him on to vigorous exploit.

9 Auspicious are thy hands, thine arms well-fashioned which proffer bounty, Indra, to thy praiser.
What sloth is this ? Why dost thou not rejoice thee ? Why dost thou not delight thyself with giving ?

10 So Indra is the truthful Lord of treasure. Freedom he gave to man by slaying Vṛtra.
Much-lauded ! help us with thy power to riches : may I be sharer of thy Godlike favour.

11 Now, Indra ! lauded, glorified with praises, let power swell high, like rivers, for the singer.
For thee a new hymn, Lord of Bays ! is fashioned. May we, care-borne, through song be victors ever.

HYMN XXII. *Indra.*

1. THAT gift of ours which Indra loves and welcomes, even that he makes for us, the Great and Strong One.
He who comes wielding in his might the thunder, Maghavan, gives prayer, praise, and laud, and Soma.

2 Bull, hurler of the four-edged rain-producer with both his arms, strong, mighty, most heroic;

3 *From a distance, from the seat of Order* : perhaps, from the farthest limit of the ordered universe. According to Sāyaṇa, from the region of cloud, *meghalokāt*.

4 *Where the herds are gathered* : in places where cattle, the prize of victory, abound.

5 *The Priest* : apparently Agni. *Fixing reverence on reverence* : urging man to continual adoration.

6 *Auśija* is generally a patronymic of the Ṛsi Kakṣivān and others. According to Sāyaṇa the instructor of the sacrifice is meant. The stanza is obscure.

7 *Bhārvara* : according to sāyaṇa, a name of Indra as son of Bhārvara, the supporter of the world, that is Prajāpati. Professor Grassmann thinks that Agni is meant and Professor Ludwig considers it tolerably clear that Bhārvara is identical with Auśija. The exact meaning of the stanza is doubtful, but its general purport appears to be that Bhārvara, whether he be Auśija, or Indra, or Agni, has a store of wealth or power to protect the worshipper and assist him in the performance of his religious duties.

8 *When he unbars* : when Indra lays open the interior of the mountain of clouds within which the rain is imprisoned.

The buffalo and wild-ox : the Gaura (Bos gaurus) and the Gavaya (Bos gavaeus) are two kinds of wild cattle. The *gaurásya* and *gavayásya* of the text must be taken as partitive genitives after *vidát*, he finds. 'The purport of the expression, according to the scholiast, is, that Indra obtains these two animals *tau dvau paśū labhate*, either for himself as sacrificial flesh, or for his worshippers, some of whom, at least, even now, would not object to eat the flesh of the wild oxen.—Wilson.

---

2 *Rain-producer* : the thunderbolt or lightning which is supposed to cause rain by opening the cloud.

Paruṣṇī : one of the rivers of the Panjāb, called in later times Irāvatī, the modern Rāvī. Indra appears to be represented as clothing himself in the wool-like waves, or fleecy vapours, of the river, and lovingly covering or uniting in one stream her several joints, limbs, or branches. 'The phraseology here,' Professor Wilson remarks, 'is somewhat obscure and the scholiast does not materially enlighten us.'

Wearing as wool Paruṣṇī for adornment, whose joints for sake of friendship he hath covered.

3 God who of all the Gods was born divinest, endowed with ample strength and mighty powers,
And bearing in his arms the yearning thunder, with violent rush caused heaven and earth to tremble.

4 Before the High God, at his birth, heaven trembled, earth, many floods and all the precipices.
The Strong One bringeth nigh the Bull's two Parents : loud sing the winds, like men, in air's mid-region.

5 These are thy great deeds, Indra, thine, the Mighty, deeds to be told aloud at all libations,
That thou, O Hero, bold and boldly daring, didst with thy bolt, by strength, destroy the Dragon.

6 True are all these thy deeds, O Most Heroic. The Milch-kine issued from the streaming udder.
In fear of thee, O thou of manly spirit, the rivers swiftly set themselves in motion.

7 With joy, O Indra, Lord of Tawny Coursers, the Sisters then, these Goddesses, extolled thee,
When thou didst give the prisoned ones their freedom to wander at their will in long succession.

8 Pressed is the gladdening stalk as 'twere a river : so let the rite, the toiler's power, attract thee
To us-ward, of the Bright One, as the courser strains his exceedingly strong leather bridle.

9 Ever by us perform thy most heroic, thine highest, best victorious deeds, O Victor.
For us make Vṛtras easy to be conquered : destroy the weapon of our mortal foeman.

10 Graciously listen to our prayer, O Indra, and strength of varied sort bestow thou on us.
Send to us all intelligence and wisdom : O Maghavan, be he who gives us cattle.

11 Now, Indra ! lauded, glorified with praises, let wealth swell high like rivers to the singer.
For thee a new hymn, Lord of Bays ! is fashioned. May we, car-borne, through song be victors ever.

HYMN XXIII. *Indra.*

1. How, what priest's sacrifice hath he made mighty, rejoicing in the Soma and its fountain ?
Delighting in juice, eagerly drinking, the Lofty One hath waxed for splendid riches.

2 What hero hath been made his feast-companion ? Who hath been partner in his loving-kindness ?
What know we of his wondrous acts ? How often comes he to aid and speed the pious toiler ?

3 How heareth Indra offered invocation ? How, hearing, marketh he the invoker's wishes ?
What are his ancient acts of bounty ? Wherefore call they him One who filleth full the singer ?

4 How doth the priest who laboureth, ever longing, win for himself the wealth which he possesseth ?
May he, the God, mark well my truthful praises, having received the homage which he loveth.

5 How, and what bond of friendship with a mortal hath the God chosen as this morn is breaking ?
How, and what love hath he for those who love him, who have entwined in him their firm affection ?

6 Is then thy friendship with thy friends most mighty? Thy brotherhood with us, —when may we tell it ?

4 The meaning of the second line is, Indra brings near, but holds apart, the heaven and the earth, the parents of the mighty Sun, and the winds sing in the intermediate space which has thus provided for them.

6 *The Milch-kine* : streams of fertilizing rain. The *udder* is the cloud.

7 *The Sisters* : the rivers.

8 The construction of the middle portion of the stanza is very difficult.

The general meaning appears to be, 'The Soma has been pressed and the juice flows copiously. Let our sacrifice draw thee hither with all the strength of a hard-pulling horse.' Who '*the Bright One*' is not clear; probably Agni is meant.

1 *Mighty* : effectual. *Its fountain* : more literally, udder; the sacrifice, the source from which the Soma flows as milk from the udder of the cow.

For splendid riches : in order to bestow splendid wealth on the sacrificer, according to Sāyaṇa.

2 *What hero, etc.* : no one is allowed to share the offerings made to Indra or to know his benevolent intentions.

6 *The streams of milk* : this line is difficult. Indra's close connexion with the Sun is referred to, and the general purport may be, as Professor Ludwig suggests : When thou risest up as the Sun, then we declare thy brotherhood with us ; or in other words, Indra's beauty

The streams of milk move, as most wondrous sunlight, the beauty of the Lovely One for glory.

7 About to slay the Indra-less destructive spirit he sharpens his keen arms to strike her.
Whereby the Strong, although our debts' exactor, drives in the distant mornings that we know not.

8 Eternal Law hath varied food that strengthens ; thought of eternal Law, removes transgressions.
The praise-hymn of eternal Law, arousing, glowing, hath oped the deaf ears of the living.

9 Firm-seated are eternal Law's foundations ; in its fair form are many splendid beauties.
By holy Law long lasting food they bring us ; by holy Law have cows come to our worship.

10 Fixing eternal Law he, too, upholds it : swift moves the might of Law and wins the booty.
To Law belong the vast deep Earth and Heaven : Milch-kine supreme, to Law their milk they render.

11 Now, Indra ! lauded, glorified with praises, let power swell high like rivers to the singer.
For thee a new hymn, Lord of Bays, is fashioned. May we, car-borne, through song be victors ever.

is made known as the light of the sun. Sāyaṇa explains *sárgāḥ* as, the efforts, (*udycgāḥ*), *góḥ*, of the moving one (Indra).

7 *Spirit* : the Druh, or mischievous female sprite who does not acknowledge Indra. The purport of the second line is: Indra, although the punisher of our sins, does not suffer us to be destroyed by evil spirits, but continuing to rise as the Sun, urges on a succession of mornings in the light of which the demons of the night disappear.

8 *Eternal Law* : here, Sāyaṇa says, the word *ṛtá* means Āditya, or Indra, or sacrifice. Its meaning varies slightly in this and the two following stanzas, but the original idea of regularity, conformity to, or establishment by, eternal order or law, is found throughout. In the second line *eternal Law* is the regular law-ordained sacrifice. *Glowing* : brilliant, or clearly sounding. *The living* : the worshipper.

9 *They bring us* : that is, the cows which *have come to our worship*, to be presented to the priests as payment of their services.

10 *Fixing eternal Law* : the establisher of the law is also its upholder or administrator. Professor Wilson translates : 'The (worshipper) subjecting Ṛta (to his will) verily enjoys Ṛta.'

To Law belong : or, were made for the sake of order or law-ordained sacrifice. *Milch-kine supreme* : bounteous heaven and earth, which cherish and support sacrifice or eternal order in general.

HYMN XXIV. *Indra.*

1. WHAT worthy praise will bring before us Indra, the Son of Strength, that he may grant us riches ;
For he the Hero, gives the singer treasures : he is the Lord who sends us gifts, ye people.

2 To be invoked and hymned in fight with Vṛtra, that well-praised Indra gives us real bounties.
That Maghavan brings comfort in the foray to the religious man who pours libations.

3 Him, verily, the men invoke in combat ; risking their lives they make him their protector,
When heroes, foe to foe, give up their bodies, fighting, each side, for children and their offspring.

4 Strong God ! the folk at need put forth their vigour, striving together in the whirl of battle.
When warrior bands encounter one another some in the grapple quit themselves like Indra.

5 Hence many a one worships the might of Indra : hence let the brew succeed the meal-oblation.
Hence let the Soma banish those who pour not : even hence I joy to pay the Strong One worship.

6 Indra gives comfort to the man who truly presses, for him who longs fot it, the Soma,
Not disaffected, with devoted spirit this man he takes to be his friend in battles.

7 He who this day for Indra presses Soma, prepares the brew and fries the grains of barley—
Loving the hymns of that devoted servant, to him may Indra give heroic vigour.

8 When the impetuous chief hath sought the conflict, and the lord looked upon the long-drawn battle,

1 *The Son of Strength* : the Mighty One.

5 *Let the brew succeed the meal-oblation* : or, let the offering of cooked viands follow that of the sacrificial cake; let varied offerings be made in rapid succession. *Let the Soma banish* : let those who pour no Soma libations to Indra be kept at a distance from those who thus worship him.

8 When the chieftain has gone out to fight, his wife calls on Indra to protect him. According to Sāyaṇa, the 'impetuous chief,' 'the lord,' is Indra whom his consort recalls to drink the Soma juice which has been prepared for him by men.

The matron calls to the Strong God whom pressers of Soma have encouraged in the dwelling.

9 He bid a small price for a thing of value : I was content, returning, still unpurchased.
He heightened not his insufficient offer. Simple and clever, both milk out the udder.

10 Who for ten milch-kine purchaseth from me this Indra who is mine ?
When he hath slain the Vṛtras let the buyer give him back to me.

11 Now, Indra ! lauded, glorified with praises, let wealth swell high like rivers for the singer.
For thee a new hymn, Lord of Bays, is fashioned. May we, car-borne, through song be victors ever.

HYMN XXV. *Indra.*

1. WHAT friend of man, God-loving, hath delighted, yearning therefor, this day in Indra's friendship ?
Who with enkindled flame and flowing Soma laudeth him for his great protecting favour ?

2 Who hath with prayer bowed to the Soma-lover ? What pious man endues the beams of morning ?
Who seeks bond, friendship, brotherhood with Indra ? Who hath recourse unto the Sage for succour ?

3 Who claims to-day the Deities' protection, asks Aditi for light, or the Ādityas ?
Of whose pressed stalk of Soma drink the Aśvins, Indra, and Agni, well-inclined in spirit ?

4 To him shall Agni Bhārata give shelter : long shall he look upon the Sun uprising,
Who sayeth, Let us press the juice for Indra, man's Friend, the Hero manliest of heroes.

5 Him neither few men overcome, nor many : to him shall Aditi give spacious shelter.
Dear is the pious, the devout, to Indra ; dear is the zealous, dear the Soma-bringer.

6 This Hero curbs the mighty for the zealous : the presser's brew Indra possesses solely:
No brother, kin, or friend to him who pours not, destroyer of the dumb who would resist him.

7 Not with the wealthy churl who pours no Soma doth Indra, Soma-drinker, bind alliance.
He draws away his wealth and slays him naked, own Friend to him who offers, for oblation.

8 Highest and lowest, men who stand between them, going, returning, dwelling in contentment,
Those who show forth their strength when urged to battle—these are the men who call for aid on Indra.

HYMN XXVI. *Indra.*

1. I WAS aforetime Manu, I was Sūrya : I am the sage Kakṣivān, holy singer.
Kutsa the son of Ārjuni I master. I am the sapient Uśanā behold me.

2 I have bestowed the earth upon the Ārya, and rain upon the man who brings oblation.
I guided forth the loudly-roaring waters, and the Gods moved according to my pleasure.

3 In the wild joy of Soma I demolished Śambara's forts, ninety-and-nine, together;
And, utterly, the hundredth habitation, when helping Divodāsa Atithigva.

9 *I was content* : spoken by Indra. *Both milk out the udder* : both the simple, or needy, buyer and the shrewd seller make as much as they can out of the bargain ; that is, the buying and selling of Indra, meaning the settlement of the fee to be paid to the priest for obtaining Indra's favour by sacrifice. Professor Grassmann banishes stanzas 9 and 10 to an appendix, as not originally belonging to the hymn.

2 *Endues the beams of morning* : the expression means, apparently, 'betakes himself to prayer, at day-break.' Sāyaṇa's interpretation is, 'Who covers that is, supports, the cows given by Indra?'

4 *Agni Bhāra'a* : Agni as the especial God of the Bharata family to which Vāmadeva the Ṛṣi of the hymn belonged.

6 *Curbs the mighty* : the meaning of *prāśuṣāṭ* is somewhat uncertain ; 'prompt discomfiter of foes.'—Sāyaṇa. 'Bridling, leading, driving or having swift horses.'—Prof. Roth. 'Conqueror of the mighty.'—Prof. Ludwig. *The dumb* : the man who has no voice to praise him.

7 *Naked* : stripped of all his property; destitute. *To him who offers, for oblation* : according to Sāyaṇa, 'to the man who pours the libation and prepares the dressed food; 'to him who presents the libation and oblation.'— Wilson.

The deity of the first three stanzas is said to be either Indra or Paramātmā (the Supreme Spirit or Soul of the universe): the deity or deified object of the other stanzas is the Śyena or Falcon.

1 Indra is the speaker of the first three verses, although it is not clear what he means by saying that he is Kakṣivān and Uśanā, unless he intends to identify himself with all existence.

3 *Śambara* ; *Divodāsa*; *Atithigva* (here an adname or epithet of Divodāsa): see Index of Names.

4 Before all birds be ranked this Bird, O Maruts ; supreme of falcons be this fleet-winged Falcon,
Because, strong-pinioned, with no car to bear him, he brought to Manu the God-loved oblation.

5 When the Bird brought it, hence in rapid motion sent on the wide path fleet as thought he hurried.
Swift he returned with sweetness of the Soma, and hence the Falcon hath acquired his glory.

6 Bearing the stalk, the Falcon speeding onward, Bird bringing from afar the draught that gladdens,
Friend of the Gods, brought, grasping fast, the Soma which he had taken from yon loftiest heaven.

7 The Falcon took and brought the Soma, bearing thousand libations with him, yea, ten thousand.
The Bold One left Malignities behind him, wise, in wild joy of Soma, left the foolish.

HYMN XXVII. *The Falcon.*

1. I, As I lay within the womb, considered all generations of these Gods in order.
A hundred iron fortresses confined me but forth I flew with rapid speed a Falcon.

2 Not at his own free pleasure did he bear me : he conquered with his strength and manly courage.
Straightway the Bold One left the fiends behind him and passed the winds as he grew yet more mighty.

3 When with loud cry from heaven down sped the Falcon, thence hasting like the wind he bore the Bold One.
Then, wildly raging in his mind, the archer Kṛśānu aimed and loosed the string to strike him.

4 The Falcon bore him from heaven's lofty summit as the swift car of Indra's Friend bore Bhujyu.
Then downward hither fell a flying feather of the Bird hasting forward in his journey.

5 And now let Maghavan accept the beaker, white, filled with milk, filled with the shining liquid;
The best of sweet meath which the priests have offered : that Indra to his joy may drink, the Hero, that he may take and drink it to his rapture.

HYMN XXVIII. *Indra-Soma.*

1. ALLIED with thee, in this thy friendship, Soma, Indra for man made waters flow together,
Slew Ahi, and sent forth the Seven Rivers, and opened as it were obstructed fountains.

2 Indu, with thee for his confederate, Indra swiftly with might pressed down the wheel of Sūrya.
What rolled, all life's support, on heaven's high summit was separated from the great oppressor.

3 Indra smote down, Agni consumed, O Indu, the Dasyus ere the noontide in the conflict.
Of those who gladly sought a hard-won dwelling he cast down many a thousand with his arrow.

4 Lower than all besides hast thou, O Indra, cast down the Dasyus, abject tribes of Dāsas.

4 *With no car to bear him* : literally, 'with his own wheel-less nature,' that is, by his own natural impulse. *Oblation* : the Soma.

6 *The draught that gladdens* : the plant that yields the exhilarating juice.

7 *The Bold One* : Indra.

---

1 *The womb* : of the rain cloud. *A hundred fortresses*: cf. 'Śambara's hundred ancient castles' (II. 14. 6,) *Considered*: or reviewed, in hope of finding a deliverer.

The speaker is Agni, that is, the lightning which rends the cloud and brings down the sweet rain—the fleet Falcon who brings Soma from heaven. See Prof. Bloomfield, The Myth of Soma and the Eagle, Festgruss an Rudolf von Roth, 1893, pp 149—155. Cf. Hymns of the Atharva-veda, VI. 48. 1.

2 *Not at his own free pleasure* : the falcon's mere will was not enough, says Soma ; he had first to fight and conquer my keepers.

The Bold One : Indra. See stanza 7 of the preceding hymn.

3 *The Bold One* : meaning Soma. The construction of the first line is difficult. *Kṛśānu* : one of the guards of the celestial Soma. See I. 155. 2.

4 The allusion in the first line is to the rescue of Bhujyu, by the Aśvins (see I. 112. 6), and we should therefore expect *índrāvatoḥ*, 'of Indra's two friends,' instead of *índrāvato*. *Feather* : *parṇám* ; which became on earth the sacred Parṇa or Palāśa tree, the beautiful Butea Frondosa.

5 The metrical form and the ritual application indicate the comparatively recent addition of this stanza to the ancient hymn.

The hymn has been discussed by Weber, Vedische Beiträge, pp. 4 ff.

1 *The Seven Rivers* : perhaps the five rivers of the Panjāb, the Indus, and the Sarasvat . See I. 32. 12.

2 *Pressed down the wheel of Sūrya* : probably an eclipse of the sun is intended. *What rolled* : the sun's wheel. From the *great oppressor* : '*maho druho, prabhūtasya drogdhuḥ*, of the very mighty oppressor or tyrant, alluding probably to his heat.'—Wilson. Cf. VI. 20 5. *Indu* : a drop, especially a drop of Soma juice, is a frequently occurring name of the God Soma.

3 *Ere the noontide* : in the forenoon, when they have inspirited themselves with draughts of Soma juice.

Ye drave away, ye put to death the foemen, and took great vengeance with your murdering weapons.

5 So, of a truth, Indra and Soma, Heroes, ye burst the stable of the kine and horses,
The stable which the bar of stone obstructed; and piercing through set free the habitations.

HYMN XXIX. *Indra.*

1. COME, lauded, unto us with powers and succours, O Indra, with thy Tawny Steeds; exulting,
Past even the foeman's manifold libations, glorified with our hymns, true Wealth-bestower.

2 Man's Friend, to this our sacrifice he cometh marking how he is called by Soma-pressers.
Fearless, and conscious that his Steeds are noble, he joyeth with the Soma-pouring heroes.

3 Make his ears hear, that he may show his vigour and may be joyful in the way he loveth.
May mighty Indra pouring forth in bounty bestow on us good roads and perfect safety;

4 He who with succour comes to his implorer, the singer here who with his song invites him;
He who himself sets to the pole swift Coursers, he who hath hundreds, thousands, Thunder-wielder.

5 O Indra Maghavan, by thee protected may we be thine, princes and priests and singers,
Sharing the riches sent from lofty heaven which yields much food, and all desire its bounty.

5 *Ye burst the stable of the king and horses*: liberated the kine, that is, the imprisoned waters which fertilized the earth and caused cattle and horses to multiply.

---

1 *Past* : or, over, that is, let not the offerings of our enemies detain thee.

2 *Heroes* : eminent men who institute sacrifices.

4 *Hundreds, thousands* : apparently, of treasures, and not horses as Sāyaṇa explains.

5 *Princes* : the institutors of the sacrifice, the *Sūris*. The phraseology of the second line is somewhat obscure. Professor Wilson renders it 'participant with thee for the sake of distributing brilliant wealth, and abundant food, entitled to (our) commendation ' Professor Ludwig in his Commentary suggests that the meaning may be that the institutors of the sacrifice are to distribute the wealth, and the priests to receive it.

HYMN XXX. *Indra.*

1. O INDRA, Vṛtra-slayer, none is better, mightier than thou :
Verily there is none like thee.

2 Like chariot-wheels these people all together follow after thee :
Thou ever art renowned as Great.

3 Not even all the gathered Gods conquered thee, Indra, in the war,
When thou didst lengthen days by night.

4 When for the sake of those oppressed, and Kutsa as he battled,
Thou stolest away the Sun's car-wheel.

5 When, fighting singly, Indra, thou o'ercamest all the furious Gods, thou slewest those who strove with thee.

6 When also for a mortal man, Indra, thou speddest forth the Sun,
And holpest Etaśa with might.

7 What ? Vṛtra-slayer, art not thou, Maghavan, fiercest in thy wrath ?
So hast thou quelled the demon too.

8 And this heroic deed of might thou, Indra, also hast achieved,
That thou didst smite to death the Dame, Heaven's Daughter, meditating ill.

9 Thou, Indra, Mighty One, didst crush Uṣas, though Daughter of the Sky.
When lifting up herself in pride.

10 Then from her chariot Uṣas fled, affrighted, from her ruined car.
When the strong God had shattered it.

11 So there this car of Uṣas lay, broken to pieces, in Vipāś,
And she herself fled far away.

3 This seems to be the meaning of the text,—a contest between Indra and the rest of the Gods—and stanza 5 appears to confirm this interpretation. Professor Wilson, following Sāyaṇa, translates : 'Verily all the gods with thee (for) their strength, have warred (with the *Asuras*) ; wherefore thou hast destroyed them by day and by night.'

When thou didst lengthen days : didst prolong the day into the night. Cf. Joshua X 1.3.

4 *Stolest away the Sun's car-wheel* : an eclipse of the Sun, perhaps, is intended ; or the meaning may be merely that the Sun's course was stayed, as in stanza 3.

5 *All the furious Gods* : according to Sāyaṇa, 'all those who strove against the Gods.'

6 *And holpest Etaśa* : that is, the return of day on some particular occasion is attributed to Indra's intervention on behalf of his favourite. See Index.

7 *The demon* : Vṛtra, the son of Danu.

8 The destruction by Indra of the chariot of Uṣas or Dawn appears to mean the extinction of her light after the rising of the Sun. So in II. 15. 6. Indra is said to have 'crushed with his thunderbolt the car of Uṣas, rending her slow steeds with his rapid Coursers.' The myth is alluded to in other passages also. See X. 138. 5.

11 *In Vipāś* : or on the bank of that river.

12 Thou, Indra, didst with magic power resist the overflowing stream
Who spread her waters o'er the land.
13 Valiantly didst thou seize and take the store which Śuṣṇa had amassed,
When thou didst crush his fortresses.
14 Thou, Indra, also smotest down Kulitara's son Śambara,
The Dāsa, from the lofty hill.
15 Of Dāsa Varcin's thou didst slay the hundred thousand and the five,
Crushed like the fellies of a car.
16 So Indra, Lord of Heroes, Powers, caused the unwedded damsel's son,
The castaway, to share the lauds.
17 So sapient Indra, Lord of Might, brought Turvaśa and Yadu, those
Who feared the flood, in safety o'er.
18 Arṇa and Citraratha, both Āryas, thou, Indra, slewest swift,
On yonder side of Sarayu,
19 Thou, Vṛtraslayer, didst conduct those two forlorn, the blind, the lame:
None may attain this bliss of thine.
20 For Divodāsa, him who brought oblations, Indra overthrew
A hundred fortresses of stone.
21 The thirty thousand Dāsas he with magic power and weapons sent
To slumber, for Dabhīti's sake.
22 As such, O Vṛtra-slayer, thou art general Lord of kine for all,
Thou Shaker of all things that be.
23 Indra, whatever deed of might thou hast this day to execute,
None be there now to hinder it.
24 O Watchful One, may Aryaman the God give thee all goodly things.
May Pūṣan, Bhaga, and the God Karūḷatī give all things fair.

12 *The overflowing stream* : or, possibly, some stream called Vibāli, the exact meaning of the word being doubtful.

14 *Kulitara's son* : this is Sāyaṇa's explanation of *kaulitarám*.

15 *Of Dāsa Varcin's*: of the followers of the demon or savage Varcin. See II. 14. 6. *And the five* : the position of *pañca* in the stanza seems to indicate that it is taken separately. Sāyaṇa prefixes it to *śatā*, making the number slain a thousand and five hundred.

Crushed like the fellies of a car : '(surrounding) him like the fellies (round the spokes of a wheel).'—Wilson.

The unwedded damsel's son : the son of Agrū, according to Sāyaṇa. See IV. 19. 9.

17 *Turvaśa and Yadu* : so I. 174. 9 'When o'er the flood thou broughtest them, O Hero, thou keptest Turvaśa and Yadu safely.'

Who feared the flood : literally, 'non-bathers' (*asnātārā*), meaning probably unable to swim.

18 *Arṇa and Citraratha* : two kings, says the Scholiast, 'presuming on their dignity as Āryas and devoid of faith in, or devotion to, Indra.' *Sarayu* here is probably some river in the Panjāb, and not the Sarayu of Oudh the modern Sarjū. Turvaśa and Yadu may perhaps have crossed the river, and under the protection of Indra conquered two Āryan chiefs whose lands lay beyond it.

19 *The blind, the lame* : see II. 13. 12. where one man only, the outcast, of Parāvṛj, is spoken of as 'the halt and blind.'

20 *Divodāsa* : see Index.

21 *Dabhīti* : a Ṛṣi favoured by Indra. See Index.

24 *Karūḷatī* : from the position of the word in the stanza would appear to be the name of a separate God, but Sāyaṇa (who is followed by Professors Roth and Grassmann as well as Wilson) takes it as an epithet of Pūṣan, i.e. the broken-toothed or toothless God. 'According to the Purāṇas, Pūṣan had his teeth knocked out by Vīrabhadra's followers at Dakṣa's sacrifice.'—Wilson. The institutor of the sacrifice appears to be addressed in this verse which is probably a later addition to the original hymn.

HYMN XXXI. *Indra.*

1. WITH what help will he come to us, wonderful, ever-waxing Friend;
With what most mighty company?
2 What genuine and most liberal draught will spirit thee with juice to burst
Open e'en strongly-guarded wealth?
3 Do thou who art Protector of us thy friends who praise thee
With hundred aids approach us.
4 Like as a courser's circling wheel, so turn thee hitherward to us,
Attracted by the hymns of men.
5 Thou seekest as it were thine own stations with swift descent of powers:
I share thee even with the Sun.
6 What time thy courage and his wheels together, Indra, run their course
With thee and with the Sun alike,
7 So even, Lord of Power and Might, the people call thee Maghavan,
Giver, who pauses not to think.
8 And verily to him who toils and presses Soma juice for thee
Thou quickly givest ample wealth.

2 *Genuine and most liberal* : producing good results and causing thee to be most bountiful. *Strongly-guarded wealth*: to burst open the treasure-houses of our enemies and give us their contents ; or the allusion may be to the waters shut up in the clouds.

4 *By the hymns* : literally, 'by the teams,' *niyúdbhiḥ*, that is, strings of verses, hymns, or praises.

5 *With swift descent of powers* : by the natural and spontaneous outflow of divine strength, as water pours down a precipice.

I share thee : 'I glorify thee together with the Sun.'—Wilson.

7 *Maghavan* : the rich and munificent One.

9 No, not a hundred hinderers can check thy gracious bounty's flow,
Nor thy great deeds when thou wilt act.
10 May thine assistance keep us safe, thy hundred and thy thousand aids:
May all thy favours strengthen us.
11 Do thou elect us this place for friendship and prosperity,
And great celestial opulence.
12 Favour us, Indra, evermore with overflowing store of wealth:
With all thy succours aid thou us.
13 With new protections, Indra, like an archer, open thou for us
The stables that are filled with kine.
14 Our chariot, Indra, boldly moves endued with splendour, ne'er repulsed,
Winning for us both kine and steeds.
15 O Sūrya, make our fame to be most excellent among the Gods,
Most lofty as the heaven on high.

HYMN XXXII. *Indra.*

1. O THOU who slewest Vṛtra, come, O Indra, hither to our side,
Mighty One with thy mighty aids.
2 Swift and impetuous art thou, wondrous amid the well-dressed folk:
Thou doest marvels for our help.
3 Even with the weak thou smitest down him who is stronger, with thy strength
The mighty, with the Friends thou hast.
4 O Indra, we are close to thee; to thee we sing aloud our songs:
Help and defend us, even us.
5 As such, O Caster of the Stone, come with thy succours wonderful,
Blameless, and irresistible.
6 May we be friends of one like thee, O Indra, with the wealth of kine,
Comrades for lively energy.
7 For thou, O Indra, art alone the Lord of strength that comes from kine:
So grant thou us abundant food.
8 They turn thee not another way, when, lauded, Lover of the Song,
Thou wilt give wealth to those who praise.
9 The Gotamas have sung their song of praise to thee that thou mayst give,
Indra, for lively energy.
10 We will declare thy hero deeds, what Dāsa forts thou brakest down,
Attacking them in rapturous joy.
11 The sages sing those manly deeds which, Indra, Lover of the Song,
Thou wroughtest when the Soma flowed.
12 Indra, the Gotamas who bring thee praises have grown strong by thee.
Give them renown with hero sons.
13 For, Indra, verily thou art the general treasure even of all:
Thee, therefore, do we invocate.
14 Excellent Indra, turn to us: glad thee among us with the juice
Of Somas, Soma-drinker thou.
15 May praise from us who think on thee, O Indra, bring thee near to us.
Turn thy two Bay Steeds hitherward.
16 Eat of our sacrificial cake: rejoice thee in the songs we sing.
Even as a lover in his bride.
17 To Indra for a thousand steeds well-trained and fleet of foot we pray,
And hundred jars of Soma juice.
18 We make a hundred of thy kine, yea, and a thousand, hasten nigh:
So let thy bounty come to us.
19 We have obtained, a gift from thee, ten water-ewers wrought of gold:
Thou, Vṛtra-slayer, givest much.
20 A bounteous Giver, give us much, bring much and not a trifling gift:
Much, Indra, wilt thou fain bestow.
21 O Vṛtra-slayer, thou art famed in many a place as bountiful
Hero, thy bounty let us share.
22 I praise thy pair of Tawny Steeds, wise Son of him who giveth kine
Terrify not the cows with these.

2 *Amid the well-dressed folk*: the adjective *chitriṇīṣu*, feminine plural in the locative case, stands without a substantive, and Sāyaṇa supplies *prajāsu*, people; well-dressed, perhaps, for a religious ceremony, or possibly, armed for war.

5 *Caster of the Stone*: wielder of the thunderbolt.

10 *In rapturous joy*: in exhilaration produced by the Soma juice.

17 *Jars*: a *khārī* is properly a measure of grain, and by metonymy a vessel, jar, or pitcher, containing that quantity, which is said to be equal to about three of our bushels.

22. *Wise Son of him who giveth kine*: Indra himself is the special giver of cattle, and this attribute of his may perhaps, as Professor Ludwig conjectures, be personified in an imaginary father Goṣā, the winner or bestower of kine. Sāyaṇa would force on *napāt*, son, the meaning *na pātayitaḥ* 'thou who dost not cast down' (thy worshippers). *With these*: two horses of thine. The meaning of this last Pāda is uncertain.

23 Like two slight images of girls, unrobed, upon a new-wrought post,
So shine the Bay Steeds in their course.

24 For me the Bays are ready when I start, or start not, with the dawn, Innocuous in the ways they take.

HYMN XXXIII. *Ṛbhus.*

1. I SEND my voice as herald to the Ṛbhus; I crave the white cow for the overspreading.
Wind-sped, the Skilful Ones in rapid motion have in an instant compassed round the heaven.

2 What time the Ṛbhus had with care and marvels done proper service to assist their Parents,
They won the friendship of the Gods; the Sages carried away the fruit of their devotion.

3 May they who made their Parents, who were lying like posts that moulder, young again for ever,—
May Vāja, Vibhvan, Ṛbhu, joined with Indra, protect our sacrifice, the Soma-lovers.

4 As for a year the Ṛbhus kept the Milch-cow, throughout a year fashioned and formed her body,
And through a year's space still sustained her brightness, through these their labours they were made immortal.

5 Two beakers let us make,—thus said the eldest. Let us make three,—this was the younger's sentence.
Four beakers let us make,—thus spoke the youngest. Tvaṣṭar approved this rede of yours, O Ṛbhus.

6 The men spake truth and even so they acted : this Godlike way of theirs the Ṛbhus followed.
And Tvaṣṭar, when he looked on the four beakers resplendent as the day, was moved with envy.

7 When for twelve days the Ṛbhus joyed reposing as guests of him who never may be hidden,
They made fair fertile fields, they brought the rivers. Plants spread o'er deserts, waters filled the hollows.

8 May they who formed the swift car, bearing Heroes, and the Cow omniform and all-impelling,
Even may they form wealth for us,—the Ṛbhus, dexterous-handed, deft in work and gracious.

9 So in their work the Gods had satisfaction, pondering it with thought and mental insight.
The Gods' expert artificer was Vāja, Indra's Ṛbhukṣan, Varuṇa's was Vibhvan.

10 They who, made glad with sacrifice and praises, wrought the two Bays, his docile Steeds, for Indra,—
Ṛbhus, as those who wish a friend to prosper, bestow upon us gear and growth of riches.

11 This day have they set gladdening drink before you. Not without toil are Gods inclined to friendship.
Therefore do ye who are so great, O Ṛbhus, vouchsafe us treasures at this third libation.

HYMN XXXIV. *Ṛbhus.*

1. To this our sacrifice come Ṛbhu, Vibhvan, Vāja, and Indra with the gift of riches,
Because this day hath Dhiṣaṇā the Goddess set drink for you : the gladdening draughts have reached you.

23 *Images of girls* : perhaps as caryatids, but the passage is obscure. Professor Wilson translates : 'Like two puppets on an arranged, new, and slender stage '

24 According to Sāyaṇa, Let thy inoffensive bay horses give me a sufficiency at sacrifices whether I go to them in a car drawn by oxen or without a car so drawn, that is, on foot.

---

1 *For the overspreading* : a technical expression for pouring the milk into or over the Soma juice. 'For the dilution (of the *Soma* libation).'—Wilson. For the *Ṛbhus,* see Index.

5 *Two beakers* : or sacrificial ladles. See I. 20. 6.

7 *Him who never may be hidden* : the Sun; Savitar.

8 *The swift car* : the three-wheeled chariot which bears the Aśvins.

The Cow omniform : or of every hue. 'Indra hath yoked his Bays, the Aśvins' car is horsed, Bṛhaspati hath brought the Cow of every hue.'—I. 161. 6.

11 *At this third libation* : in the evening, the proper time for drink-offerings to the Ṛbhus.

The myth of the Ṛbhus is exceedingly obscure. They are regarded as ancient sacrificers who attained immortality as the reward of their pious labours. The parents whom they restored to youth appear to be the universal parents, heaven and earth, rejuvenated each morning and especially in the spring. The milch-cow (stanza 4) is perhaps the earth, regarded as the productive soil. The twelve days (stanza 7) are perhaps, as Ludwig suggests, the twelve nights *vratyāḥ prajāpateḥ*, or 'holy to Prajāpati.' See Hymns of the Atharva-veda, IV. 11. 11. For careful study and ingenious interpretations of the myth, see F. Nève, *Essai sur le mythe des Ṛbhavas* : Paris : 1847 : and M. Bergaigne, *La Religion Védique,* II. 406—413; III. 51—55.

Dhiṣaṇā : a divinity closely connected with Soma and presiding over prosperity.

2 Knowing your birth and rich in gathered treasure, Ṛbhus, rejoice together with the Ṛtus.
The gladdening draughts and wisdom have approached you : send ye us riches with good store of heroes.

3 For you was made this sacrifice, O Ṛbhus, which ye, like men, won for yourselves aforetime.
To you come all who find in you their pleasure : ye all were—even the two elder—Vājas.

4 Now for the mortal worshipper, O Heroes, for him who served you, was the gift of riches.
Drink, Vājas, Ṛbhus ! unto you is offered, to gladden you, the third and great libation.

5 Come to us, Heroes, Vājas and Ṛbhukṣans, glorified for the sake of mighty treasure.
These draughts approach you as the day is closing, as cows, whose calves are newly-born, their stable.

6 Come to this sacrifice of ours, ye Children of Strength, invoked with humble adoration.
Drink of this meath, Wealth-givers, joined with Indra with whom ye are in full accord, ye Princes.

7 Close knit with Varuṇa drink the Soma, Indra; close-knit, Hymn-lover ! with the Maruts drink it :
Close-knit with drinkers first, who drink in season; close-knit with heavenly Dames who give us treasures.

8 Rejoice in full accord with the Ādityas, in concord with the Parvatas, O Ṛbhus;
In full accord with Savitar, Divine One; in full accord with floods that pour forth riches.

9 Ṛbhus, who helped their Parents and the Aśvins, who formed the Milch-cow and the pair of horses,
Made armour, set the heaven and earth asunder,—far-reaching Heroes, they have made good offspring.

10 Ye who have wealth in cattle and in booty, in heroes, in rich sustenance and treasure,
Such, O ye Ṛbhus, first to drink, rejoicing, give unto us and those who laud our present.

11 Ye were not far : we have not left you thirsting, blameless in this our sacrifice, O Ṛbhus.
Rejoice you with the Maruts and with Indra, with the Kings, Gods ! that ye may give us riches.

HYMN XXXV. *Ṛbhus.*

1. Come hither, O ye Sons of Strength, ye Ṛbhus; stay not afar, ye Children of Sudhanvan.
At this libation is your gift of treasure. Let gladdening draughts approach you after Indra's.

2 Hither is come the Ṛbhus' gift of riches; here was the drinking of the well-pressed Soma,
Since by dexterity and skill as craftsmen ye made the single chalice to be fourfold.

3 Ye made fourfold the chalice that was single : ye spake these words and said, O Friend, assist us;
Then, Vājas ! gained the path of life eternal, deft-handed Ṛbhus, to the Gods' assembly.

4 Out of what substance was that chalice fashioned which ye made fourfold by your art and wisdom?
Now for the gladdening draught press out the liquor, and drink, O Ṛbhus, of the meath of Soma.

5 Ye with your cunning made your Parents youthful; the cup, for Gods to drink, ye formed with cunning;
With cunning, Ṛbhus, rich in treasure, fashioned the two swift Tawny Steeds who carry Indra.

2 *Knowing your birth* : knowing how you have attained immortality and deification. *The Ṛtus* : the seasons personified and honoured as deities. The Ṛbhus as cosmic powers are closely connected with them.

3 *Vājas* : that is, although Vāja is strictly the name of the youngest of the three only, you are all entitled to that appellation which means active, strong, or spirited. Professor Grassmann translates : 'ihr alle seid die ersten hier, O Vadscha's;' ye are all the first (entitled to precedence) here, O V. jas; but the word *utá* is then left untranslated.

4 *The third and great libation* : see the preceding hymn, stanza 11.

5 *Ṛbhukṣans* : Ṛbhukṣan is another name of Ṛbhu, the eldest of the three.

7 *Drinkers first* : those who claim and receive the libation first ; here, apparently, the Ṛtus or Seasons.

8 *Parvatas* : Gods presiding ever mountains and clouds.

9 *Made armour* : for the Gods.

10 *Those who laud our present* : who accompany with hymns, and so recommend to the Gods, our oblation.

11 *The Kings* : the other Gods, or the Gods in general.

---

1 *After Indra's* : libations having been offered to Indra at dawn and at noonday. See stanza 7.

3 *O Friend* : Agni.

5 *Cunning* : power and skill as craftsmen ; *śácyā*.

6 Whoso pours out for you, when days are closing, the sharp libation for your joy, O Vājas,
For him, O mighty Ṛbhus, ye, rejoicing, have fashioned wealth with plenteous store of heroes.

7 Lord of Bay Steeds, at dawn the juice thou drankest : thine, only thine, is the noonday libation.
Now drink thou with the wealth-bestowing Ṛbhus, whom for their skill thou madest friends, O Indra.

8 Ye, whom your artist skill hath raised to Godhead have set you down above in heaven like falcons.
So give us riches, Children of Sudhanvan, O Sons of Strength; ye have become immortal.

9 The third libation, that bestoweth treasure, which ye have won by skill, ye dexterous-handed,—
This drink hath been effused for you, O Ṛbhus : drink it with high delight, with joy like Indra's.

HYMN XXXVI. *Ṛbhus.*

1. THE car that was not made for horses or for reins, three-wheeled, worthy of lauds, rolls round the firmament.
That is the great announcement of your Deity, that, O ye Ṛbhus, ye sustain the earth and heaven.

2 Ye Sapient Ones who made the lightly-rolling car out of your mind, by thought, the car that never errs,
You, being such, to drink of this drink-offering, you, O ye Vājas, and ye Ṛbhus, we invoke.

3 O Vājas, Ṛbhus, reaching far, among the Gods this was your exaltation gloriously declared,
In that your aged Parents, worn with length of days, ye wrought again to youth so that they moved at will.

4 The chalice that was single ye have made fourfold, and by your wisdom brought the Cow forth from the hide.
So quickly, mid the Gods, ye gained immortal life. Vājas and Ṛbhus, your great work must be extolled.

5 Wealth from the Ṛbhus is most glorious in renown, that which the Heroes, famed for vigour, have produced.
In synods must be sung the car which Vibhvan wrought: that which ye favour, Gods ! is famed among mankind.

6 Strong is the steed, the man a sage in eloquence, the bowman is a hero hard to beat in fight,
Great store of wealth and manly power hath he obtained whom Vāja, Vibhvan, Ṛbhus have looked kindly on.

7 To you hath been assigned the fairest ornament, the hymn of praise : Vājas and Ṛbhus, joy therein;
For ye have lore and wisdom and poetic skill : as such, with this our prayer we call on you to come.

8 According to the wishes of our hearts may ye, who have full knowledge of all the delights of men,
Fashion for us, O Ṛbhus, power and splendid wealth, rich in high courage, excellent, and vital strength.

9 Bestowing on us here riches and offspring, here fashion fame for us befitting heroes.
Vouchsafe us wealth of splendid sort, O Ṛbhus, that we may make us more renowned than others.

HYMN XXXVII. *Ṛbhus.*

1. COME to our sacrifice, Vājas, Ṛbhukṣans, Gods, by the paths which Gods are wont to travel,
As ye, gay Gods, accept in splendid weather the sacrifice among these folk of Manus.

2 May these rites please you in your heart and spirit; may the drops clothed in oil this day approach you.
May the abundant juices bear you onward to power and strength, and, when imbibed, delight you.

3 Your threefold going near is God-appointed, so praise is given you, Vājas and Ṛbhukṣans.

6 *Fashioned wealth* : made or fabricated as craftsmen.

---

1 *The car* : the three-wheeled chariot of the Aśvins, drawn by asses, *i.e.* the grey clouds of morning twilight.

3 *Ye wrought again to youth* : forms of the verb *takṣ*, to form, fabricate, fashion, as a carpenter does with wood, are used in this and other hymns to the Ṛbhus, the artificers, instead of words signifying, restoring, giving, producing, and the like.

5 *The car which Vibhvan wrought* : or the sacrificial cup; the text has only *vibhvataṣṭáḥ*, that which was fabricated by Vibhvan, or as Sāyaṇa says, by the Ṛbhus.

8 *According to the wishes of our hearts* : or, according to S yaṇa, on account of the praises which we have offered to you.

---

1 *In splendid weather* : after the rains, when protracted sacrifices are not interrupted by storms. *These folk of Manus* : Āryan men.

3 *Threefold going near* : coming to the altar at the three daily sacrifices.

So, Manus-like, mid younger folk I offer, to you who are aloft in heaven, the Soma.

4 Strong, with fair chains of gold and jaws of iron, ye have a splendid car and well-fed horses.
Ye Sons of Strength, ye progeny of Indra, to you the best is offered to delight you.

5 Ṛbhukṣans ! him, for handy wealth, the mightiest comrade in the fight,
Him, Indra's equal, we invoke, most bounteous ever, rich in steeds.

6 The mortal man whom, Ṛbhus, ye and Indra favour with your help,
Must be successful, by his thoughts, at sacrifice and with the steed.

7 O Vājas and Ṛbhukṣans, free for us the paths to sacrifice,
Ye Princes, lauded, that we may press forward to each point of heaven.

8 O Vājas and Ṛbhukṣans, ye Nāsatyas, Indra, bless this wealth,
And, before other men's, the steed, that ample riches may be won.

HYMN XXXVIII. *Dadhikrās.*

1. From you two came the gifts in days aforetime which Trasadasyu granted to the Pūrus.
Ye gave the winner of our fields and plough-lands, and the strong smiter who subdued the Dasyus.

2 And ye gave mighty Dadhikrās, the giver of many gifts, who visiteth all people,
Impetuous hawk, swift and of varied colour, like a brave King whom each true man must honour.

3 Whom, as 'twere down a precipice, swift rushing, each Pūru praises and his heart rejoices,—
Springing forth like a hero fain for battle, whirling the car and flying like the tempest.

4 Who gaineth precious booty in the combats and moveth, winning spoil, among the cattle;
Shown in bright colour, looking on the assemblies, beyond the churl, to worship of the living.

5 Loudly the folk cry after him in battles, as 'twere a thief who steals away a garment;
Speeding to glory, or a herd of cattle, even as a hungry falcon swooping downward.

6 And, fain to come forth first amid these armies, this way and that with rows of cars he rushes,
Gay like a bridesman, making him a garland, tossing the dust, champing the rein that holds him.

7 And that strong Steed, victorious and faithful, obedient with his body in the combat,
Speeding straight on amid the swiftly pressing, casts o'er his brows the dust he tosses upward.

8 And at his thunder, like the roar of heaven, those who attack tremble and are affrighted;
For when he fights against embattled thousands, dread is he in his striving; none may stay him.

5 *Him* : Ṛbhu, as representing his brothers also.

6 *By his thoughts* : referring to the worshipper who by his devout thoughts and acts will obtain success in sacrifice. *With the steed* : referring to the warrior who will be victorious in battle with his war-chariot.

7 *Press onward to each point of heaven* : that is, be everywhere victorious, achieve, what was in later times the object of great kings' highest ambition, the *digvijaya* or conquest of lands in every direction.

8 *Nāsatyas* : Aśvins. *The steeds* : either the war-horses in general, or, as Professor Ludwig suggests, a particular horse that is to be sacrificed.

Dadhikrās, in the nominative case, or Dadhikrā in the crude form, is the name of a mythical being often mentioned in the Ṛgveda and the actual subject of this hymn and three others. He is described as a kind of divine horse and probably, like Tārkṣya, is a personification of the morning sun ; sometimes he is considered as a creation of heaven and earth, sometimes of Mitra Varuṇa, and is invoked in the morning together with Agni, Uṣas, and the Aśvins. The name is probably derived from *dadhi*, thickened milk, and *kṛī* to scatter, in allusion to the rising sun spreading dew and hoar-frost like milk. Aeschylus. See St. P. Lexicon, or M. Williams's Dictionary. Professor Ludwig thinks that the hymn is a fragment, referring not to the mythical being but to an actual war-horse bearing his name.

1 *From you two* : Mitra and Varuṇa, according to stanza 2 of the following hymn ; Heaven and Earth, according to Sāyaṇa. *Trasadasyu* : the king has been mentioned before (I. 112. 14.) as a favourite of the Aśvins. Professor Ludwig points out that, to accord with what is said in IV. 42. 8., the reading should be Trasadasyum ; 'ye who gave Trasadasyu to the Pūrus,' the verb *nitośé* standing for the dual *nitośethe*.. *The Pūrus*: one of the Āryan tribes. See Index.

4 *Beyond the churl* : passing by the niggard who offers no oblations, and looking kindly on the sacrifice of the living man or devout worshipper. The word *aratim* apparently = *árātim*.

5 *Speeding* : referring to Dadhikrās seeking fame and booty.

6 *Making him a garland* : of the chariots that surround him.

7 *Amid the swiftly pressing* : the text has no substantive : *senāsu*, hosts, or *vikṣu*, people, may be understood.

9 The people praise the overpowering swiftness of this fleet Steed who giveth men abundance.
Of him they say when drawing back from battle. Dadhikrās hath sped forward with his thousands.

10 Dadhikrās hath o'erspread the Fivefold People with vigour, as the Sun lightens the waters.
May the strong Steed who winneth hundreds, thousands, requite with sweetness these my words and praises.

HYMN XXXIX *Dadhikrās.*

1. Now give we praise to Dadhikrās the rapid, and mention in our laud the Earth and Heaven.
May the Dawns flushing move me to exertion, and bear me safely over every trouble.

2 I praise the mighty Steed who fills my spirit, the Stallion Dadhikrāvan rich in bounties,
Whom, swift of foot and shining bright as Agni, ye, Varuṇa and Mitra, gave to Pūrus.

3 Him who hath honoured, when the flame is kindled at break of dawn, the Courser Dadhikrāvan,
Him, of one mind with Varuṇa and Mitra may Aditi make free from all transgression.

4 When we remember mighty Dadhikrāvan our food and strength, then the blest name of Maruts,
Varuṇa, Mitra, we invoke for welfare, and Agni, and the thunder-wielding Indra.

5 Both sides invoke him as they call on Indra when they stir forth and turn to sacrificing.
To us have Varuṇa and Mitra granted the Courser Dadhikrās, a guide for mortals.

6 So have I glorified with praise strong Dadhikrāvan, conquering Steed.
Sweet may he make our mouths ; may he prolong the days we have to live.

2 *Dadhikrāvan* : a lengthened, interchangeable form of Dadhikrās.

3 *Aditi* : here a male deity, probably Agni.

5 *When they stir forth and turn to sacrificing* : when men who are going out on a foray, or to battle, offer sacrifices for their success Or the meaning may be, both those who go out to battle and those who remain at home and sacrifice.

6 *Sweet may he make our mouths* : purify our lips if we have spoken wicked words.

HYMN XL. *Dadhikrāvan.*

1. LET us recite the praise of Dadhikrāvan : may all the Mornings move me to exertion ;
Praise of the Lord of Waters, Dawn, and Agni, Bṛhaspati Son of Aṅgiras, and Sūrya.

2 Brave, seeking war and booty, dwelling with the good and with the swift, may he hasten the food of Dawn.
May he the true, the fleet, the lover of the course, the bird-like Dadhikrāvan, bring food, strength, and light.

3 His pinion, rapid runner, fans him on his way, as of a bird that hastens onward to its aim,
And, as it were a falcon's gliding through the air, strikes Dadhikrāvan's side as he speeds on with might.

4 Bound by the neck and by the flanks and by the mouth, the vigorous Courser lends new swiftness to his speed.
Drawing himself together, as his strength allows, Dadhikrās springs along the windings of the paths.

5 The Haṁsa homed in light, the Vasu in mid-air, the priest beside the altar, in the house the guest,
Dweller in noblest place, mid men, in truth, in sky, born of flood, kine, truth, mountain, he is holy Law.

HYMN XLI. *Indra-Varuṇa.*

1. WHAT laud, O Indra-Varuṇa, with oblation, hath like the Immortal Priest obtained your favour ?

1. *The Lord* : literally, the conqueror, that is, the winner, the obtainer.

2 *Hasten the food of Dawn* : 'accept the (sacrificial) food at the time of the desirable dawn.'—Wilson. This line is difficult, and the meaning is somewhat obscure.

4 *Lends new swiftness to his speed* : I adopt Sāyaṇa's interpretation, *tvarayati, gantum.* Prof Eggeling translates more literally 'speedeth after the whip' (Śatapatha-Brāhmaṇa, V. 1. 5. 19).

5 In this stanza Dadhikrās is identified with the eternal Law of the universe and with all types or forms of the Supreme Being. He is the Haṁsa, the Swan of heaven, or the Sun, the Vasu in mid-air or the Wind, Agni as the priest and guest of men. As the Sun he is born from, or amid, kine or rays of light and springs up from the celestial ocean and the mountains of cloud behind which he rises. See Professor Wilson's note on the passage. The stanza is explained also in Śatapatha Brāhmaṇa VI. 7. 3. 11 (Sacred Books of the East, XLI. p. 281).

The hymn is addressed to Indra-Varuṇa, that is, Indra and Varuṇa, conjointly.

1 *The Immortal Priest* : Agni.

Hath our effectual laud, addressed with homage, touched you, O Indra-Varuṇa, in spirit ?

2 He who with dainty food hath won you, Indra and Varuṇa, Gods, as his allies to friendship,
layeth the Vṛtras and his foes in battles, and through your mighty favours is made famous.

3 Indra and Varuṇa are most liberal givers of treasure to the men who toil to serve them,
When they, as Friends inclined to friendship, honoured with dainty food, delight in flowing Soma.

4 Indra and Varuṇa, ye hurl, O Mighty, on him your strongest flashing bolt of thunder
Who treats us ill, the robber and oppressor : measure on him your overwhelming vigour.

5 O Indra-Varuṇa, be ye the lovers of this my song, as steers who love the milch-cow.
Milk may it yield us as, gone forth to pasture, the great Cow pouring out her thousand rivers.

6 For fertile fields, for worthy sons and grandsons, for the Sun's beauty and for steer-like vigour,
May Indra-Varuṇa with gracious favours work marvels for us in the stress of battle.

7 For you, as Princes, for your ancient kindness, good comrades of the man who seeks for booty,
We choose to us for the dear bond of friendship, most liberal Heroes bringing bliss like parents.

8 Showing their strength, these hymns for grace, Free-givers ! have gone to you, devoted, as to battle.
For glory have they gone, as milk to Soma, to Indra-Varuṇa my thoughts and praises.

9 To Indra and to Varuṇa, desirous of gaining wealth have these my thoughts proceeded.
They have come nigh to you as treasure-lovers, like mares, fleet-footed, eager for the glory.

10 May we ourselves be lords of during riches, of ample sustenance for car and horses.
So may the Twain who work with newest succours bring yoked teams hitherward to us and riches.

11 Come with your mighty succours, O ye Mighty ; come, Indra-Varuṇa, to us in battle.
What time the flashing arrows play in combat, may we through you be winners in the contest.

HYMN XLII. *Indra-Varuṇa.*

1. I AM the royal Ruler, mine is empire, as mine who sway all life are all Immortals.
Varuṇa's will the Gods obey and follow. I am the King of men's most lofty cover.

2 I am King Varuṇa. To me were given these first existing high celestial powers.
Varuṇa's will the Gods obey and follow. I am the King of men's most lofty cover.

3 I Varuṇa am Indra : in their greatness, these the two wide deep fairly-fashioned regions,
These the two world-halves have I, even as Tvaṣṭar knowing all beings, joined and held together.

4 I made to flow the moisture-shedding waters, and set the heaven firm in the seat of Order.
By Law the Son of Aditi, Law Observer, hath spread abroad the world in threefold measure.

5 Heroes with noble horses, fain for battle, selected warriors, call on me in combat.
I Indra Maghavan, excite the conflict ; I stir the dust, Lord of surpassing vigour.

6 All this I did. The Gods' own conquering power never impedeth me whom none opposeth.

5 *Milk may it yield us* : bring us a rich reward. *The great Cow*: of plenty.

6 *For the Sun's beauty* : for long life wherein we may continue to see the glory of the sun.

8 *For glory* : to glorify you.

9 *Eager for the glory* : of winning the prize in the chariot-race.

11 The hymn is a prayer for aid in a coming battle.

Varuṇa and his supersessor Indra severally urge their claims to superiority, and the poet decides between them. Cf. X. 124.

1 Varuṇa is the speaker of the first four stanzas. *Men's most lofty cover* : the highest heaven.

3 *Indra* : all that Indra represents, Prince and King of all. *As Tvaṣṭar* : or, as their great artificer.

4 *In the seat of Order* : in the place appointed by Law or the eternal Order of the universe. *The Son of Aditi* : I, Varuṇa.

5 Indra is the speaker of this and of the following stanza.

When lauds and Soma juice have made me joyful, both the unbounded regions are affrighted.

7 All beings know these deeds of thine : thou tellest this unto Varuṇa, thou great Disposer !
Thou art renowned as having slain the Vṛtras. Thou madest flow the floods that were obstructed.

8 Our fathers then were these, the Seven Ṛṣis, what time the son of Durgaha was captive.
For her they gained by sacrifice Trasadasyu, a demi-god, like Indra, conquering foemen.

9 The spouse of Purukutsa gave oblations to you, O Indra-Varuṇa, with homage.
Then unto her ye gave King Trasadasyu, the demi-god, the slayer of the foeman.

10 May we, possessing much, delight in riches, Gods in oblations and the kine in pasture ;
And that Milch-cow who shrinks not from the milking, O Indra-Varuṇa, give to us daily.

HYMN XLIII. *Aśvins.*

1. Who will hear, who of those who merit worship, which of all Gods take pleasure in our homage?
On whose heart shall we lay this laud celestial, rich with fair offerings, dearest to Immortals ?

2 Who will be gracious ? Who will come most quickly of all the Gods ? Who will bring bliss most largely ?
What car do they call swift with rapid coursers ? That which the Daughter of the Sun elected.

3 So many days do ye come swiftly hither, as Indra to give help in stress of battle.
Descended from the sky, divine, strong-pinioned, by which of all your powers are ye most mighty ?

4 What is the prayer that we should bring you, Aśvins, whereby ye come to us when invocated ?
Whether of you confronts e'en great betrayal ? Lovers of sweetness, Dasras, help and save us.

5 In the wide space your chariot reacheth heaven, what time it turneth hither from the ocean.
Sweets from your sweet shall drop, lovers of sweetness ! These have they dressed for you as dainty viands.

6 Let Sindhu with his wave bedew your horses : in fiery glow have the red birds come hither.
Observed of all was that your rapid going, whereby ye were the Lords of Sūrya's Daughter.

7 Whene'er I gratified you here together, your grace was given us, O ye rich in booty.
Protect, ye Twain, the singer of your praises : to you, Nāsatyas, is my wish directed.

HYMN XLIV. *Aśvins.*

1. We will invoke this day your car, far-spreading, O Aśvins, even the gathering, of the sunlight,—
Car praised in hymns, most ample, rich in treasure, fitted with seats, the car that beareth Sūryā.

2 Aśvins, ye gained that glory by your Godhead, ye Sons of Heaven, by your own might and power.
Food followeth close upon your bright appearing when stately horses in your chariot draw you.

3 Who bringeth you to-day for help with offered oblation, or with hymns to drink the juices ?
Who, for the sacrifice's ancient lover, turneth you hither, Aśvins, offering homage?

7 The poet speaks.

8 *Our fathers then were these* : 'The seven *Ṛṣis* were the protectors of this our (kingdom).'—Wilson. The meaning is obscure. Professor Grassmann banishes stanzas 8, 9, and 10 to the appendix as late additions to the hymn. Sāyaṇa says that Purukutsa, son of Durgaha, being in captivity, his wife propitiated the Seven Ṛṣis, who by the favour of Indra and Varuṇa obtained for her a son named Trasadasyu. *For her* : the wife of Purukutsa.

10 *That Milch-cow* : wealth.

2 *The Daughter of the Sun* : Sūryā, bride of the Aśvins. See I. 116. 17.

4 *Dasras* : workers of marvels, mighty ones, a common appellation of the Aśvins.

6 *Birds* : flying steeds. Cf. IV. 45. 4.

1 *The gathering of the sunlight* : Professor Wilson translates, after Sāyaṇa, 'the associator of the solar ray,' and observes : '*Saṅgatim goḥ*, is only explained, *goḥ saṅgamayitāram*, the bringer into union, or associator, of *Go* : what the latter is intended for is not explained, and the translation is purely conjectural, founded upon the connection of the *Aśvins* with light or the sun.' Professor Grassmann translates : 'der zur Milch eilt,' 'which hastens to the milk.'

4 Borne on your golden car, ye omnipresent ! come to this sacrifice of ours, Nāsatyas.
Drink of the pleasant liquor of the Soma : give riches to the people who adore you.

5 Come hitherward to us from earth, from heaven, borne on your golden chariot rolling lightly.
Suffer not other worshippers to stay you : here are ye bound by earlier bonds of friendship.

6 Now for us both, mete out, O Wonder-Workers, riches exceeding great with store of heroes,
Because the men have sent you praise, O Aśvins, and Ajamīlhas come to the laudation.

7 Whene'er I gratified you here together, your grace was given us, O ye rich in booty.
Protect, ye Twain, the singer of your praises : to you, Nāsatyas, is my wish directed.

HYMN XLV. *Aśvins*

1. YONDER goes up that light : your chariot is yoked that travels round upon the summit of this heaven.
Within this car are stored three kindred shares of food, and a skin filled with meath is rustling as the fourth.

2 Forth come your viands rich with store of pleasant meath, and cars and horses at the flushing of the dawn,
Stripping the covering from the surrounded gloom, and spreading through mid-air bright radiance like the Sun.

3 Drink of the meath with lips accustomed to the draught ; harness for the meath's sake the chariot that ye love.
Refresh the way ye go, refresh the paths with meath : hither, O Aśvins, bring the skin that holds the meath.

4 The swans ye have are friendly, rich in store of meath, gold-pinioned, strong to draw, awake at early morn,
Swimming the flood, exultant, fain for draughts that cheer : ye come like flies to our libations of the meath.

5 Well knowing solemn rites and rich in meath, the fires sing to the morning Aśvins at the break of day,
When with pure hands the prudent energetic priest hath with the stones pressed out the Soma rich in meath.

6 The rays advancing nigh, chasing with day the gloom, spread through the firmament bright radiance like the Sun ;
And the Sun harnessing his horses goeth forth : ye through your Godlike nature let his paths be known.

7 Devout in thought I have declared, O Aśvins, your chariot with good steeds, which lasts for ever,
Wherewith ye travel swiftly through the regions to the prompt worshipper who brings oblation.

HYMN XLVI. *Vāyu. Indra-Vāyu*

1. DRINK the best draught of Soma juice, O Vāyu, at our holy rites :
For thou art he who drinketh first.

2 Come, team-drawn, with thy hundred helps, with Indra seated in the car,
Vāyu, and drink your fill of juice.

3 May steeds a thousand bring you both, Indra and Vāyu, hitherward
To drink the Soma, to the feast.

4 For ye, O Indra-Vāyu, mount the golden-seated car that aids
The sacrifice, that reaches heaven.

5 On far-refulgent chariot come unto the man who offers gifts :
Come, Indra-Vāyu, hitherward.

6 Here, Indra-Vāyu, is the juice : drink it, accordant with the Gods,
Within the giver's dwelling-place.

7 Hither, O Indra-Vāyu, be your journey : here unyoke your steeds,
Here for your draught of Soma juice.

HYMN XLVII. *Vāyu. Indra-Vāyu.*

1. VĀYU, the bright is offered thee, best of the meath at holy rites.
Come thou to drink the Soma juice, God, longed-for, on thy team-drawn car.

6 *Both* : priests and patrons. *Ajamīlhas* : men of the Ṛṣi's family

The Ṛṣi of this and the remaining hymns of this Book is Vāmadeva.

1 *Three kindred shares* : shares of similar food, for both Aśvins and Sūryā, the skin of meath being intended for earthly beings.—Ludwig.

4 *Swans* : the Aśvins, chariot steeds.

6 *The rays advancing nigh* : I follow the interpretation of Sāyaṇa who supplies 'the rays' and 'the gloom;' but the exact meaning of the half-line is uncertain.

2 *Drink your fill* : the verb is in the dual number, Indra being included.

1 *The bright* : juice, understood.

2 O Vāyu, thou and Indra are meet drinkers of these Soma-draughts,
For unto you the drops proceed as waters gather to the vale.

3 O Indra-Vāyu, mighty Twain, speeding together, Lords of Strength,
Come to our succour with your team, that ye may drink the Soma juice.

4 The longed-for teams which ye possess, O Heroes, for the worshipper,
Turn to us, Indra-Vāyu, ye to whom the sacrifice is paid.

HYMN XLVIII. *Vāyu.*

1. TASTE offerings never tasted yet, as bards enjoy the foeman's wealth.
O Vāyu, on refulgent car come to the drinking of the juice.

2 Removing curses, drawn by teams, with Indra seated by thy side,
O Vāyu, on refulgent car come to the drinking of the juice.

3 The two dark treasuries of wealth that wear all beauties wait on thee.
O Vāyu, on refulgent car come to the drinking of the juice.

4 May nine-and-ninety harnessed steeds who yoke them at thy will bring thee.
O Vāyu, on refulgent car come to the drinking of the juice.

5 Harness, O Vāyu, to thy car a hundred well-fed tawny steeds,
Yea, or a thousand steeds, and let thy chariot come to us with might.

HYMN XLIX. *Indra-Bṛhaspati.*

1. DEAR is this offering in your mouth, O Indra and Bṛhaspati:
Famed is the laud, the gladdening draught.

2 This lovely Soma is effused, O Indra and Bṛhaspati,
For you, to drink it and rejoice.

3 As Soma-drinkers to our house come, Indra and Bṛhaspati—and Indra—to drink Soma juice.

4 Vouchsafe us riches hundredfold, O Indra and Bṛhaspati,
With store of horses, thousandfold.

5 O Indra and Bṛhaspati, we call you when the meath is shed,
With songs, to drink the Soma juice.

6 Drink, Indra and Bṛhaspati, the Soma in the giver's house:
Delight yourselves abiding there.

HYMN L. *Bṛhaspati.*

1. HIM who with might hath propped earth's ends, who sitteth in threefold seat, Bṛhaspati, with thunder,
Him of the pleasant tongue have ancient sages, deep-thinking, holy singers, set before them.

2 Wild in their course, in well-marked wise rejoicing were they, Bṛhaspati, who pressed around us.
Preserve Bṛhaspati, the stall uninjured, this company's raining, ever-moving birthplace.

3 Bṛhaspati, from thy remotest distance have they sat down who love the law eternal.
For thee were dug wells springing from the mountain, which murmuring round about pour streams of sweetness.

4 Bṛhaspati, when first he had his being from mighty splendour in supremest heaven,
Strong, with his sevenfold mouth, with noise of thunder, with his seven rays, blew and dispersed the darkness.

---

1 *As bards enjoy the foeman's wealth*: *vípo ná rāyo aryáḥ*: Sāyaṇa explains *vípo ná* as 'like a king who makes his enemies tremble, and *rāyo aryáḥ* as 'bestow wealth upon the worshipper.' Professor Grassmann translates: 'gleich Reisern spriess des Frommen Gut,' 'May the pious man's wealth sprout like twigs or suckers.' *Vípo* (*vípaḥ*) may mean either inspired singers, bards, or twigs, and *aríḥ*, of which *aryaḥ* is the genitive, means both an enemy and a pious man, a worshipper. I follow Professor Ludwig's interpretation. The 'bards' are the inspired singers of the victorious party who share the booty after the battle.

3 *The two dark treasuries of wealth*: heaven and earth, not yet illuminated by the sun.

---

3 *And Indra*: the words *indraśca* of the text are manifestly superfluous.

Indra and Bṛhaspati conjointly are the deities of stanzas 10 and 11, which, with 7, 8, and 9, are evidently a late addition to the original hymn.

1 *In threefold seat*: heaven, mid-air, and earth. *Set before them*: for adoration; or given them the foremost place in sacrifice.

2 *They ..who pressed around us*: apparently the Maruts. *The stall*: like the boundless stall' of III. 1 14, the aerial home of the Maruts.

This company's: the text has only *asya*, 'of this.' I follow Professor Ludwig in his interpretation of this very difficult stanza, and supply *gaṇasya*, troop or company, i.e. of the Maruts. According to Sāyaṇa, Bṛhaspati is asked to protect the worshipper or institutor of the sacrifice.

3 *Have they sat down*: probably the Maruts are intended, and not horses as Sāyaṇa says. *Wells springing from the mountain*: reservoirs of Soma juice, pressed out by the stones, have been prepared.

5 With the loud-shouting band who sang his praises, with thunder, he destroyed obstructive Vala.
Bṛhaspati thundering drave forth the cattle, the lowing cows who make oblations ready.

6 Serve we with sacrifices, gifts, and homage even thus the Steer of all the Gods, the Father.
Bṛhaspati, may we be lords of riches, with noble progeny and store of heroes.

7 Surely that King by power and might heroic hath made him lord of all his foes' possessions,
Who cherishes Bṛhaspati well-tended, adorns and worships him as foremost sharer.

8 In his own house he dwells in peace and comfort : to him for ever holy food flows richly.
To him the people with free will pay homage—the King with whom the Brahman hath precedence.

9 He, unopposed, is master of the riches of his own subjects and of hostile people.
The Gods uphold that King with their protection who helps the Brahman when he seeks his favour.

10 Indra, Bṛhaspati, rainers of treasure, rejoicing at this sacrifice drink the Soma.
Let the abundant drops sink deep within you : vouchsafe us riches with full store of heroes.

11 Bṛhaspati and Indra, make us prosper : may this be your benevolence to us-ward.
Assist our holy thoughts, wake up our spirit : weaken the hatred of our foe and rivals.

HYMN LI. *Dawn.*

1. FORTH from the darkness in the region eastward this most abundant splendid light hath mounted.
Now verily the far-refulgent Mornings, Daughters of Heaven, bring welfare to the people.

2 The richly-coloured Dawns have mounted eastward, like pillars planted at our sacrifices,
And, flushing far, splendid and purifying, unbarred the portals of the fold of darkness.

3 Dispelling gloom this day the wealthy Mornings urge liberal givers to present their treasures.
In the unlightened depth of darkness round them let niggard traffickers sleep unawakened.

4 O Goddesses, is this your car, I ask you, ancient this day, or is it new, ye Mornings,
Wherewith, rich Dawns, ye seek with wealth Navagva, Daśagva Aṅgira, the seven-toned singer ?

5 With horses harnessed by eternal Order, Goddesses, swiftly round the worlds ye travel,
Arousing from their rest, O Dawns, the sleeping, and all that lives, man, bird, and beast, to motion.

6 Which among these is eldest, and where is she through whom they fixed the Ṛbhus' regulations ?
What time the splendid Dawns go forth for splendour, they are not known apart, alike, unwasting.

7 Blest were these Dawns of old, shining with succour, true with the truth that springs from holy Order ;
With whom the toiling worshipper, by praises, hymning and lauding, soon attained to riches.

8 Hither from eastward all at once they travel, from one place spreading in the selfsame manner.
Awaking, from the seat of holy Order the Godlike Dawns come nigh like troops of cattle.

Sevenfold mouth ..seven rays : as identified with Agni.

5 *Obstructive* : or retentive; the meaning of *phaligám* is somewhat uncertain : probably, reservoir, i.e. holder and withholder of the rain. *The loudshouting band* : the Maruts.

10 *Rainers of treasure* : the meaning of *vṛṣaṇvasū* is uncertain ; 'strong or excellent as bulls,' according to Ludwig and Grassmann. Perhaps 'strong with treasures.'

3 *Niggard traffickers* : wealthy churls who offer no sacrifices.

4 *Navagva, Daśagva* : individual members of the so-named mythical priestly families which are frequently associated with the Aṅgirases. *Aṅgira* : a member of the family of Aṅgiras. *Seven-toned* : literally, 'seven-mouthed,' using in his hymns the seven metres of the Veda, or repeating hymns of seven kinds .

6 *The Ṛbhus' regulations* : the seasons of the year, the Ṛbhus being cosmic powers and closely connected with the Ṛtus.

8 *Like troops of cattle* : going forth to pasture at day-break.

9 Thus they go forth with undiminished colours, these Mornings similar, in self-same fashion,
Concealing the gigantic might of darkness with radiant bodies bright and pure and shining.

10 O Goddesses, O Heaven's refulgent Daughters, bestow upon us wealth with store of children.
As from our pleasant place of rest ye rouse us may we be masters of heroic vigour.

11 Well-skilled in lore of sacrifice, ye Daughters of Heaven, refulgent Dawns, I thus address you.
May we be glorious among the people. May Heaven vouchsafe us this, and Earth the Goddess.

HYMN LII. *Dawn.*

1. This Lady, giver of delight, after her Sister shining forth, Daughter of Heaven, hath shown herself.

2 Unfailing, Mother of the Kine, in colour like a bright red mare,
The Dawn became the Aśvins' Friend.

3 Yea, and thou art the Aśvins' Friend, the Mother of the Kine art thou :
O Dawn thou rulest over wealth.

4 Thinking of thee, O Joyous One, as her who driveth hate away,
We woke to meet thee with our lauds.

5 Our eyes behold thy blessed rays like troops of cattle loosed to feed.
Dawn hath filled full the wide expanse.

6 When thou hast filled it, Fulgent One ! thou layest bare the gloom with light.
After thy nature aid us, Dawn.

7 Thou overspreadest heaven with rays, the dear wide region of mid-air.
With thy bright shining lustre, Dawn.

HYMN LIII. *Savitar.*

1. Of Savitar the God, the sapient Asura, we crave this great gift which is worthy of our choice,
Wherewith he freely grants his worshipper defence. This with his rays the Great God hath vouchsafed to us.

2 Sustainer of the heaven, Lord of the whole world's life, the Sage, he putteth on his golden-coloured mail.
Clear-sighted, spreading far, filling the spacious realm, Savitar hath brought forth bliss that deserveth laud.

3 He hath filled full the regions of the heaven and earth : the God for his own strengthening waketh up the hymn.
Savitar hath stretched out his arms to cherish life, producing with his rays and lulling all that moves.

4 Lighting all living creatures, ne'er to be deceived, Savitar, God, protects each holy ordinance.
He hath stretched out his arms to all the folk of earth, and, with his laws observed, rules his own mighty course.

5 Savitar thrice surrounding with his mightiness mid-air, three regions, and the triple sphere of light,
Sets the three heavens in motion and the threefold earth, and willingly protects us with his triple law.

6 Most gracious God, who brings to life and lulls to rest, he who controls the world, what moves not and what moves,
May he vouchsafe us shelter,—Savitar the God,—for tranquil life, with triple bar against distress.

7 With the year's seasons hath Savitar, God, come nigh : may he prosper our home, give food and noble sons.
May he invigorate us through the days and nights, and may he send us opulence with progeny.

HYMN LIV. *Savitar.*

1. Now must we praise and honour Savitar the God : at this time of the day the men must call to him,
Him who distributes wealth to Manu's progeny, that he may grant us here riches most excellent.

2 For thou at first producest for the holy Gods the noblest of all portions, immortality :
Thereafter as a gift to men, O Savitar, thou openest existence, life succeeding life.

1 *After her Sister* : when Night has departed.

3 *The Kine* : the early rays of light, or fleecy clouds of morning. *Friend of the Aśvins*: as being worshipped at the same time.

4 *Driveth hate away* : especially the malignity of the evil spirits of the night.

1 *Savitar* : the Sun as the great vivifier, generator, and producer.

3 *Lulling* : the word in the text, *niveśáyan*, means 'bringing to rest.' Sāyaṇa explains it by 'establishing in their several duties.'

5 *Triple law* : according to Sāyaṇa, his functions as distributor of heat, rain, and cold. *Three heavens* : See I. 105. 5.

3 If we, men as we are, have sinned against the Gods through want of thought, in weakness, or through insolence,
Absolve us from the guilt and make us free from sin, O Savitar, alike among both Gods and men.

4 None may impede that power of Savitar the God whereby he will maintain the universal world.
What the fair-fingered God brings forth on earth's expanse or in the height of heaven, that work of his stands sure.

5 To lofty hills thou sendest those whom Indra leads, and givest fixed abodes with houses unto these.
However they may fly and draw themselves apart, still, Savitar, they stand obeying thy behest.

6 May the libations poured to thee thrice daily, day after day, O Savitar, bring us blessing.
May Indra, Heaven, Earth, Sindhu with the Waters, Aditi with Ādityas, give us shelter.

HYMN LV. *Viśvedevas.*

1. WHO of you, Vasus, saveth ? who protecteth? O Heaven and Earth and Aditi, preserve us,
Varuṇa, Mitra, from the stronger mortal. Gods, which of you at sacrifice giveth comfort ?

2 They who with laud extol the ancient statutes, when they shine forth infallible dividers,
Have ordered as perpetual Ordainers, and beamed as holy-thoughted Wonder-Workers.

3 The Housewife Goddess, Aditi, and Sindhu, the Goddess Svasti I implore for friendship :
And may the unobstructed Night and Morning both, day and night, provide for our protection.

4 Aryaman, Varuṇa have disclosed the pathway, Agni as Lord of Strength the road to welfare.
Lauded in manly mode may Indra-Viṣṇu grant us their powerful defence and shelter.

5 I have besought the favour of the Maruts, of Parvata, of Bhaga God who rescues.
From trouble caused by man the Lord preserve us; from woe sent by his friend let Mitra save us.

6 Agree, through these our watery oblations, Goddesses, Heaven and Earth, with Ahibudhnya.
As if to win the sea, the Gharma-heaters have opened, as they come anear, the rivers.

7 May Goddess Aditi with Gods defend us, save us the saviour God with care unceasing.
We dare not stint the sacred food of Mitra and Varuṇa upon the back of Agni.

8 Agni is Sovran Lord of wealth, Agni of great prosperity :
May he bestow these gifts on us.

9 Hither to us, rich pleasant Dawn, bring many things to be desired,
Thou who hast ample store of wealth.

10 So then may Bhaga, Savitar, Varuṇa, Mitra, Aryaman, Indra, with bounty come to us.

HYMN LVI. *Heaven and Earth.*

1. MAY mighty Heaven and Earth, most meet for honour, be present here with light and gleaming splendours;

5 *To lofty hills* : 'Thou elevatest those, of whom Indra is chief, above the vast clouds : for these, (thy worshippers), thou providest dwelling (places) filled with habitations.'—Wilson. 'The difficulties in connection with this verse are very great, and perhaps insuperable,' says Professor Peterson, in whose *Hymns from the Rgveda* (Bombay Sanskrit Series, No. XXXVI.) the Sanskrit student will find a full statement of these difficulties, and the interpretations proposed by Sāyaṇa and by European scholars, not one of which is convincing.

---

2 *They* : the deities of light ; 'dividers, as separating day from night, and Ordainers, as fixing and regulating the year and the seasons.

3 *Housewife Goddess* : as being the mother of the Gods. *Svasti* : Prosperity.

5 *The Lord* : Varuṇa. *Sent by his Friend* : Varuṇa, as the great chastiser of men. Professor Roth, whom Professor Grassmann follows, takes *jányāt* to mean caused by strangers, and *mitriyāt* caused by friends.

6 This stanza is difficult and its meaning is obscure. The words *ápyebhir iṣṭaíḥ* 'through watery oblations' are rendered by Professor Grassmann, 'nebst den erwünschten Wassergottern,' 'together with the wished-for Water-Gods.' *Ahibudhnya* : the Dragon of the Deep, is a divine being who dwells in the depths of the ocean of air. Cf. I. 186. 5 ; II. 31. 6. *As if to win the sea* : as if wishing to gain the ocean of abundant wealth. *The Gharma-heaters* : the priests who prepare the oblation of hot milk or other hot beverage which is offered especially to the Aśvins. Or Gharma may mean the cauldron or vessel in which the oblation is boiled. The meaning seems to be, as Professor Ludwig explains it, that the priests, sacrificing, and hymning lead down towards themselves the rivers of the ocean of plenty.

7 *The saviour God* : Indra. *Upon the back of Agni* : poured upon the flames.

---

1 *The Steer* : according to Sāyaṇa, Parjanya the God of rain-clouds.

When, fixing them apart, vast, most extensive, the Steer roars loudly in far-reaching courses.

2 The Goddesses with Gods, holy with holy, the Two stand pouring out their rain, exhaustless:
Faithful and guileless, having Gods for children, leaders of sacrifice with shining splendours.

3 Sure in the worlds he was a skilful Craftsman, he who produced these Twain the Earth and Heaven.
Wise, with his power he brought both realms, together spacious and deep, well-fashioned, unsupported.

4 O Heaven and Earth, with one accord promoting, with high protection as of Queens, our welfare,
Far-reaching, universal, holy, guard us. May we, car-borne, through song be victors ever.

5 To both of you, O Heaven and Earth, we bring our lofty song of praise,
Pure Ones ! to glorify you both.

6 Ye sanctify each other's form, by your own proper might ye rule,
And from of old observe the Law.

7 Furthering and fulfilling, ye, O Mighty, perfect Mitra's Law.
Ye sit around our sacrifice.

HYMN LVII. *Kṣetrapati, Etc.*

1. We through the Master of the Field, even as through a friend, obtain
What nourisheth our kine and steeds. In such may he be good to us.

2 As the cow yieldeth milk, pour for us freely, Lord of the Field, the wave that beareth sweetness,
Distilling meath, well-purified like butter, and let the Lords of holy Law be gracious.

3 Sweet be the plants for us, the heavens, the waters, and full of sweets for us be air's mid-region.
May the Field's Lord for us be full of sweetness, and may we follow after him uninjured.

4 Happily work our steers and men, may the plough furrow happily.
Happily be the traces bound; happily may he ply the goad.

5 Śuna and Sīra, welcome ye this laud, and with the milk which ye have made in heaven
Bedew ye both this earth of ours.

6 Auspicious Sītā, come thou near : we venerate and worship thee
That thou mayst bless and prosper us and bring us fruits abundantly.

7 May Indra press the furrow down, may Pūṣan guide its course aright.
May she, as rich in milk, be drained for us through each succeeding year.

8 Happily let the shares turn up the plough-land, happily go the ploughers with the oxen.
With meath and milk Parjanya make us happy. Grant us prosperity, Śuna and Sīra.

HYMN LVIII. *Ghṛta.*

1. Forth from the ocean sprang the wave of sweetness : together with the stalk it turned to Amṛta,

2 *Pouring out their rain* : bestowing good gifts.

4 *As of Queens* : I follow with some hesitation Professor Ludwig's interpretation of *pátnivadbh.r.* Professor Wilson, following Sāyaṇa, translates, 'with our spacious dwellings, *inhabited by our wives.*'

5 These three concluding verses form in reality another hymn.

In this hymn various agricultural personifications are addressed, the deity of the first three stanzas being called Kṣetrapati, of the fourth Śuna, of the fifth and eighth Śunāsīra, of the sixth and seventh Sītā. 'It is said in the Gṛhya-Sūtras that each verse is to be silently repeated, with an oblation to fire, at the commencement of ploughing.'—Wilson.

1 *The Master of the Field* : *Kṣetrapati*, the popular Genius Loci, said to mean either Rudra or Agni.

5 *Śuna and Sīra* : two deities or deified objects who bless or are closely connected with agriculture. According to Yāska Śuna (the auspicious) is Vāyu, and Sira (plough) is Āditya or the Sun. Professor Roth conjectures that the words mean here ploughshare and plough. Professor Grassmann translates; 'O Pflug und Lenker,' 'plough and ploughman.'

6 *Sītā* : the Furrow or Husbandry personified and addressed as a deity ; in after time the heroine of the Rāmāyaṇa.

7 *Indra* : as the God who sends the necessary rain, Indra is prayed to bless the work by pressing down and deepening the furrow 'May *Indra* take hold of *Sītā*.'—Wilson. *May she, as rich in milk* : according to the Scholiast, *sá*, she, here means the sky.

The hymn is in praise of *Ghṛta*, the clarified butter or oil used in sacrifices, but a choice of deities is offered in the Index—Agni or Sūrya, Waters, Cows, or Ghṛta. It is, as Professor Wilson observes, 'a good specimen of Vaidik vagueness, and mystification, and of the straits to which commentators are put to extract an intelligible meaning from the text.'

1 It would be fruitless, as Professor Ludwig remarks, to repeat all the various explanations which Sāyaṇa gives of the first line of this stanza : they only show the utter uncertainty of tradition in reference to the passage. For instance, *samudrá*, ocean, is said to mean, sacrificial

That which is holy oil's mysterious title: but the Gods' tongue is truly Amṛta's centre.

2 Let us declare aloud the name of Ghṛta, and at this sacrifice hold it up with homage.

So let the Brahman hear the praise we utter. This hath the four-horned Buffalo emitted.

3 Four are his horns, three are the feet that bear him; his heads are two, his hands are seven in number.

Bound with a triple bond the Steer roars loudly : the mighty God hath entered in to mortals.

4 That oil in triple shape the Gods discovered laid down within the Cow, concealed by Paṇis.

Indra produced one shape, Sūrya another: by their own power they formed the third from Vena.

5 From inmost reservoir in countless channels flow down these rivers which the foe beholds not.

I look upon the streams of oil descending, and lo ! the Golden Reed is there among them.

6 Like rivers our libations flow together, cleansing themselves in inmost heart and spirit.

The streams of holy oil pour swiftly downward like the wild beasts that fly before the bowman.

7 As rushing down the rapids of a river, flow swifter than the wind the vigorous currents,

The streams of oil in swelling fluctuation like a red courser bursting through the fences.

8 Like women at a gathering fair to look on and gently smiling, they incline to Agni.

The streams of holy oil attain the fuel, and Jātavedas joyfully receives them.

9 As maidens deck themselves with gay adornment to join the bridal feast, I now behold them.

Where Soma flows and sacrifice is ready, thither the streams of holy oil are running.

10 Send to our eulogy a herd of cattle : bestow upon us excellent possessions.

Bear to the Gods the sacrifice we offer : the streams of oil flow pure and full of sweetness.

11 The universe depends upon thy power and might within the sea, within the heart, within all life.

May we attain that sweetly-flavoured wave of thine, brought, at its gathering, o'er the surface of the floods.

fire ; or celestial fire ; or the firmament; or the udder of the cow; and *ūrmi*, wave, may accordingly mean reward; or rain; or butter. Professor Ludwig thinks that the sense of the stanza may be : the life-giving essence which develops itself out of the world-ocean turns into Soma in the Moon, but it is neither of these two, but the tongue of the Gods (Agni?) from which the Amṛta proceeds and to which it returns. But see A. Hillebrandt. Vedische Mythologie, I. 321, 322.

The Brahman : according to Mahīdhara, the *ṛtvij* or priest. Probably Agni is meant. The last half-line of the stanza is translated, after Sāyaṇa, by Professor Wilson : 'the fair-complexioned deity perfects this rite,' the epithet 'four-horned' being transferred to 'Brahman.' The God may be called a *buffalo* (*gaurá*, Bos Gaurus) as a type of extraordinary strength. Mahīdhara explains *gaurá* by *yajña*, sacrifice, having four horns, that is, four officiating priests.

3 *Four are his horns* : the four horns of Agni as identified with sacrifice are said by Sāyaṇa to be the four Vedas, and, if identified with Āditya, the four cardinal points. The *three feet* are, in the former case, the three daily sacrifices, in the latter, morning, noon, and evening. The two heads are, in the former case, the *Brahmaudana* and the *Pravargya* ceremonies, in the latter, day and night. Similarly, the *seven hands* are explained, alternatively, as the seven metres of the Veda or the seven rays of the Sun ; and the *triple bond* as the *Mantra*, *Kalpa*, and *Brāhmaṇa*, prayer, ceremonial, and rationale, of the Veda, or the three regions, heaven, firmament, and earth. *The Steer* is, either as sacrifice of Āditya, the pourer down of rewards, and the loud roaring is the sound of the repetition of the texts of the Veda. Mahīdhara's explanation differs from that of Sāyaṇa. The four horns are priests ; or nouns, verbs, prepositions, and particles ; the three feet are the Vedas, or the first, second, and third persons, or the past, present, and future tenses; the two heads are two sacrifices, or the agent and object ; the seven hands are the metres or the cases of the noun ; and the three bonds are the three daily sacrifices, or the singular, dual, and plural numbers. See Wilson's note.

4 *In triple-shape* : as milk, curds, and butter, according to Sāyaṇa. The meaning seems to be that Indra, Sūrya, and Vena (who is probably Agni), restored the power of the elements of sacrifice respectively in heaven the firmament, and the earth, after they had been rendered ineffectual for a time by the malignant Paṇis.

5 *The Golden Reed* : Celestial Agni.

10 *Send to our eulogy a herd of cattle* : this is Sāyaṇa's interpretation. The Gods are addressed, and asked to reward the singers.

11 *Thy power* : Agni's. *In the sea* : in the aerial ocean, the firmament, in which Agni is present as lightning. *Within the heart* : as Vaiśvānara, belonging to all men. *Within all life* : as the vital principle, or heat. The *wave* is the butter of the oblation.

BOOK THE FIFTH

HYMN I. *Agni.*

1. AGNI is wakened by the people's fuel to meet the Dawn who cometh like a milch-cow.
Like young trees shooting up on high their branches, his flames are rising to the vault of heaven.

2 For worship of the Gods the Priest was wakened: at morning gracious Agni hath arisen.
Kindled, his radiant might is made apparent, and the great Deity set free from darkness.

3 When he hath stirred the line of his attendants, with the pure milk pure Agni is anointed.
The strength-bestowing gift is then made ready, which spread in front, with tongues, erect, he drinketh.

4 The spirits of the pious turn together to Agni, as the eyes of all to Sūrya.
He, when both Dawns of different hues have borne him, springs up at daybreak as a strong white charger.

5 The noble One was born at days' beginning, laid red in colour mid the well-laid fuel.
Yielding in every house his seven rich treasures, Agni is seated, Priest most skilled in worship.

6 Agni hath sat him down, a Priest most skilful, on a sweet-smelling place, his Mother's bosom.
Young, faithful, sage, preëminent o'er many, kindled among the folk whom he sustaineth.

7 This Singer excellent at sacrifices, Agni the Priest, they glorify with homage.
Him who spread out both worlds by Law Eternal they balm with oil, strong Steed who never faileth.

8 He, worshipful House-Friend, in his home is worshipped, our own auspicious guest, lauded by sages.
That strength the Bull with thousand horns possesses. In might, O Agni, thou excellest others.

9 Thou quickly passest by all others, Agni, for him to whom thou hast appeared most lovely,
Wondrously fair, adorable, effulgent, the guest of men, the darling of the people.

10 To thee, Most Youthful God! to thee, O Agni from near and far the people bring their tribute.
Mark well the prayer of him who best extols thee. Great, high, auspicious, Agni, is thy shelter.

11 Ascend to-day thy splendid car, O Agni, in splendour, with the Holy Ones around it.
Knowing the paths by mid-air's spacious region bring hither Gods to feast on our oblation.

12 To him adorable, sage, strong and mighty we have sung forth our song of praise and homage.
Gaviṣṭhira hath raised with prayer to Agni this laud far-reaching, like gold light to heaven.

HYMN II. *Agni.*

1. THE youthful Mother keeps the Boy in secret pressed to her close, nor yields him to the Father.
But, when he lies upon the arm, the people see his unfading countenance before them.

1 *Young trees*: the meaning of '*yahvāḥ*' here is uncertain. 'Like birds (?) flying up (or like strong men reaching up) to a branch' (M. Müller).

3 *The line of his attendants*: the row of ministering priests, the people of st. 1. But the exact meaning of the words of the text is uncertain.

4 *To Sūrya*: to the Sun. *Both Dawns*: Night and Morning.

5 *Seven rich treasures*: wealth of various sorts.
His Mother's bosom: the altar raised above the ground.

8 *The Bull with thousand horns*: Agni as the Sun with his countless rays.

1 The kindling of the sacrificial fire is figuratively described. The lower piece of wood retains the latent spark and will not give it up to the *yajamāna* or worshipper until he has generated it by attrition. When the fire has been produced, and is shown like a child that is carried on the arm, its brightness is apparent to all. This seems to be the meaning of the stanza; but to arrive at it *aratnaú* must be read instead of the *aratau* of the text; and this or some similar alteration is required by the metre. But see Ludwig's Commentary.

2 What child is this thou carriest as handmaid, O Youthful One? The Consort-Queen hath borne him.
The Babe unborn increased through many autumns. I saw him born what time his Mother bare him.

3 I saw him from afar gold-toothed, bright-coloured, hurling his weapons from his habitation,
What time I gave him Amṛta free from mixture. How can the Indraless, the hymnless harm me?

4 I saw him moving from the place he dwells in, even as with a herd, brilliantly shining.
These seized him not: he had been born already. They who were grey with age again grow youthful.

5 Who separate my young bull from the cattle, they whose protector was in truth no stranger?
Let those whose hands have seized upon them free them. May he, observant, drive the herd to us-ward.

6 Mid mortal men godless have secreted the King of all who live, home of the people.
So may the prayers of Atri give him freedom. Reproached in turn be those who now reproach him.

7 Thou from the stake didst loose e'en Śunaḥśepa bound for a thousand; for he prayed with fervour.
So, Agni, loose from us the bonds that bind us, when thou art seated here, O Priest who knowest.

8 Thou hast sped from me, Agni, in thine anger: this the protector of Gods' Laws hath told me.
Indra who knoweth bent his eye upon thee: by him instructed am I come, O Agni.

9 Agni shines far and wide with lofty splendour, and by his greatness makes all things apparent.
He conquers godless and malign enchantments, and sharpens both his horns to gore the Rakṣas.

10 Loud in the heaven above be Agni's roarings with keen-edged weapons to destroy the demons.
Forth burst his splendours in the Soma's rapture. The godless bands press round but cannot stay him.

11 As a skilled craftsman makes a car, a singer I, Mighty One! this hymn for thee have fashioned.
If thou, O Agni, God, accept it gladly, may we obtain thereby the heavenly Waters.

12 May he, the strong-necked Steer, waxing in vigour, gather the foeman's wealth with none to check him.
Thus to this Agni have the Immortals spoken. To man who spreads the grass may he grant shelter, grant shelter to the man who brings oblation.

HYMN III. *Agni.*

1. THOU at thy birth art Varuṇa, O Agni; when thou art kindled thou becomest Mitra.
In thee, O Son of Strength, all Gods are centred. Indra art thou to man who brings oblation.

2 Aryaman art thou as regardeth maidens: mysterious is thy name, O Self-sustainer.
As a kind friend with streams of milk they

2 The meaning is obscure. The *handmaid* and the *Consort-Queen* (*mahiṣī*) are perhaps the two fire-sticks. The fire thus produced is not the genuine Agni, who is born as lightning from the cloud.

3 I offered sweet libations of Soma juice to Agni when I beheld him in the form of lightning, and consequently the godless who do not acknowledge Indra are unable to injure me.

4 *Even as with a herd*: Agni is here represented as the Sun with his host of rays. *These seized him not*: the Dawns could not detain him: the Sun was too powerful. But the meaning of *tāḥ*, 'these,' without a substantive, is somewhat uncertain. *They who were grey*: the ancient flames of the Sun recover their youth and strength. Or the half-line may be rendered: 'The Dawns, the youthful Maidens, grow decrepit'. This is Professor Ludwig's interpretation, and it has much to recommend it.

5 This stanza is extremely obscure. It may refer to some actual occurrence to which a mythical colouring has been added. 'What enemies have despoiled my kingdom?' is Sāyaṇa's explanation of the first half-line.

6 This stanza appears to refer to some contention between the descendants of Atri and some other priestly family, perhaps the Bhṛgus, as Professor Ludwig thinks, regarding the worship of Agni. *Home of the people*: Agni; the asylum of men.'—Wilson.

7 *Śunaḥśepa*: see I. 24. *Bound for a thousand*: bought for a thousand cows in order that he might be bound to the sacrificial post. Sāyaṇa, who is followed by Professors Wilson, Roth, and Grassmann, take *sahásrādyūpād* together, 'from a thousand stakes.'

9 *Rakṣas*: a collective noun signifying the whole race of Rākṣasas; originally, harm, injury.

---

1 *Varuṇa*: regarded as the type of royalty. *Mitra*: the friendly, beneficent God. *Indra*: the chief of all the Gods.

2 *Ary man*: in connexion with marriage; *aryaman* meaning also a companion, especially a friend who asks a girl in marriage for another, and Agni being, as the Sun, the regulator of the season for marriage, and its consecrator as the sacrificial fire.

balm thee what time thou makest wife and lord one-minded.

3 The Maruts deck their beauty for thy glory, yea, Rudra ! for thy birth fair, brightly-coloured.
That which was fixed as Viṣṇu's loftiest station—therewith the secret of the Cows thou guardest.

4 Gods through thy glory, God who art so lovely ! granting abundant gifts gained life immortal.
As their own Priest have men established Agni ; and serve him fain for praise from him who liveth.

5 There is no priest more skilled than thou in worship; none Self-sustainer pass thee in wisdom.
The man within whose house as guest thou dwellest, O God, by sacrifice shall conquer mortals.

6 Aided by thee, O Agni may we conquer through our oblation, fain for wealth, awakened :
May we in battle, in the days' assemblies, O Son of Strength, by riches conquer mortals.

7 He shall bring evil on the evil-plotter whoever turns against us sin and outrage.
Destroy this calumny of him, O Agni, whoever injures us with double-dealing.

8 At this dawn's flushing, God ! our ancient fathers served thee with offerings, making thee their envoy,
When, Agni, to the store of wealth thou goest, a God enkindled with good things by mortals.

9 Save, thou who knowest, draw thy father near thee, who counts as thine own son, O Child of Power.
O sapient Agni, when wilt thou regard us ? When, skilled in holy Law, wilt thou direct us ?

10 Adoring thee he gives thee many a title, when thou, Good Lord ! acceptest this as Father.
And doth not Agni, glad in strength of Godhead, gain splendid bliss when he hath waxen mighty ?

11 Most Youthful Agni, verily thou bearest thy praiser safely over all his troubles.
Thieves have been seen by us and open foemen : unknown have been the plottings of the wicked.

12 To thee these eulogies have been directed: or to the Vasu hath this sin been spoken.
But this our Agni, flaming high, shall never yield us to calumny, to him who wrongs us.

HYMN IV. *Agni.*

1. O Agni, King and Lord of wealth and treasures, in thee is my delight at sacrifices.
Through thee may we obtain the strength we long for, and overcome the fierce attacks of mortals.

2 Agni, Eternal Father, offering-bearer, fair to behold, far-reaching, far-refulgent,
From well-kept household fire beam food to feed us, and measure out to us abundant glory.

3 The Sage of men, the Lord of human races, pure, purifying Agni, balmed with butter,
Him the Omniscient as your Priest ye stablish : he wins among the Gods things worth the choosing.

4 Agni, enjoy, of one accord with Iḷā, striving in rivalry with beams of Sūrya,
Enjoy, O Jātavedas, this our fuel, and bring the Gods to us to taste oblations.

5 As dear House-Friend, guest welcome in the dwelling, to this our sacrifice come thou who knowest.

3 *Rudra* : here, as in other places, a name of Agni. *Viṣṇu's loftiest station* : the height of the firmament, which supplies milk to the celestial Cows, and, as mysteriously connected with them, to the cows of earth. *The secret of the Cows* : apparently, their udder—the cloud—is meant by *gúhyam nāma gónām*, 'the cows' secret name.'

4 *Gained life immortal* : Agni alone, it is said, was originally immortal, and the other Gods obtained immortality through him.
From him who liveth : Agni, the special representant of vital power.

6 *In the days' assemblies* : gatherings on days appointed for sacrifice.

8 *The store of wealth* : according to Sāyaṇa, the place containing the riches of sacrificial offerings.

9 *Thy father* : the sacrificer, who supports Agni with oblations, and in his turn is loved and cherished as a son.

10 *Acceptest this* : the homage of the worshipper. *When he hath waxen mighty* : or been exalted by our praise.

11 *Thieves have been seen* : although we have seen thieves and enemies we have been saved by Agni from suffering injury from their evil designs.

12 *Hath this sin been spoken* : if my praise be not acceptable to Agni, it is an offence and a sin. Or the meaning may be, this sin of our enemies who plot against us has been declared to Agni.

4. *Iḷā* : prayer and praise, personified. *With beams of Sūrya* : putting forth thy power at day-break and so vying with the sun.

And, Agni, having scattered all assailants, bring to us the possessions of our foemen.

6 Drive thou away the Dasyu with thy weapon. As, gaining vital power for thine own body,
O Son of Strength, the Gods thou satisfiest, so in fight save us, most heroic Agni.

7 May we, O Agni, with our lauds adore thee, and with our gifts, fair-beaming Purifier!
Send to us wealth containing all things precious: bestow upon us every sort of riches.

8 Son of Strength, Agni, dweller in three regions, accept our sacrifice and our oblation.
Among the Gods may we be counted pious: protect us with a triply-guarding shelter.

9 Over all woes and dangers, Jātavedas, bear us as in a boat across a river.
Praised with our homage even as Atri praised thee, O Agni, be the guardian of our bodies.

10 As I, remembering thee with grateful spirit, a mortal, call with might on thee Immortal,
Vouchsafe us high renown, O Jātavedas, and may I be immortal by my children.

11 The pious man, O Jātavedas Agni, to whom thou grantest ample room and pleasure,
Gaineth abundant wealth with sons and horses, with heroes and with kine for his well-being.

HYMN V. *Āprīs.*

1. To Agni, Jātavedas, to the flame, the well-enkindled God,
Offer thick sacrificial oil.

2 He, Narāśaṁsa, ne'er beguiled, inspiriteth this sacrifice:
For sage is he, with sweets in hand.

3 Adored, O Agni, hither bring Indra the Wonderful, the Friend,
On lightly-rolling car to aid.

4 Spread thyself out, thou soft as wool! The holy hymns have sung to thee.
Bring gain to us, O beautiful!

5 Open yourselves, ye Doors Divine, easy of access for our aid:
Fill, more and more, the sacrifice.

6 Fair strengtheners of vital power, young Mothers of eternal Law,
Morning and Night we supplicate.

7 On the wind's flight come, glorified, ye two celestial Priests of man:
Come ye to this our sacrifice.

8 Iḷā, Sarasvatī, Mahī, three Goddesses who bring us weal,
Be seated harmless on the grass.

9 Rich in all plenty, Tvaṣṭar, come auspicious of thine own accord:
Help us in every sacrifice.

10 Vanaspati, wherever thou knowest the Gods' mysterious names,
Send our oblations thitherward.

11 To Agni and to Varuṇa, Indra, the Maruts, and the Gods,
With Svāhā be oblation brought.

HYMN VI. *Agni.*

1. I VALUE Agni that good Lord, the home to which the kine return:
Whom fleet-foot coursers seek as home, and strong enduring steeds as home. Bring food to those who sing thy praise.

2 'Tis Agni whom we laud as good, to whom the milch-kine come in herds,
To whom the chargers swift of foot, to whom our well-born princes come. Bring food to those who sing thy praise.

3 Agni the God of all mankind, gives, verily, a steed to man.
Agni gives precious gear for wealth, treasure he gives when he is pleased. Bring food to those who sing thy praise.

4 God, Agni, we will kindle thee, rich in thy splendour, fading not,

---

6 *As, gaining vital power*: as the oblations of men which thou carriest to the Gods increase thine own strength also. Sāyaṇa takes the second half-line in connexion with the first: 'Drive thou away the Dasyu with thy weapon, obtaining vital strength for thine own body.'

8 *Dweller in three regions*: heaven, firmament and earth, as the sun, the lightning, and terrestrial fire.

9 *Atri*: the famous Ṛṣi, ancestor of Vasuśruta the Ṛṣi or seer of this hymn.

Āprīs: is the collective name of the Gods and deified objects addressed in the hymn. See I, 13; 142; 188; II. 3; III. 4.

4 *Thou soft as wool*: the *Barhis* or sacred grass, on which the Gods are to sit, is addressed.

5 *Doors Divine*: of the sacrificial hall, types of the portals of the East. See I. 188. 5.

Eternal Law: law-ordained sacrifice.

7 *Two celestial Priests*: See I. 13. 8.

10 *Vanaspati*: the sacrificial stake, regarded as a form of Agni.

11 *Svāhā*: Hail! Glory! is here an Āprī, as a personification of Agni. See I. 13. 12.

1 *Strong enduring steeds*: or constant worshippers, according to Sāyaṇa: and this interpretation is supported by stanza 2, which is a slightly-varied repetition of this stanza.

So that this glorious fuel may send forth by day its light for thee. Bring food to those who sing thy praise.

5 To thee the splendid, Lord of flame, bright, wondrous, Prince of men, is brought.
Oblation with the holy verse, O Agni, bearer of our gifts.
Bring food to those who sing thy praise.

6 These Agnis in the seats of the fire nourish each thing most excellent.
They give delight, they spread abroad, they move themselves continually. Bring food to those who sing thy praise.

7 Agni, these brilliant flames of thine wax like strong chargers mightily,
Who with the treadings of their hoofs go swiftly to the stalls of kine. Bring food to those who sing thy praise.

8 To us who laud thee, Agni, bring fresh food and safe and happy homes.
May we who have sung hymns to thee have thee for envoy in each house. Bring food to those who sing thy praise.

9 Thou, brilliant God, within thy mouth warmest both ladles of the oil.
So fill us also, in our hymns, abundantly, O Lord of Strength. Bring food to those who sing thy praise.

10 Thus Agni have we duly served with sacrifices and with hymns.
So may he give us what we crave, store of brave sons and fleet-foot steeds. Bring food to those who sing thy praise.

HYMN VII. *Agni.*

1. OFFER to Agni, O my friends, your seemly food, your seemly praise;
To him supremest o'er the folk, the Son of Strength, the mighty Lord:

2 Him in whose presence, when they meet in full assembly, men rejoice;
Even him whom worthy ones inflame, and living creatures bring to life.

3 When we present to him the food and sacrificial gifts of men,
He by the might of splendour grasps the holy Ordinance's rein.

4 He gives a signal in the night even to him who is afar,
When he, the Bright, unchanged by eld, consumes the sovrans of the wood.

5 He in whose service on the ways they offer up their drops of sweat,
On him as their high kin have they mounted, as ridges on the earth.

6 Whom, sought of many, mortal man hath found to be the Stay of all;
He who gives flavour to our food, the home of every man that lives.

7 Even as a herd that crops the grass he shears the field and wilderness,
With flashing teeth and beard of gold, deft with his unabated might.

8 For him, to whom, bright as an axe he, as to Atri, hath flashed forth,
Hath the well-bearing Mother borne, producing when her time is come.

9 Agni to whom the oil is shed by him thou lovest to support,
Bestow upon these mortals fame and splendour and intelligence.

10 Such zeal hath he, resistless one: he gained the cattle given by thee.
Agni, may Atri overcome the Dasyus who bestow no gifts, subdue the men who give no food.

HYMN VIII. *Agni.*

1. O AGNI urged to strength, the men of old who loved the Law enkindled thee, the Ancient, for their aid,
Thee very bright, and holy, nourisher of all, most excellent, the Friend and Master of the home.

6 *These Agnis* : the original flames of Agni manifested in the three fire-altars, each fire being regarded as an independent representative of Agni.

7 *To the stalls of kine* : the flames of Agni who longs for oblations of milk and butter are compared to the horses of raiders who seize the cattle of their enemies.

The Ṛṣi of this and of the following hymn is said to be iṣa of the family of Atri. But this name appears to have been formed from the word *iṣám* (food) in stanza 1, or *iṣáḥ* in stanza 1, and not to be the name of a real person.

3 *Grasps the holy Ordinance's rein* : assumes the direction of the sacrifice as invoker of the Gods and conveyer of men's oblations.

5 *On the ways* : in the course of sacrifice. The toil of the ministering priests is often regarded as their offering to the Gods. *On him* : the meaning of this line is obscure. Professor Wilson, following Sāyaṇa, translates : 'and (the drops) mount upon the fire as if they were its own numerous offspring as (boys ride) upon the back (of a father).' The meaning may be that the drops mount upon Agni, who bears the oblations to heaven, as the backs or ridges (of the hills) raise themselves above the ground. My version, which follows Professor Ludwig's explanation, is only conjectural.

8 This stanza also is obscure. *The well-bearing Mother* is the lower fire-stick which at the proper time produces the spark for the man to whom Agni, keen and bright as an axe, is manifested as he was to the ancient sage Atri, the ancestor of the Ṛṣi of the hymn.

10 The last Pāda is difficult. Professor Wilson, after Sāyaṇa, renders it : 'may iṣa overcome (hostile) men.' But *iṣaḥ* is evidently 'food', and not the name of a man.

2 Thee, Agni, men have stablished as their guest of old, as Master of the household, thee, with hair of flame;
High-bannered, multiform, distributor of wealth, kind helper, good protector, drier of the floods.

3 The tribes of men praise thee, Agni, who knowest well burnt offerings, the Discerner, lavishest of wealth,
Dwelling in secret, Blest One ! visible to all, loud-roaring, skilled in worship, glorified with oil.

4 Ever to thee, O Agni, as exceeding strong have we drawn nigh with songs and reverence singing hymns.
So be thou pleased with us, Aṅgiras ! as a God enkindled by the noble with man's goodly light.

5 Thou, Agni ! multiform, God who art lauded much ! givest in every house subsistence as of old.
Thou rulest by thy might o'er food of many a sort : that light of thine when blazing may not be opposed.

6 The Gods, Most Youthful Agni, have made thee, inflamed, the bearer of oblations and the messenger.
Thee, widely-reaching, homed in sacred oil, invoked, effulgent, have they made the Eye that stirs the thought.

7 Men seeking joy have lit thee worshipped from of old, O Agni, with good fuel and with sacred oil.
So thou, bedewed and waxing mighty by the plants, spreadest thyself abroad over the realms of earth.

HYMN IX. *Agni.*

1. Bearing oblations mortal men, O Agni, worship thee the God.
I deem thee Jātavedas : bear our offerings, thou, unceasingly.

2 In the man's home who offers gifts, where grass is trimmed, Agni is Priest,
To whom all sacrifices come and strengthenings that win renown.

3 Whom, as an infant newly-born, the kindling-sticks have brought to life,
Sustainer of the tribes of men, skilled in well-ordered sacrifice.

4 Yea, very hard art thou to grasp, like offspring of the wriggling snakes,
When thou consumest many woods like an ox, Agni, in the mead.

5 Whose flames, when thou art sending forth the smoke, completely reach the mark,
When Tṛta in the height of heaven, like as a smelter fanneth thee, e'en as a smelter sharpeneth thee.

6 O Agni, by thy succour and by Mitra's friendly furtherance,
May we, averting hate, subbue the wickedness of mortal men.

7 O Agni, to our heroes bring such riches, thou victorious God.
May he protect and nourish us, and help in gaining strength : be thou near us in fight for our success.

HYMN X. *Agni.*

1. Bring us most mighty splendour thou, Agni, resistless on thy way.
With overflowing store of wealth mark out for us a path to strength.

2 Ours art thou, wondrous Agni, by wisdom and bounteousness of power.
The might of Asuras rests on thee, like Mitra worshipful in act.

3 Agni, increase our means of life, increase the house and home of these,
The men, the princes who have won great riches through our hymns of praise.

4 Bright Agni, they who deck their songs for thee have horses as their meed.
The men are mighty in their might, they whose high laud, as that of heaven, awakes thee of its own accord.

5 O Agni, those resplendent flames of thine go valorously forth,
Like lightnings flashing round us, like a rattling car that seeks the spoil.

6 Now, Agni, come to succour us; let priests draw nigh to offer gifts;

3 *Dwelling in secret* : latent in the fire-sticks, or dwelling in men's hearts.

4 *The noble* : the patron of the sacrifice.

7 *Bedewed* : anointed with clarified butter. *By the plants* : which supply fuel.

---

1 *I deem thee Jātavedas* : I hold thee to be the knower of all created beings.

4 *Like an ox* : as an ox eats up the grass.

5 *Tṛta* : here perhaps Vāyu, the Wind. According to Sāyaṇa, Tṛta here means Agni himself *diffused in the three regions*. See Macdonell, J.R.A.S. July, 1893, p. 446.

---

4 *Awakes thee of its own accord* : the meaning of this last Pāda is doubtful. Sāyaṇa disconnects *bódhati tmánā* from the preceding words and supplies the name of the Ṛṣi Gaya : Gaya of his own accord arouses thee.

6 *Subdue all regions of the earth* : an allusion to the *digvijaya*, universal conquest, or subjugation of all neighbouring princes. Sāyaṇa explains *áśāḥ* alternatively as 'wishes' ; 'compass all their desires.'

And let the patrons of our rites subdue all regions of the earth.

7 Bring to us, Agni, Aṅgiras, lauded of old and lauded now,
Invoker! wealth to quell the strong, that singers may extol thee. Be near us in fight for our success.

HYMN XI. *Agni.*

1. THE watchful Guardian of the people hath been born, Agni, the very strong, for fresh prosperity.
With oil upon his face, with high heaven-touching flame, he shineth splendidly, pure, for the Bharatas.

2 Ensign of sacrifice, the earliest Household-Priest, the men have kindled Agni in his threefold seat,
With Indra and the Gods together on the grass let the wise Priest sit to complete the sacrifice.

3 Pure, unadorned, from thy two Mothers art thou born: thou camest from Vivasvān as a charming Sage.
With oil they strengthened thee, O Agni, worshipped God: thy banner was the smoke that mounted to the sky.

4 May Agni graciously come to our sacrifice. The men bear Agni here and there in every house.
He hath become an envoy, bearer of our gifts: electing Agni, men choose one exceeding wise.

5 For thee, O Agni, is this sweetest prayer of mine: dear to thy spirit be this product of my thought.
As great streams fill the river so our songs of praise fill thee, and make thee yet more mighty in thy strength.

6 O Agni, the Aṅgirases discovered thee what time thou layest hidden, fleeing back from wood to wood.
Thou by attrition art produced as conquering might, and men, O Aṅgiras, call thee the Son of Strength.

HYMN XII. *Agni.*

1. To Agni, lofty Asura, meet for worship, Steer of eternal Law, my prayer I offer;
I bring my song directed to the Mighty like pure oil for his mouth at sacrifices.

2 Mark the Law, thou who knowest, yea, observe it: send forth the full streams of eternal Order.
I use no sorcery with might or falsehood: the sacred Law of the Red Steer I follow.

3 How hast thou, follower of the Law eternal, become the knower of a new song, Agni?
The God, the Guardian of the seasons, knows me: the Lord of him who won this wealth I know not.

4 Who, Agni, in alliance with thy foeman, what splendid helpers won for them their riches?
Agni, who guard the dwelling-place of falsehood? Who are protectors of the speech of liars?

5 Agni, those friends of thine have turned them from thee: gracious of old, they have become ungracious.
They have deceived themselves by their own speeches, uttering wicked words against the righteous.

6 He who pays sacrifice to thee with homage, O Agni, keeps the Red Steer's Law eternal;
Wide is his dwelling. May the noble offspring of Nahuṣa who wandered forth come hither.

HYMN XIII. *Agni.*

1. WITH songs of praise we call on thee, we kindle thee with songs of praise,
Agni, with songs of praise, for help.

2 Eager for wealth, we meditate Agni's effectual praise to-day,
Praise of the God who touches heaven.

3 May Agni, Priest among mankind, take pleasure in our songs of praise,
And worship the Celestial Folk.

4 Thou, Agni, art spread widely forth, Priest dear and excellent; through thee
Men make the sacrifice complete.

1 *For the Bharatas*: for the sake of the priests, according to Sāyaṇa and Mahīdhara.

2 *In his threefold seat*; the three fire-altars.

3 *Thy two Mothers*: the fire-sticks. *Vivasvān*: the sacrificer, according to Sāyaṇa. But see Index.

4 *Here and there*: or in different places; from one altar to another.

6 *Thou layest hidden*: alluding to the legend of the flight and capture of Agni. See 1. 65. 1.

3 *Knower of a new song*: according to Professor Ludwig, the new song is one in which for the first time we have been obliged to remind thee of thy duties as the champion of eternal Law, whereas formerly we had only thanks and prayers to offer thee. *The Guardian of the seasons*: thou, Agni, who, as the Sun, regulatest the seasons, knowest me; but I know nothing of the God who has befriended my wealthy enemy.

4 Who are the Gods who have enriched the wicked who hate both thee and me?

6 The meaning of the second line is obscure. Professor Wilson, following Sāyaṇa, translates: 'and may a virtuous successor of the man who diligently worships thee come in his place.' I adopt Professor Ludwig's rendering.

5 Singers exalt thee, Agni, well lauded, best giver of our strength :
So grant thou us heroic might.

6 Thou, Agni, as the felly rings the spokes, encompassest the Gods.
I yearn for bounty manifold.

HYMN XIV. *Agni.*

1. ENKINDLING the Immortal, wake Agni with song of praise : may he bear our oblations to the Gods.

2 At high solemnities mortal men glorify him the Immortal, best
At sacrifice among mankind.

3 That he may bear their gifts to heaven, all glorify him Agni, God,
With ladle that distilleth oil.

4 Agni shone bright when born, with light killing the Dasyus and the dark :
He found the Kine, the Floods, the Sun.

5 Serve Agni, God adorable, the Sage whose back is balmed with oil :
Let him approach, and hear my call.

6 They have exalted Agni, God of all mankind, with oil and hymns
Of praise, devout and eloquent.

HYMN XV. *Agni.*

1. To him, the far-renowned, the wise Ordainer, ancient and glorious, a song I offer.
Enthroned in oil, the Asura, bliss-giver, is Agni, firm support of noble riches.

2 By holy Law they kept supporting Order, by help of sacrifice, in loftiest heaven,—
They who attained with born men to the unborn, men seated on that stay, heaven's firm sustainer.

3 Averting woe, they labour hard to bring him, the ancient, plenteous food as power resistless.
May he, born newly, conquer his assailants: round him they stand as round an angry lion.

4 When, like a mother, spreading forth to nourish, to cherish and regard each man that liveth,—
Consuming all the strength that thou hast gotten, thou wanderest round, thyself, in varied fashion.

5 May strength preserve the compass of thy vigour, God ! that broad stream of thine that beareth riches.
Thou, like a thief who keeps his refuge secret, hast holpen Atri to great wealth, by teaching.

HYMN XVI. *Agni.*

1. GREAT power is in the beam of light, sing praise to Agni, to the God
Whom men have set in foremost place like Mitra with their eulogies.

2 He by the splendour of his arms is Priest of every able man.
Agni conveys oblation straight, and deals, as Bhaga deals, his boons.

3 All rests upon the laud and love of him the rich, high-flaming God,
On whom, loud-roaring, men have laid great strength as on a faithful friend.

4 So, Agni, be the Friend of these with liberal gift of hero strength.
Yea, Heaven and Earth have not surpassed this Youthful One in glorious fame.

5 O Agni, quickly come to us, and, glorified, bring precious wealth.
So we and these our princes will assemble for the good of all. Be near in fight to prosper us.

HYMN XVII. *Agni.*

1. GOD, may a mortal call the Strong hither, with solemn rites, to aid,
A man call Agni to protect when sacrifice is well prepared.

2 Near him thou seemest mightier still in native glory, set to hold
Apart yon flame-hued vault of heaven, lovely beyond the thought of man.

The Ṛṣi of Hymn XV, is said to be Dharuṇa of the family of Atri, but this name is evidently taken from the words *dharúṇaḥ* (firm) in stanza 1, and *dharúṇam* in stanza 2.

2 *They who attained* : our ancestors, or the Fathers, who with, or by the aid of, the priests, were raised to seats in the firmament.

4 *Thou wanderest round* : seeking fresh wood to burn in order to restore thy exhausted strength.

5 *May strength preserve* : mayest thou ever find fresh fuel or strengthening food.

Thou, like a thief : 'This may, perhaps, imply that the wealth bestowed upon the *Ṛṣi* is deposited in a secure receptacle, like the hidden booty of a thief, but the whole *Sukta* is obscurely worded.'—Wilson.

---

1 *Like Mitra* : or as a friend.

2 *Every able man* : who has means, will, and skill as a sacrificer.

4 *Of these* : institutors of the sacrifice. *This Youthful One* : Agni. The exact meaning of the second line is somewhat uncertain.

---

1 *The Strong* : Agni.

2 *Near him* : Sūrya.

3 Yea, this is by the light of him whom powerful song hath bound to act,
Whose beams of splendour flash on high as though they sprang from heavenly seed.

4 Wealth loads the Wonder-Worker's car through his, the very wise One's power.
Then, meet to be invoked among all tribes, is Agni glorified.

5 Now, too, the princes shall obtain excellent riches by our lips.
Protect us for our welfare: lend thy succour, O thou Son of Strength. Be near in fight to prosper us.

HYMN XVIII. *Agni.*

1. At dawn let Agni, much-beloved guest of the house, be glorified;
Immortal who delights in all oblations brought by mortal men.

2 For Dvita who receives through wealth of native strength maimed offerings,
Thy praiser even gains at once the Soma-drops, Immortal Gods!

3 Nobles, with song I call that car of yours that shines with lengthened life,
For, God who givest steeds! that car hither and thither goes unharmed.

4 They who have varied ways of thought, who guard the lauds within their lips,
And strew the grass before the light, have decked themselves with high renown.

5 Immortal Agni, give the chiefs, heroes who institute the rite,
Heroes' illustrious, lofty fame, who at the synod met for praise presented me with fifty steeds.

HYMN XIX. *Agni.*

1. One state begets another state: husk is made visible from husk:
Within his Mother's side he speaks.

2 Discerning, have they offered gifts: they guard the strength that never wastes.
To a strong fort have they pressed in.

3 Śvaitreya's people, all his men, have gloriously increased in might.
A gold chain Bṛhaduktha wears, as, through this Soma, seeking spoil.

4 I bring, as 'twere, the longed-for milk, the dear milk of the Sister-Pair.
Like to a caldron filled with food is he, unconquered, conquering all.

5 Beam of light, come to us in sportive fashion, finding thyself close to the wind that fans thee.
These flames of his are wasting flames, like arrows keen-pointed, sharpened, on his breast.

---

3 *This is by the light of him*: this Sūrya, or the Sun, shines only by the light of Agni.

4 When the wonder-working Sun brings us wealth, the merit is due to Agni.—Ludwig. According to Sāyaṇa, the meaning is, as given by Professor Wilson: 'By the worship of him who is pleasing of aspect the provident (heap) wealth in their cars.' The absence of a verb makes the exact meaning uncertain.

The hymn is ascribed to a Ṛṣi Dvita of the family of Atri, but the name seems to be borrowed from the Dvita of stanza 2.

2 The meaning of this stanza is obscure. According to Sāyaṇa, Dvita is the Ṛṣi of the hymn, and the first line is rendered by Professor Wilson: 'Be (willing to make) a grant of thine own strength to Dvita, the bearer of the pure libation.' But *mṛktávāhase* must mean the bearer or receiver of a maimed or imperfect oblation, and Dvita then would be the mythical personage of that name to whom, together with Tṛta, it was customary to wish away and consign any threatened calamity or unpleasantness (To Tṛta and to Dvita, Dawn! bear thou away the evil dream ṚV. X. 47. 16). In the present case, any possible imperfection in the offering made to Agni is previously removed by a libation to Dvita. See Professor Ludwig's Commentary, Part I. 338. M. Bergaigne (Religion Védique, II. 327) gives a different explanation.

3 *Nobles*: wealthy institutors of the sacrifice; Maghavans. *That car of yours*: apparently Agni, who carries oblations to the Gods.

4 *Varied ways of thought*: manifold modes of showing their devotion. *Guard the lauds*: perpetuate hymns of praise by frequent repetition. *Before the light*: according to Sāyaṇa, *svárṇare* means, 'in the sacrifice which leads man to heaven.' Professor Grassmann renders the word by 'Dem Glanzesherrn,' for the Lord of Light.'

---

1 We know only outward forms and circumstances, and the real nature of the God is concealed from us.

The God speaks only in the bosom of his mother.—Ludwig. Sāyaṇa gives a totally different interpretation, the word *vavrí* (husk or covering) in the first stanza being taken as the name of the Ṛṣi of the hymn.

2 *Discerning*: perhaps, as Prof. Ludwig suggests, distinguishing thy essence from thy appearance. The *strong fort* which the worshippers have entered and settled in is, perhaps, their religious knowledge.

3 Śvaitreya's people have conquered, and their priest Bṛhaduktha has been rewarded for his services with a chain of gold, won for him by the Soma-libations which he has offered.—Ludwig. Śvaitreya (son of Śvitrā See I. 33. 14) and Bṛhaduktha are, apparently, proper names. Sāyaṇa explains the former as Agni or lightning 'abiding in the white firmament,' and the latter as 'zealously or highly praising.'

4 *The dear milk of the Sister-Pair*: the Soma dear to Heaven and Earth. The exact meaning of the line is uncertain.

5 This stanza is very difficult, and, like much of the rest of the hymn, can be only conjecturally translated.

HYMN XX. *Agni.*

1. Agni, best winner of the spoil, cause us to praise before the Gods
As our associate meet for lauds, wealth which thou verily deemest wealth.

2 Agni, the great who ward not off the anger of thy power and might
Stir up the wrath and hatred due to one who holds an alien creed.

3 Thee, Agni, would we choose as Priest, the perfecter of strength and skill;
We who bring sacred food invoke with song thee Chief at holy rites.

4 Here as is needful for thine aid we toil, O Conqueror, day by day,
For wealth, for Law. May we rejoice, Most Wise One! at the feast, with kine, rejoice, with heroes, at the feast.

HYMN XXI. *Agni.*

1. We stablish thee as Manus used, as Manus used we kindle thee.
Like Manus, for the pious man, Aṅgiras, Agni, worship Gods.

2 For well, O Agni, art thou pleased when thou art kindled mid mankind.
Straight go the ladles unto thee, thou high-born God whose food is oil.

3 Thee have all Gods of one accord established as their messenger.
Serving at sacrifices men adore thee as a God, O Sage.

4 Let mortal man adore your God, Agni, with worship due to Gods.
Shine forth enkindled, Radiant One. Sit in the chamber of the Law, sit in the chamber of the food.

HYMN XXII. *Agni.*

1. Like Atri, Viśvasāman! sing to him of purifying light,
Who must be praised in holy rites, the Priest most welcome in the house.

2 Set Jātavedas in his place, Agni the God and Minister.
Let sacrifice proceed to-day duly, comprising all the Gods.

3 All mortals come to thee for aid, the God of most observant mind.
Of thine excelling favour we bethink us as we long for it.

4 Mark with attention this our speech, O Agni, thou victorious One.
Thee, Strong-jawed! as the homestead's Lord, the Atris with their lauds exalt, the Atris beautify with songs.

HYMN XXIII. *Agni.*

1. By thy fair splendour's mighty power, O Agni, bring victorious wealth,
Wealth that o'ercometh all mankind, and, near us, conquereth in fight.

2 Victorious Agni, bring to us the wealth that vanquisheth in war;
For thou art wonderful and true, giver of strength in herds of kine.

3 For all the folk with one accord, whose sacred grass is trimmed and strewn,
Invite thee to their worship-halls, as a dear Priest, for choicest wealth.

4 For he, the God of all men, hath gotten him might that quelleth foes.
O Agni, in these homes shine forth, bright God! for our prosperity, shine, Purifier! splendidly.

HYMN XXIV. *Agni.*

1. O Agni, be our nearest Friend, be thou a kind deliverer and a gracious Friend.

2 Excellent Agni, come thou nigh to us, and give us wealth most splendidly renowned.

3 So hear us, listen to this call of ours, and keep us far from every sinful man.

4 To thee then, O Most Bright, O Radiant God, we come with prayer for happiness for our friends.

The Ṛṣis of the hymn are said to be certain members of the family of Atri called Prayasvats, that is, bringers or possessors of sacred food, a word which occurs in stanza 3.

2 *Who holds an alien creed*: who follows other than Vedic observances.

4 *For Law*: to maintain the holy law, and especially the eternally-ordained sacrifice. *With kine*: possessing plenty of cattle. *With heroes*: with brave sons about us.

The hymn is ascribed to a Ṛṣi Sasa, this name being taken from the word *sasásya* in the last Pāda of stanza 4.

1 *Manus* another form of Manu.

4 *The chamber of the Law*: the sacrificial chamber or hall. *Of the food*: or, as Professor Roth explains it, where the sacred grass is strewn; according to Sāyaṇa, of Sasa, the supposed Ṛṣi of the hymn.

The Ṛṣi is Viśvasāman, of the family of Atri.

The Ṛṣi is said to be Dyumna Viśvacarṣaṇi—both these names being words occurring in the hymn.

1 *By thy fair splendour's mighty power*: the words of the text are *dyumnásya prāsahā*.

4 *The God of all men*: *viśvácarṣaṇiḥ*, a common epithet of Agni.

The legend connected with this hymn is discussed by Prof Max Müller in Journal of the Royal Asiatic Society, New Series, II. 441 f. See Lanman's Sanskrit Reader, p. 368.

HYMN XXV. *Agni.*

1. I WILL sing near, for grace, your God Agni, for he is good to us.
Son of the Brands, may he give gifts, and, righteous, save us from the foe.

2 For he is true, whom men of old enkindled, and the Gods themselves,
The Priest with the delicious tongue, rich with the light of glorious beams.

3 With wisdom that surpasseth all, with gracious will most excellent,
O Agni, worthy of our choice, shine wealth on us through hymns of praise.

4 Agni is King, for he extends to mortals and to Gods alike.
Agni is bearer of our gifts. Worship ye Agni with your thoughts.

5 Agni gives to the worshipper a son, the best, of mightiest fame,
Of deep devotion, ne'er subdued, bringer of glory to his sire.

6 Agni bestows the hero-lord who conquers with the men in fight.
Agni bestows the fleet-foot steed, the victor never overcome.

7 The mightiest song is Agni's: shine on high, thou who art rich in light.
Like the Chief Consort of a King, riches and strength proceed from thee.

8 Resplendent are thy rays of light: loud is thy voice like pressing-stones.
Yea, of itself thy thunder goes forth like the roaring of the heaven.

9 Thus, seeking riches, have we paid homage to Agni Conqueror.
May he, most wise, as with a ship, carry us over all our foes.

The Ṛṣis of the hymn are members of the family of Atri called Vasūyus (seekers of riches). Cf. stanza 9.

1 *I will sing near*: I will invite and bring near with my song.

2 *For he is true*: the faithful rewarder of his worshippers.

7 The exact meaning of the stanza is uncertain. Professor Wilson, following Sāyaṇa, paraphrases the first line: 'That (praise) which best conveys (our veneration is due) to Agni: affluent in splendour, grant us, (Agni), great (wealth).'

Like the Chief Consort of a King: as the chief queen proceeds from her home in royal state. Professor Ludwig translates *máhiṣīva* by 'as a strong cow,' but gives in his Commentary the alternative rendering 'as a king's wife.' Sāyaṇa makes *máhiṣī* an adjective agreeing with *rayiḥ*, and says that *iva* like, is pleonastic. I have followed Mahīdhara.

8 *Loud is thy voice*: the meaning of this half-line is not certain.

HXMN XXVI. *Agni.*

1. O AGNI, Holy and Divine, with splendour and thy pleasant tongue
Bring hither and adore the Gods.

2 We pray thee, thou who droppest oil, bright-rayed! who lookest on the Sun,
Bring the Gods hither to the feast.

3 We have enkindled thee, O Sage, bright caller of the Gods to feast.
O Agni, great in Sacrifice.

4 O Agni, come with all the Gods, come to our sacrificial gift:
We choose thee as Invoking Priest.

5 Bring, Agni, to the worshipper who pours the juice, heroic strength:
Sit with the Gods upon the grass.

6 Victor of thousands, Agni, thou, enkindled, cherishest the laws,
Laud-worthy, envoy of the Gods.

7 Set Agni Jātavedas down, the bearer of our sacred gifts,
Most Youthful, God and Minister.

8 Duly proceed our sacrifice, comprising all the Gods, to-day:
Strew holy grass to be their seat.

9 So may the Maruts sit thereon, the Aśvins, Mitra, Varuṇa:
The Gods with all their company.

HYMN XXVII. *Agni.*

1. THE Godlike hero, famousest of nobles, hath granted me two oxen with a wagon.
Tṛvṛṣaṇ's son Tryaruṇa hath distinguished himself, Vaiśvānara Agni! with ten thousands.

2 Protect Tryaruṇa, as thou art waxing strong and art highly praised, Vaiśvānara Agni!
Who granteth me a hundred kine and twenty, and two bay horses, good at draught, and harnessed.

3 So Trasadasyu served thee, God Most Youthful, craving thy favour for the ninth time, Agni;
Tryaruṇa who with attentive spirit accepteth many a song from me the mighty.

6 *Cherishest the laws*: especially religious ordinances, sacrifices.

The Ṛṣis are said to be Tryaruṇa, Trasadasyu, and Aśvamedha; or Atri alone. The metre is Triṣṭup in stanzas 1, 2, 3, and Anuṣṭup in 4, 5, 6; and, correspondingly, the hymn is made up of two separate and independent eulogies of munificent princes.

3 *Trasadasyu*: Terror of Dasyus; apparently, as Ludwig suggests, an honorary name or title of several princes. *Accepteth*: rewards with gifts.

4 He who declares his wish to me, to Aśvamedha, to the Prince,
Pays him who with his verse seeks gain, gives power to him who keeps the Law.

5 From whom a hundred oxen, all of speckled hue, delight my heart,
The gifts of Aśvamedha, like thrice-mingled draughts of Soma juice.

6 To Aśvamedha who bestows a hundred gifts grant hero power,
O Indra-Agni ! lofty rule like the unwasting Sun in heaven.

HYMN XXVIII. *Agni.*

1. AGNI inflamed hath sent to heaven his lustre : he shines forth widely turning unto Morning.
Eastward the ladle goes that brings all blessing, praising the Gods with homage and oblation.

2 Enkindled, thou art King of the immortal world : him who brings offerings thou attendest for his weal.
He whom thou urgest on makes all possessions his : he sets before thee, Agni, gifts that guests may claim.

3 Show thyself strong for mighty bliss, O Agni, most excellent be thine effulgent splendours.
Make easy to maintain our household lordship, and overcome the might of those who hate us.

4 Thy glory, Agni, I adore, kindled, exalted in thy strength.
A Steer of brilliant splendour, thou art lighted well at sacred rites.

5 Agni, invoked and kindled, serve the Gods, thou skilled in sacrifice :
For thou art bearer of our gifts.

6 Invoke and worship Agni while the sacrificial rite proceeds :
For offering-bearer choose ye him.

4 The stanza is difficult. Aśvamedha apparently says that the man who requests him to institute a sacrifice is by so doing the enricher of the priests.

5 *Thrice-mingled* : mixed with milk, curds, and parched grain.

The hymn is ascribed to a supposed Viśvavārā, a lady of the family of Atri.

1 *The ladle* : the sacrificial ladle with which the oil or clarified butter is taken up and poured out. The text has the feminine adjective *ghṛtācī only, juhū́* being understood. *That brings all blessing* : Sāyaṇa takes *viśvávārā* to be the name of a woman. *Praising the Gods* : said figuratively of the ladle held by the priest who praises.

3 *Make easy to maintain* : or, to follow Sāyaṇa : Perfect the well-knit bond of wife and husband.

HYMN XXIX. *Agni.*

1. MAN's worship of the Gods hath three great lustres, and three celestial lights have they established
The Maruts gifted with pure strength adore thee, for thou, O Indra, art their sapient Ṛṣi.

2 What time the Maruts sang their song to Indra, joyous when he had drunk of Soma juices,
He grasped his thunderbolt to slay the Dragon, and loosed, that they might flow, the youthful Waters.

3 And, O ye Brahmans, Maruts, so may Indra drink draughts of this my carefully pressed Soma ;
For this oblation found for man the cattle, and Indra, having quaffed it, slew the Dragon.

4 Then heaven and earth he sundered and supported : wrapped even in these he struck the Beast with terror.
So Indra forced the Engulfer to disgorgement, and slew the Dānava panting against him.

5 Thus all the Gods, O Maghavan, delivered to thee of their free will the draught of Soma ;
When thou for Etaśa didst cause to tarry the flying mares of Sūrya racing forward.

6 When Maghavan with the thunderbolt demolished his nine-and-ninety castles all together,
The Maruts, where they met, glorified Indra : ye with the Triṣṭup hymn obstructed heaven.

7 As friend to aid a friend, Agni dressed quickly three hundred buffaloes, even as he willed it.
And Indra, from man's gift, for Vṛtra's

1 *Three great lustres* : this is Sāyaṇa's explanation of the *tryaryamā* of the text. Professor Ludwig suggests that human relationships, such as *Maghavans* or nobles, priests, and *viśas* or the people, may be intended. *The three celestial lights* : the Sun, the Wind, the Fire, according to Sāyaṇa. *They* : the Maruts, says Sāyaṇa. *Ṛṣi* : here meaning beholder, according to Sāyaṇa.

3 *Brahmans* : priests. Sāyaṇa explains the word as meaning lofty or mighty in this passage.

4 *The Beast* : the demon Vṛtra. *The Engulfer* : Vṛtra, who had swallowed the celestial waters. *The Dānava* : the son of Danu, Vṛtra.

For Etaśa : See II. 19. 5.

6 *His nine-and-ninety castles* : the aerial castles of Śambara, the demon of drought. *Obstructed heaven* : made the loud hymn strike the sky.

slaughter, drank off at once three lakes of pressed-out Soma.

8 When thou three hundred buffaloes' flesh hadst eaten, and drunk, as Maghavan, three lakes of Soma,
All the Gods raised as 'twere a shout of triumph to Indra praise because he slew the Dragon.

9 What time ye came with strong steeds swiftly speeding, O Uśanā and Indra, to the dwelling,
Thou camest thither conquering together with Kutsa and the Gods : thou slewest Śuṣṇa.

10 One car-wheel of the Sun thou rolledst forward, and one thou settest free to move for Kutsa.
Thou slewest noseless Dasyus with thy weapon, and in their home o'erthrewest hostile speakers.

11 The lauds of Gaurivīti made thee mighty : to Vidathin's son, as prey, thou gavest Pipru.
Ṛjiśvan drew thee into friendship dressing the sacred food, and thou hast drunk his Soma.

12 Navagvas and Daśagvas with libations of Soma juice sing hymns of praise to Indra.
Labouring at their task the men laid open the stall of Kine though firmly closed and fastened.

13 How shall I serve thee, Maghavan, though knowing full well what hero deeds thou hast accomplished ?
And the fresh deeds which thou wilt do, Most Mighty ! these, too, will we tell forth in sacred synods.

14 Resistless from of old through hero courage, thou hast done all these many acts, O Indra.
What thou wilt do in bravery, Thunder-wielder ! none is there who may hinder this thy prowess.

15 Indra, accept the prayers which now are offered, accept the new prayers, Mightiest ! which we utter.
Like fair and well-made robes, I, seeking riches, as a deft craftsman makes a car, have wrought them.

7 *Three lakes* : large vessels or tubs are probably intended.

9 *Uśanā* : Indra's special friend. See Index. *To the dwelling* : of Kutsa.

10 *One car wheel* : an eclipse of the sun appears to be referred to. *Noseless* : that is, the flat-nosed barbarians, *a-nāsaḥ* ; or the word may be, as Sāyaṇa explains it, *an-āsaḥ*, *i.e.* mouthless, voiceless, unintelligibly speaking. See Muir, *Original Sanskrit Texts*, II. 377.

11 *Gaurivīti* : the Ṛṣi of the hymn. *Vidathin's son* : Ṛjiśvan, mentioned in Book I, as a favourite of Indra.

12 *Navagvas and Daśagvas* : priestly families connected or identified with the Aṅgirases.

HYMN XXX. *Indra.*

1. WHERE is that Hero ? Who hath looked on Indra borne on light-rolling car by Tawny Coursers,
Who, Thunderer, seeks with wealth the Soma-presser, and to his house goes, much-invoked, to aid him ?

2 I have beheld his strong and secret dwelling, longing have sought the Founder's habitation.
I asked of others, and they said in answer, May we, awakened men, attain to Indra.

3 We will tell, Indra, when we pour libation, what mighty deeds thou hast performed to please us.
Let him who knows not learn, who knows them listen : hither rides Maghavan with all his army.

4 Indra, when born, thou madest firm thy spirit : alone thou seekest war to fight with many.
With might thou clavest e'en the rock asunder, and foundest out the stable of the Milch-kine.

5 When thou wast born supremest at a distance, bearing a name renowned in far-off regions,
Since then e'en Gods have been afraid of Indra : he conquered all the floods which served the Dāsa.

6 These blissful Maruts sing their psalm to praise thee, and pour to thee libation of the Soma.
Indra with wondrous powers subdued the Dragon, the guileful lurker who beset the waters.

7 Thou, Maghavan, from the first didst scatter foemen, speeding, while joying in the milk, the Giver.

2 *I have beheld* : meaning, perhaps, I have tried to behold, I have looked for. *The Founder's habitation* : the dwelling-place of Indra who established the world.

5 *Which served the Dāsá* : which were subject to the demon Vṛtra.

7 *The giver* : the offerer of oblations. But the meaning of *dānam* is uncertain. Professor Ludwig translates it by 'the splitting (thunderbolt),' and Sāyaṇa explains it as 'the assailant of the Gods (Vṛtra).'

Namuci : one of the malignant demons of the atmosphere who withhold the rain.

There, seeking man's prosperity, thou torest away the head of Namuci the Dāsa.

8 Pounding the head of Namuci the Dāsa, me, too thou madest thine associate, Indra !
Yea, and the rolling stone that is in heaven both worlds, as on a car, brought to the Maruts.

9 Women for weapons hath the Dāsa taken. What injury can his feeble armies do me ?
Well he distinguished his two different voices, and Indra then advanced to fight the Dasyu.

10 Divided from their calves the Cows went lowing around, on every side, hither and thither.
These Indra re-united with his helpers, what time the well-pressed Soma made him joyful.

11 What time the Somas mixed by Babhru cheered him, loud the Steer bellowed in his habitations.
So Indra drank thereof, the Fort-destroyer, and gave him guerdon, in return, of milch-kine.

12 This good deed have the Ruśamas done, Agni ! that they have granted me four thousand cattle.
We have received Ṛṇañcaya's wealth, of heroes the most heroic, which was freely offered.

13 The Ruśamas, O Agni, sent me homeward with fair adornment and with kine in thousands.
The strong libations have made Indra joyful, when night, whose course was ending, changed to morning.

14 Night, well-nigh ended, at Ṛṇañcaya's coming, King of the Ruśamas, was changed to morning.
Like a strong courser, fleet of foot, urged onward, Babhru hath gained four thousand as his guerdon.

15 We have received four thousand head of cattle presented by the Ruśamas, O Agni.
And we, the singers, have received the caldron of metal which was heated for Pravargya.

HYMN XXXI. *Indra.*

1. MAGHAVAN Indra turns his chariot downward, the strength-displaying car which he hath mounted.
Even as a herdsman driveth forth his cattle, he goeth, first, uninjured, fain for treasure.

2. Haste to us, Lord of Bays; be not ungracious : visit us, lover of gold-hued oblation.
There is naught else better than thou art, Indra : e'en to the wifeless hast thou given spouses.

3 When out of strength arose the strength that conquers, Indra displayed all powers that he possesses.
Forth from the cave he drove the milky mothers, and with the light laid bare investing darkness.

4. Anus have wrought a chariot for thy Courser, and Tvaṣṭar, Much-invoked ! thy bolt that glitters.
The Brahmans with their songs exalting Indra increased his strength that he might slaughter Ahi.

5 When heroes sang their laud to thee the Hero, Indra ! and stones and Aditi accordant,

8 *The rolling stone* : perhaps the thunderbolt ; or if the thunderbolt is supposed to be the speaker of this stanza, as Professor Ludwig is inclined to think, the Sun must be meant ; that is, heaven and earth brought the Sun to the Maruts to aid Indra in his fight with the demon.

9 Indra is the speaker of the first line. *Women* : perhaps the subject waters. *His two different voices* : the meaning may be that Indra heard the voices of the women as well as the voice of Namuci, and so knew that he had not an army of demon-warriors to fight against. Professor Wilson, following Sāyaṇa, translates : 'the two his best beloved, (Indra) confined in the inner apartments.'

10 *With his helpers* : with the aid of the Maruts.

11 *Babhru* : the Ṛṣi of the hymn, who appears to have assisted the Ruśamas, a neighbouring people, in a successful foray, and to have been rewarded with a large portion of the booty. Ṛṇañcaya was the king of of this people.

15 *Heated for Pravargya*: a ceremony introductory to the Soma-sacrifice, in which fresh milk was poured into a heated vessel called *mahāvīrá* or, as in this place, *gharmá*.

1 *Even as a herdsman driveth forth his cattle* : so, says Sāyaṇa, Indra drives his enemies before him. *Fain for treasure* : wishing to obtain the riches of his enemies.

2 *Gold-hued oblation* : consisting of yellow Soma juice. *Spouses* : carried off in raids favoured by the Warrior-God.

4 *Anus* : probably meaning Bhṛgus, who belonged to that tribe.

The Brahmans : according to Sāyaṇa, the Aṅgirases, or the Maruts.

5 *Stones*: used for pressing the Soma juice. *Without or steed or chariot* : that is, the worshippers of Indra overcame their enemies by prayer and the favour of their God.

Without or steed or chariot were the fellies which, sped by Indra, rolled upon the Dasyus.

6 I will declare thine exploits wrought aforetime, and, Maghavan, thy deeds of late achievement,
When, Lord of Might, thou sunderedst earth and heaven, winning for man the moistly-gleaming waters.

7 This is thy deed, e'en this, Wonderful ! Singer ! that, slaying Ahi, here thy strength thou showedst,
Didst check and stay e'en Śuṣṇa's wiles and magic, and, drawing nigh, didst chase away the Dasyus.

8 Thou, Indra, on the farther bank for Yadu and Turvaśa didst stay the gushing waters.
Ye both assailed the fierce : thou barest Kutsa : when Gods and Uśanā came to you together.

9 Let the steeds bring you both, Indra and Kutsa, borne on the chariot within hearing-distance.
Ye blew him from the waters, from his dwelling, and chased the darkness from the noble's spirit.

10 Even this sage hath come looking for succour even to Vāta's docile harnessed horses.
Here are the Maruts, all thy dear companions : prayers have increased thy power and might, O Indra.

11 When night was near its close he carried forward e'en the Sun's chariot backward in its running.
Etaśa brought his wheel and firmly stays it : setting it eastward he shall give us courage.

12 This Indra, O ye men, hath come to see you, seeking a friend who hath expressed the Soma.
The creaking stone is laid upon the altar, and the Adhvaryus come to turn it quickly.

13 Let mortals who were happy still be happy ; let them not come to sorrow, O Immortal.
Love thou the pious, and to these thy people—with whom may we be numbered—give thou vigour.

8 *Yadu and Turvaśa*: See Index. *Ye both* : Indra and Kutsa. *The fierce* : Śuṣṇa, a demon of drought. *Thou barest Kutsa* : to his home.

9 *Ye blew him from the waters* : drave Śuṣṇa from the atmosphere in which he dwelt, and thus removed the grief of the eminent men who instituted sacrifices.

10 *Looking for succour* : Sāya a takes *avasyúḥ* here as the name of a Ṛṣi the seer of the hymn.

11 The return of the lingering morning sun appears to be attributed, on some particular occasion, to the special intervention of Indra on his favourite's behalf. The stanza is hardly intelligible as it stands. Sāyaṇa explains Etaśa by 'for Etaśa' The verse is discussed by Prof. Geldner (Vedische Studien, II. 162f), and his explanation is criticised by Prof. Ludwig (Ueber die Neuesten Arbeiten &c. p. 171).

12 *The creaking stone* : the upper press-stone.

HYMN XXXII. *Indra.*

1. THE well thou clavest, settest free the fountains, and gavest rest to floods that were obstructed.
Thou, Indra, laying the great mountain open, slaying the Dānava, didst loose the torrents.

2 The fountain-depths obstructed in their seasons, thou, Thunderer ! madest flow, the mountain's udder.
Strong Indra, thou by slaying e'en the Dragon that lay extended there hast shown thy vigour.

3 Indra with violence smote down the weapon, yea, even of that wild and mighty creature.
Although he deemed himself alone unequalled, another had been born e'en yet more potent.

4 Him, whom the heavenly food of these delighted, child of the mist, strong waxing, couched in darkness,
Him the bolt-hurling Thunderer with his lightning smote down and slew, the Dānava's wrath-fire, Śuṣṇa.

5 Though he might ne'er be wounded still his vitals felt that, the God's bolt, which his powers supported,
When, after offered draughts, Strong Lord, thou laidest him, fain to battle, in the pit in darkness.

6 Him as he lay there huge in length extended, still waxing in the gloom which no sun lightened,
Him, after loud-voiced threats, the Hero Indra, rejoicing in the poured libation, slaughtered.

7 When 'gainst the mighty Dānava his weapon Indra uplifted, power which none could combat,
When at the hurling of his bolt he smote him, he made him lower than all living creatures.

1 *The well* : the rain-cloud. *The fountains* : the sources of the waters of the firmament. *The mountain* : the massive cloud.

The Dānava : Vṛtra, the son of Danu.

4 *Of these* : of living creatures.

8 The fierce God seized that huge and restless coiler, insatiate, drinker of the sweets, recumbent,
And with his mighty weapon in his dwelling smote down the footless evil-speaking ogre.

9 Who may arrest his strength or check his vigour ? Alone, resistless, he bears off all riches.
Even these Twain, these Goddesses, through terror of Indra's might, retire from his dominion.

10 E'en the Celestial Axe bows down before him, and the Earth, lover-like, gives way to Indra.
As he imparts all vigour to these people, straightway the folk bend them to him the Godlike.

11 I hear that thou wast born sole Lord of heroes of the Five Races, famed among the people.
As such my wishes have most lately grasped him, invoking Indra both at eve and morning.

12 So, too, I hear of thee as in due season urging to action and enriching singers.
What have thy friends received from thee, the Brahmans who, faithful, rest their hopes on thee, O Indra ?

HYMN XXXIII. *Indra.*

1. Great praise to Indra, great and strong mid heroes, I ponder thus, the feeble to the Mighty,
Who with his band shows favour to this people, when lauded, in the fight where spoil is gathered.

2 So made attentive by our hymns, Steer ! Indra ! thou fastenedst the girth of thy Bay Coursers,
Which, Maghavan, at thy will thou drivest hither. With these subdue for us the men who hate us.

3 They were not turned to us-ward, lofty Indra ! while yet through lack of prayer they stood unharnessed.
Ascend this chariot, thou whose hand wields thunder, and draw the rein, O Lord of noble horses.

4 Thou, because many lauds are thine, O Indra, wast active warring in the fields for cattle.
For Sūrya in his own abode thou, Hero, formedst in fights even a Dāsa's nature.

5 Thine are we, Indra; thine are all these people, conscious of might, whose cars are set in motion.
Some hero come to us, O Strong as Ahi ! beauteous in war, to be invoked like Bhaga.

6 Strength much to be desired is in thee, Indra : the Immortal dances forth his hero exploits.
Such, Lord of Treasure, give us splendid riches. I praise the Friend's gift, his whose wealth is mighty.

7 Thus favour us, O Indra, with thy succour; Hero, protect the bards who sing thy praises.
Be friendly in the fray to those who offer the skin of beautiful and well-pressed Soma.

8 And these ten steeds which Trasadasyu gives me, the goldrich chief, the son of Purukutsa,
Resplendent in their brightness shall convey me. Gairikṣita willed it and so came I hither.

9 And these, bestowed as sacrificial guerdon, the powerful tawny steeds of Mārutāśva;
And thousands which kind Cyavatāna gave me, abundantly bestowed for my adornment.

10 And these commended horses, bright and active, by Dhvanya son of Lakṣmaṇa presented,
Came unto me, as cows into the Ṛṣi Saṁvaraṇa's stall, with magnitude of riches.

9 *These Goddesses* : Heaven and Earth.

10 *E'en the Celestial Axe* : perhaps the thunderbolt, which is one of the meanings assigned to *svádhitiḥ*. Sāyaṇa explains the word in this passage as 'the self-supported heaven,' and Professor Roth thinks that a tree of very hard wood, called Svadhiti, is intended, as we might say, even the oak bends down before him.

11 *Of the Five Races* : belonging to the five Āryan tribes. But see Muir, *Original Sanskrit Texts*, Vol I. 178.

4 The second half of the stanza refers to an eclipse of the sun. Indra is said to have formed for Sūrya *in his own abode*, that is, in the eastern heaven, the nature of a Dāsa, *i. e.* made him a slave or dark.

6 *Dances forth his hero exploits* : battle being regarded as a war dance, as in the Old German poetry, and in Homer's.—Ludwig.

8 *Son of Purukutsa* : Paurukutsya and Gairikṣita are both patronymics of Trasadasyu.

9 This stanza is obscure. Nothing further is known of Mārutāśva or Cyavatāna.

10 Dhvanya and his father Lakṣmaṇa are also unknown to fame. These three concluding stanzas are banished to the appendix by Professor Grassmann as being a later addition to the original hymn.

HYMN XXXIV. *Indra.*

1. BOUNDLESS and wasting not, the heavenly food of Gods goes to the foeless One, doer of wondrous deeds.
Press out, make ready, offer gifts with special zeal to him whom many laud, accepter of the prayer.

2 He who filled full his belly with the Soma's juice, Maghavan, was delighted with the meath's sweet draught,
When Uśanā, that he might slay the monstrous beast, gave him the mighty weapon with a thousand points.

3 Illustrious is the man whoever presseth out Soma for him in sunshine or in cloud and rain.
The mighty Maghavan who is the sage's Friend advanceth more and more his beauteous progeny.

4 The Strong God doth not flee away from him whose sire, whose mother or whose brother he hath done to death.
He, the Avenger, seeketh this man's offered gifts : this God, the source of riches, doth not flee from sin.

5 He seeks no enterprise with five or ten to aid, nor stays with him who pours no juice though prospering well.
The Shaker conquers or slays in this way or that, and to the pious gives a stable full of kine.

6 Exceeding strong in war he stays the chariot wheel, and, hating him who pours not, prospers him who pours.
Indra the terrible, tamer of every man, as Ārya leads away the Dāsa at his will.

7 He gathers up for plunder all the niggards' gear : excellent wealth he gives to him who offers gifts.
Not even in wide stronghold may all the folk stand firm who have provoked to anger his surpassing might.

8 When Indra Maghavan hath marked two wealthy men fighting for beauteous cows with all their followers,
He who stirs all things takes one as his close ally, and, Shaker, with his Heroes, sends the kine to him.

9 Agni ! I laud the liberal Āgniveśi, Śatri the type and standard of the pious.
May the collected waters yield him plenty, and his be powerful and bright dominion.

2 *Uśanā* : See I. 51. 10. *The monstrous beast* : Vṛtra or Ahi ; according to Sāyaṇa, a demon called Mṛga.

3 The meaning of the second half of this stanza is somewhat uncertain. Professor Wilson, following Sāyaṇa, renders it : 'Śakra disregards the man who is proud of his descendants and vain of his person, and who, though wealthy, is a friend of the base.' Professor Grassmann, following Professor Roth's interpretation of the doubtful words, translates similarly : 'Den Prahler stösst zurück der starke, mächtige den eitlen Stutzer, der dem Kargen sich gesellt.' Professor Ludwig, whom I here follow with hesitation, explains *kavāsakháḥ*, or *kavā sakhā* (like Agnāviṣṇu, Agnāmarut, Nabhānediṣṭha, etc.) as, friend with the wise.

4 Śakra or the Strong God does not fear the vengeance of those whose nearest relations he has killed for neglect of his worship.

Doth not flee from sin : perhaps, as Dr. Muir suggests, does not fear to punish the offender against him.

5 *The Shaker* : he who makes his enemies tremble, according to Sāyaṇa.

6 *The chariot wheel* : of his enemies.

9 *Āgniveśi* : son of Agniveśa, Śatri, a prince or chief whose name does not occur again in the Ṛgveda.

HYMN XXXV. *Indra.*

1. INDRA, for our assistance bring that most effectual power of thine,
Which conquers men for us, and wins the spoil, invincible in fight.

2 Indra, whatever aids be thine, four be they, or, O Hero, three,
Or those of the Five Tribes of men, bring quickly all that help to us.

3 The aid most excellent of thee the Mightiest hitherward we call,
For thou wast born with hero might, conquering, Indra, with the Strong.

4 Mighty to prosper us wast thou born, and mighty is the strength thou hast.
In native power thy soul is firm: thy valour, Indra, slays a host.

5 O Śatakratu, Lord of Strength, O Indra, Caster of the Stone.
With all thy chariot's force assail the man who shows himself thy foe.

6 For, Mightiest Vṛtra-slayer, thee, fierce, foremost among many, folk
Whose sacred grass is trimmed invite to battle where the spoil is won.

7 Indra, do thou protect our car that mingles foremost in the fights,
That bears its part in every fray, invincible and seeking spoil.

2 *Four be they* : according to Sāyaṇa, the favours or succours given to the four castes : *three*, similarly meaning the succours given to the three worlds.

3 *With the Strong* : the Maruts.

8 Come to us, Indra, and protect our car with thine intelligence.
May we, O Mightiest One, obtain excellent fame at break of day, and meditate our hymn at dawn.

HYMN XXXVI. *Indra.*

1. May Indra come to us, he who knows rightly to give forth treasures from his store of riches.
Even as a thirsty steer who roams the deserts may he drink eagerly the milked-out Soma.

2 Lord of Bay Horses, Hero, may the Soma rise to thy cheeks and jaws like mountain-ridges.
May we, O King, as he who driveth coursers, all joy in thee with hymns, invoked of many!

3 Invoked of many, Caster of the Stone! my heart quakes like a rolling wheel for fear of penury.
Shall not Purūvasu the singer give thee praise, O ever-prospering Maghavan, mounted on thy car?

4 Like the press-stone is this thy praiser, Indra. Loudly he lifts his voice with strong endeavour.
With thy left hand, O Maghavan, give us riches: with thy right, Lord of Bays, be not reluctant.

5 May the strong Heaven make thee the Strong wax stronger: Strong, thou art borne by thy two strong Bay Horses.
So, fair of cheek, with mighty chariot, mighty, uphold us, strong-willed, thunder-armed, in battle.

6 Maruts, let all the people in obeisance bow down before this youthful Śrutaratha,
Who, rich in steeds, gave me two dark red horses together with three hundred head of cattle.

HYMN XXXVII. *Indra.*

1. Bedewed with holy oil and meetly worshipped, the Swift One vies with Sūrya's beam in splendour.
For him may mornings dawn without cessation who saith, Let us press Soma out for Indra.

2 With kindled fire and strewn grass let him worship, and, Soma-presser, sing with stones adjusted:
And let the priest whose press-stones ring forth loudly, go down with his oblation to the river.

3 This wife is coming near who loves her husband who carries to his home a vigorous consort.
Here may his car seek fame, here loudly thunder, and his wheel make a thousand revolutions.

4 No troubles vex that King in whose home Indra drinks the sharp Soma juice with milk commingled.
With heroes he drives near, he slays the foeman: Blest, cherishing that name, he guards his people.

5 May he support in peace and win in battle: he masters both the hosts that meet together.
Dear shall he be to Sūrya, dear to Agni, who with pressed Soma offers gifts to Indra.

HYMN XXXVIII. *Indra.*

1. Wide, Indra Śatakratu, spreads the bounty of thine ample grace:
So, Lord of fair dominion, Friend of all men, give us splendid wealth.

2 The food which, Mightiest Indra, thou possessest worthy of renown
Is bruited as most widely famed, invincible, O Golden-hued!

3 O Darter of the Stone, the powers which readily obey thy will,—
Divinities, both thou and they, ye rule, to guard them, earth and heaven.

4 And from whatever power of thine, O Vṛtra-slayer, it may be,
Bring thou to us heroic strength: thou hast a man's regard for us.

5 In thy protection, with these aids of thine, O Lord of Hundred Powers,
Indra, may we be guarded well, Hero, may we be guarded well.

---

3 *Purūvasu*: I, the Ṛṣi; apparently the same as Prabhūvasu, the seer of the hymn.

1 *The Swift One*: Agni.

2 *To the river*: for ablution before sacrificing.

3 *This wife*: according to Sāyaṇa, the wife of Indra who accompanies him to the sacrifice.

The foeman: or the wicked man, or his enemy, *pāpam vairiṇam vā*.—Sāyaṇa.

3 *The powers*: according to Sāyaṇa, the strong Maruts.

HYMN XXXIX. *Indra.*

1. STONE-DARTING Indra, Wondrous One, what wealth is richly given from thee,
That bounty, Treasure-Finder ! bring filling both thy hands, to us.

2 Bring what thou deemest worth the wish, O Indra, that which is in heaven.
So may we know thee as thou art, boundless in thy munificence.

3 Thy lofty spirit, far-renowned as fain to give and prompt to win,—
With this thou rendest e'en the firm, Stone-Darter ! so to gain thee strength.

4 Singers with many songs have made Indra propitious to their fame,
Him who is King of human kind, most liberal of your wealthy ones.

5 To him, to Indra must be sung the poet's word, the hymn of praise.
To him, accepter of the prayer, the Atris raise their songs on high, the Atris beautify their songs.

HYMN XL. *Indra. Sūrya. Atri.*

1. COME thou to what the stones have pressed, drink Soma, O thou Soma's Lord,
Indra best Vṛtra-slayer Strong One, with the Strong.

2 Strong is the stone, the draught is strong, strong is this Soma that is pressed,
Indra, best Vṛtra-slayer, Strong One with the Strong.

3 As strong I call on thee the Strong, O Thunder-armed, with various aids,
Indra, best Vṛtra-slayer, Strong One with the Strong.

4 Impetuous, Thunderer, Strong, quelling the mighty, King, potent, Vṛtra-slayer, Soma-drinker,
May he come hither with his yoked Bay Horses; may Indra gladden him at the noon libation.

5 O Sūrya, when the Asura's descendant, Svarbhānu, pierced thee through and through with darkness,
All creatures looked like one who is bewildered, who knoweth not the place where he is standing.

6 What time thou smotest down Svarbhānu's magic that spread itself beneath the sky, O Indra,
By his fourth sacred prayer Atri discovered Sūrya concealed in gloom that stayed his function.

7 Let not the oppressor with this dread, through anger swallow me up, for I am thine, O Atri.
Mitra art thou, the sender of true blessings: thou and King Varuṇa be both my helpers.

8 The Brahman Atri, as he set the press-stones, serving the Gods with praise and adoration,
Established in the heaven the eye of Sūrya, and caused Svarbhānu's magic arts to vanish.

9 The Atris found the Sun again, him whom Svarbhānu of the brood
Of Asuras had pierced with gloom. This none besides had power to do.

The hymn is not homogeneous. The first part (1—4) is a separate invocation of Indra, and the subject of the second part is the Sun's eclipse by Svarbhānu and release by Atri.

1 *With the Strong* : together with the Maruts.

5 *Svarbhānu* : the Asura or demon who causes eclipses of the sun and moon, the Rāhu of later times. The name does not occur again in the Ṛgveda.

6 *By his fourth sacred prayer* : according to Sāyaṇa, by four stanzas (5—8) of this hymn. Probably, as Ludwig suggests, a fourth prayer in addition to the usual liturgy of three prayers against an eclipse. Prof. Lanman discusses and translates the latter portion of the hymn in Festgruss an R. von Roth, pp, 187 f. and adduces an interesting Buddhist parallel from the Saṁyutta Nikāya, I. ii. 1.

7 Sūrya or the Sun is the speaker. *The oppressor* : Svarbhānu.

9 *Of the brood of Asuras* : the word *āsuráḥ* in this hymn means belonging to, or descendant of, Asuras, demons or evil spirits. This use of the word is unknown in the earliest portions of the Ṛgveda.

HYMN XLI. *Viśvedevas*

1. WHO, Mitra-Varuṇa, is your pious servant to give you gifts from earth or mighty heaven ?
Preserve us in the seat of holy Order, and give the offerer power that winneth cattle.

2 May Mitra, Varuṇa, Aryaman, and Āyu, Indra Ṛbhukṣan, and the Maruts, love us,
And they who of one mind with bounteous Rudra accept the hymn and laud with adorations.

3 You will I call to feed the car-horse, Aśvins, with the wind's flight swiftest of those who travel :

2 *Āyu* : here said to mean Vāyu, the God of wind. See I. 162. I. The celestial Agni is probably intended. *Ṛbhu ṣan* : a name of Indra, as Lord of the Ṛbhus.

And they who : the Maruts especially, as being Rudra's sons.

3 *The Asura of heaven* : or the Lord of heaven. According to Sāyaṇa, Asura means here either the destroyer of life, Rudra, or the giver of life, Sūrya or Vāyu.

Or also to the Asura of heaven, Worshipful, bring a hymn as 'twere libation.

4 The heavenly Victor, he whose priest is Kaṇva, Tṛta with Dyaus accordant, Vāta, Agni,
All-feeding Pūṣan, Bhaga sought the oblation, as they whose steeds are fleetest seek the contest.

5 Bring ye your riches forward borne on horses: let thought be framed for help and gain of treasure.
Blest be the priest of Auśija through courses, the courses which are yours the fleet, O Maruts.

6 Bring hither him who yokes the car, your Vāyu, who praises with his songs, the God and Singer;
And, praying and devout, noble and prudent, may the Gods' Spouses in their thoughts retain us.

7 I speed to you with powers that should be honoured, with songs distinguishing Heaven's mighty Daughters,
Morning and Night, the Two, as 'twere all-knowing: these bring the sacrifice unto the mortal.

8 You I extol, the nourishers of heroes, bringing you gifts, Vāstoṣpati and Tvaṣṭar—
Rich Dhiṣaṇā accords through our obeisance—and Trees and Plants, for the swift gain of riches.

9 Ours be the Parvatas, even they, for offspring, free-moving, who are Heroes like the Vasus.
May holy Āptya, Friend of man, exalted, strengthen our word for ever and be near us.

10 Tṛta praised him, germ of the earthly hero, with pure songs him the Offspring of the Waters.
Agni with might neighs loudly like a charger: he of the flaming hair destroys the forests.

11 How shall we speak to the great might of Rudra? How speak to Bhaga who takes thought for riches?
May Plants, the Waters, and the Sky preserve us, and Woods and Mountains with their trees for tresses.

12 May the swift Wanderer, Lord of refreshments, listen to our songs, who speeds through cloudy heaven:
And may the Waters, bright like castles, hear us, as they flow onward from the cloven mountain.

13 We know your ways, ye Mighty Ones: receiving choice meed, ye Wonderful, we will proclaim it.
Even strong birds descend not to the mortal who strives to reach them with swift blow and weapons.

14 Celestial and terrestrial generations, and Waters will I summon to the feasting.
May days with bright dawns cause my songs to prosper, and may the conquered streams increase their waters.

15 Duly to each one hath my laud been offered. Strong be Varūtrī with her powers to succour.

4 *The heavenly Victor*: Indra. *Tṛta*: according to Sāyaṇa Tṛta here is not the name of a separate deity (Tṛta Āptya), but an epithet of Vāyu, 'pervading the three regions of earth, firmament, and heaven.'

5 *The priest of Auśija*: Atri, the ministrant priest of Kakṣivān the son of Uśij.—Sāyaṇa.

8 *Vāstoṣpati*: Lord of the Homestead, Indra.

Dhiṣaṇā: a Goddess presiding over prosperity and gain; according to Sāyaṇa, Vāgdevatā, the Goddess of speech.

9 *The Parvatas*: the genii who preside over mountains and clouds. *For offspring*: that they may give us children and children's children.

Holy Āptya: Tṛta Āptya, a divinity or mythical being who dwells in the remotest part of the heavens.

10 *Germ of the earthly hero*: Agni, the Offspring of the Waters, who develops into the strong God, or Hero, who appears on earth in the form of terrestrial fire.

12 *Swift Wanderer*: Vāyu, God of the circumambient wind.

As they flow onward: the text has *pári srúco*. Sāyaṇa explains *sruco* (ladles) by *saraṇaśīlāḥ*, inclined or accustomed to flow. Professor Ludwig suggests *parisruto* (flowing round or over) as the original reading.

Cloven mountain: according to Sāyaṇa, the increasing, *i. e.* the towering, or swelling, mountain, or cloud.

13 This stanza is exceedingly difficult. I follow Professor Ludwig in his interpretation, and understand the meaning to be: we know what your ways are, and we glorify you because you reward us for doing so. If you appeared to us only as hostile and terrible deities we should not praise you any more than birds allow themselves to be lured down by the man who shoots at them. Professor Wilson, following Sāyaṇa, paraphrases the stanza: 'Mighty Maruts, of goodly aspect, quickly hear (the praises) that we who repair to you repeat, offering acceptable (oblations): (the Maruts) coming hither, well disposed, come down to us (destroying) with their weapons the mortals opposed to them, (overcome) by agitation.

14 *The conquered streams*: won from the hostile barbarians.

15 *Varūtrī*: one of a class of guardian Goddesses. See I. 22. 10. and III. 62. 3

Rasā a mythical stream which flows round the earth and the atmosphere, here personified as a benignant Goddess: earth, according to Sāyaṇa. See I. 112. 12. *Straight-handed*: holding out her hand to guide and help us.

May the great Mother Rasā here befriend us, straight-handed, with the princes, striving forward.

16 How may we serve the Liberal Ones with worship, the Maruts swift of course in invocation, the Maruts far-renowned in invocation ?
Let not the Dragon of the Deep annoy us, and gladly may he welcome our addresses.

17 Thus thinking, O ye Gods, the mortal wins you to give him increase of his herds of cattle : the mortal wins him, O ye Gods, your favour.
Here he wins wholesome food to feed this body : as for mine old age, Nirṛti consume it !

18 O Gods, may we obtain from you this favour, strengthening food through the Cow's praise, ye Vasus.
May she who gives good gifts, the gracious Goddess, come speeding nigh to us for our well-being.

19 May Iḷā, Mother of the herds of cattle, and Urvaśī with all the streams accept us;
May Urvaśī in lofty heaven accepting, as she partakes the oblation of the living,

20 Visit us while she shares Ūrjavya's food.

HYMN XLII. *Viśvedevas.*

1. Now may our sweetest song with deep devotion reach Varuṇa, Mitra, Aditi, and Bhaga.
May the Five Priests' Lord, dwelling in oblations, bliss-giving Asura, hear, whose paths are open.

2 May Aditi welcome, even as a mother her dear heart-gladdening son, my song that lauds her.
The prayer they love, bliss-giving, God-appointed, I offer unto Varuṇa and Mitra.

3 Inspirit him, the Sagest of the Sages; with sacrificial oil and meath bedew him.
So then let him, God Savitar, provide us excellent, ready, and resplendent treasures.

4 With willing mind, Indra, vouchsafe us cattle, prosperity, Lord of Bays ! and pious patrons;
And, with the sacred prayer by Gods appointed, give us the holy Deities' loving-kindness.

5 God Bhaga, Savitar who deals forth riches, Indra, and they who conquer Vṛtra's treasures,
And Vāja and Ṛbhukṣan and Purandhi, the Mighty and Immortal Ones, protect us !

6 Let us declare his deeds, the undecaying unrivalled Victor whom the Maruts follow.
None of old times, O Maghavan, nor later, none of these days hath reached thy hero prowess.

7 Praise him the Chief who gives the boon of riches, Bṛhaspati distributor of treasures,
Who, blessing most the man who sings and praises, comes with abundant wealth to his invoker.

8 Tended, Bṛhaspati, with thy protections, the princes are unharmed and girt by heroes.
Wealth that brings bliss is found among the givers of horses and of cattle and of raiment.

9 Make their wealth flee who, through our hymns enjoying their riches, yield us not an ample guerdon.
Far from the sun keep those who hate devotion, the godless, prospering in their vocation.

10 With wheelless chariots drive down him, O Maruts, who at the feasts of Gods regards the demons.
May he, though bathed in sweat, form empty wishes, who blames his sacred rite who toils to serve you.

11 Praise him whose bow is strong and sure his arrow, him who is Lord of every balm that healeth.

16 *The Dragon of the Deep* : Ahibudhnya, the regent of the depths of the firmament.

17 *Nirṛti* : the Goddess of destruction. 'May Nirṛti (he thinks) swallow up my old age (not me).' —Ludwig.

Iḷā : here meaning Earth, according to Sāyaṇa. *Urvaśī* : apparently Fervour or Enthusiasm personified as a divine being.

20 *Ūrjavya's food* : the viands provided by Ūrjavya, the prince or patron who institutes the sacrifice.

The hymn is generally difficult and obscure ; and parts of the translation are, and must at present be, conjectural.

---

1 *The Five Priests' Lord* : apparently Varuṇa, the five priests who serve him being five Ādityas. According to Sāyaṇa Vāyu is meant.

3 *The Sagest of the Sages* : Savitar, perhaps as identified with Agni.

5 *Ṛbhukṣan* : in this place is said by Sāyaṇa to mean Ṛbhu, and *Purandhi* (the intelligent) to mean Vibhvan.

11 *Praise him* : Rudra.

Worship thou Rudra for his great good favour : adore the Asura, God, with salutations.

12 May the House-friends, the cunning-handed Artists, may the Steer's Wives, the streams carved out by Vibhvan,
And may the fair Ones honour and befriend us, Sarasvatī, Bṛhaddivā, and Rākā.

13 My newest song, thought that now springs within me, I offer to the Great, the Sure Protector,
Who made for us this All, in fond love laying each varied form within his Daughter's bosom.

14 Now, even now, may thy fair praise, O Singer, attain Iḍaspati who roars and thunders,
Who, rich in clouds and waters with his lightning speeds forth bedewing both the earth and heaven.

15 May this my laud attain the troop of Maruts, those who are youths in act, the Sons of Rudra.
The wish calls me to riches and well-being: praise the unwearied Ones whose steeds are dappled.

16 May this my laud reach earth and air's mid-region, and forest trees and plants to win me riches.
May every Deity be swift to listen, and Mother Earth with no ill thought regard me.

17 Gods, may we dwell in free untroubled bliss.

18 May we obtain the Aśvins' newest favour, and gain their health-bestowing happy guidance.
Bring riches hither unto us, and heroes, and all felicity and joy, Immortals !

HYMN XLIII. *Viśvedevas.*

1. MAY the Milch-cows who hasten to their object come harmless unto us with liquid sweetness.
The Singer, lauding, calls, for ample riches, the Seven Mighty Ones who bring enjoyment.

2 With reverence and fair praise will I bring hither, for sake of strength, exhaustless Earth and Heaven.
Father and Mother, sweet of speech, fair-handed, may they, far-famed, in every fight protect us.

3 Adhvaryus, make the sweet libations ready, and bring the beautiful bright juice to Vāyu.
God, as our Priest, be thou the first to drink it : we give thee of the mead to make thee joyful.

4 Two arms—the Soma's dexterous immolators—and the ten fingers set and fix the press-stone.
The stalk hath poured, fair with its spreading branches, the mead's bright glittering juice that dwells on mountains.

5 The Soma hath been pressed for thee, its lover, to give thee power and might and high enjoyment.
Invoked, turn hither in thy car, O Indra, at need, thy two well-trained and dear Bay Horses.

6 Bring by God-traversed paths, accordant, Agni, the great Aramati, Celestial Lady,
Exalted, worshipped with our gifts and homage, who knoweth holy Law, to drink sweet Soma.

7 As on his father's lap the son, the darling, so on the fire is set the sacred caldron,
Which holy singers deck, as if extending and heating that which holds the fatty membrane.

8 Hither, as herald to invite the Aśvins, come the great lofty song, most sweet and pleasant !
Come in one car, Joy-givers ! to the

12 *The cunning-handed Artists* : the Ṛbhus. *The Steer's Wives* : the spouses of the mighty Indra. *Carved out by Vibhvan* : whose channels were formed by him as the artificer of Varuṇa.

Bṛhaddivā : a Goddess frequently associated with Iḷā, Sarasvatī, and others. Sāyaṇa takes the word in this place as an epithet, 'very brilliant,' of *Rākā*, the Goddess who presides over the day of full moon.

13 *The Great, the Sure Protector* : Indra. *His Daughter*: Earth. Here, as Ludwig observes, we have the germ of the myth of Prajāpati and his daughter. Cf. X .61.

14 *Iḍaspati* : the Lord of the libation; here Parjanya, God of the rain-clouds.

---

1 *The Milch-cows* : the rivers. *The Seven Mighty Ones* : probably the Indus, the five rivers of the Panjāb, and the Sarasvatī, or the Kubhā. See I. 32.12.

4 *Immolators* : or preparers.

6 *Aramati* : the Goddess who presides over worship and active piety, and also personifies the Earth ; the Spenta-Armaiti, or Holy Piety, and Spirit of Earth, of the Zoroastrians.

7 *As if extending* : perhaps, stretching (over the fire) and so roasting, as Prof. Roth explains. *Heating that which holds the fatty membrane* : 'roasting a marrow-yielding animal.'—Wilson. The *vapā* is the omentum or membrane enfolding the intestines of the victim, specially offered to Gods in the *Vapāhuti* sacrifice.

8 *Joy-givers* : ye beneficent Aśvins. *Like the bolt* : 'As the cart cannot move if the axle of the wheel is not fastened by the pin or bolt, so the offering of the *Soma* is without efficacy unless the *Aśvins* be present.'—Wilson, from Sāyaṇa.

banquet, like the bolt binding pole and nave, come hither.

9 I have declared this speech of adoration to mightiest Pūṣan and victorious Vāyu,
Who by their bounty are the hymns' inspirers, and of themselves give power as a possession.

10 Invoked by us bring hither, Jātavedas! the Maruts all under their names and figures.
Come to the sacrifice with aid all Maruts, all to the songs and praises of the singer!

11 From high heaven may Sarasvatī the Holy visit our sacrifice, and from the mountain.
Eager, propitious, may the balmy Goddess hear our effectual speech, our invocation.

12 Set in his seat the God whose back is dusky, Bṛhaspati the lofty, the Disposer.
Him let us worship, set within the dwelling, the red, the golden-hued, the all-resplendent.

13 May the Sustainer, high in heaven, come hither, the Bounteous One, invoked, with all his favours,
Dweller with Dames divine, with plants, unwearied, the Steer with triple horn, the life-bestower.

14 The tuneful eloquent priests of him who liveth have sought the Mother's bright and loftiest station.
As living men, with offered gifts and homage they deck the most auspicious Child to clothe him.

15 Agni, great vital power is thine, the mighty: pairs waxing old in their devotion seek thee.
May every Deity be swift to listen, and Mother Earth with no ill thought regard me.

16 Gods, may we dwell in free untroubled bliss.

17 May we obtain the Aśvins' newest favour, and gain their health-bestowing happy guidance.
Bring riches hither unto us, and heroes, and all felicity and joy, Immortals!

HYMN XLIV. *Viśvedevas.*

1. As in the first old times, as all were wont, as now, he draweth forth the power turned hitherward with song,
The Princedom throned on holy grass, who findeth light, swift, conquering in the plants wherein he waxeth strong.

2 Shining to him who leaves heaven's regions undisturbed, which to his sheen who is beneath show fair in light,
Good guardian art thou, not to be deceived, Most Wise! Far from deceits thy name dwelleth in holy Law.

3 Truth waits upon oblation present and to come: naught checks him in his way, this victory-bringing Priest:
The Mighty Child who glides along the sacred grass, the undecaying Youth set in the midst of plants.

4 These come, well-yoked, to you for furtherance in the rite: down come the twin-born strengtheners of Law for him,

11 *Balmy*: literally, filled with, or sprinkling *ghṛta*, oil, fatness, or fertilizing fluid. 'The showerer of water.'—Wilson.

12 *Whose back is dusky*: darkened by enveloping smoke, Bṛhaspati being here identified with Agni.

13 *The Sustainer*: or the very strong One, Agni. *With triple horn*: according to Sāyaṇa, having horns or flames of three colours, red, white, and black (with smoke).

14 *Eloquent*: the meaning of *rāspirāsaḥ* is uncertain. Sāyaṇa explains it by 'holders of sacrificial ladles.' *The Mother* is the earth, and her *loftiest station* is the altar. *Of him who liveth*: of the living man, the worshipper. *The Child* is Agni.

15 *Pairs*: human pairs of worshippers; husbands and wives. The second half of this stanza is repeated from stanza 16 of the preceding hymn.

16 This line and the following stanza are identical with 17 and 18 of the preceding hymn.

1 *He draweth forth*: the Agnīdh, or priest who kindles the sacrificial fire, draws, or literally milks out, Agni from the fire-sticks by attrition. I follow Professor Ludwig in taking *dohase* and *várdhase* as third persons singular. Professor Grassmann banishes to his Appendix this 'most bombastic and intentionally obscure hymn,' which he considers to be a later interpolation. *The Princedom*: the Prince, Agni; *jyeṣṭátātim* the abstract being used for the concrete.

2 *Shining to him*: apparently, to the Sun; but the meaning is uncertain.

Who is beneath: the Sun when he is setting, or perhaps Agni. *Thou*: Indra.

3 *Truth waits upon oblation*: the hopes and wishes of the sacrificer are realized. It seems impossible to get any meaning out of *ātyam* (courser) and I follow Professor Ludwig in reading *satyám* (truth or realization). *The victory-bringing Priest, the Mighty Child, the undecaying Youth*, is Agni.

4 *These come, well-yoked*: probably the priests, closely associated in their sacred duties, who bring the waters used in the preparation of the Soma and so are called *strengtheners of Law*, *i. e.* furtherers of the law-appointed sacrifice *for him*, for Agni the Child of the Waters.

The hide stealeth away their names: according to Sāyaṇa, Āditya or the Sun steals (that is, absorbs) the waters in low places; or Agni appropriates the offerings presented to him. Professor Ludwig is of opinion ...

With reins easily guided and commanding all. In the deep fall the hide stealeth away their names.

5 Thou, moving beauteously in visibly pregnant ones, snatching with trees the branching plant that grasps the juice,
Shinest, true Singer ! mid the upholders of the voice. Increase thy Consorts thou, lively at sacrifice.

6 Like as he is beheld such is he said to be. They with effectual splendour in the floods have made
Earth yield us room enough and amply wide extent, great might invincible, with store of hero sons.

7 Sūrya the Sage, as if unwedded, with a Spouse, in battle-loving spirit moveth o'er the foes.
May he, self-excellent, grant us a sheltering home, a house that wards the fierce heat off on every side.

8 Thy name, sung forth by Ṛṣis in these hymns of ours, goes to the loftier One with this swift mover's light.
By skill he wins the boon whereon his heart is set : he who bestirs himself shall bring the thing to pass.

9 The chief and best of these abideth in the sea, nor doth libation fail wherein it is prolonged.
The heart of him who praiseth trembleth not in fear there where the hymn is found connected with the pure.

10 For it is he : with thoughts of Kṣatra, Manasa, of Yajata, and Sadhri, and Evāvada,
With Avatsāra's sweet songs will we strive to win the mightiest strength which even he who knows should gain.

11 The Hawk is their full source, girth-stretching rapturous drink of Viśvavāra, of Māyin, and Yajata.
They ever seek a fresh draught so that they may come, know when thy time to halt and drink thy fill is near.

12 Sadāpṛṇa the holy, Tarya, Śrutavit, and Bāhuvṛkta, joined with you, have slain the foes.
He gains his wish in both the worlds and brightly shines—when he adores the host with well-advancing steeds.

13 The worshipper's defender is Sutambhara, producer and uplifter of all holy thoughts.
The milch-cow brought, sweet-flavoured milk was dealt around. Who speaks the bidding text knows this, not he who sleeps.

14 The sacred hymns love him who wakes and watches : to him who watches come the Sāma verses.
This Soma saith unto the man who watches, I rest and have my dwelling in thy friendship.

15 Agni is watchful, and the Ṛcas love him; Agni is watchful, Sāma verses seek him.
Agni is watchful, to him saith this Soma, I rest and have my dwelling in thy friendship.

krivíḥ (literally, leather bottle or bag, and metaphorically cloud, cistern, or well) in this place=*samudrá* in its twofold signification as Soma reservoir and sea. The meaning then would be that the names of the waters, *i. e.* the waters themselves, fall into the reservoir and into the sea. According to Sāyaṇa the whole stanza refers to the Sun, the *well-yoked* being his 'well-combined rays.'

5 This stanza is addressed to Agni. *Visibly pregnant ones* : perhaps the waters. *With trees* : with burning fuel. *Thy Consorts* : the flames.

7 *As if unwedded* : Sūrya the Sun-God, although wedded to Uṣas or Dawn, is courageous as an unmarried man untroubled by care for wife and child ; may he give us assurance of security as he himself knows how delightful that is.

8 *Thy name* : the name of the institutor of the sacrifice. *The loftier One* : Sūrya. *This swift mover's light* : the flames of Agni. *He who bestirs himself* : the restless Agni.

9 *Of these* : hymns of praise. *Abideth in the sea* : is closely connected with the vat or reservoir of Soma. According to Sāyaṇa the meaning is that the best of the hymns proceed to the ocean-like Sun (*samudravatparyavasānabhūtam sūryam*).

10 *For it is he* : 'He verily (is to be glorified).'—Wilson. *Kṣatra, Manasa, etc.* are said to be the names of Ṛṣis associated with Avatsāra to whom especially the hymn is ascribed.

11 *The Hawk*: who brought the Soma from heaven. See IV. 27. *Viśvavāra, Māyin,* and *Yajata* are said to be Ṛṣis.

12 *Sadāpṛṇa* and the others mentioned in this verse are also Ṛṣis. *He* : each of the Ṛṣis. *The host* : of Gods.

13 *Sutambhara* : said to be the name of a Ṛṣi. The word means the bearer of the juice or libation. Professor Ludwig says that the Hawk (st. 11) is intended.

15 *The Ṛcas* : the hymns and verses of the Ṛgveda.

The hymn is exceedingly difficult and obscure, and in parts it seems to be hopelessly unintelligible. Professor Wilson's paraphrase and Professor Grassmann's translation differ very widely from the version—founded mainly on Professor Ludwig's interpretation—which I offer as a temporary makeshift.

HYMN XLV. *Viśvedevas.*

1. Bards of approaching Dawn who know the heavens are come with hymns to throw the mountain open.
The Sun hath risen and oped the stable portals: the doors of men, too, hath the God thrown open.

2 Sūrya hath spread his light as splendour: hither came the Cows' Mother, conscious, from the stable,
To streams that flow with biting waves to deserts; and heaven is stablished like a firm-set pillar.

3 This laud hath won the burden of the mountain. To aid the ancient birth of mighty waters
The mountain parted, Heaven performed his office. The worshippers were worn with constant serving.

4 With hymns and God-loved words will I invoke you, Indra and Agni, to obtain your favour,
For verily sages, skilled in sacrificing, worship the Maruts and with lauds invite them.

5 This day approach us: may our thoughts be holy, far from us let us cast away misfortune.
Let us keep those who hate us at a distance, and haste to meet the man who sacrifices.

6 Come, let us carry out, O friends, the purpose wherewith the Mother threw the Cow's stall open,
That wherewith Manu conquered Viśiśipra, wherewith the wandering merchant gained heaven's water.

7 Here, urged by hands, loudly hath rung the press-stone wherewith Navagvas through ten months sang praises.
Saramā went aright and found the cattle. Aṅgiras gave effect to all their labours.

8 When at the dawning of this mighty Goddess, Aṅgirases all sang forth with the cattle,—
Their spring is in the loftiest place of meeting,—Saramā found the kine by Order's pathway.

9 Borne by his Coursers Seven may Sūrya visit the field that spreadeth wide for his long journey.
Down on the Soma swooped the rapid Falcon. Bright was the young Sage moving mid his cattle.

10 Sūrya hath mounted to the shining ocean when he hath yoked his fair-backed Tawny Horses.
The wise have drawn him like a ship through water: the floods obedient have descended hither.

11 I lay upon the Floods your hymn, light-winning, wherewith Navagvas their ten months completed.
Through this our hymn may we have Gods to guard us: through this our hymn pass safe beyond affliction.

HYMN XLVI. *Viśvedevas.*

1. Well knowing I have bound me, horse-like, to the pole: I carry that which bears us on and gives us help.

1 *Bards*: the Aṅgirases who sing the praises of Uṣas and who know the exact time when morning rites are to be celebrated. *The mountain*: the cloud in which the stolen Cows, or vanished rays of light, have been concealed.

2 *The Cows' Mother*: Dawn; the parent of the rays of light.

3 *The burden of the mountain*: the store of water which lies like an unborn babe in the bosom of the mountain-like cloud. *Performed his office*: aided the production of the rain. *The worshippers*: the Aṅgirases.

6 *Wherewith*: I follow Professor Grassmann in taking *yā* as instrumental—*yáyā*. *The Mother*: Dawn. *Viśiśipra*: meaning, perhaps, jawless or chinless, may, Sāyaṇa says, be Vṛtra, and *Manu* here may mean Indra. Manu probably represents the victorious Āryan invader and Viśiśipra the conquered barbarian

The wandering merchant: Sāyaṇa says that this refers to the story of Kakṣīvān to whom the Aśvins sent rain. See I. 112. 11.

7 *Through ten months*: referring to the sacrifices of nine and ten months' duration performed by the Navagvas and the Daśagvas, priestly families frequently mentioned in connexion with the Aṅgirases. These names mean, respectively, nine-month ministrants and ten-month ministrants, and are translated in the St. Petersburg Lexicon by Neuner and Zehner, Niners and Tenners. *Saramā*: see Index. *Aṅgiras*: Agni.

8 *Their spring*: the source of the Cows, that is the Cows themselves. *The loftiest place of meeting*: the height of heaven. The half-line is apparently parenthetical.

9 *The rapid Falcon*: which brought the Soma from heaven. *The young Sage*: 'ever young and far-seeing.' The Sun is intended, moving in the midst of his rays.

10 *The shining ocean*: the luminous firmament.

11 *I lay upon the floods*: I offer to the Waters. *Light-winning*: which gains for the worshipper the light of heaven.

The Consorts of the Gods are the deities of the last two stanzas.

1: The Ṛṣi Pratikṣatra. *The pole*: a metaphorical expression for sacrificial duties. *That which bears us on*: the pole, the performance of sacrifice. 'I

I seek for no release, no turning back therefrom. May he who knows the way, the Leader, guide me straight.

2 O Agnī, Indra, Varuṇa, and Mitra, give, O ye Gods, and Marut host, and Viṣṇu.
May both Nāsatyas, Rudra, heavenly Matrons, Pūṣan, Sarasvatī, Bhaga, accept us.

3 Indra and Agni, Mitra, Varuṇa, Aditi, the Waters, Mountains, Maruts, Sky, and Earth and Heaven,
Viṣṇu I call, Pūṣan, and Brahmaṇaspati, and Bhaga, Śaṁsa, Savitar that they may help.

4 May Viṣṇu also and Vāta who injures none, and Soma granter of possessions give us joy ;
And may the Ṛbhus and the Aśvins, Tvaṣṭar and Vibhvan remember us so that we may have wealth.

5 So may the band of Maruts dwelling in the sky, the holy, come to us to sit on sacred grass ;
Bṛhaspati and Pūṣan grant us sure defence, Varuṇa, Mitra, Aryaman guard and shelter us.

6 And may the Mountains famed in noble eulogies, and the fair-gleaming Rivers keep us safe from harm.
May Bhaga the Dispenser come with power and grace, and far-pervading Aditi listen to my call.

7 May the Gods' Spouses aid us of their own free will, aid us to offspring and the winning of the spoil.
Grant us protection, O ye gracious Goddesses, ye who are on the earth or in the waters' realm.

8 May the Dames, wives of Gods, enjoy our presents, Rāṭ, Aśvinī, Agnāyī, and Indrāṇī.
May Rodasī and Varuṇānī hear us, and Goddesses come at the Matrons' season.

support that transcendant and preservative load.'—Wilson. *He who knows the way* : the divine inner guide: *mārgābhijño'ntaryāmī devaḥ*—Sāyaṇa.

3 *Śaṁsa* : prayer or wish, personified. Or *śáṁsam* may be a verbal form, I praise.

8 *Rāṭ* : the name of a Goddess, or, as Sāyaṇa takes it, bright, qualifying *Aśvinī*, the Consort of the Aśvins. *Rodasī* : the Spouse of Rudra. See Index.

At the Matrons' season : at the time appointed for the celestial dames, the Consorts of the Gods.

HYMN XLVII. *Viśvedevas.*

1. URGING to toil and making proclamation, seeking Heaven's Daughter comes the Mighty Mother :
She comes, the youthful Hymn, unto the Fathers, inviting to her home and loudly calling.

2 Swift in their motion, hasting to their duty, reaching the central point of life immortal,
On every side about the earth and heaven go forth the spacious paths without a limit.

3 Steer, Sea, Red Bird with strong wings, he hath entered the dwelling-place of the Primeval Father.
A gay-hued Stone set in the midst of heaven, he hath gone forth and guards mid-air's two limits.

4 Four bear him up and give him rest and quiet, and ten invigorate the Babe for travel.
His kine most excellent, of threefold nature, pass swiftly round the boundaries of heaven.

5 Wondrous, O people, is the mystic knowledge that while the waters stand the streams are flowing :
That, separate from his Mother, Two support him, closely-united, twins, here made apparent.

1 *Heaven's Daughter* : Uṣas or Dawn. *The Mighty Mother* : perhaps, as Professor Ludwig suggests, Vāk or Speech is intended, who appears in the second line as the Hymn personified.

2 *The central point of life immortal* : the Sun. *The paths* : the long lines of light.

3 *Sea* : as the great attracter and receptacle of the waters.

He : the Sun. *The Primeval Father* : Dyaus, or Heaven.

A gay-hued Stone : Professor Ludwig would read *pṛśniraśmá*, 'with variegated rays,' instead of the *pṛśnir-áśmā* of the text. But the alteration seems to be unnecessary.

4 *Four* : according to Sāyaṇa, the four chief priests. Possibly Varuṇa, Mitra, Aryaman, Bhaga are intended.—Ludwig.

Ten : the regions of space ; as the Sun attracts the waters from all sides. *His kine* : his rays. *Of threefold nature* : producing heat, cold (by their absence), and rain.

5 The marvel is that the waters stand still in the sea while the rivers are continually flowing into it. Cf. Eclesiastes, I.7. *Separate from his Mother* : Sūrya's Mother is the invisible Aditi ; and he is supported by Heaven and Earth, the closely-connected pair who are visible in this world.—Ludwig.

6 For him they lenghten prayers and acts of worship : the Mothers weave garments for him their offspring.
Rejoicing, for the Steer's impregning contact, his Spouses move on paths or heaven to meet him.

7 Be this our praise, O Varuṇa and Mitra ; may this be health and force to us, O Agni.
May we obtain firm ground and room for resting : Glory to Heaven, the lofty habitation !

HYMN XLVIII. *Viśvedevas.*

1. WHAT may we meditate for the beloved Power, mighty in native strength and glorious in itself,
Which as a magic energy seeking waters spreads even to the immeasurable middle region's cloud ?

2 O'er all the region with their uniform advance these have spread out the lore that giveth heroes strength.
Back, with their course reversed, the others pass away : the pious lengthens life with those that are before.

3 With pressing-stones and with the bright beams of the day he hurls his broadest bolt against the Guileful One.
Even he whose hundred wander in his own abode, driving the days afar and bringing them again.

4 I, to enjoy the beauty of his form, behold that rapid rush of his as 'twere an axe's edge,
What time he gives the man who calls on him in fight wealth like a dwelling-house filled full with store of food.

5 Four-faced and nobly clad, Varuṇa, urging on the pious to his task, stirs himself with the tongue.
Naught by our human nature do we know of him, him from whom Bhaga Savitar bestows the boon.

HYMN XLIX. *Viśvedevas.*

1. THIS day I bring God Savitar to meet you, and Bhaga who allots the wealth of mortals.
You, Aśvins, Heroes rich in treasures, daily seeking your friendship fain would I turn hither.

2 Knowing full well the Asura's time of coming, worship God Savitar with hymns and praises.
Let him who rightly knoweth speak with homage to him who dealeth out man's noblest treasure.

3 Not for reward doth Pūṣan send his blessings, Bhaga, or Aditi : his garb is splendour.
May Indra, Viṣṇu, Varuṇa, Mitra, Agni produce auspicious days, the Wonder-Workers.

4 Sending the shelter which we ask, the foeless Savitar and the Rivers shall approach us.
When I, the sacrifice's priest, invite them, may we be lords of wealth and rich possessions.

5 They who devote such worship to the Vasus, singing their hymns to Varuṇa and Mitra,
Vouchsafe them ample room, far off be danger. Through grace of Heaven and Earth may we be happy.

HYMN L. *Viśvedevas.*

1. LET every mortal man elect the friendship of the guiding God.
Each one solicits him for wealth and seeks renown to prosper him.

6 *They* : worshippers. *The Mothers* : the Dawns, or the regions of space, which clothe the Sun with light. *His Spouses* : the solar rays.

7 *Firm ground and room for resting* : 'stability and permanence.'—Wilson.

1 *Which as a magic energy* : or, what time the magic energy, that is Vāk, Voice or Speech.

2 *These* : Dawns. *Before* : yet to come.

3 *With pressing-stones* : in alliance with, and strengthened by them, that is, the libations which they aid. *He* : Indra. *The Guileful One*: Vṛtra. *Even he* : Indra as the Sun. *Whose hundred* : Sāyaṇa supplies, rays.

4 *His form* : Agni's.

5 *Varuṇa* : according to Sāyaṇa, *vāruṇaḥ* here is an adjective=*tamovārakaḥ*, darkness-repelling, and an epithet of Agni.

With the tongue : causing the worshipper to speak of him.

Naught by our human nature : all our knowledge of the God comes by his inspiration.

Bhaga : according to Sāyaṇa *bhágaḥ* here is an epithet of Savitar, mighty or adorable.

2 *The Asura's time of coming* : the approach of the divine Savitar.

3 *Aditi* : according to Sāyaṇa=*akhaṇḍanīyaḥ*, who cannot be impaired, used here as an epithet of Agni, understood, as are also *pūṣā*, 'nourishing, and *bhágaḥ*, 'adorable.' But Sāyaṇa gives also the alternative interpretation of the words as three deities.

The Ṛṣi is said to be Svasti (a name apparently borrowed from *svastaye* for weal, in stanza 5).

1 *The guiding God* : Savitar.

2 These, leading God, are thine, and these here ready to speak after us.
As such may we attain to wealth and wait with services on thee.
3 So further honour as our guests the Hero Gods and then the Dames.
May he remove and keep afar our foes and all who block our path.
4 Where fire is set, and swiftly runs the victim dwelling in the trough,
He wins, with heroes in his home, friendly to man, like constant streams.
5 May these thy riches, Leader God ! that rule the car, be blest to us,
Yea, blest to us for wealth and weal. This will we ponder praising strength, this ponder as we praise the God.

HYMN LI. *Viśvedevas.*

1. WITH all assistants, Agni, come hither to drink the Soma-juice;
With Gods unto our sacred gifts.
2 Come to the sacrifice, O ye whose ways are right, whose laws are true,
And drink the draught with Agni's tongue.
3 O Singer, with the singers, O Gracious, with those who move at dawn,
Come to the Soma-draught with Gods.
4 To Indra and to Vāyu dear, this Soma, by the mortar pressed,
Is now poured forth to fill the jar.
5 Vāyu, come hither to the feast, well-pleased unto our sacred gifts :
Drink of the Soma juice effused : come to the food.
6 Ye, Indra, Vāyu, well deserve to drink the juices pressed by us.
Gladly accept them, spotless Pair : come to the food.
7 For Indra and for Vāyu pressed are Soma juices blent with curd,
As rivers to the lowland flow : come to the food.
8 Associate with all the Gods, come, with the Aśvins and with Dawn,
Agni, as erst with Atri, so enjoy the juice.
9 Associate with Varuṇa, with Mitra, Soma, Viṣṇu, come,
Agni, as erst with Atri, so enjoy the juice.
10 Associate with Vasus, with Ādityas, Indra, Vāyu, come, Agni as erst with Atri, so enjoy the juice.
11 May Bhaga and the Aśvins grant us health and wealth, and Goddess Aditi and he whom none resist.
The Asura Pūṣan grant us all prosperity, and Heaven and Earth most wise vouchsafe us happiness.
12 Let us solicit Vāyu for prosperity, and Soma who is Lord of all the world for weal ;
For weal Bṛhaspati with all his company. May the Ādityas bring us health and happiness.
13 May all the Gods, may Agni the beneficent, God of all men, this day be with us for our weal.
Help us the Ṛbhus, the Divine Ones, for our good. May Rudra bless and keep us from calamity.
14 Prosper us, Mitra, Varuṇa. O wealthy Pathyā, prosper us.
Indra and Agni, prosper us; prosper us thou, O Aditi.
15 Like Sun and Moon may we pursue in full prosperity our path,
And meet with one who gives again, who knows us well and slays us not.

HYMN LII *Maruts.*

1. SING boldly forth, Śyāvāśva, with the Maruts who are loud in song,
Who, holy, as their wont is, joy in glory that is free from guile.

2 *These* : worshippers.
3 *The Dames* : Consorts of the Gods. *May he* : Savitar.
4 This stanza is obscure. *Dronyaḥ paśuḥ*, the victim or beast connected with, or dwelling in, the *droṇa*, tub or trough, is apparently the Soma. The meaning may be that the man who causes the sacrificial fire to be kindled and libations of Soma juice to be prepared is rewarded with brave sons and general prosperity.

---

1 *With all assistants* : 'with all the protecting deities.'—Wilson.
2 *O ye* : other Gods.
3 *O Singer* . Agni. *With the singers*: with the human priests. *Those who move at dawn* : the Gods who come to the morning sacrifice.
8 *As erst with Atri* : as thou wast accustomed to enjoy the libation offered by the ancient Atri, the progenitor of the Ṛṣi of the hymn.
11 *Health and wealth* : *svasti* ; well-being, prosperity. I have slightly varied the translation of the word, which recurs in every line of stanzas 11—14 and in the first line of 15. *The Asura* : the divine and immortal being. Sāyaṇa explains the word as the expeller of enemies, or the giver of life and strength.'
12 *With all his company* : with all the host of heaven.
14 *Wealthy Pathyā* : 'the rich path,' personified as a deity of happiness and welfare.
15 *Who gives again* : who repays the kindness we have shown him when he was our guest. These, as Professor Ludwig observes, are the wishes of a man who is starting on a journey to a distant place.

---

2 For in their boldness they are friends of firm and sure heroic strength.
They in their course, bold-spirited, guard all men of their own accord.

3 Like steers in rapid motion they advance and overtake the nights;
And thus the Maruts' power in heaven and on the earth we celebrate.

4 With boldness to your Maruts let us offer laud and sacrifice :
Who all, through ages of mankind, guard mortal man from injury.

5 Praiseworthy, givers of good gifts, Heroes with full and perfect strength—
To Maruts, Holy Ones of heaven, will I extol the sacrifice.

6 The lofty Heroes cast their spears and weapons bright with gleaming gold.
After these Maruts followed close, like laughing lightning from the sky, a splendour of its own accord.

7 They who waxed mighty, of the earth, they who are in the wide mid-air,
Or in the rivers' compass, or in the abode of ample heaven.

8 Praise thou the Maruts' company, the valorous and truly strong,
The Heroes, hasting, by themselves have yoked their deer for victory.

9 Fair-gleaming, on Paruṣṇī they have clothed themselves in robes of wool,
And with their chariot tires they cleave the rock asunder in their might.

10 Whether as wanderers from the way or speeders on or to the path,
Under these names the spreading band tend well the sacrifice for me.

11 To this the Heroes well attend, well do their teams attend to this.
Visible are their varied forms. Behold, they are Pārāvatas.

12 Hymn-singing, seeking water, they, praising, have danced about the spring.
What are they unto me? No thieves, but helpers, splendid to behold.

13 Sublime, with lightnings for their spears, Sages and Orderers are they.
Ṛsi, adore that Marut host, and make them happy with thy song.

14 Ṛṣi, invite the Marut band with offerings, as a maid her friend.
From heaven, too, Bold Ones, in your might haste hither glorified with songs.

15 Thinking of these now let him come, as with the escort of the Gods,
And with the splendid Princes, famed for rapid courses, to the gifts.

16 Princes, who, when I asked their kin, named Pṛśni as their Mother-cow,
And the impetuous Rudra they, the Mighty Ones, declared their Sire.

17 The mighty ones, the seven times seven, have singly given me hundred gifts.
I have obtained on Yamunā famed wealth in kine and wealth in steeds.

HYMN LIII. *Maruts.*

1. Who knows the birth of these, or who lived in the Maruts' favour in the days of old

9 *Paruṣṇī* : one of the rivers of the Panjāb, now called the Rāvī. *Robes of wool* : the fleecy vapours which rise from the waters. See IV. 22. 2.

11 *Pārāvatas* : a tribe who dwelt on the banks of the Paruṣṇī who may have been in the habit of making sudden incursions into the country through which the Sindhu or Indus flows.

12 *Seeking water* : this is Sāyaṇa's explanation of *kubhanyavaḥ*, the meaning of which is uncertain. *The spring*: apparently, the cloud. According to Sāyaṇa the reference is to the water—or the well—which was miraculously brought to the thirsting Gotama by the Maruts. See I. 85. 11. The stanza is difficult and obscure.

14 *As a maid her friend* : this seems to be the meaning of *mitrám ná yoṣáṇā*, which Sāyaṇa explains, as a friend (or as Āditya, the Sun) with praise.

15 The three concluding stan as are very difficult, and attempts at translation and explanation must be purely conjectural. The following is the substance of Professor Ludwig's note. Śākins [mighty ones] in stanza 17 are apparently a clan (yajamānāḥ, or instititors of sacrifice) whose number consisting of a multiple of seven, gave occasion to their comparison to the Maruts, and an easy transition to the *dānastuti* or eulogy of their liberality. The construction is : now thinking of these sacrificers [or, Maruts] may he [the Ṛṣi] come together, as with the escort of the Gods (invited in stanza 14,) in company with [the Maruts or the] Sūris to the sacrificial offerings.

Stanza 16 is to be understood figuratively as eulogy of the Śākins who are here directly identified with the Maruts. The priest must know the lineage of the sacrificers, because in certain ceremonies he must proclaim their names, and here Śākins are considered to have inherited their liberality from Pṛśni as their mother and their power from Rudra as their father.

17 *The Mighty Ones* : or the Śākins, as Professor Ludwig explains.

The seven times seven : there are said to be seven troops of the Maruts, each consisting of seven. The Śākins, or powerful institutors of sacrifice, appear to be intended here (see preceding note) as compared to, or identified with the Maruts. *On Yamunā* : on the banks of the river now known as the Jumna.

This and all Ṛgveda hymns addressed to the Maruts have been translated and thoroughly discussed by Professor Max Müller in Vedic Hymns, Part I. (Sacred Books of the East, Vol. XXXII.)

1 *Of these* : Gods : the Maruts.

What time their spotted deer were yoked?

2 Who, when they stood upon their cars, hath heard them tell the way they went?
Who was the bounteous man to whom their kindred rains flowed down with food of sacrifice?

3 To me they told it, and they came with winged steeds radiant to the draught,
Youths, Heroes free from spot or stain: Behold us here and praise thou us;

4 Who shine self-luminous with ornaments and swords, with breastplates, armlets, and with wreaths,
Arrayed on chariots and with bows.

5 O swift to pour your bounties down, ye Maruts, with delight I look upon your cars,
Like splendours coming through the rain.

6 Munificent Heroes, they have cast heaven's treasury down for the worshipper's behoof:
They set the storm-cloud free to stream through both the worlds, and rainfloods flow o'er desert spots.

7 The bursting streams in billowy flood have spread abroad, like milch-kine, o'er the firmament.
Like swift steeds hasting to their journey's resting-place, to every side run glittering brooks.

8 Hither, O Maruts, come from heaven, from mid-air, or from near at hand:
Tarry not far away from us.

9 So let not Rasā, Krumu, or Anitabhā, Kubhā, or Sindhu hold you back.
Let not the watery Sarayu obstruct your way. With us be all the bliss ye give.

10 That brilliant gathering of your cars, the company of Maruts, of the Youthful Ones,
The rain-showers, speeding on, attend.

11 With eulogies and hymns may we follow your army, troop by troop, and band by band,
And company by company.

12 To what oblation-giver, sprung of noble ancestry, have sped
The Maruts on this course to-day?

13 Vouchsafe to us the bounty, that which we implore, through which, for child and progeny,
Ye give the seed of corn that wasteth not away, and bliss that reacheth to all life.

14 May we in safety pass by those who slander us, leaving behind disgrace and hate.
Maruts, may we be there when ye, at dawn, in rest and toil, rain waters down and balm.

15 Favoured by Gods shall be the man, O Heroes, Maruts! and possessed of noble sons,
Whom ye protect. Such may we be.

16 Praise the Free-givers. At this liberal patron's rite they joy like cattle in the mead.
So call thou unto them who come as ancient Friends: hymn those who love thee with a song.

HYMN LIV. *Maruts.*

1. THIS hymn will I make for the Marut host who bright in native splendour cast the mountains down.
Sing the great strength of those illustrious in renown, who stay the heat, who sacrifice on heights of heaven.

2 O Maruts, rich in water, strengtheners of life are your strong bands with harnessed steeds, that wander far.
Trita roars out at him who aims the lightning-flash. The waters sweeping round are thundering on their way.

3 They gleam with lightning, Heroes, Casters of the Stone, wind-rapid Maruts, overthrowers of the hills,
Oft through desire to rain coming with storm of hail, roaring in onset, violent and exceeding strong.

4 When, mighty Rudras, through the nights and through the days, when through the sky and realms of air, shakers of all,

9 *Rasā*: a river, probably an affluent of the Sindhu or Indus as *Anita hā* also seems to have been. *Krumu*: a tributary of the Indus, identified by some with the Kurum. *Kukhā*: the Kophen, or Kābul river which falls into the Indus near Attock. *Sarayu*: probably a river in the Panjāb which gave its name to the Sarayu or Sarjū of Oudh.

1 *Who sacrifice on heights of heaven*: 'to whom solemn rites are familiar; by whom the sacrifices called *Pṛṣtha* are made.'—Wilson. The word *pṛṣthá* is ambiguous, signifying both height or ridge and a certain arrangement of hymns (see IV. 20. 4). So also *gharmá* in the same half-line signifies both heat and an oblation of hot milk or other heated beverage, and the meaning of the compound *gharmastúbhe* is accordingly ambiguous.

2 *Trita*: the Vedic God who frequently appears in connexion with the Maruts. According to Sāyaṇa, *Trita* is the cloud or company of Maruts stationed in three places.

When over the broad fields ye drive along like ships, e'en to strongholds ye come, Maruts, but are not harmed.

5 Maruts, this hero strength and majesty of yours hath, like the Sun, extended o'er a lengthened way,
When in your course like deer with splendour unsubdued ye bowed the hill that gives imperishable rain.

6 Bright shone your host, ye Sages, Maruts, when ye smote the waving tree as when the worm consumeth it.
Accordant, as the eye guides him who walks, have ye led our devotion onward by an easy path.

7 Never is he, O Maruts, slain or overcome, never doth he decay ne'er is distressed or harmed;
His treasures, his resources, never waste away, whom, whether he be prince or Ṛṣi, ye direct.

8 With harnessed team like heroes overcoming troops, the friendly Maruts, laden with their water-casks,
Let the spring flow, and when impetuous they roar they inundate the earth with floods of pleasant meath.

9 Free for the Maruts is the earth with sloping ways, free for the rushing Ones is heaven with steep descents.
The paths of air's mid-region are precipitous, precipitous the mountains with their running streams.

10 When, as the Sun hath risen up, ye take delight, O bounteous radiant Maruts, Heroes of the sky,
Your coursers weary not when speeding on their way, and rapidly ye reach the end of this your path.

11 Lances are on your shoulders, anklets on your feet, gold chains are on your breasts, gems, Maruts, on your car.
Lightnings aglow with flame are flashing in your hands, and visors wrought of gold are laid upon your heads.

12 Maruts, in eager stir ye shake the vault of heaven, splendid beyond conception, for its shining fruit.
They gathered when they let their deeds of might flash forth. The Pious Ones send forth a far-resounding shout.

13 Sage Maruts, may we be the drivers of the car of riches full of life that have been given by you.
O Maruts, let that wealth in thousands dwell with us which never vanishes like Tiṣya from the sky.

14 Maruts, ye further wealth with longed-for heroes, further the Ṛṣi skilled in chanted verses.
Ye give the Bharata as his strength, a charger, and ye bestow a king who quickly listens.

15 Of you, most swift to succour! I solicit wealth wherewith we may spread forth mid men like as the Sun.
Accept, O Maruts, graciously this hymn of mine that we may live a hundred winters through its power.

HYMN LV. *Maruts.*

1. WITH gleaming lances, with their breasts adorned with gold, the Maruts, rushing onward, hold high power of life.
They hasten with swift steeds easy to be controlled. Their cars moved onward as they went to victory.

2 Ye, as ye wist, have gained of your own selves your power: high, O ye Mighty Ones, and wide ye shine abroad.
They with their strength have even measured out the sky.
Their cars moved onward as they went to victory.

3 Strong, born together, they together have waxed great: the Heroes more and more have grown to majesty
Resplendent as the Sun's beams in their light are they. Their cars moved onward as they went to victory.

4 Maruts, your mightiness deserves to be adored, sight to be longed for like the shining of the Sun.
So lead us with your aid to immortality.

12 *For its shining fruit*: the bright water.
13 *The drivers of the car*: that is, the controllers. May we by our prayers and sacrifices bring down and enjoy the riches which you give.

Tiṣya: an asterism regarded as shaped like an arrow and containing three stars. According to Sāyaṇa *Tiṣya* here is synonymous with Āditya.

14 *The Bharata*: a warrior, or one of family of Bharata. See Index. According to Sāyaṇa, Śyāvāśva the Ṛṣi of the hymn is intended: 'to (me) the ministrant priest.' Wilson.

Who quickly listens: to his people's prayers. Sāyaṇa explains *śruṣṭimántam* as *sukhavantam*, happy and prosperous.

15 *A hundred winters*: a frequently occurring expression, 'from which we might infer,' says Dr. J. Muir, 'that the Indians still retained some recollection of their having at one time occupied a colder country.' See *Original Sanskrit Texts*, II. 323.

Their cars moved onward as they went to victory.

5 O Maruts, from the Ocean ye uplift the rain, and fraught with vaporous moisture pour the torrents down.
Never, ye Wonder-Workers, are your Milch-kine dry. Their cars moved onward as they went to victory.

6 When to your car-poles ye have yoked your spotted deer to be your steeds, and put your golden mantles on,
O Maruts, ye disperse all enemies abroad. Their cars moved onward as they went to victory.

7 Neither the mountains nor the rivers keep you back: whither ye have resolved thither ye, Maruts, go.
Ye compass round about even the heaven and earth. Their cars moved onward as they went to victory.

Whate'er is ancient, Maruts, what of recent time, whate'er is spoken, Vasus, what is chanted forth,
They who take cognizance of all of this are ye. Their cars moved onward as they went to victory.

9 Be gracious unto us, ye Maruts, slay us not: extend ye unto us shelter of many a sort.
Pay due regard unto our friendship and our praise. Their cars moved onward as they went to victory.

10 O Maruts, lead us on to higher fortune: deliver us, when lauded, from afflictions.
Accept, ye Holy Ones, the gifts we bring you. May we be masters of abundant riches.

HYMN LVI. *Maruts.*

1. Agni, that valorous company adorned with ornaments of gold,
The people of the Maruts, I call down to-day even from the luminous realm of heaven.

2 Even as thou thinkest in thy heart, thither my wishes also tend.
Those who have come most near to thine invoking calls, strengthen them fearful to behold.

3 Earth, like a bounteous lady, liberal of her gifts, struck down and shaken, yet exultant, comes to us.
Impetuous as a bear, O Maruts, is your rush terrible as a dreadful bull.

4 They who with mighty strength o'erthrow like oxen difficult to yoke,
Cause e'en the heavenly stone to shake, yea, shake the rocky mountain as they race along.

5 Rise up! even now with lauds I call the very numerous company,
Unequalled, of these Maruts, like a herd of kine, grown up together in their strength.

6 Bind to your car the bright red mares, yoke the red coursers to your car.
Bind to the pole, to draw, the fleet-foot tawny steeds, the best at drawing, to the pole.

7 Yea, and this loudly-neighing bright red vigorous horse who hath been stationed, fair to see,
Let him not cause delay, O Maruts, in your course, urge ye him onward in your cars.

8 The Maruts' chariot, ever fain to gather glory, we invoke,
Which Rodasī hath mounted, bringing pleasant gifts, with Maruts in her company.

9 I call that brilliant band of yours, adorable, rapid on the car
Whereon the bounteous Dame, auspicious, nobly born, shows glorious with the Marut host.

HYMN LVII. *Maruts.*

1. Of one accord, with Indra, O ye Rudras, come borne on your golden car for our prosperity.
An offering from us, this hymn is brought to you, as, unto one who thirsts for water, heavenly springs.

5 *Your Milch-kine*: the rain-clouds.

---

2 *Strengthen them*: that is, the Maruts, with oblations.

3 The exact meaning of the first line is somewhat uncertain. Sāyaṇa explains it: 'As the earth—that is the people of the earth—having a powerful master, when oppressed by others, has recourse to him her own master, so the army of Maruts comes exulting to us.' But *mīḷhuṣmatī* (bounteous, liberal, bringing forth abundant fruit) cannot mean *prabalasvāmikā*, having a powerful master.

Struck down: by the rain sent by the Maruts.

7 *Who hath been stationed*: or harnessed to the car.

8 *Rodasī*: the Consort of Rudra and mother of the Maruts.

9 *The bounteous Dame*: Rodasī. *Shows glorious*: or, is glorified.

---

1 *O ye Rudras*: or Sons of Rudra. *For our prosperity*: 'to the accessible (sacrifice).'—Wilson. *Heavenly springs*: an allusion, says Sāyaṇa, to the well, that is, the cloud which was brought by the Maruts to thirsty Gotama. See I. 85. 11.

2 Armed with your daggers, full of wisdom, armed with spears, armed with your quivers, armed with arrows, with good bows,
Good horses and good cars have ye, O Pṛśni's Sons : ye, Maruts, with good weapons go to victory.

3 From hills and heaven ye shake wealth for the worshipper : in terror at your coming low the woods bow down.
Ye make the earth to tremble, Sons of Pṛśni, when for victory ye have yoked, fierce Ones ! your spotted deer.

4 Bright with the blasts of wind, wrapped in their robes of rain, like twins of noble aspect and of lovely form,
The Maruts, spotless, with steeds tawny-hued and red, strong in their mightiness and spreading wide like heaven.

5 Rich in adornment, rich in drops, munificent, bright in their aspect, yielding bounties that endure,
Noble by birth, adorned with gold upon their breasts, the Singers of the sky have won immortal fame.

6 Borne on both shoulders, O ye Maruts, are your spears : within your arms is laid your energy and strength.
Bold thoughts are in your heads, your weapons in your cars, all glorious majesty is moulded on your forms.

7 Vouchsafe to us, O Maruts, splendid bounty in cattle and in steeds, in cars and heroes.
Children of Rudra, give us high distinction : may I enjoy your Godlike help and favour.

8 Ho ! Maruts, Heroes, skilled in Law, immortal, be gracious unto us, ye rich in treasures,
Ye hearers of the truth, ye sage and youthful, grown mighty, dwelling on the lofty mountains.

HYMN LVIII. *Maruts.*

1. Now do I glorify their mighty cohort, the company of these the youthful Maruts,
Who ride impetuous on with rapid horses, and radiant in themselves, are Lords of Amṛta.

2 The mighty glittering band, arm-bound with bracelets, givers of bliss, unmeasured in their greatness,
With magical powers, bountiful, ever-roaring,—these, liberal Heroes, venerate thou singer.

3 This day may all your water-bringers, Maruts, they who impel the falling rain, approach us.
This fire, O Maruts, hath been duly kindled ; let it find favour with you, youthful Sages.

4 Ye raise up for the folk an active ruler whom, Holy Ones ! a Master's hand hath fashioned.
Ye send the fighter hand to hand, arm-mighty, and the brave hero, Maruts ! with good horses.

5 They spring forth more and more, strong in their glories, like days, like spokes where none are last in order.
Highest and mightiest are the Sons of Pṛśni. Firm to their own intention cling the Maruts.

6 When ye have hastened on with spotted coursers, O Maruts, on your cars with strong-wrought fellies,
The waters are disturbed, the woods are shattered. Let Dyaus the Red Steer send his thunder downward.

7 Even Earth hath spread herself wide at their coming, and they as husbands have with power impregned her.
They to the pole have yoked the winds for coursers: their sweat have they made rain, these Sons of Rudra.

8 Ho ! Maruts, Heroes, skilled in Law, immortal, be gracious unto us, ye rich in treasures,
Ye hearers of the truth, ye sage and youthful, grown mighty, dwelling on the lofty mountains.

4 *Like twins* : all alike.

5 *The Singers of the sky* : chanters of their thunder-psalm.

6 *Bold thoughts* : Sāyaṇa explains *nṛmṇā=nṛmṇāni* as golden tiaras. The word *uṛmṇá* in one or another of its cases occurs some thirty times in the Ṛgveda, and always in the sense of manly power, valour, or valorous deed.

8 *Ye hearers of the truth* : or, famous for your truth, for the realization of your promises.

1 *Lords of Amṛta* : controllers of the sweet life-giving rain.

2 *Arm-bound with bracelets* : or, rather, 'adorned with quoits on their hands.'—M. Müller.

4 *Whom...a Master's hand hath fashioned* : according to Sāyaṇa *vibhvataṣṭám* means fabricated or modelled by Vibhvan, the second of the three Ṛbhus, i. e. *atyantarūpavantam* or exceedingly handsome. *The fighter hand to hand* : the man who fights on foot is your gift as well as the warrior who is borne to battle in a chariot.

HYMN LIX. *Maruts.*

1. YOUR spy hath called to you to give prosperity. I sing to Heaven and Earth and offer sacrifice.
They bathe their steeds and hasten through the firmament : they spread abroad their radiance through the sea of cloud.

2 Earth shakes and reels in terror at their onward rush, like a full ship which, quivering, lets the water in.
Marked on their ways are they, visible from afar : the Heroes press between in mighty armament.

3 As the exalted horn of bulls for splendid might, as the Sun's eye set in the firmament's expanse,
Like vigorous horses ye are beauteous to behold, and for your glory show like bridegrooms, O ye Men.

4 Who, O ye Maruts, may attain the mighty lore of you the mighty, who may reach your manly deeds?
Ye, verily, make earth tremble like a ray of light what time ye bring your boons to give prosperity.

5 Like steeds of ruddy colour, scions of one race, as foremost champions they have battled in the van.
The Heroes have waxed strong like well-grown manly youths; with floods of rain they make the Sun's eye fade away.

6 Having no eldest and no youngest in their band, no middlemost, preëminent they have waxed in might,
These Sons of Pṛśni, sprung of noble ancestry : come hitherward to us, ye bridegrooms of the sky.

7 Like birds of air they flew with might in lengthened lines from heaven's high ridges to the borders of the sky.
The steeds who carry them, as Gods and mortals know, have caused the waters of the mountains to descend.

8 May Dyaus, the Infinite, roar for our banquet : may Dawns toil for us, glittering with moisture.
Lauded by thee, these Maruts, Sons o Rudra, O Ṛṣi, have sent down the heavenly treasure.

1 *Your spy* : Agni, as the lightning. According to Sāyana *spất* is for *spraṣṭā*, one who touches (the oblation), the Hotar or presenting priest.

2 *Press between* : rush through the air between heaven and earth.

7 *Gods and mortals* : the text has only *ubhấye*, both (sides or parties). The word generally means Gods and men; but perhaps, as Professor Ludwig suggests, Heaven and Earth may be intended here.

8 *Dyaus, the Infinite* : Cf. X. 63. 3.

HYMN LX. *Maruts.*

1. I LAUD with reverence the gracious Agni : here may he sit and part our meed among us.
As with spoil-seeking cars I bring oblation: turned rightward I will swell the Marut's praise-song.

2 The Maruts, yea, the Rudras, who have mounted their famous spotted deer and cars swift-moving,—
Before you, fierce Ones ! woods bow down in terror : Earth, even the mountain, trembles at your coming.

3 Though vast and tall, the mountain is affrighted, the height of heaven is shaken at your roaring
When, armed with lances, ye are sporting, Maruts, and rush along together like the waters.

4 They, like young suitors, sons of wealthy houses, have with their golden natures decked their bodies.
Strong on their cars, the lordly Ones, for glory, have set their splendours on their forms for ever.

5 None being eldest, none among them youngest, as brothers they have grown to happy fortune.
May their Sire Rudra, young and deft, and Pṛśni pouring much milk, bring fair days to the Maruts.

6 Whether, O blessed Maruts, ye be dwelling in highest, midmost, or in lowest heaven,
Thence, O ye Rudras, and thou also, Agni, notice the sacrificial food we offer.

7 O Maruts, Lords of all, when Agni and when ye drive downward from sublimest heaven along the heights,
Shakers of all, rejoicing, slayers of the foe, give riches to the Soma pressing worshipper.

1 *Turned rightward* : making reverential salutation by circumambulation from left to right ; the Gaelic *deasil*.

4 *With their golden natures* : with some hesitation I follow Professor Ludwig in taking *hiraṇyaiḥ*, as an old form of the feminine, with *svadhấbhiḥ*. Professor Wilson, following Sāyaṇa, translates : 'with golden (ornaments) and purifying waters.'

5 *Pouring much milk* : Pṛśni, the mother of the Maruts, the cloud of the firmament, being represented as a cow.

Bring fair days to the Maruts : perhaps the bright weather which follows the Rains. 'Grant favourable days for (the sake of) the Maruts.'—Wilson.

8 O Agni, with the Maruts as they gleam and sing, gathered in troop, rejoicing drink the Soma juice;
With these the living ones who cleanse and further all, joined with thy banner, O Vaiśvānara, from of old.

HYMN LXI. *Maruts.*

1. O HEROES lordliest of all, who are ye that have singly come
Forth from a region most remote?

2 Where are your horses, where the reins? How came ye? how had ye the power?
Rein was on nose and seat on back.

3 The whip is laid upon the flank. The heroes stretch their thighs apart,
Like women when the babe is born.

4 Go ye, O Heroes, far away, ye bridegrooms with a lovely Spouse
That ye may warm you at the fire.

5 May she gain cattle for her meed, hundreds of sheep and steeds and kine,
Who threw embracing arms around the hero whom Śyāvāśva praised.

6 Yea, many a woman is more firm and better than the man who turns
Away from Gods, and offers not.

7 She who discerns the weak and worn, the man who thirsts and is in want:
She sets her mind upon the Gods.

8 And yet full many a one, unpraised, mean niggard, is entitled man:
Only in weregild is he such.

9 And she, the young, the joyous-spirited, divulged the path to Śyāva, yea, to me.
Two red steeds carried me to Purumīḷha's side, that sage of far-extended fame,

10 Him who, like Vaidadaśvi, like Taranta, hath bestowed on me
A hundred cows in liberal gift.

11 They who are borne by rapid steeds, drinking the meath that gives delight,
They have attained high glories here.

12 They by whose splendour both the worlds are over-spread they shine on cars
As the gold gleams above in heaven.

13 That Marut band is ever young, borne on bright cars, unblamable,
Moving to victory, checked by none.

14 Who knoweth, verily, of these where the All-shakers take delight,
Born, spotless, after sacred Law?

15 Guides are ye, lovers of the song to mortal man through holy hymn,
And hearers when he cries for help.

16 Do ye, destroyers of the foe, worshipful and exceeding bright,
Send down the treasures that we crave.

17 O Ūrmyā, bear thou far away to Dārbhya this my hymn of praise,
Songs, Goddess, as if chariot-borne.

18 From me to Rathavīti say, when he hath pressed the Soma juice,
The wish I had departeth not.

19 This wealthy Rathavīti dwells among the people rich in kine,
Among the mountains, far withdrawn.

HYMN LXII. *Mitra-Varuṇa.*

1. By your high Law firm order is established there where they loose for travel Sūrya's horses.
Ten hundred stood together: there I looked on this the most marvellous Deities' one chief glory.

2 This, Mitra-Varuṇa, is your special greatness: floods that stood there they with the days attracted.

---

8 *Joined with thy banner*: closely connected with thy ensign or banner of flame.

4 *With a lovely Spouse*: apparently Rodasī, who is sometimes regarded as the wife of the whole band of Maruts.

5 *She*: according to Sāyaṇa, the wife of Taranta (stanza 10) who is 'the hero whom Śyāvāśva praised.'

6 *More firm*: the word thus rendered, *śáśīyasī*, is taken by Sāyaṇa to be the name of Taranta's wife.

8 *Only in weregild*: only as regards the fine to be paid for manslaughter, either by him or for him, can he be accounted a man. The verse is obscure. See Vedic Hymns (Sacred Books of the East), Part I. p. 360, and Ludwig. Ueber die neuesten Arbeiten, &c., p. 40.

9 *And she*: Taranta's wife. *Śyāva* = Śyāvāśva, the Ṛṣi of the hymn.

10 *Vaidadaśvi*: Purumīḷha, son of Vidadaśva.

11 This stanza is apparently the beginning of a separate hymn, in honour of the Maruts.

12 *As the gold*: the golden Sun.

17 *Ūrmyā*: Goddess of Night. *Dārbhya*: Rathavīti, son of Darbha.

18 *The wish I had*: to perform a sacrifice for the rich and liberal Rathavīti.

---

1 *By your high Law*: the eternal order of the universe, which in the region of the Sun regulates the starting and the journeying of his horses, depends on, or is identical with, the everlasting statutes of Mitra and Varuṇa. *Ten hundred*: rays of the Sun. *One chief glory*: the orb of the Sun, the noblest visible form of Agni and other Gods.

2 *Floods that stood there*: they, that is the sunbeams, have in the course of days milked out or attracted to themselves the waters that stood apart from the Sun *Tasthuṣīḥ* (standing, stationary) has no substantive expressed, and the meaning of the milch-kine of the firmament. The *voices* are probably the thunder and the roar of the

Ye cause to flow all voices of the cow-pen : your single chariotfelly hath rolled hither.

3 O Mitra-Varuṇa, ye by your greatness, both Kings, have firmly stablished earth and heaven,
Ye caused the cows to stream, the plants to flourish, and, scattering swift drops, sent down the rain-flood.

4 Let your well-harnessed horses bear you hither : hitherward let them come with reins drawn tightly.
A covering cloud of sacred oil attends you, and your streams flow to us from days aforetime.

5 To make the lustre wider and more famous, guarding the sacred grass with veneration,
Ye, Mitra-Varuṇa, firm, strong, awe-inspiring, are seated on a throne amid oblations.

6 With hands that shed no blood, guarding the pious, whom, Varuṇa, ye save amid oblations.
Ye Twain, together, Kings of willing spirit, uphold dominion based on thousand pillars.

7 Adorned with gold, its columns are of iron : in heaven it glitters like a whip for horses;
Or stablished on a field deep-spoiled and fruitful. So may we share the meath that loads your car-seat.

8 Ye mount your car gold-hued at break of morning, and iron-pillared when the Sun is setting,
And from that place, O Varuṇa and Mitra, behold infinity and limitation.

9 Bountiful guardians of the world ! the shelter that is impenetrable, strongest, flawless,
Aid us with that, O Varuṇa and Mitra, and when we long to win may we be victors.

HYMN LXIII. *Mitra-Varuṇa.*

1. Guardians of Order, ye whose Laws are ever true, in the sublimest heaven your chariot ye ascend.
O Mitra-Varuṇa whomsoe'er ye favour, here, to him the rain with sweetness streameth down from heaven.

2 This world's imperial Kings, O Mitra-Varuṇa, ye rule in holy synod, looking on the light.
We pray for rain, your boon, and immortality. Through heaven and over earth the thunderers take their way.

3 Imperial Kings, strong, Heroes, Lords of earth and heaven, Mitra and Varuṇa, ye ever active Ones,
Ye wait on thunder with the many-tinted clouds, and by the Asura's magic power cause Heaven to rain.

4 Your magic, Mitra-Varuṇa, resteth in the heaven. The Sun, the wondrous weapon, cometh forth as light.
Ye hide him in the sky with cloud and flood of rain, and water-drops, Parjanya! full of sweetness flow.

5 The Maruts yoke their easy car for victory, O Mitra-Varuṇa, as a hero in the wars.
The thunderers roam through regions varied in their hues. Imperial Kings, bedew us with the milk of heaven.

6 Refreshing is your voice, O Mitra-Varuṇa : Parjanya sendeth out a wondrous mighty voice.
With magic power the Maruts clothe them with the clouds. Ye Two cause Heaven to rain, the red, the spotless One.

rushing rain. *Your single chariot-felly* : the circumference or felly of the wheel being, by metonymy, put for the chariot.

4 *A covering cloud of sacred oil* : of *ghṛta*, butter, *i. e.* fertilizing rain.

5 *On a throne* : or on your car.

6 *Ye save amid oblations* : the sacrificial hall with its precincts being regarded as an inviolable asylum.

7 *Adorned with gold* :—the chariot of Mitra and Varuṇa. *Like a whip for horses* : according to Sāyaṇa, the whip is the lightning and the horses are the flying clouds.

Or stablished : the meaning of this third Pāda is not clear. Professor Wilson, following Sāyaṇa, translates : 'may we load the vehicle with the libation in an auspicious pace, or in the sacrificial hall, (where the columns) are erected.'

8 *Iron-pillared* : the chariot which shines like gold in the light of the rising sun looks dim and dark like bronze or iron at sunset.

Infinity and limitation : *áditim ditim ca* ; according to Sāyaṇa, Aditi or the Earth as an indivisible whole, and Diti as representing the divisible people and living creatures inhabiting it. Aditi appears to mean infinite Nature, and Diti to be a Goddess connected with Aditi without any distinct conception, and merely as a contrast to her. The two words may perhaps mean the eternal and the perishable, yonder boundless space and the bounded space near us, or Sky and Earth, or Nature by day and Nature by night. 'At all events, as Dr. Muir observes, 'the two together appear to be put by the poet for the entire aggregate of visible nature.' See *Original Sanskrit Texts*, V. pp. 42, 43.

The hymn is a prayer for rain.

2 *The thunderers* : the roaring winds.

3 *The Asnra's magic power* : the Asura or divine Being here is either Dyaus or Parjanya.

7 Wise, with your Law and through the Asura's magic power ye guard the ordinances, Mitra-Varuṇa.
Ye by eternal Order govern all the world. Ye set the Sun in heaven as a refulgent car.

HYMN LXIV. *Mitra-Varuṇa*

1. You, foeman-slaying Varuṇa and Mitra, we invoke with song,
Who, as with penfold of your arms, encompass round the realm of light.

2 Stretch out your arms with favouring love unto this man who singeth hymns,
For in all places is sung forth your ever-gracious friendliness.

3 That I may gain a refuge now, may my steps be on Mitra's path.
Men go protected in the charge of this dear Friend who harms us not.

4 Mitra and Varuṇa, from you may I, by song, win noblest meed.
That shall stir envy in the homes of wealthy chiefs and those who praise.

5 With your fair splendours, Varuṇa and Mitra, to our gathering come,
That in their homes the wealthy chiefs and they who are your friends may thrive.

6 With those, moreover, among whom ye hold your high supremacy,
Vouchsafe us room that we may win strength for prosperity and wealth.

7 When morning flushes, Holy Ones ! in the Gods' realm where white Cows shine,
Supporting Arcanānas, speed, ye Heroes, with your active feet hither to my pressed Soma juice.

HYMN LXV. *Mitra-Varuṇa.*

1. Full wise is he who hath discerned : let him speak to us of the Gods,—
The man whose praise-songs Varuṇa the beautiful, or Mitra, loves.

2 For they are Kings of noblest might, of glorious fame most widely spread;
Lords of the brave, who strengthen Law, the Holy Ones with every race.

3 Approaching you with prayer for aid, together I address you first
We who have good steeds call on you, Most Sage, to give us strength besides.

4 E'en out of misery Mitra gives a way to dwelling at our ease,
For he who worships hath the grace of Mitra, fighter in the van.

5 In Mitra's shelter that extends to utmost distance may we dwell,
Unmenaced, guarded by the care, ever as sons of Varuṇa.

6 Ye, Mitra, urge this people on, and to one end direct their ways.
Neglect not ye the wealthy chiefs, neglect not us the Ṛṣis : be our guardians when ye quaff the milk.

HYMN LXVI. *Mitra-Varuṇa.*

1. O sapient man, call the Two Gods, the very wise, who slay the foe.
For Varuṇa, whose form is Law, place offerings for his great delight.

2 For they have won unbroken sway in full perfection, power divine.
And, like high laws, the world of man hath been made beautiful as light.

3 Therefore we praise you that your cars may travel far in front of ours—
You who accept the eulogy of Rātahavya with his hymns.

4 And ye show wisdom, Wondrous Gods ! with fulness of intelligence.
By men's discernment are ye marked, O ye whose might is purified.

---

1 *With penfold of your arms* : I follow Professor Ludwig in taking *vrajā* as an instrumental case.

3 *May my steps be* : may I walk in the way of Mitra, that is, may I keep his holy law.

5 *The wealthy chiefs* : the institutors of sacrifice. *Your friends* : we, the priests.

6 *With those* : with the Gods.

7 *White Cows* : the white clouds of early morning. *Arcanānas* : the Ṛṣi of the hymn. *With your active feet*: the literal translation of *hastibhiḥ padbhiḥ* would be, with feet provided with hands : 'With rapid steeds.' —Wilson. See M. Bloomfield, Contributions to the Interpretation of the Veda, Second Series, p. 35.

1 *Of the Gods* : regarding Mitra and Varuṇa.

5 *As sons of Varuṇa* : or perhaps, as Professor Ludwig suggests, with Varuṇa as our son, that is with kingly descendants.

6 *Ye, Mitra* : and Varuṇa.

When ye quaff the milk : 'in the presenting of the libation.'—Wilson.

1 *O Sapient man* : thou who knowest how to praise the Gods.

Whose form is Law : according to Sāyaṇa, 'whose form is water.'

2 *Like high laws* : Professor Ludwig would read *vratena* instead of *vratéva*, that is, through holy ordinance.

3 *Rātahavya* : the Ṛṣi of the hymn. I can make nothing out of this stanza, and I follow Sāyaṇa in despair of finding a reasonable interpretation.

4 This stanza also is difficult and obscure.

5 This is the Law sublime, O Earth : to aid the Ṛṣis' toil for fame
The Two, wide-spreading, are prepared. They come with ample overflow.

6 Mitra, ye Gods with wandering eyes, would that the worshippers and we
Might strive to reach the realm ye rule, most spacious and protected well.

HYMN LXVII. *Mitra-Varuṇa.*

1. YE Gods, Ādityas, Varuṇa, Aryaman, Mitra, verily
Have here obtained supremest sway, high, holy, set apart for you.

2 When, Varuṇa and Mitra, ye sit in your golden dwelling-place,
Ye Twain, supporters of mankind, foe-slayers, give felicity.

3 All these, possessors of all wealth, Varuṇa, Mitra, Aryaman,
Follow their ways, as if with feet, and guard from injury mortal man.

4 For they are true, they cleave to Law, held holy among every race,
Good leaders, bounteous in their gifts, deliverers even from distress.

5 Which of your persons, Varuṇa or Mitra, merits not our praise ?
Therefore our thought is turned to you, the Atris' thought is turned to you.

HYMN LXVIII. *Mitra-Varuṇa.*

1. SING forth unto your Varuṇa and Mitra with a song inspired.
They, Mighty Lords, are lofty Law :

2 Full springs of fatness, Sovran Kings, Mitra and Varuṇa, the Twain,
Gods glorified among the Gods.

3 So help ye us to riches, great terrestrial and celestial wealth :
Vast is your sway among the Gods.

4 Carefully tending Law with Law they have attained their vigorous might.
The two Gods wax devoid of guile.

5 With rainy skies and streaming floods, Lords of the strength that bringeth gifts,
A lofty seat have they attained.

HYMN LXIX. *Mitra-Varuṇa.*

1. THREE spheres of light, O Varuṇa, three heavens, three firmaments ye comprehend, O Mitra:
Waxed strong, ye keep the splendour of dominion, guarding the Ordinance that lasts for ever.

2 Ye, Varuṇa, have kine who yield refreshment; Mitra, your floods pour water full of sweetness.
There stand the Three Steers, splendid in their brightness, who fill the three world-bowls with genial moisture.

3 I call at dawn on Aditi the Goddess, I call at noon and when the Sun is setting.
I pray, O Mitra-Varuṇa, for safety, for wealth and progeny, in rest and trouble.

4 Ye who uphold the region, sphere of brightness, ye who support earth's realm, Divine Ādityas,
The Immortal Gods, O Varuṇa and Mitra, never impair your everlasting statutes.

HYMN LXX. *Mitra-Varuṇa.*

1. EVEN far and wide, O Varuṇa and Mitra, doth your grace extend.
May I obtain your kind good-will.

2 From you, benignant Gods, may we gain fully food for sustenance.
Such, O ye Rudras, my we be.

3 Guard us, O Rudras, with your guards, save us, ye skilled to save, my we
Subdue the Dasyus, we ourselves,

5 *O Earth* : Pṛthivī, or Earth, is quite out of place here. Professor Ludwig suspects a corruption of the text, and Professor Grassmann thinks that the whole stanza has been inserted by mistake. The two wide-spreading or far-reaching Gods, Mitra and Varuna, are said to be ready to listen to the Ṛṣis' prayers and so to increase their renown. The copious fall of rain is proof that their prayers have been heard.

6 *Ye Gods* : Mitra and Varuṇa, Mitra only being named.

2 *Your golden dwelling-place* : the delightful place of sacrifice, according to Sāyaṇa.

3 *Follow their ways* : their royal ordinances, *vratā*, that is *vratāni*.

1 *They, Mighty Lords, are lofty Law* : '(come)mighty deities, to the great sacrifice.'—Wilson.

2 *Full springs of fatness* : originators of streams of fertilizing rain; or *ghṛtáyonī* may mean here as it does elsewhere, dwelling or having their home with *ghṛtá*, clarified butter or oil used in sacrifice.

5 *Lords of the strength that bringeth gifts* : 'lords of sustenance, suited to the liberal donors (of oblations).' —Wilson.

1 *Three firmaments* : according to Sāyaṇa, three realms of earth, an interpretation which is more in accordance with the second half of stanza 2.

2 *The Three Steers* : Agni as terrestrial fire on earth, Vāyu as the wind in the firmament, and Sūrya as the Sun in heaven. *World bowls* : Ludwig explains differently. See his Ueber die neuesten Arbeiten auf dem Gebiete der Ṛgveda forschung, p. 85. *Genial moisture* : the fertilizing rain.

2 *O ye Rudras* : O Mitra and Varuṇa.

4 Or ne'er may we, O Wondrous Strong, enjoy another's solemn feast,
Ourselves, our sons, or progeny.

HYMN LXXI. *Mitra-Varuṇa.*

1. O VARUṆA and Mitra, ye who slay the foemen, come with might
To this our goodly sacrifice.

2 For, Varuṇa and Mitra, ye Sages are Rulers over all. Fill full our songs, for this ye can.

3 Come to the juice that we have pressed. Varuṇa, Mitra, come to drink
This Soma of the worshipper.

HYMN LXXII. *Mitra-Varuṇa.*

1 To Varuṇa and Mitra we offer with songs, as Atri did. Sit on the sacred grass to drink the Soma juice.

2 By Ordinance and Law ye dwell in peace secure, bestirring men.
Sit on the sacred grass to drink the Soma juice.

3 May Varuṇa and Mitra, for our help, accept the sacrifice.
Sit on the sacred grass to drink the Soma juice.

HYMN LXXIII. *Aśvins.*

1. WHETHER, O Aśvins, ye this day be far remote or near at hand,
In many spots or in mid-air, come hither, Lords of ample wealth.

2 These here, who show o'er widest space, bringing full many a wondrous act,
Resistless, lovingly I seek, I call the Mightiest to enjoy.

3 Another beauteous wheel have ye fixed there to decorate your car.
With others through the realms ye roam in might unto the neighbouring tribes.

4 That deed of yours that is extolled, Viśvas ! hath all been done with this.
Born otherwise, and spotless, ye have entered kinship's bonds with us.

5 When Sūryā mounted on your car that rolls for ever rapidly,
Birds of red hue were round about and burning splendours compassed you.

6 Atri bethinks himself of you, O Heroes, with a friendly mind,
What time, Nāsatyas, with his mouth he stirs the spotless flame for you.

7 Strong is your swiftly moving steed, famed his exertion in the course
When by your great deeds, Aśvins, Chiefs, Atri is brought to us again.

8 Lovers of sweetness, Rudras, she who streams with sweetness waits on you.
When ye have travelled through the seas men bring you gifts of well-dressed food.

9 Aśvins, with truth they call you Twain bestowers of felicity ;
At sacrifice most prompt to hear, most gracious ye at sacrifice.

10 Most pleasing to the Aśvins be these prayers which magnify their might,
Which we have fashioned, even as cars : high reverence have we spoken forth.

4 *Or ne'er may we* : I adopt Professor Ludwig's explanation. We will overcome the Dasyus by our own power. or we will never again participate in any man's solemn festival held in honour of the Gods : a self-imprecation in case of failing to carry out their purpose.

---

1 *With might* : Sāyaṇa explains *barhaṇā* as *hantārau śatrūṇām*, destroyers of enemies.

2 *Fill full our songs* : let them overflow with, or produce abundantly, the results for which we pray.

---

1 *As Atri did* : after the manner of Atri, the founder of our family.

---

1 *In many spots* : the *purū* in the text is thus explained by Sāyaṇa.

2 *To enjoy* : the libation offered to you. According to Sāyaṇa, *bhuje* here means for enjoyment, or for protection.

3 *There* : the third wheel of their chariot, standing by itself in front, is especially ornamental. *With others* : Sāyaṇa explains *anyā* by *anyena cakreṇa, i. e.* with another, or the other, wheel ; but the two hind wheels must be intended, or *anyā* must be in agreement with *yugā*. *The neighbouring tribes* : the meaning of *nāhuṣā yugā* is not clear. Professor Ludwig translates the words by 'zu den geschlechtern der Nahuṣa,' 'to the tribes of the [people called] Nahuṣas.' Professor Wilson, following Sāyaṇa, translates the stanza differently : 'You have arrested one luminous wheel of (your) car for illumining the form (of the sun), whilst with the other you traverse the spheres (to regulate) by your power the ages of mankind.'

4 *Viśvas !* : Sāyaṇa explains *viśvā*, by *vyāptau*, the two who spread through or pervade : 'universal (deities).'—Wilson. *With this* : according to Sāyaṇa, with this Paura (the Ṛṣi of the hymn). Or 'this' may mean, as Professor Ludwig thinks, the third of the car, in which mysterious virtue more especially resides. *Born otherwise* : of divine and not human origin.

5 *Sūryā* : the Daughter of the Sun. See I. 116. 17.

7 *Atri is brought to us again* : See I. 112. 7.

8 *She who streams with sweetness* : Vāk, Voice or Speech, or our praise, *stutirasmatkṛtā*. 'Our nutritious (adoration).'—Wilson. *The seas* : of air.

HYMN LXXIV. *Aśvins.*

1. WHERE in the heavens are ye to-day, Gods, Aśvins, rich in constancy?
Hear this, ye excellent as Steers: Atri inviteth you to come.

2 Where are they now? Where are the Twain, the famed Nāsatyas, Gods in heaven?
Who is the man ye strive to reach? Who of your suppliants is with you?

3 Whom do ye visit, whom approach? to whom direct your harnessed car?
With whose devotions are ye pleased? We long for you to further us.

4 Ye, Strengtheners, for Paura stir the filler swimming in the flood,
Advancing to be captured like a lion to the ambuscade.

5 Ye from cyavāna worn with age removed his skin as 'twere a robe.
So, when ye made him young again, he stirred the longing of a dame.

6 Here is the man who lauds you both: to see your glory are we here.
Now hear me, come with saving help, ye who are rich in store of wealth.

7 Who among many mortal men this day hath won you to himself?
What bard, accepters of the bard? Who, rich in wealth! with sacrifice?

8 O Aśvins, may your car approach, most excellent of cars for speed.
Through many regions may our praise pass onward among mortal men.

9 May our laudation of you Twain, lovers of meath! be sweet to you.
Fly hitherward, ye wise of heart, like falcons with your winged steeds.

10 O Aśvins, when at any time ye listen to this call of mine,
For you is dainty food prepared: they mix refreshing food for you.

HYMN LXXV. *Aśvins.*

1. To meet your treasure-bringing car, the mighty car most dear to us,
Aśvins, the Ṛṣi is prepared, your praiser, with his song of praise. Lovers of sweetness, hear my call.

2 Pass, O ye Aśvins, pass away beyond all tribes of selfish men,
Wonderful, with your golden paths, most gracious, bringers of the flood. Lovers of sweetness, hear my call.

3 Come to us, O ye Aśvin Pair, bringing your precious treasures, come
Ye Rudras, on your paths of gold, rejoicing, rich in store of wealth. Lovers of sweetness, hear my call.

1 *Rich in constancy*: faithful friends of your worshippers. *Excellent as Steers*: 'liberal showerers (of benefits).'—Wilson.

2 *Of your suppliants*: this, although not entirely satisfactory, seems to be the only possible explanation of *nadīnām* in this place. Professor Ludwig remarks, truly enough, that if *ko* (quis?) could be taken as *kā* (quae), the passage would present no difficulty. The meaning would then be, which of the rivers (of the Panj b) rejoices in your presence? Sāyaṇa paraphrases the passage: *kaḥ stotā vām yuvayornadīnām stutīnām sacā sahāyaḥ syāt*; 'what praiser may be the associate of the praises of you twain'?

4 This stanza is desperately difficult. Professor Wilson translates in accordance with Sāyaṇa's explanation: '*Pauras*, *send* to *Paura* the rain-shedding cloud; drive it to him who is engaged in sacrifice, as (hunters chase) a lion in a forest.' Professor Wilson remarks: 'The name of the Ṛṣi is here, according to the scholiast, arbitrarily applied, first to the *Aśvins*, because they are in relation with *Paura* as the author of the *Sūkta*; and although the text gives *Paura* in the vocative singular, it is to be understood in the dual *Paura*, therefore, being *Aśvins*: next it implies, as *Pauram*, a cloud, from its being solicited by the *Ṛṣi* for the fall of rain, as implied by the last term, *Paurāya*, to me the Ṛṣi so called.' Professor Roth is of opinion that Paúra, in the vocative case, means the Aśvins, as fillers, increasers or strengtheners; and that *paurám*, in the accusative case, means the Soma, the filler or satisfying juice (cf. II. 11. 11, The juice that satisfies hath holpen Indra), said to be swimming in the flood, *i. e.* mixed with water. The second half of the stanza would then probably mean that the Soma flows on in order to be taken up and used in libations as a lion goes to the place where men lie in wait to capture him or where a pitfall has been prepared to entrap him. Still there remains the very great difficulty of Paúra in the singular being used instead of the dual Paurau. Professor Ludwig remarks: 'Paura: S. etad aśvinoḥ sambodhanam; but it is to be taken direct as a cry of warning. Paura is to mean the Aśvins, Paura is to mean the Ṛṣi of the hymn, Paura is to mean the cloud. This is naturally too much. The word udaprutam (swimming in water) shows that Paura had been enticed to a place where his enemies intended to drown him. He had gone to the spot as unsuspiciously as a lion approaches the pitfall, and was already in the water when the Aśvins called out to him and stopped him. According to this explanation the translation would be: 'For Paura ye cried, Paura! and saved him when swimming in the flood, Him who had reached the ambush as a lion to the capture goes.

5 *Cyavāna*: See I. 116. 10.

6 *Rich in store of wealth*: 'affluent in food,'—Wilson, after Sāyaṇa; 'lords of swift horses,'—Roth; 'possessors of excellent mares,'—Ludwig.

---

1 *Lovers of sweetness*: drinkers of the sweet Soma juice: according to Sāyaṇa, masters of the Madhuvidyā, or knowledge of sweetness, that is, the knowledge that teaches where the Soma is to be found. See I. 84. 13.

2 *Selfish men*: reading *ahaṁsanāḥ* for *ahaṁ sanā*. See Aufrecht, R. V. II. XLII. note.

3 *Rich in store of wealth*: or, Lords of rapid steeds. See note on stanza 6 of the preceding hymn.

4 O strong and Good, the voice of him who lauds you well cleaves to your car.
And that great beast, your chariot-steed, fair, wonderful, makes dainty food. Lovers of sweetness, hear my call.

5 Watchful in spirit, born on cars, impetuous, listing to his cry,
Aśvins, with winged steeds ye speed down to cyavāna void of guile. Lovers of sweetness, hear my call.

6 Hither, O Heroes, let your steeds, of dappled hue, yoked at the thought,
Your flying steeds, O Aśvins, bring you hitherward, with bliss, to drink. Lovers of sweetness, hear my call.

7 O Aśvins, hither come to us ; Nāsatyas, be not disinclined.
Through longing for the pious turn out of the way to reach our home. Lovers of sweetness, hear my call.

8 Ye Lords of Splendour, free from guile, come, stand at this our sacrifice.
Beside the singer, Aśvins, who longs for your grace and lauds you both. Lovers of sweetness, hear my call.

9 Dawn with her white herd hath appeared, and in due time hath fire been placed.
Harnessed is your immortal car, O Wonder-Workers, strong and kind. Lovers of sweetness, hear my call.

HYMN LXXVI. *Aśvins*

1. AGNI, the bright face of the Dawns, is shining ; the singers' pious voices have ascended.
Borne on your chariot, Aśvins, turn you hither, and come unto our full and rich libation.

2 Most frequent guests, they scorn not what is ready : even now the lauded Aśvins are beside us.
With promptest aid they come at morn and evening, the worshipper's most blessed guards from trouble.

3 Yea, come at milking-time, at early morning, at noon of day and when the Sun is setting,
By day, by night, with favour most auspicious. Not only now the draught hath drawn the Aśvins.

4 For this place, Aśvins, was of old your dwelling, these were your houses, this your habitation.
Come to us from high heaven and from the mountain. Come from the waters bringing food and vigour.

5 May we obtain the Aśvins' newest favour, and gain their health-bestowing happy guidance.
Bring riches hither unto us, and heroes, and all felicity and joy, Immortals !

HYMN LXXVII. *Aśvins.*

1. FIRST worship those who come at early morning : let the Twain drink before the giftless niggard.
The Aśvins claim the sacrifice at day-break : the sages yielding the first share extol them.

2 Worship at dawn and instigate the Aśvins : nor is the worshipper at eve rejected.
Besides ourselves another craves and worships : each first in worship is most highly favoured.

3 Covered with gold, meath-tinted, dropping fatness, your chariot with its freight of food comes hither,
Swift as thought, Aśvins, rapid as the tempest, wherewith ye travel over all obstructions.

4 He who hath served most often the Nāsatyas, and gives the sweetest food at distribution,

4 *And that great beast* : the chariot of the Aśvins is sometimes said to be drawn by a stallion ass (see I. 34. ; 116. 2; 162. 21), the dun-coloured animal representing the grey tints of early morning.

5 *Cyavāna* : See I 116. 10.

8 *Who longs for your grace* : Sāyana takes *avasyum* here to be a proper name, Avasyu, who is said to be the Ṛṣi of the hymn.

9 *In due time* : for the morning libation.

———

1 *The bright face* : making his first appearance at early morning. *Libation* : *gharmám*, the offering of hot milk or other heated beverage.

3 'The Aśvins are invited to come at different times, at morning, mid-day and sunset ; and in VIII. 22. 14, it is similarly said that they are invoked in the evening as well as at dawn. It need not, however, surprise us that they should be invited to attend the different ceremonies of the worshippers, and therefore conceived to appear at hours distinct from the supposed natural periods of their manifestation.'—J. Muir, *O. Sanskrit Texts*, V. 239.

5 This stanza is identical with V. 42. 18.

———

1 *Before the giftless niggard* : 'before the greedy withholders (of the offering).'—Wilson.

2 *Nor is the worshipper at eve rejected* : literally, a thing unaccepted or rejected. Sāyaṇa explains differently : 'the evening is not for the gods; it is unacceptable to them.'—Wilson. This explanation, though supported by the text *pūrvāhṇo vai devānām*, the forenoon verily belongs to the Gods, is not in accordance with the use of Vedic times.

Furthers with his own holy works his offspring, and ever passes those whose flames ascend not.

5 May we obtain the Aśvins' newest favour, and gain their health-bestowing happy guidance.
Bring riches hither unto us, and heroes, and all felicity and joy, Immortals !

HYMN LXXVIII. *Aśvins.*

1. Ye Aśvins, hither come to us : Nāsatyas, be not disinclined.
Fly hither like two swans unto the juice we shed.

2 O Aśvins, like a pair of deer, like two wild cattle to the mead :
Fly hither like two swans unto the juice we shed.

3 O Aśvins rich in gifts, accept our sacrifice to prosper it :
Fly hither like two swans unto the juice we shed.

4 As Atri when descending to the cavern called on you loudly like a wailing woman,
Ye came to him, O Aśvins, with the freshest and most auspicious fleetness of a falcon.

5 Tree, part asunder like the side of her who bringeth forth a child.
Ye Aśvins, listen to my call : loose Saptavadhri from his bonds.

6 For Saptavadhri, for the seer affrighted when he wept and wailed,
Ye, Aśvins, with your magic powers rent up the tree and shattered it.

7 Like as the wind on every side ruffles a pool of lotuses,
So stir in thee the babe unborn, so may the ten-month babe descend.

8 Like as the wind, like as the wood, like as the sea is set astir,
So also, ten-month babe, descend together with the after-birth.

9 The child who hath for ten months' time been lying in his mother's side,—
May he come forth alive, unharmed, yea, living from the living dame.

HYMN LXXIX. *Dawn.*

1. O heavenly Dawn, awaken us to ample opulence to-day
Even as thou hast wakened us with Satyaśravas, Vayya's son, high-born ! delightful with thy steeds !

2 Daughter of Heaven, thou dawnedst on Sunītha Śucadratha's son,
So dawn thou on one mightier still, on Satyaśravas, Vayya's son, high-born ! delightful with thy steeds !

3 So, bringing treasure, dawn to-day on us thou Daughter of the Sky,
As thou, O mightier yet, didst shine for Satyaśravas, Vayya's son, high-born ! delightful with thy steeds !

4 Here round about thee are the priests who laud thee, Bright One, with their hymns,
And men with gifts, O Bounteous Dame, splendid with wealth and offering much, high-born ! delightful with thy steeds !

5 Whatever these thy bands perform to please thee or to win them wealth,
E'en fain they gird us round and give rich gifts which ne'er are reft away, high-born ! delightful with thy steeds !

2 *Wild cattle* : Gauras, or Boves Cauri.

4 *The cavern* : the abyss or deep pit into which he was cast by Asuras or evil spirits. See I. 112. 7; 116. 8: 117. 3.

5 *Tree, part asunder* : Saptavadhri appears to have got his hand or foot jammed in a split tree, and to have been extricated when he called on the Aśvins to aid him.

9 'This and the two stanzas preceding are termed by Sāyaṇa the *garbhasrāviṇyupaniṣad*, the liturgy of child-birth.'—Wilson.

The connexion between 1—6, and 7—9 is not clear. By *yoṣā nādhamānā* (a wailing woman) a parturient woman may perhaps, Professor Ludwig thinks, be intended. Atri, as he descended into the pit, invoked the Aśvins that they might release him as a woman releases the child she bears. A tree—which is much harder and firmer than a woman's body—unclosed itself when Saptavadhri invoked the Aśvins. So shall the parturient woman bring forth her child through the help of the Aśvins and at Atri's intercession. A connexion may thus be established, though here and there it would be rather forced.

---

1 *Satyaśravas* : the Ṛṣi of the hymn. *Delightful with thy steeds* : pleasant to those whom thou favourest on account of the horses which thou bestowest. The word *áśvasūnṛte* is variously rendered *e. g.* by Professor Wilson, after Sāyaṇa, 'praised sincerely for (the gift of) horses;' by Prof. Ludwig, 'an rossen trefliches besitzende,' 'having an excellent possession in horses;' by Prof. Roth 'vom jubel der Rosse begleitete,' 'accompanied by the joyous neigh of horses;' and by Prof. Grassmann, 'rossereiche,' 'rich in horses.'

4 *Men with gifts* : the Maghavans, or wealthy householders, who institute the sacrifice and provide offerings for the Gods and presents for the officiating priests.

5 *These thy bands* : the congregation of worshippers. *Which ne'er are reft away* : or which are never in vain, never fail to obtain their due reward from heaven : 'Sāyaṇa,' Professor Wilson remarks, 'seems rather dubious as to the proper sense of several of these words :...........the sum of the meaning, agreeably to

6 Give to these wealthy patrons fame, O affluent Dawn, with hero sons,
To these our princes who have brought rich gifts ne'er to be reft away, high-born ! delightful with thy steeds !

7 Bring lofty and resplendent fame, O thou munificent Dawn, to these
Our wealthy patrons who bestow rich gifts on us of steeds and kine, high-born! delightful with thy steeds !

8 Bring us, O Daughter of the Sky, subsistence in our herds of kine,
Together with the sunbeams, with the shine of pure refulgent flames, high-born ! delightful with thy steeds !

9 O Daughter of the Sky, shine forth ; delay not to perform thy task.
Let not the Sun with fervent heat consume thee like a robber foe, high-born ! delightful with the steeds !

10 So much, and more exceedingly, O Dawn, it suits thee to bestow,
Thou Radiant One who ceasest not to shine for those who sing thy praise, high-born ! delightful with thy steeds !

HYMN LXXX. *Dawn.*

1. THE singers welcome with their hymns and praises the Goddess Dawn who bringeth in the sunlight,
Sublime, by Law true to eternal Order, bright on her path, red-tinted, far-refulgent.

2 She comes in front, fair, rousing up the people, making the pathways easy to be travelled.
High, on her lofty chariot, all-impelling, Dawn gives her splendour at the days' beginning.

3 She, harnessing her car with purple oxen, injuring none, hath brought perpetual riches.
Opening paths to happiness, the Goddess shines, praised by all, giver of every blessing.

4 With changing tints she gleams in double splendour while from the eastward she displays her body.
She travels perfectly the path of Order, nor fails to reach, as one who knows, the quarters.

5 As conscious that her limbs are bright with bathing, she stands, as 'twere, erect that we may see her.
Driving away malignity and darkness, Dawn, Child of Heaven, hath come to us with lustre.

6 The Daughter of the Sky, like some chaste woman, bends, opposite to men, her forehead downward.
The Maid, disclosing boons to him who worships, hath brought again the daylight as aforetime.

HYMN LXXXI. *Savitar.*

1. THE priests of him the lofty Priest well-skilled in hymns harness their spirit, yea, harness their holy thoughts.
He only knowing works assigns their priestly tasks. Yea, lofty is the praise of Savitar the God.

2 The Sapient One arrays himself in every form : for quadruped and biped he hath brought forth good.
Excellent Savitar hath looked on heaven's high vault, and shineth after the outgoing of the Dawn.

3 Even he, the God whose going-forth and majesty the other Deities have followed with their might,
He who hath measured the terrestrial regions out by his great power, he is the Courser Savitar.

4 To the three spheres of light thou goest, Savitar, and with the rays of Sūrya thou combinest thee.
Around, on both sides thou encompassest the night : yea, thou, O God, art Mitra through thy righteous laws.

---

the scholiast, is, all they who, offering oblations, worship the dawn receive the reward for the benefit of us, of me, that is the author of the hymn, *ye tvám havir-dadataḥ stuvanti te sarve apy-asmadartham phalaṁ dhārayanti.*'

9 *Delay not to perform thy task* : 'delay not our (sacred) rite.'—Wilson.

---

2 *In front* of the Sun ; *sūryasya purastāt.*—Sāyaṇa.

4 *The quarters* : the regions of the sky which she visits in obedience to the eternal law of the universe.

5 *With bathing* : in the dews of heaven.

---

1. *The lofty Priest* : Savitar. *Knowing works* : skilled in rules which regulate religious functions, or perhaps understanding the intentions or wishes of the worshippers : 'he alone knowing their functions directs the priests.'—Wilson.

2 *Arrays himself in every form* : makes all eternal objects clearly visible at sunrise.

3 *The Courser Savitar* : Sāyaṇa explains *étaśaḥ* as white, bright shining. It also means a horse, especially one of the horses of the Sun, and here designates the Sun himself under that form. See Śatapatha-Brāhmaṇa, VI. 3. 1. 18; Sacred Books of the East, XLI. p. 19 .

4 According to Sāyaṇa, Savitar is especially the Sun before rising, and Sūrya is the Sun in general.

5 Over all generation thou art Lord alone : Pūṣan art thou, O God, in all thy goings-forth.
Yea, thou hast domination over all this world. Śyāvāśva hath brought praise to thee, O Savitar.

HYMN LXXXII. *Savitar.*

1. WE crave of Savitar the God this treasure much to be enjoyed.
The best, all-yielding, conquering gift of Bhaga we would gladly win.

2 Savitar's own supremacy, most glorious and beloved of all,
No one diminisheth in aught.

3 For Savitar who is Bhaga shall send riches to his worshipper.
That wondrous portion we implore.

4 Send us this day, God Savitar, prosperity with progeny.
Drive thou the evil dream away.

5 Savitar, God, send far away all sorrows and calamities,
And send us only what is good.

6 Sinless in sight of Aditi through the God Savitar's influence,
May we obtain all lovely things.

7 We with our hymns this day elect the general God, Lord of the good,
Savitar whose decrees are true.

8 He who for ever vigilant precedes these Twain, the Day and Night,
Is Savitar the thoughtful God.

9 He who gives glory unto all these living creatures with the song,
And brings them forth, is Savitar.

3 *Shall send* : *suvāti*, from the root *su* or *sū*, from which Savitar also is formed. The principal significations of the root are (1) to generate or bring forth; (2) to pour forth a libation ; and (3) to send or impel. See Muir, *O. S. Texts*, V. 165.

4 *Send us* : *sāvīḥ*, from the same root : *Drive thou away* : *párā suva*.

5 *Send far away* : *párā suva*.

6 *Influence* : *savé*.

7 *The general God* : *viśvádevam* : 'who possesses all divine attributes.'—Muir; '(identical with) all the gods,'—Wilson; 'den allgott,' 'the all-god,'—Ludwig; 'den allgottlichen,' 'the all-divine,'—Grassmann. *Whose decrees are true* : *satyásavam* : 'who possesses true energy.'—Muir.

9 *He who gives glory* : 'he who by his creative power produces the objects of the song of praise.'—Ludwig.

HYMN LXXXIII. *Parjanya.*

1. SING with these songs thy welcome to the Mighty, with adoration praise and call Parjanya.
The Bull, loud roaring, swift to send his bounty, lays in the plants the seed for germination.

2 He smites the trees apart, he slays the demons : all life fears him who wields the mighty weapon.
From him exceeding strong flees e'en the guiltless, when thundering Parjanya smites the wicked.

3 Like a car-driver whipping on his horses, he makes the messengers of rain spring forward.
Far off resounds the roaring of the lion, what time Parjanya fills the sky with rain-cloud.

4 Forth burst the winds, down come the lightning-flashes : the plants shoot up, the realm of light is streaming.
Food springs abundant for all living creatures, what time Parjanya quickens earth with moisture.

5 Thou at whose bidding earth bows low before thee, at whose command hoofed cattle fly in terror,
At whose behest the plants assume all colours, even thou Parjanya, yield us great protection.

6 Send down for us the rain of heaven, ye Maruts, and let the Stallion's flood descend in torrents.
Come hither with this thunder while thou pourest the waters down, our heavenly Lord and Father.

7 Thunder and roar : the germ of life deposit. Fly round us on thy chariot water-laden.
Thine opened water-skin draw with thee downward, and let the hollows and the heights be level.

8 Lift up the mighty vessel, pour down water, and let the liberated streams rush forward.

1 *Parjanya* : God of thunderstorms and rain, the generator and nourisher of plants and living creatures. See Muir. *O. S. Texts*, V. 140 ff., and, especially, M. Müller, India, What can it Teach us pp. 186—194.

2 *The wicked* : *duṣkṛtaḥ*, evil-doers. 'There does not seem to be any sufficient reason to understand evil-doers here, and, in verse 9, of the cloud demons, or simply of the malignant clouds, as Sāyaṇa in his explanation of verse 9 does. The poet may naturally have supposed that it was exclusively or principally the wicked who were struck down by thunderbolts.'—Muir, *O.S. Texts*, V. 141.

Saturate both the earth and heaven with fatness, and for the cows let there be drink abundant.

9 When thou, with thunder and with roar, Parjanya, smitest sinners down,
This universe exults thereat, yea, all that is upon the earth.

10 Thou hast poured down the rain-flood: now withhold it. Thou hast made desert places fit for travel.
Thou hast made herbs to grow for our enjoyment: yea, thou hast won thee praise from living creatures.

HYMN LXXXIV. *Pṛthivī.*

1. Thou, of a truth, O Pṛthivī, bearest the tool that rends the hills:
Thou rich in torrents, who with might quickenest earth, O Mighty One.

2 To thee, O wanderer at will, ring out the lauds with beams of day,
Who drivest, like a neighing steed, the swelling cloud, O bright of hue.

3 Who graspest with thy might on earth e'en the strong sovrans of the wood,
When from the lightning of thy cloud the rain-floods of the heaven descend.

HYMN LXXXV. *Varuṇa.*

1. Sing forth a hymn sublime and solemn, grateful to glorious Varuṇa, imperial Ruler,
Who hath struck out, like one who slays the victim, earth as a skin to spread in front of Sūrya.

2 In the tree-tops the air he hath extended, put milk in kine and vigorous speed in horses,
Set intellect in hearts, fire in the waters, Sūrya in heaven and Soma on the mountain.

3 Varuṇa lets the big cask, opening downward, flow through the heaven and earth and air's mid-region.
Therewith the universe's Sovran waters earth as the shower of rain bedews the barley.

4 When Varuṇa is fain for milk he moistens the sky, the land, and earth to her foundation.
Then straight the mountains clothe them in the rain-cloud: the Heroes, putting forth their vigour, loose them.

5 I will declare this mighty deed of magic, of glorious Varuṇa the Lord Immortal,
Who standing in the firmament hath meted the earth out with the Sun as with a measure.

6 None, verily, hath ever let or hindered this the most wise God's mighty deed of magic,
Whereby with all their flood, the lucid rivers fill not one sea wherein they pour their waters.

7 If we have sinned against the man who loves us, have ever wronged a brother, friend, or comrade,
The neighbour ever with us, or a stranger, O Varuṇa, remove from us the trespass.

8 If we, as gamesters cheat at play, have cheated, done wrong unwittingly or sinned of purpose,
Cast all these sins away like loosened fetters, and, Varuṇa let us be thine own beloved.

HYMN LXXXVI. *Indra-Agni.*

1. The mortal man whom ye, the Twain, Indra and Agni, help in fight,

---

10 *Thou hast won thee praise*: or, perhaps, 'thou hast fulfilled the longing of the people.'

---

1. *Pṛthivī*: in this place not the Goddess Earth or earth personified, but a deity of the middle air or firmament. '*Dvirūpā Pṛthivī*,' says Sāyaṇa, 'Pṛthivī has two forms.' *The tool that rends the hills*: the instrument that strikes and pierces the mountains and opens the water-springs, the thunderbolt or the power that produces similar results.

2 *The swelling cloud*: *perúm*; the exact meaning of the word is doubtful Professor Ludwig thinks that the lightning is intended.

---

1 *Sing forth*: *prá......arcā.* The Ṛṣi addresses himself. Or *arcā* may be the first person singular, I sing. *Like one who slays the victim*: 'not the ordinary Immolator, but the priest who spreads out the skin of the slaughtered victim to receive its disjointed members.' —Ludwig.

2 *In the tree-tops*: *vánеṣu*, explained by Sāyaṇa as *vṛkṣāgreṣu*: 'in the clouds,' according to the St. Petersburg Lexicon. *Soma on the mountain*: 'the Soma creeper.' *Mahīdhara* observes, grows in the clefts of the stones of mountains, *parvatānām páṣṇa and iṣu somavallyā utpādyamānatvāt.*'—Wilson.

4 *Is fain for milk*: wishes for libations of milk ; or the meaning may be, when he wishes to draw forth the milk, the fertilizing rain, of the clouds *Earth to her foundation*: the text has only *pṛthivím*, meaning earth in its full extent (terra) as distinguished from *bhúmim*, the land, soil, or ground (humus or solum), Or *pṛthivím* may perhaps mean the firmament here as Sāyaṇa explains it. See note on *Pṛthivī* in the preceding hymn. *The Heroes*: the strong Maruts. *Loose them*: loosen the roots of the mountains and make them tremble.

5 *Deed of magic*: *māyām*: or the word may be rendered by 'device' or design.' See Wallis, *Cosmology of the Ṛgveda*, pp. 102, 103.

Breaks through e'en strongly-guarded wealth as Tṛta burst his way through reeds.

2 The Twain invincible in war, worthy to be renowned in frays;
Lords of the Fivefold People, these, Indra and Agni, we invoke.

3 Impetuous is their strength, and keen the lightning of the mighty Pair,
Which from their arms speeds with the car to Vṛtra's slayer for the kine.

4 Indra and Agni, we invoke you both, as such, to send your cars :
Lords of quick-coming bounty, ye who know, chief lovers of the song.

5 These who give increase day by day, Gods without guile for mortal man,
Worthy themselves, I honour most, Two Gods as partners, for my horse.

6 The strength-bestowing offering thus to Indra-Agni hath been paid, as butter, purified by stones.
Deal to our princes high renown, deal wealth to those who sing your praise, deal food to those who sing your praise.

HYMN LXXXVII. *Maruts.*

1. To Viṣṇu, to the Mighty whom the Maruts follow let your hymns born in song go forth, Evayāmarut;
To the impetuous, strong band, adorned with bracelets, that rushes on in joy and ever roars for vigour.

2 They who with might were manifest, and who willingly by their own knowledge told it forth, Evayāmarut.
Maruts, this strength of yours no wisdom comprehendeth : through their gifts' greatness they are moveless as the mountains.

3 Who by the psalm they sing are heard, from lofty heaven, the strong, the brightly shining Ones, Evayāmarut;
In whose abode there is no mightier one to move them, whose lightnings are as fires, who urge the roaring rivers.

4 He of the Mighty Stride forth strode, Evayāmarut, out of the spacious dwelling-place, their home in common.
When he, himself, hath yoked his emulous strong horses on heights, he cometh forth, joy-giving, with the Heroes.

5 Like your tremendous roar, the rainer with light flashing, strong, speeding, hath made all tremble, Evayāmarut,
Wherewith victorious ye, self-luminous, press onward, with strong reins, decked with gold, impetuous and well-weaponed.

6 Unbounded is your greatness, ye of mighty power : may your bright vigour be our aid, Evayāmarut;
For ye are visible helpers in the time of trouble : like fires, aglow with light, save us from shame and insult.

7 So may the Rudras, mighty warriors, Evayāmarut, with splendid brilliancy, like fires, be our protectors;

1 *Through reeds* : so Professor Roth interprets the *vāṇiḥ* of the text. See I. 52. 5. According to Sāyaṇa the meaning is, as Tṛta the Ṛṣi breaks down and refutes the words or arguments of his opponents. See Macdonell, J.R.A.S, July 1893, p. 426.

2 *The Fivefold People* : the five Āryan tribes.

5 *I honour most* : *puró dadhé* ; I set in front, in the most honourable place. *For my horse* : that I may win the chariot-race. 'For (the sake of obtaining) horses.'—Wilson.

6 *As butter* : Sāyaṇa explains *ghṛtám*, sacrificial oil or clarified butter, by Soma juice ; but *pūtám*, purified, qualifies *havyám*, the offering, and not *ghṛtám*. The libation of Soma juice which has been purified by the operation of the press-stones, strainer, etc., has been offered like clarified butter or holy oil.

The hymn is ascribed to a Ṛṣi Evayāmarut, a name which is evidently borrowed from the refrain.

1 *Born in song* : developing themselves and taking form in song : *vāci niṣpannā* :—Sāyaṇa. 'Voice-born.' —Wilson. Or *girijā* may have its usual meaning, mountain-born, with reference to the close connexion of the hymns with the pressing-stones which came from the hills. *Evayāmarut* : Professor Wilson, following Sāyaṇa translates : 'May the voice-born praises of Evayāmarut reach you, Viṣṇu, attended by the Maruts,' and observes that 'the name of the *Ṛṣi, Evayāmarut*, remains unaltered in its case termination, whatever may be its syntactical connexion with the rest of the sentence.' This is manifestly impossible, and the word is certainly not a proper name. *Evayā*, in I. 156. I, 'going thy wonted way,' is an epithet of Viṣṇu, and Professor Roth thinks that *Evayāmarut* is an exclamation meaning, O Viṣṇu and Maruts ! or, O Maruts who speed around ! But in both these cases it would be necessary to change the accent, both in this hymn and in the Sāmaveda where stanza 1 occurs again. Professor Grassmann suggests, 'speeding (like Viṣṇu) is the Marut host,' or, 'The speeding Viṣṇu is the true Marut, or lord of the Maruts,' as the probable meaning of the word. I find *Evayāmarut* unintelligible, and, as Professor Ludwig has done, leave it untranslated, as a mere sacrificial exclamation. See Vedic Hymns (Sacred Books of the East) Part 1. p. 365.

4 *He of the Mighty Stride* : Viṣṇu. According to Sāyaṇa, the wide-spreading (band of Maruts). *Their home* : Viṣṇu's and Indra's. *With the Heroes* : with the Maruts.

6 *In the time of trouble* : the meaning of *prásitau* is uncertain. Professor Wilson, after Sāyaṇa, translates : 'for you are regulators for overseeing (what is fit for) the limits of the sacrifice.'

They whose terrestrial dwelling-place is wide-extended, whom none suspect of sin, whose bands have lofty courage.

8 Come in a friendly spirit, come to us, O Maruts, and hear his call who praises you, Evayāmarut.

Like car-borne men, one-minded with the mighty Viṣṇu, keep enmity far from us with your deeds of wonder.

9 Come to our sacrifice, ye Holy Ones, to bless it, and, free from demons, hear our call, Evayāmarut.

Most excellent, like mountains in the air's mid-region, be irresistible, ye Wise, to this man's hater.

9 *This man's hater* : him who hates the institutor of the sacrifice, or derides and reviles the holy ceremony.

BOOK THE SIXTH

HYMN I. *Agni.*

1. Thou, first inventor of this prayer, O Agni, Worker of Marvels, hast become our Herald.
Thou, Bull, hast made us strength which none may conquer, strength that shall overcome all other prowess.

2 As Priest thou sattest at the seat of worship, furthering us, best Offerer, meet for honour.
So first to thee have pious men resorted, turning thy mind to thoughts of ample riches.

3 In thee, still watching, they have followed riches, who goest with much wealth as with an army,
The radiant Agni, lofty, fair to look on, worshipped with marrow, evermore resplendent.

4 They who approached the God's abode with homage, eager for glory, won them perfect glory :
Yea, they gained even sacrificial titles, and found delight in thine auspicious aspect.

5 On earth the people magnify thee greatly, thee their celestial and terrestrial riches.
Thou, Helper, must be known as our Preserver, Father and Mother of mankind for ever.

6 Dear priest among mankind, adorable Agni hath seated him, joy-giver, skilled in worship.
Let us approach thee shining in thy dwelling, kneeling upon our knees, with adoration.

7 Longing for bliss, pure-minded, God-devoted, Agni, we seek thee, such, meet to be lauded.
Thou, Agni, leddest forth our men to battle, refulgent with the heaven's exalted splendour.

8 Sage of mankind, all peoples' Lord and Master, the Bull of men, the sender down of blessings,
Still pressing on, promoting, purifying, Agni the Holy One, the Lord of riches.

9 Agni, the mortal who hath toiled and worshipped, brought thee oblations with his kindled fuel,
And well knows sacrifice with adoration, gains every joy with thee to guard and help him.

10 Mightily let us worship thee the Mighty, with reverence, Agni! fuel and oblations,
With songs, O Son of Strength, with hymns, with altar : so may we strive for thine auspicious favour.

11 Thou who hast covered heaven and earth with splendour and with thy glories, glorious and triumphant.
Continue thou to shine on us, O Agni, with strength abundant, rich, and long-enduring.

12 Vouchsafe us ever, as man needs, O Vasu, abundant wealth of kine for son and offspring.
Food noble, plenteous, far from sin and evil, be with us, and fair fame to make us happy.

13 May I obtain much wealth in many places by love of thee and through thy grace, King Agni;
For in thee, Bounteous One, in thee the Sovran, Agni, are many boons for him who serves thee.

HYMN II. *Agni.*

1. Thou, Agni, even as Mitra, hast a princely glory of thine own.
Thou, active Vasu, makest fame increase like full prosperity.

2 For, verily, men pray to thee with sacrifices and with songs.
To thee the Friendly Courser, seen of all, comes speeding through the air.

3 Of one accord men kindle thee Heaven's signal of the sacrifice,
When, craving bliss, this race of man invites thee to the solemn rite.

The Ṛṣi of the hymn is Bharadvāja, to whom, with a few exceptions, all the hymns of this Book are attributed.

1 *Our Herald* : or Invoking Priest who calls the Gods to the sacrifice.

3 *Worshipped with marrow* : to whom especially the fat covering of the inwards of the victims was offered.

4 *They who approached the God's abode* : the Ṛbhus, Maruts, or Aṅgirases may be meant.

5 *Their celestial and terrestrial riches* : *rāyáḥ ubháyāsaḥ*; literally, riches of both kinds. According to Sāyaṇa, consisting in cattle and in possessions other than cattle.

8 *Sage of mankind, etc.* : Sage, Lord, Bull, etc. are in the accusative case, in apposition with 'thee' in stanza 7, though separated by an intervening half-stanza.

—

2 *The Friendly Courser* : the Sun.

3 Or, possibly, as suggested by Professor Ludwig, 'The men accordant with the heaven light thee the sign of sacrifice;' that is, understanding the signs in heaven and so knowing the proper time for the ceremony.

4 Let the man thrive who travails sore, in prayer, far thee the Bountiful.
He with the help of lofty Dyaus comes safe through straits of enmity.

5 The mortal who with fuel lights thy flame and offers unto thee,
Supports a house with many a branch, Agni, to live a hundred years.

6 Thy bright smoke lifts itself aloft, and far-extended shines in heaven.
For, Purifier ! like the Sun thou beamest with thy radiant glow.

7 For in men's houses thou must be glorified as a well-loved guest,
Gay like an elder in a fort, claiming protection like a son.

8 Thou, Agni, like an able steed, art urged by wisdom in the wood.
Thou art like wind; food, home art thou, like a young horse that runs astray.

9 E'en things imperishable, thou, O Agni, like a grazing ox,
Eatest, when hosts, Eternal One ! of thee the Mighty rend the woods.

10 Agni, thou enterest as Priest the home of men who sacrifice.
Lord of the people, prosper them. Accept the offering, Aṅgiras !

11 O Agni, God with Mitra's might, call hither the favour of the Gods from earth and heaven.
Bring weal from heaven, that men may dwell securely. May we o'ercome the foe's malign oppressions, may we o'ercome them, through thy help o'ercome them.

HYMN III. *Agni.*

1. TRUE, guardian of the Law, thy faithful servant wins ample light and dwells in peace, O Agni,
Whom thou, as Varuṇa in accord with Mitra, guardest, O God, by banishing his trouble.

2 He hath paid sacrifices, toiled in worship, and offered gifts to wealth-increasing Agni.
Him the displeasure of the famous moves not, outrage and scorn affect not such a mortal.

3 Bright God, whose look is free from stain like Sūrya's, thou, swift, what time thou earnestly desirest,
Hast gear to give us. Come with joy at evening, where, Child of Wood, thou mayest also tarry.

4 Fierce is his gait and vast his wondrous body : he champeth like a horse with bit and bridle,
And, darting forth his tongue, as 'twere a hatchet, burning the woods, smelteth them like a smelter.

5 Archer-like, fain to shoot, he sets his arrow, and whets his splendour like the edge of iron :
The messenger of night with brilliant pathway, like a tree-roosting bird of rapid pinion.

6 In beams of morn he clothes him like the singer, and bright as Mitra with his splendour crackles.
Red in the night, by day the men's possession : red, he belongs to men by day, Immortal.

7 Like Heaven's when scattering beams his voice was uttered : among the plants the radiant Hero shouted,
Who with his glow in rapid course came hither to fill both worlds, well-wedded Dames, with treasure.

8 Who, with supporting streams and rays that suit him, hath flashed like lightning with his native vigour.

7 *Gay like an elder* : Agni must be respected and cared for like a father as well as protected like a son.

8 *In the wood* : wherein fire is produced by attrition. The exact meaning of the stanza is somewhat uncertain. *Like wind* : moving everywhere.

9 *Eatest* : this or some similar verb must be supplied.

1 *As Varuṇa in accord with Mitra* : that is, Agni, Varuṇa, and Mitra as one.—Ludwig.

3 I gratefully adopt Professor Pischel's interpretation of this very difficult stanza which I had regarded as hopelessly obscure. See *Vedische Studien*, I. pp. 37—50.

4 *With bit and bridle* : *yamasānā āsā*; 'champing fodder with his mouth.'—Wilson. *As 'twere a hatchet* : Agni, and not his tongue, is likened to the hatchet.

5 *Of iron* : or metal, the exact meaning of *áyas* being uncertain.

6 *In beams of morn* : the light of early morning shines on the fire and the singer alike and simultaneously. *Bright as Mitra* : 'diffusing friendly light.'—Wilson. *The men's possession* : I take *nṛīn* as a shortened form of *nṛṇām* ; but it is difficult to make sense of the half-stanza. Professor Wilson, following Sāyaṇa, translates : '(he it is) who is luminous by night, and who lights men (to their work) by day ; who is immortal and radiant ; who lights men by day.' The verb is supplied by Sāyaṇa.

7 *Like Heaven's* : like the voice of Dyaus, the thunder. *Well-wedded Dames* . having excellent Lords, perhaps Indra and Agni.

Like the deft Maker of the band of Maruts, the bright impetuous One hath shone refulgent.

HYMN IV. *Agni.*

1. As at man's service of the Gods, Invoker, thou, Son of Strength, dost sacrifice and worship,
So bring for us to-day all Gods together, bring willingly the willing Gods, O Agni.

2 May Agni, radiant Herald of the morning, meet to be known, accept our praise with favour.
Dear to all life, mid mortal men Immortal, our guest, awake at dawn, is Jātavedas.

3 Whose might the very heavens regard with wonder : bright as the Sun he clothes himself with lustre.
He who sends forth, Eternal Purifier, hath shattered e'en the ancient works of Aśna.

4 Thou art a Singer, Son ! our feast-companion : Agni at birth prepared his food and pathway.
Therefore vouchsafe us strength, O Strength-bestower. Win like a King : foes trouble not thy dwelling.

5 Even he who eats his firm hard food with swiftness,and overtakes the nights as Vāyu kingdoms.
May we o'ercome those who resist thine orders, like a steed casting down the flying foemen.

6 Like Sūrya with his fulgent rays, O Agni, thou overspreadest both the worlds with splendour.
Decked with bright colour he dispels the darkness, like Auśija, with clear flame swiftly flying.

7 We have elected thee as most delightful for thy beams' glow : hear our great laud, O Agni.
The best men praise thee as the peer of Indra in strength, mid Gods, like Vāyu in thy bounty.

8 Now, Agni, on the tranquil paths of riches come to us for our weal : save us from sorrow.
Grant chiefs and bard this boon. May we live happy, with hero children, through a hundred winters.

HYMN V. *Agni.*

1. I INVOCATE your Son of Strength, the Youthful, with hymns, the Youngest God, whose speech is guileless;
Sage who sends wealth comprising every treasure, bringer of many boons, devoid of malice.

2 At eve and morn thy pious servants bring thee their precious gifts, O Priest of many aspects,
On whom, the Purifier, all things living, as on firm ground their happiness have stablished.

3 Thou from of old hast dwelt among these people, by mental power the charioteer of blessings.
Hence sendest thou, O sapient Jātavedas, to him who serves thee treasures in succession.

4 Agni, whoever secretly attacks us, the neighbour, thou with Mitra's might ! who harms us,
Burn him with thine own Steers for ever youthful, burning with burning heat, thou fiercest burner.

5 He who serves thee with sacrifice and fuel, with hymn, O Son of Strength, and chanted praises,
Shines out, Immortal ! in the midst of mortals, a sage, with wealth, with splendour and with glory.

8 *The deft Maker of the band of Maruts* : Dyaus is probably intended.

---

1 *Invoker* : *Hotar*, herald or inviter of the Gods.

3 *Aśna* : apparently one of the demons of drought.

4 *His food and pathway* : or his pathway to his food may be intended.

5 *His firm hard food* : *vāraṇám ánnam*; the food of elephants, *i. e.* trees, acording to Professor Ludwig. Professor Wilson, following Sāyaṇa, translates the first half-line : 'He who whets his (gloom)—dispersing (radiance), who eats the (offered) oblation.' *As Vāyu kingdoms* : *rāṣṭrī* standing, perhaps, for *rāṣṭryā* (*rāṣṭryāṇi*), but the exact meaning is uncertain. Perhaps, as Professor Ludwig suggests, as Vāyu or the wind blows uninterrupted through the whole land, so Agni is kindled at night-fall and again at early dawn before the night has entirely passed away.

6 *Like Auśija* : perhaps some contemporary priest, who is regarded as bringing back the daylight by prayer and sacrifice. 'Like the adored (sun).'—Wilson.

8 *Tranquil* : *avṛkébhiḥ*; literally untroubled by wolves, or enemies. *Grant chiefs and bard* : the wealthy men who institute the sacrifice and the priest who sings. Or it may be rendered, 'Grant the chiefs' bard,' that is, the priest who sings for his wealthy patrons. *A hundred winters* : see V. 54. 15, note.

---

2 *Priest of many aspects* : *purvaṇīka*, having many faces, aspects, or manifestations. According to Sāyaṇa, having many flames instead of faces.

4 *Thine own Steers* : thy strong flames. *Burn him, etc* : *tápā tapiṣṭha tápasā tápasvān.*

6 Do this, O Agni, when we urge thee, quickly, triumphant in thy might subdue our foemen.
When thou art praised with words and decked with brightness, accept this chanted hymn, the singer's worship.

7 Help us, that we may gain this wish, O Agni, gain riches, Wealthy One ! with store of heroes.
Desiring strength from thee may we be strengthened, and win, Eternal ! thine eternal glory.

HYMN VI. *Agni.*

1. He who seeks furtherance and grace to help him goes to the Son of Strength with newest worship,
Calling the heavenly Priest to share the banquet, who rends the wood, bright, with his blackened pathway.

2 White-hued and thundering he dwells in splendour, Most Youthful, with the loud-voiced and eternal—
Agni, most variform, the Purifier, who follows crunching many ample forests.

3 Incited by the wind thy flames, O Agni, move onward, Pure One ! pure, in all directions.
Thy most destructive heavenly Navagvas break the woods down and devastate them boldly.

4 Thy pure white horses from their bonds are loosened : O Radiant One, they shear the ground beneath them,
And far and wide shines out thy flame, and flickers rapidly moving over earth's high ridges.

5 Forth darts the Bull's tongue like the sharp stone weapon discharged by him who fights to win the cattle.
Agni's fierce flame is like a hero's onset: dread and resistless he destroys the forests.

6 Thou with the sunlight of the great Impeller hast boldly over-spread the earth's expanses.
So drive away with conquering might all perils : fighting out foemen burn up those who harm us.

2 *The loud-voiced and eternal* : the Maruts.

3 *Navagvas* : the flames of fire being regarded as the ministers of Agni, who is the best or oldest of the Aṅgirases of whom the Navagvas are a class.

4 *Earth's high ridges* : *ádhi sānu pṛśneḥ*; Pṛśni here being the multiform earth.

5 *Who fights to win the cattle* : Indra who wars with demons of drought and darkness.

6 *The great Impeller* : Sūrya, the vivifying Sun.

7 Wondrous ! of wondrous power ! give to the singer wealth wondrous, marked, most wonderful, life-giving.
Wealth bright, O Bright One, vast, with many heroes, give with thy bright flames to the man who lauds thee.

HYMN VII. *Agni.*

1. Him, messenger of earth and head of heaven, Agni Vaiśvānara, born in holy Order,
The Sage, the King, the guest of men, a vessel fit for their mouths, the Gods have generated.

2 Him have they praised, mid-point of sacrifices, great cistern of libations, seat of riches.
Vaiśvānara, conveyer of oblations, ensign of worship, have the Gods engendered.

3 From thee, O Agni, springs the mighty singer, from thee come heroes who subdue the foeman.
O King, Vaiśvānara, bestow thou on us excellent treasures worthy to be longed for.

4 To thee, Immortal ! when to life thou springest, all the Gods sing for joy as to their infant.
They by thy mental powers were made immortal, Vaiśvānara, when thou shonest from thy Parents.

5 Agni Vaiśvānara, no one hath ever resisted these thy mighty ordinances,
When thou, arising from thy Parents' bosom, foundest the light for days' appointed courses.

6 The summits of the heaven are traversed through and through by the Immortal's light, Vaiśvānara's brilliancy.
All creatures in existence rest upon his head. The Seven swift-flowing Streams have grown like branches forth,

7 Vaiśvānara, who measured out the realms of air, Sage very wise who made the lucid spheres of heaven,

7 *Sá citra citrám citáyantam asmé citrakṣatra citrátamam vasodhām* | *Candrám rayim puruvīram bṛhántam cándra candrābhir gṛṇaté yuvasva.*

---

1 *A vessel fit for their mouths* : through whose means they receive men's offerings.

2 *Mid-point of sacrifices* : 'the bond of sacrifices.'—Wilson. Agni or fire is essential in all sacrifices.

6 *The Seven swift-flowing Streams* : the five rivers of the Panjāb, the Indus and the Sarasvatī or the Kubhā. *Have grown* : from Vaiśvānara Agni.

7 *Of immortality* : according to Sāyaṇa, of water which is the cause of immortality 'Of ambrosial (rain).'—Wilson.

The Undeceivable who spread out all the worlds, keeper is he and guard of immortality.

HYMN VIII. *Agni.*

1. At Jātavedas' holy gathering I will tell aloud the conquering might of the swift red-hued Steer.
A pure and fresher hymn flows to Vaiśvānara, even as for Agni lovely Soma is made pure.

2 That Agni, when in loftiest heaven he sprang to life, Guardian of Holy Laws, kept and observed them well.
Exceeding wise, he measured out the firmament. Vaiśvānara attained to heaven by mightiness.

3 Wonderful Mitra propped the heaven and earth apart, and covered and concealed the darkness with his light.
He made the two bowls part asunder like two skins. Vaiśvānara put forth all his creative power.

4 The Mighty seized him in the bosom of the floods : the people waited on the King who should be praised.
As envoy of Vivasvān Mātariśvan brought Agni Vaiśvānara hither from far away.

5 In every age bestow upon the singers wealth, worthy of holy synods, glorious, ever new.
King, undecaying, as it were with sharpened bolt, smite down the sinner like a tree with lightning-flash.

6 Do thou bestow, O Agni, on our wealthy chiefs, rule, with good heroes, undecaying, bending not.
So may we win for us strength, O Vaiśvānara, hundredfold, thousandfold, O Agni, by thy help.

7 O thou who dwellest in three places, Helper, keep with effective guards our princely patrons.
Keep our band, Agni, who have brought thee presents. Lengthen their lives, Vaiśvānara, when lauded.

3 *The two bowls* : the heaven and earth, called *dhiṣáṇe* or bowls from their hemispherical appearance.

4 *The Mighty* : the Gods who followed and found the fugitive Agni. *The people* : or the subjects, *viśaḥ*. *Of Vivasvān* : according to Sāyaṇa, from Āditya or the Sun.

7 *Who dwellest in three places* : in heaven as the Sun, in the firmament as lightning, and on earth as fire.

HYMN IX. *Agni.*

1. One half of day is dark, and bright the other : both atmospheres move on by sage devices.
Agni Vaiśvānara, when born as Sovran, hath with his lustre overcome the darkness.

2 I know not either warp or woof, I know not the web they weave when moving to the contest.
Whose son shall here speak words that must be spoken without assistance from the Father near him?

3 For both the warp and woof he understandeth, and in due time shall speak what should be spoken,
Who knoweth as the immortal world's Protector, descending, seeing with no aid from other.

4 He is the Priest, the first of all : behold him. Mid mortal men he is the light immortal.
Here was he born, firm-seated in his station, Immortal, ever waxing in his body.

5 A firm light hath been set for men to look on : among all things that fly the mind is swiftest.

The hymn is somewhat obscure; but the general purport appears to be; Agni is the priests' guide and teacher. As sunlight dispels the darkness so he enlightens our understandings. I know nothing of the mysteries of sacrifice ; but I look to Agni for light, and prepare the ear and eye of my mind to receive knowledge and inspiration from him.

1 *Both atmospheres* . the *rájas* or atmosphere is divided into two parts, one half belonging to the sky and the other to the earth. See Wallis, *The Cosmology of the Ṛgveda*, pp. 115, 116.

2 *I know not either warp or woof* : 'The first half of the stanza...implies, according to those who know tradition, *samp adāyavidaḥ*, says *Sāyana*, a figurative allusion to the mysteries of sacrifice : the threads of the warp, *tantu*, are the metres of the Vedas, those of the woof, *otu*, the liturgic prayers and ceremonial, the combination of which two is the cloth, or sacrifice : the *ātmavidaḥ*, or, *Vedāntis*, understand it as alluding to the mysteries of creation, the threads of the warp being the subtle elements, those of the woof the gross, and their com ination the universe.'—Wilson. Professor Grassmann and the translators of the *Siebenzig Lieder* think that a young singer is preparing himself for a contest with older bards, and, being distrustful of his own unaided powers to find material for his song, expresses his reliance upon Agni, and seeks inspiration from him. *To the contest* : the sacrifice is here intended : a meeting for religious worship; *saṅgamane devayajane*.—Sāyaṇa,

Whose son : Agni is the Father whose aid every one requires, however excellent his own human father may be.

5 *A firm light* : Agni remains in his place, and the effectual performance of the sacrifice depends upon the activity of his mind.

'According to the *Vedānti* view of the text, the light is *Brahma*, seated spontaneously in the heart as

All Gods of one accord, with one intention, move unobstructed to a single purpose.

6 Mine ears unclose to hear, mine eye to see him ; the light that harbours in my spirit broadens.
Far roams my mind whose thoughts are in the distance. What shall I speak, what shall I now imagine ?

7 All the Gods bowed them down in fear before thee, Agni, when thou wast dwelling in the darkness.
Vaiśvānara be gracious to assist us, may the Immortal favour us and help us.

HYMN X. *Agni.*

1. INSTALL at sacrifice, while the rite advances, your pleasant, heavenly Agni, meet for praises.
With hymns—for he illumines us—install him. He, Jātavedas, makes our rites successful.

2 Hear this laud, Radiant Priest of many aspects, O Agni with the fires of man enkindled,
Laud which bards send forth pure as sacred butter, strength to this man, as 'twere for self-advantage.

3 Mid mortal men that singer thrives in glory who offers gifts with hymns of praise to Agni,
And the God, wondrous bright, with wondrous succours helps him to win a stable filled with cattle.

4 He, at his birth, whose path is black behind him, filled heaven and earth with far-apparent splendour :
And he himself hath been, through night's thick darkness, made manifest by light, the Purifier.

5 With thy most mighty aid, confer, O Agni, wonderful wealth on us and on our princes,
Who stand preëminent, surpassing others in liberal gifts, in fame, and hero virtues.

6 Agni, accept this sacrifice with gladness, which, seated here, the worshipper presenteth.
Fair hymns hadst thou among the Bharadvājas, and holpest them to gain abundant vigour.

7 Scatter our foes, increase our store. May we be glad a hundred winters with brave sons.

HYMN XI. *Agni.*

1. EAGERLY sacrifice thou, most skilful, Agni ! Priest, pressing on as if the Maruts sent thee.
To our oblation bring the two Nāsatyas, Mitra and Varuṇa and Earth and Heaven.

2 Thou art our guileless, most delightful Herald, the God, among mankind, of holy synods.
A Priest with purifying tongue, O Agni, sacrifice with thy mouth to thine own body.

3 For even the blessed longing that is in thee would bring the Gods down to the singer's worship,
When the Aṅgirases' sagest Sage, the Poet, sings the sweet measure at the solemn service.

4 Bright hath he beamed, the wise, the far-refulgent. Worship the two wide-spreading Worlds, O Agni,
Whom as the Living One rich in oblations the Five Tribes, bringing gifts, adorn with homage.

5 When I with reverence clip the grass for Agni, when the trimmed ladle, full of oil, is lifted,
Firm on the seat of earth is based the altar : eye-like, the sacrifice is directed Sun-ward.

the means of true knowledge, to which all the senses, together with the mind and consciousness, refer, as to the one cause of creation, or *Paramātmā*, supreme spirit.'—Wilson. The stanza is translated by Prof. Wilson, after Sāyaṇa : 'A steady light, swifter than thought, stationed among moving beings to show (the way) to happiness : all the gods being of one mind and of like wisdom, proceed respectfully to the presence of the one (chief) agent. (Vaiśvānara)'.

---

1 *Install* : establish him as your *Purohita* or Chief Priest ; or set him in front as the Āhavanīya fire.

2 *Strength to this man* : the hymn is to give strength to the worshipper, and the priests are to sing with vigour as though their own interests were immediately concerned. Sāyaṇa takes *mamátā* (out of self-interest) as a proper name, 'As Mamatā (formerly offered it).'—Wilson.

3 *A stable filled with cattle* : the expression includes the waters of heaven, the light of day, and booty in cattle-lifting expeditions.

6 *Bharadvājas* : the family of the great Ṛṣi to whom the hymn was revealed.

7 *A hundred winters* : See note on VI. 4. 8.

---

2 *Of holy synods* : I follow Professor Ludwig in taking *vidáthā* as an old genitive plural, and not = *vidáthe*, as Sāyaṇa does. *Sacrifice......to thine own body* : or, sacrifice......thy proper body ; or, (keep thine own body near us to be worshipped.

6 Enrich us, O thou Priest of many aspects, with the Gods, Agni, with thy fires, enkindled.
O Son of Strength, clad in the robe of riches, may we escape from woe as from a prison.

HYMN XII. *Agni.*

1. KING of trimmed grass, Herald within the dwelling, may Agni worship the Impeller's World-halves.
He, Son of Strength, the Holy, from a distance hath spread himself abroad with light like Sūrya.

2 In thee, most wise, shall Dyaus, for full perfection, King ! Holy One ! pronounce the call to worship.
Found in three places, like the Speeder's footstep, come to present men's riches as oblations !

3 Whose blaze most splendid, sovran in the forest, shines waxing on his way like the Impeller.
He knows himself, like as a guileless smelter, not to be stayed among the plants, Immortal.

4 Our friends extol him like a steed for vigour, even Agni in the dwelling, Jātavedas.
Tree-fed, he fights with power as doth a champion, like Dawn's Sire to be praised with sacrifices.

5 Men wonder at his shining glows when, paring the woods with ease, o'er the broad earth he goeth,
And, like a rushing flood, loosed quickly, burneth, swift as a guilty thief, o'er desert places.

6 So mighty thou protectest us from slander, O Champion, Agni ! with all fires enkindled.
Bring opulence and drive away affliction. May brave sons gladden us through a hundred winters.

HYMN XIII. *Agni.*

1. FROM thee, as branches from a tree, O Agni, from thee, Auspicious God ! spring all our blessings—
Wealth swiftly, strength in battle with our foemen, the rain besought of heaven, the flow of waters.

2 Thou art our Bhaga to send wealth : thou dwellest, like circumambient air, with wondrous splendour.
Friend art thou of the lofty Law, like Mitra, Controller, Agni ! God ! of many a blessing.

3 Agni ! the hero slays with might his foeman ; the singer bears away the Paṇi's booty—
Even he whom thou, Sage, born in Law, incitest by wealth, accordant with the Child of Waters.

4 The man who, Son of Strength ! with sacrifices, hymns, lauds, attracts thy fervour to the altar,
Enjoys each precious thing, O God, O Agni, gains wealth of corn and is the lord of treasures.

5 Grant, Son of Strength, to men for their subsistence such things as bring high fame and hero children.
For thou with might givest much food in cattle even to the wicked wolf when he is hungry.

6 Eloquent, Son of Strength, Most Mighty, Agni, vouchsafe us seed and offspring, full of vigour.
May I by all my songs obtain abundance. May brave sons gladden us through a hundred winters.

HYMN XIV. *Agni.*

1. WHOSO to Agni hath endeared his thought and service by his hymns,
That mortal eats before the rest, and finds sufficiency of food.

1 *The Impeller's World-halves* : the heaven and earth, illumined by, and so belonging to, the all-vivifying Sun.

2. *In thee* : or by thee, in thy lightning form, Dyaus or Heaven shall pronounce the *yājyā*, the consecrating text used at sacrifices and thus invite the Gods to be present. *Found in three places* : in heaven, atmosphere, and earth, and in the corresponding fire-receptacles at sacrifice. *The Speeder's footstep* : the threefold step of Viṣṇu as the Sun, traversing the three worlds of earth, air, and sky.

3 *A guileless smelter* : he knows his power to consume what he attacks, like a melter of metal who knows what he can do and does not deceive himself. According to Sāyaṇa, *dravitā* here means runner, 'rushing like the innoxious (wind).'—Wilson.

4 *Dawn's Sire* : Dyaus or Heaven, the Father of Uṣas or Dawn.

3 *His foeman* : *vṛtrám* signifying any enemy : *dvarakam śatrum*—Sāyaṇa. *The Child of Waters* : here said to mean the lightning, born of the watery cloud.

5 *To the wicked wolf* : or, perhaps, even to the foe Vṛka. Cf. VII. 68. 8.

1 *That mortal eats before the rest* : 'May the mortal... quickly become distinguished as first (amongst men).'—Wilson.

2 Agni, in truth, is passing wise, most skilled in ordering, a Seer.
At sacrifices Manus' sons glorify Agni as their Priest.

3 The foeman's wealth in many a place, Agni, is emulous to help.
Men fight the fiend, and seek by rites to overcome the riteless foe.

4 Agni bestows the hero chief, winner of waters, firm in fray.
Soon as they look upon his might his enemies tremble in alarm.

5 For with his wisdom Agni, God, protects the mortal from reproach,
Whose conquering wealth is never checked, is never checked in deeds of might.

6 O Agni, God with Mitra's might call hither the favour of the Gods from earth and heaven.
Bring weal from heaven that men may dwell securely. May we o'ercome the foe's malign oppressions, may we o'ercome them, through thy help o'ercome them.

HYMN XV. *Agni.*

1. WITH this my song I strive to reach this guest of yours, who wakes at early morn, the Lord of all the tribes.
Each time he comes from heaven, the Pure One from of old : from ancient days the Child eats everlasting food.

2 Whom, well-disposed, the Bhṛgus stablished as a Friend, whom men must glorify, high-flaming in the wood.
As such, most friendly, thou art every day extolled in lauds by Vītahavya, O thou wondrous God.

3 Be thou the foeless helper of the skilful man, subduer of the enemy near or far away.
Bestow a wealthy home on men, O Son of Strength. Give Vītahavya riches spreading far and wide, give Bharadvāja wide-spread wealth.

4 Him, your refulgent guest, Agni who comes from heaven, the Herald of mankind, well-skilled in sacred rites,
Who, like a holy singer, utters heavenly words, oblation-bearer, envoy, God, I seek with hymns.

5 Who with his purifying, eye-attracting form hath shone upon the earth as with the light of Dawn ;
Who speeding on, as in the fight of Etaśa, cometh, untouched by age, as one athirst in heat.

6 Worship ye Agni, Agni, with your log of wood; praise your beloved, your beloved guest with songs.
Invite ye the Immortal hither with your hymns. A God among the Gods, he loveth what is choice, loveth our service, God mid Gods.

7 Agni inflamed with fuel in my song I sing, pure, Cleanser, steadfast, set in front at sacrifice.
Wise Jātavedas we implore with prayers for bliss the Priest, the holy Singer, bounteous, void of guile.

8 Men, Agni, in each age have made thee, Deathless One, their envoy, offering-bearer, guard adorable.
With reverence Gods and mortals have established thee, the ever-watchful, omnipresent Household Lord.

9 Thou, Agni, ordering the works and ways of both, as envoy of the Gods traversest both the worlds.
When we lay claim to thy regard and gracious care, be thou to us a thrice-protecting friendly guard.

10 Him fair of face, rapid, and fair to look on, him very wise may we who know not follow.
Let him who knows all rules invite for worship, Agni announce our offering to the Immortals.

11 Him, Agni, thou deliverest and savest who brings him prayer to thee the Wise, O Hero,
The end of sacrifice or its inception ; yea, thou endowest him with power and riches.

12 Guard us from him who would assail us,

2 *Most skilled in ordering* : the chief regulator of religious rites.

3 *Emulous to hlep* : waiting for us to seize and use.

1 *The Child* : born of the fire sticks, or of Heaven and Earth. *Everlasting food* : the Amṛta contained in the sacrificial offerings.

2 *Vītahavya* : either the name of the Ṛṣi, as Sāyaṇa takes it, or an epithet 'whose oblations are enjoyed,' qualifying Bharadvāja understood.

5 *In the fight of Etaśa* : when he contended with Sūrya. See II. 19. 5, where Indra is said to have assisted Etaśa.

9 *Of both* : of Gods and men.

11 The second half of the stanza is not clear. Professor Wilson paraphrases it after Sāyaṇa : 'thou rewardest with strength and with riches him (who undertakes) the institution, (who effects) the accomplishment, of the sacrifice.

Agni ; preserve us, O thou Victor, from dishonour.
Here let the place of darkening come upon thee : may wealth be ours, desirable in thousands.

13 Agni, the Priest, is King, Lord of the homestead, he, Jātavedas, knows all generations.
Most skilful worshipper mid Gods and mortals, may he begin the sacrifice, the Holy.

14 Whate'er to-day thou, bright-flamed Priest, enjoyest from the man's rite—for thou art sacrificer—
Worship, for duly dost thou spread in greatness : bear off thine offerings of to-day, Most Youthful.

15 Look thou upon the viands duly laid for thee. Fain would he set thee here to worship Heaven and Earth.
Help us, O liberal Agni, in the strife for spoil, so that we may o'ercome all things that trouble us, o'ercome, o'ercome them with thy help.

16 Together with all Gods, O fair-faced Agni, be seated first upon the wool-lined altar,
Nest-like, bedewed with oil. Bear this our worship to Savitar who sacrifices rightly.

17 Here the arranging priests, as did Atharvan, rub this Agni forth,
Whom, not bewildered, as he moved in winding ways, they brought from gloom.

18 For the Gods' banquet be thou born, for full perfection and for weal.
Bring the Immortal Gods who strengthen holy Law : so let our sacrifice reach the Gods.

19 O Agni, Lord and Master of men's homesteads, with kindled fuel we have made thee mighty.
Let not our household gear be found defective. Sharpen us with thy penetrating splendour.

12 *The place of darkening* : this passage is very obscure. Professor Ludwig thinks that the time of battle is meant. May the foes who attack us find that they have to deal with thee as our ally. Sāyaṇa explains *pāthaḥ* as food offered in sacrifice, and *dhvasmanvát* as *dhvastadoṣam*, freed from defects : 'May the food reach thee free from imperfection.' Professor Grassmann translates : 'Es dring mit dir dein rauchumhüllter Gang vor;' 'Thy smoke-enveloped course press forward with thee.'

13 *Knows all generations* : *víśvā veda jánimā* ; etymology of Jātavedas.—Ludwig.

14 *The man's* : who institutes the sacrifice.

15 *Fain would he* : the patron of the sacrifice.

The original hymn seems to end with this stanza, as the repetition, o'ercome...o'ercome, o'ercome, *tarema*... *tarema*......*tarema* also indicates.

16 *Wool-lined altar* : built up like the nest of a bird with layers of wool, in which wool and resins for incense are placed. See Aitareya-Brāhmaṇa, I. 5. 28 (Haug's translation p. 62). *To Savitar* : according to Sāyaṇa, Savitar means the originator, the institutor of the sacrifice, and the dative case is used in the sense of the genitive, 'the sacrifice of the institutor of the rite.' In another place he explains *savitré yájamānāya* by 'for the sake of the benefit of the sacrificing institutor of the ceremony.'

17 *Atharvan* : the priest who first obtained fire and offered Soma and prayers to the Gods. *As he moved in winding ways* : when he fled and tried to hide himself from the Gods.

HYMN XVI. *Agni.*

1. PRIEST of all sacrifices hast thou been appointed by the Gods,
Agni, amid the race of man.

2 So with thy joyous tongues for us sacrifice nobly in this rite.
Bring thou the Gods and worship them.

3 For well, O God, Disposer, thou knowest, straight on, the paths and ways,
Agni, most wise in sacrifice.

4 Thee, too, hath Bharata of old, with mighty men, implored for bliss.
And worshipped thee the worshipful.

5 Thou givest these abundant boons to Divodāsa pouring forth,
To Bharadvāja offering gifts.

6 Do thou, Immortal Messenger, bring hither the Celestial Folk;
Hearing the singer's eulogy.

7 Mortals with pious thought implore thee, Agni, God, at holy rites,
To come unto the feast of Gods.

8 I glorify thine aspect and the might of thee the Bountiful.
All those who love shall joy in thee,

9 Invoker placed by Manus, thou, Agni, art near, the wisest Priest :
Pay worship to the Tribes of Heaven.

10 Come, Agni, lauded, to the feast ; come to the offering of the gifts.
As Priest be seated on the grass.

11 So, Aṅgiras, we make thee strong with fuel and with holy oil.
Blaze high, thou youngest of the Gods.

12 For us thou winnest, Agni, God, heroic strength exceeding great,
Far-spreading and of high renown.

4 *Bharata* : according to Sāyaṇa the King of that name, son of Duṣyanta and Śakuntalā.

13 Agni, Atharvan brought thee forth, by rubbing, from the lotus-flower,
The head of Viśva, of the Priest.

14 Thee, Vṛtra's slayer, breaker down of castles, hath Atharvan's son,
Dadhyac the Ṛṣi, lighted up.

15 The hero Pāthya kindled thee the Dasyus' most destructive foe,
Winner of spoil in every fight.

16 Come, here, O Agni, will I sing verily other songs to thee,
And with these drops shalt thou grow strong.

17 Where'er thy mind applies itself, vigour preëminent hast thou :
There wilt thou gain a dwelling-place.

18 Not for a moment only lasts thy bounty, good to many a one !
Our service therefore shalt thou gain.

19 Agni, the Bhārata, hath been sought, the Vṛtra-slayer, marked of all,
Yea, Divodāsa's Hero Lord.

20 For he gave riches that surpass in greatness all the things of earth,
Fighting untroubled, unsubdued.

21 Thou, Agni, as in days of old, with recent glory, gathered light,
Hast overspread the lofty heaven.

22 Bring to your Agni, O my friends, boldly your laud and sacrifice :
Give the Disposer praise and song.

23 For as sagacious Herald he hath sat through every age of man,
Oblation-bearing messenger.

24 Bring those Two Kings whose ways are pure, Ādityas, and the Marut host,
Excellent God ! and Heaven and Earth.

25 For strong and active mortal man, excellent, Agni, is the look
Of thee Immortal, Son of Strength !

26 Rich through his wisdom, noblest be the giver serving thee to-day :
The man hath brought his hymn of praise.

27 These, Agni, these are helped by thee, who strong and active all their lives,
O'ercome the malice of the foe, fight down the malice of the foe.

28 May Agni with his pointed blaze cast down each fierce devouring fiend :
May Agni win us wealth by war.

29 O active Jātavedas, bring riches with store of hero sons :
Slay thou the demons, O Most Wise.

30 Keep us, O Jātavedas, from the troubling of the man of sin :
Guard us thou Sage who knowest prayer.

31 Whatever sinner, Agni, brings oblations to procure our death,
Save us from woe that he would work.

32 Drive from us with thy tongue, O God, the man who doeth evil deeds,
The mortal who would strike us dead.

33 Give shelter reaching far and wide to Bharadvāja, conquering Lord !
Agni, send wealth most excellent.

34 May Agni slay the Vṛtras,—fain for riches, through the lord of song,
Served with oblation, kindled, bright.

35 His Father's Father, shining in his Mother's everlasting side,
Set on the seat of holy Law.

36 O active Jātavedas, bring devotion that wins progeny, Agni, that it may shine to heaven.

37 O Child of Strength, to thee whose look is lovely we with dainty food,
O Agni, have poured forth our songs.

38 To thee for shelter are we come, as to the shade from fervent heat,
Agni, who glitterest like gold.

39 Mighty as one who slays with shafts, or like a bull with sharpened horn,
Agni, thou breakest down the forts.

40 Whom, like an infant newly born, devourer, in their arms they bear,
Men's Agni, skilled in holy rites.

41 Bear to the banquet of the Gods the God best finder-out of wealth,
Let him be seated in his place.

13 *The lotus-flower* : apparently a figurative expression for heaven. *Viśva* : Heaven, personified.

14 *Dadhyac* : See I. 84. 13, note.

15 *Pāthya* : probably some celebrated sacrificer. Dr. Garbe (Vaitāna-Sūtra II. 14) translates *pāthyó vṛṣā* in this text by 'der Hengst auf der Strasse, the Stallion on the way.'

18 *Not for a moment only lasts thy bounty* : Sāyaṇa understands this differently : 'Let not thy full (blaze) be distressing to the eye.'—Wilson.

19 *The Bhārata* : the especial protector of the Bharatas. According to Sāyaṇa the word means either 'descended from the priests called Bharatas,' or 'the bearer of oblations.'

24 *Those Two Kings* : Mitra and Varuṇa.

35 *His Father's Father* : 'here, as before, the mother of *Agni* is the earth, the father is heaven : Agni is said to be the father or fosterer of his parent heaven by transmitting to it the flame and smoke of burnt-offerings.'—Wilson.

37 *Child of Strength* : *sahaskṛta* ; literally, made or produced by strength, *i.e.* the violent agitation of the fire-stick.

42 In Jātavedas kindle ye the dear guest who hath now appeared
In a soft place, the homestead's Lord.
43 Harness, O Agni, O thou God, thy steeds which are most excellent :
They bear thee as thy spirit wills.
44 Come hither, bring the Gods to us to taste the sacrificial feast,
To drink the draught of Soma juice.
45 O Agni of the Bharatas, blaze high with everlasting might,
Shine forth and gleam, Eternal One.
46 The mortal man who serves the God with banquet, and, bringing gifts at sacrifice, lauds Agni,
May well attract, with prayer and hands uplifted, the Priest of Heaven and Earth, true Sacrificer.
47 Agni, we bring thee, with our hymn, oblation fashioned in the heart.
Let these be oxen unto thee, let these be bulls and kine to thee.
48 The Gods enkindle Agni, best slayer of Vṛtra, first in rank,
The Mighty One who brings us wealth and crushes down the Rākṣasas.

HYMN XVII. *Indra.*

1. DRINK Soma, Mighty One, for which, when lauded, thou breakest through the cattle-stall, O Indra ;
Thou who, O Bold One, armed with thunder smotest Vṛtra with might, and every hostile being.
2 Drink it thou God who art impetuous victor, Lord of our hymns, with beauteous jaws, the Hero,
Render of kine-stalls, car-borne, thunder-wielding, so pierce thy way to wondrous strength, O Indra.
3 Drink as of old, and let the draught delight thee : hear thou our prayer and let our songs exalt thee.
Make the Sun visible, make food abundant, slaughter the foes, pierce through and free the cattle.
4 These gladdening drops, O Indra, Self-sustainer, quaffed shall augment thee in thy mighty splendour.
Yea, let the cheering drops delight thee greatly, great, perfect, strong, powerful, all-subduing.
5 Gladdened whereby, bursting the firm enclosures, thou gavest splendour to the Sun and Morning.
The mighty rock that compassed in the cattle, ne'er moved, thou shookest from its seat, O Indra.
6 Thou with thy wisdom, power, and works of wonder, hast stored the ripe milk in the raw cows' udders,
Unbarred the firm doors for the kine of Morning, and, with the Aṅgirases, set free the cattle.
7 Thou hast spread out wide earth, a mighty marvel, and, high thyself, propped lofty heaven, O Indra.
Both worlds, whose Sons are Gods, thou hast supported, young, Mothers from old time of holy Order.
8 Yea, Indra, all the Deities installed thee their one strong Champion in the van for battle.
What time the godless was the Gods' assailant, Indra they chose to win the light of heaven.
9 Yea, e'en that heaven itself of old bent backward before thy bolt, in terror of its anger,
When Indra, life of every living creature, smote down within his lair the assailing Dragon.
10 Yea, Strong One ! Tvaṣṭar turned for thee, the Mighty, the bolt with thousand spikes and hundred edges,
Eager and prompt at will, wherewith thou crushedst the boasting Dragon, O impetuous Hero.
11 He dressed a hundred buffaloes, O Indra, for thee whom all accordant Maruts strengthen.
He, Pūṣan Viṣṇu, poured forth three great vessels to him, the juice that cheers, that slaughters Vṛtra.

42 *In Jātavedas kindle ye* : the meaning is said to be, that the fire of burnt-offerings is to be kindled by the fire produced by attrition.

46 *True Sacrificer* : whose sacrifices are always effectual.

47 *Let these be oxen* : let our oblations be as acceptable to thee as herds of cattle are to men.

6 *The ripe milk* : the cows are called raw as contrasted with the warm milk matured in their udders. See I. 62. 9. This miracle is ascribed to the Aśvins also. See I. 180. 3.

7 *Whose Sons are Gods* : Heaven and Earth are frequently called the parents of the Gods. So in Greek mythology the Gods sprang from the union of Uranus and Gaia. 'Cent mythologies,' M. Réville remarks, 'sont fondées sur le mariage du ciel et de la terre.' See Muir, *O. S. Texts*, V. p. 24.

8 *The godless* : the demon Vṛtra.

11 *He* : Agni. See V. 29. 7. *Three great vessels* : literally, lakes. See V. 29. 7. *That slaughters Vṛtra* : inspirits Indra to slay him.

12 Thou settest free the rushing wave of waters, the floods' great swell encompassed and obstructed.
Along steep slopes their course thou turnedst, Indra, directed downward, speeding to the ocean.
13 So may our new prayer bring thee to protect us, thee well-armed Hero with thy bolt of thunder,
Indra, who made these worlds, the Strong, the Mighty, who never groweth old, the victory-giver.
14 So, Indra, form us brilliant holy singers for strength, for glory, and for food and riches.
Give Bharadvāja hero patrons, Indra! Indra, be ours upon the day of trial.
15 With this may we obtain strength God-appointed, and brave sons gladden us through a hundred winters.

HYMN XVIII. *Indra.*

1. GLORIFY him whose might is all-surpassing, Indra the much-invoked who fights uninjured.
Magnify with these songs the never-vanquished, the Strong, the Bull of men, the Mighty Victor.
2 He, Champion, Hero, Warrior, Lord of battles, impetuous, loudly roaring, great destroyer,
Who whirls the dust on high, alone, o'erthrower, hath made all races of mankind his subjects.
3 Thou, thou alone, hast tamed the Dasyus; singly thou hast subdued the people for the Ārya.
In this, or is it not, thine hero exploit, Indra? Declare it at the proper season.
4 For true, I deem, thy strength is, thine the Mighty, thine, O Most Potent, thine the Conquering Victor;
Strong, of the strong, Most Mighty, of the mighty, thine, driver of the churl to acts of bounty.
5 Be this our ancient bond of friendship with you and with Aṅgirases here who speak of Vala.
Thou, Wondrous, Shaker of things firm, didst smite him in his fresh strength, and force his doors and castles.
6 With holy thoughts must he be called, the Mighty, showing his power in the great fight with Vṛtra.
He must be called to give us seed and offspring, the Thunderer must be moved and sped to battle.
7 He in his might, with name that lives for ever, hath far surpassed all human generations.
He, most heroic, hath his home with splendour, with glory and with riches and with valour.
8 Stranger to guile, who ne'er was false or faithless, bearing a name that may be well remembered,
Indra crushed Cumuri, Dhuni, Śambara, Pipru, and Śuṣṇa, that their castles fell in ruin.
9 With saving might that must be praised and lauded, Indra, ascend thy car to smite down Vṛtra.
In thy right hand hold fast thy bolt of thunder, and weaken, Bounteous Lord, his art and magic.
10 As Agni, as the dart burns the dry forest, like the dread shaft burn down the fiends, O Indra;
Thou who with high deep-reaching spear hast broken, hast covered over mischief and destroyed it.
11 With wealth, by thousand paths come hither, Agni, paths that bring ample strength, O thou Most Splendid.
Come, Son of Strength, o'er whom, Invoked of many! the godless hath no power to keep thee distant.
12 From heaven, from earth is bruited forth the greatness of him the firm, the fiery, the resplendent.
No foe hath he, no counterpart, no refuge is there from him the Conqueror full of wisdom
13 This day the deed that thou hast done is famous, when thou, for him, with many thousand others
Laidest low Kutsa, Āyu, Atithigva, and boldly didst deliver Tūrvayāṇa.

14 *The day of trial*: the decisive day of battle.
15 *With this*: *stutyā*, praise, is understood.

3 *At the proper season*: show that thou hast this power by aiding us before it is too late and when our enemies have conquered us.
5 *With you*: with Indra and his allies, the Maruts.

8 *Cumuri, etc.*: demons of drought. See Index.
10 The exact meaning of the second half-stanza is uncertain, as *gambhrīáyā* and *ṛṣváyā*, deep and high, have no substantive.
13 *For him*: for Tūrvayāṇa: who appears to have been an especial favourite of Indra. According to Sāyaṇa, *tūrvayāṇa*, 'quickly going,' is an epithet of Divodāsa. Sāyaṇa represents the exploit as having been achieved *for* Kutsa, Āyu, and Atithigva, but this is not the meaning of the words of the text. *A new hymn*: of praise for some new favour shown to us.

14 In thee, O God, the wisest of the Sages, all Gods were joyful when thou slewest Ahi.
When, lauded for thyself, thou gavest freedom to sore-afflicted Heaven and to the people.

15 This power of thine both heaven and earth acknowledge, the deathless Gods acknowledge it, O Indra.
Do what thou ne'er hast done, O Mighty Worker : beget a new hymn at thy sacrifices.

HYMN XIX. *Indra.*

1. GREAT, hero-like controlling men is Indra, unwasting in his powers, doubled in vastness.
He, turned to us, hath grown to hero vigour : broad, wide, he hath been decked by those who serve him.

2 The bowl made Indra swift to gather booty, the High, the Lofty, Youthful, Undecaying,
Him who hath waxed by strength which none may conquer, and even at once grown to complete perfection.

3 Stretch out those hands of thine, extend to us-ward thy wide capacious arms, and grant us glory.
Like as the household herdsman guards the cattle, so move thou round about us in the combat.

4 Now, fain for strength, let us invite your Indra hither, who lieth hidden with his Heroes,—
Free from all blame, without reproach, uninjured, e'en as were those who sang, of old, his praises.

5 With steadfast laws, wealth-giver, strong through Soma, he hath much fair and precious food to feed us.
In him unite all paths that lead to riches, like rivers that commingle with the ocean.

6 Bring unto us the mightiest might, O Hero, strong and most potent force, thou great Subduer !
All splendid vigorous powers of men vouchsafe us, Lord of Bay Steeds, that they may make us joyful.

7 Bring us, grown mighty in its strength, O Indra, thy friendly rapturous joy that wins the battle,
Wherewith by thee assisted and triumphant, we may laud thee in gaining seed and offspring.

8 Indra, bestow on us the power heroic, skilled and exceeding strong, that wins the booty,
Wherewith, by thine assistance, we may conquer our foes in battle, be they kin or stranger.

9 Let thine heroic strength come from behind us, before us, from above us or below us.
From every side may it approach us, Indra. Give us the glory of the realm of splendour.

10 With most heroic aid from thee, like heroes, Indra, may we win wealth by deeds of glory.
Thou, King, art Lord of earthly, heavenly treasure : vouchsafe us riches vast, sublime, and lasting.

11 The Bull, whose strength hath waxed, whom Maruts follow, free-giving Indra, the Celestial Ruler,
Mighty, all-conquering, the victory-giver, him let us call to grant us new protection.

12 Give up the people who are high and haughty to these men and to me, O Thunder-wielder !
Therefore upon the earth do we invoke thee, where heroes win, for sons and kine and waters.

13 Through these thy friendships, God invoked of many ! may we be victors over every foeman.
Slaying both kinds of foe, may we, O Hero, be happy, helped by thee, with ample riches.

HYMN XX. *Indra.*

1. GIVE us wealth, Indra, that with might, as heaven o'ertops the earth, o'ercomes our foes in battle,
Wealth that brings thousands and that wins the corn-lands, wealth, Son of Strength ! that vanquishes the foeman.

1 *Controlling men* : or, satisfier of men. 'Fulfiller (of the desires) of men.'—Wilson.

2 *The bowl* : that is, the libation of Soma juice. But see Ludwig, Ueber die neuesten Arbeiten, &c., p. 87.

4 *Who lieth hidden* : Sāyaṇa explains *catinam* as *śatrūṇām cātakam nāśakam* ; 'the destroyer (of enemies)'. —Wilson.

9 *From behind us, etc.* : or, from the west, from the north, from the south, from the east

11 This stanza has occurred in III. 47. 5.

12 *Where heroes win* : *śūrasātau* ; in battle.

13 *Both kinds of foe* : kinsmen and strangers. See stanza 8.

—

2 Even as the power of Dyaus, to thee, O Indra, all Asura sway was by the Gods entrusted,
When thou, Impetuous! leagued with Viṣṇu, slewest Vṛtra the Dragon who enclosed the waters.

3 Indra, Strong, Victor, Mightier than the mighty, addressed with prayer and perfect in his splendour,
Lord of the bolt that breaketh forts in pieces, became the King of the sweet juice of Soma.

4 There, Indra, while the light was won, the Paṇis fled, 'neath a hundred blows, for wise Daśoṇi,
And greedy Śuṣṇa's magical devices: nor left he any of their food remaining.

5 What time the thunder fell and Śuṣṇa perished, all life's support from the great Druh was taken.
Indra made room for his car-driver Kutsa who sate beside him, when he gained the sunlight.

6 As the Hawk rent for him the stalk that gladdens, he wrenched the head from Namuci the Dāsa.
He guarded Nam, Sayya's son, in slumber, and sated him with food, success, and riches.

7 Thou, thunder-armed, with thy great might hast shattered Pipru's strong forts who knew the wiles of serpents.
Thou gavest to thy worshipper Ṛjiśvan imperishable wealth, O Bounteous Giver.

8 The crafty Vetasu, the swift Daśoṇi, and Tugra speedily with all his servants,
Hath Indra, gladdening with strong assistance, forced near as 'twere to glorify the Mother.

9 Resistless, with the hosts he battles, bearing in both his arms the Vṛtra-slaying thunder.
He mounts his Bays, as the car-seat an archer: yoked at a word they bear the lofty Indra.

10 May we, O Indra, gain by thy new favour: so Pūrus laud thee, with their sacrifices,
That thou hast wrecked seven autumn forts, their shelter, slain Dāsa tribes and aided Purukutsa.

11 Favouring Uśanā the son of Kavi, thou wast his ancient strengthener, O Indra.
Thou gavest Navavāstva as a present, to the great father gavest back his grandson.

12 Thou, roaring Indra, drovest on the waters that made a roaring sound like rushing rivers,
What time, O Hero, o'er the sea thou broughtest, in safety broughtest Turvaśa and Yadu.

13 This Indra, was thy work in war: thou sentest Dhuni and Cumuri to sleep and slumber.
Dabhīti lit the flame for thee, and worshipped with fuel, hymns, poured Soma, dressed oblations.

HYMN XXI. *Indra. Viśvedevas.*

1. THESE the most constant singer's invocations call thee who art to be invoked, O Hero;
Hymns call anew the chariot-borne, Eternal: by eloquence men gain abundant riches.

2 I praise that Indra, known to all men, honoured with songs, extolled with hymns at sacrifices,
Whose majesty, rich in wondrous arts, surpasseth the magnitude of earth, and heaven in greatness.

3 He hath made pathways, with the Sun

4 *For wise Daśoṇi*: Daśoṇi would appear in this place to be the name of some man whom Indra protected. Sāyaṇa says that the dative case is put for the ablative, and that the meaning is, 'from the sage who offers many oblations,' that is, from Kutsa. Ludwig takes Daśoṇi here to be the priest of the Paṇis: 'fled or fell for or to him' meaning that he was powerless to save them.

5 *Druh*: or, oppressor. Cf. IV. 28. 2.

6 *The Hawk*: which brought the Soma from heaven. See I. 93. 6; IV. 27. *Namī*: See X. 48. 9.

8 Vetasu, Daśoṇi, and Tugra appear to be names of enemies conquered by Indra. But *swift*, *tūtujim*, may be a Proper Name, Tūtuji Tuji (VI. 26. 4), and Daśoṇi (*daśoṇim*) may be an adjective, 'having ten arms or helpers.' Cf. X. 49. 4, and see Ludwig, Der Ṛgveda, III. p. 156. *As 'twere to glorify the Mother*: Sāyaṇa takes *dyotanāya* as the name of a rājā, and according to his interpretation Indra compelled the conquered foes to approach Dyotana submissively as a son comes before a mother. *The Mother*: the great Mother Aditi.

10 *Autumn forts*: probably strong places on elevated ground occupied by the Dāsas or original inhabitants during the rains and autumn. According to Sāyaṇa, cities or strongholds of Śarat, a demon.

11 *Navavāstva*: an Asura, or a mysterious being who perhaps represents the Sun, released from captivity or eclipse by Indra and by him restored to his own or to Indra's father—apparently to Uśanā or Heaven. Cf. X. 49. 6: Bergaigne, II. 223; Pischel (Vedische Studien, II. 128); Ludwig, Ueber dien. Arbeiten auf dem Gebiete der Ṛgveda-forschung, 160.

12 See I. 174. 9.

13 *Dhuni and Cumuri*: Asuras or demons, sent to sleep, that is slain, by Indra. 'Thou, with sleep whelming Cumuri and Dhuni, slewest the Dasyu, keptest safe Dabhīti' (II. 15. 9). Cf. VI. 18. 8.

to aid him, throughout the darkness that extended pathless.
Mortals who yearn to worship ne'er dishonour, O Mighty God, thy Law who art Immortal.

4 And he who did these things, where is that Indra? among what tribes? what people doth he visit?
What sacrifice contents thy mind and wishes? What priest among them all? what hymn, O Indra?

5 Yea, here were they who, born of old, have served thee, thy friends of ancient time, thou active Worker.
Bethink thee now of these, Invoked of many! the midmost and the recent, and the youngest.

6 Inquiring after him, thy later servants, Indra, have gained thy former old traditions.
Hero, to whom the prayer is brought, we praise thee as great for that wherein we know thee mighty.

7 The demon's strength is gathered fast against thee: great as that strength hath grown, go forth to meet it.
With thine own ancient friend and companion, the thunderbolt, brave Champion! drive it backward.

8 Hear, too, the prayer of this thy present beadsman, O Indra, Hero, cherishing the singer.
For thou wast aye our fathers' Friend aforetime, still swift to listen to their supplication.

9 Bring to our help this day, for our protection, Varuṇa, Mitra, Indra, and the Maruts,
Pūṣan and Viṣṇu, Agni and Purandhi, Savitar also, and the Plants and Mountains.

10 The singers here exalt with hymns and praises thee who art very Mighty and Most Holy.
Hear, when invoked, the invoker's invocation. Beside thee there is none like thee, Immortal!

11 Now to my words come quickly thou who knowest, O Son of Strength, with all who claim our worship,
Who visit sacred rites, whose tongue is Agni, Gods who made Manu stronger than the Dasyu.

9 *Purandhi* : 'the intelligent,' or 'the bold' may be either an epithet of Agni or the name of a separate deity.

---

12 On good and evil ways be thou our Leader, thou who art known to all as Path-preparer.
Bring power to us, O Indra, with thy Horses, Steeds that are best to draw, broad-backed, unwearied.

HYMN XXII. *Indra.*

1. WITH these my hymns I glorify that Indra who is alone to be invoked by mortals,
The Lord, the Mighty One, of manly vigour, victorious, Hero, true, and full of wisdom.

2 Our sires of old, Navagvas, sages seven, while urging him to show his might, extolled him,
Dwelling on heights, swift, smiting down opponents, guileless in word, and in his thoughts most mighty.

3 We seek that Indra to obtain his riches that bring much food, and men, and store of heroes.
Bring us, Lord of Bay Steeds, to make us joyful, celestial wealth, abundant, undecaying.

4 Tell thou us this, if at thy hand aforetime the earlier singers have obtained good fortune,
What is thy share and portion, Strong Subduer, Asura-slayer, rich, invoked of many?

5 He who for car-borne Indra, armed with thunder, hath a hymn, craving, deeply-piercing, fluent,
Who sends a song effectual, firmly-grasping, and strength-bestowing, he comes near the mighty.

6 Strong of thyself, thou by this art hast shattered, with thought-swift Parvata, him who waxed against thee,
And, Mightiest! roaring! boldly rent in pieces things that were firmly fixed and never shaken.

7 Him will we fit for you with new devotion, the strongest Ancient One, in ancient manner.

2 *Navagvas* : here, apparently, identified with the Aṅgirases.

4 *What is thy share and portion* : 'what is the portion, what the offering (due) to thee.'—Wilson. *Asura-slayer*: possibly, the smiter and conqueror of the Asura Dyaus.

5 *Comes near the mighty* : 'encounters (with confidence) the malevolent.'—Wilson.

6 *Parvata* : the Genius of the mountains and clouds, frequently associated with Indra. According to Sāyaṇa (*bahuparvaṇā vajreṇa*), the many-knotted thunderbolt is intended. *Him who waxed against thee* : Vṛtra.

So may that Indra, boundless, faithful Leader, conduct us o'er all places hard to traverse.

8 Thou for the people who oppress hast kindled the earthly firmament and that of heaven.
With heat, O Bull, on every side consume them : heat earth and flood for him who hates devotion.

9 Of all the Heavenly Folk, of earthly creatures thou art the King, O God of splendid aspect.
In thy right hand, O Indra, grasp the thunder : Eternal ! thou destroyest all enchantments.

10 Give us confirmed prosperity, O Indra, vast and exhaustless for the foe's subduing.
Strengthen therewith the Ārya's hate and Dāsa's, and let the arms of Nahuṣas be mighty.

11 Come with thy team which brings all blessings hither, Disposer, much-invoked, exceeding holy.
Thou whom no fiend, no God can stay or hinder, come swiftly with these Steeds in my direction.

HYMN XXIII. *Indra.*

1. THOU art attached to pressed-out Soma, Indra, at laud, at prayer, and when the hymn is chanted ;
Or when with yoked Bays, Maghavan, thou comest, O Indra, bearing in thine arms the thunder.

2 Or when on that decisive day thou holpest the presser of the juice at Vṛtra's slaughter ;
Or when thou, while the strong one feared, undaunted, gavest to death, Indra, the daring Dasyus.

3 Let Indra drink the pressed-out Soma, Helper and mighty Guide of him who sings his praises.
He gives the hero room who pours oblations, and treasure even to the lowly singer.

4 E'en humble rites with his Bay steeds he visits : he wields the bolt, drinks Soma, gives us cattle.
He makes the valiant rich in store of heroes, accepts our praise and hears the singer's calling.

5 What he hath longed for we have brought to Indra, who from the days of old hath done us service.
While Soma flows we will sing hymn, and laud him, so that our prayer may strengthen Indra's vigour.

6 Thou hast made prayer the means of thine exalting, therefore we wait on thee with hymns, O Indra.
May we, by the pressed Soma, Soma-drinker ! bring thee, with sacrifice, blissful sweet refreshment.

7 Mark well our sacrificial cake, delighted : Indra, drink Soma and the milk commingled.
Here on the sacrificer's grass be seated : give ample room to thy devoted servant.

8 O Mighty One, be joyful as thou willest. Let these our sacrifices reach and find thee ;
And may this hymn and these our invocations turn thee, whom many men invoke, to help us.

9 Friends, when the juices flow, replenish duly your own, your bounteous Indra with the Soma.
Will it not aid him to support us ? Indra spares him who sheds the juice to win his favour.

10 While Soma flowed, thus Indra hath been lauded, Ruler of nobles, mid the Bharadvājas,
That Indra may become the singer's patron and give him wealth in every kind of treasure.

HYMN XXIV. *Indra.*

1. STRONG rapturous joy, praise, glory are with Indra : impetuous God, he quaffs the juice of Soma :
That Maghavan whom men must laud with singing, Heaven-dweller, King of songs, whose help is lasting.

2 He, Friend of man, most wise, victorious Hero, hears, with far-reaching aid, the singer call him.
Excellent, Praise of Men, the bard's Supporter, Strong, he gives strength, extolled in holy synod.

8 *The people who oppress* : the Rākṣasas and other enemies.

10 *Nahuṣas* : See VI. 46. 7, note.

1 *Strong rapturous joy* : produced by drinking Soma-libations.

2 *Praise of Men* : *śáṅso narām,* as Agni is called Narāśaṁsa.

3 The lofty axle of thy wheels, O Hero, is not surpassed by heaven and earth in greatness.
Like branches of a tree, Invoked of many! manifold aids spring forth from thee, O Indra.

4 Strong Lord, thine energies, endowed with vigour, are like the paths of kine converging homeward.
Like bonds of cord, Indra, that bind the younglings, no bonds are they, O thou of boundless bounty.

5 One act to-day, another act tomorrow: oft Indra makes what is not yet existent.
Here have we Mitra, Varuṇa, and Pūṣan to overcome the foeman's domination.

6 By song and sacrifice men brought the waters from thee, as from a mountain's ridge, O Indra.
Urging thy might, with these fair lauds they seek thee, O theme of song, as horses rush to battle.

7 That Indra whom nor months nor autumn seasons wither with age, nor fleeting days enfeeble,—
Still may his body wax, e'en now so mighty, glorified by the lauds and hymns that praise him.

8 Extolled, he bends not to the strong, the steadfast, nor to the bold incited by the Dasyu.
High mountains are as level plains to Indra: even in the deep he finds firm ground to rest on.

9 Impetuous Speeder through all depth and distance, give strengthening food, thou drinker of the juices.
Stand up erect to help us, unreluctant, what time the gloom of night brightens to morning.

10 Hasting to help, come hither and protect him, keep him from harm when he is here, O Indra.
At home, abroad, from injury preserve him. May brave sons gladden us through a hundred winters.

HYMN XXV. *Indra.*

1. WITH thine assistance, O thou Mighty Indra, be it the least, the midmost, or the highest,—
Great with those aids and by these powers support us, Strong God! in battle that subdues our foemen.

2 With these discomfit hosts that fight against us, and check the opponent's wrath, thyself uninjured.
With these chase all our foes to every quarter: subdue the tribes of Dāsas to the Ārya.

3 Those who array themselves as foes to smite us, O Indra, be they kin or be they strangers,—
Strike thou their manly strength that it be feeble, and drive in headlong flight our foemen backward.

4 With strength of limb the hero slays the hero, when bright in arms they range them for the combat.
When two opposing hosts contend in battle for seed and offspring, waters, kine, or corn-lands.

5 Yet no strong man hath conquered thee, no hero, no brave, no warrior trusting in his valour.
Not one of these is match for thee, O Indra. Thou far surpassest all these living creatures.

6 He is the Lord of both these armies' valour when the commanders call them to the conflict:

4 *Converging homeward*: all Indra's great deeds indicate their divine author as the tracks made by grazing cows may be traced back to the common pen from which they have come forth.

Like bonds: the ties by which Indra's worshippers are bound to him are ties of love and not fetters of slavery. There is a play on the word *dāman* in the text which derived from *dā*, to give, means gift or bounty, and derived from *dā*, to bind, means, cord, rope, bond, or fetter: *vatsānām ná tantáyah te Indra dā́manvantaḥ adamānaḥ sudāman* (Pada text). The word *vatsá* also means a youngling, especially a calf, and a dear child, a darling, so that Indra's favoured worshippers are also intended.

5 *Here*: that is, in Indra we have a champion equal to the three Gods mentioned.

10 *Hasting to help*: I follow Professor Pischel (*Vedische Studien*, I. p. 41) in his explanation of *nāyám* in this passage. Professor Ludwig translates somewhat similarly. Sāyaṇa (followed by Professors Wilson and Grassmann) takes *nāyám* in the signification of leader; 'accompany the leader.' Professor Roth thinks it may be a proper name. *Him*: the institutor of the sacrifice.

The poet prays for victory in a coming battle.

1 *By these powers*: on account of, or by means of, the sacrificial food which increases thy strength.

6 *He is the Lord*: Indra can give valour and victory to either side as he chooses. Sāyaṇa explains the first half-stanza differently: 'Of both these (disputants), that one acquires wealth whose priests invoke (Indra) at the sacrifice.'—Wilson.

When with their ranks expanded they are fighting with a great foe or for a home with heroes.

7 And when the people stir themselves for battle, be thou their saviour, Indra, and protector,
And theirs, thy manliest of our friends, the pious, the chiefs who have installed us priests, O Indra.

8 To thee for high dominion hath been given, for evermore, for slaughtering the Vṛtras,
All lordly power and might, O Holy Indra, given by Gods for victory in battle.

9 So urge our hosts together in the combats : yield up the godless bands that fight against us.
Singing, at morn may we find thee with favour, yea, Indra, and e'en now, we Bharadvājas.

HYMN XXVI. *Indra.*

1. O INDRA, hear us. Raining down the Soma, we call on thee to win us mighty valour.
Give us strong succour on the day of trial, when the tribes gather on the field of battle.

2 The warrior, son of warrior sire, invokes thee, to gain great strength that may be won as booty :
To thee, the brave man's Lord, the fiends' subduer, he looks when fighting hand to hand for cattle.

3 Thou didst impel the sage to win the daylight, didst ruin Śuṣṇa for the pious Kutsa.
The invulnerable demon's head thou clavest when thou wouldst win the praise of Atithigva.

4 The lofty battle-car thou broughtest forward; thou holpest Daśadyu the strong when fighting.
Along with Vetasu thou slewest Tugra, and madest Tuji strong, who praised thee, Indra.

5 Thou madest good the laud, what time thou rentest a hundred thousand fighting foes, O Hero,
Slewest the Dāsa Śambara of the mountain, and with strange aids didst succour Divodāsa.

6 Made glad with Soma-draughts and faith, thou sentest Cumuri to his sleep, to please Dabhīti.
Thou, kindly giving Raji to Piṭhīnas. slewest with might, at once, the sixty thousand.

7 May I too, with the liberal chiefs, O Indra, acquire thy bliss supreme and domination,
When, Mightiest ! Hero-girt ! Nahuṣa heroes boast them in thee, the triply-strong Defender.

8 So may we be thy friends, thy best beloved, O Indra, at this holy invocation.
Best be Prātardani, illustrious ruler, in slaying foemen and in gaining riches.

HYMN XXVII. *Indra.*

1. WHAT deed hath Indra done in the wild transport, in quaffing or in friendship with, the Soma ?
What joys have men of ancient times or recent obtained within the chamber of libation ?

2 In its wild joy Indra hath proved him faithful, faithful in quaffing, faithful in its friendship.
His truth is the delight that in this chamber the men of old and recent times have tasted.

3 All thy vast power, O Maghavan, we know not, know not the riches of thy full abundance.
No one hath seen that might of thine, productive of bounty every day renewed, O Indra.

4 This one great power of thine our eyes have witnessed, wherewith thou slewest Varaśikha's children,

3 *The sage* : *bhārgavam ṛṣim* : Sāyaṇa ; the Ṛṣi, descendant of Bhṛgu.

4 *Vetasu* : according to Sāyaṇa, either a king aided by him or a demon slain by him. Cf. VI. 20. 8.

Tuji : a rājā of that name, says Sāyaṇa.

6 *Raji* : a maiden of that name.—Sāyaṇa. *Piṭhīnas* : a man so called.—Sāyaṇa.

8 *Prātardani* : son of a prince named Pratardana.

The other names have occurred before. See Index.

The liberality of Abhyāvartin Cāyamāna is said to be the deified object of stanza 8.

1 'According to *Sāyaṇa* the Ṛṣi here expresses his impatience at the delay of the reward of his praises : in the next verse he sings his recantation.'—Wilson.

4 *Varaśikha* : a certain Asura or demon, says Sāyaṇa. He seems to have been the leader of the Vṛcīvans.

When by the force of thy descending thunder, at the mere sound, their boldest was demolished.

5 In aid of Abhyāvartin Cāyamāna, Indra destroyed the seed of Varaśikha.
At Hariyūpīyā he smote the vanguard of the Vṛcīvans, and the rear fled frighted.

6 Three thousand, mailed, in quest of fame, together, on the Yavyāvatī, O much-sought Indra,
Vṛcīvan's sons, falling before the arrow, like bursting vessels went to their destruction.

7 He, whose two red Steers, seeking goodly pasture, plying their tongues move on 'twixt earth and heaven,
Gave Turvaśa to Sṛñjaya, and, to aid him, gave the Vṛcīvans up to Daivavāta.

8 Two wagon-teams, with damsels, twenty oxen, O Agni, Abhyāvartin Cāyamāna,
The liberal Sovran, giveth me. This guerdon of Pṛthu's seed is hard to win from others.

HYMN XXVIII. *Cows.*

1. THE Kine have come and brought good fortune : let them rest in the cow-pen and be happy near us.
Here let them stay prolific, many-coloured, and yield through many morns their milk for Indra.

2 Indra aids him who offers sacrifice and gifts : he takes not what is his, and gives him more thereto.
Increasing ever more and ever more his wealth, he makes the pious dwell within unbroken bounds.

3 These are ne'er lost, no robber ever injures them : no evil-minded foe attempts to harass them.
The master of the Kine lives many a year with these, the Cows whereby he pours his gifts and serves the Gods.

4 The charger with his dusty brow o'ertakes them not, and never to the shambles do they take their way.
These Cows, the cattle of the pious worshipper, roam over widespread pasture where no danger is.

5 To me the Cows seem Bhaga, they seem Indra, they seem a portion of the first-poured Soma.
These present Cows, they, O ye men, are Indra. I long for Indra with my heart and spirit.

6 O Cows, ye fatten e'en the worn and wasted, and make the unlovely beautiful to look on.
Prosper my house, ye with auspicious voices. Your power is glorified in our assemblies.

7 Crop goodly pasturage and be prolific : drink pure sweet water at good drinking-places.
Never be thief or sinful man your master, and may the dart of Rudra still avoid you.

8 Now let this close admixture be close intermigled with these Cows,
Mixt with the Steer's prolific flow, and, Indra, with thy hero might.

HYMN XXIX. *Indra.*

1. YOUR men have followed Indra for his friendship, and for his loving-kindness glorified him.

5 *Abhyāvartin Cāyamāna* : a king, apparently the leader of the Pārthavas, the enemies of Varaśikha and the Vṛcīvans.

Hariyūpīyā : (having golden sacrificial posts), the name of a town, or, according to others, of a river.

Vṛcīvān's : Vṛcīvan is said to have been the eldest son of Varaśikha, and to have given his name to the family or tribe. The name does not occur again in the Hymns.

6 *Yavyāvatī* : the name of a river, according to Sāyaṇa identical with the Hariyūpīyā of stanza 5.

7 *He* : Indra. *Red Steers* : bright horses, according to Sāyaṇa.

Gave Turvaśa to Sṛñjaya : gave up the Turvaśas, a tribe apparently settled in the north-west of India, to their neighbours and enemies the Sṛñjayas. *Daivavāta* : Abhyāvartin Cāyamāna, son of Devavāta.

8 *With damsels* : accompanied with slave-girls ; or, drawn by mares. Cf. I. 126 3. *Of Pṛthu's seed* : or 'bestowed by Pārthavas,' that is, presented by Abhyāvartin, one of the descendants of Pṛthu.

3 *Are ne'er lost* ; *ná tā́ naśanti* : Sāyaṇa assigns an imperative meaning to *naśanti* and the other verbs in the indicative mood which occur in this and the following stanzas : 'Let not the *Cows* be lost : let no thief, etc.'—Wilson.

4 *The charger......o'ertakes them not* : they are not, or, according to Sāyaṇa, let them not be, carried off in predatory incursions.

5 The worshipper regards the Cows as the deities, Bhaga and Indra, who bring him happiness. *They, O ye men, are Indra* : an allusion, apparently, to the refrain of hymn 12 of Book II., He, O men, is Indra.

7 *May the dart of Rudra still avoid you* : so, I. 114. 10. 'Far be thy dart that killeth men or cattle,' and II. 33. 14. 'May Rudra's missile turn aside and spare us, the great wrath of the Impetuous One avoid us.'

8 This stanza appears to refer to the mingling of the milk (the cows) with the juice of strong Soma (the steer), which when offered as a libation to Indra will increase his heroic strength. But the phraseology is somewhat obscure.

For he bestows great wealth, the Thunder-wielder : worship him, Great and Kind, to win his favour.

2 Him to whose hand, men closely cling, and drivers stand on his golden chariot firmly stationed.

With his firm arms he holds the reins; his Horses, the Stallions, are yoked ready for the journey.

3 Thy devotees embrace thy feet for glory. Bold, thunder-armed, rich, through thy strength, in guerdon,

Robed in a garment fair as heaven to look on, thou hast displayed thee like an active dancer.

4 That Soma when effused hath best consistence, for which the food is dressed and grain is mingled;

By which the men who pray, extolling Indra, chief favourites of Gods, recite their praises.

5 No limit of thy might hath been appointed, which by its greatness sundered earth and heaven.

These the Prince filleth full with strong endeavour, driving, as 'twere, with help his flocks to waters.

6 So be the lofty Indra prompt to listen, Helper unaided, golden-visored Hero.

Yea, so may he, shown forth in might unequalled, smite down the many Vṛtras and the Dasyus.

HYMN XXX. *Indra.*

1. INDRA hath waxed yet more for hero prowess, alone, Eternal, he bestoweth treasures.

Indra transcendeth both the worlds in greatness : one half of him equalleth earth and heaven.

2 Yea, mighty I esteem his Godlike nature : none hindereth what he hath once determined.

Near and afar he spread and set the regions, and every day the Sun became apparent.

3 E'en now endures thine exploit of the Rivers, when, Indra, for their floods thou clavest passage.

Like men who sit at meat the mountains settled: by thee, Most Wise ! the regions were made steadfast.

4 This is the truth, none else is like thee, Indra, no God superior to thee, no mortal.

Thou slewest Ahi who besieged the waters, and lettest loose the streams to hurry seaward.

5 Indra, thou breakest up the floods and portals on all sides, and the firmness of the mountain.

Thou art the King of men, of all that liveth, engendering at once Sun, Heaven, and Morning.

HYMN XXXI. *Indra.*

1. SOLE Lord of wealth art thou, O Lord of riches : thou in thine hands hast held the people, Indra !

Men have invoked thee with contending voices for seed and waters, progeny and sunlight.

2 Through fear of thee, O Indra, all the regions of earth, though naught may move them, shake and tremble.

All that is firm is frightened at thy coming,—the earth, the heaven, the mountain, and the forest.

3 With Kutsa, Indra ! thou didst conquer Śuṣṇa, voracious, bane of crops, in fight for cattle.

5 *The Prince* : Indra appears to be meant. *Driving... his flocks* : cp. I. 10. 2. 'And the Ram hastens with his troop,' that is, Indra comes with his band of Maruts. Sāyaṇa takes *sūriḥ* in its more usual signification of worshipper or institutor of the sacrifice ; and Professor Wilson translates : 'the pious worshipper, hastening (to sacrifice), and earnestly performing worship, gratifies thee with the offering, as (the cowkeeper satisfies) the herds with water.'

6 *Helper unaided* : this seems to be the meaning of *ūtī ánūʼī*, with help that needs no other help. Sāyaṇa explains the words, 'by coming or by not coming,' whether he be present or absent.

Golden-visored : 'Azure-chinned.'—Wilson. 'With yellow-coloured jaws.'—Ludwig. I have followed Professor Roth.

---

1 Indra hath grown stronger and stronger for the performance of his mighty deeds.

3 *Like men who sit at meat* : or, perhaps, like flies who settle on food. See Geldner, Vedische Studien, II. 180.

---

1 *Men......with contending voices* : the combatants on both sides invoke Indra's aid in battle.

According to Prof. Pischel, *Vedische Studien*, I. 34, the meaning is as follows:—

Alone wast thou, Lord of all wealth and riches, yet hast thou made the folk submissive, Indra,

When with uplifted voice the tribes invoked thee for water, sons, posterity and sunlight.'

'The folk,' *kṛṣṭīḥ* meaning the speaker's enemies, and 'the tribes, *carṣaṇáyo*, meaning the five Āryan tribes.

3 *Kutsa* : the special favourite of Indra. *Bane of crops* : or Kuyava may be the name of another demon of drought or savage enemy. See Index. *Thou rentest*

In the close fray thou rentest him : thou stolest the Sun's wheel and didst drive away misfortunes.

4 Thou smotest to the ground the hundred castles, impregnable, of Śambara the Dasyu,
When, Strong, with might thou holpest Divodāsa who poured libations out, O Soma-buyer, and madest Bharadvāja rich who praised thee.

5 As such, true Hero, for great joy of battle mount thy terrific car, O Brave and Manly.
Come with thine help to me, thou distant Roamer, and, glorious God, spread among men my glory.

HYMN XXXII. *Indra.*

1. I WITH my lips have fashioned for this Hero words never matched, most plentiful and auspicious,
For him the Ancient, Great, Strong, Energetic, the very mighty Wielder of the Thunder.

2 Amid the sages, with the Sun he brightened the Parents : glorified, he burst the mountain;
And, roaring with the holy-thoughted singers, he loosed the bond that held the beams of Morning.

3 Famed for great deeds, with priests who kneel and laud him, he still hath conquered in the frays for cattle,
And broken down the forts, the Fort-destroyer, a Friend with friends, a Sage among the sages.

4 Come with thy girthed mares, with abundant vigour and plenteous strength to him who sings thy praises.
Come hither, borne by mares with many heroes, Lover of song ! Steer ! for the people's welfare.

5 Indra with rush and might, sped by his Coursers, hath swiftly won the waters from the southward.
Thus set at liberty the rivers daily flow to their goal, incessant and exhaustless.

HYMN XXXIII. *Indra.*

1. GIVE us the rapture that is mightiest, Indra, prompt to bestow and swift to aid, O Hero,
That wins with brave steeds where brave steeds encounter, and quells the Vṛtras and the foes in battle.

2 For with loud voice the tribes invoke thee, Indra, to aid them in the battle-field of heroes.
Thou, with the singers, hast pierced through the Paṇis : the charger whom thou aidest wins the booty.

3 Both races, Indra, of opposing foemen, O Hero, both the Ārya and the Dāsa,
Hast thou struck down like woods with well-shot lightnings : thou rentest them in fight, most manly Chieftain !

4 Indra, befriend us with no scanty succour, prosper and aid us, Loved of all that liveth,
When, fighting for the sunlight, we invoke thee, O Hero, in the fray, in war's division.

5 Be ours, O Indra, now and for the future, be graciously inclined and near to help us.
Thus may we, singing, sheltered by the Mighty, win many cattle on the day of trial.

HYMN XXXIV. *Indra.*

1. FULL many songs have met in thee, O Indra, and many a noble thought from thee proceedeth.
Now and of old the eulogies of sages, their

him : literally, 'bittest' : *dáśa*, according to Sāyaṇa, standing for *adaśaḥ*. *Stolest the Sun's wheel* : see I. 175. 4.

Misfortunes : according to Sāyaṇa, 'disturbing or injurious Rākṣasas, etc.

4 *The hundred castles* : probably the castles of cloud which retain the rain. So, II. 19. 6, 'And Indra, for the sake of Divodāsa, demolished Śambara's nine-and-ninety castles.'

4 *Soma-buyer* : purchaser of Soma-libations with the help which he gives to the worshipper.

---

2 *He brightened the Parents* : illuminated the universal parents, Heaven and Earth. *The sages* : the Aṅgirases, *the holy-thoughted singers* of the next line.

4 *With thy girthed mares* : the meaning of *nīvyābhiḥ*, a feminine plural adjective in the instrumental case, standing without a substantive, is uncertain. Sāyaṇa explains the word by *navyābhirnavatarābhiḥ*, 'very new or young,' and supplies *vaḍavābhiḥ*, 'mares.' Professor Roth thinks that *nīvyābhiḥ* may be a substantive meaning 'with garments,' and Professor Grassmann translates 'mit Gaben,' 'with gifts,' that is, presents carried in a *nīvī* or apron. *With many heroes* : *puruvīrābhiḥ* again is an adjective without a substantive, in the same gender, number, and case as *nīvyābhiḥ*. According to Sāyaṇa, it also qualifies *vaḍavābhiḥ*, 'with mares,' understood, and means 'having many colts.'

5 *From the southward* : from the quarter whence the Rains come.

---

1 *Give us the rapture* : let us be benefited by the transport which draughts of Soma juice produce in thee.

---

holy hymns and lauds, have yearned for Indra.

2 He, praised of many, bold, invoked of many, alone is glorified at sacrifices.
Like a car harnessed for some great achievement, Indra must be the cause of our rejoicing.

3 They make their way to Indra and exalt him, him whom no prayers and no laudations trouble;
For when a hundred or a thousand singers laud him who loves the song their praise delights him.

4 As brightness mingles with the Moon in heaven, the offered Soma yearns to mix with Indra.
Like water brought to men in desert places, our gifts at sacrifice have still refreshed him.

5 To him this mighty eulogy, to Indra hath this our laud been uttered by the poets,
That in the great encounter with the foemen, Loved of all life, Indra may guard and help us.

HYMN XXXV. *Indra.*

1. WHEN shall our prayers rest in thy car beside thee? When dost thou give the singer food for thousands?
When wilt thou clothe this poet's laud with plenty, and when wilt thou enrich our hymns with booty?

2 When wilt thou gather men with men, O Indra, heroes with heroes, and prevail in combat?
Thou shalt win triply kine in frays for cattle, so, Indra, give thou us celestial glory.

3 Yea, when wilt thou, O Indra, thou Most Mighty, make the prayer all-sustaining for the singer?
When wilt thou yoke, as we yoke songs, thy Horses, and come to offerings that bring wealth in cattle?

4 Grant to the Singer food with store of cattle, splendid with horses and the fame of riches.
Send food to swell the milch-cow good at milking: bright be its shine among the Bharadvājas.

5 Lead otherwise this present foeman, Śakra! Hence art thou praised as Hero, foe-destroyer
Him who gives pure gifts may I praise unceasing. Sage, quicken the Āṅgirases by devotion.

HYMN XXXVI. *Indra.*

1. THY raptures ever were for all men's profit: so evermore have been thine earthly riches.
Thou still hast been the dealer-forth of vigour, since among Gods thou hast had power and Godhead.

2 Men have obtained his strength by sacrificing, and ever urged him on to hero valour.

3 *They make their way*: that is, prayers and laudations reach Indra and strengthen him. They do not vex him as they would vex a man who would be unable to fulfil the prayers and would be conscious that he did not deserve the laudations.

4 *As brightness mingles with the Moon*: I follow Professor Ludwig in his interpretation of this difficult passage; but its exact meaning still seems doubtful. '*Arcā* is the nominative singular. We have here the later Jyotsnā or Kaumudī as the wife or feminine power of the Moon. Sūryā, the daughter of the Sun, *i. e.* the Moon's light which is borrowed from the Sun is an earlier conception.'—Ludwig.

5 *By the poets*: by those who sing hymns of praise. *Matibhiḥ=stotṛbhiḥ*—Sāyaṇa. *In the great encounter with the foemen*: *mahatí vṛtratū́rye*: in the great victory over Vṛtra: that is, generally, in battle with enemies; *saṅgrāme*.—Sāyaṇa.

---

1 *Rest in thy car beside thee?*: when shall our prayers reach thee as thou standest on thy chariot? The poet expresses impatience at Indra's inattention to his petitions.

5 I find this stanza hopelessly obscure, and do not attempt to translate it, giving instead of a conjectural translation a reproduction of the substance of Sāyaṇa's absolutely worthless paraphrase. *Lead otherwise*: according to Sāyaṇa, 'consign to death, to a course different from that of living beings.'—Wilson.

The Āṅgirases: the descendants of Aṅgirases, that is the Bharadvājas.

Professor Ludwig translates: 'Also at another time (I wish) hither this strong (defence), when thou as a hero, Śakra, singest open [aufsingst] the doors; may I never lose the cow that yields bright juice, cause thou her to hasten through the prayer of the Āṅgirases. In his Commentary Prof. Ludwig alters 'lose the cow, etc.' into 'lose the seed-pouring (bull) of the milch-cow.' Professor Aufrecht would read *vri janam* instead of *vṛjanam* and *vṛṇīṣe* instead of *gṛṇīṣe*, and Prof. Grassmann translates accordingly: 'Now too, as formerly, I choose for myself this man, when, Strong One, as hero thou openest the doors. Never then may the steer whose seed streams fail me. Quicken, O Sage, the singers through prayer.'

---

1 *Thy raptures*: produced by drinking the Soma juice. *Power and Godhead*: *asuryám*: Asura-hood, the nature and power of an Asura or High God. Some give a different meaning to *dhāráyathāḥ*: 'thou maintainest vigour among the gods.'—Wilson. 'Indra is said to give divine power to the other gods.'—Muir, *O. S. T.*, V. 92.

2 *His strength*: the powerful aid of Indra. *Charger*: Indra, impetuous as a war-horse who takes the bit between his teeth. Sāyaṇa explains *syūma gṛbhe*: as 'seizer of enemies who are in uninterrupted lines'. 'They offer sacrifices to him as seizer of an uninterrupted series

For the rein-seizing, the impetuous Charger they furnished power even for Vṛtra's slaughter.

3 Associate with him, as teams of horses, help, manly might, and vigour follow Indra.
As rivers reach the sea, so, strong with praises, our holy songs reach him the Comprehensive.

4 Lauded by us, let flow the spring, O Indra, of excellent and brightly-shining riches.
For thou art Lord of men, without an equal : of all the world thou art the only Sovran.

5 Hear what thou mayst hear, thou who, fain for worship, as heaven girds earth, guardest thy servant's treasure;
That thou mayst be our own, joying in power, famed through thy might in every generation.

HYMN XXXVII *Indra.*

1. Let thy Bay Horses, yoked, O mighty Indra, bring thy car hither fraught with every blessing.
For thee, the Heavenly, e'en the poor invoketh : may we this day, thy feast-companions, prosper.

2 Forth to the vat the brown drops flow for service, and purified proceed directly forward.
May Indra drink of this, our guest aforetime, Celestial King of the strong draught of Soma.

3 Bringing us hitherward all-potent Indra on well-wheeled chariot, may the Steeds who bear him
Convey him on the road direct to glory, and ne'er may Vāyu's Amṛta cease and fail him.

4 Supreme, he stirs this man to give the guerdon,—Indra, most efficacious of the princes,—
Wherewith, O Thunderer, thou removest sorrow, and, Bold One ! partest wealth among the nobles.

5 Indra is he who gives enduring vigour : may our songs magnify the God Most Mighty.
Best Vṛtra-slayer be the Hero Indra : these things he gives as Prince, with strong endeavour.

HYMN XXXVIII. *Indra.*

1. He hath drunk hence, Most Marvellous, and carried away our great and splendid call on Indra.
The Bounteous, when we serve the Gods, accepteth song yet more famous and the gifts we bring him.

2 The speaker filleth with a cry to Indra his ears who cometh nigh e'en from a distance.
May this my call bring Indra to my presence, this call to Gods composed in sacred verses.

3 Him have I sung with my best song and praises, Indra of ancient birth and Everlasting.
For prayer and songs in him are concentrated : let laud wax mighty when addressed to Indra :

4 Indra, whom sacrifice shall strengthen, Soma, and song and hymn, and praises and devotion,
Whom Dawns shall strengthen when the night departeth, Indra whom days shall strengthen, months, and autumns.

5 Him, born for conquering might in full perfection, and waxen strong for bounty and for glory,
Great, Powerful, will we to-day, O singer, invite to aid us and to quell our foemen.

---

of foes, their assailant, their subduer, and also for the destruction of Vṛtra.—Wilson.

1 *Thee, the Heavenly* : *svarvān* appears to apply to *tvā*, thee, Indra, and to stand for *svarvantam*. See Pischel, *Vedische Studien*, I. 198, 218.

3 *To glory* : 'to the prize of battle.'—Grassmann. 'To our rite.'—Wilson.

Vāyu's Amṛta : 'Vāyu is possessor of the Amṛta probably as being Tvaṣṭar's son-in-law. VIII. 26. 21.—Ludwig.

4 *This man* : the institutor of the sacrifice. *Wherewith* : on account of which guerdon. The liberal guerdon given by the nobles who defray the expenses of the sacrifice causes Indra in his turn to be gracious and liberal of his gifts to them.

5 *With strong endeavour* : exerting his power on behalf of his worshippers.

1 *He hath drunk hence* : Professor Ludwig thinks that the first line must refer to Agni, who receives the libation *hence*, that is, from the priest's cup, and conveys to Indra the invocation addressed to him. But Indra himself may be intended in the first line as well as in the second.

3 *Let laud wax mighty* : when the power of Indra is celebrated, the song should be lofty as the dignity of the subject demands.

5 *To quell our foemen* : or, to conquer Vṛtras, that is, Vṛtra and similar fiends.

HYMN XXXIX *Indra.*

1. Of this our charming, our celestial Soma, eloquent, wise, Priest, with inspired devotion,
Of this thy close attendant, hast thou drunken. God, send the singer food with milk to grace it.

2 Craving the kine, rushing against the mountain led on by Law, with holy-minded comrades,
He broke the never-broken ridge of Vala. With words of might Indra subdued the Paṇis.

3 This Indu lighted darksome nights, O Indra, throughout the years, at morning and at evening.
Him have they stablished as the days' bright ensign. He made the Mornings to be born in splendour.

4 He shone and caused to shine the worlds that shone not. By Law he lighted up the host of Mornings.
He moves with Steeds yoked by eternal Order, contenting men with nave that finds the sunlight.

5 Now, praised, O Ancient King ! fill thou the singer with plenteous food that he may deal forth treasures.
Give waters, herbs that have no poison, forests, and kine, and steeds, and men, to him who lauds thee.

HYMN XL. *Indra*

1. Drink, Indra ; juice is shed to make thee joyful : loose thy Bay Steeds and give thy friends their freedom.
Begin the song, seated in our assembly. Give strength for sacrifice to him who singeth.

2 Drink thou of this whereof at birth, O Indra, thou drankest, Mighty One ! for power and rapture.
The men, the pressing-stones, the cows, the waters have made this Soma ready for thy drinking.

3 The fire is kindled, Soma pressed, O Indra: let thy Bays, best to draw, convey thee hither.
With mind devoted, Indra, I invoke thee. Come, for our great prosperity approach us.

4 Indra, come hither : evermore thou camest through our great strong desire to drink the Soma.
Listen and hear the prayers which now we offer, and let this sacrifice increase thy vigour.

5 Mayst thou, O Indra, on the day of trial, present or absent, wheresoe'er thou dwellest,
Thence, with thy team, accordant with the Maruts, Song-lover ! guard our sacrifice, to help us.

HYMN XLI. *Indra.*

1. Come gracious to our sacrifice, O Indra : pressed Soma-drops are purified to please thee.
As cattle seek their home, so, Thunder-wielder, come, Indra, first of those who claim our worship.

2 With that well-formed most wide-extending palate, wherewith thou ever drinkest streams of sweetness,
Drink thou; the Adhvaryu standeth up before thee : let thy spoil-winning thunderbolt attend thee.

3 This drop, steer-strong and omniform, the Soma, hath been made ready for the Bull, for Indra.
Drink this, Lord of the Bays, thou Strong Supporter, this that is thine of old, thy food for ever.

4 Soma when pressed excels the unpressed Soma, better, for one who knows, to give him pleasure.
Come to this sacrifice of ours, O Victor : replenish all thy powers with this libation.

1 *Our celestial Soma* : as Professor Wilson observes, 'Several of the epithets in the text are unusual, and agreeably to European notions, very inapplicable to a beverage.' The Soma is called *eloquent* and *wise* as giving eloquence and wisdom, and *priest* because it is employed in offerings to the Gods.

With milk to grace it : that is, of which milk and butter constitute the most excellent part.

2 *Holy-minded comrades* : the Aṅgirases. *Vala* : a demon who stole away the cows of the Gods, *i. e.* the rays of light. See Index.

3 *This Indu* : Indu is here the Moon, which is identified with Soma.

The days' bright ensign : the standard by which time is measured.

4 *Nave* : used by synecdoche for chariot.

1 *Thy friends* : thy dear horses.

1 *Gracious* : more literally, 'without anger'. 'Unirascible.'—Wilson.

2 *The Adhvaryu* : the ministering priest.

3 *Supporter* : *sthātar*=Stator in Jupiter Stator, one who causes to stay or stand, rallier of men in battle.

4 *Replenish all thy powers* : or, 'give us all powers in full.'

5 We call on thee, O Indra : come thou hither : sufficient be the Soma for thy body.
Rejoice thee, Śatakratu ! in the juices : guard us in wars, guard us among our people.

HYMN XLII. *Indra.*

1. BRING sacrificial gifts to him, Omniscient, for he longs to drink,
The Wanderer who comes with speed, the Hero ever in the van.

2 With Soma go ye nigh to him chief drinker of the Soma's juice :
With beakers to the Impetuous God, to Indra with the drops effused.

3 What time, with Soma, with the juice effused, ye come before the God,
Full wise he knows the hope of each, and, Bold One, strikes this foe and that.

4 To him, Adhvaryu ! yea, to him give offerings of the juice expressed.
Will he not keep us safely from the spiteful curse of each presumptuous high-born foe ?

HYMN XLIII. *Indra.*

1. IN whose wild joy thou madest once Śambara Divodāsa's prey,
This Soma is pressed out for thee, O Indra : drink !

2 Whose gladdening draught, shed from the points, thou guardest in the midst and end,
This Soma is pressed out for thee, O Indra : drink !

3 In whose wild joy thou settest free the kine held fast within the rock,
This Soma is pressed out for thee, O Indra : drink !

4 This, in whose juice delighting thou gainest the might of Maghavan,
This Soma is pressed out for thee, O Indra : drink !

HYMN XLIV. *Indra.*

1. THAT which is wealthiest, Wealthy God ! in splendours most illustrious,
Soma is pressed : thy gladdening draught, Indra ! libation's Lord ! is this.

2 Effectual, Most Effectual One ! thine, as bestowing wealth of hymns,
Soma is pressed : thy gladdening draught, Indra ! libation's Lord ! is this.

3 Wherewith thou art increased in strength, and conquerest with thy proper aids,
Soma is pressed : thy gladdening draught, Indra ! libation's Lord ! is this.

4 Him for your sake I glorify as Lord of Strength who wrongeth none,
The Hero Indra, conquering all, Most Bounteous, God of all the tribes.

5 Those Goddesses, both Heaven and Earth, revere the power and might of him,
Him whom our songs increase in strength, the Lord of bounty swift to come.

6 To seat your Indra, I will spread abroad with power this song of praise.
The saving succours that abide in him, like songs, extend and grow.

7 A recent Friend, he found the skilful priest : he drank, and showed forth treasure from the Gods.
He conquered, borne by strong all-shaking mares, and was with far-spread power his friends' Protector.

8 In course of Law the sapient juice was quaffed : the Deities to glory turned their mind.
Winning through hymns a lofty title, he,

5 *Śatakratu* : Lord of a hundred, *i. e.* countless, powers.

3 *Strikes this foe and that* : there is no substantive in the text. Sāyaṇa makes *tám tam* refer to *kāmam*, hope or wish : 'And the suppressor (of enemies) assuredly grants it, whatever it may be.'—Wilson.

1 *Śambara* : a demon of draught. *Divodāsa* : called also Atithigva : 'Thou savedst Kutsa when Śuṣṇa was smitten down ; to Atithigva gavest Śambara for a prey.' —I. 51. 6.

2 *From the points* : from the sharp ends of the branchlets of the plant. See Hillebrandt, V. Mythologie, p. 232. *In the midst and end* : according to Sāyaṇa, at noon and at the evening libation.

4 *Gainest the might of Maghavan* : Indra acquires his power from libations of Soma juice.

6 *To seat your Indra* : as Indra's seat is on the *barhiś* or sacred grass that is spread on the floor of the chamber of sacrifice, so the hymn also, as his spiritual seat, is supposed to have the power of inducing him to come.

7 *He found the skilful priest* : 'Indra appreciates him who is skilled (in holy rites).'—Wilson. The word *yaṣṭāram*, sacrificer, is supplied by Sāyaṇa.

Borne by strong, all-shaking mares : this is Sāyaṇa's first explanation of *staulābhir dhantárībhiḥ*, two feminine plurals in the instrumental case, *vaḍavābhiḥ*, 'with mares, being understood. Brought by his robust agitators (of the earth, his steeds).'—Wilson. Or, Sāyaṇa says, although the words are feminine, the Maruts may be intended. Other conjectural explanations have been attempted, but they are not convincing.

the Lovely, made his beauteous form apparent.

9 Bestow on us the most illustrious strength: ward off men's manifold malignities.
Give with thy might abundant vital force, and aid us graciously in gaining riches.

10 We turn to thee as Giver, liberal Indra. Lord of the Bay Steeds, be not thou ungracious.
No friend among mankind have we to look to: why have men called thee him who spurs the niggard?

11 Give us not up, Strong Hero! to the hungry: unharmed be we whom thou, so rich, befriendest.
Full many a boon hast thou for men: demolish those who present no gifts nor pour oblations.

12 As Indra thundering impels the rain-clouds, so doth he send us store of kine and horses.
Thou art of old the Cherisher of singers: let not the rich who bring no gifts deceive thee.

13 Adhvaryu, hero, bring to mighty Indra—for he is King thereof—the pressed-out juices;
To him exalted by the hymns and praises, ancient and modern, of the singing Ṛṣis.

14 In the wild joy of this hath Indra, knowing full many a form, struck down resistless Vṛtras.
Proclaim aloud to him the savoury Soma so that the Hero, strong of jaw, may drink it.

15 May Indra drink this Soma poured to please him, and cheered therewith slay Vṛtra with his thunder.
Come to our sacrifice even from a distance, good lover of our songs, the bard's Supporter.

16 The cup whence Indra drinks the draught is present: the Amṛta dear to Indra hath been drunken,
That it may cheer the God to gracious favour, and keep far from us hatred and affliction.

17 Therewith enraptured, Hero, slay our foemen, the unfriendly, Maghavan! be they kin or strangers,
Those who still aim their hostile darts to smite us, turn them to flight, O Indra, crush and kill them.

18 O Indra Maghavan, in these our battles win easy paths for us and ample freedom.
That we may gain waters and seed and offspring, set thou our princes on thy side, O Indra.

19 Let thy Bay Stallions, harnessed, bring thee hither, Steeds with strong chariot and strong reins to hold them,
Strong Horses, speeding hither, bearing thunder, well-harnessed, for the strong exciting potion

20 Beside the vat, Strong God! stand thy strong Horses, shining with holy oil, like waves exulting.
Indra, they bring to thee, the Strong and Mighty, Soma of juices shed by mighty press-stones.

21 Thou art the Bull of earth, the Bull of heaven, Bull of the rivers, Bull of standing waters.
For thee, the Strong, O Bull, hath Indu swollen juice pleasant, sweet to drink, for thine election.

22 This God, with might, when first he had his being, with Indra for ally, held fast the Paṇi.
This Indu stole away the warlike weapons, and foiled the arts of his malignant father.

23 The Dawns he wedded to a glorious Consort, and set within the Sun the light that lights him.

10 *Who spurs the niggard*: urges even the niggardly to be liberal. See Pischel, *Vedische Studien*, I p. 124.

12 *The Cherisher of singers*: or, 'he whom the singers nourish, that is, strengthen by their hymns.

14 *Knowing full many a form*: detecting and not deceived by the various forms assumed by the demon Vṛtra and his crew.

15 *The bard's Supporter*: or, 'whom singers nourish,' as in stanza 12.

19 In this and the two following stanzas we have the repetition, so dear to some of the Vedic poets, of *vṛṣa* in composition, *vṛṣan* and *vṛṣabhá*, so commonly applied in the hymns to living beings and things preëminent for strength.

22 *This God*: Indu or Soma, the Moon. *Of his malignant father*: Tvaṣṭar appears to be meant. Sāyaṇa's paraphrase is non-natural: 'of the malignant secreter of (the stolen) wealth, (the cattle).'—Wilson. Sāyaṇa makes *pituḥ*, as derived from *pā*, to protect, = *pālayituḥ*, 'the safe keeper, and *svásya* = Lat. *sui*, 'of his property. This safe keeper, secreter, and robber would be the demon Vala.

23 *Glorious Consort*: the Sun. *In the third lucid regions*: perhaps, as Professor Ludwig suggests, in the spheres of the Sun, the Moon, and the stars. 'According to the scholiast, this may merely mean that the Soma becomes as it were ambrosia when received or concealed in the vessels at the three diurnal ceremonies, which ambrosia is properly deposited with the gods

He found in heaven, in the third lucid regions, the threefold Amṛta in its close concealment.

24 He stayed and held the heaven and earth asunder: the chariot with the sevenfold reins he harnessed.
This Soma set with power within the milch-kine a spring whose ripe contents ten fingers empty.

HYMN XLV. *Indra.*

1. THAT Indra is our youthful Friend, who with his trusty guidance led
Turvaśa, Yadu from afar.

2 Even to the dull and uninspired Indra gives vital power, and wins
Even with slow steed the offered prize.

3 Great are his ways of guiding us, and manifold are his eulogies:
His kind protections never fail.

4 Friends, sing your psalm and offer praise to him to whom the prayer is brought:
For our great Providence is he.

5 Thou, Slaughterer of Vṛtra, art Guardian and Friend of one and two,
Yea, of a man like one of us.

6 Beyond men's hate thou leadest us, and givest cause to sing thy praise:
Good Hero art thou called by men.

7 I call with hymns, as 'twere a cow to milk, the Friend who merits praise,
The Brahman who accepts the prayer.

8 Him in whose hands they say are stored all treasures from the days of old,
The Hero, conquering in the fight.

9 Lord of Strength, Caster of the Stone, destroy the firm forts built by men,
And foil their arts, unbending God!

10 Thee, thee as such, O Lord of Power, O Indra, Soma-drinker, true,
We, fain for glory, have invoked.

11 Such as thou wast of old, and art now to be called on when the prize
Lies ready, listen to our call.

12 With hymns and coursers we will gain, Indra, through thee, both steeds and spoil
Most glorious, and the proffered prize.

13 Thou, Indra, Lover of the Song, whom men must stir to help, hast been
Great in the contest for the prize.

14 Slayer of foes, whatever aid of thine imparts the swiftest course,
With that impel our car to speed.

15 As skilfullest of those who drive the chariot, with our art and aim,
O Conqueror, win the proffered prize.

16 Praise him who, Matchless and Alone, was born the Lord of living men,
Most active, with heroic soul.

17 Thou who hast been the singers' Friend, a Friend auspicious with thine aid,
As such, O Indra, favour us.

18 Grasp in thine arms the thunderbolt, O Thunder-armed, to slay the fiends:
Mayst thou subdue the foemen's host.

19 I call the ancient Friend, allied with wealth, who speeds the lowly man,
Him to whom chiefly prayer is brought.

20 For he alone is Lord of all the treasures of the earth: he speeds
Hither, chief Lover of the Song.

21 So with thy yoked teams satisfy our wish with power and wealth in steeds
And cattle, boldly, Lord of kine!

22 Sing this, what time the juice is pressed, to him your Hero, Much-invoked,
To please him as a mighty Steer.

23 He, Excellent, withholdeth not his gift of power and wealth in kine,
When he hath listened to our songs.

24 May he with might unclose for us the cow's stall, whosesoe'er it be,
To which the Dasyu-slayer goes.

25 O Indra Śatakratu, these our songs have called aloud to thee,
Like mother cows to meet their calves.

abiding in the third bright sphere, or in heaven.—Wilson.

24 *The chariot*: of the Sun, drawn by seven horses. *Whose ripe contents ten fingers empty*: this appears to be the meaning of the *pakvám dáṣayantram útsam* of the text, literally, 'the ripe spring with ten engines.' 'The mature deeply-organized secretion.'—Wilson.

---

1 *Turvaśa, Yadu*: the names of these two eponymi of Āryan tribes are frequently associated. See Index. An expedition against Divodāsa appears to be referred to.

2 *Even to the dull and uninspired*: he favours whom he will, and the race is not always to the swift.

7 *As 'twere a cow to milk*: like the cow that is brought to give the milk that is to be mingled with the Soma libation. *The Brahman*: Indra regarded as a Priest.

11 *When the prize lies ready*: to be given to the victor in the chariot race, the chief object of the hymn being to secure victory in the approaching contest through the favour of the God.

24 *Whosesoe'er it be*; the meaning of *kuvitsasya* here is somewhat uncertain. Sāyaṇa explains it as, of Kuvitsa, a certain person who does much harm. The meaning appears to be, may Indra open for us the cow-stall and give us the cattle of any Dasyu whom he, that is, we under his guidance, may attack.

26 Hard is thy love to win : thou art a Steer to him who longs for steers :
Be to one craving steeds a Steed.

27 Delight thee with the juice we pour for thine own great munificence :
Yield not thy singer to reproach.

28 These songs with every draught we pour come, Lover of the Song, to thee,
As milch-kine hasten to their young :

29 To thee most oft invoked, amid the many singers' rivalry
Who beg with all their might for wealth.

30 Nearest and most attractive may our laud, O Indra, come to thee.
Urge thou us on to ample wealth.

31 Bṛbu hath set himself above the Paṇis, o'er their highest head,
Like the wide bush on Gaṅgā's bank.

32 He whose good bounty, thousandfold, swift as the rushing of the wind,
Suddenly offers as a gift.

33 So all our singers ever praise the pious Bṛbu's noble deed,
Chief, best to give his thousands, best to give a thousand liberal gifts.

HYMN XLVI. *Indra.*

1. THAT we may win us wealth and power we poets, verily, call on thee :
In war men call on thee, Indra, the hero's Lord, in the steed's race-course call on thee.

26 *Thou art a Steer* : *gavām pradātā*,, 'a giver of cattle.'—Sāyaṇa. *A Steed* : *aśvapradaḥ*, a giver of horses.—Sāyaṇa.

27 This stanza is repeated, word for word, from III. 41. 6.

31 *Bṛbu* : according to Sāyaṇa, the carpenter or artificer of the Paṇis.

The *Paṇis* here are, in accordance with the original meaning of the words, merchants or traders, and the merchant Bṛbu is eulogized for his piety and liberality, qualities which were not the usual characteristics of the class to which he belonged. A legend, referred to by Sāyaṇa, and recorded in the *Mānava-dharma-śāstra* or *Laws of Manu*, 10. 107, relates that Bharadvāja, when distressd by hunger in a lonely forest, accepted many cows from the carpenter Bṛbu ; the moral being that men of inferior caste and low condition may distinguish themselves by their liberality. See Wilson's Note, Vol. III. p. 466. *The wide bush* : the belt of underwood. Others would read *urukakṣaḥ* as one word instead of *urúḥ kákṣaḥ*, and explain it as the name of a man, son of a woman called Gaṅgā.

33 *Chief* : *sūri*, as institutor of the sacrifice. See, on stanzas 31—33, Prof. Weber's Episches im vedischen Ritual (Sitzungsberichte der K. P. Akademie der Wissenschaften, XXXVIII. pp. 28 sqq.), and M. Müller, Chips from a German Workshop, IV. 138 (new edition).

2 As such, O Wonderful, whose hand holds thunder, praised as mighty, Caster of the Stone !
Pour on us boldly, Indra, kine and chariot-steeds, ever to be the conqueror's strength.

3 We call upon that Indra, who, most active, ever slays the foe :
Lord of the brave, Most Manly, with a thousand powers, help thou and prosper us in fight.

4 Ṛcīṣama, thou forcest men as with a bull, with anger, in the furious fray.
Be thou our Helper in the mighty battle fought for sunlight, water, and for life.

5 O Indra, bring us name and fame, enriching, mightiest, excellent,
Wherewith, O Wondrous God, fair-visored, thunder-armed, thou hast filled full this earth and heaven.

6 We call on thee, O King, Mighty amid the Gods, Ruler of men, to succour us.
All that is weak in us, Excellent God, make firm: make our foes easy to subdue.

7 All strength and valour that is found, Indra, in tribes of Nahuṣas, and all the splendid fame that the Five Tribes enjoy
Bring, yea, all manly powers at once.

8 Or, Maghavan, what vigorous strength in Tṛkṣi lay, in Druhyus or in Pūru's folk,
Fully bestow on us, that, in the conquering fray, we may subdue our foes in fight.

9 O Indra, grant a happy home, a triple refuge triply strong.
Bestow a dwelling-place on the rich lords and me, and keep thy dart afar from these.

3 *With a thousand powers* : *sáhasramuṣka*, literally, mille testiculos habens. The reading of the Sāmaveda, *sáhasramanyo*, full of boundless ardour, is, as Professor Ludwig remarks, much more aesthetic.

4 *Ṛcīṣama* : or, worthy of praise ! But the exact meaning of the epithet is somewhat uncertain.

5 *Fair-visored* : or, fair of cheek.

7 *Nahuṣas* : people, apparently distinct from the five Āryan tribes *par excellence*, and dwellers on or near the Indus. According to Sāyaṇa, human beings in general are meant, and Professor Roth explains the word as men generally, but with the special sense of stranger, or neighbour. See Muir, *O.S. Texts*, I. 179, 180.

8 *Tṛkṣi* : a king so named, says Sāyaṇa. In another place (VIII. 22. 7) he has the patronymic Trāsadasyava, son *i. e.* peer of, Trasadasyu. *In Druhyus* or *in Pūru's folk* : literally, 'in Druhyu or in Pūru,' the names of the eponymi of these tribes being used for the tribes themselves.

10 They who with minds intent on spoil subdue the foe, boldly attack and smite him down,—
From these, O Indra Maghavan who lovest song, be closest guardian of our lives.

11 And now, O Indra, strengthen us: come near and aid us in the fight,
What time the feathered shafts are flying in the air, the arrows with their sharpened points.

12 Give us, where heroes strain their bodies in the fight, the shelter that our fathers loved.
To us and to our sons give refuge: keep afar all unobserved hostility.

13 When, Indra, in the mighty fray thou urgest chargers to their speed,
On the uneven road and on a toilsome path, like falcons, eager for renown,

14 Speeding like rivers rushing down a steep descent, responsive to the urging call,
That come like birds attracted to the bait, held in by reins in both the driver's hands.

HYMN XLVII. *Indra, Etc.*

1. YEA, this is good to taste and full of sweetness, verily it is strong and rich in flavour.
No one may conquer Indra in the battle when he hath drunken of the draught we offer.

2 This sweet juice here had mightiest power to gladden: it boldened Indra when he slaughtered Vṛtra,
When he defeated Śambara's many onslaughts, and battered down his nine-and ninety ramparts.

3 This stirreth up my voice when I have drunk it: this hath aroused from sleep my yearning spirit.
This Sage hath measured out the six expanses from which no single creature is excluded.

4 This, even this, is he who hath created the breadth of earth, the lofty height of heaven.
He formed the nectar in three headlong rivers. Soma supports the wide mid-air above us.

5 He found the wavy sea of brilliant colours in forefront of the Dawns who dwell in brightness.
This Mighty One, the Steer begirt by Maruts, hath propped the heavens up with a mighty pillar.

6 Drink Soma boldly from the beaker, Indra, in war for treasures, Hero, Vṛtra-slayer!
Fill thyself full at the mid-day libation, and give us wealth, thou Treasury of riches.

7 Look out for us, O Indra, as our Leader, and guide us on to gain yet goodlier treasure.
Excellent Guardian, bear us well through peril, and lead us on to wealth with careful guidance.

8 Lead us to ample room, O thou who knowest, to happiness, security, and sunlight.
High, Indra, are the arms of thee the Mighty: may we betake us to their lofty shelter.

9 Set us on widest chariot-seat, O Indra, with two steeds best to draw, O Lord of Hundreds!
Bring us the best among all sorts of viands: let not the foe's wealth, Maghavan, subdue us.

10 Be gracious, Indra, let my days be lengthened: sharpen my thought as 'twere a blade of iron
Approve whatever words I speak, dependent on thee, and grant me thy divine protection.

11 Indra the Rescuer, Indra the Helper, Hero who listens at each invocation,
Śakra I call, Indra invoked of many. May Indra Maghavan prosper and bless us.

12 May helpful Indra as our good Protector, Lord of all treasures, favour us with succour,

12 *To us and to our sons give refuge*: the Commentator takes *acittam* 'unobserved' with *cardiḥ*, and explains the words as 'armour unknown by the enemies.'

---

3 *This Sage hath measured out*: the creative acts of Indra are ascribed to Soma which inspirits him to perform them. *The six expanses*, are the two worlds, heaven and earth, and the three subdivisions of each; or, according to the Commentator, heaven, earth, day, night, water, and plants.

4 *In three headlong rivers*: perhaps the three unknown rivers Añjasī, Kuliśī, and Vīrapatnī, of I. 104. 4, which Benfey considers to be personifications of the clouds; but the meaning of the half-line is uncertain. 'This Soma has deposited the ambrosia in its three principal (receptacles).'—Wilson. Soma in stanzas 4 and 5 is probably the Moon-God.

9 *Let not the foe's wealth, Maghavan, subdue us*: it seems necessary to follow Professor Ludwig in taking *rāyaḥ* in the plural as the subject of the singular verb *tārīt*. Other examples of such an irregularity are found in the Veda.

Baffle our foes, and give us rest and safety, and may we be the lords of hero vigour.

13 May we enjoy the grace of him the Holy, yea, may we dwell in his auspicious favour.
May helpful Indra as our good Preserver drive from us, even from afar, our foemen.

14 Like rivers rushing down a slope, O Indra, to thee haste songs and prayers and linked verses.
Thou gatherest, Thunderer ! like wide-spread bounty, kine, water, drops, and manifold libations.

15 Who lauds him, satisfies him, pays him worship ? E'en the rich noble still hath found him mighty.
With power, as when one moves his feet alternate, he makes the last precede, the foremost follow.

16 Famed is the Hero as each strong man's tamer, ever advancing one and then another.
King of both worlds, hating the high and haughty, Indra protects the men who are his people.

17 He loves no more the men he loved aforetime : he turns and moves away allied with others.
Rejecting those who disregard his worship, Indra victorious lives through many autumns.

18 In every figure he hath been the model : this is his only form for us to look on.
Indra moves multiform by his illusions; for his Bay Steeds are yoked, ten times a hundred.

19 Here Tvaṣṭar, yoking to the car the Bay Steeds, hath extended sway.
Who will for ever stand upon the foeman's side, even when our princes sit at ease?

20 Gods, we have reached a country void of pasture the land, though spacious, was too small to hold us.
Bṛhaspati, provide in war for cattle; find a path, Indra, for this faithful singer.

21 Day after day far from their seat he drove them, alike, from place to place, those darksome creatures.
The Hero slew the meanly-huckstering Dāsas, Varcin and Śambara, where the waters gather.

22 Out of thy bounty, Indra, hath Prastoka bestowed ten coffers and ten mettled horses.
We have received in turn from Divodāsa Śambara's wealth, the gift of Atithigva.

23 Ten horses and ten treasure-chests, ten garments as an added gift,
These and ten lumps of gold have I received from Divodāsa's hand.

24 Ten cars with extra steed to each, for the Atharvans hundred cows,
Hath Aśvatha to Pāyu given.

25 Thus Sṛñjaya's son honoured the Bharadvājas, recipients of all noble gifts and bounty.

26 Lord of the wood, be firm and strong in body : be, bearing us, a brave victorious hero
Show forth thy strength, compact with straps of leather, and let thy rider win all spoils of battle.

27 Its mighty strength was borrowed from the heaven and earth : its conquering force was brought from sovrans of the wood.
Honour with holy gifts the Car like Indra's bolt, the Car bound round with straps, the vigour of the floods.

13 This stanza is apparently the conclusion of the original hymn ; a new hymn or fragment of a hymn begins with the following stanza.—Ludwig.

15 *With power* : he rules the fortunes of men according to his pleasure, setting up one and putting down another, making the first last and the last first.

18 '*Indra* presents himself as *Agni*, *Viṣṇu*, or *Rudra*, or any other deity who is the actual object of worship, and is really the deity to be adored : he is identifiable with each.'—Wilson.

Ten times a hundred : 'His chariots and horses are multiplied according to the forms in which he manifests himself : agreeably to the *Vaidāntika* interpretation of the stanza, *Indra* is here identified with Parameśvara, the supreme first cause, identical with creation.'—Wilson.

19 *Tvaṣṭar* : supposed by the Commentator to be identified with Indra ; but this is unnecessary. The *sway* may be merely the authority which Tvaṣṭar exercises in yoking the chariot-steeds for Indra.

Who will for ever stand upon the foeman's side ? : that is, Indra will not always favour our enemies, even when, as is now the case, our nobles are not engaged in war.—Ludwig.

21 Indra is represented as having put to flight the dark aborigines and slain the niggardly demons or savages Varcin and Śambara. See IV. 30. 14, 15.

22 *Prastoka*, *Divodāsa*, and *Atithigva* are names of one and the same prince, who is called also Aśvatha, and Sārñjaya or son of Sṛñjaya.

24 *For the Atharvans* : for the Ṛṣis of the family of Atharvan, says Sāyaṇa. *Pāyu* : the brother of Garga the Ṛṣi of the hymn.

This stanza consists of two Pādas only instead of four.

26 *Lord of the wood* : forest tree, that is the timber of which the car is made. This car is the deified object of this and the two following stanzas.

28 Thou Bolt of Indra, Vanguard of the Maruts, close knit to Varuṇa and Child of Mitra,—
As such, accepting gifts which here we offer, receive, O Godlike Chariot, these oblations.

29 Send forth thy voice aloud through earth and heaven, and let the world in all its breadth regard thee;
O Drum, accordant with the Gods and Indra, drive thou afar, yea, very far, our foemen.

30 Thunder out strength and fill us full of vigour : yea, thunder forth and drive away all dangers.
Drive hence, O War-drum, drive away misfortune : thou art the Fist of Indra : show thy firmness.

31 Drive hither those, and these again bring hither : the War-drum speaks aloud as battle's signal.
Our heroes, winged with horses, come together. Let our car-warriors, Indra, be triumphant.

HYMN XLVIII. *Agni and Others.*

1. SING to your Agni with each song, at every sacrifice, for strength.
Come, let us praise the Wise and Everlasting God, even as a well-beloved Friend,

2 The Son of Strength; for is he not our gracious Lord ? Let us serve him who bears our gifts.
In battle may he be our help and strengthener, yea, be the saviour of our lives.

3 Agni, thou beamest forth with light, great Hero, never changed by time.
Shining, pure Agni ! with a light that never fades, beam with thy fair beams brilliantly.

4 Thou worshippest great Gods : bring them without delay by wisdom and thy wondrous power.
O Agni, make them turn hither to succour us. Give strength, and win it for thyself.

5 He whom floods, stones, and trees support, the offspring of eternal Law;
He who when rubbed with force is brought to life by men upon the lofty height of earth;

6 He who hath filled both worlds full with his brilliant shine, who hastens with his smoke to heaven;
He made himself apparent through the gloom by night, the Red Bull in the darksome nights, the Red Bull in the darksome nights.

7 O Agni, with thy lofty beams, with thy pure brilliancy, O God,
Kindled, Most Youthful One ! by Bharadvāja's hand, shine on us, O pure God, with wealth, shine, Purifier ! splendidly.

8 Thou art the Lord of house and home of all the tribes, O Agni, of all tribes of men.
Guard with a hundred forts thy kindler from distress, through hundred winters, Youngest God ! and those who make thy singers rich.

9 Wonderful, with thy favouring help, send us thy bounties, gracious Lord.
Thou art the Charioteer, Agni, of earthly wealth : find rest and safety for our seed.

10 With guards unfailing never negligent speed thou our children and our progeny.
Keep far from us, O Agni, all celestial wrath and wickedness of godless men.

11 Hither, O friends, with newest song drive her who freely pours her milk;
Loose her who never turns away;

12 Who, for the host of Maruts bright with native sheen, hath shed immortal fame like milk;
Whom the impetuous Maruts look upon with love, who moves in splendour on their ways.

29 *O Drum* : the *dundubhī* addressed and glorified in these concluding verses was a sort of loud kettle-drum, like that still used.

31 Drive to us the cows of the enemy and send our own cows home in safety. *Gāḥ*, cows, is understood with *amū́ḥ*, those, and *imāḥ*, these.

---

1 *Come, let us sing* : it seems necessary to take the singular verb with the plural pronoun.

2 *Who bears our gifts* : conveys our sacrificial offerings to the Gods.

5 *Floods, stones, and trees* : the waters that are mixed with the Soma juice, the press-stones which crush the plant, and the wood which, produces the fire by attrition or feeds it as fuel. *The lofty height of earth* : the altar.

11 *Who freely pours her milk* : *sabárdughā* ; the general name of the cow or cows milked at sacrifices.

12 The sacrificial cow is here identified with Pṛśni' the mother of the Maruts.

13 For Bharadvāja she poured down in days of old
The milch-cow yielding milk for all, and food that gives all nourishment.

14 Your friend like Indra passing wise, with magic power like Varuṇa.
Like Aryaman joy-giving, bringing plenteous food like Viṣṇu for my wish, I praise,

15 Bright as the host of Maruts mighty in their roar. May they bring Pūṣan free from foes;
May they bring hither hundreds, thousands for our men : may they bring hidden stores to light, and make wealth easy to be found.

16 Haste to me, Pūṣan, in thine ear, bright Deity : I fain would speak :
Most sinful is our foeman's hate.

17 Tear not up by the roots the Kākambīra tree : destroy thou all malignity.
Let them not snare by day the neck of that Celestial Bird the Sun.

18 Uninjured let thy friendship be, like the smooth surface of a skin,
A flawless skin, containing curds, full to the mouth, containing curds.

19 For thou art high above mankind, in glory equal to the Gods.
Therefore, O Pūṣan, look upon us in the fight : now help us as in days of old.

20 May the kind excellence of him the Kind, loud Roarers ! be our guide,
Be it the God's, O Maruts, or a mortal man's who worships, ye impetuous Ones!

21 They whose high glory in a moment like the God, the Sun, goes round the space of heaven,
The Maruts have obtained bright strength, a sacred name, strength that destroys the Vṛtras, strength Vṛtra-destroying excellent.

22 Once, only once, the heaven was made, once only once, the earth was formed-
Once, only Pṛśni's milk was shed : no second, after this, is born.

13 According to my version, which follows that of Professor Ludwig, Pṛśni should be the deity of this stanza. Sāyaṇa explains it differently : O Maruts, milk, etc.

14 *Your friend* : Pūṣan. *For my wish* : that I may obtain my wish ; 'for the distribution of wealth,'—Wilson.

17 *The Kākambīra tree* : according to Sāyaṇa, *kākambīra* means literally 'crow-bearer:' 'with its progeny of crows.'—Wilson. It is apparently the name of some umbrageous tree, and in this place implies metaphorically Śamyu the Ṛṣi of the hymn with his many branches of sons and grandsons.

Let them not snare : let not our enemies deprive us of the sunlight : the Sun being frequently called a bird, those who would deprive the speaker of the light of day are regarded as fowlers.

18 *Containing curds* : 'Such a skin of curds, *Sāyaṇa* says, is always carried in *Pūṣan's* chariot.'—Wilson.

20 *The God's* : Agni's.

22 Heaven and Earth, having once been made or brought forth, are permanent. Pṛśni, the mother of the Maruts, has once for all given birth to her brood. *No second* : *śárdhaḥ*, host (of Maruts) is understood with *anyáḥ*.

HYMN XLIX. *Viśvedevas.*

1. I LAUD with newest songs the Righteous People, Mitra and Varuṇa who make us happy.
Let them approach, here let them listen,—Agni, Varuṇa, Mitra, Lords of fair dominion.

2 Him, to be praised at each tribe's sacrifices, the Two young Matrons' sober-minded Herald,
The Son of Strength, the Child of Heaven, the signal of sacrifice, red Agni will I worship.

3 Unlike in form are the Red God's two Daughters : one is the Sun's, and stars bedeck the other.
Apart, the Sanctifiers, in succession, come to the famed hymn, praised in holy verses.

4 I with a lofty song call hither Vāyu, all-bounteous, filler of his car, most wealthy.
Thou, Sage, with bright path, Lord of harnessed horses, impetuous, promptly honourest the prudent.

5 That chariot of the Aśvins, fair to look on, pleaseth me well, yoked with a thought, refulgent,
Wherewith, Nāsatyas, Chiefs, ye seek our dwelling, to give new strength to us and to our children.

6 Bulls of the Earth, O Vāta and Parjanya, stir up for us the regions of the water.

2 *The Two young Matrons* : Heaven and Earth. *The Child of Heaven* : or of Dyaus or Dyu.

3 *Two Daughters* : Day and Night.

4 *Filler of his car* : with wealth to reward his worshippers. *The prudent* : the wise worshipper.

6 *Bulls of the Earth* : or of Pṛthivī as identified with Pṛśni. *Vāta* is another name of Vāyu, the Wind-God; and *Parjanya* is the Rain-cloud personified. *Hearers of truth* : the Maruts are thus addressed, as making true or realizing the prayers of men to which they listen. I follow Sāyaṇa's interpretation of the second half of the stanza.

Hearers of truth, ye, Sages, World-Supporters, increase his living wealth whose songs delight you.

7 So may Sarasvatī, the Hero's Consort, brisk with rare life, the lightning's Child, inspire us,
And, with the Dames accordant, give the singer a refuge unassailable and flawless.

8 I praise with eloquence him who guards all pathways. He, when his love impelled him, went to Arka.
May he vouchsafe us gear with gold to grace it : may Pūṣan make each prayer of ours effective.

9 May Herald Agni, fulgent, bring for worship Tvaṣṭar adored, in homes and swift to listen,
Glorious, first to share, the life-bestower, the ever active God, fair-armed, fair-handed.

10 Rudra by day, Rudra at night we honour with these our songs, the Universe's Father.
Him great and lofty, blissful, undecaying let us call specially as the Sage impels us.

11 Ye who are youthful, wise, and meet for worship, come, Maruts, to the longing of the singer.
Coming, as erst to Aṅgiras, O Heroes, ye animate and quicken e'en the desert.

12 Even as the herdsman driveth home his cattle, I urge my songs to him the strong swift Hero
May he, the glorious, lay upon his body the singer's hymns, as stars bedeck the heaven.

13 He who for man's behoof in his affliction thrice measured out the earthly regions, Viṣṇu—
When one so great as thou affordeth shelter, may we with wealth and with ourselves be happy.

14 Sweet be this song of mine to Ahibudhnya, Parvata, Savitar, with Floods and Lightnings;
Sweet, with the Plants, to Gods who seek oblations. May liberal Bhaga speed us on to riches.

15 Give riches borne on cars, with many heroes, contenting men, the guard of mighty Order.
Give us a lasting home that we may battle with godless bands of men who fight against us, and meet with tribes to whom the Gods are gracious.

7 *The Hero's Consort* : *vīrápatnī* : according to Sāyaṇa, she whose husband is the hero Prajāpati, or, the protectress of heroes. The River-God Sarasvān or Sarasvat is more usually considered to be the consort of Sarasvatī, who originally a River-Goddess, appears in this place in her later and present-day character of the Goddess of learning and eloquence. See note, borrowed from Muir, on I. 3. 10. *The Dames* : Gnās, or Consorts of the Gods.

8 *Him who guards all pathways* : Pūṣan, the special protector of travellers and guardian of roads and paths. See I. 42. *Arka* : the Sun, to whom Pūṣan appears to have gone both as an envoy on behalf of the other Gods when Sūryā was to be given in marriage, and as a suitor on his own account. Sūryā, it may be remembered, chose the Aśvins to be her husbands. See I. 116. 17. I follow Professor Pischel (*Vedische Studien*, I. pp. 1—52) in his interpretation of this difficult stanza.

10 *The Sage* : the wise, that is, wisdom-giving, Soma.

11 *As erst to Aṅgiras* : *a girasvát* ; 'like rays (of light).'—Wilson; 'like the Aṅgirasas.'—Roth ; 'like messengers of the Gods.'—Grassmann.

12. *The strong swift Hero* : Viṣṇu seems to be intended, and not the company of Maruts as Sāyaṇa explains the passage, taking *virāya* as an adjective=heroic or powerful.

14 *Ahibudhnya* : the Dragon of the Deep, or 'leviathan of the Sea of Heaven,' the distant, invisible and deified being who presides over the firmament.

15 *The guard of mighty Order* : the wealth that enables men to institute the law-ordained sacrifices. *To whom the Gods are gracious* : 'to whom the Gods come to accept libations.' I follow Sāyaṇa in thus distinguishing *ā́devīḥ* from *ádevīḥ*, godless.

HYMN L. *Viśvedevas.*

1. I call with prayers on Aditi your Goddess, on Agni, Mitra, Varuṇa for favour,
On Aryaman who gives unasked, the gracious, on Gods who save, on Savitar and Bhaga.

2 Visit, to prove us free from sin, O Sūrya, Lord of great might, the bright Gods sprung from Dakṣa,
Twice-born and true, observing sacred duties, Holy and full of light, whose tongue is Agni.

3 And, O ye Heaven and Earth, a wide dominion, O ye most blissful Worlds, our lofty shelter,

2 *Visit, to prove us free from sin* : visit and invite the Gods to come and bear witness to our innocence before the all-seeing Sun. The word *anāgāstvé* in the locative case (in sinlessness) is used with a dative signification. *Sprung from Dakṣa* : Dakṣa is a creative Power associated with Aditi, and therefore sometimes identified with Prajāpati. Sāyaṇa explains *dákṣapitṛn* in his commentary on VII. 66. 2, as 'preservers or lords of strength,' and the compound may mean Lords of vigour, or fathers of strength in this passage also. *Twice-born* : having two births or manifestations, dwelling in heaven and appearing also on earth : *Whose tongue is Agni* : who consume oblations by means of fire.

Give ample room and freedom for our dwelling, a home, ye Hemispheres, which none may rival.

4 This day invited may the Sons of Rudra, resistless, excellent, stoop down to meet us;
For, when beset with slight or sore affliction, we ever call upon the Gods, the Maruts;

5 To whom the Goddess Rodasī clings closely, whom Pūṣan follows bringing ample bounty.
What time ye hear our call and come, O Maruts, upon your separate path all creatures tremble.

6 With a new hymn extol, O thou who singest, the Lover of the Song, the Hero Indra.
May he, exalted, hear our invocation, and grant us mighty wealth and strength when lauded.

7 Give full protection, Friends of man, ye Waters, in peace and trouble, to our sons and grandsons.
For ye are our most motherly physicians, parents of all that standeth, all that moveth.

8 May Savitar come hither and approach us, the God who rescues, Holy, golden-handed,
The God who, bounteous as the face of Morning, discloses precious gifts for him who worships.

9 And thou, O Son of Strength, do thou turn hither the Gods to-day to this our holy service.
May I for evermore enjoy thy bounty, and, Agni, by thy grace be rich in heroes.

10 Come also to my call, O ye Nāsatyas, yea, verily, through my prayers, ye Holy Sages.
As from great darkness ye delivered Atri, protect us, Chiefs, from danger in the conflict.

11 O Gods, bestow upon us riches, splendid with strength and heroes, bringing food in plenty.
Be gracious, helpful Gods of earth, of heaven, born of the Cow, and dwellers in the waters.

12 May Rudra and Sarasvatī, accordant, Viṣṇu and Vāyu, pour down gifts and bless us;
Ṛbhukṣan, Vāja, and divine Vidhātar, Parjanya, Vāta make our food abundant.

13 May this God Savitar, the Lord, the Offspring of Waters, pouring down his dew be gracious,
And, with the Gods and Dames accordant, Tvaṣṭar; Dyaus with the Gods and Pṛthivī with oceans.

14 May Aja-Ekapād and Ahibudhnya, and Earth and Ocean hear our invocation;
All Gods who strengthen Law, invoked and lauded, and holy texts uttered by sages, help us.

15 So with my thoughts and hymns of praise the children of Bharadvājā sing aloud to please you.
The Dames invoked, and the resistless Vasus, and all ye Holy Ones have been exalted.

HYMN LI. *Viśvedevas.*

1. THAT mighty eye of Varuṇa and Mitra, infallible and dear, is moving upward.
The pure and lovely face of holy Order hath shone like gold of heaven in its arising.

2 The Sage who knows these Gods' three ranks and orders, and all their generations near and distant,
Beholding good and evil acts of mortals, Sūra marks well the doing of the pious.

3 *Ye Hemispheres* : *dhiṣane* ; literally, 'two bowls,' a frequently-occurring expression for heaven and earth.

5 *Rodasī* : the Consort of Rudra.

11 *Born of the Cow* : the Maruts, sons of the Cow Pṛśni, according to Sāyaṇa. The Gods of heaven are said to be the Ādityas, those of earth the Vasus, and those of water, that is, the firmament, the Rudras. Roth explains *gojātāḥ* as 'born of the starry heaven.'

12 This and the four following stanzas form a new hymn, or are a recapitulation with additions, of the preceding verses. *And divine Vidhātar* : or 'the divine Disposer.'

14 *Aja-Ekapād* ; according to Roth, probably a genius of the storm, 'the stormer of one foot.' See II. 31. 6. But *ajá* may signify 'unborn' rather than 'driver,' and the Sun may be intended, in accordance with the explanation of the Commentators. Aja-Ekapād is called in X. 65. 13. the bearer of heaven, 'and the ascription of one foot to the Sun might be due to his appearance alone in the sky as opposed to the Dawns and Aśvins.' See Wallis, *Cosmology of the Ṛgveda*, p. 54. M. Bergaigne says : 'Aja-Ekapād, then is the 'unborn who has only one foot,' that is to say, 'who dwells in the single isolated world, the place of mystery,' in opposition to the god who manifests himself in divers worlds, to Agni or Soma in their various visible forms.' See *La Religion Védique*, III. pp. 20—25.

15 Sāyaṇa interprets the first line somewhat differently : 'Thus do my sons the Bharadvājas worship the Gods with sacred rites and hymns'

1 *Eye of Varuṇa and Mitra* : the Sun.

2 *Three ranks and orders* : according to Sāyaṇa, the three cognizable worlds or stations of the Gods, the earth of the Vasus, the firmament of the Rudras, and heaven of the Ādityas. *Sūra* : Sūrya ; the Sun.

3 I praise you Guards of mighty Law eternal, Aditi, Mitra, Varuṇa, the noble,
Aryaman, Bhaga, all whose thoughts are faithful : hither I call the Bright who share in common.

4 Lords of the brave, infallible, foe-destroyers, great Kings, bestowers of fair homes to dwell in,
Young, Heroes, ruling heaven with strong dominion, Ādityas, Aditi I seek with worship.

5 O Heaven our Father, Earth our guileless Mother, O Brother Agni, and ye Vasus, bless us.
Grant us, O Aditi and ye Ādityas, all of one mind, your manifold protection.

6 Give us not up to any evil creature, as spoil to wolf or she-wolf, O ye Holy.
For ye are they who guide aright our bodies, ye are the rulers of our speech and vigour.

7 Let us not suffer for the sin of others, nor do the deed which ye, O Vasus, punish.
Ye, Universal Gods ! are all-controllers : may he do harm unto himself who hates me.

8 Mighty is homage : I adopt and use it. Homage hath held in place the earth and heaven.
Homage to Gods ! Homage commands and rules them. I banish even committed sin by homage

9 You Furtherers of Law, pure in your spirit, infallible, dwellers in the home of Order,
To you all Heroes mighty and far-seeing I bow me down, O Holy Ones, with homage.

10 For these are they who shine with noblest splendour; through all our troubles these conduct us safely—
Varuṇa, Mitra, Agni, mighty Rulers, true-minded, faithful to the hymn's controllers.

11 May they, Earth, Aditi, Indra, Bhaga, Pūṣan increase our laud, increase the Fivefold people.
Giving good help, good refuge, goodly guidance, be they our good deliverers, good protectors.

12 Come now, O Gods, to your celestial station : the Bharadvājas' priest entreats your favour.
He, sacrificing, fain for wealth, hath honoured the Gods with those who sit and share oblations.

13 Agni, drive thou the wicked foe, the evil-hearted thief away,
Far, far, Lord of the brave ! and give us easy paths.

14 Soma, these pressing-stones have called aloud to win thee for our Friend.
Destroy the greedy Paṇi, for a wolf is he.

15 Ye, O most bountiful, are they who, led by Indra, seek the sky.
Give us good paths for travel : guard us well at home.

16 Now have we entered on the road that leads to bliss, without a foe,
The road whereon a man escapes all enemies and gathers wealth.

3 *Who share in common* : *sadhanyāḥ*; ; according to Sāyaṇa, *dhanasahitān*, 'accompanied by wealth.'

7 *Let us not suffer for the sin of others* : so, VII. 86. 5. 'Loose us from sins committed by our fathers.' Compare also Taittirīya Brāhmaṇa, III. 7. 12. 3. cited by Muir, *O. S. T.*, V. 66. 'May Agni free me from the sin which my mother or my father committed when I was a babe unborn.'

10 *The hymn's controllers* : 'those who are prominent in (their) praise.'—Wilson.

11 *The Fivefold People* : *páñca jánāḥ* ; the five Āryan tribes ; 'the five orders of beings.'—Wilson.

12 This stanza is difficult, and I do not thoroughly understand it.

14 *Paṇi* : either one of the envious demons who steal away the light, or the avaricious and niggardly trafficker who offers no sacrifices to the Gods.

15 *Ye, O Most Bountiful* : all ye Gods.

16 These four concluding stanzas, in changed metres, are a prayer for protection on a journey. Professor Grassmann banishes them, together with stanzas 11 and 12, to the Appendix as being in his opinion later additions to the original hymn.

HYMN LII. *Viśvedevas.*

1. This I allow not in the earth or heaven, at sacrifice or in these holy duties.
May the huge mountains crush him down : degraded be Atiyāja's sacrificing patron.

2 Or he who holds us in contempt, O Maruts, or seeks to blame the prayer that we are making,
May agonies of burning be his portion. May the sky scorch the man who hates devotion.

3 Why then, O Soma, do they call thee keeper of prayer ? Why then our guardian from reproaches ?

1 According to Sāyaṇa Ṛjiśvan curses a rival Ṛṣi Atiyāja : but the name Atiyāja (from *ati* and *yaj*) seems to be employed expressly to signify one who over-sacrifices, that is, sacrifices more than is necessary or prescribed, superfluity, as well as deficiency, being a fault that causes a sacrifice to fail. See Ludwig, IV. 220.

3 *Soma* : the Moon-God.

Why then beholdest thou how men revile us? Cast thy hot dart at him who hates devotion.

4 May Mornings as they spring to life protect me, and may the Rivers as they swell preserve me.
My guardians be the firmly-seated mountains: the Fathers, when I call on Gods, defend me!

5 Through all our days may we be healthy-minded, and look upon the Sun when he arises.
Grant this the Treasure-Lord of treasures, coming, observant, oftenest of Gods, with succour!

6 Most near, most oft comes Indra with protection, and she Sarasvatī, who swells with rivers:
Parjanya, bringing health with herbs, and Agni, well lauded swift to listen, like a father.

7 Hear this mine invocation; come hither, O Universal Gods,
Be seated on this holy grass.

8 To him who comes to meet you, Gods, with offerings bathed in holy oil—
Approach ye, one and all, to him.

9 All Sons of Immortality shall listen to the songs we sing,
And be exceeding good to us.

10 May all the Gods who strengthen Law, with Ṛtus, listening to our call,
Be pleased with their appropriate draught.

11 May Indra with the Marut host, with Tvaṣṭar, Mitra, Aryaman,
Accept the laud and these our gifts.

12 O Agni, Priest, as rules ordain, offer this sacrifice of ours,
Remembering the Heavenly Folk.

13 Listen, All-Gods, to this mine invocation, ye who inhabit heaven, and air's mid regions,
All ye, O Holy Ones, whose tongue is Agni, seated upon this sacred grass, be joyful.

14 May the All-Gods who claim our worship hear my thought; may the two World-halves hear it, and the Waters' Child.
Let me not utter words that ye may disregard. Closely allied with you may we rejoice in bliss.

15 And those who, Mighty, with the wiles of serpents, were born on earth, in heaven, where waters gather—
May they vouchsafe us life of full duration. May the Gods kindly give us nights and mornings.

16 At this my call, O Agni and Parjanya, help, swift to hear, my thought and our laudation.
One generates holy food, the other offspring, so grant us food enough with store of children.

17 When holy grass is strewn and fire enkindled, with hymn and lowly homage I invite you.
All-Gods, to day in this our great assembly rejoice, ye Holy, in the gifts we offer.

5 *Treasure-Lord of treasures*: Agni, from whom, or through whom, all blessings come to the pious.

9 *Sons of Immortality*: according to the Scholiast, 'sons of the immortal' (Prajāpati, regarded as the progenitor of Gods and men).

10 *With Ṛtus*: together with the Seasons personified; or, at the prescribed seasons, as Sāyaṇa explains.

13 *All Gods*: *Viśve devāḥ*, or Universal Gods.

15 *With the wiles of serpents*: *áhimāyāḥ*: according to Sāyaṇa, 'possessed of the wisdom or knowledge that kills.' Cf. I. 3. 9, note.

16 *The other offspring*: Parjanya, the personified Rain-cloud, produces corn and food offered in sacrifice, and Agni promotes the procreation of children.

HYMN LIII. *Pūṣan.*

1. LORD of the path, O Pūṣan, we have yoked and bound thee to our hymn,
Even as a car, to win the prize.

2 Bring us the wealth that men require, a manly master of a house,
Free-handed with the liberal meed.

3 Even him who would not give, do thou, O glowing Pūṣan, urge to give,
And make the niggard's soul grow soft.

4 Clear paths that we may win the prize; scatter our enemies afar.
Strong God, be all our thoughts fulfilled.

5 Penetrate with an awl, O Sage, the hearts of avaricious churls,
And make them subject to our will.

6 Thrust with thine awl, O Pūṣan: seek that which the niggard's heart holds dear,
And make him subject to our will.

———

1 *Lord of the path*: custodian of roads and guide of travellers. *To win the prize*: or, to win us wealth or food.

2 *Master of a house*: a householder who will institute sacrifices and liberally reward the officiating priests.

4 *Win the prize*: or win us wealth, or food.

5 *With an awl*: 'with a goad.'—Wilson.

7 Tear up and rend in pieces, Sage, the hearts of avaricious churls,
And make them subject to our will.

8 Thou, glowing Pūṣan, carriest an awl that urges men to prayer;
Therewith do thou tear up and rend to shreds the heart of every one.

9 Thou bearest, glowing Lord ! a goad with horny point that guides the cows :
Thence do we seek thy gift of bliss.

10 And make this hymn of ours produce kine, horses, and a store of wealth
For our delight and use as men.

HYMN LIV. *Pūṣan.*

1. O PŪṢAN, bring us to the man who knows, who shall direct us straight,
And say unto us, It is here.

2 May we go forth with Pūṣan who shall point the houses out to us,
And say to us, These same are they.

3 Unharmed is Pūṣan's chariot wheel; the box ne'er falleth to the ground,
Nor doth the loosened felly shake.

4 Pūṣan forgetteth not the man who serveth him with offered gift :
That man is first to gather wealth.

5 May Pūṣan follow near our kine; may Pūṣan keep our horses safe :
May Pūṣan gather gear for us.

6 Follow the kine of him who pours libations out and worships thee;
And ours who sing thee songs of praise.

7 Let none be lost, none injured, none sink in a pit and break a limb.
Return with these all safe and sound.

8 Pūṣan who listens to our prayers, the Strong whose wealth is never lost,
The Lord of riches, we implore.

9 Secure in thy protecting care, O Pūṣan, never may we fail :
We here are they who sing thy praise.

10 From out the distance, far and wide, may Pūṣan stretch his right hand forth,
And drive our lost again to us.

HYMN LV. *Pūṣan.*

1. SON of Deliverance, come, bright God ! Let us twain go together : be our charioteer of sacrifice.

2 We pray for wealth to thee most skilled of charioteers, with braided hair,
Lord of great riches, and our Friend.

3 Bright God whose steeds are goats, thou art a stream of wealth, a treasure-heap,
The Friend of every pious man.

4 Pūṣan, who driveth goats for steeds, the Strong and Mighty, who is called
His Sister's lover, will we laud.

5 His Mother's suitor I address. May he who loves his Sister hear,
Brother of Indra, and my Friend.

6 May the sure-footed goats come nigh, conveying Pūṣan on his car,
The God who visiteth mankind.

9 *With horny point* : the exact meaning of *goopaśā* is uncertain. Others explain it as 'director of cattle,' 'furnished with leathern thongs;' 'cow tailed.'

This hymn and the five following have been translated by Dr. Muir, *Original Sanskrit Texts*, V. 176—180. Professor Peterson also gives a translation of Hymns LIII—LVII in his *Hymns from the Ṛgveda* (Bombay Sanskrit Series No. XXXVI).

1 This stanza, Sāyaṇa says, is to be muttered by one who seeks his lost property. *The man who knows* : the wise man or wizard.

2 *These same are they* : these are the houses in which the stolen property is concealed.

3 *The box* : basket, or inner part of the car. Professor Wilson, following Sāyaṇa, translates : 'The discus of Pūṣan does not destroy ; its sheath is not discarded, its edge harms not us.' But the three things mentioned are evidently parts of Pūṣan's chariot.

7 *With these* : cows.

8 We pray to Pūṣan for the safety of our property because he is the Lord of wealth ; he himself loses nothing that is his, and he always listens to our prayers.

1 *Son of Deliverance* : that is, 'Deliverer,' one who gives men ample room and freedom. Sāyaṇa explains *vimuco napāt* in another place as 'offspring of the cloud.' See I. 42. 1. Here, he says, the meaning is, 'son of Prajāpati, who at the creation sends forth from himself all creatures'. Roth explains *vimúc* as 'unyoking' horses at the end of a journey. Pūṣan would then be 'the son of return,' the God who brings travellers safely home, which is one of his especial functions.

2 *With braided hair* : *kapardínam* ; an epithet of Rudra also. See I. 114. 1.

3 *Whose steeds are goats* : cf. I. 138. 4.

4 *His Sister's lover* : according to Sāyaṇa, Pūṣan's sister is Uṣas or Dawn.

5 *His Mother's suitor* : Sāyaṇa explains *mātúr didhiṣúm* as *rātreḥ patim*, lord or husband of Night. Probably Sūryā is intended. See Bergaigne, *La Religion Védique*, II. 428. Compare also Book VI. 48. 8. *Brother of Indra* as an Āditya or son of Aditi.

6 *Sure-footed* : *niṣṭmbhāḥ* : this word does not occur elsewhere and its meaning is uncertain. Wilson renders it 'harnessed,' and other explanations have been proposed, but as Dr. Muir observes : 'All seems guess work.'

HYMN LVI. *Pūṣan.*

1. Whoso remembers Pūṣan as eater of mingled curd and meal
Need think no more upon the God.

2 And he is best of charioteers. Indra, the hero's Lord, allied
With him as Friend, destroys the foes.

3 And there the best of charioteers hath guided through the speckled cloud
The golden wheel of Sūra's car.

4 Whate'er we speak this day to thee, Wise, Wondrous God whom many praise,
Give thou fulfilment of our thought.

5 Lead on this company of ours, that longs for kine, to win the spoil:
Thou, Pūṣan, art renowned afar.

6 Prosperity we crave from thee, afar from sin and near to wealth,
Tending to perfect happiness both for tomorrow and to-day.

HYMN LVII. *Indra and Pūṣan.*

1. Indra and Pūṣan will we call for friendship and prosperity
And for the winning of the spoil.

2 One by the Soma sits to drink juice which the mortar hath expressed:
The other longs for curd and meal.

3 Goats are the team that draws the one : the other hath Bay Steeds at hand;
With both of these he slays the fiends.

4 When Indra, wondrous strong, brought down the streams, the mighty waterfloods,
Pūṣan was standing by his side.

5 To this, to Pūṣan's favouring love, and Indra's, may we closely cling,
As to a tree's extended bough.

6 As one who drives a car draws in his reins, may we draw Pūṣan near,
And Indra, for our great success.

HYMN LVIII. *Pūṣan.*

1. Like heaven art thou : one form is bright, one holy, like Day and Night dissimilar in colour.
All magic powers thou aidest, self-dependent ! Auspicious be thy bounty here, O Pūṣan.

2 Goat-borne, the guard of cattle, he whose home is strength, inspirer of the hymn, set over all the world;
Brandishing here and there his lightly-moving goad, beholding every creature, Pūṣan, God, goes forth.

3 O Pūṣan, with thy golden ships that travel across the ocean, in the air's mid-region,
Thou goest on an embassy to Sūrya, subdued by love, desirous of the glory.

4 Near kinsman of the heaven and earth is Pūṣan, liberal, Lord of food, of wondrous lustre,
Whom strong and vigorous and swiftly-moving, subdued by love, the Deities gave to Sūryā.

HYMN LIX. *Indra-Agni.*

1. I will declare, while juices flow, the manly deeds that ye have done :

1 *Eater of mingled curd and meal* : *karambhád* ; *karambhá* was some soft food, a sort of gruel offered especially to Pūṣan.

I have followed Professor Ludwig in my translation of this difficult passage, the meaning seeming to be that in setting before Pūṣan the food that he loves the worshipper has done all that is necessary to secure his help. Sāyaṇa's explanation is much the same if 'a God' be substituted for 'the God' in line 2, that is, Pūṣan alone is sufficient : the worshipper need think upon no other God.

3 Pūṣan seems to be intended. He is said to have driven the Sun's wheel *paruṣe gávi*, literally, in the brindled bull,' meaning apparently, the speckled cloud, or train of variegated clouds. He, the impeller, the chief of charioteers (Pūṣan), ever urges on that golden wheel (of his car) for the radiant Sun. While the others think that the verse refers to Indra's pressing down the wheel of the Sun from the mountain of cloud and bringing back the light. See Peterson, *Hymns from the Ṛgveda*, p. 171.

---

3 *The fiends* : the Vṛtras, the demons of drought, or enemies in general.

---

1 *One holy* : 'venerable'.—Wilson. This is apparently a euphemism for 'dark.' Pūṣan is here regarded as the Sun present by day and even in his absence regulating the night also. According to Professor Ludwig, he is represented as the summer Sun and the winter Sun. *Thou aidest* : 'thou exercisest.'—Muir.

3 *Subdued by love* : of Sūryā, the daughter of the Sun. See VI. 49. 8. *Of the glory* : of winning Sūryā for his bride.

4 *The Deities gave to Sūryā* : 'the formula of the verse gives the idea rather of a birth than of a marriage. But Pūṣan is the lover of his mother, VI. 55. 5; Sūryā then might be the spouse as well as the mother of Pūṣan. She is doubtlessly also the sister with whom Pūṣan is united, VI. 55. 4.5.'—Bergaigne, *La Religion Védique*, II. 428.

Your Fathers, enemies of Gods, were smitten down, and, Indra-Agni, ye survive.

2 Thus, Indra-Agni, verily your greatness merits loftiest praise,
Sprung from one common Father, brothers, twins are ye; your Mother is in every place.

3 These who delight in flowing juice, like fellow horses at their food,
Indra and Agni, Gods armed with the thunderbolt, we call this day to come with help.

4 Indra and Agni, Friends of Law, served with rich gifts, your speech is kind
To him who praises you while these libations flow: that man, O Gods, ye ne'er consume.

5 What mortal understands, O Gods, Indra and Agni, this your way ?
One of you, yoking Steeds that move to every side, advances in your common car.

6 First, Indra-Agni, hath this Maid come footless unto those with feet.
Stretching her head and speaking loudly with her tongue, she hath gone downward thirty steps.

7 E'en now, O Indra-Agni, men hold in their arms and stretch their bows.
Desert us not in this great fray, in battles for the sake of kine.

8 The foeman's sinful enmities, Indra and Agni, vex me sore.
Drive those who hate me far away, and keep them distant from the Sun.

9 Indra and Agni, yours are all the treasures of the heavens and earth.
Here give ye us the opulence that prospers every living man.

10 O Indra-Agni, who accept the laud, and hear us for our praise,
Come near us, drawn by all our songs, to drink of this our Soma juice.

1 *Your Fathers......were smitten down* : *hatā́so vām pitā́ro* : the meaning is obscure. Sāyaṇa explains *pitā́ro* as Asuras or demons, deriving the word from a root *pi*, to injure : 'The Pitṛs the enemies of the gods, have been slain by you.'—Wilson. Prof. Grassmann reads, conjecturally, *pīyavo*,' 'scorners,' 'instead of the unsuitable *pitaro*.' Gods of an elder generation, the fathers of Indra and Agni, appear to be intended, and the words as they stand can hardly bear any other meaning. *Hatā́so* then would mean, 'not were slain,' but were struck down, degraded, and deprived of their power, like the earlier Hellenic Gods. Professor Ludwig suggests other possible explanations. See also Bergaigne, La Religion Védique, III. 75, and Ehni, Der Mythus des Yama, p. 80.

2 *One common Father* : Dyaus. According to Sāyaṇa, Prajāpati.

Your Mother : Aditi, infinite and omnipresent ; according to Sāyaṇa, identified with the wide-extended earth. But see Ehni, Der Mythus des Yama, p. 79.

4 *Ye ne'er consume* : Prof. Ludwig suggests the reading *bhartsathaḥ*, 'threaten,' instead of *bhasáthaḥ*.

5 *One of you* : Indra, as the Sun, whose horses here are the spreading beams of light, pursues his appointed way through heaven.

6 *This Maid* : the text has only the feminine pronoun *iáym* (haec); Uṣas or Dawn is intended. *Footless* : moving unsupported in the sky. Cf. I. 152. 3. *Stretching her head* : according to one of Sāyaṇa's explanations, 'having abandoned the head, being herself headless,' which is hardly consistent with what follows. *Thirty steps* : the thirty divisions of the Indian day and night through which Dawn passes before she reappears. But cf. I. 123. 8.

7 The hymn is a prayer for aid in a fray.

HYMN LX. *Indra-Agni.*

1. He slays the foe and wins the spoil who worships Indra and Agni, strong and mighty Heroes,
Who rule as Sovrans over ample riches, victorious, showing forth their power in conquest.

2 So battle now, O Indra and thou, Agni, for cows and waters, sunlight, stolen Mornings.
Team-borne, thou makest kine thine own, O Agni : thou, Indra, light, Dawns, regions, wondrous waters.

3 With Vṛtra-slaying might, Indra and Agni, come, drawn by homage, O ye Vṛtra-slayers.
Indra and Agni, show yourselves among us with your supreme and unrestricted bounties.

4 I call the Twain whose deeds of old have all been famed in ancient days :
O Indra-Agni, harm us not.

5 The Strong, the scatterers of the foe, Indra and Agni, we invoke;
May they be kind to one like me.

6 They slay our Ārya foes, these Lords of heroes, slay our Dasyu foes :
And drive our enemies away.

7 Indra and Agni, these our songs of praise have sounded forth to you :
Ye who bring blessings ! drink the juice.

8 Come, Indra-Agni, with those teams, desired of many, which ye have,

2 *Stolen Mornings* : the Dawns and light that have been carried away and concealed by the Paṇis or demons of darkness.

3 *Vṛtra-slaying* : or, generally, 'foeman slaying.'

O Heroes, for the worshipper.
9 With those to this libation poured, ye Heroes, Indra-Agni, come:
Come ye to drink the Soma juice.
10 Glorify him who compasses all forests with his glowing flame,
And leaves them blackened with his tongue.
11 He who gains Indra's bliss with fire enkindled finds an easy way
Over the floods to happiness.
12 Give us fleet coursers to convey Indra and Agni, and bestow
Abundant strengthening food on us.
13 Indra and Agni, I will call you hither and make you joyful with the gifts I offer.
Ye Twain are givers both of food and riches: to win me strength and vigour I invoke you.
14 Come unto us with riches, come with wealth in horses and in kine.
Indra and Agni, we invoke you both, the Gods, as Friends for friendship, bringing bliss.
15 Indra and Agni, hear his call who worships with libations poured.
Come and enjoy the offerings, drink the sweetly-flavoured Soma juice.

HYMN LXI. *Sarasvatī.*

1. To Vadhryaśva when he worshipped her with gifts she gave fierce Divodāsa, canceller of debts.
Consumer of the churlish niggard, one and all, thine, O Sarasvatī, are these effectual boons.
2 She with her might, like one who digs for lotus-stems, hath burst with her strong waves the ridges of the hills.
Let us invite with songs and holy hymns for help Sarasvatī who slayeth the Pārāvatas.
3 Thou castest down, Sarasvatī, those who scorned the Gods, the brood of every Bṛsaya skilled in magic arts.
Thou hast discovered rivers for the tribes of men, and, rich in wealth! made poison flow away from them.
4 May the divine Sarasvatī, rich in her wealth, protect us well,
Furthering all our thoughts with might;
5 Whoso, divine Sarasvatī, invokes thee where the prize is set,
Like Indra when he smites the foe.
6 Aid us, divine Sarasvatī, thou who art strong in wealth and power:
Like Pūṣan, give us opulence.
7 Yea, this divine Sarasvatī, terrible with her golden path,
Foe-slayer, claims our eulogy.
8 Whose limitless unbroken flood, swift-moving with a rapid rush,
Comes onward with tempestuous roar.
9 She hath spread us beyond all foes, beyond her Sisters, Holy One,
As Sūrya spreadeth out the days.
10 Yea, she most dear amid dear streams, Seven-sistered, graciously inclined,
Sarasvatī hath earned our praise.
11 Guard us from hate Sarasvatī, she who hath filled the realms of earth,
And that wide tract, the firmament!
12 Seven-sistered, sprung from threefold source, the Five Tribes' prosperer, she must be
Invoked in every deed of might.
13 Marked out by majesty among the Mighty Ones, in glory swifter than the other rapid Streams,
Created vast for victory like a chariot, Sarasvatī must be extolled by every sage.
14 Guide us, Sarasvatī, to glorious treasure: refuse us not thy milk, nor spurn us from thee.
Gladly accept our friendship and obedience: let us not go from thee to distant countries.

10 *Glorify*: addressed to the *stotar* or praise-singer.
11 *Over the floods*: the dangers and troubles that bar his way.
12 *To convey Indra and Agni*: to bring you, Indra and Agni, to our sacrifice.

1 *Vadhryaśva*: a celebrated Ṛṣi. See X. 69. *She*: Sarasvatī, the River Goddess. *Gave*: as a son. *Canceller of debts*: acquitting, by his birth, the debt which his father owed to his progenitors, the religious obligation of begetting a son who should perform the ceremonies which they require. *Churlish niggard*: who offers no sacrifices. The meaning of *avasám* is uncertain. Sāyaṇa explains it as 'gratifying himself only.' Professor Ludwig regards it as compounded of *a* + *vasā* = thin or meagre. *These effectual boons*: the gift of a son.
2 *She*: Sarasvatī as the river. The description given in the text can hardly apply to the small stream generally known under that name; and from this and other passages which will be noticed as they occur it seems probable that Sarasvatī is also another name of Sindhu or the Indus. See Zimmer, *Altindisches Leben*, pp. 6 ff. *Pārāvatas*: See V. 52. 11.
3 *Every Bṛsaya*: every demon like Bṛsaya, who is said to have been the father of Vṛtra. See I. 93. 4. *Rich in wealth*: *vājinīvati*: according to Sāyaṇa, 'giver of sustenance.'
9 *Her Sisters*: the other rivers of the Panjāb.
12 *Sprung from threefold source*: 'abiding in the three worlds,' that is, pervading heaven, earth, and hell, according to Sāyaṇa, like Gaṅgā in later times.

HYMN LXII. *Aśvins.*

1. I LAUD the Heroes Twain, this heaven's Controllers: singing with songs of praise I call the Aśvins,
Fain in a moment, when the morns are breaking, to part the earth's ends and the spacious regions.

2 Moving to sacrifice through realms of lustre they light the radiance of the car that bears them.
Traversing many wide unmeasured spaces, over the wastes ye pass, and fields, and waters.

3 Ye to that bounteous path of yours, ye mighty, have ever borne away our thoughts with horses,
Mind-swift and full of vigour, that the trouble of man who offers gifts might cease and slumber.

4 So ye, when ye have yoked your chariot-horses, come to the hymn of the most recent singer.
Our true and ancient Herald Priest shall bring you, the Youthful, bearing splendour, food, and vigour.

5 With newest hymn I call those Wonder-Workers, ancient and brilliant, and exceeding mighty,
Bringers of bliss to him who lauds and praises, bestowing varied bounties on the singer.

6 So ye, with birds, out of the sea and waters bore Bhujyu, son of Tugra, through the regions.
Speeding with winged steeds through dustless spaces, out of the bosom of the flood they bore him.

7 Victors, car-borne, ye rent the rock asunder: Bulls, heard the calling of the eunuch's consort.
Bounteous, ye filled the cow with milk for Śayu: thus, swift and zealous Ones, ye showed your favour.

8 Whate'er from olden time, Heaven, Earth! existeth great object of the wrath of Gods and mortals,
Make that, Ādityas, Vasus, sons of Rudra, an evil brand to one allied with demons.

9 May he who knows, as Varuṇa and Mitra, air's realm, appointing both the Kings in season,
Against the secret fiend cast forth his weapon, against the lying words that strangers utter.

10 Come to our home with friendly wheels, for offspring; come on your radiant chariot rich in heroes.
Strike off, ye Twain, the heads of our assailants who with man's treacherous attack approach us.

11 Come hitherward to us with teams of horses, the highest and the midmost and the lowest.
Bountiful Lords, throw open to the singer doors e'en of the firm-closed stall of cattle.

HYMN LXIII. *Aśvins.*

1. WHERE hath the hymn with reverence, like an envoy, found both fair Gods to-day, invoked of many—
Hymn that hath brought the two Nāsatyas hither? To this man's thought be ye, both Gods, most friendly.

2 Come readily to this mine invocation, lauded with songs, that ye may drink the juices.
Compass this house to keep it from the foeman, that none may force it, either near or distant.

3 Juice in wide room hath been prepared to feast you: for you the grass is strewn, most soft to tread on.
With lifted hands your servant hath adored you. Yearning for you the press-stones shed the liquid.

1 *To part the earth's ends*: as heralds of light to define the limits of earth and sky and so separate one from the other.

3 This stanza is very obscure. Sāyaṇa's paraphrase is inconsistent with the plain meaning of several of the words of the text. 'Fierce Aśvins, from that humble mansion to which (you have repaired), you have ever borne with your desirable horses, as swift as thought, the pious worshippers in some manner (to heave: Let the injurer of the liberal man (be consigned by you) to (final) repose.'—Wilson.

6 *Bhujyu*: See I. 116. 3—5.

7 *The eunuch's consort*: Vadhrimatī. See I. 116. 13. *Śayu*: See I. 116. 22.

9 Mitra and Varuṇa appear here as comprehended in a third God, who must be the Asura Dyaus. He, comprising the heaven of night as well as the heaven of day, assigns to Mitra and Varuṇa the charge, respectively of day and night. See Ludwig's Commentary.

10 *For offspring*: *tánayāya*; to give us offspring. The second line of the stanza might be rendered: 'Turn back, ye Twain, the heads, with secret onslaught, even of those who seek to harm the mortal.'

11 *The highest and the midmost or the lowest*: or, as Professor Ludwig translates; 'the earliest, the midmost, and the latest.'

---

2 *Either near or distant*: neighbour or stranger.

3 *In wide room*: where there is ample space for the sacrificial ceremonies.

4 Agni uplifts him at your sacrifices : forth goes the oblation dropping oil and glowing.
Up stands the grateful-minded priest, elected, appointed to invoke the two Nāsatyas.

5 Lords of great wealth ! for glory Sūrya's Daughter mounted your car that brings a hundred succours.
Famed for your magic arts were ye, magicians ! amid the race of Gods, ye dancing Heroes !

6 Ye Twain, with these your glories fair to look on, brought, to win victory, rich gifts for Sūryā.
After you flew your birds, marvels of beauty : dear to our hearts ! the song, well lauded, reached you.

7 May your winged coursers, best to draw, Nāsatyas ! convey you to the object of your wishes.
Swift as the thought, your car hath been sent onward to food of many a sort and dainty viands.

8 Lords of great wealth, manifold is your bounty : ye filled our cow with food that never faileth.
Lovers of sweetness ! yours are praise and singers, and poured libations which have sought your favour.

9 Mine were two mares of Puraya, brown, swift-footed; a hundred with Sumīḍha, food with Peruk
Śāṇḍa gave ten gold-decked and well-trained horses, tame and obedient and of lofty stature.

10 Nāsatyas ! Purupanthās offered hundreds, thousands of steeds to him who sang your praises,
Gave, Heroes ! to the singer Bharadvāja. Ye-Wonder-Workers, let the fiends be slaughtered.

11 May I with princes share your bliss in freedom.

HYMN LXIV. *Dawn.*

1. THE radiant Dawns have risen up for glory, in their white splendour like the waves of waters.
She maketh paths all easy, fair to travel, and, rich, hath shown herself benign and friendly.

2 We see that thou art good : far shines thy lustre ; thy beams, thy splendours have flown up to heaven.
Decking thyself, thou makest bare thy bosom, shining in majesty, thou Goddess Morning.

3 Red are the kine and luminous that bear her the Blessed One who spreadeth through the distance.
The foes she chaseth like a valiant archer, like a swift warrior she repelleth darkness.

4 Thy ways are easy on the hills : thou passest Invincible ! Self-luminous ! through waters.
So lofty Goddess with thine ample pathway, Daughter of Heaven, bring wealth to give us comfort.

5 Dawn, bring me wealth : untroubled, with thine oxen thou bearest riches at thy will and pleasure ;
Thou who, a Goddess, Child of Heaven, hast shown thee lovely through bounty when we called thee early.

6 As the birds fly forth from their resting-places, so men with store of food rise at thy dawning.

5 *Sūrya's Daughter* : See I. 116. 17. *Dancing Heroes* : ye who dance through the air. Cf. VIII. 20. 22, and 'Day's harbinger comes dancing from the east' (Milton—Song On May Morning).

6 *Rich gifts for Sūryā* : who chose the Aśvins to be her husbands.

9 This and the following stanza eulogize the liberality of several wealthy institutors of sacrifice ; but it is difficult to make out what were the gifts they gave as the verses are filled with epithets without nouns. *Vaḍave*, mares, suits the dual epithets *ṛjre*, and *raghvī*, brown and swift. After *śatám*, a hundred. Sāyaṇa supplies *gāvaḥ*, cows. Instead of 'well-trained' Sāyaṇa's rendering is 'handsome,' and he supplies *aśvān*, 'horses,' or *rathān*, 'chariots' for the absent noun. 'Obedient, gallant, and well-favoured servants' would represent his rendering of the last half-line of the stanza. The translations given by Professors Ludwig and Grassmann differ from each other and from Sāyaṇa's version. As Professor Wilson remarks : 'If we render the stanza literally, it is utterly unintelligible : the greater part of the *Sūkta* is very obscure.' Puraya, Sumīḍha, and Peruka are the names of liberal patrons.

10 *Purupanthās* : another of these generous nobles. In this case *áśvānām*, of horses, appears in the text.

11 *Your bliss* : the felicity which the Aśvins bestow.

---

1 *Dawns* : the plural may be honorific, or may signify Dawn and her rays of light.

3 *Warrior* : borne on a chariot.

4 *Through waters* : of the firmament.

6 This stanza occurs in a hymn to Dawn ascribed to the Ṛṣi Kakṣivān' I. 124. 12. *With store of food* : *pitubhājāḥ*, 'enjoying or sharing food,' is explained by Sāyaṇa as *annasyopāyakāḥ*, 'who have to gain their sustenance.' The wealthy may be meant, who sharet their store with others and must work to replenish it.

Yea, to the liberal mortal who remaineth at home, O Goddess Dawn, much good thou bringest.

HYMN LXV. *Dawn.*

1. Shedding her light on human habitations this Child of Heaven hath called us from our slumber;
She who at night-time with her argent lustre hath shown herself e'en through the shades of darkness.

2 All this with red-rayed steeds have they divided: the Dawns on bright cars shine in wondrous fashion.
They, bringing near the stately rite's commencement, drive far away the night's surrounding shadows.

3 Dawns, bringing hither, to the man who worships, glory and power and might and food and vigour,
Opulent, with imperial sway like heroes, favour your servant and this day enrich him.

4 Now is there treasure for the man who serves you, now for the hero, Dawns! who brings oblation;
Now for the singer when he sings the praise-song. Even to one like me ye brought aforetime.

5 O Dawn who standest on the mountain ridges, Aṅgirases now praise thy stalls of cattle.
With prayer and holy hymn they burst them open: the heroes' calling on the Gods was fruitful.

6 Shine on us as of old, thou Child of Heaven, on him, rich Maid! who serves like Bharadvāja.
Give to the singer wealth with noble heroes, and upon us bestow wide-spreading glory.

HYMN LXVI. *Maruts.*

1. E'en to the wise let that be still a wonder to which the general name of Cow is given.
The one hath swelled among mankind for milking: Pṛśni hath drained but once her fair bright udder.

2 They who like kindled flames of fire are glowing, the Maruts, twice and thrice have waxen mighty.
Golden and dustless were their cars, invested with their great strength and their heroic vigour.

3 They who are Sons of the rain-pouring Rudra, whom the long-lasting One had power to foster:
The Mighty Ones whose germ great Mother Pṛśni is known to have received for man's advantage.

4 They shrink not from the birth; in this same manner still resting there they purge away reproaches.
When they have streamed forth, brilliant, at their pleasure, with their own splendour they bedew their bodies.

5 Even those who bear the brave bold name of Maruts, whom not the active quickly wins for milking.
Even the liberal wards not off those fierce ones, those who are light and agile in their greatness.

6 When, strong in strength and armed with potent weapons, they had united well-formed earth and heaven,

The liberal mortal: the man who sacrifices to the Gods. To bring out this meaning more clearly the last line may be translated: 'To him who stays at home and pours oblations, O Goddess Dawn, thou givest ample riches.'

---

1 *At night-time*: an allusion, perhaps, to the 'false dawn' before the appearance of the real dawn, although this faint glimmer can hardly be called lustre. Or the light of stars may be intended, as belonging to Dawn rather than to Night.

2 *All this......have they divided*: separated light from darkness. *The stately rite*: the Agnihotra, or great morning sacrifice.

5 *Aṅgirases here praise*: 'What we are doing here is in reality only a repetition of what the Aṅgirasas did in ancient times.'—Ludwig.

6 *Bharadvāja*: the great ancestor of the priestly family of which the Ṛṣi of the hymn was a member.

---

1 This meaning may be that while things of different nature are designated by the name of Cow, all that is so called has a claim to our wonder and admiration. The Cow of earth yields her milk frequently and in abundance: Pṛśni, the Cow of the firmament, has given milk but once, when she brought forth her offspring, the Maruts. 'Once only Pṛśni's milk was shed: no second, after this, is born' (VI. 48. 22). Sāyaṇa's interpretation is utterly inconsistent with the plain meaning of the words of the text.

2 *Twice and thrice*: perhaps in relation to earth and heaven, and to earth, firmament, and heaven.

4 *Still resting there*: while yet unborn they free their mother from the reproach of barrenness.

5 *Wins for milking*: persuades to grant his petitions. The version of the second line is merely conjectural as the meaning of *staunāḥ* (explained by Sāyaṇa as = *stenāḥ* robbers) is unknown. 'The liberal donor pacifies the angry Maruts who are otherwise in their might the resistless plunderers of their wealth).'—Wilson.

6 *United*: by obscuring the horizon with cloud and rain.

Rodasī stood among these furious Heroes like splendour shining with her native brightness.

7 No team of goats shall draw your car, O Maruts, no horse no charioteer be he who drives it.
Halting not, reinless, through the air it travels, speeding alone its paths through earth and heaven.

8 None may obstruct, none overtake, O Maruts, him whom ye succour in the strife of battle
For sons and progeny, for kine and waters: he bursts the cow-stall on the day of trial.

9 Bring a bright hymn to praise the band of Maruts, the Singers, rapid, strong in native vigour,
Who conquer mighty strength with strength more mighty: earth shakes in terror at their wars, O Agni.

10 Bright like the flashing flames of sacrifices, like tongues of fire impetuous in their onset,
Chanting their psalm, singing aloud, like heroes, splendid from birth, invincible, the Maruts.

11 That swelling band I call with invocation, the brood of Rudra, armed with glittering lances.
Pure hymns are meet for that celestial army : like floods and mountains have the Strong Ones battled.

HYMN LXVII. *Mitra-Varuṇa.*

1. Now Mitra-Varuṇa shall be exalted high by your songs, noblest of all existing;
They who, as 'twere with reins are best Controllers, unequalled with their arms to check the people.

2 To you Two Gods is this my thought extended, turned to the sacred grass with loving homage.
Give us, O Mitra-Varuṇa, a dwelling safe from attack, which ye shall guard, Boon-Givers !

3 Come hither, Mitra-Varuṇa, invited with eulogies and loving adoration,
Ye who with your might, as Work-Controllers, urge even men who quickly hear to labour.

4 Whom, of pure origin, like two strong horses, Aditi bore as babes in proper season,
Whom, Mighty at your birth, the Mighty Goddess brought forth as terrors to the mortal foeman.

5 As all the Gods in their great joy and gladness gave you with one accord your high dominion,
As ye surround both worlds, though wide and spacious, your spies are ever true and ne'er bewildered.

6 So, through the days maintaining princely power, ye prop the height as 'twere from loftiest heaven.
The Star of all the Gods, established, filleth the heaven and earth with food of man who liveth.

7 Take the strong drink, to quaff till ye are sated, when he and his attendants fill the chamber.
The young Maids brook not that none seeks to win them, when, Quickeners of all ! they scatter moisture.

8 So with your tongue come ever, when your envoy, faithful and very wise, attends our worship.
Nourished by holy oil ! be this your glory : annihilate the sacrificer's trouble.

9 When, Mitra-Varuṇa, they strive against you and break the friendly laws ye have established,
They, neither Gods nor men in estimation, like Apī's sons have godless sacrifices.

7 No feeble or ordinary team must convey you ; no common charioteer must drive your chariot.

8 *Bursts the cow-stall* : carries away the enemy's cattle.

10 *Singing aloud* : 'causing their opponents to tremble,' according to Sāyaṇa, who derives the word from the root *dhū*, to shake. Derived from *dhvan*, to sound, *dhunayaḥ* means singers, musicians, minstrels, leaders of the wild music of the wind and storm (stürmer.—Ludwig). See *Vedische Studien*, I. 269.

11 *Like floods and mountains* : perhaps, with the impetuosity of rushing waters and the firm strength of mountains. But the meaning of this last half-line, as of many other passages of the hymn, is very obscure.

The hymn has been translated and thoroughly discussed by Peter von Bradke (Festgrutss an R. von Roth, 1893, pp. 117—125). See also Vedic Hymns, I. 368—372 (Sacred Books of the East, XXXII).

5 *Your spies* : messengers or angels, probably the rest of the Ādityas. See I. 25. 13.

6 *The height* : the high ridge or summit of heaven. *The Star of all the Gods* : representing all the Gods : the Sun. He draws up the waters which descend to fertilize the earth.

7 *He* : the worshipper ; or, perhaps, Soma. *The chamber* : of sacrifice. *The Young Maids* : the water, necessary for the preparation of the Soma libation, is ready and impatiently waiting to be used.

8 *With your tongue* : Agni, by whose tongue of fire they consume the oblations. *Your envoy* : Agni.

9 *Like Apī's sons* : 'sons of the Waters.'—Grassmann. The meaning is uncertain. *Godless sacrifices* : unattended by Gods, and therefore fruitless.

10 When singers in their song uplift their voices, some chant the Nivid texts with steady purpose.
Then may we sing you lauds that shall be fruitful : do ye not rival all the Gods in greatness?

11 O Mitra-Varuṇa, may your large bounty come to us hither, near to this our dwelling,
When the kine haste to us, and when they harness the fleet-foot mettled stallion for the battle.

HYMN LXVIII. *Indra-Varuṇa.*

1. HIS honouring rite whose grass is trimmed is offered swiftly to you, in Manu's wise, accordant,
The rite which Indra-Varuṇa shall carry this day to high success and glorious issue.

2 For at Gods' worship they are best through vigour; they have become the strongest of the Heroes;
With mighty strength, most liberal of the Princes, Chiefs of the host, by Law made Vṛtra's slayers.

3 Praise those Twain Gods for powers that merit worship, Indra and Varuṇa, for bliss, the joyous.
One with his might and thunderbolt slays Vṛtra; the other as a Sage stands near in troubles.

4 Though dames and men have waxen strong and mighty, and all the Gods self-praised among the Heroes,
Ye, Indra-Varuṇa, have in might surpassed them, and thus were ye spread wide, O Earth and Heaven.

5 Righteous is he, and liberal and helpful who, Indra-Varuṇa, brings you gifts with gladness.
That bounteous man through food shall conquer foemen, and win him opulence and wealthy people.

6 May wealth which ye bestow in food and treasure on him who brings you gifts and sacrifices,
Wealth, Gods! which breaks the curse of those who vex us, be, Indra-Varuṇa, e'en our own possession.

7 So also, Indra-Varuṇa, may our princes have riches swift to save, with Gods to guard them—
They whose great might gives victory in battles, and their triumphant glory spreads with swiftness.

8 Indra and Varuṇa, Gods whom we are lauding. mingle ye wealth with our heroic glory.
May we, who praise the strength of what is mighty, pass dangers, as with boats we cross the waters.

9 Now will I sing a dear and far-extending hymn to Varuṇa the God, sublime, imperial Lord,
Who, mighty Governor, Eternal, as with flame, illumines both wide worlds with majesty and power.

10 True to Law, Indra-Varuṇa, drinkers of the juice, drink this pressed Soma which shall give you rapturous joy.
Your chariot cometh to the banquet of the Gods, to sacrifice, as it were home, that ye may drink.

11 Indra and Varuṇa, drink your fill, ye Heroes, of this invigorating sweetest Soma.
This juice is shed by us that ye may quaff it : on this trimmed grass be seated, and rejoice you.

HYMN LXIX. *Indra-Viṣṇu*

1. INDRA and Viṣṇu, at my task's completion I urge you on with food and sacred service.
Accept the sacrifice and grant us riches, leading us on by unobstructed pathways.

2 Ye who inspire all hymns, Indra and Viṣṇu, ye vessels who contain the Soma juices,
May hymns of praise that now are sung address you, the lauds that are recited by the singers.

10 *Nivid texts* : short formularies of invocation inserted in a liturgy.

11 *When the kine haste to us* : when the cattle of the men whom we are about to attack are ready and eager to be carried off. Sāyaṇa's interpretation of the last line is totally different : 'when (your) praises are uttered, and the sacrificers add in the ceremony the *Soma* that inspires straightforwardness and resolution, and is the showerer (of benefits).)'—Wilson.

---

3 *In troubles* : 'in deeds of might.'—Ludwig. 'With snares, or nooses,' according to Professor Geldner, *Vedische studien* I. 142.

4 *Self-praised* : on account of their own deeds, or their own nature.

8 *Of what is mighty* : apparently, riches.

9 This stanza, in honour of Varuṇa alone, appears to be the beginning of another hymn. Professor Grassmann banishes stanzas 9 and 10 to his Appendix.

---

1 *At my task's completion* : when all arrangements for the sacrifice have been made.

2 *Who inspire* : literally, 'the generators,' *janitārā*. *By the singers* : or, with laudations.'

3 Lords of joy-giving draughts, Indra and Viṣṇu, come, giving gifts of treasure, to the Soma.
With brilliant rays of hymns let chanted praises, repeated with the lauds, adorn and deck you.

4 May your foe-conquering horses bring you hither, Indra and Viṣṇu, sharers of the banquet.
Of all our hymns accept the invocations : list to my prayers and hear the songs I sing you.

5 This your deed, Indra-Viṣṇu, must be lauded : widely ye strode in the wild joy of Soma.
Ye made the firmament of larger compass, and made the regions broad for our existence.

6 Strengthened with sacred offerings, Indra-Viṣṇu, first eaters, served with worship and oblation,
Fed with the holy oil, vouchsafe us riches : ye are the lake, the vat that holds the Soma.

7 Drink of this meath, O Indra, thou, and Viṣṇu; drink ye your fill of Soma, Wonder-Workers.
The sweet exhilarating juice hath reached you. Hear ye my prayers, give ear unto my calling.

8 Ye Twain have conquered, ne'er have ye been conquered : never hath either of the Twain been vanquished.
Ye, Indra-Viṣṇu, when ye fought the battle, produced this infinite with three divisions.

HYMN LXX. *Heaven and Earth.*

1. FILLED full of fatness, compassing all things that be, wide, spacious, dropping meath, beautiful in their form,
The Heaven and the Earth by Varuṇa's decree, unwasting, rich in germs, stand parted each from each.

2 The Everlasting Pair, with full streams, rich in milk, in their pure rule pour fatness for the pious man.
Ye who are Regents of this world, O Earth and Heaven, pour into us the genial flow that prospers men.

3 Whoso, for righteous life, pours offerings to you, O Heaven and Earth, ye Hemispheres, that man succeeds.
He in his seed is born again and spreads by Law : from you flow things diverse in form, but ruled alike.

4 Enclosed in fatness, Heaven and Earth are bright therewith : they mingle with the fatness which they still increase.
Wide, broad, set foremost at election of the priest, to them the singers pray for bliss to further them.

5 May Heaven and Earth pour down the balmy rain for us, balm-dropping, yielding balm, with balm upon your path,
Bestowing by your Godhead sacrifice and wealth, great fame and strength for us and good heroic might.

6 May Heaven and Earth make food swell plenteously for us, all-knowing Father, Mother, wondrous in their works.
Pouring out bounties, may, in union, both the Worlds, all beneficial, send us gain, and power, and wealth.

HYMN LXXI. *Savitar.*

1. FULL of effectual wisdom Savitar the God hath stretched out golden arms that he may bring forth life.
Young and most skilful, while he holds the region up, the Warrior sprinkles fatness over both his hands.

2 May we enjoy the noblest vivifying force of Savitar the God, that he may give us wealth :
For thou art mighty to produce and lull to rest the world of life that moves on two feet and on four.

3 Protect our habitation, Savitar, this day, with guardian aids around, auspicious, firm and true.
God of the golden tongue, keep us for newest

8 *Produced this infinite* : brougnt into existence the world with all its creatures, the three divisions being heaven, firmament, and earth. See Professor Wilson's note for Sāyaṇa's explanation of the passage.

The deities are Dyāvāpṛthivī, that is Dyaus, Heaven, and Pṛthivī, Earth, combined in a compound dual.

1 *Full of fatness* : containing *ghṛta*, *ghī*, clarified butter, fatness in general, especially the fertilizing rain.

3 *Ye Hemispheres* : *dhiṣaṇe* ; two bowls. 'Firm-set,' —Wilson. *By Law* : in the course of nature.

4 *Set foremost at election of the priest* : 'first propitiated at the sacrifice.'—Wilson.

vi 1 *Savitar* : the Sun as the great generator or viisfier. *Sprinkles fatness* : Professor Ludwig thinks that thn may by somewhat ironical. 'The god sprinkles his haids, probably, as a preparation for the hard work whch he is about to perform; but there is an underlying thought that a good deal of the fatness [in the shape of fertilizing rain] also falls down to the earth.'

bliss : let not the evil-wisher have us in his power.

4 This Savitar the God, the golden-handed, Friend of the home, hath risen to meet the twilight.
With cheeks of brass, with pleasant tongue, the Holy, he sends the worshipper rich gifts in plenty.

5 Like a Director, Savitar hath extended his golden arms, exceeding fair to look on.
He hath gone up the heights of earth and heaven, and made each monster fall and cease from troubling.

6 Fair wealth, O Savitar, to-day, to-morrow, fair wealth produce for us each day that passes.
May we through this our song be happy gainers, God, of a fair and spacious habitation.

HYMN LXXII. *Indra-Soma.*

1. GREAT is this might of yours, Indra and Soma : the first high exploits were your own achievements.
Ye found the Sun, ye found the light of heaven : ye killed all darkness and the Gods' blasphemers.

2 Ye, Indra-Soma, gave her light to Morning, and led the Sun on high with all his splendour.
Ye stayed the heaven with a supporting pillar, and spread abroad apart, the Earth, the Mother.

3 Ye slew the flood-obstructing serpent Vṛtra, Indra and Soma: Heaven approved your exploit.
Ye urged to speed the currents of the rivers, and many seas have ye filled full with waters.

4 Ye in the unripe udders of the milch-kine have set the ripe milk, Indra, thou, and Soma.

Ye have held fast the unimpeded whiteness within these many-coloured moving creatures.

5 Verily ye bestow, Indra and Soma, wealth, famed, victorious, passing to our children.
Ye have invested men, ye Mighty Beings, with manly strength that conquers in the battle.

HYMN LXXIII. *Bṛhaspati.*

1. SERVED with oblations, first-born, mountain-render, Aṅgiras' son, Bṛhaspati, the Holy,
With twice-firm path, dwelling in light, our Father, roars loudly, as a bull, to Earth and Heaven.

2 Bṛhaspati, who made for such a people wide room and verge when Gods were invocated,
Slaying his enemies, breaks down their castles, quelling his foes and conquering those who hate him.

3 Bṛhaspati in war hath won rich treasures, hath won, this God, the great stalls filled with cattle.
Striving to win waters and light, resistless, Bṛhaspati with lightning smites the foeman.

HYMN LXXIV. *Soma-Rudra.*

1. HOLD fast your Godlike sway, O Soma-Rudra : let these our sacrifices quickly reach you.
Placing in every house your seven great treasures, bring blessing to our quadrupeds and bipeds.

2 Soma and Rudra, chase to every quarter the sickness that hath visited our dwelling.
Drive Nirṛti away into the distance, and give us excellent and happy glories.

3 Provide, O Soma-Rudra, for our bodies all needful medicines to heal and cure us.

4 *To meet the twilight*: 'at the close of night.'—Wilson. *Cheeks of brass* : *áyóhanuḥ*; according to Sāyaṇa. 'golden-jawed.'

5 *A Director* ; a priest who directs others. Or, perhaps, 'an Invoker,' as Professor Ludwig suggests. *Each monster* : every terror of the night. Sāyaṇa's, interpretation of the last line is totally different : 'and,' moving along, delights every thing that is.'—Wilson.

4 *Ye in the unripe udders* : the unripe, that is raw, udders are contrasted with the warm milk that is cooked or matured in them. See I. 62. 9. *The unimpeded whiteness* : the milk which is not prevented from flowing. The colour of the milk is contrasted with the colour of the cows that produce it.

1 *Bṛhaspati* : Lord of Prayer ; the Deity in whom the action of the worshipper upon the Gods is personified. See I. 14. 3. *Mountain-render* : 'Bṛhaspati *cleft the mountain*' (I. 62. 3). *Dwelling in light* : or, perhaps, in the Sun. The meaning of *prāgharmasád* is uncertain.

2 *Such a people* : so good a people. *When Gods were invocated* : in battle.

3 *With lightning* : or with Sunlight : 'with sacred prayers.'—Wilson.

1 *Quadrupeds and bipeds* : or, 'bless all of us, men and four-footed creatures.

2 *Nirṛti* : the Goddess of Death and Destruction.

Set free and draw away the sin committed which we have still inherent in our persons.

4 Armed with keen shafts and weapons, kind and loving, be gracious unto us, Soma and Rudra.

Release us from the noose of Varuṇa; keep us from sorrow, in your tender loving-kindness.

HYMN LXXV. *Weapons of War.*

1. THE warrior's look is like a thunderous rain-cloud's, when, armed with mail, he seeks the lap of battle.

Be thou victorious with unwounded body: so let the thickness of thy mail protect thee.

2 With Bow let us win kine, with Bow the battle, with Bow be victors in our hot encounters.

The Bow brings grief and sorrow to the foeman : armed with the Bow may we subdue all regions.

3 Close to his ear, as fain to speak, She presses, holding her well-loved Friend in her embraces.

Strained on the Bow, She whispers like a woman—this Bowstring that preserves us in the combat.

4 These, meeting like a woman and her lover, bear, mother-like, their child upon their bosom.

May the two Bow-ends, starting swift asunder, scatter, in unison, the foes who hate us.

5 With many a son, father of many daughters, He clangs and clashes as he goes to battle.

Slung on the back, pouring his brood, the Quiver vanquishes all opposing bands and armies.

6 Upstanding in the Car the skilful Charioteer guides his strong Horses on whithersoe'er he will.

See and admire the strength of those controlling Reins which from behind declare the will of him who drives.

7 Horses whose hoofs rain dust are neighing loudly, yoked to the Chariots, showing forth their vigour,

With their forefeet descending on the foemen, they, never flinching, trample and destroy them.

8 Car-bearer is the name of his oblation, whereon are laid his Weapons and his Armour.

So let us here, each day that passes, honour the helpful Car with hearts exceeding joyful.

9 In sweet association lived the fathers who gave us life, profound and strong in trouble,

Unwearied, armed with shafts and wondrous weapons, free, real heroes, conquerors of armies.

10 The Brāhmans, and the Fathers meet for Soma-draughts, and, graciously inclined, unequalled Heaven and Earth.

Guard us from evil, Pūṣan, guard us strengtheners of Law : let not the evil-wisher master us.

11 Her tooth a deer, dressed in an eagle's feathers, bound with cow-hide, launched forth, She flieth onward.

There where the heroes speed hither and thither, there may the Arrows shelter and protect us.

12 Avoid us thou whose flight is straight, and let our bodies be as stone.

May Soma kindly speak to us, and Aditi protect us well.

4 *The noose of Varuṇa* : Varuṇa, the moral Governor of the world, is represented as armed with a noose or lasso for the capture and destruction of the wicked.

---

3 *She* : the bowstring. *Her well-loved friend* : the arrow. *Whispers like a woman* : 'twangs like the scream of a woman.'—Muir. But the faint sound made by the string while it is being drawn to the ear is intended. Homer likens the sound to the voice of a swallow.

4 *These* : the two ends of the bow. *Like a woman and her lover* : or, 'drawing close like two women to their lovers'. *Their child* : the arrow.

5 *With many a son* : the quiver is called the father of sons and daughters, it is said, because the words signifying arrow are both masculine and feminine.

8 *Car-bearer* : *rathavāhanam* : a platform, stand, or truck on which the chariot is placed when not in use. The word seems in this place to mean also the oblation offered by the warrior to the ideal war-chariot personified, or to a tutelary deity of chariots.

9 There is no verb in this stanza, and the only substantive, *pitáraḥ*, fathers, is explained by both Commentators as *pālayitāraḥ*, guards, defenders, that is, apparently, those who attend the chariot of the chief. Professor Wilson, following Sāyaṇa, translates : 'The guards (of the chariot), revelling in the savoury (spoil), distributors of food, protectors in calamity, armed with spears, resolute, beautifully arranged, strong in arrows, invincible, of heroic valour, robust, and conquerors of numerous hosts.'

10 *The Brāhmans and the Fathers* : or, perhaps, the sacerdotal Fathers. The stanza, which is grammatically difficult, seems out of place.

11 *Her tooth a deer* : the point of the arrow is made of a piece of deer's horn attached to the shaft with leather strings. The butt of the arrow is feathered.

13 He lays his blows upon their backs, he deals his blows upon their thighs.
Thou, Whip, who urgest horses, drive sagacious horses in the fray.

14 It compasses the arm with serpent windings, fending away the friction of the bowstring:
So may the Brace, well-skilled in all its duties, guard manfully the man from every quarter.

15 Now to the Shaft with venom smeared, tipped with deer-horn, with iron mouth,
Celestial, of Parjanya's seed, be this great adoration paid.

16 Loosed from the Bowstring fly away, thou Arrow, sharpened by our prayer.
Go to the foemen, strike them home, and let not one be left alive.

17 There where the flights of Arrows fall like boys whose locks are yet unshorn.
Even there may Brahmaṇaspati, and Aditi protect us well, protect us well through all our days.

18 Thy vital parts I cover with thine Armour: with immortality King Soma clothe thee.
Varuṇa give thee what is more than ample, and in thy triumph may the Gods be joyful.

19 Whoso would kill us, whether he be a strange foe or one of us,
May all the Gods discomfit him. My nearest, closest Mail is prayer.

13 *He* : the whip.

14 *It* : the brace or guard worn on the archer's left arm, fastened on with leather straps.

15 *With venom smeared* : by the Laws of Manu, that is, the ideal Code of the Mānavas, Kṣatriyas were forbidden to poison their arrows. Arrows appear to have been of two kinds, one, the older and less effective, *tipped with deer-horn*, and the other *with iron mouth*, pointed with *áyas*, bronze or iron. *Celestial, of Parjanya's seed* : made of the tall reeds that grow in the Rains under the influence of Parjanya the God of the rain-cloud.

16 *Sharpened by our prayer* : 'whetted by charm.'—Wilson.

17 *Like boys whose locks are yet unshorn*: : 'the point of the comparison is not very obvious, but it may mean that the arrows fall where they list, as boys before they are left with the lock of hair, before the religious tonsure, play about wherever they like'—Wilson. Professor Roth separates *viśikhā* from *kumārā́*, and translates : 'Where the arrows fly, young and old : that is, feathered and unfeathered.'

18 *Thy vital parts* : the *várman,* or coat of mail, protected the shoulders, back, chest, and lower parts of the body. If not made of metal, it was strengthened and adorned with metal of some kind. The Indians in the army of Xerxes are said by Herodotus to have worn clothes made out of the bark of trees (VII. 65); but he probably meant the common soldiers only, and not the chiefs. For a full description of the arms, offensive and defensive, used in Vedic times, see Muir, *O. S. Texts*, V. 469 ; *Altindisches Leben*, pp. 293—301; or Dutt's *History of Civilization in Ancient India*, I. p. 88.

BOOK THE SEVENTH

HYMN I. *Agni.*

1. THE men from fire-sticks, with their hands' swift movement, have, in deep thought, engendered glorious Agni,
Far-seen, with pointed flame, Lord of the homestead.

2 The Vasus set that Agni in the dwelling, fair to behold, for help from every quarter :
Who, in the home for ever, must be honoured.

3 Shine thou before us, Agni, well-enkindled, with flame, Most Youthful God, that never fadeth.
To thee come all our sacrificial viands.

4 Among all fires these fires have shone most brightly, splendid with light, begirt by noble heroes,
Where men of lofty birth sit down together.

5 Victorious Agni, grant us wealth with wisdom, wealth with brave sons, famous and independent,
Which not a foe who deals in magic conquers.

6 To whom, the Strong, at morn and eve comes, maid-like, the ladle dropping oil, with its oblation :
Wealth-seeking comes to him his own devotion.

7 Burn up all malice with those flames, O Agni, wherewith of old thou burntest up Jarūtha,
And drive away in silence pain and sickness.

8 With him who lighteth up thy splendour, Agni, excellent, pure, refulgent, Purifier,
Be present, and with us through these our praises.

9 Agni, the patriarchal men, the mortals who have in many places spread thy lustre,—
Be gracious to us here for their sake also.

10 Let these men, heroes in the fight with foemen, prevail against all godless arts of magic,—
These who approve the noble song I sing thee.

11 Let us not sit in want of men, O Agni, without descendants, heroless, about thee :
But, O House-Friend, in houses full of children.

12 By sacrifice which the Steeds' Lord ever visits, there make our dwelling rich in seed and offspring,
Increasing still with lineal successors.

13 Guard us, O Agni, from the hated demon, guard us from malice of the churlish sinner :
Allied with thee may I subdue assailants.

14 May this same fire of mine surpass all others, this fire where offspring, vigorous and firm-handed,
Wins, on a thousand paths, what ne'er shall perish.

15 This is that Agni, saviour from the foeman, who guards the kindler of the flame from sorrow :
Heroes of noble lineage serve and tend him.

16 This is that Agni, served in many places, whom the rich lord who brings oblation kindles,
And round him goes the priest at sacrifices.

17 Agni, may we with riches in possession bring thee continual offerings in abundance,
Using both means to draw thee to our worship.

18 Agni, bear thou, Eternal, these most welcome oblations to the Deities' assembly :
Let them enjoy our very fragrant presents.

19 Give us not up, Agni, to want of heroes, to wretched clothes, to need, to destitution.

All the hymns of this Book are ascribed to the Ṛṣi Vasiṣṭha, with whom his sons are associated as the seers of parts of two hymns.

1 *In deep thought* : 'with their fingers,' according to Sāyaṇa, this meaning having been attributed without any philological grounds to the word *dīdhitibhiḥ* from its use in this and similar passages.

6 *His own devotion* : the worship which belongs especially to him.

7 *Jarūtha* : a Rākṣasa or demon with a loud harsh voice.—Sāyaṇa.

12 *Tho Steeds' Lord* : Agni, whose swift flames are called horses.

17 *Both means* : prayer and praise.

Yield us not, Holy One, to fiend or hunger; injure us not at home or in the forest.

20 Give strength and power to these my prayers, O Agni; O God, pour blessings on our chiefs and nobles.
Grant that both we and they may share thy bounty. Ye Gods, protect us evermore with blessings.

21 Thou Agni, swift to hear, art fair of aspect : beam forth, O Son of Strength, in full effulgence.
Let me not want, with thee, a son for ever : let not a manly hero ever fail us.

22 Condemn us not to indigence, O Agni, beside these flaming fires which Gods have kindled;
Nor, even after fault, let thy displeasure, thine as a God, O Son of Strength, o'ertake us.

23 O Agni, fair of face, the wealthy mortal who to the Immortal offers his oblation.
Hath him who wins him treasure by his Godhead, to whom the prince, in need, goes supplicating.

24 Knowing our chief felicity, O Agni, bring hither ample riches to our nobles,
Wherewith we may enjoy ourselves, O Victor, with undiminished life and hero children.

25 Give strength and power to these my prayers, O Agni; O God, pour blessings on our chiefs and nobles.
Grant that both we and they may share thy bounty. Ye Gods, protect us evermore with blessings.

HYMN II. *Āprīs.*

1. Gladly accept, this day, our fuel, Agni : send up thy sacred smoke and shine sublimely.
Touch the celestial summits with thy columns, and overspread thee with the rays of Sūrya.

2 With sacrifice to these we men will honour the majesty of holy Narāśaṁsa—
To these the pure, most wise, the thought-inspirers, Gods who enjoy both sorts of our oblations.

3 We will extol at sacrifice for ever, as men may do, Agni whom Manu kindled,
Your very skilful Asura, meet for worship, envoy between both worlds, the truthful speaker.

4 Bearing the sacred grass, the men who serve him strew it with reverence, on their knees, by Agni.
Calling him to the spotted grass, oil-sprinkled, adorn him, ye Adhvaryus, with oblation.

5 With holy thoughts the pious have thrown open Doors fain for chariots in the Gods' assembly.
Like two full mother cows who lick their youngling, like maidens for the gathering, they adorn them.

6 And let the two exalted Heavenly Ladies, Morning and Night, like a cow good at milking,
Come, much-invoked, and on our grass be seated, wealthy, deserving worship, for our welfare.

7 You, Bards and Singers at men's sacrifices, both filled with wisdom, I incline to worship.
Send up our offerings when we call upon you, and so among the Gods obtain us treasures.

8 May Bhāratī with all her Sisters, Ilā accordant with the Gods, with mortals Agni,
Sarasvatī with all her kindred Rivers, come to this grass, Three Goddesses, and seat them.

21 *For ever*: *nitye*; perpetual ; who shall live for ever in his posterity.

22 *Which Gods have kindled* : lighted by the ministering priests.

23 *Hath him* : possesses, or enjoys the favour of, Agni. 'That deity (Agni) favours the presenter of (sacrificial) wealth.'—Wilson.

24 *Knowing our chief felicity* : understanding what we want to make us happy, that is, riches.

The Āprīs are the divine or deified beings and objects to which the propitiatory verses are addressed. For other Āprī hymns see I. 13; 188; II. 3; III. 4; V. 5; IX. 5; X. 70; 110.

2 *Narāśaṁsa* : 'the Praise of Men' ; Agni. *Both sorts of our oblations* : offerings of *ghṛta*, *ghī*, or clarified butter, and libations of Soma juice.

5 *Doors* : the deified doors of the hall of sacrifice where the Gods assemble. *Fain for chariots* : welcoming the approach of the cars in which the priests come to the ceremony. The latter half of the stanza is obscure : '(the ladles) placed to the east are plying the fire with *ghī* at sacrifices, as the mother cows lick the calf, or as rivers (water the fields).'—Wilson.

6 *Like a cow* : the dual *dhenū*, two cows, instead of *dhenuḥ*, would, as Ludwig suggests, seem to us to be preferable.

7 *Bards and Singers* : the *hotārā*, or 'two Invokers' of I. 13. 8; perhaps Agni and Varuṇa and Āditya.

8 Stanzas 8—11 are identical with stanzas 8—11 of Book III. 4.

9 Well pleased with us do thou, O God, O Tvaṣṭar, give ready issue to our procreant vigour,
Whence springs the hero, powerful, skilled in action, lover of Gods, adjuster of the press-stones.

10 Send to the Gods the oblation, Lord of Forests, and let the Immolator, Agni, dress it.
He as the truer Priest shall offer worship, for the God'sgenerations well he knoweth.

11 Come thou to us, O Agni, duly kindled, together with the potent Gods and Indra.
On this our grass sit Aditi, happy Mother, and let our Hail! delight the Gods Immortal.

HYMN III. *Agni.*

1. ASSOCIATE with fires, make your God Agni envoy at sacrifice, best skilled in worship,
Established firm among mankind, the Holy, flame-crowned and fed with oil, the Purifier.

2 Like a steed neighing eager for the pasture, when he hath stepped forth from the great enclosure:
Then the wind following blows upon his splendour, and, straight, the path is black which thou hast travelled.

3 From thee a Bull but newly born, O Agni, the kindled everlasting flames rise upward.
Aloft to heaven thy ruddy smoke ascendeth: Agni, thou speedest to the Gods as envoy.

4 Thou whose fresh lustre o'er the earth advanceth when greedily with thy jaws thy food thou eatest.
Like a host hurried onward comes thy lasso: fierce, with thy tongue thou piercest, as 'twere barley.

5 The men have decked him both at eve and morning, Most Youthful Agni, as they tend a courser.
They kindle him, a guest within his dwelling: bright shines the splendour of the worshipped Hero.

6 O fair of face, beautiful is thine aspect when, very near at hand, like gold thou gleamest,
Like Heaven's thundering roar thy might approaches, and like the wondrous Sun thy light thou showest.

7 That we may worship, with your Hail to Agni! with sacrificial cakes and fat oblations,
Guard us, O Agni, with those boundless glories as with a hundred fortresses of iron.

8 Thine are resistless songs for him who offers, and hero-giving hymns wherewith thou savest;
With these, O Son of Strength, O Jātavedas, guard us, preserve these princes and the singers.

9 When forth he cometh, like an axe newsharpened, pure in his form, resplendent in his body,
Sprung, sought with eager longing, from his Parents, for the Gods' worship, Sage and Purifier:

10 Shine this felicity on us, O Agni: may we attain to perfect understanding.
All happiness be theirs who sing and praise thee. Ye Gods, preserve us evermore with blessings.

HYMN IV. *Agni.*

1. BRING forth your gifts to his refulgent splendour, your hymn as purest offering to Agni,
To him who goes as messenger with knowledge between all songs of men and Gods in heaven.

2 Wise must this Agni be, though young and tender, since he was born, Most Youthful, of his Mother;
He who with bright teeth seizeth fast the forests, and eats his food, though plenteous, in a moment.

3 Before his presence must we all assemble, this God's whom men have seized in his white splendour.

1 *Associate*: *sajoṣāḥ* being a shortened form of *sajoṣasaḥ*, the nominative plural. Sāyaṇa explains it as an accusative singular, qualifying Agni.

2 *From the great enclosure*: 'from the vast enclosing (forest).'—Wilson. Others understand it as the enclosure in which the horse is confined.

4 *Thou piercest as 'twere barley*: the comparison is somewhat compressed: the meaning is, thou penetratest and fellest the trees of the forest with thy tongue as men cut down barley with a reaping-hook.

9 *From his Parents*: the two fire-sticks.

3 *Must we all assemble*: I follow Ludwig in his interpretation of *saṁsádi*: as we are forsaken, and our protector is far away (st. 6, 7, 8), we must crowd to the God of Fire for defence.

This Agni who hath brooked that men should seize him hath shone for man with glow insufferable.

4 Far-seeing hath this Agni been established, deathless mid mortals, wise among the foolish.
Here, O victorious God, forbear to harm us : may we for ever share thy gracious favour.

5 He who hath occupied his God-made dwelling, Agni, in wisdom hath surpassed Immortals.
A Babe unborn, the plants and trees support him, and the earth beareth him the All-sustainer.

6 Agni is Lord of Amṛta in abundance, Lord of the gift of wealth and hero valour,
Victorious God, let us not sit about thee like men devoid of strength, beauty, and worship.

7 The foeman's treasure may be won with labour : may we be masters of our own possessions.
Agni, no son is he who springs from others: lengthen not out the pathways of the foolish.

8 Unwelcome for adoption is the stranger, one to be thought of as another's offspring,
Though grown familiar by continual presence. May our strong hero come, freshly triumphant.

9 Guard us from him who would assail us, Agni; preserve us O thou Victor, from dishonour.
Here let the place of darkening come upon thee : may wealth be ours, desirable, in thousands.

10 Shine this felicity on us, O Agni : may we attain to perfect understanding.
All happiness be theirs who sing and praise thee. Ye Gods, preserve us evermore with blessings.

6 In the second line I have borrowed from Prof. Max Müller, *Vedic Hymns*, I. p. 80.

7 Let us remain in undisturbed possession of our own property, and let us have sons of our own begetting and not the adopted children of others.

8 Men do not look with pleasure and affection on adopted sons ; but we are longing to see our absent protector return to us.—Ludwig. Others explain the last half-verse differently : 'therefore let there come to us (a son) new-born, possessed of food, victorious over foes.'—Wilson.

9 This stanza is a repetition of VI. 15, 12, where see note.

10 Repeated from stanza 10 of the preceding hymn.

HYMN V. *Agni.*

1. BRING forth your song of praise to mighty Agni, the speedy messenger of earth and heaven,
Vaiśvānara, who, with those who wake, hath waxen great in the lap of all the Gods Immortal.

2 Sought in the heavens, on earth is Agni stablished, leader of rivers, Bull of standing waters.
Vaiśvānara, when he hath grown in glory, shines on the tribes of men with light and treasure.

3 For fear of thee forth fled the dark-hued races, scattered abroad, deserting their possessions,
When, glowing, O Vaiśvānara, for Pūru, thou Agni didst light up and rend their castles.

4 Agni Vaiśvānara, both Earth and Heaven submit them to thy threefold jurisdiction.
Refulgent in thine undecaying lustre thou hast invested both the worlds with splendour.

5 Agni, the tawny horses, loudly neighing our resonant hymns that drop with oil, attend thee;
Lord of the tribes, our Charioteer of riches, Ensign of days, Vaiśvānara of mornings.

6 In thee, O bright as Mitra, Vasus seated the might of Asuras, for they loved thy spirit.
Thou dravest Dasyus from their home, O Agni, and broughtest forth broad light to light the Ārya.

7 Born in the loftiest heaven thou in a moment reachest, like wind, the place where Gods inhabit.
Thou, favouring thine offspring, roaredst loudly when giving life to creatures, Jātavedas.

The hymn is addressed to Agni as Vaiśvānara, the God who is present with, and benefits, all Āryan men.

1 *With those who wake* : tended by the priests. According to Sāyaṇa 'associated with the wakened Gods.'

2 *Bull of standing waters* : the meaning of *stiyānām* is uncertain. Perhaps, as Ludwig suggests, plants and bushes are intended which Agni like a bull levels with the ground.

3 *The dark-hued races* : according to von Roth, the spirits of darkness. *For Pūru* : or, for man.

4 *Threefold jurisdiction* : in heaven, mid-air, and earth.

5 *The tawny horses* : the hymns that hasten to Agni like eager horses. Ludwig translates the *haritaḥ* of the text by 'gold-yellow,' qualifying 'hymn's; that is, hymns with libations of yellow Soma juice.

6 *Thou dravest* : cf. I. 117. 21.

8 Send us that strength, Vaiśvānara, send it, Agni, that strength, O Jātavedas, full of splendour,
Wherewith, all-bounteous God, thou pourest riches, as fame wide-spreading, on the man who offers.

9 Agni, bestow upon our chiefs and nobles that famous power, that wealth which feedeth many.
Accordant with the Vasus and the Rudras, Agni, Vaiśvānara, give us sure protection.

HYMN VI. *Agni.*

1. PRAISE of the Asura, high imperial Ruler, the Manly One in whom the folk shall triumph—
I laud his deeds who is as strong as Indra, and lauding celebrate the Fort-destroyer.

2 Sage, Sing, Food, Light,—they bring him from the mountain, the blessed Sovran of the earth and heaven.
I decorate with songs the mighty actions which Agni, Fort-destroyer, did aforetime.

3 The foolish, faithless, rudely-speaking niggards, without belief or sacrifice or worship,—
Far far sway hath Agni chased those Dasyus, and, in the east, hath turned the godless westward.

4 Him who brought eastward, manliest with his prowess, the Maids rejoicing in the western darkness,
That Agni I extol, the Lord of riches, unyielding tamer of assailing foemen.

5 Him who brake down the walls with deadly weapons, and gave the Mornings to a noble Husband,
Young Agni, who with conquering strength subduing the tribes of Nahus made them bring their tribute.

6 In whose protection all men rest by nature, desiring to enjoy his gracious favour—
Agni Vaiśvānara in his Parents' bosom hath found the choicest seat in earth and heaven.

7 Vaiśvānrara the God, at the sun's setting, hath taken to himself deep-hidden treasures :
Agni hath taken them from earth and heaven, from the sea under and the sea above us.

HYMN VII. *Agni.*

1. I SEND forth even your God, victorious Agni, like a strong courser, with mine adoration.
Herald of sacrifice be he who knoweth : he hath reached Gods, himself, with measured motion.

2 By paths that are thine own come hither, Agni, joyous, delighting in the Gods' alliance,
Making the heights of earth roar with thy fury, burning with eager teeth the woods and forests.

3 The grass is strewn; the sacrifice advances : adored as Priest, Agni is made propitious,
Invoking both All-boon-bestowing Mothers of whom, Most Youthful ! thou wast born to help us.

4 Forthwith the men, the best of these for wisdom, have made him leader in the solemn worship.
As Lord in homes of men is Agni stablished, the Holy One, the joyous, sweetly speaking.

5 He hath come, chosen bearer, and is seated in man's home, Brahman, Agni, the Supporter,
He whom both Heaven and Earth exalt and strengthen, whom, Giver of all boons, the Hotar worships.

6 These have passed all in glory, who, the manly, have wrought with skill the hymn of adoration ;

1 *Fort-destroyer* : demolisher of the cloud-castles of the demons of drought, or of the strongholds of the non-Āryan tribes.

2 *Form the mountain* : from the cloud, as lightning.

3 *Westward* : into the darkness of night.

4 *Who brought eastward* : brought back the vanished lights of dawn.

5 *To a noble Husband*: the Sun, or Agni himself. *The tribes of Nahus* : or, according to von Roth, neighbouring people.

7 Agni becomes the representative of the Sun, and in his absence gives light and other blessings to man. *The sea above us* : the ocean of air.

---

1 *Like a strong courser* : glorified with my praises, like a horse that has been groomed and adorned. Or, perhaps, merely, rapid as a horse. *With measured motion* : or, a speedy runner. Sāyaṇa explains the word *mitédruḥ*, in this place as 'consumer of trees,' but in IV. 6. 5 as *parimitagatiḥ*, 'with measured motion.'

3 *Both......Mothers* : Heaven and Earth.

Who, listening, have advanced the people's welfare, and set their thoughts on this my holy statute.

7 We, the Vasiṣṭhas, now implore thee, Agni, O Son of Strength, the Lord of wealth and treasure.

Thou hast brought food to singers and to nobles. Ye Gods, preserve us evermore with blessings.

HYMN VIII. *Agni*

1. THE King whose face is decked with oil is kindled with homage offered by his faithful servant.
The men, the priests adore him with oblations. Agni hath shone forth when the dawn is breaking.

2 Yea, he hath been acknowledged as most mighty, the joyous Priest of men, the youthful Agni.
He, spreading o'er the earth, made light around him, and grew among the plants with blackened fellies.

3 How dost thou decorate our hymn, O Agni ? What power dost thou exert when thou art lauded ?
When, Bounteous God, may we be lords of riches, winners of precious wealth which none may conquer ?

4 Far famed is this the Bharata's own Agni : he shineth like the Sun with lofty splendour.
He who hath vanquished Pūru in the battle, the heavenly guest hath glowed in full refulgence.

5 Full many oblations are in thee collected : with all thine aspects thou hast waxen gracious.
Thou art already famed as praised and lauded, yet still, O nobly born, increase thy body.

6 Be this my song, that winneth countless treasure, engendered with redoubled force for Agni,
That, splendid, chasing sickness, slaying demons, it may delight our friend and bless the singers.

7 We, the Vasiṣṭhas, now implore thee, Agni, O Son of Strength, the Lord of wealth and riches.
Thou hast brought food to singers and to nobles. Ye Gods, preserve us evermore with blessings.

HYMN IX. *Agni.*

1. ROUSED from their bosom is the Dawns' beloved, the joyous Priest, most sapient, Purifier.
He gives a signal both to Gods and mortals, to Gods oblations, riches to the pious.

2 Most wise is he who, forcing doors of Paṇis, brought the bright Sun to us who feedeth many.
The cheerful Priest, men's Friend and home-companion, through still night's darkness he is made apparent.

3 Wise, ne'er deceived, uncircumscribed, refulgent, our gracious guest, a Friend with good attendants,
Shines forth with wondrous light before the Mornings ; the young plants hath he entered, Child of Waters.

4 Seeking our gatherings, he, your Jātavedas, hath shone adorable through human ages,
Who gleams refulgent with his lovely lustre : the kine have waked to meet him when enkindled.

5 Go on thy message to the Gods, and fail not, O Agni, with their band who pray and worship.
Bring all the Gods that they may give us riches, Sarasvatī, the Maruts, Aśvins, Waters.

6 Vasiṣṭha, when enkindling thee, O Agni, hath slain Jarūtha. Give us wealth in plenty.
Sing praise in choral song, O Jātavedas. Ye Gods, preserve us evermore with blessings.

6 *Who set their thoughts on this my holy statute* : that is, apparently, who duly observe the law which requires us to worship Agni. 'Who are glorifiers of this truthful (deity).'—Wilson.

2 *With blackened fellies* : leaving black tracks behind him : 'dark-pathed.'—Wilson.

4 *The Bharata* : Vasiṣṭha, the *purohita* of the Bharatas. *Pūru* : the Pūrus, (one of the Five Āryan Tribes) who opposed the Bharatas.

6 *Countless treasure* : literally, hundreds, thousands. *Our friend* : the institutor of the sacrifice.

1. *The Dawns' beloved* : Agni, as lighted up at day-break. *A signal* : of sacrifice, which men are to offer and Gods are to receive.

6 *Jarūtha* : See VII. 1. 7, where the destruction of Jarūtha, is ascribed to Agni himself. Jarūtha, said by Sāyaṇa to have been a Rākṣasa or demon, was probably an enemy who was slain in a battle at which Vasiṣṭha was present as *purohita*.—Ludwig.

HYMN X. *Agni.*

1. He hath sent forth, bright, radiant, and refulgent, like the Dawn's Lover, his far-spreading lustre.
Pure in his splendour shines the golden Hero: our longing thoughts hath he aroused and wakened.

2 He, like the Sun, hath shone while Morn is breaking, and priests who weave the sacrifice sing praises,
Agni, the God, who knows their generations and visits Gods, most bounteous, rapid envoy.

3 Our songs and holy hymns go forth to Agni, seeking the God and asking him for riches,
Him fair to see, of goodly aspect, mighty, men's messenger who carries their oblations.

4 Joined with the Vasus, Agni, bring thou Indra bring hither mighty Rudra with the Rudras,
Aditi good to all men with Ādityas, Bṛhaspati All-bounteous, with the Singers.

5 Men eagerly implore at sacrifices Agni, Most Youthful God, the joyous Herald.
For he is Lord and Ruler over riches, and for Gods' worship an unwearied envoy.

HYMN XI. *Agni.*

1. Graet art thou, Agni, sacrifice's Herald: not without thee are deathless Gods made joyful.
Come hither with all Deities about thee: here take thy seat, the first, as Priest, O Agni.

2 Men with oblations evermore entreat thee, the swift, to undertake an envoy's duty.
He on whose sacred grass with Gods thou sittest, to him, O Agni, are the days propitious.

3 Three times a day in thee are shown the treasures sent for the mortal who presents oblation.
Bring the Gods hither like a man, O Agni: be thou our envoy, guarding us from curses.

4 Lord of the lofty sacrifice is Agni, Agni is Lord of every gift presented.
The Vasus were contented with his wisdom, so the Gods made him their oblation-bearer.

5 O Agni, bring the Gods to taste our presents: with Indra leading, here let them be joyful.
Convey this sacrifice to Gods in heaven. Ye Gods, preserve us evermore with blessings.

HYMN XII. *Agni.*

1. We with great reverence have approached The Youngest who hath shone forth well-kindled in his dwelling,
With wondrous light between wide earth and heaven, well-worshipped, looking forth in all directions.

2 Through his great might o'ercoming all misfortunes, praised in the house is Agni Jātavedas.
May he protect us from disgrace and trouble, both us who laud him and our noble patrons.

3 O Agni, thou art Varuṇa and Mitra: Vasiṣṭhas with their holy hymns exalt thee.
With thee be most abundant gain of treasure. Ye Gods, preserve us evermore with blessings.

HYMN XIII. *Agni.*

1. Bring song and hymn to Agni, Asura-slayer, enlightener of all and thought-bestower.
Like an oblation on the grass, to please him, I bring this to Vaiśvānara, hymn-inspirer.

2 Thou with thy flame, O Agni, brightly glowing, hast at thy birth filled full the earth and heaven.
Thou with thy might, Vaiśvānara Jātavedas, settest the Gods free from the curse that bound them.

1 *Like the Dawn's Lover*: the Sun. See I. 69. 1.
2 *And priests*: I adopt Sāyaṇa's interpretation of this half-line.
4 *Singers*: or Ṛkvans, deities who attend and sing the praises of some God: 'the adorable (Aṅgirasas).'—Wilson.

---

3 *Three times a day*: at the morning, the noon, and the evening libation. Or the meaning may be, in the three fire-receptacles. *Like a man*: acting like a human priest. The Commentators explain *manuṣvát* by 'as (at the sacrifice) of Manu.'

---

1 *The Youngest*: Agni, most youthful of the Gods, as being continually reproduced.

---

2 *The curse that bound them*: the Gods seem to have been subject to the infirmities of old age until Indra, or, as is here said, Agni, freed them. See IV. 19. 2.

3 Agni, when, born thou lookedst on all creatures, like a brisk herdsman moving round his cattle.
The path to prayer, Vaiśvānara, thou foundest. Ye Gods, preserve us evermore with blessings.

HYMN XIV *Agni.*

1. With reverence and with offered gifts serve we the God whose flame is bright:
Let us bring Jātavedas fuel, and adore Agni when we invoke the Gods.

2 Agni, may we perform thy rites with fuel, and honour thee, O Holy one, with praises :
Honour thee, Priest of sacrifice ! with butter, thee, God of blessed light ! with our oblation.

3 Come, Agni, with the Gods to our invoking, come, pleased, to offerings sanctified with Vaṣaṭ.
May we be his who pays thee, God, due honour. Ye Gods, preserve us evermore with blessings.

HYMN XV. *Agni.*

1. Offer oblations in his mouth, the bounteous God's whom we must serve.
His who is nearest kin to us :

2 Who for the Fivefold People's sake hath seated him in every home,
Wise, Youthful, Master of the house.

3 On all sides may that Agni guard our household folk and property;
May he deliver us from woe.

4 I have begotten this new hymn for Agni, Falcon of the sky :
Will he not give us of his wealth ?

5 Whose glories when he glows in front of sacrifice are fair to see,
Like wealth of one with hero sons.

6 May he enjoy this hallowed gift, Agni accept our songs, who bears
Oblations, best of worshippers.

7 Lord of the house, whom men must seek, we set thee down, O Worshipped One!
Bright, rich in heroes, Agni ! God !

8 Shine forth at night and morn : through thee with fires are we provided well.
Thou, rich in heroes, art our Friend.

9 The men come near thee for their gain, the singers with their songs of praise :
Speech, thousandfold, comes near to thee.

10 Bright, Purifier, meet for praise, Immortal with refulgent glow,
Agni drives Rākṣasas away.

11 As such, bring us abundant wealth, young Child of Strength, for this thou canst :
May Bhaga give us what is choice.

12 Thou, Agni, givest hero fame : Bhaga and Savitar the God,
And Diti give us what is good.

13 Agni, preserve us from distress : consume our enemies, O God,
Eternal, with the hottest flames.

14 And, irresistible, be thou a mighty iron fort to us,
With hundred walls for man's defence.

15 Do thou preserve us, eve and morn, from sorrow, from the wicked men,
Infallible ! by day and night.

HYMN XVI. *Agni.*

1. With this my reverent hymn I call Agni for you, the Son of Strength,
Dear, wisest envoy, served with noble sacrifice, immortal messenger of all.

2 His two red horses, all-supporting, let him yoke : let him, well-worshipped, urge them fast.
Then hath the sacrifice good prayers and happy end, and heavenly gift of wealth to men.

3 The flame of him the Bountiful, the Much-invoked, hath mounted up,
And his red-coloured smoke-clouds reach and touch the sky : the men are kindling Agni well.

4 Thee, thee Most Glorious One we make our messenger. Bring the Gods hither to the feast.
Give us, O Son of Strength, all food that feedeth man : give that for which we pray to thee.

5 Thou, Agni, art the homestead's Lord, our Herald at the sacrifice.

---

3 *Sanctified with Vaṣaṭ*: Vaṣaṭ (may he bear it to the Gods) is the exclamation used at the moment of pouring the sacrificial oil or clarified butter on the fire.

9 *Speech* : *ákṣarā*, the imperishable ; here speech in the shape of praise and prayer.

12 *Diti* : generally regarded as the opposite of Aditi, which may have been the word used by the poet, changed by later reciters, who considered the metre irregular, into Diti. *See Vedic Hymns*, I. p. 256.

5 *Herald* : *Hotar*, or invoking priest. *Cleanser* : *Potar*, or purifier, another of the officiating priests. Agni performs the duties of all human priests.

Lord of all boons, thou art the Cleanser and a Sage. Pay worship, and enjoy the good.

6 Give riches to the sacrificer, O Most Wise, for thou art he who granteth wealth.
Inspire with zeal each priest at this our solemn rite; all who are skilled in singing praise.

7 O Agni who art worshipped well, dear let our princes be to thee,
Our wealthy patrons who are governors of men, who part, as gifts, their stalls of kine.

8 They in whose home, her hand bearing the sacred oil, Iḷā sits down well-satisfied—
Guard them, Victorious God, from slander and from harm : give us a refuge famed afar.

9 Do thou, a Priest with pleasant tongue, most wise, and very near to us,
Agni, bring riches hither to our liberal chiefs, and speed the offering of our gifts.

10 They who bestow as bounty plenteous wealth of steeds, moved by desire of great renown—
Do thou with saving help preserve them from distress, Most Youthful ! with a hundred forts.

11 The God who gives your wealth demands a full libation poured to him.
Pour ye it forth, then fill the vessel full again : then doth the God pay heed to you.

12 Him have the Gods appointed Priest of sacrifice, oblation-bearer, passing wise.
Agni gives wealth and valour to the worshipper, to folk who offer up their gifts.

HYMN XVII. *Agni.*

1. AGNI, be kindled well with proper fuel, and let the grass be scattered wide about thee.

2 Let the impatient Portals be thrown open : bring thou the Gods impatient to come hither.

3 Taste, Agni : serve the Gods with our oblation. Offer good sacrifices, Jātavedas !

4 Let Jātavedas pay fair sacrifices, worship and gratify the Gods Immortal.

5 Wise God, win for us things that are all-goodly, and let the prayers we pray to-day be fruitful.

6 Thee, even thee, the Son of Strength, O Agni, those Gods have made the bearer of oblations.

7 To thee the God may we perform our worship : do thou, besought, grant us abundant riches.

HYMN XVIII. *Indra.*

1. ALL is with thee, O Indra, all the treasures which erst our fathers won who sang thy praises.
With thee are milch-kine good to milk, and horses : best winner thou of riches for the pious.

2 For like a King among his wives thou dwellest : with glories, as a Sage, surround and help us.
Make us, thy servants, strong for wealth, and honour our songs with kine and steeds and decoration.

3 Here these our holy hymns with joy and gladness in pious emulation have approached thee.
Hitherward come thy path that leads to riches : may we find shelter in thy favour, Indra.

4 Vasiṣṭha hath poured forth his prayers, desiring to milk thee like a cow in goodly pasture.
All these my people call thee Lord of cattle : may Indra come unto the prayer we offer.

5 What though the floods spread widely, Indra made them shallow and easy for Sudās to traverse.
He, worthy of our praises, caused the Śimyu, foe of our hymn, to curse the rivers' fury.

8 *Iḷā* : the Goddess who is regarded as the sacrificial food or oblation personified : *annarūpā havirlakṣaṇā devī.*—Sāyaṇa.

2 *The impatient Portals* : the doors of the sacrificial chamber which long to bear their part in the holy ceremony.

6 *Those Gods* : the famous Gods.

The hymn glorifies Indra as the protector of Sudās, the King of the Tṛtsus, and praises the liberality of that prince. See *Vedic India* (Story of the Nations Series), pp. 319—332.

4 *Vasiṣṭha* : the Ṛṣi of the hymn and the chief priest who had accompanied the warlike expedition of Sudās. *To milk thee* : to obtain riches through thy favour by means of my hymn, as men milk the cow at sacrifice for the milk which is required for libations.

5 The poet begins to recount the events of Sudās's victorious expedition. These are not always intelligible partly on account of the obscure phraseology employed, and partly on account of our ignorance of details which are vaguely alluded to. In this stanza Sudās, king or chief of the Tṛtsu tribe, has, with the aid of

6 Eager for spoil was Turvaśa Puroḍās, fain to win wealth, like fishes urged by hunger.
The Bhṛgus and the Druhyus quickly listened : friend rescued friend mid the two distant peoples.

7 Together came the Pakthas, the Bhalānas, the Alinas, the Śivas, the Viṣāṇins.
Yet to the Tṛtsus came the Ārya's Comrade, through love of spoil and heroes' war, to lead them.

8 Fools, in their folly fain to waste her waters, they parted inexhaustible Paruṣṇī.
Lord of the Earth, he with his might repressed them : still lay the herd and the affrighted herdsman.

9 As to their goal they sped to their destruction : they sought Paruṣṇī ; e'en the swift returned not.
Indra abandoned, to Sudās the manly, the swiftly flying foes, unmanly babblers.

10 They went like kine unherded from the pasture, each clinging to a friend as chance directed.
They who drive spotted steeds, sent down by Pṛśni, gave ear, the Warriors and the harnessed horses.

11 The King who scattered one-and-twenty people of both Vaikarṇa tribes through lust of glory—
As the skilled priest clips grass within the chamber, so hath the Hero Indra wrought their downfall.

12 Thou, thunder-armed, o'erwhelmedst in the waters famed ancient Kavaṣa and then the Druhyu.
Others here claiming friendship to their friendship, devoted unto thee, in thee were joyful.

13 Indra at once with conquering might demolished all their strong places and their seven castles.
The goods of Anu's son he gave to Tṛtsu. May we in sacrifice conquer scornful Pūru.

14 The Anavas and Druhyus, seeking booty, have slept, the sixty hundred, yea, six thousand,
And six-and-sixty heroes. For the pious were all these mighty exploits done by Indra.

15 These Tṛtsus under Indra's careful guidance came speeding like loosed waters rushing downward.
The foemen, measuring exceeding closely, abandoned to Sudās all their provisions.

Indra, crossed a deep river (the Paruṣṇī which is now called the Rāvī), and put the Śimyus to flight, some of the fugitives being drowned in its waters. The Śimyus are mentioned together with the Dasyus, in I. 100. 18, as hostile barbarians slain by Indra. The second half of the stanza is difficult, the meaning of two of the words being uncertain.

6 *Turvaśa Puroḍās* : Turvaśa appears here as one of the enemies of Sudās. I follow, with much hesitation, Ludwig in taking Puroḍās as an appellative of Turvaśa : 'Turvaśa, who was preceding (at solemn rites).'—Wilson. *The Bhṛgus and the Druhyus* : here, apparently, allies of Turvaśa. *Friends* : according to others, Matsyas, a people.

7 *The Pakthas*, and the rest mentioned in the first line of the stanza appear to have been non-Āryan tribes opposed to the Tṛtsus. According to the Scholiast these names are the denominations of various ministers at religious rites, and following this interpretation Wilson translates the stanza as follows : 'Those who dress the oblation, those who pronounce auspicious words, those who abstain from penance, those who bear horns (in their hands), those who bestow happiness (on the world by sacrifice), glorify that Indra who recovered the cattle of the *Ārya* from the plunderers, who slew the enemies in battle,' *The Ārya's Comrade* : Indra, the ally of Tṛtsu against the non-Āryan confederacy.

8 The confederates, who were on the right or farther bank of the Paruṣṇī, intending to attack Sudās and the Tṛtsus, appear to have attempted to make the river fordable by digging channels and so diverting the water, which, it seems, rushed back into its natural bed and drowned the men who were crossing the stream. The second line of the stanza is obscure and the translation is conjectural. Wilson translates : 'but he by his greatness pervades the earth, Kavi, the son of Cayamāna, like a falling victim, sleeps (in death).' *The herd* and *the herdsman* are, of course, the hostile band and its leader.

10 *They went* : the fugitives who escaped drowning. *They who drive spotted steeds*: the Maruts, sent down by their mother Pṛśni to aid Sudās.

11 *People* : or, houses, *i. e.* families. *Both Vaikarṇa tribes*: perhaps some allies of the Druhyus; but the meaning of *vaikarṇáyoḥ* is uncertain. See Zimmer, *Altindisches Leben*, p. 103. Ludwig thinks that the reference is to a mythic battle at some place called Vaikarṇau between Indra (the King) and the Maruts (the one-and-twenty people). *Clips grass* : with one clean cut.

12 *Kavaṣa* : perhaps the priest of one of the two Vaikarṇa tribes which Zimmer is inclined to identify with the Kuru-Krivis. See *Altindisches Leben*, p. 127. *Others here* : 'for they, Indra, who are devoted to thee and glorify thee, preferring thy friendship, enjoy it.'—Wilson. The exact meaning is uncertain.

13 *To Tṛtsu* : to Sudās, the King of the Tṛtsus.

14 *The Anavas* : men of the Anu tribe. *The sixty hundred* : 'The enumeration is very obscurely expressed, *ṣaṣṭiḥ śatā ṣaṭsahasrā ṣaṣṭir adhi ṣaṭ*, literally, six hundreds, six thousands, sixty, with six more : Sāyaṇa understands by *śatāni*, thousands, *sahasrāṇītyarthaḥ*.'—Wilson. 'Sixty-six thousand six hundred and six.' Ludwig suggests that *daśā* should be read instead of *śatā*, which would make the number 6666. See Benfey, *Vedica und Linguistica*, pp. 139—162.

15 *Measuring exceeding closely* : though taking great care of their goods and reluctantly giving them up.

16 The hero's side who drank the dressed oblation, Indra's denier, far o'er earth he scattered.
Indra brought down the fierce destroyer's fury. He gave them various roads, the path's Controller.

17 E'en with the weak he wrought this matchless exploit : e'en with a goat he did to death a lion.
He pared the pillar's angles with a needle. Thus to Sudās Indra gave all provisions.

18 To thee have all thine enemies submitted: e'en the fierce Bheda hast thou made thy subject.
Cast down thy sharpened thunderbolt, O Indra, on him who harms the men who sing thy praises.

19 Yamunā and the Tṛtsus aided Indra. There he stripped Bheda bare of all his treasures.
The Ajas and the Śigrus and the Yakṣus brought in to him as tribute heads of horses.

20 Not to be scorned, but like Dawns past and recent, O Indra, are thy favours and thy riches.
Devaka, Manyamāna's son, thou slewest, and smotest Śambara from the lofty mountain.

21 They who, from home, have gladdened thee, thy servants Parāśara, Vasiṣṭha, Śatayātu,
Will not forget thy friendship, liberal Giver. So shall the days dawn prosperous for the princes.

22 Priest-like, with praise, I move around the altar, earning Paijavana's reward, O. Agni,
Two hundred cows from Devavān's descendant, two chariots from Sudās with mares to draw them.

23 Gift of Paijavana, four horses bear me in foremost place, trained steeds with pearl to deck them.
Sudās's brown steeds, firmly-stepping, carry me and my son for progeny and glory.

24 Him whose fame spreads between wide earth and heaven, who, as dispenser, gives each chief his portion,
Seven flowing Rivers glorify like Indra. He slew Yudhyāmadhi in close encounter.

25 Attend on him O ye heroic Maruts as on Sudās's father Divodāsa.
Further Paijavana's desire with favour. Guard faithfully his lasting firm dominion.

HYMN XIX. *Indra.*

1. He like a bull with sharpened horns, terrific, singly excites and agitates all the people :
Thou givest him who largely pours libations his goods who pours not, for his own possession.

2 Thou, verily, Indra, gavest help to Kutsa, willingly giving ear to him in battle,
When, aiding Ārjuneya, thou subduedst to him both Kuyava and the Dāsa Śuṣṇa.

3 O Bold One, thou with all thine aids hast boldly holpen Sudās whose offerings were accepted,
Pūru in winning land and slaying foemen, and Trasadasyu son of Purukutsa.

16 *The hero's side* : the party of the hostile leader, the non-Āryans who denied Indra, and themselves devoured the oblations that should have been presented to him. *He gave them various roads* : made them fly in all directions.

17 *E'en with a goat* : impossible deeds mentioned as illustrations of Indra's miraculous power.

18 *Bheda* : an enemy of Sudās, or an unbeliever, says Sāyaṇa.

19 *Yamunā* : the Jumna. But it is not easy to see how the expedition reached so far. The Ajas, Śigrus, and Yakṣus were perhaps subject to Bheda, but nothing is known regarding them. *Heads of horses* : which had been killed in battle.

20 *Like Dawns* : renewed every day. *Devaka* : not mentioned elsewhere. According to Grassmann *devákam mānyamānám* refers to Śambara 'thinking himself a God.'

21 *Parāśara* is said by one authority to have been the son, and by another the grandson of the Ṛṣi Vasiṣṭha. *Śatayātu* is said to be Śakti, Vasiṣṭha's son.

22 Here begins the *dānastuti* or praise of the prince's liberality. *Paijavana* : Sudās, descendant of Pijavana. *Devavān's descendant* : Sudās, Devavān being either the same as Divodāsa, the father of Sudās, or one of his forefathers.

24 *Seven flowing Rivers glorify* : the seven chief rivers of the Panjāb glorify him as they glorify Indra. Or, they (men) praise him as the seven rivers praise Indra. 'The seven rivers bear his glory far and wide' (I. 102-2). *Yudhyāmidhi* : not mentioned elsewhere.

25 *Maruts* : here, perhaps, the Maghavans or wealthy nobles are intended who stand in the same relation to Sudās as the Maruts to Indra.

---

1 *Excites and agitates* : as God of battles. *Thou*: Indra. This abrupt change from the third person to the second is not unusual in the Veda.

2 *Ārjuneya* : Kutsa, descendant of Arjuna. See I. 112. 23. *Kuyava* : See I. 103.8.

4 At the Gods' banquet, hero-souled ! with Heroes, Lord of Bay Steeds, thou slewest many foemen.
Thou sentest in swift death to sleep the Dasyu, both Cumuri and Dhuni, for Dabhīti.

5 These were thy mighty powers that, Thunder-wielder, thou swiftly crushedst nine-and-ninety castles :
Thou capturedst the hundredth in thine onslaught; thou slewest Namuci, thou slewest Vṛtra.

6 Old are the blessings, Indra, which thou gavest Sudās the worshipper who brought oblations.
For thee, the Strong, I yoke thy strong Bay Horses : may our prayers reach thee and win strength, Most Mighty !

7 Give us not up, Lord of Bay Horses, Victor, in this thine own assembly, to the wicked.
Deliver us with true and faithful succours: dear may we be to thee among the princes.

8 May we men, Maghavan, the friends thou lovest, near thee be joyful under thy protection.
Fain to fulfil the wish of Atithigva humble the pride of Turvaśa and Yādva.

9 Swiftly, in truth, O Maghavan, about thee men skilled in hymning sing their songs and praises.
Elect us also into their assembly who by their calls on thee despoiled the niggards.

10 Thine are these lauds, O manliest of heroes, lauds which revert to us and give us riches.
Favour these, Indra, when they fight with foemen, as Friend and Hero and the heroes' Helper.

11 Now, lauded for thine aid, Heroic Indra, sped by our prayer, wax mighty in thy body.
Apportion to us strength and habitations. Ye Gods, protect us evermore with blessings.

4 *For Cumuri, Dhuni,* and *Dabhīti.* See Vol. I. Index.

5 *Namuci* : another demon of drought. See I. 53. 7. *In thine onslaught* : according to Sāyaṇa, for thy dwelling : 'thou hast occupied the hundredth as a place of abode.'—Wilson.

6 *Sudās* : the King of the Tṛtsus, celebrated in the preceding hymn.

8 *Atithigva* : probably a descendant of Sudās who must have lived long before the composition of this hymn, as the favour bestowed upon him by Indra is spoken of as old in stanza 6. *Yādva* : or Yadu's son.

9 *Elect us also* : that is, let us share the blessings which thou withholdest from the illiberal churls who offer no oblations and givest to those who call upon thee and worship thee.

HYMN XX. *Indra.*

1. Strong, Godly-natured, born for hero exploit, man's Friend, he doth whatever deed he willeth.
Saving us e'en from great transgression, Indra, the Youthful, visiteth man's home with favour.

2 Waxing greatness Indra slayeth Vṛtra : the Hero with his aid hath helped the singer.
He gave Sudās wide room and space, and often hath granted wealth to him who brought oblations.

3 Soldier unchecked, war-rousing, battling Hero, unconquered from of old, victorious ever,
Indra the very strong hath scattered armies; yea, he hath slain each foe who fought against him.

4 Thou with thy greatness hast filled full, O Indra, even both the worlds with might, O thou Most Mighty.
Lord of Bays, Indra, brandishing his thunder, is gratified with Soma at the banquet.

5 A Bull begat the Bull for joy of battle, and a strong Mother brought forth him the manly.
He who is Chief of men, their armies' Leader, is strong Hero, bold, and fain for booty.

6 The people falter not, nor suffer sorrow, who win themselves this God's terrific spirit.
He who with sacrifices worships Indra is lord of wealth, law-born and law's protector.

7 Whene'er the elder fain would help the younger the greater cometh to the lesser's present.

5 *A Bull begat the Bull* : 'A vigorous (god) begot a vigorous (son).'—Muir. The father of Indra is Kaśyapa, according to Sāyaṇa; but probably Dyaus is intended. *A strong Mother* : Aditi.

6 *Law-born* : born in accordance with the law.

7 The relations between Gods and men resemble those between elders and juniors, superiors and inferiors among men. The inferior comes to his superior with some offering in his hand and is assisted by him in return. So Indra should accept our oblations, and reward us with wealth.

Shall the Immortal sit aloof inactive? O Wondrous Indra, bring us wondrous riches.

8 Thy dear folk, Indra, who present oblations, are, in chief place, thy friends, O Thunder-wielder.
May we be best content in this thy favour, sheltered by One who slays not, but preserves us.

9 To thee the mighty hymn hath clamoured loudly, and, Maghavan, the eloquent hath besought thee.
Desire of wealth hath come upon thy singer: help us then, Śakra, to our share of riches.

10 Place us by food which thou hast given, O Indra, us and the wealthy patrons who command us.
Let thy great power bring good to him who lauds thee. Ye Gods, preserve us evermore with blessings.

HYMN XXI. *Indra.*

1. PRESSED is the juice divine with milk commingled: thereto hath Indra ever been accustomed.
We wake thee, Lord of Bays, with sacrifices: mark this our laud in the wild joy of Soma.

2 On to the rite they move, the grass they scatter, these Soma-drinkers eloquent in synod.
Hither, for men to grasp, are brought the press-stones, far-thundering, famous, strong, that wait on heroes.

3 Indra, thou settest free the many waters that were encompassed, Hero, by the Dragon.
Down rolled, as if on chariots borne, the rivers: through fear of thee all things created tremble.

4 Skilled in all manly deeds the God terrific hath with his weapons mastered these opponents.
Indra in rapturous joy shook down their castles: he slew them in his might, the Thunder-wielder.

5 No evil spirits have impelled us, Indra, nor fiends, O Mightiest God, with their devices.
Let our true God subdue the hostile rabble: let not the lewd approach our holy worship.

6 Thou in thy strength surpassest Earth and Heaven: the regions comprehend not all thy greatness.
With thine own power and might thou slewest Vṛtra: no foe hath found the end of thee in battle.

7 Even the earlier Deities submitted their powers to thy supreme divine dominion.
Indra wins wealth and deals it out to others: men in the strife for booty call on Indra.

8 The humble hath invoked thee for protection, thee, Lord of great felicity, O Indra.
Thou with a hundred aids hast been our Helper: one who brings gifts like thee hath his defender.

9 May we, O Indra, be thy friends for ever, eagerly, Conqueror, yielding greater homage.
May, through thy grace, the strength of us who battle quell in the shock the onset of the foeman.

10 Place us by food which thou hast given, O Indra, us and the wealthy patrons who command us.
Let thy great power bring good to him who lauds thee. Ye Gods, preserve us evermore with blessings.

HYMN XXII. *Indra.*

1. DRINK Soma, Lord of Bays, and let it cheer thee: Indra, the stone, like a well-guided courser,
Directed by the presser's arms hath pressed it.

2 So let the draught of joy, thy dear companion, by which, O Lord of Bays, thou slayest foemen,
Delight thee, Indra, Lord of princely treasures.

3 Mark closely, Maghavan, the words I utter, this eulogy recited by Vasiṣṭha:
Accept the prayers I offer at thy banquet.

9 *The eloquent* :stāmúḥ ; according to Ludwig, mouthy, talkative, and, in a good sense, fluent, eloquent. The Commentators explain the word as 'praiser.'

1 *We wake thee* : or, we think of thee, serve thee.
4 *These opponents* : according to Sāyaṇa, the demons of the air. The text has no noun for 'these.'

5 *The lewd* : those who do not follow Vedic observances, according to Yāska. For a full discussion of the meaning of *śiśnádevāḥ*, see Muir, *O. S. Texts*, IV. 406—411.

8 *One who brings gifts like thee* : Sāyaṇa interprets differently : 'be our defender against every overpowering (assailant) like to thee.'—Wilson.

4 Hear thou the call of the juice-drinking press-stone: hear thou the Brahman's hymn who sings and lauds thee.
Take to thine inmost self these adorations.

5 I know and ne'er forget the hymns and praises of thee, the Conqueror, and thy strength immortal.
Thy name I ever utter. Self-Refulgent!

6 Among mankind many are thy libations, and many a time the pious sage invokes thee.
O Maghavan, be not long distant from us.

7 All these libations are for thee, O Hero: to thee I offer these my prayers that strengthen.
Ever, in every place, must men invoke thee.

8 Never do men attain, O Wonder-Worker, thy greatness, Mighty One, who must be lauded,
Nor, Indra, thine heroic power and bounty.

9 Among all Ṛṣis, Indra, old and recent, who have engendered hymns as sacred singers,
Even with us be thine auspicious friendships. Ye Gods, preserve us evermore with blessings.

HYMN XXIII. *Indra.*

1. Prayers have been offered up through love of glory: Vasiṣṭha, honour Indra in the battle.
He who with might extends through all existence hears words which I, his faithful servant, utter.

2 A cry was raised which reached the Gods, O Indra, a cry to them to send us strength in combat.
None among men knows his own life's duration: bear us in safety over these our troubles.

3 The Bays, the booty-seeking car I harness: my prayers have reached him who accepts them gladly.
Indra, when he had slain resistless foemen, forced with his might the two world-halves asunder.

4 Like barren cows, moreover, swelled the waters: the singers sought thy holy rite, O Indra.
Come unto us as with his team comes Vāyu: thou, through our solemn hymns bestowest booty.

5 So may these gladdening draughts rejoice thee, Indra, the Mighty, very bounteous to the singer.
Alone among the Gods thou pitiest mortals: O Hero, make thee glad at this libation.

6 Thus the Vasiṣṭhas glorify with praises Indra the Powerful whose arm wields thunder.
Praised, may he guard our wealth in kine and heroes. Ye Gods, preserve us evermore with blessings.

HYMN XXIV. *Indra.*

1. A home is made for thee to dwell in, Indra: O Much-invoked, go thither with the heroes.
That thou, to prosper us, mayst be our Helper, vouchsafe us wealth, rejoice with draughts of Soma.

2 Indra, thy wish, twice-strong, is comprehended: pressed is the Soma, poured are pleasant juices.
This hymn of praise, from loosened tongue, made perfect, draws Indra to itself with loud invoking.

3 Come, thou Impetuous; God, from earth or heaven; come to our holy grass to drink the Soma.
Hither to me let thy Bay Horses bring thee to listen to our hymns and make thee joyful.

4 Come unto us with all thine aids, accordant, Lord of Bay Steeds, accepting our devotions,
Fair-helmeted, o'ercoming with the mighty, and lending us the strength of bulls, O Indra.

5 As to the chariot pole a vigorous courser, this laud is brought to the great strong Upholder.
This hymn solicits wealth of thee: in heaven, as 'twere above the sky, set thou our glory.

4 *Juice-drinking*: that presses out the juice of the plant, and so may be said to drink it. The Scholiast inserts *mama*, of me: 'Hear the invocation of the (grinding) stone (of me) repeatedly drinking (the *Soma*).'—Wilson.

2 *A cry was raised*: I follow Pischel's interpretation of this very difficult stanza. See *Vedische Studien*, I. pp. 34—36.

4 *Barren cows*: which are fatter than others.

1 *A home*: in the sacrificial chamber. *Heroes*: or, men; the priests.

4 *Fair-helmeted*: or fair-cheeked, or handsome-chinned.

6 With precious things. O Indra, thus content us : may we attain to thine exalted favour.
Send our chiefs plenteous food with hero children. Preserve us evermore, ye Gods, with blessings.

HYMN XXV. *Indra.*

1 WHEN with thy mighty help, O potent Indra, the armies rush together in their fury.
When from the strong man's arm the lightning flieth, let not the mind go forth to side with others.

2 O Indra, where the ground is hard to traverse, smite down our foes, the mortals who assail us.
Keep far from us the curse of the reviler: bring us accumulated store of treasures.

3 God of the fair helm, give Sudās a hundred succours, a thousand blessings, and thy bounty.
Strike down the weapon of our mortal foeman : bestow upon us splendid fame and riches.

4 I wait the power of one like thee, O Indra, gifts of a Helper such as thou art, Hero.
Strong, Mighty God, dwell with me now and ever : Lord of Bay Horses, do not thou desert us.

5 Here are the Kutsas supplicating Indra for might, the Lord of Bays for God-sent conquest.
Make our foes ever easy to be vanquished: may we, victorious, win the spoil, O Hero.

6 With precious things, O Indra, thus content us: may we attain to thine exalted favour.
Send our chiefs plenteous food with hero children. Preserve us evermore, ye Gods, with blessings.

HYMN XXVI. *Indra.*

1. SOMA unpressed ne'er gladdened liberal Indra, no juices pressed without a prayer have pleased him.
I generate a laud that shall delight him, new and heroic, so that he may hear us.

2 At every laud the Soma gladdens Indra : pressed juices please him as each psalm is chanted,
What time the priests with one united effort call him to aid, as sons invoke their father.

3 These deeds he did; let him achieve new exploits, such as the priests declare at their libations.
Indra hath taken and possessed all castles, like as one common husband doth his spouses.

4 Even thus have they declared him. Famed is Indra as Conqueror, sole distributer of treasures;
Whose many succours come in close succession. May dear delightful benefits attend us.

5 Thus, to bring help to men, Vasiṣṭha laudeth Indra, the peoples' Hero, at libation.
Bestow upon us strength and wealth in thousands. Preserve us evermore, ye Gods, with blessings.

HYMN XXVII. *Indra.*

1. MEN call on Indra in the armed encounter that he may make the hymns they sing decisive.
Hero, rejoicing in thy might, in combat give us a portion of the stall of cattle,

2 Grant, Indra Maghavan, invoked of many, to these my friends the strength which thou possessest.
Thou, Maghavan, hast rent strong places open : unclose for us, Wise God, thy hidden bounty.

3 King of the living world, of men, is Indra, of all in varied form that earth containeth.
Thence to the worshipper he giveth riches: may he enrich us also when we laud him.

4 Maghavan Indra, when we all invoke him, bountiful ever sendeth strength to aid us :

The battle has begun, and the singer prays to Indra for aid.

1 *The lightning* : the swift and flashing arrow. *Others* : the enemy.

3 *Sudās* : according to Sāyaṇa, 'the liberal donor (of oblations).' Wilson.

5 *The Kutsas* : apparently the priests of the hostile party.

---

1 *Soma unpressed* : cp. VI. 41. 4, Soma when (properly) pressed excels the unpressed (or ill-pressed) Soma. Not only must the juice be duly expressed, but it must be expressed and offered with prayer.

3 *All castles* : all the strongholds of the demons of drought, the cloud-castles in which the rain is imprisoned.

---

1 *Give us a portion, etc.* : aid us to capture and carry off the cattle of the enemy.

Whose perfect guerdon, never failing, bringeth wealth to the men, to friends the thing they covet.

5 Quick, Indra, give us room and way to riches, and let us bring thy mind to grant us treasures,
That we may win us cars and steeds and cattle. Preserve us evermore, ye Gods, with blessings.

HYMN XXVIII. *Indra.*

1. COME to our prayers, O Indra, thou who knowest: let thy Bay Steeds be yoked and guided hither.
Though mortal men on every side invoke thee, still give thine ear to us, O All-impeller.

2 Thy greatness reacheth to our invocation, the sages' prayer which, Potent God, thou guardest.
What time thy hand, O Mighty, holds the thunder, awful in strength thou hast become resistless.

3 What time thou drewest both world-halves together, like heroes led by thee who call each other—
For thou wast born for strength and high dominion—then e'en the active overthrew the sluggish.

4 Honour us in these present days, O Indra, for hostile men are making expiation.
Our sin that sinless Varuṇa discovered, the Wondrous-Wise hath long ago forgiven.

5 We will address this liberal Lord, this Indra, that he may grant us gifts of ample riches,
Best favourer of the singer's prayer and praises. Preserve us evermore, ye Gods, with blessings.

2 *Thy greatness reacheth to our invocation* : thou hast the power to come to our call if thou wilt.

3 *Drewest both world-halves together* : settest heaven and earth opposite to each other, like armies arrayed for battle. *E'en the active* : the meaning of the half-line is doubtful, and *cit*, even, seems to be out of place. Wilson translates, after Sāyaṇa : 'whence the presenter of offerings overcomes him who offers them not.' According to Professor Grassmann, 'the active' is Indra, and 'the inactive' is the sluggish demon. Ludwig suggests an alteration of the text.

4 *Are making expiation* : or, possibly, set themselves in order, that is, equip and prepare themselves for battle. *The Wondrous-Wise* : *māyī́*; Varuṇa.

HYMN XXIX *Indra.*

1. THIS Soma hath been pressed for thee, O Indra: come hither, Lord of Bays, for this thou lovest.
Drink of this fair, this well-effused libation: Maghavan, give us wealth when we implore thee.

2 Come to us quickly with thy Bay Steeds, Hero, come to our prayer, accepting our devotion.
Enjoy thyself aright at this libation, and listen thou unto the prayers we offer.

3 What satisfaction do our hymns afford thee? When, Maghavan? Now let us do thee service.
Hymns, only hymns, with love for thee, I weave thee: then hear, O Indra, these mine invocations.

4 They, verily, were also human beings whom thou wast wont to hear, those earlier sages.
Hence I, O Indra Maghavan, invoke thee: thou art our Providence, even as a Father.

5 We will address this liberal Lord, this Indra, that he may grant us gifts of ample riches,
Best favourer of the singer's prayer and praises. Preserve us evermore, ye Gods, with blessings.

HYMN XXX. *Indra.*

1. WITH power and strength, O Mighty God, approach us: be the augmenter, Indra, of these riches;
Strong Thunderer, Lord of men, for potent valour, for manly exploit and for high dominion.

2 Thee, worth invoking, in the din of battle, heroes invoke in fray for life and sunlight.
Among all people thou art foremost fighter: give up our enemies to easy slaughter.

3 When fair bright days shall dawn on us, O Indra, and thou shalt bring thy banner near in battle,
Agni the Asura shall sit as Herald, cal-

3 *Now let us do thee service* : *nūnám* : 'no time like the present.'—Ludwig.

1 *For potent valour* : that is, to give us potent valour.

2 *Foremost fighter* : caster of the spear, warrior, according to von Roth; but the meaning of *sényaḥ* is somewhat uncertain.

ling Gods hither for our great good fortune.

4 Thine are we, Indra, thine, both these who praise thee, and those who give rich gifts, O God and Hero.
Grant to our princes excellent protection, may they wax old and still be strong and happy.

5 We will address this liberal Lord, this Indra, that he may grant us gifts of ample riches,
Best favourer of the singer's prayer and praises. Preserve us evermore, ye Gods, with blessings.

HYMN XXXI. *Indra.*

1. SING ye a song, to make him glad, to Indra, Lord of Tawny Steeds,
The Soma-drinker, O my friends.

2 To him the Bounteous say the laud, and let us glorify, as men May do, the Giver of true gifts.

3 O Indra, Lord of boundless might, for us thou winnest strength and kine,
Thou winnest gold for us, Good Lord.

4 Faithful to thee we loudly sing, heroic Indra, songs to thee : Mark, O Good Lord, this act of ours.

5 Give us not up to man's reproach, to foeman's hateful calumny : In thee alone is all my strength.

6 Thou art mine ample coat of mail, my Champion, Vṛtra-Slayer, thou :
With thee for Friend I brave the foe.

7 Yea, great art thou whose conquering might two independent Powers confess.
The Heaven, O Indra, and the Earth.

8 So let the voice surround thee, which attends the Maruts on their way,
Reaching thee with the rays of light.

9 Let the ascending drops attain to thee, the Wondrous God, in heaven :
Let all the folk bow down to thee.

10 Bring to the Wise, the Great, who waxeth mighty, your offerings, and make ready your devotion ;
To many clans he goeth, man's controller.

11 For Indra, the sublime, the far-pervading, have singers generated prayer and praises :
The sages never violate his statutes.

12 The choirs have stablished Indra King for ever, for victory, him whose anger is resistless :
And, for the Bays' Lord, strengthened those he loveth.

7 *Independent* : *svadhāvarī* ; 'abounding in food.'—Wilson.

8 *The voice* : 'the praises of thine adorers.—Wilson.

12 *Strengthened* : 'barhayā : for abarhayan, as is clear from what precedes.'—Ludwig. Sāyaṇa takes *barhayā* as the imperative : 'urge thy kinsmen, (worshipper, to glorify) the lord of bay steeds.'—Wilson.

HYMN XXXII. *Indra.*

1. LET none, no, not thy worshippers, delay thee far away from us.
Even from far away come thou unto our feast, or listen if already here.

2 For here, like flies on honey, these who pray to thee sit by the juice that they have poured.
Wealth-craving singers have on Indra set their hope, as men set foot upon a car.

3 Longing for wealth I call on him, the Thunderer with the strong right hand,
As a son calleth on his sire.

4 These Soma juices, mixed with curd, have been expressed for Indra here.
Come with thy Bay Steeds, Thunder-wielder, to our home, to drink them till they make thee glad.

5 May he whose ear is open hear us. He is asked for wealth : will he despise our prayer ?
Him who bestows at once a hundred thousand gifts none shall restrain when he would give.

6 The hero never checked by men hath gained his strength through Indra, he
Who presses out and pours his deep libations forth, O Vṛtra-slayer, unto thee.

7 When thou dost drive the fighting men together be, thou Mighty One, the mighty's shield.
May we divide the wealth of him whom thou hast slain : bring us, Unreachable, his goods.

8 For Indra, Soma-drinker, armed with thunder, press the Soma juice.
Make ready your dressed meats : cause him to favour us. The Giver blesses him who gives.

I am indebted to Max Müller's translation of this hymn in his *Ancient Sanskrit Literature* for many of the renderings which I have adopted.

3 *With the strong right hand* : or giver of good gifts.

7 *The mighty's shield* : 'the shield of the mighty (Vasiṣṭhas).'—M.M.; 'a protection of the Maghavans,' *i. e.* the institutors of the sacrifice—Ludwig.

8 *The Giver blesses him who gives* : Indra rewards the liberal worshipper.

9 Grudge not, ye Soma-pourers ; stir you, pay the rites, for wealth, to the great Conqueror.
Only the active conquers, dwells in peace, and thrives : not for the niggard are the Gods.

10 No one hath overturned or stayed the car of him who freely gives.
The man whom Indra and the Marut host defend comes to a stable full of kine.

11 Indra, that man when fighting shall obtain the spoil, whose strong defender thou wilt be.
Be thou the gracious helper, Hero ! of our cars, be thou the helper of our men.

12 His portion is exceeding great like a victorious soldier's spoil.
Him who is Indra, Lord of Bays, no foes subdue. He gives the Soma-pourer strength.

13 Make for the Holy Gods a hymn that is not mean, but well-arranged and fair of form.
Even many snares and bonds subdue not him who dwells with Indra through his sacrifice.

14 Indra, what mortal will attack the man who hath his wealth in thee ?
The strong will win the spoil on the decisive day through faith in thee, O Maghavan.

15 In battles with the foe urge on our mighty ones who give the treasures dear to thee,
And may we with our princes, Lord of Tawny Steeds ! pass through all peril, led by thee.

16 Thine, Indra, is the lowest wealth, thou cherishest the mid-most wealth,
Thou ever rulest all the highest : in the fray for cattle none resisteth thee.

17 Thou art renowned as giving wealth to every one in all the battles that are fought.
Craving protection, all these people of the earth, O Much-invoked, implore thy name.

18 If I, O Indra, were the Lord of riches ample as thine own,
I should support the singer, God who givest wealth ! and not abandon him to woe.

19 Each day would I enrich the man who sang my praise, in whatsoever place he were.
No kinship is there better, Maghavan, than thine : a father even is no more.

20 With Plenty for his true ally the active man will gain the spoil.
Your Indra, Much-invoked, I bend with song, as bends a wright his wheel of solid wood.

21 A moral wins no riches by unworthy praise: wealth comes not to the niggard churl.
Light is the task to give, O Maghavan, to one like me on the decisive day.

22 Like kine unmilked we call aloud, Hero, to thee, and sing thy praise,
Looker on heavenly light, Lord of this moving world, Lord, Indra, of what moveth not.

23 None other like to thee, of earth or of the heavens, hath been or ever will be born.
Desiring horses, Indra Maghavan ! and kine, as men of might we call on thee.

24 Bring, Indra, the Victorious Ones; bring, elder thou, the younger host.
For, Maghavan, thou art rich in treasures from of old, and must be called in every fight.

25 Drive thou away our enemies, O Maghavan : make riches easy to be won.
Be thou our good Protector in the strife for spoil : Cherisher of our friends be thou.

26 O Indra, give us wisdom as a sire gives wisdom to his sons.
Guide us, O Much-invoked, in this our way may we still live and look upon the light.

27 Grant that no mighty foes, unknown, malevolent, unhallowed, tread us to the ground.
With thine assistance, Hero, may we pass through all the waters that are rushing down.

HYMN XXXIII *Vasiṣṭha.*

1. THESE who wear hair-knots on the right, the movers of holy thought, white-robed, have won me over.

10 *Comes to a stable full of kine* : carries off rich booty.

20 *Plenty* : or, Spirit, Boldness.

24 *Bring, Indra, the Victorious Ones* : these would be the Maruts. 'Elder Indra, bring that (wealth to me) being the junior.'—Wilson. 'Bring all this to those who are good, O Indra, be they old or young.'—M. Müller.

The hymn is a glorification of Vasiṣṭha and his family the latter part relating his birth and the earlier verses, referring to his connexion with King Sudās.

1 *Hair-knots* : *kaparda* is the *cūḍa* or single lock of

I warned the men, when from the grass I raised me,—Not from afar can my Vasiṣṭhas help you.

2 With soma they brought Indra from a distance, over Vaiśanta, from the strong libation.
Indra preferred Vasiṣṭhas to the Soma pressed by the son of Vayatā, Pāśadyumna.

3 So, verily, with these he crossed the river, in company with these he slaughtered Bheda.
So in the fight with the Ten Kings, Vasiṣṭhas ! did Indra help Sudās through your devotions.

4 I gladly, men ! with prayer prayed by our fathers have fixed your axle : ye shall not be injured :
Since, when ye sang aloud the Śakvarī verses, Vasiṣṭhas ! ye invigorated Indra.

5 Like thirsty men they looked to heaven, in battle with the Ten Kings, surrounded and imploring.
Then Indra heard Vasiṣṭha as he praised him, and gave the Tṛtsus ample room and freedom.

6 Like sticks and staves wherewith they drive the cattle, stripped bare, the Bharatas were found defenceless:
Vasiṣṭha then became their chief and leader : then widely were the Tṛtsus' clans extended.

7 Three fertilize the worlds with genial moisture : three noble Creatures cast a light before them.
Three that give warmth to all attend the morning. All these have they discovered, these Vasiṣṭhas.

8 Like the Sun's growing glory is their splendour, and like the sea's is their unfathomed greatness.
Their course is like the wind's. Your laud, Vasiṣṭhas, can never be attained by any other.

9 They with perceptions of the heart in secret resort to that which spreads a thousand branches.
The Apsaras brought hither the Vasiṣṭhas wearing the vesture spun for them by Yama.

10 A form of lustre springing from the lightning wast thou, when Varuṇa and Mitra saw thee.
Thy one and only birth was then, Vasiṣṭha, when from thy stock Agastya brought thee hither.

11 Born of their love for Urvaśī, Vasiṣṭha thou, priest, art son of Varuṇa and Mitra ;
And as a fallen drop, in heavenly fervour, all the Gods laid thee on a lotus-blossom.

12 He, thinker, knower both of earth and heaven, endowed with many a gift, bestowing thousands,
Destined to wear the vesture spun by Yama, sprang from the Apsaras to life, Vasiṣṭha.

13 Born at the sacrifice, urged by adorations,

hair left on the head at tonsure, which, according to the Scholiast, it was characteristic of the *Vasiṣṭhas* to wear on the right of the crown of the head. *White-robed* : white-coloured, according to Sāyaṇa. *Me* : Vasiṣṭha, who is the speaker of stanzas 1—6. 'Von Roth (under the word *av*) regards Indra as the speaker. May it not be Sudās?'—Muir, *O.S. Text*, I. 319, 320, where stanzas 1—13 are translated. *From the grass* : the sacred grass laid on the floor of the sacrificial chamber.

2 *Vaiśanta* : probably the name of a river. *Pāśadyumna* : another king who was sacrificing to Indra at the same time as Sudās.

3 *The river* Yamunā See VII. 18. 19. *Ten Kings* : of the confederate tribes who opposed Sudās. See VII. 18.

4 *Śakvarī verses* : hymns of praise in the Śakvarī metre (14 × 4).

5 *Tṛtsus* : the tribe of which Sudās was King.
6 *Bharatas* : apparently the same as the Tṛtsus.

7 Indra is the speaker of the rest of the hymn. 'In explanation of this, Sāyaṇa quotes a passage from the Śāṭyāyana Brāhmaṇa : (1) Agni produces a fertilizing fluid on the earth, Vāyu in the air, the Sun in the sky. (2) The 'three noble creatures' are the Vasus, Rudras, and Ādityas. The Sun is their light. (3) Agni, Vāyu, and the Sun each attend the Dawn.'—Muir. *O. S. Texts*, 1. 320.

9 *That which spreads a thousand branches* : according to Ludwig's Translation, the Sun-God is meant ; according to his later view, the reference is to the mystic tree sustained by Varuṇa in the baseless region (I. 24. 7). *The vesture* ; the body. The stanza is very obscure, and Sāyaṇa's explanation, which overrides grammar, is not satisfactory : 'By the wisdom seated in the heart the *Vasiṣṭhas* traverse the hidden thousand-branched world, and the *Apsarasas* sit down, wearing the vesture spread out by Yama.'—Wilson.

10 Vasiṣṭha appears here as an embodiment of lightning, light, or fire and to have been brought down to men by Agastya who was born in the same way as Vasiṣṭha.

11 *Urvaśī* : the most celebrated of the Apsarases or nymphs of heaven *On a lotus-blossom* : or, according to others, 'in the sacred pitcher,' or water-jar used in sacrifice. 'In the lake.'—Wilson.

For a full account of this production of Vasiṣṭha, the curious reader is referred to Muir. *O. S. Texts*, I. 321. See M. Müller, *Chips*, IV. 108, 109, and Hillebrandt. *Varuṇa und Mitra*, 148, 149.

12 *The Apsaras* : Urvaśī.

both with a common flow bedewed the pitcher.
Then from the midst thereof there rose up Māna, and thence they say was born the sage Vasiṣṭha.

14 He brings the bearer of the laud and Sāman : first shall he speak bringing the stone for pressing.
With grateful hearts in reverence approach him : to you, O Pratṛdas, Vasiṣṭha cometh.

HYMN XXXIV *Viṣvedevas.*

1. MAY our divine and brilliant hymn go forth, like a swift chariot wrought and fashioned well.

2 The waters listen as they flow along : they know the origin of heaven and earth.

3 Yea, the broad waters swell their flood for him : of him strong heroes think amid their foes.

4 Set ye for him the coursers to the pole: like Indra Thunderer is the Golden-armed.

5 Arouse you, like the days, to sacrifice : speed gladly like a traveller on the way.

6 Go swift to battles, to the sacrifice : set up a flag, a hero for the folk.

7 Up from his strength hath risen as 'twere a light : it bears the load as earth bears living things.

8 Agni, no demon I invoke the Gods : by law completing it, I form a hymn.

9 Closely about you lay your heavenly song, and send your voice to where the Gods abide.

10 Varuṇa, Mighty, with a thousand eyes, beholds the paths wherein these rivers run.

11 He, King of kings, the glory of the floods, o'er all that liveth hath resistless sway.

12 May he assist us among all the tribes, and make the envier's praise devoid of light.

13 May the foes' threatening arrow pass us by : may he put far from us our bodies' sin.

14 Agni, oblation-eater, through our prayers aid us : to him our dearest laud is brought.

15 Accordant with the Gods choose for our Friend the Waters' Child : may he be good to us.

16 With lauds I sing the Dragon born of floods : he sits beneath the streams in middle air.

17 Ne'er may the Dragon of the Deep harm us : ne'er fail this faithful servant's sacrifice.

18 To these our heroes may they grant renown: may pious men march boldly on to wealth.

19 Leading great hosts, with fierce attacks of these, they burn their foes as the Sun burns the earth.

20 What time our wives draw near to us, may he, left-handed Tvaṣṭar, give us hero sons.

21 May Tvaṣṭar find our hymn acceptable, and may Aramati, seeking wealth, be ours.

22 May they who lavish gifts bestow those treasures : may Rodasī and Varuṇānī listen.
May he, with the Varūtrīs, be our refuge, may bountiful Tvaṣṭar give us store of riches.

23 So may rich Mountains and the liberal Waters, so may all Herbs that grow on ground, and Heaven,
And Earth accordant with the Forest-Sovrans, and both the World-halves round about protect us.

24 To this may both the wide Worlds lend

13 *Māna* : said to be another name of Agastya.

14 *The bearer of the laud and Sāman* : the pressing-stone, which was worked du ing the recitation of sacred verses. *Pratṛdás* : a name used here to designate the Tṛtsus

This difficult and obscure hymn has been translated and thoroughly discussed by Geldner (*Vedische Studien*, II. pp. 129—155, criticized by Prof. Ludwig, *Ueber die neuesten Arbeiten auf dem Gebiete der Ṛgveda-forschung*, pp. 163—167).

---

2 'An allusion, perhaps, to the subsequently received cosmogony, as in *Manu*, that water was the first of created things.'—Wilson.

3 *For him* : Indra.

4 *The Golden-armed* : Savitar.

6 *A hero* : a sort of personification of the sacrifice. 'An expiatory sacrifice for (the good of) mankind.'—Wilson.

16 *The Dragon born of floods* : Ahibudhnya, or the Dragon of the Deep of the following stanza ; the regent of the sea of air.

18 *They* : the Gods.

19 *Of these* : Gods, or Maruts, according to the Scholiast.

21 *Aramati* : the Genius of Devotion and active piety.

22 *Varūtrīs* : protecting Goddesses.

23 *Forest-Sovrans* : tall timber trees.

---

approval, and Varuṇa in heaven, whose Friend is Indra.
May all the Maruts give consent, the Victors, that we may hold great wealth in firm possession.

25 May Indra, Varuṇa, Mitra, and Agni, Waters, Herbs, Trees accept the praise we offer.
May we find refuge in the Marut's bosom. Protect us evermore, ye Gods, with blessings.

HYMN XXXV. *Viśvedevas.*

1. Befriend us with their aids Indra and Agni, Indra and Varuṇa who receive oblations !
Indra and Soma give health, strength and comfort, Indra and Pūṣan be our help in battle.

2 Auspicious Friends to us be Bhaga, Śaṁsa, auspicious be Purandhi and all Riches ;
The blessing of the true and well-conducted, and Aryaman in many forms apparent.

3 Kind unto us be Maker and Sustainer, and the far-reaching Pair with God-like natures.
Auspicious unto us be Earth and Heaven, the Mountain, and the Gods' fair invocations.

4 Favour us Agni with his face of splendour, and Varuṇa and Mitra and the Aśvins.
Favour us noble actions of the pious, impetuous vāta blow on us with favour.

5 Early invoked, may Heaven and Earth be friendly, and Air's mid-region good for us to look on.
To us may Herbs and Forest-Trees be gracious, gracious the Lord Victorious of the region.

6 Be the God Indra with the Vasus friendly, and, with Ādityas, Varuṇa who blesseth.
Kind, with the Rudras, be the Healer Rudra, and, with the Dames, may Tvaṣṭar kindly listen.

7 Blest unto us be Soma, and devotions, blest be the Sacrifice, the Stones for pressing.
Blest be the fixing of the sacred Pillars, blest be the tender Grass and blest the Altar.

8 May the far-seeing Sun rise up to bless us : be the four Quarters of the sky auspicious.
Auspicious be the firmly-seated Mountains, auspicious be the Rivers and the Waters.

9 May Aditi through holy works be gracious, and may the Maruts, loud in song, be friendly.
May Viṣṇu give felicity, and Pūṣan, the Air that cherisheth our life, and Vāyu.

10 Prosper us Savitar, the God who rescues, and let the radiant Mornings be propitious.
Auspicious to all creatures be Parjanya, auspicious be the field's benign Protector.

11 May all the fellowship of Gods befriend us, Sarasvatī, with Holy Thoughts, be gracious.
Friendly be they, the Liberal Ones who seek us, yea, those who dwell in heaven, on earth, in waters.

12 May the great Lords of Truth protect and aid us : blest to us be our horses and our cattle.
Kind be the pious skilful-handed Ṛbhus, kind be the Fathers at our invocations.

13 May Aja-Ekapād, the God, be gracious, gracious the Dragon of the Deep, and Ocean.
Gracious be he the swelling Child of Waters, gracious be Pṛśni who hath Gods to guard her.

14 So may the Rudras, Vasus, and Ādityas accept the new hymn which we now are making.
May all the Holy Ones of earth and heaven, and the Cow's offspring hear our invocation.

15 They who of Holy Gods are very holy, Immortal, knowing Law, whom man must worship,—
May these to-day give us broad paths to travel. Preserve us evermore, ye Gods, with blessings.

1 *Befriend us* : *śám no bhavatām*. The indeclinable word *śám*, signifying happy, auspicious, pleasant, sweet, kind, agreeable, etc., etc., is used with or without the verb *bhū*, in the first thirteen stanzas. I have varied the expression here and there.

2 *Śaṁsa* : Prayer or Wish personified. Or it may be Narāśaṁsa, Agni. *Purandhi*: Plenty, or Spirit, Boldness personified.

3 *Far-reaching Pair* : Heaven and Earth.

5 *The Lord Victorious* : Indra.

10 *The field's benign Protector* : Agni, or Rudra. See IV. 57. 1.

13 *Aja-Ekapād* : the Sun. See VI. 50. 14, and footnote.

The Dragon of the Deep : Ahibudhnya, regent of the depths of the firmament.

14 *Cow's offspring* : the Maruts. According to von Roth those who are born and live in radiant heaven.

15 *Broad paths to travel* : perhaps, generally, an easy road to prosperity.

HYMN XXXVI. *Viśvedevas*

1. Let the prayer issue from the seat of Order, for Sūrya with his beams hath loosed the cattle.
With lofty ridges earth is far extended, and Agni's flame hath lit the spacious surface.

2 O Asuras, O Varuṇa and Mitra, this hymn to you, like food, anew I offer.
One of you is a strong unerring Leader, and Mitra, speaking, stirreth men to labour.

3 The movements of the gliding wind come hither : like cows, the springs are filled to overflowing.
Born in the station e'en of lofty heaven the Bull hath loudly bellowed in this region.

4 May I bring hither with my song, O Indra, wise Aryaman who yokes thy dear Bay Horses,
Voracious, with thy noble car, O Hero, him who defeats the wrath of the malicious.

5 In their own place of sacrifice adorers worship to gain long life and win his friendship.
He hath poured food on men when they have praised him; be this, the dearest reverence, paid to Rudra.

6 Coming together, glorious, loudly roaring—Sarasvatī, Mother of Floods, the seventh—
With copious milk, with fair streams, strongly flowing, full swelling with the volume of their water ;

7. And may the mighty Maruts, too, rejoicing, aid our devotion and protect our offspring.
Let not swift-moving Akṣarā neglect us: they have increased our own appropriate riches,

8 Bring ye the great Aramati before you, and Pūṣan as the Hero of the synod,
Bhaga who looks upon this hymn with favour, and, as our strength, the bountiful Purandhi.

9 May this our song of praise reach you, O Maruts, and Viṣṇu guardian of the future infant.
May they vouchsafe the singer strength for offspring. Preserve us evermore, ye Gods, with blessings.

HYMN XXXVII. *Viśvedevas.*

1. Let your best-bearing car that must be lauded, ne'er injured, bring you Vājas and Ṛbhukṣans.
Fill you, fair-helmeted ! with mighty Soma, thrice-mixed, at our libations, to delight you.

2 Ye who behold the light of heaven, Ṛbhukṣans, give our rich patrons unmolested riches.
Drink, heavenly-natured, at our sacrifices, and give us bounties for the hymns we sing you.

3 For thou, O Bounteous One, art used to giving, at parting treasure whether small or ample.
Filled full are both thine arms with great possessions : thy goodness keeps thee not from granting riches.

4 Indra, high-famed, as Vāja and Ṛbhu-

1 *The seat of Order* : 'the hall of the sacrifice.'—Wilson. *The cattle* : rays of light.

2 'One of you (Varuṇa) is the lord and unassailable guide, and he who is called Mitra, (*i.e.* the friend) calls men to activity. Here so much at least is declared (and the same thing is expressed in nearly the same words in other places), that the light of day, which awakens life, and brings joy and activity into the world, is the narrower sphere of Mitra's power ; though, however, Varuṇa is not relegated to the night alone, for he continues to be the lord and the first.'—Von Roth, quoted by Muir *O. S. Texts*, V. 70. The meaning of *ináḥ* translated by 'lord' in this extract, is, in the Veda, rather 'strong,' 'energetic,' and is so given in the St. Petersburg Lexicon, the meaning 'lord' belonging to later literature. The second half of the second line is repeated, with a variation, from III. 59. 1.

3 *The springs* : the fountains of rain ; the clouds. *The Bull* : Parjanya, God of the rain-cloud. *This region* : literally, this udder ; the firmament.

4 *Voracious* : epithet of horses ; but the meaning of *dhāyú* is uncertain. According to Sāyaṇa, it means 'holding,' 'vigorous;' according to Ludwig, 'pouring forth rain;' according to Grassmann, 'thirsty.'

5 *His friendship* : Rudra's.

6 *The seventh* : with the six other celebrated rivers. See I. 32. 12.

7 *Akṣarā* : Vāk, or Voice; 'the imperishable goddess of speech.'—Wilson. Cf. VII. 15. 9.

8 *Aramati* : the personification of religious worship, or active piety. See VII. 34. 21. According to Sāyaṇa, *arámatim* here is an epithet of *mahīm*, 'the never-resting Earth.' For the various meanings assigned by Sāyaṇa to this word in the various places in which it occurs, See Muir, *O. S. Texts*, IV. 317.

9 *Viṣṇu* : Cf. X. 184. 1.

---

1 *Vājas and Ṛbhukṣans* : that is, Ṛbhukṣan or Ṛbhu, Vibhvan, and Vāja, commonly called the Ṛbhus from the name of the first of the three. *Fair-helmeted*: 'handsome-chinned.'—Wilson ; 'Strong-jawed.'—Ludwig. *Thrice-mixed* : with milk, curds, and meal.

3 *Bounteous One* : Maghavan; Indra.

kṣan, thou goest working, singing to the dwelling.
Lord of Bay Steeds, this day may we Vasiṣṭhas offer our prayers to thee and bring oblations.

5 Thou winnest swift advancement for thy servant, through hymns, Lord of Bay Steeds, which thou hast favoured.
For thee with friendly succour have we battled, and when, O Indra, wilt thou grant us riches?

6 To us thy priests a home, as 'twere, thou givest : when, Indra wilt thou recognize our praises ?
May thy strong Steed, through our ancestral worship, bring food and wealth with heroes to our dwelling.

7 Though Nirṛti the Goddess reigneth round him, Autumns with food in plenty come to Indra.
With three close Friends to length of days he cometh, he whom men let not rest at home in quiet.

8 Promise us gifts, O Savitar : may riches come unto us in Parvata's full bounty.
May the Celestial Guardian still attend us. Preserve us evermore, ye Gods, with blessings.

HYMN XXXVIII. *Savitar.*

1. On high hath Savitar, this God, extended the golden lustre which he spreads around him.
Now, now must Bhaga be invoked by mortals, Lord of great riches who distributes treasures.

2 Rise up, O Savitar whose hands are golden, and hear this man while sacrifice is offered,
Spreading afar thy broad and wide effulgence, and bringing mortal men the food that feeds them.

3 Let Savitar the God be hymned with praises, to whom the Vasus, even, all sing glory.
Sweet be our lauds to him whose due is worship : may he with all protection guard our princes.

4 Even he whom Aditi the Goddess praises, rejoicing in God Savitar's incitement:
Even he who praise the high imperial Rulers, Varuṇa, Mitra, Aryaman, sing in concert.

5 They who come emulous to our oblation, dispensing bounty, from the earth and heaven.
May they and Ahibudhnya hear our calling: guard us Varūtrī with the Ekadhenus.

6 This may the Lord of Life, entreated, grant us,—the wealth which Savitar the God possesses.
The mighty calls on Bhaga for protection, on Bhaga calls the weak to give him riches.

7 Bless us the Vājins when we call, while slowly they move, strong Singers, to the Gods' assembly.
Crushing the wolf, the serpent, and the demons, may they completely banish all affliction.

8 Deep-skilled in Law eternal, deathless, Singers, O Vājins, help us in each fray for booty.
Drink of this meath, be satisfied, be joyful: then go on paths which Gods are wont to travel.

HYMN XXXIX *Viśvedevas.*

1. Agni, erect, hath shown enriching favour: the flame goes forward to the Gods' assembly.
Like car-borne men the stones their path have chosen : let the priest, quickened, celebrate our worship.

4 *Working* : 'the fulfiller (of wishes).'—Wilson. The first line is somewhat obscure.

7 *Nirṛti* : the Goddess of Death and Destruction, who has no power over Indra. *Three close Friends* : the Ṛbhus, who represent the year, the annual course of Indra as the Sun. Sāyaṇa's explanation is different; 'Indra, the upholder of the three regions, whom the divine Nirṛti acknowledges as ruler, whom abundant years pass over, whom mortals detain from his own abode, approaches to (recruit) his decaying strength.'—Wilson; who observes : 'the explanation is not very clear.'

8 *Parvata's full bounty* : the Genius of mountain and cloud.

3 *The Vasus* : the Gods in general, according to Sāyaṇa.

5 *Varūtrī* : 'the protectress (the goddess of speech).'—Wilson. *Ekadhenus* : the Waters are probably meant: 'excellent cattle,'—Wilson.

7 *Vājins* : a class of divinities so named, according to Sāyaṇa ; but according to Mahīdhara, horses, *i.e.* the teams which draw the chariots of the Gods. *The wolf,* or the robber. *The serpent* : or the assassin. *The demons* : the Rākṣasas. See *Śatapatha-Brāhmaṇa*, V. I. 5. 21—24, (S. Books of the East, XLI. 27) for a different version of stanzas 6 and 7.

1 *The stones* : the pressing-stones have begun their course.

2 Soft to the tread, their sacred grass is scattered: these go like Kings amid the band around them,
At the folk's early call on Night and Morning,—Vāyu, and Pūṣan with his team, to bless us.

3 Here on their path the noble Gods proceeded: in the wide firmament the Beauteous decked them.
Bend your way hither, ye who travel widely: hear this our envoy who hath gone to meet you.

4 For they are holy aids at sacrifices: all Gods approach the place of congregation.
Bring these, desirous, to our worship, Agni, swift the Nāsatyas, Bhaga, and Purandhi.

5 Agni, to these men's hymns, from earth, from heaven, bring Mitra, Varuṇa, Indra, and Agni,
And Aryaman, and Aditi, and Viṣṇu. Sarasvatī be joyful, and the Maruts.

6 Even as the holy wish, the gift is offered: may he, unsated, come when men desire him.
Give never-failing ever-conquering riches: with Gods for our allies may we be victors.

7 Now have both worlds been praised by the Vasiṣṭhas; and holy Mitra, Varuṇa, and Agni.
May they, bright Deities, make our song supremest. Preserve us evermore, ye Gods, with blessings.

HYMN XL. *Viśvedevas.*

1. Be gathered all the audience of the synod: let us begin their praise whose course is rapid.
Whate'er God Savitar this day produces, may we be where the Wealthy One distributes.

2 This, dealt from heaven, may both the Worlds vouchsafe us, and Varuṇa, Indra, Aryaman, and Mitra.
May Goddess Aditi assign us riches, Vāyu and Bhaga make them ours for ever.

3 Strong be the man and full of power, O Maruts, whom ye, borne on by spotted coursers, favour.
Him, too, Sarasvatī and Agni further, and there is none to rob him of his riches.

4 This Varuṇa is guide of Law, he, Mitra, and Aryaman, the Kings, our work have finished.
Divine and foeless Aditi quickly listens. May these deliver us unharmed from trouble.

5 With offerings I propitiate the branches of this swift-moving God, the bounteous Viṣṇu.
Hence Rudra gained his Rudra-strength: O Aśvins, ye sought the house that hath celestial viands.

6 Be not thou angry here, O glowing Pūṣan, for what Varūtrī and the Bounteous gave us.
May the swift-moving Gods protect and bless us, and Vāta send us rain, who wanders round us.

7 Now have both worlds been praised by the Vasiṣṭhas, and holy Mitra, Varuṇa, and Agni.
May they, bright Deities, make our song supremest. Preserve us evermore, ye Gods, with blessings.

HYMN XLI. *Bhaga.*

1. Agni at dawn, and Indra we invoke at dawn, and Varuṇa and Mitra, and the Aśvins twain:
Bhaga at dawn, Pūṣan, and Brahmaṇaspati, Soma at dawn, Rudra we will invoke at dawn.

2 *These go like Kings*: according to Sāyaṇa, 'may the two lords of people (Vāyu and Pūṣan)...appear now.'

3 *Our envoy*: Agni.

5 *Agni*; in his own form as a celestial God, not in that of terrestrial fire.

6 *He, unsated*: Agni.

———

1 *Their praise*: praise of the Gods.

2 *Dealt from heaven*: or, distributed by Dyu or Dyaus.

4 *Our work*: the sacrifice.

5 *The branches*: '*vayā́ḥ*, branches: all other deities are, as it were, branches of *Viṣṇu*, *anye devāḥ, śākhā iva bhavanti*: as by a text cited by the scholiast, *Viṣṇu* is all divinities, *Viṣṇu sarvā devatā iti śruteḥ*.'—Wilson. This, Ludwig remarks, gives no satisfactory interpretation; but I am unable to offer any thing better at present. Grassmann alters *vayā́ḥ* into *vayāma*: 'we with our offerings approach the banquet of this swift-moving God, the bounteous Viṣṇu; *i.e.* come to offer him sacrificial food.'

———

The hymn is addressed chiefly to Bhaga the bountiful, whose name, slightly corrupted, survives in the Slavonic languages as a general name for God; but the Gods mentioned in stanza 1, and Uṣas, Dawn or Morning, are also regarded as the deities of the verses in which their names occur.

2 We will invoke strong, early-conquering Bhaga, the Son of Aditi, the great supporter:
Thinking of whom, the poor, yea, even the mighty, even the King himself says, Give me Bhaga.

3 Bhaga our guide, Bhaga whose gifts are faithful, favour this song, and give us wealth, O Bhaga.
Bhaga, augment our store of kine and horses, Bhaga, may we be rich in men and heroes.

4 So may felicity be ours at present, and when the day approaches, and at noon-tide;
And may we still, O Bounteous One, at sunset be happy in the Deities' loving-kindness.

5 May Bhaga verily be bliss-bestower, and through him, Gods! may happiness attend us.
As such, O Bhaga, all with might invoke thee: as such be thou our Champion here, O Bhaga.

6 To this our worship may all Dawns incline them, and come to the pure place like Dadhikrāvan.
As strong steeds draw a chariot may they bring us hitherward Bhaga who discovers treasure.

7 May blessed Mornings dawn on us for ever, with wealth of kine, of horses, and of heroes,
Streaming with all abundance, pouring fatness. Preserve us evermore, ye Gods, with blessings.

HYMN XLII. *Viśvedevas.*

1. LET Brahmans and Aṅgirases come forward, and let the roar of cloudy heaven surround us.
Loud low the Milch-kine swimming in the waters: set be the stones that grace our holy service.

2 Fair, Agni, is thy long-known path to travel: yoke for the juice thy bay, thy ruddy horses,
Or red steeds, Hero-bearing, for the chamber. Seated, I call the Deities' generations.

3 They glorify your sacrifice with worship, yet the glad Priest near them is left unequalled.
Bring the Gods hither, thou of many aspects: turn hitherward Aramati the Holy.

4 What time the Guest hath made himself apparent, at ease reclining in the rich man's dwelling,
Agni, well-pleased, well-placed within the chamber gives to a house like this wealth worth the choosing.

5 Accept this sacrifice of ours, O Agni; glorify it with Indra and the Maruts.
Here on our grass let Night and Dawn be seated: bring longing Varuṇa and Mitra hither.

6 Thus hath Vasiṣṭha praised victorious Agni, yearning for wealth that giveth all subsistence.
May he bestow on us food, strength, and riches. Preserve us evermore, ye Gods, with blessings.

HYMN XLIII. *Viśvedevas.*

1. SING out the pious at your sacrifices to move with adorations Earth and Heaven—
The Holy Singers, whose unmatched devotions, like a tree's branches, part in all directions.

2 Let sacrifice proceed like some fleet courser: with one accord lift ye on high the ladles.
Strew sacred grass meet for the solemn service: bright flames that love the Gods have mounted upward.

3 Like babes in arms reposing on their mother, let the Gods sit upon the grass's summit.
Let general fire make bright the flame of

2 *Give me Bhaga*: or riches.

6 *The pure place*: the chamber of sacrifice *Like Dadhikrāvan*: swift as Dadhikrāvan, the famous horse, the type and model of racers. See IV. 39. 3; 40. 1—3.

1 *Aṅgirases*: Ṛṣis so named, according to Sāyaṇa. *The Milch-kine*: the clouds in the watery firmament, with allusion also to the milk and water mixed with the Soma juice. *The stones*: the press-stones. Sāyaṇa's explanation is different: 'may the pious couple, (the *Yajamāna* and his wife) conjointly appreciate the beauty of the sacrifice.'—Wilson.

2 *Thy bay, thy ruddy horses*: or the Harits and the Rohits. *Red steeds*: or Aruṣas. *Hero-bearing*: carrying the Hero Agni. *For the chamber*: the sacrificial hall; 'in thy stable.'—M. Müller.

3 The human priests cannot equal Agni in efficiency. *Aramati*: the Genius of Devotion. See VII. 36. 8.

4 *The Guest*: Agni.

3 *Let general fire*: or, according to Sāyaṇa, 'Let the full ladle balm the fire of worship.' The exact

worship : scorn us not, Agni, in the Gods' assembly.

4 Gladly the Gods have let themselves be honoured, milking the copious streams of holy Order.
The highest might to-day is yours, the Vasus': come ye, as many as ye are, one-minded.

5 So, Agni, send us wealth among the people: may we be closely knit to thee, O Victor,
Unharmed, and rich, and taking joy together. Preserve us evermore, ye Gods, with blessings.

HYMN XLIV. *Dadhikrās.*

1. I CALL on Dadhikrās, the first, to give you aid, the Aśvins, Bhaga, Dawn, and Agni kindled well,
Indra, and Viṣṇu, Pūṣan, Brahmaṇaspati, Ādityas, Heaven and Earth, the Waters, and the Light.

2 When, rising, to the sacrifice we hasten, awaking Dadhikrās with adorations.
Seating on sacred grass the Goddess Iḷā, let us invoke the sage swift-hearing Aśvins.

3 While I am thus arousing Dadhikrāvan I speak to Agni, Earth, and Dawn, and Sūrya,
The red, the brown of Varuṇa ever mindful : may they ward off from us all grief and trouble.

4 Foremost is Dadhikrāvan, vigorous courser; in forefront of the cars, his way he knoweth,

meaning is uncertain as both subject and object are adjectives without substantives.

4 *Milking the copious streams* : enjoying the libations of law-ordained sacrifice. 'Who are the bestowers of water, the shedders of showers.'—Wilson.

1 *Dadhikrās* : See. IV. 38. 1.

3 *Dadhikrāvan* : a lengthened form of Dadhikrās. See IV. 39. 2, and 40. *The red, the brown* : apparently the horse of Varuṇa, that is, the Sun, is intended. *Ever mindful* : 'who is mindful of his adorers,—Wilson. The meaning of the word *maṁśćatoḥ*, or *māṁśćatoḥ*, is uncertain. Von Roth thinks that a colour, dun or yellow is meant. Ludwig would explain it as 'knotting snares or nooses.' Grassmann translates it by, 'des Mondverascheuchers, 'who scares away the Moon.'

4 *In forefront of the cars* : according to Sāyaṇa, the chariots of the Gods are intended. But, as Pischel observes (*Vedische Studien*, I. 124), Dadhikrāvan, the famous race-horse, was for 'the gentlemen of the turf' in King Trasadasyu's time what the matchless English horse Eclipse was in recent days. It seems probable that Dahhikrāvan may have been originally only a most distinguished racer, glorified and deified by the exaggerated praises of the bards of a people who ware passionately fond of chariot-racing.

Closely allied with Sūrya and with Morning, Ādityas, and Aṅgirases, and Vasus.

5 May Dadhikrās prepare the way we travel that we may pass along the path of Order.
May Agni hear us, and the Heavenly Army : hear us all Mighty Ones whom none deceiveth.

HYMN XLV. *Savitar.*

1. MAY the God Savitar, rich in goodly treasures, filling the region, borne by steeds, come hither,
In his hand holding much that makes men happy, lulling to slumber and arousing creatures.

2 Golden, sublime, and easy in their motion, his arms extend unto the bounds of heaven.
Now shall that mightiness of his be lauded: even Sūra yields to him in active vigour.

3 May this God Savitar, the Strong and Mighty, the Lord of precious wealth, vouchsafe us treasures.
May he, advancing his far-spreading lustre, bestow on us the food that feedeth mortals.

4 These songs praise Savitar whose tongue is pleasant, praise him whose arms are full, whose hands are lovely.
High vital strength, and manifold, may he grant us. Preserve us evermore, ye Gods, with blessings.

HYMN XLVI. *Rudra.*

1. To Rudra bring these songs, whose bow is firm and strong, the self-dependent God with swiftly-flying shafts,
The Wise, the Conqueror whom none may overcome, armed with sharp-pointed weapons : may he hear our call.

2 He through his lordship thinks on beings of the earth, on heavenly beings through his high imperial sway.
Come willingly to our doors that gladly welcome thee, and heal all sickness, Rudra, in our families.

3 May thy bright arrow which, shot down by thee from heaven, flieth upon the earth, pass us uninjured by.

2 *Sūra* : the Sun as distinguished from, or a different form of, Savitar who is said by Sāyaṇa to be the Sun before his rising.

Thou, very gracious God, hast thousand medicines: inflict no evil on our sons or progeny.

4 Slay us not, nor abandon us, O Rudra: let not thy noose, when thou art angry, seize us.

Give us trimmed grass and fame among the living. Preserve us evermore, ye Gods, with blessings.

HYMN XLVII. *Waters.*

1. MAY we obtain this day from you, O Waters, that wave of pure refreshment, which the pious

Made erst the special beverage of Indra, bright, stainless, rich in sweets and dropping fatness.

2 May the Floods' Offspring, he whose course is rapid, protect that wave most rich in sweets, O Waters,

That shall make Indra and the Vasus joyful. This may we gain from you to-day, we pious.

3 All-purifying, joying in their nature, to paths of Gods the Goddesses move onward.

They never violate the laws of Indra. Present the oil-rich offering to the Rivers.

4 Whom Sūrya with his bright beams hath attracted, and Indra dug the path for them to travel,

May these Streams give us ample room and freedom. Preserve us evermore, ye Gods, with blessings.

3 *Very gracious God*; *svapivāta*. 'This word is not explained in the printed text of Sāyaṇa, although in the "Varietas Lectionis," appended to his preface, Prof. Müller notes that in one MS., B. 4, *svapivāta* is rendered by *jitaprāṇa*, "he by whom life (or breath) is conquered." In the Nirukta, X. 7, it is explained by *svāpta-vacana*, "thou whose words are very suitable or authoritative."—Muir, *O. S. Texts*, IV. 314, where an exhaustive note on the word will be found. Wilson renders *svapivāta* by 'wind-appeaser,' and Grassmann by 'vielbegehrter,' 'much-desired.'

4 *Give us trimmed grass*: let us share in sacrifice. *Fame among the living*: the St. Petersburg Lexicon takes *jīvaśaṁse* to mean rule over the living. Others take the word as qualifying *barhiṣi*, trimmed grass, *i.e.* sacrifice, and signifying 'desired by the living,' 'to be praised among men,' 'promising (long) life.' See *Vedic Hymns*, Part I. p. 439.

---

1 *Wave of pure refreshment*: 'sweet essence of the earth; '*ūrmi* is said here to imply the *Soma* juice produced from the earth.'—Wilson.

3 *All-purifying*: *śatápavitrāḥ*; literally, with a hundred, that is, countless, means of purification. *The Goddesses*: the divine Waters.

HYMN XLVIII. *Ṛbhus.*

1. YE liberal Heroes, Vājas and Ṛbhukṣans, come and delight you with our flowing Soma.

May your strength, Vibhus, as ye come to meet us, turn hitherward your car that brings men profit.

2 May we as Ṛbhu with your Ṛbhus conquer strength with our strength, as Vibhus with the Vibhus.

May Vāja aid us in the fight for booty, and helped by Indra may we quell the foeman.

3 For they rule many tribes with high dominion, and conquer all their foes in close encounter.

May Indra, Vibhvan, Vāja, and Ṛbhukṣan destroy by turns the wicked foeman's valour.

4 Now, Deities, give us ample room and freedom: be all of you, one-minded, our protection.

So let the Vasus grant us strength and vigour. Preserve us evermore, ye Gods, with blessings.

HYMN XLIX. *Waters.*

1. FORTH from the middle of the flood the Waters—their chief the Sea—flow cleansing, never sleeping.

Indra, the Bull, the Thunderer, dug their channels: here let those Waters, Goddesses, protect me.

2 Waters which come from heaven, or those that wander dug from the earth, or flowing free by nature,

Bright, purifying, speeding to the Ocean, here let those Waters, Goddesses, protect me.

3 Those amid whom goes Varuṇa the Sovran, he who discriminates men's truth and falsehood—

Distilling meath, the bright, the purifying, here let those Waters, Goddesses, protect me.

4 They from whom Varuṇa the King, and

1 *Vājas and Ṛbhukṣans*: ye three, Ṛbhu, Vibhvan, and Vāja.

2 The meaning is, may we be as powerful as Ṛbhu, as mighty as the company of the Vibhus (another name of the Ṛbhus). Sāyaṇa explains *ṛbhu* as great, and *vibhvaḥ* as powerful. *In the fight for booty*: *vājasātau*; a play on the word and name *vāja*.

4 *The Vasus*: according to Sāyaṇa *vásavaḥ* here is an epithet of *Ṛbhávaḥ*, understood; the exalted (Ṛbhus).'—Wilson.

---

1 *The flood*: the ocean of air, the firmament.

Soma, and all the Deities drink strength and vigour,
They into whom Vaiśvānara Agni entered, here let those Waters, Goddesses, protect me.

HYMN L. *Various Deities.*

1. O MITRA-VARUṆA, guard and protect me here : let not that come to me which nests within and swells.
I drive afar the scorpion hateful to the sight : let not the winding worm touch me and wound my foot.

2 Eruption that appears upon the twofold joints, and that which overspreads the ankles and the knees,
May the refulgent Agni banish far away : let not the winding worm touch me and wound my foot.

3 The poison that is formed upon the Śalmali, that which is found in streams, that which the plants produce,
All this may all the Gods banish and drive away : let not the winding worm touch me and wound my foot.

4 The steep declivities, the valleys, and the heights, the channels full of water, and the waterless—
May those who swell with water, gracious Goddesses, never afflict us with the Śipada disease, may all the rivers keep us free from Śimidā.

HYMN LI. *Ādityas.*

1. THROUGH the Ādityas' most auspicious shelter, through their most recent succour may we conquer.
May they, the Mighty, giving ear, establish this sacrifice, to make us free and sinless.

2 Let Aditi rejoice and the Ādityas, Varuṇa, Mitra, Aryaman, most righteous.
May they, the Guardians of the world, protect us, and, to show favour, drink this day our Soma.

3 All Universal Deities, the Maruts, all the Ādityas, yea, and all the Ṛbhus,
Indra, and Agni, and the Aśvins, lauded. Preserve us evermore, ye Gods, with blessings.

HYMN LII. *Ādityas.*

1. MAY we be free from every bond, Ādityas ! a castle among Gods and men, ye Vasus.
Winning, may we win Varuṇa and Mitra, and, being, may we be, O Earth and Heaven.

2 May Varuṇa and Mitra grant this blessing, our Guardians, shelter to our seed and offspring.
Let us not suffer for another's trespass, nor do the thing that ye, O Vasus, punish.

3 The ever-prompt Aṅgirases, imploring riches from Savitar the God, obtained them.
So may our Father who is great and holy, and all the Gods, accordant, grant this favour.

HYMN LIII. *Heaven and Earth.*

1. As priest with solemn rites and adorations I worship Heaven and Earth, the High and Holy.
To them, great Parents of the Gods, have sages of ancient time, singing, assigned precedence.

2 With newest hymns set in the seat of Order, those the Two Parents, born before all others,
Come, Heaven and Earth, with the Celestial People, hither to us, for strong is your protection.

3 Yea, Heaven and Earth, ye hold in your possession full many a treasure for the liberal giver.

The deities are (1) Mitra and Varuṇa, (2) Agni, (3) Viśve Devāḥ, (4) Praise of the Rivers. Each stanza of the hymn is to be repeated as an antidote to the poison or disease which it specifies.

1 *That which nests within and swells* : 'the insidious and spreading (poison).—Wilson. Sāyaṇa supplies the substantive *viṣam*. *The scorpion* : *ajakāvám* ; the exact meaning is uncertain.

2 *Twofold joints* : of the arms and legs. Sāyaṇa's interpretation is different: 'the poison which is generated in the manifold knots (of trees).'—Wilson.

3 *The Śalmali* : the silk-cotton tree. *All the Gods*: or, the All-Gods or Viśvedevas.

4 *The Śipada disease* : 'perhaps the Vedic form of *Ślipada*, the Cochin leg.'—Wilson. *Śimidā* : apparently a female demon, or a disease, attributed to her malevolence.

3 *Universal Deities* : *viśve devāḥ* ; the All-Gods. *Lauded* : the sentence is incomplete, the substantives in the nominative case having no verb.

1 *Being* : really and truly being, rich, powerful, and distinguished.

3 *Our Father* : Varuṇa, the father of Vasiṣṭha; or Savitar, or Prajāpati may be intended.

3 *For the liberal giver* : or, for Sudās.

Grant us that wealth which comes in free abundance. Preserve us evermore, ye Gods, with blessings.

HYMN LIV. *Vāstoṣpati.*

1. Acknowledge us, O Guardian of the Homestead : bring no disease, and give us happy entrance.
Whate'er we ask of thee, be pleased to grant it, and prosper thou quadrupeds and bipeds.

2 Protector of the Home, be our promoter : increase our wealth in kine and steeds, O Indu.
May we be ever-youthful in thy friendship: be pleased in us as in his sons a father.

3 Through thy dear fellowship that bringeth welfare, may we be victors, Guardian of the Dwelling !
Protect our happiness in rest and labour. Preserve us evermore, ye Gods, with blessings.

HYMN LV. *Vāstoṣpati.*

1. Vāstoṣpati, who killest all disease and wearest every form,
Be an auspicious Friend to us.

2 When, O bright Son of Saramā, thou showest, tawny-hued ! thy teeth,
They gleam like lances' points within thy mouth when thou wouldst bite ; go thou to sleep.

3 Saramā's Son, retrace thy way : bark at the robber and the thief.
At Indra's singers barkest thou ? Why dost thou seek to terrify us ? Go to sleep.

4 Be on thy guard against the boar, and let the boar beware of thee.
At Indra's singers barkest thou ? Why dost thou seek to terrify us ? Go to sleep.

5 Sleep mother, let the father sleep, sleep dog and master of the house.
Let all the kinsmen sleep, sleep all the people who are round about.

6 The man who sits, the man who walks, and whosoever looks on us,
Of these we closely shut the eyes, even as we closely shut this house.

7 The Bull who hath a thousand horns, who rises up from out the sea,—
By him the Strong and Mighty One we lull and make the people sleep.

8 The women sleeping in the court, lying without, or stretched on beds,
The matrons with their odorous sweets—these, one and all, we lull to sleep.

HYMN LVI. *Maruts.*

1. Who are these radiant men in serried rank, Rudra's young heroes borne by noble steeds ?

2 Verily no one knoweth whence they sprang : they, and they only, know each other's birth.

3 They strew each other with their blasts, these Hawks : they strove together, roaring like the wind.

4 A sage was he who knew these mysteries, what in her udder mighty Pṛśni bore.

Vāstoṣpati is the Genius or tutelary God of the house. In this hymn he is addressed also as Indu, another name of Soma the Moon-God.

Vāstoṣpati is the deity of the first stanza, and Indra of the rest.

The metre is Gāyatrī in stanza I, Upariṣṭādbṛhatī ($8 \times 3 + 12$) in 2—4, and Anuṣṭup in 5—8, and the hymn appears to be made up of three corresponding pieces unconnected by their subjects.

2 *Son of Saramā* : Saramā, the hound of Indra, is mother of the two Sārameyas, the brindled watch-dogs of Yama, God of the Dead. This stanza and the two following appear to be addressed by the spirits of Indra's worshippers to one of the dogs who would prevent their entering the home of the pious.

5 This and the three following stanzas form a lullaby or sleep-song, probably sung as a charm by a lover on a secret visit to his love.

7 *The Bull who hath a thousand horns* : the Sun, whose setting brings the time of rest and sleep ; or perhaps the starry heaven is intended.

8 *With their odorous sweets* : wearing garlands of fragrant flowers on festive occasions, according to Sāyaṇa : 'decorated with holiday perfumes.'—Wilson. According to a legend mentioned by Sāyaṇa, Vasiṣṭha, having fasted for three days was entering the house of Varuṇa in hope of food, when the watch-dog set upon him and was put to sleep by the repetition of the last four verses, which are to be recited on similar occasions by thieves and house-breakers. See Wilson's note. The hymn has been discussed by Aufrecht, *Indische Studien*, IV. 337f, and by Lanman, *Sanskrit Reader*, p. 370.

---

3 *They strew each other with their blasts* : the meaning of *svapū́bhiḥ* is uncertain. 'They go together by their own pure paths.'—Wilson. 'They plucked each other with their beaks (?)'—M. Müller. 'They bestrew each other with light.'—Grassmann. 'They scatter dust over each other with besoms.'—Roth. I follow Professor Ludwig. The meaning appears to be that the Hawks or rapid Maruts are so crowded in their onward sweep that those in front feel the quick breath of those who follow. Similarly (VIII. 20. 21), the crowded Maruts are likened to cattle who lick each other's heads or humps.

4 *What in her udder* : according to Sāyaṇa, what beings (Maruts, etc.) mighty Pṛśni bore at her udder or in the firmament.

5 Ever victorious, through the Maruts, be this band of Heroes, nursing manly strength,
6 Most bright in splendour, fleetest on their way, close-knit to glory, strong with varied power.
7 Yea, mighty is your power and firm your strength : so, potent, with the Maruts, be the band.
8 Bright is your spirit, wrathful are your minds : your bold troop's minstrel is like one inspired.
9 Ever avert your blazing shaft from us, and let not your displeasure reach us here.
10 Your dear names, conquering Maruts, we invoke, calling aloud till we are satisfied.
11 Well-armed, impetuous in their haste, they deck themselves, their forms, with oblations : to you, the pure, ornaments made of gold.
12 Pure, Maruts, pure yourselves, are your oblations: to you, the pure, pure sacrifice I offer.
By Law they came to truth, the Law's observers, bright by their birth, and pure, and sanctifying.
13 Your rings, O Maruts, rest upon your shoulders, and chains of gold are twined upon your bosoms.
Gleaming with drops of rain, like lightning-flashes, after your wont ye whirl about your weapons.
14 Wide in the depth of air spread forth your glories, far, most adorable, ye bear your titles.
Maruts, accept this thousandfold allotment of household sacrifice and household treasure.
15 If, Maruts, ye regard the praise recited here at this mighty singer invocation,
Vouchsafe us quickly wealth with noble heroes, wealth which no man who hateth us may injure.
16 The Maruts, fleet as coursers, while they deck them like youths spectators of a festal meeting,
Linger, like beauteous colts, about the dwelling, like frisking calves, these who pour down the water.
17 So may the Maruts help us and be gracious, bringing free room to lovely Earth and Heaven.
Far be your bolt that slayeth men and cattle. Ye Vasus, turn yourselves to us with blessings.
18 The priest, when seated, loudly calls you, Maruts, praising in song your universal bounty.
He, Bulls ! who hath so much in his possession, free from duplicity, with hymns invokes you.
19 These Maruts bring the swift man to a stand-still, and strength with mightier strength they break and humble
These guard the singer from the man who hates him and lay their sore displeasure on the wicked.
20 These Maruts rouse even the poor and needy : the Vasus love him as an active champion.
Drive to a distance, O ye Bulls, the darkness : give us full store of children and descendants.
21 Never, O Maruts, may we lose your bounty, nor, car-borne Lords ! be hindmost when ye deal it.
Give us a share in that delightful treasure, the genuine wealth that, Bulls ! is your possession.
22 What time the men in fury rush together for running streams, for pastures, and for houses.
Then, O ye Maruts, ye who spring from Rudra, be our protectors in the strife with foemen.
23 Full many a deed ye did for our forefathers worthy of lauds which, even of old, they sang you.
The strong man, with the Maruts, wins in battle, the charger, with the Maruts, gains the booty.
24 Ours, O ye Maruts, be the vigorous Hero, the Lord Divine of men, the strong Sustainer,
With whom to fair lands we may cross the waters, and dwell in our own home with you beside us.

8 *Your bold troop's minstrel* : the leader of the Maruts' thunder-psalm. *Like one inspired* : *munírivа*, like a Muni or inspired saint. 'The sounds produced by the shaking of the trees are like the varied intonations of a reciter of praises, is Sāyaṇa's explanation.'—Wilson. Lanman translates differently : Clear is your whistling. Your hearts are wrathful as the wild onward-rush of a doughty troop.'

14 *Ye bear your titles* : you make yourselves known. 'You send down (the waters) that beat down (the dust).'—Wilson. *Nấmāni*, names, according to Sāyaṇa, means waters, because they bend down the dust, *pāṁsūn namayanti*.

24 *The Lord Divine* : literally, the Asura. *We may cross the waters* : the Maruts are besought to favour an expedition for the acquisition of new settlements on the farther side of a river.

25 May Indra, Mitra, Varuṇa and Agni, Waters, and Plants, and Trees accept our praises.
May we find shelter in the Marut's bosom. Preserve us evermore, ye Gods, with blessings.

HYMN LVII. *Maruts.*

1. YEA, through the power of your sweet juice, ye Holy ! the Marut host is glad at sacrifices.
They cause even spacious heaven and earth to tremble, they make the spring flow when they come, the Mighty.

2 The Maruts watch the man who sings their praises, promoters of the thought of him who worships.
Seat you on sacred grass in our assembly, this day, with friendly minds, to share the banquet.

3 No others gleam so brightly as these Maruts with their own forms, their golden gauds, their weapons.
With all adornments, decking earth and heaven, they heighten, for bright show, their common splendour.

4 Far from us be your blazing dart, O Maruts, when we, through human frailty, sin against you.
Let us not be exposed to that, ye Holy ! May your most loving favour still attend us.

5 May even what we have done delight the Maruts, the blameless Ones, the bright, the purifying.
Further us, O ye Holy, with your kindness : advance us mightily that we may prosper.

6 And may the Maruts, praised by all their titles, Heroes, enjoy the taste of our oblations.
Give us of Amṛta for the sake of offspring: awake the excellent fair stores of riches.

1 *Ye Holy* : according to Sāyaṇa, the Maruts are addressed. *The Marut host* : *nâma Mârutam* : the Marut name, *i.e.* those who are called Maruts.

This hymn, and all the hymns to the Maruts have been translated and explained in Max Müller's *Vedic Hymns*, I. (Sacred Books of the East, Vol. XXXII.)

6 *Give us of Amṛta* : the secret essence which pervades the world and nourishes and sustains all must naturally also be the element that promotes reproduction.—Ludwig. Von Roth explains the passage differently : 'Add us to (the number of) the people of eternity, *i.e.* to the blessed.' 'Vouchsafe our children long life.'—Grassmann. 'Bestow water upon our progeny.'—Wilson.

7 Hither, ye Maruts, praised, with all your succours, with all felicity come to our princes,
Who, of themselves, a hundredfold increase us. Preserve us evermore, ye Gods, with blessings.

HYMN LVIII. *Maruts.*

1. SING to the troop that pours down rain in common, the Mighty Company of celestial nature.
They make the world-halves tremble with their greatness : from depths of earth and sky they reach to heaven.

2 Yea, your birth, Maruts, was with wild commotion, ye who move swiftly, fierce in wrath, terrific.
Ye all-surpassing in your might and vigour, each looker on the light fears at your coming.

3 Give ample vital power unto our princes : let our fair praises gratify the Maruts.
As the way travelled helpeth people onward, so further us with your delightful succours.

4 Your favoured singer counts his wealth by hundreds : the strong steed whom ye favour wins a thousand.
The Sovran whom ye aid destroys the foeman. May this your gift, ye Shakers, be distinguished.

5 I call, as such, the Sons of bounteous Rudra : will not the Maruts turn again to us-ward ?
What secret sin or open stirs their anger, that we implore the Swift Ones to forgive us.

6 This eulogy of the Bounteous hath been spoken : accept, ye Maruts, this our hymn of praises.
Ye Bulls, keep those who hate us at a distance. Preserve us evermore, ye Gods, with blessings.

HYMN LIX. *Maruts.*

1. WHOMSO ye rescue here and there, whomso ye guide, O Deities,

1 *From depths of earth and sky* : *nirṛti* here is said to be synonymous with *bhūmi*, earth, and *avaṁśá*, the unsupported, with *antarikṣa*, firmament. But *nirṛti*, Death, Destruction, as identified with *bhūmi*, may be the Pṛthivī of the atmosphere (See V. 84.), which must originally have been considered to be the place of departed spirits.

2 *Each looker on the light* : *viśvaḥ svardṛk* : according to Sāyaṇa, every tree.

To him give shelter, Agni, Mitra, Varuṇa, ye Maruts, and thou Aryaman.

2 Through your kind favour, Gods, on some auspicious day, the worshipper subdues his foes.
That man increases home and strengthening ample food who brings you offerings as ye list.

3 Vasiṣṭha will not overlook the lowliest one among you all.
O Maruts, of our Soma juice effused to-day drink all of you with eager haste.

4 Your succour in the battle injures not the man to whom ye, Heroes, grant your gifts.
May your most recent favour turn to us again. Come quickly, ye who fain would drink.

5 Come hitherward to drink the juice, O ye whose bounties give you joy.
These offerings are for you, these, Maruts, I present. Go not to any place but this.

6 Sit on our sacred grass, be graciously inclined to give the wealth for which we long,
To take delight, ye Maruts, Friends of all, with Svāhā, in sweet Soma juice.

7 Decking the beauty of their forms in secret the Swans with purple backs have flown down hither.
Around me all the Company hath settled, like joyous Heroes glad in our libation.

8 Maruts, the man whose wrath is hard to master, he who would slay us ere we think, O Vasus,
May he be tangled in the toils of mischief; smite ye him down with your most flaming weapon.

9 O Maruts, ye consuming Gods, enjoy this offering brought for you,
To help us, ye who slay the foe.

10 Sharers of household sacrifice, come, Maruts, stay not far away,
That ye may help us, Bounteous Ones.

11 Here, Self-strong Maruts, yea, even here, ye Sages with your sunbright skins !
I dedicate your sacrifice.

12 Tryambaka we worship, sweet augmenter of prosperity.
As from its stem the cucumber, so may I be released from death, not reft of immortality.

HYMN LX. *Mitra-Varuṇa.*

1. When thou, O Sun, this day, arising sinless, shalt speak the truth to Varuṇa and Mitra,
O Aditi, may all the Deities love us, and thou, O Aryaman, while we are singing.

2 Looking on man, O Varuṇa and Mitra, this Sun ascendeth up by both the pathways,
Guardian of all things fixt, of all that moveth, beholding good and evil acts of mortals.

3 He from their home hath yoked the Seven gold Coursers who, dropping oil and fatness, carry Sūrya.
Yours, Varuṇa and Mitra, he surveyeth the worlds and living creatures like a herdsman.

4 Your coursers rich in store of sweets have mounted : to the bright ocean Sūrya hath ascended,
For whom the Ādityas make his pathway ready, Aryaman, Mitra, Varuṇa, accordant.

5 For these, even Aryaman, Varuṇa and Mitra, are the chastisers of all guile and falsehood.
These, Aditi's Sons, infallible and mighty, have waxen in the home of law Eternal.

4 *Injures not* : a litotes for, is of the greatest advantage to.

5 *Whose bounties give you joy* : or follow each other closely, and are ever fresh and ready.

6 *Svāhā* : an exclamation, like Ave ! or Hail ! used in making oblations to the Gods.

7 *With purple backs* : *nīlapṛṣṭhāḥ*: cf. Horace's 'purpurei olores.'

8 *Mischief* : or one of the malicious spirits called Druhs.

12 *Tryambaka* : a name of Rudra. *Sweet* : according to Sāyaṇa, *sugándhim*, sweet-smelling, means here, 'whose fame is fragrant.' 'The verse occurs in the *Yajur-Veda*, 6. 30, and is, in some instances, differently interpreted; *Tryambaka* is termed *netratrayopetam Rudram* the triocular Rudra : *sugandhim*, *divyagandhopetam*, of celestial fragrance : the *urváruka* is said to mean the *karkandhu* [fruit of the jujube-tree), which, when ripe, falls of itself from its stalk.'—Wilson.

The hymn is addressed chiefly to Mitra and Varuṇa, but Sūrya or the Sun is the deity of the first stanza.

1 *Sinless* : Sāyaṇa makes *ánāgāḥ*=*anāgasaḥ* : 'declare the truth...that we are void of sin.'—Wilson. But this seems forced, and the implied meaning of the poet is clear enough if the word is taken in its usual signification.

2 *Both the pathways* : near the earth and high in the firmament.

6 These, Mitra, Varuṇa whom none deceiveth, with great power quicken even the fool to wisdom,
And, wakening, moreover, thoughtful insight, lead it by easy paths o'er grief and trouble.

7 They ever vigilant, with eyes that close not, caring for heaven and earth, lead on the thoughtless.
Even in the river's bed there is a shallow: across this broad expanse may they conduct us.

8 When Aditi and Varuṇa and Mitra, like guardians, give Sudās their friendly shelter,
Granting him sons and lineal succession, let us not, bold ones ! move the Gods to anger.

9 May he with offerings purify the altar from any stains of Varuṇa's reviler.
Aryaman save us from all those who hate us : give room and freedom to Sudās, ye Mighty.

10 Hid from our eyes is their resplendent meeting : by their mysterious might they hold dominion.
Heroes ! we cry trembling in fear before you, even in the greatness of your power have mercy.

11 He who wins favour for his prayer by worship, that he may gain him strength and highest riches,
That good man's mind the Mighty Ones will follow : they have brought comfort to his spacious dwelling.

12 This priestly task, Gods ! Varuṇa and Mitra ! hath been performed for you at sacrifices.
Convey us safely over every peril. Preserve us evermore, ye Gods, with blessings.

HYMN LXI. *Mitra-Varuṇa.*

1. O VARUṆA and Mitra, Sūrya spreading the beauteous light of you Twain Gods ariseth.
He who beholdeth all existing creatures observeth well the zeal that is in mortals.

2 The holy sage, renowned afar, directeth his hymns to you, O Varuṇa and Mitra,—
He whose devotions, sapient Gods, ye favour so that ye fill, as 'twere, with power his autumns.

3 From the wide earth, O Varuṇa and Mitra, from the great lofty heaven, ye Bounteous Givers,
Have in the fields and houses set your warders who visit every spot and watch unceasing.

4 I praise the strength of Varuṇa and Mitra : that strength, by mightiness, keeps both worlds asunder.
Heroless pass the months of the ungodly : he who loves sacrifice makes his home enduring.

5 Steers, all infallible are these your people in whom no wondrous thing is seen, no worship.
Guile follows close the men who are untruthful : no secrets may be hidden from your knowledge.

6 I will exalt your sacrifice with homage : as priest, I, Mitra-Varuṇa, invoke you.
May these new hymns and prayers that I have fashioned delight you to the profit of the singer.

7 This priestly task, Gods ! Varuṇa and Mitra ! hath been performed for you at sacrifices.
Convey us safely over every peril. Preserve us evermore, ye Gods, with blessings.

6 *Mitra, Varuṇa* : and Aryaman, understood : the verbs are in the plural.

8 *Bold ones* : the warning is addressed to the people of Sudās, who has been frequently mentioned in preceding hymns.

9 *May he* : Agni may be intended. *Varuṇa's reviler*: those who speak evil of princes like Sudās, Varuṇa being the king's prototype.—Ludwig.

10 *Their resplendent meeting* : that of Mitra, Varuṇa, and Aryaman.

11 *Have brought comfort to his spacious dwelling* : 'bestow a spacious mansion for a dwelling upon him.'—Wilson.

2 *Autumns* : years of his life.

5 This stanza is difficult. Sāyaṇa's interpretation as given by Wilson is : 'Unperplexed, all-pervading showerers (of benefits), these praises are for you, in which nothing surprising, no adoration (worthy of you), is beheld : the insincere commendations of men serve as offences : eulogies of you, although offered in secret are not unappreciated.' The version of the *Seventy Hymns* is somewhat as follows : 'All your avenging spirits, O ye Mighty, follow unerringly the sinner's traces. They have no sign that men may mark, no figure. Naught is so secret that ye fail to know it.' This latter involves a slight alteration of the text. I prefer Ludwig's interpretation, although it is not absolutely convincing.

6 *To the profit of the singer* : See *Vedische Studien*, I. 43.

HYMN LXII. *Mitra-Varuṇa.*

1\. Sūrya hath sent aloft his beams of splendour o'er all the tribes of men in countless places.
Together with the heaven he shines apparent, formed by his Makers well with power and wisdom.

2 So hast thou mounted up before us, Sūrya, through these our praises, with fleet dappled horses.
Declare us free from all offence to Mitra, and Varuṇa, and Aryaman, and Agni.

3 May holy Agni, Varuṇa, and Mitra send down their riches upon us in thousands.
May they, the Bright Ones, make our praise-song perfect, and, when we laud them, grant us all our wishes.

4 O undivided Heaven and Earth, preserve us, us, Lofty Ones ! your nobly-born descendants.
Let us not anger Varuṇa, nor Vāyu, nor him, the dearest Friend of mortals, Mitra.

5 Stretch forth your arms and let our lives be lengthened : with fatness dew the pastures of our cattle.
Ye Youthful, make us famed among the people : hear, Mitra-Varuṇa, these mine invocations.

6 Now Mitra, Varuṇa, Aryaman vouchsafe us freedom and room, for us and for our children.
May we find paths all fair and good to travel. Preserve us evermore, ye Gods, with blessings.

HYMN LXIII. *Mitra-Varuṇa.*

1\. Common to all mankind, auspicious Sūrya, he who beholdeth all, is mounting upward ;
The God, the eye of Varuṇa and Mitra, who rolled up darkness like a piece of leather.

2 Sūrya's great ensign, restless as the billow, that urgeth men to action, is advancing :
Onward he still would roll the wheel well-rounded, which Etaśa, harnessed to the car-pole, moveth.

3 Refulgent from the bosom of the Mornings, he in whom singers take delight ascendeth.
This Savitar, God, is my chief joy and pleasure, who breaketh not the universal statute.

4 Golden, far-seeing, from the heaven he riseth : far is his goal, he hasteth on resplendent.
Men, verily, inspirited by Sūrya speed to their aims and do the work assigned them.

5 Where the immortals have prepared his pathway he flieth through the region like a falcon.
With homage and oblations will we serve you, O Mitra-Varuṇa, when the Sun hath risen.

6 Now Mitra, Varuṇa, Aryaman vouchsafe us freedom and room, for us and for our children.
May we find paths all fair and good to travel. Preserve us evermore, ye Gods, with blessings.

---

2 *Etaśa* : or the bright or dappled steed ; one of the horses of the Sun.

3 *Breaketh not* : faithfully observes and supports.

HYMN LXIV. *Mitra-Varuṇa.*

1\. Ye Twain who rule, in heaven and earth, the region, clothed be your clouds in robes of oil and fatness.
May the imperial Varuṇa, and Mitra, and high-born Aryaman accept our presents.

2 Kings, guards of mighty everlasting Order, come hitherward, ye Princes, Lords of Rivers.
Send us from heaven, O Varuṇa and Mitra, rain and sweet food, ye who pour down your bounties.

3 May the dear God, and Varuṇa and Mitra conduct us by the most effective pathways,
That foes may say unto Sudās our chieftain, May, we, too, joy in food with Gods to guard us.

4 Him who hath wrought for you this car in spirit, who makes the song rise upward and sustains it,
Bedew with fatness, Varuṇa and Mitra : ye Kings, make glad the pleasant dwelling-places.

5 To you this laud, O Varuṇa and Mitra is offered like bright Soma juice to Vāyu.

1 *Clothed be your clouds* : 'A covering cloud of sacred oil attends you (V. 62. 4). 'Impelled by you, (the clouds) assume the form of rain.'—Wilson.

3 The second half of the stanza is obscure. The meaning appears to be that even our foes, the godless who offer no sacrifices, shall envy the prosperity which we enjoy through the liberality of Sudās, and shall wish to follow our example, to sacrifice to the Gods and to enjoy their protection and the blessings which they send.

4 *This car* : this carefully-formed hymn which goes, like a chariot, to the Gods.

5 *To Vāyu* : who receives the first draught of Soma juice at the morning libation.

Favour our songs of praise, wake thought and spirit. Preserve us evermore, ye Gods, with blessings.

HYMN LXV. *Mitra-Varuṇa.*

1. WITH hymns I call you, when the Sun hath risen, Mitra, and Varuṇa whose thoughts are holy,
Whose Power Divine, supreme and everlasting, comes with good heed at each man's supplication.

2 For they are Asuras of Gods, the friendly: make, both of you, our lands exceeding fruitful.
May we obtain you, Varuṇa and Mitra, wherever Heaven and Earth and days may bless us.

3 Bonds of the sinner, they bear many nooses: the wicked mortal hardly may escape them.
Varuṇa-Mitra, may your path of Order bear us o'er trouble as a boat o'er waters.

4 Come, taste our offering, Varuṇa and Mitra: bedew our pasture with sweet food and fatness.
Pour down in plenty here upon the people the choicest of your fair celestial water.

5 To you this laud, O Varuṇa and Mitra, is offered, like bright Soma juice to Vāyu.
Favour our songs of praise, wake thought and spirit. Preserve us evermore, ye Gods, with blessings.

HYMN LXVI *Mitra-Varuṇa.*

1. LET our strong hymn of praise go forth, the laud of Mitra-Varuṇa,
With homage to that high-born Pair;

2 The Two exceeding wise, the Sons of Dakṣa, whom the gods ordained
For lordship, excellently great.

3 Such, Guardians of our homes and us, O Mitra-Varuṇa, fulfil
The thoughts of those who sing your praise.

4 So when the Sun hath risen to-day, may sinless Mitra, Aryaman,
Bhaga, and Savitar send us forth.

5 May this our home be guarded well: forward, ye Bounteous, on the way,
Who bear us safely o'er distress.

6. And those Self-reigning, Aditi, whose statute is inviolate,
The Kings who rule a vast domain.

7 Soon as the Sun hath risen, to you, to Mitra-Varuṇa, I sing,
And Aryaman who slays the foe.

8 With wealth of gold may this my song bring unmolested power and might,
And, Brahmans, gain the sacrifice.

9 May we be thine, God Varuṇa, and with our princes, Mitra, thine:
Food and Heaven's light will we obtain.

10 Many are they who strengthen Law, Sun-eyed, with Agni for their tongue,
They who direct the three great gatherings with their thoughts, yea, all things with surpassing might.

11 They who have stablished year and month and then the day, night, sacrifice and holy verse,
Varuṇa, Mitra, Aryaman, the Kings, have won dominion which none else may gain.

12 So at the rising of the Sun we think of you with hymns to-day,
Even as Varuṇa, Mitra, Aryaman deserve: ye are the charioteers of Law.

13 True to Law, born in Law, the strengtheners of Law, terrible, haters of the false,
In their felicity which gives the best defence may we men and our princes dwell.

The hymn appears to be composed of fragments of other hymns with a few original additions. Cf. VII 63. 5; 66. 7. 12; VI. 68. 8; VII. 62. 5; III. 62. 16. See von Bradke, *Dyaus Asura*, 3—5.

1 *Power Divine*: *asuryám*: Asurahood. *Whose*: refers to Mitra and Varuṇa.

2 *Asuras of Gods*: the high or ruling Gods of all the deities.

3 *Bonds*: binders. *Many nooses*: 'Your guiles, ye Holy Ones, to quell oppressors, your snares spread out against the foe, Ādityas' (II. 27. 16).

———

2 *Sons of Dakṣa*: See VI. 50. 2. *For lordship*: literally for Asurahood.

4 *Sinless*: Sāyaṇa here, as in VII. 60. 1, takes *ánāgāḥ* as = *anāgasaḥ*, as that, according to his interpretation, the translation would be: may Savitar, Mitra, Aryaman, and Bhaga send us sinless forth.

6 *Aditi* is out of place here, as there is no copulative in the text: whose mother is Aditi, seems to be intended.

8 *And, Brahmans, gain the sacrifice*: the exact meaning is uncertain: 'May it (be effective), sages, for the fulfilment of (the objects of) the sacrifice.'—Wilson.

10 *The three great gatherings*: or three assemblies. The meaning it not clear. Ludwig is of opinion that the three castes are intended.

The meaning of stanzas 10 and 11 is that although there be many deities, Varuṇa, Mitra, and Aryaman are supreme.

14 Uprises, on the slope of heaven, that marvel that attracts the sight,
As swift celestial Etaśa bears it away, prepared for every eye to see.
15 Lord of each single head, of fixt and moving things, equally through the whole expanse,
The Seven sister Bays bear Sūrya on his car, to bring us wealth and happi
16 A hundred autumns may we see that bright Eye, God-ordained, arise :
A hundred autumns may we live.
17 Infallible through your wisdom, come hither, resplendent Varuṇa,
And Mitra, to the Soma draught.
18 Come as the laws of Heaven ordain, Varuṇa, Mitra, void of guile :
Press near and drink the Soma juice.
19 Come, Mitra, Varuṇa, accept, Heroes, our sacrificial gift :
Drink Soma, ye who strengthen Law.

HYMN LXVII. *Aśvins.*

1. I WITH a holy heart that brings oblation will sing forth praise to meet your car, ye Princes,
Which, Much-desired ! hath wakened as your envoy. I call you hither as a son his parents.
2 Brightly hath Agni shone by us enkindled: the limits even of darkness were apparent.
Eastward is seen the Banner of the Morning, the Banner born to give Heaven's Daughter glory.
3 With hymns the deft priest is about you, Aśvins, the eloquent priest attends you now, Nāsatyas.
Come by the paths that ye are wont to travel, on car that finds the light, laden with treasure.
4 When, suppliant for your help, Lovers of Sweetness ! I seeking wealth call you to our libation,
Hitherward let your vigorous horses bear you : drink ye with us the well-pressed Soma juices.
5 Bring forward, Aśvins, Gods, to its fulfilment my never-wearied prayer that asks for riches.
Vouchsafe us all high spirit in the combat, and with your powers, O Lords of Power, assist us.
6 Favour us in these prayers of ours, O Aśvins. May we have genial vigour, ne'er to fail us.
So may we, strong in children and descendants, go, wealthy, to the banquet that awaits you.
7 Lovers of Sweetness, we have brought this treasure to you as 'twere an envoy sent for friendship.
Come unto us with spirits free from anger, in homes of men enjoying our oblation.
8 With one, the same, intention, ye swift movers, o'er the Seven Rivers hath your chariot travelled.
Yoked by the Gods, your strong steeds never weary while speeding forward at the pole they bear you.
9 Exhaustless be your bounty to our princes who with their wealth incite the gift of riches,
Who further friendship with their noble natures, combining wealth in kine with wealth in horses.
10 Now hear, O Youthful Twain, mine invocation : come, Aśvins, to the home where food aboundeth.
Vouchsafe us wealth, do honour to our nobles. Preserve us evermore, ye Gods, with blessings.

HYMN LXVIII. *Aśvins.*

1. COME, radiant Aśvins, with your noble horses : accept your servant's hymns, ye Wonder-Workers :
Enjoy oblations which we bring to greet you.
2 The gladdening juices stand prepared before you : come quickly and partake of mine oblation.
Pass by the calling of our foe and hear us.
3 Your chariot with a hundred aids, O Aśvins, beareth you swift as thought across the regions,
Speeding to us, O ye whose wealth is Sūryā.

15 *Sister Bays* : the Harits. See IV. 6. 9; 13.3.

18 *Come as the laws of Heaven ordain* : 'Come with your glories from the sky.'—Sāyaṇa. 'Come hither with the hosts of heaven.'– Grassmann.

1 *Much-desired* : 'adorable.'—Wilson.

9 *Incite the gift of riches* : move the Gods to give riches in return.

Friendship : or, a kinsman, meaning, apparently, the priest.

3 *Whose wealth is Sūryā* : having Sūryā for your possession or treasure. Sūryā, the daughter of the Sun, is the consort of the Aśvins. See I. 116. 17.

4 What time this stone of yours, the Gods' adorer, upraised sounds forth for you as Soma-presser,
Let the priest bring you, Fair Ones, through oblations.

5 The nourishment ye have is, truly, wondrous : ye gave thereof a quickening store to Atri,
Who, being dear to you, receives your favour.

6 That gift, which all may gain, ye gave Cyavāna, when he grew old, who offered you oblations,
When ye bestowed on him enduring beauty.

7 What time his wicked friends abandoned Bhujyu, O Aśvins, in the middle of the ocean,
Your horse delivered him, your faithful servant.

8 Ye lent your aid to Vṛka when exhausted, and listened when invoked to Śayu's calling.
Ye made the cow pour forth her milk like water, and, Aśvins, strengthened with your strength the barren.

9 With his fair hymns this singer, too, extols you, waking with glad thoughts at the break of morning.
May the cow nourish him with milk to feed him. Preserve us evermore, ye Gods, with blessings.

4 *The Gods' adorer* ; *devayā́ḥ* : literally, turning or going to the Gods, inasmuch as it is employed in preparing the Soma juice. *The priest* : here, perhaps, the pressing-stone.

5 *A quickening store* : the meaning of *mā́hiṣvantam*, which does not occur elsewhere, is uncertain. According to Sāyaṇa it means a pit or cavern : ye liberated Atri from the cavern, or, literally, ye separated the cavern from Atri. For the legend, See I. 116. 12.

6 *Which all may gain* ; which you Aśvins are ready to grant to every worshipper who needs it. For the story of Cyavāna, See I. 116. 10; 117. 13; 118. 6.

7 *Bhujyu* : See Vol. I., Index. *Your horse* : this meaning is suggested by von Roth for the uncertain word *árāvā*, which generally appears to mean hostile or illiberal but may perhaps stand in this passage for *arvā*, a common word signifying horse. See I. 117. 14:—'With horses brown of hue that flew with swift wings ye brought back Bhujyu from the sea of billows.' See also VII. 69. 7.

8 *Vṛka* : literally wolf, or robber. Some man so named seems to be meant. *Śayu*: See I. 118. 8; VI. 13.5.

9 *This singer* : the Ṛṣi Vasiṣṭha. *The cow* : that is brought to supply the milk required for libations.

HYMN LXIX. *Aśvins.*

1. May your gold chariot, drawn by vigorous horses, come to us, blocking up the earth and heaven,
Bright with its fellies while its way drops fatness, food-laden, rich in coursers, man's protector.

2 Let it approach, yoked by the will, three-seated, extending far and wide o'er fivefold beings,
Whereon ye visit God-adoring races, bending your course whither ye will, O Aśvins.

3 Renowned, with noble horses, come ye hither : drink, Wondrous Pair, the cup that holds sweet juices.
Your car whereon your Spouse is wont to travel marks with its track the farthest ends of heaven.

4 When night was turning to the grey of morning the Maiden, Sūrya's Daughter, chose your splendour.
When with your power and might ye aid the pious he comes through heat to life by your assistance.

5 O Chariot-borne, this car of yours invested with rays of light comes harnessed to our dwelling.
Herewith, O Aśvins, while the dawn is breaking, to this our sacrifice bring peace and blessing.

6 Like the wild cattle thirsty for the lightning, Heroes, come nigh this day to our libations.
Men call on you with hymns in many places, but let not other worshippers detain you.

7 Bhujyu, abandoned in the midst of ocean, ye raised from out the water with your horses,
Uninjured, winged, flagging not, undaunted, with deeds of wonder saving him, O Aśvins.

8 Now hear, O Youthful Twain, mine invocation : come, Aśvins, to the home where food aboundeth.

2 *Fivefold beings* : '*sarvaprāṇinaḥ*,' all living beings, says Sāyaṇa.

3 *Your Spouse* : Sūryā, daughter of the Sun.

4 *Chose your splendour* : See I. 116. 17.

6 *Thirsty for the lightning* : which immediately precedes, or accompanies, the rain they long for.

7 *Horses* : not in the text, but supplied by Sāyaṇa and obviously understood. See preceding hymn, 7, note.

Vouchsafe us wealth, do honour to our nobles. Preserve us evermore, ye Gods, with blessings.

HYMN LXX. *Aśvins.*

1. Rich in all blessings, Aśvins come ye hither: this place on earth is called your own possession,
Like a strong horse with a fair back it standeth, whereon, as in a lap, ye seat you firmly.

2 This most delightful eulogy awaits you: in the man's house drink-offering hath been heated,
Which bringeth you over the seas and rivers, yoking as 'twere two well-matched shining horses.

3 Whatever dwellings ye possess, O Aśvins, in fields of men or in the streams of heaven,
Resting upon the summit of the mountain, or bringing food to him who gives oblation,

4 Delight yourselves, ye Gods, in plants and waters when Ṛṣis give them and ye find they suit you.
Enriching us with treasures in abundance ye have looked back to former generations.

5 Aśvins, though ye have heard them oft aforetime, regard the many prayers which Ṛṣis offer.
Come to the man even as his heart desireth: may we enjoy your most delightful favour.

6 Come to the sacrifice offered you, Nāsatyas, with men, oblations, and prayer duly uttered.
Come to Vasiṣṭha as his heart desireth, for unto you these holy hymns are chanted.

7 This is the thought, this is the song, O Aśvins: accept this hymn of ours, ye Steers, with favour.
May these our prayers addressed to you come nigh you. Preserve us evermore, ye Gods, with blessings.

1 *This place*: the altar.

2 *Drink-offering*: *gharmá*: the libation of hot milk; or, the caldron in which it is prepared.

4 *Ye have looked back to former generations*: Sāyaṇa explains *yugāni* differently: '(favour us) as you have favoured former couples [*i.e.* sacrificers and their wives].' —Wilson.

5 *The man*: the institutor of the sacrifice.

HYMN LXXI. *Aśvins.*

1. The Night retireth from the Dawn her Sister; the Dark one yieldeth to the Red her pathway.
Let us invoke you rich in steeds and cattle: by day and night keep far from us the arrow.

2 Bearing rich treasure in your car, O Aśvins, come to the mortal who presents oblation.
Keep at a distance penury and sickness; Lovers of Sweetness, day and night preserve us.

3 May your strong horses, seeking bliss, bring hither your chariot at the earliest flush of morning.
With coursers yoked by Law drive hither, Aśvins, your car whose reins are light, laden with treasure.

4 The chariot, Princes, that conveys you, moving at daylight, triple-seated, fraught with riches,
Even with this come unto us, Nāsatyas, that laden with all food it may approach us.

5 Ye freed Cyavāna from old age and weakness: ye brought the courser fleet of food to Pedu.
Ye rescued Atri from distress and darkness, and loosed for Jāhuṣa the bonds that bound him.

6 This is the thought, this is the song, O Aśvins: accept this hymn of ours, ye Steers, with favour.
May these our prayers addressed to you come nigh you. Preserve us evermore, ye Gods, with blessings.

HYMN LXXII. *Aśvins.*

1. Come, O Nāsatyas, on your car resplendent, rich in abundant wealth of kine and horses.
As harnessed steeds, all our laudations follow you whose forms shine with most delightful beauty.

2 Come with the Gods associate, come ye hither to us, Nāsatyas, with your car accordant.

1 *The Red*: the Sun. *The arrow*: of disease and death.

3 *Seeking bliss*: for men.

5 For *Cyavāna*, *Pedu*, *Atri*, and *Jāhuṣa*, See Vol. I. Index. The re-appearance, heralded by the Aśvins or Gods of Twilight, of the departed Sun appears to be symbolized in all these legends.

'Twixt you and us there is ancestral friendship and common kin : remember and regard it.

3 Awakened are the songs that praise the Aśvins, the kindred prayers and the Celestial Mornings.
Inviting those we long for, Earth and Heaven, the singer calleth these Nāsatyas hither.

4 What time the Dawns break forth in light, O Aśvins, to you the poets offer their devotions.
God Savitar hath sent aloft his splendour, and fires sing praises with the kindled fuel.

5 Come from the west, come from the east, Nāsatyas, come, Aśvins, from below and from above us.
Bring wealth from all sides for the Fivefold People. Preserve us evermore, ye Gods, with blessings.

HYMN LXXIII. *Aśvins.*

1. We have o'erpassed the limit of this darkness while, worshipping the Gods, we sang their praises.
The song invoketh both Immortal Aśvins far-reaching, born of old, great Wonder-Workers.

2 And, O Nāsatyas, man's dear Priest is seated, who brings to sacrifice and offers worship,
Be near and taste the pleasant juice, O Aśvins : with food, I call you to the sacrifices.

3 We choosing you, have let our worship follow its course : ye Steers, accept this hymn with favour.
Obeying you as your appointed servant, Vasiṣṭha singing hath with lauds aroused you.

4 And these Two Priests come nigh unto our people, united, demon-slayers, mighty-handed.
The juices that exhilarate are mingled. Injure us not, but come with happy fortune.

5 Come from the west, come from the east, Nāsatyas, come, Aśvins, from below and from above us.
Bring wealth from all sides for the Fivefold People. Preserve us evermore, ye Gods, with blessings.

HYMN LXXIV. *Aśvins.*

1. These morning sacrifices call you, Aśvins, at the break of day.
For help have I invoked you rich in power and might : for, house by house ye visit all.

2 O Heroes, ye bestow wonderful nourishment: send it to him whose songs are sweet.
Accordant, both of you, drive your car down to us, and drink the savoury Soma juice.

3 Approach ye and be near to us : drink, O ye Aśvins, of the meath.
Draw forth the milk, ye Mighty, rich in genuine wealth : injure us not, and come to us.

4 The horses that convey you in their rapid flight down to the worshipper's abode,
With these your speedy coursers, Heroes, Aśvins, come, ye Gods, come well-inclined to us.

5 Yea, verily, our princes seek the Aśvins in pursuit of food.
These shall give lasting glory to our liberal lords, and, both Nāsatyas, shelter us.

6 Those who have led the way, like cars, offending none, those who are guardians of the men—
Also through their own might the heroes have grown strong, and dwell in safe and happy homes.

HYMN LXXV. *Dawn.*

1. Born in the heavens the Dawn hath flushed, and showing her majesty is come as Law ordaineth.
She hath uncovered fiends and hateful darkness ; best of Aṅgirases, hath waked the pathways.

2 Rouse us this day to high and happy fortune : to great felicity, O Dawn, promote us.

---

5 *The Fivefold People* : the five Āryan tribes. See I. 7. 9.

The first half-line has occurred before in I. 92. 6, and 183. 6.

2 *Man's dear Priest* : Agni.

4 *These Two Priests* : the Aśvins. *Demon-slayers* : slayers of Rākṣasas and evil spirits of the night which disappear at the coming of the heralds of day.

---

3 *Draw forth the milk* : milk the sweet rain from the firmament.

6 *Who have led the way, like cars* : wealthy nobles or princes, 'the heroes' of the second line.

---

1 *Best of Aṅgirases* : endowed with the noblest characteristics of the holy Aṅgirases. *Waked the pathways*: lighted them for men to use.

Vouchsafe us manifold and splendid riches, famed among mortals, man-befriending Goddess!

3 See, lovely Morning's everlasting splendours, bright with their varied colours, have approached us.

Filling the region of mid-air, producing the rites of holy worship, they have mounted.

4 She yokes her chariot far away, and swiftly visits the lands where the Five Tribes are settled,

Looking upon the works and ways of mortals, Daughter of Heaven, the world's Imperial Lady.

5 She who is rich in spoil, the Spouse of Sūrya, wondrously opulent, rules all wealth and treasures.

Consumer of our youth, the seers extol her: lauded by priests rich Dawn shines out refulgent.

6 Apparent are the steeds of varied colour, the red steeds carrying resplendent Morning.

On her all-lovely car she comes, the Fair One, and brings rich treasure for her faithful servant.

7 True with the True and Mighty with the Mighty, with Gods a Goddess, Holy with the Holy,

She brake strong fences down and gave the cattle: the kine were lowing as they greeted Morning.

8 O Dawn, now give us wealth in kine and heroes, and horses, fraught with manifold enjoyment.

Protect our sacred grass from man's reproaches. Preserve us evermore, ye Gods, with blessings.

HYMN LXXVI. *Dawn.*

1. Savitar God of all men hath sent upward his light, designed for all mankind, immortal.

Through the Gods' power that Eye was first created. Dawn hath made all the universe apparent.

2 I see the paths which Gods are wont to travel, innocuous paths made ready by the Vasus.

Eastward the flag of Dawn hath been uplifted; she hath come hither o'er the tops of houses.

3 Great is, in truth, the number of the Mornings which were aforetime at the Sun's uprising.

Since thou, O Dawn, hast been beheld repairing as to thy love, as one no more to leave him.

4 They were the Gods' companions at the banquet, the ancient sages true to Law Eternal.

The Fathers found the light that lay in darkness, and with effectual words begat the Morning.

5 Meeting together in the same enclosure, they strive not, of one mind, one with another.

They never break the Gods' eternal statutes, and injure none, in rivalry with Vasus.

6 Extolling thee, Blest Goddess, the Vasiṣṭhas, awake at early morn, with lauds implore thee.

Leader of kine and Queen of all that strengthens, shine, come as first to us, O high-born Morning.

7 She bringeth bounty and sweet charm of voices. The flushing Dawn is sung by the Vasiṣṭhas,

Giving us riches famed to distant places. Preserve us evermore, ye Gods, with blessings.

HYMN LXXVII. *Dawn.*

1. She hath shone brightly like a youthful woman, stirring to motion every living creature.

Agni hath come to feed on mortals' fuel. She hath made light and chased away the darkness.

2 Turned to this All, far-spreading, she hath risen and shone in brightness with white robes about her.

She hath beamed forth lovely with golden colours, Mother of kine, Guide of the days she bringeth.

---

7 *Gave the cattle*: restored the rays of light that had been imprisoned by the demons of darkness.

---

3 *As to thy love*: to the Sun, who is sometimes called the lover and sometimes the husband of Uṣas or Dawn.

4 *The Fathers*: the ancestors of the Ṛṣis in the spirit-world are associated with the Gods as companions, friends, and assistants. See M. Müller, *India, What can it Teach us?* pp. 223, 224.

5 *In the same enclosure*: the vast aerial hall in which the Gods assemble.

---

1 *Agni hath come to feed on mortals' fuel*: 'Agni is to be kindled for the good of men.'—Wilson.

2 *Kine*: rays of light.

3 Bearing the Gods' own Eye, auspicious Lady, leading her Courser white and fair to look on,
Distinguished by her beams Dawn shines apparent, come forth to all the world with wondrous treasure.

4 Draw nigh with wealth and dawn away the foeman : prepare for us wide pasture free from danger.
Drive away those who hate us, bring us riches : pour bounty, opulent Lady, on the singer.

5 Send thy most excellent beams to shine and light us, giving us lengthened days, O Dawn, O Goddess,
Granting us food, thou who hast all things precious, and bounty rich in chariots, kine, and horses.

6 O Uṣas, nobly-born, Daughter of Heaven, whom the Vasiṣṭhas with their hymns make mighty,
Bestow thou on us vast and glorious riches. Preserve us evermore, ye Gods, with blessings.

HYMN LXXVIII. *Dawn.*

1. We have beheld her earliest lights approaching : her many glories part, on high, asunder.
On car sublime, refulgent, wending hither, O Uṣas, bring the wealth that makes us happy.

2 The fire well-kindled sings aloud to greet her, and with their hymns the priests are chanting welcome.
Uṣas approaches in her splendour, driving all evil darkness far away, the Goddess.

3 Apparent eastward are those lights of Morning, sending out lustre, as they rise, around them.
She hath brought forth Sun, sacrifice, and Agni, and far away hath fled detested darkness.

4 Rich Daughter of the Sky, we all behold her, yea, all men look on Dawn as she is breaking.
Her car that moves self-harnessed hath she mounted, the car drawn onward by her well-yoked horses.

5 Inspired with loving thoughts this day to greet thee, we and our wealthy nobles have awakened.
Show yourselves fruitful, Dawns, as ye are rising. Preserve us evermore, ye Gods, with blessings.

HYMN LXXIX. *Dawn.*

1. Rousing the lands where men's Five Tribes are settled, Dawn hath disclosed the pathways of the people.
She hath sent out her sheen with beauteous oxen. The Sun with light hath opened earth and heaven.

2 They paint their bright rays on the sky's far limits : the Dawns come on like tribes arrayed for battle.
Thy cattle, closely shutting up the darkness, as Savitar spreads his arms, give forth their lustre.

3 Wealthy, most like to Indra, Dawn hath risen, and brought forth lauds that shall promote our welfare.
Daughter of Heaven, a Goddess, she distributes, best of Aṅgirases, treasures to the pious.

4 Bestow on us, O Dawn, that ample bounty which thou didst send to those who sang thy praises;
Thou whom with bellowings of a bull they quickened : thou didst unbar the firm-set mountain's portals.

5 Impelling every God to grant his bounty sending to us the charm of pleasant voices,
Vouchsafe us thoughts, for profit, as thou breakest. Preserve us evermore, ye Gods, with blessings.

HYMN LXXX. *Dawn.*

1 The priests, Vasiṣṭhas, are the first awakened to welcome Uṣas with their songs and praises,
Who makes surrounding regions part asunder,and shows apparent all existing creatures.

3 *The Gods' own Eye,* and Dawn's *white Courser* are the Sun.

1. *Five Tribes* : of Āryans. *Pathways* : *pathyā* here has apparently the same meaning as in VII. 75. 1. But according to the Pada text and Sāyaṇa it is an adjective agreeing with *Uṣāḥ* (Dawn), and signifying beneficial.

2 *They* : the Dawns. *For battle* : supplied by Sāyaṇa.

3 *Best of Aṅgirases* : See VII. 75. 1.

4 The second line is translated by Prof. Wilson : 'thou whom (thy worshippers) welcomed with clamour (loud as the bellowing) of a bull.'

Portals : the doors of the mountain or cloud in which the cows or rays of light were imprisoned. Uṣas is by implication entreated to open these doors now for the singer of the hymn.

2 Giving fresh life when she hath hid the darkness, this Dawn hath wakened there with new-born lustre.
Youthful and unrestrained she cometh forward : she hath turned thoughts to Sun and fire and worship.

3 May blessed Mornings shine on us for ever, with wealth of kine, of horses, and of heroes,
Streaming with all abundance, pouring fatness. Preserve us evermore, ye Gods, with blessings.

HYMN LXXXI. *Dawn.*

1. ADVANCING, sending forth her rays, the Daughter of the Sky is seen.
Uncovering, that we may see, the mighty gloom, the friendly Lady makes the light.

2 The Sun ascending, the refulgent Star, pours down his beams together with the Dawn.
O Dawn, at thine arising, and the Sun's, may we attain the share allotted us.

3 Promptly we woke to welcome thee, O Uṣas, Daughter of the Sky,
Thee, Bounteous One, who bringest all we long to have, and to the offerer health and wealth.

4 Thou, dawning, workest fain to light the great world, yea, heaven, Goddess ! that it may be seen.
We yearn to be thine own, Dealer of Wealth : may we be to this Mother like her sons.

5 Bring us that wondrous bounty, Dawn, that shall be famed most far away.
What, Child of Heaven, thou hast of nourishment for man, bestow thou on us to enjoy.

6 Give to our princes opulence and immortal fame, and strength in herds of kine to us.
May she who prompts the wealthy, Lady of sweet strains, may Uṣas dawn our foes away.

2 *She hath turned thoughts* : or, with Sāyaṇa, 'she hath made manifest sacrifice, Sun, and Agni.' Cf. VII. 78. 3.

3 This stanza is repeated from VII. 41. 7.

6 *Lady of sweet strains* : *sūnṛtāvatī* : according to Sāyaṇa, 'speaker of truth.' 'Possessing all that is excellent.'—Ludwig.

HYMN LXXXII. *Indra-Varuṇa*

1. GRANT us your strong protection, Indra-Varuṇa, our people, and our family, for sacrifice.
May we subdue in fight our evil-hearted foes, him who attacks the man steadfast in lengthened rites.

2 O Indra-Varuṇa, mighty and very rich ! One of you is called Monarch and One Autocrat.
All Gods in the most lofty region of the air have, O ye Steers, combined all power and might in you.

3 Ye with your strength have pierced the fountains of the floods : the Sun have ye brought forward as the Lord in heaven.
Cheered by this magic draught ye, Indra-Varuṇa, made the dry places stream, made songs of praise flow forth.

4 In battels and in frays we ministering priests, kneeling upon our knees for furtherance of our weal,
Invoke you, only you, the Lords of twofold wealth, you prompt to hear, we bards, O Indra-Varuṇa.

5 O Indra-Varuṇa, as ye created all these creatures of the world by your surpassing might,
In peace and quiet Mitra waits on Varuṇa, the Other, awful, with the Maruts seeks renown.

6 That Varuṇa's high worth may shine preëminent, these Twain have measured each his proper power and might.
The One subdueth the destructive enemy; the Other with a few furthereth many a man.

7 No trouble, no misfortune, Indra-Varuṇa, no woe from any side assails the mortal man
Whose sacrifice, O Gods, ye visit and enjoy : ne'er doth the crafty guile of mortal injure him.

8 With your divine protection, Heroes, come to us : mine invocation hear, if ye be pleased therewith.

2 *One of you* : Varuṇa is called *samrāj* or universal ruler (thoroughly resplendent, according to Sāyaṇa), and Indra *svarāj*, independent ruler, or, according to Sāyaṇa, self-resplendent.

4 *Twofold wealth* : celestial and terrestrial.

5 *Waits on Varuṇa* : and so acknowledges his supremacy. *The Other* : Indra.

6 *The One* : Varuṇa.

Bestow ye upon us, O Indra-Varuṇa, your friendship and your kinship and your favouring grace.

9 In battle after battle, Indra-Varuṇa, be ye our Champions, ye who are the peoples' strength,
When both opposing bands invoke you for the fight, and men that they may gain offspring and progeny.

10 May Indra, Varuṇa, Mitra, and Aryaman vouchsafe us glory and great shelter spreading far.
We think of the beneficent light of Aditi, and Savitar's song of praise, the God who strengthens Law.

HYMN LXXXIII. *Indra-Varuṇa.*

1. LOOKING to you and your alliance, O ye Men, armed with broad axes they went forward, fain for spoil.
Ye smote and slew his Dāsa and his Āryan enemies, and helped Sudās with favour, Indra-Varuṇa.

2 Where heroes come together with their banners raised, in the encounter where is naught for us to love,
Where all things that behold the light are terrified, there did ye comfort us, O Indra-Varuṇa.

3 The boundaries of earth were seen all dark with dust : O Indra-Varuṇa, the shout went up to heaven.
The enmities of the people compassed me about. Ye heard my calling and ye came to me with help.

4 With your resistless weapons, Indra-Varuṇa, ye conquered Bheda and ye gave Sudās your aid.
Ye heard the prayers of these amid the cries of war : effectual was the service of the Tṛtsus' priest.

5 O Indra-Varuṇa, the wickedness of foes and mine assailants' hatred sorely trouble me.
Ye Twain are Lords of riches both of earth and heaven : so grant to us your aid on the decisive day.

6 The men of both the hosts invoked you in the fight, Indra and Varuṇa, that they might win the wealth,
What time ye helped Sudās, with all the Tṛtsu folk, when the Ten Kings had pressed him down in their attack.

7 Ten Kings who worshipped not, O Indra-Varuṇa, confederate, in war prevailed not o'er Sudās.
True was the boast of heroes sitting at the feast : so at their invocations Gods were on their side.

8 O Indra-Varuṇa, ye gave Sudās your aid when the Ten Kings in battle compassed him about,
There where the white-robed Tṛtsus with their braided hair, skilled in song worshipped you with homage and with hymn.

9 One of you Twain destroys the Vṛtras in the fight, the Other evermore maintains his holy Laws.
We call on you, ye Mighty, with our hymns of praise. Vouchsafe us your protection, Indra-Varuṇa.

10 May Indra, Varuṇa, Mitra, and Aryaman vouchsafe us glory and great shelter spreading far.
We think of the beneficent light of Aditi, and Savitar's song of praise, the God who strengthens Law.

HYMN LXXXIV. *Indra-Varuṇa.*

1. KINGS, Indra-Varuṇa, I would turn you hither to this our sacrifice with gifts and homage,
Held in both arms the ladle, dropping fatness, goes of itself to you whose forms are varied.

2 Dyaus quickens and promotes your high dominion who bind with bonds not wrought of rope or cordage.
Far from us still be Varuṇa's displeasure : may Indra give us spacious room to dwell in.

Indra and Varuṇa are praised by the Vasiṣṭhas, the family priests of Sudās, King of the Tṛtsus, for having given him the victory over the ten confederate Kings. See VII. 33. 3.

1 *O ye Men* : or Heroes; Indra and Varuṇa. *Armed with broad axes* 'armed with large sickles.'—Wilson. Ludwig maintains that the former meaning is perfectly impossible, and argues that *pṛthupárśavaḥ* must mean 'the Pṛthus and the Parśus.'

2 *Where is naught for us to love* : Prof. Grassmann, whom Prof. Peterson follows, explains differently : 'where all that is dear is at stake.'

4 *Bheda* : See VII. 18. 19.

5 *Both of earth and heaven* : or perhaps, belonging to both sides.

8 *With their braided hair* : See VII. 33. 1.

10 This stanza is repeated from the preceding hymn.

———

2 *Dyaus* : cf. VI. 62. 9. *Not wrought of rope* : moral and figurative, no material.

3 Make ye our sacrifice fair amid the assemblies : make ye our prayers approved among our princes.
May God-sent riches come for our possession : further ye us with your delightful succours.

4 O Indra-Varuṇa, vouchsafe us riches with store of treasure, food, and every blessing;
For the Āditya, banisher of falsehood, the Hero, dealeth wealth in boundless plenty.

5 May this my song reach Varuṇa and Indra, and, strongly urging, win me sons and offspring.
To the Gods' banquet may we go with riches. Preserve us evermore, ye Gods, with blessings.

HYMN LXXXV. *Indra-Varuṇa.*

1. For you I deck a harmless hymn, presenting the Soma juice to Varuṇa and Indra—
A hymn that shines like heavenly Dawn with fatness. May they be near us on the march and guard us.

2 Here where the arrows fall amid the banners both hosts invoke the Gods in emulation.
O Indra-Varuṇa, smite back those—our foemen, yea, smite them with your shaft to every quarter.

3 Self-lucid in their seats, e'en heavenly Waters endowed with Godhead Varuṇa and Indra.
One of these holds the folk distinct and sundered, the Other smites and slays resistless foemen.

4 Wise be the priest and skilled in Law Eternal, who with his sacred gifts and adoration.
Brings you to aid us with your might, Ādityas : let him have viands to promote his welfare.

4 *The Āditya* : Varuṇa.

1 *On the march* : the Ṛṣi prays for aid in an expected battle.

3 *With Godhead* : libations of Soma juice, with which water is mingled, support the Gods in their several stations : *somenāpyāyitā hi devatāḥ sve sve sthāne 'vatiṣṭhante.*—Sāyaṇa. *Distinct and sundered* : differently treated, rewarded or punished in accordance with their deserts. 'The other sustains the separate creatures.' —Muir. 'The one protects the tribes which are scattered abroad.'—Grassmann.

4 *Wise be the priest* : or, wise must the priest be, skilled, etc. *He* : the institutor of sacrifice. *Viands*: sacrificial food to be offered to the Gods.

5 May this my song reach Varuṇa and Indra, and, strongly urging, win me sons and offspring.
To the Gods' banquet may we go with riches. Preserve us evermore, ye Gods with blessings.

HYMN LXXXVI. *Varuṇa.*

1. Wise, verily, are creatures through his greatness who stayed even spacious heaven and earth asunder;
Who urged the high and mighty sky to motion, the Star of old, and spread the earth before him.

2 With mine own heart I commune on the question how Varuṇa and I may be united.
What gift of mine will he accept unangered? When may I calmly look and find him gracious?

3 Fain to know this my sin I question others: I seek the wise, O Varuṇa, and ask them.
This one same answer even the sages gave me, "Surely this Varuṇa is angry with thee."

4 What, Varuṇa, hath been my chief transgression, that thou wouldst slay the friend who sings thy praises ?
Tell me, Unconquerable Lord, and quickly sinless will I approach thee with mine homage.

5 Free us from sins committed by our fathers, from those wherein we have ourselves offended.
O King, loose, like a thief who feeds the cattle, as from the cord a calf, set free Vasiṣṭha.

6 Not our own will betrayed us, but seduction, thoughtlessness, Varuṇa ! wine, dice, or anger.
The old is near to lead astray the younger : even sleep removeth not all evil-doing.

7 Slavelike may I do service to the Bounteous, serve, free from sin, the God inclined to anger.

1 *The Star* : the Sun.

5 *Like a thief who feeds the cattle* : who has performed penance for his theft, and, at the completion of the service, offered fodder to the stolen animal : 'who has feasted on stolen cattle '—M. Müller. But See Pischel, *Vedische Studien*, I. p. 106.

6. *Seduction* : or, as Sāyaṇa explains, 'the settled course of fate.'
The old is near : 'The stronger perverts the weaker.'—Muir. 'There is a senior [God] in the proximity of the junior [man].'—Wilson.

This gentle Lord gives wisdom to the simple : the wiser God leads on the wise to riches.

8 O Lord, O Varuṇa, may this laudation come close to thee and lie within thy spirit.
May it be well with us in rest and labour. Preserve us ever-more, ye Gods, with blessings.

HYMN LXXXVII. *Varuṇa.*

1. VARUṆA cut a path way out for Sūrya, and led the watery floods of rivers onward.
The Mares, as in a race, speed on in order. He made great channels for the days to follow.

2 The wind, thy breath, hath sounded through the region like a wild beast that seeks his food in pastures.
Within these two, exalted Earth and Heaven, O Varuṇa, are all the forms thou lovest.

3 Varuṇa's spies, sent forth upon their errand, survey the two world-halves well formed and fashioned.
Wise are they, holy, skilled in sacrifices, the furtherers of the praise-songs of the prudent.

4 To me who understand hath Varuṇa spoken, the names borne by the Cow are three times seven.
The sapient God, knowing the place's secret, shall speak as 'twere to teach the race that cometh.

5 On him three heavens rest and are supported, and the three earths are there in sixfold order.
The wise King Varuṇa hath made in heaven that Golden Swing to cover it with glory.

6 Like Varuṇa from heaven he sinks in Sindhu, like a white-shining spark, a strong wild creature.
Ruling in depths and meting out the region, great saving power hath he, this world's Controller.

7 Before this Varuṇa may we be sinless—him who shows mercy even to the sinner—
While we are keeping Aditi's ordinances. Preserve us evermore, ye Gods, with blessings.

1 *The Mares* : the swift rivers. The half-line is difficult. 'Hastening (to his task) as a horse let loose rushes to (a flock of) mares, he divided the great nights from the days.'—Wilson. 'Like a troop (of horses) let loose, following the mares, he has made great channels for the days.'—Muir.

3 *Varuṇa's spies* : the other Ādityas, or perhaps the Fathers.

4 *The Cow* : according to Sāyaṇa, Vāk or Speech in the form of a cow having twenty-one metres attached to her breast, throat, and head, or holding the names of twenty-one kinds of sacrifice. Aditi may be intended, or Pṛśni with the thrice seven Maruts.

The sapient God : 'The wise god, though he knows them, has not revealed the mysteries of (her) place, which he desires to grant to a future generation.'—Muir. According to Sāyaṇa, *ná* in this line is not negative.

5 For the *three heavens* and *three earths*, See Vol. I., Index. *In sixfold order* : perhaps referring to the heavens and earths or else the three earths arbitrarily doubled. 'The three earths with their six seasons.'—Wilson. *That Golden Swing* : the Sun.

6 *He* : the Sun. *Sindhu* : or the sea. *Ruling in depths*: referring to Varuṇa whose dominion following the setting sun, reaches to the depths of the ocean. *Meting out the region* : or, who measured out the firmament. Sāyaṇa's interpretation of this stanza is different : '(Radiant) as the sun, Varuṇa placed the ocean (in its bed), white as a drop (of water), vigorous as an antelope, object of profound praise, distributor of water, the powerful transporter beyond sin, the ruler of this existing (world).'—Wilson.

7 *Aditi's ordinances* : according to Sāyaṇa, Aditi here means 'the Mighty.' that is, Varuṇa.

HYMN LXXXVIII. *Varuṇa.*

1. PRESENT to Varuṇa thine hymn, Vasiṣṭha, bright, most delightful to the Bounteous Giver,
Who bringeth on to us the Bull, the lofty, the Holy, laden with a thousand treasures.

2 And now, as I am come before his presence, I take the face of Varuṇa for Agni's.
So might he bring—Lord also of the darkness—the light in heaven that I may see its beauty !

3 When Varuṇa and I embark together and urge our boat into the midst of ocean,
We, when we ride o'er ridges of the

---

1 *The Bull* : the Sun.

2 *For Agni's* : that is it appears to me to be flaming with anger.

3 'The kernel of the hymn lies in verses 3 to 6. The singer believes that he has been forsaken by his helper Varuṇa ; with anguish he remembers his communion with the God in former times. In a vision he sees himself translated into Varuṇa's realm, he goes sailing with the God, is called to be Ṛṣi or holy singer to the God, and is in his palace with him. Now, Varuṇa has withdrawn his favour, yet let him have mercy on his singer, and not punish him so grievously for his sin. The hymn perhaps originally closed with verse 6'—Prof. von Roth's note in the *Siebenzig Lieder*, translated by Prof. Peterson. But See Hillebrandt, *Varuṇa und Mitra*, pp. 25, 26.

waters, will swing within that swing and there be happy.

4 Varuṇa placed Vasiṣṭha in the vessel, and deftly with his might made him a Ṛṣi.
When days shone bright the Sage made him a singer, while the heavens broadened and the Dawns were lengthened.

5 What hath become of those our ancient friendships, when without enmity we walked together?
I, Varuṇa, thou glorious Lord, have entered thy lofty home, thine house with thousand portals.

6 If he, thy true ally, hath sinned against thee, still, Varuṇa, he is the friend thou lovedst.
Let us not, Living One, as sinners, know thee : give shelter, as a Sage, to him who lauds thee.

7 While we abide in these fixed habitations, and from the lap of Aditi win favour,
May Varuṇa untie the bond that binds us. Preserve us evermore, ye Gods, with blessings.

HYMN LXXXIX. *Varuṇa.*

1. LET me not yet, King Varuṇa, enter into the house of clay :
Have mercy, spare me, Mighty Lord.

2 When, Thunderer ! I move along tremulous like a wind-blown skin,
Have mercy, spare me, Mighty Lord.

3 O Bright and Powerful God, through want of strength I erred and went astray :
Have mercy, spare me, Mighty Lord.

4 Thirst found thy worshipper though he stood in the midst of water-floods :
Have mercy, spare me, Mighty Lord.

5 O Varuṇa, whatever the offence may be which we as men commit against the heavenly host,
When through our want of thought we violate thy laws, punish us not, O God, for that iniquity.

HYMN XC. *Vāyu.*

1. To you pure juices, rich in meath, are offered by priests through longing for the Pair of Heroes.
Drive, Vāyu, bring thine harnessed horses hither : drink the pressed Soma till it make thee joyful.

2 Whoso to thee, the Mighty, brings oblation, pure Soma unto thee, pure-drinking Vāyu,
That man thou makest famous among mortals : to him strong sons are born in quick succession.

3 The God whom both these worlds brought forth for riches, whom heavenly Dhiṣaṇā for our wealth appointeth,
His team of harnessed horses waits on Vāyu, and, foremost, on the radiant Treasure-bearer.

4 The spotless Dawns with fair bright days have broken; they found the spacious light when they were shining.
Eagerly they disclosed the stall of cattle: floods streamed for them as in the days aforetime.

5 These with their truthful spirit, shining brightly, move on provided with their natural insight.
Viands attend the car that beareth Heroes, your car, ye Sovran Pair, Indra and Vāyu.

6 May these who give us heavenly light, these rulers, with gifts of kine and horses, gold and treasures.
These princes, through full life, Indra and

7 *Aditi* : here said to mean earth.

The hymn has been translated by Dr. Muir *O.S. Texts*, V. 67, Prof. M. Müller, *Anc. Sansk. Lit.*, 540, the authors of *Siebenzig Lieder*, p. 12, and Prof. Peterson, *Hymns from the Ṛgveda*, p. 287.

1 *The house of clay* : the grave. Cf. Atharva-veda, V. 30. 14.

2 *Thunderer* : *adrivaḥ*, Caster of the Stone, a common epithet of Indra, but not suitable to Varuṇa. *Tremulous* : Sāyaṇa adds *śaityena*, with cold : and Prof. Wilson observes that 'the *Varuṇa-pāśa*, a kind of dropsy, seems to be referred to.' Cf. Atharva-veda, IV. 16. 7.

4 *Thirst* : avarice. *In the midst of water-floods* : when surrounded by abundant wealth. According to the Commentator, the allusion is to Vasiṣṭha's sea-voyage; or perhaps the perpetual thirst of dropsy may be intended.

The last three stanzas are addressed to Indra and Vāyu as a dual Deity.

1 *The Pair of Heroes* : Indra and Vāyu.

3 *The God* : apparently, Indra. *Dhiṣaṇā* : a Goddess of prosperity and gain. *The radiant Treasure-bearer* : perhaps Soma.

4 *They found* : the Aṅgirases. 'They are not named in the text, but Sāyaṇa refers the whole to them ; by their praise of *Vāyu* the dawn broke, the stolen cattle were rescued, and the obstructed rain set at liberty.'—Wilson.

5 *These* : the institutors of sacrifice.

6 *These rulers, these princes*, are the wealthy nobles who defray the expenses and reward the priests.

Vāyu ! o'ercome in battle with their steeds and heroes.

7 Like coursers seeking fame will we Vasiṣṭhas, O Indra-Vāyu, with our fair laudations.
Exerting all our power call you to aid us. Preserve us evermore, ye Gods, with blessings.

HYMN XCI. *Vāyu.*

1. WERE not in sooth, the Gods aforetime blameless, whose pleasure was increased by adoration ?
For Vāyu and for man in his affliction they caused the Morning to arise with Sūrya.

2 Guardians infallible, eager as envoys, preserve us safe through many months and autumns.
Addressed to you, our fair praise, Indra-Vāyu, implores your favour and renewed well-being.

3 Wise, bright, arranger of his teams, he seeketh men with rich food whose treasures are abundant.
They have arranged them of one mind with Vāyu : the men have wrought all noble operations.

4 So far as native power and strength permit you, so far as men behold whose eyes have vision,
O ye pure-drinkers, drink with us pure Soma : sit on this sacred grass, Indra and Vāyu.

5 Driving down teams that bear the lovely Heroes, hitherward, Indra-Vāyu, come together.
To you this prime of savoury juice is offered : here loose your horses and be friendly-minded.

6 Your hundred and your thousand teams, O Indra and Vāyu, all-munificent, which attend you,
With these most gracious-minded come ye hither, and drink, O Heroes of the meath we offer.

7 Like coursers seeking fame will we Vasiṣṭhas, O Indra-Vāyu, with our fair laudations,
Exerting all our power, call you to aid us. Preserve us evermore, ye Gods, with blessings.

Indra is associated with Vāyu in almost every stanza.

1 *For Vāyu* : I translate the *vāyáve* of the text, but it is evident that *Āyáve*, for Āyu, or the living one, should be read in its stead.

3 *He seeketh* : Vāyu. The meaning of the stanza is obscure.

5 *The lovely Heroes* : Indra and Vāyu.

HYMN XCII. *Vāyu.*

1. O VĀYU, drinker of the pure, be near us : a thousand teams are thine, All-bounteous Giver.
To thee the rapture-bringing juice is offered, whose first draught, God, thou takest as thy portion.

2 Prompt at the holy rites forth came the presser with Soma-draughts for Indra and for Vāyu,
When ministering priests with strong devotion bring to you Twain the first taste of the Soma.

3 The teams wherewith thou seekest him who offers, within his home, O Vāyu, to direct him,
Therewith send wealth: to us with full enjoyment, a hero son and gifts of kine and horses.

4 Near to the Gods and making Indra joyful, devout and offering precious gifts to Vāyu,
Allied with princes, smiting down the hostile, may we with heroes conquer foes in battle.

5 With thy yoked teams in hundreds and in thousands come to our sacrifice and solemn worship.
Come, Vāyu, make thee glad at this libation. Preserve us evermore, ye Gods, with blessings.

1 *Drinker of the pure* : or bright, Soma.

4 *Allied* : the priests are the allies and moral supporters of the princes in war.

5 *In hundreds and in thousands* : Cf. I. 135. 3.

HYMN XCIII. *Indra-Agni.*

1. SLAYERS of enemies, Indra and Agni, accept this day our new-born pure laudation.
Again, again I call you prompt to listen, best to give quickly strength to him who craves it.

2 For ye were strong to gain, exceeding mighty, growing together, waxing in your vigour.

Lords of the pasture filled with ample riches, bestow upon us strength both fresh and lasting.

3 Yea when the strong have entered our assembly, and singers seeking with their hymns your favour,
They are like steeds who come into the race-course, those men who call aloud on Indra-Agni.

4 The singer, seeking with his hymns your favour, begs splendid riches of their first possessor.
Further us with new bounties, Indra-Agni, armed with strong thunder, slayers of the foeman.

5 When two great hosts, arrayed against each other, meet clothed with brightness, in the fierce encounter
Stand ye beside the godly, smite the godless; and still assist the men who press the Soma.

6 To this our Soma-pressing, Indra-Agni, come ye prepared to show your loving-kindness,
For not at any time have ye despised us. So may I draw you with all strengthenings hither.

7 So Agni, kindled mid this adoration, invite thou Mitra, Varuṇa, and Indra.
Forgive whatever sin we have committed: may Aryaman and Aditi remove it.

8 While we accelerate these our sacrifices, may we win strength from both of you, O Agni:
Ne'er may the Maruts, Indra, Viṣṇu slight us. Preserve us evermore, ye Gods, with blessings.

HYMN XCIV. *Indra-Agni.*

1. As rain from out the cloud, for you, Indra and Agni, from my soul
This noblest praise hath been produced.

2 Do ye, O Indra-Agni, hear the singer's call: accept his songs.
Ye Rulers, grant his heart's desire.

3 Give us not up to poverty, ye Heroes, Indra-Agni, nor
To slander and reproach of men.

4 To Indra and to Agni we bring reverence, high and holy hymn,
And, craving help, soft words with prayer.

5 For all these holy singers here implore these Twain to succour them,
And priests that they may win them strength.

6 Eager to laud you, we with songs invoke you, bearing sacred food,
Fain for success in sacrifice.

7 Indra and Agni, come to us with favour, ye who conquer men:
Let not the wicked master us.

8 At no time let the injurious blow of hostile mortal fall on us:
O Indra-Agni, shelter us.

9 Whatever wealth we crave of you, in gold, in cattle, or in steeds,
That, Indra-Agni, let us gain;

10 When heroes prompt in worship call Indra and Agni, Lords of steeds,
Beside the Soma juice effused.

11 Call hither with the song and lauds those who best slay the foemen, those
Who take delight in hymns of praise.

12 Slay ye the wicked man whose thought is evil of the demon kind.
Slay him who stays the waters, slay the Serpent with your deadly dart.

HYMN XCV. *Sarasvatī.*

1. THIS stream Sarasvatī with fostering current comes forth, our sure defence, our fort of iron.
As on a car, the flood flows on, surpassing in majesty and might all other waters.

3 *The strong*: the nobles who institute sacrifices.

4 *Their first possessor*: each God who is invoked.

5 *Great hosts*: 'hosts' must be supplied. The feminine dual adjectives have no substantive in the text.

7 *Aryaman and Aditi*: Mitra and others being understood, as the verb is plural.

8 *O Agni*: that is, Indra and Agni.

---

1 *As rain*: the hymn of praise is copious in its flow, and is doubly beneficial, gratifying the Gods and bringing blessings to the worshipper. *From my soul*: *mánmanaḥ*: explained by the Commentator here and in the corresponding passage of the Sāmaveda by *stotuḥ*, praiser or worshipper.

11 *Call hither*: I follow Prof. Ludwig in reading *āvivāsata*, instead of *āvivāsataḥ* which involves a very harsh construction.

12 *Him who stays the waters*: *udadhím*: according to Sāyaṇa, like an *udadhiḥ*, water-holder or pitcher. *The Serpent*: *ābhogám*, 'the coiler,' explained differently by Sāyaṇa, as 'one who enjoys good things from the worshippers.'

---

1 *Sarasvatī*: Sindhu or Indus appears to be intended under this name. See VI. 61. 2, and *Vedic Hymns*, I. p. 60.

2 Pure in her course from mountains to the ocean, alone of streams Sarasvatī hath listened.
Thinking of wealth and the great world of creatures, she poured for Nāhuṣa her milk and fatness.

3 Friendly to man he grew among the women, a strong young Steer amid the Holy Ladies.
He gives the fleet steed to our wealthy princes, and decks their bodies for success in battle.

4 May this Sarasvatī be pleased and listen at this our sacrifice, auspicious Lady,
When we with reverence, on our knees, implore her close-knit to wealth, most kind to those she loveth

5 These offerings have ye made with adoration : say this, Sarasvatī, and accept our praises;
And, placing us under thy dear protection, may we approach thee, as a tree, for shelter.

6 For thee, O Blest Sarasvatī, Vasiṣṭha hath here unbarred the doors of sacred Order.
Wax, Bright One, and give strength to him who lauds thee. Preserve us evermore, ye Gods, with blessings.

HYMN XCVI. *Sarasvatī.*

1. I SING a lofty song, for she is mightiest, most divine of Streams.
Sarasvatī will I exalt with hymns and lauds, and, O Vasiṣṭha, Heaven and Earth.

2 When in the fulness of their strength the Pūrus dwell, Beauteous One, on thy two grassy banks,
Favour us thou who hast the Maruts for thy friends : stir up the bounty of our chiefs.

3 So may Sarasvatī auspicious send good luck; she, rich in spoil, is never niggardly in thought,
When praised in Jamadagni's way and lauded as Vasiṣṭha lauds.

4 We call upon Sarasvān, as unmarried men who long for wives,
As liberal men who yearn for sons.

5 Be thou our kind protector, O Sarasvān, with those waves of thine
Laden with sweets and dropping oil.

6 May we enjoy Sarasvān's breast, all-beautiful, that swells with streams,
May we gain food and progeny.

HYMN XCVII. *Bṛhaspati.*

1. WHERE Heaven and Earth combine in men's assembly, and those who love the Gods delight in worship,
Where the libations are effused for Indra, may he come first to drink and make him stronger.

2 We crave the heavenly grace of Gods to guard us—so may Bṛhaspati, O friends, exalt us—
That he, the Bounteous God, may find us sinless, who giveth from a distance like a father.

3 That Brahmaṇaspati, most High and Gracious, I glorify with offerings and with homage.
May the great song of praise divine, reach Indra who is the King of prayer the Gods' creation.

4 May that Bṛhaspati who brings all blessings, most dearly loved, be seated by our altar.
Heroes and wealth we crave; may he bestow them, and bear us safe beyond the men who vex us.

2 *Nāhuṣa* : according to the legend, a King who prayed to Sarasvatī who gave him butter and milk sufficient for the thousand-year sacrifice which he was about to perform. The Nahuṣas, the people living on the banks of the river, are probably intended.

3 *He grew* : Sarasvān, the consort of Sarasvatī.

5 *These offerings* : this half-line is very obscure. Prof. Ludwig thinks that these words may be supposed to be spoken by Sarasvatī to her worshippers, but he is not satisfied of the correctness of his conjecture. 'Presenting to thee, Sarasvatī these oblations with reverence (may we receive from thee affluence).'—Wilson.

---

1. *Heaven and Earth* : heaven as the home of the Goddess, and earth where she flows as a river.

2 *The Pūrus* : an Āryan tribe settled on both banks of the Sarasvatī or Indus. See Vol. I., Index. *Grassy banks* : this, as von Roth has suggested, seems to be the meaning of *ándhasi*, but the expression is difficult. See Hillebrandt, *Vedische Mythologie*, p. 254.

3 *Jamadagni* : a celebrated ancient Ṛṣi.

Indra is the deity of stanza I, Indra and Brahmaṇaspati are the deities of 3 and 9, Indra and Bṛhaspati of 10, and the rest of the hymn is addressed to Bṛhaspati. Bṛhaspati and Brahmaṇaspati are one and the same God, the Lord of Prayer. See I, 14. 3.

1 *Where Heaven and Earth combine* : where Gods and men meet at the the place of sacrifice. *And make him stronger* : Sāyaṇa explains *vāyaśca* differently : '(may his) swift (horses approach).'—Wilson.

2 *Like a father* : although he is far away he gives us what we ask like a father who is near at hand.—Ludwig.

3 *The Gods' creation* : *devákṛtasya* : inspired, or, literally, made, by the Gods.

5 To us these Deathless Ones, erst born, have granted this laud of ours which gives the Immortal pleasure.
Let us invoke Bṛhaspati, the foeless, the clear-voiced God, the Holy One of households

6 Him, this Bṛhaspati, his red-hued horses, drawing together, full of strength, bring hither.
Robed in red colour like the cloud, they carry the Lord of Might whose friendship gives a dwelling.

7 For he is pure, with hundred wings, refulgent, with sword of gold, impetuous, winning sunlight.
Sublime Bṛhaspati, easy of access granteth his friends most bountiful refreshment.

8 Both Heaven and Earth, divine, the Deity's Parents, have made Bṛhaspati increase in grandeur.
Glorify him, O friends, who merits glory: may he give prayer fair way and easy passage.

9 This, Brahmaṇaspati, is your laudation : prayer hath been made to thunder-wielding Indra.
Favour our songs, wake up our thought and spirit : destroy the godless and our foemen's malice.

10 Ye Twain are Lords of wealth in earth and heaven, thou, O Bṛhaspati, and thou, O Indra.
Mean though he be, give wealth to him who lauds you. Preserve us evermore, ye Gods, with blessings.

HYMN XCVIII. *Indra.*

1. Priests, offer to the Lord of all the people the milked-out stalk of Soma, radiant-coloured.
No wild-bull knows his drinking-place like Indra who ever seeks him who hath pressed the Soma,

2 Thou dost desire to drink, each day that passes, the pleasant food which thou hast had aforetime,
O Indra, gratified in heart and spirit, drink eagerly the Soma set before thee.

3 Thou, newly-born, for strength didst drink the Soma; the Mother told thee of thy future greatness.
O Indra, thou hast filled mid-air's wide region, and given the Gods by battle room and freedom.

4 When thou hast urged the arrogant to combat, proud in their strength of arm, we will subdue them.
Or, Indra, when thou fightest girt by heroes, we in the glorious fray with thee will conquer.

5 I will declare the earliest deeds of Indra, and recent acts which Maghavan hath accomplished.
When he had conquered godless wiles and magic, Soma became his own entire possession.

6 Thine is this world of flocks and herds around thee, which with the eye of Sūrya thou beholdest.
Thou, Indra, art alone the Lord of cattle; may we enjoy the treasure which thou givest.

7 Ye Twain are Lords of wealth in earth and heaven, thou, O Bṛhaspati, and thou, O Indra.
Mean though he be, give wealth to him who lauds you. Preserve us evermore, ye Gods, with blessings.

HYMN XCIX. *Viṣṇu.*

1. Men come not nigh thy majesty who growest beyond all bound and measure with thy body.
Both thy two regions of the earth, O Viṣṇu, we know : thou God, knowest the highest also.

2 None who is born or being born, God Viṣṇu, hath reached the utmost limit of thy grandeur.
The vast high vault of heaven hast thou supported, and fixed earth's eastern pinnacle securely.

5 Our hymns of praise which are acceptable to the immortal God have been given to us by the everlasting deities themselves. Sāyaṇa's explanation is different : 'may the first born immortals' (by his command) bestow upon us the food that is necessary for existence.' —Wilson.

6 *Whose friendship gives a dwelling* : I adopt the interpretation given by Professor Cowell in his note on the passage in Wilson's translation.

7 *With hundred wings* : 'borne by numerous conveyances.'—Wilson.

8 *In grandeur* : or, by their might.

10 *Mean* : or, poor.

---

1 *Radiant-coloured* : *aruṇám*, red, ruddy, here explained by the Commentator as *ārocamānam*, shining.

3 *Thy future greatness* : See VI. 18. 4, where Aditi says :—'No peer hath he among born already, nor among those who shall be born hereafter.'

---

1 *Two regions of the earth*: that is, the earth and the firmament. 'The two lower regions are within the range of our perception ; the third belongs to Viṣṇu, whither he stepped with the third of his ascending strides.'—Wallis, *Cosmology of the Ṛgveda*, p. 115.

3 Rich in sweet food be ye, and rich in milch-kine, with fertile pastures, fain to do men service.
Both these worlds, Viṣṇu, hast thou stayed asunder, and firmly fixed the earth with pegs around it.

4 Ye have made spacious room for sacrificing by generating Sūrya, Dawn, and Agni.
O Heroes, ye have conquered in your battles even the bull-jawed Dāsa's wiles and magic.

5 Ye have destroyed, thou, Indra, and thou, Viṣṇu, Śambara's nine-and-ninety fenced castles.
Ye Twain smote down a hundred times a thousand resistless heroes of the royal Varcin.

6 This is the lofty hymn of praise, exalting the Lords of Mighty Stride, the strong and lofty.
I laud you in the solemn synods, Viṣṇu: pour ye food on us in our camps, O Indra.

7 O Viṣṇu, unto thee my lips cry Vaṣaṭ! Let this mine offering, Śipiviṣṭa, please thee.
May these my songs of eulogy exalt thee. Preserve us evermore, ye Gods, with blessings.

HYMN C. *Viṣṇu.*

1 NE'ER doth the man repent, who, seeking profit, bringeth his gift to the far-striding Viṣṇu.
He who adoreth him with all his spirit winneth himself so great a benefactor.

2 Thou, Viṣṇu, constant in thy courses, gavest good-will to all men, and a hymn that lasteth,
That thou mightst move us to abundant comfort of very splendid wealth with store of horses.

3 Three times strode forth this God in all his grandeur over this earth bright with a hundred splendours.
Foremost be Viṣṇu, stronger than the strongest: for glorious is his name who lives for ever.

4 Over this earth with mighty step strode Viṣṇu, ready to give it for a home to Manu.
In him the humble people trust for safety: he, nobly born, hath made them spacious dwellings.

5 To-day I laud this name, O Śipiviṣṭa, I, skilled in rules, the name of thee the Noble.
Yea, I the poor and weak praise thee the Mighty who dwellest in the realm beyond this region.

6 What was there to be blamed in thee, O Viṣṇu, when thou declaredst, I am Śipiviṣṭa?
Hide not this form from us, nor keep it secret, since thou didst wear another shape in battle.

7 O Viṣṇu, unto thee my lips cry Vaṣaṭ! Let this mine offering, Śipiviṣṭa, please thee.
May these my songs of eulogy exalt thee. Preserve us evermore, ye Gods, with blessings.

HYMN CI. *Parjanya.*

1 SPEAK forth three words, the words which light precedeth, which milk this udder that produceth nectar.
Quickly made manifest, the Bull hath bellowed, engendering the germ of plants, the Infant.

---

3 The first line appears to be Viṣṇu's blessing on heaven and earth when be parted and supported them.

4 *Bull-jawed*: or Vṛṣaśipra may be the name of the Dāsa.

5 *Royal Varcin*: See II. 14. 6.

7 *Vaṣaṭ*: the exclamation used on making an oblation. *Śipiviṣṭa*: a name of Viṣṇu of uncertain etymology and meaning 'Invested with rays of light,' according to Sāyaṇa. See Muir, *O.S. Texts*, IV. 87, 88, *note*.

---

2 *A hymn that lasteth*: continually recurring occasion to praise thee.

3 *This earth*: meaning, says the Commentator, earth, firmament, and heaven.

6 This stanza is unintelligible. The Commentator on the corresponding passage of the Sāmaveda says: 'Viṣṇu formerly abandoning his own form, and assuming another artificial shape, succoured Vasiṣṭha in battle. Recognizing the god, the Ṛṣi addresses him with the verse.' *Śipiviṣṭa* is said to be a word of equivocal meaning, 'clothed with rays of light, and 'denuded.' See Wilson's note, and *O. S. Texts*, IV. 87, 88, *note*. The passage looks like the germ of the later incarnations of the God which occur in the *Śatapatha Brāhmaṇa* and the *Purāṇas*.

---

1 *Three words*: or texts of the three Vedas. *Which light precedeth*: introduced by the sacred syllable OM. More probably Parjanya is addressed, the three words being his voice, the thunder (V. 63. 6), heard in heaven, air, and earth, and preceded by the lightning-flash. See Bergaigne, *Quarante Hymnes du Ṛgveda*, p. 79. *Milk this udder*: draw down the sweet rain from the cloud. *The Bull*: Parjanya. *The Infant*: Agni in the form of lightning.

2 Giver of growth to plants, the God who ruleth over the waters and all moving creatures,
Vouchsafe us triple shelter for our refuge, and threefold light to succour and befriend us.

3 Now he is sterile, now begetteth offspring, even as he willeth doth he change his figure.
The Father's genial flow bedews the Mother; therewith the Sire, therewith the son is nourished.

4 In him all living creatures have their being, and the three heavens with triply-flowing waters.
Three reservoirs that sprinkle down their treasure shed their sweet streams around him with a murmur.

5 May this my song to Sovran Lord Parjanya come near unto his heart and give him pleasure.
May we obtain the showers that bring enjoyment, and God-protected plants with goodly fruitage.

6 He is the Bull of all, and their impregner: he holds the life of all things fixed and moving.
May this rite save me till my hundredth autumn. Preserve us evermore, ye Gods, with blessings.

HYMN CII *Parjanya.*

1 SING forth and laud Parjanya, son of Heaven, who sends the gift of rain:
May he provide our pasturage.
2 Parjanya is the God who forms in kine, in mares, in plants of earth,
And womankind, the germ of life.
3 Offer and pour into his mouth oblation rich in savoury juice:
May he for ever give us food.

2 *Threefold light*: with reference to the divisions of the day and the seasons.

3 *He is sterile*: sends no rain, like a barren cow that gives no milk.

The Father's genial flow: 'The father is the sky, earth the mother, who receives the rain from the former, which, producing the means of offering libations and oblations, returns again to the parent heaven, as well as supports his offspring—all living creatures.'—Wilson.

4 *Three reservoirs*: according to Sāyaṇa, clouds in the east, west, and north

6 *The Bull of all*: the plants, understood.

---

3 *Into his mouth*: that is, Agni, who is the mouth by which the other Gods consume the offerings that are made to them.

HYMN CIII. *Frogs.*

1. THEY who lay quiet for a year, the Brāhmans who fulfil their vows,
The Frogs have lifted up their voice, the voice Parjanya hath inspired.

2 What time on these, as on a dry skin lying in the pool's bed, the floods of heaven descended,
The music of the Frogs comes forth in concert like the cows lowing with their calves beside them.

3 When at the coming of the Rains the water has poured upon them as they yearned and thirsted,
One seeks another as he talks and greets him with cries of pleasure as a son his father.

4 Each of these twain receives the other kindly, while they are revelling in the flow of waters,
When the Frog moistened by the rain springs forward, and Green and Spotty both combine their voices.

5 When one of these repeats the other's language, as he who learns the lesson of the teacher,
Your every limb seems to be growing larger as ye converse with eloquence on the waters.

6 One is Cow-bellow and Goat-bleat the other, one Frog is Green and one of them is Spotty.
They bear one common name, and yet they vary, and, talking, modulate the voice diversely.

7 As Brāhmans, sitting round the brimful vessel, talk at the Soma-rite of Atirātra,
So, Frogs, ye gather round the pool to honour this day of all the year, the first of Rain-time.

The hymn has been translated by Dr. Muir, *O. S. Texts*, V. 436, and by Professor F. Max Müller in his *Ancient Sanskrit Literature*, pp. 494f, who remarks: 'The hymn......which is called a panegyric of the frogs, is clearly a satire on the priests; and it is curious to observe that the same animal should have been chosen by the Vedic satirist to represent the priests, which, by the earliest satirist of Greece, was selected as the representative of the Homerio heroes.' But see Oldenberg, *Die Religion des Veda*, p. 70. The hymn evidently belongs to a late period of Vedic poctry.

3 *With cries of pleasure*: *akhkhalīkṛtya*: uttering the imitative exclamation *akhkhala*.

5 *Your every limb*: this abrupt change of person is not unfrequent in the Veda.

7 *Atirātra*: a ceremony accompanied by three nocturnal recitations.

8 These Brāhmans with the Soma juice, performing their year-long rite, have lifted up their voices ;
And these Adhvaryus, sweating with their kettles, come forth and show themselves, and none are hidden.

9 They keep the twelve month's God-appointed order, and never do the men neglect the season.
Soon as the Rain-time in the year returneth, these who were heated kettles gain their freedom.

10 Cow-bellow and Goat-bleat have granted riches, and Green and Spotty have vouchsafed us treasure.
The Frogs who give us cows in hundreds lengthen our lives in this most fertilizing season.

HYMN CIV. *Indra-Soma.*

1. INDRA and Soma, burn, destroy the demon foe, send downward, O ye Bulls, those who add gloom to gloom.
Annihilate the fools, slay them and burn them up : chase them away from us, pierce the voracious ones.

8 *Year-long rite* : 'Sāyaṇa makes it refer to *Gavām ayanam*, a sacrificial session, which commences and ends with the *atirātra*, and lasts a whole year.'—Cowell, in Wilson's Translation. *Sweating with their kettles* : 'There is a quibble on the word *gharmiṇaḥ*, having or bearing the vessel, or performing the rite so termed; or suffering from *gharma*, heat, or the hot season '— Wilson. *And none are hidden* : *guhyā ná ké cit* : some take *ná* here as like' : 'issue forth like persons who have been hidden.' —Muir. 'Pop out like hermits.'—M. Müller.

9 *The men*: the priest-like frogs. *These who were heated kettles* : the frogs who had been burnt and scorched by the hot weather.

10 *Have granted riches* : as the earliest proclaimers of the advent of the Rains which revive and fertilize the earth.

'It is possibly an echo of this production that we find in a description of autumn in the Harivaṁśa, V 8803, where the poet compares the noise made by a frog, after his rest of sixteen half months, along with his wives, to the recitation of the Ṛgveda by a Brāhman surrounded by his pupils...On this verse the late M. Langlois somewhat naively remarks as follows : Dans noe moeurs rien n' egalerait l' impertinence d' une comparaison dans laquelle une grenouille serait assimilee a un respectable ecclesiastique. Les Indiens, a ce qu' il parait, ne voyaient daus telle espece de rapprochement aucune teinte d' impiete.'—Muir, *O. S. Texts*, V. 433. But See Bergaigne, *La Religion Vedique*, I. 292.

The hymn consists chiefly of imprecations directed against demons and evil spirits, Rākṣasas and Yātudhānas. The deities are various.

1 *The demon foe* : *rákṣaḥ* : the Rākṣasas, fiends, demons, goblins, going about at night, disturbing sacrifices and devout men, ensnaring and even devouring human beings, and generally hostile to the human race.

2 Indra and Soma, let sin round the wicked boil like as a caldron set amid the flames of fire.
Against the foe of prayer, devourer of raw flesh, the vile fiend fierce of eye, keep ye perpetual hate.

3 Indra and Soma, plunge the wicked in the depth, yea, cast them into darkness that hath no support,
So that not one of them may ever thence return : so may your wrathful might prevail and conquer them.

4 Indra and Soma, hurl your deadly crushing bolt down on the wicked fiend from heaven and from the earth.
Yea, forge out of the mountains your celestial dart wherewith ye burn to death the waxing demon race.

5 Indra and Soma, cast ye downward out of heaven your deadly darts of stone burning with fiery flame,
Eternal, scorching darts ; plunge the voracious ones within the depth, and let them sink without a sound.

6 Indra and Soma, let this hymn control you both, even as the girth encompasses two vigorous steeds—
The song of praise which I with wisdom offer you : do ye, as Lords of men, animate these my prayers.

7 In your impetuous manner think ye both thereon : destroy these evil beings, slay the treacherous fiends.
Indra and Soma, let the wicked have no bliss who evermore assails us with malignity.

8 Whoso accuses me with words of falsehood when I pursue my way with guileless spirit,
May he, the speaker of untruth, be, Indra, like water which the hollowed hand compresses.

9 Those who destroy, as is their wont, the simple, and with their evil natures harm the righteous,
May Soma give them over to the serpent, or to the lap of Nirṛti consign them.

2 *The vile fiend* : *kimídine* : explained by the Commentator as one who goes about saying, *Kimidānīm* or What now ! A qu d...unc, a vile and treacherous spy and informer. The word is used as the name of a class of evil spirits.

5 *Without a sound* : so suddenly that they have not time to cry out.

9 *To the serpent* : or to death by serpents' bites. *Nirṛti* : Death and Destruction.

10 The fiend, O Agni, who designs to injure the essence of our food, kine, steeds, or bodies,
May he, the adversary, thief, and robber, sink to destruction, both himself and offspring.

11 May he be swept away, himself and children : may all the three earths press him down beneath them.
May his fair glory, O ye Gods, be blighted, who in the day or night would fain destroy us.

12 The prudent finds it easy to distinguish the true and false : their words oppose each other.
Of these two that which is the true and honest, Soma protects, and brings the false to nothing.

13 Never doth Soma aid and guide the wicked or him who falsely claims the Warrior's title.
He slays the fiend and him who speaks untruly : both lie entangled in the noose of Indra.

14 As if I worshipped deities of falsehood, or thought vain thoughts about the Gods, O Agni.
Why art thou angry with us, Jātavedas ? Destruction fall on those who lie against thee !

15 So may I die this day if I have harassed any man's life or if I be a demon.
Yea, may he lose all his ten sons together who with false tongue hath called me Yātudhāna.

16 May Indra slay him with a mighty weapon, and let the vilest of all creatures perish,
The fiend who says that he is pure, who calls me a demon though devoid of demon nature.

17 She too who wanders like an owl at night-time, hiding her body in her guile and malice,
May she fall downward into endless caverns. May press-stones with loud ring destroy the demons.

18 Spread out, ye Maruts, search among the people : seize ye and grind the Rākṣasas to pieces,
Who fly abroad, transformed to birds, at night-time, or sully and pollute our holy worship.

19 Hurl down from heaven thy bolt of stone, O Indra : sharpen it, Maghavan, made keen by Soma.
Forward, behind, and from above and under, smite down the demons with thy rocky weapon.

20 They fly, the demon dogs, and, bent on mischief, fain would they harm indomitable Indra.
Śakra makes sharp his weapon for the wicked : now let him cast his bolt at fiendish wizards.

21 Indra hath ever been the fiends' destroyer who spoil oblations of the Gods' invokers :
Yea, Śakra, like an axe that spilts the timber, attacks and smashes them like earthen vessels.

22 Destroy the fiend shaped like an owl or owlet, destroy him in the form of dog or cuckoo.
Destroy him shaped as eagle or as vulture : as with a stone, O Indra, crush the demon.

23 Let not the fiend of witchcraft-workers reach us : may Dawn drive off the couples of Kimīdins.
Earth keep us safe from earthly woe and trouble : from grief that comes from heaven mid-air preserve us.

13 *The Warrior's title* : the rank of a Kṣatriya or prince of the military order.

The first eleven stanzas 'are considered to be a malediction upon the *Rákṣasas* by the *Ṛṣi*. To account for the change of tone (in 12—16), *Sāyaṇa* gives an unusual version of the legend told in the *Mahābhārata* of king *Kalmāṣapāda* being transformed to a *Rākṣasa*, and devouring the 100 sons of Vasiṣṭha : here it is said that a *Rākṣasa*, having devoured the *Ṛṣi's* sons, assumed his shape, and said to him, "I am *Vasiṣṭha*, thou art the *Rākṣasa*;" to which Vasiṣṭha replied by repeating this verse (stanza 12), declaratory of his discriminating between truth and falsehood.'—Wilson.

'The verses may, as Professor Max Müller supposes, have arisen out of Vasiṣṭha's contest with Viśvāmitra [See III. 53. 21. note], and it may have been the latter personage who brought those charges of heresy, and of murderous and demoniacal character against his rival.'—Muir, *O. S. Texts*, I. 327, 328.

15 *Yātudhāna* : explained by Sāyaṇa as = Rākṣasa. The Yātudhāna probably was rather the goblin or sorcerer while the Rākṣasa was the violent and voracious ogre.

17 Here the malediction on evil spirits in general is resumed and continued to the end of the hymn. *She too* : the *Rākṣasī*, or she-fiend.

23 *Kimīdins* : or vile spirits. See note on stanza 2.

24 Slay the male demon, Indra! slay the female, joying and triumphing in arts of magic.
Let the fools' gods with bent necks fall and perish, and see no more the Sun when he arises.

25 Look each one hither, look around: Indra and Soma, watch ye well.
Cast forth your weapon at the fiends; against the sorcerers hurl your bolt.

24 *Fools' gods* : *mū́radevāḥ* : explained by Sāyaṇa as=*māraṇakrīḍāḥ*, 'those who make killing their sport.' According to the St. Petersburg Lexicon, *mū́radevāḥ*=*mūladevāḥ*, a species of demons or goblins.

BOOK THE EIGHTH

HYMN I. *Indra.*

1. Glorify naught besides, O friends ; so shall no sorrow trouble you.
Praise only mighty Indra when the juice is shed, and say your lauds repeatedly :

2 Even him, eternal, like a bull who rushes down, men's Conqueror, bounteous like a cow ;
Him who is cause of both, of enmity and peace, to both sides most munificent.

3 Although these men in sundry ways invoke thee to obtain thine aid,
Be this our prayer, addressed, O Indra, unto thee, thine exaltation every day.

4 Those skilled in song, O Maghavan, among these men o'ercome with might the foeman's songs.
Come hither, bring us strength in many a varied form most near that it may succour us.

5 O Caster of the Stone, I would not sell thee for a mighty price,
Not for a thousand, Thunderer ! nor ten thousand, nor a hundred, Lord of countless wealth !

6 O Indra, thou art more to me than sire or niggard brother is.
Thou and my mother, O Good Lord, appear alike, to give me wealth abundantly.

7 Where art thou ? Whither art thou gone ? For many a place attracts thy mind.
Haste, Warrior, Fort-destroyer, Lord of battle's din, haste, holy songs have sounded forth.

8 Sing out the psalm to him who breaks down castles for his faithful friend,
Verses to bring the Thunderer to destroy the forts and sit on Kāṇva's sacred grass.

9 The Horses which are thine in tens, in hundreds, yea, in thousands thine,
Even those vigorous Steeds, fleet-footed in the course, with those come quickly near to us.

10 This day I call Sabardughā who animates the holy song,
Indra the richly-yielding Milch-cow who provides unfailing food in ample stream.

11 When Sūra wounded Etaśa, with Vāta's rolling winged car.
Indra bore Kutsa Ārjuneya off, and mocked Gandharva the unconquered One.

12 He without ligature, before making incision in the neck,
Closed up the wound again, most wealthy Maghavan, who maketh whole the injured part.

13 May we be never cast aside, and strangers, as it were, to thee.
We, Thunder-wielding Indra, count ourselves as trees rejected and unfit to burn.

14 O Vṛtra-slayer, we were thought slow and unready for the fray.
Yet once in thy great bounty may we have delight, O Hero, after praising thee.

15 If he will listen to my laud, then may our Soma-drops that flow
Rapidly through the strainer gladden Indra, drops due to the Tugryas' Strengthener.

16 Come now unto the common laud of thee and of thy faithful friend.
So may our wealthy nobles' praise give

2 *Bounteous like a cow* : the adjective is not in the text, but must be supplied in order to make the comparison intelligible. See *Vedische Studien*, I. 103. *To both sides* : to the singers and the institutors of sacrifice.

5 *A hundred* : meaning 'infinite,' according to the Commentator.

8 *For his faithful friend* : Ludwig takes Vāvātar to be the name of a king who has been deserted by Indra and consequently defeated in battle. *Kāṇva's sacred grass* : trimmed and prepared by Medhātithi and Medhyātithi, each of whom is a son of Kaṇva.

10 *Sabardughā* : the general name of cows which supply the milk required for sacrificial purposes. See VI. 48. 11, note. Here Indra himself is intended, as is shown in the following line.

11 *Sūra*: Sūrya, the Sun-God. *Wounded* : 'harassed.' —Wilson. *Etaśa*: a *protégé* of Indra. See Vol. I. Index. *Vāta* : the Wind-God. *Kutsa* : See Vol. I., Index. *Gandharva*: the Sun. The meaning of the stanza is somewhat obscure.

12 *Closed up the wound again* : healed Etaśa who had been wounded by Sūrya.

13 *Count ourselves as trees* : or, 'count us not as trees,' the meaning of *na*, 'not' and 'like' being ambiguous.

15 *Due to the Tugryas' Strengthener* : that belong to Indra the protector of the chiefs of the race of Tugra, who appear to have been the patrons of the Ṛsis of Kaṇva's family.

16 *Faithful friend* : See stanza 8.

joy to thee. Fain would I sing thine eulogy.

17 Press out the Soma with the stones, and in the waters wash it clean.
The men investing it with raiment made of milk shall milk it forth from out the stems.

18 Whether thou come from earth or from the lustre of the lofty heaven,
Wax stronger in thy body through my song of praise : fill full all creatures, O most Wise.

19 For Indra press the Soma out, most gladdening and most excellent.
May Śakra make it swell sent forth with every prayer and asking, as it were, for strength.

20 Let me not, still beseeching thee with earnest song at Soma rites,
Anger thee like soma wild beast. Who would not beseech him who hath power to grant his prayer ?

21 The draught made swift with rapturous joy, effectual with its mighty strength,
All-conquering, distilling transport, let him drink : for he in ecstasy gives us gifts.

22 Where bliss is not, may he, All-praised, God whom the pious glorify,
Bestow great wealth upon the mortal worshipper who sheds the juice and praises him.

23 Come, Indra, and rejoice thyself, O God, in manifold affluence.
Thou fillest like a lake thy vast capacious bulk with Soma and with draughts besides.

24 A thousand and a hundred Steeds are harnessed to thy golden car.
So may the long-maned Bays, yoked by devotion, bring Indra to drink the Soma juice.

25 Yoked to thy chariot wrought of gold, may thy two Bays with peacock tails,
Convey thee hither, Steeds with their white backs, to quaff sweet juice that makes us eloquent.

26 So drink, thou Lover of the Song, as the first drinker, of this juice.
This the outpouring of the savoury sap prepared is good and meet to gladden thee.

27 He who alone by wondrous deed is Mighty, Strong by holy works
May he come, fair of cheek ; may he not stay afar, but come and turn not from our call.

28 Śuṣṇa's quick moving castle thou hast crushed to pieces with thy bolts.
Thou, Indra, from of old, hast followed after light, since we have had thee to invoke.

29 My praises when the Sun hath risen, my praises at the time of noon,
My praises at the coming of the gloom of night, O Vasu, have gone forth to thee.

30 Praise yea, praise him. Of princes these are the most liberal of their gifts,
These, Paramajyā, Ninditāśva, Prapathī, most bounteous, O Medhyātithi.

31 When to the car, by faith, I yoked the horses longing for the way—
For skilled is Yadu's son in dealing precious wealth, he who is rich in herds of kine.

32 May he who gave me two brown steeds together with their cloths of gold,

17 *From out the stems* : See *Vedische Studien,* I. 133, 178. Sāyaṇa explains the second line differently : '(for by so doing) the leaders (of the rain, the *Maruts*) clothing (the sky with clouds) as with a vesture of the hide of the cow, milk forth (the water) for the rivers.'—Wilson.

21 *Let him drink* : *pibatu* : supplied by the Scholiast; there being no verb in the text.

22 *Where bliss is not* : that is, in defeat and trouble. But the meaning of *śevāre* is uncertain. 'At the sacrifice,' is Sāyaṇa's explanation. Von Roth suggests 'in the treasure-chamber.' I adopt Ludwig's interpretation.

23 *With draughts besides* : with thy fellow-topers (the Maruts).'—Wilson.

26 *As the first drinker* : 'According to the Scholiast, *pūrvapāḥ* means *Vāyu*, who, having arrived first in the race, drank the *Soma* before the other gods. The allusion is to the principal *graha* libation, called *Aindravāyava*, which *Indra* and *Vāyu* share together.'—Wilson.

28 *Castle* : of cloud. *Followed after light* : to find and bring it back.

30 *Praise him* : Indra, Paramajyā, Ninditāśva, and Prapathī appear to be the names of the chiefs who are praised for their liberality. Sāyaṇa makes Āsaṅga the speaker : 'Praise me, for we are the most liberal givers : (praise me as one) who bears the best arms (*paramajyā*), follows the right path (*prapathī*), and outstrips a horse in speed (*ninditāśva*).'

31 *The horses* : presented by the prince. The sentence is incomplete. The Scholiast supplies at the end of the line *tadānīm evammām stuhi*, then praise me thus. *Yadu's son* : Āsaṅga, descendant of the ancient eponymous hero Yadu. See Vol. I., Index. *Rich in herds of kine* : *paśuḥ* which appears to be in apposition with *yādvaḥ*, is hardly intelligible here. Sāyaṇa explains it as *paśumān*, having beasts or cattle, or as a derivative of *paś*, to see, and meaning one who sees what is subtle, *ūkṣmasya draṣṭā*. Neither of these explanations has anything but Sāyaṇa's name to recommend it, but I adopt the former as a makeshift.

May he, Āsaṅga's son Svanadratha, obtain all joy and high felicities.

33 Playoga's son Āsaṅga, by ten thousand, O Agni, hath surpassed the rest in giving.
For me ten bright-hued oxen have come forward like lotus-stalks from out a lake upstanding.

34 What time her husband's perfect restoration to his lost strength and manhood was apparent,
His consort Śaśvatī with joy addressed him, Now art thou well, my lord, and shalt be happy.

HYMN II. *Indra.*

1. HERE is the Soma juice expressed; O Vasu, drink till thou art full :
Undaunted God, we give it thee.

2 Washed by the men, pressed out with stones, strained through the filter made of wool,
'Tis like a courser bathed in stream.

3 This juice have we made sweet for thee like barley, blending it with milk.
Indra, I call thee to our feast.

4 Beloved of all, Indra alone drinks up the flowing Soma juice
Among the Gods and mortal men.

5 The Friend, whom not the brilliant-hued, the badly-mixt or bitter draught,
Repels, the far-extending God;

6 While other men than we with milk chase him as hunters chase a deer,
And with their kine inveigle him.

7 For him, for Indra, for the God, be pressed three draughts of Soma juice
In the juice-drinker's own abode.

8 Three reservoirs exude their drops, filled are three beakers to the brim,
All for one offering to the God.

9 Pure art thou, set in many a place, and blended in the midst with milk
And curd, to cheer the Hero best.

10 Here, Indra, are thy Soma-draughts pressed out by us, the strong, the pure:
They crave admixture of the milk.

11 O Indra, pour in milk, prepare the cake, and mix the Soma-draught :
I hear them say that thou art rich.

12 Quaffed juices fight within the breast. The drunken praise not by their wine,
The naked praise not when it rains.

13 Rich be the praiser of one rich, munificent and famed like thee:
High rank be his, O Lord of Bays.

14 Foe of the man who adds no milk, he heeds not any chanted hymn
Or holy psalm that may be sung.

15 Give us not, Indra, as a prey unto the scornful or the proud :
Help, Mighty One, with power and might.

16 This, even this, O Indra, we implore : as thy devoted friends,
The Kaṇvas praise thee with their hymns.

17 Naught else, O Thunderer, have I praised in the skilled singer's eulogy :

33 *Ten bright-hued oxen* : meaning ten thousand, according to Sāyaṇa.

34 Āsaṅga, the King whose liberality, with that of his son (32), and perhaps his grandsons (30), has been eulogized in the four preceding stanzas, had, the legend says, been changed to a woman by the imprecation of the Gods and afterwards restored to his manhood in consequence of his repentance and the intercession of Medhātithi and Medhyātithi whom he richly rewarded. In this stanza Śaśvatī congratulates him on his restoration. Professors Ludwig and Grassmann have translated the stanza more literally.

---

1 *O Vasu* : Good Lord, 'Giver of dwellings,' according to Sāyaṇa.

2 *Strained through the filter made of wool* more literally, 'cleansed by the tail-wool of the sheep,' the material of which the sieve, strainer, or filter used for clearing and purifying the Soma juice was made.

3 *Like barley* : or, like the sacrificial cake made of barley-meal.

4 *Alone drinks up* : he alone is to receive the entire libation, which other Gods only share among them.

5 *Brilliant-hued* : without sufficient mixture with milk to thicken it and change its colour. The meaning of this and the following stanza is : Indra prefers our libations, imperfectly prepared as they may be, to the milk-offerings with which other men endeavour to attract him.

8 *Three reservoirs* : or troughs used in the preparation of the Soma-libations. They are called severally, *droṇakalaśa*, *pūtabhṛt*, and *ādhavanīya*.

9 *In the midst* : 'in the middle (of the day ?).'—Hillebrandt.

12 This stanza breaks the connexion between stanzas 11 and 13, and is in itself almost unintelligible. Wilson paraphrases, after Sāyaṇa : 'The potations (of Soma) contend in thy interior (for thine exhilaration) like the ebriety caused by wine : thy worshippers praise thee (filled full of *Soma*) like the udder (of a cow with milk).' Sāyaṇa's explanation of *nagnāḥ*, naked men, as worshippers, *stotāraḥ*, 'who do not desert the verses of the Veda,' is obviously impossible. *Ūdhaḥ* udder, frequently means the rainy sky, and it may have this meaning here ; so that the sense of the passage may possibly be, as Ludwig suggests, that neither great wealth nor abject poverty tends to make a man devout. The rich man when he drinks his wine at home and the ill-clad wretch exposed to the drenching rain are equally regardless of the Gods.

13 *Rich be the praiser of the rich* : this appears to be the continuation of 'thou art rich' of stanza 11.

14 Indra will not accept worship without oblation.

On thy laud only have I thought.

18 The Gods seek him who presses out the Soma; they desire not sleep :
They punish sloth unweariedly.

19 Come hither swift with gifts of wealth— be not thou angry with us—like
A great man with a youthful bride.

20 Let him not, wrathful with us, spend the evening far from us to-day,
Like some unpleasant son-in-law.

21 For well we know this Hero's love, most liberal of the boons he gives,
His plans whom the three worlds display.

22 Pour forth the gift which Kaṇvas bring, for none more glorious do we know
Than the Strong Lord with countless aids.

23 O presser, offer Soma first to Indra, Hero, Śakra, him
The Friend of man, that he may drink;

24 Who, in untroubled ways, is best provider, for his worshippers.
Of strength in horses and in kine.

25 Pressers, for him blend Soma juice, each draught most excellent, for him
The Brave, the Hero, for his joy.

26 The Vṛtra-slayer drinks the juice. May he who gives a hundred aids
Approach, nor stay afar from us.

27 May the strong Bay Steeds, yoked by prayer, bring hither unto us our Friend,
Lover of Song, renowned by songs.

28 Sweet are the Soma juices, come ! Blent are the Soma juices, come !
Ṛṣi-like, mighty, fair of cheek, come hither quickly to the feast.

29 And lauds which strengthen thee for great bounty and valour, and exalt
Indra who doeth glorious deeds,

30 And songs to thee who lovest song, and all those hymns addressed to thee—
These evermore confirm thy might.

31 Thus he, sole doer of great deeds whose hand holds thunder, gives us strength,
He who hath never been subdued.

32 Vṛtra he slays with his right hand, even Indra, great with mighty power,
And much-invoked in many a place.

33 He upon whom all men depend, all regions, all achievements, he
Takes pleasure in our wealthy chiefs.

34 All this hath he accomplished, yea, Indra, most gloriously renowned,
Who gives our wealthy princes strength.

35 Who drives his chariot seeking spoil, even from afar, to him he loves :
For swift is he to bring men wealth.

36 The Sage who, winning spoil with steeds, slays Vṛtra, Hero with the men,
His servant's faithful succourer.

37 O Priyamedhas, worship with collected mind this Indra whom
The Soma hath full well inspired.

38 Ye Kaṇvas, sing the Mighty One, Lord of the Brave, who loves renown,
All-present, glorified by song.

39 Strong Friend, who, with no trace of feet, restores the cattle to the men,
Who rest their wish and hope on him.

40 Shaped as a Ram, Stone-hurler ! once thou camest hither to the son
Of Kaṇva, wise Medhyātithi.

41 Vibhindu, thou hast helped this man, giving him thousands four times ten,
And afterward eight thousand more.

42 And these twain pouring streams of milk, creative, daughters of delight,
For wedlock sake I glorify.

19 *A great man* : the exact meaning of *mahā́n*, great, is not certain. Sāyaṇa explains it by *guṇairadhikaḥ*, eminent on account of his good qualities. 'Be not bashful, like the ardent husband of a new bride.'—Wilson. 'Like a rich man, newly married.'—Grassmann.

20 *Like some unpleasant son-in-law* : who sees that his company is unwelcome and consequently stays at home.

23 *First to Indra* : See VIII. 1. 26. *Śakra* : Indra, the Mighty One.

34 *All this hath he accomplished* : the slaughter of Vṛtra and other great deeds ; or, he made all these creatures.

36 *The Sage* : Indra. *With the men* : accompanied by the Maruts.

37 *Priyamedhas* : members of the family of one of the Ṛṣis.

39 *With no trace of feet* : without tracking the lost cattle (the rays of light) by their footsteps.

40 *Shaped as a Ram* : See I. 51. 1. The legend is told in the *Ṣaḍviṁśa Brāhmaṇa*, I. 1.

41 *Vibhindu* : the prince, the institutor of the sacrifice.

42 The stanza is obscure, the meaning of *mākī́*, a feminine dual which Sāyaṇa explains by *nirmātryau*, makers or creators, *i.e.* heaven and earth, being uncertain. Sāyaṇa's paraphrase of the stanza is : 'I glorify these two (heaven and earth), the augmenters of water, the originators (of beings), the benefactors of the worshipper, on account of their generation (of the wealth so given to me).'—Wilson.

———

HYMN III. *Indra.*

1. DRINK, Indra, of the savoury juice, and cheer thee with our milky draught.
Be, for our weal, our Friend and sharer of the feast, and let thy wisdom guard us well.

2 In thy kind grace and favour may we still be strong: expose us not to foe's attack.
With manifold assistance guard and succour us, and bring us to felicity.

3 May these my songs of praise exalt thee, Lord, who hast abundant wealth.
Men skilled in holy hymns, pure, with the hues of fire, have sung them with their lauds to thee.

4 He, with his might enhanced by Ṛṣis thousandfold, hath like an ocean spread himself.
His majesty is praised as true at solemn rites, his power where holy singers rule.

5 Indra for worship of the Gods, Indra while sacrifice proceeds,
Indra, as worshippers in battle-shock, we call, Indra that we may win the spoil.

6 With might hath Indra spread out heaven and earth, with power hath Indra lighted up the Sun.
In Indra are all creatures closely held; in him meet the distilling Soma-drops.

7 Men with their lauds are urging thee, Indra, to drink the Soma first.
The Ṛbhus in accord have lifted up their voice, and Rudras sung thee as the first.

8 Indra increased his manly strength at sacrifice, in the wild rapture of this juice.
And living men to-day, even as of old, sing forth their praises to his majesty.

9 I crave of thee that hero strength, that thou mayst first regard this prayer,
Wherewith thou holpest Bhṛgu and the Yatis and Praskaṇva when the prize was staked.

10 Wherewith thou sentest mighty waters to the sea, that, Indra, is thy manly strength.
For ever unattainable is this power of him to whom the worlds have cried aloud.

11 Help us, O Indra, when we pray to thee for wealth and hero might.
First help thou on to strength the man who strives to win, and aid our laud, O Ancient One.

12 Help for us, Indra, as thou holpest Paura once, this man's devotions bent on gain.
Help, as thou gavest Ruśama and Śyāvaka and Svarṇara and Kṛpa aid.

13 What newest of imploring prayers shall, then, the zealous mortal sing?
For have not they who laud his might, and Indra-power won for themselves the light of heaven?

14 When shall they keep the Law and praise thee mid the Gods? Who counts as Ṛṣi and as sage?
When ever wilt thou, Indra Maghavan, come nigh to presser's or to praiser's call?

15 These songs of ours exceeding sweet, these hymns of praise ascend to thee,
Like ever-conquering chariots that display their strength, gain wealth, and give unfailing aid.

16 The Bhṛgus are like Suns, like Kaṇvas, and have gained all that their thoughts were bent upon.
The living men of Priyamedha's race have sung exalting Indra with their lauds.

17 Best slayer of the Vṛtras, yoke thy Bay Steeds, Indra, from afar.
Come with the High Ones hither, Maghavan, to us, Mighty, to drink the Soma juice.

18 For these, the bards and singers, have cried out to thee with prayer, to gain the sacrifice.
As such, O Maghavan, Indra, who lovest song, even as a lover hear my call.

19 Thou from the lofty plains above, O Indra, hurledst Vṛtra down.
Thou dravest forth the kine of guileful Mṛgaya and Arbuda from the mountain's hold.

3 *With the hues of fire*: or, radiant as Agni.

7 *The Ṛbhus*: as deities connected with the seasons which are regulated by the Sun whom Indra has caused to shine.

9 *Bhṛgu*: See Vol. I., Index. *Yatis*: an ancient race of ascetics connected with the Bhṛgus, and, according to one legend, said to have taken part in the creation of the world. *Praskaṇva*: a Ṛṣi, son of Kaṇva, the seer of some hymns of Book I.

10 *The worlds*: all men, or all living creatures.

12 *Paura*: the son of King Puru. *Ruśama*, *Śyāvaka*, *Svarṇara*, and *Kṛpa* appear to have been princes especially favoured by Indra. Cf. stanza 2 of the following hymn.

17 *High Ones*: the Maruts.

18 *To gain the sacrifice*: to ensure its proper performance and the blessings which flow from it.

19 *Mṛgaya*: See IV. 16 13. *Arbuda*: See Vol. I., Index.

20 Bright were the flaming fires, the Sun gave forth his shine, and Soma, Indra's juice, shone clear.
Indra, thou blewest the great Dragon from the air : men must regard that valorous deed.

21 The fairest courser of them all, who runneth on as 'twere to heaven.
Which Indra and the Maruts gave, and Pākasthāman Kaurayāṇ.

22 To me hath Pākasthāman given, a ruddy horse, good at the pole,
Filling his girth and rousing wealth;

23 Compared with whom no other ten strong coursers, harnessed to the pole,
Bear Tugrya to his dwelling place.

24 Raiment is body, food is life, and healing ointment giveth strength.
As the free-handed giver of the ruddy steed, I have named Pākasthāman fourth.

HYMN IV. *Indra.*

1. THOUGH, Indra, thou art called by men eastward and westward, north and south,
Thou chiefly art with Ānava and Turvaśa, brave Champion ! urged by men to come.

2 Or, Indra, when with Ruma, Ruśama, Śyāvaka, and Kṛpa thou rejoicest thee,
Still do the Kaṇvas, bringing praises, with their prayers, O Indra, draw thee hither : come.

3 Even as the wild-bull, when he thirsts, goes to the desert's watery pool,
Come hither quickly both at morning and at eve, and with the Kaṇvas drink thy fill.

4 May the drops gladden thee, rich Indra, and obtain bounty for him who pours the juice.
Soma pressed in the mortar didst thou take and drink, and hence hast won surpassing might.

5 With mightier strength he conquered strength, with energy he crushed their wrath.
O Indra, Strong in youth, all those who sought the fray bent and bowed down to thee like trees.

6 He who wins promise of thine aid goes girt as with a thousand mighty men of war.
He makes his son preëminent in hero might : he serves with reverential prayer.

7 With thee, the Mighty, for our Friend, we will not fear or feel fatigue.
May we see Turvaśa and Yadu : thy great deed, O Hero, must be glorified.

8 On his left hip the Hero hath reclined himself : the proffered feast offends him not.
The milk is blended with the honey of the bee : quickly come hither, haste, and drink.

9 Indra, thy friend is fair of form and rich in horses, cars, and kine.
He evermore hath food accompanied by wealth, and radiant joins the company.

10 Come like a thirsty antelope to the drinking-place : drink Soma to thy heart's desire.
Raining it down, O Maghavan, day after day, thou gainest thy surpassing might.

11 Priest, let the Soma juice flow forth, for Indra longs to drink thereof.
He even now hath yoked his vigorous Bay Steeds : the Vṛtra-slayer hath come near.

12 The man with whom thou fillest thee with Soma deems himself a pious worshipper.
This thine appropriate food is here poured out for thee : come, hasten forward. drink of it.

13 Press out the Soma juice, ye priests, for Indra borne upon his car.
The pressing-stones speak loud of Indra, while they shed the juice which, offered, honours him.

14 To the brown juice may his dear vigorous Bay Steeds bring Indra, to our holy task.

20 *The great Dragon* : or Serpent, Ahi.

21 *Kaurayāṇ* : Kaurayāṇa, the son of Kuruyāṇa. Pākasthāman, whose liberality is praised in stanzas 21—24, is not mentioned elsewhere.

23 *Tugrya* : Bhujyu, son of Tugra See Vol. I., Index.

---

1 *Ānava* : descendant of the eponymous Anu, *Turvaśa* : See Vol. I., Index.

2 *Ruśama*, *Śyāvaka*, and *Kṛpa* have been mentioned in stanza 12 of the preceding hymn. *Ruma* was another of Indra's favourites.

3 *The wild-bull* : or Gaura (Bos Gaurus), a kind of buffalo.

7 *May we see Turvaśa and Yadu* : enjoying happiness through thy favour.—Sāyaṇa.

9 *Thy friend* : the man whom thou favourest. *Joins the company* : the assembly of his equals.

10 *Raining it down* : pouring down the transformed Soma in the shape of rain. See *Vedische Studien*, I. 88.

Hither let thy Car-steeds who seek the sacrifice bring thee to our drink-offerings.

15 Pūṣan, the Lord of ample wealth, for firm alliance we elect.
May he with wisdom, Śakra ! Looser ! Much-invoked ! aid us to riches and to seed.

16 Sharpen us like a razor in the barber's hands : send riches thou who settest free.
Easy to find with thee are treasures of the Dawn for mortal man whom thou dost speed.

17 Pūṣan, I long to win thy love, I long to praise thee, Radiant God.
Excellent Lord, 'tis strange to me, no wish have I to sing the psalm that Pajra sings.

18 My kine, O Radiant God, seek pasture where they will, my during wealth, Immortal One.
Be our protector, Pūṣan ! be, most liberal Lord, propitious to our gathering strength.

19 Rich was the gift Kuruṅga gave, a hundred steeds at morning rites.
Among the gifts of Turvaśas we thought of him, the opulent, the splendid King.

20 What by his morning songs Kāṇva, the powerful, hath, with the Priyamedhas, gained—
The herds of sixty thousand pure and spotless kine, have I, the Ṛṣi, driven away.

21 The very trees were joyful at my coming : kine they obtained in plenty, steeds in plenty.

HYMN V. *Aśvins.*

1. WHEN, even as she were present here, red Dawn hath shone from far away,
She spreadeth light on every side.

2 Like Heroes on your will-yoked car far-shining, Wonder-Workers ! ye
Attend, O Aśvins, on the Dawn.

3 By you, O Lords of ample wealth, our songs of praise have been observed :
As envoy have I brought the prayer.

4 Kaṇvas must praise the Aśvins dear to many, making many glad,
Most rich, that they may succour us.

5 Most liberal, best at winning strength, inciters, Lords of splendour who
Visit the worshipper's abode.

6 So for devout Sudeva dew with fatness his unfailing mead,
And make it rich for sacrifice.

7 Hitherward running speedily with horses, as with rapid hawks,
Come, Aśvins, to our song of praise :

8 Wherewith the three wide distances, and all the lights that are in heaven.
Ye traverse, and three times of night.

9 O Finders of the Day, that we may win us food of kine and wealth,
Open the paths for us to tread.

10 O Aśvins, bring us wealth in kine, in noble heroes, and in cars :
Bring us the strength that horses give.

11 Ye Lords of splendour, glorified, ye Wonder-Workers borne on paths
Of gold, drink sweets with Soma juice.

12 To us, ye Lords of ample wealth, and to our wealth chiefs extend
Wide shelter, ne'er to be assailed.

13 Come quickly downward to the prayer of people whom ye favour most :
Approach not unto other folk.

14 Ye Aśvins whom our minds perceive, drink of this lovely gladdening draught,
The meath which we present to you.

15 Bring riches hither unto us in hundreds and in thousands, source
Of plenteous food, sustaining all.

16 Verily sages call on you, ye Heroes, in full many a place.
Moved by the priests, O Aśvins, come.

17 Men who have trimmed the sacred grass, bringing oblations and prepared,

15 *Pūṣan* : may here be a name of Indra. *Looser* : of the chariot-horses when thou comest to sacrifices ; or, according to Sāyaṇa, liberator (from sin).

17 *Pajra* : one of the Pajras, a celebrated priestly family, with whom the Kaṇvas appear to have been on hostile terms.

19 *Kuruṅga* : this prince's name does not occur again.

20 *Pure and spotless* : I follow Sāyaṇa's interpretation of *nirmajām*, but its correctness is at least doubtful. Von Roth suggests 'to the watering-place' as the meaning of the word, and Ludwig 'so that none remained behind.'

3 *Lords of ample wealth* : 'affluent in sacrifices.'—Wilson. See V. 74 7. *As envoy* : as the messenger of the patron of the sacrifice.

8 *Times of night* : *yāmas*, night-watches of three hours each.

11 *Sweets* : or meath, *mádhu* ; here, perhaps, the milk.—Ludwig.

16 *By the priests* : *vāghádbhiḥ* : according to Sāyaṇa, 'with horses.'

O Aśvins, are invoking you.

18 May this our hymn of praise to-day, most powerful to bring you, be,
O Aśvins, nearest to your hearts.

19 The skin filled full of savoury meath, laid in the pathway of your car—
O Aśvins, drink ye both therefrom.

20 For this, ye Lords of ample wealth, bring blessing for our herd, our kine,
Our progeny, and plenteous food.

21 Ye too unclose to us like doors the strengthening waters of the sky,
And rivers, ye who find the day.

22 When did the son of Tugra serve you, Men? Abandoned in the sea,
That with winged steeds your car might fly.

23 Ye, O Nāsatyas, ministered to Kaṇva with repeated aid,
When cast into the heated pit.

24 Come near with those most recent aids of yours which merit eulogy,
When I invoke you, Wealthy Gods.

25 As ye protected Kaṇva erst, Priyamedha and Upastuta,
Atri, Śiñjāra, Aśvins Twain!

26 And Aṁśu in decisive fight, Agastya in the fray for kine.
And, in his battles, Sobhari.

27 For so much bliss, or even more, O Aśvins, Wealthy Gods, than this,
We pray while singing hymns to you.

28 Ascend your car with golden seat, O Aśvins, and with reins of gold,
That reaches even to the sky.

29 Golden is its supporting shaft, the axle also is of gold,
And both the wheels are made of gold.

30 Thereon, ye Lords of ample wealth, come to us even from afar,
Come ye to this mine eulogy.

31 From far away ye come to us, Aśvins, enjoying plenteous food
Of Dāsas, O Immortal Ones.

32 With splendour, riches, and renown, O Aśvins, hither come to us,
Nāsatyas, shining brilliantly.

33 May dappled horses, steeds who fly with pinions, bring you hitherward
To people skilled in sacrifice.

34 The wheel delayeth not that car of yours accompanied by song,
That cometh with a store of food.

35 Borne on that chariot wrought of gold, with coursers very fleet of foot,
Come, O Nāsatyas, swift as thought.

36 O Wealthy Gods, ye taste and find the brisk and watchful wild beast good.
Associate wealth with food for us.

37 As such, O Aśvins, find for me my share of new-presented gifts,
As Kaśu, Cedi's son, gave me a hundred head of buffaloes, and ten thousand kine.

38 He who hath given me for mine own ten Kings like gold to look upon.
At Caidya's feet are all the people round about, all those who think upon the shield.

39 No man, not any, goes upon the path on which the Cedis walk.
No other prince, no folk is held more liberal of gifts than they.

19 The Aśvins appear to be invited to halt and drink the libations prepared for them by their worshippers, and not, as Sāyaṇa explains, to drink from the skin suspended in their own car.—Ludwig.

22 *The son of Tugra*: Bhujyu, whose rescue by the Aśvins has frequently been related and referred to. The meaning is, I do not honour you only when I am in distress, as others whom you have aided have done.

23 *Ministered to Kaṇva*: See I. 112. 5, and 118. 7.

24 *Wealthy Gods*: the meaning of *vṛṣaṇvasū* is uncertain: 'rich in showers' is Sāyaṇa's explanation, and 'excellent as steers' Prof. Ludwig's. I follow von Roth, but his interpretation is conjectural.

25 *Kaṇva, Priyamedha, Upastuta* and *Atri* have been mentioned in Book I. Sāyaṇa takes *śiñjāram* to be an epithet of Atri, 'repeating praises.'

26 *Aṁśu*: a worshipper so named.—Sāyaṇa. *Agastya*: appears in I. 117. 11, where he is said to have been the family-priest of Khela. The great Ṛṣi Agastya is the seer of Hymns 166—191 of Book I. See also VII. 33. 10. *Sobhari*: a Ṛṣi, the seer of Hymns 19—22 of this Book.

31 *Plenteous food of Dāsas*: the meaning appears to be that even far away in the east the Dāsas or non-Āryan inhabitants sacrifice to the Aśvins. Sāyaṇa explains the stanza differently: 'Immortal Aśvins, destroyers of the cities of the *Dāsas*, ye bring to us food from afar.'—Wilson.

36 According to Sāyaṇa the *watchful wild beast* is the Soma which must be chased or sought after by the Gods. Ludwig would read *svapatho*, with a transitive and causal meaning, instead of *svádatho*, *i. e.*, ye when ye appear in the morning *send to sleep* the wild beasts that have been awake all night. The stanza is obscure.

37 *Buffaloes*: or camels.

38 This stanza appears to be spoken by Kaśu who is called Caidya or son of Cedi. *Who think upon the shield*: who are practised in wearing armour of leather, according to Sāyaṇa.

HYMN VI *Indra*

1. INDRA, great in his power and might, and like Parjanya rich in rain,
Is magnified by Vatsa's lauds.

2 When the priests, strengthening the Son of Holy Law, present their gifts,
Singers with Order's hymn of praiser.

3 Since Kaṇvas with their lauds have made Indra complete the sacrifice
Words are their own appropriate arms.

4 Before his hot displeasure all the peoples, all the men, bow down,
As rivers bow them to the sea.

5 This power of his shone brightly forth when Indra brought together, like
A skin, the worlds of heaven and earth.

6 The fiercely-moving Vṛtra's head he severed with his thunderbolt,
His mighty hundred-knotted bolt.

7 Here are—we sing them loudly forth—our thoughts among the best of songs.
Even lightnings like the blaze of fire.

8 When hidden thoughts, spontaneously advancing, glow, and with the stream
Of sacrifice the Kaṇvas shine.

9 Indra, may we obtain that wealth in horses and in herds of cows,
And prayer that may be noticed first.

10 I from my Father have received deep knowledge of the Holy Law :
I was born like unto the Sun.

11 After the lore of ancient time I make, like Kaṇva, beauteous songs,
And Indra's self gains strength thereby.

12 Whatever Ṛṣis have not praised thee, Indra, or have lauded thee,
By me exalted wax thou strong.

13 When his wrath thundered, when he rent Vṛtra to pieces, limb by limb,
He sent the waters to the sea.

14 Against the Dasyu Śuṣṇa thou, Indra, didst hurl thy during bolt :
Thou, Dread one, hast a hero's fame.

15 Neither the heavens nor firmaments nor regions of the earth contain
Indra, the Thunderer with his might.

16 O Indra him who lay at length staying thy copious waters thou,
In his own footsteps, smotest down.

17 Thou hiddest deep in darkness him, O Indra, who had set his grasp
On spacious heaven and earth conjoined.

18 Indra, whatever Yatis and Bhṛgus have offered praise to thee,
Listen, thou Mighty, to my call.

19 Indra, these spotted cows yield thee their butter and the milky draught;
Aiders, thereby, of sacrifice;

20 Which, teeming, have received thee as a life-germ, Indra, with their mouth,
Like Sūrya who sustaineth all

21 O Lord of Might, with hymns of praise the Kaṇvas have increased thy power,
The drops poured forth have strengthened thee.

22 Under thy guidance, Indra, mid thy praises, Lord of Thunder, shall
The sacrifice be soon performed.

23 Indra, disclose much food for us, like a stronghold with store of kine:
Give progeny and heroic strength.

24 And, Indra, grant us all that wealth of fleet steeds which shone bright of old
Among the tribes of Nahuṣas.

25 Hither thou seemest to attract heaven's fold which shines before our eyes,
When, Indra, thou art kind to us.

26 Yea, when thou puttest forth thy power, Indra, thou governest the folk.
Mighty, unlimited in strength.

27 The tribes who bring oblations call to thee, to thee to give them help,
With drops to thee who spreadest far.

28 There where the mountains downward slope, there by the meeting of the streams
The Sage was manifest with song.

3 *Words are their own appropriate arms* : 'they declare all weapons needless.'—Wilson.

10 *From my Father*: 'from Indra, the true protector,' according to Sāyaṇa.

12 *Have not praised thee* : have not praised thee yet, that is, will praise thee hereafter.—Ludwig.

16 *In his own footsteps* : or, in the (waters) at his feet. 'Into the rushing streams.'—Wilson.

17 *Conjoined* : like two bowls turned towards each other.

18 *Yatis* : 'pious sages.'—Wilson. Aṅgirases, according to Sāyaṇa.

20 The stanza is unintelligible to me. Sāyaṇa says that 'thee' means Indra in the shape of the grass which his fertilizing energy causes to grow, and by feeding on which the cows multiply. This energy of Indra's is all-supporting like the sun. See Wilson's note. Ludwig proposes an alteration of the text.

24 *Tribes of Nahuṣas* : or, perhaps, the neighbouring tribes.

28 *The Sage* : Indra. 'Sāyaṇa's conclusion of the purport of the verse is, that men ought to sacrifice in those places where *Indra* is said to be manifested.'—Wilson.

29 Thence, marking, from his lofty place
    downward he looks upon the sea,
  And thence with rapid stir he moves.

30 Then, verily, they see the light refulgent
    of primeval seed,
  Kindled on yonder side of heaven.

31 Indra, the Kaṇvas all exalt thy wisdom
    and thy manly power,
  And, Mightiest ! thine heroic strength.

32 Accept this eulogy of mine, Indra, and
    guard me carefully :
  Strengthen my thought and prosper it.

33 For thee, O Mighty, Thunder-armed, we
    singers through devotion have
  Fashioned the hymn that we may live.

34 To Indra have the Kaṇvas sung, like waters
    speeding down a slope :
  The song is fain to go to him.

35 As rivers swell the ocean, so our hymns
    of praise make Indra strong,
  Eternal, of resistless wrath.

36 Come with thy lovely Bay Steeds, come
    to us from regions far away :
  O Indra, drink this Soma juice.

37 Best slayer of Vṛtras, men whose sacred
    grass is ready trimmed
  Invoke thee for the gain of spoil.

38 The heavens and earth come after thee
    as the wheel follows Etaśa :
  To thee flow Soma-drops effused.

39 Rejoice, O Indra, in the light, rejoice in
    Śaryaṇāvān, be Glad in the sacrificer's
    hymn.

40 Grown strong in heaven, the Thunder-armed
    hath bellowed, Vṛtra-slayer, Bull,
  Chief drinker of the Soma juice.

41 Thou art a Ṛṣi born of old, sole Ruler
    over all by might :
  Thou, Indra, guardest well our wealth.

42 May thy Bay Steeds with beauteous backs,
    a hundred, bring thee to the feast,
  Bring thee to these our Soma-draughts.

43 The Kaṇvas with their hymns of praise
    have magnified this ancient thought
  That swells with streams of meath and
    oil.

44 Mid mightiest Gods let mortal man choose
    Indra at the sacrifice,
  Indra, whoe'er would win, for help.

45 Thy steeds, by Priyamedhas praised, shall
    bring thee, God whom all invoke,
  Hither to drink the Soma juice.

46 A hundred thousand have I gained from
    Parśu, from Tirindira,
  And presents of the Yādavas.

47 Ten thousand head of kine, and steeds three
    times a hundred they bestowed
  On Pajra for the Sāma-song.

48 Kakuha hath reached up to heaven, bes-
    towing buffaloes yoked in fours,
  And matched in fame the Yādavas.

HYMN VII.   *Maruts.*

1. O MARUTS, when the sage hath poured the
    Tṛṣṭup forth as food for you,
  Ye shine amid the mountain-clouds.

2 When, Bright Ones, fain to show your might
    ye have determined on your course,
  The mountain-clouds have bent them down.

3 Loud roaring with the winds the Sons of
    Pṛśni have upraised themselves :
  They have poured out the streaming food.

4 The Maruts spread the mist abroad and
    make mountains rock and reel,
  When with the winds they go their way ;

5 What time the rivers and the hills before
    your coming bowed them down,
  So to sustain your mighty force.

6 We call on you for aid by night, on you
    for succour in the day,
  On you while sacrifice proceeds.

7 These, verily, wondrous, red of hue, speed
    on their courses with a roar
  Over the ridges of the sky.

8 With might they drop the loosened rein so
    that the Sun may run his course,
  And spread themselves with beams of light.

---

46 *From Parśu, from Tirindira :* 'from Tirindira the son of Parśu.'—Wilson. Both names are Iranian (cf. Tiridates, Persa). See Weber's *Episches im Vedischen Ritual,* pp. 36—38 (Sitzungsberichte der K. P. Akademie der Wissenschaften, 1891, XXXVIII).

  Yādavas : or Yadus, descendants of the hero Yadu.

  47 *Pajra :* See VIII. 4. 17.

  48 *Kakuha :* or, the lofty one, meaning Tirindira. *Buffaloes :* or camels.

---

  1 *The Tṛṣṭup :* according to one of Sāyaṇa's three interpretations, the Soma offering at the midday libation accompanied by hymns in the Tṛṣṭup metre.

  8 *They drop the loosened rein :* they speed forward to prepare the way for the Sun.

---

  29 *The sea :* the reservoir of Soma juice.

  30 *The light :* the Sun which is lighted up beyond the range of men's sight.

  38 *As the wheel follows Etaśa :* as the chariot of the Sun follows the horse that draws it.

  39 *Śaryaṇāvān :* said to be a lake and district in Kurukṣetra. See I. 84. 14, note.

9 Accept, ye Maruts, this my song, accept ye this mine hymn of praise,
Accept, Ṛbhukṣans, this my call.

10 The dappled Cows have poured three lakes, meath for the Thunder-wielding God,
From the great cask, the watery cloud.

11 O Maruts, quickly come to us when, longing for felicity,
We call you hither from the sky.

12 For, Rudras and Ṛbhukṣans, ye, Most Bountiful, are in the house,
Wise when the gladdening draught is drunk.

13 O Maruts, send us down from heaven riches distilling rapturous joy,
With plenteous food, sustaining all.

14 When, Bright Ones, hither from the hills ye have resolved to take your way,
Ye revel in the drops effused.

15 Man should solicit with his lauds happiness which belongs to them,
So great a band invincible.

16 They who like fiery sparks with showers of rain blow through the heaven and earth,
Milking the spring that never fails.

17 With chariots and tumultuous roar, with tempests and with hymns of praise
The Sons of Pṛśni hurry forth.

18 For wealth, we think of that whereby ye aided Yadu, Turvaśa,
And Kaṇva who obtained the spoil.

19 May these our viands Bounteous Ones! that flow in streams like holy oil,
With Kāṇva's hymns, increase your might.

20 Where, Bounteous Lords for whom the grass is trimmed, are ye rejoicing now?
What Brahman is adoring you?

21 Is it not there where ye of old, supplied with sacred grass, for lauds
Inspired the strong in sacrifice?

22 They brought together both the worlds, the mighty waters, and the Sun,
And, joint by joint, the thunderbolt.

23 They sundered Vṛtra limb from limb and split the gloomy mountain-clouds,
Performing a heroic deed.

24 They reinforced the power and strength of Trita as he fought, and helped
Indra in battle with the foe.

25 They deck themselves for glory, bright, celestial, lightning in their hands,
And helms of gold upon their heads.

26 When eagerly ye from far away came to the cavern of the Bull,
He bellowed in his fear like Heaven.

27 Borne by your golden-footed steeds, O Gods, come hither to receive
The sacrifice we offer you.

28 When the red leader draws along their spotted deer yoked to the car.
The Bright Ones come, and shed the rain.

29 Suṣoma, Śaryaṇāvān, and Ārjīka full of homes, have they,
These Heroes, sought with downward car.

30 When, Maruts, ye come to him, the singer who invokes you thus,
With favours to your suppliant?

31 What now? where have ye still a friend since ye left Indra all alone?
Who counteth on your friendship now?

32 The Kaṇvas sing forth Agni's praise together with our Maruts' who
Wield thunder and wear swords of gold.

33 Hither for new felicity may I attract the Impetuous Ones,
The Heroes with their wondrous strength.

34 Before them sink the very hills deeming themselves abysses: yea,
Even the mountains bend them down.

35 Steeds flying on their tortuous path through mid-air carry them, and give
The man who lauds them strength and life.

9 *Ṛbhukṣans*: Mighty Ones, according to Sāyaṇa.

10 *The dappled Cows*; the Maruts. *Three lakes*: three large Soma receptacles, the *Droṇakalaśa* the *Ādhavanīya*, and the *Pūtabhṛt*. The meaning is, the Maruts have poured down abundant water from the rain-cloud.

19 *With Kāṇva's hymns*: hymns of the Ṛṣi Punarvatsa, a descendant of Kaṇva.

21 *The strong in sacrifice*: the *Maghavans*, wealthy worshippers.

24 *Trita*: a Vedic deity, perhaps Agni in his third form, generally associated with Indra, Vāyu, and the Maruts. See. Vol. I., index. *In battle with the foe*: or, to overcome Vṛtra.

26 *The cavern of the Bull*: perhaps, the hollow of the rain-cloud: 'the opening of the rainy (firmament).'—Wilson.

28 *Leader*: or side-horse.

29 *Śaryaṇāvān*: Has occurred before (See I. 84. 14 and VIII 6. 39) as the name of a lake. *Ārjīka* is said by Sāyaṇa to be the name of a district, and he takes *Suṣoma* (containing excellent Soma) to be an adjective qualifying it, see Zimmer, *Altindisches Leben*, p. 19.

31 *Left Indra all alone?*: This is merely a rhetorical question meaning, ye never did desert him. The Maruts alone stood by him when he fought with Vṛtra.

36 Agni was born the first of all, like Sūrya lovely with his light :
With lustre these have spread abroad.

HYMN VIII. *Aśvins.*

1. WITH all the succours that are yours, O Aśvins, hither come to us :
Wonderful, borne on paths of gold, drink ye the meath with Soma juice.

2 Come now, ye Aśvins, on your car decked with a sun-bright canopy,
Bountiful, with your golden forms, Sages with depth of intellect.

3 Come hither from the Nahuṣas, come, drawn by pure hymns, from mid-air.
O Aśvins, drink the savoury juice shed in the Kaṇvas' sacrifice.

4 Come to us hither from the heavens, come from mid-air, well-loved by us :
Here Kaṇva's son hath pressed for you the pleasant meath of Soma juice.

5 Come, Aśvins, to give ear to us, to drink the Soma, Aśvins, come.
Hail, Strengtheners of the praise-song ! speed onward, ye Heroes, with your thoughts.

6 As, Heroes, in the olden time the Ṛṣis called you to their aid,
So now, O Aśvins, come to us, come near to this mine eulogy.

7 Even from the luminous sphere of heaven come to us, ye who find the light,
Carers for Vatsa, through our prayers and lauds, O ye who hear our call.

8 Do others more than we adore the Aśvins with their hymns of praise ?
The Ṛṣi Vatsa, Kaṇva's son, hath magnified you with his songs.

9 The holy singer with his hymns hath called you, Aśvins, hither-ward;
Best Vṛtra-slayers, free from stain, as such bring us felicity.

10 What time, ye Lords of ample wealth, the Lady mounted on your car,
Then, O ye Aśvins, ye attained all wishes that your hearts desired.

11 Come thence, O Aśvins, on your car that hath a thousand ornaments :
Vatsa the sage, the sage's son, hath sung a song of sweets to you.

12 Cheerers of many, rich in goods, discoverers of opulence,
The Aśvins, Riders through the sky, have welcomed this my song of praise.

13 O Aśvins, grant us all rich gifts wherewith no man mav interfere.
Make us observe the stated times : give us not over to reproach.

14 Whether, Nāsatyas, ye be nigh, or whether ye be far away,
Come thence, O Aśvins, on your car that hath a thousand ornaments.

15 Vatsa the Ṛṣi with his songs, Nāsatyas, hath exalted you :
Grant him rich food distilling oil, graced with a thousand ornaments.

16 Bestow on him, O Aśvins, food that strengthens, and that drops with oil,
On him who praises you for bliss, and, Lords of bounty, prays for wealth.

17 Come to us, ye who slay the foe, Lords of rich treasure, to this hymn.
O Heroes, give us high renown and these good things of earth for help.

18 The Priyamedhas have invoked you with all succours that are yours,
You, Aśvins, Lords of solemn rites, with calls entreating you to come.

19 Come to us, Aśvins, ye who bring felicity, auspicious Ones,
To Vatsa who with prayer and hymn, lovers of song, hath honoured you.

20 Aid us, O Heroes, for those hymns for which ye helped Gośarya erst,
Gave Vaśa, Daśavraja aid, and Kaṇva and Medhātithi:

21 And favoured Trasadasyu, ye Heroes, in spoil-deciding fray :
For these, O Aśvins, graciously assist us in acquiring strength.

22 O Aśvins, may pure hymns of ours, and songs and praises, honour you:
Best slayers everywhere of foes, as such we fondly yearn for you.

36 *With lustre these have spread abroad* : 'then they (the Maruts) stood round in their radiance.' 'The Scholiast intimates that this verse refers to the ceremony called *Āgnimāruta*, when *Agni* is first worshipped, then the *Maruts*.'—Wilson.

---

3 *From the Nahuṣas* : or, according to others, from the neighbouring people.

7 *Carers for Vatsa* : ye who favour and provide for Vatsa, the Ṛṣi of Hymn VI. of this Book.

10 *The Lady* : Sūryā, Daughter of the Sun. See, I. 116. 17.

20 *Gośarya* : said by Sāyaṇa to be a name of Śayu. See I. 116, 22. *Vaśa* and *Daśavraja* are known only as *protégés* of the Aśvins.

21 *Trasadasyu* : See Vol. I., Index.

23 Three places of the Aśvins, erst concealed, are made apparent now.
Both Sages, with the flight of Law come hither unto those who live.

HYMN IX. *Aśvins.*

1. To help and favour Vatsa now, O Aśvins, come ye hitherward.
Bestow on him a dwelling spacious and secure, and keep malignities away.

2 All manliness that is in heaven, with the Five Tribes, or in mid-air,
Bestow, ye Aśvins, upon us.

3 Remember Kāṇva first of all among the singers, Aśvins, who
Have thought upon your wondrous deeds.

4 Aśvins, for you with song of praise this hot oblation is effused,
This your sweet Soma juice, ye Lords of ample wealth, through which ye think upon the foe.

5 Whatever ye have done in floods, in the tree, Wonder-Workers, and in growing plants,
Therewith, O Aśvins, succour me.

6 What force, Nāsatyas, ye exert, whatever, Gods, ye tend and heal,
This your own Vatsa gains not by his hymns alone : ye visit him who offers gifts.

7 Now hath the Ṛṣi splendidly thought out the Aśvins' hymn of praise.
Let the Atharvan pour the warm oblation forth, and Soma very rich in sweets.

8 Ye Aśvins, now ascend your car that lightly rolls upon its way.
May these my praises make you speed hitherward like a cloud of heaven.

9 When, O Nāsatyas, we this day make you speed hither with our hymns,
Or, Aśvins, with our songs of praise, remember Kāṇva specially.

10 As erst Kakṣīvān and the Ṛṣi Vyaśva, as erst Dīrghatamas invoked your presence,
Or, in the sacrificial chambers, Vainya Pṛthī, so be ye mindful of us here, O Aśvins.

11 Come as home-guardians, saving us from foemen, guarding our living creatures and our bodies,
Come to the house to give us seed and offspring,

12 Whether with Indra ye be faring, Aśvins, or resting in one dwelling-place with Vāyu,
In concord with the Ṛbhus or Ādityas, or standing still in Viṣṇu's striding-places.

13 When I, O Aśvins, call on you to-day that I may gather strength,
Or as all-conquering might in war, be that the Aśvins' noblest grace.

14 Now come, ye Aśvins, hitherward : here are oblations set for you;
These Soma-draughts to aid Yadu and Turvaśa, these offered you mid Kaṇva's Sons.

15 Whatever healing balm is yours, Nāsatyas, near or far away,
Therewith, great Sages, grant a home to Vatsa and to Vimada.

16 Together with the Goddess, with the Aśvins' Speech have I awoke.
Thou, Goddess, hast disclosed the hymn, and holy gift from mortal men.

17 Awake the Aśvins, Goddess Dawn ! Up Mighty Lady of sweet strains !
Rise, straightway, priest of sacrifice ! High glory to the gladdening draught !

18 Thou, Dawn, approaching with thy light shinest together with the Sun,

23 *Three places* : according to Sāyaṇa, the three wheels of the Aśvins' chariot are intended. The three places can only be heaven, firmament, and earth, hidden during the darkness of night and made visible by the coming of the Aśvins and Dawn.

---

1 *Vatsa* : apparently another name of Śaśakarṇa, called also Kāṇva or descendant of Kaṇva, the Ṛṣi of the hymn.

3 *Thought upon* : or touched upon, handled.

4 *Think upon the foe* : plan the destruction of the demon of darkness.

5 *Whatever ye have done* : Professor Wilson paraphrases after Sāyaṇa : 'preserve me with that (healing virtue) deposited by you in the waters, in the trees, in the herbs.'

7 *The Atharvan* : the priest who has special charge of the fire and the Soma. I follow Ludwig in taking *átharvaṇi* as a nominative and not as a locative as Sāyaṇa does ; 'the will sprinkle the sweet-flavoured *Soma* and the *gharma* (oblation) on the *Atharvan* fire.'—Wilson.

10 *Kakṣīvān* : See I. 18. 1. *Vyaśva* : See I. 112. 15. *Dīrghatamas* : See Vol. I., Index. *Vainya* : Son of Vena. *Pṛthī* : the first anointed king.

11 *Our living creatures* : our dependents and our cattle

12 *Viṣṇu's striding-places* : from which he made his three great strides through earth, firmament, and heaven

13 *That* : the granting of my request.

15 *And to Vimada* : as ye did to Vimada.—Sāyaṇa. See Vol. I., Index.

16 *The Goddess* : Dawn. *The Aśvins' Speech* : Vāk or Speech who glorifies the Aśvins ; *i. e.* the hymn that praises them.

And to this man-protecting home the chariot of the Aśvins comes.
19 When yellow stalks give forth the juice, as cows from udders pour their milk,
And voices sound the song of praise, the Aśvins' worshippers show first.
20 Forward for glory and for strength, protection that shall conquer men,
And power and skill, most sapient Ones !
21 When Aśvins, worthy of our lauds, ye seat you in the father's house.
With wisdom or the bliss ye bring.

HYMN X. *Aśvins.*

1. WHETHER ye travel far away or dwell in yonder light of heaven,
Or in a mansion that is built above the sea, come thence, ye Aśvins, hitherward.
2 Or if for Manu ye prepared the sacrifice, remember also Kaṇva's son.
I call Bṛhaspati, Indra, Viṣṇu, all the gods, the Aśvins borne by rapid steeds.
3 Those Aśvins I invoke who work marvels, brought hither to receive,
With whom our friendship is most famed, and kinship passing that of Gods.
4 On whom the solemn rites depend, whose worshippers rise without the Sun :
These who foreknow the holy work of sacrifice, and by their Godhead drink the sweets of Soma juice.
5 Whether ye, Lords of ample wealth, now linger in the east or west,
With Druhyu, or with Anu, Yadu, Turvaśa, I call you hither; come to me.
6 Lords of great riches, whether through the firmament ye fly or speed through heaven and earth,
Or with your Godlike natures stand upon your cars, come thence, O Aśvins, hitherward.

19 *Yellow stalks* : of Soma plants.

20 *Forward for glory* : advance and come to give us glory, etc.

21 *In the father's house* : in the sacrificial hall of the father of the family, the wealthy householder who institutes the sacrifice. This stanza is a continuation of 19, although the connexion is interrupted by the intervening stanza.

1 *Above the sea* : above the ocean of air.

3 *To receive* : our oblations.

4 *Without the sun* : Sāyaṇa explains *asūre* differently, connecting in with *sūri* instead of *sūra* : 'of whom there are worshippers in a place where there is no worship.'—Wilson.

5 *Druhyu* and the other names stand for the tribes called after these ancient chieftains. See Vol. I., Index.

HYMN XI. *Agni.*

1. THOU Agni, God mid mortal men, art guard of sacred rites, thou art
To be adored at sacrifice.
2 O Mighty Agni, thou must be glorified at our festivals,
Bearing our offerings to the Gods.
3 O Jātavedas Agni, fight and drive our foes afar from us,
Them and their godless enmities.
4 Thou, Jātavedas, seekest not the worship of a hostile man,
However nigh it be to thee.
5 We sages, mortals as we are, adore the mighty name of thee,
Immortal Jātavedas' name.
6 Sages, we call the Sage to help, mortals, we call the God to aid :
We call on Agni with our songs.
7 May Vatsa draw thy mind away even from thy loftiest dwelling-place,
Agni, with song that yearns for thee.
8 Thou art the same in many a place : mid all the people thou art Lord.
In fray and fight we call on thee.
9 When we are seeking strength we call Agni to help us in the strife,
The giver of rich gifts in war.
10 Ancient, adorable at sacrifices, Priest from of old, meet for our praise, thou sittest.
Fill full and satisfy thy body, Agni, and win us happiness by offering worship.

The hymn is translated in Max Müller's *History of Ancient Sanskrit Literature.*

2 *Bearing our offerings to the Gods* : literally, 'the charioteer of solemn rites.'

HYMN XII. *Indra.*

1. JOY, Mightiest Indra, known and marked, sprung most from Soma-draughts, wherewith
Thou smitest down the greedy fiend, for that we long.

1 *Joy* : *mádaḥ*, **the rapturous** exhilaration **produced in Indra by drinking the Soma juice.** *For that we long* : the short refrain or burden which generally concludes each stanza of each triplet of this hymn is sometimes rather loosely attached and cannot always be clearly brought out in the proper place in translation.

2 Wherewith thou holpest Adhrigu, the great Daśagva, and the God
Who stirs the sunlight, and the sea, for that we long.

3 Wherewith thou dravest forth like cars Sindhu and all the mighty floods
To go the way ordained by Law, for that we long.

4 Accept this laud for aid, made pure like oil, thou Caster of the Stone,
Whereby even in a moment thou hast waxen great.

5 Be pleased, Song-lover, with this song : it flows abundant like the sea.
Indra, with all thy succours thou hast waxen great.

6 The God who from afar hath sent gifts to maintain our friendship's bond,
Thou, spreading them like rain from heaven, hast waxen great.

7 The beams that mark him have grown strong, the thunder rests between his arms,
When, like the Sun, he hath increased both Heaven and Earth.

8 When, Mighty Lord of Heroes, thou didst eat a thousand buffaloes,
Then grew and waxed exceeding great thine Indra-power.

9 Indra consumeth with the rays of Sūrya the malicious man :
Like Agni conquering the woods, he hath grown strong.

10 This newest thought of ours that suits the time approaches unto thee :
Serving, beloved in many a place it metes and marks.

11 The pious germ of sacrifice directly purifies the soul.
By Indra's lauds it waxes great, it metes and marks.

12 Indra who wins the friend hath spread himself to drink the Soma-draught :
Like worshipper's dilating praise; it metes and marks.

13 He whom the sages, living men, have gladdened, offering up their hymns,
Hath swelled like oil of sacrifice in Agni's mouth.

14 Aditi also hath brought forth a hymn for Indra, Sovran Lord :
The work of sacrifice for help is glorified.

15 The ministering priests have sung their songs for aid and eulogy :
God, thy Bays turn not from the rite which Law ordains.

16 If, Indra, thou drink Soma by Viṣṇu's or Tṛta Āptya's side,
Or with the Maruts take delight in flowing drops;

17 Or, Śakra, if thou gladden thee afar or in the sea of air,
Rejoice thee in this juice of ours, in flowing drops.

18 Or, Lord of Heroes, if thou aid the worshipper who sheds the juice,
Or him whose laud delights thee, and his flowing drops.

19 To magnify the God, the God, Indra, yea, Indra for your help,
And promptly end the sacrifice—this have they gained.

20 With worship, him whom men adore, with Soma, him who drinks it most,
Indra with lauds have they increased—this have they gained.

21 His leadings are with power and might and his instructions manifold :
He gives the worshipper all wealth : this have they gained.

22 For slaying Vṛtra have the Gods set Indra in the foremost place.

2 *Adhrigu* : according to Sāyaṇa a Ṛṣi so named. See I. 112. 20. *Daśagva* : one of the priestly family connected with, or identical with, the Aṅgirases, 'the accomplisher of the ten (months' rite).'—Wilson Ludwig thinks that *Daśagva* here may mean the Sun. *The sea* : of air.

8 *Didst eat a thousand buffaloes* : the buffaloes probably represent the clouds which the Sun dissipates or consumes.—Ludwig. 'When thou hast slain thousands of mighty foes.'—Wilson.

10 *It metes and marks* : defines and discriminates Indra's good qualities.—Sāyaṇa.

11 The *germ of sacrifice* is probably the wish that prompts the offering.

Sāyaṇa explains differently : 'The devout praiser of the adorable (Indra purifies in due succession the offering (of the Soma); with sacred hymns he magnifies (the might of Indra; he verily proclaims the measure (of his merits).

12 *Worshipper's dilating praise* : I follow Sāyaṇa : but the stanza is unintelligible to me. 'Indra the benefactor of his friend (the worshipper). has enlarged himself to drink the Soma, in like manner as the pious praise dilates and proclaims the measure of his merits.'—Wilson. The meaning of *vāśī* (praise, according to Sāyaṇa) is uncertain. Von Roth thinks that the two press-stones are meant, and others explain it as the sword, knife, or axe used in sacrifice.

16 *Tṛta Āptya* : See VIII. 7. 24, note. Here he appears as the preparer of celestial Soma for Indra.

Indra the choral bands have sung, for vigorous strength.

23 We to the Mighty with our might, with lauds to him who hears our call,
With holy hymns have sung aloud, for vigorous strength.

24 Not earth, nor heaven, nor firmaments contain the Thunder-wielding God :
They shake before his violent rush and vigorous strength.

25 What time the Gods, O Indra, set thee foremost in the furious fight,
Then thy two beautiful Bay Steeds carried thee on.

26 When Vṛtra, stayer of the floods, thou slewest, Thunderer with might,
Then thy two beautiful Bay Steeds carried thee on.

27 When Viṣṇu, through thine energy, strode wide those three great steps of his,
Then thy two beautiful Bay Steeds carried thee on.

28 When thy two beautiful Bay Steeds grew great and greater day by day,
Even then all creatures that had life bowed down to thee.

29 When, Indra, all the Marut folk humbly submitted them to thee,
Even then all creatures that had life bowed down to thee.

30 When yonder Sun, that brilliant light, thou settest in the heaven above,
Even then all creatures that had life bowed down to thee.

31 To thee, O Indra, with this thought the sage lifts up this eulogy,
Akin and leading as on foot to sacrifice.

32 When in thine own dear dwelling all gathered have lifted up the voice
Milk-streams at worship's central spot, for sacrifice,

33 As Priest, O Indra, give us wealth in brave men and good steeds and kine
That we may first remember thee for sacrifice.

31 The second line is difficult. Wilson, following Sāyaṇa, paraphrases the stanza: 'The wise (worshipper), Indra, offers thee this gratifying sincere praise along with pious rites at the sacrifice, as (a man places) a kinsman in (a prominent) position.'

32 *Milk-streams* : the sweetly-flowing hymns.

Wilson remarks : 'This is probably an ancient hymn, both by its repetitions and combination of simplicity and obscurity.'

HYMN XIII. *Indra.*

1. INDRA, when Soma juices flow, makes his mind pure and meet for lauds.
He gains the power that brings success, for great is he.

2 In heaven's first region, in the seat of Gods, is he who brings success,
Most glorious, prompt to save, who wins the water-floods.

3 Him, to win strength, have I invoked, even Indra mighty for the fray.
Be thou most near to us for bliss, a Friend to aid.

4 Indra, Song-lover, here for thee the worshipper's libation flows.
Rejoicing in this sacred grass thou shinest forth.

5 Even now, O Indra, give us that which, pressing juice, we crave of thee.
Bring us wealth manifold which finds the light of heaven.

6 What time the zealous worshipper hath boldly sung his songs to thee,
Like branches of a tree up-grows what they desire.

7 Generate songs even as of old, give ear unto the singer's call :
Thou for the pious hast grown great at each carouse.

8 Sweet strains that glorify him play like waters speeding down a slope,
Yea, him who in this song is called the Lord of Heaven;

9 Yea, who alone is called the Lord, the single Ruler of the folk,
By worshippers seeking aid : may he joy in the draught.

10 Praise him, the Glorious, skilled in song, Lord of the two victorious Bays :
They seek the worshipper's abode who bows in prayer.

11 Put forth thy strength : with dappled Steeds come, thou of mighty intellect,
With swift Steeds to the sacrifice, for 'tis thy joy.

12 Grant wealth to those who praise thee, Lord of Heroes, Mightiest Indra : give
Our princes everlasting fame and opulence.

13 I call thee when the Sun is risen, I call thee at the noon of day:
With thy car-horses, Indra, come well-pleased to us.

7 *Generate songs* : by granting the prayers of the singers.

14 Speed forward hither, come to us, rejoice thee in the milky draught:
Spin out the thread of ancient time, as well is known.

15 If, Śakra, Vṛtra-slayer, thou be far away or near to us.
Or in the sea, thou art the guard of Soma juice.

16 Let songs we sing and Soma-drops expressed by us make Indra strong:
The tribes who bring oblations find delight in him.

17 Him sages longing for his aid, with offerings brought in eager haste,
Him. even as branches, all mankind have made to grow.

18 At the Tṛkadrukas the Gods span sacrifice that stirred the mind:
May our songs strengthen him who still hath strengthened us.

19 When, true to duty, at due times the worshipper offers lauds to thee,
They call him Purifier, Pure, and Wonderful.

20 That mind of Rudra, fresh and strong, moves conscious in he ancient ways,
With reference whereto the wise have ordered this.

21 If thou elect to be my Friend drink of this sacrificial juice,
By help whereof we may subdue all enemies.

22 O Indra, Lover of the song, when shall thy praiser be most blest?
When wilt thou grant us wealth in herds of kine and steeds?

23 And thy two highly-lauded Bays, strong stallions, draw thy car who art
Untouched by age, most gladdening car for which we pray.

24 With ancient offerings we implore the Young and Strong whom many praise.
He from of old hath sat upon dear sacred grass.

25 Wax mighty, thou whom many laud for aids which Ṛṣis have extolled.
Pour down for us abundant food and guard us well.

26 O Indra, Caster of the Stone, thou helpest him who praises thee:
From sacrifice I send to thee a mind-yoked hymn.

27 Here, yoking for the Soma-draught these Horses, sharers of thy feast,
Thy Bay Steeds, Indra, fraught with wealth, consent to come.

28 Attendants on thy glory, let the Rudras roar assent to thee,
And all the Marut companies come to the feast.

29 These his victorious followers hold in the heavens the place they love,
Leagued in the heart of sacrifice, as well we know.

30 That we may long behold the light, what time the ordered rite proceeds,
He duly measures, as he views, the sacrifice.

31 O Indra, strong is this thy car, and strong are these Bay Steeds of thine:
O Śatakratu, thou art strong, strong is our call.

32 Strong is the press-stone, strong thy joy, strong is the flowing Soma juice:
Strong is the rite thou furtherest, strong is our call.

33 As strong I call on thee the Strong, O Thunderer with thy thousand aids:
For thou hast won the hymn of praise. Strong is our call.

14 *Spin out the thread of ancient times*: 'extend the ancient sacrifice.'—Wilson.

The due performance of sacrifice is regarded as an unbroken thread reaching through a succession of Ṛṣis from ancient to modern times.

15 *In the sea*: in the firmament, or ocean of air.

17 *All mankind*: *kṣoṇiḥ*. But see M. Müller, *Vedic Hymns*, I. 310.

18 *At the Tṛkadrukas*: according to Sāyaṇa these are the first three days of the Abhiplava ceremony. According to some modern scholars they are probably three peculiar Soma-vessels, or an oblation consisting of three offerings of Soma. *Span sacrifice*: See above note on 14. *That stirred the mind*: that urged others to follow the example.

19 *Him*: a change of person, Indra being meant.

20 *Have ordered this*: song of praise, or holy ceremony.—Ludwig.

26 *Mind-yoked*: made ready by the poet's mind, as a chariot—to which the hymn is frequently compared—is equipped for a journey.

28 *The Rudras*: the sons of Rudra, the Maruts.

29 *The heart,* literally navel, that is the central point, *of sacrifice,* is the receptacle on which oblations are placed, or the *uttaravedī* or north altar.

31 *Strong*: *vṛṣā*: as has been noticed before (See I. 177. 2.3. some of the Vedic poets delight in the repetition of this word and derivatives from the same root. Sāyaṇa explains *vṛṣā*: as 'showerer of benefits,' and Ludwig translates it by 'stierkräftig,' strong as a bull. The original meaning of the word is male, masculine, and, hence, strong.

HYMN XIV. *Indra.*

1. If I, O Indra, were, like thee, the single Sovran of all wealth,
My worshipper should be rich in kine.

2 I should be fain, O Lord of Power, to strengthen and enrich the sage,
Were I the Lord of herds of kine.

3 To worshippers who press the juice thy goodness, Indra, is a cow
Yielding in plenty kine and steeds.

4 None is there, Indra, God or man, to hinder thy munificence,
The wealth which, lauded, thou wilt give.

5 The sacrifice made Indra strong when he unrolled the earth, and made
Himself a diadem in heaven.

6 Thine aid we claim, O Indra, thine who after thou hast waxen great
Hast won all treasures for thine own.

7 In Soma's ecstasy Indra spread the firmament and realms of light,
When he cleft Vala limb from limb.

8 Showing the hidden he drave forth the cows for the Aṅgirases,
And Vala he cast headlong down.

9 By Indra were the luminous realms of heaven established and secured,
Firm and immovable from their place.

10 Indra, thy laud moves quickly like a joyous wave of water-floods :
Bright shine the drops that gladden thee.

11 For thou, O Indra, art the God whom hymns and praises magnify:
Thou blessest those who worship thee.

12 Let the two long-maned Bay Steeds bring Indra to drink the Soma juice,
The Bountiful to our sacrifice.

13 With waters' foam thou torest off, Indra, the head of Namuci,
Subduing all contending hosts.

14 The Dasyus, when they fain would climb by magic arts and mount to heaven,
Thou, Indra, castest down to earth.

15 As Soma-drinker conquering all, thou scatteredst to every side
Their settlement who poured no gifts.

13 *With waters' foam* : with a thunderbolt in the form of foam, according to a later legend. See Lanman, *Sanskrit Reader*, p. 375, who takes Namuci to be a waterspout in a lake, and 'with foam' to mean 'accompanied by foam.'

HYMN XV. *Indra.*

1. Sing forth to him whom many men invoke, to him whom many laud :
Invite the powerful Indra with your songs of praise.

2 Whose lofty might—for doubly strong is he—supports the heavens and earth,
And hills and plains and floods and light with manly power.

3 Such, Praised by many ! thou art King : alone thou smitest Vṛtras dead,
To gain, O Indra, spoils of war and high renown.

4 We sing this strong and wild delight of thine which conquers in the fray,
Which, Caster of the Stone ! gives room and shines like gold.

5 Wherewith thou also foundest lights for Āyu and for Manu's sake :
Now joying in this sacred grass thou beamest forth.

6 This day too singers of the hymn praise, as of old, this might of thine :
Win thou the waters day by day, thralls of the strong.

7 That lofty Indra-power of thine, thy strength and thine intelligence,
Thy thunderbolt for which we long, the wish makes keen.

8 O Indra, Heaven and Earth augment thy manly power and thy renown ;
The waters and thy mountains stir and urge thee on.

9 Viṣṇu the lofty ruling Power, Varuṇa, Mitra sing thy praise :
In thee the Maruts' company have great delight.

10 O Indra, thou wast born the Lord of men, most liberal of thy gifts :
Excellent deeds for evermore are all thine own.

11 Ever, alone, O highly-praised, thou sendest Vṛtras to their rest :
None else than Indra executes the mighty deed.

12 Though here and there, in varied hymns, Indra, men call on thee for aid,

4 *Wild delight* : Soma juice, the cause of thy rapture.

5 *For Āyu and for Manu's sake* : that is for man. Āyu was the son of Purūravas and Urvaśī.

6 *Thralls of the strong* : controlled and imprisoned by Vṛtra.

7 *The wish* : our wishes expressed in prayer and praise.

Still with our heroes fight and win the
light of heaven.

13 Already have all forms of him entered
our spacious dwelling-place :
For victory stir thou Indra, up, the Lord
of Might.

HYMN XVI. *Indra.*

1. Praise Indra whom our songs must laud,
sole Sovran of mankind, the Chief
Most liberal who controlleth men.

2 In whom the hymns of praise delight, and
all the glory-giving songs.
Like the floods' longing for the sea.

3 Him I invite with eulogy, best King,
effective in the fight,
Strong for the gain of mighty spoil.

4 Whose perfect ecstasies are wide, profound,
victorious, and give
Joy in the field where heroes win.

5 Him, when the spoils of war are staked,
men call to be their advocate :
They who have Indra win the day.

6 Men honour him with stirring songs and
magnify with solemn rites :
Indra is he who giveth ease.

7 Indra is priest and Ṛṣi, he is much
invoked by many men,
And mighty by his mighty powers.

8 Meet to be lauded and invoked, true Hero
with his deeds of might,
Victorious even when alone.

9 The men, the people magnify that Indra
with their Sāma songs,
With hymns and sacred eulogies :

10 Him who advances them to wealth, sends
light to lead them in the war,
And quells their foemen in the fray.

11 May he, the saviour much-invoked, may
Indra bear us in a ship
Safely beyond all enemies.

12 As such, O Indra, honour us with gifts
of booty, further us,
And lead us to felicity.

13 *All forms of him* : the various qualities of Indra have been celebrated.

Stir thou : the Ṛṣi addresses himself. *Lord of Might*: *śácipatim* : in later literature, lord or husband of Śacī or his might personified and regarded as his cons

———

7 *Priest* : *brahmā*, meaning, according to Sāyaṇa, greater than all. See VI. 45. 7, 'The Brahman who accepts the prayer,' that is, Indra regarded as a priest. *Ṛṣi* : according to Sāyaṇa, 'the beholder of all the Āryan race.'

———

HYMN XVII *Indra.*

1. Come, we have pressed the juice for thee;
O Indra, drink this Soma here :
Sit thou on this my sacred grass.

2 O Indra, let thy long-maned Bays, yoked
by prayer, bring thee hitherward :
Give ear and listen to our prayers.

3 We Soma-bearing Brāhmans call thee
Soma-drinker with thy friend,
We, Indra, bringing Soma juice.

4 Come unto us who bring the juice, come
unto this our eulogy,
Fair-visored ! drink thou of the juice.

5 I pour it down within thee, so through
all thy members let it spread :
Take with thy tongue the pleasant drink.

6 Sweet to thy body let it be, delicious be
the savoury juice :
Sweet be the Soma to thine heart.

7 Like women, let this Soma-draught,
invested with its robe, approach,
O active Indra, close to thee.

8 Indra, transported with the juice, vast in
his bulk, strong in his neck
And stout arms, smites the Vṛtras down.

9 O Indra, go thou forward, thou who
rulest over all by might :
Thou Vṛtra-slayer slay the fiends.

10 Long be thy grasping-hook wherewith
thou givest ample wealth to him
Who sheds the juice and worships thee.

11 Here, Indra, is thy Soma-draught, made
pure upon the sacred grass :
Run hither, come and drink thereof.

12 Famed for thy radiance, worshipped well !
this juice is shed for thy delight :
Thou art invoked, Ākhaṇḍala !

13 To Kuṇḍapāyya, grandson's son, grandson
of Śṛṅgavṛṣ ! to thee,

3 *With thy friend* : Indra's companion, the thunderbolt. 'With suitable praise.'—Wilson.

7 *Like women* : dressed in white garments and moving slowly. *Its robe* : the milk that colours it.

12 *Famed for thy radiance, worshipped well* : the words thus rendered, *śácigo* and *śácipūjana*, have not been satisfactorily explained by the Commentator, and their meaning is still uncertain. According to Sāyaṇa, the former may mean 'thou whose cattle are strong,' or 'thou whose radiance is renowned,' and the latter 'thou of renowned adoration' or 'whose hymns are renowned.' See Wilson's note. *Thou art invoked, Ākhaṇḍala*: or, 'Thou O Destroyer, art invoked.' This appellation of Indra does not occur again in the Ṛgveda. See Muir, *O. S. Texts*, IV. 190.

13 *Kuṇḍapāyya* and *Śṛṅgavṛṣ* appear here to be names of men. According to Sāyaṇa, *kuṇḍapāyya* is the name

To him have I addressed my thought.

14 Strong pillar thou, Lord of the home! armour of Soma-offerers:
The drop of Soma breaketh all the strongholds down, and Indra is the Ṛsis' Friend.

15 Holy Pṛdākusānu, winner of the spoil, one eminent o'er many men,
Lead on the wild horse Indra with his vigorous grasp forward to drink the Soma juice.

HYMN XVIII. *Ādityas.*

1. Now let the mortal offer prayer to win the unexampled grace
Of these Ādityas and their aid to cherish life.

2 For not an enemy molests the paths which these Ādityas tread:
Infallible guards, they strengthen us in happiness.

3 Now soon may Bhaga, Savitar, Varuṇa, Mitra, Aryaman
Give us the shelter widely spread which we implore.

4 With Gods come thou whose fostering care none checks, O Goddesss Aditi:
Come, dear to many, with the Lords who guard us well.

5 For well these Sons of Aditi know to keep enmities aloof,
Unrivalled, giving ample room, they save from woe.

6 Aditi guard our herd by day, Aditi, free from guile, by night,
Aditi, ever strengthening, save us from grief!

7 And in the day our hymn is this: May Aditi come nigh to help,
With loving-kindness bring us weal and chase our foes.

8 And may the Aśvins, the divine Pair of Physicians, send us health:
May they remove iniquity and chase our foes.

9 May Agni bless us with his fires, and Sūrya warm us pleasantly:
May the pure Wind breathe sweet on us, and chase our foes.

10 Drive ye disease and strife away, drive ye away malignity:
Ādityas, keep us ever far from sore distress.

11 Remove from us the arrow, keep famine, Ādityas! far away:
Keep enmities afar from us, Lords of all wealth!

12 Now, O Ādityas, grant to us the shelter that lets man go free,
Yea, even the sinner from his sin, ye Bounteous Gods!

13 Whatever mortal with the power of demons fain would injure us,
May he, impetuous, suffer harm by his own deeds.

14 May sin o'ertake our human foe, the man who speaketh evil thing,
Him who would cause our misery, whose heart is false.

15 Gods, ye are with the simple ones, ye know each mortal in your hearts;
Ye, Vasus, well discriminate the false and true.

16 Fain would we have the sheltering aid of mountains and of water-floods:
Keep far from us iniquity, O Heaven and Earth.

17 So with auspicious sheltering aid do ye, O Vasus, carry us
Beyond all trouble and distress, borne in your ship.

18 Ādityas, ye Most Mighty Ones, grant to our children and their seed
Extended term of life that they may live long days.

of a particular Soma ceremony, and the offspring of *Śṛṅgavṛṣ*, is Indra himself. '(Indra), who wast the offspring of Śṛṅgavṛṣ, of whom the *kuṇḍapāyya* rite was the protector, (the sages) have fixed (of old) their minds upon this ceremony.' See Wilson's note who observes that 'the construction is loose, and the explanation not very satisfactory.'

14 *Lord of the home*: apparently the householder who institutes the sacrifice is addressed. *he vāstoṣpate gṛhapate.* —Sāyaṇa. *The Ṛsis' Friend*: *munīnāṁ sákhā*, the friend of the Munis, sages, saintly men or ascetics; of us Ṛṣis, according to Sāyaṇa.

15 *Pṛdākusānu*: I follow Ludwig in taking this to be the name of the institutor of the sacrifice. According to Sāyaṇa who explains it as 'lifting up the head or back like a serpent,' or 'to be propitiated, as a serpent is, with gems, charms, medicaments, etc.,' it is an epithet of Indra; and the leader forward of Indra in the second line is the worshipper, understood. Grassmann banishes the last three stanzas to his Appendix as not originally forming part of the hymn.

1 *Ādityas*: See I. 14. 3.

4 *With the Lords*: *sūríbhiḥ*; that is, the Gods.

13 *With the power of demons*: 'from his diabolical nature.'—Wilson.

19 Sacrifice, O Ādityas, is your inward monitor : be kind,
For in the bond of kindred we are bound to you.

20 The Maruts' high protecting aid, the Aśvins, and the God who saves,
Mitra and Varuṇa for weal we supplicate.

21 Grant us a home with triple guard, Aryaman, Mitra, Varuṇa !
Unthreatened, Maruts ! meet for praise, and filled with men.

22 And as we human beings, O Ādityas, are akin to death,
Graciously lengthen ye our lives that we may live.

HYMN XIX. *Agni.*

1. SING praise to him, the Lord of Light. The Gods have made the God to be their messenger,
And sent oblation to Gods.

2 Agni, the Bounteous Giver, bright with varied flames, laud thou, O singer Sobhari—
Him who controls this sacred food with Soma blent, who hath first claim to sacrifice.

3 Thee have we chosen skilfullest in sacrifice, Immortal Priest among the Gods,
Wise finisher of this holy rite :

4 The Son of Strength, the blessed, brightly-shining One, Agni whose light is excellent.
May he by sacrifice win us in heaven the grace of Mitra, Varuṇa, and the Floods.

5 The mortal who hath ministered to Agni with oblation, fuel, ritual lore,
And reverence, skilled in sacrifice.

6 Verily swift to run are his fleet-footed steeds, and most resplendent fame is his.
No trouble caused by Gods or wrought by mortal man from any side o'ertaketh him.

7 May we by thine own fires be well supplied with fire, O Son of Strength, O Lord of Might :
Thou as our Friend hast worthy men.

8 Agni, who praises like a guest of friendly mind, is as a car that brings us gear.
Also in thee is found perfect security : thou art the Sovran Lord of wealth.

9 That man, moreover, merits praise who brings, auspicious Agni, sacrificial gifts :
May he win riches by his thoughts.

10 He for whose sacrifice thou standest up erect is prosperous and rules o'er men.
He wins with coursers and with singers skilled in song : with heroes he obtains the prize.

11 He in whose dwelling Agni is chief ornament, and, all-desired, loves his laud well,
And zealously tends his offerings—

12 His, or the lauding sage's word, his, Son of Strength ! who is most prompt with sacred gifts,
Set thou beneath the Gods, Vasu, above mankind, the speech of the intelligent.

13 He who with sacrificial gifts or homage bringeth very skilful Agni nigh,
Or him who flashes fast with song,

14 The mortal who with blazing fuel, as his laws command, adores the Perfect God,
Blest with his thoughts in splendour shall exceed all men, as though he overpassed the floods.

15 Give us the splendour, Agni, which may overcome each greedy fiend in our abode,
The wrath of evil-hearted folk.

16 That, wherewith Mitra, Varuṇa, and

19 *Your inward monitor* : or near remembrancer, not suffering you to rest until you have rewarded men for their devotions. Ludwig says that the *hiḷáḥ* of the text is really *hi īḷaḥ* : For sacrifice, Ādityas, is your nearest dwelling-place.

20 *The God who saves* : Indra, who is especially the tutelary God of Āryans.

21 *With triple guard* : or, triply defending or defended. According to Sāyaṇa, protecting from heat, cold, and wet; or three-storeyed.

22 *Akin to death* : born subject to death.

1 *The Gods* : in the first line are, according to Sāyaṇa, the priests, *i. e.* those who praise : *dīvyanti stuvantīti devā ṛtvijo* ; but the word may be taken in its ordinary signification.

5 *Ritual lore* : *vedena* here can hardly mean, as Sāyaṇa explains it, 'by studying the Veda.' It may perhaps mean 'by knowledge of the proper use of the sacred formulas,' or as M. Müller says, 'by the bundle of grass' used in sacrifice. See *Anc. S. Literature*. p. 28, note, and p. 205.

7 *Hast worthy men* : in us thy worshippers.

10 *With coursers and with singers* : is successful in chariot-races and is rewarded by the Gods for his sacrifices.

12 *Set thou beneath the Gods* and *above mankind*, is said to mean 'spread through all the sky.' The meaning of this and the preceding stanza is somewhat obscurely expressed.

14 *The Perfect God* : *áditim*, explained by Sāyaṇa as *akhaṇḍanīyam*, indivisible, complete.

16 *That* : radiance or splendour.

Aryaman, the Aśvins, Bhaga give us light,
That may we, by thy power finding best furtherance, worship,
O Indra, helped by thee.

17 O Agni, most devout are they, the sages who have set thee Sage exceeding wise,
O God, for men to look upon :

18 Who have arranged thine altar Blessed God, at morn, brought thine oblation, pressed the juice.
They by their deeds of strength have won them mighty wealth, who have set all their hope in thee.

19 May Agni worshipped bring us bliss, may the gift, Blessed One, and sacrifice bring bliss ;
Yea, may our praises bring us bliss.

20 Show forth the mind that brings success in war with fiends, wherewith thou conquerest in fight.
Bring down the many firm hopes of our enemies, and let us vanquish with thine aid.

21 I praise with song the Friend of man, whom Gods sent down to be herald and messenger,
Best worshipper, bearer of our gifts.

22 Thou unto sharp-toothed Agni, Young and Radiant God, proclaimest with thy song the feast—
Agni, who for our sweet strains moulds heroic strength when sacred oil is offered him,

23 While, served with sacrificial oil, now upward and now downward Agni moves his sword,
As doth the Asura his robe.

24 The God, the Friend of man, who bears our gifts to heaven, the God with his sweet-smelling mouth,
Distributes, skilled in sacrifice, his precious things, Invoking Priest, Immortal God.

25 Son of Strength, Agni, if thou wert the mortal, bright as Mitra ! worshipped with our gifts !
And I were the Immortal God,

26 I would not give thee up, Vasu, to calumny, or misery, O Bounteous One.
My worshipper should feel no hunger or distress, nor, Agni, should he live in sin.

27 Like a son cherished in his father's house, let our oblation rise unto the Gods.

28 With thine immediate aid may I, excellent Agni, ever gain my wish,
A mortal with a God to help.

29 O Agni, by thy wisdom, by thy bounties, by thy leading may I gather wealth.
Excellent Agni, thou art called my Providence : delight thou to be liberal.

30 Agni, he conquers by thine aid that brings him store of noble heroes and great strength,
Whose bond of friendship is thy choice.

31 Thy spark is black and crackling, kindled in due time, O Bounteous, it is taken up.
Thou art the dear Friend of the mighty Mornings : thou shinest in glimmerings of the night.

32 We Sobharis have come to him, for succour, who is good to help with thousand powers,
The Sovran, Trasadasyu's Friend.

33 O Agni, thou on whom all other fires depend, as branches on the parent stem,
I make the treasures of the folk, like songs, mine own, while I exalt thy sovran might.

34 The mortal whom, Ādityas, ye, Guileless, lead to the farther bank
Of all the princes, Bounteous Ones !—

35 Whoe'er he be, Man-ruling Kings ! the Regent of the race of men—
May we, O Mitra, Varuṇa, and Aryaman, like him be furtherers of your law.

36 A gift of fifty female slaves hath Trasadasyu given me, Purukutsa's son,
Most liberal, kind, lord of the brave.

37 And Śyāva too for me led forth a strong steed at Suvāstu's ford :

20 *Bring down the many firm hopes* : there is no substantive in the text, and hopes, resolves, thoughts or something similar must be supplied.

21 *The Friend of man* : or *mánurhitam* may mean 'him who was established by Manus.'

23 *His sword* : the flashing flame. *The Asura* : the Sun, according to Sāyaṇa. *Robe* : outward form.

26 *In sin* : such as neglect of the Gods in consequence of poverty.

33 The meaning of the second line appears to be : 'I praise Agni better than other men. I overpower their hymns and secure for myself the rewards which they were intended to obtain.'

36 *Female slaves* : *vadhū́nām* : *vadhū́* means usually a bride, a wife, a woman in general, and here handmaids or female slaves, the wives or daughters of conquered Dāsas, appear to be meant. According to von Roth, mares or other female draught-animals are intended.

37 *Suvā́stu* is in all probability the Soastos of Arrian (Suwad or Swat) near the Kophen or Kābul river. *Kine* : there is no substantive in the text. The stanza, which has no comment in the printed edition,

A herd of three times seventy kine, good lord of gifts, he gave to me.

HYMN XX. *Maruts.*

1. LET none, Swift Travellers ! check you : come hither, like-spirited, stay not far away,
Ye benders even of what is firm.

2 Maruts, Ṛbhukṣans, Rudras come ye with your cars strong-fellied and exceeding bright.
Come, ye for whom we long, with food, to sacrifice, come ye with love to Sobhari.

3 For well we know the vigorous might of Rudra's Sons, the Maruts, who are passing strong,
Swift Viṣṇu's band, who send the rain.

4 Islands are bursting forth and misery is stayed : the heaven and earth are joined in one.
Decked with bright rings, ye spread the broad expanses out, when ye, Self-luminous, stirred yourselves.

5 Even things immovable shake and reel, the mountains and the forest trees at your approach,
And the earth trembles as ye come.

6 To lend free course, O Maruts, to your furious rush, heaven high and higher still gives way,
Where they, the Heroes mighty with their arms, display their gleaming ornaments on their forms.

7 After their Godlike nature they, the bull-like Heroes, dazzling and impetuous, wear
Great splendour as they show erect.

8 The pivot of the Sobharis' chariot within the golden box is balmed with milk.
May they the Well-born, Mighty, kindred of the Cow, aid us to food and to delight.

9 Bring, ye who sprinkle balmy drops, oblations to your vigorous Marut company,
To those whose leader is the Bull.

10 Come hither, O ye Maruts, on your strong-horsed car, solid in look, with solid naves.
Lightly like winged falcons, O ye Heroes, come, come to enjoy our offerings.

11 Their decoration is the same : their ornaments of gold are bright upon their arms;
Their lances glitter splendidly.

12 They toil not to defend their bodies from attack, strong Heroes with their mighty arms.
Strong are your bows and strong the weapons in your cars, and glory sits on every face.

13 Whose name extendeth like a sea, alone, resplendent, so that all have joy in it,
And life-power like ancestral might.

14 Pay honour to these Maruts and sing praise to them, for of the wheel-spokes of the car
Of these loud roarers none is last : this is their power, this moves them to give mighty gifts.

15 Blest by your favouring help was he, O Maruts, at the earlier flushings of the morn,
And even now shall he be blest.

16 The strong man to whose sacrifice, O Heroes, ye approach that ye may taste thereof,
With glories and with war that winneth spoil shall gain great bliss, ye Shakers of the world.

17 Even as Rudra's Sons, the brood of the Creator Dyaus, the Asura, desire,
O Youthful Ones, so shall it be :

is very obscure and can be only conjecturally translated. See Ludwig's Translation and Commentary, I. 427, and IV. 380.

---

4 Sāyaṇa seems to explain this verse, 'The islands fall asunder, the firmest (trees) experience distress ; they (the winds) distress heaven and earth ; the waters hurry onward, O bright weaponed, self-shining ones, when you agitate them '—E.B.C.'s note in Wilson's Translation. The stanza is difficult. I have followed, generally, Ludwig's version. *Islands* : the higher unsubmerged grounds. *Misery* : caused by the preceding hot and dry weather. *Are joined in one* : as the heavy rain cures the horizon. *Bright rings* : worn on the arms or the ankles or carried by the Maruts on their shoulders. See I. 166. 9.

7 *Bull-like* : the exact meaning of *vṛṣapsavaḥ* is uncertain. *Show erect* : *dhrutapsavaḥ* is conjecturally translated.

8 *Box* : the interior of the chariot. *With milk* : with fertilizing rain sent by the Maruts. *The Cow* : Pṛśni.

9 *Ye who sprinkle balmy drops* : priests who offer libations. *Whose leader is the Bull* : whom Indra leads. Or, it may be, whose chariot is drawn by bulls, as in the following stanza.

10 *Solid in look* : or with bull-like, or strong look.

14 *None is last* : no part of their chariot wheel is behind the rest in speed. *This moves them to give mighty gifts* : or, this (characteristic belongs to them) through greatness of their gifts.

15 *He* : your worshipper.

18 And these the bounteous, worthy of the Maruts who move onward pouring down the rain—
Even for their sake, O Youthful Ones, with kindest heart take us to you to be your own.

19 O Sobhari, with newest song sing out unto the youthful purifying Bulls,
Even as a plougher to his steers.

20 Who, like a celebrated boxer, overcome the challengers in every fight :
They who, like shining bulls, are most illustrious—honour those Maruts with thy song.

21 Allied by common ancestry, ye Maruts, even the Cows, alike in energy,
Lick, all by turns, each other's head.

22 Even mortal man, ye Dancers breast-adorned with gold, attains to brotherhood with you.
Mark ye and notice us, O Maruts ; evermore your friendship is secured to us.

23 O Maruts, rich in noble gifts, bring us a portion of the Maruts' medicine,
Ye Coursers who are Friends to us.

24 Haters of those who serve you not, bliss-bringers, bring us bliss with those auspicious aids
Wherewith ye are victorious and guard Sindhu well, and succour Kṛvi in his need.

25 Maruts, who rest on fair trimmed grass, what balm soever Sindhu or Asiknī hath,
Or mountains or the seas contain.

26 Ye carry on your bodies, ye who see it all : so bless us graciously therewith.
Cast, Maruts, to the ground our sick man's malady : replace the dislocated limb.

18 *The bounteous* : the liberal institutors of sacrifice.

19 *Purifying bulls* : the strong Maruts who send the sweet rain.

21 *Allied by common ancestry* : as the offspring of Pṛśni. *The Cows* : the Maruts. *Lick...each other's head* : as they crowd together in their course. According to Sāyaṇa, 'the cows severally lick up the quarters of the sky.'

22 *Ye Dancers* : ye who dance through the air.

24 *Kṛvi* : the eponymus of a warrior tribe in the Panjāb, in later times combined with, or identical with the Pañcālas. Sāyaṇa takes *kṛvim* here to mean a well : 'with which you provided a well (for Gotama).' —Wilson.

25 *Asiknī* : the Acesines of Quintus Curtius, the Vedic name of the Candrabhāgā, the modern Cenāb.

26 *Replace the dislocated limb* : 're-establish his enfeebled frame.'—Wilson

HYMN XXI. *Indra.*

1. We call on thee, O Matchless One ! We seeking help, possessing nothing firm ourselves,
Call on thee wonderful in fight :

2 On thee for aid in sacrifice. This youth of ours, the bold, the mighty, hath gone forth.
We therefore, we thy friends, Indra, have chosen thee, free-giver, as our Guardian God.

3 Come hither, for the drops are here, O Lord of corn-lands. Lord of horses, Lord of kine :
Drink thou the Soma, Soma's Lord !

4 For we the kinless singers have drawn hither thee, O Indra, who hast numerous kin.
With all the forms thou hast, come thou of bull-like strength, come near to drink the Soma juice.

5 Sitting like birds beside thy meath, mingled with milk, that gladdeneth and exalteth thee,
Indra, to thee we sing aloud.

6 We speak to thee with this our reverential prayer. Why art thou pondering yet awhile ?
Here are our wishes ; thou art liberal, Lord of Bays : we and our hymns are present here.

7 For not in recent times alone, O Indra, Thunder-armed, have we obtained thine aid.
Of old we knew thy plenteous wealth.

8 Hero, we knew thy friendship and thy rich rewards : these, Thunderer, now we crave of thee.
O Vasu, for all wealth that cometh of the kine, sharpen our powers, fair-visored God.

9 Him who of old hath brought to us this and that blessing, him I magnify for you,
Even Indra, O my friends, for help :

10 Borne by Bay Steeds, the Lord of heroes, ruling men, for it is he who takes delight.
May Maghavan bestow on us his worshippers hundreds of cattle and of steeds.

11 Hero, may we, with thee for Friend, withstand the man who pants against us in his wrath,

2 *This youth of ours* : the noble who has instituted the sacrifice.

In fight with people rich in kine.

12 May we be victors in the singer's battle-song, and meet the wicked, Much-invoked !
With heroes smite the foeman and show forth our strength. O Indra, further thou our thoughts.

13 O Indra, from all ancient time rivalless ever and companionless art thou :
Thou seekest comradeship in war.

14 Thou findest not the wealthy man to be thy friend : those scorn thee who are flown with wine.
What time thou thunderest and gatherest, then thou, even as a Father, art invoked.

15 O Indra, let us not, like fools who waste their lives at home, with friendship such as thine
Sit idly by the poured-out juice.

16 Giver of kine, may we not miss thy gracious gifts : let us not rob thee of thine own.
Strip even the strong places of the foe, and bring : thy gifts can never be made vain.

17 Indra or blest Sarasvatī alone bestows such wealth, treasure so great, or thou, O Citra, on the worshipper.

18 Citra is King, and only kinglings are the rest who dwell beside Sarasvatī.
He, like Parjanya with his rain, hath spread himself with thousand, yea, with myriad gifts.

HYMN XXII. *Aśvins.*

1. HITHERWARD have I called to-day, for succour, that most wondrous car
Which ye ascended, Aśvins, ye whose paths are red, swift to give ear, for Sūryā's sake.

2 Car ever young, much longed-for, easily invoked, soon guided, first in deeds of might,
Which waits and serves, O Sobhari, with benevolence, without a rival or a foe.

3 These Aśvins with our homage, these Two Omnipresent Deities
Hitherward will we bring for kind help, these who seek the dwelling of the worshipper.

4 One of your chariot wheels is moving swiftly round, one speeds for you its onward course.
Like a milch-cow, O Lords of splendour, and with haste let your benevolence come to us.

5 That chariot of yours which hath a triple seat and reins of gold,
The famous car that traverseth the heaven and earth, thereon Nāsatyas, Aśvins, come.

6 Ye with your plough, when favouring Manu with your help, ploughed the first harvest in the sky.
As such will we exalt you, Lords of splendour, now, O Aśvins, with our prayer and praise.

7 Come to us, Lords of ample wealth, by paths of everlasting Law,
Whereby to high dominion ye with mighty strength raised Tṛkṣi, Trasadasyu's son.

8 This Soma pressed with stones is yours, ye Heroes, Lords of plenteous wealth.
Approach to drink the Soma, come, drink in the worshipper's abode.

9 O Aśvins, mount the chariot, mount the golden seat, ye who are Lords of plenteous wealth,
And bring to us abundant food.

10 The aids wherewith ye helped Paktha and Adhrigu, and Babhru severed from his friends,—
With those, O Aśvins, come hither with speed and soon, and heal whatever is diseased.

13 *Thou seekest comradeship in war* : befriendest thy worshippers when they need thine assistance in battle.

14 *Gatherest* : the clouds.—M. Müller.

17 *Citra* : the name of this king does not occur elsewhere in the Ṛgveda.

18 *King* : *rājā*. *Kinglings* : *rājakáḥ*. *Parjanya* : God of the rain-cloud, regarded as the type of liberal beneficence.

---

1 *Ye whose paths are red* : *rudravartanī* : this epithet of the Aśvins is variously explained : 'having a path which causes weeping in battle,' or 'whose paths are praised,'—Sāyaṇa; 'advancing on the path to battle.'—Wilson ; 'proceeding on terrible roads.'—Muir ; 'going on Rudra's path.'—Ludwig; 'on your light path.'—Grassmann, 'going on a reddish path.'—Pischel. See *Vedische Studien*, I., pp. 15 and 55—60. *For Sūryā's sake* : who chose the Aśvins as her husbands. See I. 116. 17.

4 The movements of the two wheels are not very intelligibly decribed. See I. 30. 19, and V. 73. 3. *Like a milch-cow* : a common type of liberality.

6 *Ploughed the first harvest* : first ploughed the ground and sowed and reaped : that is, taught, by example, men to do so. Cp. I. 117. 21 : 'Ploughing and sowing barley, O ye Aśvins, milking out food for men, ye wonder-workers, Blasting away the Dasyu with your trumpet, ye have bestowed wide light upon the Ārya.'

7 *Tṛkṣi* : See VI. 46. 8.

10 *Paktha*, *Adhrigu*, and *Babhru* are said to have been kings.

11 When we continually invoke the Aśvins, the resistless, at this time of day,
We lovers of the song, with songs.

12 Through these, ye Mighty Ones, come hither to my call which brings all blessings, wears all forms,—
Through which, All-present Heroes, lavishest of food ye strengthened Kṛvi, come through these.

13 I speak to both of these as such, these Aśvins whom I reverence at this time of day:
With homage we entreat them both.

14 Ye who are Lords of splendour, ye whose paths are red, at eve, at morn, at sacrifice,
Give us not utterly as prey to mortal foe, ye Rudras, Lords of ample wealth.

15 For bliss I call the blissful car, at morn the inseparable Aśvins with their car
I call, like Sobhari our sire.

16 Rapid as thought, and strong, and speeding to the joy, bringing your swiftly-coming help,
Be to us a protection even from far away, Lords of great wealth, with many aids.

17 Come, Wonder-Workers, to our home, our home, O Aśvins, rich in cattle, steeds, and gold,
Chief drinkers of the Soma's juice!

18 Choice-worthy strength, heroic, firm and excellent, uninjured by the Rakṣas foe,
At this your coming nigh, ye Lords of ample wealth and all good things, may we obtain.

HYMN XXIII. *Agni.*

1. WORSHIP thou Jātavedas, pray to him who willingly accepts,
Whose smoke wanders at will, and none may grasp his flame.

2 Thou, all men's friend, Viśvamanas, exaltest Agni with thy song,
The Giver, and his flames with which no cars contend.

3 Whose resolute assault, to win vigour and food, deserves our praise,—
Through whose discovering power the priest obtaineth wealth.

4 Up springs the imperishable flame, the flame of the Refulgent One
Most bright, with glowing jaws and glory in his train.

5 Skilled in fair sacrifice, extolled, arise in Godlike loveliness,
Shining with lofty splendour, with effulgent light.

6 Called straight to our oblations, come, O Agni, through our eulogies,
As thou hast been our envoy bearing up our gifts.

7 I call your Agni, from of old Invoking Priest of living men:
Him with this song I laud and magnify for you.

8 Whom, wondrous wise, they animate with solemn rites and his fair form,
Kind as a friend to men who keep the holy Law.

9 Him, true to Law, who perfecteth the sacrifice, Law-loving ones!
Ye with your song have gratified in the place of prayer.

10 May all our sacrifices go to him the truest Aṅgiras,
Who is among mankind the most illustrious Priest.

11 Imperishable Agni, thine are all these high enkindled lights,
Like horses and like stallions showing forth their strength.

12 So give us, Lord of Power and Might, riches combined with hero strength,
And guard us with our sons and grandsons in our frays.

13 Soon as the eager Lord of men is friendly unto Manu's race,
Agni averteth from us all the demon host.

14 O Hero Agni, Lord of men, on hearing this new laud of mine,
Burn down the Rākṣasas, enchanters, with thy flame.

15 No mortal foe can e'er prevail by arts of magic over him

12 *Kṛvi*: See VIII. 20. 24.

14 *Ye Rudras*: ye red-hued or bright Gods.

17 *Rich in cattle*: proleptic; which your coming will make rich.

The Ṛṣi is Viśvamanas the son of Vyaśva.

1 *Who willingly accepts*: *pratīvyam*: according to Sāyaṇa, 'disposed to encounter enemies.'

2 The second line is difficult, as the adjective *viṣpa dhasaḥ* stands without a substantive and may be either the accusative plural or the genitive singular: 'who is the giver of chariots to the unenvious (worshipper).' —Wilson.

3 *Assault*: on the oblations which the fire consumes.

9 *Law-loving ones*: 'pious worshippers.'—Wilson. *Have gratified*: or must gratify.

Who serveth Agni well with sacrificial gifts.

16 Vyaśva the sage, who sought the Bull, hath won thee, finder of good things :
As such may we enkindle thee for ample wealth.

17 Uśanā Kāvya stablished thee, O Agni, as Invoking Priest :
Thee, Jātavedas, Sacrificing Priest for man.

18 All Deities of one accord appointed thee their messenger :
Thou, God, through hearing, hadst first claim to sacrifice.

19 Him may the mortal hero make his own immortal messenger.
Far-spreading, Purifier, him whose path is black.

20 With lifted ladles let us call him splendid with his brilliant flame,
Men's ancient Agni, wasting not, adorable.

21 The man who pays the worship due to him with sacrificial gifts
Obtains both plenteous nourishment and hero fame.

22 To Jātavedas Agni, chief in sacrifices, first of all
With homage goes the ladle rich with sacred gifts.

23 Even as Vyaśva did, may we with these most high and liberal hymns
Pay worship unto Agni of the splendid flame.

24 Now sing, as Sthūrayūpa sang, with lauds to him who spreadeth far,
To Agni of the home, O Ṛṣi, Vyaśva's son.

25 As welcome guest of human kind, as offspring of the forest kings,
The sages worship ancient Agni for his aid.

26 For men's oblations brought to him who is the mighty Lord of all,
Sit, Agni, mid our homage, on the sacred grass.

27 Grant us abundant treasures, grant the opulence which many crave,
With store of heroes, progeny, and high renown.

28 Agni, Most Youthful of the Gods, send evermore the gift of wealth
Unto Varosuṣāman and to all his folk.

29 A mighty Conqueror art thou, O Agni, so disclose to us
Food in our herds of kine and gain of ample wealth.

30 Thou, Agni, art a glorious God : bring hither Mitra, Varuṇa,
Imperial Sovrans, holy-minded, true to Law.

HYMN XXIV. *Indra.*

1. COMPANIONS, let us learn a prayer to Indra whom the thunder arms,
To glorify your bold and most heroic Friend.

2 For thou by slaying Vṛtra art the Vṛtra-slayer, famed for might.
Thou, Hero, in rich gifts surpassest wealthy chiefs.

3 As such, when glorified, bring us riches of very wondrous fame,
Set in the highest rank, Wealth-giver, Lord of Bays !

4 Yea, Indra, thou disclosest that preëminent dear wealth of men :
Boldly, O Bold One, glorified, bring it to us.

5 The workers of destruction stay neither thy right hand nor thy left :
Nor hosts that press about thee, Lord of Bays, in fight.

6 O Thunder-armed, I come with songs to thee as to a stall with kine :
Fulfil the wish and thought of him who sings thy praise.

7 Chief Vṛtra-slayer, through the hymn of Viśvamanas think of all,
All that concerneth us, Excellent, Mighty Guide.

8 May we, O Vṛtra-slayer, O Hero, find this thy newest boon, Longed-for, and excellent, thou who art much invoked !

16 *Who sought the Bull* : the strong Agni. According to Sāyaṇa, 'the showerer (of rain).'

17 *Uśanā Kāvya* : See Vol. I., Index.

18 *Through hearing* : and, by causing the Gods to hear, men's prayers.

24 *Sthūrayūpa* : said by Sāyaṇa to be the name of of a Ṛṣi.

25 *Forest kings* : tall trees, or trees in general.

28 *Varosuṣāman* : I follow the St. Petersburg Lexicon in joining *varo* to *suṣāmṇe* and taking the whole as one word and the name of a chief. Ludwig translates somewhat as follows : 'Agni, send quickly to the folk who know the goodly Sāman well. the gift of wealth, for ever, Youngest God ! to all.' But in a later volume of his work (III. p. 162 he comes to the conclusion that Suṣāman is a proper name, and that *varo* (which may, he thinks, be an interjection) must not be combined with it.

9 O Indra, Dancer, Much-invoked ! as thy great power is unsurpassed,
So be thy bounty to the worshipper unchecked.

10 Most Mighty, most heroic One, for mighty bounty fill thee full.
Though strong, strengthen thyself to win wealth, Maghavan !

11 O Thunderer, never have our prayers gone forth to any God but thee :
So help us, Maghavan, with thine assistance now.

12 For, Dancer, verily I find none else for bounty, saving thee,
For splendid wealth and power, thou Lover of the Song.

13 For Indra pour ye out the drops ; meath blent with Soma let him drink :
With bounty and with majesty will he further us.

14 I spake to the Bay Coursers' Lord, to him who gives ability :
Now hear the son of Aśva as he praises thee.

15 Never was any Hero born before thee mightier than thou :
None certainly like thee in goodness and in wealth.

16 O ministering priest, pour out of the sweet juice what gladdens most :
So is the Hero praised who ever prospers us.

17 Indra, whom Tawny Coursers bear, praise such as thine, preëminent,
None by his power or by his goodness hath attained.

18 We, seeking glory, have invoked this Master of all power and might
Who must be glorified by constant sacrifice.

19 Come, sing we praise to Indra, friends, the Hero who deserves the laud,
Him who with none to aid o'ercomes all tribes of men.

20 To him who wins the kine, who keeps no cattle back, Celestial God,
Speak wondrous speech more sweet than butter and than meath.

21 Whose hero powers are measureless, whose bounty ne'er may be surpassed,
Whose liberality, like light, is over all.

22 As Vyaśva did, praise Indra, praise the Strong unfluctuating Guide,
Who gives the foe's possessions to the worshipper.

23 Now, son of Vyaśva, praise thou him who to the tenth time still is new,
The very Wise, whom living men must glorify

24 Thou knowest, Indra, Thunder-armed, how to avoid destructive powers,
As one secure from pitfalls each returning day.

25 O Indra, bring that aid wherewith of old, Most Wondrous ! thou didst slay
His foes for active Kutsa : send it down to us.

26 So now we seek thee fresh in might, Most Wonderful in act ! for gain :
For thou art he who conquers all our foes for us.

27 Who will set free from ruinous woe, or Ārya on the Seven Streams :
O valiant Hero, bend the Dāsa's weapon down.

28 As to Varosuṣāman thou broughtest great riches, for their gain,
To Vyaśva's sons, Blest Lady, rich in ample wealth !

29 Let Nārya's sacrificial meed reach Vyaśva's Soma-bearing sons :
In hundreds and in thousands be the great reward.

30 If one should ask thee, Where is he who sacrificed ? Whither lookest thou ?

9 *Dancer* : of the dance of war. According to Sāyaṇa, 'dancer, or who causes to dance, *i.e.* agitator, exciter, from Indra's faculty of internal impulse in all beings.'—Wilson.

14 *Son of Aśva* : *i.e.* of Vyaśva, the Ṛṣi Viśvamanas.

20 *Who keeps no cattle back* : either literally who aids his worshippers to win cattle in their raids and gives them all the booty ; or, who sends forth all the kine or rays of light that he has recovered from the powers of darkness. According to Sāyaṇa, 'who rejects no praise.'

23 *Who to the tenth time still is new* : continually renews his liberality to us. This seems to be the meaning of the *daśamám návam* (tenth new) of the text. Sāyaṇa explains differently : 'who is the tenth (of the pervading vital principles), the adorable.'

24 *Destructive powers* : the plural of Nirṛti, Death or Destruction. I adopt Ludwig's interpretation of the second line

27 *Ārya on the Seven Streams* : from any Āryan enemy in the land of the Seven Rivers, probably the Indus, the five rivers of the Panjāb, and the Kubhā.

28 *Varosuṣāman* : See VIII. 23. 28. *Blest Lady* : Uṣas or Dawn is addressed.

29 *Nārya's sacrificial meed* : Nārya appears to be the name of the institutor of the sacrifice.

30 Ludwig observes : 'This stanza clearly refers to the greatness of the reward given by Nārya, and its meaning is : here are so many cows (presented by Nārya) that one might think that, in consequence of the sacrifice, Vala had given up his cows [which he had stolen from the Gods, and hidden in a cave], and taken his departure.' Uṣas says also, 'my cows are quite superfluous here, and I will drive them away to some other place.' The stanza is addressed to Uṣas,

Like Vala he hath passed away and dwelleth now on Gomatī.

HYMN XXV. *Mitra-Varuṇa.*

1. I WORSHIP you who guard this All, Gods, holiest among the Gods,
You, faithful to the Law, whose power is sanctified.

2 So, too, like charioteers are they, Mitra and sapient Varuṇa,
Sons high-born from of old, whose holy laws stand fast.

3 These Twain, possessors of all wealth, most glorious, for supremest sway
Aditi, Mighty Mother, true to Law, brought forth.

4 Great Varuṇa and Mitra, Gods, Asuras and imperial Lords,
True to Eternal Law proclaim the high decree.

5 The offspring of a lofty Power, Dakṣa's Two Sons exceeding strong,
Who, Lords of flowing rain, dwell in the place of food.

6 Ye who have gathered up your gifts, celestial and terrestrial food,
Let your rain come to us fraught with the mist of heaven.

7 The Twain, who from the lofty sky seem to look down on herds below,
Holy, imperial Lords, are set to be revered.

8 They, true to Law, exceeding strong, have sat them down for sovran rule :
Princes whose laws stand fast, they have obtained their sway.

9 Pathfinders even better than the eye, with unobstructed sight,
Even when they close their lids, observant, they perceive.

10 So may the Goddess Aditi, may the Nāsatyas guard us well,
The Maruts guard us well, endowed with mighty strength.

11 Do ye, O Bounteous Gods, protect our dwelling-place by day and night :
With you for our defenders may we go unharmed.

12 May we, unharmed, serve bountiful Viṣṇu, the God who slayeth none :
Self-moving Sindhu hear and be the first to mark.

13 This sure protection we elect, desirable and reaching far,
Which Mitra, Varuṇa, and Aryaman afford.

14 And may the Sindhu of the floods, the Maruts, and the Aśvin Pair,
Boon Indra, and boon Viṣṇu have one mind with us.

15 Because these warring Heroes stay the enmity of every foe,
As the fierce water-flood repels the furious ones.

16 Here this one God, the Lord of men, looks forth exceeding far and wide :
And we, for your advantage, keep his holy laws.

17 We keep the old accustomed laws, the statutes of supremacy,
The long-known laws of Mitra and of Varuṇa.

18 He who hath measured with his ray the boundaries of heaven and earth,
And with his majesty hath filled the two worlds full,

19 Sūrya hath spread his light aloft up to the region of the sky,
Like Agni all aflame when gifts are offered him.

20 With him who sits afar the word is lord of food that comes from kine,
Controller of the gift of unempoisoned food.

21 So unto Sūrya, Heaven, and Earth at morning and at eve I speak.
Bringing enjoyments ever rise thou up for us.

and the second line is the answer she is to give to the question contained in the first. *Gomatī* some affluent of the Indus, which in later times lent its name to the Gomatī, or Gumti, which flows through Oudh and falls into the Ganges.

---

2 *Charioteers* : furtherers of eternal Law. See VII. 66. 12.

5 *Dakṣa's Two Sons* : or sons of power or energy, according to Sāyaṇa. Dakṣa as a creative power, is frequently associated with Aditi. *Place of food* : heaven from which the food-producing rain comes.

12 *Sindhu* : the Indus. According to Sāyaṇa, Viṣṇu who causes wealth to flow to his worshippers.

20 Varuṇa has only to command and men have milk and wholesome food. Sāyaṇa explains differently: 'Raise your voice in the spacious hall of sacrifice to him who is lord over food derived from cattle.'—Wilson

21 *Thou* : Sūrya, that is, according to Sāyaṇa, Mitra and Varuṇa in Sūrya's shape.

22 From Ukṣaṇyāyana a bay, from Harayāṇa a white steed,
And from Suṣāman we obtained a harnessed car.

23 These two shall bring me further gain of troops of tawny-coloured steeds,
The carriers shall they be of active men of war.

24 And the two sages have I gained who hold the reins and bear the whip,
And the two great strong coursers, with my newest song.

22 *Suṣāman* : here without *Varo*, the prefix or interjection or whatever it may be. See VIII. 23. 28.

23 *These two* : horses.

24 *Two sages* : *viprā* : the meaning is uncertain. According to Sāyaṇa the word is an epithet of 'coursers': 'sagacious.'—Wilson. Ludwig thinks that the grooms (probably enslaved enemies) are ironically called sages, or as he translates, Brāhmans. Dr. Muir translates the stanza differently ; 'I have celebrated at the same time with a new hymn, these two sages and mighty [princes], strong, swift, and carrying whips.' But this rendering has little to recommend it.

HYMN XXVI. *Aśvins.*

1. I CALL your chariot to receive united praise mid princely men,
Strong Gods who pour down wealth, of never vanquished might !

2 Ye to Varosuṣāman come, Nāsatyas, for this glorious rite.
With your protecting aid, Strong Gods, who pour down wealth.

3 So with oblations we invoke you, rich in ample wealth, to-day,
When night hath passed, O ye who send us plenteous food.

4 O Aśvins, Heroes, let your car, famed, best to travel, come to us,
And, for his glory, mark your zealous servant's lauds.

5 Aśvins, who send us precious gifts, even when offended, think of him :
For ye, O Rudras, lead us safe beyond our foes.

6 For, Wonder-Workers, with fleet steeds ye fly completely round this All,
Stirring our thoughts, ye Lords of splendour, honey-hued.

7 With all-sustaining opulence, Aśvins, come hitherward to us,
Ye rich and noble Heroes, ne'er to be o'erthrown.

8 To welcome this mine offering, O ye Indra-like Nāsatyas, come
As Gods of best accord this day with other Gods.

9 For we, like Vyaśva, lifting up our voice like oxen, call on you :
With all your loving kindness, Sages, come to us.

10 O Ṛṣi, laud the Aśvins well. Will they not listen to thy call ?
Will they not burn the Paṇis who are nearer them ?

11 O Heroes, listen to the son of Vyaśva, and regard me here,
Varuṇa, Mitra, Aryaman, of one accord.

12 Gods whom we yearn for, of your gifts, of what ye bring to us, bestow
By princes' hands on me, ye Mighty, day by day.

13 Him whom your sacrifices clothe, even as a woman with her robe,
The Aśvins help to glory honouring him well.

14 Whoso regards your care of men as succour widest in its reach,
About his dwelling go, ye Aśvins, loving us.

15 Come to us ye who pour down wealth, come to the home which men must guard :
Like shafts, ye are made meet for sacrifice by song.

16 Most fetching of all calls, the laud, as envoy, Heroes, called to you :
Be it your own, O Aśvin Pair.

17 Be ye in yonder sea of heaven, or joying in the home of food,
Listen to me, Immortal Ones.

18 This river with his lucid flow attracts you, more than all the streams,—
Even Sindhu with his path of gold.

19 O Aśvins, with that glorious fame come hither, through our brilliant song,

1 *Princely men* : the *Sūris* or institutors of the sacrifice.

2 *Varosuṣāman* : See VIII. 23. 28. *Who pour down wealth* : *vṛṣaṇvasū* ; See IV. 50. 10, note.

5 *Rudras* : bright Gods.

6 *Honey-hued* : *mádhuvarṇā* : 'of fascinating complexion.'—Wilson.

15 *Like shafts* : as arrows are sharpened for their work, so the Aśvins are prepared for the sacrifice by the Ṛṣi's hymn. The word *viṣudrúhā*, explained by Sāyaṇa as two arrows, is difficult, and other readings and explanations have been suggested.

18 *With his lucid flow* : *śvetayā́varī* : taken by Sāyaṇa as the name of a river.

Come ye whose ways are marked with light.

20 Harness the steeds who draw the car, O Vasu, bring the well-fed pair.
O Vāyu, drink thou of our meath : come unto our drink-offerings.

21 Wonderful Vāyu, Lord of Right, thou who art Tvaṣṭar's son-in-law,
Thy saving succour we elect.

22 To Tvaṣṭar's son-in-law we pray for wealth whereof he hath control :
For glory we seek Vāyu, men with juice effused.

23 From heaven, auspicious Vāyu, come ; drive hither with thy noble steeds :
Come on thy mighty car with wide-extending seat.

24 We call thee to the homes of men, thee wealthiest in noble food,
And liberal as a press-stone with a horse's back.

25 So, glad and joyful in thine heart, do thou, God, Vāyu, first of all
Vouchsafe us water, strength, and thought.

HYMN XXVII. *Viśvedevas.*

1. CHIEF Priest is Agni at the laud, as stones and grass at sacrifice :
With song I seek the Maruts, Brahmaṇaspati, Gods for help much to be desired.

2 I sing to cattle and to Earth, to trees, to Dawns, to Night, to plants.
O all ye Vasus, ye possessors of all wealth, be ye the furtherers of our thoughts.

3 Forth go, with Agni, to the Gods our sacrifice of ancient use,
To the Ādityas, Varuṇa whose Law stands fast, and the all-lightening Marut troop.

4 Lords of all wealth, may they be strengtheners of man, destroyers of his enemies.
Lords of all wealth, do ye, with guards which none may harm, preserve our dwelling free from foes.

5 Come to us with one mind to-day, come to us all with one accord,
Maruts with holy song, and, Goddess Aditi, Mighty One, to our house and home.

6 Send us delightful things, ye Maruts, on your steeds : come ye, O Mitra, to our gifts.
Let Indra, Varuṇa, and the Ādityas sit, swift Heroes, on our sacred grass.

7 We who have trimmed the grass for you, and set the banquet in array,
And pressed the Soma, call you, Varuṇa, like men, with sacrificial fires aflame.

8 O Maruts, Viṣṇu, Aśvins, Pūṣan, haste away with minds turned hitherward to me.
Let the Strong Indra, famed as Vṛtra's slayer, come first with the winners of the spoil.

9 Ye Guileless Gods, bestow on us a refuge strong on every side,
A sure protection, Vasus, unassailable from near at hand or from afar.

10 Kinship have I with you, and close alliance, O ye Gods, destroyers of our foes.
Call us to our prosperity of former days, and soon to new felicity.

11 For now have I sent forth to you, that I may win a fair reward,
Lords of all wealth, with homage, this my song of praise like a milch-cow that faileth not.

12 Excellent Savitar hath mounted up on high for you, ye sure and careful Guides.
Bipeds and quadrupeds, with several

21 *Tvaṣṭar's son-in-law* : the Commentators give no satisfactory explanation. Saraṇyū, Tvaṣṭar's daughter, was the wife of Vivasvān, who cannot be identified with Vāyu. See Hillebrandt, *Vedische Mythologie*, I. p. 521.

24 The second line is difficult. The press-stone which produces the Soma juice which makes the Gods bountiful is regarded as a type of liberality; it may be called *áśvapṛṣṭham*, literally, horse-backed, because it bears its load of Soma stalks like a horse. 'Sharp-backed', 'with sharp ridges', as suggested by Pischel, gives a a better meaning.

1 *Chief Priest* : according to Sāyaṇa, *puróhitaḥ* here is taken in its primary sense of 'placed in front,' that is, set by the priests on the *uttaravedī* or northern altar or fire-receptacle. *The laud* : *ukthá* : a kind of religious service consisting of the recitation of certain eulogistic verses.

2 *I sing to* : or I glorify, in order that I may win or propitiate them.

6 *Come ye, O Mitra* : Varuṇa and Aryaman being understood.

7 *Like men* : *manuṣvát* : or after the manner of Manus.

11 *Like a milch-cow that faileth not* : the meaning of *ányām* here is somewhat uncertain. Sāyaṇa explains it by *adṛṣṭapūrvām* unprecedented, and Grassmann by 'a stream that never dries up.' I have adopted Ludwig's interpretation.

hopes and aims, and birds have settled to their tasks.

13 Singing their praise with God-like thought let us invoke each God for grace,
Each God to bring you help, each God to strengthen you.

14 For of one spirit are the Gods with mortal man, co-sharers all of gracious gifts.
May they increase our strength hereafter and to-day, providing ease and ample room.

15 I laud you, O ye Guileless Gods, here where we meet to render praise.
None, Varuṇa and Mitra, harms the mortal man who honours and obeys your laws.

16 He makes his house endure, he gathers plenteous food who pays obedience to your will.
Born in his sons anew he spreads as Law commands, and prospers every way unharmed.

17 E'en without war he gathers wealth, and goes his way on pleasant paths,
Whom Mitra, Varuṇa and Aryaman protect, sharing the gift, of one accord.

18 E'en on the plain for him ye make a sloping path, an easy way where road is none :
And far away from him the ineffectual shaft must vanish, shot at him in vain.

19 If ye appoint the rite to-day, kind Rulers, when the Sun ascends,
Lords of all wealth, at sunset or at waking-time, or be it at the noon of day,

20 Or, Asuras, when ye have sheltered the worshipper who goes to sacrifice, at eve,
May we, O Vasus, ye possessors of all wealth, come then into the midst of you.

21 If ye to-day at sunrise, or at noon, or in the gloom of eve,
Lords of all riches, give fair treasure to the man, the wise man who hath sacrificed,

22 Then we, imperial Rulers, claim of you this boon, your wide protection, as a son.
May we, Ādityas, offering holy gifts, obtain that which shall bring us greater bliss.

HYMN XXVIII. *Viśvedevas.*

1. The Thirty Gods and Three besides, whose seat hath been the sacred grass,
From time of old have found and gained.

2 Varuṇa, Mitra, Aryaman, Agnis, with Consorts, sending boons,
To whom our Vaṣaṭ ! is addressed :

3 These are our guardians in the west, and northward here, and in the south,
And on the east, with all the tribe.

4 Even as the Gods desire so verily shall it be. None minisheth this power of theirs,
No demon, and no mortal man.

5 The Seven carry seven spears; seven are the splendours they possess,
And seven the glories they assume.

HYMN XXIX *Viśvedevas.*

1. One is a youth brown, active, manifold : he decks the golden one with ornament.

2 Another, luminous, occupies the place of sacrifice, Sage, among the Gods.

3 One brandishes in his hand an iron knife, firm, in his seat amid the Deities.

4 Another holds the thunderbolt, wherewith he slays the Vṛtras, resting in his hand.

5 Another bears a pointed weapon : bright is he, and strong, with healing medicines.

1 *Thirty Gods and Three* : See I. 139. 11.

2 *Agnis* : Agni in his various forms and under different names. *With Consorts* : with the Gnās, Celestial Dames, wives of the Gods. *Vaṣaṭ !* : the exclamation made when the oblation is offered.

4 *No demon and no mortal man* : or no mortal who presents no offerings to the Gods.

5 *The Seven* : the Maruts, seven, or seven times nine, or seven times seven in number. Sāyaṇa mentions the legend of their birth, which will be found in the *Rāmāyaṇa*, Book I., Cantos 46, 47. The meaning is merely that the Maruts carry lances, that is, their lightnings, and are splendidly adorned. See I. 37. The connexion of this stanza with the preceding is not obvious.

---

1 *One* : Soma. 'The yellow Soma juice is itself an ornament to the gold on the finger (Atharvaveda, XVIII. 3. 18, hiranyapāvāḥ) of the priest.'—Ludwig. According to others. Soma as the Moon is intended, who 'decorates (himself) with golden ornaments.'—Wilson.

2 *Another, luminous* : Agni.

3 *One brandishes* : Tvaṣṭar, as the Artificer of the Gods.

4 *Another holds the thunderbolt* : Indra.

5 *Another*: Rudra. See I. 43. 4.

6 Another, thief-like, watches well the ways, and knows the places where the treasures lie.

7 Another with his mighty stride hath made his three steps thither where the Gods rejoice.

8 Two with one Dame ride on with winged steeds, and journey forth like travellers on their way.

9 Two, highest, in the heavens have set their seat, worshipped with holy oil, Imperial Kings.

10 Some, singing lauds, conceived the Sāma-hymn, great hymn whereby they caused the Sun to shine.

HYMN XXX. *Viśvedevas.*

1. Not one of you, ye Gods, is small, none of you is a feeble child :
All of you, verily, are great.

2 Thus be ye lauded, ye destroyers of the foe, ye Three-and-Thirty Deities,
The Gods of man, the Holy Ones.

3 As such defend and succour us, with benedictions speak to us :
Lead us not from our fathers' and from Manu's path into the distance far away.

4 Ye Deities who stay with us, and all ye Gods of all mankind,
Give us your wide protection, give shelter for cattle and for steed.

HYMN XXXI. *Various Deities.*

1. That Brahman pleases Indra well, who worships, sacrifices, pours Libation, and prepares the meal.

2 Śakra protects from woe the man who gives him sacrificial cake.
And offers Soma blent with milk.

3 His chariot shall be glorious, sped by Gods, and mighty shall he be,
Subduing all hostilities.

4 Each day that passes, in his house flows his libation, rich in milk,
Exhaustless, bringing progeny.

5 O Gods, with constant draught of milk, husband and wife with one accord
Press out and wash the Soma juice.

6 They gain sufficient food : they come united to the sacred grass,
And never do they fail in strength.

7 Never do they deny or seek to hide the favour of the Gods :
They win high glory for themselves.

8 With sons and daughters by their side they reach their full extent of life,
Both decked with ornaments of gold.

9 Serving the Immortal One with gifts of sacrificial meal and wealth,
They satisfy the claims of love and pay due honour to the Gods.

10 We claim protection from the Hills, we claim protection of the Floods,
Of him who stands by Viṣṇu's side.

11 May Pūṣan come, and Bhaga, Lord of wealth, All-bounteous, for our weal :
Broad be the path that leads to bliss :

12 Aramati, and, free from foes, Viśva with spirit of a God,
And the Ādityas' peerless might.

13 Seeing that Mitra, Aryaman, and Varuṇa are guarding us,
The paths of Law are fair to tread.

14 I glorify with song, for wealth, Agni the God, the first of you.

6 *Another* : Pūṣan. See I. 42.

7 *Another with his mighty stride* : Viṣṇu. *Thither* : to his station in the height of heaven.

8 *Two with one Dame* : the Aśvins with Sūryā. See I. 116. 17.

9 *Two, highest* : Mitra and Varuṇa.

10 *Some, singing lauds* : the Aṅgirases, or, according to Sāyaṇa, the Atris.

---

2 *Three-and-Thirty Deities* ; See I. 139. 11. *The Gods of man* : or, God whom Manu worshipped, which interpretation is supported by stanza 3.

4 *Who stay with us* : or are present at this sacrifice.

---

1 *Brahman* : here any pious worshipper, not one of the regular professional priests, but the institutor of sacrifice who during the ceremony may be regarded as their chief. *Prepares the meal* : *paśupuroḍāśādikam pacati*: Sāyaṇa ; 'cooks the cake which is an essential part of the animal sacrifice, etc.

9 *The Immortal One* : *amṛtāya* : Agni, or the Immortal (host), that is, the Gods in general. According to Sāyaṇa, 'that they may obtain immortality (in their sons and descendants).' *They satisfy* : this *pāda* is considered by some, on metrical and other grounds, to be an interpolation. According to Pischel (*Vedische Studien*, I p. 178), the half-line refers to the beating and preparation of the rough stalks of the Soma plant.

10 *Of him who stands by Viṣṇu's side* : of Viṣṇu and his associate Indra.'—Ludwig.

12 *Aramati* : the Genius of Devotion. *Viśva* : Dyaus ?—Ludwig. 'All the worshippers,' according to Sāyaṇa.

14 *Who prospereth our fields* : *kṣetrasādhasam* : Sāyaṇa explains *kṣetra* (the modern Hindi *khet*, a field), as sacrifice ; 'the bountiful perfecter of the sacrifice.'—Wilson.

We honour as a well-loved Friend the God who prospereth our fields.

15 As in all frays the hero, so swift moves his car whom Gods attend.
The man who, sacrificing, strives to win the heart of Deities will conquer those who worship not.

16 Ne'er are ye injured, worshipper, presser of juice, or pious man.
The man who, sacrificing, strives to win the heart of Deities will conquer those who worship not.

17 None in his action equals him, none holds him far or keeps him off.
The man who, sacrificing, strives to win the heart of Deities will conquer those who worship not.

18 Such strength of heroes shall be his, such mastery of fleet-foot steeds.
The man who, sacrificing, strives to win the heart of Deities will conquer those who worship not.

HYMN XXXII. *Indra.*

1. KAṆVAS, tell forth with song the deeds of Indra, the Impetuous,
Wrought in the Soma's wild delight.

2 Strong God, he slew Anarśani, Sṛbinda, Pipru, and the fiend,
Ahīśuva, and loosed the floods.

3. Thou broughtest down the dwelling-place, the height of lofty Arbuda.
That exploit, Indra, must be famed.

4 Bold, to your famous Soma I call the fair-visored God for aid,
Down like a torrent from the hill.

5 Rejoicing in the Soma-draughts, Hero, burst open, like a fort,
The stall of horses and of kine.

6 If my libation gladdens, if thou takest pleasure in my laud,
Come with thy Godhead from afar.

7 O Indra, Lover of the Song, the singers of thy praise are we :
O Soma-drinker, quicken us.

8 And, taking thy delight with us bring us still undiminished food:
Great is thy wealth, O Maghavan.

9 Make thou us rich in herds of kine, in steeds, in gold : let us exert
Our strength in sacrificial gifts.

10 Let us call him to aid whose hands stretch far, to whom high laud is due.
Who worketh well to succour us.

11 He, Śatakratu, even in fight acts as a Vṛtra-slayer still :
He gives his worshippers much wealth.

12 May he, this Śakra, strengthen us, Boon God who satisfies our needs,
Indra, with all his saving helps.

13 To him, the mighty stream of wealth, the Soma-presser's rescuing Friend,
To Indra sing your song of praise ;

14 Who bringeth what is great and firm, who winneth glory in his wars,
Lord of vast wealth through power and might.

15 There liveth none to check or stay his energies and gracious deeds :
None who can say, He giveth not.

16 No debt is due by Brahmans now, by active men who press the juice :
Well hath each Soma-draught been paid.

17 Sing ye to him who must be praised, say lauds to him who must be praised,
Bring prayer to him who must be praised.

18 May he, unchecked, strong, meet for praise, bring hundreds, thousands forth to light,
Indra who aids the worshipper.

19 Go with thy God-like nature forth, go where the folk are calling thee :
Drink, Indra, of the drops we pour.

20 Drink milky draughts which are thine own, this too which was with Tugrya once,
This is it, Indra, that is thine.

21 Pass him who pours libations out in angry mood or after sin :
Here drink the juice we offer thee.

1 *The Impetuous* : *ṛjīṣiṇaḥ* : 'the drinker of the stale *Soma*.'—Wilson.

2 *The fiend* : the Dāsa, or savage. All the names are names of demons of drought of whom Pipru has been mentioned frequently in preceding Books.

3 *Arbuda*: See I. 51. 6; II. 11. 20; 14. 4.

4 *Like a torrent from the hill* : 'as (a traveller invokes) the water from a cloud.'—Wilson.

11 *Śatakratu* : Lord of a Hundred Powers.

12 *Śakra* : the Mighty.

16 The Brahmans or worshippers have, by offering libations, discharged their obligations to the Gods, and the Gods have repaid them, or will soon repay them for their offerings.

18 *Hundreds, thousands* : countless treasures for us to enjoy.

20 *Which was with Tugrya* : like that which thy favourite Bhujyu (See Vol. I, Index) formerly offered thee.

22 Over the three great distances, past the Five Peoples go thy way,
O Indra, noticing our voice.

23 Send forth thy ray like Sūrya : let my songs attract thee hitherward,
Like waters gathering to the vale.

24 Now to the Hero fair of cheek, Adhvaryu, pour the Soma forth :
Bring of the juice that he may drink :

25 Who cleft the water-cloud in twain, loosed rivers for their downward flow,
And set the ripe milk in the kine.

26 He, meet for praise, slew Vṛtra, slew Ahīśuva, Ūrṇavābha's son,
And pierced through Arbuda with frost.

27 To him your matchless Mighty One, unconquerable Conqueror,
Sing forth the prayer which Gods have given :

28 Indra, who in the wild delight of Soma juice considers here
All holy Laws among the Gods.

29 Hither let these thy Bays who share thy banquet, Steeds with golden manes,
Convey thee to the feast prepared.

30 Hither, O thou whom many laud, the Bays whom Priyamedha praised,
Shall bring thee to the Soma-draught.

HYMN XXXIII. *Indra.*

1. We compass thee like waters, we whose grass is trimmed and Soma pressed.
Here where the filter pours its stream, thy worshippers round thee, O Vṛtra-slayer, sit.

2 Men, Vasu ! by the Soma, with lauds call thee to the foremost place :
When comest thou athirst unto the juice as home, O Indra, like a bellowing bull ?

3 Boldly, Bold Hero, bring us spoil in thousands for the Kaṇvas' sake :
O active Maghavan, with eager prayer we crave the yellow-hued with store of kine.

4 Medhyātithi, to Indra sing, drink of the juice to make thee glad.
Close-knit to his Bay Steeds, bolt-armed, beside the juice is he : his chariot is of gold.

5 He who is praised as strong of hand both right and left, most wise and bold :
Indra who, rich in hundreds, gathers thousands up, honoured as breaker-down of forts.

6 The bold of heart whom none provokes, who stands in bearded confidence;
Much-lauded, very glorious, overthrowing foes, strong Helper, like a bull with might.

7 Who knows what vital power he wins, drinking beside the flowing juice ?
This is the fair-cheeked God who, joying in the draught, breaks down the castles in his strength.

8 As a wild elephant rushes on, this way and that way, mad with heat,
None may compel thee, yet come hither to the draught : thou movest mighty in thy power.

9 When he, the Mighty, ne'er o'erthrown, steadfast, made ready for the fight,
When Indra Maghavan lists to his praiser's call, he will not stand aloof, but come.

10 Yea, verily, thou art a Bull, with a bull's rush, whom none may stay :
Thou, Mighty One, art celebrated as a Bull, famed as a Bull both near and far.

22 *The three great distances* : the space in front of thee, behind thee, and at thy side. *Noticing our voice* : hearing and attending to our invocations. Come to us who are thy true worshippers, and pass by others who worship thee in the hope of being avenged upon their enemies or of obtaining pardon for some sin.

26 *Ūrṇavābha's son* : Aurṇavābha : a demon of drought. See II. 11. 18. *With frost* : making the piercing cold of winter his weapon.

---

1 *The filter* : or woollen strainer through which the Soma juice is run to purify it.

2 *As home* : as familiar to thee as thine own home.

3 *The yellow-hued* : there is no substantive, but gold must be intended.

6 *In bearded confidence* : a conjectural paraphrase. *Śmaśruṣu* [in (his) beard] is said by Sāyaṇa to mean here 'in combats,' that is, perhaps, as Ludwig suggests, among ranks of men bristling with spears. But this can hardly be the meaning of the word which 'is probably an idiomatic expression for the fierce look of a warrior who challenges the foe.'—Ludwig. So, in the Edda, Thorr, when about to meet a foe, is said to have 'raised his beard's voice.' See Grimm, *Teutonic Mythology*, I. 177 (English Translation).

8 *Mad with heat* : that is, *mast*, or as phonetically spelt, *must*.

10 *Thou art a Bull* : *vṛṣā* : or strong and mighty. As has been observed before (VIII. 13. 31, note), some of the Vedic poets delight in the repetition of this word and its derivatives.

11 Thy reins are very bulls in strength, bulls' strength is in thy golden whip.
Thy car, O Maghavan, thy Bays are strong as bulls : thou, Śatakratu, art a Bull.

12 Let the strong presser press for thee. Bring hither, thou straight-rushing Bull.
The mighty makes the mighty run in flowing streams for thee whom thy Bay Horses bear.

13 Come, thou most potent Indra, come to drink the savoury Soma juice.
Maghavan, very wise, will quickly come to hear the songs, the prayer, the hymns of praise.

14 When thou hast mounted on thy car let thy yoked Bay Steeds carry thee,
Past other men's libations, Lord of Hundred Powers, thee, Vṛtra-slayer, thee our Friend.

15 O thou Most Lofty One, accept our laud as nearest to thine heart.
May our libations be most sweet to make thee glad, O Soma-drinker, Heavenly Lord.

16 Neither in thy decree nor mine, but in another's he delights,—
The man who brought us unto this.

17 Indra himself hath said, The mind of woman brooks not discipline,
Her intellect hath little weight.

18 His pair of horses, rushing on in their wild transport, draw his car :
High-lifted is the stallion's yoke.

19 Cast down thine eyes and look not up. More closely set thy feet. Let none
See what thy garment veils, for thou, a Brahman, hast become a dame.

HYMN XXXIV. *Indra.*

1. Come hither, Indra, with thy Bays, come thou to Kaṇva's eulogy.
Ye by command of yonder Dyaus, God bright by day ! have gone to heaven.

2 May the stone draw thee as it speaks, the Soma-stone with ringing voice.
Ye by command of yonder Dyaus, etc.

3 The stones' rim shakes the Soma here like a wolf worrying a sheep.
Ye, etc.

4 The Kaṇvas call thee hitherward for succour and to win the spoil.
Ye, etc.

5 I set for thee, as for the Strong, the first draught of the juices shed.

6 Come with abundant blessings, come with perfect care to succour us.

7 Come, Lord of lofty thought, who hast infinite wealth and countless aids.

8 Adorable mid Gods, the Priest good to mankind shall bring thee near.

9 As wings the falcon, so thy Bays rushing in joy shall carry thee.

10 Come from the enemy to us, to Svāhā ! and the Soma-draught.

11 Come hither with thine ear inclined to hear, take pleasure in our lauds.

12 Lord of well-nourished Horses, come with well-fed Steeds alike in hue.

13 Come hither from the mountains, come from regions of the sea of air.

14 Disclose to us, O Hero, wealth in thousands both of kine and steeds.

15 Bring riches hitherward to us in hundreds, thousands, myriads.
Ye by command of yonder Dyaus, God bright by day ! have gone to heaven.

16 The thousand steeds, the mightiest troop, which we and Indra have received
From Vasurocis as a gift,

17 The brown that match the wind in speed, and bright bay coursers fleet of foot,
Like Suns, resplendent are they all.

11 *Golden whip* : the lightning, with which Indra lashes the clouds, his horses.

12 *The mighty makes the mighty run* : the priest makes the Soma juice flow.

16 The last four stanzas of the hymn are not very intelligible, nor is their connexion with the preceding verses obvious. Stanzas 16 and 18 appear to be spoken by a woman and 17 by a man. Stanza 19 is said to be addressed by Indra to Āsaṅga son of Playoga, who had been changed to a woman by the imprecation of the Gods, and who was afterwards restored to manhood.

The Ṛṣi is Nipātithi of the family of Kaṇva, but stanzas 16—18 are ascribed in the Index to the thousand Vasurocişas who are said to have been a division of the family of Aṅgiras.

1 The exact meaning of the second line, which is the burden of the first fifteen stanzas, is obscure. *Ye* probably means Indra's horses, and *God bright by day* ! (*divāvaso*) Indra himself ; that is, ye, horses and thou, Indra, have gone to heaven. The Scholiast offers two different explanations, in one case boldly altering two words of the text. See Wilson's Translation, note.

8 *The Priest good to mankind* : or, the Invoking Priest, Invoker or Herald established by Manu, namely Agni.

10 *Svāhā* : an exclamation used in sacrifice ; Ave ! or Hail !

16 *Vasurocis* : *vásurocişaḥ* is probably the ablative singular, and not the nominative plural, of the name of the institutor of the sacrifice. Wilson, following Sāyaṇa, translates : 'We, the thousand Vasurocişas, and Indra (our leader), when we obtain vigorous herds of horses,—.'

18 Mid the Pārāvata's rich gifts, swift steeds whose wheels run rapidly,
I seemed to stand amid a wood.

HYMN XXXV. *Aśvins.*

1. WITH Agni and with Indra, Viṣṇu. Varuṇa, with the Ādityas, Rudras, Vasus, closely leagued ;
Accordant, of one mind with Sūrya and with Dawn, O Aśvins, drink the Soma juice.

2 With all the Holy Thoughts, all being, Mighty Ones ! in close alliance with the Mountains, Heaven, and Earth ;
Accordant of one mind with Sūrya and with Dawn, O Aśvins, drink the Soma juice.

3 With all the Deities, three times eleven, here, in close alliance with the Maruts, Bhṛgus, Floods ;
Accordant, of one mind with Sūrya and with Dawn, O Aśvins, drink the Soma juice.

4 Accept the sacrifice, attend to this my call : come nigh, O ye Twain Gods, to all libations here.
Accordant, of one mind with Sūrya and with Dawn, O Aśvins, bring us strengthening food.

5 Accept our praise-song as a youth accepts a maid. Come nigh, O ye Twain Gods, to all libations here.
Accordant, of one mind with Sūrya and with Dawn, O Aśvins, bring us strengthening food.

6 Accept the songs we sing, accept the solemn rite. Come nigh, O ye Twain Gods, to all libations here.
Accordant, of one mind with Sūrya and with Dawn, O Aśvins, bring us strengthening food.

7 Ye fly as starlings fly unto the forest trees ; like buffaloes ye seek the Soma we have shed.
Accordant, of one mind with Sūrya and with Dawn, come thrice, O Aśvins, to our home.

8 Ye fly like swans, like those who travel on their way ; like buffaloes ye seek the Soma we have shed.
Accordant, of one mind with Sūrya and with Dawn, come thrice, O Aśvins, to our home.

9 Ye fly to our oblation like a pair of hawks ; like buffaloes ye seek the Soma we have shed.
Accordant, of one mind with Sūrya and with Dawn, come thrice, O Aśvins, to our home.

10 Come hitherward and drink and satisfy yourselves, bestow upon us progeny and affluence.
Accordant, of one mind with Sūrya and with Dawn, O Aśvins, grant us vigorous strength.

11 Conquer your foes, protect us, praise your worshippers ; bestow upon us progeny and affluence.
Accordant, of one mind with Sūrya and with Dawn, O Aśvins, grant us vigorous strength.

12 Slay enemies, animate men whom ye befriend ; bestow upon us progeny and affluence.
Accordant, of one mind with Sūrya and with Dawn, O Aśvins, grant us vigorous strength.

13 With Mitra, Varuṇa, Dharma, and the Maruts in your company approach unto your praiser's call.
Accordant, of one mind with Sūrya and with Dawn, and with the Ādityas, Aśvins ! come.

14 With Viṣṇu and the Aṅgirases attending you, and with the Maruts come unto your praiser's call.
Accordant, of one mind with Sūrya and with Dawn, and with the Ādityas, Aśvins ! come.

15 With Ṛbhus and with Vājas. O ye Mighty Ones, leagued with the Maruts come ye to your praiser's call.
Accordant, of one mind with Sūrya and with Dawn, and with the Ādityas, Aśvins ! come.

16 Give spirit to our prayer and animate our thoughts; slay ye the Rākṣasas and drive away disease.

18 *The Pārāvata* : is Vasurocis. The Pārāvatas are probably the Paruētaí of Ptolemy, who were settled northwards of Arachosia.—Ludwig.

5 *A youth* : literally two youths. 'As youths are delighted (by the voices of maidens).'—Wilson.

8 Ye come eagerly to the Soma as thirsty *haṁsas* (swans, geese, or flamingoes) travellers, and buffaloes hasten to the water.

13 *Dharma* : Right, Justice, Law, Virtue or Duty personified.

Accordant, of one mind with Sūrya and with Dawn, the presser's Soma, Aśvins! drink.

17 Strengthen the Ruling Power, strengthen the men of war; slay ye the Rākṣasas and drive away disease.
Accordant, of one mind with Sūrya and with Dawn, the presser's Soma, Aśvins! drink.

18 Give strength unto the milch-kine, give the people strength, slay ye the Rākṣasas and drive away disease.
Accordant, of one mind with Sūrya and with Dawn, the presser's Soma, Aśvins! drink.

19 As ye heard Atri's earliest eulogy, so hear Śyāvāśva, Soma-presser, ye who reel in joy.
Accordant, of one mind with Sūrya and with Dawn, drink juice, O Aśvins, three days old.

20 Further like running streams Śyāvāśva's eulogies who presses out the Soma, ye who reel in joy.
Accordant, of one mind with Sūrya and with Dawn, drink juice, O Aśvins, three days old.

21 Seize, as ye grasp the reins, Śyāvāśva's solemn rites who presses out the Soma, ye who reel in joy.
Accordant, of one mind with Sūrya and with Dawn, drink juice, O Aśvins, three days old.

22 Drive down your chariot hitherward: drink ye the Soma's savoury juice.
Approach, ye Aśvins, come to us: I call you, eager for your aid. Grant treasures to the worshipper.

23 When sacrifice which tells our reverence hath begun. Heroes! to drink the gushing juice,
Approach, ye Aśvins, come to us: I call you, eager for your aid. Grant treasures to the worshipper.

24 Sate you with consecrated drink, with juice effused, ye Deities.
Approach, ye Aśvins, come to us: I call you, eager for your aid. Grant treasures to the worshipper.

17 *The Ruling Power*: *kṣatrám*: hence *Kṣatriya*, a man of the princely or military order.

18 *The people*: *viśas*: hence *Vaiśya*, a man of the mercantile class or order.

19 *Atri's*: as he was the progenitor of the Ṛṣi of the Hymn. See Vol. I., Index.

21 *Solemn rites*: that is, the oblations presented thereat.

24 *Consecrated drink*: libations offered with the sacrificial exclamation Svāhā! Ave! or Hail!

HYMN XXXVI. *Indra.*

1. THOU helpest him whose grass is trimmed, who sheds the juice, O Śatakratu, drink Soma to make thee glad.
The share which they have fixed for thee, thou, Indra, Victor o'er all hosts and space, begirt with Maruts, Lord of Heroes, winner of the floods.

2 Maghavan, help thy worshipper: let him help thee. O Śatakratu, drink Soma to make thee glad.
The share which they have fixed for thee, etc.

3 Thou aidest Gods with food, and that with might aids thee,
O Śatakratu, drink Soma to make thee glad.

4 Creator of the heaven, creator of the earth, O Śatakratu, drink Soma to make thee glad.

5 Father of cattle, father of all steeds art thou. O Śatakratu, drink Soma to make thee glad.

6 Stone-hurler, glorify the Atris' hymn of praise. O Śatakratu, drink Soma to make thee glad.

7 Hear thou Śyāvāśva while he pours to thee, as erst thou heardest Atri when he wrought his holy rites.
Indra, thou only gavest Trasadasyu aid in the fierce fight with heroes, strengthening his prayers.

1 *Which they have fixed*: which all the Gods have assigned. This half-verse is the refrain of stanzas 1—6. *And space, begirt*: or, and wide space, girt. *The floods*: the waters of heaven, the rain.

2 *Let him help thee*: according to Sāyaṇa, 'protect thyself (by drinking the Soma).' 'The mutual relation between the God and his worshipper is expressed, and the translation 'help thyself' is ridiculous.'—Ludwig.

3 *Food*: sacrificial food. *That*: food, especially in the shape of Soma.

7 *Trasadasyu*: an especial favourite of Indra and the Aśvins, celebrated for his victories and liberality. See Index.

HYMN XXXVII. *Indra.*

1. THIS prayer, and those who shed the juice, in wars with Vṛtra thou holpest, Indra, Lord of Strength, with all thy succours.
O Vṛtra-slayer, from libation poured at

1 *O Vṛtra-slayer, etc.*: this half-verse is repeated as a refrain in the five following stanzas.

noon, drink of the Soma juice, thou blameless Thunderer.

2 Thou mighty Conqueror of hostile armaments, O Indra, Lord of Strength, with all thy saving help.

3 Sole Ruler, thou art Sovran of this world of life, O Indra, Lord of Strength, with all thy saving help.

4 Thou only sunderest these two consistent worlds, O Indra, Lord of Strength, with all thy saving help.

5 Thou art the Lord supreme o'er rest and energy, O Indra, Lord of Strength, with all thy saving help.

6 Thou helpest one to power, and one thou hast not helped, O Indra, Lord of Strength, with all thy saving aid.

7 Hear thou Śyāvāśva while he sings to thee, as erst thou heardest Atri when he wrought his holy rites.
Indra, thou only gavest Trasadasyu aid in the fierce fight with heroes, strengthening his powers.

HYMN XXXVIII. *Indra-Agni.*

1. YE Twain are Priests of sacrifice, winners in war and holy works:
Indra and Agni, mark this well.

2 Ye bounteous riders on the car, ye Vṛtra-slayers unsubdued:
Indra and Agni, mark this well.

3 The men with pressing-stones have pressed this meath of yours which gives delight:
Indra and Agni, mark this well.

4 Accept our sacrifice for weal, sharers of praise! the Soma shed:
Indra and Agni, Heroes, come.

5 Be pleased with these libations which attract you to our sacred gifts:
Indra and Agni, Heroes, come.

6 Accept this eulogy of mine whose model is the Gāyatrī: Indra and Agni, Heroes, come.

7 Come with the early-faring Gods, ye who are Lords of genuine wealth:
Indra-Agni, to the Soma-draught!

8 Hear ye the call of Atris, hear Śyāvāśva as he sheds the juice:
Indra-Agni to the Soma-draught!

9 Thus have I called you to our aid as sages called on you of old:
Indra-Agni to the Soma draught!

10 Indra's and Agni's grace I claim, Sarasvatī's associates
To whom this psalm of praise is sung.

HYMN XXXIX. *Agni.*

1. THE glorious Agni have I praised, and worshipped with the sacred food.
May Agni deck the Gods for us. Between both gathering-places he goes on his embassy, the Sage. May all the others die away.

2 Agni, burn down the word within their bodies through our newest speech,
All hatreds of the godless, all the wicked man's malignities. Away let the destroyers go. May all the others die away.

3 Agni, I offer hymns to thee, like holy oil within thy mouth.
Acknowledge them among the Gods, for thou art the most excellent, the worshipper's blissful messenger. Let all the others die away.

4 Agni bestows all vital power even as each man supplicates.
He brings the Vasus strengthening gifts, and grants delight, in rest and stir, for every calling on the Gods. Let all the others die away.

4 *Consistent worlds*: there is no substantive in the text, and *lokau* (worlds) is supplied by Sāyaṇa.

5 *Rest and energy*: or peace and war. 'Prosperity and gains.'—Wilson.

6 *To power*: *kṣatrāya*: the rule exercised by princes.

7 Repeated from the preceding hymn with the alteration of two words—*rébhataḥ*, singing, instead of *sunvatáḥ*, pouring (libations), and *kṣatrāni* (princely) powers instead of *bráhmāṇi*, prayers, 'as if,' observes Dr. Muir, 'the former (*brahmāṇi*,) contained a reference to the functions of the priest, and the latter to those of the prince.'—*O.S. Texts*, I. 263.

1 *Mark this well*: 'hear (the praise) of this (thy worshipper).'—Wilson.

2 *Bounteous*: *tośā́sā*: according to Sāyaṇa, 'destroyers of foes.'

6 *Whose model is the Gāyatrī*: composed in Gāyatrī metre.

7 *Early-faring Gods*: 'But Thou wast up at break of day.'—George Herbert.

10 *Sarasvatī's associates*: according to Sāyaṇa, 'to whom praise belongs.'

1 *Deck the Gods for us*: 'brighten the gods with the oblations at our sacrifice.'—Wilson. *Both gathering-places*: heaven and earth. *All the others*: *anyaké same*: meaning, according to Sāyaṇa, all our enemies.

2 *All hatreds of the godless*: *arātīr arāvṇām* must be read instead of *arātī rarāvṇām*.—Ludwig.

5 Agni hath made himself renowned by wonderful victorious act.
  He is the Priest of all the tribes, chosen with sacrificial meeds. He urges Deities to receive. Let all the others die away.

6 Agni knows all that springs from Gods, he knows the mystery of men.
  Giver of wealth is Agni, he uncloses both the doors to us when worshipped with our newest gift. Let all the others die away.

7 Agni inhabiteth with Gods and men who offer sacrifice.
  He cherisheth with great delight much wisdom, as all things that be, God among Gods adorable. May all the others die away.

8 Agni who liveth in all streams, Lord of the Sevenfold Race of men,
  Him dweller in three homes we seek, best slayer of the Dasyus for Mandhātar, first in sacrifice. Let all the others die away.

9 Agni the Wise inhabiteth three gathering-places, triply formed.
  Decked as our envoy let the Sage bring hither and conciliate the Thrice Eleven Deities. Let all the others die away.

10 Our Agni, thou art first among the Gods, and first mid living men.
  Thou only rulest over wealth. Round about thee, as natural dams, circumfluous the waters run. Let all the others die away.

HYMN XL.   *Indra-Agni.*

1. INDRA and Agni, surely ye as Conquerors will give us wealth,
  Whereby in fight we may o'ercome that which is strong and firmly fixed, as

Agni burns the woods with wind. Let all the others die away.

2 We set no snares to tangle you; Indra we worship and adore, Hero of heroes mightiest.
  Once may he come unto us with his Steed, come unto us to win us strength, and to complete the sacrifice.

3 For, famous Indra-Agni, ye are dwellers in the midst of frays.
  Sages in wisdom, ye are knit to him who seeketh you as friends. Heroes, bestow on him his wish.

4 Nabhāka-like, with sacred song Indra's and Agni's praise I sing,
  Theirs to whom all this world belongs, this heaven and this mighty earth which bear rich treasure in their lap.

5 To Indra and to Agni send your prayers, as was Nabhāka's wont,—
  Who oped with sideway opening the sea with its foundations seven—Indra all powerful in his might.

6 Tear thou .asunder, as of old, like tangles of a creeping plant,
  Demolish thou the Dāsa's might. May we with Indra's help divide the treasure he hath gathered up.

7 What time with this same song these men call Indra-Agni sundry ways,
  May we with our own heroes quell those who provoke us to the fight, and conquer those who strive with us.

8 The Two refulgent with their beams rise and come downward from the sky.
  By Indra's and by Agni's hest, flowing away, the rivers run which they released from their restraint.

9 O Indra, many are thine aids, many thy ways of guiding us,

---

5 *With sacrificial meeds* : *dākṣiṇābhiḥ* : his *dakṣiṇās* or honoraria as Priest are the oblations which he receives as a God.

6 *That springs from Gods* : 'the past and the present, while *the mystery of men* is the future.'—Ludwig. *Both the doors* : of wealth, or, perhaps of heaven also.

8 *Lord of the Sevenfold Race of men* : perhaps meaning, God of all men, like Vaiśvānara ; or the reference may be to the seven priests : 'Who is ministered to by seven priests.'—Wilson. 'Acting as seven priests.'—M. Müller. *Mandhātar* : said to be the same as Māndhātar, son of Yuvanāśva, and Ṛṣi of X. 134.

9 *Three gathering-places* : heaven, firmament, and earth.

10 *Round about thee the waters run* : Cf. 'Him, pure, resplendent, Offspring of the Waters, the waters pure have on all sides encompassed.' (II. 35. 3).

———

1 *Let all the others die away* : this   refrain recurs in all stanzas of the hymn except the final.

2 *Once* : *kadācit*: expressive of impatience.—Ludwig.

4 *Nabhāka-like* : Nabhāka may have been the father of Nābhāka the Ṛṣi of the hymn.

5 *Who oped* : 'who overspread (with their lustre).'—Wilson. The Commentator does not explain the passage.

7 *This same song* : a hymn like our own, for victory in battle.

8 *The Two refulgent with their beams* : apparently the Sun and Moon. According to Sāyaṇa, Indra and Agni are intended.

Lord of the Bay Steeds, Hinva's Son. To a Good Hero come our prayers, which soon shall have accomplishment.

10 Inspire him with your holy hymns, the Hero bright and glorious,
Him who with might demolisheth even the brood of Śuṣṇa, and winneth for us the heavenly streams.

11 Inspire him worshipped with fair rites, the glorious Hero truly brave.
He brake in pieces Śuṣṇa's brood who still expected not the stroke, and won for us the heavenly streams. Let all the others die away.

12 Thus have we sung anew to Indra-Agni, as sang our sires, Aṅgirases, and Mandhātar.
Guard us with triple shelter and preserve us : may we be masters of a store of riches.

HYMN XLI. *Varuṇa.*

1. To make this Varuṇa come forth, sing thou a song unto the band of Maruts wiser than thyself,—
This Varuṇa who guardeth well the thoughts of men like herds of kine.
Let all the others die away.

2 Him altogether praise I with the song and hymns our fathers sang, and with Nābhāka's eulogies,—
Him dwelling at the rivers' source, surrounded by his Sisters Seven.

3 The nights he hath encompassed, and stablished the morns with magic art : visible over all is he.
His dear Ones, following his Law, have prospered the Three Dawns for him.

4 He, visible o'er all the earth, stablished the quarters of the sky :
He measured out the eastern place, that is the fold of Varuṇa : like a strong herdsman is the God.

5 He who supports the worlds of life, he who well knows the hidden names mysterious of the morning beams,
He cherishes much wisdom, Sage, as heaven brings forth each varied form.

6 In whom all wisdom centres, as the nave is set within the wheel.
Haste ye to honour Trita, as kine haste to gather in the fold, even as they muster steeds to yoke.

7 He wraps these regions as a robe; he contemplates the tribes of Gods and all the works of mortal men.
Before the home of Varuṇa all the Gods follow his decree.

8 He is an Ocean far-removed, yet through the heaven to him ascends the worship which these realms possess.
With his bright foot he overthrew their magic, and went up to heaven.

9 Ruler, whose bright far-seeing rays, pervading all three earths, have filled the three superior realms of heaven.
Firm is the seat of Varuṇa : over the Seven he rules as King.

10 Who, after his decree, o'erspread the Dark Ones with a robe of light;
Who measured out the ancient seat, who

9 *Hinva's Son*: Hinva (the driver, impeller, instigator of actions), a father invented for Indra by the poet. *To a Good Hero* : to Indra. 'The meaning of the verse, even with the help of the scholiast, is far from intelligible.'—Wilson.

1 *To make this Varuṇa come forth* : Sāyaṇa explains *prábhūtaye* as an adjective=*prakṛṣṭadhanāya* : 'to that opulent Varuṇa.'—Wilson. *Wiser* : more skilled in singing. *The thoughts* : holy thoughts and devotions. The refrain, Let all, etc., recurs at the end of every stanza.

2 *Nābhāka's* : that is, mine own. *Sisters Seven* : the five rivers of the Panjab, the Indus and perhaps the Kubhā. See I. 32, note.

3 *His dear Ones* : apparently the nights, which give place to the mornings. *Three Dawns* : according to Sāyaṇa, morning, noon, and evening.

4 *The fold* : or. perhaps, the course, meaning the place from which he starts.

6 *Trita* : Varuṇa, here, apparently, identified with this ancient God who represents the expanse of heaven. According to Sāyaṇa, (Varuṇa) 'who abides in the three worlds.'

7 This stanza is very obscure, and my rendering is conjectural. The commentary is defective, and von Roth and Ludwig think that the correctness of one word in the text is doubtful. According to the slight alteration suggested by the latter scholar, 'under the lead' would stand instead of 'before the home.'

8 The first line of this stanza also is difficult. Wilson, following Sāyaṇa, translates : 'He is the hidden ocean ; swift he mounts (the heaven) as (the sun) the sky ; when he has placed the sacrifice in those (regions of the firmament).' Ludwig's interpretation, which I follow, requires *tiráḥ* to be read instead of *turáḥ* (swift). *Their magic* : the magical arts of the fiends of darkness.

9 *Firm* : So Hesiod (Theog. V. 127) calls Ouranos = Varuṇa the firm seat of the Gods. See M. Müller, *Chips from a German Workshop*, IV. xx (new edition). *The Seven* : rivers, understood.

10 *The Dark Ones* : the nights, which Varuṇa turns into days. But see *Chips*, IV. xxii. *The Unborn* : the primeval, everlasting, uncreated Divine Being. According to Sāyaṇa, the Sun.

pillared both the worlds apart as the Unborn supported heaven. Let all the others die away.

HYMN XLII. *Varuṇa.*

1. Lord of all wealth, the Asura propped the heavens, and measured out the broad earth's wide expanses.
He, King supreme, approached all living creatures. All these are Varuṇa's holy operations.

2 So humbly worship Varuṇa the Mighty: revere the wise Guard of World Immortal.
May he vouchsafe us triply-barred protection. O Earth and Heaven, within your lap preserve us.

3 Sharpen this song of him who strives his utmost, sharpen, God Varuṇa, his strength and insight;
May we ascend the ship that bears us safely, whereby we may pass over all misfortune.

4 Aśvins, with songs the singer stones have made you hasten hitherward,
Nāsatyas, to the Soma-draught. Let all the others die away.

5 As the sage Atri with his hymns, O Aśvins, called you eagerly,
Nāsatyas, to the Soma-draught. Let all the others die away.

6 So have I called you to our aid, even as the wise have called of old,
Nāsatyas, to the Soma-draught. Let all the others die away.

HYMN XLIII. *Agni.*

1. These songs of mine go forth as lauds of Agni, the disposing Sage,
Whose worshipper is ne'er o'erthrown.

2 Wise Agni Jātavedas, I beget a song of praise for thee.
Who willingly receivest it.

3 Thy sharpened flames, O Agni, like the gleams of light that glitter through,
Devour the forests with their teeth.

4 Gold-coloured, bannered with the smoke, urged by the wind, aloft to heaven
Rise, lightly borne, the flames of fire.

5 These lightly kindled fiery flames are all around made visible,
Even as the gleamings of the Dawns.

6 As Jātavedas speeds along, the dust is black beneath his feet,
When Agni spreads upon the earth.

7 Making the plants his nourishment, Agni devours and wearies not,
Seeking the tender shrubs again.

8 Bending him down with all his tongues, he flickers with his fiery glow:
Splendid is Agni in the woods.

9 Agni, thine home is in the floods: into the plants thou forcest way,
And as their Child art born anew.

10 Worshipped with offerings shines thy flame, O Agni, from the sacred oil,
With kisses on the ladle's mouth.

11 Let us serve Agni with our hymns, Disposer, fed on ox and cow,
Who bears the Soma on his back.

12 Yea, thee, O Agni, do we seek with homage and with fuel, Priest
Whose wisdom is most excellent.

13 O worshipped with oblations, pure Agni, we call on thee as erst,
Did Bhṛgu, Manus, Aṅgiras.

14 For thou, O Agni, by the fire, Sage by the Sage, Good by the Good,
Friend by the Friend, art lighted up.

15 So wealth in thousands, food with store of heroes give thou to the sage,
O Agni, to the worshipper.

16 O Agni, Brother, made by strength, Lord of red steeds and brilliant sway,
Take pleasure in this laud of mine.

17 My praises, Agni, go to thee, as the cows seek the stall to meet,
The lowing calf that longs for milk.

1 *The Asura*: the High God, Varuṇa. 'The wise spirit.'—M. Müller.

2 *Of the World Immortal*: *amṛtasya*: according to Sāyaṇa, of amrita or ambrosia.

3 *The ship*: a metaphorical expression for hymn and sacrifice. Cf. I. 46. 7; 140. 12; IX. 89. 2; X. 44. 6; 63. 10; 101. 2; 105. 9.

11 *Fed on ox and cow*: 'the eater of the ox, the eater of the marrow.'—Wilson. *Who bears the Soma on his back*: *sómapṛṣṭāya*: 'on whose back the libation is poured.'—Wilson.

14 Sāyaṇa refers to the *Aitareya Brāhmaṇa*, I. 16, 'which describes how the fire produced by friction from the two *araṇis* [fire-sticks] is thrown into the Āhavanīya fire, in the Atithyeṣṭi ceremony. "In the verse *tvam hyagne* [For thou, O Agni] etc., the one *vipra* (a sage) means one Agni, the other *vipra* the other Agni; the one *san* (being, existing) means the one, the other *san* (in *satā*) the other Agni.' (Haug's trans.).—Note by E. B. C. in Wilson's Translation. *Sán* and *satā́* may also mean 'good.'

16 *Made by strength*: produced by violent agitation of the fire-stick.

18 Agni, best Aṅgiras, to thee all people who have pleasant homes,
Apart, have turned as to their wish.

19 The sages skilled in holy song and thinkers with their thoughts have urged
Agni to share the sacred feast.

20 So, Agni, unto thee the Priest, Invoker, strong in forays, pray
Those who spin out the sacrifice.

21 In many a place, the same in look art thou, a Prince o'er all the tribes :
In battles we invoke thine aid.

22 Pray thou to Agni, pray to him who blazes served with sacred oil :
Let him give ear to this our call.

23 We call on thee as such, as one who hears, as Jātavedas, one,
Agni ! who beats away our foes.

24 I pray to Agni, King of men, the Wonderful, the President
Of holy Laws : may he give ear.

25 Him like a bridegroom, him who stirs all people, like a noble horse,
Like a fleet steed, we instigate.

26 Slaying things deadly, burning up foes, Rākṣasas, on every side,
Shine, Agni, with thy sharpened flame.

27 Thou whom the people kindle even as Manus did, best Aṅgiras !
O Agni, mark thou this my speech.

28 O Agni, made by strength ! be thou born in the heavens or born in floods,
As such we call on thee with songs.

29 Yea, all the people, all the folk who have good dwellings, each apart,
Send food for thee to eat thereof.

30 O Agni, so may we, devout, gazed at by men, throughout our days,
Pass lightly over all distress.

31 We venerate with cheerful hearts the cheerful Agni, dear to all,
Burning, with purifying flame.

32 So thou, O Agni rich in light, beaming like Sūrya with thy rays
Boldly demolishest the gloom.

33 We pray to thee for this thy gift, Victor ! the gift that faileth not,
O Agni, choicest wealth from thee.

28 *In the heavens* : as the Sun. *In floods* : in the waters of the firmament as lightning.

30 *Gazed at by men* : objects of their admiration. 'Beholding men.'—Wilson. 'Living (among men).'—St. Petersburg Lexicon.

HYMN XLIV. *Agni.*

1. PAY service unto Agni with your fuel, rouse your Guest with oil :
In him present your offerings.

2 Agni, do thou accept my laud, be magnified by this my song :
Welcome my sweetly-spoken words.

3 Agni, envoy, I place in front ; the oblation-bearer I address :
Here let him seat the Deities.

4 Agni, the lofty flames of thee enkindled have gone up on high,
Thy bright flames, thou Refulgent One.

5 Beloved ! let my ladles full of sacred oil come near to thee :
Agni, accept our offerings.

6 I worship Agni—may he hear !—the cheerful, the Invoker, Priest,
Of varied splendour, rich in light.

7 Ancient Invoker, meet for praise, beloved Agni, wise and strong,
The visitant of solemn rites.

8 Agni, best Aṅgiras, accept straightway these offerings, and guide
The seasonable sacrifice.

9 Excellent God, with brilliant flames, enkindled bring thou hitherward,
Knowing the way, the Heavenly Host.

10 Him, Sage and Herald, void of guile, ensign of sacrifices, him
Smoke-bannered, rich in light, we seek.

11 O Agni, be our Guardian thou, God, against those who injure us :
Destroy our foes, thou Son of Strength.

12 Making his body beautiful, Agni the Sage hath waxen by
The singer and his ancient hymn.

13 I invocate the Child of Strength, Agni with purifying flame,
At this well-ordered sacrifice.

14 So Agni, rich in many friends, with fiery splendour, seat thyself
With Gods upon our sacred grass.

15 The mortal man who serves the God Agni within his own abode,
For him he causes wealth to shine.

16 Agni is head and height of heaven, the Master of the earth is he :

14 *Rich in many friends* : 'thou who hast Mitra's splendour.'—Ludwig.

15 *For him he causes wealth to shine* : or, 'To him he shines forth opulence.' 'To him he gives riches.'—Wilson.

He quickeneth the waters' seed.

17 Upward, O Agni, rise thy flames, pure and resplendent, blazing high,
Thy lustres, fair effulgences.

18 For, Agni, thou as Lord of Light rulest o'er choicest gifts : may I,
Thy singer, find defence in thee.

19 O Agni, they who understand stir thee to action with their thoughts :
So let our songs enhance thy might.

20 We ever claim the friendship of Agni, the singing messenger,
Of God-like nature, void of guile.

21 Agni who bears most holy sway, the holy Singer, holy Sage,
Shines holy when we worship him.

22 Yea, let my meditations, let my songs exalt thee evermore.
Think, Agni, of our friendly bond,

23 If I were thou and thou wert I, O Agni, every prayer of thine
Should have its due fulfilment here.

24 For Excellent and Lord of wealth art thou O Agni, rich in light :
May we enjoy thy favouring grace.

25 Agni, to thee whose laws stand fast our resonant songs of praise speed forth,
As rivers hasten to the sea.

26 Agni, the Youthful Lord of men, who stirreth much and eateth all,
The Sage, I glorify with hymns.

27 To Agni let us haste with lauds, the Guide of sacrificial rites,
Armed with sharp teeth, the Mighty One.

28 And let this man, good Agni, be with thee the singer of thy praise :
Be gracious, Holy One, to him.

29 For thou art sharer of our feast, wise, ever watchful as a Sage :
Agni, thou shinest in the sky.

30 O Agni, Sage, before our foes, before misfortunes fall on us,
Excellent Lord, prolong our lives.

16 *The waters' seed* : as lightning, he impregnates the waters of the air.

26 *Eateth all* : consumes the entire oblation.—Sāyaṇa. But the meaning is probably general.

28 *This man* : the Ṛṣi or singer himself.

29 *In the sky* : or, up to heaven.

HYMN XLV. *Indra*

1. HITHERWARD ! they who light flame and straightway trim the sacred grass,
Whose Friend is Indra ever young.

2 High is their fuel, great their laud, wide is their splinter from the stake,
Whose Friend is Indra ever young.

3 Unequelled in fight the hero leads his army with the warrior chiefs.
Whose Friend is Indra ever young.

4 The new-born Vṛtra-slayer asked his Mother, as he seized his shaft,
Who are the fierce ? Who are renowned ?

5 Śavasī answered, He who seeks thine enmity will battle like
A stately elephant on a hill.

6 And hear, O Maghavan ; to him who craves of thee thou grantest all :
Whate'er thou makest firm is firm.

7 What time the Warrior Indra goes to battle, borne by noble steeds,
Best of all charioteers is he.

8 Repel, O Thunder-armed, in all directions all attacks on us :
And be our own most glorious God.

9 May Indra set our car in front, in foremost place to win the spoil,
He whom the wicked injure not.

10 Thine enmity may we escape, and, Śakra, for thy bounty, rich
In kine, may we come near to thee ;

11 Softly approaching, Thunder-armed ! wealthy by hundreds, rich in steeds,
Unrivalled, ready with our gifts.

12 For thine exalted excellence gives to thy worshippers each day
Hundreds and thousands of thy boons.

13 Indra, we know thee breaker-down even of strong forts, winner of spoil,
As one who conquers wealth for us.

14 Though thou art highest, Sage and Bold ! let the drops cheer thee when we come

2 *Splinter* : the first shaving, splinter, or strip of wood, cut from the *yūpa* or sacrificial post, and used in the sacrifice.

4 As soon as he was born Indra showed his warlike disposition, and asked what worthy opponents he should have.

5 *Śavasī*, or, the Strong Dame ; his mother Aditi. *A stately elephant* : I follow Sāyaṇa who explains *ápsaḥ* as *darśanīyo gajaḥ*, a beautiful elephant, although in other places the word seems to mean beauty (I. 124 7), and forehead (V. 80. 6). The allusion is to the size and strength of Vṛtra, Indra's future antagonist.

To thee as to a trafficker.
15 Bring unto us the treasure of the opulent man who, loth to give,
Hath slighted thee for gain of wealth.

16 Indra, these friends of ours, supplied with Soma, wait and look to thee,
As men with fodder to the herd.

17 And thee who art not deaf, whose ears are quick to listen, for our aid,
We call to us from far away.

18 When thou hast listened, make our call one which thou never wilt forget,
And be our very nearest Friend.

19 When even now, when we have been in trouble, we have thought of thee,
O Indra, give us gifts of kine.

20 O Lord of Strength, we rest on thee, as old men rest upon a staff:
We long to have thee dwell with us.

21 To Indra sing a song of praise, Hero of mighty valour, him
Whom no one challenges to war.

22 Hero, the Soma being shed, I pour the juice for thee to drink:
Sate thee and finish thy carouse.

23 Let not the fools, or those who mock, beguile thee when they seek thine aid:
Love not the enemies of prayer.

24 Here let them with rich milky draught cheer thee to great munificence:
Drink as the wild-bull drinks the lake.

25 Proclaim in our assemblies what deeds, new and ancient, far away,
The Vṛtra-slayer hath achieved.

26 In battle of a thousand arms Indra drank Kadrū's Soma juice:
There he displayed his manly might.

27 True undeniable strength he found in Yadu and in Turvaśa,
And conquered through the sacrifice.

28 Him have I magnified, our Lord in common, Guardian of your folk,
Discloser of great wealth in kine;

29 Ṛbhukṣan, not to be restrained, who strengthened Tugra's son in lauds,
Indra beside the flowing juice;

30 Who for Triśoka clave the hill that formed a wide receptacle,
So that the cows might issue forth.

31 Whate'er thy plan or purpose be, whate'er, in transport, thou wouldst do,
Do it not, Indra, but be kind.

32 But little hath been heard of done upon the earth by one like thee:
Let thine heart, Indra, turn to us.

33 Thine then shall be this high renown, thine shall these lofty praises be,
When, Indra, thou art kind to us.

34 Not for one trespass, not for two, O Hero, slay us, nor for three,
Nor yet for many trespasses.

35 I fear one powerful like thee, the crusher-down of enemies,
Mighty, repelling all attacks.

36 O wealthy God, ne'er may I live to see my friend or son in need:
Hitherward let thy heart be turned.

37 What friend, O people, unprovoked, hath ever said unto a friend,
He turns and leaves us in distress?

38 Hero, insatiate enjoy this Soma juice so near to thee,
Even as a hunter rushing down.

39 Hither I draw those Bays of thine yoked by our hymn, with splendid car,
That thou mayst give unto the priests.

40 Drive all our enemies away, smite down the foes who press around,

14 *As to a trafficker*: as to one who knows the value of our worship and oblations and will give us something in return.

23 *The enemies of prayer*: according to Sāyaṇa those who hate Brāhmans.

24 *The wild-bull*: the *gaura*.

26 *Kadrū's Soma juice*: Kadrū here is apparently the name of a Ṛṣi or of one of the officiating priests. The St. Petersburg Lexicon takes it to mean, from a *kadrū* or Soma vessel.

27 *Undeniable*: *ahnavāyyám*, according to Sāyaṇa, is the name of the enemy of Turvaśa and Yadu: 'he overcame Ahnavāyya in battle.'—Wilson.

29 *Ṛbhukṣan*: Indra, Lord of the Ṛbhus. *Tugra's son*: Bhujyu. According to Sāyaṇa, *tugryavṛdham* means 'augmenter of water.'

30 *The hill* is the massive rain-cloud, and *the cows* are streams of water.

31 *Do it not*: 'Sāyaṇa understands this, "do it not for thou hast done it for us,—only make us happy." Could it be that the worshipper had a feeling of nemesis? or would he monopolize all?'—Note by E. B. C. in Wilson's Translation.

32 'In the following verses (32—36) the poet seems to express disappointment at the inadequate manifestation of Indra's power, while he at the same time entreats his grace and forgiveness.'—*O. S. Texts*, V. p. 111.

37 This stanza is Indra's answer to the poet's complaint. The meaning seems to be: no friend without good cause calls his friend a traitor. What then have I done, or left undone, that thou shouldst say that I have forsaken thee? See Ludwig's Commentary on the very difficult *jah káḥá* or *jahākaḥ*.

———

And bring the wealth for which we long :
41 O Indra, that which is concealed in strong firm place precipitous :
Bring us the wealth for which we long :
42 Great riches which the world of men shall recognize as sent by thee :
Bring us the wealth for which we long.

HYMN XLVI. *Indra.*

1. We, Indra, Lord of ample wealth, our Guide, depend on one like thee,
Thou driver of the Tawny Steeds.
2 For, Hurler of the Bolt, we know thee true, the giver of our food,
We know the giver of our wealth.
3 O thou whose majesty the bards celebrate with their songs, thou Lord,
Of hundred powers and hundred aids.
4 Fair guidance hath the mortal man whom Aryaman, the Marut host,
And Mitra, void of guile, protect.
5 Kine, steeds, and hero strength he gains, and prospers, by the Ādityas sped,
Ever in wealth which all desire.
6 We pray to Indra for his gift, to him the Fearless and the Strong,
We pray to him the Lord of wealth.
7 For verily combined in him are all the fearless powers of aid.
Him, rich in wealth, let swift Steeds bring to us, his Bays, to Soma juice for his carouse :
8 Yea, that most excellent carouse, Indra, which slays most enemies,
With Heroes wins the light of heaven, and is invincible in war :
9 Which merits fame, all-bountiful ! and, unsubdued, hath victory in deeds of might.
So come to our libations, Strongest ! Excellent ! May we obtain a stall of kine.
10 Responding to our wish for cows, for steeds, and chariots, as of old,
Be gracious, Greatest of the Great !
11 For, Hero, nowhere can I find the bounds of thy munificence.
Still do thou favour us, O Bolt-armed Maghavan : with strength hast thou rewarded hymns.
12 High, glorifier of his friend, he knows all generations, he whom many praise.
All races of mankind with ladles lifted up invoke that Mighty Indra's aid.
13 Be he our Champion and Protector in great deeds, rich in all wealth, the Vṛtra-slayer, Maghavan.
14 In the wild raptures of the juice sing to your Hero with high laud, to him the Wise,
To Indra, glorious in his name, the Mighty One, even as the hymn alloweth it.
15 Thou givest wealth to me myself, thou givest treasure, Excellent ! and the strong steed,
O Much-invoked, in deeds of might, yea, even now.
16 Him, Sovran Ruler of all precious things, who even hath power o'er this fair form of his,
As now it taketh shape, and afterward,
17 We praise, so that the Mighty One may speed to you, Pourer of bounties, Traveller, prepared to go.
Thou favourest the Maruts known to all, by song and sacrifice.
With song and praise I sing to thee.
18 We in the sacrifice perform their will whose voice is lifted high,
The worship of those Thundering Ones who o'er the ridges of these mountains fly in troops.
19 O Indra, Mightiest, bring us that which crushes men of evil minds,
Wealth suited to our needs, O Stirrer of the thought, best wealth, O thou who stirrest thought.

The hymn appears to be composed of two or more originally separate hymns (see Pischel, *Vedische Studien*, I. pp. 7-9). There are seventeen varieties of metre (see Index of Hymns). The hymn is difficult and obscure in parts, where only conjectural translations can be given.

7 *Powers of aid* : or, succourers ; the Maruts may be intended.

13 This stanza may have been the conclusion of one of the original hymns.

14 *As the hymn alloweth it* : in due accordance with the metre.

16 Sāyaṇa explains the latter part of the first line and the following part of the second as, 'who overcomes this obstructor (the enemy) as he wages war.' I follow Ludwig's interpretation who refers to III. 53. 8, 'Maghavan weareth every shape at pleasure, effecting magic changes in his body; 'and VI. 47. 18, 'Indra moves multiform by his illusions.'

18 *Their will* : the pleasure of the Maruts.

20 O Winner, noble winner, strong, wondrous, most splendid, excellent,
Sole Lord of victory, bring all-overpowering wealth, joy-giving, chief in deeds of might.

21 Now let the godless man approach who hath received reward so great
As Vaśa, Aśvya, when this light of morning dawned, received from Pṛthuśravas, from Kanīta's son.

22 Steeds sixty thousand and ten thousand kine, and twenty hundred camels I obtained ;
Ten hundred brown in hue, and other ten red in three spots : in all, ten thousand kine.

23 Ten browns that make my wealth increase, fleet steeds whose tails are long and fair,
Turn with swift whirl my chariot wheel ;

24 The gifts which Pṛthuśravas gave, Kanīta's son munificent.
He gave a chariot wrought of gold : the prince was passing bountiful, and won himself most lofty fame.

25 Come thou to this great rite of ours, Vāyu ! to give us vigorous light.
We have served thee that thou mightest give much to us, yea, mightest quickly give great wealth.

26 Who with thrice seven times seventy horses comes to us, invested with the rays of morn,
Through these our Soma-draughts and those who press, to give, drinker of pure bright Soma juice.

27 Who hath inclined this glorious one, bounteous himself, to give me gifts.
Borne on firm chariot with the prosperous Nahuṣa, wise, to a man yet more devout.

28 Sole Lord in beauty meet for praise, O Vāyu, dropping fatness down,
Hurried along by steeds, by camels, and by hounds, spreads forth thy train : even this it is.

29 So, as a prize dear to the strong, the sixty thousand have I gained,
Bulls that resemble vigorous steeds.

30 To me come oxen like a herd, yea, unto me the oxen come.

31 And in the grazing herd he made a hundred camels bleat for me,
And twenty hundred mid the white.

32 A hundred has the sage received, Dāsa Balbūtha's and Tarukṣa's gifts.
These are thy people, Vāyu, who rejoice with Indra for their guard, rejoice with Gods for guards.

33 And now to Vaśa Aśvya here this stately woman is led forth,
Adorned with ornaments of gold.

HYMN XLVII. *Ādityas.*

1. GREAT help ye give the worshipper, Varuṇa, Mitra, Mighty Ones ! No sorrow ever reaches him whom ye, Ādityas, keep from harm. Yours are incomparable aids, and good the succour they afford.

2 O Gods, Ādityas, well ye know the way to keep all woes afar.
As the birds spread their sheltering wings, spread your protection over us.

3 As the birds spread their sheltering wings let your protection cover us.
We mean all shelter and defence, ye who have all things for your own.

4 To whomsoever they, Most Wise, have given a home and means of life,
O'er the whole riches of this man they, the Ādityas, have control.

5 As drivers of the car avoid ill roads, let sorrows pass us by.
May we be under Indra's guard, in the Ādityas' favouring grace.

20 *O winner* : of wealth to be given to thy worshippers. 'O bountiful, most bountiful.'—Wilson.

21 *Vaśa Aśvya* : the Ṛṣi of the hymn. See I. 112. 10. *Pṛthuśravas* : See I. 116. 21.

22 *In all, ten thousand kine* : the exact meaning is not very clear. The last line is rendered differently in Wilson's Translation : 'a thousand brown mares,—and ten times ten thousand cows with three red patches.'

26 *Who* : apparently Vāyu, but, according to Sāyaṇa, Pṛthuśravas.

27 *On firm chariot* : literally, on a car made of the wood of the Araḍu tree (Galosanthes Indica). But Sāyaṇa makes two proper names of the words, 'with Āraḍva and Akṣa.'

28 The *steeds, camels,* and *hounds* are apparently the fantastic forms of the clouds that fly before Vāyu or the wind.

31 *Mid the white*: herds of cows.

32 *Dāsa Balbūtha* : probably an aboriginal ally of Pṛthuśravas. See Weber, *Episches im Vedischen Ritual*, p. 30.

33 *This stately woman* : probably the wife of the conquered King.—Ludwig.

1 *Yours are, etc* : the refrain recurs in every verse of the hymn.

6 For verily men sink and faint through loss of wealth which ye have given.
Much hath he gained from you, O Gods, whom ye, Ādityas, have approached.

7 On him shall no fierce anger fall, no sore distress shall visit him,
To whom, Ādityas, ye have lent your shelter that extendeth far.

8 Resting in you, O Gods, we are like men who fight in coats of mail.
Ye guard us from each great offence, ye guard us from each lighter fault.

9 May Aditi defend us, may Aditi guard and shelter us,
Mother of wealthy Mitra and of Aryaman and Varuṇa.

10 The shelter, Gods, that is secure, auspicious, free from malady,
A sure protection, triply strong, even that do ye extend to us.

11 Look down on us, Ādityas, as a guide exploring from the bank.
Lead us to pleasant ways as men lead horses to an easy ford.

12 Ill be it for the demons' friend to find us or come near to us.
But for the milch-cow be it well, and for the man who strives for fame.

13 Each evil deed made manifest, and that which is concealed, O Gods,
The whole thereof remove from us to Trita Āptya far away.

14 Daughter of Heaven, the dream that bodes evil to us or to our kine,
Remove, O Lady of the Light, to Trita Āptya far away.

15 Even if, O Child of Heaven, it make a garland or a chain of gold,
The whole bad dream, whate'er it be, to Trita Āptya we consign.

16 To him whose food and work is this, who comes to take his share therein,
To Trita, and to Dvita, Dawn! bear thou the evil dream away.

17 As we collect the utmost debt, even the eighth and sixteenth part,
So unto Āptya we transfer together all the evil dream.

18 Now have we conquered and obtained, and from our trespasses are free.
Shine thou away the evil dream, O Dawn, whereof we are afraid. Yours are incomparable aids, and good the succour they afford.

HYMN XLVIII. *Soma.*

1. Wisely have I enjoyed the savoury viand, religious-thoughted, best to find out treasure,
The food to which all Deities and mortals, calling it meath, gather themselves together.

2 Thou shalt be Aditi as thou hast entered within, appeaser of celestial anger.
Indu, enjoying Indra's friendship, bring us—as a swift steed the car—forward to riches.

3 We have drunk Soma and become immortal; we have attained the light, the Gods discovered.
Now what may foeman's malice do to harm us? What, O Immortal, mortal man's deception?

4 Absorbed into the heart, be sweet, O Indu, as a kind father to his son, O Soma,
As a wise Friend to friend: do thou, wide-ruler, O Soma, lengthen out our days for living.

5 These glorious drops that give me freedom have I drunk. Closely they knit my joints as straps secure a car.
Let them protect my foot from slipping on the way: yea, let the drops I drink preserve me from disease.

6 Make me shine bright like fire produced by friction: give us a clearer sight and make us better.

13 *To Trita Āptya far away*: Trita Āptya is a divinity dwelling in the remotest part of the heavens to whom it was customary to wish away and consign any threatened calamity or unpleasantness. As Sāyaṇa regards Trita Āptya as the Ṛṣi of the hymn, he is compelled to force a different interpretation on the first half of the second line: '(let it not be found) in Trita Āptya, keep it far from us.'—Wilson.

14 *Daughter of Heaven*: Uṣas or Dawn.

15 "The sense would then be 'even though parts of it be pleasant, we put the whole of the evil dream away."—Macdonell, Journal of R.A.S., July, 1893. p. 461.

16 *To him*: to Trita whose business it is to receive these consignments. *To Dvita*: a similar being, sometimes associated with Trita. See V. 18. 2.

1 *Meath*: *mádhu*: or, sweet.

2 *Within*: within my heart. *Indu*: Soma.

3 *We have drunk Soma*: See Muir, *O. S. Texts*. III. 264, 265.

5 *From slipping on the way*: 'may they keep us from a loosely knit worship.'—Wilson.

For in carouse I think of thee, O Soma, Shall I, as a rich man, attain to comfort ?

7 May we enjoy with an enlivened spirit the juice thou givest, like ancestral riches.
O Soma, King, prolong thou our existence as Sūrya makes the shining days grow longer.

8 King Soma, favour us and make us prosper : we are thy devotees ; of this be mindful.
Spirit and power are fresh in us, O Indu : give us not up unto our foeman's pleasure.

9 For thou hast settled in each joint, O Soma, aim of men's eyes and guardian of our bodies.
When we offend against thine holy statutes, as a kind Friend, God, best of all, be gracious.

10 May I be with the Friend whose heart is tender, who, Lord of Bays ! when quaffed will never harm me—
This Soma now deposited within me. For this, I pray for longer life to Indra.

11 Our maladies have lost their strength and vanished : they feared, and passed away into the darkness.
Soma hath risen in us, exceeding mighty, and we are come where men prolong existence.

12 Fathers, that Indu which our hearts have drunken, Immortal in himself, hath entered mortals.
So let us serve this Soma with oblation, and rest securely in his grace and favour.

13 Associate with the Fathers thou, O Soma, hast spread thyself abroad through earth and heaven.
So with oblation let us serve thee, Indu, and so let us become the lords of riches,

14 Give us your blessing, O ye Gods, preservers. Never may sleep or idle talk control us.
But evermore may we, as friends of Soma, speak to the synod with brave sons around us.

9 *Aim of men's eyes* : or beholder of men.
12 *Immortal in himself* : See note on I. 18. 4.
13 *Soma* : here the Moon-God, who is intimately connected with the Pitṛs or Fathers. See *Hymns of the Atharva-veda*, XVIII. 4. 72.

15 On all sides, Soma, thou art our life-giver : aim of all eyes, light-finder, come within us.
Indu, of one accord with thy protections both from behind and from before preserve us.

HYMN XLIX. *Agni.*

1. AGNI, come hither with thy fires ; we choose thee as Invoking Priest.
Let the extended ladle full of oil balm thee, best Priest, to sit on sacred grass.

2 For unto thee, O Aṅgiras, O Son of Strength, move ladles in the sacrifice.
To Agni, Child of Force, whose locks drop oil, we seek, foremost in sacrificial rites.

3 Agni, thou art Disposer, Sage, Herald, bright God ! and worshipful,
Best offerer, cheerful, to be praised in holy rites, pure Lord ! by singers with their hymns.

4 Most Youthful and Eternal, bring the longing Gods to me, the guileless, for the feast.
Come, Vasu, to the banquet that is well-prepared : rejoice thee, gracious, with our songs.

5 Famed art thou, Agni, far and wide, Preserver, righteous, and a Sage.
The holy singers, O refulgent kindled God ! arrangers, call on thee to come.

6 Shine, Most Resplendent ! blaze, send bliss unto the folk, and to thy worshipper : Great art thou.
So may my princes, with good fires, subduing foes, rest in the keeping of the Gods.

I place at the end of this Book the eleven hymns, called the Vālakhilya, which are usually inserted after Hymn XLVIII. These hymns are not reckoned in the division of the Ṛgveda into Maṇḍalas (Books) and Anuvākas (Chapters), and Sāyaṇa does not notice them in his Commentary. See Wilson's Translation, V. p. 96, note by Cowell. See also Max Müller's *Vedic Hymns* I, (Sacred Books of the East, Vol. XXXII.), pp. xlvi—xlviii.

Eleven must be added to the number of this hymn and of all that follow in this Book to make them correspond with the numbers in Max Müller's edition of the text.

2 *Whose locks drop oil* : 'butter-haired.'—Wilson.

5 *The arrangers* : of the ritual of sacrifice.

6 *Princes* : wealthy patrons. According to Sāyaṇa, the Ṛṣi's own sons and others may be intended.

7 O Agni, as thou burnest down to earth even high-grown underwood,
So, bright as Mitra is, burn him who injures us, him who plots ill against thy friend.

8 Give us not as a prey to mortal enemy, nor to the wicked friend of fiends.
With conquering guards, auspicious, unassailable, protect us, O Most Youthful God.

9 Protect us, Agni, through the first, protect us through the second hymn,
Protect us through three hymns, O Lord of Power and Might, through four hymns, Vasu, guard thou us.

10 Preserve us from each fiend who brings the Gods no gift, preserve thou us in deeds of strength:
For we possess in thee the nearest Friend of all, for service of the Gods and weal.

11 O Holy Agni, give us wealth renowned with men and strengthening life.
Bestow on us, O Helper, that which many crave, more glorious still by righteousness;

12 Wherewith we may o'ercome our rivals in the war, o'erpowering the foe's designs.
So wax thou by our food, O Excellent in strength. Quicken our thoughts that find out wealth.

13 Agni is even as a bull who whets and brandishes his horns.
Well-sharpened are his jaws which may not be withstood: the Child of Strength hath powerful teeth.

14 Not to be stayed, O Bull, O Agni, are thy teeth when thou art spreading far and wide.
Make our oblations duly offered up, O Priest, and give us store of precious things.

15 Thou liest in the wood: from both thy Mothers mortals kindle thee.
Unweariedly thou bearest up the offerer's gifts, then shinest bright among the Gods.

16 And so the seven priests, O Agni, worship thee, Free-giver, Everlasting One.
Thou cleavest through the rock with heat and fervent glow. Agni, rise up above the men.

17 For you let us whose grass is trimmed call Agni, Agni, restless God.
Let us whose food is offered call to all the tribes Agni the Invoking Priest of men.

18 Agni, with noble psalm that tells his wish he dwells, thinking on thee who guardest him.
Speedily bring us strength of many varied sorts to be most near to succour us.

19 Agni, Praise-singer! Lord of men, God! burner-up of Rākṣasas,
Mighty art thou, the ever-present Household-Lord, Home-friend and Guardian from the sky.

20 Let no fiend come among us, O thou rich in light, no spell of those who deal in spells.
To distant pastures drive faint hunger: far away, O Agni, chase the demons' friends.

HYMN L. *Indra.*

1. BOTH boons,—may Indra, hitherward turned, listen to this prayer of ours,
And mightiest Maghavan with thought inclined to us come near to drink the Soma juice.

2 For him, strong, independent Ruler, Heaven and Earth have fashioned forth for power and might.
Thou seatest thee as first among thy peers in place, for thy soul longs for Soma juice.

3 Fill thyself full, O Lord of wealth, O Indra, with the juice we shed.
We know thee, Lord of Bay Steeds! victor in the fight, vanquishing e'en the invincible.

9 The numbers probably have reference to the four quarters of the sky.—Ludwig.

12 *Wherewith*: referring to the wealth which Agni is asked to give.

15 *In the wood*: in the pieces of wood used for the production of Agni.

16 *Seven priests*: minor Hotar priests, such as the Maitrāvaruṇa and others. *The rock*: *ádrim*, explained by Sāyaṇa as *megham*, the cloud.

17 *The restless God*: or, 'the irresistible.'—Wilson.

18 *He dwells*: that is, the pious institutor of sacrifice.

20 *Spell of those who deal in spells*: *yāturyātumávatām*: 'torment of the evil spirits.'—Wilson.

1 *Both boons*: Indra is asked to bear the prayer and to drink the Soma.

4 Changeless in truth, O Maghavan Indra, let it be as thou in wisdom willest it.
May we, O fair of cheek, win booty with thine aid, O Thunderer, swiftly seeking it.

5 Indra, with all thy saving helps give us assistance, Lord of power.
For after thee we follow even as glorious bliss, thee, Hero, finder-out of wealth.

6 Increaser of our steeds and multiplying kine, a golden well, O God, art thou,
For no one may impair the gifts laid up in thee. Bring me whatever thing I ask.

7 For thou,—come to the worshipper !—wilt find great wealth to make us rich.
Fill thyself full, O Maghavan, for gain of kine, full, Indra, for the gain of steeds.

8 Thou as thy gift bestowest many hundred herds, yea, many thousands dost thou give.
With singers' hymns have we brought the Fort-render near, singing to Indra for his grace.

9 Whether the simple or the sage, Indra, have offered praise to thee,
He Śatakratu ! by his love hath gladdened thee, ambitious ! ever pressing on !

10 If he the Strong of arm, the breaker-down of forts, the great Destroyer, hear my call,
We, seeking riches cry to Indra, Lord of wealth, to Śatakratu with our lauds.

11 We count not then as sinners, nor as niggardly or foolish men,
When with the Soma juice which we have shed we make Indra, the Mighty One, our Friend.

12 Him have we yoked in fight, the powerful Conqueror, debt-claimer, not to be deceived.
Best charioteer, the Victor marks each fault, he knows the strong to whom he will come near.

13 Indra, give us security from that whereof we are afraid.
Help us, O Maghavan, let thy succour give us this : drive away foes and enemies.

14 For thou, O liberal Lord of bounty, strengthenest his ample home who worships thee.
So Indra, Maghavan, thou Lover of the Song, we with pressed Soma call on thee,

15 Indra is Vṛtra-slayer, guard, our best defender from the foe.
May he preserve our last and middlemost, and keep watch from behind us and before.

16 Defend us from behind, below, above, in front, on all sides, Indra, shield us well.
Keep far away from us the terror sent from heaven : keep impious weapons far away.

17 Protect us, Indra, each to-day, each morrow, and each following day.
Our singers, through all days, shalt thou, Lord of the brave, keep safely both by day and night.

18 A crushing Warrior, passing rich is Maghavan, endowed with all heroic might.
Thine arms, O Śatakratu, are exceeding strong, arms which have grasped the thunderbolt.

HYMN LI. *Indra.*

1. OFFER ye up as praise to him that wherein Indra takes delight.
The Soma-bringers magnify Indra's great energy with hymns. Good are the gifts that Indra gives.

2 Sole among chiefs, companionless, impetuous, and peerless, he
Hath waxen great o'er many folk, yea, over all things born, in might.

3 Lord of swift bounty, he will win e'en with a steed of worthless sort.
This, Indra, must be told of thee who wilt perform heroic deeds.

4 Come to us hither : let us pay devotions that enhance thy might,

9 *The simple or the sage* : 'the unskilled or the skilled.'—Wilson.

12 *Marks each fault* : the meaning of *bhṛmám* is uncertain : according to Ludwig it is 'his supporter or feeder', that is, the worshipper who presents him with sacrificial food. Sāyaṇa takes it with *vājinam* : 'the strong racer.'—Wilson. *The strong* : the rich and powerful worshipper.

15 *Our last and middlemost* : *putram*, son, being understood, according to Sāyaṇa. The expression probably means 'all of us.'

16 *The terror sent from heaven* : 'supernatural alarm.'—Wilson.

1 *Good are, etc*: the refrain is repeated in each verse.

2 *Chiefs* : *nṛbhiḥ* : men, meaning Gods, according to Sāyaṇa. *Folk* : or, tribes.

3 *He will win e'en with a steed of worthless sort* : 'He......wishes to bestow blessings (upon us) with his unurged courser.'—Wilson.

For which, Most Potent ! thou wouldst fain bless the man here who strives for fame.
5 For thou, O Indra, makest yet more bold the spirit of the bold
Who with strong Soma serveth thee, still ready with his reverent prayers.
6 Worthy of song, he looketh down as a man looketh into wells.
Pleased with the Soma-bringer's skill he maketh him his mate and friend.
7 In strength and wisdom all the Gods, Indra, have yielded unto thee.
Be thou the Guard of all, O thou whom many praise.
8 Praised, Indra, is this might of thine, best for the service of the Gods,
That thou with power dost slay Vṛtra, O Lord of Strength.
9 He makes the races of mankind like synods of the Beauteous One.
Indra knows this his manifest deed, and is renowned.
10 Thy might, O Indra, at its birth, thee also, and thy mental power,
In thy care, Maghavan rich in kine ! they have increased exceedingly.
11 O Vṛtra-slayer, thou and I will both combine for winning spoil.
Even malignity will consent, O Bolt-armed Hero, unto us.
12 Let us extol this Indra as truthful and never as untrue.
Dire is his death who pours no gifts ; great light hath he who offers them. Good are the gifts that Indra gives.

HYMN LII. *Indra.*

1. WITH powers of Mighty Ones hath he, Ancient, Beloved, been equipped,
Through whom the Father Manu made prayers efficacious with the Gods.
2 Him, Maker of the sky, let stones wet with the Soma ne'er forsake,
Nor hymns and prayer that must be said.
3 Indra who knew full well disclosed the kine to the Aṅgirases.
This his great deed must be extolled.
4 Indra, promoter of the song, the sage's Strengthener as of old,
Shall come to bless and succour us at presentation of this laud.
5 Now after their desire's intent the pious singers with the cry
Of Hail ! have sung loud hymns to thee, Indra, to gain a stall of kine.
6 With Indra rest all deeds of might, deeds done and yet to be performed,
Whom singers know devoid of guile.
7 When the Five Tribes with all their men to Indra have sent out their voice,
And when the priest hath strewn much grass, this is the Friend's own dwelling-place.
8 This praise is verily thine own : thou hast performed these manly deeds,
And sped the wheel upon its way.
9 At the o'erflowing of this Steer, boldly he strode for life, and took
Soma as cattle take their corn.
10 Receiving this and craving help, we, who with you are Dakṣa's sons,
Would fain exalt the Maruts' Lord.
11 Yea, Hero, with the singers we sing to the duly-coming Band.
Allied with thee may we prevail.
12 With us are raining Rudras, clouds accordant in call to battle, at the death of Vṛtra,
The strong assigned to him who sings and praises. May Gods with Indra at their head protect us.

6 *He looketh down* : kindly on us as a thirsty man looks eagerly into a well.

9 *Like synods of the Beauteous One* : like assemblies that meet to honour him ; but the meaning is obscure.

10 *They* : thy worshippers.

11 *Malignity* : or the malignant man. 'The niggard.' —Wilson.

12 *Dire is his death* : or, great is his destruction.

---

1 This difficult verse is variously interpreted both by Indian commentators and by European scholars. I follow partly Aufrecht's translation as given by Dr. Muir, and partly Ludwig's Commentary. See *O.S. Texts*, I. pp. 163—164; Ludwig's *Ṛgveda*, V. pp. 167—168; and Wilson's Translation, V. p. 107. The *Ancient, Beloved* appears to be Soma and not Indra.

7 *The Friend's* : Indra's. The second line is very obscure. See Bergaigne, I. vi., and *Vedic Hymns*, I., p. 226. I adopt Ludwig's interpretation.

8 *The wheel* : the Sun.

9 *This Steer* : Soma ; that is, when abundant libations had been offered. *He* : Indra.

10 *Dakṣa's sons* : of the same origin with you. 'Lords of food,' according to Sāyaṇa.

11 *Duly-coming Band* : of Maruts, led by Indra.

12 *The strong* : perhaps the thunderbolt with which Indra aids the worshipper.

HYMN LIII. *Indra.*

1. May our hymns give thee great delight.
Display thy bounty, Thunderer.
Drive off the enemies of prayer.

2 Crush with thy foot the niggard churls who bring no gifts. Mighty art thou :
There is not one to equal thee.

3 Thou art the Lord of Soma pressed, Soma unpressed is also thine.
Thou art the Sovran of the folk.

4 Come, go thou forth, dwelling in heaven and listening to the prayers of men :
Thou fillest both the heavens and earth.

5 Even that hill with rocky heights, with hundreds, thousands, held within.
Thou for thy worshippers brakest through.

6 We call on thee both night and day to taste the flowing Soma juice :
Do thou fulfil our heart's desire.

7 Where is that ever-youthful Steer, strong-necked and never yet bent down ?
What Brahman ministers to him ?

8 To whose libation doth the Steer, betake him with delight therein ?
Who takes delight in Indra now ?

9 Whom, Vṛtra-slayer, have thy gift and hero powers accompanied ?
Who is thy dearest in the laud ?

10 For thee among mankind, among the Pūrus is this Soma shed.
Hasten thou hither : drink thereof.

11 This, growing by Suṣomā and by Śaryaṇāvān, dear to thee,
In Ārjīkīya, cheers thee best.

12 Hasten thou hitherward, and drink this for munificence to-day,
Delightful for thine eager draught.

3 *Unpressed* : in its natural state in the stalks of the plant. Or, as Ludwig suggests, the Soma which Indra drinks in heaven may be meant. See VII. 26. 1.

5 *That hill* : the cloud with its countless treasures of rain.

6 *Night* : just before dawn.

10 *Among the Pūrus* : among men, or among Kings named Pūrus.—Sāyaṇa.

11 *Suṣomā* : apparently a river which cannot now be identified. *Ārjīkīya* : probably a country or district. *Śaryaṇāvān* is said to be a lake in the district of Kurukṣetra. See Vol. I., Index. For conjectures regarding Suṣomā and Ārjīkīya, see Zimmer, *Altindisches Leben*, pp. 12, 13. Cf. VIII. 7. 29.

HYMN LIV. *Indra.*

1. Though, Indra, thou art called by men from east and west, from north and south,
Come hither quickly with fleet steeds ;

2 If in the effluence of heaven, rich in its light, thou takest joy,
Or in the sea in Soma juice.

3 With songs I call thee, Great and Wide, even as a cow to profit us,
Indra, to drink the Soma-draught.

4 Hither, O Indra, let thy Bays bear up and bring upon thy car
Thy glory, God ! and majesty.

5 Thou, Indra, wouldst be sung and praised as great, strong, lordly in thy deeds :
Come hither, drink our Soma juice.

6 We who have shed the Soma and prepared the feast are calling thee.
To sit on this our sacred grass.

7 As, Indra, thou art evermore the common Lord of all alike,
As such we invocate thee now.

8 The men with stones have milked for thee this nectar of the Soma juice :
Indra, be pleased with it, and drink.

9 Neglect all pious men with skill in sacred song : come hitherward,
With speed, and give us high renown.

10 Gods, may the mighty rest unharmed, the King who gives me spotted kine,
Kine decked with golden ornaments.

11 Beside a thousand spotted kine I have received a gift of gold,
Pure, brilliant, and exceeding great.

12 Durgaha's grandsons, giving me a thousand kine, munificent,
Have won renown among the Gods.

2 *The effluence of heaven* : or the place in heaven from which the Amṛta flows. *In the sea* : of air ; the firmament.

3 *As a cow* : as the most useful of all animals.

9 *All pious men* : all other worshippers.

10 *The King* : who instituted the sacrifice. According to Sāyaṇa, Indra is meant ; but this is impossible.

12 *Durgaha's grandsons* : Sāyaṇa explains *durgáhasya* by *duḥkham gāhamānasya me*, of me plunged in grief, and *náptāḥ* (nepotes) as *arakṣitasya*, unprotected : 'Unprotected as I am, and plunged in sorrow (my dependents) by the favour of the gods obtain food, and are blessed with abundance in a thousand cattle.' See Wilson's Translation, and Cowell's note.

HYMN LV. *Indra.*

1. Loud singing at the sacred rite where Soma flows we priests invoke
With haste, that he may help, as the bard's Cherisher, Indra who findeth wealth for you.

2. Whom with fair helm, in rapture of the juice, the firm resistless slayers hinder not :
Giver of glorious wealth to him who sing his praise, honouring him who toils and pours :

3 Śakra, who like a curry-comb for horses or a golden goad,
Indra, the Vṛtra-slayer, urges eagerly the opening of the stall of kine :

4 Who for the worshipper scatters forth ample wealth, even though buried, piled in heaps :
May Indra, Lord cf Bay Steeds, fair-helmed Thunderer, act at his pleasure, as he lists.

5 Hero whom many praise, what thou hast longed for, even of old, from men.
All that we offer unto thee, O Indra, now, sacrifice, laud, effectual speech.

6 To Soma, Much-invoked, Bolt-armed ! for thy carouse, Celestial, Soma-drinker ! come.
Thou to the man who prays and pours the juice hast been best giver of delightful wealth.

7 Here, verily, yesterday we let the Thunder-wielder drink his fill.
So in like manner offer him the juice today. Now range you by the Glorious One.

8 Even the wolf, the savage beast that rends the sheep, follows the path of his decrees.
So graciously accepting, Indra, this our praise, with wondrous thought come forth to us.

9 What manly deed of vigour now remains that Indra hath not done ?
Who hath not heard his glorious title and his fame, the Vṛtra-slayer from his birth ?

10 How great his power resistless ! how invincible the Vṛtra-slayer's matchless might !
Indra excels all usurers who see the day, excels all traffickers in strength.

11 O Indra, Vṛtra-slayer, we, thy very constant worshippers,
Bring prayers ne'er heard before to thee, O Much-invoked, O Thunder-armed, to be thy meed.

12 O thou of mighty acts, the aids that are in thee call forward many an eager hope.
Past the drink-offerings, Vasu, even of the good, hear my call, Strongest God, and come.

13 Verily, Indra, we are thine, we worshippers depend on thee.
For there is none but only thou to show us grace, O Maghavan, thou much invoked.

14 From this our misery and famine set us free, from this dire curse deliver us.
Succour us with thine help and with thy wondrous thought. Most Mighty, finder of the way.

15 Now let your Soma juice be poured ; be not afraid, O Kali's sons.
This darkening sorrow goes away ; yea, of itself it vanishes.

1 *We priests invoke* : the construction is difficult. I follow Ludwig and take *huvé*, an infinitive, as equivalent to the first person plural.

3 *Curry-comb for horses* : the purifier of his worshippers and well-skilled in horses, according to Sāyaṇa. *Golden goad* : wonderful and golden-bodied, according to Sāyaṇa. The meaning of *kíjaḥ*, as well as of *mṛkṣáḥ*, is uncertain, but both seem to signify instruments connected with horses.

4 *Buried* : : as gold, precious stones etc.

8 *The wolf* : according to Sāyaṇa, the robber. The reason of mentioning either in this place is not obvious.

10 *Who see the day* : who live. According to Sāyaṇa, who look upon the Sun in their present life, but will be sunk in darkness after death.

14 *From this our misery* : the hymn was 'seen' and employed in a time of dearth and famine. *Finder of the way* : to prosperity.

15 *Kali's sons* : Kali is the Ṛṣi or seer of the hymn.

HYMN LVI. *Ādityas.*

1. Now pray we to these Kṣatriyas, to the Ādityas for their aid,
These who are gracious to assist.

2 May Mitra bear us o'er distress, and Varuṇa and Aryaman,
Yea, the Ādityas, as they know.

3 For wonderful and meet for praise is these Ādityas' saving help
To him who offers and prepares.

4 The mighty aid of you, the Great, Varuṇa, Mitra, Aryaman,
We claim to be our sure defence.

1 *Kṣatriyas* : royal princes.

5 Guard us, Ādityas, still alive, before the deadly weapon strike :
Are ye not they who hear our call ?

6 What sheltering defence ye have for him who toils in pouring gifts,
Graciously bless ye us therewith.

7 Ādityas, Gods, from sorrow there is freedom; for the sinless, wealth,
O ye in whom no fault is seen.

8 Let not this fetter bind us fast : may he release us for success ;
For strong is Indra and renowned.

9 O Gods who fain would lend your aid, destroy not us as ye destroy
Your enemies who go astray.

10 And thee too, O Great Aditi, thee also, Goddess, I address,
Thee very gracious to assist.

11 Save us in depth and shallow from the foe, thou Mother of Strong Sons :
Let no one of our seed be harmed.

12 Far-spread ! wide-ruling ! grant that we, unharmed by envy, may expand :
Grant that our progeny may live.

13 Those who, the Princes of the folk, in native glory, ne'er deceived,
Maintain their statutes, void of guile—

14 As such, from mouth of ravening wolves, O ye Ādityas, rescue us,
Like a bound thief, O Aditi.

15 Ādityas, let this arrow, yea, let this malignity depart
From us or e'er it strike us dead.

16 For, Bountiful Ādityas, we have evermore enjoyed your help,
Both now and in the days of old.

17 To every one, O ye Most Wise, who turneth even from sin to you,
Ye Gods vouchsafe that he may live.

18 May this new mercy profit us, which, ye Ādityas, frees like one,
Bound from his bonds, O Aditi.

19 O ye Ādityas, this your might is not to be despised by us :
So be ye graciously inclined.

20 Let not Vivasvān's weapon nor the shaft, Ādityas, wrought with skill,
Destroy us ere old age be nigh.

21 On every side dispel all sin, Ādityas, all hostility,
Indigence, and combined attack.

HYMN LVII. *Indra.*

1. Even as a car to give us aid, we draw thee hither for our bliss,
Strong in thy deeds, checking assault, Lord, Mightiest Indra, of the brave !

2 Great in thy power and wisdom, Strong, with thought that comprehendeth all !
Thou hast filled full with majesty.

3 Thou very Mighty One, whose hands by virtue of thy greatness grasp,
The golden bolt that breaks its way.

4 Your Lord of might that ne'er hath bent, that ruleth over all mankind,
I call, that he, as he is wont, may aid the chariots and the men.

5 Whom, ever furthering, in frays that win the light, in both the hosts
Men call to succour and to help.

6 Indra, the Strong, the measureless, worthy of praise, Most Bountiful,
Sole Ruler even over wealth.

7 Him, for his ample bounty, him, this Indra do I urge to drink,
Who, as his praise was sung of old, the Dancer, is the Lord of men.

8 Thou Mighty One, whose friendship none of mortals ever hath obtained :
None will attain unto thy might.

9 Aided by thee, with thee allied, in frays for water and for sun,
Bolt-armed ! may we win ample spoil.

10 So seek we thee with sacrifice and songs, chief Lover of the Song,
As, in our battles Indra, thou to Purumāyya gavest help.

11 O Thunderer, thou whose friendship and whose onward guidance both are sweet,
Thy sacrifice must be prepared.

12 To us, ourselves, give ample room, give for our dwelling ample room :
Give ample room to us to live.

11 *Of Strong Sons* : the Ādityas.

17 *Who turneth even from sin* : who comes to you for forgiveness.

20 *Vivasvān's weapon* : the deadly bolt of the Sun, or perhaps, metaphorically, of the sacrificer.

21 *Combined attack* : 'the closely drawn net.'—Wilson.

2 *Thou hast filled full* : the universe.

7 *The Dancer* : in the dance of war.

10 *Purumāyya* : according to Sāyaṇa, 'me (the Ṛṣi) the possessor of much wisdom.'

13 We count the banquet of the Gods a spacious pathway for the men,
And for the cattle, and the car.

14 Six men, yea, two and two, made glad with Soma juice, come near to me
With offerings pleasant to the taste.

15 Two brown-hued steeds, Indrota's gift, two bays from Ṛkṣa's son were mine,
From Aśvamedha's son two red.

16 From Atithigva good car-steeds, from Ārkṣa rein-obeying steeds,
From Āśvamedha beauteous ones.

17 Indrota, Atithigva's son, gave me six horses matched with mares :
And Pūtakratu gave besides.

18 Marked above all, amid the brown, is the red mare Vṛṣaṇvatī,
Obedient to the rein and whip.

19 O bound to me by deeds of might, not even the man who loves to blame,
Hath found a single fault in you.

HYMN LVIII. *Indra.*

1. I SEND you forth the song of praise for Indu, hero-gladdener.
With hymn and plenty he invites you to complete the sacrifice.

2 Thou wishest for thy kine a bull, for those who long for his approach,
For those who turn away from him, lord of thy cows whom none may kill.

3 The dappled kine who stream with milk prepare his draught of Soma juice :
Clans in the birth-place of the Gods, in the three luminous realms of heaven.

4 Praise, even as he is known, with song Indra the guardian of the kine,
The Son of Truth, Lord of the brave.

5 Hither his Bay Steeds have been sent, red Steeds are on the sacred grass,
Where we in concert sing our songs.

6 For Indra Thunder-armed the kine have yielded mingled milk and meath,
What time he found them in the vault.

7 When I and Indra mount on high up to the Bright One's place and home,
We, having drunk of meath, will reach his seat whose Friends are three times seven.

8 Sing, sing ye forth your songs of praise, ye Priyamedhas, sing your songs :
Yea, let young children sing their lauds : as a strong castle praise ye him.

9 Now loudly let the viol sound, the lute send out its voice with might,
Shrill be the music of the string. To Indra is the hymn up-raised.

10 When hither speed the dappled cows, unflinching, easy to be milked,
Seize quickly, as it bursts away, the Soma juice for Indra's drink.

11 Indra hath drunk, Agni hath drunk : all Deities have drunk their fill.
Here Varuṇa shall have his home, to whom the floods have sung aloud as mother-kine unto their calves.

13 Sacrifice to the Gods procures freedom and security for us and all who belong to us.

15 'These princes with their respective fathers are the six of V. 14. The sons of *Ṛkṣa* and *Aśvamedha* had originally commenced the sacrifice, but *Indrota* and his father *Atithigva* came to see it and added their gifts. The sons alone are mentioned : the son is the father's second self, *pitṛ-putrayor abhedāt*.'—Cowell's note in Wilson's Translation.

16 *Ārkṣa* : the son of Ṛkṣa. *Āśvamedha* : the son of Aśvamedha.

17 *Pūtakratu* : son of Aśvamedha.

18 *Vṛṣaṇvatī* : according to von Roth, 'perhaps, that may be found among stallions.'

19 *O bound to me* : this stanza is addressed to the princes who instituted the sacrifice and gave the rewards which have been mentioned.

---

1 *The song of praise* : *triṣṭubham* : used in a general sense for any hymn of praise. *Indu* : Soma. According to Sāyaṇa, Indra is meant.

2 The stanza is difficult. I adopt Pischel's explanation of *nadám* and *odatīnām*.

3 *Clans*: *viśaḥ*: possibly the cows are meant. Eggelings translates: 'At his birth the well-like, milking speckled one mix the Soma (draught), the clans of the gods in the three spheres of the heavens' (Sacred Books of the East, XLI. p. 307). Pischel observes: 'The connexion of the first three stanzas is probably this: Soma shall be celebrated by you in your song of praise in order that he may liberally reward you. What thou wishest for thyself is a bull for the cows, in order that they may be propagated and provide Indra with milk to be mixed with his Soma juice, while they serve the race of Gods in all three realms of heaven. —*Vedische Studien*, I. p. 197.

6 *In the vault* : 'in the cavity of the Soma-vessel.'—von Roth; 'on the horizon.'—Ludwig ; 'near at hand.'—Sāyaṇa.

7 *The Bright One's place* : the station of the Sun. *Whose Friends are three times seven* : Indra who is the friend of the Maruts. I follow Ludwig in combining the *triḥ saptá sákhyuḥ* of the text into one compound word. Sāyaṇa's explanation is different : 'let us be united in the twenty-first sphere of the (universal) friend.'—See note in Wilson's Translation.

9 *The viol* ; *gárgaraḥ* : 'a kind of musical instrument,' says Sāyaṇa. *Godhá*, originally the leather guard worn by bowmen on the left arm, and *piṅgā* (said to mean bowstring) are also, apparently, names of musical instruments.

12 Thou, Varuṇa, to whom belong Seven Rivers, art a glorious God.
The waters flow into thy throat as 'twere a pipe with ample mouth.

13 He who hath made the fleet steeds spring, well-harnessed, to the worshipper,
He, the swift Guide, is that fair form that loosed the horses near at hand.

14 Indra, the very Mighty, holds his enemies in utter scorn.
He, far away, and yet a child, cleft the cloud smitten by his voice.

15 He, yet a boy exceeding small, mounted his newly-fashioned car.
He for his Mother and his Sire cooked the wild mighty buffalo.

16 Lord of the home, fair-helmeted, ascend thy chariot wrought of gold.
We will attend the Heavenly One, the thousand-footed, red of hue, matchless, who blesses where he goes.

17 With reverence they come hitherward to him as to a Sovran lord,
That they may bring him near for this man's good success, to prosper and bestow his gifts.

18 The Priyamedhas have observed the offering of the men of old,
Of ancient custom, while they strewed the sacred grass, and spread their sacrificial food.

HYMN LIX. *Indra.*

1. He who, as Sovran Lord of men, moves with his chariots unrestrained,
The Vṛtra-slayer vanquisher, of fighting hosts, preëminent, is praised with song.

2 Honour that Indra, Puruhanman ! for his aid, in whose sustaining hand of old,
The splendid bolt of thunder was deposited, as the great Sun was set in heaven.

3 No one by deed attains to him who works and strengthens evermore :
No, not by sacrifice, to Indra praised o all, resistless, daring, bold in might.

4 The potent Conqueror, invincible in war, him at whose birth the Mighty Ones,
The Kine who spread aftar, sent their loud voices out, heavens, earths sent their loud voices out,

5 O Indra, if a hundred heavens and if a hundred earths were thine—
No, not a thousand Suns could match thee at thy birth, not both the worlds, O Thunderer.

6 Thou, Hero, hast performed thy hero deeds with might, yea, all with strength, O Strongest One.
Maghavan, help us to a stable full of kine, O Thunderer, with wondrous aids.

7 Let not a godless mortal gain this food, O thou whose life is long !
But one who yokes the bright-hued steeds, the Etaśas, even Indra yoker of the Bays.

8 Urge ye the Conqueror to give, your Indra greatly to be praised,
To be invoked in shallow waters and in depths, to be invoked in deeds of might.

9 O Vasu, O thou Hero, raise us up to ample opulence.
Raise us to gain of mighty wealth, O Maghavan, O Indra, to sublime renown.

10 Indra, thou justifiest us, and tramplest down thy slanderers.
Guard thyself, valiant Hero, in thy vital parts : strike down the Dāsa with thy blows.

11 The man who brings no sacrifice, inhuman, godless, infidel,
Him let his friend the mountain cast to rapid death, the mountain cast the Dasyu down.

12 O Mightiest Indra, loving us, gather thou up, as grains of corn,
Within thine hand, of these their kine, to give away, yea, gather twice as loving us.

12 Varuṇa's throat, or palate, is said to mean the sea, into which the seven rivers flow.

15 *His Mother and his Sire* : Earth and Heaven. The *buffalo* is the dark rain-cloud which Indra pierces with his lightning, or perhaps the demon Vala is intended.

16 *The Heavenly One* : the Sun, which is Indra's chariot. *Thousand-footed* : bright with countless rays of light.

17 *This man's* : who institutes the sacrifice.

---

2 *Puruhanman* : the Ṛṣi of the hymn addresses himself. *Sustaining* : or *vidhartári* may (with Ludwig) be taken as a nominative with *vájraḥ*, the bolt of thunder as a sustainer (of Order).

4 *The Kine* : the heavens and the earths.

7 *Etaśas* : the horses of the Sun.

10 *In thy vital parts* : literally, between thy thighs. 'Shelter us between thy thighs.'—Wilson.

11 *His friend* : in which he hopes to find refuge : according to Sāyaṇa. Parvata (mountain) is a Ṛṣi, the friend of Indra.

12 *Their kine* : the property of the hostile aborigines.

13 O my companions, wish for power. How may we perfect Śara's praise,
The liberal princely patron, never to be harmed ?

14 By many a sage whose grass is trimmed thou art continually praised,
That thou, O Śara, hast bestowed here one and here another calf.

15 The noble, Śūradeva's son, hath brought a calf, led by the ear to three of us.
As a chief brings a goat to milk.

HYMN LX. *Agni.*

1. O AGNI, with thy mighty wealth guard us from all malignity,
Yea, from all hate of mortal man.

2 For over thee, O Friend from birth, the wrath of man hath no control :
Nay, Guardian of the earth art thou.

3 As such, with all the Gods, O Son of Strength, auspicious in thy flame.
Give us wealth bringing all things good.

4 Malignities stay not from wealth the mortal man whom, Agni, thou
Protectest while he offers gifts.

5 Sage Agni, he whom thou dost urge, in worship of the Gods, to wealth,
With thine assistance winneth kine.

6 Riches with many heroes thou hast for the man who offers gifts :
Lead thou us on to higher bliss.

7 Save us, O Jātavedas, nor abandon us to him who sins,
Unto the evil-hearted man.

8 O Agni, let no godless man avert thy bounty as a God :
Over all treasures thou art Lord.

9 So, Son of Strength, thou aidest us to what is great and excellent.
Those, Vasu ! Friend ! who sing thy praise.

10 Let our songs come anear to him beauteous and bright with piercing flame,
Our offerings, with our homage, to the Lord of wealth, to him whom many praise, for help :

11 To Agni Jātavedas, to the Son of Strength, that he may give us precious gifts,
Immortal, from of old Priest among mortal men, the most delightful in the house :

12 Agni, made yours by sacrifice, Agni, while holy rites advance ;
Agni, the first in songs, first with the warrior steed ; Agni to win the land for us.

13 May Agni who is Lord of wealth vouchsafe us food for friendship sake.
Agni we ever seek for seed and progeny, the Vasu who protects our lives.

14 Solicit with your chants, for help, Agni the God with piercing flame,
For riches famous Agni, Purumīlha and ye men ! Agni to light our dwelling well.

15 Agni we laud that he may keep our foes afar, Agni to give us health and strength.
Let him as Guardian be invoked in all the tribes, the lighter-up of glowing brands.

HYMN LXI. *Agni.*

1. PREPARE oblation : let him come ; and let the minister serve again
Who knows the ordering thereof.

2 Rejoicing in his friendship, let the priest be seated over man,
Beside the shoot of active power.

3 Him, glowing bright beyond all thought, they seek among the race of man ;

---

13 *Śara's praise* : Śara must be the institutor of the sacrifice : according to Sāyaṇa he is Indra, 'the destroyer.'

14 *Here one and here another* : *ékam-ekam* : meaning many.

15 *Śūradeva's son* : Śara. Sāyaṇa explains *śauradevyáḥ* as cows won in battle. 'May Maghavan, taking them by the ears, lead the cows with their calves from our three (destructive enemies), as the owner leads a goat to drink.'—Wilson.

---

2 *Guardian of the earth* : *kṣápāvān* : 'Lord of the night.'—Sāyaṇa.

5 *Winneth kine* : literally, is a goer among cows : 'walks (lord) among crowds of cattle.'—Wilson.

12 *With the warrior steed* : *árvati* : the fierce and rapid fire that clears the jungle for the advance of the Āryan settlers.

14 *To light our dwelling well* : I follow Ludwig's explanation. Sāyaṇa takes *suditáye* as a proper name : 'a house for (me) Suditi.'—Wilson.

15 *The lighter-up of glowing brands* : *vásturrṣūṇām* : according to Sāyaṇa, 'the giver of homes to us Ṛṣis.'

The language of the hymn is intentionally obscure, and much of my translation (in which I generally follow Ludwig) must be regarded as conjectural.

1 *Let him come* : Agni. *The minister* : or, the Adhvaryu.

2 *The shoot* : Agni, according to Sāyaṇa : the stalks of the Soma-plant, according to von Roth.

3 *They seek* : that is, the Gods.

With him for tougue they seize the food.

4 He hath inflamed the twofold plain : life-giving, he hath climbed the wood,
And with his tongue hath struck the rock.

5 Wandering here the radiant Calf finds none to fetter him, and seeks
The Mother to declare his praise.

6 And now that great and mighty team, the team of horses that are his,
And traces of his car, are seen.

7 The seven milk a single cow ; the two set other five to work,
On the stream's loud-resounding bank.

8 Entreated by Vivasvān's ten, Indra cast down the water-jar
With threefold hammer from the sky.

9 Three times the newly-kindled flame proceeds around the sacrifice :
The priests anoint it with the meath.

10 With reverence they drain the fount that circles with its wheel above,
Exhaustless, with the mouth below.

11 The pressing-stones are set at work : the meath is poured into the tank,
At the out-shedding of the fount.

12 Ye cows, protect the fount : the two Mighty Ones bless the sacrifice.
The handles twain are wrought of gold.

13 Pour on the juice the ornament which reaches both the heaven and earth :
Supply the liquid to the Bull.

14 These know their own abiding-place : like calves beside the mother cows
They meet together with their kin.

15 Devouring in their greedy jaws, they make sustaining food in heaven,
To Indra, Agni light and prayer.

16 The Pious One milked out rich food, sustenance dealt in portions seven,
Together with the Sun's seven rays.

17 I took some Soma when the Sun rose up, O Mitra, Varuṇa.
That is the sick man's medicine.

18 From where oblations must be laid, which is the Well-beloved's home,
He with his tongue hath compassed heaven.

HYMN LXII. *Aśvins.*

1. ROUSE ye for him who keeps the Law, yoke your steeds, Aśvins, to your car :
Let your protecting help be near.

2 Come, Aśvins, with your car more swift than is the twinkling of an eye :
Let your protecting help be near.

3 Aśvins, ye overlaid with cold the fiery pit for Atri's sake :
Let your protecting help be near.

4 Where are ye ? whither are ye gone ? whither, like falcons, have ye flown ?
Let your protecting help be near.

5 If ye at any time this day are listening to this my call,
Let your protecting help be near.

6 The Aśvins, first to hear our prayer, for closest kinship I approach :
Let your protecting help be near.

7 For Atri ye, O Aśvins, made a dwelling-place to shield him well,

4 *The twofold plain* : the expanses of earth and heaven. *Climbed the wood* : a forest conflagration is referred to.

5 *The radiant Calf* : Agni in the form of lightning. *Here* : in the sky above us. *The Mother* : the cloud, which will praise him with a thunder-psalm.

7 *The seven* : officiating priests, or assistants. See II. 1. 2. *A single cow* : the text has only *ekām*. Sāyaṇa supplies, cow, which he explains as the *gharma*, pitcher or caldron used for heating milk, etc., in the Pravargya ceremony. *Loud-resounding bank* : with reference to the sacrificial exclamations, uttered by the officiating priests. *The two* : the Adhvaryu and the Pratiprasthātar, his Assistant, direct the five others in the performance of the ceremony.

8 *Entreated by Vivasvān's ten* : according to Sāyaṇa, the ten fingers of the worshipper. Ten priests are probably meant. *Indra* : Agni or Āditya may be meant. —Sāyaṇa. *The water-jar* : the rainy cloud. *Hammer* : meaning, probably, the zigzag lightning. Sāyaṇa explains it by *raśminā*, with his ray.

10 *The fount* : *avatám* : the *gharma* or *mahāvira*, the contents of which are poured into the fire. *Its wheel* : apparently, the circular rim on which it usually stands and which is now inverted that all the liquid may flow out. According to Hillebrandt (*Vedische Mythologie* I. 325) *the fount* is the Moon.

12 *The two Mighty Ones* : Heaven and Earth. But as the meaning of *rapsudā* is unknown, the sentence can be only conjecturally translated : '(The two kinds of milk) in the sacrifice are plentiful and fruit-giving.'—Wilson.

13 *The ornament* : the milk which is mingled with the Soma. *To the Bull* : to Agni.

14 *These know* : the cows know, and come to, the place where they are to be milked for sacrificial purposes as well as they know their own stable.

15 *Devouring* : perhaps the flames ; but the stanza is obscure.

16 *The Pious One* : Agni. *Dealt in portions seven* : one for each priest.

18 *The Well-beloved's home* : 'the place which I, the eager offerer, choose.—Wilson. *Haryatá*, 'the well-beloved,' is perhaps the Soma.

---

1 *Who keeps the Law* : which enjoins sacrifice. The Ṛṣi means himself.

3 *For Atri's sake* : See I. 116. 8.

Let your protecting help be near.
8 Ye warded off the fervent heat for Atri when he sweetly spake :
Let your protecting help be near.
9 Erst Saptavadhri by his prayer obtained the trenchant edge of fire :
Let your protecting help be near.
10 Come hither, O ye Lords of wealth, and listen to this call of mine :
Let your protecting help be near.
11 What is this praise told forth of you as Elders in the ancient way ?
Let your protecting help be near.
12 One common brotherhood is yours, Aśvins your kindred is the same :
Let your protecting help be near.
13 This is your chariot, Aśvins, which speeds through the regions, earth and heaven :
Let your protecting aid be near.
14 Approach ye hitherward to us with thousands both of steeds and kine :
Let your protecting help be near.
15 Pass us not by, remember us with thousands both of kine aud steeds :
Let your protecting help be near.
16 The purple-tinted Dawn hath risen, and true to Law hath made the light :
Let your protecting help be near.
17 He looked upon the Aśvins, as an axe-armed man upon a tree :
Let your protecting help be near.
18 By the black band encompassed round, break it down, bold one, like a fort.
Let your protecting help be near.

HYMN LXIII. *Agni.*

1. EXERTING all our strength with thoughts of power we glorify in speech
Agni your dear familiar Friend, the darling Guest in every home.
2 Whom, served with sacrificial oil like Mitra, men presenting gifts
Eulogize with their songs of praise ;
3 Much-lauded Jātavedas, him who bears oblations up to heaven
Prepared in service of the Gods.
4 To noblest Agni, Friend of man, best Vṛtra-slayer, are we come,
Him in whose presence Ṛkṣa's son, mighty Śrutarvan, waxes great ;
5 To deathless Jātavedas, meet for praise, adored, with sacred oil,
Visible through the gloom of night ;
6 Even Agni whom these priestly men worship with sacrificial gifts,
With lifted ladles offering them.
7 O Agni, this our newest hymn hath been addressed from us to thee,
O cheerful Guest, well-born, most wise, worker of wonders, ne'er deceived.
8 Agni, may it be dear to thee, most grateful, and exceeding sweet :
Grow mightier, eulogized therewith.
9 Splendid with splendours may it be, and in the battle with the foe
Add loftier glory to thy fame.
10 Steed, cow, a lord of heroes, bright like Indra, who shall fill the car.
Whose high renown ye celebrate, and people praise each glorious deed.
11 Thou whom Gopavana made glad with song, O Agni Aṅgiras,
Hear this my call, thou Holy One.
12 Thou whom the priestly folk implore to aid the gathering of the spoil,
Such be thou in the fight with foes.
13 I, called to him who reels with joy, Śrutarvan, Ṛkṣa's son, shall stroke
The heads of four presented steeds, like the long wool of fleecy rams.
14 Four coursers with a splendid car, Śaviṣṭha's horses, fleet of foot,
Shall bring me to the sacred feast, as flying steeds brought Tugra's son.

9 *Saptavadhri* : See V. 78. 6. His release seems to have been effected by employing fire. But see Myriantheus, *Die Aśvins*, pp. 88, 90.

11 'Why is this (repeated invocation) addressed to you as if you were decrepit like old men?'—Wilson.

12. *One common brotherhood* : as twin children of the consort of Vivasvān, the Sun.

17 The meaning is obscure. 'Aśvins, the splendidly-brilliant (sun cleaves the darkness) as the woodman with his axe a tree.'—Wilson. He (the demon) looked at the Aśvins.'—Grassmann.

18 The first line is said by Sāyaṇa to be addressed to Saptavadhri. It seems to express self-encouragement before an attack upon a Dāsa enemy. But see Myriantheus, *Die Aśvins*, p. 90.

———

1 I follow Ludwig in his interpretation of this stanza the construction of which is difficult.

2 *Like Mitra* : or as a friend ; or like the Sun—Sāyaṇa.

10 *Steed, cow* : there is no verb to govern these accusatives. Perhaps, let it, that is, the hymn, give, may be understood. Sāyaṇa explains *gām.* cow, by *gantāram*, goer. '(Worship) ye men, the bright (Agni) who goes like a horse and fills our chariots (with spoil).'—Wilson.

14 *Tugra's son* : Bhujyu. See Vol. I., Index.

15 The very truth do I declare to thee, Paruṣṇī, mighty flood.
Waters ! no man is there who gives more horses than Śaviṣṭha gives.

HYMN LXIV. *Agni.*

1. Yoke, Agni, as a charioteer, thy steeds who best invite the Gods: As ancient Herald seat thyself.
2 And, God, as skilfullest of all, call for us hitherward the Gods:
Give all our wishes sure effect.
3 For thou, Most Youthful, Son of Strength, thou to whom sacrifice is paid,
Art holy, faithful to the Law.
4 This Agni, Lord of wealth and spoil hundredfold, thousandfold, is head
And chief of riches and a Sage.
5 As craftsmen bend the felly, so bend at our general call: come nigh,
Aṅgiras, to the sacrifice.
6 Now, O Virūpa, rouse for him, Strong God who shines at early morn,
Fair praise with voice that ceases not.
7 With missile of this Agni, his who looks afar, will we lay low
The thief in combat for the kine.
8 Let not the Companies of Gods fail us, like Dawns that float away,
Like cows who leave the niggardly.
9 Let not the sinful tyranny of any fiercely-hating foe
Smite us, as billows smite a ship.
10 O Agni, God, the people sing reverent praise to thee for strength :
With terrors trouble thou the foe.
11 Wilt thou not, Agni, lend us aid in winning cattle, winning wealth ?
Maker of room, make room for us.
12 In this great battle cast us not aside as one who bears a load :
Snatch up the wealth and win it all.
13 O Agni, let this plague pursue and fright another and not us :
Make our impetuous strength more strong.
14 The reverent or unwearied man whose holy labour he accepts,
Him Agni favours with success.
15 Abandoning the foeman's host pass hither to this company :
Assist the men with whom I stand.
16 As we have known thy gracious help, as of a Father, long ago,
So now we pray to thee for bliss.

HYMN LXV. *Indra.*

1. Not to forsake me, I invoke this Indra girt by Maruts,
Lord Of magic power who rules with might.
2 This Indra with his Marut Friends clave into pieces Vṛtra's head
With hundred-knotted thunderbolt.
3 Indra, with Marut Friends grown strong, hath rent asunder Vṛtra, and
Released the waters of the sea.
4 This is that Indra who, begirt by Maruts, won the light of heaven
That he might drink the Soma juice.
5 Mighty, impetuous, begirt by Maruts, him who loudly roars,
Indra we invocate with songs.
6 Indra begirt by Maruts we invoke after the ancient plan,
That he may drink the Soma juice.
7 O liberal Indra, Marut-girt, much-lauded Śatakratu, drink
The Soma at this sacrifice.
8 To thee, O Indra, Marut-girt, these Soma juices, Thunderer !
Are offered from the heart with lauds.
9 Drink, Indra, with thy Marut Friends, pressed Soma at the morning rites,
Whetting thy thunderbolt with strength.
10 Arising in thy might, thy jaws thou shookest, Indra, having quaffed
The Soma which the mortar pressed.
11 Indra, both worlds complained to thee when uttering thy fearful roar,

15 *Paruṣṇī* : now the Rāvī, the river on whose bank Śrutarvan offered his sacrifice.

---

1 *Ancient Herald* : or, chief Invoker.

6 *Virūpa* : the Ṛṣi of the hymn who addresses himself. *Who shines at early morn* : or, aspiring heavenward.

7 *The thief* : the hymn is a prayer for aid in an expedition for the recovery of stolen cattle.

8 *Like Dawns that float away* : 'like cows that bathe them in the stream,' according to the explanation given in the St. Petersburg Lexicon. *Like cows who leave the niggardly* : 'the kine abandon not a little (calf).'—Wilson.

---

3 *Of the sea* : of the firmament or ocean of air.

11 *Complained to thee* : in terror. *When uttering thy fearful roar* : the meaning of *krákṣamāṇam*, rendered thus conjecturally, is uncertain.

What time thou smotest Dasyus dead.
12 From Indra have I measured out a song eight-footed with nine parts,
Delicate, faithful to the Law.

HYMN LXVI. *Indra.*

1. SCARCELY was Śatakratu born when of his Mother he inquired,
Who are the mighty? Who are famed ?
2. Then Śavasī declared to him Aurṇavābha, Ahīśuva:
Son, these be they thou must o'erthrow.
3 The Vṛtra-slayer smote them all as spokes are hammered into naves:
The Dasyu-killer waxed in might.
4 Then Indra at a single draught drank the contents of thirty pails,
Pails that were filled with Soma juice.
5 Indra in groundless realms of space pierced the Gandharva through, that he
Might make Brahmans' strength increase.
6 Down from the mountains Indra shot hither his well-directed shaft :
He gained the ready brew of rice.
7 One only is that shaft of thine, with thousand feathers, hundred barbs,
Which, Indra, thou hast made thy friend.
8 Strong as the Ṛbhus at thy birth, therewith to those who praise thee, men
And women, bring thou food to eat.
9 By thee these exploits were achieved, the mightiest deeds, abundantly:
Firm in thy heart thou settest them.
10 All these things Viṣṇu brought, the Lord of ample stride whom thou hadst sent—
A hundred buffaloes, a brew of rice and milk : and Indra slew the ravening boar.
11 Most deadly is thy bow, successful, fashioned well : good is thine arrow, decked with gold.
Warlike and well equipped thine arms are, which increase sweetness for him who drinks the sweet.

12 *Eight-footed with nine parts* : the hymn consists of triplets, each of which contains nine Pādas, parts or half-lines, of eight feet or syllables each. That is, the metre is octosyllabic (8×3), and the triplet contains three stanzas in that metre, or nine octosyllabic Pādas. *From Indra* : originating in him as its subject or inspirer. *Faithful to the Law* : closely connected with sacrifice.

1 Cp. VIII. 45. 4.

2 *Śavasī* : or, the Mighty One. Indra's Mother. *Aurṇavābha* or Urṇavābha's son. See VIII. 32. 26. *These*: and other fiends, as *té*, these, is plural.

4 *Pails* : or, bowls : literally, lakes. The meaning of the word *kāṇukā* in this stanza is uncertain. It appears to be an adjective qualifying *sarāṅsi* pails or lakes. See note in Wilson's Translation.

5 *The Gandharva* : a heavenly being who dwells in the region of the air and guards the celestial Soma, that is, the rain. See I. 22. 14, and 163. 2. According to Sāyaṇa, the Gandharva is the rain-cloud itself, which Indra shattered, and so released the fertilizing water.

6 The stanza is similarly explained by Sāyaṇa. Indra smote the rain from the clouds, and obtained food for men.

7 *One only* : Indra alone is the wielder of the thunderbolt.

10 *All these things* : the buffaloes or dark clouds, and the rice and milk or fertilizing rain. *Slew* : the verb is supplied by Sāyaṇa. *The ravening boar* : Vṛtra. Cf. I. 61. 7, where the deed is similarly related. See Prof. A.A. Macdonell, *Journal R. A. Society*, 1895, i 186.

11 *Which increase sweetness for him who drinks the sweet* : this is Ludwig's interpretation of two very difficult words which mean according to Wilson's Translation, 'destructively overthrowing, destructively piercing; according to the St. Petersburg Lexicon, 'like two bees delighting in sweetness;' and according to Grassmann, 'sweetness loves thy two lips.'

HYMN LXVII. *Indra.*

1. BRING us a thousand, Indra, as our guerdon for the Soma juice :
Hundreds of kine, O Hero, bring.
2 Bring cattle, bring us ornament, bring us embellishment and steeds,
Give us, besides, two rings of gold.
3 And, Bold One, bring in ample store rich jewels to adorn the ear,
For thou, Good Lord, art far renowned.
4 None other is there for the priest, Hero ! but thou, to give him gifts,
To win much spoil and prosper him.
5 Indra can never be brought low, Śakra can never be subdued :
He heareth and beholdeth all.
6 He spieth out the wrath of man, he who can never be deceived :
Ere blame can come he marketh it.
7 He hath his stomach full of might, the Vṛtra-slayer, Conqueror,
The Soma-drinker, ordering all.

1 *A thousand* : cows, understood.

2 *Two rings* : the meaning of *manā* here is somewhat uncertain. See Max Müller, *India, What can it Teach us* ? pp. 125, 126; Weber, *Episches im Vedichen Ritual*, p. 30; and Zimmer, *Altindisches Leben*, pp. 50, 51.

8 In thee all treasures are combined, Soma ! all blessed things in thee,
Uninjured, easy to bestow.

9 To thee speeds forth my hope that craves the gift of corn, and kine and gold,
Yea, craving horses, speeds to thee.

10 Indra, through hope in thee alone even this sickle do I grasp.
Fill my hand, Maghavan, with all that it can hold of barley cut or gathered up.

HYMN LXVIII. *Soma.*

1. THIS here is Soma, ne'er restrained, active, all-conquering bursting forth,
Ṛṣi and Sage by sapience.

2 All that is bare he covers o'er, all that is sick he medicines ;
The blind man sees, the cripple walks.

3 Thou, Soma, givest wide defence against the hate of alien men,
Hatreds that waste and weaken us.

4 Thou by thine insight and thy skill, Impetuous One, from heaven and earth
Drivest the sinner's enmity.

5 When to their task they come with zeal, may they obtain the Giver's grace,
And satisfy his wish who thirsts.

6 So may he find what erst was lost, so may he speed the pious man,
And lengthen his remaining life.

7 Gracious, displaying tender love, unconquered, gentle in thy thoughts,
Be sweet, O Soma, to our heart.

8 O Soma, terrify us not ; strike us not with alarm, O King :
Wound not our heart with dazzling flame.

9 When in my dwelling-place I see the wicked enemies of Gods,
King, chase their hatred far away, thou Bounteous One, dispel our foes.

8 *Soma* : here said to mean Indra himself.

10 'It would appear as if the field were a barren one and the poet sought from *Indra* a harvest which he had not sown.'—Wilson.

---

1 *Bursting forth* : according to Sāyaṇa, causing (fruit) to spring forth.

4 *Impetuous One* : *ṛjīṣin* : according to Sāyaṇa, 'possessed of the remains or dregs of the Soma juice offered in the third *savana*.'

5 *They* : the priests. *The Giver's* : bountiful Indra's. *His wish* : Indra's longing for Soma libations.

9 *The wicked enemies* : or, the enmities; that is, when I see that the Gods are displeased with me.

HYMN LXIX. *Indra.*

1. O ŚATAKRATU, truly I have made none else my Comforter.
Indra, be gracious unto us.

2 Thou who hast ever aided us kindly of old to win the spoil,
As such, O Indra, favour us.

3 What now ? As prompter of the poor thou helpest him who sheds the juice.
Wilt thou not, Indra, strengthen us ?

4 O Indra, help our chariot on, yea, Thunderer, though it lag behind :
Give this my car the foremost place.

5 Ho there ! why sittest thou at ease ? Make thou my chariot to be first :
And bring the fame of victory near.

6 Assist our car that seeks the prize. What can be easier for thee ?
So make thou us victorious.

7 Indra, be firm : a fort art thou. To thine appointed place proceeds
The auspicious hymn in season due.

8 Let not our portion be disgrace. Broad is the course, the prize is set,
The barriers are opened wide.

9 This thing we wish, that thou mayst take thy fourth, thy sacrificial name.
So art thou held to be our Lord.

10 Ekadyū hath exalted you, Immortals: both Goddesses and Gods hath he delighted.
Bestow upon him bounty meet for praises. May he, enriched with prayer, come soon and early.

HYMN LXX. *Indra.*

1. INDRA, God of the mighty arm, gather for us with thy right hand
Manifold and nutritious spoil.

2 We know thee mighty in thy deeds, of mighty bounty, mighty wealth,
Mighty in measure, prompt to aid.

3 Hero, when thou art fain to give, neither may Gods nor mortal men

4 The hymn is a prayer for success in a coming chariot race.

7 *To thine appointed place* : 'to thee the repeller (of enemies).'—Wilson.

9 *Thy fourth, thy sacrificial name* : the other three, according to Sāyaṇa, are the constellation-names, the secret name, and the revealed name.

10 The Gods in general are the deities of this stanza. *Ekadyū* is the seer of the hymn. *He, enriched with prayer*: Indra, exalted by our hymn.

Restrain thee like a fearful Bull.

4 Come, let us glorify Indra, Lord supreme of wealth, Self-ruling King :
In bounty may he harm us not.

5 Let prelude sound and following chant : so let him hear the Sāman sung,
And with his bounty answer us.

6 O Indra, with thy right hand bring, and with thy left remember us :
Let us not lose our share of wealth.

7 Come nigh, O Bold One, boldly bring hither the riches of the churl
Who giveth least of all the folk.

8 Indra, the booty which thou hast with holy singers to receive,
Even that booty win with us.

9 Indra, thy swiftly-coming spoil, the booty which rejoices all,
Sounds quick in concert with our hopes.

HYMN LXXI. *Indra.*

1. HASTE forward to us from afar, or, Vṛtra-slayer, from anear,
To meet the offering to the meath.

2 Strong are the Soma-draughts; come nigh : the juices fill thee with delight :
Drink boldly even as thou art wont.

3 Joy, Indra, in the strengthening food : let it content thy wish and thought,
And be delightful to thine heart.

4 Come to us thou who hast no foe : we call thee down to hymns of praise,
In heaven's sublimest realm of light.

5 This Soma here expressed with stones and dressed with milk for thy carouse,
Indra, is offered up to thee.

6 Graciously, Indra, hear my call. Come and obtain the draught, and sate
Thyself with juices blent with milk.

7 The Soma, Indra, which is shed in chalices and vats for thee,
Drink thou, for thou art Lord thereof.

8 The Soma seen within the vats, as in the flood the Moon is seen,
Drink thou, for thou art Lord thereof.

9 That which the Hawk brought in his claw, inviolate, through the air to thee,
Drink thou, for thou art Lord thereof.

HYMN LXXII. *Viśvedevas.*

1. WE choose unto ourselves that high protection of the Mighty Gods
That it may help and succour us.

2 May they be ever our allies, Varuṇa, Mitra, Aryaman,
Far-seeing Gods who prosper us.

3 Ye furtherers of holy Law, transport us safe o'er many woes,
As over water-floods in ships.

4 Dear wealth be Aryaman to us, Varuṇa dear wealth meet for praise :
Dear wealth we choose unto ourselves.

5 For Sovrans of dear wealth are ye, Ādityas, not of sinner's wealth,
Ye sapient Gods who slay the foe.

6 We in our homes, ye Bounteous Ones, and while we journey on the road,
Invoke you, Gods, to prosper us.

7 Regard us, Indra, Viṣṇu, here, ye Aśvins and the Marut host,
Us who are kith and kin to you.

8 Ye Bounteous Ones, from time of old we here set forth our brotherhood,
Our kinship in the Mother's womb.

9 Then come with Indra for your chief, as early day, ye Bounteous Gods
Yea, I address you now for this.

HYMN LXXIII. *Agni.*

1. AGNI, your dearest Guest, I laud, him who is loving as a friend,
Who brings us riches like a car.

2 Whom as a far-foreseeing Sage the Gods have, from the olden time,
Established among mortal men.

3 Do thou, Most Youthful God, protect the men who offer, hear their songs,
And of thyself preserve their seed.

5 *Let prelude sound* : *prá stoṣad upagāsiṣat* : let the *prastotar* and the *udgātar*, two of the officiating priests at the chanting of a Sāman, discharge their functions : the former singing the prelude and the latter the accompaniment.

8 *Win with us* : make us thy allies.

9 *Sounds in concert with our hopes* : answers to our expectation. Perhaps as Ludwig thinks, the word 'sounds' refers to the herd of cattle which probably constituted the spoil that is spoken of.

8 *The Moon* : in allusion to the double meaning of Soma, the plant and its juice, and the Moon.

9 *The Hawk* : See I. 80. 2, and 93. 6.

8 *In the Mother's womb* : as common children of Aditi the General Mother of all living beings.

3 *And of thyself preserve their seed* : or, and guard our offspring and ourselves.

4 What is the praise wherewith, O God,
Aṅgiras, Agni, Son of Strength,
We, after thine own wish and thought,

5 May serve thee, O thou Child of Power, and with what sacrifice's plan?
What prayer shall I now speak to thee ?

6 Our God, make all of us to dwell in happy habitations, and
Reward our songs with spoil and wealth.

7 Lord of the house, what plenty fills the songs which thou inspirest now,
Thou whose hymn helps to win the kine ?

8 Him Wise and Strong they glorify, the foremost Champion in the fray,
And mighty in his dwelling-place.

9 Agni, he dwells in rest and peace who smites and no one smites again:
With hero sons he prospers well

HYMN LXXIV. *Aśvins.*

1. To this mine invocation, O ye Aśvins, ye Nāsatyas, come,
To drink the savoury Soma juice.

2 This laud of mine, ye Aśvins Twain, and this mine invitation hear,
To drink the savoury Soma juice.

3 Here Kṛṣṇa is invoking you, O Aśvins, Lords of ample wealth.
To drink the savoury Soma juice.

4 List, Heroes, to the singer's call, the call of Kṛṣṇa lauding you,
To drink the savoury Soma juice.

5 Chiefs, to the sage who sings your praise grant an inviolable home,
To drink the savoury Soma juice.

6 Come to the worshipper's abode, Aśvins, who here is lauding you,
To drink the savoury Soma juice.

7 Yoke to the firmly jointed car the ass which draws you, Lords of wealth.
To drink the savoury Soma juice.

8 Come hither, Aśvins, on your car of triple form with triple seat,
To drink the savoury Soma juice.

9 O Aśvins, O Nāsatyas, now accept with favouring grace my songs,
To drink the savoury Soma juice.

9 *He* : the faithful worshipper.

5 *To drink*: so that ye may drink.
7 *The ass* : cf. I. 34. 9; 116. 2; and 162. 21.
8 *Of triple form with triple seat* : See I. 34. 2, 9.

HYMN LXXV. *Aśvins.*

1. YE Twain are wondrous strong, well-skilled in arts that heal, both bringers of delight, ye both won Dakṣa's praise.
Viśvaka calls on you as such to save his life. Break ye not off our friendship, come and set me free.

2 How shall he praise you now who is distraught in mind ? Ye Twain give wisdom for the gain of what is good.
Viśvaka calls on you as such to save his life. Break ye not off our friendship, come and set me free.

3 Already have ye Twain, possessors of great wealth, prospered Viṣṇāpū thus for gain of what is good.
Viśvaka calls on you as such to save his life. Break ye not off our friendship, come and set me free.

4 And that Impetuous Hero, winner of the spoil, though he is far away, we call to succour us,
Whose gracious favour, like a father's, is most sweet. Break ye not off our friendship, come and set me free.

5 About the holy Law toils Savitar the God : the horn of holy Law hath he spread far and wide.
The holy Law hath quelled even mighty men of war. Break ye not off our friendship, come and set me free.

HYMN LXXVI. *Aśvins.*

1. SPLENDID, O Aśvins, is your praise. Come fountain-like, to pour the stream.
Of the sweet juice effused—dear is it, Chiefs, in heaven—drink like two wild bulls at a pool.

The Ṛṣi is Viśvaka son of Kṛṣṇa.

1 *Dakṣa's praise* : on the occasion mentioned in I. 116. 2; or when the Aśvins won Sūryā for their bride, I. 116. 17. *To save his life* : according to Sāyaṇa, 'for the sake of his son.' *Come and set me free* : 'flying loose (your reins and gallop hither).'—Wilson. 'Unyoke your horses.'Grassmann.

2 *Distraught in mind* : referring either to Viśvaka himself, or the man for whom he invokes the Aśvins' aid. According to Sāyaṇa, Vimanāḥ (distraught in mind) here is the name of a Ṛṣi.

3 *Viṣṇāpū* : the Ṛṣi's son or grandson.

4 *That Impetuous Hero* : Indra. 'These two verses,' says Grassmann, 'are taken from another hymn. Verse 5 is addressed to Savitar, and verse 4, as it appears, to Indra. The refrain, which is altogether unsuitable here, has been added in order to connect the verses with the preceding hymn.'

2 Drink the libation rich in sweets, O Aśvins Twain: sit. Heroes, on the sacred grass.
Do ye with joyful heart in the abode of man preserve his life by means of wealth.

3 The Priyamedhas bid you come with all the succours that are yours.
Come to his house whose holy grass is trimmed, to dear sacrifice at the morning rites.

4 Drink ye the Soma rich in meath, ye Aśvins Twain : sit gladly on the sacred grass.
So, waxen mighty, to our eulogy from heaven come ye as wild-bulls to the pool.

5 Come to us, O ye Aśvins, now with steeds of many a varied hue,
Ye Lords of splendour, wondrous, borne on paths of gold, drink Soma, ye who strengthen Law.

6 For we the priestly singers, fain to hymn your praise, invoke you for the gain of strength.
So, wondrous, fair, and famed for great deeds come to us, through our hymn, Aśvins, when ye hear.

HYMN LXXVII. *Indra.*

1. As cows low to their calves in stalls, so with our songs we glorify
This Indra, even your Wondrous God who checks attack, who joys in the delicious juice.

2 Celestial, bounteous Giver, girt about with might, rich, mountain-like, in precious things,
Him swift we seek for foodful booty rich in kine, brought hundredfold and thousandfold.

3 Indra, the strong and lofty hills are powerless to bar thy way.
None stay that act of thine when thou wouldst fain give wealth to one like me who sings thy praise.

4 A Warrior thou by strength, wisdom, and wondrous deed, in might excellest all that is.
Hither may this our hymn attract thee to our help, the hymn which Gotamas have made.

5 For in thy might thou stretchest out beyond the boundaries of heaven.
The earthly region, Indra, comprehends thee not. After thy Godhead hast thou waxed.

6 When, Maghavan, thou honourest the worshipper, no one is there to stay thy wealth.
Most liberal Giver thou, do thou inspire our song of praise, that we may win the spoil.

HYMN LXXVIII. *Indra.*

1. To Indra sing the lofty hymn, Maruts ! that slays the Vṛtras best.
Whereby the Holy Ones created for the God the light divine that ever wakes.

2 Indra who quells the curse blew curses far away, and then in splendour came to us.
Indra, refulgent with thy Marut host ! the Gods strove eagerly to win thy love.

3 Sing to your lofty Indra, sing, Maruts, a holy hymn of praise.
Let Śatakratu, Vṛtra-slayer, kill the foe with hundred-knotted thunderbolt.

4 Aim and fetch boldly forth, O thou whose heart is bold : great glory will be thine thereby.
In rapid torrent let the mother waters spread. Slay Vṛtra, win the light of heaven.

5 When thou, unequalled Maghavan, wast born to smite the Vṛtras dead,
Thou spreadest out the spacious earth and didst support and prop the heavens.

6 Then was the sacrifice produced for thee, the laud, and song of joy,
Thou in thy might surpassest all, all that now is and yet shall be.

2 *The libation* : *gharmám* : the heated milk or other beverage, or the vessel in which it is heated.

3 *The Priyamedhas* : Priyamedha and his family.

---

1 *As cows* : the cows who are milked for sacrificial purposes, whose calves are shut up during the ceremony.

5 *The earthly region* : the *rajas* region, middle air, or firmament is frequently divided into two, one half belonging to the earth and the other half to the sky. See Wallis, *Cosmology of the Ṛgveda*, pp. 114, 115.

---

1 *Maruts* : here meaning the singers of the hymn of praise. 'Priests.'—Wilson. *The light divine* : the Sun, which the Viśvedevas generated or created for Indra.

7 Raw kine thou filledst with ripe milk. Thou madest Sūrya rise to heaven.
Heat him as milk is heated with pure Sāma hymns, great joy to him who loves the song.

HYMN LXXIX. *Indra.*

1. May Indra, who in every fight must be invoked, be near to us.
May the most mighty Vṛtra-slayer, meet for praise, come to libations and to hymns.

2 Thou art the best of all in sending bounteous gifts, true art thou, lordly in thine act.
We claim alliance with the very Glorious One, yea, with the Mighty Son of Strength.

3 Prayers unsurpassed are offered up to thee the Lover of the Song.
Indra, Lord of Bay Steeds, accept these fitting hymns, hymns which we have thought out for thee.

4 For thou, O Maghavan, art truthful, ne'er subdued and bringest many a Vṛtra low.
As such, O Mightiest Lord, Wielder of Thunder, send wealth hither to the worshipper.

5 O Indra, thou art far-renowned, impetuous, O Lord of Strength.
Alone thou slayest with the guardian of mankind resistless never-conquered foes.

6 As such we seek thee now, O Asura, thee most wise, craving thy bounty as our share.
Thy sheltering defence is like a mighty cloak. So may thy glories reach to us.

7 *Raw kine* ; cf. I. 62. 9; 180. 3; II. 40. 2; IV 3. 9; VI. 72. 4; 17. 6; 44. 24; VIII. 32. 25. *Thou madest Sūrya rise to heaven* : Sāyaṇa relates a legend that when the Paṇis had carried off the cows of the Aṅgirases and placed them in a mountain enveloped in darkness, Indra, at the prayer of the Ṛṣis, set the sun in heaven in order that he might see and recover their cattle. *Heat him as milk is heated* : this line is difficult. '(Priests) excite (Indra) with your praises as men heat the *Gharma* with *Sāman*-hymns.' —Wilson. *Gharma* means either the hot milk or other beverage offered in the Pravargya ceremony, or the vessel in which it is heated. *Great joy to him who loves the song* : or perhaps the meaning is, the Bṛhat-Sāman (one of the most important Sāma hymns, the first and second verses of R.V. VI. 46), is dear to him who loves song.

---

3 *Fitting hymns* : *yojanā* : See Wilson's Translation and note.

5 *The guardian of mankind* : Indra's thunderbolt with which he slays the demons of drought.

HYMN LXXX. *Indra.*

1. Down to the stream a maiden came, and found the Soma by the way.
Bearing it to her home she said, For Indra will I press thee out, for Śakra will I press thee out.

2 Thou roaming yonder, little man, beholding every house in turn,
Drink thou this Soma pressed with teeth, accompanied with grain and curds, with cake of meal and song of praise.

3 Fain would we learn to know thee well, nor yet can we attain to thee.
Still slowly and in gradual drops, O Indu, unto Indra flow.

4 Will he not help and work for us? Will he not make us wealthier ?
Shall we not, hostile to our lord, unite ourselves to Indra now ?

5 O Indra, cause to sprout again three places, these which I declare,—
My father's head, his cultured field, and this the part below my waist.

6 Make all of these grow crops of hair, you cultivated field of ours,
My body, and my father's head.

7 Cleansing Apālā, Indra ! thrice, thou gavest sunlike skin to her,
Drawn, Śatakratu ! through the hole of car, of wagon, and of yoke.

The Ṛṣi is Apālā of the family of Atri.

1 *A maiden* : Apālā.

2 *Little man* : *vīrakáḥ* : according to Sāyaṇa, hero. Indra is intended perhaps as Sūrya the Sun-God.

3 *Indu* : Soma.

4 *He* : Indra. *Hostile to our lord* : Apālā, it is said, was afflicted with a cutaneous disease and was consequently repudiated by her husband.

7 *Sunlike* : bright and clear. 'Sāyaṇa says that Indra dragged her through the wide hole of his chariot, the narrower hole of the cart and the small hole of the yoke, and she cast off three skins. The first skin became a hedgehog, the second an alligator, the third a chameleon. I suppose, with Prof. Aufrecht, that the hole or space of the chariot and cart represents the opening between the four wheels; the hole of the yoke seems to me to mean the opening through which the animal's head passed, corresponding to Homer's ἐξζυγλη II. 19. 406.'—Cowell.

For the legend from the Śāṭyāyana Brāhmaṇa, founded on the hints contained in this hymn and repeated by Sāyaṇa in his Commentary, see also Wilson's Translation, Vol. V.

Prof. Aufrecht has published the text and commentary of this hymn in *Indische Studien*, IV. p. 1 sqq. See M. Müller's Ṛgveda Saṁhitā, Vol. III., 2nd edition, p. 33 sqq.

HYMN LXXXI. *Indra.*

1. INVITE ye Indra with a song to drink your draught of Soma juice,
All-conquering Śatakratu, most munificent of all who live.

2 Lauded by many, much-invoked, leader of song, renowned of old :
His name is Indra, tell it forth.

3 Indra the Dancer be to us the giver of abundant strength :
May he, the mighty, bring it near.

4 Indra whose jaws are strong hath drunk of worshipping Sudakṣa's draught,
The Soma juice with barley mixt.

5 Call Indra loudly with your songs of praise to drink the Soma juice,
For this is what augments his strength.

6 When he hath drunk its gladdening drops, the God with vigour of a God
Hath far surpassed all things that are.

7 Thou speedest down to succour us this ever-conquering God of yours,
Him who is drawn to all our songs ;

8 The Warrior not to be restrained, the Soma-drinker ne'er o'erthrown,
The Chieftain of resistless might.

9 O Indra, send us riches, thou Omniscient, worthy of our praise :
Help us in the decisive fray.

10 Even thence, O Indra, come to us with food that gives a hundred powers,
With food that gives a thousand powers.

11 We sought the wisdom of the wise. Śakra, Kine-giver, Thunder-armed !
May we with steeds o'ercome in fight.

12 We make thee, Śatakratu, find enjoyment in the songs we sing,
Like cattle in the pasture lands.

13 For, Śatakratu, Thunder-armed, all that we craved, as men are wont,
All that we hoped, have we attained.

14 Those, Son of Strength, are come to thee who cherish wishes in their hearts :
O Indra, none excelleth thee.

15 So, Hero, guard us with thy care, with thy most liberal providence,
Speedy, and terrible to foes.

16 O Śatakratu Indra, now rejoice with that carouse of thine
Which is most splendid of them all ;

17 Even, Indra, that carouse which slays the Vṛtras best, most widely famed,
Best giver of thy power and might.

18 For that which is thy gift we know, true Soma-drinker, Thunder-armed,
Mighty One, amid all the folk.

19 For Indra, Lover of Carouse, loud be our songs about the jūice :
Let poets sing the song of praise.

20 We summon Indra to the draught, in whom all glories rest, in whom
The seven communities rejoice.

21 At the Trikadrukas the Gods span sacrifice that stirs the mind :
Let our songs aid and prosper it.

22 Let the drops pass within thee as the rivers flow into the sea :
O Indra, naught excelleth thee.

23 Thou, wakeful Hero, by thy might hast taken food of Soma juice,
Which, Indra, is within thee now.

24 O Indra, Vṛtra-slayer, let Soma be ready for thy maw,
The drops be ready for thy forms.

25 Now Śrutakaksa sings his song that cattle and the steed may come,
That Indra's very self may come.

26 Here, Indra, thou art ready by our Soma juices shed for thee,
Śakra, at hand that thou mayst give.

27 Even from far away our songs reach thee, O Caster of the Stone :
May we come very close to thee.

3 *The Dancer* : active in battle, dancer of the war dance. *Near* : *abhijñú* : or, up to our knees.

4 *Sudakṣa's draught* : offered by a Ṛṣi of that name.

7 According to Sāyaṇa this stanza is addressed by the *Yajamāna* or sacrificer to the *Stotar* or praising priest, and he gives an imperative sense to the indicative, thou speedest down : 'Bring hither.' —Wilson.

10 *Even thence* : from where thou art ; from heaven.

11 *Of the wise* : Indra. *Kine-giver* : *godare* : perhaps, 'burster open of the cow-stall;' 'cleaver of mountains.' —Wilson.

12 *Like cattle* : as the cowherd refreshes his cattle.—Sāyaṇa.

18 *Thy gift* : the wealth which thou givest. *Amid all the folk* : among all the worshippers who offer thee Soma.—Sāyaṇa.

20 *Seven communities* : *saptá saṁsádaḥ* : probably=all the folk, in stanza 18; 'the seven associated priests.'—Wilson.

21 *At the Trikadrukas* : See VIII. 13. 18, and note.

24 *Thy forms* : thy various bodies or splendours.—Sāyaṇa.

25 *Śrutakakṣa* : the Ṛṣi of the hymn.

28 For so thou art the hero's Friend, a Hero, too, art thou, and strong :
So may thine heart be won to us.

29 So hath the offering, wealthiest Lord, been paid by all the worshippers :
So dwell thou, Indra, even with me.

30 Be not thou like a slothful priest, O Lord of spoil and wealth : rejoice
In the pressed Soma blent with milk.

31 O Indra, let not ill designs surround us in the sunbeams' light :
This may we gain with thee for Friend.

32 With thee to help us, Indra, let us answer all our enemies :
For thou art ours and we are thine.

33 Indra, the poets and thy friends, faithful to thee, shall loudly sing
Thy praises as they follow thee.

HYMN LXXXII. *Indra.*

1. SŪRYA, thou mountest up to meet the Hero famous for his wealth,
Who hurls the bolt and works for man :

2 Him who with might of both his arms brake nine-and-ninety castles down,
Slew Vṛtra and smote Ahi dead.

3 This Indra is our gracious Friend. He sends us in a full broad stream
Riches in horses, kine, and corn.

4 Whatever, Vṛtra-slayer ! thou, Sūrya, hast risen upon to-day,
That, Indra, all is in thy power.

5 When, Mighty One, Lord of the brave, thou thinkest thus, I shall not die,
That thought of thine is true indeed.

6 Thou, Indra, goest unto all Soma libations shed for thee,
Both far away and near at hand.

7 We make this Indra very strong to strike the mighty Vṛtra dead :
A vigorous Hero shall he be.

8 Indra was made for giving, set, most mighty, o'er the joyous draught.
Bright, meet for Soma, famed in song.

9 By song as 'twere, the powerful bolt which none may parry was prepared :
Lofty, invincible he grew.

10 Indra, Song-lover, lauded, make even in the wilds fair ways for us,
Whenever, Maghavan, thou wilt.

11 Thou whose commandment and behest of sovran sway none disregards,
Neither audacious man nor God.

12 And both these Goddesses, Earth, Heaven, Lord of the beauteous helm ! revere
Thy might which no one may resist.

13 Thou in the black cows and the red and in the cows with spotted skin
This white milk hast deposited.

14 When in their terror all the Gods shrank from the Dragon's furious might,
Fear of the monster fell on them.

15 Then he was my Defender, then, Invincible, whose foe is not,
The Vṛtra-slayer showed his might.

16 Him your best Vṛtra-slayer, him the famous Champion of mankind
I urge to great munificence,

17 To come, Much-lauded ! Many-named ! with this same thought that longs for milk,
Whene'er the Soma juice is shed.

18 Much-honoured by libations, may the Vṛtra-slayer wake for us :
May Śakra listen to our prayers.

19 O Hero, with that aid dost thou delight us, with what succour bring
Riches to those who worship thee ?

20 With whose libation joys the Strong, the Hero with his team who quells
The foe, to drink the Soma juice ?

21 Rejoicing in thy spirit bring thousandfold opulence to us :
Enrich thy votary with gifts.

22 These juices with their wedded wives flow to enjoyment lovingly :

30 *Priest* : *brahmā* : Brahman or praying priest.

31 *In the sunbeams' light* : as Indra stands in the closest relationship to the Sun.

---

2 *Nine-and-ninety castles* : cloud-castles of the demon Śambara.

8 *Was made* : was created by Prajāpati.—Sāyaṇa.

12 *Lord of the beauteous helm* : or 'deity of the handsome jaw.'—Wilson.

13 *In the black cows* : cf I. 62. 9.

14 *The Dragon's furious might* : the fierce attack of the demon Ahi. *Of the monster* : or, of the wild beast, Ahi.

16 *Champion* : I join *prá* to *śárdham*, as suggested in the St. Petersburg Lexicon.

17 *To come* : that is, that thou, Indra, mayst come. This abrupt change of person is not uncommon in the Veda.

22 The *wedded wives*: of the Soma juices are said to be the two waters called *vasatīvaryaḥ* and *ekadhanāḥ*, used in the Soma ceremonies. *To enjoyment* : to be drunk by Indra. *To waters speeds the restless one* : or, with Grassmann, 'The lover of the waters speeds.' The exact meaning of *nicumpuṇáḥ* is uncertain, Yāska deriving it from *cam*, to eat, and Mahīdhara from *cup*, to creep or move slowly. The meaning of the sentence

To waters speeds the restless one.
23 Presented strengthening gifts have sent Indra away at sacrifice,
With might, unto the cleansing bath.
24 These two who share his feast, Bay Steeds with golden manes, shall bring him to
The banquet that is laid for him.
25 For thee, O Lord of Light, are shed these Soma-drops, and grass is strewn :
Bring Indra to his worshippers.
26 May Indra give thee skill, and lights of heaven, wealth to his votary
And priests who praise him : laud ye him.
27 O Śatakratu, wondrous strength and all our lauds I bring to thee :
Be gracious to thy worshippers.
28 Bring to us all things excellent, O Śatakratu, food and strength :
For, Indra, thou art kind to us.
29 O Śatakratu, bring to us all blessings, all felicity :
For, Indra, thou art kind to us.
30 Bearing the Soma juice we call, best Vṛtra-slayer, unto thee :
For, Indra, thou art kind to us.
31 Come, Lord of rapturous joys, to our libation with thy Bay Steeds, come
To our libation with thy Steeds.
32 Known as best Vṛtra-slayer erst, as Indra Śatakratu, come
With Bay Steeds to the juice we shed.
33 O Vṛtra-slayer, thou art he who drinks these drops of Soma : come
With Bay Steeds to the juice we shed.
34 May Indra give, to aid us, wealth handy that rules the Skilful Ones :
Yea, may the Strong give potent wealth.

is, according to the Scholiast, that, at the time of the concluding purificatory ceremony which is to atone for errors and omissions in the principal sacrifice, the stale Soma is thrown into the waters. See Cowell's note in Wilson's Translation.

23 *The cleansing bath* : the *avabhṛtha*, here, apparently, the bath or vessel in which the Soma plants were rinsed and purified.

34 *Handy* : *ṛbhúm. That rules the Skilful Ones* : *ṛbhukṣáṇam. The Strong* : *vājí.* These words are used as plays upon the names of the Ṛbhus, or as Grassmann says, the verse may have been taken from a hymn addressed to the Ṛbhus. 'May Indra bring to us the bounteous Ṛbhu Ṛbhukṣaṇa to partake of our sacrificial viands; may he, the mighty, bring the mighty (Vāja)'—Wilson. Cowell remarks : 'Ṛbhukṣaṇa was the eldest and Vāja the youngest of the three brothers. The Ṛbhus have a share in the evening libation between Prajāpati and Savitṛ, see Ait. Brāhm. iii. 30. This verse is addressed to the Ṛbhus in the evening libation on the ninth day of the Dvādaśāha ceremony (*ib.* v. 21).'

HYMN LXXXIII. *Maruts.*

1. The Cow, the famous Mother of the wealthy Maruts, pours her milk :
Both horses of the cars are yoked,—
2 She in whose bosom all the Gods, and Sun and Moon for men to see,
Maintain their everlasting Laws.
3 This all the pious sing to us, and sacred poets evermore :
The Maruts to the Soma-draught !
4 Here is the Soma ready pressed : of this the Maruts drink, of this
Self-luminous the Aśvins drink.
5 Of this, moreover, purified, set in three places, procreant,
Drink Varuṇa, Mitra, Aryaman.
6 And Indra, like the Herald Priest, desirous of the milky juice,
At early morn will quaff thereof.
7 When have the Princes gleamed and shone through waters as through troops of foes ?
When hasten they whose might is pure ?
8 What favour do I claim this day of you great Deities, you who are
Wondrously splendid in yourselves ?
9 I call, to drink the Soma, those Maruts who spread all realms of earth
And luminous regions of the sky.
10 You, even such, pure in your might, you, O ye Maruts, I invoke
From heaven to drink this Soma juice.
11 The Maruts, those who have sustained and propped the heavens and earth apart,
I call to drink this Soma juice.
12 That vigorous band of Maruts that abideth in the mountains, I
Invoke to drink this Soma juice.

HYMN LXXXIV. *Indra.*

1. Song-lover ! like a charioteer come songs to thee when Soma flows.
O Indra, they have called to thee as mother-kine unto their calves.

1 *The Cow* : Pṛśni.

2 *In whose bosom* : 'in whose presence.'—Wilson.

3 *The Maruts* : are to be invoked, understood.

5 *Set in three places* : first, in a trough ; then in a straining cloth ; then in a third trough or vessel called *Pūtabhṛt. Procreant* : granting progeny to the worshipper.

6 *The Herald Priest* : Agni.

1 *Like a charioteer* : straight and swift to their object.

2 Bright juices hitherward have sped thee, Indra, Lover of the Song.
Drink, Indra, of this flowing sap : in every house 'tis set for thee.

3 Drink Soma to inspirit thee, juice, Indra, which the Falcon brought :
For thou art King and Sovran Lord of all the families of men.

4 O Indra, hear Tiraścī's call, the call of him who serveth thee.
Satisfy him with wealth of kine and valiant offspring : Great art thou.

5 For he, O Indra, hath produced for thee the newest gladdening song,
A hymn that springs from careful thought, ancient, and full of sacred truth.

6 That Indra will we laud whom songs and hymns of praise have magnified.
Striving to win, we celebrate his many deeds of hero might.

7 Come now and let us glorify pure Indra with pure Sāma hymns.
Let the pure milky draught delight him strengthened by pure songs of praise.

8 O Indra, come thou pure to us, with pure assistance, pure thyself.
Pure, send thou riches down to us, and, meet for Soma, pure, be glad.

9 O Indra, pure, vouchsafe us wealth, and, pure, enrich the worshipper.
Pure, thou dost strike the Vṛtras dead, and strivest, pure, to win the spoil.

HYMN LXXXV. *Indra.*

1. For him the Mornings made their courses longer, and Nights with pleasant voices spake to Indra.
For him the Floods stood still, the Seven Mothers, Streams easy for the heroes to pass over.

2 The Darter penetrated, though in trouble, thrice-seven close-pressed ridges of the mountains.
Neither might God nor mortal man accomplish what the Strong Hero wrought in full-grown vigour.

3 The mightiest force is Indra's bolt of iron when firmly grasped in both the arms of Indra.
His head and mouth have powers that pass all others, and all his people hasten near to listen.

4 I count thee as the Holiest of the Holy, the caster-down of what hath ne'er been shaken.
I count thee as the Banner of the heroes, I count thee as the Chief of all men living.

5 What time, O Indra, in thine arms thou tookest thy wildly rushing bolt to slay the Dragon,
The mountains roared, the cattle loudly bellowed, the Brāhmans with their hymns drew nigh to Indra.

6 Let us praise him who made these worlds and creatures, all things that after him sprang into being.
May we win Mitra with our songs, and Indra, and wait upon our Lord with adoration.

7 Flying in terror from the snort of Vṛtra, all Deities who were thy friends forsook thee.
So, Indra, be thy friendship with the Maruts : in all these battles thou shalt be the victor.

8 Thrice-sixty Maruts, waxing strong, were with thee, like piles of beaming light, worthy of worship.
We come to thee : grant us a happy portion. Let us adore thy might with this oblation.

9 A sharpened weapon is the host of Maruts. Who, Indra, dares withstand thy bolt of thunder?

3 *Which the Falcon brought* : See I. 80. 2, and 93. 6.

5 *Newest......ancient* : recent in form and expression, but ancient in substance. See Muir, *O. S. Texts*, III. 238, 239.

7 *Pure Indra with pure Sāma hymns* : according to Sāyaṇa, 'Indra, purified with pure Sāma-hymns,' from the pollution he had incurred by killing the Brāhman Vṛtra. See Wilson's Translation, note.

---

1 *The heroes* : perhaps Turvaśa and Yadu.—Ludwig.

2 *The Darter* : of the thunderbolt ; Indra. *Though in trouble* : because he had none to aid him What the *thrice-seven close-pressed ridges of the mountains* are, is uncertain. See Wilson's Translation, note. Ludwig thinks that the battle of the Sun with the demons of winter may be meant.

3 *To listen* : to the commands which issue from his mouth.

5 *Wildly rushing* : this is M. Müller's translation of *madacyutam*. It might be rendered also 'sped in thy rapturous joy.' 'Rauschbeschleunigten '—Ludwig. *The Dragon* : Ahi.

7 *With the Maruts* : as they alone stood by him in the conflict.

8 *Thrice-sixty* : or sixty-three, according to Sāyaṇa, nine companies consisting of seven each. See Cowell's note in Wilson's Translation. *Like piles of beaming light* : 'like cows gathered together.'—Wilson; 'like morning stars.'—Grassmann. I have followed Ludwig.

Weaponless are the Asuras, the godless : scatter them with thy wheel, Impetuous Hero.

10 To him the Strong and Mighty, most auspicious, send up the beauteous hymn for sake of cattle.
Lay on his body many songs for Indra invoked with song, for will not he regard them ?

11 To him, the Mighty, who accepts laudation, send forth thy thought as by a boat o'er rivers,
Stir with thy hymn the body of the Famous and Dearest One, for will not he regard it ?

12 Serve him with gifts of thine which Indra welcomes : praise with fair praise, invite him with thine homage.
Draw near, O singer, and refrain from outcry. Make thy voice heard, for will not he regard it ?

13 The Black Drop sank in Aṁśumatī's bosom, advancing with ten thousand round about it.
Indra with might longed for it as it panted : the hero-hearted laid aside his weapons.

14 I saw the Drop in the far distance moving, on the slope bank of Aṁśumatī's river,
Like a black cloud that sank into the water. Heroes, I send you forth. Go, fight in battle.

15 And then the Drop in Aṁśumatī's bosom, splendid with light, assumed its proper body ;
And Indra, with Bṛhaspati to aid him, conquered the godless tribes that came against him.

16 Then, at thy birth, thou wast the foeman, Indra, of those the seven who ne'er had met a rival.
The hidden Pair, the Heaven and Earth, thou foundest, and to the mighty worlds thou gavest pleasure.

17 So, Thunder-armed ! thou with thy bolt of thunder didst boldly smite that power which none might equal ;
With weapons broughtest low the might of Śuṣṇa, and, Indra, foundest by thy strength the cattle.

18 Then wast thou, Chieftain of all living mortals, the very mighty slayer of the Vṛtras.
Then didst thou set the obstructed rivers flowing, and win the floods that were enthralled by Dāsas.

19 Most wise is he, rejoicing in libations, splendid as day, resistless in his anger.
He only doth great deeds, the only Hero, sole Vṛtra-slayer he, with none beside him.

20 Indra is Vṛtra's slayer, man's sustainer : he must be called ; with fair praise let us call him.
Maghavan is our Helper, our Protector, giver of spoil and wealth to make us famous.

21 This Indra, Vṛtra-slayer, this Ṛbhukṣan, even at his birth, was meet for invocation.
Doer of many deeds for man's advantage, like Soma quaffed, for friends we must invoke him.

9 *With thy wheel* : or discus, a sharp-edged quoit used as a weapon of war.

12 *Draw near, O singer, and refrain from outcry* : 'O priest, adorn thyself grieve not (for poverty).'—Wilson.

13 *The Black Drop*: the darkened Moon. *Aṁśumatī* : a mystical river of the air into which the Moon dips to recover its vanished light. *Ten thousand* : probably, demons of darkness ; the numerals are without a substantive. *As it panted* : while striving against its assailants. *Laid aside his weapons* : after conquering the demons and restoring the darkened Moon.

14 Indra addresses the Maruts.

Sāyaṇa explains stanzas 13—15 differently, in accordance with a legend which was probably suggested by this passage. He takes *drapsáḥ kṛṣṇáḥ*, black drop, to mean 'the swift moving Kṛṣṇaḥ,' an Asura or demon who with ten thousand of his kind had occupied the banks of the river Aṁśumatī, which, he says, is the Yamunā or Jumna, and was there defeated by Indra, Bṛhaspati, and the Maruts. See Cowell's note in Wilson's Translation.

16 *The seven* : Kṛṣṇa, Vṛtra, Namuci, Śambara, and others.'—Sāyaṇa.

21 *Ṛbhukṣan* : or, Lord of Ṛbhus.

HYMN LXXXVI. *Indra.*

1. O INDRA, Lord of Light, what joys thou broughtest from the Asuras,
Prosper therewith, O Maghavan, him who lauds that deed, and those whose grass is trimmed for thee.

2 The unwasting share of steeds and kine which, Indra, thou hast fast secured,
Grant to the worshipper who presses Soma and gives guerdon, not unto the churl.

1 *Joys* : riches.—Sāyaṇa. *From the Asuras* : from the powerful Rākṣasas.—Sāyaṇa.

2 *Gives guerdon* : liberally rewards the priests.

3 The riteless, godless man who sleeps, O Indra, his unbroken sleep,—
May he by following his own devices die. Hide from him wealth that nourishes.

4 Whether, O Śakra, thou be far, or, Vṛtra-slayer, near at hand,
Thence by heaven-reaching songs he who hath pressed the juice invites thee with thy long-maned Steeds.

5 Whether thou art in heaven's bright sphere, or in the basin of the sea;
Whether, chief Vṛtra-slayer, in some place on earth, or in the firmament, approach.

6 Thou Soma-drinker, Lord of Strength, beside our flowing Soma juice
Delight us with thy bounty rich in pleasantness, O Indra, with abundant wealth.

7 O Indra, turn us not away: be the companion of our feast.
For thou art our protection, yea, thou art our kin: O Indra, turn us not away.

8 Sit down with us, O Indra, sit beside the juice to drink the meath.
Show forth great favour to the singer, Maghavan; Indra, with us, beside the juice.

9 O Caster of the Stone, nor Gods nor mortals have attained to thee.
Thou in thy might surpassest all that hath been made: the Gods have not attained to thee.

10 Of one accord they made and formed for kingship Indra, the Hero who in all encounters overcometh,
Most eminent for power, destroyer in the conflict, fierce and exceeding strong, stalwart and full of vigour.

11 Bards joined in song to Indra so that he might drink the Soma juice,
The Lord of Light, that he whose laws stand fast might aid with power and with the help he gives.

12 The holy sages form a ring, looking and singing to the Ram.
Inciters, full of vigour, not to be deceived, are with the chanters, nigh to hear.

13 Loudly I call that Indra, Maghavan the Mighty, who evermore possesses power, ever resistless.
Holy, most liberal, may he lead us on to riches, and, Thunder-armed, make all our pathways pleasant for us.

14 Thou knowest well, O Śakra, thou Most Potent, with thy strength, Indra, to destroy these castles.
Before thee, Thunder-armed! all beings tremble: the heavens and earth before thee shake with terror,

15 May thy truth, Indra, Wondrous Hero! be my guard: bear me o'er much woe, Thunderer! as over floods.
When, Indra, wilt thou honour us with opulence, all-nourishing and much-to-be-desired, O King?

12 *The Ram*: Indra See I. 51. 1. and VIII 2. 40. *Inciters*: apparently, the Gods themselves.

HYMN LXXXVII. *Indra.*

1. To Indra sing a Sāma hymn, a lofty song to Lofty Sage,
To him who guards the Law, inspired, and fain for praise.

2 Thou, Indra, art the Conqueror: thou gavest splendour to the Sun.
Maker of all things, thou art Mighty and All-God.

3 Radiant with light thou wentest to the sky, the luminous realm of heaven.
The Deities, Indra strove to win thee for their Friend.

4 Come unto us, O Indra, dear, still conquering, unconcealable,
Vast as a mountain spread on all sides, Lord of Heaven.

5 O truthful Soma-drinker, thou art mightier than both the worlds.
Thou strengthenest him who pours libation, Lord of Heaven.

6 For thou art he, O Indra, who stormeth all castles of the foe,
Slayer of Dasyus, man's Supporter, Lord of Heaven.

7 Now have we, Indra, Friend of Song, sent our great wishes forth to thee,
Coming like floods that follow floods.

8 As rivers swell the ocean, so, Hero, our prayers increase thy might,
Though of thyself, O Thunderer, waxing day by day.

9 With holy song they bind to the broad wide-yoked car the Bay Steeds of the rapid God,
Bearers of Indra, yoked by word.

2 *All-God*: *viśvádevaḥ*: 'the lord of all the gods.'—Wilson.

4 *Unconcealable*: as the Sun-God.

7 *Coming like floods*: in crowds. But the half-line is very obscure. 'As men going by water (splash their friends) with handfuls.'—Wilson.

10 O Indra, bring great strength to us, bring valour, Śatakratu, thou most active, bring
A hero conquering in war.

11 For, gracious Śatakratu, thou hast ever been a Mother and a Sire to us,
So now for bliss we pray to thee.

12 To thee, Strong, Much-invoked, who showest forth thy strength, O Śatakratu, do I speak :
So grant thou us heroic strength.

HYMN LXXXVIII. *Indra.*

1. O THUNDERER, zealous worshippers gave thee drink this time yesterday.
So, Indra, listen here to those who bring the laud : come near unto our dwelling-place.

2 Lord of Bay Steeds, fair-helmed, rejoice thee : this we crave. Here the disposers wait on thee.
Thy loftiest glories claim our lauds beside the juice, O Indra, Lover of the Song.

3 Turning, as 'twere, to meet the Sun, enjoy from Indra all good things.
When he who will be born is born with power we look to treasures as our heritage.

4 Praise him who sends us wealth, whose bounties injure none : good are the gifts which Indra grants.
He is not worth with one who satisfies his wish : he turns his mind to giving boons.

5 Thou in thy battles, Indra, art subduer of all hostile bands.
Father art thou, all-conquering, cancelling the curse, thou victor of the vanquisher.

6 The Earth and Heaven clung close to thy victorious might, as to their calf two mother-cows.
When thou attackest Vṛtra all the hostile bands shrink and faint, Indra, at thy wrath.

7 Bring to your aid the Eternal One, who shoots and none may shoot at him,
Inciter, swift, victorious, best of Charioteers. Tugrya's unvanquished Strengthener ;

8 Arranger of things unarranged, e'en Śatakratu, source of might,
Indra, the Friend of all, for succour we invoke, Guardian of treasure, sending wealth.

HYMN LXXXIX *Indra. Vāk.*

1. I MOVE before thee here present in person, and all the Deities follow behind me.
When, Indra, thou securest me my portion, with me thou shalt perform heroic actions.

2 The food of meath in foremost place I give thee, thy Soma shall be pressed, thy share appointed.
Thou on my right shalt be my friend and comrade : then shall we two smite dead full many a foeman.

3 Striving for strength bring forth a laud to Indra, a truthful hymn if he in truth existeth.
One and another say, There is no Indra. Who hath beheld him ? Whom then shall we honour ?

4 Here am I, look upon me here, O singer. All that existeth I surpass in greatness.
The Holy Law's commandments make me mighty. Rending with strength I rend the worlds asunder.

5 When the Law's lovers mounted and approached me as I sate lone upon the dear sky's summit.
Then spake my spirit to the heart within me, My friends have cried unto me with their children.

6 All these thy deeds must be declared at Soma-feasts, wrought, Indra, Bounteous Lord, for him who sheds the juice,

---

10 *A hero* : a heroic son.

---

2 *Disposers* : the priests who order religious ceremonies.

3 This stanza is difficult and obscure. Mahīdhara's explanation is : 'The gathering (rays) proceeding to the sun distribute all Indra's treasures (to living beings, sc. as rain, corn, etc.) ; may we too by our power leave those treasures as an inheritance to him who has been or will be born.' See Cowell's note in Wilson's Translation.

6 *As to their calf* : or the translation may be, as sire and mother to their child.

7 *Tugrya* is Bhujyu, the son of Tugra. See Vol. I., Index.

8 *Arranger of things unarranged* : 'the consecrator of others but himself consecrated by none.'—Wilson.

---

1 This stanza is spoken by Agni.

2 Indra answers.

3 Addressed to the priests. *One and another* : *néma* : but according to Sāyaṇa, Nema is the name of the Ṛṣi. Nema says, "verily there is no Indra."—Wilson.

4 Indra speaks this and the following stanza.

5 *The Law's lovers* : the priests who in sacrifice ascend to Indra. According to Hillebrandt (*V. Mythologie*, I. 354), the Maruts; *śiśumantaḥ* meaning not 'with their children,' but 'with the Infant (Soma).'

When thou didst open wealth heaped up by many, brought from far away to Śarabha, the Ṛṣi's kin.

7 Now run ye forth your several ways : he is not here who kept you back.
For hath not Indra sunk his bolt deep down in Vṛtra's vital part ?

8 On-rushing with the speed of thought within the iron fort he pressed :
The Falcon went to heaven and brought the Soma to the Thunderer.

9 Deep in the ocean lies the bolt with waters compassed round about,
And in continuous onward flow the floods their tribute bring to it.

10 When, uttering words which no one comprehended, Vāk, Queen of Gods, the Gladdener, was seated,
The heaven's four regions drew forth drink and vigour : now whither hath her noblest portion vanished ?

11 The Deities generated Vāk the Goddess, and animals of every figure speak her.
May she, the Gladdener, yielding food and vigour, the Milch-cow Vāk, approach us meetly lauded.

12 Step forth with wider stride, my comrade Viṣṇu ; make room, Dyaus, for the leaping of the lightning.
Let us slay Vṛtra, let us free the rivers : let them flow loosed at the command of Indra.

HYMN XC. *Various.*

1. YEA, specially that mortal man hath toiled for service of the Gods,

6 The priest addresses Indra. *Śarabha* : a Ṛṣi of that name.—Sāyaṇa. The original hymn appears to end with this stanza.

7 Addressed to the waters of heaven after Indra's battle with Vṛtra.

8 *He* : the Falcon. *The iron fort* : the stronghold or cloud in which the Soma or ambrosial rain was imprisoned. Cf. IV. 27. 2.

9 *In the ocean* : as produced naturally in the sea of air.

10 This and the following stanza have no apparent connexion with what precedes. *Vāk* : or Vāc, vox, voice, or Speech personified. Her unintelligible words are the thunder. *Her noblest portion* : according to Sāyaṇa, the rain which follows thunder. Or the thunder itself may be intended. See Cowell's note in Wilson's Translation. *Was seated* : at the sacrifice offered to her.

11 *Speak her* : articulately-speaking men and lower animals all derive their voices from her.

12 This stanza, which is out of place here, is spoken by Indra when he is about to attack Vṛtra. See IV. 18. 11.

Who quickly hath brought near Mitra and Varuṇa to share his sacrificial gifts.

2 Supreme in sovran power, far-sighted, Chiefs and Kings, most swift to hear from far away,
Both, wondrously, set them in motion as with arms, in company with Sūrya's beams.

3 The rapid messenger who runs before you, Mitra-Varuṇa, with iron head, swift to the draught,

4 He whom no man may question, none may summon back, who stands not still for colloquy,—
From hostile clash with him keep ye us safe this day : keep us in safety with your arms.

5 To Aryaman and Mitra sing a reverent song, O pious one,
A pleasant hymn that shall protect to Varuṇa : sing forth a laud unto the Kings.

6 The true, Red Treasure they have sent, one only Son born of the Three.
They, the Immortal Ones, never deceived, survey the families of mortal men.

7 My songs are lifted up, and acts most splendid are to be performed.
Come hither, ye Nāsatyas, with accordant mind, to meet and to enjoy my gifts.

8 Lords of great wealth, when we invoke your bounty which no demon checks,
Both of you, furthering our eastward-offered praise, come, Chiefs whom Jamadagni lauds !

9 Come, Vāyu, drawn by fair hymns, to our sacrifice that reaches heaven.
Poured on the middle of the straining-cloth, and cooked, this bright drink hath been offered thee.

10 He comes by straightest paths, as ministering Priest, to taste the sacrificial gifts.
Then, Lord of harnessed teams ! drink of the twofold draught, bright Soma mingled with the milk.

11 Verily, Sūrya, thou art great ; truly, Āditya, thou art great.
As thou art great indeed, thy greatness is admired : yea, verily, thou, God, art great.

3 *The rapid messenger* : the lightning, as one of the forms of Agni.

6 *The true, Red Treasure* : the Sun. *The Three* : heaven, mid-air, and earth.

12 Yea, Sūrya, thou art great in fame : thou evermore, O God, art great.
Thou by thy greatness art the Gods' High Priest, divine, far-spread unconquerable light.

13 She yonder, bending lowly down, clothed in red hues and rich in rays,
Is seen, advancing as it were with various tints, amid the ten surrounding arms.

14 Past and gone are three mortal generations : the fourth and last into the Sun hath entered.
He mid the worlds his lofty place hath taken. Into green plants is gone the Purifying.

15 The Rudras' Mother, Daughter of the Vasus, centre of nectar, the Ādityas' Sister—
To folk who understand will I proclaim it—injure not Aditi, the Cow, the sinless.

16 Weak-minded men have as a cow adopted me who came hither from the Gods, a Goddess,
Who, skilled in eloquence, her voice uplifteth, who standeth near at hand with all devotions.

HYMN XCI. *Agni.*

1. LORD of the house, Sage, ever young, high power of life, O Agni, God,
Thou givest to thy worshipper.

2 So with our song that prays and serves, attentive, Lord of spreading light,
Agni, bring hitherward the Gods.

3 For, Ever-Youthful One, with thee, best Furtherer, as our ally,
We overcome, to win the spoil.

4 As Aurva Bhṛgu used, as Apnavāna used, I call the pure
Agni who clothes him with the sea.

5 I call the Sage who sounds like wind, the Might that like Parjanya roars,
Agni who clothes him with the sea.

6 As Savitar's productive Power, as him who sends down bliss, I call
Agni who clothes him with the sea.

7 Hither, for powerful kinship, I call Agni, him who prospers you,
Most frequent at our solemn rites ;

8 That through this famed One's power, he may stand by us even as Tvaṣṭar comes
Unto the forms that must be shaped.

9 This Agni is the Lord supreme above all glories mid the Gods :
May he come nigh to us with strength.

10 Here praise ye him the most renowned of all the ministering Priests,
Agni, the Chief at sacrifice ;

11 Piercing, with purifying flame, enkindled in our homes, most high,
Swiftest to hear from far away.

12 Sage, laud the Mighty One who wins the spoil of victory like a steed,
And, Mitra-like, unites the folk.

13 Still turning to their aim in thee, the oblation-bearer's sister hymns
Have come to thee before the wind.

14 The waters find their place in him, for whom the threefold sacred grass
Is spread unbound, unlimited.

15 The station of the Bounteous God hath, through his aid which none impair,
A pleasant aspect like the Sun.

13 *She yonder* : Uṣas or Dawn. *The ten surrounding arms* : the ten regions of the world.

14 *Three mortal generations* : according to the legend, Prajāpati produced in succession three kinds of creatures who all died. The fourth generation lived and enjoyed the light and warmth of the Sun. See Cowell's note in Wilson's Translation, or *Śatapatha-Brāhmaṇa*, II. 5. 1. *Into green plants* : Sāyaṇa explains *harítaḥ* as the quarters of the sky, and *pávamānaḥ* (the Purifying) as Vāyu or the Wind. Grassmann takes *pávamānaḥ* to be the Soma, and *harítaḥ* to be the horses of the Sun. I have followed Ludwig's interpretation; but I find the stanza almost unintelligible.

15 *Centre of nectar* : or, of amṛta, or immortality, or the world of the immortal Gods. *The cow* ; the earthly cow, as the type of Aditi or universal Nature, must not be offended. The stanza is spoken by the priest who has received the cow as his reward.

16 *Weak-minded men* : 'Men are too feeble in their intellect to comprehend me in my true form and my real nature : they can only understand my worth in the shape of a cow.'—See Ludwig, *R. V.*, IV. 245, 246.

The concluding stanza is spoken by Aditi as a cow.

4 *Aurva Bhṛgu* : or, perhaps, Aurva, and Bhṛgu. The ancient Ṛṣi Aurva is said to have been the grandson of Bhṛgu. *Apnavāna* : another ancient Ṛṣi, mentioned in connexion with the Bhṛgus and the earliest worshipper of Agni, in Book IV. 7. 1.

12 *Sage* : the priest is addressed.

13 *Before the wind* : or, in front of the wind, with which the flame is fanned.

14 'The waters rest in Agni, who abides as lightning in the firmament.'—Note in Wilson's Translation which I have followed closely in this stanza.

15 Or, a comma being substituted for the full stop at the end of the preceding stanza, and *padám* (station) taken as in apposition to *padám* (place) in 14 : 'The station of the bounteous : he hath, through his aid which none impair, A pleasant aspect like the Sun.'

16 Blazing with splendour, Agni, God, through pious gifts of sacred oil,
Bring thou the Gods and worship them.

17 The Gods as mothers brought thee forth, the Immortal Sage, O Aṅgiras,
The bearer of our gifts to heaven.

18 Wise Agni, Gods established thee, the Seer, noblest messenger,
As bearer of our sacred gifts.

19 No cow have I to call mine own, no axe at hand wherewith to work,
Yet what is here I bring to thee.

20 O Agni, whatsoever be the fuel that we lay for thee,
Be pleased therewith, Most Youthful God.

21 That which the white-ant eats away, that over which the emmet crawls—
May all of this be oil to thee.

22 When he enkindles Agni, man should with his heart attend the song :
I with the priests have kindled him.

HYMN XCII. *Agni*

1. THAT noblest Furtherer hath appeared, to whom men bring their holy works.
Our songs of praise have risen aloft to Agni who was born to give the Ārya strength.

2 Agni of Divodāsa turned, as 'twere in majesty, to the Gods.
Onward he sped along the mother earth, and took his station in the height of heaven.

3 Him before whom the people shrink when he performs his glorious deeds,
Him who wins thousands at the worship of the Gods, himself, that Agni, serve with songs.

4 The mortal man whom thou wouldst lead to opulence, O Vasu, he who brings thee gifts.
He, Agni, wins himself a hero singing lauds, yea, one who feeds a thousand men.

5 He with the steed wins spoil even in the fenced fort, and gains imperishable fame.
In thee, O Lord of wealth, continually we lay all precious offerings to the Gods.

6 To him who dealeth out all wealth, who is the cheerful Priest of men,
To him, like the first vessels filled with savoury juice, to Agni go the songs of praise.

7 Votaries, richly-gifted, deck him with their songs, even as the steed who draws the car.
On both, Strong Lord of men ! on child and grandson pour the bounties which our nobles give.

8 Sing forth to him, the Holy, most munificent, sublime with his refulgent glow,
To Agni, ye Upastutas.

9 Worshipped with gifts, enkindled, splendid, Maghavan shall win himself heroic fame.
And will not his most newly shown benevolence come to us with abundant strength ?

10 Priest, presser of the juice ! praise now the dearest Guest of all our friends,
Agni, the driver of the cars.

11 Who, finder-out of treasures open and concealed, bringeth them hither, Holy One ;
Whose waves, as in a cataract, are hard to pass, when he, through song, would win him strength.

12 Let not the noble Guest, Agni, be wroth with us : by many a man his praise is sung,
Good Herald, skilled in sacrifice.

19 As Prayoga, the Ṛṣi of the hymn, has no cow and no axe to cut wood, Agni is asked in this and the two following stanzas to dispense with the customary offerings of milk, and to accept such wood as the worshipper can pick up.

22 *With his heart* : a devout spirit will compensate the want of milk and properly prepared fuel.

---

2 *Of Divodāsa* : whom Divodāsa especially worshipped and claimed as his tutelary God. The stanza is obscure, and my translation founded on von Roth's interpretation of *prá vi vāvṛte*, which has been accepted by Cowell, must be regarded as conjectural. See Wilson's Translation and note.

4 *A hero* : a brave son.

7 The second line is obscure. 'Graceful lord of men, grant wealth to us rich in children and grandchildren.' —Wilson.

8 *Upastutas* : singers so named after the Ṛṣi Upastuta. See I. 36. 10.

10 *Priest, presser of the juice* : *āsāva* : *stotaḥ*—Sāyaṇa. 'Singer of hymns'—Wilson.

11 *Whose waves* : billowy floods of flame rushing on like waters falling down a precipice 'Whose (flames), as he hastens to wage the battle by means of our sacred rite, are hard to be passed through as waves rushing down a declivity.'—Wilson. See also Pischel, *Vedische Studien*, I. p. 184. *Through song* : inspirited and strengthened by our hymns.

13 O Vasu, Agni, let not them be harmed who come in any way with lauds to thee.
Even the lowly, skilled in rites, with offered gifts, seeketh thee for the envoy's task.

14 Friend of the Maruts, Agni, come with Rudras to the Soma-draught,
To Sobhari's fair song of praise, and be thou joyful in the light.

13 *For the envoy's task* : to bear his oblations to the Gods.

VĀLAKHILYA

(Book VIII. Hymns 49—59. *M. Müller.*)

HYMN I. *Indra.*

1. To you will I sing Indra's praise who gives good gifts as well we know ;
The praise of Maghavan who, rich in treasure, aids his singers with wealth thousandfold.

2 As with a hundred hosts, he rushes boldly on, and for the offerer slays his foes.
As from a mountain flow the water-brooks, thus flow his gifts who feedeth many a one.

3 The drops effused, the gladdening draughts, O Indra, Lover of the Song,
As waters seek the lake where they are wont to rest, fill thee, for bounty, Thunderer.

4 The matchless draught that strengthens and gives eloquence, the sweetest of the meath drink thou,
That in thy joy thou mayst scatter thy gifts o'er us, plenteously, even as the dust.

5 Come quickly to our laud, urged on by Soma-pressers like a horse—
Laud, Godlike Indra, which milch-kine make sweet for thee : with Kaṇva's sons are gifts for thee.

6 With homage have we sought thee as a Hero, strong, preëminent, with unfailing wealth.
O Thunderer, as a plenteous spring pours forth its stream, so,
Indra, flow our songs to thee.

7 If now thou art at sacrifice, or if thou art upon the earth,
Come thence, high-thoughted ! to our sacrifice with the Swift, come, Mighty with the Mighty Ones.

See Book VIII., Hymn XLIX., note. Professor Cowell's version of these eleven hymns will be found in Appendix I. of Wilson's Translation, Vol. V. I am indebted to him for some improvements on the version which I had previously prepared.

8 The active, fleet-foot, tawny Coursers that are thine are swift to victory, like the Wind,
Wherewith thou goest round to visit Manus' seed, wherewith all heaven is visible.

9 Indra, from thee so great we crave prosperity in wealth of kine,
As, Maghavan, thou favouredst Medhyātithi, and, in the fight, Nīpātithi.

10 As, Maghavan, to Kaṇva, Trasadasyu, and to Paktha and Daśavraja ;
As, Indra, to Gośarya and Ṛjiśvan, thou vouchsafedst wealth in kine and gold.

HYMN II. *Indra.*

1. Śakra I praise, to win his aid, far-famed, exceeding bountiful,
Who gives, as 'twere in thousands, precious wealth to him who sheds the juice and worships him.

2 Arrows with hundred points, unconquerable, are this Indra's mighty arms in war.
He streams on liberal worshippers like a hill with springs, when juices poured have gladdened him.

3 What time the flowing Soma-drops have gladdened with their taste the Friend,
Like water, gracious Lord ! were my libations made, like milch-kine to the worshipper.

4 To him the peerless, who is calling you to give you aid, forth flow the drops of pleasant meath.
The Soma-drops which call on thee, O gracious Lord, have brought thee to our hymn of praise.

5 He rushes hurrying like a steed to Soma that adorns our rite,

2 *As with a hundred hosts* : 'like a weapon with a hundred edges.'—Cowell.

4 *That...gives eloquence* : *vivákṣaṇam* from *vac* ; 'swelling,' from *vakṣ=ukṣ*.—von Roth. and Cowell. *Plenteously. even as the dust*: the meaning of the text is obscure. The St. Petersburg Lexicon takes *dhṛṣád=dṛṣad*, the nether millstone : 'just as the mill-stone pours out meal.—Cowell.

7 *The Swift* and *the Mighty Ones*, are Indra's horses.

9 *Medhyātithi* : a Ṛṣi whose name has frequently occurred. *Nīpātithi* : mentioned only here and Vālakhilya Hymn III.

10 *Trasadasyu* : See. Vol. I., Index. *Paktha* : a favourite of the Aśvins. See VIII. 22. 10. *Daśavraja* : See VIII. 8. 20. *Gośarya* : See VIII. 8. 20. *Ṛjiśvan* : See Vol. I., Index.

Which hymns make sweet to thee, lover of pleasant food. The call to Paura thou dost love.

6 Praise the strong, grasping Hero, winner of the spoil, ruling supreme o'er mighty wealth.
Like a full spring, O Thunderer, from thy store hast thou poured on the worshipper evermore.

7 Now whether thou be far away, or in the heavens, or on the earth,
O Indra, mighty-thoughted, harnessing thy Bays, come Lofty with the Lofty Ones.

8 The Bays who draw thy chariot, Steeds who injure none, surpass the wind's impetuous strength—
With whom thou silencest the enemy of man, with whom thou goest round the sky.

9 O gracious Hero, may we learn anew to know thee as thou art :
As in decisive fight thou holpest Etaśa, or Vaśa 'gainst Daśavraja,

10 As, Maghavan, to Kaṇva at the sacred feast, to Dīrghanītha thine home-friend,
As to Gośarya thou, Stone-darter, gavest wealth, give me a gold-bright stall of kine.

HYMN III. *Indra.*

1. As with Manu Sāmvaraṇi, Indra, thou drankest Soma juice,
And, Maghavan, with Nīpātithi, Medhyātithi, with Puṣṭigu and Śruṣṭigu,—

2 The son of Pṛṣadvāna was Praskaṇva's host, who lay decrepit and forlorn.
Aided by thee the Ṛṣi Dasyave-vṛka strove to obtain thousands of kine.

3 Call hither with thy newest song Indra who lacks not hymns of praise,
Him who observes and knows, inspirer of the sage, him who seems eager to enjoy.

4 He unto whom they sang the seven-headed hymn, three-parted, in the loftiest place,
He sent his thunder down on all these living things, and so displayed heroic might.

5 We invocate that Indra who bestoweth precious things on us.
Now do we know his newest favour ; may we gain a stable that is full of kine.

6 He whom thou aidest, gracious Lord, to give again, obtains great wealth to nourish him.
We with our Soma ready, Lover of the Song ! call, Indra Maghavan, on thee.

7 Ne'er art thou fruitless, Indra ; ne'er dost thou desert the worshipper :
But now, O Maghavan, thy bounty as a God is poured forth ever more and more.

8 He who hath overtaken Kṛvi with his might, and silenced Śuṣṇa with deathbolts,—
When he supported yonder heaven and spread it out, then first the son of earth was born.

9 Good Lord of wealth is he to whom all Āryas, Dāsas here belong.
Directly unto thee, the pious Ruśama Pavīru, is that wealth brought nigh.

10 In zealous haste the singers have sung forth a song distilling oil and rich in sweets.
Riches have spread among us and heroic strength, with us are flowing Soma-drops.

HYMN IV. *Indra.*

1. As, Śakra, thou with Manu called Vivasvān drankest Soma juice,
As, Indra, thou didst love the hymn by

5 *The Call to Paura* : the invitation to Paura's house. According to von Roth *paurá* means the filler, the satisfier ; 'thou approvest the summons to the satisfying beverage.'—Cowell. See V. 74. 4.

7 This stanza is almost a repetition of stanza 7 of Hymn I.

9 *Etaśa* : See I. 61. 15. *Vaśa* : mentioned as a favourite of the Aśvins in X. 40. 7. *Daśavraja* : said in stanza 10 of Hymn I, to have been helped by Indra.

10 *Dīrghanītha* : Ludwig takes this word to be an adjective qualifying *médhe adhvaré*, 'at the sacrificial feast of long duration.' *A gold-bright stall of kine* : according to Ludwig, a stall graced with bay steeds, would be a better translation.

---

1 *Sāṁvaraṇi* : son of the Vedic Ṛṣi Savaraṇa. See V. 33. 10. At the end of the stanza, 'so drink with us,' is to be understood.

2 *Forlorn* : rejected and cast out by his kindred. *Dasyave-vṛka* : literally, the Wolf-to-the-Dasyu, that is, Destroyer of fiends or barbarians.

4 *The seven-headed* : sung by seven heavenly singers.

8 *The son of earth* : man.

9 *Ruśama Pavīru* : the Ruśamas are mentioned in V. 30. 13—15. The name of Pavīru does not occur again.

---

1 *Vivasvān* : or Vivasvat, was the father of Manu who is generally called Vaivasvata. *Āyu* : the Ṛṣi of the hymn, or the sacrificer.

Trita's side, so dost thou joy with Āyu now.

2 As thou with Mātariśvan, Medhya, Pṛṣadhra, hast cheered thee Indra, with pressed juice,
Drunk Soma with Ṛjūnas, Syūmaraśmi, by Daśoṇya's Daśaśipra's side.

3 'Tis he who made the lauds his own and boldly drank the Soma juice,
He to whom Viṣṇu came striding his three wide steps, as Mitra's statutes ordered it.

4 In whose laud thou didst joy, Indra, at the great deed, O Śatakratu, Mighty One!
Seeking renown we call thee as the milkers call the cow who yields abundant milk.

5 He is our Sire who gives to us, Great, Mighty, ruling as he wills.
Unsought, may he the Strong, Rich, Lord of ample wealth, give us of horses and of kine.

6 He to whom thou, Good Lord, givest that he may give increases wealth that nourishes.
Eager for wealth we call on Indra, Lord of wealth, on Śatakratu with our lauds.

7 Never art thou neglectful : thou guardest both races with thy care.
The call on Indra, fourth Āditya ! is thine own. Amṛta is stablished in the heavens.

8 The offerer whom thou, Indra, Lover of the Song, liberal Maghavan, favourest,—
As at the call of Kaṇva so, O gracious Lord, hear, thou our songs and eulogy.

9 Sung is the song of ancient time : to Indra have ye said the prayer.
They have sung many a Bṛhatī of sacrifice, poured forth the worshipper's many thoughts.

10 Indra hath tossed together mighty stores of wealth, and both the worlds, yea, and the Sun.
Pure, brightly-shining, mingled with the milk, the draughts of Soma have made Indra glad.

2 *Mātariśvan* : the Ṛṣi of Hymn VI, of the Vālakhilya. *Medhya* : the Ṛṣi of Hymns V, IX, and X. *Pṛṣadhra* : the Ṛṣi of Hymn VIII. *Syūmaraśmi* : mentioned, as a favourite of the Aśvins, in I. 112. 16. The names of Ṛjūnas, Daśoṇya, and Daśaśipra do not occur again in the Ṛgveda.

5 *Ruling as he wills* : 'he who acts as the sovereign.'—Cowell.

7 *Both races* : Gods and men. *Fourth Āditya* : Varuṇa, Mitra, and Aryaman being the other three. *Amṛta* : 'ambrosia.'—Cowell.

8 As thou hearest, must be supplied at the beginning of the stanza.

9 *Bṛhatī* : verse in the Bṛhatī metre.

HYMN V. *Indra.*

1. As highest of the Maghavans, preëminent among the Bulls,
Best breaker-down of forts, kine-winner, Lord of wealth, we seek thee, Indra Maghavan.

2 Thou who subduedst Āyu, Kutsa, Atithigva, waxing daily in thy might,
As such, rousing thy power, we invocate thee now, thee Śatakratu, Lord of Bays.

3 The pressing-stones shall pour for us the essence of the meath of all,
Drops that have been pressed out afar among the folk, and those that have been pressed near us.

4 Repel all enmities and keep them far away : let all win treasure for their own.
Even among Śiṣṭas are the stalks that make thee glad, where thou with Soma satest thee.

5 Come, Indra, very near to us with aids of firmly-based resolve ;
Come, most auspicious, with thy most auspicious help, good Kinsman, with good kinsmen, come !

6 Bless thou with progeny the chief of men, the lord of heroes, victor in the fray.
Aid with thy powers the men who sing thee lauds and keep their spirits ever pure and bright.

7 May we be such in battle as are surest to obtain thy grace :
With holy offerings and invocations of the Gods, we mean, that we may win the spoil.

8 Thine, Lord of Bays, am I. Prayer longeth for the spoil. Still with thy help I seek the fight.
So, at the raiders' head, I, craving steeds

1 *Highest* : or, nearest. *The Bulls* : strong heroes.

2 *Āyu, Kutsa, Atithigva* : See I. 53. 10.

4 *Śiṣṭas* : apparently a tribe of no great importance. *Stalks* : of the Soma-plant.

8 *At the raiders' head*: at the head of the band who are going forth to seize the cattle of their enemies. Von Roth thinks that *matīnām* should be read in stead

and kine, unite myself with thee alone.

HYMN VI. *Indra.*

1. INDRA, the poets with their hymns extol this hero might of thine :
They strengthened, loud in song, thy power that droppeth oil. With hymns the Pauras came to thee.

2 Through piety they came to Indra for his aid, they whose libations give thee joy.
As thou with Kṛśa and Saṁvarta hast rejoiced, so, Indra, be thou glad with us.

3 Agreeing in your spirit, all ye Deities, come nigh to us.
Vasus and Rudras shall come near to give us aid, and Maruts listen to our call.

4 May Pūṣan, Viṣṇu, and Sarasvatī befriend, and the Seven Streams, this call of mine :
May Waters, Wind, the Mountains, and the Forest-Lord, and Earth give ear unto my cry.

5 Indra, with thine own bounteous gift, most liberal of the Mighty Ones,
Be our boon benefactor, Vṛtra-slayer, be our feast-companion for our weal.

6 Leader of heroes, Lord of battle, lead thou us to combat, thou Most Sapient One.
High fame is theirs who win by invocations, feasts and entertainment of the Gods.

7 Our hopes rest on the Faithful One : in Indra is the people's life.
O Maghavan, come nigh that thou mayst give us aid : make plenteous food stream forth for us.

8 Thee would we worship, Indra, with our songs of praise : O Śatakratu, be thou ours.
Pour down upon Praskaṇva bounty vast and firm, exuberant, that shall never fail.

of *mathīnām*, and Grassmann translates accordingly, 'in Anfang meiner Bitten,' 'at the beginning of my prayers.'

1 *Pauras* : 'the offerers.'—Cowell. See Vālakhilya, II. 5.

2 *Kṛśa* : the Ṛṣi of Hymn VII. of the Vālakhilya. *Saṁvarta* : not mentioned elsewhere.

4 *The Forest Lord* : *vanaspati* : the tall timber tree, frequently meaning the Sacrificial Post.

5 *Benefactor* : or Bhaga, the God who distributes wealth.

HYMN VII. *Praskaṇva's Gift.*

1. GREAT, verily, is Indra's might. I have beheld, and hither comes
Thy bounty, Dasyave-vṛka !

2 A hundred oxen white of hue are shining like the stars in heaven,
So tall, they seem to prop the sky.

3 Bamboos a hundred, hundred dogs, a hundred skins of beasts well-tanned,
A hundred tufts of Balbaja, four hundred red-hued mares are mine.

4 Blest by the Gods, Kāṇvāyanas ! be ye who spread through life on life:
Like horses have ye stridden forth.

5 Then men extolled the team of seven : not yet full-grown, its fame is great.
The dark mares rushed along the paths, so that no eye could follow them.

HYMN VIII. *Praskaṇva's Gift.*

1. THY bounty, Dasyave-vṛka, exhaustless hath displayed itself :
Its fulness is as broad as heaven.

2 Ten thousand Dasyave-vṛka, the son of Pūtakratā, hath
From his own wealth bestowed on me.

3 A hundred asses hath he given, a hundred head of fleecy sheep,

1 'Great is Indra's power, and the gifts which I have received from thee, O destroyer of the Dasyus, can be compared only to his bounty.' Dasyavevṛka, here, is the name, not of the Ṛṣi, but of a hero who in alliance with the Kaṇvas has been victorious in his attack on the hostile barbarians. See Ludwig, Vol. III. p. 164.

3 *Balbaja* : a kind of coarse grass (Eleusine Indica), used in religious ceremonies, and for other purposes when plaited.

4 *Kāṇvāyanas* : descendants of Kaṇva.

5 *The team of seven* : 'siebengespannes.'—Grassmann; 'seven-yoked team.'—Cowell. But the exact meaning here of *sāptásya* is uncertain. Von Roth thinks that it is probably a proper name. Ludwig takes it in the sense of a bond of friendship or alliance. *The dark mares* : there is no substantive, and 'mares' is conjecturally supplied. According to Ludwig, the dark hosts of the Dasyus conquered by Dasyave-vṛka are intended, and the whole stanza would be more correctly translated :

'Then no more thought they of the great renown of the collective bond.
The dark tribes rushed along the paths so that no eye could reach to them.' See Ludwig's Commentary, Vol. V. p. 552.

2 *The son of Pūtakratā* : or, more probably, called Pautakrata after his father Pūtakratu—Ludwig.

3 *Slaves* : *dāsán* : conquered barbarians.

A hundred slaves, and wreaths besides.

4 There also was a mare led forth, picked out for Pūtakratā's sake,
Not of the horses of the herd.

5 Observant Agni hath appeared, oblation-bearer with his car.
Agni with his resplendent flame hath shone on high as shines the Sun, hath shone like Sūrya in the heavens.

HYMN IX. *Aśvins.*

1. ENDOWED, O Gods, with your primeval wisdom, come quickly with your chariot, O ye Holy.
Come with your mighty powers, O ye Nāsatyas; come hither, drink ye this the third libation.

2 The truthful Deities, the Three-and-Thirty, saw you approach before the Ever-Truthful.
Accepting this our worship and libation, O Aśvins bright with fire, drink ye the Soma.

3 Aśvins, that work of yours deserves our wonder,—the Bull of heaven and earth and air's mid region;
Yea, and your thousand promises in battle,—to all of these come near and drink beside us.

4 Here is your portion laid for you, ye Holy: come to these songs of ours, O ye Nāsatyas.
Drink among us the Soma full of sweetness, and with your powers assist the man who worships.

HYMN X. *Viśvedevas.*

1. HE whom the priests in sundry ways arranging the sacrifice, of one accord, bring hither,
Who was appointed as a learned Brāhman,—what is the sacrificer's knowledge of him?

2 Kindled in many a spot, still One is Agni; Sūrya is One though high o'er all he shineth.
Illumining this All, still One is Uṣas. That which is One hath into All developed.

3 The chariot bright and radiant, treasure-laden, three-wheeled, with easy seat, and lightly rolling,
Which She of Wondrous Wealth was born to harness,—this car of yours I call. Drink what remaineth.

HYMN XI. *Indra-Varuṇa.*

1. IN offerings poured to you, O Indra-Varuṇa, these shares of yours stream forth to glorify your state.
Ye haste to the libations at each sacrifice when ye assist the worshipper who sheds the juice.

2 The waters and the plants, O Indra-Varuṇa, had efficacious vigour, and attained to might:
Ye who have gone beyond the path of middle air,—no godless man is worthy to be called your foe.

3 True is your Kṛśa's word, Indra and Varuṇa: The seven holy voices pour a wave of meath.
For their sake, Lords of splendour! aid the pious man who, unbewildered, keeps you ever in his thoughts.

4 Dropping oil, sweet with Soma, pouring forth their stream, are the Seven Sisters in the seat of sacrifice.
These, dropping oil, are yours, O Indra-Varuṇa: with these enrich with gifts and help the worshipper.

---

4 *Picked out* or, adorned. *Pūtakratā*: the wife of Pūtakratu.

---

1 *Nāsatyas*; 'truthful ones.'—Cowell. See Vol I., Index.

2 *The Three-and-Thirty*: or, Thrice-Eleven. See I. 34. 11. *The Ever-Truthful*: the Sun, whose approach is heralded by the Aśvins.

3 *The Bull*: the Sun, whom, as his heralds and revealers, they may be said to have created. *Thousand promises*: 'a characteristic periphrasis for the Maghavans, or wealthy nobles.'—Ludwig.

---

1 The hymn appears to consist of unconnected fragments, and the purport of this stanza is not obvious.

3 *She of Wondrous Wealth*: Uṣas or Dawn. *Was born to harness*: or, as Prof. Cowell translates: 'At whose yoking the Dawn was born.' The chariot of the Aśvins precedes that of the Dawn.

---

2 *The waters and the plants*: used in sacrifice; the Soma-plants and the water employed in preparing the juice for libation. The meaning of the stanza seems to be: although you are far away in the most distant firmament, our libations have had power to attract you. Regard us only: the godless man is unworthy of your consideration even as an enemy.

3 *The seven holy voices*: the voices of the seven priests or sacred bards. See IX. 103. 3. *A wave of meath*: 'a stream of honey.'—Cowell.

4 *The Seven Sisters*: 'sister-streams of the Soma.'—Cowell.

5 To our great happiness have we ascribed to these Two Bright Ones truthfulness, great strength, and majesty.
O Lords of splendour, aid us through the Three-times-Seven, as we pour holy oil, O Indra-Varuṇa.

6 What ye in time of old, Indra and Varuṇa, gave Ṛṣis—revelation, thought, and power of song,
And places which the wise made, weaving sacrifice,—these through my spirit's fervid glow have I beheld.

7 O Indra-Varuṇa, grant to the worshippers cheerfulness void of pride, and wealth to nourish them.
Vouchsafe us food, prosperity, and progeny, and lengthen out our days that we may see long life.

5 *The Three-times-Seven* : perhaps the Maruts, thrice-seven being used indefinitely for a larger number consisting of troops of seven. See I. 133. 6.

6 *Revelation* : *śrutám* : that which was heard (from the beginning); sacred knowledge. 'Fame.'—Cowell. *Places* : perhaps, as Ludwig suggests, homes in the world to come, which the wise Ṛṣis have prepared for themselves by performing sacrifice here below. *Through my spirit's fervid glow* : *tápasā*: according to Grassmann and Cowell, this *tápas* means 'the holy austerities' of the Ṛṣis, and not the sacred fervour of the seer of the hymn. I have followed Ludwig.

BOOK THE NINTH

HYMN I. *Soma Pavamāna.*

1. In sweetest and most gladdening stream flow pure, O Soma, on thy way,
Pressed out for Indra, for his drink.

2 Fiend-queller, Friend of all men, he hath with the wood attained unto
His place, his iron-fashioned home.

3 Be thou best Vṛtra-slayer, best granter of bliss, most liberal :
Promote our wealthy princes' gifts.

4 Flow onward with thy juice unto the banquet of the Mighty Gods :
Flow hither for our strength and fame.

5 O Indu, we draw nigh to thee, with this one object day by day :
To thee alone our prayers are said.

6 By means of this eternal fleece may Sūrya's Daughter purify
Thy Soma that is foaming forth.

7 Ten sister maids of slender form seize him within the press and hold
Him firmly on the final day.

8 The virgins send him forth : they blow the skin musician-like and fuse
The triple foe-repelling meath.

9 Inviolable milch-kine round about him blend for Indra's drink,
The fresh young Soma with their milk.

10 In the wild raptures of this draught, Indra slays all the Vṛtras : he,
The Hero, pours his wealth on us.

HYMN II. *Soma Pavamāna.*

1. Soma, flow on, inviting Gods, speed to the purifying cloth :
Pass into Indra, as a Bull.

2 As mighty food speed hitherward, Indu, as a most splendid Steer :
Sit in thy place as one with strength.

3 The well-loved meath was made to flow, the stream of the creative juice :
The Sage drew waters to himself.

4 The mighty waters, yea, the floods accompany thee Mighty One,
When thou wilt clothe thee with the milk.

5 The lake is brightened in the floods. Soma, our Friend, heaven's prop and stay,
Falls on the purifying cloth.

6 The tawny Bull hath bellowed, fair as mighty Mitra to behold:
He shines together with the Sun.

7 Songs, Indu, active in their might are beautified for thee, wherewith
Thou deckest thee for our delight.

8 To thee who givest ample room we pray, to win the joyous draught :
Great are the praises due to thee.

9 Indu as, Indra's Friend, on us pour with a stream of sweetness, like
Parjanya sender of the rain.

10 Winner of kine, Indu, art thou, winner of heroes, steeds, and strength :
Primeval Soul of sacrifice.

Nearly all the hymns of this Book are addressed to the deified Soma juice, or to Soma, or Indu, the Moon, who as containing the celestial nectar, the drink of the Gods, is identified with the Soma-plant and its exhilarating juice. As the Moon-God pours down his ambrosial rain through the sieve of heaven, he is addressed and worshipped as Pavamāna (Self-Purifying), represented by the Soma juice as it undergoes purification by flowing through the wool which is used as a filter or strainer. See Muir, *O. S. Texts*, V. 258 sqq., Hillebrandt, *Vedische Mythologie*, I. 385 sqq., and Max Müller, *Chips*, IV. 353—367. But cf. Oldenberg, *Religion des Veda*, 599—612.

1 *Flow pure* : *pávasva* : 'purify thyself.'—Ludwig.

2 *With the wood* : some wooden vessel or implement, perhaps the *sruva* or dipping-spoon. *Iron-fashioned home*: receptacle that has been hammered or formed with a tool of *áyas*, iron or other metal. It is not clear what vessel is intended.

6 *Sūrya's Daughter* : Śraddhā or Faith. See *Śatapatha-Brāhmaṇa*, XII. 7. 3. 11.

7 *Ten sister maids* : the priest's fingers. *The final day* : on which the Soma is effused.

8 *Virgins* : the unwedded ones : the fingers. *Musician-like* : or, as men blow a bagpipe ; but the meaning of *bākurám* and the second half-line is not clear. 'They seize it glittering like a water skin.'—Wilson.

3 *The Sage* : the Soma. *Waters* : with which the stalks or the plant are sprinkled.

5 *The lake* : the Soma juice.

6 *The tawny Bull* : 'the golden-hued showerer of blessings.'—Wilson. The strong greenish-yellow Soma juice. *Hath bellowed* : an exaggerated expression for the sound made by the juice as it drops, but in keeping with its representation as a bull.

9 *Like Parjanya* : enriching and blessing us as the rain-cloud fertilizes the ground.

HYMN III. *Soma Pavamāna.*

1. HERE present this Immortal God flies, like a bird upon her wings,
To settle in the vats of wood.

2 This God, made ready with the hymn, runs swiftly through the winding ways,
Inviolable as he flows.

3 This God while flowing is adorned, like a bay steed for war, by men
Devout and skilled in holy songs.

4 He, like a warrior going forth with heroes, as he flows along
Is fain to win all precious boons.

5 This God, as he is flowing on, speeds like a car and gives his gifts:
He lets his voice be heard of all.

6 Praised by the sacred bards, this God dives into waters, and bestows
Rich gifts upon the worshipper.

7 Away he rushes with his stream, across the regions, into heaven,
And roars as he is flowing on.

8 While flowing, meet for sacrifice, he hath gone up to heaven across
The regions, irresistible.

9 After the way of ancient time, this God, pressed out for Deities,
Flows tawny to the straining-cloth.

10 This Lord of many Holy Laws, even at his birth engendering strength,
Effused, flows onward in a stream.

HYMN IV. *Soma Pavamāna.*

1. O SOMA flowing on thy way, win thou and conquer high renown;
And make us better than we are.

2 Win thou the light, win heavenly light, and, Soma, all felicities;
And make us better than we are.

3 Win skilful strength and mental power. O Soma, drive away our foes;
And make us better than we are.

4 Ye purifiers, purify Soma for Indra, for his drink:
Make thou us better than we are.

5 Give us our portion in the Sun through thine own mental power and aids;
And make us better than we are.

6 Through thine own mental power and aid long may we look upon the Sun;
Make thou us better than we are.

7 Well-weaponed Soma, pour to us a stream of riches doubly great;
And make us better than we are.

8 As one victorious unsubdued in battle pour forth wealth to us;
And make us better than we are.

9 By worship, Pavamāna! men have strengthened thee to prop the Law:
Make thou us better than we are.

10 O Indu, bring us wealth in steeds, manifold, quickening all life;
And make us better than we are.

HYMN V. *Āprīs.*

1. ENKINDLED, Pavamāna, Lord, sends forth his light on every side
In friendly show, the bellowing Bull.

2 He, Pavamāna, Self-produced, speeds onward sharpening his horns:
He glitters through the firmament.

3 Brilliant like wealth, adorable, with splendour Pavamāna shines,
Mightily with the streams of meath.

4 The tawny Pavamāna, who strews from of old the grass with might,
Is worshipped, God amid the Gods.

5 The golden, the Celestial Doors are lifted with their frames on high,
By Pavamāna glorified.

---

1 *The vats of wood*: *droṇāni*: large wooden vessels, tubs or troughs which receive the Soma juice.

2 *The winding ways*: of the wool which forms the strainer.—Ludwig. 'Rushes against the enemies.'—Wilson.

6 *Dives into waters*: called *vasatīvaryaḥ*, with which the stalks of the Soma-plant are sprinkled.

9 *Pressed out for Deities*: the Soma juice being identified with the Amṛta or nectar, the drink of the Gods, contained in the Moon.

1 *Better than we are*: or, happier than we are.

4 *Purifiers*: priests whose business is to purify the juice. *Make thou*: O Soma.

9 *To prop the Law*: *vidharmaṇi*: 'for their own upholding.'—Wilson.

10 *Quickening all life*: *viśvāyum*: explained by Sāyaṇa as = *sarvagāminam*: 'all-reaching.'—Wilson.

In this Āprī hymn attributes of Agni are transferred to Soma Pavamāna.

1 *Enkindled*: *sámiddhaḥ*: properly applicable to Agni. *The bellowing Bull*: 'the showerer of blessings, uttering a loud sound.'—Wilson.

2 *Self-produced*: *Tanūnápāt*; properly a name of Agni; here, the Moon.

5 *The Celestial Doors*: the doors of the hall of sacrifice are here identified with the portals of the east through which light comes into the world. See II. 3. 5.

6 With passion Pavamāna longs for the great lofty Pair, well-formed,
Like beauteous maidens, Night and Dawn.

7 Both Gods who look on men I call, Celestial Heralds : Indra's Self
Is Pavamāna, yea, the Bull.

8 This, Pavamāna's sacrifice, shall the three beauteous Goddesses,
Sarasvatī and Bhāratī and Ilā, Mighty One, attend.

9 I summon Tvaṣṭar hither, our protector, champion, earliest-born,
Indu is Indra, tawny Steer; Pavamāna is Prajāpati.

10 O Pavamāna, with the meath in streams anoint Vanaspati,
The ever-green, the golden-hued, refulgent, with a thousand boughs.

11 Come to the consecrating rite of Pavamāna, all ye Gods,—
Vāyu, Sūrya, Bṛhaspati, Indra, and Agni, in accord.

HYMN VI. *Soma Pavamāna.*

1. SOMA, flow on with pleasant stream, a Bull devoted to the Gods,
Our Friend, unto the woollen sieve.

2 Pour hitherward, as Indra's Self, Indu, that gladdening stream of thine,
And send us coursers full of strength.

3 Flow to the filter hitherward, pouring that ancient gladdening juice,
Streaming forth power and high renown.

4 Hither the sparkling drops have flowed, like waters down a steep descent :
They have reached Indra purified.

5 Whom, having passed the filter, ten dames cleanse, as 'twere a vigorous steed,
While he disports him in the wood,—

6 The steer-strong juice with milk pour forth, for feast and service of the Gods,
To him who bears away the draught.

7 Effused, the God flows onward with his stream to Indra, to the God,
So that his milk may strengthen him.

8 Soul of the sacrifice, the juice effused flows quickly on : he keeps
His ancient wisdom of a Sage.

9 So pouring forth, as Indra's Friend, strong drink, best Gladdener ! for the feast,
Thou, even in secret, storest hymns.

HYMN VII. *Soma Pavamāna.*

1. FORTH on their way the glorious drops have flowed for maintenance of Law,
Knowing this sacrifice's course.

2 Down in the mighty waters sinks the stream of meath, most excellent,
Oblation best of all in worth.

3 About the holy place, the Steer true, guileless, noblest, hath sent forth
Continuous voices in the wood.

4 When, clothed in manly strength, the Sage flows in celestial wisdom round,
The Strong would win the light of heaven.

5 When purified, he sits as King above the hosts, among his folk,
What time the sages bring him nigh.

6 Dear, golden-coloured, in the fleece he sinks and settles in the wood :
The Singer shows his zeal in hymns.

7 He goes to Indra, Vāyu, to the Aśvins, as his custom is,
With gladdening juice which gives them joy.

8 The streams of pleasant Soma flow to Bhaga, Mitra-Varuṇa,—
Well-knowing through his mighty powers.

---

7 *Celestial Heralds* : See I. 13. 8. *Indra's Self*: *índraḥ* here is explained by Sāyaṇa as=*dīptaḥ* ; 'radiant.'—Wilson.

10 *Vanaspati* : the sacrificial stake.

11 *The consecrating rite* : *sv́āhākṛtim* : oblation accompanied with the utterance of the sacred formula Svāhā.

---

5 *Whom* : relative to juice in the following stanza. *Ten dames* : the fingers. *The wood* : the vat or trough.

6 *To him who bears away the draught* : to Indra. Others take *bhdrāya* to mean 'for strength or prowess in battle.'

9 *Even in secret* : wisdom lies hidden in the Soma, and cannot be recognized until one drinks the juice.—Ludwig.

---

2 *The mighty waters* : the holy waters called *vasatīvaryaḥ*.

3 *In the wood* : according to Sāyaṇa, *váne* here=*udake*, in the water. The stanza is very difficult, and I am unable to offer a satisfactory translation.

4 *The Strong* : Indra. 'Then the mighty (Indra) in heaven is eager to repair to the oblation.'—Wilson.

5 *Above the hosts, among his folk* : or, as preferred by Prof. Ludwig in his Commentary, above the contending tribes or people (*viśaḥ*)

8 *Well-knowing, through his mighty powers* : that is, the streams that, through the power of Soma, know the way they should go. 'The worshippers knowing its (virtues are rewarded) with happiness.'—Wilson.

9 Gain for us, O ye Heaven and Earth, riches of meath to win us wealth:
Gain for us treasures and renown.

HYMN VIII. *Soma Pavamāna.*

1. Obeying Indra's dear desire these Soma juices have flowed forth,
Increasing his heroic might.

2 Laid in the bowl, pure-flowing on to Vāyu and the Aśvins, may
These give us great heroic strength.

3 Soma, as thou art purified, incite to bounty Indra's heart,
To sit in place of sacrifice.

4 The ten swift fingers deck thee forth, seven ministers impel thee on :
The sages have rejoiced in thee.

5 When through the filter thou art poured, we clothe thee with a robe of milk
To be a gladdening draught for Gods.

6 When purified within the jars, Soma, bright-red and golden-hued,
Hath clothed him with a robe of milk.

7 Flow on to us and make us rich. Drive all our enemies away.
O Indu, flow into thy Friend.

8 Send down the rain from heaven, a stream of opulence from earth. Give us,
O Soma, victory in war.

9 May we obtain thee, Indra's drink, who viewest men and findest light,
Gain thee, and progeny and food.

HYMN IX. *Soma Pavamāna.*

1. The Sage of Heaven whose heart is wise, when laid between both hands and pressed,
Sends us delightful powers of life.

2 On, onward to a glorious home; dear to the people void of guile,
With excellent enjoyment, flow.

3 He, the bright Son, when born illumed his Parents who had sprung to life,
Great Son great Strengtheners of Law.

4 Urged by the seven devotions he hath stirred the guileless rivers which
Have magnified the Single Eye.

5 These helped to might the Youthful One, high over all, invincible,
Even Indu, Indra ! in thy law.

6 The Immortal Courser, good to draw, looks down upon the Seven : the fount
Hath satisfied the Goddesses

7 Aid us in holy rites, O Man : O Pavamāna, drive away
Dark shades that must be met in fight.

8 Make the paths ready for a hymn newer and newer evermore :
Make the lights shine as erst they shone.

9 Give, Pavamāna, high renown, give kine and steeds and hero sons :
Win for us wisdom, win the light.

HYMN X. *Soma Pavamāna.*

1. Like cars that thunder on their way, like coursers eager for renown,
Have Soma-drops flowed forth for wealth.

2 Forth have they rushed from holding hands, like chariots that are urged to speed,
Like joyful songs of singing-men.

3 The Somas deck themselves with milk, as Kings are graced with eulogies,
And, with seven priests, the sacrifice.

4 Pressed for the gladdening draught, the drops flow forth abundantly with song,
The Soma juices in a stream.

5 Winning Vivasvān's glory and producing Morning's light, the Suns
Pass through the openings of the cloth.

6 The singing-men of ancient time open the doors of sacred songs,—
Men, for the mighty to accept.

7 *Flow on to us and make us rich* : or, 'Flow to us wealthy worshippers.' *Thy Friend* : Indra. Cf. IX. 2. 1.

---

1 *The Sage of Heaven* : the Soma. *Both hands* : *naptyoḥ* : literally, two granddaughters. According to Sāyaṇa, two boards used in pressing the Soma are intended. See Cowell's note in Wilson's Translation.

3 *His Parents* : *mātarā* : literally, his two mothers; Heaven and Earth.

4 *Seven devotions* : practised in the preparation of the Soma. Sāyaṇa takes *saptá* with *nadyáḥ* : 'gladdens the seven guileless rivers.'—Wilson. *Single Eye* : Soma, the Moon.

6 *Courser* : the flowing Soma. *The Seven* : rivers. *The fount* : 'Full, as a well, he has satisfied the divine streams.'—Wilson.

7 *O Man* : manly Soma.

---

5 *The Suns* : so called as being creators of the light: 'the sun-bright juices.'—Wilson. *Vivasvān* : the morning Sun.

6 *Men, for the mighty to accept* : 'men, offerers of Soma,' according to Sāyaṇa.

7 Combined in close society sit the seven priests, the brother-hood,
Filling the station of the One.

8 He gives us kinship with the Gods, and with the Sun unites our eye :
The Sage's offspring hath appeared.

9 The Sun with his dear eye beholds that quarter of the heavens which priests
Have placed within the sacred cell.

HYMN XI. *Soma Pavamāna.*

1. SING forth to Indu, O ye men, to him who is purified,
Fain to pay worship to the Gods.

2 Together with thy pleasant juice the Atharvans have commingled milk,
Divine, devoted to the God.

3 Bring, by thy flowing, weal to kine, weal to the people, weal to steeds.
Weal, O thou King, to growing plants.

4 Sing a praise-song to Soma brown of hue, of independent might,
The Red, who reaches up to heaven.

5 Purify Soma when effused with stones which hands move rapidly,
And pour the sweet milk in the meath.

6 With humble homage draw ye nigh; blend the libation with the curds :
To Indra offer Indu up.

7 Soma, foe-queller, chief o'er men, doing the will of Gods, pour forth
Prosperity upon our kine.

8 Heart-knower, Sovran of the heart, thou art effused, O Soma, that Indra may drink thee and rejoice.

9 O Soma Pavamāna, give us riches and heroic strength,—
Indu ! with Indra for ally.

HYMN XII. *Soma Pavamāna.*

1. To Indra have the Soma drops, exceeding rich in sweets, been poured,
Shed in the seat of sacrifice.

2 As mother kine low to their calves, to Indra have the sages called,
Called him to drink the Soma juice.

3 In the stream's wave wise Soma dwells, distilling rapture, in his seat,
Resting upon a wild-cow's hide.

4 Far-sighted Soma, Sage and Seer, is worshipped in the central point
Of heaven, the straining-cloth of wool.

5 In close embraces Indu holds Soma when poured within the jars.
And on the purifying sieve.

6 Indu sends forth a voice on high to regions of the sea of air,
Shaking the vase that drops with meath.

7 The Tree whose praises never fail yields heavenly milk among our hymns,
Urging men's generations on.

7 *The seven priests* : the *adhvaryus* who bring the water with which the stalks of the Soma-plants are sprinkled. *The One* : Soma.—Sāyaṇa

8 *He gives us kinship with the Gods* : I follow Prof. Pischel's interpretation of this difficult passage. 'Soma unites our navel with the navel of the Gods, our eye with the Sun, that is, he brings us into union with the Gods in heaven.'—*Vedische Studien*, I., p. 6 . 'I take into my navel the navel of the sacrifice (the Soma).'—Wilson. 'He (Soma as kinsman has brought us a kinsman (Sūrya).'—Ludwig. *The Sage's offspring* : a periphrasis for the Sage himself, that is, Soma.—Ludwig.

9 This stanza is very obscure. I have adopted Benfey's explanation who 'here follows an occasional interpretation of *div* or *dyuloka*, given by the Scholiast, which identifies it with the *droṇakalaśa* or large *Soma*-trough. He takes it as meaning that the Sun looks towards the place where the Soma lies while it is pressed...Sāyaṇa seems to interpret this verse as meaning that Indra views the Soma with affection even after it has been drunk by the priests (fixed in the heart).'—Cowell, in Wilson's Translation.

2 *The Atharvans* : the priests, who perform the duties of the Adhvaryus.

3 *King* : the usual designation of Soma in the Brāhmaṇa.

4 *The Red* : *kadācidaruṇavarṇāya* : 'sometimes red-coloured.'—Sāyaṇa.

3 *In the stream's wave* : in the water with which the stalks are sprinkled. *Upon a wild-cow's hide* : this, which is Benfey's explanation of *gaurī*, seems to be borne out by *gor ádhi tvací*, upon the ox-hide, of IX. 101. 11. Sāyaṇa's interpretation is different : 'to a chant in the middle tone.'—Wilson.

4 *Of heaven* : *divaḥ* : See IX. 10. 9, and note.

5 *Indu holds Soma* : 'the deity seems to be thus opposed to the mere plant.'—Cowell's note. Ludwig suggests that Indu here may be the Moon, as the time of important liturgical ceremonies depends upon the Moon's phases. So also Hillebrandt, *V. M.*, I., p. 316.

6 *To regions of the sea of air* : or *samudrásya* here may mean, of the sea or water into which the Soma juice falls. *Shaking* : or, perhaps, stirring (with joy). *The vase* : *kóśam* : the *droṇakalaśa*, the large wooden vessel for holding the juice. According to Sāyaṇa, whose interpretation I have followed in the first line, *kóśam* here means the cloud.

7 *The Tree* : Soma. *Men's generations* : sacrificial seasons, according to Sāyaṇa.

8 The Wise One, with the Sage's stream, the Soma urged to speed, flows on
To the dear places of the sky.
9 O Pavamāna, bring us wealth bright with a thousand splendours. Yea.
O Indu, give us ready help.

HYMN XIII. *Soma Pavamāna.*

1. PASSED through, the fleece in thousand streams the Soma, purified, flows on
To Indra's, Vāyu's special place.
2 Sing forth, ye men who long for help, to Pavamāna, to the Sage,
Effused to entertain the Gods.
3 The Soma-drops with thousand powers are purified for victory,
Hymned to become the feast of Gods.
4 Yea, as thou flowest bring great store of food that we may win the spoil:
Indu, bring splendid manly might.
5 May they in flowing give us wealth in thousands, and heroic power,—
These Godlike Soma-drops effused.
6 Like coursers by their drivers urged, they were poured forth, for victory,
Swift through the woollen straining-cloth.
7 Noisily flow the Soma-drops, like milch-kine lowing to their calves:
They have run forth from both the hands.
8 As Gladdener whom Indra loves, O Pavamāna, with a roar
Drive all our enemies away.
9 O Pavamānas, driving off the godless, looking on the light,
Sit in the place of sacrifice.

HYMN XIV. *Soma Pavamāna.*

1. REPOSING on the river's wave the Sage hath widely flowed around,
Bearing the hymn which many love.
2 When the Five kindred Companies, active in duty, with the song
Establish him, the Powerful,
3 Then in his juice whose strength is great, have all the Gods rejoiced themselves,
When he hath clothed him in the milk.
4 Freeing himself he flows away, leaving his body's severed limbs,
And meets his own Companion here.
5 He by the daughters of the priest, like a fair youth, hath been adorned,
Making the milk, as 'twere, his robe.
6 O'er the fine fingers, through desire of milk, in winding course he goes,
And utters voice which he hath found.
7 The nimble fingers have approached, adorning him the Lord of Strength:
They grasp the vigorous Courser's back.
8 Comprising all the treasures that are in the heavens and on the earth,
Come, Soma, as our faithful Friend.

HYMN XV. *Soma Pavamāna.*

1. THROUGH the fine fingers, with the song, this Hero comes with rapid ears,
Going to Indra's special place.
2 In holy thought he ponders much for the great worship of the Gods.
Where the Immortals have their seat.
3 Like a good horse is he led out, when on the path that shines with light
The mettled steeds exert their strength.
4 He brandishes his horns on high, and whets them, Bull who leads the herd,
Doing with might heroic deeds.
5 He moves, a vigorous Steed, adorned with beauteous rays of shining gold,

1 *Indra's, Vāyu's special place*: the vessels especially prepared to hold libations intended for Indra and Vāyu.

3 *For victory*: *vājasātaye*: 'for the attainment of food'—Wilson. So explains Sāyaṇa in stanzas 3 and 4; but in 6 the word is explained by *saṁgrāmāmāya* to battle, in the first clause where he inserts it after *hiyānāḥ*, urged, and by *annalābhāya*, for the attainment of food, in the second clause.

8 *With a roar*: making a loud noise in dropping.

———

1 *On the river's wave*: in the *vasatīvarī* waters, which are used to sprinkle the stalks. *Bearing the hymn*: Prof. Geldner explains this as meaning, 'Bearing away the much coveted prize,' Soma being regarded as a courser or race-horse. See *Vedische Studien*, I., p. 120

2 *Five kindred Companies*: referring, probably, to some sacrifice instituted in common by representatives of the five Āryan tribes.

4 *His own Companion*: Indra. *He meets*: this (*saṅgato bhavati*) is Sāyaṇa's explanation of *samjighnate*; but it is not easy to see how the word can bear this signification.

5 *Daughters*: or granddaughters; the fingers.

6 *Which he hath found*: 'which the worshipper recognizes.'—Wilson.

———

1 *Indra's special place*: 'Indra's abode'.—Wilson. In Hymn XIII. 1, *niṣkṛtám* is explained by Sāyaṇa as the vessel prepared and set apart

3 *Like a good horse*: the text has only *hitáḥ* which may mean either good or placed. 'Placed (in the cart) he is brought.'—Wilson.

4 *Horns*: cf. IX. 5. 2.

5 *Rays of shining gold*: as the Moon.

Becoming Sovran of the streams.

6 He, over places rough to pass, bringing rich treasures closely packed.
Descends into the reservoirs.

7 Men beautify him in the vats, him worthy to be beautified,
Him who brings forth abundant food.

8 Him, even him, the fingers ten and the seven songs make beautiful,
Well-weaponed, best of gladdeners.

HYMN XVI. *Soma Pavamāna.*

1. THE pressers from the Soma-press send forth thy juice for rapturous joy :
The speckled sap runs like a flood.

2 With strength we follow through the sieve him who brings might and wins the kine,
Enrobed in water with his juice.

3 Pour on the sieve the Soma, ne'er subdued in waters, waterless,
And make it pure for Indra's drink.

4 Moved by the purifier's thought, the Soma flows into the sieve:
By wisdom it hath gained its home.

5 With humble homage, Indra, have the Soma-drops flowed forth to thee,
Contending for the glorious prize.

6 Purified in his fleecy garb, attaining every beauty, he
Stands, hero-like, amid the kine.

7 Swelling, as 'twere, to heights of heaven, the stream of the creative juice
Falls lightly on the cleansing sieve.

8 Thus, Soma, purifying him who knoweth song mid living men,
Thou wanderest through the cloth of wool.

6 *Places rough to pass* : the wool of the strainer. Sāyaṇa gives a totally different explanation of this stanza. See Wilson's Translation. I have followed Prof. Ludwig.

8 *Seven songs* : the songs of the seven priests.

———

1. *From the Soma-press* : *oṇyoḥ*, ablative dual of *oṇi*, signifying apparently an implement or a vessel, consisting of two pieces, used in the preparation of the Soma juice. The word is said to be employed to denote, metaphorically, heaven and earth. 'They who express thee, the juice of heaven and earth '—Wilson.

3 *Waterless* : *ánaptam*, which Sāyaṇa explains by *anāptam*, not reached, or overtaken, by enemies. The meaning is not clear.

4 *Its home* : in the large wooden vessel called *droṇakalaśa*.

5 *Contending for the glorious prize* : like race-horses. 'Giving thee vigour for the great conflict.'—Wilson.

HYMN XVII. *Soma Pavamāna.*

1. LIKE rivers down a steep descent, slaying the Vṛtras, full of zeal,
The rapid Soma-streams have flowed.

2 The drops of Soma juice effused fall like the rain upon the earth :
To Indra flow the Soma-streams.

3 With swelling wave the gladdening drink, the Soma, flows into the sieve,
Loving the Gods and slaying fiends.

4 It hastens to the pitchers, poured upon the sieve it waxes strong
At sacrifices through the lauds.

5 Soma, thou shinest mounting heaven as 'twere above light's triple realm,
And moving seem'st to speed the Sun.

6 To him, the head of sacrifice, singers and bards have sung their songs,
Offering what he loves to see.

7 The men, the sages with their hymns, eager for help, deck thee strong steed,
Deck thee for service of the Gods.

8 Flow onward to the stream of meath : rest efficacious in thy home,
Fair, to be drunk at sacrifice.

HYMN XVIII. *Soma Pavamāna.*

1. THOU, Soma, dweller on the hills, effused, hast flowed into the sieve :
All-bounteous art thou in carouse.

2 Thou art a sacred Bard, a Sage; the meath is offspring of thy sap :
All-bounteous art thou in carouse.

3 All Deities of one accord have come that they may drink of thee :
All-bounteous art thou in carouse.

4 He who containeth in his hands all treasures much to be desired :
All-bounteous art thou in carouse.

5 Who milketh out this mighty Pair, the Earth and Heaven, like mother kine :
All-bounteous art thou in carouse.

5 Addressed to Soma as the Moon.

6 *The head of sacrifice* : the most important element of the ceremony. According to Sāyaṇa, at the head, that is, on the last and most important day of the effusion of the Soma juice. *Offering what he loves to see*: 'entertaining affection for him the all-beholding.'—Wilson.

8 *Meath* : or honey. *In thy home* : in the *droṇakalaśa*.

———

1 *Dweller on the hills* : 'pressed between the stones.'—Wilson.

6 Who in a moment mightily floweth around these two world-halves :
All-bounteous art thou in carouse.

7 The Strong One, being purified, hath in the pitchers cried aloud :
All-bounteous art thou in carouse.

HYMN XIX. *Soma Pavamāna.*

1. O Soma, being purified bring us the wondrous treasure, meet
For lauds, that is in earth and heaven.

2 For ye Twain, Indra, Soma, are Lords of the light, Lords of the kine :
Great Rulers, prosper ye our songs.

3 The tawny Steer, while cleansed among the living, bellowing on the grass,
Hath sunk and settled in his home.

4 Over the Steer's productive flow the sacred songs were resonant,
The mothers of the darling Son.

5 Hath he not, purified, impregned the kine who long to meet their Lord,
The kine who yield the shining milk?

6 Bring near us those who stand aloof : strike fear into our enemies:
O Pavamāna, find us wealth.

7 Soma, bring down the foeman's might, his vigorous strength and vital power,
Whether he be afar or near.

HYMN XX. *Soma Pavamāna.*

1. Forth through the straining-cloth the Sage flows to the banquet of the Gods,
Subduing all our enemies.

2 For he, as Pavamāna, sends thousandfold treasure in the shape
Of cattle to the singing-men.

3 Thou graspest all things with thy mind, and purifiest thee with thoughts :
As such, O Soma, find us fame.

4 Pour lofty glory on us, send sure riches to our liberal lords,
Bring food to those who sing thy praise.

5 As thou art cleansed, O Wondrous Steed, O Soma, thou hast entered, like
A pious King, into the songs.

6 He, Soma, like a courser in the floods invincible, made clean
With hands, is resting in the jars.

7 Disporting, like a liberal chief, thou goest, Soma, to the sieve,
Lending the laud a Hero's strength.

HYMN XXI. *Soma Pavamāna.*

1. To Indra flow these running drops, these Somas frolicsome in mood.
Exhilarating, finding light;

2 Driving off foes, bestowing room upon the presser, willingly
Bringing their praiser vital force.

3 Lightly disporting them, the drops flow to one common reservoir,
And fall into the river's wave.

4 These Pavamānas have obtained all blessings much to be desired,
Like coursers harnessed to a car.

5 With view to us, O Soma-drops, bestow his manifold desire
On him who yet hath given us naught.

6 Bring us our wish with this design, as a wright brings his new-wrought wheel:
Flow pure and shining with the stream.

7 These drops have cried with resonant voice: like swift steeds they have run the course,
And roused the good man's hymn to life.

HYMN XXII. *Soma Pavamāna.*

1. These rapid Soma-streams have stirred themselves to motion like strong steeds,
Like cars, like armies hurried forth.

2 Swift as wide winds they lightly move, like rain-storms of Parjanya, like
The flickering flames of burning fire.

3 These Soma juices, blent with curds, purified, skilled in sacred hymns,
Have gained by song their hearts' desire.

4 Hymns are sung over the Soma-stream, and are called mothers of the precious juice because it is prepared while they are sung.

5 *The kine* : the vasatīvarī waters which long to mingle with the Soma.

5 *Steed* : *vahne* : 'bearer (of our offerings).'—Wilson.

6 *Like a courser* : 'the bearer (of oblations).'—Wilson.

7 *Chief* : Sāyaṇa explains *maṁháḥ* by *dānam, gift*.

5 This stanza is obscure, and Sāyaṇa's commentary is imperfect. It seems that the Soma-drops are prayed to enrich the institutor of the sacrifice who has not as yet rewarded the priests.

7 *Run the course* : reached the *droṇakalaśa*.

3 *By song* : *vipā́* : by knowledge, according to Sāyaṇa. 'The St. Petersb. Dict. explains *vip* as the twigs (cf. *vepres*) which form the bottom of the funnel and support the filtering-cloth.' Cowell, in Wilson's Translation.

4 Immortal, cleansed, these drops, since first they flowed, have never wearied, fain
To reach the regions and their paths.

5 Advancing they have travelled o'er the ridges of the earth and heaven,
And this the highest realm of all.

6 Over the heights have they attained the highest thread that is spun out,
And this which must be deemed most high.

7 Thou, Soma, holdest wealth in kine which thou hast seized from niggard churls:
Thou calledst forth the outspun thread.

HYMN XXIII. *Soma Pavamāna.*

1. SWIFT Soma drops have been effused in streams of meath, the gladdening drink,
For sacred lore of every kind.

2 Hither to newer resting-place the ancient Living Ones are come.
They made the Sun that he might shine.

3 O Pavamāna, bring to us the unsacrificing foeman's wealth,
And give us food with progeny.

4 The living Somas being cleansed diffuse exhilarating drink,
Turned to the vat which drips with meath.

5 Soma flows on intelligent, possessing sap and mighty strength,
Brave Hero who repels the curse.

6 For Indra, Soma! thou art cleansed, a feast-companion for the Gods:
Indu, thou fain wilt win us strength

7 When he had drunken draughts of this, Indra smote down resistless foes:
Yea, smote them, and shall smite them still.

6 Or, 'Streams rushing down have filled the threads, most excellent, spread out beneath'; that is, the threads of the straining-cloth. See note in Wilson. According to Sāyaṇa 'the thread' is sacrifice; and 'this which must be deemed most high' may be, as Ludwig suggests, the place of sacrifice which is also to be held holy. Wilson translates the second line:—'this rite is glorified thereby.'

7 *From niggard churls*: or from the Paṇis. *Thou calledst out the outspun thread*: 'thou hast called aloud at the outspread sacrifice.'—Wilson.

---

2 *Newer resting-place*: a newly-prepared place of sacrifice. *The ancient Living Ones*: the Soma-drops.

HYMN XXIV. *Soma Pavamāna.*

1. HITHERWARD have the Soma streamed, the drops while they are purified:
When blent, in waters they are rinsed.

2 The milk hath run to meet them like floods rushing down a precipice:
They come to Indra, being cleansed.

3 O Soma Pavamāna, thou art flowing to be Indra's drink:
The men have seized and lead thee forth.

4 Victorious, to be hailed with joy, O Soma, flow, delighting men,
To him who ruleth o'er mankind.

5 Thou, Indu, when, effused by stones, thou runnest to the filter, art,
Ready for Indra's high decree.

6 Flow on, best Vṛtra-slayer; flow meet to be hailed with joyful lauds.
Pure, purifying, wonderful.

7 Pure, purifying is he called the Soma of the meath effused,
Slayer of sinners, dear to Gods.

HYMN XXV. *Soma Pavamāna.*

1. GREEN-HUED! as one who giveth strength flow on for Gods to drink, a draught
For Vāyu and the Marut host.

2 O Pavamāna, sent by song, roaring about thy dwelling-place,
Pass into Vāyu as Law bids.

3 The Steer shines with the Deities, dear Sage in his appointed home,
Foe-Slayer, most beloved by Gods.

4 Taking each beauteous form, he goes, desirable, while purified,
Thither where the Immortals sit.

5 To Indra Soma flows, the Red, engendering song, exceeding wise,
The visitor of living men.

4 *To him who ruleth o'er mankind*: to Indra.

5 *Ready for Indra's high decree*: Wilson, following Sāyaṇa, translates: 'an ample portion for Indra's belly.' See Bergaigne, *La Religion Védique*, III. 210 ff., for the meaning of *dhāman* in the Ṛgveda.

---

2 *Into Vāyu*: into the vessel appropriated to Vāyu—Sāyaṇa.

5 *The Red*: *aruṣáḥ*: here explained by Sāyaṇa as= *ārocamānaḥ*, shining or radiant. *The visitor of living men*: *āyuṣák*: the meaning of this word is uncertain. The St. Petersburg Lexicon explains it as, conjointly with men; with human co-operation. Ludwig in his translation renders it by 'der den lebenden besucht,' who visits the living man; but in his Commentary suggests that it may mean, during the whole of life. 'Constantly.'—Wilson.

The visitor of living men.
6 Flow, best exhilarator, Sage, flow to the filter in a stream
To seat thee in the place of song.

HYMN XXVI. *Soma Pavamāna.*

1. THE sages with the fingers' art have dressed and decked that vigorous Steed
Upon the lap of Aditi.
2 The kine have called aloud to him exhaustless with a thousand streams,
To Indu who supporteth heaven.
3 Him, nourisher of many, Sage, creative Pavamāna, they
Have sent, by wisdom, to the sky.
4 Him, dweller with Vivasvān, they with use of both arms have sent forth,
The Lord of Speech infallible.
5 Him, green, beloved, many eyed, the Sisters with pressing stones
Send down to ridges of the sieve.
6 O Pavamāna, Indu, priests hurry thee on to Indra, thee
Who aidest song and cheerest him.

HYMN XXVII. *Soma Pavamāna.*

1. THIS Sage, exalted by our lauds, flows to the purifying cloth,
Scattering foes as he is cleansed.
2 As giving power and winning light, for Indra and for Vāyu he
Is poured upon the filtering-cloth.
3 The men conduct him, Soma, Steer, Omniscient, and the Head of Heaven,
Effused into the vats of wood.
4 Longing for kine, longing for gold hath Indu Pavamāna lowed,
Still Conqueror, never overcome.
5 This Pavamāna, gladdening draught, drops on the filtering cloth, and then
Mounts up with Sūrya to the sky.
6 To Indra in the firmament this mighty tawny Steer hath flowed,
This Indu, being purified.

HYMN XXVIII. *Soma Pavamāna.*

1. URGED by the men, this vigorous Steed, Lord of the mind, Omniscient,
Runs to the woollen straining-cloth.
2 Within the filter hath he flowed, this Soma for the Gods effused,
Entering all their essences.
3 He shines in beauty there, this God Immortal in his dwelling-place,
Foe-slayer, dearest to the Gods.
4 Directed by the Sisters ten, bellowing on his way this Steer
Runs onward to the wooden vats.
5 This Pavamāna, swiftand strong, Omniscient, gave splendour to
The Sun and all his forms of light.
6 This Soma, being purified, flows mighty and infallible,
Slayer of sinners, dear to Gods.

HYMN XXIX. *Soma Pavamāna.*

1. FORWARD with mighty force have flowed the currents of this Steer effused,
Of him who sets him by the Gods.
2 The singers praise him with their song, and learned priests adorn the Steed,
Brought forth as light that merits laud.
3 These things thou winnest lightly while purified, Soma, Lord of wealth:
Fill full the sea that claims our praise.
4 Winning all precious things at once, flow on, O Soma, with thy stream:
Drive to one place our enemies.

6 *Of song* : *arkásya* : *arcanīyasyendrasya*, of the adorable Indra, according so Sāyaṇa. *Arka* has two meanings in the Ṛgveda (1) song or hymn of praise and (2) light or splendour. See Pischel, *Vedische Studien*, I. pp. 23—26.

---

1 *Aditi* : the earth.

2 *The kine* : who supply the milk that is mixed with the Soma juice.

4 *Vivasvān* : meaning here the sacrificer. *Of both arms* : *bhurijoḥ* : according to Sāyaṇa = *bāhvoḥ* the arms of the body. The St. Petersburg Lexicon explains the word as meaning a sort of vice or implement for holding wood while it is being cut. *Lord of speech* : making men eloquent.

5 *Many-eyed* : 'far beholding.'—Wilson. *The Sisters* : the fingers of the officiating priest.

---

3 *Omniscient* : or, all-possessing. *Vats of wood* : *vánesu* : according to Benfey, into the streams of water.

4 *Longing for kine* : who supply milk to mix with the Soma juice. *Gold* : worn on the finger of the priest who presses out the juice. *Lowed* : made a noise in dropping.

5 *Mounts up* : as the Moon.

---

1 *Who sets him by the Gods* : or, who decorates the Gods. 'Who seeks to surpass the gods.'—Wilson.

3 *These things* : for which we pray. *The sea* : the Soma-vat or reservoir.

5 Preserve us from the godless, from ill-omened voice of one and all,
That so we may be freed from blame.

6 O Indu, as thou flowest on bring us the wealth of earth and heaven,
And splendid vigour, in thy stream.

HYMN XXX. *Soma Pavamāna.*

1. STREAMS of this Potent One have flowed easily to the straining-cloth :
While he is cleansed he lifts his voice.

2 Indu, by pressers urged to speed, bellowing out while beautified.
Sends forth a very mighty sound.

3 Pour on us, Soma, with thy stream man-conquering might which many crave,
Accompanied with hero sons.

4 Hither hath Pavamāna flowed, Soma flowed hither in a stream,
To settle in the vats of wood.

5 To waters with the stones they drive thee tawny-hued, most rich in sweets,
O Indu, to be Indra's drink.

6 For Indra, for the Thunderer press the Soma very rich in sweets,
Lovely, inspiriting, for strength.

HYMN XXXI. *Soma Pavamāna.*

1. THE Soma-drops, benevolent, come forth as they are purified,
Bestowing wealth which all may see.

2 O Indu, high o'er heaven and earth be thou, increaser of our might :
The Master of all strength be thou.

3 The winds are gracious in their love to thee, the rivers flow to thee :
Soma, they multiply thy power.

4 Soma, wax great. From every side may vigorous powers unite in thee :
Be in the gathering-place of strength.

5 For thee, brown-hued ! the kine have poured imperishable oil and milk.
Aloft on the sublimest height.

6 Friendship, O Indu, we desire with thee who bearest noble arms,
With thee, O Lord of all that is.

HYMN XXXII. *Soma Pavamāna.*

1. THE rapture-shedding Soma-drops, effused in our assembly, have
Flowed forth to glorify our prince.

2 Then Trita's Maidens onward urge the Tawny-coloured with the stones,
Indu for Indra, for his drink.

3 Now like a swan he maketh all the company sing each his hymn :
He, like a steed, is bathed in milk.

4 O Soma, viewing heaven and earth, thou runnest like a darting deer :
Set in the place of sacrifice.

5 The cows have sung with joy to him, even as a woman to her love :
He came as to a settled race.

6 Bestow illustrious fame on us, both on our liberal lords and me,
Glory, intelligence, and wealth.

HYMN XXXIII. *Soma Pavamāna.*

1. LIKE waves of waters, skilled in song the juices of the Soma speed
Onward, as buffaloes to woods.

2 With stream of sacrifice the brown bright drops have flowed with strength in store
Of kine into the wooden vats.

3 To Indra, Vāyu, Varuṇa, to Viṣṇu, and the Maruts, flow
The drops of Soma juice effused.

---

5 *Ill-omened voice* : *svanā́t*, explained by Sāyaṇa as = *śabdā́nnindārūpāt*, sound or word in the form of blame; the raging fury of the demon or the godless man, according to Grassmann.

---

2 *A very mighty sound*: or, a sound which Indra loves.

---

1 *Wealth which all may see* : 'intellectual wealth.'—Wilson.

3 *The winds*: cf. 'Vāyu is Soma's guardian God' (X. 85. 5).

4 This stanza has occurred before. See I. 91. 16. *Be in the gathering place of strength* : be the central point and source of all power.

5 *The kine* : of the clouds, the waters. *Oil and milk*: sweet and fertilizing rain. Or the cows who supply for the libation may be intended, in which case 'the sublimest' would be the place of sacrifice.

---

1 *Our prince* : the noble who institutes the sacrifice.

2 *Trita's Maidens* : the fingers of the priest. See IX 38. 2.

3 *Like a swan*: as a sentinel *haṁsa* (swan, wild-goose, or flamingo) at the approach of danger sounds a note of alarm which is answered by all the rest.—Ludwig.

4 *Darting* ; Sāyaṇa takes *taktáḥ* with 'thou,' Soma, and explains it by *gavyaiḥ payaādibhirmiśritaḥ san*, being mixed with milk, curds, etc. Elsewhere Sāyaṇa explains it by 'swift.'

5 *Cows* : praises, according to Sāyaṇa. *As to a settled race* : as a horse is brought to run a race that has been arranged. 'As a hero hastens to the welcome contest.'—Wilson.

4 Three several words are uttered : kine are lowing, cows who give their milk :
The Tawny-hued goes bellowing on.

5 The young and sacred mothers of the holy rite have uttered praise :
They decorate the Child of Heaven.

6 From every side, O Soma, for our profit, pour thou forth four seas
Filled full of riches thousandfold.

HYMN XXXIV. *Soma Pavamāna.*

1. The drop of Soma juice effused flows onward with this stream impelled.
Rending strong places, with its might.

2 Poured forth to Indra, Varuṇa, to Vāyu and the Marut host,
To Viṣṇu, flows the Soma juice.

3 With stones they press the Soma forth, the Strong conducted by the strong :
They milk the liquor out with skill.

4 'Tis he whom Trita must refine, 'tis he who shall make Indra glad :
The Tawny One is decked with tints.

5 Him do the Sons of Pṛśni milk, the dwelling-place of sacrifice,
Oblation lovely and most dear.

6 To him in one united stream these songs flow on straight forward : he,
Loud voiced, hath made the milch-kine low.

HYMN XXXV. *Soma Pavamāna.*

1. Pour forth on us abundant wealth, O Pavamāna, with thy stream.
Wherewith thou mayest find us light.

2 O Indu, swayer of the sea, shaker of all things, flow thou on,
Bearer of wealth to us with might.

3 With thee for Hero, Valiant One ! may we subdue our enemies :
Let what is precious flow to us.

4 Indu arouses strength, the Sage who strives for victory, winning power,
Discovering holy works and means.

5 Mover of speech, we robe him with our songs as he is purified
Soma, the Guardian of the folk;

6 On whose way, Lord of Holy Law, most rich, as he is purified.
The people all have set their hearts.

HYMN XXXVI. *Soma Pavamāna.*

1. Forth from the mortar is the juice sent, like a car-horse, to the sieve :
The Steed steps forward to the goal.

2 Thus, Soma, watchful, bearing well, cheering the Gods, flow past the sieve,
Turned to the vat that drops with meath.

3 Excellent Pavamāna, make the lights shine brightly out for us :
Speed us to mental power and skill.

4 He, beautified by pious men, and coming from their hands adorned,
Flows through the fleecy straining-cloth.

5 May Soma pour all treasures of the heavens, the earth, the firmament
Upon the liberal worshipper.

6 Thou mountest to the height of heaven, O Soma, seeking steeds and kine,
And seeking heroes, Lord of Strength !

HYMN XXXVII. *Soma Pavamāna.*

1. Soma, the Steer, effused for draught, flows to the purifying sieve,
Slaying the fiends, loving the Gods.

4 *Three several words* : according to Sāyaṇa, *trividhā stutiḥ*, praise of three kinds, from the three Vedas. 'The priests utter the three sacred texts.'—Wilson. Probably three triplets chanted during the ceremony. See Bergaigne, I. 288.

5 *Mothers of the holy rite* : apparently, the cows who supply milk for libations. *The Child of Heaven* : the Soma, which, according to a text quoted by Sāyaṇa, 'was in the third heaven from hence.'

6 *Four seas* : imaginary seas, to correspond with the four quarters of heaven.

---

1 *Strong places* : the strongholds of enemies, the fiends who withhold the rain.

4 *Trita* : the preparer of the Celestial Soma.

5 *The dwelling-place of sacrifice* : the Soma-plant contains within itself the chief element of sacrifice, and the preparation of the juice is only the development of its nature.—Ludwig.

---

2 *The sea* : The reservoir of Soma juice.

4 *Discovering holy works and means* : acquainted with sacred rites and arms.—Wilson.

6 *On whose way* : on whose statutes or decrees.

---

1 *To the goal*: *kārṣman* : apparently, a line or furrow drawn across the end of the race-course. In I. 116. 17, Sāyaṇa explains *kārṣman* as a piece of wood serving as a goal, but in this place he takes it to mean, 'the God-attracting battle-field called a sacrifice,' *devānāmākarṣaṇavati yajñākhye saṅgrāme*. See Cowell's note in Wilson's Translation.

---

2 *The vat* : the *droṇakalaśa*.

---

1 *For draught* : *pītáye* : 'for the drinking (of the gods).'—Wilson.

2 Far-sighted, tawny-coloured, he flows to the sieve, intelligent,
Bellowing, to his place of rest.

3 This vigorous Pavamāna runs forth to the luminous realm of heaven,
Fiend-slayer, through the fleecy sieve.

4 This Pavamāna up above Trita's high ridge hath made the Sun,
Together with the Sisters, shine.

5 This Vṛtra-slaying Steer, effused, Soma room-giver, ne'er deceived,
Hath gone, as 'twere, to win the spoil.

6 Urged onward by the sage, the God speeds forward to the casks of wood,
Indu to Indra willingly.

HYMN XXXVIII. *Soma Pavamāna.*

1. THIS Steer, this Chariot, rushes through the woollen filter, as he goes
To war that wins a thousand spoils.

2 The Dames of Trita with the stones onward impel this Tawny One,
Indu to Indra for his drink.

3 Ten active fingers carefully adorn him here; they make him bright
And beauteous for the gladdening draught.

4 He like a falcon settles down amid the families of men.
Speeding like lover to his love.

5 This young exhilarating juice looks downward from its place in heaven,
This Soma-drop that pierced the sieve.

6 Poured for the draught, this tawny juice flows forth, intelligent, crying out,
Unto the well-beloved place.

2 *Intelligent* : or, endowed with strength.

4 *Trita's high ridge* : according to Sāyaṇa, 'the high place (of the sacrifice) of Trita' the Ṛṣi. But the heavenly home of Trita, the celestial preparer of the Soma for Indra, is intended. *The Sisters* : the Dawns.

6 *Willingly* : *maṁhánā* : 'plenteously.'—Ludwig. 'In his might.'—Cowell.

———

1 *To war that wins a thousand spoils* : more literally, to thousandfold booty, or deed of might.

2 *The Dames of Trita* : as Trita is the celestial purifier of the Soma, the fingers of the earthly purifiers are called his dames, or his maidens as in IX. 32. 2.

5 *From its place in heaven* : or *diváḥ* may be the genitive case, taken with *śiśuḥ*, the Child of Heaven, as in IX. 33. 5.

6 *The well beloved place* : the *droṇakalaśa* or vat in which it rests.

———

HYMN XXXIX. *Soma Pavamāna.*

1. FLOW on, O thou of lofty thought, flow swift in thy beloved form,
Saying, I go where dwell the Gods.

2 Preparing what is unprepared, and bringing store of food to man,
Make thou the rain descend from heaven.

3 With might, bestowing power, the juice enters the purifying sieve,
Far-seeing, sending forth its light.

4 This is it which in rapid course hath with the river's wave flowed down
From heaven upon the straining cloth.

5 Inviting him from far away, and even from near at hand, the juice
For Indra is poured forth as meath.

6 In union they have sung the hymn : with stones they urge the Tawny One.
Sit in the place of sacrifice.

HYMN XL. *Soma Pavamāna.*

1. THE Very Active hath assailed, while purified, all enemies :
They deck the Sage with holy songs.

2 The Red hath mounted to his place; to Indra goes the mighty juice:
He settles in his firm abode.

3 O Indu, Soma, send us now great opulence from every side, Pour on us treasures thousandfold.

4 O Soma Pavamāna, bring, Indu, all splendours hitherward :
Find for us food in boundless store.

5 As thou art cleansed, bring hero strength and riches to thy worshipper,
And prosper thou the singer's hymns.

6 O Indu, Soma, being cleansed, bring hither riches doublypiled,
Wealth, mighty Indu, meet for lauds.

HYMN XLI. *Soma Pavamāna.*

1. ACTIVE and bright have they come forth, impetuous in speed like bulls,
Driving the black skin far away.

2 *Preparing what is unprepared* : 'consecrating the unconsecrated worshipper or place' is Sāyaṇa's explanation.

6 *Sit* : O Gods.—Sāyaṇa.

———

2 *The Red* : Soma. *His place* : the *droṇakalaśá*, or reservoir. *His firm abode* : heaven.

6 *Doubly-piled* : *dvibárhasam* : according to Sāyaṇa, 'from both worlds, heaven and earth.'

———

1 *They* : the Soma juices. *The black skin* : meaning, apparently, both the black pall or covering of night and the Rākṣasas or dark-skinned Dasyus or hostile aborigines.

2 Quelling the riteless Dasyu, may we think upon the bridge of bliss,
Leaving the bridge of woe behind.

3 The mighty Pavamāna's roar is heard as 'twere the rush of rain
Lightnings are flashing to the sky.

4 Pour out on us abundant food, when thou art pressed, O Indu wealth
In kine and gold and steeds and spoil.

5 Flow on thy way, Most Active, thou: fill full the mighty heavens and earth,
As Dawn, as Sūrya with his beams.

6 On every side, O Soma, flow round us with thy protecting stream,
As Rasā flows around the world.

HYMN XLII. *Soma Pavamāna.*

1. ENGENDERING the Sun in floods, engendering heaven's lights, green-hued,
Robed in the waters and the milk,

2 According to primeval plan this Soma, with his stream, effused
Flows purely on, a God for Gods.

3 For him victorious, waxen great, the juices with a thousand powers
Are purified for winning spoil.

4 Shedding the ancient fluid he is poured into the cleansing sieve:
He, thundering, hath produced the Gods.

5 Soma, while purifying, sends hither all things to be desired,
He sends the Gods who strengthen Law.

6 Soma, effused, pour on us wealth in kine, in heroes, steeds, and spoil,
Send us abundant store of food.

HYMN XLIII. *Soma Pavamāna.*

1. WE will enrobe with sacred song the Lovely One who, as a Steed,
Is decked with milk for rapturous joy.

2 All songs of ours desiring grace adorn him in the ancient way,
Indu for Indra, for his drink.

3 Soma flows on when purified, beloved and adorned with songs,
Songs of the sage Medhyātithi.

4 O Soma Pavamāna, find exceeding glorious wealth for us,
Wealth, Indu, fraught with boundless might.

5 Like courser racing to the prize Indu, the lover of the Gods,
Roars, as he passes, in the sieve.

6 Flow on thy way to win us strength, to speed the sage who praises thee:
Soma, bestow heroic power.

HYMN XLIV. *Soma Pavamāna.*

1. INDU, to us for this great rite, bearing as 'twere thy wave to Gods,
Unwearied, thou art flowing forth.

2 Pleased with the hymn, impelled by prayer, Soma is hurried far away,
The Wise One in the Singer's stream.

3 Watchful among the gods, this juice advances to the cleansing sieve :
Soma, most active, travels on.

4 Flow onward, seeking strength for us, embellishing the sacrifice :
The priest with trimmed grass calleth thee.

5 May Soma, ever bringing power to Bhaga and to Vāyu, Sage
And Hero, lead us to the Gods.

6 So, to increase our wealth to-day, Inspirer, best of Furtherers,
Win for us strength and high renown.

HYMN XLV. *Soma Pavamāna.*

1. FLOW, thou who viewest men, to give delight, to entertain the Gods,
Indu, to Indra for his drink.

3 The cleansing of the terrestrial Soma is identified with the purification of the celestial nectar accompanied by rain and lightning. See Hillebrandt, *V. M.* 343, 362.

6 *Rasā* : a mythical stream that flows round the atmosphere and the earth. See V. 41. 15, and X. 108. 1.

---

1 *In floods* : in the waters on high; in the firmament.

4 *Hath produced the Gods* : *yatra somo 'bhiṣūyate tatra devā niyatam prādurbhavanti* ; where Soma is effused, there the gods constantly appear.—Sāyaṇa.

---

1 *As a steed* : is bathed in water. *For rapturous joy* : 'for the exhilaration (of the gods).'—Wilson.

3 *Medhyātithi* : the Ṛṣi of the hymn.

5 *Racing to the prize* : *vājasṛt* : 'rushing into battle.'—Wilson.

6 *Heroic power* : 'excellent male offspring.'—Wilson.

---

1 *For this great rite* : 'to give us abundant wealth.'—Wilson. *Unwearied* : *ayāsyaḥ* : according to Sāyaṇa, this is the name of the Ṛṣi : 'Ayāsya (goeth) towards the gods (in sacrifice).'—Wilson.

2 Stream to thine embassy for us: thou hastenest, for Indra, to
The Gods, O better than our friends.

3 We balm thee, red of hue, with milk to fit thee for the rapturous joy:
Unbar for us the doors of wealth.

4 He through the sieve hath passed, as comes a courser to the pole, to run:
Indu belongs unto the Gods.

5 All friends have lauded him as he sports in the wood, beyond the fleece:
Singers have chanted Indu's praise.

6 Flow, Indu, with that stream wherein steeped thou announcest to the man
Who worships thee heroic strength.

HYMN XLVI. *Soma Pavamāna.*

1. LIKE able coursers they have been sent forth to be the feast of Gods,
Joying in mountains, flowing on.

2 To Vāyu flow the Soma-streams, the drops of juice made beautiful
Like a bride dowered by her sire.

3 Pressed in the mortar, these, the drops of juice, the Somas rich in food,
Give strength to Indra with their work.

4 Deft-handed men, run hither, seize the brilliant juices blent with meal,
And cook with milk the gladdening draught.

5 Thus, Soma, Conqueror of wealth! flow, finding furtherance for us,
Giver of ample opulence.

6 This Pavamāna, meet to be adorned, the fingers ten adorn,
The draught that shall make Indra glad.

HYMN XLVII. *Soma Pavamāna.*

1. GREAT as he was, Soma hath gained strength by this high solemnity:
Joyous he riseth like a bull.

2 His task is done: his crushings of the Dasyus are made manifest:
He sternly reckoneth their debts.

3 Soon as his song of praise is born, the Soma, Indra's juice, becomes
A thousand-winning thunderbolt.

4 Seer and Sustainer, he himself desireth riches for the sage
When he embellisheth his songs.

5 Fain would they both win riches as in races of the steeds. In war
Thou art upon the conquerors' side.

HYMN XLVIII. *Soma Pavamāna.*

1. WITH sacrifice we seek to thee kind Cherisher of manly might
In mansions of the lofty heavens;

2 Gladdening crusher of the bold, ruling with very mighty sway,
Destroyer of a hundred forts.

3 Hence, Sapient One! the Falcon, strong of wing, unwearied, brought thee down,
Lord over riches, from the sky.

2 *Thou hastenest*: Sāyaṇa gives a different explanation of this part of the stanza: 'thou (who) art drunk for Indra, (pour) on the gods wealth for (us) their friends.'—Wilson. I have adopted Ludwig's interpretation.

3 *We balm thee, red of hue*: or, 'Yea, we adorn thee, red.' *For the rapturous joy*: *mádāya*: 'for the purpose of exhilaration.'—Wilson.

4 *To the pole*: the meaning of *dhúram* here is not clear, and the comparison is not obvious. 'As a horse in going passes the shaft (of the chariot).'—Wilson. 'As a horse (presses) through the yoke,' Grassmann. Ludwig suggests 'hedge' or 'barrier' as the probable meaning of the word in this place.

5 *In the wood, beyond the fleece*: when he has passed through the woollen strainer and fallen into the wooden trough or vat. *Singers*: *nāváḥ*: shouts of joy, according to the St. Petersburg Lexicon.

---

1 *They have been sent forth*: *ásṛgran* (effusi sunt) is applicable both to the effused Soma-drops and to horses loosed or started for a race. *Joying in mountains*: coming from plants grown on hills.

2 *Dowered by her sire*: meaning, perhaps, possessed of property inherited from her father.

4 *Deft-handed*: *suhastyaḥ* cannot be satisfactorily accounted for. *Suhastyā*, a dual, may have been the original reading. See Ludwig's Commentary, Vol. V., pp. 347, 348.

---

1 *Riseth*: or, roareth *Śabdam karoti*.—Sāyaṇa.

2 *He sternly reckoneth their debts*: 'resolute he acquits the debts (of the worshipper).'—Wilson.

3 *A thousand-winning thunderbolt*: all powerful to slay the wicked and to reward worshippers.

4 *Sustainer*: I follow Ludwig in taking *vidhartári* as a nominative singular. But see Cowell's note in Wilson's Translation.

5 *They both*: Soma and the sage of singer.—Ludwig. Sāyaṇa interprets the stanza differently: 'Thou desirest to give wealth to those who conquer in combat as (men offer fodder) to horses in battle.' Wilson.

---

1 *Kind Cherisher of manly might*: 'auspicious bearing wealth.'—Wilson.

2 *Hundred forts*: cf. IV. 26. 3.

3 *The Falcon*: See IV. 26 and 27.

4 That each may see the light, the Bird brought us the guard of Law, the Friend
Of all, the speeder through the air.
5 And now, sent forth, it hath attained to mighty power and majesty,
Most active, ready to assist.

HYMN XLIX. *Soma Pavamāna.*

1. Pour down the rain upon us, pour a wave of waters from the sky,
And plenteous store of wholesome food.
2 Flow onward with that stream of thine, whereby the cows have come to us,
The kine of strangers to our home.
3 Chief Friend of Gods in sacred rites, pour on us fatness with thy stream,
Pour down on us a flood of rain.
4 To give us vigour, with thy stream run through the fleecy straining-cloth :
For verily the Gods will hear.
5 Onward hath Pavamāna flowed and beaten off the Rākṣasas,
Flashing out splendour as of old.

HYMN L. *Soma Pavamāna.*

1. Loud as a river's roaring wave thy powers have lifted up themselves :
Urge on thine arrow's sharpened point.
2 At thine effusion upward rise three voices full of joy, when thou
Flowest upon the fleecy ridge.
3 On to the fleece they urge with stones the tawny well-beloved One,
Even Pavamāna, dropping meath.
4 Flow with thy current to the sieve, O Sage most powerful to cheer,
To seat thee in the place of song.
5 Flow, Most Exhilarating ! flow anointed with the milk for balm,
Indu, for Indra, for his drink.

HYMN LI. *Soma Pavamāna.*

1. Adhvaryu, on the filter pour the Soma juice expressed with stones,
And make it pure for Indra's drink.
2 Pour out for Indra, Thunder-armed, the milk of heaven, the Soma's juice,
Most excellent, most rich in sweets.
3 These Gods and all the Marut host, Indu ! enjoy this juice of thine,
This Pavamāna's flowing meath.
4 For, Soma, thou hast been effused, strengthening for the wild carouse,
O Steer, the singer, for our help.
5 Flow with thy stream, Far-sighted One, effused, into the cleansing sieve :
Flow on to give us strength and fame.

HYMN LII. *Soma Pavamāna.*

1. Wealth-winner, dwelling in the sky, bringing us vigour with the juice,
Flow to the filter when effused.
2 So, in thine ancient ways, may he, beloved, with a thousand streams
Run o'er the fleecy straining-cloth.
3 Him who is like a caldron shake : O Indu, shake thy gift to us
Shake it, armed Warrior ! with thine arms.
4 Indu, invoked with many a prayer, bring down the vigour of these men,
Of him who threatens us with war.

4 *The Friend of all* : or, the common possession. *The speeder through the air* : *rajastúram* : 'the showerer of water.'—Wilson.

4 *The Gods will hear* : the sound that thou makest in flowing.—Sāyaṇa.

5 *Flashing out splendour as of old* : or, 'Making lights shine as erst they shone.'

1 *Urge on thine arrow's sharpened point* : *vāṇásya codayā pavim* : apparently a bold metaphorical expression for 'make a noise like that of a discharged arrow.' 'Emit thy sound like that of a (rushing) arrow.'—Wilson. Or *vāṇásya* may mean of (thy) reed, pipe, flute, or other musical instrument, and Sāyaṇa explains *pavim* by *śabdam*. Benfey accordingly (Sāmaveda, II. 5. 1. 5. 1.) renders the passage : 'Erhebe deiner Flote Schall.' 'Lift up the music of thy flute.' According to Hillebrandt, *V. M.*, I. p. 43, the reed or arrow means the sharp-pointed stalk of the Soma-plant.

2 *Three voices full of joy* : or, three several joyful words. See IX. 33. 4. *The fleecy ridge* : 'the summit of the fleece.'—Wilson.

4 *In the place of song* : See IX. 25. 6. 'On Indra's lap.'—Wilson.

4 *For the wild carouse* : 'for speedy exhilaration.'—Wilson.

2 *May he* : the juice, regarded as distinct from Soma who is addressed.

3 *Him who is like a caldron* : beat or bruise the Soma that is full of juice as a caldron is of water. *With thine arms* : or, with the blows (of the pressing-stones). The meaning of the second and third 'shake' seems to be 'send rapidly.' '(Soma), send (us) him who is like a pot; Indu, send us now wealth ; swift-flowing (Soma) send it with blows (of the stones).'—Wilson. Professor Grassmann says that by 'him who is like a caldron' the wealthy-enemy is intended, whose possessions are to be poured out upon the pious worshippers.

5 Indu, Wealth-giver, with thine help pour out for us a hundred, yea,
A thousand of thy pure bright streams.

HYMN LIII. *Soma Pavamāna.*

1. O THOU with stones for arms, thy powers, crushing the fiends, have raised themselves :
Chase thou the foes who compass us.

2 Thou conquerest thus with might when car meets car, and when the prize is staked:
With fearless heart will I sing praise.

3 No one with evil thought assails this Pavamāna's holy laws :
Crush him who fain would fight with thee.

4 For Indra to the streams they drive the tawny rapture-dropping Steed,
Indu the bringer of delight.

HYMN LIV. *Soma Pavamāna.*

1. AFTER his ancient splendour, they, the bold, have drawn the bright milk from
The Sage who wins a thousand gifts.

2 In aspect he is like the Sun; he runneth forward to the lakes,
Seven currents flowing through the sky.

3 He, shining in his splendour, stands high over all things that exist—
Soma, a God as Sūrya is.

4 Thou, Indu, in thy brilliancy, pourest on us, as Indra's Friend,
Wealth from the kine to feast the Gods.

HYMN LV. *Soma Pavamāna.*

1. POUR on us with thy juice all kinds of corn, each sort of nourishment,
And, Soma, all felicities.

2 As thine, O Indu, is the praise, and thine what springeth from the juice,
Seat thee on the dear sacred grass.

3 And, finding for us kine and steeds, O Soma, with thy juice flow on
Through days that fly most rapidly.

4 As one who conquers, ne'er subdued, attacks and slays the enemy,
Thus, Vanquisher of thousands ! flow.

HYMN LVI. *Soma Pavamāna.*

1. SWIFT to the purifying sieve flows Soma as exalted Law,
Slaying the fiends, loving the Gods.

2 When Soma pours the strengthening food a hundred ever-active streams
To Indra's friendship win their way.

3 Ten Dames have sung to welcome thee, even as a maiden greets her love:
O Soma, thou art decked to win.

4 Flow hitherward, O Indu, sweet to Indra and to Viṣṇu : guard
The men, the singers, from distress.

HYMN LVII. *Soma Pavamāna.*

1. THY streams that never fail or waste flow forth like showers of rain from heaven,
To bring a thousand stores of strength.

2 He flows beholding on his way all well-beloved sacred lore,
Green-tinted, brandishing his arms.

3 He, when the people deck him like a docile king of elephants.
Sits as a falcon in the wood.

4 So bring thou hitherward to us, Indu, while thou art purified,
All treasures both of heaven and earth.

1 *With stones for arms* : *adrivaḥ* : generally an appellative of Indra, the slinger or caster of the stone or thunderbolt ; here, according to Sāyaṇa,=*grāvavan soma*, O Soma, possessor of, that is expressed by, the stones.

2 *When car meets car* : in battle. *When the prize is staked* : in the chariot-race ; or the reference may be also to battle.

4 *To the streams* : the *vasatīvarī* waters.

1 *They, the bold* : the Soma-pressers. *The Sage* or Ṛṣi ; Soma.

2 *The lakes* : of air. *Seven currents* : corresponding to the seven earthly rivers. 'He unites with the seven down-descending rivers of heaven.'—Wilson.

4 *From the kine* : consisting of milk, curds, etc.

4 *Vanquisher of thousands* : or, thou who winnest thousands, *i.e.* countless spoils or treasures.

3 *Ten Dames* : the fingers, whose sound is heard in the operation of pressing the Soma juice.

3 *Like a docile king of elephants* : von Roth, in the St. Petersburg Lexicon, suggests *íbhe* for *íbhaḥ*, 'like a pious king among his retinue;' but no alteration is necessary, *íbhaḥ* and *rā́jā* being taken together in the sense of elephant king or stately and noble elephant. See *Vedische Studien*, I. p. XV. *Sit as a falcon in the wood*: in the wood, as referring to the Soma, meaning the wooden trough or vat. 'Sits on the waters like a hawk.' —Wilson.

HYMN LVIII. *Soma Pavamāna.*

1. SWIFT runs this giver of delight, even the stream of flowing juice:
Swift runs this giver of delight.

2 The Morning knows all precious things, the Goddess knows her grace to man:
Swift runs this giver of delight.

3 We have accepted thousands from Dhvasra's and Puruṣanti's hands :
Swift runs this giver of delight.

4 From whom we have accepted thus thousands and three times ten besides:
Swift runs this giver of delight.

HYMN LIX. *Soma Pavamāna.*

1. FLOW onward, Soma, winning kine, and steeds, and all that gives delight:
Bring hither wealth with progeny.

2 Flow onward from the waters, flow, inviolable, from the plants:
Flow onward from the pressing-boards.

3 Soma, as Pavamāna, pass over all trouble and distress :
Sit on the sacred grass, a Sage.

4 Thou, Pavamāna, foundest light; thou at thy birth becamest great:
O Indu, thou art over all.

HYMN LX. *Soma Pavamāna.*

1. SING forth and laud with sacred song most active Pavamāna, laud
Indu who sees with thousand eyes.

2 Thee who hast thousand eyes to see, bearer of thousand burthens, they
Have filtered through the fleecy cloth.

3 He, Pavamāna, hath streamed through the fleece then: he runs into the jars,
Finding his way to Indra's heart.

4 That Indra may be bounteous, flow, most active Soma, for our weal :
Bring genial seed with progeny.

HYMN LXI. *Soma Pavamāna.*

1. FLOW onward, Indu, with this food for him who in thy wild delight
Battered the nine-and-ninety down,

2 Smote swiftly forts, and Śambara, then Yadu and that Turvaśa,
For pious Divodāsa's sake.

3 Finder of horses, pour on us horses and wealth in kine and gold,
And, Indu, food in boundless store.

4 We seek to win thy friendly love, even Pavamāna's flowing o'er
The limit of the cleansing sieve.

5 With those same waves which in their stream o'erflow the purifying sieve,
Soma, be gracious unto us.

6 O Soma, being purified, bring us from all sides,—for thou canst,—
Riches and food with hero sons.

7 Him here, the Child whom streams have borne, the ten swift fingers beautify :
With the Ādityas is he seen.

8 With Indra and with Vāyu he, effused, flows onward with the beams
Of Sūrya to the cleansing sieve.

9 Flow rich in sweets and lovely for our Bhaga, Vāyu, Pūṣan flow
For Mitra and for Varuṇa.

10 High is thy juice's birth : though set in heaven, on earth it hath obtained
Strong sheltering power and great renown.

11 Striving to win, with him we gain all wealth from the ungodly man,
Yea, all the glories of mankind.

1 *Swift* : *tárat* : 'rescuing (his worshippers from sin).' —Wilson.

3 *Dhvasra* and *Puruṣanti* were 'two kings who conferred great wealth on *Taranta* and *Purumīḷha*, two ṛṣis of the family of *Vidadaśva*. See p. XXXIII. of Max-Müller's Ṛgveda, Vol. V.' Cowell's note in Wilson's Translation.

4 *Thus thousands and three times ten* : Sāyaṇa, taking *tánā* (thus, in this manner) to mean 'garments,' mistaking *triṁśátam*, thirty, for *triśatam*, three hundred, and neglecting the *cá* (and), interprets 'three hundred thousand garments.' 'Thirty robes and thousands.'—E. B. Cowell. Grassmann places this hymn in his Appendix as a composition of fragments and out of place where it stands in the text.

2 *The waters*: the *vasatīvarī* waters. *The pressing-boards* : *dhiṣáṇābhyaḥ* : according to Sāyaṇa, *grā́vābhyaḥ*, the pressing-stones.

1 *With sacred song* : *gāyatréṇa* : 'with a Gāyatrī hymn.' —Wilson.

2 *Bearer of thousand burthens* : or, bringer of thousand bounties.

1 *The nine-and-ninety* : 'ninety-nine (cities of the foe).'—Wilson.

3 *In boundless store* : literally, in thousands.

7 *Whom streams have borne* : *sindhumātaram* : 'whose parents are the rivers.' Wilson. Born as the Moon in the ocean of air. *With the Ādityas is he seen* : that is, he is counted as one of the Ādityas.

12 Finder of room and freedom, flow for
Indra whom we must adore,
For Varuṇa and the Marut host.

13 The Gods have come to Indu well-descended, beautified with milk,
The active crusher of the foe.

14 Even as mother cows their calf, so let our praise-songs strengthen him,
Yea, him who winneth Indra's heart.

15 Soma, pour blessings on our kine, pour forth the food that streams with milk :
Increase the sea that merits laud.

16 From heaven hath Pavamāna made, as 'twere, the marvellous thunder, and
The lofty light of all mankind.

17 The gladdening and auspicious juice of thee, of Pavamāna, King !
Flows o'er the woollen straining-cloth.

18 Thy juice, O Pavamāna, sends its rays abroad like splendid skill,
Like lustre, all heaven's light, to see.

19 Flow onward with that juice of thine most excellent, that brings delight,
Slaying the wicked, dear to Gods.

20 Killing the foeman and his hate, and winning booty every day,
Gainer art thou of steeds and kine.

21 Red-hued, be blended with the milk that seems to yield its lovely breast,
Falcon-like resting in thine home.

22 Flow onward thou who strengthenedst Indra to slaughter Vṛtra who
Compassed and stayed the mighty floods.

23 Soma who rainest gifts, may we win riches with our hero sons :
Strengthen, as thou art cleansed, our hymns.

24 Aided by thee, and through thy grace, may we be slayers when we war :
Watch, Soma, at our solemn rites.

25 Chasing our foemen, driving off the godless, Soma floweth on,
Going to Indra's special place.

26 O Pavamāna, hither bring great riches, and destroy our foes :
O Indu, grant heroic fame.

27 A hundred obstacles have ne'er checked thee when fain to give thy boons,
When, being cleansed, thou combatest.

28 Indu, flow on, a mighty juice; glorify us among the folk :
Drive all our enemies away.

29 Indu, in this thy friendship most lofty and glorious may we
Subdue all those who war with us.

30 Those awful weapons that thou hast, sharpened at point to strike men down—
Guard us therewith from every foe.

HYMN LXII. *Soma Pavamāna.*

1. THESE rapid Soma-drops have been poured through the purifying sieve
To bring us all felicities.

2 Dispelling manifold mishap, giving the courser's progeny,
Yea, and the warrior steed, success.

3 Bringing prosperity to kine, they make perpetual Iḷā flow
To us for noble eulogy.

4 Strong, mountain-born, the stalk hath been pressed in the streams for rapturous joy :
Hawk-like he settles in his home.

5 Fair is the God-loved juice; the plant is washed in waters, pressed by men :
The milch-kine sweeten it with milk.

6 As drivers deck a courser, so have they adorned the meath's juice for
Ambrosia, for the festival.

13 *Well-descended* : literally, well-born or well-produced; '(who is) completely generated.'—Wilson.

15 *The sea* : *samudrám* : according to Sāyaṇa, water generally.

16 'The purified (Soma) has generated the great light which is common to all mankind, like the wonderful thundering of the sky.' Muir, *O.S. Texts*, IV. 112. The great light common to all men, or *vaiśvānarám* or *the lofty light of all mankind*, is Agni Vaiśvānara.

20 *The foeman and his hate* : 'the hostile Vṛtra.'—Wilson.

25 *The godless* : *árāvṇaḥ* : those who present no sacrificial offerings; 'the withholders (of wealth).'—Wilson. *Special place* : that is, the vessel set apart for his libations.

26 *Heroic fame* : or, fame with brave sons.

27 *Obstacles* : or, enemies, according to Sāyaṇa. *Thou combatest* : *makhasyáse* : according to Sāyaṇa, 'when thou wishest to give us wealth.' 'The meanings "fight," "strive," etc., are foreign to Sāyaṇa, being derived from a comparison of macto, etc.'—Editor's note in Wilson's Translation.

30 *Weapons* : the Moon being the warrior who overcomes the darkness of night. See Hillebrandt, *V.M.*, I 340. Cf 'The moon...advances like an indignant warrior through a fleeing army.'—S.T. Coleridge.

3 *Iḷā* ; here, according to Sāyaṇa, meaning 'food.' 'Labetrank,' refreshing draught.—Grassmann.

4 *The stalk* : the Soma-plant, which is said to have grown on the mountains.

5 *In waters* : the *vasatīvarī* waters.

6 *For ambrosia* : *amṛtāya* : 'for the sake of immortality.'—Wilson.

7 Thou, Indu, with thy streams that drop sweet juices, which were poured for help,
Hast settled in the cleansing sieve.

8 So flow thou onward through the fleece, for Indra flow, to be his drink,
Finding thine home in vats of wood.

9 As giving room and freedom, as most sweet, pour butter forth and milk,
O Indu, for the Aṅgirases.

10 Most active and benevolent, this Pavamāna, sent to us
For lofty friendship, meditates.

11 Queller of curses, mighty, with strong sway, this Pavamāna shall
Bring treasures to the worshipper.

12 Pour thou upon us thousandfold possessions, both of kine and steeds,
Exceeding glorious, much-desired.

13 Wandering far, with wise designs, the juice here present is effused,
Made beautiful by living men.

14 For Indra flows the gladdening drink, the measurer of the region, Sage,
With countless wealth and endless help.

15 Born on the mountain, lauded here, Indu for Indra is set down,
As in her sheltering nest a bird.

16 Pressed by the men, as 'twere to war hath Soma Pavamāna sped,
To test with might within the vats.

17 That he may move, they yoke him to the three-backed triple-seated car
By the Seven Ṛṣis' holy songs.

18 Drive ye that Tawny Courser, O ye pressers, on his way to war,
Swift Steed who carries off the spoil.

19 Pouring all glories hither, he, effused and entering the jar,
Stands like a hero mid the kine.

20 Indu, the living men milk out the juice to make the rapturous draught:
Gods for the Gods milk out the meath.

21 Pour for the Gods into the sieve our Soma very rich in sweets,
Him whom the Gods most gladly hear.

22 Into his stream who gladdens best these Soma juices have been poured,
Lauded with songs for lofty fame.

23 Thou flowest to enjoy the milk, and bringest valour, being cleansed:
Winning the spoil flow hitherward.

24 And, hymned by Jamadagnis, let all nourishment that kine supply,
And general praises, flow to us.

25 Soma, as leader of the song flow onward with thy wondrous aids,
For holy lore of every kind.

26 Do thou as leader of the song, stirring the waters of the sea,
Flow onward, thou who movest all.

27 O Soma, O thou Sage, these worlds stand ready to attest thy might:
For thy behoof the rivers flow.

28 Like showers of rain that fall from heaven thy streams perpetually flow
To the bright fleece spread under them.

29 For potent Indra purify Indu effectual and strong,
Enjoyment-giver, Mighty Lord.

30 Soma, true, Pavamāna, Sage, is seated in the cleansing sieve,
Giving his praiser hero strength.

HYMN LXIII. *Soma Pavamāna.*

1. Pour hitherward, O Soma, wealth in thousands and heroic strength,
And keep renown secure for us.

2 Thou makest food and vigour swell for Indra, best of gladdeners!
Within the cups thou seatest thee.

3 For Indra and for Viṣṇu poured, Soma hath flowed into the jar:
May Vāyu find it rich in sweets.

4 These Somas swift and brown of hue, in stream of solemn sacrifice

9 *For the Aṅgirases*: or, from the Aṅgirases. The Jamadagnis were not members of that family.—Ludwig.

10 *Meditates*: 'is known (to all).' Wilson.

13 *Wandering far*: *urugāyāḥ*: according to Sāyaṇa, much-lauded, or praised by many.

14 *The measurer of the region*: who measured out and made the firmament.

15 *Born on the mountain*: or, perhaps, as Sāyaṇa takes it, 'made manifest by song.'

17 *By the Seven Ṛṣis' holy songs*: or 'Of Ṛṣis, with seven holy songs'; the *car* being the sacrifice, the three backs or ridges being the three daily libations, the three seats being the three Vedas.

19 *Mid the kine*: among the enemy's cattle, for whose possession he is fighting. So, says Sāyaṇa, Soma stands among the sacrifices.

20 *The living men*: the worshippers, according to Sāyaṇa; but perhaps, as Ludwig suggests, his *stotārah* should be *sotāraḥ*, pressers. *Gods*: *devāḥ*: the priests.

26 *Waters of the sea*: of the sea of air, the firmament.

Have flowed through twisted obstacles,
5 Performing every noble work, active, augmenting Indra's strength,
Driving away the godless ones.
6 Brown Soma-drops, effused that seek Indra, to their appropriate place
Flow through the region hitherward.
7 Flow onward with that stream of thine wherewith thou gavest Sūrya light,
Urging on waters good to men.
8 He, Pavamāna, high o'er man yoked the Sun's courser Etaśa
To travel through the realm of air.
9 And those ten Coursers, tawny-hued, he harnessed that the Sun might come :
Indu, he said, is Indra's self.
10 Hence, singers, pour the gladdening juice to Vāyu and to Indra, pour
The drops upon the fleecy cloth.
11 O Soma Pavamāna, find wealth for us not to be assailed,
Wealth which the foeman may not win.
12 Send riches hither with thy stream in thousands, both of steeds and kine,
Send spoil of war and high renown.
13 Soma the God, expressed with stones, like Sūrya, floweth on his way,
Pouring the juice within the jar.
14 These brilliant drops have poured for us, in stream of solemn sacrifice,
Worshipful laws and strength in kine.
15 Over the cleansing sieve have flowed the Somas, blent with curdled milk,
Effused for Indra Thunder-armed.
16 Soma, do thou most rich in sweets, a gladdening drink most dear to Gods,
Flow to the sieve to bring us wealth.
17 For Indra, living men adorn the Tawny Courser in the streams, Indu, the giver of delight.
18 Pour for us, Soma, wealth in gold, in horses and heroic sons,
Bring hither strength in herds of kine.
19 For Indra pour ye on the fleece him very sweet to taste, who longs.
For battle as it were in war.
20 The singers, seeking help, adorn the Sage who must be decked with songs :
Loud bellowing the Steer comes on.
21 The singers with their thoughts and hymns have, in the stream of sacrifice,
Caused Soma, active Steer, to roar.
22 God, working with mankind, flow on; to Indra go thy gladdening juice :
To Vāyu mount as Law commands
23 O Soma, Pavamāna, thou pourest out wealth that brings renown :
Enter the lake, as one we love.
24 Soma thou flowest chasing foes and bringing wisdom and delight :
Drive off the folk who love not Gods.
25 The Pavamānas have been poured, the brilliant drops of Soma juice,
For holy lore of every kind.
26 The Pavamānas have been shed, the beautiful swift Soma-drops,
Driving all enemies afar.
27 From heaven, from out the firmament, hath Pavamāna been effused
Upon the summit of the earth.
28 O Soma, Indu, very wise, drive, being purified, with thy stream
All foes, all Rākṣasas away.
29 Driving the Rākṣasas afar, O Soma, bellowing, pour for us
Most excellent and splendid strength.
30 Soma, do thou secure for us the treasures of the earth and heaven,
Indu, all boons to be desired.

HYMN LXIV. *Soma Pavamāna.*

1. SOMA, thou art a splendid Steer, a Steer, O God, with steerlike sway :
Thou as a Steer ordainest laws.
2 Steer-strong thy might is as a steer's, steer-strong thy wood, steer-like thy drink :
A Steer indeed, O Steer, art thou.
3 Thou, Indu, as a vigorous horse, hast neighed together steeds and kine :

4 *Twisted obstacles* : either the twigs of which the frame of the filter was made, or the rough surface of the wool of the strainer. 'Are let loose upon the *Rākṣasas*.'—Wilson.

8 In this and the following stanza Soma is identified with the Sun.

9 *Coursers* : or Harits. Cf. IV. 6. 9 and 13. 3.

10 *Hence* : from this vessel.

14 *Worshipful laws* : the meaning of *dhā́mānyā́ryā* is not clear. '(Flowing) towards the dwellings of respectable (worshippers).'—Wilson. 'Venerable might.'—Ludwig.

23 *The lake* : the *droṇakalaśa*, vat or reservoir.

27 *The summit of the earth* : the raised altar.

1 *Steer* : Sāyaṇa, as usual, explains *vṛṣā* by *varṣakaḥ* 'Sprinkler.'—Wilson.

3 *Neighed together* : collected, through the efficacy of the sound thou makest in dropping through the filter, and enriched us with steeds and kine.

Unbar for us the doors to wealth.

4 Out of desire of cows and steeds and horses potent Soma-drops,
Brilliant and swift, have been effused.

5 They purified in both the hands, made beautiful by holy men,
Flow onward to the fleecy cloth.

6 These Soma juices shall pour forth all treasures for the worshipper
From heaven and earth and firmament.

7 The streams of Pavamāna, thine, Finder of all, have been effused,
Even as Sūrya's rays of light.

8 Making the light that shines from heaven thou flowest on to every form :
Soma, thou swellest like a sea.

9 Urged on thou sendest out thy voice, O Pavamāna; thou hast moved,
Like the God Sūrya, to the sieve.

10 Indu, Enlightener, Friend, hath been purified by the sages' hymns :
So starts the charioteer his steed—

11 Thy God-delighting wave which hath flowed to purifying seive,
Alighting in the home of Law.

12 Flow to our sieve, a gladdening draught that hath most intercourse with Gods,
Indu, to Indra for his drink.

13 Flow onward with a stream for food, made beautiful by sapient men :
Indu with sheen approach the milk.

14 While thou art cleansed, Song-Lover, bring comfort and vigour to the folk,
Poured, Tawny One ! on milk and curds.

15 Purified for the feast of Gods, go thou to Indra's special place,
Resplendent, guided by the strong.

16 Accelerated by the hymn, the rapid drops of Soma juice
Have flowed, urged onward, to the lake.

17 Easily have the living drops, made beautiful, approached the lake,
Yea, to the place of sacrifice.

18 Compass about, our faithful Friend, all our possessions with thy might :
Guard, hero like, our sheltering home.

19 Loud neighs the Courser Etaśa, with singers, harnessed for the place,
Guided for travel to the lake.

20 What time the Swift One resteth in the golden place of sacrifice,
He leaves the foolish far away.

21 The friends have sung in unison, the prudent wish to sacrifice :
Down sink the unintelligent.

22 For Indra girt by Maruts, flow, thou Indu, very rich in sweets,
To sit in place of sacrifice.

23 Controlling priests and sages skilled in holy song adorn thee well :
The living make thee beautiful.

24 Aryaman, Mitra, Varuṇa drink Pavamāna's juice, yea, thine :
O Sage, the Maruts drink thereof.

25 O Soma, Indu, thou while thou art purified urgest onward speech.
Thousandfold, with the lore of hymns.

26 Yea, Soma, Indu, while thou art purified do thou bring to us
Speech thousandfold that longs for war.

27 O Indu, Much-invoked, while thou art purifying, as the Friend.
Of these men enter thou the lake.

28 Bright are these Somas blent with milk, with light that flashes brilliantly.
And form that utters loud acclaim.

29 Led by his drivers, and sent forth, the Strong Steed hath come nigh for spoil,
Like warriors when they stand arrayed.

30 Specially, Soma, coming as a Sage from heaven to prosper us,
Flow like the Sun for us to see.

HYMN LXV. *Soma Pavamāna.*

1. THE glittering maids send Sūra forth, the glorious sisters, close-allied,
Send Indu forth, their mighty Lord.

8 *To every form* : to bring us blessings in every shape.

9 *To the sieve* : *vidharmaṇi* : 'in observance of the law,' according to M. Bergaigne. See *La Religion Védique*, III. 218, note.

16 *The Lake* : *samudrám* : acccording to Sāyaṇa, the sea of air, the firmament. The *droṇakalaśa*, vat or reservoir, is probably intended.

19 *The Courser Etaśa* : here meaning Soma. *Váhniḥ* (from *vah*, Lat. veh-o) is properly a horse of burden, or draught-horse.

21 *The friends* : the priests ; or perhaps the Maruts. *Down sink* : *narake*, into hell, says Sāyaṇa.

26 *That longs for war* : *makhasyúvam* 'desiring wealth.' —Wilson. See IX. 6 . 27, note.

28 *Form* : *kṛpā* : stream, according to Sāyaṇa.

30 *Specially* : *ṛdhák* : said by Yāska to be the Vedic form of *pṛthak*, and to be used in the sense of prospering. See Wilson's Translation, Editor's note. Or *ṛdhák* may mean, lightly, easily, without effort.

---

1 *The glittering maids* : the fingers, perhaps with reference to the gold rings worn by the priests when they press the Soma *Sūra* : here said to mean Soma; 'the invigorating.'—Wilson. *The glorious sisters* : the fingers.

2 Pervade, O Pavamāna, all our treasures with repeated light,
God, coming hither from the Gods.

3 Pour on us, Pavamāna, rain, as service and rain praise for Gods :
Pour all to be our nourishment.

4 Thou art a Steer by lustre : we, O Pavamāna, faithfully
Call upon thee the Splendid One.

5 Do thou, rejoicing, nobly-armed ! pour upon us heroic strength :
O Indu, come thou hitherward.

6 When thou art cleansed with both the hands and dipped in waters, with the wood.
Thou comest to the gathering-place.

7 Sing forth your songs, as Vyaśva sang, to Soma Pavamāna, to,
The Mighty One with thousand eyes;

8 Whose coloured sap they drive with stones, the yellow meath-distilling juice,
Indu for Indra, for his drink.

9 We seek to gain the friendly love of thee that Strong and Mighty One,
Of thee the winner of all wealth.

10 Flow onward with thy stream, a Steer, inspiriting the Maruts' Lord,
Winning all riches by thy might.

11 I send thee forth to battle from the press, O Pavamāna, Strong,
Sustainer, looker on the light.

12 Acknowledged by this song of mine, flow, tawny-coloured, with thy stream :
Incite to battle thine ally.

13 O Indu, visible to all pour out for us abundant food:
Soma, be thou our prosperer.

14 The pitchers, Indu, with thy streams have sung aloud in vigorous might :
Enter them, and let Indra drink.

15 O thou whose potent gladdening juice they milk out with the stones, flow on,
Destroyer of our enemies.

16 King Pavamāna is implored with holy songs, on man's behalf,
To travel through the firmament.

17 Bring us, O Indu, hundredfold increase of kine, and noble steeds,
The gift of fortune for our help.

18 Pressed for the banquet of the Gods, O Soma, bring us might, and speed,
Like beauty for a brilliant show.

19 Soma, flow on exceeding bright with loud roar to the wooden vats,
Falcon-like resting in thine home.

20 Soma, the Water-winner flows to Indra, Vāyu, Varuṇa,
To Viṣṇu and the Marut host.

21 Soma, bestowing food upon our progeny, from every sides,
Pour on us riches thousandfold !

22 The Soma juices which have been expressed afar or near at hand,
Or there on Śaryaṇāvān's bank,

23 Those pressed among Ārjīkas, pressed among the active, in men's homes,
Or pressed among the Races Five—

24 May these celestial drops, expressed, pour forth upon us, as they flow,
Rain from the heavens and hero strength.

25 Urged forward o'er the ox-hide flows the Lovely One of tawny hue,
Lauded by Jamadagni's song.

26 Like horses urged to speed, the drops, bright, stirring vital power, when blent
With milk, are beautified in streams.

27 So they who toil with juices send thee forward for the Gods' repast :
So with this splendour flow thou on.

28 We choose to-day that chariot-steed of thine, the Strong, that brings us bliss,
The Guardian, the desire of all,

29 The Excellent, the Gladdener, the Sage with heart that understands,
The Guardian, the desire of all;

30 Who for ourselves, O thou Most Wise, is wealth and fair intelligence,
The Guardian, the desire of all.

HYMN LXVI. *Soma Pavamāna.*

1. For holy lore of every sort, flow onward thou whom all men love.
A Friend to be besought by friends.

3 *As service* : as the cause of worship.

6 *With the wood* : '(taken up) with the wooden vessel.'—Wilson. Cf. IX. 1. 2.

7 *Vyaśva* : a Ṛṣi frequently mentioned in Book VIII.

12 *Thine ally* : Indra.

22 *Śaryaṇāvān's bank* : this lake is said to be on the borders of the Kurukṣetra country.

23 *Ārjīkas* : apparently a non-Āryan people in the North-West, See VIII. 53. 11.

25 *O'er the ox-hide* : the leather sheet that received the droppings of the Soma.

28 *The guardian* : *pāntam* : according to Pischel, 'den schwellenden,' 'the swelling one.' See his exhaustive excursus on the word in *Vedische Studien*, I. pp. 191—194.

The Ṛṣis are the hundred Vaikhānasas, said to have been a race of saintly hermits sprung from the nails of Prajāpati.

2 O'er all thou rulest with these Two which, Soma Pavamāna, stand,
Turned, as thy stations, hitherward.

3 Wise Soma Pavamāna, thou encompassest on every side
Thy stations as the seasons come.

4 Flow onward, generating food, for precious boons of every kind,
A Friend for friends, to be our help.

5 Upon the lofty ridge of heaven thy bright rays with their essences,
Soma, spread purifying power.

6 O Soma, these Seven Rivers flow, as being thine, to give command:
The Streams of milk run forth to thee.

7 Flow onward, Soma in a stream, effused to gladden Indra's heart,
Bringing imperishable fame.

8 Driving thee in Vivasvān's course, the Seven Sisters with their hymns
Made melody round thee the Sage.

9 The virgins deck thee o'er fresh streams to drive thee to the sieve when thou,
A singer, bathest in the wood.

10 The streams of Pavamāna, thine, Sage, Mighty One, have poured them forth.
Like coursers eager for renown.

11 They have been poured upon the fleece towards the meath-distilling vat :
The holy songs have sounded forth.

12 Like milch-kine coming home, the drops of Soma juice have reached the lake,
Have reached the place of sacrifice.

13 O Indu, to our great delight the running waters flow to us,
When thou wilt robe thyself in milk.

14 In this thy friendship, and with thee to help us, fain to sacrifice,
Indu, we crave thy friendly love.

15 Flow on, O Soma, for the great Viewer of men, for gain of kine
Enter thou into Indra's throat.

16 Best art thou, Soma, of the great, Strongest of strong ones, Indu : thou
As Warrior ever hast prevailed.

17 Mightier even than the strong, more valiant even than the brave,
More liberal than the bountiful,

18 Soma, as Sūra, bring us food, win offspring of our bodies : we.
Elect thee for our friendship, we elect thee for companionship.

19 Agni, thou pourest life; send down upon us food and vigorous strength ;
Drive thou misfortune far away,

20 Agni is Pavamāna, Sage, Chief Priest of all the Races Five :
To him whose wealth is great we pray.

21 Skilled in thy task, O Agni, pour splendour with hero strength on us,
Granting me wealth that nourishes.

22 Beyond his enemies away to sweet praise Pavamāna flows,
Like Sūrya visible to all.

23 Adorned by living men, set forth for entertainment, rich in food,
Far-sighted Indu is a Steed.

24 He, Pavamāna, hath produced the lofty Law, the brilliant light,
Destroying darkness black of hue.

25 From tawny Pavamāna, the Destroyer, radiant streams have sprung,
Quick streams from him whose gleams are swift.

26 Best rider of the chariot, praised with fairest praise mid beauteous ones,
Gold-gleaming with the Marut host,

27 May Pavamāna, best to win the booty, penetrate with rays,
Giving the singer hero strength.

28 Over the fleecy sieve hath flowed the drop effused : to Indra comes
Indu while he is purified

29 This Soma, through the pressing-stones, is sporting on the oxhide, and
Summoning Indra to the draught.

2 *With these Two* : probably a double asterism. See Hillebrandt, *V. M.* p. 446 ; and Gaidicke, *Der Accusativ im Veda*, p. 199.

8 The stream of Soma is likened to the course of Vivasvān or the Sun.

The Seven Sisters are probably the *Seven Rivers* of stanza 6. According to Sāyaṇa 'the seven kindred (priests)' are intended

9 *The virgins* : the fingers.

12 *The lake* : the *droṇakalaśa* or reservoir.

15 *For gain of kine* : *gáviṣṭaye* : according to Sāyaṇa, 'for the seeker of the kine of the Aṅgirases.'

18 *As Sūra*: See IX. 65. 1. 'Who art a hero.'—Wilson. 'From the Sun.' —Ludwig.

19. *Misfortune* : *ducchunām* : frequently personified as an evil power; 'the *Rākṣasas*.'—Wilson.

23 *Is a Steed* : 'one who continually goes to the Gods,' is Sāyaṇa's explanation of *ātyaḥ*, horse or courser.

25 *The Destroyer* : of darkness. Cf. IX. 61. 30.

27 *Penetrate* : the whole world.—Sāyaṇa.

29 *On the ox-hide* : See IX. 65. 25.

30 O Pavamāna, bless us, so that we may live, with that bright milk
Of thine which hath been brought from heaven.

HYMN LXVII. *Soma and Others.*

1. THOU, Soma, hast a running stream, joyous, most strong at sacrifice :
Flow bounteously bestowing wealth.
2 Effused as cheerer of the men, flowing best gladdener, thou art
A Prince to Indra with thy juice.
3 Poured forth by pressing-stones, do thou with loud roar send us in a stream
Most excellent illustrious might.
4 Indu, urged forward, floweth through the fleecy cloth : the Tawny One
With his loud roar hath brought as strength.
5 Indu, thou flowest through the fleece, bringing felicities and fame,
And, Soma, spoil and wealth in kine.
6 Hither, O Indu, bring us wealth in steeds and cattle hundredfold :
Bring wealth, O Soma, thousandfold.
7 In purifying, through the sieve the rapid drops of Soma juice
Come nigh to Indra in their course.
8 For Indra floweth excellent Indu, the noblest Soma juice
The Living for the Living One.
9 The glittering maids send Sūra forth : they with their song have sung aloud
To Pavamāna dropping meath.
10 May Pūṣan, drawn by goats, be our protector, and on all his paths
Bestow on us our share of maids.
11 This Soma flows like gladdening oil for him who wears the braided locks :
He shall give us our share of maids.
12 This Soma juice, O glowing God, flows like pure oil, effused for thee :
He shall give us our share of maids.
13 Flow onward, Soma, in thy stream, begetter of the sages' speech :
Wealth-giver among Gods art thou.
14 The Falcon dips within the jars : he wraps him in his robe and goes
Loud roaring to the vats of wood.
15 Soma, thy juice hath been effused and poured into the pitcher : like
A rapid hawk it rushes on.
16 For Indra flow most rich in sweets, O Soma, bringing him delight.
17 They were sent forth to feast the Gods, like chariots that display their strength.
18 Brilliant, best givers of delight, these juices have sent Vāyu forth.
19 Bruised by the press-stones and extolled, Soma, thou goest to the sieve,
Giving the worshipper hero strength.
20 This juice bruised by the pressing-stones and lauded passes through the sieve,
Slayer of demons, through the fleece.
21 O Pavamāna, drive away the danger, whether near at hand
Or far remote, that finds me here.
22 This day may Pavamāna cleanse us with his purifying power,
Most active purifying Priest.
23 O Agni, with the cleansing light diffused through all thy fiery glow,
Purify thou this prayer of ours.
24 Cleanse us with thine own cleansing power, O Agni, that is bright with flame,
And by libations poured to thee.
25 Savitar, God, by both of these, libation, purifying power,
Purify me on every side.
26 Cleanse us, God Savitar, with Three, O Soma, with sublimest forms,
Agni, with forms of power and might.
27 May the Gods' company make me clean, and Vasus make me pure by song.
Purify me, ye General Gods; O Jātavedas, make me pure.
28 Fill thyself full of juice, flow forth, O Soma, thou with all thy stalks,
The best oblation to the Gods.
29 We with our homage have approached the Friend who seeks our wondering praise,
Young, strengthener of the solemn rite.

2 *A Prince*: *sūriḥ* : a rich and liberal patron.

9 *The glittering maids send Sūra forth* : repeated from IX. 65. 1.

10 *Our share of maids* : desirable and approved wives.—Sāyaṇa.

11 *For him who wears the braided locks* : *kapardine* See I. 114. 1. and VII. 83. 8. Here Pūṣan is intended.

12 *O glowing God*. Pūṣan.

14 *The Falcon* : the falcon-like Soma.

18 *Have sent Vāyu forth* : have drawn him down from heaven 'Are let forth for Vāyu.'—Wilson.

26 The *Three sublimest forms* are said to be Agni, Vāyu, and Sūrya, or Fire, Wind, and Sun.

27 *The Gods' company* : the *yajamānas* or sacrificers, or the troop of Gods, Indra and others.—Sāyaṇa. *General Gods* : *viśve devāḥ* : or, all ye Gods.

30 Lost is Alāyya's axe. O Soma, God : do thou send it back hither in thy flow
Even, Soma, God, if 'twere a mole.

31 The man who reads the essence stored by saints, the Pāvamānī hymns,
Tastes food completely purified, made sweet by Mātariśvan's touch.

32 Whoever reads the essence stored by saints, the Pāvamānī hymns,
Sarasvatī draws forth for him water and butter, milk and meath.

HYMN LXVIII. *Soma Pavamāna.*

1. THE drops of Soma juice like cows who yield their milk have flowed forth, rich in meath, unto the Shining One,
And, seated on the grass, raising their voice, assumed the milk, the covering robe wherewith the udders stream.

2 He bellows with a roar around the highest twigs : the Tawny One is sweetened as he breaks them up.
Then, passing through the sieve into the ample room, the God throws off the dregs according to his wish.

3 The gladdening drink that measured out the meeting Twins fills full with milk the Eternal Ever-waxing Pair.
Bringing to light the Two great Regions limitless, moving above them he gained sheen that never fades.

4 Wandering through the Parents, strengthening the floods, the Sage makes his place swell with his own native might.
The stalk is mixed with grain : he comes led by the men together with the sisters, and preserves the Head.

5 With energetic intellect the Sage is born, deposited as germ of Law, far from the Twins.
They being young at first showed visibly distinct the Creature that is half-concealed and half-exposed.

6 The sages knew the form of him the Gladdener, what time the Falcon brought the plant from far away.
Him who assures success they beautified in streams, the stalk who yearned therefor, mighty and meet for praise.

7 Together with the Ṛsis, with their prayers and hymns ten women deck thee, Soma, friendly when effused.
Led by the men, with invocations of the Gods, through the fleece, thou hast given us strength to win the spoil.

8 Songs resonant with praise have celebrated him. Soma, Friend, springing forth with his fair company.
Even him who rich in meath, with undulating stream, Winnner of Wealth, Immortal, sends his voice from heaven.

9 He sends it into all the region forth from heaven. Soma, while he is filtered, settles in the jars.
With milk and waters is he decked when pressed with stones : Indu, when purified, shall find sweet rest and room.

10 Even thus poured forth flow on thy way, O Soma, vouchsafing us most manifold lively vigour.
We will invoke benevolent Earth and Heaven. Give us, ye Gods, riches with noble heroes.

30 This stanza is well-nigh unintelligible. Alāyya may, as is suggested in the St. Petersburg L xicon, be a name of Indra, and the lost axe may be the thunderbolt which the poet thinks has long lain idle, and which Soma is prayed to replace in the hands of the Thunderer, even though it were worthless and mischievous like a mole. Sāyaṇa's interpretation is different.—'May the battle-axe of the foe destroy the foe alone: flow to us, bright Soma; (slay) the villain only, bright Soma.'—Wilson.

31 *By saints* : by the Ṛsis to whom they were revealed. *Pāvamānī hymns* : the hymns in this Book dedicated to the purification of the Soma juice. *By Mātariśvan's touch* : 'Sāyaṇa says *Mātariśvan* means *Vāyu* because it breathes in the atmosphere *antarikṣe śvasiti*: the food is sweetened and purified by the purifying wind and the man eats it.'—Wilson. Mātariśvan probably represents Agni.

1 *The Shining One devám* : the radiant Indra. The second line is obscure. According to Sāyaṇa, *usriyāḥ* here means 'cows' and not milk :— 'the lowing kine sitting on the *barhis* grass hold in their udders the pure (juice) welling up.'—Wilson.

2 *The highest twigs*: of the Soma-plant, which as being the tenderest and juiciest are crushed first.—Ludwig. 'He with a noise reëchoes the principal (praises): separating the growing herbs, the green tinted (Soma) sweetens them. —Wilson.

3 *The meeting Twins* : Soma is called the Creator and Preserver of heaven and earth.

4 *The Parents* : heaven and earth. *The floods* : the waters of the firmament. *Grain* : especially barley. *Makes his place swell* ; enriches his own station, the *uttaravedi* or northward altar. *The sisters* : the fingers. *The Head* : apparently Sūrya. 'Sāyaṇa's explanation of *śiraḥ*, viz., *śīrṇam bhūtajātam* (the withered world?), needs explaining more than the original itself.'—Wilson.

5 *The Sage* : the Sun. *Far from the Twins* : rising in a distant region beyond heaven and earth. *The Creature that is half-concealed and half exposed* : the meaning appears to be, as Ludwig says, that heaven and earth while they were yet unseparated, produced the Moon : the Sun came into being only when they had been separated through Soma's energetic agency.

7 *Ten women* : the fingers.

HYMN LXIX. *Soma Pavamāna.*

1. LAID like an arrow on the bow the hymn hath been loosed like a young calf to the udder of its dam.
As one who cometh first with full stream she is milked the Soma is impelled to this man's holy rites.

2 The thought is deeply fixed; the savoury juice is shed; the tongue with joyous sound is stirring in the mouth;
And Pavamāna, like the shout of combatants, the drop rising in sweet juice, is flowing through the fleece.

3 He flows about the sheep-skin, longing for a bride : he looses Aditi's Daughters for the worshipper.
The sacred drink hath come, gold-tinted, well-restrained : like a strong Bull he shines, whetting his manly might.

4 The Bull is bellowing; the Cows are coming nigh : the Goddesses approach the God's own resting-place.
Onward hath Soma passed through the sheep's fair bright fleece, and hath, as 'twere, endued a garment newly washed.

5 The golden-hued, Immortal, newly bathed, puts on a brightly shining vesture that is never harmed.
He made the ridge of heaven to be his radiant robe, by sprinkling of the bowls from moisture of the sky.

6 Even as the beams of Sūrya, urging men to speed, that cheer and send to sleep, together rush they forth,
These swift outpourings in long course of holy rites : no form save only Indra shows itself so pure.

7 As down the steep slope of a river to the vale, drawn from the Steer the swift strong draughts have found a way.
Well be it with the men and cattle in our home. May powers, O Soma, may the people stay with us.

8 Pour out upon us wealth in goods, in gold, in steeds, in cattle and in corn, and great heroic strength.
Ye, Soma, are my Fathers, lifted up on high as heads of heaven and makers of the strength of life.

9 These Pavamānas here, these drops of Soma, to Indra have sped forth like cars to booty.
Effused, they pass the cleansing fleece, while, gold-hued, they cast their covering off to pour the rain down.

10 O Indu, flow thou on for lofty Indra, flow blameless, very gracious, foe-destroyer.
Bring splendid treasures to the man who lauds thee. O Heaven and Earth, with all the Gods protect us.

1 *Hath been loosed, &c.* : 'is let loose to (Indra) the fosterer as a calf to the udder of its mother, 'Sāyaṇa takes *ūdhani* [to the udder] twice over : he says it is used of *Indra* because he is the nourisher of everything.' —Wilson. *As one who cometh first* : according to Sāyaṇa, as a cow coming before her calf yields her milk, (so Indra coming before his worshippers pours vast blessings upon them). *First* : *ágre*: at the head; at the beginning of religious ceremony.

2 *The tongue with joyous sound is stirring in the mouth* : probably priest's tongue influenced by the exhilarating Soma juice. 'The *Soma* stream emitting pleasant juice is driven into (Indra's) mouth.'—Wilson.

3 *Longing for a bride* : seeking the waters with which he is to be united. *Aditi's Daughters*: probably, the plants, whose buds Soma as the Moon opens and fertilizes with his nectareous beams. 'The daughters of Infinity (Aditi (are probably the quarters of the sky.'—Ludwig.

4 *The Bull* : Soma. According to Sāyaṇa, *the Cows* are the propitiatory hymns of praise, which are called also *Goddesses* or divine.

5 *Brightly-shining vesture*: the milk with which the Soma juice is mixed. Sāyaṇa explains the second half of the stanza differently, taking *chamvaḥ* bowls or beakers into which the Soma juice is poured, as meaning metaphorically the two great receptacles of all living beings, or heaven and earth, and introducing Āditya what is not mentioned in the text :—'he has created Āditya who stands on the back of the sky for the destruction (of sin) and purification (and has created) Āditya's brilliance, the cover of the two worlds.'—Wilson.

7 *Vājāḥ* and *kṛṣṭáyaḥ*, *powers* and *people*, are explained by Sāyaṇa as 'food' and 'offspring.'

8 *Ye, Soma* : '*Soma* is treated as plural by attraction; or, as Sāyaṇa puts it, the plurality of the *pitṛs* is applied to Soma.'—Wilson. Probably Moon and Stars are intended. See Hillebrandt, *V. M.* I. p 398.

10 *With all the Gods* : *devaiḥ* : '*subhagairdhanaiḥ* with auspicious riches.'—Sāyaṇa.

HYMN LXX. *Soma Pavamāna.*

1. THE three times seven Milch-kine in the eastern heaven have for this Soma poured the genuine milky draught.
Four other beauteous Creatures hath he made for his adornment, when he waxed in strength through holy rites.

1 *The three times seven Milch-kine* are, according to Sāyaṇa, the twelve months, the five seasons, the three worlds, and Āditya or the Sun. Probably, as Ludwig says, the seven celestial rivers, multiplied by three to correspond with the threefold division of the heavens, are intended. These supply the genuine draught, in contrast to the *four other beauteous creatures*, the Vasatīvarī and the three Ekadhanā waters, which are terrestrial and factitious, made to adorn or purify Soma.

2 Longing for lovely Amṛta, by his wisdom he divided, each apart from other, earth and heaven.
He gladly wrapped himself in the most lucid floods, when through their glory they found the God's resting-place.

3 May those his brilliant rays be ever free from death, inviolate, for both classes of created things,—
Rays wherewith powers of men and Gods are purified. Yea, even for this have sages welcomed him as King.

4 He, while he is adorned by the ten skilful ones, that he too in the Midmost Mothers may create,
While he is watching o'er the lovely Amṛta's ways, looks on both races as Beholder of mankind.

5 He, while he is adorned to stream forth mighty strength, rejoices in his place between the earth and heaven.
The Steer dispels the evil-hearted with his might, aiming at offerings as an archer at the game.

6 Beholding, as it were, Two Mother Cows, the Steer goes roaring on his way even as the Maruts roar.
Knowing Eternal Law, the earliest light of heaven, he, passing wise, was chosen out to tell it forth.

7 The fearful Bull is bellowing with violent might, far-sighted, sharpening his yellow-coloured horns.
Soma assumes his seat in the well-fashioned place: the cowhide and the sheepskin are his ornament.

8 Bright, making pure his body free from spot and stain, on the sheep's back the Golden-coloured hath flowed down.
Acceptable to Mitra, Vāyu, Varuṇa, he is prepared as threefold meath by skilful men.

9 Flow on for the God's banquet, Soma, as a Steer, and enter Indra's heart, the Soma's reservoir.
Bear us beyond misfortune ere we be oppressed: the man who knows the land directs the man who asks.

10 Urged like a car-steed, flow to strength, O Soma: Indu, flow onward to the throat of Indra.
Skilled, bear us past, as in a boat o'er water: as battling Hero save us from the foeman.

HYMN LXXI. *Soma Pavamāna.*

1. THE guerdon is bestowed: the Mighty takes his seat, and, ever-watchful, guards from fiend and evil sprite.
Gold-hued, he makes the cloud his diadem, the milk his carpet in both worlds, and prayer his robe of state.

2 Strong, bellowing, he goes, like one who slays the folk; he lets this hue of Asuras flow off from him,
Throws off his covering, seeks his father's meeting-place, and thus makes for himself the bright robe he assumes.

3 Onward he flows, from both the hands, pressed out with stones: excited by the prayer, the water makes him wild.

3 *Both classes*: animate and inanimate. Or Gods and men.

4 *The ten skilful ones*: the fingers. *The Midmost Mothers*: the clouds that hang between heaven and earth, in which, perhaps, Soma aids in producing the rain. But the meaning is uncertain. Sāyaṇa explains *pramé* by *lokān pramātum*, 'to measure out, or create, the worlds.' *Both races*: Gods and men.

6 *As it were, Two Mother Cows*: Heaven and Earth. Sāyaṇa explains the second Pāda of the second line differently:—'the intelligent (*Pavamāna*) chose man to be the offerer of his praise.'—Wilson.

8 *Threefold*: according to Sāyaṇa, mixed with the Vasatīvarī water, curds, and milk. Probably, poured into three separate vessels, one for each of the three deities mentioned.

9 *The man who knows the Land*: who is acquainted with the roads or ways. 'Sāyaṇa completes the simile: "as by telling him he protects (helps) him, so do thou who knowest the roads of the sacrifice protect us by telling us the sacrificial paths." '—Wilson. But, of course, the application is intended to be general.

10 *Bear us past*: carry us over all difficulties and dangers. *From the foeman*: *nidáḥ*: from the reviling (of the foe).'—Wilson.

1 *The guerdon*: the honorarium given to the priests, consisting originally of a cow. *The Mighty*: Soma. *His carpet*: *upastíre*: that which is spread, scattered, or sprinkled. Cp. IX. 69. 5, where *upastáraṇam* is translated by 'sprinkling.'

2 *Hue of Asuras*: or, celestial brightness; 'Himmelsglanz.'—Grassmann. 'He puts forth that *Asura*-slaying tint of his'.—Wilson. *Seeks his father's meeting-place*: goes to meet the *yajamāna* or sacrificer. According to Sāyaṇa: 'the food (*pituḥ*), that is, the Soma, goes to the prepared reservoir.'

3 *The water makes him wild*: *vṛṣāyáte nábhasā*: *nábhas* in the Soma-hymns is used to signify either the rain-water in which, or the cloud from which, the Soma flows to the earth. Here it means the water with which the Soma-plant is sprinkled. See *Vedische Studien*, I. p 135. According to Ludwig: 'he acts like a bull in the sea of cloud.' *To satisfy the worshipper*: I adopt Ludwig's suggestion and take *yájate* as a dative of the participle. Wilson translates, after Sāyaṇa:—'he is honoured at the (god—) protected (sacrifice).'

He frolics and draws near, completes his work with song, and bathes in streams to satisfy the worshipper.

4 They pour out meath around the Master of the house, Celestial Strengthener of the mountain that gives might;
In whom, through his great powers, oblation-eating cows in their uplifted udder mix their choicest milk.

5 They, the ten sisters, on the lap of Aditi, have sent him forward like a car from both the arms.
He wanders and comes near the Cow's mysterious place, even the place which his inventions have produced.

6 Like as a falcon to his home, so speeds the God to his own golden wisely-fashioned place to rest.
With song they urge the darling to the sacred grass : the Holy One goes like a courser to the Gods.

7 From far away, from heaven, the red-hued noted Sage, Steer of the triple height, hath sung unto the kine.
With thousand guidings he, leading this way and that, shines, as a singer, splendidly through many a morn.

8 His covering assumes a radiant hue; where'er he comes into the fight he drives the foe afar.
The Winner of the Floods, with food he seeks the host of heaven, he comes to praises glorified with milk.

9 Like a bull roaming round the herds he bellows : he hath assumed the brilliancy of Sūrya.
Down to the earth hath looked the heavenly Falcon : Soma with wisdom views all living creatures.

4 *The Master of the house* : according to Sāyaṇa, the conqueror of the fort of the enemy. See IX. 78. 3. *The mountain that gives might* : the cloud. In the second half of this stanza I adopt Sāyaṇa's interpretation as a makeshift, although it seems impossible that *mūrdhán*, 'head,' should here mean 'uplifted.' Ludwig takes *ū́dhani*, 'udder,' in the sense of 'behälter,' or receptacle into which the Soma flows.

5 *On the lap of Aditi* : on the earth. 'near to the ground.'—Wilson. *The Cow's mysterious place* : or, distant place, is the udder of heaven, the cloud.

7 *Of the triple height* : working in heaven, firmament and earth.—Ludwig. See IX. 75. 3.

9 *The heavenly Falcon* : *divyāḥ suparṇāḥ* : 'celestial, flying gracefully.'—Wilson. Soma, says Sāyaṇa, is said to go gracefully, 'because it is carried off by *Gāyatrī* in the shape of a hawk.'

HYMN LXXII. *Soma Pavamāna.*

1. THEY cleanse the Gold-hued : like a red Steed is he yoked, and Soma in the jar is mingled with the milk.
He sendeth out his voice, and many loving friends of him the highly-lauded hasten with their songs.

2 The many sages utter words in unison, while into Indra's throat they pour the Soma juice,
When, with the ten that dwell together closely joined, the men whose hands are skilful cleanse the lovely meath.

3 He goes upon his way, unresting, to the cows, over the roaring sound which Sūrya's Daughter loves.
The Falcon brought it to him for his own delight : now with the twofold kindred sisters is his home.

4 Washed by the men, stone-pressed, dear on the holy grass, faithful to seasons, Lord of cattle from of old,
Most liberal, completing sacrifice for men, O Indra, pure bright Soma, Indu, flows for thee.

5 O Indra, urged by arms of men and poured in streams, Soma flows on for thee after his Godlike kind.
Plans thou fulfillest, gatherest thoughts for sacrifice : in the bowls sits the Gold-hued like a roosting bird.

6 Sages well-skilled in work, intelligent, drain out the stalk that roars, the Sage, the Everlasting One.
The milk, the hymns unite them with him in the place of sacrifice, his seat who is produced anew.

7 Earth's central point, sustainer of the mighty heavens, distilled into the streams, into the waters' wave,
As Indra's thunderbolt, Steer with far-spreading wealth, Soma is flowing on to make the heart rejoice.

2 *Indra's throat* : literally, belly ; the *droṇakalaśá* or reservoir. *The ten* : the fingers.

3 *The cows* : the milk and curds. *The roaring sound* of the effused Soma is said to be dear to Sūrya's Daughter, Uṣas or Dawn, because it is chiefly heard in the early morning. *The Falcon* : I adopt Ludwig's interpretation of the strange word *vinaṁgṛsáḥ* as no other meaning seems suitable here. According to Sāyaṇa, the word means praiser, or worshipper. *The twofold kindred sisters* : the fingers of both hands.

7 *The heart* : of Indra. *As Indra's thunderbolt* : cp. IX. 77. 1.

8 Over the earthly region flow thou on thy way, helping the praiser and the pourer, thou Most Wise.
Let us not lack rich treasure reaching to our home, and may we clothe ourselves in manifold bright wealth.

9 Hither, O Indu, unto us a hundred gifts of steeds, a thousand gifts of cattle and of gold,
Measure thou forth, yea, splendid ample strengthening food do thou, O Pavamāna, heed this laud of ours.

HYMN LXXIII. *Soma Pavamāna.*

1. THEY from the spouting drop have sounded at the rim : naves speed together to the place of sacrifice.
That Asura hath formed, to seize, three lofty heights. The ships of truth have borne the pious man across.

2 The strong Steers, gathering, have duly stirred themselves, and over the stream's wave the friends sent forth the song.
Engendering the hymn, with flowing streams of meath, Indra's dear body have they caused to wax in strength.

3 With sanctifying gear they sit around the song : their ancient Father guards their holy work from harm.
Varuṇa hath o'erspread the mighty sea of air. Sages had power to hold him in sustaining floods.

4 Sweet-tongued, exhaustless, they have sent their voices down together, in heaven's vault that pours a thousand streams.
His wildly-restless warders never close an eye : in every place are found the bonds that bind man fast.

5 O'er Sire and Mother they have roared in unison, bright with the verse of praise, burning up riteless men,
Blowing away with supernatural might from earth and from the heavens the swarthy skin which Indra hates.

6 Those which, as guides of song and counsellors of speed, were manifested from their ancient dwelling place,—
From these the eyeless and the deaf have turned aside : the wicked travel not the pathway of the Law.

7 What time the filter with a thousand streams is stretched, the thoughtful sages purify their song therein.
Bright-coloured are their spies, vigorous, void of guile, excellent, fair to see, beholders of mankind.

8 Guardian of Law, most wise, he may not be deceived : three Purifiers hath he set within his heart.
With wisdom he beholds all creatures that exist : he drives into the pit the hated riteless ones.

9 The thread of sacrifice spun in the cleansing sieve, on Varuṇa's tongue-tip, by supernatural might,—
This, by their striving, have the prudent ones attained : he who hath not this power shall sink into the pit.

HYMN LXXIV. *Soma Pavamāna*

1. BORN like a youngling he hath clamoured in the wood, when he, the Red, the Strong, would win the light of heaven.
He comes with heavenly seed that makes

1 *They* : the pressing-stones, from whose rim or edge the Soma-drops fall noisily. *Naves*: by synecdoche wheels, again by the same figure, chariots, and then by metaphor the swiftly-running Soma-drops. *That Asura* : the divine Soma. *To seize* : to be held and used. *Three lofty heights* : the three elevated worlds. *The ships of truth* or, of the truthful (Soma). According to Sāyaṇa, the four vessels which hold the Āditya, Āgrayaṇa, Ukthya, and Dhruva libations.

2 *The strong Steers* : the priests.

3 *Their ancient Father* : Soma ; or, perhaps, Agni. *Varuṇa* : 'Soma the all-enveloper.'—Wilson. *Him* : Soma. *In sustaining floods* : in the Vasatīvarī waters.—Sāyaṇa.

4 *They* : the beams that radiate from Soma : *somaraśmayaḥ* : Soma-rays.—Sāyaṇa.

5 *Sire and Mother* : the general parents, Heaven and Earth. *The swarthy skin* : 'the black skinned (*Rākṣasas*).' —Wilson.

6 *Those* : rays. I follow Sāyaṇa's interpretation. The first line is very obscure.

7 *The filter* : the tip of their tongue. Cf. stanza 9, and hymn 75. 2. See Bergaigne, *La Religion Védique*, I. 283. *Bright coloured* : *rudrāsaḥ* : sons of Rudra, according to Sāyaṇa. But see *Vedische Studien*, I. pp. 55, 56.

8 *Of Law* : of law-ordained sacrifice. The *three Purifiers* whom Soma sets within his heart and combines in his own being are Agni, Vāyu, Sūrya, the purifying powers of fire, wind, and sun.

9 *On Varuṇa's tongue-tip* : the Vasatīvarī waters in which Soma dwells (vasati) stand on the tip of Varuṇa's tongue—Sāyaṇa. *He who hath not this power* : 'he who is incompetent for the rite.'—Wilson.

1 *In the wood* : in the wooden vat. According to Sāyaṇa, 'in the water.'

the water swell : him for wide-spreading shelter we implore with prayer.

2 A far-extended pillar that supports the sky, the Soma-stalk, filled full, moves itself every way.
He shall bring both these great worlds while the rite proceeds : the Sage holds these who move together and all food.

3 Wide space hath he who follows Aditi's right path, and mighty, well-made food, meath blent with Soma juice;
He who from hence commands the rain, Steer of the kine, Leader of floods, who helps us hence, who claims our laud.

4 Butter and milk are drawn from animated cloud; thence Amṛta is produced, centre of sacrifice.
Him the Most Bounteous Ones, ever united, love; him as our Friend the Men who make all swell rain down.

5 The Soma-stalk hath roared, following with the wave : he swells with sap for man the skin which Gods enjoy.
Upon the lap of Aditi he lays the germ, by means whereof we gain children and progeny.

6 In the third region which distils a thousand streams, may the Exhaustless Ones descend with procreant power.
The kindred Four have been sent downward from the heavens : dropping with oil they bring Amṛta and sacred gifts.

7 Soma assumes white colour when he strives to gain : the bounteous Asura knows full many a precious boon.
Down the steep slope, through song, he comes to sacrifice, and he will burst the water-holding cask of heaven,

8 Yea, to the shining milk-anointed beaker, as to his goal, hath stepped the conquering Courser.
Pious-souled men have sent their gifts of cattle unto Kakṣīvān of the hundred winters.

9 Soma, thy juice when thou art blended with the streams, flows, Pavamāna, through the long wool of the sheep.
So, cleansed by sages, O best giver of delight, grow sweet for Indra, Pavamāna ! for his drink.

2 *He shall bring both these great worlds* : shall bring Heaven and Earth to the sacrifice.

3 *He who follows Aditi's right path* : the regularly moving moon. Sāyaṇa takes *áditeḥ* with *gávyūtiḥ* : 'the way to earth is broad.'—Wilson Somewhat similarly Hillebrandt, V.M., I. 360.

4 *The Most Bounteous Ones, the Men who make all swell*, are, probably, the Maruts who fertilize the earth, and send Soma down in the rain. Sāyaṇa's explanation is different :—'the assembled liberal givers [the *yajamānas* or sacrificers] delight him : (the Soma juices) the leaders, the protectors shower down the accumulated (water).'—Wilson. For the meaning of *péravaḥ* those who swell, or cause to swell, 'protectors' according to Sāyaṇa, see *Vedische Studien, I.* p. 85

5 *For man* : for the sacrificer. *The skin* : his own body.—Sāyaṇa. *Upon the lap of Aditi* : of the earth, according to Sāyaṇa. The meaning is that Soma is the source of all Nature's productive power.

6 *In the third region*; dwelling in heaven. *The Exhaustless Ones* ; these are *the kindred Four* of the following line, meaning according to Sāyaṇa, four rays or digits of Soma. It is most probable that the four Goddesses Sinivālī, Kuhū or Gungū, Rākā, and Anumati are meant. Cp. II. 32. 6, 7.'—Ludwig.

7 *Strives to gain* : seeks to enjoy heaven.—Sāyaṇa. *The water-holding cask* : the water-laden cloud.

8 *The conquering Courser* : the swiftly-flowing Soma. *Kakṣivān* : the Ṛṣi of the hymn.

HYMN LXXV. *Soma Pavamāna.*

1. Graciously-minded he is flowing on his way to win dear names o'er which the Youthful One grows great.
The Mighty and Far-seeing One hath mounted now the mighty Sūrya's car which moves to every side.

2 The Speaker, unassailable Master of this hymn, the Tongue of sacrifice pours forth the pleasant meath.
Within the lustrous region of the heavens the Son makes the third secret name of Mother and of Sire.

3 Sending forth flashes he hath bellowed to the jars, led by the men into the golden reservoir.
The milky streams of sacrifice have sung to him : he of the triple height shines brightly through the morns.

4 Pressed by the stones, with hymns, and

1 *O'er which* : that is the Youthful One, the fresh and strong Soma, exceeds in greatness even the high titles which he wins by his gracious deeds.

2 *Speaker* ; *Master* ; *Tongue of sacrifice* : Soma, the giver of eloquence. *The Son* : Soma. *Of Mother and of Sire* : of his parents, Heaven and Earth. What *the third secret name*, that is, probably, a name in addition to those of Heaven and Earth, and comprising both deities, may be, does not appear. Sāyaṇa's explanation is different : 'the son (the sacrificer) assumes a third name unknown to his parents ;' that is, Wilson adds, 'a name not given at birth...He (Sāyaṇa) cites Baudhāyana, who gives *Somayājin* [Somayāga sacrificer] as an instance of a third name.

3 *The milky streams* : cf. I. 144. 2. *Of the triple height* : dwelling in three high places, heaven, the firmament or the mountain-top, and the place of sacrifice. Cf. IX. 71. 7.

graciously inclined, illuminating both the Parents, Heaven and Earth,
He flows in ordered season onward through the fleece, a current of sweet juice still swelling day by day.

5 Flow onward, Soma, flow to bring prosperity : cleansed by the men, invest thee with the milky draught.
What gladdening drinks thou hast, foaming, exceeding strong, even with these incite Indra to give us wealth.

HYMN LXXVI. *Soma Pavamāna.*

1. On flows the potent juice, sustainer of the heavens, the strength of Gods, whom men must hail with shouts of joy.
The Gold-hued, started like a courser by brave men, impetuously winneth splendour in the streams.

2 He takes his weapons, like a hero, in his hands, fain to win light, car-borne, in forays for the kine.
Indu, while stimulating Indra's might, is urged forward and balmed by sages skilful in their task.

3 Soma, as thou art purified with flowing wave, exhibiting thy strength enter thou Indra's throat.
Make both worlds stream for us, as lightning doth the clouds : mete out exhaustless powers for us, as 'twere through song.

4 Onward he flows, the King of all that sees the light : the Ṛṣis' Lord hath raised the song of sacrifice;
Even he who is adorned with Sūrya's arrowy beam, Father of hymns, whose wisdom is beyond our reach.

5 Like as a bull to herds, thou flowest to the pail, bellowing as a steer upon the water's lap.
So, best of Cheerers, thou for Indra flowest on that we, with thy protection, may o'ercome in fight.

HYMN LXXVII. *Soma Pavamāna.*

1. More beauteous than the beautiful, as Indra's bolt, this Soma, rich in sweets, hath clamoured in the vat.
Dropping with oil, abundant, streams of sacrifice flow unto him like milch-kine, lowing, with their milk.

2 On flows that Ancient One whom, hitherward, from heaven, sped through the region of the air, the Falcon snatched.
He, quivering with alarm and terrified in heart before bow-armed Kṛśānu, holdeth fast the sweet.

3 May those first freshest drops of Soma juice effused flow on their way to bring us mighty strength in kine.
Beauteous as serpents, worthy to be looked upon, they whom each sacred gift and all our prayers have pleased.

4 May that much-lauded Indu, with a heart inclined to us, well-knowing, fight against our enemies.
He who hath brought the germ beside the Strong One's seat moves onward to the widely-opened stall of kine.

5 The active potent juice of heaven is flowing on, great Varuṇa whom the forward man can ne'er deceive.
Mitra, the Holy, hath been pressed for troubled times, neighing like an impatient horse amid the herd.

HYMN LXXVIII. *Soma Pavamāna.*

1. Raising his voice the King hath flowed upon his way : invested with the waters he would win the kine.
The fleece retains his solid parts as though impure, and bright and cleansed he seeks the special place of Gods.

2 Thou, Soma, art effused for Indra by the men, balmed in the wood as wave, Sage, Viewer of mankind.

---

3 *As 'twere through song* : 'now with the rite, *i.e.* at the very time the rite is being performed.'—Wilson.

---

2 *The Falcon*: See I. 93. 5. *He*: Soma, according to Sāyaṇa, but more probably the falcon. *Kṛśānu* : the archer who guards the celestial Soma. See I. 112. 21.

3 *Serpents* : the meaning of *ahyāḥ* is uncertain here. Sāyaṇa explains it by *striyaḥ*, women :—'pleasing to look upon like beautiful well-adorned (women).'—Wilson.

4. *He who hath brought the germ* : here the sacrificer and not Soma is meant.—Ludwig. *The Strong One* : Agni.

5 In this stanza Soma is compared to, or mystically identified with, Varuṇa and Mitra. Sāyaṇa leaves *Varuṇa* unexplained, but interprets *Mitra* by *sarveṣām mitrabhūtaḥ*, '(Soma) the friend of all.'

---

1 *The fleece* : literally, the sheep; the filter made of wool. *Solid parts* : *tānvā* : the fragments of stalk which will not pass through the strainer. According to Sāyaṇa, 'with its own covering,'— the sheep with its fleece.'—Wilson. *The special place of Gods* : the vessels which hold the libations assigned to various Gods.

2 *Balmed in the wood* : according to Sāyaṇa, 'art driven into the water.' *Bay steeds*: swiftly-running tawny drops.

Full many are the paths whereon thou mayest go: a thousand bay steeds hast thou resting in the bowls.

3 Apsarases who dwell in waters of the sea, sitting within, have flowed to Soma wise of heart.
They urge the Master of the house upon his way, and to the Eternal Pavamāna pray for bliss.

4 Soma flows on for us as winner of the kine, winner of thousands, cars, water, and light, and gold;
He whom the Gods have made a gladdening draught to drink, the drop most sweet to taste, weal-bringing, red of hue.

5 Soma, as Pavamāna thou, our faithful Friend, making for us these real treasures, flowest on.
Slay thou the enemy both near and far away: grant us security and ample pasturage.

HYMN LXXIX. *Soma Pavamāna.*

1. Spontaneous let our drops of Soma juice flow on, pressed, golden-hued, among the Gods of lofty heaven.
Perish among us they who give no gifts of food! perish the godless! May our prayers obtain success.

2 Forward to us the drops, distilling meath, shall flow, like riches for whose sake we urge the horses on.
Beyond the crafty hindering of all mortal men may we continually bear precious wealth away.

3 Yea, verily, foe of hate shown to himself is he, yea, verily, destroyer too of other hate.
As thirst subdueth in the desert, conquer thou, O Soma Pavamāna, men of evil thoughts.

4 Near kin to thee is he, raised loftiest in the heavens: upon the earth's high ridge thy scions have grown forth.
The press-stones chew and crunch thee on the ox's hide: sages have milked thee with their hands into the streams.

5 So do they hurry on thy strong and beauteous juice, O Indu, as the first ingredient of the draught.
Bring low, thou Pavamāna, every single foe, and be thy might shown forth as sweet and gladdening drink.

HYMN LXXX. *Soma Pavamāna.*

1. On flows the stream of Soma who beholds mankind: by everlasting Law he calls the Gods from heaven.
He lightens with the roaring of Bṛhaspati: the lakes have not contained the pourings of juice.

2 Thou, powerful Soma, thou to whom the cows have lowed, ascendest bright with sheen, thine iron-fashioned home.
Thou, lengthening our princes' life and high renown, flowest for Indra as his might to gladdening drink.

3 Best giver of delight, he flows to Indra's throat, robing himself in might, Auspicious One, for fame.
He spreads himself abroad to meet all things that be: the vigorous Tawny Steed flows sporting on his way.

4 The men, the ten swift fingers, milk thee out for Gods, even thee most rich in meath, with thousand flowing streams.
Soma who winnest thousands, driven by the men, expressed with stones, bring, as thou flowest, all the Gods.

3 *Apsarases who dwell in waters of the sea*: 'nymphs of the firmament.—Wilson. The nymphs are identified with their element, and represent the water with which the Soma juice is mixed. *The Master of the house*: *harmyásya sakṣáṇim*: Soma. In IX. 71. 4, Sāyaṇa explains these words as 'overpowerer, or stormer of the fort of the enemy,' and in this place as the sprinkler of the hall of sacrifice.' *Sakṣáṇi*, from the root *sah*, means overpowerer, and from the root *sac*, connected with, especially as master and possessor.

---

1 *They who give no gifts of food*: I can find no satisfactory explanation of *iṣáḥ drātiyah*, so I give Sāyaṇa's interpretation as a makeshift. 'May they be destroyed who are the withholders of food from us.'—Wilson.

2 *Urge the horses on*: Sāyaṇa explains *árvataḥ*, horses, by, 'strong enemy.' 'By whose aid we encounter the powerful (enemy).'—Wilson.

3 'Soma knows how to defend not only himself, but us also.'—Ludwig. *Destroyer*: literally, the wolf.

4 *He*: 'the Moon.'—Ludwig. 'Thy best juice dwells in the navel of heaven, that which receives (the oblation).' Wilson. *On the ox's hide*: Although men of the present time pour out the Soma upon the skin of a black antelope and not on a cowhide or oxhide, still it is measured out for sale on an oxhide.'—Sāyaṇa.

---

1 *The roaring of Bṛhaspati*: that is, says Sāyaṇa, the voice or praise of the worshipper. Agni may be intended, as Ludwig suggests. *The lakes*: or seas (*samudrásaḥ*), probably the Soma-reservoirs. Sāyaṇa takes *ná* as a particle of comparison: 'the libations cover (the earth) like rivers.' Wilson.

2 *Iron-fashioned home*: See IX. 1. 2.

5 Deft-handed men with stones, the ten swift fingers, drain thee into waters, thee, the Steer enriched with sweets.
Thou, Soma, gladdening Indra and the Heavenly Host, flowest as Pavamāna like a river's wave.

HYMN LXXXI. *Soma Pavamāna.*

1. ONWARD to Indra's throat move, beauteously adorned, the waves of Soma as he purifies himself,
When they, brought forward with the lovely curd of kine, effused, have cheered the Hero to bestow his gifts.

2 Hither hath Soma flowed unto the beakers, like a chariot-horse, a stallion swift upon his way.
Thus, knowing both the generations, he obtains the rights and dues of Gods from yonder and from hence.

3 While thou art cleansed, O Soma, scatter wealth on us; Indu, bestow great bounty as a liberal Prince.
Giver of life, with wisdom help to opulence; strew not our home possessions far away from us.

4 Hither let Pūṣan Pavamāna come to us, Varuṇa, Mitra, bountiful, of one accord,
The Maruts, Aśvins, Vāyu, and Bṛhaspati, Savitar, Tvaṣṭar, tractable Sarasvatī.

5 Both Heaven and Earth, the all-invigorating Pair, Vidhātar, Aditi, and Aryaman the God,
Bhaga who blesses men, the spacious Firmament,—let all the Gods in Pavamāna take delight.

HYMN LXXXII. *Soma Pavamāna.*

1. EVEN as a King hath Soma, red and tawny Bull, been pressed : the Wondrous One hath bellowed to the kine.
While purified he passes through the filtering fleece to seat him hawk-like on the place that drops with oil.

2. To glory goest thou, Sage with disposing skill, like a groomed steed thou rushest forward to the prize.
O Soma, be thou gracious, driving off distress : thou goest, clothed in butter, to a robe of state.

3 Parjanya is the Father of the Mighty Bird : on mountains, in earth's centre hath he made his home.
The waters too have flowed, the Sisters, to the kine : he meets the pressing-stones at the beloved rite.

4 Thou givest pleasure as a wife delights her lord. Listen, O Child of Pajrā, for to thee I speak.
Amid the holy songs go on that we may live : in time of trouble, Soma, watch thou free from blame.

5 As to the men of old thou camest, Indu unharmed, to strengthen, winning hundreds, thousands,
So now for new felicity flow onward : the waters follow as thy law ordaineth.

HYMN LXXXIII. *Soma Pavamāna.*

1. SPREAD is thy cleansing filter, Brahmaṇaspati : as Prince, thou enterest its limbs from every side.
The raw, whose mass hath not been heated gains not this : they only which are dressed, which bear, attain to it.

2 High in the seat of heaven is spread the Scorcher's sieve : its threads are standing separate, glittering with light.
The Swift Ones favour him who purifieth this : with consciousness they stand upon the height of heaven.

2 *Both the generations* : of Gods and men. Sāyaṇa takes *ubháyasya jánmanaḥ* with *devā́nām* :—'and knowing both races of gods—those who come to (the sacrifice) from the other world and those who (come) from this world.' —Wilson.

3 *Help to opulence* : according to Sāyaṇa, 'help Vasu (the Ṛṣi of the hymn) to prosperity.'

4 *Tractable* : *suyámā* : easily led by prayer). According to Sāyaṇa=*suvigrahā*, beautiful in form.

5 *All-invigorating* : *viśvaminvé* : 'all-pervading.'—Sāyaṇa. *Vidhātar* : the Disposer, regarded as a separate deity, as Dhātar is the Maker, Ordainer, or Establisher.

1 *As a King* : 'magnificent as a king.'—Wilson. *That drops with oil* : Sāyaṇa here explains *ghṛtávantam* by *udakavantam*, watery.

2 *To a robe of state*: *nirṇijam* : 'to the cleansing (vessel).' —Wilson.

3 *Parjanya* : the God of the rain-cloud and waters of the air in which the mighty Bird, the Moon, is born. *In earth's centre* : at the altar, in the oblation.

4 *Pajrā* : according to Sāyaṇa, the earth. The St. Petersburg Lexicon explains the word as meaning the moist fresh Soma-plant of which Soma, the juice, is the child. Perhaps, as Ludwig suggests, Pajrā may be the name of the sacrificer's wife.

1 Brahmaṇaspati's filter appears to be the heavenly filter through which the rain descends to earth. See Bergaigne, *La Religion Védique*, I. 79, 201. *The raw* : uncooked oblation. *Which bear* : 'bearing (the sacrifice.)'—Wilson. *This* : according to Sāyaṇa, to this filter. Ludwig thinks that Agni or Sūrya is meant by '*tat.*'

2 *The Scorcher's sieve*: 'The filter of the foe-scorching (Soma).'—Wilson. *The Swift Ones* : 'his swift-flowing (juices) protect the purifier (the worshipper).'—Wilson

3 The foremost spotted Steer hath made the Mornings shine, and yearning after strength sustains all things that be.
By his high wisdom have the mighty Sages wrought : the Fathers who behold mankind laid down the germ,

4 Gandharva verily protects his dwelling-place; Wondrous, he guards the generations of the Gods.
Lord of the snare, he takes the foeman with the snare : those who are most devout have gained a share of meath.

5 Rich in oblations ! robed in cloud, thou compassest oblation, sacrifice, the mighty seat of Gods.
King, on thy chariot-sieve thou goest up to war, and with a thousand weapons winnest lofty fame.

HYMN LXXXIV. *Soma Pavamāna.*

1. Flow, cheering Gods, most active, winner of the flood, for Indra, and for Vāyu, and for Varuṇa.
Bestow on us to-day wide room with happiness, and in thine ample dwelling laud the Host of Heaven.

2 He who hath come anear to creatures that have life, Immortal Soma flows onward to all of them.
Effecting, for our aid, both union and release, Indu, like Sūrya, follows closely after Dawn.

3 He who is poured with milk, he who within the plants hastes bringing treasure for the happiness of Gods,
He, poured forth in a stream flows with the lightning's flash, Soma who gladdens Indra and the Host of Heaven.

4 Winner of thousands, he, this Soma, flows along, raising a vigorous voice that wakens with the dawn.
Indu with winds drives on the ocean of the air, he sinks within the jars, he rests in Indra's heart.

5 The kine with milk dress him who makes the milk increase, Soma, amid the songs, who finds the light of heaven.
Winner of wealth, the effectual juice is flowing on, Singer and Sage by wisdom, dear as heaven itself.

HYMN LXXXV. *Soma Pavamāna.*

1. Flow on to Indra, Soma, carefully effused: let sickness stay afar together with the fiends.
Let not the double-tongued delight them with thy juice : here be thy flowing drops laden with opulence.

2 O Pavamāna, urge us forward in the fight : thou art the vigour of the Gods, the well-loved drink.
Smite thou our enemies who raise the shout of joy : Indra, drink Soma juice, and drive away our foes.

3 Unharmed, best Cheerer, thou, O Indu, flowest on : thou, even thou thyself, art Indra's noblest food.
Full many a wise man lifts to thee the song of praise, and hails thee with a kiss as Sovran of this world.

4 Wondrous, with hundred streams, hymned in a thousand songs, Indu pours out for Indra his delightful meath.
Winning us land and waters, flow thou hitherward : Rainer of bounties, Soma, make broad way for us.

5 Roaring within the beaker thou art balmed with milk : thou passest through the fleecy filter all at once.
Carefully cleansed and decked like a prize-winning steed, O Soma, thou hast flowed down within Indra's throat.

6 Flow onward sweet of flavour for the Heavenly Race, for Indra sweet, whose name is easily invoked :
Flow sweet for Mitra, Varuṇa, and Vāyu, rich in meath, inviolable for Bṛhaspati.

7 Ten rapid fingers deck the Courser in the jar : with hymns the holy singers send their voices forth.
The filtering juices hasten to their eulogy, the drops that gladden find their way to Indra's heart.

---

3 *The Mighty Sages* : those who possess supernatural wisdom; the Gods. *The Fathers*: 'The fruitfulness of heaven and earth, which give birth to gods and men, is described as produced by the fathers.'—Wallis, *Cosmology of the RV.*, p. 72. See X. 64. 14.

4 *Gandharva* : here, the Sun. *His* : Soma's.

5 *Robed in cloud* : *nábhaḥ* : meaning, water from the clouds. *With a thousand weapons* : more literally, having a thousand, that is, countless sharp points 'Thousand-raved.'—Ludwig.

---

1 *In thine ample dwelling* : 'on the spacious sacrificial ground.'—Sāyaṇa.

2 The second line is obscure. Wilson translates, after Sāyaṇa :—'Indu, binding and loosing, accompanies the sacrifice (for its protection) as the Sun the Dawn ;' that is, binding or connecting the sacrifice with the gods and loosing or separating it from the Asuras or evil spirits. But this explanation is unsatisfactory. Ludwig suggests that 'union' refers to Soma's binding together heaven and earth, Gods and men, and for the meaning of 'release' he refers to IX. 68. 5.

8 While thou art purified pour on us hero strength, great, far-extended shelter, spacious pasturage.
Let no oppression master this our holy work : may we, O Indu, gain all opulence through thee.

9 The Steer who sees afar hath risen above the sky : the Sage hath caused the lights of heaven to give their shine.
The King is passing through the filter with a roar : they drain the milk of heaven from him who looks on men.

10 High in the vault of heaven, unceasing, honey-tongued, the Loving Ones drain out the mountain-haunting Steer,—
The drop that hath grown great in waters, in the lake, meath-rich, in the stream's wave and in the cleansing sieve.

11 The Loving Ones besought with many voices the Eagle who had flown away to heaven.
Hymns kiss the Youngling worthy of laudation, resting on earth, the Bird of golden colour.

12 High to heaven's vault hath the Gandharva risen, beholding all his varied forms and figures.
His ray hath shone abroad with gleaming splendour : pure, he hath lighted both the worlds, the Parents.

HYMN LXXXVI. *Soma Pavamāna.*

1. Thy gladdening draughts, O Pavamāna, urged by song flow swiftly of themselves like sons of fleet-foot mares.
The drops of Soma juice, those eagles of the heavens, most cheering, rich in meath, rest in the reservoir.

2 As rapid chariot-steeds, so turned in several ways have thine exhilarating juices darted forth,
Soma-drops rich in meath, waves, to the Thunder-armed, to Indra, like milch-kine who seek their calf with milk.

3 Like a steed urged to battle, finder of the light, speed onward to the cloud-born reservoir of heaven,
A Steer that o'er the woolly surface seeks the sieve, Soma while purified for Indra's nourishment.

4 Fleet as swift steeds, thy drops, divine, thought-swift, have been, O Pavamāna, poured with milk into the vat.
The Ṛṣis have poured in continuous Soma drops, ordainers who adorn thee, Friend whom Ṛṣis love.

5 O thou who seest all things, Sovran as thou art and passing strong, thy rays encompass all abodes.
Pervading with thy natural powers thou flowest on, and as the whole world's Lord, O Soma, thou art King.

6 The beams of Pavamāna, sent from earth and heaven, his ensigns who is ever steadfast, travel round.
When on the sieve the Golden-hued is cleansed, he rests within the vats as one who seats him in his place.

7 Served with fair rites he flows, ensign of sacrifice : Soma advances to the special place of Gods.
He speeds with thousand currents to the reservoir, and passes through the filter bellowing as a bull.

8 The Sovran dips him in the seain and the streams, and set in rivers with the waters' wave moves on.
High heaven's Sustainer at the central point of earth, raised on the fleecy surface Pavamāna stands.

9 He on whose high decree the heavens and earth depend hath roared and thundered like the summit of the sky.
Soma flows on obtaining Indra's friendly love, and, as they purify him, settles in the jars.

10 He, light of sacrifice distils delicious meath, most wealthy, Father and begetter of the Gods.

9 *The Steer who sees afar* : wise Soma, the Moon.

10 *The Loving Ones* : *venāḥ* : the Gods or, specially, the Maruts. According to Sāyaṇa, great Ṛṣis, called Venas. *The mountain-haunting Steer* : Soma, first seen over the mountain heights. See Hillebrandt, *V. M.*, I. 389.

11 Soma in this stanza is *the Eagle, the Youngling* or infant, and *the Bird of golden colour.*

12 *The Gandharva* : here Soma, the Moon. See Hillebrandt, *V. M.*, I. 429.

3 *Speed onward* : hasten to pour down the rain from the cloud.

4 *Friend whom Ṛṣis love* : *ṛṣiṣāṇa* : the word does not occur elsewhere, and its precise meaning is uncertain. '*O ṛṣi*-enjoyed.'—Wilson. 'Thou who playest the part of a Ṛṣi.'—Ludwig.

8 *The sea* and *the streams* are the firmament and its waters. Soma, who is at the same time the God in heaven and the earthly beverage, is said to combine with the solar rays in the clouds, and thus to cause the rain to descend. See Hillebrandt, *V. M.*, I. 215. *Central point of earth* : the place of sacrifice.

He, gladdening, best of Cheerers, juice that Indra loves, enriches with mysterious treasure earth and heaven.

11 The vigorous and far-seeing one, the Lord of heaven, flows, shouting to the beaker, with his thousand streams.
Coloured like gold he rests in seats where Mitra dwells, the Steer made beautiful by rivers and by sheep.

12 In forefront of the rivers Pavamāna speeds, in forefront of the hymn, foremost among the kine.
He shares the mighty booty in the van of war : the well-armed Steer is purified by worshippers.

13 This heedful Pavamāna, like a bird sent forth, hath with his wave flowed onward to the fleecy sieve.
O Indra, through thy wisdom, by thy thought, O Sage, Soma flows bright and pure between the earth and heaven.

14 He, clad in mail that reaches heaven, the Holy One, filling the firmament, stationed amid the worlds,
Knowing the realm of light, hath come to us in rain : he summons to himself his own primeval Sire.

15 He who was first of all to penetrate his form bestowed upon his race wide shelter and defence.
From that high station which he hath in loftiest heaven he comes victorious to all encounters here.

16 Indu hath started for Indra's special place and slights not as a Friend the promise of his Friend.
Soma speeds onward like a youth to youthful maids, and gains the beaker by a course of hundred paths.

17 Your songs, exhilarating, tuneful, uttering praise, are come into the places where the people meet.
Worshippers have exalted Soma with their hymns, and milch kine have come near to meet him with their milk.

18 O Soma, Indu, while they cleanse thee, pour on us accumulated, plentiful, nutritious food,
Which, ceaseless, thrice a day shall yield us hero power enriched with store of nourishment, and strength, and meath.

19 Far-seeing Soma flows, the Steer, the Lord of hymns, the Furtherer of day, of morning, and of heaven.
Mixt with the streams he caused the beakers to resound, and with the singers' aid they entered Indra's heart.

20 On, with the prudent singers, flows the ancient Sage and guided by the men hath roared about the vats.
Producing Trita's name, may he pour forth the meath, that Vāyu and that Indra may become his Friends.

21 He, being purified, hath made the Mornings shine : this, even this is he who gave the rivers room.
He made the Three Times Seven pour out the milky flow : Soma, the Cheerer, yields whate'er the heart finds sweet.

22 Flow onward, Soma, in thine own celestial forms, flow, Indu, poured within the beaker and the sieve.
Sinking into the throat of Indra with a roar, led by the men thou madest Sūrya mount to heaven.

23 Pressed out with stones thou flowest onward to the sieve, O Indu, entering the depths of Indra's throat.
Far-sighted Soma, now thou lookest on mankind : thou didst unbar the cow-stall for the Aṅgirases.

24 In thee, O Soma, while thou purifiedst thee, high-thoughted sages, seeking favour, have rejoiced.
Down from the heavens the Falcon brought thee hitherward, even thee, O Indu, thee whom all our hymns adorn.

11 *By rivers and by sheep* : by the purifying waters and the woollen strainer.

14 *His own primeval Sire* : or, the ancient Father of this (All). Indra is meant.

15 *He* : Soma. *His form* : Indra's. *His race* : Indra and the Gods.

16 *Slights not as a Friend the promise of his Friend* : 'the friend leaves not the stomach of his friend.'—Wilson. Sāyaṇa derives *saṁgiram* from *saṁgṝ*, to swallow, instead of from *saṁgṝ*, to assent. *Hundred paths* : through the interstices of the wool.

18 *Thrice a day* : at the three appointed sacrifices.

20 *Producing Trita's name* : literally, begetting, that is, making (*janáyan*) the name of Trita; meaning probably, as Prof. Ludwig suggests, reminding us of Trita, with whom he is closely connected. 'Generating the water of the threefold (Indra).'—Wilson.

21 *The Three Times Seven* : the seven celestial rivers, corresponding to the rivers of earth, multiplied by three to accord with the threefold division of the heavens. According to Sāyaṇa, cows are meant.

23 *Thou didst unbar the cow-stall* : didst recover the cattle stolen by the Paṇis, that is the rays of light that the fiends of darkness had carried off; the great deed of Indra being ascribed to Soma his inspirer.

25 Seven Milch-kine glorify the Tawny-coloured One while with his wave in wool he purifies himself.
The living men, the mighty, have impelled the Sage into the waters' lap, the place of sacrifice.

26 Indu, attaining purity, plunges through the foe, making his ways all easy for the pious man.
Making the kine his mantle, he, the lovely Sage, runs like a sporting courser onward through the fleece.

27 The ceaseless watery fountains with their hundred streams sing, as they hasten near, to him the Golden-hued.
Him, clad in robes of milk, swift fingers beautify on the third height and in the luminous realm of heaven.

28 These are thy generations of celestial seed : thou art the Sovran Lord of all the world of life.
This universe, O Pavamāna, owns thy sway; thou, Indu, art the first establisher of Law.

29 Thou art the sea, O Sage who bringest all to light : under thy Law are these five regions of the world.
Thou reachest out beyond the earth, beyond the heavens : thine are the lights, O Pavamāna, thine the Sun.

30 Thou in the filter, Soma Pavamāna, art purified to support the region for the Gods.
The chief, the longing ones have sought to hold thee fast, and all these living creatures have been turned to thee.

31 Onward the Singer travels o'er the fleecy sieve : the Tawny Steer hath bellowed in the wooden vats.
Hymns have been sung aloud in resonant harmony, and holy songs kiss him, the Child who claims our praise.

32 He hath assumed the rays of Sūrya for his robe, spinning, as he knows how, the triply-twisted thread.
He, guiding to the newest rules of Holy Law, comes as the Women's Consort to the special place.

33 On flows the King of rivers and the Lord of heaven : he follows with a shout the paths of Holy Law.
The Golden-hued is poured forth with his hundred streams, Wealth-bringer, lifting up his voice while purified.

34 Fain to be cleansed, thou, Pavamāna, pourest out, like wondrous Sūra, through the fleece, an ample sea.
Purified with the hands, pressed by the men with stones, thou speedest on to mighty booty-bringing war.

35 Thou, Pavamāna, sendest food and power in streams : thou sittest in the beakers as a hawk on trees,
For Indra poured as cheering juice to make him glad, as nearest and far-seeing bearer-up of heaven.

36 The Sisters Seven, the Mothers, stand around the Babe, the noble, new-born Infant, skilled in holy song,
Gandharva of the floods, divine, beholding men, Soma, that he may reign as King of all the world.

37 As Sovran Lord thereof thou passest through these worlds, O Indu, harnessing thy tawny well-winged Mares.
May they pour forth for thee milk and oil rich in sweets : O Soma, let the folk abide in thy decree.

38 O Soma, thou beholdest men from every side : O Pavamāna, Steer, thou wanderest through these.
Pour out upon us wealth in treasure and in gold : may we have strength to live among the things that be.

39 Winner of gold and goods and cattle flow thou on, set as impregner, Indu, mid the worlds of life.
Rich in brave men art thou, Soma, who winnest all : these holy singers wait upon thee with the song.

25 *Seven Milch-kine* : the celestial rivers.

26 *Making the kine his mantle*: he who is afterwards covered or mingled with milk.

29 *Thou art the sea* : Soma and the sea being alike producers of rain. *Lights* : stars.

30 *The region* : mid-air; the firmament. *The chief, the longing ones* : the Venas, the Maruts.

32 *Spinning...the triply-twisted thread* : bearing his part in morning, noon-day and evening sacrifice. *The Women's Consort* : Lord and husband of the Waters of heaven. *The special place* : 'the consecrated (vessel).'—Wilson.

34 *Like wondrous Sūra* : adorable like the Sun.

36 *The Sisters Seven* : the great rivers which may provide water for Soma-sacrifices. *Gandharva* : frequently identified with the Sun, here means Soma, the Moon.

37 *Tawny...Mares* : *harítaḥ*; Harits. Cf. IV. 6. 9; 13. 3; VII. 66. 15; IX. 63. 9.

38 *Through these* : there is no substantive. Sāyaṇa supplies *apaḥ*, waters.

40 The wave of flowing meath hath wakened up desires : the Steer enrobed in milk plunges into the streams.
Borne on his chariot-sieve the King hath risen to war, and with a thousand rays hath won him high renown.

41 Dear to all life, he sends triumphant praises forth, abundant, bringing offspring, each succeeding day.
From Indra crave for us, Indu, when thou art quaffed, the blessing that gives children, wealth that harbours steeds.

42 When days begin, the strong juice, lovely, golden-hued, is recognized by wisdom more and more each day,
He, stirring both the Races, goes between the two, the bearer of the word of men and word of Gods.

43 They balm him, balm him over, balm him thoroughly, caress the mighty strength and balm it with the meath.
They seize the flying Steer at the stream's breathing-place : cleansing with gold they grasp the Animal herein.

44 Sing forth to Pavamāna skilled in holy song : the juice is flowing onward like a mighty stream.
He glideth like a serpent from his ancient skin, and like a playful horse the Tawny Steer hath run.

45 Dweller in floods, King, foremost, he displays his might, set among living things as measurer of days.
Distilling oil he flows, fair, billowy, golden-hued, borne on a car of light, sharing one home with wealth.

46 Loosed is the heavens' support, the uplifted cheering juice : the triply-mingled draught flows round into the worlds.
The holy hymns caress the stalk that claims our praise, when singers have approached his beauteous robe with song.

47 Thy streams that flow forth rapidly collected run over the fine fleece of the sheep as thou art cleansed.
When, Indu, thou art balmed with milk within the bowl, thou sinkest in the jars, O Soma, when expressed.

48 Winner of power, flow, Soma, worthy of our laud : run onward to the fleece as well-beloved meath.
Destroy, O Indu, all voracious Rākṣasas. With brave sons in the assembly let our speech be bold.

40 *Desires* : the meaning of *vanánāḥ* : is not certain ; 'voices (of praise).'—Wilson. *With a thousand rays* : *sahásrabhṛṣṭiḥ* : literally, having a thousand edges or sharp points. Cp. IX. 83. 5.

41 *The blessing* : this seems to be very nearly the meaning of *bráhma* here, But the word may as usual be rendered by prayer, or devotion. 'Solicit Indra (to give) us food productive of progeny.'—Wilson.

42 *When days begin* : according to Sāyaṇa, ealry in the morning. The commencement of the year is more probably intended. The second half of the stanza is obscurely expressed. It appears to mean that Soma acts as a mediator between heaven and earth, urging men to offer, and the Gods to receive, worship, bearing up to heaven the hymns and praises of human worshippers and bringing back to them the assurance that their petitions will be granted. Sāyaṇa's explanation is different : 'approaching the two men (the praiser and the worshipper or secular and sacred people) he passes in the midst (of heaven and earth, bestowing), upon the upholder (of the rite) both human and divine (riches).'—Wilson. I follow Ludwig who takes *dhartári* as nominative singular.

43 *At the stream's breathing-place* : where the stream seems to stay still for a moment to recover breath. *Cleansing with gold* : with gold-ringed fingers. *The Animal* : Soma.

45 *As measurer of days* : Soma being identified with the Moon.

46 *Triply-mingled* : or, poured into three vessels, the *droṇakalaśa*, *adhavanīya*, and *pūtabhṛt*. *Robe* : the integuments which cover the juice : that is the exterior of the stalk and shoots.

HYMN LXXXVII. *Soma Pavamāna.*

1. RUN onward to the reservoir and seat thee : cleansed by the men speed forward to the battle.
Making thee beauteous like an able courser, forth to the sacred grass with reins they lead thee.

2 Indu, the well-armed God, is flowing onward, who quells the curse and guards from treacherous onslaught,
Father, begetter of the Gods, most skilful, the buttress of the heavens and earth's supporter.

3. Ṛṣi and Sage, the Champion of the people, deft and sagacious, Uśanā in wisdom,
He hath discovered even their hidden nature, the Cows' concealed and most mysterious title.

3 *Uśanā in wisdom* : as wise as the celebrated Uśanā. Sāyaṇa explains differently, regarding Uśanā as the discoverer : '*Uśanās*—he verily by his poetic gift discovered the secret milk of those cows which was hidden and concealed.'—Wilson. By *title* or *name* of the Cows, water appears to be intended.

4 This thine own Soma rich in meath, O Indra, Steer for the Steer, hath flowed into the filter.
The strong Free-giver, winning hundreds, thousands, hath reached the holy grass that never fails him.

5 These Somas are for wealth of countless cattle, renown therefor, and mighty strength immortal.
These have been sent forth, purified by strainers, like steeds who rush to battle fain for glory.

6 He, while he cleanses him, invoked of many, hath flowed to give the people all enjoyment.
Thou whom the Falcon brought, bring dainty viands, bestir thyself and send us wealth and booty.

7 This Soma, pressed into the cleansing filter, hath run as 'twere a host let loose, the Courser;
Like a strong bull who whets his horns keen-pointed, like a brave warrior in the fray for cattle.

8 He issued forth from out the loftiest mountain, and found kine hidden somewhere in a stable.
Soma's stream clears itself for thee, O Indra, like lightning thundering through the clouds of heaven,

9 Cleansing thyself, and borne along with Indra, Soma, thou goest round the herd of cattle.
May thy praise help us, Mighty One, prompt Giver, to the full ample food which thou bestowest.

HYMN LXXXVIII. *Soma Pavamāna.*

1. For thee this Soma is effused, O Indra: drink of this juice; for thee the stream is flowing—
Soma, which thou thyself hast made and chosen, even Indu, for thy special drink to cheer thee.

2 Like a capacious car hath it been harnessed, the Mighty; to acquire abundant treasures.
Then in the sacrifice they celebrated all triumphs won by Nahus in the battle.

3 Like Vāyu with his team, moving at pleasure, most gracious when invoked like both Nāsatyas,
Thou art thyself like the Wealth-Giver, Soma! who grants all boons, like song-inspiring Pūṣan.

4 Like Indra who hath done great deeds, thou, Soma, art slayer of the Vṛtras, Fort-destroyer.
Like Pedu's horse who killed the brood of serpents, thus thou, O Soma, slayest every Dasyu.

5 Like Agni loosed amid the forest, fiercely he winneth splendour in the running waters.
Like one who fights, the roaring of the mighty, thus Soma Pavamāna sends his current.

6 These Somas passing through the fleecy filter, like rain descending from the clouds of heaven,
Have been effused and poured into the beakers, swiftly like rivers running lowly seaward.

7 Flow onward like the potent band of Maruts, like that Celestial Host whom none revileth.
Quickly be gracious unto us like waters, like sacrifice victorious, thousand-fashioned.

8 Thine are King Varuṇa's eternal statutes, lofty and deep, O Soma, is thy glory.
All-pure art thou like Mitra the beloved, adorable, like Aryaman, O Soma.

4 *Steer for the Steer*: or, Strong for the Strong.

5 *Mighty strength immortal*: 'ample food and ambrosia.'—Wilson.

8 *From out the loftiest mountain*: Sāyaṇa makes *antárdreḥ* depend upon *kúcit*, somewhere: 'This Soma stream has come from on high and has detected the cattle which were in a stall (hidden) somewhere within the mountain.'—Wilson. Grassmann translates: 'Er ist entsprungen aus dem höchsten Pressstein' 'He hath sprung forth from the most lofty press-stone.'

9 *The herd of cattle*: Soma accompanies Indra in his expedition to recover the stolen cattle.—Sāyaṇa. *Or* the cattle or cows may be the milk with which Soma is mixed.

2 I can make nothing out of the second line of this stanza. The version which I give as a temporary makeshift is founded on Ludwig's remarks in his Commentary on the passage. Vol. V. p. 308, of the *Ṛgveda*. Wilson, following Sāyaṇa, translates:—'After this (*i. e.* after the harnessing of the waggon—Note.) may all the races of men expecting our (attack) go to the desirable battle.' 'Now let the races of all men, rising up like trees, come near to him in order to obtain success,' would, according to Grassmann, be nearer the meaning.

4 *Pedu's horse*: given to him by the Aśvins. See I. 116. 6; 117. 9; 118. 9; 119. 10.

7 *Like sacrifice*: according to Sāyaṇa, *yajñáḥ*, sacrifice, means here, worthy of sacrifice:—'(thou art) of a thousand shapes, adorable like (Indra) the victor in battle.'—Wilson.

8 This stanza is found also in Book I. 91. 3.

HYMN LXXXIX. *Soma Pavamāna.*

1. THIS Chariot-horse hath moved along the pathways, and Pavamāna flowed like rain from heaven.
With us hath Soma with a thousand currents sunk in the wood, upon his Mother's bosom.

2. King, he hath clothed him in the robe of rivers, mounted the straightest-going ship of Order.
Sped by the Hawk the drop hath waxed in waters : the father drains it, drains the Father's offspring.

3 They come to him, red, tawny, Lord of Heaven, the watchful Guardian of the meath, the Lion.
First, Hero in the fight, he seeks the cattle, and with his eye the Steer is our protector.

4 They harness to the broad-wheeled car the mighty Courser whose back bears meath, unwearied, awful.
The twins, the sisters brighten him, and strengthen—these children of one dame—the vigorous Racer.

5 Four pouring out the holy oil attend him, sitting together in the same container.
To him they flow, when purified, with homage, and still, from every side, are first about him.

6 He is the buttress of the heavens, supporter of earth, and in his hand are all the people.
Be the team's Lord a well to thee the singer : cleansed is the sweet plant's stalk for deed of glory.

7 Fighting, uninjured come where Gods are feasted ; Soma, as Vṛtra-slayer flow for Indra.
Vouchsafe us ample riches very splendid : may we be masters of heroic vigour.

2 *The father drains it* : 'The scholiast finds it difficult to make sense of this : *pitā* (*pālako lokaḥ*) he supposes to mean the *Adhvaryu*, who extracts the juice of the *Soma* which is born from the heaven as from a father; or the first milker may be the *yajamāna* and the second the *Adhvaryu* ; or *duhe* may be repeated out of respect.'Wilson.

4 *Sisters......children of one dame* : the priest's fingers.

5 *Four* : the quarters of the sky. *Container* : the firmament.

6 *The team's Lord* : Soma as resembling Vāyu. Cp. IX. 88. 3. Sāyaṇa explains differently : may (*Soma*) the fountain (of desires) be possessed of horses for thee (his) adorer.'—Wilson.

HYMN XC. *Soma Pavamāna,*

1. URGED on, the Father of the Earth and Heaven hath gone forth like a car to gather booty,
Going to Indra, sharpening his weapons, and in his hand containing every treasure.

2 To him the tones of sacred song have sounded, Steer of the triple height, the Life-bestower.
Dwelling in wood as Varuṇa in rivers, lavishing treasure he distributes blessings.

3 Great Conqueror, warrior-girt, Lord of all heroes, flow on thy way as he who winneth riches ;
With sharpened arms, with swift bow, never vanquished in battle, vanquishing in fight the foemen.

4 Giving security, Lord of wide dominion, send us both earth and heaven with all their fulness.
Striving to win the Dawns, the light, the waters, and cattle, call to us abundant vigour.

5 O Soma, gladden Varuṇa and Mitra ; cheer, Indu Pavamāna ! Indra, Viṣṇu.
Cheer thou the Gods, the Company of Maruts : Indu, cheer mighty Indra to rejoicing.

6 Thus like a wise and potent King flow onward, destroying with thy vigour all misfortunes.
For our well-spoken hymn give life, O Indu. Do ye preserve us evermore with blessings.

HYMN XCI. *Soma Pavamāna.*

1. As for a chariot-race, the skilful Speaker, Chief, Sage, Inventor, hath, with song, been started.
The sisters ten upon the fleecy summit drive on the Car-horse to the resting-places.

1 *Father* : *janitā* : generator, of earth by sending rain, and of heaven by obtaining oblations for the gods.—Sāyaṇa.

2 *Of the triple height* : See IX. 71. 7.

4 *Call to us* : send us with thy shout or roar.

6 The hymn ends with the usual concluding half-line of the hymns ascribed to the Vasiṣṭhas.

1 *The skilful Speaker* : Soma who makes us eloquent. *The resting-places* : *sádanāni*: the seats, the reservoirs in which he settles.

2 The drop of Soma, pressed by wise Nahuṣyas, becomes the banquet of the Heavenly People—
Indu, by hands of mortal men made beauteous, immortal, with the sheep and cows and waters.

3 Steer roaring unto Steer, this Pavamāna, this juice runs to the white milk of the milch-cow.
Through thousand fine hairs goes the tuneful Singer, like Sūra by his fair and open pathways.

4 Break down the strong seats even of the demons : cleansing thee, Indu, robe thyself in vigour.
Rend with thy swift bolt, coming from above them, those who are near and those who yet are distant.

5 Prepare the forward paths in ancient manner for the new hymn, thou Giver of all bounties.
Those which are high and hard for foes to conquer may we gain from thee, Active ! Food-bestower !

6 So purifying thee vouchsafe us waters, heaven's light, and cows, offspring and many children.
Give us health, ample land, and lights, O Soma, and grant us long to look upon the sunshine.

HYMN XCII. *Soma Pavamāna.*

1. THE gold-hued juice, poured out upon the filter, is started like a car sent forth to conquer.
He hath gained song and vigour while they cleansed him, and hath rejoiced the Gods with entertainments.

2 He who beholdeth man hath reached the filter : bearing his name, the Sage hath sought his dwelling.
The Ṛṣis came to him, seven holy singers, when in the bowls he settled as Invoker.

3 Shared by all Gods, most wise, propitious, Soma goes, while they cleanse him, to his constant station.
Let him rejoice in all his lofty wisdom : to the Five Tribes the Sage attains with labour.

4 In thy mysterious place, O Pavamāna Soma, are all the Gods, the Thrice-Eleven.
Ten on the fleecy height, themselves, self-prompted, and seven fresh rivers, brighten and adorn thee.

5 Now let this be the truth of Pavamāna, there where all singers gather them together,
That he hath given us room and made the daylight, hath holpen Manu and repelled the Dasyu.

6 As the priest seeks the station rich in cattle, like a true King who goes to great assemblies,
Soma hath sought the beakers while they cleansed him, and like a wild bull, in the wood hath settled.

HYMN XCIII. *Soma Pavamāna.*

1. TEN sisters, pouring out the rain together, swift-moving thinkers of the sage, adorn him.
Hither hath run the gold-hued Child of Sūrya and reached the vat like a fleet vigorous courser.

2 Even as a youngling crying to his mothers, the bounteous Steer hath flowed along to waters.
As youth to damsel, so with milk he hastens on to the chose meeting-place, the beaker.

3 Yea, swollen is the udder of the milch-cow : thither in streams goes very sapient Indu.

2 *Nahuṣyas* : probably a neighbouring people. See VI. 46. 7, and note on *Nahuṣas* which has the same meaning.

3 *Sūra* : Sūrya, the Sun. *Fair and open* : *adhvasmábhiḥ* : 'imperishable.'—Wilson.

5 *Those* : portions of thee, according to Sāyaṇa.

6 In the second half of the stanza, instead of taking *urū́*, wide, ample, with *kṣetram*, field, land., Sāyaṇa joins it, as=*urūṇi*, with *jyotiṁṣi*, lights :—'make our land prosper, diffuse the luminaries widely (in the firmament).—Wilson.

---

2 *The Ṛṣis*: according to Sāyaṇa, Bharadvāja, Kaśyapa, Gotama, Atri, Viśvāmitra, Jamadagni, Vasiṣṭha.

3 *The Five Tribes* : the five Āryan tribes. According to Sāyaṇa, 'the five classes of beings.' *i. e.*, four castes and the Niṣādas.

4 *The Thrice-Eleven* : See I. 139. 11. *Ten* : the fingers.

5 *Manu* : as the representative of the Āryan race.

6 *The station rich in cattle* : 'the hall where the victim is stationed.'—Wilson. *To great assemblies* : or, to war and battle. *The wood* : the wooden vat or reservoir.

---

1 *Ten sisters* : the fingers which press out the juice of the Soma-plant. *Thinkers* : or thoughts, devotions. According to Sāyaṇa, fingers. *Child of Sūrya* : Sāyaṇa explains *jáḥ*, offspring, by *jāyāḥ* wives, *i.e.*, the quarters of the heaven, called Sūrya's wives because they are made manifest by his rays.

The kine make ready, as with new-washed treasures, the Head and Chief with milk within the vessels.

4 With all the Gods, O Indu Pavamāna, while thou art roaring send us wealth in horses.

Hither upon her car come willing Plenty, inclined to us, to give us of her treasures.

5 Now unto us mete riches, while they cleanse thee, all-glorious, swelling wealth, with store of heroes.

Long be his life who worships thee, O Indu. May he, enriched with prayer, come soon and early.

HYMN XCIV. *Soma Pavamāna.*

1. WHEN beauties strive for him as for a charger, then strive the songs like soldiers for the sunlight.

Acting the Sage, he flows enrobed in waters and song as 'twere a stall that kine may prosper.

2 The worlds expand to him who from aforetime found light to spread the law of life eternal.

The swelling songs, like kine within the stable, in deep devotion call aloud on Indu.

3 When the sage bears his holy wisdom round him, like a car visiting all worlds, the Hero,

Becoming fame, mid Gods, unto the mortal, wealth to the skilled, worth praise mid the Ever-present,

4 For glory born he hath come forth to glory: he giveth life and glory to the singers.

They, clothed in glory, have become immortal. He, measured in his course, makes frays successful.

5 Stream to us food and vigour, kine and horses: give us broad lights and fill the Gods with rapture.

All these are easy things for thee to master: thou, Pavamāna Soma, quellest foemen.

HYMN XCV *Soma Pavamāna.*

1. LOUD neighs the Tawny Steed when started, settling deep in the wooden vessel while they cleanse him.

Led by the men he takes the milk for raiment: then shall he, through his powers, engender praise-songs.

2 As one who rows drives on his boat, he, Gold-hued, sends forth his voice, loosed on the path of Order.

As God, the secret names of Gods he utters, to be declared on sacred grass more widely.

3 Hastening onward like the waves of waters, our holy hymns are pressing nigh to Soma.

To him they come with lowly adoration, and, longing, enter him who longs to meet them.

4 They drain the stalk, the Steer who dwells on mountains, even as a Bull who decks him on the upland.

Hymns follow and attend him as he bellows: Trita bears Varuṇa aloft in ocean.

5 Sending thy voice out as Director, loosen the Invoker's thought, O Indu, as they cleanse thee.

While thou and Indra rule for our advantage, may we be masters of heroic vigour.

3 *The Head and Chief*: 'the elevated *Soma*.'—Wilson.
4 *Send us*: more literally, open or disclose to us.
5 The hymn ends with the half-line which is the special conclusion of the hymns ascribed to Nodhas. See Book I. 58, 60—64.

1 The meaning is apparently: when the beautifying 'waters hasten emulously to cleanse Soma as though he were a horse, the voices of singing worshippers vie with each other like the shouts of men who are fighting for light and life. Soma flows on in his wisdom, blent with the waters, and surrounded with hymns into the midst of which he enters as into a stable full of kine in order to make them increase and multiply.

3 The stanza is somewhat obscure. *Worth praise*: or, adorable. *The Ever-present*: the Gods who come to help men. Wilson, following Sāyaṇa, translates the second line: 'then desirous of bestowing upon mortals the wealth that abides with the gods, he (is) to be glorified in the many places of sacrifice for the preservation of the riches he has given.'

5 *All these*: all the Rākṣasas, according to Sāyaṇa.

1 *Deep in the wooden vessel*: literally 'in the belly of the wood.'

2 *He utters*: reveals to the priest who is to declare them at sacrifice.

4 *Trita*: The preparer of the celestial Soma. *Varuṇa*: here meaning Soma; 'the defeater of enemies.'—Wilson *In ocean*: in the firmament.

5 *As Director*: *upavaktéva*: *upavaktā́* here appears to mean Adhvaryu: *yathādhvaryuḥ*—Sāyaṇa. *Loosen the Invoker's thought*: aid the Hotar or invoking priest to give free utterance to his thought or hymn.

HYMN XCVI. *Soma Pavamāna*

1. IN forefront of the cars forth goes the Hero, the Leader, winning spoil : his host rejoices.
Soma endues his robes of lasting colours, and blesses, for his friends, their calls on Indra.

2 Men decked with gold adorn his golden tendril, incessantly with steed-impelling homage.
The Friend of Indra mounts his car : well-knowing, he comes thereon to meet the prayer we offer.

3 O God, for service of the Gods flow onward, for food sublime, as Indra's drink, O Soma.
Making the floods, bedewing earth and heaven, come from the vast, comfort us while we cleanse thee

4 Flow for prosperity and constant vigour, flow on for happiness and high perfection.
This is the wish of these friends assembled : this is my wish, O Soma Pavamāna.

5 Father of holy hymns, Soma flows onward, the Father of the earth, Father of heaven :
Father of Agni, Sūrya's generator, the Father who begat Indra and Viṣṇu.

6 Brahman of Gods, the Leader of the poets, Ṛṣi of sages, Bull of savage creatures,
Falcon amid the vultures, Axe of forests, over the cleansing sieve goes Soma singing.

7 He, Soma Pavamāna, like a river, hath stirred the wave of voice, our songs and praises.
Beholding these inferior powers in cattle, he rests among them as a Steer well-knowing.

8 As Gladdener, Warrior never harmed in battle, with thousand genial streams, pour strength and vigour.
As thoughtful Pavamāna, urge O Indu, speeding the kine, the plant's wave on to Indra.

9 Dear, grateful to the Gods, on to the beaker moves Soma, sweet to Indra, to delight him.
With hundred powers, with thousand currents, Indu, like a strong car-horse, goes to the assembly.

10 Born in old time as finder-out of treasures, drained with the stone, decking himself in waters,
Warding off curses, King of all existence, he shall find way for prayer the while they cleanse him.

11 For our sage fathers, Soma Pavamāna, of old performed, by thee, their sacred duties.
Fighting unvanquished, open the enclosures : enrich us with large gifts of steeds and heroes.

12 As thou didst flow for Manu Life-bestowing, Foe-queller, Comforter, rich in oblations,
Even thus flow onward now conferring riches : combine with Indra, and bring forth thy weapons.

13 Flow onward, Soma, rich in sweets and holy, enrobed in waters on the fleecy summit.
Settle in vessels that are full of fatness, as cheering and most gladdening drink for Indra.

14 Pour, hundred-streamed, winner of thousands, mighty at the Gods' banquet, pour the rain of heaven,
While thou with rivers roarest in the beaker, and blent with milk prolongest our existence.

15 Purified with our holy hymns, this Soma o'ertakes malignities like some strong charger,
Like fresh milk poured by Aditi, like

1 *Of lasting colours* : *rabhasā́ni* : 'hastily made.'—Wilson. 'Brilliant.'—Grassmann.

2 *Steed-impelling*: urging him on, as a whip urges on a horse.

3 *From the vast* : from the wide firmament. There is no substantive in the text.

6 *Brahman of Gods* : thou art Bṛhaspati, the Lord of Prayer, among the Gods, or, chief among the priests. *Axe* : the handle of the axe being naturally made of the strongest wood.—M. Müller, Ludwig thinks that lightning may be intended. According to the St. Petersburg Lexicon, *svádhitiḥ* here means a tree with very hard wood. See V. 32. 10.

7 The second line is obscure. Wilson translates : 'the showerer (of benefits) beholding the hidden (treasure) presides over these irresistible powers, knowing about the cattle.'

9 *Goes to the assembly* : 'proceeds like a strong horse to battle.'—Wilson.

11 *The enclosures* : the obstructions which keep the rain from falling.

13 *Full of fatness* : *ghṛtávānti* : according to Sāyaṇa, 'water-holding .

15 *By Aditi* : regarding as the Cosmic Cow.

passage in ample room, or like a docile car-horse.

16 Cleansed by the pressers, armed with noble weapons, stream to us the fair secret name thou bearest.
Pour booty, like a horse, for love of glory : God, Soma, send us kine, and send us Vāyu.

17 They deck him at his birth, the lovely Infant, the Maruts with their troop adorn the Car-horse.
By songs a Poet and a Sage by wisdom, Soma goes singing through the cleansing filter.

18 Light-winner, Ṛṣi-minded, Ṛṣi-maker, hymned in a thousand hymns, Leader of sages,
A Steer who strives to gain his third form, Soma is, like Virāj, resplendent as a Singer.

19 Hawk seated in the bowls, Bird wide-extended, the Banner seeking kine and wielding weapons,
Following close the sea, the wave of waters, the great Bull tells his fourth form and declares it.

20 Like a fair youth who decorates his body, a courser rushing to the gain of riches,
A steer to herds, so, flowing to the pitcher, he with a roar hath passed into the beakers.

21 Flow on with might as Pavamāna, Indu : flow loudly roaring through the fleecy filter.
Enter the beakers sporting, as they cleanse thee, and let thy gladdening juice make Indra joyful.

22 His streams have been effused in all their fulness, and he hath entered, balmed with milk, the goblets.
Singing his psalm, well-skilled in song, a Chanter, he comes as 'twere to his friend's sister roaring.

23 Chasing our foes thou comest, Pavamāna ! Indu, besung, as lover to his darling.
As a bird flies and settles in the forest, thus Soma settles, purified, in goblets.

24 With full stream and abundant milk, O Soma, thy beams come, like a woman, as they cleanse thee.
He, gold-hued, rich in boons, brought to the waters, hath roared within the goblet of the pious.

HYMN XCVII.   *Soma Pavamāna*

1. MADE pure by this man's urgent zeal and impulse the God hath to the Gods his juice imparted.
He goes, effused and singing, to the filter, like priest to measured seats supplied with cattle.

2 Robed in fair raiment meet to wear in battle, a mighty Sage pronouncing invocations.
Roll onward to the beakers as they cleanse thee, far-seeing at the feast of Gods, and watchful.

3 Dear, he is brightened on the fleecy summit, a Prince among us, nobler than the noble.
Roar out as thou art purified, run forward. Do ye preserve us evermore with blessings.

4 Let us sing praises to the Gods : sing loudly, send ye the Soma forth for mighty riches.
Let him flow, sweetly-flavoured, through the filter, and let our pious one rest in the pitcher.

5 Winning the friendship of the Deities, Indu flows in a thousand streams to make them joyful.
Praised by the men after the ancient statute, he hath come nigh, for our great bliss, to Indra.

6 Flow, Gold-hued, cleansing thee, to enrich the singer : let thy juice go to Indra to support him.
Come nigh, together with the Gods, for bounty. Do ye preserve us evermore with blessings.

---

16 *Vāyu* : the breath of life, life.—Sāyaṇa.

18 *His third form* : the form that he wears in heaven; 'the third region (heaven).'—Wilson. *Virāj* : splendid or most illustrious Indra.—Sāyaṇa.

19 *The banner* : *drapsáḥ* : usually meaning, a drop, or a spark. See IV. 13. 2. *His fourth form* : the Moon. According to Sāyaṇa, the region of the Moon which is said to be above that of the Sun.

22 *As 'twere to his friend's sister* : Sāyaṇa explains *jāmím*, sister, by *jāyām*, wife : 'like (a libertine) to the wife of a friend.'—Wilson. The meaning is probably no more than 'as lover to his darling' in the following stanza.

1 *Urgent zeal and impulse* : *hemánā*, by impulse (from the root *hi*) is said by Sāyaṇa to mean 'by gold,' that is, by the gold-adorned hand of the priest. *Measured seats supplied with cattle* : 'the halls prepared (for sacrifice) containing victims.'—Wilson. *Singing* : the sound of the flowing juice is compared to the priest's recitation of sacred texts.

7 The God declares the Deities' generations, like Uṣanā, proclaiming lofty wisdom.
With brilliant kin, far-ruling, sanctifying, the Boar advances, singing, to the places.

8 The Swans, the Vṛṣagaṇas from anear us have brought their restless spirit to our dwelling.
Friends come to Pavamāna meet for praises, and sound in concert their resistless music.

9 He follows the Wide-strider's rapid movement : cows low, as 'twere, to him who sports at pleasure.
He with the sharpened horns brings forth abundance : the Silvery shines by night, by day the Golden.

10 Strong Indu, bathed in milk, flows on for Indra, Soma exciting strength, to make him joyful.
He quells malignities and slays the demons, the King of mighty power who brings us comfort.

11 Then in a stream he flows, milked out with press-stones, mingled with sweetness, through the fleecy filter—
Indu rejoicing in the love of Indra, the God who gladdens, for the God's enjoyment.

12 As he is purified he pours out treasures, a God bedewing Gods with his own juices.
Indu hath, wearing qualities by seasons, on the raised fleece engaged the ten swift fingers.

13 The Red Bull bellowing to the kine advances, causing the heavens and earth to roar and thunder.
Well is he heard like Indra's shout in battle : letting this voice be known he hastens hither.

14 Swelling with milk, abounding in sweet flavours, urging the meath-rich plant thou goest onward.
Raising a shout thou flowest as they cleanse thee, when thou, O Soma, art effused for Indra.

15 So flow thou on inspiriting, for rapture, aiming death-shafts at him who stays the waters,
Flow to us wearing thy resplendent colour, effused and eager for the kine, O Soma.

16 Pleased with us, Indu, send us as thou flowest good easy paths in ample space and comforts.
Dispelling, as 'twere with a club, misfortunes, run o'er the height, run o'er the fleecy summit.

17 Pour on us rain celestial, quickly streaming, refreshing, fraught with health and ready bounty.
Flow, Indu, send these Winds thy lower kinsmen, setting them free like locks of hair unbraided.

18 Part, like a knotted tangle, while they cleanse thee, O Soma, righteous and unrighteous conduct.
Neigh like a tawny courser who is loosened, come like a youth, O God, a house-possessor.

19 For the God's service, for delight, O Indu, run o'er the height, run o'ver the fleecy summit.
With thousand streams, inviolate, sweet-scented, flow on for gain of strength that conquers heroes.

20 Without a car, without a rein to guide them, unyoked, like coursers started in the contest,
These brilliant drops of Soma juice run forward. Do ye, O Deities, come nigh to drink them.

21 So for our banquet of the Gods, O Indu, pour down the rain of heaven into the vessels.
May Soma grant us riches sought with longing, mighty, exceeding strong, with store of heroes.

22 What time the loving spirit's word had formed him Chief of all food, by statute of the Highest,

7 *The God* : Soma, who has been called the Father of Gods. *Like Uśanā* : the sound of the flowing and dropping Soma juice is likened to the song of the famous sage and sacred poet. *The Boar* : strong, swift Soma. *Singing* : making a sound with the descending drops of juice. Sāyaṇa explains differently :—'making a noise (as) a wild boar (makes a noise) with its foot.' Wilson. *The places* : the filters.

8 *The Swans* : the singers, descendants of the Ṛṣi Vṛṣagaṇa.

9 *The Wide-strider's rapid movement* : the swift course of the Sun. *Cows low as 'twere* : Sayāṇa explains *gāvaḥ*, cows, by *anye gantāraḥ*. other goers, takes *ná* as negative, and derives *mimate* from *mā*, to measure, instead of from *mā*, to bleat or low :—'other goers cannot overtake him (though he is) moving easily.'—Wilson. *He with the sharpened horns* : Soma as the Moon : the silvery light by night and the golden-coloured juice by day.

12 *Wearing qualities by seasons* : 'clothed in pleasant radiance according to the season.'—Wilson.

15 *Him who stays the waters* : Vṛtra.

17 *Winds* : cf. 'Vāyu is Soma's guardian God' (X. 85. 5).

22 Sāyaṇa's explanation of the first line is extremely laboured :—'When the praise of the zealous worshipper

Then loudly lowing came the cows to Indu, the chosen, well-loved Master in the beaker.

23 The Sage, Celestial, liberal, raining bounties, pours as he flows the Genuine for the Truthful.

The King shall be effectual strength's upholder : he by the ten bright reins is mostly guided.

24 He who beholds mankind, made pure with filters, the King supreme of Deities and mortals,

From days of old is Treasure-Lord of riches : he, Indu, cherishes fair well-kept Order.

25 Haste, like a steed, to victory for glory, to Indra's and to Vāyu's entertainment.

Give us food ample, thousandfold : be, Soma, the finder-out of riches when they cleanse thee.

26 Effused by us let God-delighting Somas bring as they flow a home with noble heroes.

Rich in all boons like priests acquiring favour, the worshippers of heaven, the best of Cheerers.

27 So, God, for service of the Gods flow onward, flow, drink of Gods, for ample food, O Soma.

For we go forth to war against the mighty : make heaven and earth well stablished by thy cleansing.

28 Thou, yoked by strong men, neighest like a courser, swifter than thought is, like an awful lion.

By paths directed hitherward, the straightest, send thou us happiness, Indu, while they cleanse thee.

29 Sprung from the Gods, a hundred streams, a thousand, have been effused : sages prepare and purge them.

Bring us from heaven the means of winnning, Indu; thou art forerunnner of abundant riches.

30 The streams of days were poured as'twere from heaven : the wise King doth not treat his friend unkindly.

Like a son following his father's wishes, grant to this family success and safety.

31 Now are thy streams poured forth with all their sweetness, when, purified. thou goest through the filter.

The race of kine is thy gift, Pavamāna: when born thou madest Sūrya rich with brightness.

32 Bright, bellowing along the path of Order, thou shinest as the form of life eternal.

Thou flowest on as gladdening drink for Indra, sending thy voice out with the hymns of sages.

33 Pouring out streams at the Gods' feast with service, thou, Soma, lookest down, a heavenly Eagle.

Enter the Soma-holding beaker, Indu, and with a roar approach the ray of Sūrya.

34 Three are the voices that the Courser utters : he speaks the thought of prayer, the law of Order.

To the Cow's Master come the Cows inquiring : the hymns with eager longing come to Soma.

35 To Soma come the Cows, the Milch-kine longing, to Soma sages with their hymns inquiring.

Soma, effused, is purified and blended : our hymns and Tṛṣṭup songs unite in Soma.

36 Thus, Soma, as we pour thee into vessels, while thou art purified flow for our welfare.

Pass into Indra with a mighty roaring : make the voice swell, and generate abundance.

37 Singer of true songs, ever-watchful, Soma hath settled in the ladles when they cleanse him.

Him the Adhvaryus, paired and eager, follow, leaders of sacrifice and skilful-handed.

38 Cleansed near the Sun as 'twere, he as Creator hath filled full heaven and earth, and hath disclosed them.

He by whose dear help men gain all their wishes shall yield the precious meed as to a victor.

sanctifies him as that of a noisy (crowd) in front (praises) a distinguished (prince) for the support (he affords).'—Wilson.

23 *The Genuine for the Truthful* : *ṛtám ṛtā́ya* : the Soma juice for Indra. *The ten bright reins* : or rays, *i.e.*, the fingers. The half-line is difficult.

30 *The streams of days* : the libations of Soma juice which we offered every day. *Like a son* : the Soma juice is regarded as the son of the *yajamāna* or sacrificer who causes it to be prepared.

34 *The Courser* is Soma, and the three voices (*vācaḥ*) or words which he utters are according to Sāyaṇa praises or sacred texts in the form of the three Vedas. The three tones, low, middle, and high, are probably intended. Or *váhniḥ* (the courser) may mean the bearer of the oblation, *yajamāna*, as Sāyaṇa explains.

39 He, being cleansed, the Strengthener and Increaser, Soma the Bounteous, helped us with his lustre,
Wherewith our sires of old who knew the footsteps found light and stole the cattle from the mountain.

40 In the first vault of heaven loud roared the Ocean, King of all being, generating creatures.
Steer, in the filter, on the fleecy summit, Soma, the Drop effused, hath waxen mighty.

41 Soma the Steer, in that as Child of Waters he chose the Gods, performed that great achievement.
He, Pavamāna, granted strength to Indra; he, Indu, generated light in Sūrya.

42 Make Vāyu glad, for furtherance and bounty: cheer Varuṇa and Mitra, as they cleanse thee.
Gladden the Gods, gladden the host of Maruts: make Heaven and Earth rejoice, O God, O Soma.

43 Flow onward righteous slayer of the wicked, driving away our enemies and sickness,
Blending thy milk with milk which cows afford us. We are thy friends, thou art the Friend of Indra.

44 Pour us a fount of meath, a spring of treasure; send us a hero son and happy fortune.
Be sweet to Indra when they cleanse thee, Indu, and pour down riches on us from the ocean.

45 Strong Soma, pressed, like an impetuous courser, hath flowed in stream as a flood speeding downward.
Cleansed, he hath settled in his wooden dwelling: Indu hath flowed with milk and with the waters.

46 Strong, wise, for thee who longest for his coming this Soma here flows to the bowls, O Indra.
He, chariot-borne, sun-bright, and truly potent, was poured forth like the longing of the pious.

47 He, purified with ancient vital vigour, pervading all his Daughter's forms and figures,
Finding his threefold refuge in the waters, goes singing, as a priest, to the assemblies.

48 Now, chariot-borne, flow unto us, God Soma, as thou art purified flow to the saucers,
Sweetest in waters, rich in meath, and holy, as Savitar the God is, truthful-minded.

49 To feast him, flow mid song and hymn, to Vāyu, flow purified to Varuṇa and Mitra.
Flow to the song-inspiring car-borne Hero, to mighty Indra, him who wields the thunder.

50 Pour on us garments that shall clothe us meetly, send, purified, milch-kine, abundant yielders.
God Soma, send us chariot-drawing horses that they may bring us treasures bright and golden.

51 Send to us in a stream celestial riches, send us, when thou art cleansed, what earth containeth,
So that thereby we may acquire possessions and Ṛṣihood in Jamadagni's manner.

52 Pour forth this wealth with this purification: flow onward to the yellow lake, O Indu.
Here, too, the Ruddy, wind-swift, full of wisdom, shall give a son to him who cometh quickly.

53 Flow on for us with this purification to the famed ford of thee whose due is glory.
May the Foe-queller shake us down, for triumph, like a tree's ripe fruit, sixty thousand treasures.

54 Eagerly do we pray for those two exploits, at the blue lake and Pṛṣana, wrought in battle.

40 *In the first vault*: that is in the highest firmament. *The Ocean*: Soma.

47 *His Daughter's forms and figures*: Soma pervades, and imparts a share of his nutritious power to, the grass, herbs, and shrubs which are the varied forms assumed by Earth his daughter.

51 *Ṛṣihood in Jamadagni's manner*: 'make our sacred prayer (sweet) as Jamadagni.'—Wilson.

52 *Yellow*: the meaning of *māṁścatvé* is uncertain. See VII. 44. 3, note.

53 *To the famed ford*: possibly, as Ludwig suggests, the aid of Soma is craved at some ford of a neighbouring river, famous on account of a battle that has been fought there, and destined to be the scene of an approaching conflict.

54 The first line is conjecturally translated after Ludwig, who takes *Pṛśana* to be the name of a place. Sāyaṇa's elaborate explanation is different:—'These two great acts, the raining (of arrows) and the humiliation (of foes) are the givers of happiness; they are deadly either in a fight on horseback or in a hand-to-hand fight.'—Wilson. Here Sāyaṇa explains *māṁścatvé* (at the blue or

He sent our enemies to sleep and slew them, and turned away the foolish and unfriendly.

55 Thou comest unto three extended filters, and hastenest through each one as they cleanse thee.
Thou art the giver of the gift, a Bhaga, a Maghavan for liberal lords, O Indu.

56 This Soma here, the Wise, the All-obtainer, flows on his way as King of all existence.
Driving the drops at our assemblies, Indu completely traverses the fleecy filter.

57 The Great Inviolate are kissing Indu, and singing in his place like eager sages.
The wise men send him forth with ten swift fingers, and balm his form with essence of the waters.

58 Soma, may we, with thee as Pavamāna, pile up together all our spoil in battle.
This boon vouchsafe us Varuṇa and Mitra, and Aditi and Sindhu, Earth and Heaven.

HYMN XCVIII. *Soma Pavamāna*

1. STREAM on us riches that are sought by many, best at winning strength,
Riches, O Indu, thousandfold, glorious, conquering the great.

2 Effused, he hath, as on a car, invested him in fleecy mail :
Onward hath Indu flowed in streams, impelled, surrounded by the wood.

3 Effused, this Indu hath flowed on, distilling rapture, to the fleece :
He goes erect, as seeking kine in stream, with light, to sacrifice.

4 For thou thyself, O Indu, God, to every mortal worshipper
Attractest riches thousandfold, made manifest in hundred forms.

5 Good Vṛtra-slayer, may we be still nearest to this wealth of thine
Which many crave, nearest to food and happiness, Resistless One !

6 Whom, bright with native splendour, crushed between the pair of pressing-stones—
The wavy Friend whom Indra loves—the twice-five sisters dip and bathe,

7 Him with the fleece they purify, brown, golden-hued, beloved of all,
Who with exhilarating juice goes forth to all the Deities.

8 Through longing for this sap of yours ye drink what brings ability,
Even him who, dear as heaven's own light, gives to our princes high renown.

9 Indu at holy rites produced you, Heaven and Earth, the Friends of men,
Hill-haunting God the Goddesses. They bruised him where the roar was loud.

10 For Vṛtra-slaying Indra, thou, Soma, art poured that he may drink,
Poured for the guerdon-giving man, poured for the God who sitteth there.

11 These ancient Somas, at the break of day, have flowed into the sieve,
Snorting away at early morn these foolish evil-hearted ones.

12 Friends, may the princes, ye and we, obtain this Most Resplendent One.
Gain him who hath the smell of strength, win him whose home is very strength.

HYMN XCIX. *Soma Pavamāna.*

1. THEY for the Bold and Lovely One ply manly vigour like a bow :

yellow lake ?) by 'in battle with horses,' and *pṛśane* (at Pṛśana !) by 'in close, or hand-to-hand encounter.' Two victories appear to be referred to, and that is about all that can be said.

55 The *three extended filters* are said to be fire, wind, and sun, in addition to the one artificial filter of wool.

57 *The Great Inviolate* : the Gods. *Kissing* : or sipping.

58 *All our spoil in battle* : yet to be won in the approaching fight wherein we look to Soma for help and victory.

---

2 *By the wood* : the wooden vat or trough.

3 *Seeking kine* : desirous of the milk which is to be mixed with his juice.

9 This stanza is difficult. Sāyaṇa explains it differently :—'Divine heaven and earth the progeny of Manu, the *Soma* juice is generated at your sacrifices, radiant, abiding in the grinding stones; (the priests) bruise him at the loud-sounding ceremony.'— Wilson. *Hill-haunting*: cf. IX. 85. 10.

10 *For the guerdon-giving man* : for the good of the institutor of the sacrifice.

11 *Snorting away* : driving away with the bubbling sound they make

12 *Who hath the smell of strength* : *vājagandhyam* : 'fragrant and invigorating.'—Wilson. 'Forming or having a wagon-load of goods or spoil.'—S. P. Lexicon. *Him whose home is strength* : *vājapastyam* : 'food and dwellings.' —Wilson. 'Him who has a house full of goods.'—S. P. Lexicon.

---

1 *They* : the priests. *Ply manly vigour like a bow* : 'stretch the bow of manhood.'—Wilson. They exert all their manly strength, or as Benfey suggests, attack and storm the God with prayer and sacrifice, 'beseeching and besieging' as Milton says. *The Lord Divine* : the Asura (Zend, Ahura), here meaning Soma.

Joyous, in front of songs they weave bright raiment for the Lord Divine.

2 And he, made beautiful by night, dips forward into strengthening food,
What time the sacrificer's thoughts speed on his way the Golden-hued.

3 We cleanse this gladdening drink of his, the juice which Indra chiefly drinks,--
That which kine took into their mouths, of old, and princes take it now.

4 To him, while purifying, they have raised the ancient psalm of praise :
And sacred songs which bear the names of Gods have supplicated him.

5 They purify him as he drops, courageous, in the fleecy sieve.
Him they instruct as messenger to bear the sage's morning prayer.

6 Soma, best Cheerer, takes his seat, the while they cleanse him in the bowls.
He as it were impregns the cow, and babbles on, the Lord of Song.

7 He is effused and beautified, a God for Gods, by skilful men.
He penetrates the mighty floods collecting all he knows therein.

8 Pressed, Indu, guided by the men, thou art led to the cleaning sieve.
Thou, yielding Indra highest joy, takest thy seat within the bowls.

HYMN C. *Soma Pavamāna.*

1. THE Guileless Ones are singing praise to Indra's well beloved Friend,
As, in the morning of its life, the mothers lick the new-born calf.

2 O Indu, while they cleanse thee, bring, O Soma, doubly-waxing wealth :
Thou in the worshipper's abode causest all treasures to increase.

3 Set free the song which mind hath yoked, even as thunder frees the rain :
All treasures of the earth and heaven, O Soma, thou dost multiply.

4 Thy stream when thou art pressed runs on like some victorious warrior's steed,
Hastening onward through the fleece like a swift horse who wins the prize.

5 Flow on, Sage Soma, with thy stream to give us mental power and strength,
Effused for Indra, for his drink, for Mitra and for Varuṇa.

6 Flow to the filter with thy stream, effused, best winner, thou, of spoil,
O Soma, as most rich in sweets for Indra, Viṣṇu, and the Gods.

7 The mothers, void of guiles, caress thee Golden-coloured, in the sieve,
As cows, O Pavamāna, lick the new-born calf, as Law commands.

8 Thou, Pavamāna, movest on with wondrous rays to great renown.
Striving within the votary's house thou drivest all the glooms away.

9 Lord of great sway, thou liftest thee above the heavens, above the earth.
Thou, Pavamāna hast assumed thy coat of mail in majesty.

HYMN CI. *Soma Pavamāna*

1. FOR first possession of your juice, for the exhilarating drink,
Drive ye away the dog, my friends, drive ye the long-tongued dog away.

2 He who with purifying stream, effused, comes flowing hitherward,
Indu, is like an able steed.

3 The men with all-pervading song send unassailable Soma forth,
By pressing-stones, to sacrifice.

4 The Somas, very rich in sweets, for which the sieve is destined, flow,
Effused, the source of Indra's joy : may your strong juices reach the Gods.

5 Indu flows on for Indra's sake : thus have the Deities declared.
The Lord of Speech exerts himself, Ruler of all, because of might.

2 *By night* : *kṣapā* : 'at the end of the night.'—Wilson. Ludwig translates *kṣapā* by 'der fürst,' 'the prince.'

3 *Which kine took into their mouths* : in the form of the juices of grass from which the milky portion of the libation is evolved.

4 Sāyaṇa's explanation of the second line of this stanza, is different :—'and the fingers exercising their pressure are able (to prepare the oblation) for the gods.'—Wilson.

6 *He as it were impregns the cow* : meaning, perhaps, as Ludwig suggests, that the milk becomes efficacious as a libation only when it is mixed with Soma juice.

7 *Collecting all he knows therein* : the meaning of this half-line is not clear : —'when he is recognized amongst these (people) as the giver (of riches).' —Wilson.

1 *The Guileless Ones* : the *vasatīvarī* waters.

7 *As Law commands* : *vídharmaṇi* : see Bergaigne, *La Religion Védique*, III. 218. note 2. 'At the sacrifice.'—Wilson. 'In the realm of heaven.'—Grassmann.

9 *Thy coat of mail* : *drāpím* : See IX. 86. 14.

1 *Drive ye away* : prevent dogs or Rākṣasas from drinking the Soma juice.

6 Inciter of the voice of song, with thousand streams the ocean flows,
Even Soma, Lord of opulence, the Friend of Indra, day by day.

7 As Pūṣan, Fortune, Bhaga, comes this Soma while they make him pure.
He, Lord of the multitude, hath looked upon the earth and heaven.

8 The dear cows lowed in joyful mood together to the gladdening drink.
The drops as they were purified, the Soma juices, made then paths.

9 O Pavamāna, bring the juice, the mightiest, worthy to be famed,
Which the Five Tribes have over them, whereby we may win opulence.

10 For us the Soma juices flow, the drops best furtherers of our weal,
Effused as friends without a spot, benevolent, finders of the light.

11 Effused by means of pressing-stones, upon the ox-hide visible,
They, treasure-finders, have announced food unto us from every side.

12 These Soma juices, skilled in song, purified, blent with milk and curd,
When moving and when firmly laid in oil, resemble lovely Suns.

13 Let not the power of men restrain the voice of the outpouring Juice :
As Bhṛgu's sons chased Makha, so drive ye the greedy hound away.

14 The Friend hath wrapped him in his robe, as in his parents arms, a son.
He went, as lover to a dame, to take his station suitor-like.

15 That Hero who produces strength, he who hath propped both worlds apart,
Gold-hued, hath wrapped him in the sieve, to settle, priest-like, in his place.

16 Soma upon the ox's skin through the sheep's wool flows purified.
Bellowing out, the Tawny Steer goes on to Indra's special place.

HYMN CII. *Soma Pavamāna.*

1. THE Child, when blended with the streams, speeding the plan of sacrifice,
Surpasses all things that are dear, yea, from of old.

2 The place, near the two pressing-stones of Trita, hath he occupied,
Secret and dear through seven lights of sacrifice.

3 Urge to three courses, on the heights of Trita, riches in a stream .
He who is passing wise measures his courses out.

4 Even at his birth the Mothers Seven taught him, for glory, like a sage,
So that he, firm and sure, hath set his mind on wealth.

5 Under his sway, of one accord, are all the guileless Deities :
Warriors to be envied, they, when they are pleased.

6 The Babe whom they who strengthen Law have generated fair to see,
Much longed for at the sacrifice most liberal Sage,—

7 To him, united, of themselves, come the young Parents of the rite,
When they adorn him, duly weaving sacrifice.

8 With wisdom and with radiant eyes unbar to us the stall of heaven,
Speeding at solemn rite the plan of Holy Law.

HYMN CIII. *Soma Pavamāna.*

1. To Soma who is purified as ordering Priest the song is raised :
Bring meed, as 'twere, to one who makes thee glad with hymns.

13 *Makha* : apparently, a demon whose name does not occur again in the Ṛgveda.

16 *Special place* : 'prepared station.'—Wilson. The vessel containing the libation appropriated to Indra.

---

1 *The streams* : literally 'the great,' 'waters' being understood.

2 I am indebted to Prof. Macdonell (Journal of the R. A. S., July, 1893, pp. 457-8) for the translation and explanation of this and the following very difficult stanzas. *The place* : far away in heaven where Trita presses and prepares the celestial Soma for Indra. *He* : Soma. *Dear* : to Soma. *Seven lights of sacrifice* : probably the seven rays or tongues of the sacrificial fire with which Soma is closely connected. 'Through the seven ordinances of sacrifices.'—Macdonell.

3 'The main justification of my interpretation,' says Prof. Macdonell, 'is that I supply no extraneous word with 'trīṇi', but explain it by the third line. The meaning of my translation is : 'Do thou, Soma, on the heights of Trita, direct the fertilizing streams which produce wealth into the channels of Trita, for thou knowest these channels, having measured them out with thy streams.' *Three courses* : or channels, of Trita. *He who is passing wise* : Soma. *His* : Trita's.

4 *The Mothers Seven* : the Seven Rivers.

5 *Warriors to be envied* : the meaning of the line is uncertain.

6 *They who strengthen Law* : according to Sāyaṇa, the *vasativari* waters.

7 *The young Parents of the rite* : ever-young, fresh and strong Heaven and Earth.

---

2 Blended with milk and curds he flows on through the long wool of the sheep.
The Gold-hued, purified, makes him three seats for rest.

3 On through the long wool of the sheep to the meath-dropping vat he flows :
The Ṛṣis' sevenfold quire hath sung aloud to him.

4 Shared by all Gods, Infallible, the Leader of our holy hymns,
Golden-hued Soma, being cleansed, hath reached the bowls.

5 After thy Godlike qualities, associate with Indra, go,
As a Priest purified by priests, Immortal One.

6 Like a car-horse who shows his strength, a God effused for Deities.
The penetrating Pavamāna flows along.

HYMN CIV. *Soma Pavamāna.*

1. Sit down, O friends, and sing aloud to him who purifies himself :
Deck him for glory, like a child, with holy rites.

2 Unite him bringing household wealth, even as a calf, with mother kine,
Him who hath double strength, the God, delighting juice.

3 Purify him who gives us power, that he, most Blessed One, may be
A banquet for the Troop, Mitra, and Varuṇa.

4 Voices have sung aloud to thee as finder-out of wealth for us :
We clothe the hue thou wearest with a robe of milk.

5 Thou, Indu, art the food of Gods, O Sovran of all gladdening drinks :
As Friend for friend, be thou best finder of success.

6 Drive utterly away from us each demon, each voracious fiend,
The godless and the false : keep sorrow far away.

HYMN CV. *Soma Pavamāna*

1. Sing ye aloud, O friends, to him who makes him pure for gladdening drink :
They shall make sweet the Child with sacrifice and laud.

2 Like as a calf with mother cows, so Indu is urged forth and sent,
Glorified by our hymns, the God-delighting juice.

3 Effectual means of power is he, he is a banquet for the Troop,
He who hath been effused, most rich in meath, for Gods.

4 Flow to us, Indu, passing, strong, effused, with wealth of kine and steeds :
I will spread forth above the milk thy radiant hue.

5 Lord of the tawny, Indu thou who art the God's most special food,
As Friend to friend, for splendour be thou good to men.

6 Drive utterly, far away from us each godless, each voracious foe.
O Indu, overcome and drive the false afar.

HYMN CVI. *Soma Pavamāna.*

1. To Indra, to the Mighty Steer, may these gold-coloured juices go,
Drops rapidly produced, that find the light of heaven.

2 Effused, this juice victorious flows for Indra, for his maintenance.
Soma bethinks him of the Conqueror, as he knows.

3 May Indra in his raptures gain from him the grasp that gathers spoil,
And, winning waters, wield the steer-strong thunderbolt.

4 Flow vigilant for Indra, thou Soma, yea, Indu, run thou on :
Bring hither splendid strength that finds the light of heaven.

5 Do thou, all-beautiful, purify for Indra's sake the mighty juice,
Path-maker thou, far seeing, with a thousand ways.

2 *Three seats for rest* : three reservoirs in which he may settle. The *droṇakalaśa*, the *ādhavanīya*, and the *pūtabhṛt*.

3 *The Ṛṣis' sevenfold quire* : 'the seven metres of the Ṛṣis.'—Wilson.

5 *After thy Godlike qualities* : according to Sāyaṇa, 'to the hosts of the gods.'

6 *Penetrating* : *vyānaśiḥ* : 'spreading widely into the vessels.'—Wilson.

---

2 *Unite him* : 'Associate him the support of the mansion with the maternal (waters) as the calf (with the mother).' —Wilson.

3 *The Troop* : the banded Maruts.

---

5 *Lord of the tawny* : *harīṇām* : Sāyaṇa supplies *paśūnām*, cattle.

The hymn is a sort of *rifacimento of* Hymn 104.

2 *For his maintenance* : *bhárāya* : or, for battle. *The Conqueror* : Indra.

6 Best finder of prosperity for us, most rich in sweets for Gods,
Proceed thou loudly roaring on a thousand paths.

7 O Indu, with thy streams, in might, flow for the banquet of the Gods :
Rich in meath, Soma, in our beaker take thy place.

8 Thy drops that swim in water have exalted Indra to delight :
The Gods have drunk thee up for immortality.

9 Stream opulence to us, ye drops of Soma, pressed and purified,
Pouring down rain from heaven in floods, and finding light.

10 Soma, while filtered, with his wave flows through the long wool of the sheep,
Shouting while purified before the voice of song.

11 With songs they send the Mighty forth, sporting in wood, above the fleece :
Our psalms have glorified him of the triple height.

12 Into the jars hath he been loosed, like an impetuous steed for war,
And lifting up his voice, while filtered, glided on.

13 Gold-hued and lovely in his course, through tangles of the wool he flows,
And pours heroic fame upon the worshippers.

14 Flow thus, a faithful votary : the streams of meath have been effused.
Thou comest to the filter, singing, from each side.

HYMN CVII. *Soma Pavamāna.*

1. HENCE sprinkle forth the juice effused, Soma, the best of sacred gifts,
Who, friend of man, hath run amid the water-streams. He hath pressed Soma out with stones.

2 Now, being purified, flow hither through the fleece inviolate and most odorous.
We gladden thee in waters when thou art effused, blending thee still with juice and milk.

3 Pressed out for all to see, delighting Gods, Indu, Far-sighted One, is mental power.

4 Cleansing thee, Soma, in thy stream, thou flowest in a watery robe :
Giver of wealth, thou sittest in the place of Law, O God, a fountain made of gold.

5 Milking the heavenly udder for dear meath, he hath sat in the ancient gathering-place.
Washed by the men, the Strong, Far-seeing One streams forth nutritious food that all desire.

6 O Soma, while they cleanse thee, dear and watchful in the sheep's long wool,
Thou hast become a Singer most like Aṅgiras : thou madest Sūrya mount to heaven.

7 Bountiful, best of furtherers, Soma floweth on, Ṛṣi and Singer, keen of sight.
Thou hast become a Sage most welcome to the Gods : thou madest Sūrya mount to heaven.

8 Pressed out by pressers, Soma goes over the fleecy backs of sheep,
Goes, even as with a mare, in tawny-coloured stream, goes in exhilarating stream.

9 Down to the water-Soma, rich in kine, hath flowed with cows, with cows that have been milked.
They have approached the mixing-vessels as a sea : the cheerer streams for the carouse.

10 Effused by stones, O Soma, and urged through the long wool of the sheep,
Thou, entering the saucers as a man the fort, gold-hued hast settled in the wood.

11 He beautifies himself through the sheep's long fine wool, like an impetuous steed in war,
Even Soma Pavamāna who shall be the joy of sages and of holy bards.

12 O Soma,—for the feast of Gods, river-like he hath swelled with surge,

11 *Him of the triple height* : *tripṛṣṭhám* : the three heights are probably the firmament, the mountain and the altar. 'Abiding in three receptacles.'—Wilson.

---

1 *He* : the priest.

4 *In the place of Law* : in the place of Law-ordained sacrifice.

5 *Milking the heavenly udder for dear meath* : extracting the sweet and precious juice from the stalk and tendrils of the Soma plant.

9 *They have approached the mixing-vessels as a sea* : *saṃvāraṇāni*, from *saṃvṛ*, to cover, enclose, surround, must, apparently, mean the vessels that contain the juices and not the juices themselves as Sāyaṇa explains :—'his enjoyable juices go (to the pitcher as waters) to the ocean.'—Wilson.

12 *O Soma......he*, is a sort of periphrasis for Soma in the nominative case.

With the stalk's juice, exhilarating, resting not, into the vat that drops with meath.

13 Like a dear son who must be decked, the Lovely One hath clad him in a shining robe.
Men skilful at their work drive him forth, like a car, into the rivers from their hands.

14 The living drops of Soma juice pour, as they flow, the gladdening drink,
Intelligent drops above the basin of the sea, exhilarating, finding light.

15 May Pavamāna, King and God, speed with his wave over the sea the lofty rite:
May he by Mitra's and by Varuṇa's decree flow furthering the lofty rite.

16 Far-seeing, lovely, guided by the men, the God whose home is in the sea—

17 Soma, the gladdening juice, flows pressed for Indra with his Marut host:
He hastens o'er the fleece with all his thousand streams: men make him bright and beautiful.

18 Purified in the bowl and gendering the hymn, wise Soma joys among the Gods.
Robed in the flood, the Mighty One hath clad himself with milk and settled in the vats.

19 O Soma, Indu, every day thy friendship hath been my delight.
Many fiends follow me; help me, thou Tawny-hued; pass on beyond these barriers.

20 Close to thy bosom am I, Soma, day and night. O Tawny-hued, for friendship sake.
Sūrya himself refulgent with his glow have we o'ertaken in his course like birds.

21 Deft-handed! thou when purified liftest thy voice amid the sea.
Thou, Pavamāna, makest riches flow to us, yellow, abundant, much-desired.

22 Making thee pure and bright in the sheep's long wool, thou hast bellowed, steer-like, in the wood.
Thou flowest, Soma Pavamāna, balmed with milk unto the special place of Gods.

23 Flow on to win us strength, flow on to lofty lore of every kind.
Thou, Soma, as Exhilarator wast the first to spread the sea abroad for Gods.

24 Flow to the realm of earth, flow to the realm of heaven, O Soma, in thy righteous ways.
Fair art thou whom the sages, O Far-seeing One, urge onward with their songs and hymns.

25 Over the cleansing sieve have flowed the Pavamānas in a stream,
Girt by the Maruts, gladdening, Steeds with Indra's strength, for wisdom and for dainty food.

26 Urged onward by the pressers, clad in watery robes, Indu is speeding to the vat.
He gendering light, hath made the glad Cows low, while he takes them as his garb of state.

HYMN CVIII. *Soma Pavamāna.*

1. For Indra, flow thou Soma on, as gladdening juice most sweet, intelligent,
Great, cheering, dwelling most in heaven.

2 Thou, of whom having drunk the Steer acts like a steer: drinking of this that finds the light,
He, Excellently Wise, is come to strengthening food, to spoil and wealth like Etaśa.

3 For, verily, Pavamāna, thou hast, splendidest, called all the generations of
The Gods to immortality.

4 By whom Dadhyac Navagva opens fastened doors, by whom the sages gained their wish,
By whom they won the fame of lovely Amṛta in the felicity of Gods.

5 Effused, he floweth in a stream, best rapture-giver, in the long wool of the sheep,
Sporting, as 'twere the waters' wave.

14 *Of the sea*: of the firmament, or sea of air.

19 *Many fiends*: the text has only *purūṇi*, many, in the neuter plural. Sāyaṇa supplies *rakṣāṃsi* Rākṣasas *or fiends*. *Pass on beyond these barriers*: 'overcome those who surround me.' —Wilson.

20 *Close to thy bosom am I*: 'I (delight) in thy presence.' —Wilson.

21 *Amid the sea*: *antarikṣe kalaśe vā*, in the firmament or in the beaker, says Sāyaṇa.

25 *The Pavamānas*: 'thy purified juices.'—Wilson.

2 *The Steer acts like a steer*: *vṛṣabho vṛṣāyáte*: 'the showerer Indra is invigorated.'—Wilson. *Etaśa*: one of the horses of the Sun; or a horse in general);—'as a horse comes to the battle.—Sāyaṇa.

4 *Dadhyac Navagva*: Dadhyac was the son of Atharvan the priest who first obtained fire and offered Soma and prayer to the Gods. Here he is called a Navagva and consequently one of the Aṅgirases. See both names in Vol. I., Index. *Won the fame of lovely Amṛta*: 'obtained the sustenance of the delicious (ambrosial) water.' —Wilson.

6 He who from out the rocky cavern took with might the red-refulgent watery Cows,
Thou masterest the stable full of kine and steeds: burst it, brave Lord, like one in mail.

7 Press ye and pour him, like a steed, laud-worthy, speeding through the region and the flood,
Who swims in water, roars in wood;

8 Increaser of the water, Steer with thousand streams, dear to the race of Deities;
Who born in Law hath waxen mighty by the Law, King, God, and lofty Ordinance.

9 Make splendid glory shine on us, thou Lord of strengthening food, God, as the Friend of Gods:
Unclose the fount of middle air.

10 Roll onward to the bowls, O Mighty One, effused, as Prince supporter of the tribes.
Pour on us rain from heaven, send us the waters' flow: incite our thoughts to win the spoil.

11 They have drained him the Steer of heaven, him with a thousand streams, distilling rapturous joy,
Him who brings all things excellent.

12 The Mighty One was born Immortal, giving life, lightening darkness with his shine.
Well-praised by sages he hath by his wondrous power assumed the Threefold as his robe.

13 Effused is he who brings good things, who brings us bounteous gifts and sweet refreshing food,
Soma who brings us quiet homes:

14 He whom our Indra and the Marut host shall drink, Bhaga shall drink with Aryaman,
By whom we bring to us Mitra and Varuṇa and Indra for our great defence.

15 Soma, for Indra's drink do thou, led by the men, well-weaponed and most gladdening,
Flow on with greatest store of sweets.

16 Enter the Soma-holder, even Indra's heart, as rivers pass into the sea,
Acceptable to Mitra, Vāyu, Varuṇa, the noblest Pillar of the heavens.

12. *The Threefold*: the morning, noon, and evening libation.

13 The metre of this stanza is Gāyatrī Yavamadhyā, that is Gāyatrī having the middle like a barley-corn thick in the middle and tapering at both ends.: first a Pāda of eight syllables, then one of twelve, and lastly another of eight.

HYMN CIX. *Soma Pavamāna.*

1. PLEASANT to Indra's, Mitra's, Pūṣan's Bhaga's taste, sped onward, Soma, with thy flowing stream.

2 Let Indra drink, O Soma, of thy juice for wisdom, and all Deities for strength.

3 So flow thou on as bright celestial juice, flow to the vast, immortal dwelling-place.

4 Flow onward, Soma, as a mighty sea, as Father of the Gods to every form.

5 Flow on, O Soma, radiant for the Gods and Heaven and Earth and bless our progeny.

6 Thou, bright Juice, art Sustainer of the sky: flow, mighty, in accordance with true Law.

7 Soma, flow splendid with thy copious stream through the great fleece as in the olden time.

8 Born, led by men, joyous, and purified, let the Light-finder make all blessings flow:

9 Indu, while cleansed, keeping the people safe, shall give us all possessions for our own.

10 Flow on for wisdom, Soma, and for power, as a strong courser bathed, to win the prize.

11 The pressers purify this juice of thine, the Soma, for delight, and lofty fame.

12 They deck the Gold-hued Infant, newly-born, even Soma, Indu, in the sieve for Gods.

13 Fair Indu hath flowed on for rapturous joy, Sage for good fortune in the waters' lap.

14 He bears the beauteous name of Indra, that wherewith he overcame all demon foes.

15 All Deities are wont to drink of him, pressed by the men and blent with milk and curds.

The Ṛṣis are the Agnayo Dhiṣṇyāḥ, sacrificial Agnis or Fires, said to be sons of Īśvara the Supreme Deity of post-Vedic times.

3 *Flow to the vast, immortal dwelling-place*: 'flow for immortality and spacious abode.'—Wilon.

4 *To every form*: to all the forms or essences of the Gods into which he enters. Or to every power, to aid us in every way.

14 *He bears*: according to Sāyaṇa, the translation of the first half-line would be: Indra's fair body he supports, wherewith, etc.

16 He hath flowed forth with thousand streams effused, flowed through the filter and the sheep's long wool.

17 With endless genial flow the Strong hath run, purified by the waters, blent with milk.

18 Pressed out with stones, directed by the men, go forth, O Soma, into Indra's throat.

19 The mighty Soma with a thousand streams is poured to Indra through the cleansing sieve.

20 Indu they balm with pleasant milky juice for Indra, for the Steer, for his delight.

21 Lightly, for sheen, they cleanse thee for the Gods, gold-coloured, wearing water as thy robe.

22 Indu to Indra streams, yea, downward streams, Strong, flowing to the floods, and mingling there.

HYMN CX. *Soma Pavamāna.*

1. O'ERPOWERING Vṛtras, forward run to win great strength :
Thou speedest to subdue like one exacting debts.

2 In thee, effused, O Soma, we rejoice ourselves for great supremacy in fight.
Thou, Pavamāna, enterest into mighty deeds,

3 O Pavamāna, thou didst generate the Sun, and spread the moisture out with power,
Hasting to us with plenty vivified with milk.

4 Thou didst produce him, Deathless God ! mid mortal men for maintenance of Law and lovely Amṛta :
Thou evermore hast moved making strength flow to us.

5 All round about hast thou with glory pierced for us as 'twere a never-failing well for men to drink,
Borne on thy way in fragments from the presser's arms.

6 Then, beautifully radiant, certain Heavenly Ones, have sung to him their kinship as they looked thereon,
And Savitar the God opens as 'twere a stall.

7 Soma, the men of old whose grass was trimmed addressed the hymn to thee for mighty strength and for renown :
So, Hero, urge us onward to heroic power.

8 They have drained forth from out the great depth of the sky the old primeval milk of heaven that claims the laud:
They lifted up their voice to Indra at his birth.

9 As long as thou, O Pavamāna, art above this earth and heaven and all existence in thy might,
Thou standest like a Bull the chief amid the herd.

10 In the sheep's wool hath Soma Pavamāna flowed, while they cleanse him, like a playful infant,
Indu with hundred powers and hundred currents.

11 Holy and sweet, while purified, this Indu flows on, a wave of pleasant taste, to Indra,—
Strength-winner, Treasure-finder, Life-bestower.

12 So flow thou on, subduing our assailants, chasing the demons hard to be encountered,
Well-armed and conquering our foes, O Soma.

HYMN CXI. *Soma Pavamāna.*

1. WITH this his golden splendour purifying him, he with his own allies subdues all enemies, as Sūra with his own allies.
Cleansing himself with stream of juice he shines forth yellow-hued and red, when with the praisers he encompasses all forms, with praisers having seven mouths.

2 That treasure of the Paṇis thou discoveredst; thou with thy mothers deckest thee in thine abode, with songs of worship in thine home.

3 *With plenty vivified with milk* : 'with abundant wisdom that procures cattle (for thy worshippers).'—Wilson.

5 *In fragments*: in pieces of the crushed stalk and shoots of the Soma plant

6 *Beautifully radiant* : *vasurúcaḥ* : according to Sāyaṇa, a proper name, Vasurucas, plural of Vasuruc. *Opens as 'twere a stall* : 'drives away the obstructing (darkness).'—Wilson.

1 *He* : Soma. *All enemies* : the fiends of darkness. *As Sūra with his own allies* : as Sūrya or the Sun with his attendant beams of light. *All forms* : *viśvā rūpā* : all the lunar mansions, according to Sāyaṇa. According to Hillebrandt, (assumest) all beauty. *With the praisers* : *ṛkvabhiḥ* : perhaps the Aṅgirases are intended. *Having seven mouths* : that is, one mouth each, the mouth being mentioned in reference to their love of Soma juice.

2 *Treasure of the Paṇis* : the rays of light carried off and concealed by the demons of darkness. *Thy Mothers* : apparently the Dawns. According to Sāyaṇa the *vasatīvarī* waters. *Threefold* : there is no substantive in the text, and it is uncertain what *tridhā́tubhiḥ* refers to.

As 'twere from far, the hymn is heard, where holy songs resound in joy. He with the ruddy-hued, threefold hath won life-power, he, glittering, hath won life-power.

3 He moves intelligent, directed to the East. The very beauteous car rivals the beams of light, the beautiful celestial car.
Hymns, lauding manly valour, came, inciting Indra to success, that ye may be unconquered, both thy bolt and thou, both be unconquered in the war.

HYMN CXII. *Soma Pavamāna.*

1. We all have various thoughts and plans, and diverse are the ways of men.
The Brahman seeks the worshipper, wright seeks the cracked, and leech the maimed. Flow, Indu, flow for Indra's sake.

2 The smith with ripe and seasoned plants, with feathers of the birds of air,
With stones, and with enkindled flames, seeks him who hath a store of gold. Flow, Indu, flow for Indra's sake.

3 A bard am I, my dad's a leech, mammy lays corn upon the stones.
Striving for wealth, with varied plans, we follow our desires like kine. Flow, Indu, flow for Indra's sake.

4 The horse would draw an easy car, gay hosts attract the laugh and jest.
The male desires his mate's approach, the frog is eager for the flood, Flow, Indu, flow for Indra's sake.

Sāyaṇa refers it to the *vasatīvarī* waters, and explains it by 'the supporters of the three worlds.' Grassmann thinks that the beverages, consisting of three ingredients, mixed with the Soma juice are intended. Probably the Dawns sometimes spoken of as three (cf. VIII. 41.3), are meant.

3 *The very beauteous car* : of Soma. *Beams of light* : sunbeams.

The hymn appears to be an old popular song transformed into an address to Soma by attaching to each stanza a refrain which has no connexion with the subject of the song. But see *Vedische Studien* I. p. 107. The hymn is translated in Muir's *O S. Texts*, V. 424.

1 *The Brahman* : 'This verse distinctly proves that the priesthood already formed a profession.'—Muir, *O. S. Texts*, I. 252.

2 *Plants* : meaning here reeds which were made into arrows. *With stones, and with enkindled flames* : according to Sāyaṇa, with glistening stones to form the heads of the arrows. *Who hath a store of gold* : and will be able to pay well for the arrows which the artisan makes for him.

3 *My dad* : *tatáḥ* : a familiar expression, corresponding to *nanā*, mammy.

HYMN CXIII. *Soma Pavamāna.*

1. Let Vṛtra-slaying Indra drink Soma by Śaryaṇāvān's side,
Storing up vigour in his heart, prepared to do heroic deeds. Flow, Indu, flow for Indra's sake.

2 Lord of the Quarters, flow thou on, boon Soma, from Ārjika land,
Effused with ardour and with faith, and the true hymn of sacrifice. Flow, Indu, flow for Indra's sake.

3 Hither hath Sūrya's Daughter brought the wild Steer whom Parjanya nursed.
Gandharvas have seized hold of him, and in the Soma laid the juice. Flow, Indu, flow for Indra's sake.

4 Splendid by Law ! declaring Law, truth-speaking, truthful in thy works,
Enouncing faith, King Soma ! thou, O Soma, whom thy maker decks. Flow, Indu, flow for Indra's sake.

5 Together flow the meeting streams of him the Great and truly Strong.
The juices of the juicy meet. Made pure by prayer, O Golden-hued, flow, Indu, flow for Indra's sake.

6 O Pavamāna, where the priest, as he recites the rhythmic prayer,
Lords it o'er Soma with the stone, with Soma bringing forth delight, flow, Indu, flow for Indra's sake.

7 O Pavamāna, place me in that deathless, undecaying world
Wherein the light of heaven is set, and everlasting lustre shines. Flow, Indu, flow for Indra's sake.

8 Make me immortal in that realm where dwells the King, Vivasvān's Son,
Where is the secret shrine of heaven, where are those waters young and fresh. Flow, Indu, flow for Indra's sake.

1 *Śaryaṇāvān* : a lake in the Kurukṣetra district.

2 *Of the Quarters* : of the four regions of the sky. *Ārjika-land* : according to Sāyaṇa, the country of the Ṛjikas. Cf. VIII. 7 29.

3 *The wild Steer whom Parjanya nursed* : the mighty Soma-plant whose growth has been fostered by the God of the rainy cloud. *Sūrya's Daughter* : *Śraddhā* or Faith. Cf. IX. 1. 6. *Gandharvas* : guardians of the heavenly Soma. See Vol. I., Index.

4 *Thy maker* : the Soma-presser, or the institutor of the sacrifice :—'the upholder (of the rite).'—Wilson.

8 *The King* : Yama, the ruler of departed spirits, son of Vivasvān. See Vol. I., Index.

9 Make me immortal in that realm where they move even as they list,
In the third sphere of inmost heaven where lucid worlds are full of light. Flow, Indu, flow for Indra's sake.

10 Make me immortal in that realm of eager wish and strong desire,
The region of the radiant Moon, where food and full delight are found. Flow, Indu, flow for Indra's sake

11 Make me immortal in that realm where happiness and transports, where
Joys and felicities combine, and longing wishes are fulfilled. Flow, Indu, flow for Indra's sake.

9 *Where they move even as they list* : 'where action is unrestrained.'—Muir. 'Where the sun wanders at will.' —Wilson.

10 *Of the radiant Moon* : the adjective *bradhnasya*, of the ruddy or brilliant, stands without a substantive. 'Sun' is supplied by Sāyaṇa. 'Des rotstralenden.' —Ludwig. See Hillebrandt, *Vedische Mythologie*, I., 396.

As regards the joys of the departed, referred to in stanzas 7—12, Professor von Roth observes (Journ. Amer. Orient. Soc. iii. 343, quoted by Dr. Muir, *O. S. Texts*, V. 307) 'The place where these glorified ones are to live is heaven. In order to show that not merely an outer court of the divine dwellings is set apart for them, the highest heaven, the midst or innermost parts of heaven, is expressly spoken of as their seat. This is their place of rest ; and its divine splendour is not disfigured by any specification of particular beauties or enjoyments, such as those with which other religions have been wont to adorn the mansions of the blest......There they are happy : the language used to describe their condition is the same with which is denoted the most exalted felicity.'

HYMN CXIV. *Soma Pavamāna.*

1. THE man who walketh as the Laws of Indu Pavamāna bid,—
Men call him rich in children, him, O Soma, who hath met thy thought. Flow, Indu, flow for Indra's sake.

2 Kaśyapa, Ṛṣi, lifting up thy voice with hymn-composers' lauds,
Pay reverence to King Soma born the Sovran Ruler of the plants. Flow, Indu, flow for Indra's sake.

3 Seven regions have their several Suns; the ministering priests are seven;
Seven are the Āditya Deities,—with these, O Soma, guard thou us. Flow, Indu, flow for Indra's sake.

4 Guard us with this oblation which, King Soma, hath been dressed for thee.
Let not malignity conquer us, let nothing evil do us harm. Flow, Indu, flow for Indra's sake.

2 *Kaśyapa* : the seer of the hymn addresses himself.

3 *Seven regions* : the regions of the sky, the four quarters with intermediate points. They are sometimes said to be five, six, or seven in number, but more frequently eight. *Āditya Deities* : Varuṇa, Mitra, Aryaman, Bhaga, Dakṣa, Aṁśa, and perhaps Dhātar. Other enumerations also are given, and their number is sometimes said to be eight. See M. Müller, *Vedic Hymns*, I. p. 232 (Sacred Books of the East, XXXII).

BOOK THE TENTH

HYMN I. *Agni.*

1. **High** hath the Mighty risen before the dawning, and come to us with light from out the darkness.
Fair-shapen Agni with white-shining splendour hath filled at birth all human habitations.

2 Thou, being born, art Child of Earth and Heaven, parted among the plants in beauty, Agni !
The glooms of night thou, Brilliant Babe, subduest, and art come forth, loud roaring, from thy Mothers.

3 Here, being manifested, lofty Viṣṇu, full wise, protects his own supremest station.
When they have offered in his mouth their sweet milk, to him with one accord they sing forth praises.

4 Thence bearing food the Mothers come to meet thee, with food for thee who givest food its increase.
These in their altered form again thou meetest. Thou art Invoking Priest in homes of mortals.

5 Priest of the holy rite, with car that glitters, refulgent Banner of each act of worship,
Sharing in every God through might and glory, even Agni Guest of men I summon hither.

6 So Agni stands on earth's most central station, invested in well-decorated garments.
Born, red of hue, where men pour out libations, O King, as great High Priest bring the Gods hither.

7 Over the earth and over heaven, O Agni, thou, Son, hast ever spread above thy Parents.
Come, Youthfullest ! to those who long to meet thee, and hither bring the Gods, O Mighty Victor.

1 *The Mighty* : Agni.

2 *Among the plants* : according to Sāyaṇa, in the fire-sticks.

3 *Viṣṇu* : in the form of Agni who is his manifestation on earth. *They* : worshippers.

4 *The Mothers* : the plants which nourish life. *In their altered form* : as dry wood which Agni, as fire, consumes.

5 *Sharing in* : because Agni as the bearer of men's oblations supports all other Gods.

HYMN II. *Agni.*

1. **Gladden** the yearning Gods, O thou Most Youthful : bring them, O Lord of Seasons, knowing seasons,
With all the Priests Celestial, O Agni. Best worshipper art thou of all Invokers.

2 Thine is the Herald's, thine the Cleanser's office, thinker art thou, wealth-giver, true to Order.
Let us with Svāhā offer up oblations, and Agni, worthy God, pay the Gods worship.

3 To the Gods' pathway have we travelled, ready to execute what work we may accomplish.
Let Agni, for he knows, complete the worship. He is the Priest : let him fix rites and seasons.

4 When we most ignorant neglect the statutes of you, O Deities with whom is knowledge,
Wise Agni shall correct our faults and failings, skilled to assign each God his fitting season.

5 When, weak in mind, of feeble understanding, mortals bethink them not of sacrificing,
Then shall the prudent and discerning Agni worship the Gods, best worshipper, in season.

6 Because the Father hath produced thee, Leader of all our solemn rites, their brilliant Banner :
So win by worship pleasant homes abounding in heroes, and rich food to nourish all men.

7 Thou whom the Heaven and Earth, thou whom the Waters, and Tvaṣṭar, maker of fair things, created,
Well knowing, all along the Fathers' path-

1 *Seasons* : the proper times of worship. *Priests Celestial* : Agni being the Hotar, the Aśvins, the Adhvaryus, Tvaṣṭar the Agnīdh, and Mitra the Upavaktar. Āśvalāyana, as cited by Sāyaṇa, gives a different enumeration. See Wilson, note.

2 *The Herald* is the Hotar or invoking priest : *the Cleanser* is the Potar or Purifier, the assistant of the Brahman. *Svāhā* : an exclamation=Ave ! or Hail !

3 *The Gods' pathway* : 'the way that leads to the gods ' —Wilson.

6 *The father* : Prajāpati; or the institutor of the sacrifice —Sāyaṇa.

7 *The Fathers' pathway* : the way that leads to the home of the Manes or Ancestral Spirits.

way, shine with resplendent light, enkindled, Agni

HYMN III. *Agni.*

1. O KING, the potent and terrific envoy, kindled for strength, is manifest in beauty.
He shines, all-knowing, with his lofty splendour : chasing black Night he comes with white-rayed Morning.

2 Having o'ercome the glimmering Black with beauty, and bringing forth the dame the Great Sire's Daughter,
Holding aloft the radiant light of Sūrya, as messenger of heaven he shines with treasures.

3 Attendant on the Blessed Dame the Blessed hath come : the Lover followeth his Sister.
Agni, far-spreading with conspicuous lustre, hath compassed Night with whitely-shining garments.

4 His goings-forth kindle as 'twere high voices the goings of the auspicious Friend of Agni.
The rays, the bright beams of the strong-jawed, mighty, adorable Steer are visible as he cometh.

5 Whose radiant splendours flow, like sounds, about us, his who is lofty, brilliant, and effulgent,
Who reaches heaven with best and brightest lustres, sportive and piercing even to the summit.

6 His powers, whose chariot fellies gleam and glitter have loudly roared while, as with teams, he hasted.
He, the most Godlike, far-extending envoy, shines with flames ancient, resonant, whitely-shining.

7 So bring us ample wealth : seat thee as envoy of the two youthful Matrons, Earth and Heaven.
Let Agni rapid with his rapid horses, impetuous with impetuous Steeds, come hither.

1 *O King* : Ludwig takes *rājan* here as the nominative case. *With white-rayed Morning* : I follow Ludwig in taking *ruṣatīm* as instrumental for *ruṣutyām*.

2 *Glimmering Black* : dark night, faintly lighted by stars. *The Great Sire's Daughter* : Uṣas or Dawn, daughter of Dyaus or Heaven.

3 *The lover* : Agni who appears together with Dawn.

4 The first line is almost unintelligible. 'The blazing flames of that mighty Agni do not (deter) his adorers.' —Wilson.

HYMN IV. *Agni.*

1. To thee will I send praise and bring oblation, as thou hast merited lauds when we invoked thee.
A fountain in the desert art thou, Agni, O Ancient King, to man who fain would worship,

2 Thou unto whom resort the gathered people, as the kine seek the warm stall, O Most Youthful.
Thou art the messenger of Gods and mortals, and goest glorious with thy light between them.

3 Making thee grow as 'twere some noble infant, thy Mother nurtures thee with sweet affection.
Over the desert slopes thou passest longing, and seekest, like some beast set free, thy fodder.

4 Foolish are we, O Wise and free from error : verily, Agni, thou dost know thy grandeur.
There lies the form : he moves and licks, and swallows, and, as House-Lord, kisses the Youthful Maiden.

5 He rises ever fresh in ancient fuel : smoke-bannered, gray, he makes the wood his dwelling.
No swimmer, Steer, he presses through the waters, and to his place accordant mortals bear him.

6 Like thieves who risk their lives and haunt the forest, the twain with their ten girdles have secured him.
This is a new hymn meant for thee, O Agni : yoke as it were thy car with parts that glitter.

7 Homage and prayer are thine, O Jātavedas, and this my song shall evermore exalt thee.
Agni, protect our children and descendants, and guard with ever-watchful care our bodies.

HYMN V. *Agni.*

1. HE only is the Sea, holder of treasures : born many a time he views the hearts within us.

1 *To man* : or, to Pūru.
3 *Thy Mother* : Earth.
4 *The form* : the *Āhavanīya* fire. *The Youthful Maiden* : according to Sāyaṇa, either the mixed oblation, or the young earth as compared with her withered plants.
6. *The twain* : the two arms, with their grasping fingers which produce fire by agitation of the fire-stick.

1 *He* : Agni as the Sun. *The secret couple's bosom* : the meaning is uncertain. The fire-sticks in which Agni is

He hides him in the secret couple's bosom.
The Bird dwells in the middle of the
fountain.

2 Inhabiting one dwelling-place in common,
strong Stallions and the Mares have
come together.
The sages guard the seat of Holy Order,
and keep the highest names concealed
within them.

3 The Holy Pair, of wondrous power, have
coupled : they formed the Infant, they
who bred produced him.
The central point of all that moves and
moves not, the while they wove the
Sage's thread with insight

4 For tracks of Order and refreshing viands
attend from ancient times the goodly
Infant.
Wearing him as a mantle, Earth and
Heaven grow strong by food of pleasant
drink and fatness.

5 He, calling loudly to the Seven red Sisters,
hath, skilled in sweet drink, brought
them to be looked on.
He, born of old, in middle air hath halted,
and sought and found the covering robe
of Pūṣan.

6 Seven are the pathways which the wise
have fashioned ; to one of these may
come the troubled mortal.
He standeth in the dwelling of the Highest,

a Pillar, on sure ground where paths
are parted.

7 Not Being, Being in the highest heaven,
in Aditi's bosom and in Dakṣa's birth-
place,
Is Agni, our first-born of Holy Order,
the Milch-cow and the Bull in life's
beginning.

HYMN VI   *Agni*

1. THIS is that Agni, he by whose protection, favour, and help the singer is
successful ;
Who with the noblest flames of glowing
fuel comes forth encompassed with far-
spreading lustre.

2 Agni, the Holy One, the everlasting,
who shines far beaming with celestial
splendours ;
He who hath come unto his friends with
friendship, like a fleet steed who never
trips or stumbles.

3 He who is Lord of all divine oblation,
shared by all living men at break of
morning,
Agni to whom our offerings are devoted,
in whom rests he whose car, through
might, is scatheless.

4 Increasing by his strength. while lauds
content him, with easy flight unto the
Gods he travels.
Agni the cheerful Priest, best Sacrificer,
balms with his tongue the Gods with
whom he mingles

5 With songs and adorations bring ye hither
Agni who stirs himself at dawn like
Indra,

latent may be intended. 'He waits on the cloud in the
neighbourhood of the hidden (firmament).'—Wilson.
The Bird : the Sun. *The fountain* : the source of light in
the east.

2 *Strong Stallions* : perhaps the flames of the Sun.
Mares : waters of the firmament. *The highest names* : of
Agni, such as Jātavedas and Vaiśvānara. *Concealed within
them* : in their secret hearts, for worship.

3 *The Holy Pair* : Heaven and Earth. *The Infant* : Agni.
The while they wove : *viyántaḥ* in the text is unintelligible,
and I follow Wallis in reading *vayantī* in its stead. *The
Sage's thread* : the series of sacrifices to which Agni is
entitled.

5 *The Seven red Sisters* : the seven tongues or flames of
Agni, called *kālī, karālī,* etc.—Sāyaṇa. *And found the
covering robe of Pūṣan* : and hath reappeared in the form
of Pūṣan or the Sun.

6 *Pathways* : long lines of light. *The Wise* : the Fathers.
The troubled mortal : the man who is longing for daybreak
may approach the pathway of light. Wallis, translates
the second line differently :—'The support of life in
the home of the highest, at the divergence of the ways,
standeth on sure ground.' *He* : apparently Agni as the
Sun, to whom the troubled or sinful man comes for
light or forgiveness. *Pillar* : support and stay of the universe, like the Skambha of Atharva-veda, X. 7. *Where
paths are parted* : where ends the dark road which the Sun
travels by night, and the bright path of his daily course
begins.

7 *Not Being, Being* : non-existent, existent. *asacca
sacca* 'both unevolved and evolved,' identifying Agni
with the first cause and first effect, with a reference to
such texts as *Asad eva idam agra āsit* 'the non existent
existent (or unevolved) was verily before this (creation).'—
Wilson, from Sāyaṇa. Here Agni is represented as
Prajāpati who as a yet undeveloped embryo is at the
same time both male and female.—Ludwig. Or Dakṣa
may be the Sun and Aditi the Earth. 'In fact Agni
is identified with all things. These latter hymns to
Agni are very obscure : the notions are mystical; many
of the terms are unusual, or are unusually applied;
and the construction is singularly elliptical and loose.'—
Wilson.
This Hymn has been wholly translated, with comments
by Wallis. See *The Cosmology of the Ṛgveda,* pp. 48-50.

———

3 The exact meaning of the second line is uncertain :—
'and in whom (the sacrificer), whose sacrifice is undisturbed by his foes, throws his choice oblation.'—Wilson.

5 *At dawn* : with Grassmann I take *usrám* here to be
a locative. Sāyaṇa explains it as *bhogānām utsrāviṇam,*
the bestower of enjoyments. According to Ludwig's

Whom sages laud with hymns as Jātavedas of those who wield the sacrificial ladle.

6 In whom all goodly treasures meet together, even as steeds and riders for the booty.

Inclining hither bring us help, O Agni, even assistance most desired by Indra.

7 Yea, at thy birth, when thou hadst sat in glory, thou, Agni, wast the aim of invocations.

The Gods came near, obedient to thy summons, and thus attained their rank as chief Protectors.

HYMN VII. *Agni.*

1. O AGNI, shared by all men living bring us good luck for sacrifice from earth and heaven.

With us be thine intelligence, Wonder-Worker ! Protect us, God, with thy far-reaching blessings.

2 These hymns brought forth for thee, O Agni, laud thee for bounteous gifts, with cattle and with horses.

Good Lord, when man from thee hath gained enjoyment, by hymns, O nobly-born, hath he obtained it.

3 Agni I deem my Kinsman and my Father, count him my Brother and my Friend for ever.

I honour as the face of lofty Agni in heaven the bright and holy light of Sūrya.

4 Effectual, Agni, are our prayers for profit. He whom, at home thou, Priest for ever, guardest

Is rich in food, drawn by red steeds, and holy : by day and night to him shall all be pleasant.

5 Men with their arms have generated Agni, helpful as some kind friend, adorned with splendours,

And stablished as Invoker mid the people the ancient Priest the sacrifice's lover.

6 Worship, thyself, O God, the Gods in heaven : what, void of knowledge, shall the fool avail thee ?

As thou, O God, hast worshipped Gods by seasons, so, nobly-born ! to thine own self pay worship.

7 Agni, be thou our Guardian and Protector : bestow upon us life and vital vigour.

Accept, O Mighty One, the gifts we offer, and with unceasing care protect our bodies.

HYMN VIII. *Agni.*

1. AGNI advances with his lofty banner : the Bull is bellowing to the earth and heavens.

He hath attained the sky's supremest limits : the Steer hath waxen in the lap of waters.

2 The Bull, the youngling with the hump, hath frolicked, the strong and never-ceasing Calf hath bellowed.

Bringing our offerings to the God's assembly, he moves as Chief in his own dwelling-places.

3 Him who hath grasped his Parents' head, they stablished at sacrifice a wave of heavenly lustre.

In his swift flight the red Dawns borne by horses refresh their bodies in the home of Order.

4 For, Vasu thou precedest every Morning, and still hast been the Twins' illuminator.

For sacrifice, seven places thou retainest while for thine own self thou engenderest Mitra.

5 Thou art the Eye and Guard of mighty Order, and Varuṇa when to sacrifice thou comest.

---

interpretation, the translation for the first line would be : 'With songs and adorations bring ye hither the Lord *of morning's kine*, the quivering Agni.'

6 *Riders* : *saptīvantaḥ* : the word properly means 'possessed of horses, and is applicable to drivers as well as riders. *For the booty* : to win the spoil, or to guard it from others.

1 *Thine intelligence* : the meaning of *praketaiḥ* here is not *clear*. Wilson translates it by 'indications (of favour)': Ludwig by 'wishes'; and Grassmann by 'light.'

3 The second line is remarkable as a direct declaration of the relationship of Agni and Sūrya—Ludwig.

7 *Be thou our Guardian and Protector*: *avitā*, says Sāyaṇa, is a protector from obvious dangers and *gopā* a preserver from perils that are unseen.

1 *Advances* through the firmament. *His lofty banner* : the lightning. *Waters* : of the firmament.

2 *Never-ceasing* : *asremá* : according to Sāyaṇa, 'undecaying.' 'Glorious.'—Wilson.

3 *His Parents' head* : the head or forehead of Heaven and Earth, or of the two fire-sticks. *The red Dawns* : or the flames, according to Sāyaṇa. There is no substantive in the text. *The home of Order* : probably the Sun, if the Dawns are spoken of; and the place of law-ordained sacrifice according to Sāyaṇa's explanation.

4 *The Twins' illuminator* : lighter-up of day and night, that is, of the end of night, or very early morning. But see Hillebrandt, *Varuṇa and Mitra*, p. 116. *Seven places* : seven altars for the sacrificial fire. *Mitra* : the Sun.

5 *Varuṇa* : King and Governor.

Thou art the Waters' Child O Jātavedas, envoy of him whose offering thou acceptest.

6 Thou art the Leader of the rite and region, to which with thine auspicious teams thou tendest,
Thy light-bestowing head to heaven thou liftest, making thy tongue the oblation-bearer, Agni.

7 Through his wise insight Trita in the cavern, seeking as ever the Chief Sire's intention,
Carefully tended in his Parents' bosom, calling the weapons kin, goes forth to combat.

8 Well-skilled to use the weapons of his Father, Āptya, urged on by Indra, fought the battle.
Then Trita slew the foe seven-rayed, three-headed, and freed the cattle of the Son of Tvaṣṭar.

9 Lord of the brave, Indra cleft him in pieces who sought to gain much strength and deemed him mighty.
He smote his three heads from his body, seizing the cattle of the omniform Son of Tvaṣṭar.

HYMN IX. *Waters.*

1. YE, Waters, are beneficent : so help ye us to energy
That we may look on great delight.

2 Give us a portion of the sap, the most auspicious that ye have,
Like mothers in their longing love.

3 To you we gladly come for him to whose abode ye send us on ;
And, Waters, give us procreant strength.

4 The Waters be to us for drink, Goddesses for our aid and bliss :
Let them stream to us health and strength.

5 I beg the Floods to give us balm, these Queens who rule o'er precious things,
And have supreme control of men.

6 Within the Waters—Soma thus hath told me—dwell all balms that heal,
And Agni, he who blesseth all.

7 O Waters, teem with medicine to keep my body safe from harm,
So that I long may see the Sun.

8 Whatever sin is found in me, whatever evil I have wrought,
If I have lied or falsely sworn, Waters, remove it far from me.

9 The Waters I this day have sought, and to their moisture have we come :
O Agni, rich in milk, come thou, and with thy splendour cover me.

HYMN X. *Yama Yamī.*

1. FAIN would I win my friend to kindly friendship. So may the Sage, come through the air's wide ocean,
Remembering the earth and days to follow, obtain a son, the issue of his father.

6 *And region* : thou knowest, and canst show the way through the firmament.

7 *In the cavern* : in the secret depth of the firmament. *Seeking.........the Chief Sire's intention* : wishing to carry out the design of Indra or perhaps of Dyaus or Dyu *His Parents* : 'the parental heaven and earth.'—Wilson. *Calling the weapons kin* : calling the weapons, *i. e.* the bolts which are produced from the sky, akin, simply means claiming them as belonging to his father Dyu as they are in the next stanza spoken of as paternal (pitryāṇi).—Macdonell, J. R. A. S., July, 1893, p. 428.

8 *Of his Father* : belonging to the *Chief Sire* of stanza 7. *The foe* : the special enemy of Tṛta is Triśiras, the son of Tvaṣṭar, called Viśvarūpa or the Multiform. *The cattle of the Son of Tvaṣṭar* : the cows imprisoned by him, the showers obstructed by the fiend.

For the legends founded on the last three stanzas of this hymn, see Muir, *O. S. Texts,* V. pp. 229—233. See also Bergaigne, *La Religion Védique*, II. 329, 330.

1 *Great delight* : according to the scholiast, meaning perfect knowledge of Brahma. See Wilson's note.

3 The meaning of the stanza is obscure. It appears to have been recited by the priest at the consecration of a new house.

The first three stanzas are to be repeated by Brāhmans at their morning ablutions. See Colebrooke's Essays, Essay I. *On the Religious Ceremonies of the Hindus*. See also Lanman, *Sanskrit Reader*, p. 376.

6 Stanzas 6—9 are repeated from Book I. 23. 20-23.

Yama and Yamī, son and daughter of Vivasvān, are the Ṛṣis as well as the deities of the hymn which is a dialogue between them.

Yama and Yamī are, says von Roth, 'as their names denote, twin brother and sister, and are the first human pair, the originators of the race. As the Hebrew conception closely connected the parents of mankind by making the woman formed from a portion of the body of the man, so by the Indian tradition they are placed in the relationship of twins. This thought is laid by the hymn in question in the mouth of Yamī herself, when she is made to say : 'Even in the womb the Creator made us for husband and wife.' Professor Müller, on the other hand, says (Lectures on the Science of Language, second series p. 510) : 'There is a curious dialogue between her (Yamī) and her brother, where she (the night) implores her brother (the day) to make her his wife, and where he declines her offer, 'because', as he says, 'they have called it a sin that a brother should marry his sister." Again, p. 521, 'There is not a single word in the Veda pointing to *Yama* and *Yamī* as the first couple

2 Thy friend loves not the friendship which considers her who is near in kindred as a stranger.
Sons of the mighty Asura, the Heroes, supporters of the heavens, see far around them.

3 Yea, this the Immortals seek of thee with longing, progeny of the sole existing mortal.
Then let thy soul and mine be knit together, and as a loving husband take thy consort.

4 Shall we do now what we ne'er did aforetime ? we who spake righteously now talk impurely ?
Gandharva in the floods, the Dame of Waters—such is our bond, such our most lofty kinship.

5 Even in the womb God Tvaṣṭar, Vivifier, shaping all forms, Creator, made us consorts.
None violates his holy ordinances : that we are his the heavens and earth acknowledge.

6 Who knows that earliest day whereof thou speakest ? Who hath beheld it ? Who can here declare it ?
Great is the Law of Varuṇa and Mitra. What, wanton ! wilt thou say to men to tempt them ?

7 I, Yamī, am possessed by love of Yama, that I may rest on the same couch beside him.
I as a wife would yield me to my husband. Like car-wheels let us speed to meet each other.

8 They stand not still, they never close their eyelids, those sentinels of Gods who wander round us.
Not me—go quickly, wanton, with another, and hasten like a chariot wheel to meet him.

9 May Sūrya's eye with days and nights endow him, and ever may his light spread out before him.
In heaven and earth the kindred Pair commingle. On Yamī be the unbrotherly act of Yama.

10 Sure there will come succeeding times when brothers and sisters will do acts unmeet for kinsfolk.
Not me, O fair one,—seek another husband, and make thine arm a pillow for thy consort.

11 Is he a brother when no lord is left her ? Is she a sister when Destruction cometh ?
Forced by my love these many words I utter. Come near, and hold me in thy close embraces.

12 I will not fold mine arms about thy body : they call it sin when one comes near his sister.
Not me,—prepare thy pleasures with another : thy brother seeks not this from thee, O fair one.

13 Alas ! thou art indeed a weakling, Yama ; we find in thee no trace of heart or spirit.
As round the tree the woodbine clings, another will cling about thee girt as with a girdle.

of mortals, the Indian Adam and Eve......If Yama had been the first created of men, surely the Vedic poets, in speaking of him, could not have passed this over in silence.' See, however, the passage from the Atharvaveda, XVIII. 3, 13, to be quoted further on, (Reverence ye with an oblation Yama, the son of Vivasvat, the assembler of men, who was the first of men that died, and the first that departed to this (celestial) world).' Muir, *O. S. Texts*, V. p. 288. Yama as the first man may perhaps be, as Prof. Max Müller holds, 'a later phase of religious thought.'

1 Yamī speaks *The Sage* : *vedhāḥ* : Yama, whom she wishes to give her a son. *Come* : Sāyaṇa explains the masculine participle *jaganvān* by the feminine *gatavatī*, that is, I, Yamī, who have come. *The earth* : which, otherwise, will remain without human inhabitants.

2 Yama replies . *A stranger* : of a different family, and so a lawful wife. *Sons of the mighty Asura* : the spies or sentinels spoken of in stanza 8.

3 Yamī speaks.

4 Yama replies. *Gandharva* : Vivasvān or the Sun. *In the floods* : in the waters of the firmament. *The Dame of Waters* : Saraṇyū. 'His aqueous wife.' —Muir. *Such is our bond* : these are our parents. But see Ludwig, *Ueber die neuesten Arbeiten, u. s. w*; p. 107.

5 Yamī speaks.

6 Yama replies. *To tempt them* : the meaning of *vīcyā* is uncertain. The S. P. Lexicon explains it by 'deceitfully'. 'Falsely.'—Grassmann. 'What sayest thou, who punishest men with hell ?'—Wilson.

7 *Same couch* : see Benfey, *Vedica und Verwandtes*, pp. 39—42, for a different explanation of *samáne yónau.*

8 Yama replies. *Sentinels of Gods* : recording angels who watch men's actions.

9 Yamī speaks. The meaning seems to be : if there be any guilt let me take it upon myself, and let not Yama's life be shortened by way of punishment. *The kindred Pair* : Day and Night.

10 Yama replies. 'Make thine arm a pillow.'— Wilson.

11 Yamī speaks. *Destruction* : Nirṛti; the utter extinction of the human race. 'The meaning is, a true brother will not let his sister lack a husband, and a true sister will not let her brother lack a wife.'—Wilson's Translation, Editor's note.

12 Yama replies.

13 Yamī speaks.

Sāyaṇa's interpretation of this difficult hymn differs

14 Embrace another, Yamī ; let another, even as the woodbine rings the tree, enfold thee.
Win thou his heart and let him win thy fancy, and he shall form with thee a blest alliance.

HYMN XI. *Agni*

1. THE Bull hath yielded for the Bull the milk of heaven : the Son of Aditi can never be deceived.
According to his wisdom Varuṇa knoweth all : may he, the Holy, hallow times for sacrifice.

2 Gandharvī spake : may she, the Lady of the flood, amid the river's roaring leave my heart untouched.
May Aditi accomplish all that we desire, and may our eldest Brother tell us this as Chief.

3 Yea, even this blessed Morning, rich in store of food, splendid, with heavenly lustre, hath shone out for man,
Since they, as was the wish of yearning Gods, brought forth that yearning Agni for the assembly as the Priest.

4 And the fleet Falcon brought for sacrifice from afar this flowing Drop most excellent and keen of sight,
Then when the Āryan tribes chose as Invoking Priest Agni the Wonder-Worker, and the hymn rose up.

5 Still art thou kind to him who feeds thee as with grass, and, skilled in sacrifice, offers thee holy gifts.
When thou, having received the sage's strengthening food with lauds, after long toil, comest with many more.

6 Urge thou thy Parents, as a lover, to delight : the Lovely One desires and craves it from his heart.
The priest calls out, the sacrificer shows his skill, the Asura tries his strength, and with the hymn is stirred.

7 Far-famed is he, the mortal man, O Agni, thou Son of Strength, who hath obtained thy favour.
He, gathering power, borne onward by his horses, makes his days lovely in his might and splendour.

8 When, Holy Agni, the divine assembly, the sacred synod mid the Gods, is gathered,
And when thou, Godlike One, dealest forth treasures, vouchsafe us, too, our portion of the riches.

9 Hear us, O Agni, in your common dwelling : harness thy rapid car of Amṛta.
Bring Heaven and Earth, the Deities' Parents, hither : stay with us here, nor from the Gods be distant.

HYMN XII. *Agni*

1. HEAVEN and Earth, first by everlasting Order, speakers of truth, are near enough to hear us,
When the God, urging men to worship, sitteth as Priest, assuming all his vital vigour.

in many places from that which I have adopted, and Wilson's Translation should be consulted for the views of the great Indian Commentator and the Pandits of his time. The hymn has been transliterated, translated, and annotated by Dr. Muir, *O. S. Texts*, V. 288—291. It has also been translated by the authors of the *Siebenzig Lieder*, and fully discussed by Dr. J. Ehni in Der *Vedische Mythus des Yama*. See also Hillebrandt, *Vedische Mythologie*, I. p. 495.

The subject of the hymn is the origin and institution of sacrifice, first established by Agni under the authority of Varuṇa, who must be regarded as the deity of the first stanza.

1 *The Bull* : the mighty Soma. *For the Bull* : for mighty Varuṇa. *The milk of heaven* : the divine Soma juice, to be used at sacrifice. *The Son of Aditi* : Varuṇa. *According to his wisdom* : *yáthā dhiyā́* : the two words taken together as an adverbial phrase. According to Sāyaṇa, it is Agni who milks the streams of prosperity from heaven for the worshipper. I have generally followed Pischel's interpretation of the first five stanzas (*Vedische Studien*, I. pp. 188, 189).

2 *Gandharvī* : said to be the daughter of Surabhi (one of the daughters of Dakṣa), and the mother of the race of horses. Here she appears to be an Apsarás or waternymph, haunting the banks of rivers and practising the seductive arts of a siren. The meaning seems to be, let no disturbing influence unsettle my devout thoughts. *Our eldest Brother* : Varuṇa, regarded as the founder of society united by common religious observances.

3 The poet regards the coming of the dawn as a proof that the sacrifice is successful. *Since they* : the priests.

4 *This flowing Drop* : the Soma, brought from heaven by the Falcon. See IV. 26 and 27.

5 *Thou* : Agni. *As with grass* : 'as pasture satisfies (the herds).'—Wilson. *With many more* : bringing many other Gods to the sacrifice.

6 *As a lover* : woos his mistress. Agni is called upon to entreat his parents, Heaven and Earth, to reproduce him perpetually. *The Lovely One* : Agni. *Sacrificer* makhaḥ; see *Vedic Hymns*, I. p. 47. The original hymn appears to end with this difficult stanza.

9 *Rapid* : *dravitnúm* : taken by Sāyana with *amṛtasya* and explained by 'distilling the drink of Gods.' *Nor from the Gods be distant* : 'let none of the gods be absent.'—Wilso

---

1 *First* : most exalted as well as most ancient. *T* *God* : Agni. *As Priest* : as Hotar, invoker, or herald.

2 As God comprising Gods by Law Eternal, bear, as the Chief who knoweth, our oblation,
Smoke-bannered with the fuel, radiant, joyous, better to praise and worship, Priest for ever.

3 When the cow's nectar wins the God completely, men here below are heaven's sustainers.
All the Gods came to this thy heavenly Yajus, which from the motley Pair milked oil and water.

4 I praise your work that ye may make me prosper : hear, Heaven and Earth, Twain Worlds that drop with fatness.
While days and nights go to the world of spirits, here let the Parents with sweet meath refresh us.

5 Hath the King seized us ? How have we offended against his holy ordinance ? Who knoweth ?
For even Mitra mid the Gods is angry : there are both song and strength for those who come not.

6 'Tis hard to understand the Immortal's nature, where she who is akin becomes a stranger.
Guard ceaselessly, great Agni, him who ponders Yama's name, easy to be comprehended.

7 They in the synod where the Gods rejoice them, where they are seated in Vivasvān's dwelling,
Have given the Moon his beams, the Sun his splendour—the Two unweariedly maintain their brightness.

8 The counsel which the Gods meet to consider, their secret plan,—of that we have no knowledge.
There let God Savitar, Aditi, and Mitra proclaim to Varuṇa that we are sinless.

9 Hear us, O Agni, in your common dwelling: harness thy rapid car. the car of Amṛta.
Bring Heaven and Earth, the Deities' Parents, hither : stay with us here, nor from the Gods be distant.

HYMN XIII. *Havirdhānas.*

1. I YOKE with prayer your ancient inspiration : may the laud rise as on the prince's pathway.
All Sons of Immortality shall hear it, all the possessors of celestial natures.

2 When speeding ye came nigh us like twin sisters, religious-hearted votaries brought you forward.
Take your place, ye who know your proper station : be near, be very near unto our Soma.

3 Five paces have I risen from Earth : I follow her who hath four feet with devout observance.
This by the Sacred Syllable have I measured: I purify in the central place of Order.

4 He, for God's sake, chose death to be his portion. He chose not, for men's good, a life eternal.

2 *Better to praise* : more skilled than men in praising the Gods.

3 This stanza is very obscure. The meaning seems to be that, by possessing the amṛta, ambrosia, or nectar contained in the milk of the sacrificial cow and in the Soma juice which wins and captivates Agni, men are enabled to offer acceptable sacrifices to the Gods, and thus to support the heavens and earth. *Heavenly Yajus* : divine sacrificial prayer or formula. But *divyám* by its position in the verse seems rather to belong to *ghṛtám*, butter or sacrificial oil. *The motley Pair* : *enī* : many-coloured heaven and earth.

'When the self-aggregated ambrosia of the divine Agni is generated from his radiance, then the products from it sustain both heaven and earth, all the worshippers glorify this thy oblation, the celestial nutritious water which thy white radiance milks forth.'—Wilson. According to Sāyaṇa, *the products from it* are the plants and trees which spring from the *amṛta* or rain which rewards the oblations of men, and the *vi ve deváh* of the text are *sarve stotāraḥ*, all the worshippers. Some meaning is apparent in this paraphrase, but it cannot be extracted from the words of the text.

5 *The King* : Varuṇa. *For even Mitra* : we must have committed some sin, for even Mitra, the Friend, the gracious God, is wroth with us. *Strength* : strengthening sacrificial viands. *For those who come not* : for the Gods who will not yet come to receive our worship and oblations.

6 This stanza is apparently a later addition. The latter half of the first line is taken from X. 10. 2, but its application here is not obvious.

7 *In Vivasvān's dwelling* : 'on the altar of the sacrificer.' —Wilson. Heaven or the realm of the Sun is intended.

———

'The deities are the two *Śakaṭas*, small carts or barrows used at sacrifices to carry the materials, especially the *Soma*-plant, hence called *Havirdhānas*, oblation-bearers.' —Wilson.

1 *The prince* is the noble who institutes the sacrifice. 'Like the path of the worshipper.'—Wilson.

3 This stanza is most obscure. Wilson, following Sāyaṇa, translates : 'I make the five stages of the sacrifice ascend ; I take four steps by pious observances; with the sacred syllable I perfect this (adoration); I purify (the *Soma*) on the navel of the sacrifice.' The *five stages* are, according to Sāyaṇa, the five elements of the sacrifice, grain, Soma, the kine, the Puroḍāśa cake, and the clarified butter. The *four steps* are the metres most commonly used.

The words as they stand in the text do not appear to be susceptible of any satisfactory explanation.

4 *He* : Yama. See X. 14. 1. *For Gods' sake* : his death being the type of the sacrifices which support

They sacrificed Bṛhaspati the Ṛṣi. Yama delivered up his own dear body.

5 The Seven flow to the Youth on whom the Maruts wait : the Sons unto the Father brought the sacrifice.
Both these are his, as his they are the Lords of both : both toil; belonging unto both they prosper well.

HYMN XIV. *Yama.*

1. HONOUR the King with thine oblations, Yama, Vivasvān's Son, who gathers men together,
Who travelled to the lofty heights above us, who searches out and shows the path to many.

2 Yama first found for us a place to dwell in : this pasture never can be taken from us.
Men born on earth tread their own paths that lead them whither our ancient Fathers have departed.

3 Mātalī prospers there with Kavyas, Yama with Aṅgiras' sons, Bṛhaspati with Ṛkvans :
Exalters of the Gods, by Gods exalted, some joy in praise and some in our oblation.

4 Come, seat thee on this bed of grass, O Yama, in company with Aṅgirases and Fathers.
Let texts recited by the sages bring thee : O King, let this oblation make thee joyful.

5 Come, Yama, with the Aṅgirases the Holy, rejoice thee here with children of Virūpa.
To sit on sacred grass at this our worship, I call Vivasvān, too, thy Father hither.

6 Our Fathers are Aṅgirases, Navagvas, Atharvans, Bhṛgus who deserve the Soma.
May these, the Holy, look on us with favour, may we enjoy their gracious loving-kindness.

7 Go forth, go forth upon the ancient pathways whereon our sires of old have gone before us.
There shalt thou look on both the Kings enjoying their sacred food, God Varuṇa and Yama.

8 Meet Yama, meet the Fathers, meet the merit of free or ordered acts, in highest heaven.
Leave sin and evil, seek anew thy dwelling, and bright with glory wear another body.

9 Go hence, depart ye, fly in all directions: this place for him the Fathers have provided.
Yama bestows on him a place to rest in adorned with days and beams of light and waters.

10 Run and outspeed the two dogs, Saramā's offspring, brindled, four-eyed, upon thy happy pathway.

delight the Gods. *For men's good* : See X. 90. 8—14 for the results of the sacrifice of Puruṣa, with whom Yama may be identified. *They* : the Gods. This Pāda is unintelligible as it stands. Instead of *bṛhaspátim yajñám akṛṇvato ṛṣim*, Prof. Ludwig would read *Vaivasvatam yajñam atanuta ṛṣiḥ*, the Ṛṣi performed the Vaivasvata, or funeral, sacrifice (*Ueber die neuesten, u. s. w.*, p. 110). I have mainly followed Ehni, *Der Vedische Mythus des Yama*, pp. 160—162, but the exact meaning of the stanza is still doubtful to me.

5 *The Seven* : rivers. According to Sāyaṇa, metres. *The Youth* : Indra. *The Sons* : the Maruts. *The Father* : Indra. *Both these* : *havirdhānas*. *Of both* : Gods and men. *Unto both* : to Gods and men, or to Heaven and Earth.

———

The hymn is a funeral address, partly to Yama the God of the Dead and partly to the soul of the departed whose body is being consumed on the pile.

1 *Yama* : the deified Lord of the Dead : originally the first who died and so showed the souls of his successors the way to the home of the departed. See X. 12. *Lofty heights* : of heaven, the abode of the Blest.

3 *Mātalī* : a divine being, identified by the Commentators with Indra whose charioteer was Mātali. *Kavyas* : a class of Manes, the spirits of a pious race of ancient time. *Aṅgiras' sons* : the Aṅgirases, the typical first sacrificers. See Vol. I., Index. *Ṛkvans* : or singers, a class of spirits or deities who attend and sing the praises of Bṛhaspati. See VII. 10. 4. *Some joy in praise* : the Gods delight in Svāhā, the sacrificial exclamation, worship or praise. *Some in our oblation* : the Manes delight in Svadhā, the sweet food or oblation which is presented to them.

4 *Aṅgirases and Fathers* : or, perhaps, Aṅgirases our Fathers.

5 *Children of Virūpa* : Vairūpas, a sub-division of the Aṅgirases.

6 *Navagvas, Atharvans, Bhṛgus* : priestly families of ancient times.

7 This and the following stanza are addressed to the spirit of the dead man whose funeral rites are being celebrated.

8 *Free or ordered acts* : voluntary good works and prescribed sacrifices, whose merit is stored up in heaven to be enjoyed on arrival by the spirits of the pious who have performed them.

9 According to Sāyaṇa, this stanza is addressed to the Piśācas and other evil spirits that haunt the place of cremation.

10 The spirit of the departed is addressed. *The two dogs* : offspring of Saramā, the hound of Indra. See Index.

Draw nigh then to the gracious-minded Fathers where they rejoice in company with Yama.

11 And those two dogs of thine, Yama, the watchers, four-eyed, who look on men and guard the pathway,—
Entrust this man, O King, to their protection, and with prosperity and health endow him.

12 Dark-hued, insatiate, with distended nostrils, Yama's two envoys roam among the people;
May they restore to us a fair existence here and to-day, that we may see the sunlight.

13 To Yama pour the Soma, bring to Yama consecrated gifts :
To Yama sacrifice prepared and heralded by Agni goes.

14 Offer to Yama holy gifts enriched with butter, and draw near :
So may he grant that we may live long days of life among the Gods.

15 Offer to Yama, to the King, oblation very rich in meath :
Bow down before the Ṛṣis of the ancient times, who made this path in days of old.

16 Into the six Expanses flies the Great One in Tṛkadrukas.
The Gāyatrī, the Tṛṣṭup, all metres in Yama are contained.

HYMN XV. *Fathers.*

1. MAY they ascend, the lowest, highest, midmost, the Fathers who deserve a share of Soma.
May they who have attained the life of spirits, gentle and righteous, aid us when we call them.

2 Now let us pay this homage to the Fathers, to those who passed of old and those who followed,
Those who have rested in the earthly region, and those who dwell among the Mighty Races.

3 I have attained the gracious-minded Fathers, I have gained son and progeny from Viṣṇu.
They who enjoy pressed juices with oblation seated on sacred grass, come oftenest hither.

4 Fathers who sit on sacred grass, come, help us : these offerings have we made for you; accept them.
So come to us with most auspicious favour, and give us health and strength without a trouble.

5 May they, the Fathers, worthy of the Soma, invited to their favourite oblations.
Laid on the sacred grass, come nigh and listen : may they be gracious unto us and bless us.

6 Bowing your bended knees and seated southward, accept this sacrifice of ours with favour.
Punish us not for any sin, O Fathers, which we through human frailty have committed.

7 Lapped in the bosom of the purple Mornings, give riches to the man who brings oblations.
Grant to your sons a portion of that treasure, and, present, give them energy, ye Fathers.

8 Our ancient Fathers who deserve the Soma, who came, most noble, to our Soma banquet,—
With these let Yama, yearning with the yearning, rejoicing eat our offerings at his pleasure.

9 Come to us, Agni, with the gracious Fathers who dwell in glowing light, the very Kavyas,
Who thirsted mid the Gods, who hasten hither, oblation winners, theme of singers' praises.

13 The three following stanzas are addressed to the priests.

16 The meaning appears to be that the Great Unit, Yama as All-God, broadens and fills the universe after plentiful libations of Soma juice in the Three Kadruka days, or first three days of the Abhiplava festival. See Ehni, *Yama*, pp. 154—157. For different explanations, see Bergaigne, I. 178; II 122, 127.

This hymn, with the exception of the last stanza, has been translated, and annotated by Muir, *O. S. Texts*. V. pp. 291—295, by the authors of the *Siebenzig Lieder*, and by Prof. Peterson, *Hymns from the Ṛgveda*.

1 *Ascend* : rise to higher rank; obtain the best oblation, according to Sāyaṇa. *Lowest, highest, midmost* : the Fathers are classified according to their degrees of merit acquired on earth.

2 *The earthly region* : the firmament nearest to the earth. See VIII. 77. 5. *The Mighty Races* : of the Gods.

3 *Son and progeny* : *nápātam ca vikrámaṇam ca* : the meaning appears to be, as suggested by Ludwig, that the speaker has discharged his obligation to the Fathers by begetting a son through the favour of Viṣṇu. Still *vikrámaṇam* is an unintelligible expression in this connexion. See *The Hymns of the Atharva-veda*, XVIII. 1. 45, note.

7 *Lapped in the bosom of the purple Mornings* : 'Seated in the proximity of the radiant flames (of the altar).'—Wilson

9 *Kavyas* : See X. 14. 3.

10 Come, Agni, come with countless ancient Fathers, dwellers in light, primeval, God-adorers,
Eaters and drinkers of oblations, truthful, who travel with the Deities and Indra.

11 Fathers whom Agni's flames have tasted, come ye nigh : ye kindly leaders, take ye each your proper place.
Eat sacrificial food presented on the grass: grant riches with a multitude of hero sons.

12 Thou, Agni Jātavedas, when entreated, didst bear the offerings which thou madest fragrant,
And give them to the Fathers who did eat them with Svadhā. Eat, thou God, the gifts we bring thee.

13 Thou, Jātavedas, knowest well the number of Fathers who are here and who are absent,
Of Fathers whom we know and whom we know not : accept the sacrifice well-prepared with portions.

14 They who, consumed by fire or not cremated, joy in their offering in the midst of heaven,—
Grant them, O Sovran Lord, the world of spirits and their own body, as thy pleasure wills it.

HYMN XVI. *Agni.*

1. BURN him not up, nor quite consume him, Agni : let not his body or his skin be scattered.
O Jātavedas, when thou hast matured him, then send him on his way unto the Fathers.

2 When thou hast made him ready, Jātavedas, then do thou give him over to the Fathers.
When he attains unto the life that waits him, he shall become the Deities' controller.

3 The Sun receive thine eye, the Wind thy spirit; go, as thy merit is, to earth or heaven.
Go, if it be thy lot, unto the waters; go, make thine home in plants with all thy members.

4 Thy portion is the goat : with heat consume him: let thy fierce flame, thy glowing splendour, burn him
With thine auspicious forms, O Jātavedas, bear this man to the region of the pious.

5 Again, O Agni, to the Fathers send him who, offered in thee, goes with our oblations.
Wearing new life let him increase his offspring : let him rejoin a body, Jātavedas.

6 What wound soe'er the dark bird hath inflicted, the emmet, or the serpent, or the jackal,
May Agni who devoureth all things heal it and Soma who hath passed into the Brāhmans.

7 Shield thee with flesh against the flames of Agni, encompass thee about with fat and marrow,
So will the Bold One, eager to attack thee with fierce glow fail to girdle and consume thee.

8 Forbear, O Agni, to upset this ladle : the Gods and they who merit Soma love it.
This ladle, this which serves the Gods to drink from, in this the Immortal Deities rejoice them.

9 I send afar flesh-eating Agni, bearing off stains may he depart to Yama's subjects.
But let this other Jātavedas carry oblation to the Gods, for he is skilful.

11 *Whom Agni's flames have tasted* : whose bodies have been burnt. A class of Manes called Agniṣvāttas, according to Sāyaṇa.

12 *With Svadhā* : with the sacrificial exclamation Svadhā, or, with their allotted portion.

13 *With portions* : or, with Svadhās.

14 *The world of spirits* : *ásunītim* : a difficult word whose meaning is somewhat uncertain. Sāyaṇa joins it with *tanvám*, and explains the two words by 'the body that leads to life,' 'that body that is endowed with breath.'—Wilson. See X. 12. 4

This hymn has been partially transliterated and annotated by Muir, *O. S. Texts*, V. pp. 295—297.

———

Stanzas 1—6 are to be repeated while the body of the departed is being partially consumed on the funeral pile.

2 *The life that waits him* : *ásunītim* : See X. 15. 14. *Controller* : by winning their favour.

3 *The Sun receive thine eye, the Wind thy spirit* : let like return to like. See Muir's note, *O. S. Texts*, V. 298.

4 Agni is addressed. *The goat* : that was slaughtered and laid limb by limb on the corpse.

5 *Let him increase his offspring* : when he becomes one of the Fathers to whom is ascribed the fruitfulness of heaven and earth, the parents of Gods and men. See X. 64. 14. *Let him rejoin* : or, let life rejoin his body : the nominative is not expressed.

7 The corpse is addressed. *Flesh* : the caul and other parts of a slaughtered animal which covered the corpse to prevent too quick and complete cremation.

9 *Stains* : of sin or impurity which may have attached to the departed. Cp. stanza 6.

10 I choose as God for Father-worship Agni, flesh-eater, who hath past within your dwelling,
While looking on this other Jātavedas. Let him light flames in the supreme assembly.

11 With offerings meet let Agni bring the Fathers who support the Law.
Let him announce oblations paid to Fathers and to Deities.

12 Right gladly would we set thee down, right gladly make thee burn and glow.
Gladly bring yearning Fathers nigh to eat the food of sacrifice.

13 Cool, Agni, and again refresh the spot which thou hast scorched and burnt.
Here let the water-lily grow, and tender grass and leafy herb.

14 O full of coolness, thou cool Plant, full of fresh moisture, freshening Herb,
Come hither with the female frog : fill with delight this Agni here.

HYMN XVII. *Various Deities.*

1. TVAṢṬAR prepares the bridal of his Daughter : all the world hears the tidings and assembles.
But Yama's Mother, Spouse of great Vivasvān, vanished as she was carried to her dwelling.

2 From mortal men they hid the Immortal Lady, made one like her and gave her to Vivasvān.
Saraṇyū brought to him the Aśvin brothers, and then deserted both twinned pairs of children.

3 Guard of the world, whose cattle ne'er are injured, may Pūṣan bear thee hence, for he hath knowledge.
May he consign thee to these Fathers' keeping, and to the gracious Gods let Agni give thee.

4 May Āyu, giver of all life, protect thee, and bear thee forward on the distant pathway.
Thither let Savitar the God transport thee, where dwell the pious who have passed before thee.

5 Pūṣan knows all these realms : may he conduct us by ways that are most free from fear and danger.
Giver of blessings, glowing, all-heroic, may he, the wise and watchful, go before us.

6 Pūṣan was born to move on distant pathways, on the road far from earth and far from heaven.
To both most wonted places of assembly he travels and returns with perfect knowledge.

7 The pious call Sarasvatī, they worship Sarasvatī while sacrifice proceedeth.
The pious called Sarasvatī aforetime. Sarasvatī send bliss to him who giveth.

8 Sarasvatī, who camest with the Fathers, with them rejoicing thee in our oblations,
Seated upon this sacred grass be joyful, and give us strengthening food that brings no sickness.

10 *Light flames* : typically offer sacrifice in the assembly of the Gods.

11 *With offerings* meet : literally, bearing Kavyas or Kavya-worship, that is, offerings to the *kavis*, sages, or Fathers.

12 *Thee* : Agni; the fire.

13 *Water-lily* : *kiyāmbu* : some kind of acquatic plant. *Tender grass* : *pākadūrvā* : a variety of *dūrvā* grass (Panicum Dactylon).

14 *Fill* with *delight* : meaning, euphemistically, extinguish. 'After the fire has consumed the corpse, water is poured upon it to extinguish it. Then furthermore certain water plants are put there. In addition to these a frog—here a female, elsewhere a male—is put upon the place where the fire has burned. These, as representatives of life in the waters, are symbolically supposed both to prevent and extinguish fire.' (M. Bloomfield, *Contributions to the Interpretation of the Veda*. Second Series, Baltimore : 1890).

Dr. Muir's *Original Sanskrit Texts*, V. pp. 297—299, should be consulted with regard to this funeral hymn addressed to Agni, and much additional information on the subject may be obtained from the essays, there referred to, by von Roth and Max Müller.

1 The first two stanzas are difficult, and appear to have no connexion with the rest of the hymn. *Tvaṣṭar* : a God often regarded, as here, as an agent in natural phenomena. *His Daughter* : Saraṇyū, the stormy cloud: or, perhaps, the dawn. *Vivasvān*: representing the bright heavens, or the Sun, *Yama's Mother* : Saraṇyū, who afterwards gave birth to Yama and Yamī. See X. 10, note. *Vanished* : or was stolen away. *Carried* : as a bride, in procession.

2 *They* : the Gods. *The Immortal Lady* : Saraṇyū. *Brought to him* : under another form bore to Vivasvān. *Both twinned pairs* : Yama and Yamī and the Aśvins. For the legend which has been formed out of these obscure hints, see Wilson's Translation, and Muir, *O. S. Texts*, V. 228.

3 Here the funeral hymn begins, with an address to the spirit of the departed. *Pūṣan* : as a Sun-God and the heavenly Herdsman who knows the path through the heavens and is therefore a good conductor of the spirit of the departed.

4 *Āyu* : according to Sāyaṇa, Vāyu is intended, the letter 'v' being elided. Or the meaning may be, life of full vitality.

7 *Sarasvatī* : See I. 3. 10.

9 Thou, called on as Sarasvatī by Fathers who come right forward to our solemn service,
Give food and wealth to present sacrificers, a portion, worth a thousand, of refreshment.

10 The Mother Floods shall make us bright and shining, cleansers of holy oil, with oil shall cleanse us :
For, Goddesses, they bear off all defilement: I rise up from them purified and brightened.

11 Through days of earliest date the Drop descended on this place and on that which was before it.
I offer up, throughout the seven oblations, the Drop which still to one same place is moving.

12 The Drop that falls, thy stalk which arms have shaken, which from the bosom of the press hath fallen,
Or from the Adhvaryu's purifying filter, I offer thee with heart and cry of Vaṣaṭ !

13 That fallen Drop of thine, the stalk which from the ladle fell away,
This present God Bṛhaspati shall pour it forth to make us rich.

14 The plants of earth are rich in milk, and rich in milk is this my speech;
And rich in milk the essence of the Waters : make me pure therewith.

HYMN XVIII. *Various Deities.*

1. Go hence, O Death, pursue thy special pathway apart from that which Gods are wont to travel.
To thee I say it who hast eyes and hearest: Touch not our offspring, injure not our heroes.

2 As ye have come effacing Mṛtyu's footstep, to further times prolonging your existence,
May ye be rich in children and possessions. cleansed, purified, and meet for sacrificing.

3 Divided from the dead are these, the living : now be our calling on the Gods successful.
We have gone forth for dancing and for laughter, to further times prolonging our existence.

4 Here I erect this rampart for the living; let none of these, none other, reach this limit.
May they survive a hundred lengthened autumns, and may they bury Death beneath this mountain.

5 As the days follow days in close succession, as with the seasons duly come the seasons,
As each successor fails not his foregoer, so form the lives of these, O great Ordainer.

6 Live your full lives and find old age delightful, all of you striving one behind the other.
May Tvaṣṭar, maker of fair things, be gracious and lengthen out the days of your existence.

7 Let these unwidowed dames with noble husbands adorn themselves with fragrant balm and unguent.
Decked with fair jewels, tearless, free from sorrow, first let the dames go up to where he lieth.

8 Rise, come unto the world of life, O woman : come, he is lifeless by whose side thou liest.
Wifehood with this thy husband was thy

11 This stanza is not very intelligible. *The Drop* is apparently the Soma; but Sāyaṇa explains it, alternatively, by Āditya or the Sun. See *Śatapatha-Brāhmaṇa*, VII. 4. 1. 20 (Sacred Books of the East, XLI. 368).

14 *Rich in milk* : full of sap, vigour, vital and vivifying power.

---

1 *Death* : Mṛtyu, the God of Death ; distinct from Yama, the judge and ruler of the departed. *Our offspring prajām* : meaning here, says Sāyaṇa, female offspring, *duhitṛdauhitrātmikām*, in the form of daughters and their daughters. *Our heroes* : sons and their sons.—Sāyaṇa.

2 Addressed to the kinsmen of the deceased. *Effacing Mṛtyu's footstep* : a wisp or clog was fastened to the foot of the corpse which represented Mṛtyu or Death, in order to prevent the premature return of Death to carry off the living. See *A. V.*, 19. 12. *Cleansed* : from sins of a former life. *Purified* : from sins of the present life.

3 *Dancing and laughter* : the enjoyments of ordinary life after the fulfilment of our duties to the dead.

4 *This rampart* : of stone, or earth, raised by the Adhvaryu as a line of demarcation between the dead and the living, and limiting as it were, the jurisdiction of Death until the natural time for his approach. *This mountain* : the mound or bank.

5 *So form the lives* : let them pass away in due order of seniority. *Ordainer* : *Dhātar* : the name of a divine being who is the creator, arranger, maintainer, and manager of all things.

6 *One behind the other* : the oldest reaching the end of their journey first.

7 *First* : *ágre* : to begin with; *i. e.*, before the ceremonies begin. See M. Müller, *Chips*, IV. 35—39 (edition of 1895). On the whole stanza, see Dr. F. Hall, Journal of R. A. S., Vol. III. Part I., p. 185f.

8 'This verse is to be spoken by the husband's brother, etc., to the wife of the dead man, and he is to make her leave her husband's body. See the *Āśvalāyana Gṛhya Sūtras*, IV. 2'—Editor's note, in Wilson's Translation.

portion, who took thy hand and wooed thee as a lover.

9 From his dead hand I take the bow he carried, that it may be our power and might and glory.
There art thou, there; and here with noble heroes may we o'ercome all hosts that fight against us.

10 Betake thee to the lap of Earth the Mother, of Earth far-spreading, very kind and gracious.
Young Dame, wool-soft unto the guerdon-giver, may she preserve thee from Destruction's bosom.

11 Heave thyself, Earth, nor press thee downward heavily: afford him easy access, gently tending him.
Cover him, as a mother wraps her skirt about her child, O Earth.

12 Now let the heaving earth be free from motion: yea, let a thousand clods remain above him.
Be they to him a home distilling fatness, here let them ever be his place of refuge.

13 I stay the earth from thee, while over thee I place this piece of earth. May I be free from injury.
Here let the Fathers keep this pillar firm for thee, and there let Yama make thee an abiding-place.

14 Even as an arrow's feathers, they have set me on a fitting day.
The fit word have I caught and held as 'twere a courser with the rein.

9 This stanza is applicable only when the deceased was a Kṣatriya or man of the princely and military order.

10 Addressed to the body. *Guerdon-giver* : the liberal rewarder of the priests. *Destruction's bosom* : or the lap of Nirṛti.

13 *I stay the earth* : 'I keep off the earth above thee with thy lid.' 'This is addressed to the urn containing the bones and ashes, which is buried after the corpse has been burnt.'—Wilson. *Pillar* : perhaps a beam laid over the remains.

14 This stanza, which seems to be a later addition, is not noticed in Sāyaṇa's Commentary, and the meaning of the second line is not very clear. I have followed Prof. Whitney's rendering (Lanman, p. 386). The verse, says Lanman, 'seems to express the poet's satisfaction at having made a good hymn at the right time and place, and with as good skill as a skilful horse-man has.'

The hymn has been translated by the authors of the *Siebenzig Lieder*. See Zimmer's *Altindisches Leben*, pp. 400—407, Mr. Romesh Chunder Dutt's *Civilization in Ancient India*, pp. 108, and 278, 279. Lanman's *Sanskrit Reader*, pp. 382—386, and Zenaide Ragozin's *Vedic India*, pp. 351—353. The essays of von Roth and Max Müller have already been referred to.

HYMN XIX. *Waters or Cows.*

1. TURN, go not farther on your way: visit us, O ye Wealthy Ones.
Agni and Soma, ye who bring riches again, secure us wealth.

2 Make these return to us again, bring them beside us once again.
May Indra give them back to us, and Agni drive them hither-ward.

3 Let them return to us again: under this herdsman let them feed.
Do thou, O Agni, keep them here, and let the wealth we have remain.

4 I call upon their herdsman, him who knoweth well their coming nigh,
Their parting and their home-return, and watcheth their approach and rest.

5 Yea, let the herdsman, too, return, who marketh well their driving-forth;
Marketh their wandering away, their turning back and coming home.

6 Home-leader, lead them home to us; Indra, restore to us our kine:
We will rejoice in them alive.

7 I offer you on every side butter and milk and strengthening food.
May all the Holy Deities pour down on us a flood of wealth.

8 O thou Home-leader, lead them home, restore them thou who bringest home.
Four are the quarters of the earth; from these bring back to us our kine.

HYMN XX. *Agni.*

1. SEND unto us a good and happy mind.

2 I worship Agni, Youthfullest of Gods, resistless, Friend of laws;
Under whose guard and heavenly light the Spotted seek the Mother's breast:

The hymn is a prayer for the return of strayed cows, to whom the first line is addressed.

1 *Ye who bring riches again* : *punarvasū* : 'ye who clothe (your worshippers) again.'—Wilson. See Hillebrandt, *V. M.*, I. 460.

2 *These* : cows, or waters.—Sāyaṇa. *Make return* is the imperative singular, and Sāyaṇa says that the seer of the hymn addresses himself. The address is to Indra.

4 Sāyaṇa explains this stanza somewhat differently: —'I invoke the knowledge of the place, of their going, of their coming, of their departure, of their wandering, of their returning: (I invoke) him who is their keeper.—Wilson. This is a more strictly literal rendering of the abstract nouns in the text.

2 *The Spotted* : there is no noun. The variegated oblations, as Sāyaṇa says, appear to be intended; and *the Mother's breast* may be the clouds of the firmament. The stanza is difficult, and translation must be tentative.

3 Whom with their mouth they magnify, bannered with flame and homed in light.
He glitters with his row of teeth.

4 Kind, Furtherer of men, he comes, when he hath reached the ends of heaven,
Sage, giving splendour to the clouds.

5 To taste man's offerings, he, the Strong, hath risen erect at sacrifice :
Fixing his dwelling he proceeds.

6 Here are oblation, worship, rest : rapidly comes his furtherance.
To sword-armed Agni come the Gods.

7 With service for chief bliss I seek the Lord of Sacrifice, Agni, whom
They call the Living, Son of Cloud.

8 Blest evermore be all the men who come from us, who magnify
Agni with sacrificial gifts.

9 The path he treads is black and white and red, and striped, and brown, crimson, and glorious.
His sire begat him bright with hues of gold.

10 Thus with his thoughts, O Son of Strength, O Agni, hath Vimada, accordant with the Immortals,
Offered thee hymns, soliciting thy favour. Thou hast brought all food, strength, a prosperous dwelling.

HYMN XXI. *Agni.*

1. WITH offerings of our own we choose thee, Agni, as Invoking Priest,
For sacrifice with trimmed grass,—at your glad carouse—piercing and brightly shining. Thou art waxing great.

2 The wealthy ones adorn thee, they who bring us horses as their gift :
The sprinkling ladle, Agni,—at your glad carouse—and glowing offering taste thee. Thou art waxing great.

3 The holy statutes rest by thee, as 'twere with ladles that o'erflow.
Black and white-gleaming colours,—at your glad carouse—all glories thou assumest. Thou art waxing great.

4 O Agni, what thou deemest wealth, Victorious and Immortal One !
Bring thou to give us vigour,—at your glad carouse—splendid at sacrifices. Thou art waxing great.

5 Skilled in all lore is Agni, he whom erst Atharvan brought to life.
He was Vivasvān's envoy, at your glad carouse—the well-loved friend of Yama, Thou art waxing great.

6 At sacrifices they adore thee, Agni, when the rite proceeds.
All fair and lovely treasures—at your glad carouse—thou givest him who offers. Thou art waxing great.

7 Men, Agni, have established thee as welcome Priest at holy rites,
Thee whose face shines with butter,—at your glad carouse—bright, with eyes most observant. Thou art waxing great.

8 Wide and aloft thou spreadest thee, O Agni, with thy brilliant flame.
A Bull art thou when bellowing,—at your glad carouse—thou dost impregn the Sisters. Thou art waxing great.

HYMN XXII. *Indra.*

1. WHERE is famed Indra heard of? With what folk is he renowned to-day as Mitra is,—
Who in the home of Ṛṣis and in secret is extolled with song ?

2 Even here is Indra famed, and among us this day the glorious Thunderer is praised,

3 *Homed in light*: the meaning of *kṛpanīlam* is uncertain .'Pitying prayer.' according to Ludwig. 'Sustainer of pious works'.—Wilson.

5 *He proceeds* : is carried from one fire receptacle or altar to another.

6 *Sword-armed* : armed with his sword or knife of piercing flames.

8 *The men who come from us* : sons and grandsons of the worshippers.

9 *The path he treads* : according to Sāyaṇa, his chariot.

10 *Vimada* : the Ṛṣi of the hymn.

---

1 *At your glad carouse* : apparently a Soma-drinking refrain, addressed to the Viśvedevas or All-Gods. *Thou art waxing great* ; a similar refrain or burden addressed to Agni. See Wilson's Translation, note. Grassmann omits both refrains, which he considers to be later interpolations.

2 *Taste thee* : feel the power of the fire.

3 The first line is difficult :—'The establishers (of the rite) worship thee with their ladles , (filled with the oblation), like (earth—) sprinkling (showers). —Wilson. I follow Ludwig's interpretation. Those who worship Agni according to his Law are regarded as his own statutes incarnate.

5 *Atharvan* : the priest who is said to have been the first to obtain fire and offer Soma and prayers. *Vivasvān*: the Soma-priest, or the sacrificer.

8 *The Sisters* : the plants, which Agni, descending in rain, makes fruitful.

---

1 *In secret* : in the forest, according to Sāyaṇa.

He who like Mitra mid the folk hath won complete and full renown.

3 He who is Sovran Lord of great and perfect strength, exerter of heroic might,
Who bears the fearless thunder as a father bears his darling son.

4 Harnessing to thy car, as God, two blustering Steeds of the Wind-God, O Thunderer,
That speed along the shining path, thou making ways art glorified.

5 Even to these dark Steeds of Wind thou of thyself hast come to ride,
Of which no driver may be found, none, be he God or mortal man.

6 When ye approach, men ask you, thee and Uśanā : Why come ye to our dwelling-place ?
Why are ye come to mortal man from distant realms of earth and heaven ?

7 O Indra, thou shalt speak us fair : our holy prayer is offered up.
We pray to thee for help as thou didst strike the monster Śuṣṇa dead.

8 Around us is the Dasyu, riteless, void of sense, inhuman, keeping alien laws.
Baffle, thou Slayer of the foe, the weapon which this Dāsa wields.

9 Hero with Heroes, thou art ours : yea, strong are they whom thou dost help.
In many a place are thy full gifts, and men, like vassals, sing thy praise.

10 Urge thou these heroes on to slay the enemy, brave Thunderer ! in the fight with swords
Even when hid among the tribes of Sages numerous as stars.

11 Swift come those gifts of thine whose hand is prompt to rend and burn, O Hero Thunder-armed :
As thou with thy Companions didst destroy the whole of Śuṣṇa's brood.

12 Let not thine excellent assistance come to us, O Hero Indra, profitless.
May we, may we enjoy the bliss of these thy favours, Thunderer !

13 May those soft impulses of thine, O Indra, be fruitful and innocent to us.
May we know these whose treasures are like those of milch-kine, Thunderer !

14 That Earth, through power of knowing things that may be known, handless and footless yet might thrive,
Thou slewest, turning to the right, Śuṣṇa for every living man.

15 Drink, drink the Soma, Hero Indra ; be not withheld as thou art good, O Treasure-giver.
Preserve the singers and our liberal princes, and make us wealthy with abundant riches.

HYMN XXIII. *Indra.*

1. INDRA, whose right hand wields the bolt, we worship, driver of Bay Steeds seeking sundered courses.
Shaking his beard with might he hath arisen, casting his weapons forth and dealing bounties.

2 The treasure which his Bay Steeds found at sacrifice,—this wealth made opulent Indra slayer of the foe.
Ṛbhu, Ṛbhukṣan, Vāja—he is Lord of Might. The Dāsa's very name I utterly destroy.

3 When, with the Princes, Maghavan, famed of old, comes nigh the thunderbolt of gold, and the Controller's car
Which his two Tawny Coursers draw, then Indra is the Sovran Lord of power whose glory spreads afar.

4 *Making ways* : as a God of light, making paths through the pathless darkness.

6 *Uśanā*: Uśanā or Uśanas Kāvya, who has been frequently mentioned as a favoured friend and companion of Indra.

9 *With Heroes* : the attendant Maruts.

10 *The enemy* : or Vṛtra. *Hid among the tribes of Sages*: dwelling among the wise Gods and invisible to me. *Numerous as stars* : the meaning of *nákṣatra avasām* is uncertain.

11 *Whose hand is prompt to rend and burn* : I follow Ludwig's interpretation, but the meaning which he gives to *ākṣāṇe* is doubtful.

13 *Soft impulses of thine* : 'our (praises) reaching thee.'—Wilson.

14 *For every living man* : *viśvāyave* : according to Sāyaṇa for the sake of Viśvāyu, a king, the son of Urvaśī, the Apsaras or nymph of heaven who became the wife of Purūravas. *Turning to the right* : circumambulating Śuṣṇa with the right hand towards him for good luck; performing the Gaelic deasil.

1 *Seeking sundered courses* : *vívratānām* : unruly, and pulling away from each other, or wandering. According to Sāyaṇa, having many functions.

2 *At sacrifice* : Sāyaṇa explains *váne* by 'at sacrifice, or, in the forest.' The exact meaning of the word here is not certain. *Of the foe* : or, of Vṛtra.

Ṛbhu, Ṛbhukṣan, Vāja : Indra combining the three Ṛbhus in his own person.

3 *With the Princes* : with the Maruts.

4 With him too is this rain of his that comes like herds : Indra throws drops of moisture on his yellow beard.
When the sweet juice is shed he seeks the pleasant place, and stirs the worshipper as wind disturbs the wood.

5 We laud and praise his several deeds of valour who, fatherlike, with power hath made us stronger ;
Who with his voice slew many thousand wicked ones who spake in varied manners with contemptuous cries.

6 Indra, the Vimadas have formed for thee a laud, copious, unparalleled, for thee Most Bountiful.
We know the good we gain from him the Mighty One when we attract him as a herdsman calls the kine.

7 Ne'er may this bond of friendship be dissevered, the Ṛṣi Vimada's and thine, O Indra.
We know thou carest for us as a brother : with us, O God, be thine auspicious friendship.

HYMN XXIV. *Indra. Aśvins.*

1. O INDRA, drink this Soma, pressed out in the mortar, full of sweets.
Send down to us great riches,—at your glad carouse—in thousands, O Most Wealthy. Thou art waxing great.

2 To thee with sacrifices, with oblations, and with lauds we come.
Lord of all strength and power, grant—at your glad carouse—the best choice-worthy treasure. Thou art waxing great.

3 Thou who art Lord of precious boons, inciter even of the churl,
Guardian of singers, Indra,—at your glad carouse—save us from woe and hatred. Thou art waxing great.

4 Strong, Lords of Magic power, ye Twain churned the united worlds apart,
When ye, implored by Vimada, Nāsatyas, forced apart the pair.

5 When the united pair were rent asunder all the Gods complained.
The Gods to the Nāsatyas cried, Bring these together once again.

6 Sweet be my going forth, and rich in sweets be my approach to home.
So, through your Deity, both Gods, enrich us with all pleasantness.

4 *Drops of moisture* : perhaps the rain which he pours upon the lightning which may be regarded as his beard. —Ludwig. *The pleasant place*: the chamber of sacrifice. *The worshipper*: or, according to Sāyaṇa, his own body. The text has no word to express the object here.

The double burden or refrain of Hymn XXI, is employed in the first three stanzas.

3 *Of singers* : worshippers; 'eulogists.'—Wilson.

4 *Churned......apart* : or perhaps , produced by churning or violent agitation. Sāyaṇa explains differently :— 'you have churned forth (the fire).'—Wilson.

HYMN XXV. *Soma.*

1. SEND us a good and happy mind, send energy and mental power.
Then—at your glad carouse—let men joy in thy love, Sweet Juice ! as kine in pasture. Thou art waxing great.

2 In all thy forms, O Soma, rest thy powers that influence the heart.
So also these my longings—at your glad carouse—spread themselves seeking riches. Thou art waxing great.

3 Even if, O Soma, I neglect thy laws through my simplicity,
Be gracious—at your glad carouse—as sire to son. Preserve us even from slaughter. Thou art waxing great.

4 Our songs in concert go to thee as streams of water to the wells.
Soma, that we may live, grant—at your glad carouse—full powers of mind, like beakers. Thou art waxing great.

5 O Soma, through thy might who art skilful and strong, these longing men,
These sages, have thrown open—at your glad carouse—the stall of kine and horses. Thou art waxing great.

6 Our herds thou guardest, Soma, and the moving world spread far and wide.
Thou fittest them for living,—at your glad carouse—looking upon all beings. Thou art waxing great.

7 On all sides, Soma, be to us a Guardian ne'er to be deceived.
King, drive away our foemen—at your glad carouse :—let not the wicked rule us. Thou art waxing great.

1 The first half line of this stanza has occurred before as the first line of X. 20. The double burden or refrain is again employed, with little or no connexion with the rest of the stanza.

4 *Like beakers* : filled full, like chalices of Soma juice.

5 *The longing men* : the priests. *Have thrown open, etc.* : have, by their sacrifices, opened the way to wealth.

8 Be watchful, Soma, passing wise, to give us store of vital strength.
More skilled than man to guide us,—at your glad carouse—save us from harm and sorrow. Thou art waxing great.

9 Chief slayer of our foemen, thou, Indu, art Indra's gracious Friend,
When warriors invoke him—at your glad carouse—in fight, to win them offspring. Thou art waxing great.

10 Victorious is this gladdening drink: to Indra dear it grows in strength.
This—at your glad carouse—enhanced the mighty hymn of the great sage Kakṣīvān. Thou art waxing great.

11 This to the sage who offers gifts brings power that comes from wealth in kine.
This, better than the seven, hath—at your glad carouse—furthered the blind, the cripple. Thou art waxing great.

HYMN XXVI. *Pūṣan.*

1. FORWARD upon their way proceed the ready teams, the lovely songs.
Further them glorious Pūṣan with yoked chariot, and the Mighty Twain!

2 With sacred hymns let this man here, this singer, win the God to whom
Belong this majesty and might. He hath observed our eulogies.

3 Pūṣan the Strong hath knowledge of sweet praises even as Indu hath.
He dews our corn with moisture, he bedews the pasture of our kine.

4 We will bethink ourselves of thee, O Pūṣan, O thou God, as One.
Who brings fulfilment of our hymns, and stirs the singer and the sage.

5 Joint-sharer of each sacrifice, the driver of the chariot steeds;
The Ṛṣi who is good to man, the singer's Friend and faithful Guard.

6 One who is Lord of Śuca, Lord of Sucā caring for herself:
Weaving the raiment of the sheep and making raiment beautiful.

7 The mighty Lord of spoil and wealth, Strong Friend of all prosperity;
He with light movement shakes his beard, lovely and ne'er to be deceived.

8 O Pūṣan, may those goats of thine turn hitherward thy chariot-pole.
Friend of all suppliants art thou, born in old time, and firm and sure.

9 May the majestic Pūṣan speed our chariot with his power and might.
May he increase our store of wealth and listen to this call of ours.

HYMN XXVII. *Indra.*

1. THIS, singer, is my firm determination, to aid the worshipper who pours the Soma.
I slay the man who brings no milk-oblation, unrighteous, powerful, the truth's perverter.

2 Then will I, when I lead my friends to battle against the radiant persons of the godless,
Prepare for thee at home a vigorous bullock, and pour for thee the fifteen-fold strong juices.

3 I know not him who sayeth and declareth that he hath slain the godless in the battle.
Soon as they see the furious combat raging, men speak forth praises of my vigorous horses.

10 *Kakṣīvān*: a famous Ṛṣi, the seer of some hymns of Book I. See Index, Vol. I.

11 *Better than the seven*: more effectually than the seven priests. Sāyaṇa explains differently:—'it gives wealth to the seven (priests).—Wilson. *The blind*: the Ṛṣi Dīrghatamas, according to Sāyaṇa. *The cripple*: Parāvṛj. See both names in Vol. I., Index.

---

1 *Ready teams*; ordered series of our words. *The Mighty Twain*: the Aśvins. According to Sāyaṇa, *dasrā*=*darśanīyaḥ*, of goodly aspect, applied to Pūṣan; or, the two performers of the rite, the *Yajamāna* and his wife.

6 *Śuca* and *Sucā*: names of a man and women.—Ludwig. According to Sāyaṇa and Wilson, 'the pure (he-goat) and the pure (she-goat).' *Weaving the raiment*: 'making woollen cloths such as the woollen filter, etc.'—Wilson. *And making raiment beautiful*: or, he hath made vesture pure and bright; that is, says Sāyaṇa, he hath purified all around with his heat and light.

7 *Friend*: the augmenter. *Shakes his beard*: when he drinks the Soma juice.

8 *Those goats*: Pūṣan's chariot is said to be drawn by a team of goats. Cf. I. 38. 4.

---

1 Indra addresses the Ṛṣi. *Powerful*: *ābhúm*: perhaps, possessed of the means that would enable him to offer sacrifices.

2 The Ṛṣi replies. *Fifteenfold strong juices*: according to Sāyaṇa, the juices of the Soma-plant whose leaves grow during the light half of the month and die away during the dark-half.

3 Indra speaks, rebuking the Ṛṣi and ascribing all victories to himself.

4 While yet my deeds of might were unrecorded, all passed for Maghavans though I existed.
The potent one who dwelt in peace I conquered, grasped by the foot and slew him on the mountain.

5 None hinder me in mine heroic exploits, no, not the mountains when I will and purpose.
Even the deaf will tremble at my roaring, and every day will dust be agitated.

6 To see the Indraless oblation-drinkers, mean offerers, o'ertaken by destruction!
Then shall the fellies of my car pass over those who have blamed my joyous Friend and scorned him.

7 Thou wast, thou grewest to full vital vigour: an earlier saw, a later one shall see thee.
Two canopies, as 'twere, are round about him who reacheth to the limit of this region.

8 The freed kine eat the barley of the pious. I saw them as they wandered with the herdsman.
The calling of the pious rang around them. What portion will these kine afford their owner?

9 When we who eat the grass of men are gathered I am with barley-eaters in the corn-land.
There shall the captor yoke the yokeless bullock, and he who hath been yoked seek one to loose him.

10 There wilt thou hold as true my spoken purpose, to bring together quadrupeds and bipeds.
I will divide, without a fight, his riches who warreth here, against the Bull, with women.

11 When a man's daughter hath been ever eyeless, who, knowing, will be wroth with her for blindness?
Which of the two will loose on him his anger—the man who leads her home or he who woos her?

12 How many a maid is pleasing to the suitor who fain would marry for her splendid riches?
If the girl be both good and fair of feature, she finds, herself, a friend among the people.

13 His feet have grasped: he eats the man who meets him. Around his head he sets the head for shelter.
Sitting anear and right above he smites us, and follows earth that lies spread out beneath him.

14 High, leafless, shadowless, and swift is Heaven: the Mother stands, the Youngling, loosed, is feeding.

4 *The potent one*: the powerful fiend Śambara, for instance.

5 *Dust*: of battle, stirred up by Indra.

6 *To see*: *dárśan*: according to Sāyaṇa, I, Indra, see. *Oblation-drinkers*: who themselves consume the offerings that should be presented to Indra. *Mean offerers*, *bāhukṣadaḥ*: literally, arm-cutters. According to Von Roth, parsimonious worshippers who offer the forelegs, or inferior parts of the sacrificial animal. 'Who cut (the worshippers) to pieces with their hands.'—Wilson. *Joyous Friend*: Viṣṇu.—Ludwig. Or the meaning may be, your joyous friend; Indra himself, the friend of his worshippers.

7 The Ṛṣi speaks. *An earlier saw*: the meaning of the half-line is not clear. Perhaps, foes have already felt thy power, and others yet shall feel it. 'The ancient Indra verily destroys (his foe), the other does not destroy Indra.'—Wilson. *Two canopies*: heaven and earth. *Him*: Indra.

8 Indra speaks, fearing, apparently, that the worshipper will have no milk to offer him.

9 'There is no comment on this obscure verse, and Wilson leaves a blank in his MS.'—Editor of Wilson's Translation, Vol. VI. Ludwig says that Indra declares that he has brought men and cattle together and made the latter subject to the former, to be yoked and to remain yoked when and as long as their masters please. According to this interpretation, the first half of the stanza might be rendered: 'Grass-eating beasts with men have I connected, and those who eat grain in the widespread cornland.'

10 *Against the Bull*: against me, the mighty Indra. *With women*: with weak allies.

11 'Hitherto,' says Prof. Ludwig, 'it is possible to establish a connexion and interdependence of the separate strophes; with strophe 11 the difficulty begins.' *On him*: on the father. *Who woos her*: seeks her in marriage for his friend or employer.

12 *Herself*: *svayám cit*: by her own worth, independently of her dowry.

13 *His feet have grasped*: Indra, as the Sun, has seized and drawn up the water of the rivers with the rays which are his feet. *Eats the man who meets him*: perhaps merely, scorches the man who exposes himself to his burning rays. According to Sāyaṇa, 'feeds upon, *i. e.* takes into his orb, the water that approaches him.' Another explanation is, that the pious after death go to the Sun and become sunbeams.—Ludwig. *He sets the head for shelter*: he takes the height of heaven as a covering. *Anear and right above*: in his meridian height. *Follows earth*: descends to the horizon and sets beyond it.

14 *Leafless, shadowless*: heaven being compared to a tree that overshadows the earth. According to Sāyaṇa, *árvā* here is the ever-moving Sun. *The Mother*: Uṣas or Dawn. According to Sāyaṇa, *mātā* here means 'the builder (of the world.)' *The Youngling*: or Calf; Agni who feeds on the oblations. *She*: Heaven, or the atmospheric Pṛthivi, roaring as the rain comes down. *Another's offspring*: Indra as Āditya or the Sun, the offspring of Aditi. *In what world, etc.*: that is, who knows where the rain comes from? *The Cow*: the Sky. The second half-stanza has occurred before. See III. 55. 13.

Loud hath she lowed, licking Another's offspring. In what world hath the Cow laid down her udder ?

15 Seven heroes from the nether part ascended, and from the upper part came eight together.
Nine from behind came armed with winnowing-baskets : ten from the front pressed o'er the rock's high ridges.

16 One of the ten, the tawny, shared in common, they send to execute their final purpose.
The Mother carries on her breast the Infant of noble form and soothes it while it knows not.

17 The Heroes dressed with fire the fatted wether : the dice were thrown by way of sport and gaming.
Two reach the plain amid the heavenly waters, hallowing and with means of purifying.

18 Crying aloud they ran in all directions : One half of them will cook, and not the other.
To me hath Savitar, this God, declared it : He will perform, whose food is wood and butter.

19 I saw a troop advancing from the distance, moved, not by wheels but their own God-like nature.
The Friendly One seeks human generations, destroying, still new bands of evil beings.

20 These my two Bulls, even Pramara's, are harnessed : drive them not far ; here let them often linger.
The waters even shall aid him to his object, and the all-cleansing Sun who is above us.

21 This is the thunderbolt which often whirleth down from the lofty misty realm of Sūrya.
Beyond this realm there is another glory : so through old age they pass and feel no sorrow.

22 Bound fast to every tree the cow is lowing, and thence the man-consuming birds are flying,
Then all this world, though pressing juice for Indra and strengthening the Ṛṣi, is affrighted.

23 In the Gods' mansion stood the first-created, and from their separation came the later.
Three warm the Earth while holding stores of water, and Two of these convey the murmuring moisture.

24 This is thy life : and do thou mark and know it. As such, hide not thyself in time of battle.

15 *Seven heroes* : according to Sāyaṇa, Viśvāmitra and other Ṛṣis, sons of Prajāpati. *Eight* : the Vālakhilyas, a numerous race of divine pygmies. *Nine* : the Bhṛgus. *Ten* : Aṅgirases. Or, alternatively, seven Maruts, on Indra's right, eight on his left, nine behind him, and ten in front. These explanations by Sāyaṇa cannot be accepted ; but it is hard to say what is meant. Ludwig thinks that the various classes of letters of the alphabet are intended. His ingenious explanation will be found in the Preface to his fourth volume of the Ṛgveda, pp. XXXIII—XXXV.

16 *The tawny* : *kapilám* : according to Sāyaṇa, the famous Ṛṣi Kapila. 'The Sun ?'—Grassmann. *The Mother* : Night ?—Grassmann. *The Infant* : the young Sun, if *the Mother* is Night.

17 *The fatted wether* : perhaps, the swollen rain-cloud. *The dice* : the stars. *Two* : the Sun and Moon. These are Ludwig's suggestions.

18 *They* : according to Sāyaṇa, the Aṅgirases. Perhaps the contentious priests with whom Agni the veritable priest is contrasted.—Ludwig. *He* : Agni.

19 *A troop* : the stars. *The Friendly One* : Indra as the Sun. *Evil beings* : *śiśnā* : Rākṣasas and spirits of darkness that vanish at the coming of the Sun.

20 *Bulls* : steeds according to Sāyaṇa. *Pramara's* : belonging to me, the Destroyer or Death. But the whole stanza is obscure. *All-cleansing* : so Sāyaṇa explains *markā*, which Von Roth interprets by 'obscuration.' Ludwig thinks that the Moon, 'the obscurer of the Sun' is meant.

21 *This is the thunderbolt* : the meaning, probably, is 'this *dakṣiṇā* or honorarium given to the priests is a veritable thunderbolt. '—Ludwig. But as Wilson observes, the stanza may be 'intended to express the usual theory of rain ; the moisture of the earth being drawn up into the solar region as vapour, and thence descending as rain by the action of the thunderbolt and the wind.'

22 According to Sāyaṇa, *tree* here means 'bow', *cow* means 'bowstring', and *man-consuming birds* 'deadly arrows.' The general meaning is that sacrifices to Indra and liberal gifts to priests will not free men from the fear of death.

23 *The first-created* : the clouds. *The later* : the waters of the rain. *Three* : Parjanya, Vāyu, and Āditya or the Sun. *Holding stores of water* : *anūpāḥ* : 'Sowing in succession.'—Wilson. 'Following the water.'—Ludwig. 'Rich in water.' —Grassmann. *Two* : Vāyu and Āditya.

24 According to Sāyaṇa, Indra is addressed. The following is Wilson's translation of Sāyaṇa's paraphrase of the stanza :—'That thy (divine nature identified with the sun) is the cause of life : and know such (solar form) of his (to be worthy of adoration) as the sacrifice; conceal nothing : that motion of him the all-cleansing (sun) makes manifest the universe; it absorbs the moisture; it is never discontinued.' The *robes that veil* the foot, or rays, of the Sun are the waters into which they are supposed to vanish.

The hymn is enigmatical and difficult in the highest degree, and neither Sāyaṇa nor later scholars have succeeded in making it intelligible throughout.

He manifests the light and hides the vapour : his foot is never free from robes that veil it.

HYMN XXVIII. *Indra. Vasukra.*

1. Now all my other friends are here assembled : my Sire-in-law alone hath not come hither.
So might he eat the grain and drink the Soma, and, satisfied, return unto his dwelling.

2 Loud belloweth the Bull whose horns are sharpened : upon the height above earth's breadth he standeth.
That man I guard and save in all his troubles who fills my flanks when he hath shed the Soma.

3 Men with the stone press out for thee, O Indra, strong, gladdening Soma, and thereof thou drinkest.
Bulls they dress for thee, and of these thou eatest when, Maghavan, with food thou art invited.

4 Resolve for me, O singer, this my riddle : The rivers send their swelling water backward :
The fox steals up to the approaching lion : the jackal drives the wild-boar from the brushwood.

5 How shall I solve this riddle, I, the simple, declare the thought of thee the Wise and Mighty ?
Tell us, well knowing, as befits the season : Whitherward is thy prosperous car advancing ?

6 Thus do they magnify me, me the mighty : higher than even high heaven is my car-pole.
I all at once demolish many thousands : my Sire begot me with no foe to match me.

7 Yea, and the Gods have known me also, Indra, as mighty, fierce and strong in every exploit.
Exulting with the bolt I slaughtered Vṛtra, and for the offerer oped with might the cow-stall.

8 The Deities approached, they carried axes ; splitting the wood they came with their attendants.
They laid good timber in the fire-receivers, and burnt the grass up where they found it growing.

9 The hare hath swallowed up the opposing razor : I sundered with a clod the distant mountain.
The great will I make subject to the little : the calf shall wax in strength and eat the bullock.

10 There hath the strong-winged eagle left his talon, as a snared lion leaves the trap that caught him.
Even the wild steer in his thirst is captured : the leather strap still holds his foot entangled.

11 So may the leather strap their foot entangle who fatten on the viands of the Brahman.
They all devour the bulls set free to wander, while they themselves destroy their bodies' vigour.

12 They were well occupied with holy duties who sped in person with their lauds to Soma.
Speaking like man, mete to us wealth and booty : in heaven thou hast the name and fame of Hero.

The Ṛṣi is Vasukra son of Indra, and the hymn is mainly a dialogue between the Father and the son. Vasukra's wife is the seer as well as the speaker of stanza 1.

1 This stanza is spoken by Vasukra's wife in ignorance, says the legend, that her Father-in-law Indra is present in disguise.

2 Indra speaks. *The Bull* : the mighty Indra.

3 Vasukra speaks.

4 Indra must be the speaker, although Sāyaṇa gives the stanza to Vasukra. Indra declares his power to alter the course of nature. See Wilson's Translation, note by the Editor.

5 Vasukra speaks.

6 Indra speaks. *My Sire* : or, the general Father Prajāpati.—Sāyaṇa.

7 Vasukra speaks, and tells what he has done with Indra's help.

8 This obscure stanza is probably an account of the Gods' first sacrifice. See Pischel, *Vedische Studien*, I. pp. 178—180. According to Sāyaṇa it refers to the cleaving of the clouds, and the filling of the rivers. Ludwig sees in it a reference to the beginning of agriculture. *Their attendants* : the Maruts.

9 Cf. with stanza 4.

10 The application of this stanza is not apparent. Sāyaṇa's explanation of this and the following verse is entirely different from that of most recent scholars.

HYMN XXIX. *Indra.*

1. As sits the young bird on the tree rejoicing, ye, swift Pair, have been roused by clear laudation,
Whose Herald-Priest through many days is Indra, earth's Guardian, Friend of men, the best of Heroes.

2 May we, when this Dawn and the next dance hither, be thy best servants, most heroic Hero!
Let the victorious car with triple splendour bring hitherward the hundred chiefs with Kutsa.

3 What was the gladdening draught that pleased thee, Indra? Speed through our doors to songs, for thou art mighty.
Why comest thou to me, what gift attracts thee? Fain would I bring thee food most meet to offer.

4 Indra, what fame hath one like thee mid heroes? With what plan wilt thou act? Why hast thou sought us?
As a true Friend, Wide-Strider! to sustain us, since food absorbs the thought of each among us.

5 Speed happily those, as Sūrya ends his journey, who meet his wish as bridegrooms meet their spouses;
Men who present, O Indra strong by nature, with food the many songs that tell thy praises.

6 Thine are two measures, Indra, wide-wellmeted, heaven for thy majesty, earth for thy wisdom.
Here for thy choice are Somas mixed with butter: may the sweet meath be pleasant for thy drinking.

7 They have poured out a bowl to him, to Indra, full of sweet juice, for faithful is his bounty.
O'er earth's expanse hath he grown great by wisdom, the Friend of man, and by heroic exploits.

8 Indra hath conquered in his wars, the Mighty: men strive in multitudes to win his friendship.
Ascend thy chariot as it were in battle, which thou shalt drive to us with gracious favour.

1 The meaning of the stanza is obscure, and the text of the first half-line is unintelligible. I follow the reading which Sāyaṇa gives in his Commentary, *vāyo* instead *vā yó*. 'As (the bird) who deposits its young (in its nest) in the tree (is) eagerly looking around.'—Wilson. *Swift Pair*: Aśvins.

2 *Dance hither* or, come dancing. Cp. Milton's 'Now the bright morning-star, day's harbinger, Comes dancing from the east.' *Triple splendour*: perhaps with reference to Agni, Vāyu, and Sūrya.—Ludwig. *Hundred chiefs*: the Maruts may be intended, 'hundred' being used indefinitely. *Kutsa*: Indra's favourite companion.

4 Indra is reminded that the protection of his worshippers is his special glory. *Wide-Strider!*: as identified with the Sun; 'widely renowned,' according to Sāyaṇa. *Food*: the hymn appears to have been 'seen' or revealed in a time of dearth or famine.'—Ludwig.

5 *Meet his wish*: satisfy his, Indra's, longing for Soma, libations.

6 *Thine are two measures*: Thy majesty or greatness is vast and lofty as heaven, and thy wisdom is wide as earth; or, 'with confusion of the measure and the thing measured,' thou hast measured out the heaven by thy greatness and the earth by thy wisdom. See Wallis, *Cosmology of the Ṛgveda*, p. 18.

HYMN XXX. *Waters.*

1. As 'twere with swift exertion of the spirit, let the priest speed to the celestial Waters,
The glorious food of Varuṇa and Mitra. To him who spreadeth far this laud I offer.

2 Adhvaryus, be ye ready with oblations, and come with longing to the longing Waters,
Down on which looks the purple-tinted Eagle. Pour ye that flowing wave this day, deft-handed.

3 Go to the reservoir, O ye Adhvaryus: worship the Waters' Child with your oblations.
A consecrated wave he now will give you, so press for him the Soma rich in sweetness.

4 He who shines bright in floods, unfed with fuel, whom sages worship at their sacrifices:
Give waters rich in sweets, Child of the Waters, even those which gave heroic might to Indra:

5 Those in which Soma joys and is delighted, as a young man with fair and pleasant damsels.
Go thou unto those Waters, O Adhvaryu, and purify with herbs what thou infusest.

The subject is the ceremony of fetching the sacred waters required for the preparation of the Soma juice.

1 *To him who spreadeth far*: Indra, according to Sāyaṇa.

2 *The purple-tinted Eagle*: Soma, the Moon.

3 *To the reservoir*: to fetch the holy Waters. *The Waters' Child* usually Agni, as the lightning that springs from the clouds or waters of the firmament, but here the Deity who produces the rain, the Moon. See Hillebrandt, *V. M.*, I. 374.

4 *In floods*: of the aerial ocean. Cp. II. 35. 4.

5 *With herbs*: probably Darbha or Kuśa grass.

6 So maidens bow before the youthful gallant who comes with love to them who yearn to meet him.
In heart accordant and in wish one-minded are the Adhvaryus and the heavenly Waters.
7 He who made room for you when fast imprisoned, who freed you from the mighty imprecation,—
Even to that Indra send the meath-rich current, the wave that gratifies the Gods, O Waters.
8 Send forth to him the meath-rich wave, O Rivers, which is your offspring and a well of sweetness,
Oil-balmed, to be implored at sacrifices. Ye wealthy Waters, hear mine invocation.
9 Send forth the rapture-giving wave, O Rivers, which Indra drinks, which sets the Twain in motion ;
The well that springeth from the clouds, desirous, that wandereth triple-formed, distilling transport.
10 These winding Streams which with their double current, like cattle-raiders, seek the lower pastures,—
Waters which dwell together, thrive together, Queens, Mothers of the world, these, Ṛṣi, honour.
11 Send forth our sacrifice with holy worship send forth the hymn and prayer for gain of riches.
For need of sacrifice disclose the udder. Give gracious hearing to our call, O Waters.
12 For, wealthy Waters, ye control all treasures : ye bring auspicious intellect and Amṛta.
Ye are the Queens of independent riches Sarasvatī give full life to the singer !
13 When I behold the Waters coming hither, carrying with them milk and meath and butter,
Bearing the well-pressed Soma juice to Indra, they harmonize in spirit with Adhvaryus.
14 Rich, they are come with wealth for living beings, O friends, Adhvaryus, seat them in their places.
Seat them on holy grass, ye Soma-bringers, in harmony with the Offspring of the Waters.
15 Now to this grass are come the longing Waters : the Pious Ones are seated at our worship.
Adhvaryus, press the Soma juice for Indra : so will the service of the Gods be easy.

6 The Waters bow to Soma as maidens to their lovers.
9 *The Twain* : *ubhe* : probably, Heaven and Earth. Sāyaṇa explains differently :—'which sends us both (kinds of fruit)'; that is, 'the fruit, whether reward or punishment, of the present life, and of a former life.'—Wilson, and Editor's note. *Desirous* : eager to mix with the Soma, according to Sāyaṇa; but the meaning of *auśānām* is uncertain. Ludwig and Hillebrandt translate it by 'des Uśanas,' belonging to Uśanas or Uśanā *Tripleformed* : Soma with two admixtures.—Grassmann.
10 *Double current* : meaning probably, the two kinds of waters called respectively Ekadhanā and Vasativarī.
11 *Disclose the udder* : let your streams flow.
12 *Sarasvatī* : as chief and wisest of the Water-Goddesses.

HYMN XXXI. *Viśvedevas.*

1. MAY benediction of the Gods approach us, holy, to aid us with all rapid succours.
Therewith may we be happily befriended, and pass triumphant over all our troubles.
2 A man should think on wealth and strive to win it by adoration on the path of Order,
Counsel himself with his own mental insight, and grasp still nobler vigour with his spirit.
3 The hymn is formed, poured are the allotted portions : as to a ford friends come unto the Wondrous.
We have obtained the power of ease and comfort, we have become acquainted, with Immortals.
4 Pleased be the Eternal Lord who loves the household with this man whom God Savitar created.
May Bhaga Aryaman grace him with cattle : may he appear to him, and be, delightful.
5 Like the Dawns' dwelling-place be this assembly, where in their might men rich in food have gathered.
Striving to share the praises of this singer. To us come strengthening and effectual riches !
6 This Bull's most gracious far-extended favour existed first of all in full abundance.
By his support they are maintained in common who in the Asura's mansion dwell together.

1 *Benediction* : or, the laudation ; that is, Ludwig suggests, 'May the power of praising the Gods, and at the same time the Gods themselves come to us.'
3 *The Wondrous* : meaning, perhaps, Soma.
4 *The Eternal Lord* : Agni. According to Sāyaṇa, Prajāpati. *This man* : the institutor of the sacrifice. Savitar has given him life and now let Agni bless him. *Bhaga Aryaman* : Aryaman as Bhaga who distributes wealth.
6 *This Bull* : Agni as the Sun. *The Asura* is Dyaus.

7 What was the tree, what wood, in sooth, produced it, from which they fashioned forth the Earth and Heaven ?
These Twain stand fast and wax not old for ever : these have sung praise to many a day and morning.

8 Not only here is this : more is beyond us. He is the Bull, the Heaven's and Earth's supporter.
With power divine he makes his skin a filter, when the Bay Coursers bear him on as Sūrya.

9 He passes o'er the broad earth like a Stega : he penetrates the world as Wind the mist-cloud.
He, balmed with oil, near Varuṇa and Mitra, like Agni in the wood, hath shot forth splendour.

10 When suddenly called the cow that erst was barren, she, self-protected, ended all her troubles.
Earth, when the first son sprang from sire and mother, cast up the Śamī, that which men were seeking.

11 To Nṛṣad's son they gave the name of Kaṇva, and he the brown-hued courser won the treasure.
For him dark-coloured streamed the shining udder : none made it swell for him. Thus Order willed it.

8 *Not only here* : the first half-line is obscure. 'Not such (is their power); there is another greater than they.'—Wilson. 'There is no other thing besides like unto him.'—Wallis. *A filter* : *pavítram* : which purifies the rays of light which stream through it.

9 *A Stega* : said to be a certain biting or stinging insect. According to Sāyaṇa, 'the aggregation of rays, the Sun.' Ludwig conjectures that 'plough-share' may be the meaning.

10 This stanza is very obscure. 'The cow which was barren is the *Śamī* tree, which brings forth the *Aśvattha*, and from the wood of these two trees are made the *araṇi*, the two pieces of wood which are rubbed together to produce the sacred fire—the upper and harder piece is the *Śamī* (the Acacia Suma), and the lower and soft is the *Aśvattha* (the Ficus religiosa).'—Wilson.

'The verses (7—10) deal with the formation of the three main components of the universe, heaven, earth, and the sun. Of the first two the poet has little to tell us and passes on at once to the third. The sun is identified with the bull, Agni of the sacrifice, and the earth with the lower rubbing-stick anointed with ghee, which is licked up ('devours' instead of 'cast up') as soon as fire is struck.'—Wallis, *Cosmology of the Ṛgveda*, pp. 47, 48.

11 This stanza appears to have no connexion with the hymn, and is inexplicable as it stands here. See I. 117. 8, where the son of Nṛṣad is mentioned as a favourite of the Aśvins.

HYMN XXXII. *Indra.*

1. FORTH speed the Pair to bring the meditating God, benevolent with boons sent in return for boons.
May Indra graciously accept both gifts from us, when he hath knowledge of the flowing Soma juice.

2 Thou wanderest far, O Indra, through the spheres of light and realms of earth, the region, thou whom many praise !
Let those who often bring their solemn rites conquer the noisy babblers who present no gifts.

3 More beautiful than beauty must this seem to me, when the son duly careth for his parents' line.
The wife attracts the husband : with a shout of joy the man's auspicious marriage is performed aright.

4 This beauteous place of meeting have I looked upon, where, like milch-cows, the kine order the marriage train;
Where the Herd's Mother counts as first and best of all, and round her are the seven-toned people of the choir.

5 The Pious One hath reached your place before the rest : One only moves victorious with the Rudras' band.
To these your helpers pour our meath, Immortal Gods, with whom your song of praise hath power to win their gifts.

6 He who maintains the Laws of God informed me that thou wast lying hidden in the waters.

1 *The meditating God* : Indra. My version of the first line follows the explanation given by Ludwig in his Commentary. Sāyaṇa's interpretation is different :—'Indra sends his quick-going horses to the service of the (worshipper) expectant (of his arrival).'—Wilson. *Both gifts* : oblation and praise.

3 *Careth for his parents' line*: by marrying and becoming a father; or as Sāyaṇa explains, by having his birth proclaimed according to custom in sacrifices instituted by him.

4 *Order the marriage train* : the meaning of this half-line is uncertain. According to Sāyaṇa, *the herd* is the company of sacrificers and priests, its *mother* is Stuti or Praise, the *seven-toned*, or sevenfold, are the metres, or the seasons, or the Hotar priests. *The Herd's Mother* is more probably Pṛśni, the mother of the Maruts. The whole stanza is translated by Wilson:—'Shine, Indra, upon this elegant chamber of sacrifice, when our praises desire (thy approach) as milch-kine (desire) their stalls; since the praise of me the worshipper precedes (the adoration) of the company, and this person accompanied by the seven officiating priests is the offerer of praise.'

5 *The Pious One* : Agni, the special worshipper of Gods. *One only* : Indra.

6 *He* : perhaps Soma. *Thou* : Agni, Cp. I. 23. 20.

Indra, who knoweth well, beheld and showed thee. By him instructed am I come, O Agni.

7 The stranger asks the way of him who knows it : taught by the skilful guide he travels onward.
This is, in truth, the blessing of instruction : he finds the path that leads directly forward.

8 Even now he breathed : these days hath he remembered. Concealed, he sucked the bosom of his Mother.
Yet in his youth old age hath come upon him : he hath grown gracious, good, and free from anger.

9 O Kalaśa, all these blessings will we bring them, O Kuruśravaṇa, who give rich presents.
May he, O wealthy princes, and this Soma which I am bearing in my heart, reward you.

HYMN XXXIII. *Various Deities.*

1. THE urgings of the people have impelled me, and by the nearest way I bring you Pūṣan.
The Universal Gods have brought me safely. The cry was heard, Behold, Duḥśāsu cometh !

2 The ribs that compass me give pain and trouble me like rival wives.
Indigence, nakedness, exhaustion press me sore : my mind is fluttering like a bird's.

3 As rats eat weavers' threads, cares are consuming me, thy singer, Śatakratu, me.
Have mercy on us once, O Indra, Bounteous Lord : be thou a Father unto us.

4 I the priests' Ṛṣi chose as prince most liberal Kuruśravaṇa,
The son of Trasadasyu's son,

5 Whose three bays harnessed to the car bear me straight onward : I will laud
The giver of a thousand meeds,

6 The sire of Upamaśravas, even him whose words were passing sweet,
As a fair field is to its lord.

7 Mark, Upamaśravas, his son, mark, grandson of Mitrātithi :
I am thy father's eulogist.

8 If I controlled Immortal Gods, yea, even were I Lord of men,
My liberal prince were living still.

9 None lives, even had he hundred lives, beyond the statute of the Gods :
So am I parted from my friend.

HYMN XXXIV. *Dice, Etc.*

1. SPRUNG from tall trees on windy heights, these rollers transport me as they turn upon the table.
Dearer to me the die that never slumbers than the deep draught of Mūjavān's own Soma.

2 She never vexed me nor was angry with me, but to my friends and me was ever gracious.
For the die's sake, whose single point is final, mine own devoted wife I alienated.

3 My wife holds me aloof, her mother hates me : the wretched man finds none to give him comfort.

---

8 *Even now he breathed* : began to show signs of life. The connexion between stanzas 1—4 and 5—8 is not apparent. *Sucked the bosom of his Mother* : enjoyed oblations, in the shape of Soma juice, etc., produced by the earth.

9 The meaning of *Kalaśa*, literally 'pitcher' or 'beaker,' here is uncertain. '(Indra), the possessor of the pitchers.' —Wilson. Ludwig suggests *kalāśaḥ* as the right reading : 'We will perform these holy ceremonies in their minutest details.' *Kuruśravaṇa* : according to Sāyaṇa, 'hearer of the praise of priests,' but probably the name of a prince, as in the following hymn.

---

1 *Duḥśāsu* : literally, 'the malevolent.' Perhaps, as Ludwig suggests, a hostile prince whose victory over Kuruśravaṇa has caused the distress mentioned in the following stanza.

2 The first line is taken from I. 105. 8.

3 This first line is taken from I. 105. 5. *Weavers' threads* : threads steeped in water, according to Sāyaṇa. *Once*; 'after having so often given us up to misery.' —Ludwig.

4 *The Priests' Ṛṣi* : higher in rank than the other priests. *Chose* : *i. e.* I chose to keep him as my master in order to go out to battle with him.'—Lanman, *Sanskrit Reader*, p. 386.

6 This and the three following stanzas are said to be consolatory verses addressed by the Ṛṣi Kavaṣa to Upamaśravas on the death of his father Mitrātithi.

8 *Were I Lord of men* : as one of the Gods. *My liberal prince* : Mitrātithi.

9 *Beyond the statute of the Gods* : beyond the time fixed for the duration of his life.

This hymn has been placed by Grassmann in his Appendix as a composite production consisting of incoherent fragments. See Lanman, *Sanskrit Reader*, pp. 386, 389.

---

1 *Sprung from tall trees* : the nuts of the Vibhīdaka, or, later, Vibhītaka, tree (Terminalia Bellerica) were used as dice in early times. *Rollers* : swiftly rolling dice. *Mūjavān* : said to be a mountain on which the finest Soma plants grew.

2 *Whose single point is final* : the speaker has apparently lost all by throwing aces.

As of a costly horse grown old and feeble, I find not any profit of the gamester.

4 Others caress the wife of him whose riches the die hath coveted, that rapid courser : Of him speak father, mother, brothers saying, We know him not : bind him and take him with you.

5 When I resolve to play with these no longer, my friends depart from me and leave me lonely. When the brown dice, thrown on the board, have rattled, like a fond girl I seek the place of meeting.

6 The gamester seeks the gambling-house, and wonders, his body all afire, Shall I be lucky ? Still do the dice extend his eager longing, staking his gains against his adversary.

7 Dice, verily, are armed with goads and driving-hooks, deceiving and tormenting, causing grievous woe. They give frail gifts and then destroy the man who wins, thickly anointed with the player's fairest good.

8 Merrily sports their troop, the three-and-fifty, like Savitar the God whose ways are faithful. They bend not even to the mighty's anger : the King himself pays homage and reveres them.

9 Downward they roll, and then spring quickly upward, and, handless, force the man with hands to serve them. Cast on the board, like lumps of magic charcoal, though cold themselves they burn the heart to ashes.

10 The gambler's wife is left forlorn and wretched : the mother mourns the son who wanders homeless. In constant fear, in debt, and seeking riches, he goes by night unto the home of others.

11 Sad is the gambler when he sees a matron, another's wife, and his well-ordered dwelling. He yokes the brown steeds in the early morning, and when the fire is cold sinks down an outcast.

12 To the great captain of your mighty army, who hath become the host's imperial leader, To him I show my ten extended fingers : I speak the truth. No wealth am I withholding.

13 Play not with dice : no, cultivate thy corn-land. Enjoy the gain, and deem that wealth sufficient. There are thy cattle, there thy wife, O gambler. So this good Savitar himself hath told me.

14 Make me your friend : show us some little mercy. Assail us not with your terrific fierceness. Appeased be your malignity and anger, and let the brown dice snare some other captive.

4 *Bind him* : he has staked his personal freedom, and lost; and his people renounce him.

7 *Driving-hooks* : used by mahouts or elephant-drivers. The last half-line of the stanza is difficult :—'they appear to the gambler covered with honey.'—Muir.

8 *Three-and-fifty* : or, perhaps, thrice five in number. It would appear from Sāyaṇa's Commentary that fifty-three was the usual number of dice employed; and yet this seems hardly probable. Ludwig suggests 'three times five' as the meaning here of *tripañcāśáḥ*, and Prof. Weber would read *tripañcaśaḥ* instead of *tripañcāśáḥ* (*Ueber den Rājasūya*, p. 72). *Like Savitar* : '(disposing men's destinies) like the god S.'—Muir.

10 *Riches* : wealth gained by robbery, according to Sāyaṇa.

11 *Yokes the brown steeds* : begins throwing the nut-dice. *When the fire is cold* : 'by the time when the fire goes out he has sunk into a degraded wretch.'—Muir.

12 *The great captain*: the highest numbered of all the dice. *Ten fingers*: to show that I have nothing left.

14 This stanza is a farewell address to the Dice. *Some other*: our enemy.—Sāyaṇa.

The hymn or lay has been transliterated, translated in prose, and freely reproduced in rhymed octosyllabic verse, by Dr. J. Muir, *O.S. Texts*, V. 425—429. It has also been translated by the authors of the *Siebenzig Lieder*.

HYMN XXXV. *Viśvedevas.*

1. THESE fires associate with Indra are awake, bringing their light when first the Dawn begins to shine. May Heaven and Earth, great Pair, observe our holy work. We claim for us this day the favour of the Gods.

2 Yea, for ourselves we claim the grace of Heaven and Earth, of Śaryaṇāvān, of the Hills and Mother Streams. For innocence we pray to Sūrya and to Dawn. So may the flowing Soma bring us bliss to-day.

3 May the great Twain, the Mothers, Heaven and Earth, this day preserve us free from sin for peace and happiness.

1 *With Indra* : as a God of the morning light.

2 *Of Śaryaṇāvān, of the Hills*: according to Sāyaṇa, 'of the mountains of Śaryaṇāvān,' a lake in the district of Kurukṣetra. I follow Ludwig in taking both *párvatān* and *śaryaṇāvatah* as genitives.

May Morning sending forth her light drive sin afar. We pray to kindled Agni for felicity.

4 May this first Dawn bring us the host of gracious Gods : rich, may it richly shine for us who strive for wealth.
The wrath of the malignant may we keep afar. We pray to kindled Agni for felicity.

5 Dawns, who come forward with the bright beams of the Sun, and at your earliest flushing bring to us the light,
Shine ye on us to-day auspicious, for renown. We pray to kindled Agni for felicity.

6 Free from all sickness may the Mornings come to us, and let our fires mount upward with a lofty blaze.
The Aśvin Pair have harnessed their swift-moving car. We pray to kindled Agni for felicity.

7 Send us to-day a portion choice and excellent, O Savitar, for thou art he who dealeth wealth.
I cry to Dhiṣaṇā, Mother of opulence. We pray to kindled Agni for felicity.

8 Further me this declaring of Eternal Law, the Law of Gods, as we mortals acknowledge it !
The Sun goes up beholding all the rays of morn. We pray to kindled Agni for felicity.

9 This day we pray with innocence in strewing grass, adjusting pressing-stones, and perfecting the hymn.
Thou in the Ādityas' keeping movest restlessly. We pray to kindled Agni for felicity.

10 To our great holy grass I bid the Gods at morn to banquet, and will seat them as the seven priests,—
Varuṇa, Indra, Mitra, Bhaga for our gain. We pray to kindled Agni for felicity.

11 Come hither, O Ādityas, for our perfect weal : accordant help our sacrifice that we may thrive.
Pūṣan, Bṛhaspati, Bhaga, both Aśvins, and enkindled Agni we implore for happiness.

12 Ādityas, Gods, vouchsafe that this our home may be praise-worthy, prosperous, our heroes' sure defence,
For cattle, for our sons, for progeny, for life. We pray to kindled Agni for felicity.

13 This day may all the Maruts, all be near us with aid : may all our fires be well enkindled.
May all Gods come to us with gracious favour. May spoil and wealth be ours, and all possessions.

14 He whom ye aid, O Deities, in battle, whom ye protect and rescue from affliction,
Who fears no danger at your milk-libation,—such may we be to feast the Gods, ye Mighty.

HYMN XXXVI. *Viśvedevas.*

1. THERE are the Dawn and Night, the grand and beauteous Pair, Earth, Heaven, and Varuṇa, Mitra, and Aryaman.
Indra I call, the Maruts, Mountains, and the Floods, Ādityas, Heaven and Earth, the Waters, and the Sky.

2 May Dyaus and Pṛthivi, wise, true to Holy Law, keep us in safety from distress and injury.
Let not malignant Nirṛti rule over us. We crave to-day this gracious favour of the Gods.

3 Mother of Mitra and of opulent Varuṇa, may Aditi preserve us safe from all distress.
May we obtain the light of heaven without a foe. We crave this gracious favour of the Gods to-day.

4 May ringing press-stones keep the Rākṣasas afar, ill dream, and Nirṛti, and each voracious fiend.
May the Ādityas and the Maruts shelter us. We crave this gracious favour of the Gods to-day.

5 *Your*: according to the text 'their,' the verb in the first line being in the third person.

7 *Dhiṣaṇā*: a Goddess who presides over Prosperity, according to Hillebrandt, the Earth

8 *Further me*: 'May that glorification of the gods which men repeat in connexion with the rite preserve me.'—Wilson.

9 *Movest restlessly*: performest thy duties, according to Sāyaṇa. Agni rapidly burning the fuel appears to be intended.

14 *Who fears no danger*: who feels assured that his worship of the Gods will protect him.

---

1 *The Waters*: of the firmament.

2 *Dyaus and Pṛthivi*: Heaven and Earth. *Nirṛti* Death or Destruction.

5 Full flow libations; on our grass let Indra sit; Bṛhaspati the singer laud with Sāma hymns!
Wise be our hearts' imaginings that we may live. We crave this gracious favour of the Gods to-day.

6 Ye Aśvins, make our sacrifice ascend to heaven, and animate the rite that it may send us bliss,
Offered with holy oil, with forward-speeding rein. We crave the gracious favour of the Gods to-day.

7 Hither I call the band of Maruts, swift to hear, great, purifying, bringing bliss, to be our Friends.
May we increase our wealth to glorify our name. We crave this gracious favour of the Gods to-day.

8 We bring the Stay of Life, who makes the waters swell, swift-hearing, Friend of Gods, who waits on sacrifice.
May we control that Power, Soma whose rays are bright. We crave this gracious favour of the Gods to-day.

9 Alive ourselves, with living sons, devoid of guilt, may we win this with winners by fair means to win.
Let the prayer-haters bear our sin to every side. We crave this gracious favour of the Gods to-day.

10 Hear us, O ye who claim the worship of mankind, and give us, O ye Gods, the gift for which we pray,
Victorious wisdom, fame with heroes and with wealth. We crave to-day this gracious favour of the Gods.

11 We crave the gracious favour of the Gods to-day, great favour of great Gods, sublime and free from foes,
That we may gain rich treasure sprung from hero sons. We crave this gracious favour of the Gods to-day.

12 In great enkindled Agni's keeping, and, for bliss, free from all sin before Mitra and Varuṇa.
May we share Savitar's best animating help. We crave this gracious favour of the Gods to-day.

13 All ye, the Gods whom Savitar the Father of truth, and Varuṇa and Mitra govern,
Give us prosperity with hero children, and opulence in kine and various treasure.

14 Savitar, Savitar from east and westward, Savitar, Savitar from north and southward,
Savitar send us perfect health and comfort, Savitar let our days of life be lengthened!

8 *Who makes the waters swell*: *apām perum*: 'protector of the waters.'—Sāyaṇa. 'Drinker of the waters'.—Ludwig. Soma is meant. See IX, 76, 4.

HYMN XXXVII. *Sūrya.*

1. Do homage unto Varuṇa's and Mitra's Eye: offer this solemn worship to the Mighty God,
Who seeth far away, the Ensign, born of Gods. Sing praises unto Sūrya, to the Son of Dyaus.

2 May this my truthful speech guard me on every side, wherever heaven and earth and days are spread abroad.
All else that is in motion finds a place of rest: the waters ever flow and ever mounts the Sun.

3 No godless man from time remotest draws thee down when thou art driving forth with winged dappled Steeds.
One lustre waits upon thee moving to the east, and, Sūrya, thou arisest with a different light.

4 O Sūrya, with the light whereby thou scatterest gloom, and with thy ray impellest every moving thing,
Keep far from us all feeble, worthless sacrifice, and drive away disease and every evil dream.

5 Sent forth thou guardest well the Universe's law, and in thy wonted way arisest free from wrath.
When Sūrya, we address our prayers to thee to-day, may the Gods favour this our purpose and desire.

6 This invocation, these our words may Heaven and Earth, and Indra and the Waters and the Maruts hear.
Ne'er may we suffer want in presence of the Sun, and, living happy lives, may we attain old age.

1 *Varuṇa's and Mitra's Eye*: Sūrya or the Sun. 'The eye of Mitra, Varuṇa and Agni.'—I. 115. 1.

3 *Dappled Steeds*: 'with Etaśas.'—Ludwig. *One lustre*: by night. Cf. I. 115. 5; and *Aitareya-Brāhmaṇa*, III, 4.44. 'One ancient radiance follows (thee) whilst thou risest with another.'—Wilson. See Wallis, *Cosmology of the Ṛgveda*, p. 117.

5 *In thy wonted way* : *svadhā ánu*: 'after the *svadhā* offerings.'—Wilson.

7 Cheerful in spirit, evermore, and keen of sight, with store of children, free from sickness and from sin,
Long-living, may we look, O Sūrya, upon thee uprising day by day, thou great as Mitra is !

8 Sūrya, may we live long and look upon thee still, thee, O Far-seeing One, bringing the glorious light,
The radiant God, the spring of joy to every eye, as thou art mounting up o'er the high shining flood.

9 Thou by whose lustre all the world of life comes forth, and by thy beams again returns unto its rest,
O Sūrya with the golden hair, ascend for us day after day, still bringing purer innocence.

10 Bless us with shine, bless us with perfect daylight, bless us with cold, with fervent heat and lustre.
Bestow on us, O Sūrya, varied riches, to bless us in our home and when we travel.

11 Gods, to our living creatures of both kinds vouchsafe protection, both to bipeds and to quadrupeds,
That they may drink and eat invigorating food. So grant us health and strength and perfect innocence.

12 If by some grievous sin we have provoked the Gods, O Deities, with the tongue or thoughtlessness of heart,
That guilt, O Vasus, lay upon the Evil One, on him who ever leads us into deep distress.

HYMN XXXVIII. *Indra.*

1. O INDRA, in this battle great and glorious, in this loud din of war help us to victory,
Where in the strife for kine among bold ring-decked men arrows fly all around and heroes are subdued.

2 At home disclose to us opulence rich in food, streaming with milk, O Indra, meet to be renowned.
Śakra, may we be thine, the friendly Conqueror's : even as we desire, O Vasu, so do thou.

3 The godless man, much-lauded Indra, whether he be Dāsa or be Ārya, who would war with us,—
Easy to conquer be for thee, with us, these foes : with thee may we subdue them in the clash of fight.

4 Him who must be invoked by many and by few, who standeth nigh with comfort in the war of men,
Indra, famed Hero, winner in the deadly strife, let us bring hitherward to-day to favour us.

5 For, Indra, I have heard thee called Self-capturer, One, Steer ! who never yields, who urges even the churl.
Release thyself from Kutsa and come hither. How shall one like thee sit still bound that he may not move ?

HYMN XXXIX. *Aśvins.*

1. As 'twere the name of father, easy to invoke, we all assembled here invoke this Car of yours,
Aśvins, your swiftly-rolling circumambient Car which he who worships must invoke at eve and dawn.

2 Awake all pleasant strains and let the hymns flow forth : raise up abundant fulness : this is our desire.
Aśvins, bestow on us a glorious heritage, and give our princes treasure fair as Soma is.

3 Ye are the bliss of her who groweth old at home, and helpers of the slow although he linger last.

8 *Flood*: or floor of heaven.

12 *The Evil One*: *drāvā*: here probably a kind of Diabolus or Devil.—Ludwig.

---

1 *Ring-decked*: adorned with armlets, or quoits as weapons.

5 *Self-capturer*; it is difficult to assign a reasonable and appropriate meaning to *svavṛjam*. Sāyaṇa explains it by *svayam eva cchettāram*, 'one who cuts himself:' 'self mutilator'.—Wilson. According to the St. Petersburg Lexicon, the meaning is 'one who appropriates or takes to himself;' according to Ludwig 'the self-rescuer,' and according to Geldner 'one who suffers himself to be captured.' The poet calls on Indra to tear himself away from his favourite Kutsa in order to aid his worshippers in the coming fight. 'A legend is here somewhat obscurely related, that *Kutsa* and *Luśa* having summoned Indra at the same time to their respective sacrifices, he went first to *Kutsa* who then detained him, having fastened him...with a hundred leather thongs. This verse is addressed to *Indra* and *Luśa* exhorting him to free himself.—Wilson.

The Ṛṣi is Ghoṣā, daughter of Kakṣivān.

3 *Of her who groweth old at home*: referring to Ghoṣā herself. See I. 17. 7. *Healers of the blind*: See I. 112. 8.

Men call you too, Nāsatyas, healers of the blind, the thin and feeble, and the man with broken bones.

4 Ye made Cyavāna, weak and worn with length of days, young again, like a car, that he had power to move.
Ye lifted up the son of Tugra from the floods. At our libations must all these your acts be praised.

5 We will declare among the folk your ancient deeds heroic ; yea, ye were Physicians bringing health.
You, you who must be lauded, will we bring for aid, so that this foe of ours, O Aśvins, may believe.

6 Listen to me, O Aśvins ; I have cried to you. Give me your aid as sire and mother aid their son.
Poor, without kin or friend or ties of blood am I. Save me before it be too late, from this my curse.

7 Ye, mounted on your chariot brought to Vimada the comely maid of Purumitra as a bride.
Ye, came unto the calling of the weakling's dame, and granted noble offspring to the happy wife.

8 Ye gave again the vigour of his youthful life to the sage Kali when old age was coming nigh.
Ye rescued Vandana and raised him from the pit, and in a moment gave Viśpalā power to move.

9 Ye Aśvins Twain, endowed with manly strength, brought forth Rebha when hidden in the cave and well-nigh dead,
Freed Saptavadhri, and for Atri caused the pit heated with fire to be a pleasant resting-place.

10 On Pedu ye bestowed, Aśvins, a courser white, mighty with nine-and-ninety varied gifts of strength,
A horse to be renowned, who bore his friend at speed, joy-giving, Bhaga-like to be invoked of men.

11 From no side, ye Two Kings whom none may check or stay, doth grief, distress, or danger come upon the man
Whom, Aśvins swift to hear, borne on your glowing path, ye with your Consort make the foremost in the race.

12 Come on that Chariot which the Ṛbhus wrought for you, the Chariot, Aśvins, that is speedier than thought,
At harnessing whereof Heaven's Daughter springs to birth, and from Vivasvān come auspicious Night and Day.

13 Come, Conquerors of the sundered mountain, to our home, Aśvins who made the cow stream milk for Śayu's sake,
Ye who delivered even from the wolf's deep throat and set again at liberty the swallowed quail.

14 We have prepared this laud for you, O Aśvins, and, like the Bhṛgus, as a car have framed it,
Have decked it as a maid to meet the bridegroom, and brought it as a son, our stay for ever.

HYMN XL. *Aśvins.*

1. YOUR radiant Chariot—whither goes it on its way ?—who decks it for you, Heroes, for its happy course,
Starting at daybreak, visiting each morning every house, borne hitherward through prayer unto the sacrifice ?

2 Where are ye, Aśvins, in the evening, where at morn ? Where is your halting-place, where rest ye for the night ?
Who brings you homeward, as the widow bedward draws her husband's brother, as the bride attracts the groom ?

4 *Cyavāna*: See I. 116. 10, and 117. 13. *Son of Tugra*: Bhujyu. See Vol. I., Index.

6 *My curse*: leprosy, which prevented her marriage.

7 *Vimada*: See I. 117. 20. *The weakling's dame* See I. 117. 24.

8 For *Kali*, *Vandana*, and *Viśpalā* in this stanza, and *Rebha*, *Atri*, and *Pedu* in 9 and 10, See Vol. I., Index. For *Saptavadhri* (stanza 9) See V. 78, 6.

11 *Whom none may check or stay*: *adite—adīnau.*—Sāyaṇa. *Your Consort*: Sūryā. *The foremost in the race*: that is, generally, preëminent.

12 *Heaven's Daughter*: Uṣas or Dawn. *Vivasvān*: the morning Sun.

13 *Conquerors of the sundered mountain*: probably with reference to the deliverance of Jāhuṣa—Ludwig. See I. 116. 20. *The swallowed quail*: see I. 112.8. The quail is probably Dawn delivered from the jaws of the wolf Night by the twin Light-Gods.

14 *Our stay for ever* : who will perpetuate our family; 'the eternal performer of rites.'—Wilson.

---

2 *As the widow*: in certain circumstances a widow was bound to marry her deceased husband's brother. See Manu (*Mānavadharmaśāstra*), IX 69. 70.The law of the Jews was the same. See Deuteronomy, xxv. 5.

3 Early ye sing forth praise as with a herald's voice, and, meet for worship, go each morning to the house.
Whom do ye ever bring to ruin? Unto whose libations come ye, Heroes, like two Sons of Kings?

4 Even as hunters follow two wild elephants, we with oblations call you down at morn and eve.
To folk who pay you offerings at appointed times, Chiefs, Lords of splendour, ye bring food to strengthen them.

5 To you, O Aśvins, came the daughter of a King, Ghoṣā, and said, O Heroes, this I beg of you:
Be near me in the day, be near me in the night: help me to gain a car-borne chieftain rich in steeds.

6 O Aśvins, ye are wise: as Kutsa comes to men, bring your car nigh the folk of him who sings your praise.
The bee, O Aśvins, bears your honey in her mouth, as the maid carries it purified in her hand.

7 To Bhujyu and to Vaśa ye come near with help, O Aśvins, to Śiñjāra and to Uśanā.
Your worshipper secures your friendship for himself. Through your protection I desire felicity.

8 Kṛśa and Śayu ye protect, ye Aśvins Twain: ye Two assist the widow and the worshipper;
And ye throw open, Aśvins, unto those who win the cattle-stall that thunders with its sevenfold mouth.

9 The Woman hath brought forth, the Infant hath appeared, the plants of wondrous beauty straightway have sprung up.
To him the rivers run as down a deep descent, and he this day becomes their master and their lord.

10 They mourn the living, cry aloud, at sacrifice: the men have set their thoughts upon a distant cast.
A lovely thing for fathers who have gathered here,—a joy to husbands,—are the wives their arms shall clasp

11 Of this we have no knowledge. Tell it forth to us, now the youth rests within the chambers of the bride.
Fain would we reach the dwelling of the vigorous Steer who loves the kine, O Aśvins: this is our desire.

12 Your favouring grace hath come, ye Lords of ample wealth: Aśvins, our longings are stored up within your hearts.
Ye, Lords of splendour, have become our twofold guard: may we as welcome friends reach Aryaman's abode.

13 Even so, rejoicing in the dwelling-place of man, give hero sons and riches to the eloquent.
Make a ford, Lords of splendour, where men well may drink: remove the spiteful tree-stump standing in the path.

14 O Aśvins, Wonder-Workers, Lords of lustre, where and with what folk do ye delight yourselves to-day?
Who hath detained them with him? Whither are they gone? Unto what sage's or what worshipper's abode?

HYMN XLI. *Aśvins.*

1. THAT general Car of yours, invoked by many a man, that comes to our libations, three-wheeled, meet for lauds,

3 *As with a herald's voice*: *kāpayā* is thus explained by Sāyaṇa. *The house*: of the sacrificer.

5 The second half of the second line is difficult: 'be able (to grant favour) to the son of my brother, who has horses and a chariot.'—Wilson.

6 *As Kutsa comes to men*: borne on Indra's chariot. *Bears your honey*: sips honey when the Aśvins have ushered in the day. *As the maid*: Dr. Muir and Prof. Grassmann explain this half-line differently, 'as a maid, or a woman, resorts to her rendezvous (with her lover).'

7 *Vaśa*: See I. 112, 10 *Śiñjāra*: See VIII. 5.25. *Uśanā*: see Vol. I., Index.

8 *Kṛśa*: a Ṛṣi favoured by Indra; or, as Sāyaṇa explains the word here, the feeble man in general. *Śayu*: has been mentioned frequently. *The cattle-stall*: the raincloud whose waters are the cows.

9 *The Woman*: perhaps the water of the cloud. *The Infant*: the lightning. *To him*: the sacrificer may perhaps be intended.

10 *They mourn the living*: perhaps, show their sorrow for the widower at the funeral of his wife. See Lanman (*Sanskrit Reader*. p. 387) from whom I have borrowed. *Set their thoughts upon a distant cast*: of the noose or snaring-net: apparently a periphrasis for, have taken thought for the distant future and children to live after them.

11 Ghoṣā appears to speak of herself in the plural number. She plainly expresses her wishes for marriage.

12 *Aryaman's abode*: Aryaman is here used in the original sense of the word, bosom-friend and companion, especially the friend who asks a woman in marriage for another.

Prof. Grassmann places stanzas 10—14 in his Appendix as being obscure and in his opinion forming no part of the original hymn.

1 *Three-wheeled*: See I, 34.9.

That circumambient Car, worthy of sacrifice, we call with our pure hymns at earliest flush of dawn.

2 Ye, O Nāsatyas, mount that early-harnessed Car, that travels early, laden with its freight of balm,
Wherewith ye, Heroes, visit clans who sacrifice, even the poor man's worship where the priest attends.

3 If to the deft Adhvaryu with the meath in hand, or to the Kindler firm in strength, the household friend,
Or to the sage's poured libations ye approach, come thence, O Aśvins, now to drink the offered meath.

HYMN XLII. *Indra.*

1. Even as an archer shoots afar his arrow, offer the laud to him with meet adornment.
Quell with your voice the wicked's voice, O sages. Singer, make Indra rest beside the Soma.

2 Draw thy Friend to thee like a cow at milking : O Singer, wake up Indra as a lover.
Make thou the Hero haste to give us riches even as a vessel filled brimful with treasure.

3 Why, Maghavan, do they call thee Bounteous Giver ? Quicken me : thou, I hear, art he who quickens.
Śakra, let my intelligence be active, and bring us luck that finds great wealth, O Indra.

4 Standing, in battle for their rights, together, the people, Indra, in the fray invoke thee.
Him who brings gifts the Hero makes his comrade : with him who pours no juice he seeks not friendship.

5 Whoso with plenteous food for him expresses strong Somas as much quickly-coming treasure,
For him he overthrows in early morning his swift well-weaponed foes, and slays the tyrant.

6 He unto whom we offer praises, Indra, Maghavan, who hath joined to ours his wishes,—
Before him even afar the foe must tremble : low before him must bow all human glories.

7 With thy fierce bolt, O God invoked of many, drive to a distance from afar the foeman.
O Indra, give us wealth in corn and cattle, and make thy singer's prayer gain strength and riches.

8 Indra, the swallower of strong libations rich in the boons they bring, the potent Somas,
He, Maghavan, will not restrict his bounty : he brings much wealth unto the Soma-presser.

9 Yea, by superior play he wins advantage, when he, a gambler, piles his gains in season.
Celestial-natured, he o'erwhelms with riches the devotee who keeps not back his treasure.

10 O Much-invoked, may we subdue all famine and evil want with store of grain and cattle.
May we allied, as first in rank, with princes obtain possessions by our own exertion.

11 Bṛhaspati protect us from the rearward, and from above, and from below, from sinners !
May Indra from the front, and from the centre, as Friend to friends, vouchsafe us room and freedom.

HYMN XLIII. *Indra.*

1. In perfect unison all yearning hymns of mine that find the light of heaven have sung forth Indra's praise.
As wives embrace their lord, the comely bridegroom, so they compass Maghavan about that he may help.

2 Directed unto thee my spirit never strays, for I have set my hopes on thee, O Much-invoked !
Sit, Wonderful ! as King upon the sacred grass, and let thy drinking-place be by the Soma juice.

3 *The Kindler*: the Agnīdh, the priest who kindles the sacrificial fire.

---

1 *The wicked's voice*: 'the praises of your adversaries.'—Wilson.

4 *The Hero*: Indra.

5 *As much quickly-coming treasure*: representing the wealth which the offering of the libations is expected to produce.

6 *Unto whom we offer praises*; or, in whom we have placed our hope.

9 *When he, a gambler*: cp. X 43, 5.

10 *With princes*: with men eminent for their wealth: *rājabhir-dhanānāmīśvaraiḥ*—Sāyaṇa.

3 From indigence and hunger Indra turns away : Maghavan hath dominion over precious wealth.
These the Seven Rivers flowing on their downward path increase the vital vigour of the potent Steer.

4 As on the fair-leafed tree rest birds, to Indra flow the gladdening Soma juices that the bowls contain.
Their face that glows with splendour through their mighty power hath found the shine of heaven for man, the Āryas' light.

5 As in the game a gambler piles his winnings, so Maghavan, sweeping all together, gained the Sun.
This mighty deed of thine none other could achieve, none, Maghavan, before thee, none in recent time.

6 Maghavan came by turns to all the tribes of men : the Steer took notice of the people's songs of praise.
The man in whose libations Śakra hath delight by means of potent Somas vanquisheth his foes.

7 When Soma streams together unto Indra flow like waters to the river, rivulets to the lake,
In place of sacrifice sages exalt his might, as the rain swells the corn by moisture sent from heaven.

8 He rushes through the region like a furious Bull, he who hath made these floods the dames of worthy lords.
This Maghavan hath found light for the man who brings oblation, sheds the juice, and promptly pours his gifts.

9 Let the keen axe come forth together with the light : here be, as erst, the teeming cow of sacrifice.
Let the Red God shine bright with his refulgent ray, and let the Lord of heroes glow like heaven's clear sheen.

10 O Much-invoked, may we subdue all famine and evil want with store of grain and cattle.
May we allied, as first in rank, with princes obtain possessions by our own exertion.

11 Bṛhaspati protect us from the rearward, and from above, and from below, from sinners.
May Indra from the front, and from the centre, as Friend to friends, vouchsafe us room and freedom.

HYMN XLIV. *Indra.*

1. MAY Sovran Indra come to the carousal, he who by Holy Law is strong and active,
The overcomer of all conquering forces with his great steer-like power that hath no limit.

2 Firm-seated is thy car, thy Steeds are docile ; thy hand, O King, holds, firmly grasped, the thunder.
On thy fair path, O Lord of men, come quickly : we will increase thy powers when thou hast drunken.

3 Let strong and mighty Steeds who bear this Mighty Indra, the Lord of men, whose arm wields thunder,
Bring unto us, as sharers of our banquet, the Steer of conquering might, of real vigour.

4 So like a Bull thou rushest to the Lord who loves the trough, the Sage, the prop of vigour, in the vat,
Prepare thine energies, collect them in thyself : be for our profit as the Master of the wise.

5 May precious treasures come to us—so will I pray. Come to the votary's gift offered with beauteous laud.
Thou art the Lord, as such sit on this holy grass : thy vessels are inviolate as Law commands.

6 Far went our earlist invocation of the Gods, and won us glories that can never be surpassed.

3 *Turns away*: Sāyaṇa makes *viṣuvṛ'* transitive:—'May Indra be the remover of thirst and hunger.'—Wilson.

5 *Gained the Sun*: conquers him by taking away his moisture, that is, the water that he has absorbed.—Sāyaṇa.

8 *The dames of worthy lords*: that is, subjected them to the Āryans, whereas they had been the thralls of Dāsas. See I 32. 11.

9 *The keen axe*: Agni, who is frequently likened to an axe. See I, 127. 3, and VI. 3. 4. *The Red God*: *aruṣaḥ*: according to Sāyaṇa, 'the radiant Indra'; but Agni is probably intended, or perhaps 'the red bolt' as M. Müller prefers.

10 The two concluding stanzas are identical in Hymns 52, 53, 54.

4 *The Lord*: *patim*: the Soma. *Collect them in thyself*: take us into thyself.—Wilson. *Of the wise*: *kenipānām* is thus explained by the Commentators, but the meaning seems doubtful. Ludwig thinks that 'the master *of the oars*' that is, the steersman, is intended.

6 *In desolation* : *irmā*—Ludwig. *Trembling in alarm*: or, doers of ill deeds according to Yāska's interpretation of *képayaḥ*.

They who could not ascend the ship of sacrifice, sink down in desolation, trembling with alarm.

7 So be the others, evil-hearted, far away, whose horses, difficult to harness, have been yoked.
Here in advance men stand anear to offer gifts, by whom full many a work that brings reward is done.

8 He firmly fixed the plains and mountains as they shook. Dyaus thundered forth and made the air's mid-region quake.
He stays apart the two confronting bowls; he sings lauds in the potent Soma's joy when he hath drunk.

9 I bear this deftly-fashioned goad of thine, wherewith thou, Maghavan, shalt break the strikers with the hoof.
At this libation mayst thou be well satisfied. Partake the juice, partake the worship, Maghavan.

10 O Much-invoked, may we subdue all famine and evil want with store of grain and cattle.
May we allied, as first in rank, with princes obtain possessions by our own exertion.

11 Bṛhaspati protect us from the rearward, and from above, and from below, from sinners.
May Indra from the front and from the centre, as Friend to friends, vouchsafe us room and freedom.

HYMN XLV. *Agni.*

1. First Agni sprang to life from out of Heaven : the second time from us came Jātavedas.
Thirdly the Manly-souled was in the waters. The pious lauds and kindles him the Eternal.

2 Agni, we know thy three powers in three stations, we know thy forms in many a place divided.
We know what name supreme thou hast in secret : we know the source from which thou hast proceeded.

3 The Manly-souled lit thee in sea and waters, man's Viewer lit thee in the breast of heaven,
There as thou stoodest in the third high region the Steers increased thee in the water's bosom.

4 Agni roared out, like Dyaus what time he thunders : he licked the ground, about the plants he flickered.
At once, when born, he looked around enkindled, and lightened heaven and earth within with splendour.

5 The spring of glories and support of riches, rouser of thoughts and guardian of the Soma,
Good Son of Strength, a King amid the waters, in forefront of the Dawns he shines enkindled.

6 Germ of the world, ensign of all creation, be sprang to life and filled the earth and heavens.
Even the firm rock he cleft when passing over, when the Five Tribes brought sacrifice to Agni.

7 So among mortals was Immortal Agni stablished as holy wise and willing envoy.
He waves the red smoke that he lifts above him, striving to reach the heavens with radiant lustre.

8 Like gold to look on, far he shone refulgent, beaming imperishable life for glory,
Agni by vital powers became immortal when his prolific Father Dyaus begat him.

9 Whoso this day, O God whose flames are lovely, prepares a cake, O Agni, mixt with butter,

7 *Whose horses, difficult to harness, have been yoked*: whose ill-managed attempts to perform acceptable sacrifice have failed. *In advance*: before death according to Sāyaṇa.

8 *He* Indra. *As they shook*: cp. 11. 12. 2. *Two confronting bowls*: heaven and earth.

9 *Goad*: the hymn of praise which urges Indra to action. *The strikers with the hoof*: a class of Yātudhāhas or demons. See X. 87. 12.

1 *From out of heaven*: or, from Dyaus or Heaven his father; in the shape of the Sun. *From us*: produced by men in the shape of sacrificial and domestic fire. *In the waters*: of the firmament, in the shape of lightning, the third form of Agni.

2 *In secret*: unknown to those who know not the Veda.—Sāyaṇa.

3 *The Manly souled*: or, the Friend of men: Varuṇa, according to Sāyaṇa, and Prajāpati, according to Mahīdhara. Perhaps Dyaus (cp. stanza 8) may be intended—Ludwig. Grassmann thinks that Indra, the kindler of the lightning, is meant. *The Steers*: or, the Mighty Ones ; the Maruts.

6 *The firm rock*: 'the solid cloud.'—Wilson. Some extraordinary conflagration of jungle may perhaps be referred to. *The Five Tribes*: *pañca janāh*: literally, the five men, meaning, according to Sāyaṇa, men in general, and, according to Mahīdhara, the institutor of the sacrifice and the four chief priests.

Lead thou and further him to higher fortune, to bliss bestowed by Gods, O thou Most Youthful.

10 Endow him, Agni, with a share of glory, at every song of praise sung forth enrich him.

Dear let him be to Sūrya, dear to Agni, preëminent with son and children's children.

11 While, Agni, day by day men pay thee worship they win themselves all treasures worth the wishing.

Allied with thee, eager and craving riches, they have disclosed the stable filled with cattle.

12 Agni, the Friend of men, the Soma's keeper, Vaiśvānara, hath been lauded by the Ṛṣis.

We will invoke benignant Earth and Heaven : ye Deities, give us wealth with hero children.

HYMN XLVI. *Agni.*

1. STABLISHED for thee, to lend thee vital forces, Giver of wealth, Guard of his servant's body.

The Great Priest, born, who knows the clouds, Abider with men, is seated in the lap of waters.

2 Worshipping, seeking him with adoration like some lost creature followed by its footprints,

Wise Bhṛgus, yearning in their hearts, pursued him, and found him lurking where the floods are gathered.

3 On the Cow's forehead, with laborious searching, Trita, the offspring of Vibhūvas, found him.

Born in our houses, Youthful, joy-bestower, he now becomes the central point of brightness.

4 Yearning, with homage, they have set and made him blithe Priest among mankind, oblation-bearer,

Leader of rites and Purifier, envoy of men, as sacrifice that still advances.

5 The foolish brought the ne'er-bewildered forward, great, Victor, Song-inspirer, Fort-destroyer.

Leading the Youth gold-bearded, like a courser gleaming with wealth, they turned their hymn to profit.

6 Holding his station firmly in the houses, Trita sat down within his home surrounded

Thence, as Law bids, departs the Tribes' Companion having collected men with no compulsion.

7 His are the fires, eternal, purifying, that make the houses move, whose smoke is shining,

White, waxing in their strength, for ever stirring, and sitting in the wood ; like winds are Somas.

8 The tongue of Agni bears away the praise-song, and, through his care for Earth, her operations.

Him, bright and radiant, living men have stablished as their blithe Priest, the Chief of Sacrificers.

9 That Agni, him whom Heaven and Earth engendered, the Waters. Tvaṣṭar, and with might, the Bhṛgus,

12 *Soma's keeper*: as identified with the Moon, the great receptacle of the celestial Soma, the nectar or ambrosia of the Gods. See Hillebrandt, *V. M.*, I. 330—336.

---

1 *For thee*: the Ṛṣi addresses himself *Who knows the clouds*: from which he (Agni) comes in the form of Lightning. *Of waters*: of the firmament.

2 *Wise Bhṛgus*: frequently mentioned as specially connected with the worship of Agni. Cf II. 4. 2. *Pursued him*: see I. 65. 1.

3 *On the Cow's forehead*: 'on the head of the cloud.' *Trita*: Agni in his third form as lightning. The abstract personified form of the celestial Agni is here represented as endeavouring to find the lurking fire in the sky.—Macdonell. *Offspring of Vibhūvas* : or, connected with Vibhūvasu, the very wealthy, Soma.

4 *As sacrifice that still advances* : 'als das sich vorwärts bewegende opfer.' —Ludwig. According to Sāyaṇa, 'the object of sacrifice, him who goes forward (from one fire receptacle to another).'

5 *The foolish* : human priests, weak and foolish in comparison with the wise Agni. *Gleaming with wealth* : the meaning of *dhánarcam* is uncertain. The St. Petersburg Lexicon offers *dhanarjam*, 'striving to win the prize' as probably the right reading.

6 On stanzas 3 and 6 see Macdonell (J. R. A. S., July, 1893, pp. 450—452), who translates the second half of 6 as follows : From hence the house-friend of settlers collecting (them) goes among men by distribution, not by (means of) bonds; *i. e.* carried from place, not freshly produced by cord and drill.

7 *That make the houses move* : this seems to be what the words *damām aritrā* should mean, though how flames can be thus qualified is not clear. 'The rescuers from the humiliated (spirits of ill).'—Wilson. 'Protectors of the houses.'—Mahidhara. *Like winds are Somas* : as winds fan flame, so Soma libations increase the might of Agni. According to Sāyaṇa, the flames are 'like the fast-flowing juices of the *Soma*.'—Wilson. I follow Ludwig's explanation, but the meaning of the passage is doubtful

8 *Her operations* : holy works performed by men.

Him Mātariśvan and the Gods have fashioned holy for man and first to be entreated.

10 Agni, whom Gods have made oblation-bearer, and much-desiring men regard as holy,
Give life to him who lauds thee when he worships, and then shall glorious men in troops adore thee.

HYMN XLVII. *Indra Vaikuṇṭha.*

1. THY right hand have we grasped in ours, O Indra, longing for treasure, Treasure-Lord of treasures!
Because we know thee, Hero, Lord of cattle : vouchsafe us mighty and resplendent riches.

2 Wealth, fully armed, good guard and kind protector, sprung from four seas, the prop and stay of treasures,
Fraught with great bounties, meet for praise and glory ; vouchsafe us mighty and resplendent riches.

3 Wealth, with good Brahmans, Indra ! God-attended, high, wide, and deep, and based on broad foundations,
Strong, with famed Ṛṣis, conquering our foemen : vouchsafe us mighty and resplendent riches.

4 Victorious, winning strength, with hero sages, confirmed in power, most useful, wealth-attracting,
True, Indra ! crushing forts and slaying Dasyus : vouchsafe us mighty and resplendent riches.

5 Wealthy in heroes and in cars and horses, strength hundredfold and thousandfold, O Indra,
With manly sages, happy troops, light-winning : vouchsafe us mighty and resplendent riches.

6 To Saptagu the sage, the holy-minded, to him, Bṛhaspati, the song approaches,
Aṅgiras' Son who must be met with homage : vouchsafe us mighty and resplendent riches.

7 My lauds, like envoys, craving loving-kindness, go forth to Indra with their strong entreaty,
Moving his heart and uttered by my spirit : vouchsafe us mighty and resplendent riches.

8 Grant us the boon for which I pray, O Indra, a spacious home unmatched among the people.
To this may Heaven and Earth accord approval : vouchsafe us mighty and resplendent riches.

HYMN XLVIII. *Indra Vaikuṇṭha.*

1. I WAS the first possessor of all precious gear : the wealth of every man I win and gather up.
On me as on a Father living creatures call ; I deal enjoyment to the man who offers gifts.

2 I, Indra, am Atharvan's stay and firm support : I brought forth kine to Trita from the Dragon's grasp.
I stripped the Dasyus of their manly might, and gave the cattle-stalls to Mātariśvan and Dadhyac.

3 For me hath Tvaṣṭar forged the iron thunderbolt : in me the Gods have centred intellectual power.
My sheen is like the Sun's insufferably bright : men honour me as Lord for past and future deeds.

4 I won myself these herds of cattle, steeds and kine, and gold in ample store, with my destructive bolt.
I give full many a thousand to the worshipper, what time the Somas and the lauds have made me glad.

5 Indra am I ; none ever wins my wealth from me : never at any time am I a thrall to death.
Pressing the Soma, ask riches from me alone : ye, Pūrus, in my friendship shall not suffer harm.

9 *Mātariśvan* : a divine or semi-divine being who brought Agni from heaven. See I. 31. 3, and 60. 1.

Vaikuṇṭha is said to mean son of Vikuṇṭhā, an Asurī or female demon who was allowed by Indra to become his second mother.

2 *Wealth* : Sāyaṇa gives another interpretation :—'(We know thee to be) well armed' etc.—Wilson. *Sprung from four seas* : regarded as the store-houses of jewels. '(Renowned throughout) the four oceans.'—(applied to Indra) Wilson.

6 *Bṛhaspati* : according to the Scholiast meaning Saptagu. 'the lord of much (praise)'.—Wilson. According to others, the God Bṛhaspati called Saptagu as being drawn by seven oxen : 'der fährt mit sieben Rindern'—Grassmann. *Aṅgiras' Son* : meaning apparently Bṛhaspati as especially loved and honoured by Aṅgiras and his descendants. See VI. 73. 1.

8 *Unmatched* : *ásamam* : 'not held in common.'—Wilson.

Indra Vaikuṇṭha is the Ṛṣi of this hymn, which is a self-laudatory reply to Saptagu in Hymn XLVII.

2 *Atharvan* is the name of the priest who first obtained fire and offered Soma and prayers to the Gods. See I. 80. 16, and 83. 5. *The Dragon* is apparently Ahi or Vṛtra. 'I generated the waters above the cloud for the sake of Trita.'—Wilson. *Mātariśvan and Dadhyac* : or, according to Sāyaṇa, 'Mātariśvan's son Dadhyac.'

5 *Ye, Pūrus* : 'O men.'—Wilson.

6 These, breathing loud in fury, two and two, who caused Indra to bring his bolt of thunder to the fray,
The challengers, I struck with deadly weapon down : firm stand what words the God speaks to his worshippers.

This One by stronger might I conquered singly ; yea, also two : shall three prevail against me ?
Like many sheaves upon the floor I thrash them. How can my foes, the Indraless, revile me ?

8 Against the Gungus I made Atithigva strong, and kept him mid the folk like Vṛtra-conquering strength,
When I won glory in the great foe-slaying fight, in battle where Karañja fell, and Parṇaya.

9 With food for mine enjoyment Sāpya Namī came : he joined me as a friend of old in search of kine.
As I bestowed on him an arrow for the fight I made him worthy of the song and hymn of praise.

10 One of the two hath Soma, seen within it ; the Herdsman with the bone shows forth the other.
He, fain to fight the Bull whose horns were sharpened, stood fettered in the demon's ample region.

11 I, as a God, ne'er violate the statutes of Gods, of Vasus, Rudriyas, Ādityas.
These Gods have formed me for auspicious vigour, unconquered and invincible for ever.

6 *These* : who these were is uncertain. *Two and two* : probably the warrior who fights on the chariot and the charioteer.—Ludwig. The literal translation of the last half-line of the stanza appears to be:—'the non-worshipper speaking firm words to worshippers ; *ánamasyuḥ*, he who has no other to reverence, being Indra, whose promise of victory to his worshippers is never broken.'—Ludwig.

7 *This One* : or, this one thing, that is, 'the primordial substance or unit out of which the universe was developed.' —Wallis, *Cosmology of the Ṛgveda*, p. 58.

8 *Against the Gungus* : or, to aid the Gungus, as Sāyaṇa explains. Who these people were is uncertain. *Atithigva*: Divodāsa, son of Atithigu, according to Sāyaṇa. See Vol. I., Index. *Karañja...and Parṇaya* : apparently tree-demons. See I. 53. 8.

9 *Sāpya* : a famous name of Indra's friend Nami, who in VI. 20. 6 is called Sayya's son.

10 *One of the two* : *i. e.* Moon. *The Herdsman* : Indra. *With the bone* : of Dadhyac. See I. 84. 13. *The other* : Vṛtra. *He* : Vṛtra. *The Bull* : Indra. *The demon's ample region* : mid-air, which was then dominated by the Druh or malignant spirit of drought. I follow Prof. Ludwig's interpretation of this obscure stanza which is evidently an interpolation motivated by the mention of Dadhyac in stanza 2. For a somewhat different interpretation, see Hillebrandt, *V. M.*, I. 337.

11 *Rudriyas* : the Maruts, sons of Rudra.

HYMN XLIX. *Indra Vaikuṇṭha.*

1. I HAVE enriched the singer with surpassing wealth ; I have allowed the holy hymn to strengthen me.
I, furtherer of him who offers sacrifice, have conquered in each fight the men who worship not.

2 The People of the heavens, the waters, and the earth have stablished me among the Gods with Indra's name.
I took unto myself the two swift vigorous Bays that speed on divers paths, and the fierce bolt for strength.

3 With deadly blows I smote Atka for Kavi's sake ; I guarded Kutsa well with these my saving helps.
As Śuṣṇa's slayer I brandished the dart of death : I gave not up the Āryan name to Dasyu foes.

4 Smadibha, Tugra, and the Vetasus I gave as prey to Kutsa, father-like, to succour him.
I was a worthy King to rule the worshipper, when I gave Tuji dear inviolable gifts.

5 I gave up Mṛgaya to Śrutarvan as his prey because he ever followed me and kept my laws.
For Āyu's sake I caused Veśa to bend and bow, and into Savya's hand delivered Paḍgṛbhi.

6 I, I crushed Navavāstva of the lofty car, the Dāsa, as the Vṛtra-slayer kills the fiends ;
When straightway on the region's farthest edge I brought the God who makes the lights to broaden and increase.

Indra Vaikuṇṭha is the Ṛṣi also.

3 *Atka* : mentioned again in Hymn 99 of this Book. *Kavi* : the father of Indra's friend Uśanā.

4 *Smadibha* : or, as an adjective joined with Tugra, 'with all his followers.' See VI. 20. 8, where *Vetasu* and *Tugra* are mentioned as having been conquered by Indra, and VI. 26. 4, where their names occur again together with that of Tuji.

5 *Mṛgaya* : a demon of the air. See IV. 16. 13, and VIII. 3. 19. *Śrutarvan* : a prince whose liberality is lauded in VIII. 63. *Āyu* : sometimes spoken of as a King favoured by Indra and at other times as conquered by him. See Index. The name of *Veśa* does not occur again. *Savya* : the Ṛṣi of Hymns 51—57 of Book I. *Paḍgṛbhi*: some demon or savage enemy who is not mentioned again.

6 *Navavāstva* : see I. 36. 18, and VI. 20. 11. *Of the lofty car* : or Bṛhadratha, as a name of Navavāstva. *The lights* : the stars or perhaps light in general. In the former case *the God* would be Dyaus or Varuṇa, and in the latter case Sūrya or the Sun.—Ludwig.

7 I travel round about borne onward in my might by the fleet-footed dappled Horses of the Sun.
When man's libation calls me to the robe of state I soon repel the powerful Dasyu with my blows.

8 Stronger am I than Nahus, I who slew the seven : I glorified with might Yadu and Turvaśa.
I brought another low, with strength I bent his strength : I let the mighty nine-and-ninety wax in power.

9 Bull over all the streams that flow along the earth, I took the Seven Rivers as mine own domain.
I, gifted with great wisdom, spread the floods abroad : by war I found for man the way to high success.

10 I set within these cows the white milk which no God, not even Tvaṣṭar's self, had there deposited,—
Much-longed-for, in the breasts, the udders of the kine, the savoury sweets of meath, the milk and Soma juice.

11 Even thus hath Indra Maghavan, truly bounteous, sped Gods and men with mighty operation.
The pious glorify all these thine exploits, Lord of Bay Coursers, Strong, and Self-resplendent.

HYMN L. *Indra Vaikuṇṭha.*

1. I LAUD your Mighty One who joyeth in the juice, him who is shared by all men, who created all ;
Indra, whose conquering strength is powerful in war, whose fame and manly vigour Heaven and Earth revere.

2 He with his friend is active, lauded, good to man, Indra who must be glorified by one like me.
Hero, Lord of the brave, all cars are thy delight, warring with Vṛtra, or for waters, or for spoil.

3 Who are the men whom thou wilt further, Indra, who strive to win thy bliss allied with riches?
Who urged thee forward to exert thy power divine, to valour, in the war for waters on their fields ?

4 Thou, Indra, through the holy prayer art mighty, worthy of sacrifice at all libations.
In every fight thou castest heroes on the ground : thou art the noblest song, O Lord of all the folk.

5 Help now, as Highest, those who toil at sacrifice: well do the people know thy great protecting might.
Thou shalt be Everlasing, Giver of success : yea, on all these libations thou bestowest strength.

6 All these libations thou makest effectual, of which thou art thyself supporter, Son of Power.
Therefore thy vessel is to be esteemed the best, sacrifice, holy text, prayer, and exalted speech.

7 They who with flowing Soma pray to thee, O Sage, to pour on them thy gifts of opulence and wealth,
May they come forward, through their spirit, on the path of bliss, in the wild joy of Soma juice effused.

HYMN LI. *Agni. Gods.*

1. LARGE was that covering, and firm of texture, folded wherein thou enteredst the waters.
One Deity alone, O Jātavedas Agni, saw all thy forms in sundry places.

7 *The robe of state*: apparently the milk which is the royal mantle wherewith Soma is invested.

8 *Stronger am I than Nahus* : *náhuṣo náhuṣṭaraḥ* ; literally, more Nahus than Nahus; I out-Nahus Nahus, a King who contended with Indra : 'I am nearer than the neighbour,' according to Roth whom Grassmann follows. 'I am the especial bond of bonds.'—Wilson. I follow Ludwig's interpretation. *I who slew the seven* : the seven, perhaps, are the chief of the demons destroyed by Indra. Ludwig takes *saptahā* to mean 'seven times' :— 'I am seven times stronger than Nahus.' *Another* : whom, is uncertain. *Wax in power* : until they became worthy antagonists. 'I have demolished ninety and nine powerful (foes).'—Wilson.

10 *Milk and Soma juice*: sweet ambrosial rain; *the kine* being the teeming clouds.

11 In this stanza Indra—Ṛṣi addresses himself as the deity of the hymn.

2 *His friend* : his constant companion. the thunderbolt.
3 *Allied with riches* : the happiness which Indra sends being given in return for costly sacrificial offerings.
4 *Song* : *mántraḥ* : subject of thy worshippers' songs of praise.
6 *Vessel* : *pātram* : 'protection.'—Wilson.

The legend says that Agni, fearing to share the fate of his three elder brothers who had perished in the service of the Gods, fled away and hid himself in the waters. The Gods discovered him and persuaded him to return to his sacred duties.

Stanzas 1, 3, 5, 7, 9 are spoken by the Gods, and 2, 4, 6, 8 by Agni.

1 He must have been very well wrapped up, the Gods ironically say, or the water would have extinguished him.——Ludwig. *Forms* : literally, 'bodies.'

2 What God hath seen me? Who of all their number clearly beheld my forms in many places?
Where lie, then, all the sacred logs of Agni that lead him God-ward, Varuṇa and Mitra?

3 In many places, Agni Jātavedas, we sought thee hidden in the plants and waters.
Then Yama marked thee, God of wondrous splendour! effulgent from thy tenfold secret dwelling.

4 I fled in fear from sacrificial worship, Varuṇa, lest the Gods should thus engage me.
Thus were my forms laid down in many places. This, as my goal, I Agni saw before me.

5 Come; man is pious and would fain do worship; he waits prepared: in gloom thou, Agni, dwellest.
Make pathways leading God-ward clear and easy, and bear oblations with a kindly spirit.

6 This goal mine elder brothers erst selected, as he who drives a car the way to travel.
So, Varuṇa, I fled afar through terror, as flies the wild-bull from an archer's bow-string.

7 We give thee life unwasting, Jātavedas, so that, employed, thou never shalt be injured.
So, nobly born! shalt thou with kindly spirit bear to the Gods their share of men's oblations.

8 Grant me the first oblations and the latter, entire, my forceful shares of holy presents,
The soul of plants, the fatness of the waters, and let there be long life, ye Gods, to Agni.

9 Thine be the first oblations and the latter, entire, thy forceful shares of holy presents.
Let all this sacrifice be thine, O Agni, and let the world's four regions bow before thee.

HYMN LII. *Gods.*

1. Instruct me, all ye Gods, how I, elected your Priest, must seat me here, and how address you.
Instruct me how to deal to each his portion, and by what path to bring you man's oblation.

2 I sit as Priest most skilled in sacrificing: the Maruts and all Deities impel me.
Aśvins, each day yours is the Adhvaryu's duty: Brahman and wood are here: 'tis yours to offer.

3 Who is the Priest? Is he the Priest of Yama? On whom is thrust this God-appointed honour?
He springs to life each month, each day that passes; so Gods have made him their oblation-bearer.

4 The Gods have made me bearer of oblations, who slipped away and passed through many troubles.
Wise Agni shall ordain for us the worship, whether five-wayed, threefold, or seven-threaded.

2 *Sacred logs* : pieces of Śamī and Aśvattha wood, from which alone the sacrificial fire is produced. Others explain *samídhaḥ* by 'flames.'

3 *Thy tenfold secret dwelling* : according to Sāyaṇa, 'the three worlds,—heaven, mid-air, earth ; three divinities, Agni, Vāyu, Āditya; the waters, the shrubs, the trees, and the bodies of living beings.'—Wilson. The meaning appears to be, as Ludwig conjectures that Yama knew that Agni would appear again from the fire-sticks worked by the fingers of both hands.

8 *The first oblations and the latter* : or the Prayājas and the Anuyājas, the former being texts and oblations forming part of the introductory ceremony at a Soma sacrifice, and the latter the secondary or final offerings. *Forceful share* : the potent concentrated portion. *The fatness* : *ghṛtám* : *ghī*, clarified butter.

1 Agni, having been elected Oblation-bearer, asks the Gods to instruct him in his duties.

3 The first line is spoken by some God who doubts Agni's competence. *Is he the Priest of Yama* ? : can he convey offerings to the Blest in the realms of the God of the departed ? In the second half of the first line I follow Ludwig, but the meaning is uncertain. The second line is the answer of another God. *Each month, each day*; the *Pitṛyajña*, or sacrifice to the Fathers, is offered monthly, and the *Agnihotra*, or oblation to Agni and the Gods, daily. These comprehend all other periodical rites.

4 The first line is spoken by Agni. *Slipped away* : see the preceding hymn. The second line is what the Gods said. *Five-wayed* : consisting of five courses or parts, see X. 124. 1. *Threefold* : consisting of the three daily Soma-libations, see X. 124. 1. *Seven-threaded* : performed by seven priests. See X. 124. 1.

Stanza 5 is spoken by Agni. Stanza 6 is the poet's conclusion.

For an explanation of the number of the Gods (33—305—3003) see *The Hymns of the Atharva-veda*, X. 7. 13, note.

On Hymns 51—53 see Macdonell, J. R. A. S., January, 1894, pp 11-22.

5 So will I win you strength and life for ever, O Gods, that I may give you room and freedom.
To Indra's arms would I consign the thunder; in all these battles shall he then be victor.

6 The Deities three hundred and thirty-nine, have served and honoured Agni,
Strewn sacred grass, anointed him with butter, and seated him as Priest, the Gods' Invoker.

HYMN LIII. *Agni Saucīka Gods.*

1. He hath arrived, he whom we sought with longing, who skilled in sacrifice well knows its courses.
Let him discharge his sacrificial duties: let him sit down as Friend who was before us.

2 Best Priest, he hath been won by being seated, for he hath looked on the well-ordered viands.
Come, let us worship Gods who must be worshipped, and pouring oil, laud those who should be lauded.

3 Now hath he made the feast of Gods effective: now have we found the secret tongue of worship.
Now hath he come, sweet, robed in vital vigour, and made our calling on the Gods effective.

4 This prelude of my speech I now will utter, whereby we Gods may quell our Asura foemen.
Eaters of strengthening food who merit worship, O ye Five Tribes, be pleased with mine oblation.

5 May the Five Tribes be pleased with mine oblation, and the Cow's Sons and all who merit worship.
From earthly trouble may the earth protect us, and air's mid realm from woe that comes from heaven.

6 Spinning the thread, follow the region's splendid light: guard thou the pathways well which wisdom hath prepared.
Weave ye the knotless labour of the bards who sing: be Manu thou, and bring the Heavenly People forth.

7 Lovers of Soma, bind the chariot traces fast: set ye the reins in order and embellish them.
Bring hitherward the car with seats where eight may sit, whereon the Gods have brought the treasure that we love.

8 Here flows Aśmanvatī: hold fast each other, keep yourselves up, and pass, my friends, the river.
There let us leave the Powers that brought no profit, and cross the flood to Powers that are auspicious.

9 Tvaṣṭar, most deft of workmen, knew each magic art, bringing most blessed bowls that hold the drink of Gods.
His axe, wrought of good metal, he is sharpening now, wherewith the radiant Brahmaṇaspati will cut.

10 Now, O ye Sapient Ones, make ye the axes sharp wherewith ye fashion bowls to hold the Amṛta.
Knowing the secret places make ye ready that whereby the Gods have gotten immortality.

11 Ye with a secret tongue and dark intention laid the maiden deep within, the calf within the mouth.

1 The Gods speak. *Courses* : or portions.

2 *By being seated* : 'by his seat (at the altar).'—Wilson.

3 *Tongue of worship* : Agni, by whose fiery tongues the Gods drink libations.

4 Agni speaks. *Asura foemen* : the Asuras in the later hymns of the Veda are evil spirits in perpetual hostility with the Gods, not to be confounded with the great celestial Asuras, the chiefs of the Gods, nor with the Rākṣasas, demons or ogres, who disturb the sacrifices of men.

5 *The Five Tribes* : according to some, says Yāska 'the Gandharvas, gods, Fathers, Asuras, and Rākṣasas.' See Muir, *O. S. Texts*, I. 177. But the five Āryan tribes may be intended. *The Cow's Sons* : the Maruts, children of Pṛśni. Von Roth explains *gojātāḥ* as 'born in the starry heaven.' See VII. 35. 14.

6 The Gods speak. *The region's splendid light* : the Sun. *Weave ye* : flames of Agni. Assist the singer in his holy task and let there be no difficulties in his way.

7 This stanza appears to begin a new hymn, made up of fragments. According to Sāyaṇa it is spoken by the Gods to one another.

8 *Aśmanvatī* : or, the stony stream. See *The Hymns of the Atharva-veda*, XII. 2. 26.

9 *Will cut* : perhaps, will cut and destroy demons; but the meaning is uncertain.

10 *O ye Sapient Ones* : ye Ṛbhus. *That* : perhaps Amṛta or celestial Soma juice. Cf. I. 20. 6; 110. 3.

11 The first line is obscure. '(The Maruts) placed a female in the enveloping hide (of a dead cow), and a calf in the mouth (of a dead cow).'—Wilson. According to this interpretation the miracle ascribed to them would somewhat resemble that mentioned in I. 110. 8. See Bergaigne, *La Religion Védique*, II. 27. The first half of the second line is hard to construe. Wilson paraphrases the line :—'daily the generous (fraternity of the Ṛbhus) offers suitable praise (to the gods), granting victory over our foes.' Prof. Geldner takes *kārá*, against the Pada text, as a locative, and renders the last half-line to the following effect :—"May he (the sacrificer), when he wishes to win, gain the victory in the race.'

They evermore are near us with their gracious help : successful is the song that strives for victory.

HYMN LIV. *Indra.*

1. I SING thy fame that, Maghavan, through thy Greatness the heavens and earth invoked thee in their terror,
Thou, aiding Gods, didst quell the power of Dāsas, what time thou holpest many a race, O Indra.

2 When thou wast roaming, waxen strong in body, telling thy might, Indra, among the people,
All that men called thy battles was illusion : no foe hast thou to-day, nor erst hast found one.

3 Who are the Ṛṣis, then, who comprehended before our time the bounds of all thy greatness ?
For from thy body thou hast generated at the same time the Mother and the Father.

4 Thou, Mighty Steer, hast four supremest natures, Asura natures that may ne'er be injured.
All these, O Maghavan, thou surely knowest, wherewith thou hast performed thy great achievements.

5 Thou hast all treasures in thy sole possession, treasures made manifest and treasures hidden.
Defer not thou, O Maghavan, my longing : thou. art Director, Indra, thou art Giver.

6 To him who set the light in things of splendour, and with all sweetness blent essential sweetness,
To Indra hath this welcome hymn that strengthens been uttered by the votary Bṛhaduktha.

HYMN LV. *Indra.*

1. FAR is that secret name by which, in terror, the worlds invoked thee and thou gavest vigour
The earth and heaven thou settest near each other, and Maghavan, madest bright thy Brother's Children.

2 Great is that secret name and far-extending, whereby thou madest all that is and shall be.
The Five Tribes whom he loveth well have entered the light he loveth that was made aforetime.

3 He filled the heaven and earth and all between them, Gods five times sevenfold in their proper seasons.
With four-and-thirty lights he looks around him, lights of one colour though their ways are divers.

4 As first among the lights, O Dawn, thou shonest, whereby thou broughtest forth the Stay of Increase,
Great art thou, matchless is thine Asura nature, who, high above, art kin to those beneath thee.

5 The old hath waked the young Moon from his slumber who runs his circling course with many round him.
Behold the Gods' high wisdom in its greatness : he who died yesterday to-day is living.

6 Strong is the Red Bird in his strength, great Hero, who from of old hath had no nest to dwell in.
That which he knows is truth and never idle : he wins and gives the wealth desired of many.

3 The question is rhetorical. The great Ṛṣis of the olden time could not comprehend thy greatness, much less can we comprehend it.

The Mother and the Father : Earth and Heaven, parents of all. See M. Müller, *India, What can it Teach Us* ?, p. 161.

4 *Asura* : divine, with a vague sense of supreme grandeur.

6 *Who set the light* : the first essential light.

———

1 *Far is that secret name* : thou art not present with us now. *In terror* : terrified by Vṛtra. *Thy Brother's Children* : according to Sāyaṇa, Indra's brother is Parjanya, the God of the rain-cloud, and his children are the gathered waters. Varuṇa and his stars are probably intended.—Ludwig.

3 *Gods five times sevenfold* : 'It cannot be doubted that the original Gods were the constellations.'—Ludwig. According to Sāyaṇa, the five orders of beings and the classes of seven; that is, Gods, men, Fathers and Rākṣasas, and the seven troops of Maruts, the seven rays of the Sun, the seven senses, etc. The *four-and-thirty lights* : are probably the sun, moon, and five planets, and the twenty seven lunar asterisms or mansions of the moon. According to Sāyaṇa, the *four-and-thirty* are eight Vasus, eleven Rudras, twelve Ādityas, Prajāpati, Vaṣaṭkāra, and Virāj.

4 *The Stay of Increase* : that which is the foundation and support of all subsistence; according to Sāyaṇa, the Sun. *Art kin to those beneath thee* : art allied and connected with men as provider of their food. The second line is difficult, and is differently interpreted by others.

5 Sāyaṇa explains this stanza differently, making Indra, identified with Time, the subject. I follow Ludwig's interpretation (Commentary, II. p. 203) which seems to be nearer to the sense of the words, and is simpler and more rational. *With many round him* : stars of the asterisms through which he passes.

6 *The Red Bird* : the Sun, with whom Indra is identified.

7 Through these the Thunderer gained strong manly vigour, through whom he waxed in power to smite down Vṛtra,—
Who through the might of Indra's operation came forth as Gods in course of Law and Order.

8 All-strong, performing works with his companion, All-marking, rapid Victor, Curse-averter,
The Hero, waxing, after draughts of Soma, blew far from heaven the Dasyus with his weapon.

HYMN LVI. *Viśvedevas.*

1. HERE is one light for thee, another yonder : enter the third and be therewith united.
Uniting with a body be thou welcome, dear to the Gods in their sublimest birth-place.

2 Bearing thy body, Vājin, may thy body afford us blessing and thyself protection.
Unswerving, stablish as it were in heaven thine own light as the mighty God's supporter.

3 Strong Steed art thou : go to the yearning Maidens with vigour, happily go to heaven and praises :
Fly happily to the Gods with easy passage, according to the first and faithful statutes.

4 Part of their grandeur have the Fathers also gained : the Gods have seated mental power in them as Gods.
They have embraced within themselves all energies, which, issuing forth, again into their bodies pass.

5 They strode through all the region with victorious might, establishing the old immeasurable laws.
They compassed in their bodies all existing things, and streamed forth offspring in many successive forms.

6 In two ways have the sons established in his place the Asura who finds the light, by the third act,
As fathers, they have set their heritage on earth, their offspring, as a thread continuously spun out.

7 As in a ship through billows, so through regions of air, with blessings, through toils and troubles
Hath Bṛhaduktha brought his seed with glory, and placed it here and in the realms beyond us.

HYMN LVII. *Viśvedevas.*

1. LET us not, Indra, leave the path, the Soma-presser's sacrifice :
Let no malignity dwell with us.

2 May we obtain, completely wrought, the thread spun out to reach the Gods,
That perfecteth the sacrifice.

3 We call the spirit hither with the Soma of our parted sires,
Yea, with the Fathers' holy hymns.

7 *Through these* : probably the stars are intended. '(Accompanied) by these Maruts.'—Wilson.
8 *His companion* : the thunderbolt.

'The mystical union of the Fathers with the rays of light is the fundamental idea underlying the abstruse allusions' of this funeral hymn. 'The poet bids the deceased man unite himself with the beams of the heavenly light; he takes occasion to celebrate the power and greatness of the Fathers, to whom the spirit of the departed is journeying ; and ends with a statement of the success of the journey for which he has prayed.' See Wallis, *Cosmology of the Ṛgveda*, pp. 72, 73.

1 *One light* : the earthly fire of the funeral pile. *Another* : in the firmament. *The third* : the light in the highest region above the firmament. *A body* : a new body after cremation. *Their sublimest birth-place* : the Sun.

2 *Vājin* : apparently the name of the deceased, the son of Bṛhaduktha the Ṛṣi of the hymn. The word means originally 'strong' strong steed' as in stanza 3.

3 *The yearning Maidens* : perhaps the Dawns; but the meaning of *suveniḥ* is uncertain. *To heaven and praises*: 'to the (land of) praise, and to the sky.'—Wallis.

4 *Of their grandeur* : of the greatness of the Gods.

5 *Establishing the old immeasurable laws* : or, in accordance with the more generally received interpretation of *dhāmāni* here, 'measuring ancient stations never measured out.'

6 *In two ways* : in heaven and on earth. *The sons* : explained by Sāyaṇa as the Aṅgirases, sons of Āditya. The Fathers in general appear to be intended. *The Asura* : Agni. *The third act* : or third sacred duty, that of continuing their family ; religious study and sacrifice being the first and second.—Sāyaṇa.

7 *Placed it here and in the realm beyond us* : established his offspring in heavenly regions as well as here upon earth.

Mr Wallis, from whose translation I have borrowed, remarks :—'The interpretation of one or two expressions is uncertain ; the general sense is clear. The rays of light are here the bodies of the fathers, which emanate from the sun, assume the forms of all things on the earth and of the later sacrificers, the descendants of the fathers, and again return to their birth-place in the sky from which they had extended themselves.'—*Cosmology of the Ṛgveda*, pp. 74, 75.

For Prof. Max Müller's translation of Hymns 57—60, with the legend founded upon them and ample elucidative matter, see Journal R. A. S., Vol. II. Part II., 1866, p. 426—465.

3 *The spirit* : of the deceased whose obsequies are performed. *Of our sires* : *nārāśaṁsena* : explained as meaning, suited to man; that is to deified men, the Fathers or Spirits of the Blest.

---

4 Thy spirit come to thee again for wisdom, energy, and life,
That thou mayst long behold the sun!

5 O Fathers, may the Heavenly Folk give us our spirit once again,
That we may be with those who live.

6 O Soma with the spirit still within us, blest with progeny,
May we be busied in the law.

HYMN LVIII. *Manas or Spirit.*

1. THY spirit, that went far away to Yama to Vivasvān's Son,
We cause to come to thee again that thou mayst live and sojourn here.

2 Thy spirit, that went far away, that passed away to earth and heaven,
We cause to come to thee again that thou mayst live and sojourn here.

3 Thy spirit, that went far away, away to the four-cornered earth,
We cause to come to thee again that thou mayst live and sojourn here.

4 Thy spirit, that went far away to the four quarters of the world,
We cause to come to thee again that thou mayst live and sojourn here.

5 Thy spirit, that went far away, away unto the billowy sea,
We cause to come to thee again that thou mayst live and sojourn here.

6 Thy spirit, that went far away to beams of light that flash and flow,
We cause to come to thee again that thou mayst live and sojourn here.

7 Thy spirit, that went far away, went to the waters and the plants,
We cause to come to thee again that thou mayst live and sojourn here.

8 Thy spirit, that went far away, that visited the Sun and Dawn,
We cause to come to thee again that thou mayst live and sojourn here.

9 Thy spirit, that went far away, away to lofty mountain heights,
We cause to come to thee again that thou mayst live and sojourn here.

10 Thy spirit, that went far away into this All that lives and moves,
We cause to come to thee again that thou mayst live and sojourn here.

11 Thy spirit, that went far away to distant realms beyond our ken,
We cause to come to thee again that thou mayst live and sojourn here.

12 Thy spirit, that went far away to all that is and is to be,
We cause to come to thee again that thou mayst live and sojourn here.

The hymn is an address to recall the fleeting spirit of a man at the point of death.

7 *Waters......plants* : cf. X. 16. 3.

HYMN LIX. *Nirṛti and Others.*

1. HIS life hath been renewed and carried forward as two men, car-borne, by the skilful driver.
One falls, then seeks the goal with quickened vigour. Let Nirṛti depart to distant places.

2 Here is the psalm for wealth, and food, in plenty : let us do many deeds to bring us glory.
All these our doings shall delight the singer. Let Nirṛti depart to distant places.

3 May we o'ercome our foes with acts of valour, as heaven is over earth, hills over lowlands.
All these our deeds the singer hath considered. Let Nirṛti depart to distant places.

4 Give us not up as prey to death, O Soma : still let us look upon the Sun arising.
Let our old age with passing days be kindly. Let Nirṛti depart to distant places.

5 O Asunīti, keep the soul within us, and make the days we have to live yet longer.
Grant that we still may look upon the sunlight : strengthen thy body with the oil we bring thee.

6 Give us our sight again, O Asunīti, give us again our breath and our enjoyment.
Long may we look upon the Sun uprising ;
O Anumati, favour thou and bless us.

1 *His life* : the life of Subandhu one of the Ṛsis of the hymn. According to Sāyaṇa the first line is a prayer :—'May the life of Subandhu be augmented so as to be more lasting and newer.'—Wilson. Subandhu is not mentioned in the text. *Two men* : the warrior and the charioteer. *One falls* : Sāyaṇa explains differently:—'he who falls (from life) increases (his) desire to live.'—Wilson. *Nirṛti* : the Goddess of death and destruction.

5 *Asunīti* : apparently the personification of a deity presiding over funerals. It may be a name for Yama, or it may mean 'guide to life' or 'way to life.' See Muir, *O. S. Texts*, V. 297, and Bergaigne, *La Religion Vedique* I. 96.

6 *Anumati* : a personification of the favour with which the Gods regard the sacrifices and prayers of the pious. 'Gracious (goddess).'—Wilson.

7 May Earth restore to us our vital spirit, may Heaven the Goddess and mid-air restore it.
May Soma give us once again our body, and Pūṣan show the Path of peace and comfort.

8 May both Worlds bless Subandhu, young Mothers of everlasting Law.
May Heaven and Earth uproot and sweep iniquity and shame away : nor sin nor sorrow trouble thee.

9 Health-giving medicines descend sent down from heaven in twos and threes,
Or wandering singly on the earth. May Heaven and Earth uproot and sweep iniquity and shame away : nor sin nor sorrow trouble thee.

10 Drive forward thou the wagon-ox, O Indra, which brought Uśīnarāṇī's wagon hither.
May Heaven and Earth uproot and sweep iniquity and shame away : nor sin nor sorrow trouble thee.

HYMN LX. *Asamāti and Others.*

1. BRINGING our homage we have come to one magnificent in look.
Glorified of the mighty Gods ;

2 To Asamāti, spring of gifts, lord of the brave, a radiant car,
The conqueror of Bhajeratha ;

3 Who, when the spear hath armed his hand, or even weaponless o'erthrows
Men strong as buffaloes in fight ;

4 Him in whose service flourishes Ikṣvāku, rich and dazzling-bright.
As the Five Tribes that are in heaven.

5 Indra, support the princely power of Rathaproṣṭhas matched by none,
Even as the Sun for all to see.

6 Thou for Agastya's sister's sons yokest thy pair of ruddy steeds.
Thou troddest niggards under foot, all those, O King, who brought no gifts.

7 This is the mother, this the sire, this one hath come to be thy life.
What brings thee forth is even this. Now come, Subandhu, get thee forth.

8 As with the leather thong they bind the chariot yoke to hold it fast,
So have I held thy spirit fast, held it for life and not for death, held it for thy security.

9 Even as this earth, the mighty earth, holds fast the monarchs of the wood.
So have I held thy spirit fast, held it for life and not for death, held it for thy security.

10 Subandhu's spirit I have brought from Yama, from Vivasvān's Son,
Brought it for life and not for death, yea, brought it for security.

11 The wind blows downward from on high, downward the Sun-God sends his heat,
Downward the milch-cow pours her milk : so downward go thy pain and grief.

8 *Iniquity and shame* : *rápas*, according to William's Dictionary means, defect, fault, sin, hurt, injury. In his Commentary on I. 69. 4. Sāyaṇa paraphrases *rapāṁsi*, the plural of the word, by *bādhakāni rākṣasādīni*, disturbing Rākṣasas, etc.

9 *In twos and threes* : according to Sāyaṇa, in the persons of the two Aśvins and of the three Goddesses Ilā, Sarasvatī, and Bhāratī.

10 *Uśīnarāṇī* must mean the wife of Uśīnara, chief of the Uśīnaras who are mentioned in later times as living in Madhyadeśa or the Midland country. The meaning of the line is not obvious.

Stanzas 8, 9, 10, which Prof. Grassmann places in his Appendix, are of a different character from that of the preceding part of the hymn, and seem to be a separate song or fragment of a song.

---

2 *Asamāti* : according to Sāyaṇa, the name of a King. But the word is more probably an adjective, as in stanza 5. qualifying *rátham*, car, and signifying unequalled. *Bhajeratha* : it is uncertain whether this is the name of a prince or of a country.

3 *Who* : Asamāti, according to Sāyaṇa.

4 *Ikṣvāku* : a prince or a people; the name does not occur again in the Ṛgveda. *The Five Tribes* : the deities regarded as forming five tribes corresponding to the five tribes on earth, in the same manner as the seven rivers of the land of the Āryans have their counterparts in heaven. See Muir, *O. S. Texts*, I. p. 177. Sāyaṇa explains differently :—'(so that) the five orders of men (are as happy) as if they were in heaven.'—Wilson.

5 *Rathaproṣṭhas* : the family of the prince. Asamāti or another, whose praises the poet celebrates.

6 *Agastya's sister's sons* : Bandhu and his brothers, the Ṛṣis of the hymn. Stanzas I—6 have no apparent connexion with the six stanzas that follow.

7 *This* : Agni, according to Sāyaṇa. The speaker probably means himself.—Ludwig. Subandhu seems to have been in a trance and apparently dead. 'It is supposed that the brothers of Subandhu have addressed their supplication to Agni, to restore him to life, and that he has come accordingly, being, as it were, his parent and begetter. Another interpretation explains the terms literally as, Subandhu, your father, mother, and son, have come to mourn your decease.'—Wilson.

8 *So have I held* : 'so has Agni placed,' according to Sāyaṇa.

11 *Thy pain and grief* : 'thy sin.'—Sāyaṇa.

12 Felicitous is this mine hand, yet more felicitous is this.
This hand contains all healing balms, and this makes whole with gentle touch.

HYMN LXI. *Viśvedevas.*

1. THE welcome speaker in the storm of battle uttered with might this prayer to win the Aśvins,
When the most liberal God, for Paktha, rescued his parents, and assailed the seven Hotras.

2 Cyavāna, purposing deceptive presents, with all ingredients, made the altar ready.
Most sweet-voiced Tūrvayāṇa poured oblations like floods of widely fertilizing water.

3 To his oblations, swift as thought, ye hurried, and welcomed eagerly the prayers he offered.
With arrows in his hand the Very Mighty forced from him all obedience of a servant.

4 I call on you the Sons of Dyaus, the Aśvins, that a dark cow to my red kine be added.
Enjoy my sacrifice, come to my viands, contented, not deceiving expectation.

10 Uttering praise to suit the rite Navagvas came speedily to win the damsel's friendship.
They who approached the twice-strong stable's keeper, meedless would milk the rocks that naught had shaken.

11 Swift was new friendship with the maid: they quickly accepted it as genuine seed and bounty.
Milk which the cow Sabardughā had yielded was the bright heritage which to thee they offered.

12 When afterwards they woke and missed the cattle, the speaker thus in joyful mood addressed them:
Matchless are singers through the Vasu's nature; he bringeth them all food and all possessions.

13 his followers then who dwelt in sundry places came and desired to slay the son of Nṛṣad.
Resistless foe, he found the hidden treasure of Śuṣṇa multiplied in numerous offspring.

14 Thou, called Effulgence, in whose threefold

12 *More felicitous is this* : my other hand, probably the right. *With gentle touch* : with light friction, laying on of hands, or hypnotizing passes.

This Hymn, as Ludwig observes, belongs to the most difficult, one might almost say most hopeless, portions of the Ṛgveda. It is made up of several parts which are in no intelligible connexion with one another.

1 According to the view taken by Pischel who has most carefully studied and elaborately discussed the first three stanzas (*Vedische Studien I.* pp. 71—77), they contain in brief the ancient story of Tūrvayāṇa, the young King of the Pakthas, and Cyavāna. Cyavāna, a favourite of the Aśvins who had restored him to youth (I. 116. 10, and 117. 13), intended to sacrifice to them, hoping with their aid to conquer Tūrvayāṇa and his parents. But Indra stays the sacrifice, drives the priests away, and enables Tūrvayāṇa who had poured rich libations to him to gain the victory over his opponent.

The welcome speaker : Tūrvayāṇa, whose words were welcome to the Gods. *To win the Aśvins* : *raúdram* : not addressed to Rudra,' but to the Aśvins who are called *raúdrau* in stanza 15, and, elsewhere, *rudrā* and *rudrávartanī*. *The most liberal God* ; Indra. *Paktha* : King of the Pakthas (see VII. 18.7), that is, apparently, Tūrvayāṇa, who has been mentioned in I.53. 10, and VI. 18. 13, as especially aided by Indra. *Seven Hotras* : the usual number of Hotar priests employed at important sacrifices.

2 *Deceptive presents* : his intended sacri ce was displeasing to Indra, whom, possibly, Cyavāna falsely pretended that he was about to worship. *With all ingredients* : required for the preparation of the Soma juice. *Poured oblations* : to Indra.

3 *To his oblations* : to the offerings of Cyavāna. *Ye*: Aśvins. *The Very Mighty* : Indra, who threatened Cyavāna, and made him his obedient servant.

4 The Ṛṣi now prays to the Aśvins on his own account, and asks for a dark-coloured cow as a reward. Sāyaṇa, whom Professors Ludwig and Grassmann follow, explains the second half of the first line more poetically : 'When the dark night retires before the purple oxen (of the chariot of the dawn).'—Wilson. 'When the black sits among the red cows; that is, while it is still dark, but the grey of morning is beginning to appear.'—Ludwig.

5 I pass over stanzas 5—9, which contain an ancient legend, probably the germ of the later story of Brahmā or Prajāpati and his daughter, concerning two deities or powers of nature, male and female. See Appendix.

10 *Navagvas* : 'the *Aṅgirasas*.'—Wilson. *The damsel's* : Sāyaṇa says that Pṛśni may be meant. Perhaps Saramā is intended. *The twice-strong stable's keeper* : the Paṇi or Paṇis who kept the stolen cows or vanished rays of light concealed. *Meedless* : as the Paṇis refused to give up the cows. *Would milk the rocks* : would force from the rocky prison the meed or honorarium which they deserved in the shape of the cows.

11 *Sabardughā* : 'nectar-yielding;' the general name or cows milked at sacrifices. *Which to thee they offered* : which the Aṅgirases offered to Indra.

12 The *Vasu* is Indra.

13 *The son of Nṛṣad* : Nārṣada, usually a patronymic of Kaṇva, but said to be in this place the name of a certain demon. *Resistless foe* : Indra.

14 Here begins another part of the hymn. Agni is addressed. *Effulgence* : identified with the Sun. *Threefold dwelling* : earth, firmament, and heaven.

dwelling, as in the light of heaven, the Gods are sitting,
Thou who art called Agni or Jātavedas, Priest, hear us, guileless Priest of holy worship.

15 And, Indra, bring, that I may laud and serve them, those Two resplendent glorious Nāsatyas,
Blithe, bounteous, man-like, to the sacrificer, honoured among our men with offered viands.

16 This King is praised and honoured as Ordainer: himself the bridge, the Sage speeds o'er the waters.
He hath stirred up Kakṣīvān, stirred up Agni, as the steed's swift wheel drives the felly onward.

17 Vaitaraṇa, doubly kinsman, sacrificer, shall milk the cow who ne'er hath calved, Sabardhu,
When I encompass Varuṇa and Mitra with lauds, and Aryaman in safest shelter.

18 Their kin, the Prince in heaven, thy nearest kinsman, turning his thought to thee thus speaks in kindness:
This is our highest bond: I am his offspring. How many others came ere I succeeded?

19 Here is my kinship, here the place I dwell in: these are my Gods; I in full strength am present.
Twice-born am I, the first-born Son of Order: the Cow milked this when first she had her being.

20 So mid these tribes he rests, the friendly envoy, borne on two paths, refulgent Lord of fuel.
When, like a line, the Babe springs up erectly, his Mother straight hath borne him strong to bless us.

21 Then went the milch-kine forth to please the damsel, and for the good of every man that liveth.
Hear us, O wealthy Lord; begin our worship. Thou hast grown mighty through Āśvaghna's virtues.

22 And take thou notice of us also, Indra, for ample riches, King whose arm wields thunder!
Protect our wealthy nobles, guard our princes unmenaced near thee, Lord of Tawny Coursers.

23 When he goes forth, ye Pair of Kings, for booty, speeding to war and praise to please the singer,—
I was the dearest sage of those about him,—let him lead these away and bring them safely.

24 Now for this noble man's support and comfort, singing with easy voice we thus implore thee:
Impetuous be his son and fleet his courser: and may I be his priest to win him glory.

25 If, for our strength, the priest with adoration to win your friendship made the laud accepted,
That laud shall be a branching road to virtue for every one to whom the songs are suited.

26 Glorified thus, with holy hymns and homage:—Of noble race, with Waters, God-attended—

15 *Man-like*: as men reward one who institutes a sacrifice for their benefit.

16 *This King*: Sūrya, the Sun-God. 'This royal Soma.'—Wilson. *Himself the bridge*: the long beams of light from the bridge by which Sūrya passes over the waters of the firmament or sea of air. *Kakṣīvān*: the celebrated Ṛṣi. See Vol. I., Index.

17 *Vaitaraṇa*: '(Agni), the conveyer (of all).'—Wilson. Agni is so called, probably as sacrificer for a prince Vitaraṇa. *Doubly kinsman*: closely allied to heaven and earth. *Sabardhu*: the Cow whose milk is used in sacrifice; also called Sabardughā, as in stanza 11. According to Ludwig, the New Year which has not yet distributed its treasures is meant.

18 *Their kin*: akin to Mitra, Varuṇa, and Aryaman. *The Prince*: *sūri*: Sūrya, the Sun-God. *Thy nearest kinsman*: Sūrya. I adopt Ludwig's interpretation of *nābhānédiṣṭhah*, which appears unintelligible as the name of the son of Manu who was deprived of his inheritance by his father according to the *Yajur-veda*, and by his brothers according to the *Aitareya-Brāhmaṇa*. But see Weber, *Episches im V. Ritual*, pp. 40f. *This*: Dyaus. *How many others*: many Savitars (suns that introduce the new year) have been before me.—Ludwig.

19 *These are my Gods*: 'these are my resplendent (rays).—Wilson. Probably the priests are intended.—Ludwig. *The Cow*: Aditi. *Milked this*: milked forth this universe.'—Wilson. Agni is the speaker of this stanza.

20 *He*: Agni. *Two paths*: from earth to heaven and from heaven to earth.

21 The reference in the first line is, apparently, to the imprisoned cows and Saramā (see stanza 10); but all explanations of the allusions in this hymn are more or less conjectural. Ludwig thinks that the reference may be to the actual milking of the sacrificial cows at the ceremony which this hymn accompanied. Wilson translates:—'The words of a desirable praise, of a certain tranquil person (Nābhānediṣṭha), attain the prototype (Indra). *Āśvaghna*: probably the patronymic of Vitaraṇa.—Ludwig. See note on Vaitaraṇa in stanza 17.

23 *He*: Āśvaghna Vitaraṇa. *Ye Pair of Kings*: Mitra and Varuṇa.

26 *Glorified thus*: that is, May Varuṇa glorified with song beginning, 'Of noble race, etc.,' enrich us. *Now*

May he enrich us for our prayers and praises : now can the cow be milked; the path is open.

27 Be to us, then, ye Gods who merit worship, be ye of one accord our strong protection,
Who went on various ways and brought us vigour, ye who are undeceivable explorers.

HYMN LXII. *Viśvedevas, Etc.*

1. YE who, adorned with guerdon through the sacrifice, have won you Indra's friendship and eternal life,
Even to you be happiness, Aṅgirases. Welcome the son of Manu, ye who are most wise.

2 The Fathers, who drave forth the wealth in cattle, have in the year's courses cleft Vala by Eternal Law:
A lengthened life be yours, O ye Aṅgirases. Welcome the son of Manu, ye who are most wise.

3 Ye raised the Sun to heaven by everlasting Law, and spread broad earth, the Mother, out on every side.
Fair wealth of progeny be yours, Aṅgirases. Welcome the son of Manu, ye who are most wise.

4 This kinsman in your dwellingplace speaks pleasant words: give ear to this, ye Ṛṣis, children of the Gods.
High Brahman dignity be yours, Aṅgirases. Welcome the son of Manu, ye who are most wise.

5 Distinguished by their varied form, these Ṛṣis have been deeply moved.
These are the sons of Aṅgiras : from Agni have they sprung to life.

6 Distinguished by their varied form, they sprang from Agni, from the sky.
Navagva and Daśagva, noblest Aṅgiras, he giveth bounty with the Gods.

can the cow be milked : it is now time for the morning Agnihotram.—Ludwig.

Prof. Grassmann has banished this almost unintelligible hymn to his Appendix.

1 *The son of Manu* : Nābhānediṣṭha Mānava. See X. 61. 18 note.

2 *The Fathers* : the Aṅgirases. *Vala* : the demon who stole the cows of the Gods.

3 *By everlasting Law* : 'by means of your sacrifice.' —Wilson.

4. *This kinsman* : or, this Nābhā, that is Nābhānediṣṭha.

5 *Distinguished by their varied form* : or, Virūpas. See III. 53. 7.

6 *From the sky* : or, from Dyaus. *Noblest Aṅgiras* : Agni himself, according to Sāyaṇa. He is also called Navagva and Daśagva as these priestly names or titles belong to or are closely connected with the Aṅgirases.

7 With Indra for associate the priests have cleared the stable full of steeds and kine,
Giving to me a thousand with their eight-marked ears, they gained renown among the Gods.

8 May this man's sons be multiplied ; like springing corn may Manu grow,
Who gives at once in bounteous gift a thousand kine, a hundred steeds.

9 No one attains to him, as though a man would grasp the heights of heaven.
Sāvarṇya's sacrificial meed hath broadened like an ample flood.

10 Yadu and Turva, too, have given two Dāsas, well-disposed, to serve,
Together with great store of kine.

11 Blest be the hamlet's chief, most liberal Manu, and may his bounty rival that of Sūrya.
May the God let Sāvarṇi's life be lengthened, with whom, unwearied, we have lived and prospered.

HYMN LXIII. *Viśvedevas.*

1. MAY they who would assume kinship from far away, Vivasvān's generations, dearly loved of men,
Even the Gods who sit upon the sacred grass of Nahuṣa's son Yayāti, bless and comfort us.

2 For worthy of obeisance, Gods, are all your names, worthy of adoration and of sacrifice.
Ye who were born from waters, and from Aditi, and from the earth, do ye here listen to my call.

7 *With their eight-marked ears* : having marks branded on their ears; or perhaps, with slit ears. Cf. *Hymns of the Atharva-veda*, VI. 141. 2.

8 *Manu* : here apparently the name of Sāvarṇi the prince whose munificence is the subject of stanzas 8—11. *A thousand kine, a hundred steeds* : 'kine' is conjecturally supplied. 'A thousand and a hundred horses.'—Wilson. 'A thousand times a hundred horses.'—Ludwig.

9 *Sāvarṇya* here means Sāvarṇi.

10 *Turva* : equivalent to Turvaśa; a prince of the clan called after the eponymus Turva. *Dāsas* : enslaved natives.

1 *Kinship* ; relationship with us, and the duties of protection and aid which relationship implies. Cf. I. 109. 7, note. *Vivasvān's generations* : Sāyaṇa supplies a verb, and explains differently :—(support) the generations of (Manu the son of) Vivasvat.'—Wilson. *Yayāti* : see I. 31. 17, and 108. 8, note.

2 *From waters* : the aerial waters, or intermediate region of air. *Aditi* : von Roth understands Aditi here to mean 'infinity', the boundlessness of heaven as opposed to the limitation of earth. See Muir, *O. S. Texts*, V. 39. Sāyaṇa's explanation is similar.

3 I will rejoice in these Ādityas for my weal, for whom the Mother pours forth water rich in balm,
And Dyaus the Infinite, firm as a rock, sweet milk,—Gods active, strong through lauds, whose might the Bull upholds.

4 Looking on men, ne'er slumbering, they by their deserts attained as Gods to lofty immortality.
Borne on refulgent cars, sinless, with serpents' powers, they robe them, for our welfare, in the height of heaven.

5 Great Kings who bless us, who have come to sacrifice, who, ne'er assailed, have set their mansion in the sky,—
These I invite with adoration and with hymns, mighty Ādityas, Aditi, for happiness.

6 Who offereth to you the laud that ye accept, O ye All-Gods of Manu, many as ye are?
Who, Mighty Ones, will prepare for you the sacrifice to bear us over trouble to felicity?

7 Ye to whom Manu, by seven priests, with kindled fire, offered the first oblation with his heart and soul,
Vouchsafe us, ye Ādityas, shelter free from fear, and make us good and easy paths to happiness.

8 Wise Deities, who have dominion o'er the world, ye thinkers over all that moves not and that moves,
Save us from uncommitted and committed sin, preserve us from all sin to-day for happiness.

9 In battles we invoke Indra still swift to hear, and all the holy Host of Heaven who banish grief,
Agni, Mitra, and Varuṇa that we may gain, Dyaus, Bhaga, Maruts, Pṛthivi for happiness :

10 Mightily-saving Earth, incomparable Heaven the good guide Aditi who gives secure defence
The well-oared heavenly Ship that lets no waters in, free from defect, will we ascend for happiness.

11 Bless us, all Holy Ones, that we may have your help, guard and protect us from malignant injury.
With fruitful invocation may we call on you, Gods, who give ear to us for grace, for happiness.

12 Keep all disease afar and sordid sacrifice, keep off the wicked man's malicious enmity.
Keep far away from us all hatred, O ye Gods, and give us ample shelter for our happiness.

13 Untouched by any evil, every mortal thrives, and, following the Law, spreads in his progeny.
Whom ye with your good guidance, O Ādityas, lead safely through all his pain and grief to happiness.

14 That which ye guard and grace in battle, O ye Gods, ye Maruts, where the prize is wealth, where heroes win,
That conquering Car, O Indra, that sets forth at dawn, that never breaks, may we ascend for happiness.

15 Vouchsafe us blessing in our paths and desert tracts, blessing in waters and in battle for the light ;
Blessing upon the wombs that bring male children forth, and blessing, O ye Maruts, for the gain of wealth.

16 The noblest Svasti with abundant riches, who comes to what is good by distant pathway,—
May she at home and far away preserve us, and dwell with us under the Gods' protection

17 Thus hath the thoughtful sage, the son of Plati, praised you, O Aditi and all Ādityas,
Men are made rich by those who are Immortal : the Heavenly Folk have been extolled by Gaya.

HYMN LXIV. *Viśvedevas.*

1. WHAT God, of those who hear, is he whose well-praised name we may record in this our sacrifice ; and how ?
Who will be gracious ? Who of many give us bliss ? Who out of all the Host will come to lend us aid ?

3 *The Mother* : Earth. *Dyaus* : Heaven. *The Bull* : the Sun. Sāyaṇa explains *vṛṣabharān* as 'bringers of rain.'

4 *With serpents' powers* : 'of unsurpassable wisdom'. —Wilson.

10 *The heavenly Ship* : according to Sāyaṇa, a metaphorical expression for sacrifice.

14 *For happiness* : *svastáye*, for happiness or welfare, recurs at the end of all the stanzas from 3 to 14 inclusive.

16 *Svastí* : Pathyā Svasti, according to the Index; the Goddess of prosperity and happiness.

17 *The son of Plati* : Gaya, the Ṛṣi of the hymn.

2 The will and thoughts within my breast exert their power : they yearn with love, and fly to all the regions round.
None other comforter is found save only these : my longings and my hopes are fixt upon the Gods.

3 To Narāśaṁsa and to Pūṣan I sing forth, unconcealable Agni kindled by the Gods.
To Sun and Moon, two Moons, to Yama in the heaven, to Trita, Vāta, Dawn, Night, and the Aśvins Twain.

4 How is the Sage extolled whom the loud singers praise ? What voice, what hymn is used to laud Bṛhaspati ?
May Aja-Ekapād with Ṛkvans swift to hear, and Ahi of the Deep listen unto our call.

5 Aditi, to the birth of Dakṣa and the vow thou summonest the Kings Mitra and Varuṇa.
With course unchecked, with many chariots Aryaman comes with the seven priests to tribes of varied sort.

6 May all those vigorous Coursers listen to our cry, hearers of invocation, speeding on their way ;
Winners of thousands where the priestly meed is won, who gather of themselves great wealth in every race.

7 Bring ye Purandhi, bring Vāyu who yokes his steeds, for friendship bring ye Pūṣan with your songs of praise :
They with one mind, one thought attend the sacrifice, urged by the favouring aid of Savitar the God.

8 The thrice-seven wandering Rivers, yea, the mighty floods, the forest trees, the mountains, Agni to our aid,
Kṛśānu, Tiṣya, archers to our gathering-place, and Rudra strong amid the Rudras we invoke.

9 Let the great Streams come hither with their mighty help, Sindhu, Sarasvatī, and Sarayu with waves.
Ye Goddess Floods, ye Mothers, animating all, promise us water rich in fatness and in balm.

10 And let Bṛhaddivā, the Mother, hear our call, and Tvaṣṭar, Father, with the Goddesses and Dames.
Ṛbhukṣan, Vāja, Bhaga, and Rathaspati, and the sweet speech of him who labours guard us well !

11 Pleasant to look on as a dwelling rich in food is the blest favour of the Maruts, Rudra's Sons.
May we be famed among the folk for wealth in kine, and ever come to you, ye Gods, with sacred food.

12 The thought which ye, O Maruts, Indra and ye Gods have given to me, and ye, Mitra and Varuṇa,—
Cause this to grow and swell like a milch-cow with milk. Will ye not bear away my songs upon your car ?

13 O Maruts, do ye never, never recollect and call again to mind this our relationship ?
When next we meet together at the central point, even there shall Aditi confirm our brotherhood.

14 The Mothers, Heaven and Earth, those mighty Goddesses, worthy of sacrifice, come with the race of Gods.
These Two with their support uphold both Gods and men, and with the Fathers pour the copious genial stream.

3 *Unconcealable Agni* : or, to the unconcealable (Savitar). and Agni. *Two Moons* : New Moon and Full Moon

4 *Aja-Ekapād* : see VI. 50. 14. *Ṛkvans* : singers ; minor deities who attend and sing the praises of some superior God. *Ahi of the Deep* : the great Dragon of the depths of the aerial ocean; Ahibudhnya. See Vol. I., Index.

5 *Dakṣa* : meaning here the Sun, according to Sāyaṇa. Ludwig thinks that the sacrificer, regarded as Dakṣa or Prajāpati, and said to be born again through completion of his vow, is intended. In the second line also *Aryaman* is considered by Sāyaṇa to be the Sun :—'Aryaman, whose course is not hurried, the giver of delight to many, having seven ministering (rays) proceeds in his multiform births.'—Wilson.

6 *Coursers* : the horses which bring the Gods to men's sacrifices.

7 *Purandhi* : Plenty personified as a deity. Or *purándhim* may be an adjective 'the spirited, or liberal. Pūṣan.'

8 *Thrice-seven* : the seven rivers of the Āryans having their counterparts in heaven and in the firmament. *Kṛśānu* : the archer who guards the heavenly Soma. *Tiṣya* : an asterism regarded as being in the form of an arrow, and so here identified with Kṛśānu.

10 *Bṛhaddivā* : a Goddess associated with Iḷā, Sarasvatī, and others. *Dames* : the consorts of the Gods. *Rathapati* : the God who presides over chariots of war. *Speech*: or prayer. *Who labours* : at the sacrifice.

13 *At the central point* : the place of sacrifice.

14 *With the Fathers* : 'The fruitfulness of heaven and earth, which give birth to gods and men, is described as produced by the fathers.' See Wallis, *Cosmology of the Ṛgveda*, p. 72.

15 This invocation wins all good that we desire Bṛhaspati, highly-praised Aramati, are here,
Even where the stone that presses meath rings loudly out, and where the sages make their voices heard with hymns.

16 Thus hath the sage, skilled in loud singers' duties, desiring riches, yearning after treasure,
Gaya, the priestly singer, with his praises and hymns contented the Celestial people.

17 Thus hath the thoughtful sage, the son of Plati, praised you, O Aditi and all Ādityas.
Men are made rich by those who are Immortal : the Heavenly Folk have been extolled by Gaya.

15 *Aramati* : the Genius of Devotion.
17 The concluding stanza of Hymn 63 is repeated here.

HYMN LXV. *Viśvedevas.*

1. May Agni, Indra, Mitra, Varuṇa consent, Aryaman, Vāyu, Pūṣan, and Sarasvatī, Ādityas, Maruts, Viṣṇu, Soma, lofty Sky, Rudra and Aditi, and Brahmaṇaspati.

2 Indra and Agni, Hero-lords when Vṛtra fell, dwelling together, speeding emulously on,
And Soma blent with oil, putting his greatness forth, have with their power filled full the mighty firmament.

3 Skilled in the Law I lift the hymn of praise to these, Law-strengtheners, unassailed, and great in majesty.
These in their wondrous bounty send the watery sea : may they as kindly Friends send gifts to make us great.

4 They with their might have stayed Heaven, Earth, and Pṛthivī, the Lord of Light, the firmament, the lustrous spheres.
Even as fleet-foot steeds who make their masters glad, the princely Gods are praised, most bountiful to man.

5 Bring gifts to Mitra and to Varuṇa who, Lords of all, in spirit never fail the worshipper,
Whose statute shines on high through everlasting Law, whose places of sure refuge are the heavens and earth.

6 The cow who yielding milk goes her appointed way hither to us as leader of holy rites,
Speaking aloud to Varuṇa and the worshipper, shall with oblation serve Vivasvān and the Gods.

7 The Gods whose tongue is Agni dwell in heaven, and sit, aiders of Law, reflecting, in the seat of Law.
They propped up heaven and then brought waters with their might, got sacrifice and in a body made it fair.

8 Born in the oldest time, the Parents dwelling round are sharers of one mansion in the home of Law.
Bound by their common vow Dyaus, Pṛthivī stream forth the moisture rich in oil to Varuṇa the Steer.

9 Parjanya, Vāta, mighty, senders of the rain, Indra and Vāyu, Varuṇa, Mitra, Aryaman :
We call on Aditi, Ādityas, and the Gods, those who are on the earth, in waters, and in heaven.

10 Tvaṣṭar and Vāyu, those who count as Ṛbhus, both celestial Hotar-priests, and Dawn for happiness,
Winners of wealth, we call, and wise Bṛhaspati, destroyer of our foes, and Soma Indra's Friend.

11 They generated prayer, the cow, the horse, the plants, the forest trees, the earth, the waters, and the hills.
These very bounteous Gods made the Sun mount to heaven, and spread the righteous laws of Āryas o'er the land.

12 O Aśvins, ye delivered Bhujyu from distress, ye animated Śyāva, Vadhṛmatī's son.
To Vimada ye brought his consort Kamadyū, and gave his lost Viṣṇāpū back to Viśvaka.

13 Thunder, the lightning's daughter, Aja-Ekapād, heaven's bearer, Sindhu, and the waters of the sea :
Hear all the Gods my words, Sarasvatī give ear together with Purandhi and with Holy Thoughts.

---

3 *The watery sea* : the clouds and rain.

4 *Pṛthivī* : meaning here the region of mid-air.

5 *Places of sure refuge*: Sāyaṇa explains *nādhasī* differently :—'upon whom the two *solicitous* worlds remain dependent.'

6 *The cow* : who is milked at sacrifice. According to Sāyaṇa, thunder may be meant, and by 'milk' strength may be intended.

7 *In a body* : that is, personified. Cf. X. 66. 9, note.

8 *The Parents* : Heaven and Earth.

10 *Celestial Hotar-priests* : See I. 13. 8.

12 These deeds of the Aśvins are told in I. 16 and 17.

13 *Aja-Ekapād* : see VI. 50. 14. *Holy Thoughts* : Devotions personified.

14 With Holy Thoughts and with Purandhi may all Gods, knowing the Law immortal, Manu's Holy Ones,
Boon-givers, favourers, finders of light, and Heaven, with gracious love accept my songs, my prayer, my hymn.

15 Immortal Gods have I, Vasiṣṭha, lauded, Gods set on high above all other beings.
May they this day grant us wide space and freedom : ye Gods, preserve us evermore with blessings.

HYMN LXVI. *Viśvedevas.*

1. I CALL the Gods of lofty glory for our weal, the makers of the light, well-skilled in sacrifice ;
Those who have waxen mightily, Masters of all wealth, Immortal, strengthening Law, the Gods whom Indra leads.

2 For the strong band of Maruts will we frame a hymn : the chiefs shall bring forth sacrifice for Indra's troop,
Who, sent by Indra and advised by Varuṇa, have gotten for themselves a share of Sūrya's light

3 May Indra with the Vasus keep our dwelling safe, and Aditi with Ādityas lend us sure defence.
May the God Rudra with the Rudras favour us, and Tvaṣṭar with the Dames further us to success.

4 Aditi, Heaven and Earth, the great eternal Law, Indra, Viṣṇu, the Maruts, and the lofty Sky.
We call upon Ādityas, on the Gods, for help, on Vasus, Rudras, Savitar of wondrous deeds.

5 With Holy Thoughts Sarasvān, firm-lawed Varuṇa, great Vāyu, Pūṣan, Viṣṇu, and the Aśvins Twain,
Lords of all wealth, Immortal, furtherers of prayer, grant us a triply-guarding refuge from distress.

6 Strong be the sacrifice, strong be the Holy Ones, strong the preparers of oblation, strong the Gods.
Mighty be Heaven and Earth, true to eternal Law, strong be Parjanya, strong be they who laud the Strong.

7 To win us strength I glorify the Mighty Twain, Agni and Soma, Mighty Ones whom many laud.
May these vouchsafe us shelter with a triple guard, these whom the strong have served in worship of the Gods.

8 Potent, with firm-fixt laws, arranging sacrifice, visiting solemn rites in splendour of the day,
Obeying Order, these whose priest is Agni, free from falsehood, poured the waters out when Vṛtra died.

9 The Holy Ones engendered, for their several laws, the heavens and earth, the waters, and the plants and trees.
They filled the firmament with heavenly light for help : the Gods embodied Wish and made it beautiful.

10 May they who bear up heaven, the Ṛbhus deft of hand, and Vāta and Parjanya of the thundering Bull,
The waters and the plants, promote the songs we sing : come Bhaga, Rāti, and the Vājins to my call.

11 Sindhu, the sea, the region, and the firmament, the thunder, and the ocean, Aja-Ekapād,
The Dragon of the Deep, shall listen to my words, and all the Deities and Princes shall give ear.

12 May we be yours, we men, to entertain the Gods : further our sacrifice and give it full success.
Ādityas, Rudras, Vasus, givers of good gifts, quicken the holy hymns which we are singing now

13 I follow with success upon the path of Law the two celestial Hotars, Priests of oldest time.
We pray to him who dwelleth near, Guard of the Field, to all Immortal Gods who never are remiss.

14 *Manu's Holy Ones* : deities whom Manu worshipped.

15 *Vasiṣṭha* : that is, a descendant of the great Ṛṣi Vasiṣṭha.

---

4 The names in the first line are in the nominative case and without a verb : 'are invoked', may be understood.

6 *Strong* : *vṛṣan* repeated in the way loved by some of the Vedic poets ; 'showerer of benefits,' according to Sāyaṇa. *The Gods* : meaning, says Sāyaṇa, the priests.

9 *Laws* : courses of action. *Embodied Wish* : gave a body to the wishes and hopes of worshippers, and personified them in the same manner as sacrifice is said to have been embodied and beautified in X. 65. 7.

10 *Vāta and Parjanya of the thundering Bull* : meaning the wind and storm that attend the thunderous rain-cloud. *Rāti* : divine Favour or Bounty. *Vājins*; a class of divinities according to Sāyaṇa. See VII. 38. 7.

11 *Aja-Ekapād* : See VI. 50. 14. *Dragon of the Deep*: Ahibudhnya. See VI. 49. 14.

13 *Two celestial Hotars* : Agni and Āditya, according to Sāyaṇa. *Guard of the Field* : probably Indra.

14 Vasiṣṭha's sons have raised their voices, like their sire. Ṛṣi-like praying to the Gods for happiness.
Like friendly-minded kinsmen, come at our desire, O Gods, and shake down treasures on us from above.

15 Immortal Gods have I, Vasiṣṭha, lauded, Gods set on high above all other beings.
May they this day grant us wide space and freedom : ye Gods, preserve us evermore with blessings.

HYMN LXVII. *Bṛhaspati.*

1. THIS holy hymn, sublime and seven-headed, sprung from eternal Law, our sire discovered.
Ayāsya, friend of all men, hath engendered the fourth hymn as he sang his laud to Indra.

2 Thinking aright, praising eternal Order, the sons of Dyaus the Asura, those heroes,
Aṅgirases, holding the rank of sages, first honoured sacrifice's holy statute.

3 Girt by his friends who cried with swan-like voices, bursting the stony barriers of the prison,
Bṛhaspati spake in thunder to the cattle, and uttered praise and song when he had found them.

4 Apart from one, away from two above him, he drave the kine that stood in bonds of falsehood.
Bṛhaspati, seeking light amid the darkness, drave forth the bright cows : three he made apparent.

5 When he had cleft the lairs and western castle, he cut off three from him who held the waters.
Bṛhaspati discovered, while he thundered like Dyaus, the dawn, the Sun, the cow, the lightning.

6 As with a hand, so with his roaring Indra cleft Vala through, the guardian of the cattle.
Seeking the milk-draught with sweat-shining comrades he stole the Paṇi's kine and left him weeping.

7 He with bright faithful Friends, winners of booty, hath rent the milker of the cows asunder.
Bṛhaspati with wild boars strong and mighty, sweating with heat, hath gained a rich possession.

8 They, longing for the kine, with faithful spirit incited with their hymns the Lord of cattle.
Bṛhaspati freed the radiant cows with comrades self-yoked, averting shame from one another.

9 In our assembly with auspicious praises exalting him who roareth like a lion,
May we, in every fight where heroes conquer, rejoice in strong Bṛhaspati the Victor.

10 When he had won him every sort of booty and gone to heaven and its most lofty mansions,
Men praised Bṛhaspati the Mighty, bringing the light within their mouths from sundry places.

11 Fulfil the prayer that begs for vital vigour : aid in your wonted manner even the humble.
Let all our foes be turned and driven backward. Hear this, O Heaven and Earth, ye All-producers.

12 Indra with mighty strength cleft asunder the head of Arbuda the watery monster,
Slain Ahi, and set free the Seven Rivers. O Heaven and Earth, with all the Gods protect us.

HYMN LXVIII. *Bṛhaspati.*

1. LIKE birds who keep their watch, plashing in water, like the loud voices of the thundering rain-cloud,

15 Repeated from the preceding hymn.

---

1 *Seven-headed* : having seven divisions. Accompanied by seven bands of the Maruts, or having seven metres, according to Sāyaṇa. *Our sire* : Aṅgiras. *Fourth* : or, extending to all four sides, mighty.

3 *The cattle* : the lost cows of the Aṅgirases, representing metaphorically the rays of light which had been stolen by the fiends of darkness. See I. 62. 3.

4 *Apart from one, away from two* : the meaning is uncertain. Perhaps at a distance from the earth, down from heaven and the firmament. *Falsehood* : the wickedness of the treacherous Paṇis. *Three* : heaven, firmament, and earth.

5 *Western castle* : this is obscure. Ludwig suggests that *ápācīm* may mean 'hostile' or 'detested.' *Three* : heaven, firmament, and earth. *Him who held the waters* : the demon Vala, who kept the rain, as well as the cows or rays of light, imprisoned. *The cow* : the cattle; the beams of light.

6 *Comrades* : his faithful friends the Maruts.

7 *Wild boars* : the strong fierce Maruts ; according to Sāyaṇa, 'bearers of excellent water.'

8 *The Lord of cattle* : Bṛhaspati, so called because he had released them.

10 *The light* : that is, the hymns of praise which will bring them the light of help. The stanza is difficult.

12 *The watery monster* : the fiend who dominated the ocean of air. *Ahi* : or, the Dragon, Vṛtra or his brother.

Like merry streamlets bursting from the mountain, thus to Bṛhaspati our hymns have sounded.

2 The Son of Aṅgiras, meeting the cattle, as Bhaga, brought in Aryaman among us.
As Friend of men he decks the wife and husband : as for the race, Bṛhaspati, nerve our coursers.

3 Bṛhaspati, having won them from the mountains, strewed down, like barley out of winnowing-baskets,
The vigorous, wandering cows who aid the pious, desired of all, of blameless form, well-coloured.

4 As the Sun dews with meath the seat of Order, and casts a flaming meteor down from heaven.
So from the rock Bṛhaspati forced the cattle, and cleft the earth's skin as it were with water.

5 Forth from mid air with light he drave the darkness, as the gale blows a lily from the river.
Like the wind grasping at the cloud of Vala, Bṛhaspati gathered to himself the cattle.

6 Bṛhaspati, when he with fiery lightnings cleft through the weapon of reviling Vala,
Consumed him as tongues eat what teeth have compassed : he threw the prisons of the red cows open.

7 That secret name borne by the lowing cattle within the cave Bṛhaspati discovered,
And drave, himself, the bright kine from the mountain, like a bird's young after the egg's disclosure.

8 He looked around on rock-imprisoned sweetness as one who eyes a fish in scanty water.
Bṛhaspati, cleaving through with varied clamour, brought it forth like a bowl from out the timber.

9 He found the light of heaven, and fire, and Morning : with lucid rays he forced apart the darkness.
As from a joint, Bṛhaspati took the marrow of Vala as he gloried in his cattle.

10 As trees for foliage robbed by winter, Vala mourned for the cows Bṛhaspati had taken.
He did a deed ne'er done, ne'er to be equalled, whereby the Sun and Moon ascend alternate.

11 Like a dark steed adorned with pearl, the Fathers have decorated heaven with constellations.
They set the light in day, in night the darkness. Bṛhaspati cleft the rock and found the cattle.

12 This homage have we offered to the Cloud God who thunders out to many in succession.
May this Bṛhaspati vouchsafe us fulness of life with kine and horses, men, and heroes.

2 *The Son of Aṅgiras* : Bṛhaspati, especially, worshipped and cherished by Aṅgiras. *Aryaman* : the institution of marriage, represented by Aryaman ; one meaning of the name being groomsman or matchmaker.

3 *Out of winnowing baskets* : *sthivíbhyaḥ* : the exact meaning of the word is somewhat uncertain, but it is evidently a measure, basket, or instrument connected with corn. *Sthivimántaḥ*, 'armed with *sthivis*,' occurs in X. 27. 15. and is said by Sāyaṇa to mean 'occupants of stations.' Wilson renders *sthivíbhyaḥ* in this place by 'from the granaries'. The cows bestowed by Bṛhaspati are countless as grains of barley on the threshing flour or winnowing-place.

4 *Cleft the earth's skin* : or surface, with the hoofs of many cattle.

5 *A lily* : *śāpāla* : according to Sāyaṇa the same as Śaivala, the Vallisneria Octandra, a common aquatic plant.

6 *Weapon* : I adopt Sāyaṇa's explanation of *jásum*, although in X. 33. 2, the same word means 'exhaustion.

8 *Sweetness* : the sweet milk; that is, the cows who produced it.

Like a bowl : which already exists potentially in the wood from which it is produced by cutting.

9 Wilson, following Sāyaṇa, paraphrases the second line :—'he seized (the cattle from the rock) of Vala surrounded by the kine as (one extracts) marrow from a bone.'

11 *The Fathers* : 'The connection of the fathers with the light, of which they are both the embodiments and the guardians, is alone sufficient to explain their action in placing the stars in the sky.'—Wallis, *Cosmology of the Ṛgveda*, p. 68 Or, as Ludwig remarks, the Fathers themselves may be the stars.

12 *To many* : 'cows' is, apparently, understood. Sāyaṇa supplies *ṛcas* :—'who recites in order many (sacred stanzas).'—Wilson.

HYMN LXIX. *Agni.*

1. Auspicious is the aspect of Vadhryaśva's fire good is its guidance, pleasant are its visitings.

---

1 *Vadhryaśva* has been mentioned, in VI. 61. 1, as a worshipper of Sarasvatī : here he appears as a special worshipper of Agni.

When first the people of Sumitra kindle it, with butter poured thereon it crackles and shines bright.

2 Butter is that which makes Vadhryaśva's fire grow strong : the butter is its food, the butter makes it fat.

It spreads abroad when butter hath been offered it, and balmed with streams of butter shines forth like the Sun.

3 Still newest is this face of thine, O Agni, which Manu and Sumitra have enkindled.

So richly shine, accept our songs with favour, so give us strengthening food, so send us glory.

4 Accept this offering, Agni, whom aforetime Vadhryaśva hath entreated and enkindled.

Guard well our homes and people, guard our bodies, protect thy gift to us which thou hast granted.

5 Be splendid, guard us Kinsman of Vadhryaśva : let not the enmity of men o'ercome thee.

Like the bold hero Cyavana, I Sumitra tell forth the title of Vadhryaśva's Kinsman.

6 All treasures hast thou won, of plains and mountains, and quelled the Dāsas' and Āryas' hatred.

Like the bold hero Cyavana, O Agni, mayst thou subdue the men who long for battle.

7 Deft Agni hath a lengthened thread, tall oxen, a thousand heifers, numberless devices.

Decked by the men, splendid among the splendid, shine brightly forth amid devout Sumitras.

8 Thine is the teeming cow, O Jātavedas, who pours at once her ceaseless flow, Sabardhuk.

Thou art lit up by men enriched with guerdon, O Agni, by the pious-souled Sumitras.

9 Even Immortal Gods, O Jātavedas, Vadhryaśva's Kinsman, have declared thy grandeur.

When human tribes drew near with supplication thou conqueredst with men whom thou hadst strengthened.

10 Like as a father bears his son, O Agni, Vadhryaśva bare thee in his lap and served thee.

Thou, Youngest God, having enjoyed his fuel, didst vanquish those of old though they were mighty.

11 Vadhryaśva's Agni evermore hath vanquished his foes with heroes who had pressed the Soma.

Lord of bright rays, thou burntest up the battle, subduing, as our help, e'en mighty foemen.

12 This Agni of Vadhryaśva, Vṛtra-slayer, lit from of old, must be invoked with homage.

As such assail our enemies, Vadhryaśva, whether the foes be strangers or be kinsmen.

3 *Sumitra* : son of Vadhryaśva and Ṛṣi of the hymn.

5 *Cyavana* : a son of Bhṛgu. Or the word may mean conquering, as Sāyaṇa interprets it. *Vadhryaśva's Kinsman* ; as having been especially worshipped and cherished by that Ṛṣi. See stanza 10.

7 *A lengthened thread* : continual sacrifices, from ancient to present times. *Devices* : ways of attaining his object. Or *śataniṭha* may mean, 'having a hundred or many musical modes or sacred songs ;' or 'praised by many, 'the leader of hundreds (of) burnt offerings). —Wilson.

HYMN LXX. *Āprīs.*

1. ENJOY, O Agni, this my Fuel, welcome the oil-filled ladle where we pour libation.

Rise up for worship of the Gods, wise Agni, on the earth's height, while days are bright with beauty.

2 May he who goes before the Gods come hither with steeds whose shapes are varied, Narāśaṁsa.

May he, most Godlike, speed our offered viands with homage God-ward on the path of Order.

3 Men with oblations laud most constant Agni, and pray him to perform an envoy's duty.

With lightly-rolling car and best draught-horses, bring the Gods hither and sit down as Hotar.

4 May the delight of Gods spread out transversely : may it be with us long in length and fragrant.

O Holy Grass divine, with friendly spirit bring thou the willing Gods whose Chief is Indra.

Other Āprī hymns may be compared ; I. 13, 142, and 188; II. 3; III. 4. V. 5; VII. 2, and IX. 5. The usual deities and deified objects with the exception of Tanūnapāt, are invoked.

3 *As Hotar* : 'as ministrant priest'.—Wilson.

4 *The delight of Gods* : the sacred grass.

5 Touch ye the far-extending height of heaven or spring apart to suit the wide earth's measure.
Yearning, ye Doors, with those sublime in greatness, seize eagerly the heavenly Car that cometh.

6 Here in this shrine may Dawn and Night, the Daughters of Heaven, the skilful Goddesses, be seated.
In your wide lap, auspicious, willing Ladies may the Gods seat them with a willing spirit.

7 Up stands the stone, high burns the fire enkindled : Aditi's lap contains the Friendly Natures.
Ye Two Chief Priests who serve at this our worship, may ye, more skilled, win for us rich possessions.

8 On our wide grass, Three Goddesses be seated : for you have we prepared and made it pleasant.
May Iḷā, she whose foot drops oil, the Goddess, taste, man-like, sacrifice and well-set presents.

9 Since thou, God Tvaṣṭar, hast made beauty perfect, since thou hast been the Aṅgirases' Companion,
Willing, most wealthy, Giver of possessions, grant us the Gods' assembly, thou who knowest.

10 Well-knowing, binding with thy cord, bring hither, Lord of the Wood, the Deities' assembly.
The God prepare and season our oblations : may Heaven and Earth be gracious to my calling.

11 Agni, bring hither Varuṇa to help us, Indra from heaven, from air's mid-realm the Maruts.
On sacred grass all Holy ones be seated, and let the Immortal Gods rejoice in Svāhā.

HYMN LXXI. *Jñānam*

1. WHEN-men, Bṛhaspati, giving names to objects, sent out Vāk's first and earliest utterances,
All that was excellent and spotless, treasured within them, was disclosed through their affection.

2 Where, like men cleansing corn-flour in a cribble, the wise in spirit have created language,
Friends see and recognize the marks of friendship : their speech retains the blessed sign imprinted.

3 With sacrifice the trace of Vāk they followed, and found her harbouring within the Ṛṣis.
They brought her, dealt her forth in many places : seven singers make her tones resound in concert.

4 One man hath ne'er seen Vāk, and yet he seeth : one man hath hearing but hath never heard her.
But to another hath she shown her beauty as a fond well-dressed woman to her husband.

5 One man they call a laggard, dull in friendship : they never urge him on to deeds of valour.
He wanders on in profitless illusion : the Voice he heard yields neither fruit nor blossom.

6 No part in Vāk hath he who hath abandoned his own dear friend who knows the truth of friendship.
Even if he hears her still in vain he listens: naught knows he of the path of righteous action.

5 *The heavenly Car* : which brings the Gods.

7. *The stone* : with which the Soma juice is expressed. *Aditi's lap* : the surface of the earth. *The Friendly Natures*: the Gods. According to Sāyaṇa, 'the acceptable sacrificial vessels.' *Two Chief Priests* : *purohitau* : perhaps Agni and Āditya. *More skilled* : than human priests.

8 *Three Goddesses* : Iḷā, Sarasvatī, and Bhāratī. *Taste*: the verb is plural, meaning may Iḷā and the others taste. *Man-like* : as at the sacrifice of Manu, according to Sāyaṇa.

9 *Grant us the Gods' assembly* : the Commentators explain *pāthas* some times as 'place', sometimes as 'food' or 'air' or 'water.' Here Wilson, following Sāyaṇa, translates :—'offer the food of the gods (to them).'

10 *Binding with thy cord* : it is not clear what is to be bound, or ranged in order. According to Sāyaṇa the *pāthas*, which he explains as *annaṁ devānām*, food of the Gods, is to be fastened with a rope. *Lord of the Wood* : *vánaspati* : the *yūpa* or Sacrificial Post.

11 *Svāhā* : that is, in the sacrificial offerings presented with the exclamation Svāhā, Ave, or Hail.

Jñānam or Knowledge, the subject of this very difficult hymn, is said by Sāyaṇa to mean Parama brahmajñānam, knowledge of the higher truths of Religion, which teaches man his own nature and how he may be reunited to the Supreme Spirit.

1 *Vāk* : Voice or Speech, the Sacred Word. Here specially the voice of the hymn regarded as the means of communication between men and Gods. See *Vedic India* (Story of the Nations Series), pp. 269—271).

3 *Harbouring within the Ṛṣis* : they discovered, in the course of sacrifice, that the inspired Ṛṣis alone understood Speech as required for religious purposes. *In many places* : among the Hotar-priests. *Seven singers* : 'the seven noisy (birds) meet together.'—Wilson : referring, says Sāyaṇa, to the seven metres, the Gāyatrī, etc.

7 Unequal in the quickness of their spirit are friends endowed alike with eyes and hearing.
Some look like tanks that reach the mouth or shoulder, others like pools of water fit to bathe in.

8 When friendly Brāhmans sacrifice together with mental impulse which the heart hath fashioned,
They leave one far behind through their attainments, and some who count as Brāhmans wander elsewhere.

9 Those men who step not back and move not forward, nor Brāhmans nor preparers of libations,
Having attained to Vāk in sinful fashion spin out their thread in ignorance like spinsters.

10 All friends are joyful in the friend who cometh in triumph, having conquered in assembly.
He is their blame-averter, food-provider : prepared is he and fit for deed of vigour.

11 One plies his constant task reciting verses : one sings the holy psalm in Śakvarī measures.
One more, the Brāhman, tells the lore of being, and one lays down the rules of sacrificing.

HYMN LXXII. *The Gods.*

1. LET us with tuneful skill proclaim these generations of the Gods,
That one may see them when these hymns are chanted in a future age.

2 These Brahmaṇaspati produced with blast and smelting, like a smith,
Existence, in an earlier age of Gods, from Non-existence sprang.

3 Existence, in the earliest age of Gods, from Non-existence sprang.
Thereafter were the regions born. This sprang from the Productive Power.

4 Earth sprang from the Productive Power ; the regions from the earth were born.
Dakṣa was born of Aditi, and Aditi was Dakṣa's Child.

5 For Aditi, O Daksa, she who is thy Daughter, was brought forth.
After her were the blessed Gods born sharers of immortal life.

6 When ye, O Gods, in yonder deep close-clasping one another stood,
Thence, as of dancers, from your feet a thickening cloud of dust arose.

7 When, O ye Gods, like Yatis, ye caused all existing things to grow,
Then ye brought Sūrya forward who was lying hidden in the sea.

8 Eight are the Sons of Aditi who from her body sprang to life.
With seven she went to meet the Gods : she cast Mārtāṇḍa far away.

9 So with her Seven Sons Aditi went forth to meet the earlier age.
She brought Mārtāṇḍa thitherward to spring to life and die again.

8 *Some who count as Brāhmans wander elsewhere* : 'others walk about boasting to be *Brāhmans*.'—Muir.

9 *Step not back and move not forward* : take no active part in religious ceremonies. 'Those who do not walk (with the Brāhmans) in this lower world, nor (with the gods) in the upper world, ' is Wilson's paraphrase of the text which I have rendered literally. *Like spinsters* : '(like) female weavers. Such is the sense which Prof. Aufrecht thinks may, with probability, be assigned to *siris*, a word which occurs only here.'—Muir.

11 *Reciting verses* : repeating *ṛcas* or verses of the Ṛg-veda. This is the duty of the Hotar. *The holy psalm* : the Gāyatra or Sāman. The Udgātar or Chanter, one of the four chief priests is intended. *The lore of being* : the knowledge of all that exists. *Lays down the rules* : 'prescribes the order.' —Muir. 'Measures the materials.'—Wilson. This is the duty of the Adh-varyu, another of the chief priests. The hymn has been transliterated and translated by Dr. J. Muir, *O. S. Texts*, I, pp. 254—256. It has also been metrically rendered by the authors of the *Siebenzig Lieder des Ṛgveda*, who have endeavoured, by transposing some of the stanzas, to bring them into closer connexion. According to Sāyaṇa, the subject of the whole hymn is 'the eulogy of the understanding of the Veda as essential to divine knowledge.'

2 *These* : all beings. *Like a smith* : as a blacksmith blows up his fire and melts metal.

3 *The regions*: 'the quarters (of the horizon).'—Wilson. *This* : meaning earth. *Productive Power* : the meaning of *uttānápadaḥ* is uncertain. Wallis renders it by 'the begetter (the sky); Wilson by 'the upward-growing (tree).'

4 *And Aditi was Dakṣa's Child* : 'Yāska remarks...... How can this be possible ? They may have had the same origin ; or, according to the nature of the gods, they may have been born from each other,—have derived their substance from one another.'—*O. S. Texts*. IV. 13 Aditi is Infinity or the Infinite, and Dakṣa is Force or. Power personified. See *Vedic Hymns*, I. p. 245.

6 'The two verses 6 and 7 are interesting as containing an independent story of the origin of the world : the gods are said to have kicked up in dancing the atoms which formed the earth.—Wallis, *Cosmology of the Ṛgveda* p. 43.

7 *Yatis* : devotees.

8 *Eight are the Sons* : according to the Commentator, Mitra, Varuṇa, Dhātar, Aryaman, Aṁśa, Bhaga, Vivasvān, and Āditya (the Sun). *Mārtāṇḍa* : *Sūrya*, the Sun. His exposure probably refers to his sweeping through the sky.—Ludwig. But see Bergaigne, *La Religion Védique*, III. 107.

HYMN LXXIII. *Indra.*

1. Thou wast born mighty for victorious valour, exulting, strongest, full of pride and courage.
There, even there, the Maruts strengthened Indra when his most rapid Mother stirred the Hero.

2 There with fiend's ways e'en Pṛśanī was seated: with much laudation they exalted Indra.
As if encompassed by the Mighty-footed, from darkness, near at hand, forth came the Children.

3 High are thy feet when on thy way thou goest: the strength thou foundest here hath lent thee vigour.
Thousand hyenas in thy mouth thou holdest. O Indra, mayst thou turn the Aśvins hither.

4 Speeding at once to sacrifice thou comest: for friendship thou art bringing both Nāsatyas.
Thou hadst a thousand treasures in possession. The Aśvins, O thou Hero, gave thee riches.

5 Glad, for the race that rests on holy Order, with friends who hasten to their goal, hath Indra
With these his magic powers assailed the Dasyu: he cast away the gloomy mists, the darkness.

6 Two of like name for him didst thou demolish, as Indra striking down the car of Uṣas.
With thy beloved lofty Friends thou camest, and with the assurance of thine heart thou slewest.

7 War-loving Namuci thou smotest, robbing the Dāsa of his magic for the Ṛṣi.
For man thou madest ready pleasant pathways, paths leading as it were directly God-ward.

8 These names of thine thou hast fulfilled completely: as Lord, thou holdest in thine arm, O Indra.
In thee, through thy great might, the Gods are joyful: the roots of trees hast thou directed upward.

9 May the sweet Soma juices make him happy to cast his quoit that lies in depth of waters.
Thou from the udder which o'er earth is fastened hast poured the milk into the kine and herbage.

10 When others call him offspring of the Courser, my meaning is that Mighty Power produced him.
He came from Manyu and remained in houses: whence he hath sprung is known to Indra only.

11 Like birds of beauteous wing the Priyamedhas, Ṛṣis, imploring, have come nigh to Indra:
Dispel the darkness and fill full our vision: deliver us as men whom snares entangle.

HYMN LXXIV. *Indra.*

1. I am prepared to laud with song or worship the Noble Ones who are in earth and heaven,
Or Coursers who have triumphed in the contest, or those who famed, have won the prize with glory.

1 *Mother*: Aditi. *Stirred the Hero*: gave him free motion as soon as he was born, or incited him to action by telling him of his future opponent. See VIII. 45. 5, and 66. 2.

2 This stanza is unintelligible to me *Pṛśanī*: meaning perhaps Pṛśnī, as Ludwig conjectures. *The Mighty-footed*: Indra. *The Children*: the new-born Maruts Wilson translates, after Sāyaṇa:—'The martial troop of (Indra) the injurer encamped around Indra (accompanied) by the swift-moving (Maruts): they animated him with abundant praise; like (cattle) penned up within a great stall, the embryonic (waters) issued from the (*Vṛtra*) who had arrived in the form of darkness.'

3 *High are thy feet*: as travelling through the heavens. *Hyenas* *sālávṛkān* jackals.'—Wilson.

6 *Two of like name*: or, of similar nature; gloomy mists and darkness. *The car of Uṣas*: See IV. 30. 8—11. *The assurance of thine heart*: thy trusted thunderbolt.

8 *Thou hast fulfilled*: hast acted in full accordance with the names thou bearest, such as Vṛtra-slayer, Śakra, etc. *Thou holdest*: the thunderbolt. *The roots of trees*: the clouds are often compared to trees. The rain is their fruit, and when they pour it down their roots are supposed to be turned upward.

9 *Quoit*: *cakrám*: meaning the thunderbolt. *The udder*: the firmament.

10 *The Courser*: meaning Heaven. *Manyu*: wrath, passion or ardour, personified. *My meaning is*: the speaker declares that he is raised above the common mythological explanations. He considers the God to have sprung from a transcendental Power.—Ludwig.

Grassmann banishes this hymn to his Appendix as being generally obscure and in parts absolutely unintelligible. I have, for the most part, followed Ludwig's interpretation.

The subject of the hymn is a coming horse-race, and the Ṛṣi invokes in favour of the Yajamāna. the Vasus, racers who have won the prize in former times and the men who owned them. Indra also is appealed to for help. See *Vedische Studien,* I. p. 129.

2 Their call, the call of Gods, went up to heaven : they kissed the ground with glory-seeking spirit,
There where the Gods look on for happy fortune, and like the kindly heavens bestow their bounties.

3 This is the song of those Immortal Beings who long for treasures in their full perfection.
May these, completing prayers and sacrifices, bestow upon us wealth where naught is wanting.

4 Those living men extolled thy deed, O Indra, those who would fain burst through the stall of cattle,
Fain to milk her who bare but once, great, lofty, whose Sons are many and her streams past number.

5 Śacīvan, win to your assistance Indra who never bends, who overcomes his foemen.
Ṛbhukṣan, Maghavan, the hymn's upholder, who, rich in food, bears man's kind friend, the thunder.

6 Since he who won of old anew hath triumphed, Indra hath earned his name of Vṛtra-slayer.
He hath appeared, the mighty Lord of Conquest. What we would have him do let him accomplish.

HYMN LXXV. *The Rivers.*

1. The singer, O ye Waters in Vivasvān's place, shall tell your grandeur forth that is beyond compare.
The Rivers have come forward triply, seven and seven. Sindhu in might surpasses all the streams that flow.

2 Varuṇa cut the channels for thy forward course, O Sindhu, when thou rannest on to win the race.
Thou speedest o'er precipitous ridges of the earth, when thou art Lord and Leader of these moving floods.

3 His roar is lifted up to heaven above the earth : he puts forth endless vigour with a flash of light.
Like floods of rain that fall in thunder from the cloud, so Sindhu rushes on bellowing like a bull.

4 Like mothers to their calves, like milch kine with their milk, so, Sindhu, unto thee the roaring rivers run.
Thou leadest as a warrior king thine army's wings what time thou comest in the van of these swift streams.

5 Favour ye this my laud, O Gaṅgā, Yamunā, O Śutudrī, Paruṣṇī and Sarasvatī :
With Asiknī, Vitastā, O Marudvṛdhā, O Ārjīkīyā with Suṣomā hear my call.

6 First with Tṛṣṭāmā thou art eager to flow forth, with Rasā, and Susartu, and with Śvetyā here,
With Kubhā ; and with these, Sindhu ! and Mehatnu, thou seekest in thy course Krumu and Gomatī.

7 Flashing and whitely-gleaming in her mightiness, she moves along her ample volumes through the realms,
Most active of the active, Sindhu unrestrained, like to a dappled mare, beautiful, fair to see.

2 *The call of Gods* : the Gods are imagined as present and interested in the race. *They kissed the ground* : the horses lightly touched the earth as they ran.

4 *Those living men* : the Aṅgirases. *Her who bare but once* : Heaven, according to Sāyaṇa ; Earth, according to Grassmann. Pṛśni, the mother of the Maruts, must be meant.—Ludwig. See VI. 48. 22.

5 *Śacīvan* : apparently a man's name. 'Celebrator of holy rites.'—Wilson.

6 *He who won of old* : the Yajamāna. *He hath appeared* : the poet imagines Indra himself to be present.

---

1 *O ye Waters* : apparently the Rivers are addressed as representing all the divine Waters. *Vivasvān's place* : where the singers stand when they sing hymns. *Triply, seven and seven* : twenty-one rivers ; two other sets of seven each being added to the seven chief rivers of the Panjāb. Sāyaṇa explains differently :—'they flowed by sevens through the three (worlds).'—Wilson. 'Each set of seven (streams) has followed a threefold course.'—Muir. 'By seven and seven......in three courses.'—M. Müller.

5 The poet addresses first the most distant rivers. *Gaṅgā* : the Ganges is mentioned, indirectly, in only one other verse of the *Ṛgveda*, and even there, the word is said by some to be the name of a woman. See VI. 45.31. *Yamunā* : the Jumna. *Śutudrī* : the Sutlej or Satlaj. *Paruṣṇī*: the Rāvī : *Sarasvatī* : see VI. 61. 2. *Asiknī* : the ancient Acesines : the Vedic name of the Candrabhāgā, the present Cenāb. *Vitastā* : probably the Jhelum, the Hydaspes of the Greeks. *Marudvṛdhā* : meaning, increased by the Maruts : not identified. *Ārjīkīyā* and *Suṣomā* are said by Yāska to be the Vipās and the Sindhu; but this is not possible, and it is uncertain what rivers are meant.

6 *Kubhā*, *Krumu*, and *Gomatī* have been mentioned in previous Books. The other streams whose names occur in this stanza are probably unimportant affluents of the Indus. All that is known regarding the rivers mentioned in stanzas 5 and 6 may be found in Zimmer's *Altindisches Leben*, pp. 4ff.

7 *In her mightiness* : in the preceding stanzas Sindhu appears to be a River-God, but in this and following verses the epithets are feminine.

8 Rich in good steeds is Sindhu, rich in cars and robes, rich in gold, nobly-fashioned, rich in ample wealth.
Blest Sīlamāvatī and young Ūrṇāvatī invest themselves with raiment rich in store of sweets.

9 Sindhu hath yoked her car, light-rolling, drawn by steeds, and with that car shall she win booty in this fight.
So have I praised its power, mighty and unrestrained, of independent glory, roaring as it runs.

HYMN LXXVI. *Press-stones.*

1. I GRASP at you when power and strength begin to dawn : bedew ye, Indra and the Maruts, Heaven and Earth,
That Day and Night, in every hall of sacrifice, may wait on us and bless us when they first spring forth.

2 Press the libation out, most excellent of all : the Pressing-stone is grasped like a hand-guided steed.
So let it win the valour that subdues the foe, and the fleet courser's might that speeds to ample wealth.

3 Juice that this Stone pours out removes defect of ours, as in old time it brought prosperity to man.
At sacrifices they established holy rites on Tvaṣṭar's milk-blent juice bright with the hue of steeds.

4 Drive ye the treacherous demons far away from us: keep Nirṛti afar and banish penury.
Pour riches forth for us with troops of hero sons, and bear ye up, O Stones, the song that visits Gods.

5 To you who are more mighty than the heavens themselves, who, finishing your task with more than Vibhvan's speed,
More rapidly than Vāyu seize the Soma juice, better than Agni give us food, to you I sing.

6 Stirred be the glorious Stones: let it press out the juice, the Stone with heavenly song that reaches up to heaven,
There where the men draw forth the meath for which they long, sending their voice around in rivalry of speed.

7 The Stones press out the Soma, swift as car-borne men, and, eager for the spoil, drain forth the sap thereof.
To fill the beaker, they exhaust the udder's store, as the men purify oblations with their lips.

8 Ye, present men, have been most skilful in your work, even ye, O Stones who pressed Soma for Indra's drink.
May all ye have of fair go to the Heavenly Race, and all your treasure to the earthly worshipper.

HYMN LXXVII. *Maruts.*

1. As with their voice from cloud they sprinkle treasure so are the wise man's liberal sacrifices.

8 *Sīlamāvatī* and *Ūrṇāvatī* appear to be names of rivers. According to Sāyaṇa, the words are epithets of Sindhu and mean respectively 'abounding in *Sīlamā* plants,' said to be used for cordage, and 'rich in wool'. The meaning of the second half of the second line is uncertain:—'wears (as only one river is supposed to be the subject) honey-growing (flowers).'—Wilson.

9 *In this fight* : the hymn may, as Prof. Ludwig suggests, be a prayer for aid in a battle that is to be fought on the banks of the Sindhu or Indus. The hymn has been transliterated and translated by Dr. J. Muir, *O. S. Texts*, V. 343—345, and a version of stanzas 1—8 is given by Prof. Zimmer, *Altindisches Leben*, p. 4. A complete translation, with full explanatory notes, is given in Max Müller's *India, What can it Teach Us* ?, pp. 164—168.

---

1 *I grasp at you* : 'I propitiate you.'—Wilson. *Power and strength* : the morning beams which bring new vigour. *Day and Night* : or, 'both day-halves.'

3 *To man* : or, to Manu. *Tvaṣṭar's milk-blent juice* : the Soma juice brewed by Tvaṣṭar for the year, which represents the life-sustaining power of Nature.—Ludwig. *Bright with the hue of steeds* : tawny-coloured. Sāyaṇa interprets differently :—'when the son of Tvaṣṭṛ, hidden by the (stolen) cows, and assuming the form of a horse, (was to be slain).—Wilson. Triśiras the son of Tvaṣṭar was regarded as an enemy of the Gods. Indra slew him and took possession of the Soma.

4 *Nirṛti* : the Goddess of Death and Destruction.

5 *Vibhvan* : one of the three Ṛbhus. *Vāyu* : or, the wind.

6 *The men* : meaning the press-stones. Cf. stanza 8.

7 *The udder's store* : the juice contained in the milky Soma-plant. *With their lips* : with the praises that they utter.

8 *Worshipper* : Sāyaṇa explains *sunvaté* by *yajamānāya*, to the Yajamāna or sacrificer. The more literal translation would be 'to the presser,' the man who presses out or effuses the Soma juice.

---

1 This stanza is obscure. According to Sāyaṇa, *vijānuṣaḥ* (the wise man's) is formed from *jan*, to generate, and not from *jñā*, to know :—'they are the generators (of the world) like sacrifices abounding in libations.'—Wilson. *The good Maruts' priest* : either the band of the Maruts themselves regarded as a Brahman, or a human priest specially skilled in propitiating them. Prof. M. Müller translates differently. See *Vedic Hymns*, I p. 412.

I praise their Company that merits worship as the good Maruts' priest to pay them honour.

2 The youths have wrought their ornaments for glory through many nights,—this noble band of Maruts.
Like stags the Sons of Dyaus have striven onward, the Sons of Aditi grown strong like pillars.

3 They who extend beyond the earth and heaven, by their own mass, as from the cloud spreads Sūrya;
Like mighty Heroes covetous of glory, like heavenly gallants who destroy the wicked.

4 When ye come nigh, as in the depth of waters, the earth is loosened, as it were, and shaken.
This your all-feeding sacrifice approaches: come all united, fraught, as 'twere, with viands.

5 Ye are like horses fastened to the chariot poles, luminous with your beams, with splendour as at dawn;
Like self-bright falcons, punishers of wicked men, like hovering birds urged forward, scattering rain around.

6 When ye come forth, O Maruts, from the distance, from the great treasury of rich possessions,
Knowing, O Vasus, boons that should be granted, even from afar drive back the men who hate us.

7 He who, engaged in the rite's final duty brings, as a man, oblation to the Maruts,
Wins him life's wealthy fulness, blest with heroes: he shall be present, too, where Gods drink Soma.

2 *This noble band of Maruts* : Prof. Ludwig suggests that *sumārutam* means here a festival held in honour of the Maruts at the end of the periodical rains, and that, after many nights, the Maruts adorn themselves for this. *Pillars* : I follow Ludwig ; but the meaning of *akrāḥ* is uncertain. Geldner takes it to mean 'horses, a parallelism to stags or antelopes. Sāyaṇa makes *ná*, like, negative, and explains *akrāḥ* by *ākramaṇaśīlāḥ* :—'the swift-going sons of Aditi do not increase in glory.'—Wilson.

4 *This your all-feeding sacrifice approaches* : 'this manifold sacrifice comes towards you.'—Wilson.

7 *In the rite's final duty* : Sāyaṇa explains *udṛīci yajñe* by *yajñe samāptastutike sampūrṇe sati*, when the sacrifice has its praise perfected, when the sacrifice is complete. *As a man* : according to Ludwig, 'no longer a man, that is, not in his human character but having become divine by worship. *Where the Gods drink Soma* : he, a God himself, shall be admitted to the Gods' society.

8 For these are helps adored at sacrifices, bringing good fortune by their name Ādityas.
Speeding on cars let them protect our praises, delighting in our sacrifice and worship.

HYMN LXXVIII. *Maruts.*

1. YE by your hymns are like high-thoughted singers, skilful, inviting Gods with sacrifices;
Fair to behold, like Kings, with bright adornment, like spotless gallants, leaders of the people :

2 Like fire with flashing flame, breast-bound with chains of gold, like tempest-blasts, self-moving, swift to lend your aid;
As best of all foreknowers, excellent to guide, like Somas, good to guard the man who follows Law.

3 Shakers of all, like gales of wind they travel, like tongues of burning fires in their effulgence.
Mighty are they as warriors clad in armour, and, like the Fathers' prayers, Most Bounteous Givers.

4 Like spokes of car-wheels in one nave united, ever victorious like heavenly Heroes,
Shedding their precious balm like youthful suitors, they raise their voice and chant their psalm as singers.

5 They who are fleet to travel like the noblest steeds, long to obtain the prize like bounteous charioteers,
Like waters speeding on with their precipitous floods, like omniform Aṅgirases with Sāma-hymns.

6 Born from the stream, like press-stones are the Princes, for ever like the stones that crush in pieces;
Sons of a beauteous Dame, like playful children, like a great host upon the march with splendour.

7 Like rays of Dawn, the visitors of sacrifice, they shine with ornaments as eager to be bright.

4 *Shedding their precious balm* : pouring out the fertilizing rain as liberally as young wooers give presents.

6 *Born from the stream* : from the sea of air, or from Sindhu, the Indus.

7 *They measure out the distance* : 'have traversed leagues.' —Wilson. 'They measure many miles.'—M. Müller.

Like rivers hasting on, glittering with their spears, from far away they measure out the distances.

8 Gods, send us happiness and make us wealthy, letting us singers prosper, O ye Maruts.

Bethink you of our praise and of our friendship : ye from of old have riches to vouchsafe us.

HYMN LXXIX. *Agni.*

1. I HAVE beheld the might of this Great Being. Immortal in the midst of tribes of mortals.

His jaws now open and now shut together: much they devour, insatiately chewing.

2 His eyes are turned away, his head is hidden : unsated with his tongue he eats the fuel.

With hands upraised, with reverence in the houses, for him they quickly bring his food together.

3 Seeking, as 'twere, his Mother's secret bosom, he, like a child, creeps on through wide-spread bushes.

One he finds glowing like hot food made ready, and kissing deep within the earth's recesses.

4 This holy Law I tell you, Earth and Heaven : the Infant at his birth dovours his Parents.

No knowledge of the God have I, a mortal. Yea, Agni knoweth best, for he hath wisdom.

5 This man who quickly gives him food, who offers his gifts of oil and butter and supports him,—

Him with his thousand eyes he closely looks on : thou showest him thy face from all sides, Agni.

6 Agni, hast thou committed sin or treason among the Gods ? In ignorance I ask thee.

Playing, not playing, he gold-hued and toothless, hath cut his food up as the knife a victim.

7 He born in wood hath yoked his horses rushing in all directions, held with reins that glitter.

The well-born friend hath carved his food with Vasus : in all his limbs he hath increased and prospered.

HYMN LXXX. *Agni.*

1. AGNI bestows the fleet prize-winning courser : Agni, the hero famed and firm in duty.

Agni pervades and decks the earth and heaven, and fills the fruitful dame who teems with heroes.

2 Blest be the wood that feeds the active Agni : within the two great worlds hath Agni entered.

Agni impels a single man to battle, and with him rends in pieces many a foeman.

3 Agni rejoiced the ear of him who praised him, and from the waters burnt away Jarūtha.

Agni saved Atri in the fiery cavern, and made Nṛmedha rich with troops of children.

4 Agni hath granted wealth that decks the hero, and sent the sage who wins a thousand cattle.

Agni hath made oblations rise to heaven : to every place are Agni's laws extended.

5 With songs of praise the Ṛṣis call on Agni; on Agni, heroes worsted in the foray.

Birds flying in the region call on Agni : around a thousand cattle Agni wanders.

2 *His eyes* : according to Sāyaṇa, the eyes of Agni are the distant Sun and Moon, and *his head* is hidden in mens' stomachs, in the shape of the heat which enables them to digest their food. *His food* : the sticks for fuel, which are bound up into fagots.

3 This stanza is very obscure. Agni, born from the wood of the fire-sticks, seems, as he creeps through the brushwood that he is burning, to seek entrance again into his mother's side. He then finds an old dry tree or log, which had been deeply rooted in the earth, and feeds on it as on food that has been specially prepared for him.

4 *His Parents* : the two fire-sticks from which he has been produced.

6 *Hast thou committed sin* ? : Art thou as voracious and destructive in heaven as thou art on earth ? *Playing, not playing* : playing about the fuel, and yet earnestly intent on devouring his food. 'Sporting (here), not sporting (there).—Wilson. *A victim* : *gām* : ox or cow.

7 *The well-born Friend* : Agni. *In all his limbs* : *párvabhiḥ* : 'with logs of wood.'—Wilson.

---

3 *Jarūtha* : See VII. 1. 7, and 9. 6. *Atri* : his deliverance is ascribed to the Aśvins in I. 112. 7, 116. 8, 117. 3. and 118. 7.

5 *Around a thousand cattle* : in the fires lighted to keep off wild beasts and demons of darkness.

6 Races of human birth pay Agni worship, men who have sprung from Nahus' line adore him.
Stablished in holy oil is Agni's pasture, on the Gandharva path of Law and Order.

7 The Ṛbhus fabricated prayer for Agni, and we with mighty hymns have called on Agni.
Agni, Most Youthful God, protect the singer: win us by worship, Agni, great possessions.

HYMN LXXXI. *Viśvakarman.*

1. He who sate down as Hotar-priest, the Ṛṣi, our Father, offering up all things existing,—
He, seeking through his wish a great possession, came among men on earth as archetypal.

2 What was the place whereon he took his station? What was it that supported him? How was it?
Whence Viśvakarman, seeing all, producing the earth, with mighty power disclosed the heavens.

3 He who hath eyes on all sides round about him, a mouth on all sides, arms and feet on all sides,
He, the Sole God, producing earth and heaven, weldeth them, with his arms as wings, together.

4 What was the tree, what wood in sooth produced it, from which they fashioned out the earth and heaven?
Ye thoughtful men inquire within your spirit whereon he stood when he established all things.

5 Thine highest, lowest, sacrificial natures, and these thy mid-most here, O Viśvakarman,
Teach thou thy friends at sacrifice, O Blessed, and come thyself, exalted, to our worship.

6 Bring thou thyself, exalted with oblation, O Viśvakarman, Earth and Heaven to worship.
Let other men around us live in folly: here let us have a rich and liberal patron.

7 Let us invoke to-day, to aid our labour, the Lord of Speech, the thought-swift Viśvakarman.
May he hear kindly all our invocations who gives all bliss for aid, whose works are righteous.

HYMN LXXXII. *Viśvakarman.*

1. The Father of the eye, the Wise in spirit, created both these worlds submerged in fatness.
Then when the eastern ends were firmly fastened, the heavens and the earth were far extended.

2 Mighty in mind and power is Viśvakarman, Maker, Disposer, and most lofty Presence.
Their offerings joy in rich juice where they value One, only One, beyond the Seven Ṛṣis.

6 *Gandharva path*: sublime; that which the Gandharvas in heaven use to travel.

7 *The Ṛbhus*: or Ṛṣis skilful as the Ṛbhus.

Viśvakarman, the Omnific, is represented in this hymn as the universal Father and Generator, the Creator of all things and Architect of the worlds.

1 *All things existing*: regarded as being contained in the offerings presented by Viśvakarman. *Through his wish*: through his desire to create. *Archetypal*: the meaning of *prathamachhád* is uncertain. In Wilson's Translation 'inventor' is a misprint for 'investor', that is, 'first investing Agni with the worlds,' according to Sāyaṇa's explanation. 'First appeatring'—Ludwig. The first worshipper.'—Wallis.

3 *Weldeth them*: cp. IV. 2. 17, and X. 72. 2. *With his arms as wings*: fanning the flame in which the matter is smelted. Ludwig thinks that whirlwinds, produced by the action of hands, feet, and wings, are intended.

4 The first half-line occurs also in X. 31. 7. *They*: the makers of the world directed by Parameśvara.—Sāyaṇa.

5 Or the first half-line may be rendered:—'Thy sacrificial forms, the highest, lowest.' *Come thyself, exalted, to our worship*: 'exhilarated, thyself offer up thyself.' —Muir. 'Do thou sacrifice to thyself delighting thyself.'—Wallis. 'According to Mahīdhara the meaning is that man is incompetent to worship the creator, that is, in his forms, and it must be done by himself.'—Wilson. I have adopted Prof. Ludwig's explanation of the last clause.

6 *Bring.........to worship*: or, sacrifice to Heaven and Earth.

7 *Our labour*: the arduous work of sacrificing. 'In our conflict.'—Muir. The hymn has been translated by Dr. J. Muir, *O. S. Texts*, IV. pp. 6, 7, by Mr. Wallis, *Cosmology of the Ṛgveda*, pp. 81—83, and, partly, by Prof. F. Max Müller in his *Hibbert Lectures*, p. 293f.

See also Mme. Zénaide Ragozin, *Vedic India*, pp. 263, 416.

1 *The Father of the eye*: Viśvakarman, who made the light which enables the eye to see. *Submerged in fatness*: Sāyaṇa explains *ghṛtám* here by 'water:'—'engendered the water, (and then) these two (heaven and earth) floating (on the waters).'—Wilson.

2 *Most lofty Presence*: literally, the highest apparition; the highest image or object of spiritual contemplation. *Their offerings*: the offerings, or perhaps the wishes, of the Fathers, semi-personified. *The Seven Ṛṣis*: the constellation Ursa Major, the seven stars of which are

3 Father who made us, he who, as Disposer, knoweth all races and all things existing,
Even he alone, the Deities' name-giver,—him other beings seek for information.

4 To him in sacrifice they offered treasures,—Ṛṣis of old, in numerous troops, as singers,
Who, in the distant, near, and lower region, made ready all these things that have existence.

5 That which is earlier than this earth and heaven, before the Asuras and Gods had being,—
What was the germ primeval which the waters received where all the Gods were seen together ?

6 The waters, they received that germ primeval wherein the Gods were gathered all together.
It rested set upon the Unborn's navel, that One wherein abide all things existing.

7 Ye will not find him who produced these creatures : another thing hath risen up among you.
Enwrapt in misty cloud, with lips that stammer, hymn-chanters wander and are discontented.

the great Ṛṣis Marīci, Atri, Aṅgiras, Pulastya, Pulaha, Kratu, and Vasiṣṭha. The meaning is that the spirits of the blest enjoy the fulfilment of all their desires beyond the starry heavens where the One Being, the great Creator, dwells.

3 *For information* : to learn who is the Supreme God; or what their several functions are.

4 *Distant, near, and lower region* : meaning, apparently, the heavenly, the earthly, and the intermediate atmosphere.

6 *The Unborn*, Aja, seems here to be identified with Viśvakarman. See *Vedic India*, pp. 423, 424.

7 *Another thing* : meaning according to the Commentator, 'Viśvakarman is a different entity from you who are sentient beings, who have individual consciousness, and so forth.'—See Editor's note in Wilson's translation. Sāyaṇa 'gives the general sense of the last clause (of the stanza) as "You are merely anxious for enjoyment in this world and in the next, therefore you know nothing of *Viśvakarman*," taking *ukthaśāsaḥ* as implying singing hymns with a view to gaining felicity in a future state. Mahīdhara has a similar explanation : "you who are engaged in the enjoyments of this world or the next, being subject to false knowledge or ignorance, have no knowledge of the Truth."'—Wilson.

With regard to this and the preceding hymn Mr. Wallis observes that they make no attempt to explain in what way the process of sacrifice could be regarded as an act of creation. We are told little more than that Viśvakarman was a primeval sacrificer and also a creator; we have no hint how to combine the two ideas into a harmonious unity. See *Cosmology of the Ṛgveda*, pp. 83, 84, and Muir, *O. S. Texts*, IV. 7, 8, where the hymn is translated and some of its difficulties are discussed. Prof. Ludwig's Commentary is especially full and valuable, and should be consulted by all students of the Veda.

HYMN LXXXIII. *Manyu.*

1. He who hath reverenced thee, Manyu, destructive bolt, breeds for himself forthwith all conquering energy.
Ārya and Dāsa will we conquer with thine aid, with thee the Conqueror, with conquest conquest-sped.

2 Manyu was Indra, yea, the God was Manyu, Manyu was Hotar, Varuṇa, Jātavedas.
The tribes of human lineage worship Manyu. Accordant with thy fervour, Manyu, guard us.

3 Come hither, Manyu, mightier than the mighty ; chase, with thy fervour for ally, our foemen.
Slayer of foes, of Vṛtra, and of Dasyu, bring thou to us all kinds of wealth and treasure.

4 For thou art, Manyu, of surpassing vigour, fierce, queller of the foe, and self-existent,
Shared by all men, victorious, subduer : vouchsafe to us superior strength in battles.

5 I have departed, still without a portion, wise God ! according to thy will, the Mighty.
I, feeble man, was wroth thee, O Manyu ! I am myself ; come thou to give me vigour.

6 Come hither, I am all thine own ; advancing turn thou to me, Victorious, All-supporter !
Come to me, Manyu, Wielder of the Thunder : bethink thee of thy friend, and slay the Dasyus.

7 Approach, and on my right hand hold thy station : so shall we slay a multitude of foemen.
The best of meath I offer to support thee: may we be first to drink thereof in quiet.

1 *Manyu* : Anger, Passion, personified.

3 *With thy fervour* : *tápasā* : *tápas* means 'heat', 'burning,' and, secondly, penance, rigorous abstraction.

5 *Without a portion* : without a share in thy favours. *I am myself* : I am just what I am; a weak mortal, for whose infirmity allowance should be made. 'Being (incorporated with) my body, approach me.'—Wilson

HYMN LXXXIV. *Manyu.*

1. Borne on with thee, O Manyu girt by Maruts, let our brave men, impetuous, bursting forward,
March on, like flames of fire in form, exulting, with pointed arrows, sharpening their weapons.

2 Flashing like fire, be thou, O conquering Manyu, invoked, O Victor, as our army's leader.
Slay thou our foes, distribute their possessions : show forth thy vigour, scatter those who hate us.

3 O Manyu, overcome thou our assailant : on ! breaking, slaying, crushing down the foemen.
They have not hindered thine impetuous vigour : Mighty, Sole born ! thou makest them thy subjects.

4 Alone of many thou art worshipped, Manyu : sharpen the spirit of each clan for battle.
With thee to aid, O thou of perfect splendour, we will uplift the glorious shout for conquest.

5 Unyielding bringing victory like Indra, O Manyu, be thou here our Sovran Ruler.
To thy dear name, O Victor, we sing praises : we know the spring from which thou art come hither.

6 Twin-born with power, destructive bolt of thunder, the highest conquering might is thine, Subduer !
Be friendly to us in thy spirit, Manyu, O Much-invoked, in shock of mighty battle.

7 For spoil let Varuṇa and Manyu give us the wealth of both sides gathered and collected ;
And let our enemies with stricken spirits, o'erwhelmed with terror, slink away defeated.

1 *Like flames of fire in form* : *agnírūpāḥ.*

3 *Sole born* : 'O thou who art without companion.—
—Wilson.

5 *The spring* : the source.

7 *For spoil* : the preservation of their own property and the seizure of their enemies' goods being regarded as a double conquest. Or *dhánam ubháyam* may mean wealth of both kinds, horses and cows.

This hymn and the preceding are to be repeated, Sāyaṇa says, at sacrifices to ensure the destruction of enemies.

HYMN LXXXV. *Sūryā's Bridal.*

1. Truth is the base that bears the earth ; by Sūrya are the heavens sustained.
By Law the Ādityas stand secure, and Soma holds his place in heaven.

2 By Soma are the Ādityas strong, by Soma mighty is the earth.
Thus Soma in the midst of all these constellations hath his place.

3 One thinks, when they have brayed the plant, that he hath drunk the Soma's juice ;
Of him whom Brahmans truly know as Soma no one ever tastes.

4 Soma, secured by sheltering rules, guarded by hymns in Bṛhatī,
Thou standest listening to the stones : none tastes of thee who dwells on earth.

5 When they begin to drink thee then, O God, thou swellest out again.
Vāyu is Soma's guardian God. The Moon is that which shapes the years.

6 Raibhī was her dear bridal friend, and Nārāśaṁsī led her home.
Lovely was Sūryā's robe : she came to that which Gāthā had adorned.

7 Thought was the pillow of her couch, sight was the unguent for her eyes :
Her treasury was earth and heaven when Sūryā went unto her Lord.

The main subject of this composite hymn, which is one of the latest in the Ṛgveda, is the ceremony of marriage in general and more especially the wedding of Sūryā, the Daughter of the Sun, another form of Dawn, who is regarded as the typical bride.

1 *Truth* ; or reality; *sátyam*, used interchangeably with *ṛtam*, the Law and Order of the universe.

2 *By Soma* : by the power of the deified Soma whose influence pervades, quickens, and supports all existence. In the second line *Soma* is the Moon, but perhaps there is an allusion to the other sense also of the word. *These constellations* : the *nakṣatras* or lunar mansions. 'In the centre of these stars.'—Muir.

3 *Know as Soma* : know to be the Moon, regarded as the food of Gods only.

4 *By hymns in Bṛhatī* : that is by hymns in that metre. But the meaning of *bārhataiḥ* is uncertain. According to Sāyaṇa, the Bārhatas are the seven guardians of the Soma, Svāna, Bhrāja, Aṅghāri, and others.

5 *They* : the Gods. *Thee*: the ambrosia contained in thee, which the Gods drink during the waning of the Moon. *O God* : Soma, the Moon.

6 Soma is the deity of the preceding five stanzas. Sūryā's Bridal is the subject of 6—17. *Raibhī*, *Nārāśaṁsī*, and *Gāthā* are ritual verse, eulogistic hymn, and non-Vedic song personified.

7 *Treasury* : *kośaḥ* : meaning, probably, trousseau or bridal outfit. According to some the box or body of the chariot is intended.

8 Hymns were the cross-bars of the pole, Kurīra-metre decked the car :
The bridesmen were the Aśvin Pair : Agni was leader of the train.

9 Soma was he who wooed the maid : the groomsmen were both Aśvins, when
The Sun-God Savitar bestowed his willing Sūryā on her Lord.

10 Her spirit was the bridal car ; the covering thereof was heaven :
Bright were both Steers that drew it, when Sūryā approached her husband's home.

11 Thy Steers were steady, kept in place by holy verse and Sāma-hymn :
All ear were thy two chariot wheels : thy path was tremulous in the sky,

12 Clean, as thou wentest, were thy wheels : wind was the axle fastened there.
Sūryā, proceeding to her Lord, mounted a spirit-fashioned car.

13 The bridal pomp of Sūryā, which Savitar started, moved along.
In Maghā days are oxen slain, in Arjunīs they wed the bride.

14 When on your three-wheeled chariot, O Aśvins, ye came as wooers unto Sūryā's bridal,
Then all the Gods agreed to your proposal : Pūṣan as Son elected you as Fathers.

15 O ye Two Lords of lustre, then when ye to Sūryā's wooing came,
Where was one chariot wheel of yours ? Where stood ye for the Sire's command ?

16 The Brahmans, by their seasons, know, O Sūryā, those two wheels of thine :
One kept concealed, those only who are skilled in highest truths have learned.

17 To Sūryā and the Deities, to Mitra and to Varuṇa.
Who know aright the thing that is, this adoration have I paid.

18 By their own power these Twain in close succession move ;
They go as playing children round the sacrifice.
One of the Pair beholdeth all existing things ; the other ordereth seasons and is born again.

19 He, born afresh, is new and new for ever : ensign of days he goes before the Mornings.
Coming, he orders for the Gods their portion. The Moon prolongs the days of our existence.

20 Mount this, all-shaped, gold-hued, with strong wheels, fashioned of Kiṁśuka and Śalmali, light-rolling,
Bound for the world of life immortal, Sūryā : make for thy lord a happy bridal journey.

21 Rise up from hence : this maiden hath a husband. I laud Viśvāvasu with hymns and homage.
Seek in her father's home another fair one, and find the portion from of old assigned thee.

22 Rise up from hence, Viśvāvasu : with reverence we worship thee.
Seek thou another willing maid, and with her husband leave the bride.

8 *Decked the car* : formed its canopy. But the meaning of *opaśāḥ* here is uncertain. '*Kurīra* metre was the thong of the whip.'—Wilson. *The bridesmen* : in I. 119. 7 and elsewhere the Aśvins are said to be the husbands of Sūryā. Here they are represented as the friends who had asked her in marriage for Soma.

11 *All ear* : the text has *śrotram*, an ear, which Sāyaṇa says, means *śrotre*, two ears. 'The two wheels were thy ears.'—Wilson.

13 *In Maghā days* : or in stricter accordance with the text, 'In Aghā days, when the Moon is in the lunar mansion Maghā. See Jacobi, *Festgruss* an *R. von Roth* p. 69, and Weber, *Vedische Beiträge*, p. 32f. *Slain* : only on especially festive occasions, weddings for instance. 'Are whipped along.'—Wilson. *In Arjunīs* : two asterisms or lunar mansions, more commonly called Phālgunīs. *They wed the bride* : she is escorted to her husband's home.

14 *As wooers* : on behalf of Soma. *Pūṣan* : here meaning Savitar. *Son and Fathers* : intended to express close relationship and Savitar's obligation to the Aśvins who had arranged the marriage.

15 *For the Sire's command* : to receive Savitar's invitation to take part in the bridal procession. According to Sāyaṇa, 'to offer your gift.'

16 The *two wheels* are probably heaven and earth and the third, *one kept concealed*, is the mysterious invisibl[e] world beyond them.

18 In this stanza and the following one, which are bu[t] loosely connected with the rest of the hymn, Sūrya re[-]presents the Sun, and Soma is the Moon.

20 Stanzas 20—33 contain a collection of formula[s] repeated when the bride mounts her chariot, while sh[e] is travelling to her husband's house, when she arriv[es] there, and on the following morning. *This* : chario[t]. *Kiṁśuka* : the wood of the Butea frondosa. *Śalmali* : the silk-cotton tree; Salmalia malabarica. *Sūryā* : th[e] girl is addressed by the name of Sūryā, the typical brid[e].

21 *Viśvāvasu* : one of the Gandharvas, the protect[or] of virgins. He is told to leave the bride who no long[er] needs his care, and to transfer his guardianship to som[e] marriageable maiden who has not yet found a husban[d]. *Fair one* : *vyáktām* : 'decorated with ornaments.'—Wilso[n].

23 Straight in direction be the paths, and thornless, whereon our fellows travel to the wooing.
Let Aryaman and Bhaga lead us : perfect, O Gods, the union of the wife and husband.

24 Now from the noose of Varuṇa I free thee, wherewith Most Blessed Savitar hath bound thee.
In Law's seat, to the world of virtuous action, I give thee up uninjured with thy consort.

25 Hence, and not thence, I send thee free. I make thee softly fettered there.
That, Bounteous Indra, she may live blest in her fortune and her sons.

26 Let Pūṣan take thy hand and hence conduct thee ; may the two Aśvins on their car transport thee.
Go to the house to be the household's mistress and speak as lady to thy gathered people.

27 Happy be thou and prosper with thy children here : be vigilant to rule thy household in this home.
Closely unite thy body with this man, thy lord. So shall ye, full of years, address your company.

28 Her hue is blue and red : the fiend who clingeth close is driven off.
Well thrive the kinsmen of this bride : the husband is bound fast in bonds.

29 Give thou the woollen robe away : deal treasure to the Brahman priests.
This female fiend hath got her feet, and as a wife attends her lord.

30 Unlovely is his body when it glistens with this wicked fiend,
What time the husband wraps about his limbs the garment of his wife.

31 Consumptions, from her people, which follow the bride's resplendent train,—
These let the Holy Gods again bear to the place from which they came.

32 Let not the highway thieves who lie in ambush find the wedded pair.
By pleasant ways let them escape the danger, and let foes depart.

33 Signs of good fortune mark the bride : come all of you and look at her.
Wish her prosperity, and then return unto your homes again.

34 Pungent is this, and bitter this, filled, as it were, with arrow-barbs, Empoisoned and not fit for use.
The Brahman who knows Sūryā well deserves the garment of the bride.

35 The fringe, the cloth that decks her head, and then the triply parted robe,—
Behold the hues which Sūryā wears : these doth the Brahman purify.

36 I take thy hand in mine for happy fortune that thou mayst reach old age with me thy husband.
Gods, Aryaman, Bhaga, Savitar, Purandhi, have given thee to be my household's mistress.

37 O Puṣan, send her on as most auspicious, her who shall be the sharer of my pleasures ;
Her who shall twine her loving arms about me, and welcome all my love and mine embraces.

23 *To the wooing* : to the father, to whom the interceders are to apply for his daughter's hand on behalf of their friend, according to Sāyaṇa.

24 *The noose of Varuṇa* : the girdle with which the bride is girded after she has been bathed, combed, and dressed for the marriage ceremony. See Prof. Max Müller's *Ṛgveda-Saṁhitā*, Vol. VI., Preface, p. 14. Or, as Lanman suggests, the noose may mean the tie by which a girl is bound to her father till marriage. *Law's seat* : the place of sacrifice, the altar.

Stanzas 24—26 and 32, 33 are spoken just before the bride's departure from her father's house.

25 *Hence, and not thence* : from thy father's house and not from thy husband's.

27 *Be vigilant to rule thy household* : this is Sāyaṇa's explanation. 'Be watchful over the domestic fire.' —Wilson. The verse is addressed to the bride, and to the newly-wedded pair on arrival at the bridegroom's house.

28 *Her hue* : the colour of Kṛtyā, Magic personified, a female deity or fiend.

29 *The woollen robe* : 'the garment soiled by the body.' —Wilson. *Attends her lord* : the magic, or evil spell, returns to its originator.—Ludwig.

31 *From her people* : 'a most remarkable and direct assumption of "heredity" as a lurking danger.'—Mme, Zénaïde Ragozin, *Vedic India*, p. 371.

33 Perhaps spoken, on the way, to the spectators of the procession.

34 *This* : the bride's garment. *Sūryā* : meaning here the song of Sūryā's Bridal.

35 The meaning of *āśāsanam*, *viśasanam*, and *adhivikārtanam* is uncertain. Prof. Wilson renders these words by border-cloth,' 'head-cloth,' and 'divided skirt.' Prof. Weber and the St. Petersburg Lexicon explain the passage as referring to the preparation of the carcass of the animal that has been slaughtered for the festivity. According to this view the first line might be rendered :— 'The butchering, the cutting up, the severing of limb and joint'; and for 'hues' 'forms' might be substituted.

36 The bridegroom addresses the bride.

38 For thee, with bridal train, they, first, escorted Sūryā to her home.
Give to the husband in return, Agni, the wife with progeny.

39 Agni hath given the bride again with splendour and with ample life.
Long lived be he who is her lord; a hundred autumns let him live.

40 Soma obtained her first of all; next the Gandharva was her lord.
Agni was thy third husband : now one born of woman is thy fourth.

41 Soma to the Gandharva, and to Agni the Gandharva gave :
And Agni hath bestowed on me riches and sons and this my spouse.

42 Be ye not parted; dwell ye here ; reach the full time of human life.
With sons and grandsons sport and play, rejoicing in your own abode.

43 So may Prajāpati bring children forth to us ; may Aryaman adorn us till old age come nigh.
Not inauspicious enter thou thy husband's house : bring blessing to our bipeds and our quadrupeds.

44 Not evil-eyed, no slayer of thy husband, bring weal to cattle, radiant, gentle-hearted ;
Loving the Gods, delightful, bearing heroes, bring blessing to our quadrupeds and bipeds.

45 O Bounteous Indra, make this bride blest in her sons and fortunate.
Vouchsafe to her ten sons, and make her husband the eleventh man.

46 Over thy husband's father and thy husband's mother bear full sway.
Over the sister of thy lord, over his brothers rule supreme.

47 So may the Universal Gods, so may the Waters join our hearts.
May Mātariśvan, Dhātar, and Deṣṭrī together bind us close.

HYMN LXXXVI. *Indra.*

1. MEN have abstained from pouring juice : they count not Indra as a God.
Where at the votary's store my friend Vṛṣākapi hath drunk his fill. Supreme is Indra over all.

2 Thou, Indra, heedless passest by the ill Vṛṣākapi hath wrought ;
Yet nowhere else thou findest place wherein to drink the Soma juice. Supreme is Indra over all.

3 What hath he done to injure thee, this tawny beast Vṛṣākapi,
With whom thou art so angry now ? What is the votary's foodful store ? Supreme is Indra over all.

4 Soon may the hound who hunts the boar seize him and bite him in the ear,
O Indra, that Vṛṣākapi whom thou protectest as a friend. Supreme is Indra over all.

5 Kapi hath marred the beauteous things, all deftly wrought, that were my joy.
In pieces will I rend his head ; the sinner's portion shall be woe. Supreme is Indra over all.

38 *Thee* : Agni. *They* : the Gandharvas, according to Sāyaṇa.

40 As the typical bride Sūryā was first married to Soma, so the young maid originally belongs to him, then to the Gandharva, as the guardian of virginity, then, to Agni as the sacred fire round which she walks in the marriage ceremony, and fourthly to her human husband. —Grassmann.

42 The formulae contained in stanzas 42—47 are repeated when the bridegroom has returned with his bride to his home, and offers sacrifice with fire. The wedded pair are addressed first, and then the bride is exhorted and blessed. Stanza 47 is spoken by the bridegroom for his wife and himself.

47 *Deṣṭrī* : Instructress, a female deity, not mentioned elsewhere in the Ṛgveda. According to Sāyaṇa, *dātrī phalānām sarasvatī* is meant : 'the bountiful (Sarasvatī).' —Wilson.

For a full account of the marriage ceremonies of the Hindus, derived from the ritual of Brāhmans who use the Sāma-veda, see Colebrooke's *Miscellaneous Essays*, No. III., and Weber and Hass, *Indische Studien*, V. pp. 177 ff. See also *Hymns of the Atharva-veda* Book XIV., and Dr. J. Ehni's paper. *Zeitschrift der Deutschen Morgenländischen Gesellschaft*, XXXIII. pp. 166 ff. I have relied mainly on Ludwig's Commentary. Prof. Grassmann has banished the hymn to his Appendix.

1 Sāyaṇa ascribes this stanza to Indra; others make Indrāṇī the speaker. Vṛṣākapi is said to have monopolized the offerings that should have been presented to Indra. *Vṛṣākapi*—literally 'the strong ape.' or 'the male ape' —appears to be a sort of intermediate being between a demigod and a demon; but it is not easy to determine his nature. Sāyaṇa calls him the son of Indra.

He is also said to be the setting sun, and the sun who draws up vapour and irrigates with mist. According to M. Bergaigne, *La Religion Védique*, II. 270, he was a mythical sacrificer.

2 Indrāṇī blames Indra for his apathy.

3 Indra speaks. *What is the votary's foodful store* ? why should his appropriation of the worshipper's offerings make thee so angry ?

4 Indrāṇī is the speaker of this stanza and of the two, or three, that follow.

5 *Kapi* : the ape ; an abbreviation of Vṛṣākapi. *Hath marred the beauteous things* : according to Sāyaṇa, hath spoiled the oblations prepared for me by my worshippers. But it seems more probable that Vṛṣākapi has assaulted Indrāṇī and inflicted injuries on her person.

6 No Dame hath ampler charms than I, or greater wealth of love's delights.
None with more ardour offers all her beauty to her lord's embrace. Supreme is Indra over all.

7 Mother whose love is quickly won, I say what verily will be.
My breast, O Mother, and my head and both my hips seem quivering. Supreme is Indra over all.

8 Dame with the lovely hands and arms, with broad hair-plaits add ample hips,
Why, O thou Hero's wife, art thou angry with our Vṛṣākapi ? Supreme is Indra over all.

9 This noxious creature looks on me as one bereft of hero's love,
Yet Heroes for my sons have I, the Maruts' Friend and Indra's Queen. Supreme is Indra over all.

10 From olden time the matron goes to feast and general sacrifice.
Mother of Heroes, Indra's Queen, the rite's ordainer is extolled. Supreme is Indra over all.

11 So have I heard Indrāṇī called most fortunate among these Dames,
For never shall her Consort die in future time through length of days. Supreme is Indra over all.

12 Never, Indrāṇī, have I joyed without my friend Vṛṣākapi,
Whose welcome offering here, made pure with water, goeth to the Gods. Supreme is Indra over all.

13 Wealthy Vṛṣākapāyī, blest with sons and consorts of thy sons,
Indra will eat thy bulls, thy dear oblation that effecteth much. Supreme is Indra over all.

14 Fifteen in number, then, for me a score of bullocks they prepare,
And I devour the fat thereof : they fill my belly full with food. Supreme is Indra over all.

15 Like as a bull with pointed horn, loud bellowing amid the herds,
Sweet to thine heart, O Indra, is the brew which she who tends thee pours. Supreme is Indra over all.

18 O Indra this Vṛṣākapi hath found a slain wild animal,
Dresser, and new-made pan, and knife, and wagon with a load of wood. Supreme is Indra over all.

19 Distinguishing the Dāsa and the Ārya, viewing all, I go.
I look upon the wise, and drink the simple votary's Soma juice. Supreme is Indra over all.

20 The desert plains and steep descents, how many leagues in length they spread !
Go to the nearest houses, go unto thine home, Vṛṣākapi. Supreme is Indra over all.

21 Turn thee again Vṛṣākapi : we twain will bring thee happiness.
Thou goest homeward on thy way along this path which leads to sleep. Supreme is Indra over all.

22 When, Indra and Vṛṣākapi, ye travelled upward to your home,
Where was that noisome beast, to whom went it, the beast that troubles man ? Supreme is Indra over all.

6 Indrāṇī speaks with pride of her voluptuous charms which incited Vṛṣākapi to his amorous assault.

7 This stanza is ascribed by Sāyaṇa to Vṛṣākapi. It is hardly intelligible; but, as Ludwig says, it seems to be spoken by Indrāṇī, expressing her indignation at Vṛṣākapi's audacity which makes all her body quiver with rage.

8 Indra speaks.

9 Indrāṇī speaks this and the following stanza. *Bereft of hero's love* : who has no brave husband to protect her.

10 *The matron goes to feast* : Indrāṇī means that Vṛṣākapi assaulted her when she was on her way to a festival, which women were accustomed to attend; and that her rank as Indra's consort did not preserve her from insult.

11 Indra speaks this and the following stanza.

13 Spoken by Vṛṣākapi to his wife Vṛṣākapāyī who is said to represent the dawn, or, by others, the gloaming which follows the setting sun Vṛṣākapi.

14 Indra speaks. *Fifteen* : sacrificers ; probably Vṛṣākapi and his wife, and their sons and daughters-in-law. Sāyaṇa explains differently :—'The worshippers dress for me fifteen (and) twenty bulls.'—Wilson.

15 Indrāṇī speaks, endeavouring to attract him to her own libation instead of the offerings of Vṛṣākapi.

I pass over stanzas 16 and 17, which I cannot translate into decent English.

18 Indrāṇī speaks, but her speech is difficult to understand. *Wild animal* : von Roth conjectures 'wild ass' as the meaning of *párasvantam* here. *Dresser* : or slaughter-bench. 'A fire-place (to cook it).'—Wilson. Indrāṇī seems to speak depreciatingly of a sacrifice offered by Vṛṣākapi as consisting of an unsuitable victim, prepared with instruments and means which chance has thrown in his way. Ludwig thinks that Vṛṣākapi may represent the Moon whose spots are fancifully considered to be the objects mentioned by Indrāṇī.

19 *I look* : with favour. *The simple votary* is the worshipper who offers his libation in a sincere spirit of devotion. The stanza and the two following are spoken by Indra.

20 Vṛṣākapi appears to meditate flight into distant deserts to escape from the wrathful Indrāṇi. Indra dissuades him, and promises to reconcile Indrāṇī to him.

23 Daughter of Manu, Parśu bare a score of children at a birth.
Her portion verily was bliss although her burthen caused her grief.

HYMN LXXXVII. *Agni.*

1. I BALM with oil the mighty Rakṣas-slayer ; to the most famous Friend I come for shelter
Enkindled, sharpened by our rites, may Agni protect us in the day and night from evil.

2 O Jātavedas with the teeth of iron, enkindled with thy flame attack the demons.
Seize with thy tongue the foolish gods' adorers : rend, put within thy mouth the raw-flesh eaters.

3 Apply thy teeth, the upper and the lower, thou who hast both, enkindled and destroying.
Roam also in the air, O King, around us, and with thy jaws assail the wicked spirits.

4 Bending thy shafts through sacrifices, Agni, whetting their points with song as if with whetstones,
Pierce to the heart therewith the Yātudhānas, and break their arms uplifed to attack thee.

5 Pierce through the Yātudhāna's skin, O Agni ; let the destroying dart with fire consume him.
Rend his joints, Jātavedas, let the eater of flesh, flesh-seeking, track his mangled body.

6 Where now thou seest Agni Jātavedas, one of these demons standing still or roaming,
Or flying on those paths in air's mid-region, sharpen the shaft and as an archer pierce him.

7 Tear from the evil spirit, Jātavedas, what he hath seized and with his spears hath captured.
Blazing before him strike him down, O Agni ; let spotted carrion-eating kites devour him.

8 Here tell this forth, O Agni : whosoever is, he himself, or acteth as, a demon,
Him grasp, O thou Most Youthful, with thy fuel : to the Man-seer's eye give him as booty.

9 With keen glance guard the sacrifice, O Agni : thou Sage, conduct it onward to the Vasus.
Let not the fiends, O Man-beholder, harm thee burning against the Rākṣasas to slay them.

10 Look on the fiend mid men, as Man-beholder: rend thou his three extremities in pieces.
Demolish with thy flame his ribs, O Agni, the Yātudhāna's root destroy thou triply.

11 Thrice, Agni, let thy noose surround the demon who with his falsehood injures Holy Order.
Loud roaring with thy flame, O Jātavedas, crush him and cast him down before the singer.

12 Lend thou the worshipper that eye, O Agni, wherewith thou lookest on the hoof-armed demon.
With light celestial in Atharvan's manner burn up the fool who ruins truth with falsehood.

22 The two concluding stanzas to be spoken by Indrāṇī. Stanza 22 is obscure, and stanza 23 has no discoverable connexion with the rest of the hymn.

23 *Daughter of Manu* : that is, of the progenitor of men. Nothing more is known of *Parśu,* which means a rib. Much of this hymn appears to be inexplicable. M. Bergaigne thinks that Vṛṣākapi, Indra's friend, represents Soma, and Indrāṇī the wife of Indra represents Prayer. 'This bizarre myth would symbolize the frequently expressed idea that Indra loves neither the sacred beverage without prayer nor prayer without the sacred beverage. He wishes therefore his union with Prayer to be accompanied by the union of Prayer with Soma, and he neglects sacrifice as long as this union of the two essential elements of worship remains unaccomplished.'—See *La Religion Védique,* II. 270, 271.

Prof. Geldner gives a different interpretation of the hymn, which he has translated and exhaustively discussed in *Vedische Studien,* II. pp. 22-42. See also Oldenberg, *Religion des Veda,* 172-174.

2 *The demons* : Yātudhānas, explained by Sāyaṇa as=Rākṣasas. See VII. 104. 15. *Foolish gods' adorers*: *mūradevān* : according to Sāyaṇa, a special class of evil spirits called Mūradevas because they make destruction their sport.

5 *The eater of flesh* : the wolf or other carnivorous animal.

8 *The Man-seer* here is either Agni himself or Sūrya the Sun.

9 *To the Vasus* : to the Gods to whom the oblations are made. Sāyaṇa explains *vásubhyaḥ* here by *vasūnām-arthāya*:—'to (the acquisition of) riches.'—Wilson.

10 *His three extremities* : his three heads, according to Sāyaṇa. "Kopf und Schultern,' head and shoulders.—Grassmann. *Root* : meaning his feet. *Triply*: used vaguely, to correspond with the three upper extremities. 'Cut off the triple foot of the *Yātudhāna*.'—Wilson.

12 *Hoof-armed* : striking with the hoof. According to Sāyaṇa 'having nails like hoofs.' *In Atharvan's manner* : like Atharvan, the ancient priest who is said to have been the first who obtained fire.

13 Agni, what curse the pair this day have uttered, what heated word the worshippers have spoken,
Each arrowy taunt sped from the angry spirit,—pierce to the heart therewith the Yātudhānas.

14 With fervent heat exterminate the demons; destroy the fiends with burning flame, O Agni.
Destroy with fire the foolish gods' adorers ; blaze and destroy the insatiable monsters.

15 May Gods destroy this day the evil-doer : may each hot curse of his return and blast him.
Let arrows pierce the liar in his vitals, and Viśva's net enclose the Yātudhāna.

16 The fiend who smears himself with flesh of cattle, with flesh of horses and of human bodies,
Who steals the milch-cow's milk away, O Agni,—tear off the heads of such with fiery fury.

17 The cow gives milk each year, O Man-regarder : let not the Yātudhāna ever taste it.
If one would glut him with the biesting, Agni, pierce with thy flame his vitals as he meets thee.

18 Let the fiends drink the poison of the cattle ; may Aditi cast off the evil-doers.
May the God Savitar give them up to ruin, and be their share of plants and herbs denied them.

19 Agni, from days of old thou slayest demons : never shall Rākṣasas in fight o'ercome thee.
Burn up the foolish ones, the flesh-devourers : let none of them escape thine heavenly arrow.

20 Guard us, O Agni, from above and under, protect us from behind us and before us ;
And may thy flames, most fierce and never wasting, glowing with fervent heat, consume the sinner.

21 From rear, from front, from under, from above us, O King, protect us as a Sage with wisdom.
Guard to old age thy friend, O Friend, Eternal : O Agni, as Immortal, guard us mortals.

22 We set thee round us as a fort, victorious Agni, thee a Sage,
Of hero lineage, day by day, destroyer of our treacherous foes.

23 Burn with thy poison turned against the treacherous brood of Rākṣasas,
O Agni, with thy sharpened glow, with lances armed with points of flame.

24 Burn thou the paired Kimīdins, burn, Agni, the Yātudhāna pairs.
I sharpen thee, Infallible, with hymns. O Sage, be vigilant.

25 Shoot forth, O Agni, with thy flame : demolish them on every side.
Break thou the Yātudhāna's strength, the vigour of the Rākṣasa.

HYMN LXXXVIII. *Agni.*

1. DEAR, ageless sacrificial drink is offered in light-discovering, heaven-pervading Agni.
The Gods spread forth through his Celestial Nature, that he might bear the world up and sustain it.

2 The world was swallowed and concealed in darkness : Agni was born, and light became apparent.
The Deities, the broad earth, and the heavens, and plants, and waters gloried in his friendship.

3 Inspired by Gods who claim our adoration, I now will laud Eternal Lofty Agni,
Him who hath spread abroad the earth with lustre, this heaven, and both the worlds, and air's mid-region.

4 Earliest Priest whom all the Gods accepted, and chose him, and anointed him with butter,
He swiftly made all things that fly, stand, travel, all that hath motion, Agni Jātavedas.

5 Because thou, Agni, Jātavedas, stoodest at the world's head with thy refulgent splendour,

13 *The pair* : the married pair : perhaps the sacrificer and his wife. The Ṛṣi prays that every hasty word that may have been uttered by pious people in their anger may be used as a weapon to wound the Yātudhāna.

15 *Viśva's net* : the noose of the all-pervading Agni.

18 *The poison of the cattle* : if they drink milk, let it poison them. According to Sāyaṇa, let them drink the poison of the cattle (which is kept in the house), meaning perhaps some poisonous ointment used for external application only.

24 *Kimīdins* : treacherous and malevolent spirits. See VII. 104. 2, note.

1 *Sacrificial drink* : 'swelling oblation,' according to Prof. Pischel.

5 *We sent thee forth* : the Ṛṣi glorifies the power of the priests who made Agni their messenger to the Gods.

We sent thee forth with hymns and songs and praises : thou filledst heaven and earth, God meet for worship.

6 Head of the world is Agni in the night-time ; then, as the Sun, at morn springs up and rises.
Then to his task goes the prompt Priest foreknowing the wondrous power of Gods who must be honoured.

7 Lovely is he who, kindled in his greatness, hath shone forth, seated in the heavens, refulgent.
With resonant hymns all Gods who guard our bodies have offered up oblation in this Agni.

8 First the Gods brought the hymnal into being ; then they engendered Agni, then oblation.
He was their sacrifice that guards our bodies : him the heavens know, the earth, the waters know him.

9 He, Agni, whom the Gods have generated, in whom they offered up all worlds and creatures,
He with his bright glow heated earth and heaven, urging himself right onward in his grandeur.

10 Then by the laud the Gods engendered Agni in heaven, who fills both worlds through strength and vigour.
They made him to appear in threefold essence : he ripens plants of every form and nature.

11 What time the Gods, whose due is worship, set him as Sūrya, Son of Aditi, in heaven,
When the Pair, ever wandering, sprang to being, all creatures that existed looked upon them.

12 For all the world of life the Gods made Agni Vaiśvānara to be the days' bright Banner,—
Him who hath spread abroad the radiant Mornings, and, coming with his light, unveils the darkness.

13 The wise and holy Deities engendered Agni Vaiśvānara whom age ne'er touches.
The Ancient Star that wanders on for ever, lofty and strong, Lord of the Living Being.

14 We call upon the Sage with holy verses, Agni Vaiśvānara the ever-beaming,
Who hath surpassed both heaven and earth in greatness : he is a God below, a God above us.

15 I have heard mention of two several pathways, ways of the Fathers and of Gods and mortals.
On these two paths each moving creature travels, each thing between the Father and the Mother.

16 These two united paths bear him who journeys born from the head and pondered with the spirit
He stands directed to all things existing, hasting, unresting in his fiery splendour.

17 Which of us twain knows where they speak together, upper and lower of the two rite-leaders ?
Our friends have helped to gather our assembly. They came to sacrifice ; who will announce it ?

18 How many are the Fires and Suns in number ? What is the number of the Dawns and Waters ?
Not jestingly I speak to you, O Fathers. Sages, I ask you this for information.

19 As great as is the fair-winged Morning's presence to him who dwells beside us, Mātariśvan !

6 Agni, who is the Moon by night, at dawn becomes Sūrya or the Sun-God who when he sets again becomes Agni.

9 *All worlds and creatures* : proleptically : meaning that the oblation offered by the gods was destined to produce the universe.—Ludwig. According to Sāyaṇa :—'in whom all beings have offered oblations; ' but it is clear that the oblations of the Gods are intended.

10 *Through strength and vigour* : *śáktibhiḥ* : 'by his functions :'—Wilson. *In threefold essence* : or in three conditions, or places, as the Sun, lightning, and terrestrial fire.

11 *The Pair* : the Sun and Moon. According to Sāyaṇa, Uṣas and Sūrya.

13 *Lord of the Living Being* : the meaning of *yakṣásya* is uncertain. Sāyaṇa explains it by *pūjyasya devasya*, of the adorable God. 'The observer of what is firm.'—Ludwig. 'The lord of meteors.'—Grassmann. 'Surveillant du Yakṣa.'—Bergaigne.

14 *Below* : on earth.

15 *Two several pathways* : the way to the other world and the way back to the earth. *The Father and the Mother* : heaven and earth.

16 *Him who journeys* : Agni. *From the head* : of the world. From Āditya, the head or chief of all existence, according to Sāyaṇa.

17 *Us twain* : Agni and the Ṛṣi. *Upper and lower* : according to Sāyaṇa, the upper fire is Vāyu and the lower is terrestrial Agni. *Who will announce it ?* : Agni alone will make the sacrifice known to the Gods.

19 *Morning's presence* : the light of Dawn which spreads over heaven and earth. *Him who dwells beside us* : the Yajamāna, or institutor of the sacrifice.—Ludwig. *Below the Hotar* : below the regular Hotar-priest. Sāyaṇa explains this stanza differently :—'As long, Mātariśvan, as the swiftly-moving (nights) cover the face of the dawn, (so long) the *Bráhman*, the inferior sitting down (to perform the work) of the *Hotṛ*, approaching the sacrifice supports (the ceremony).'—Wilson.

Is what the Brāhman does when he approaches to sacrifice and sits below the Hotar.

HYMN LXXXIX. *Indra.*

1. I WILL extol the most heroic Indra who with his might forced earth and sky asunder;
Who hath filled all with width as man's Upholder, surpassing floods and rivers in his greatness.

2 Sūrya is he : throughout the wide expanses shall Indra turn him, swift as car-wheels, hither,
Like a stream resting not but ever active : he hath destroyed, with light, the black-hued darkness.

3 To him I sing a holy prayer, incessant, new, matchless, common to the earth and heav en,
Who marks, as they were backs, all living creatures : ne'er doth he fail a friend, the noble Indra.

4 I will send forth my songs in flow unceasing, like water from the ocean's depth, to Indra.
Who to his car on both its sides securely hath fixed the earth and heaven as with an axle.

5 Rousing with draughts, the Shaker, rushing onward, impetuous, very strong, armed as with arrows
Is Soma ; forest trees and all the bushes deceive not Indra with their offered likeness.

6 Soma hath flowed to him whom naught can equal, the earth, the heavens, the firmament, the mountains,—
When heightened in his ire his indignation shatters the firm and breaks the strong in pieces.

7 As an axe fells the tree so he slew Vṛtra, brake down the strongholds and dug out the rivers.
He cleft the mountain like a new-made pitcher. Indra brought forth the kine with his Companions.

8 Wise art thou, Punisher of guilt, O Indra. The sword lops limbs, thou smitest down the sinner,
The men who injure, as it were a comrade, the lofty Law of Varuṇa and Mitra.

9 Men who lead evil lives, who break agreements, and injure Varuṇa, Aryaman and Mitra,—
Against these foes, O Mighty Indra, sharpen, as furious death, thy Bull of fiery colour.

10 Indra is Sovran Lord of Earth and Heaven, Indra is Lord of waters and of mountains.
Indra is Lord of prosperers and sages : Indra must be invoked in rest and effort.

11 Vaster than days and nights, Giver of increase, vaster than firmament and flood of ocean,
Vaster than bounds of earth and wind's extension, vaster than rivers and our lands is Indra.

12 Forward, as herald of refulgent Morning, let thine insatiate arrow fly, O Indra,
And pierce, as 'twere a stone launched forth from heaven, with hottest blaze the men who love deception.

13 Him, verily, the moons, the mountains followed, the tall trees followed and the plants and herbage.
Yearning with love both Worlds approached, the Waters waited on Indra when he first had being.

14 Where was the vengeful dart when thou, O Indra, clavest the demon ever bent on outrage ?

1 *With width* : with his own extended magnitude. 'With radiance.'—Wilson.

2 *Sūrya is he* : Indra is identified with the Sun whose course he directs. According to Sāyaṇa, *sūryaḥ* here = *suvīryah*, heroic.

3 *Incessant* : or unerring that is, in strict accordance with the rules of the ritual. *As they were backs* : as if they were horses or oxen, the length and shape of whose backs must be carefully considered in forming a judgment of their worth.

5 Prof. Wilson observes:—'This verse is obscure, partly because the words are unusual, partly because there is a confusion between *Indra* and *Soma*.' *Deceive not Indra* : he will not accept any substitutes : he will have nothing but the genuine Soma-plant and its juice.

7 *His Companions* : the Maruts, who assisted him in performing his exploit.

8 *Punisher of guilt* : here Indra is said to discharge the duties which in more ancient hymns are ascribed to Agni and to Mitra and Varuṇa.

9 *Thy Bull* : thy thunderbolt. 'The heavy strong red weapon.'—M. Müller.

10 *In rest and effort* : 'for the acquirement and preservation of wealth.—Wilson.

13 *The moons* : : or, the months. *Waited on Indra* : as the representative of the Sun, the originator of all life. —Ludwig.

14 *Fiends* : *mitrakrúvah* : the exact meaning of the word is uncertain. Prof. Ludwig takes it as a genitive case : 'What time they lay there on the earth extended like oxen in a demon's place of slaughter.'

When fiends lay there upon the ground extended like cattle in the place of immolation ?

15 Those who are set in enmity against us, the Oganas, O Indra, waxen mighty,—
Let blinding darkness follow those our foemen, while these shall have bright shining nights to light them.

16 May plentiful libations of the people, and singing Ṛsis' holy prayers rejoice thee.
Hearing with love this common invocation, come unto us, pass by all those who praise thee.

17 O Indra, thus may we be made partakers of thy new favours that shall bring us profit.
Singing with love, may we the Viśvāmitras win daylight even now through thee, O Indra.

18 Call we on Maghavan, auspicious Indra, best hero in the fight where spoil is gathered,
The Strong who listens, who gives aid in battles, who slays the Vṛtras, wins and gathers riches.

HYMN XC. *Puruṣa.*

1. A THOUSAND heads hath Puruṣa, a thousand eyes, a thousand feet.
On every side pervading earth he fills a space ten fingers wide.

2 This Puruṣa is all that yet hath been and all that is to be ;
The Lord of Immortality which waxes greater still by food.

3 So mighty is his greatness ; yea, greater than this is Puruṣa.
All creatures are one-fourth of him, three-fourths eternal life in heaven.

4 With three-fourths Puruṣa went up : one-fourth of him again was here.
Thence he strode out to every side over what eats not and what eats.

5 From him Virāj was born ; again Puruṣa from Virāj was born.
As soon as he was born he spread eastward and westward o'er the earth.

6 When Gods prepared the sacrifice with Puruṣa as their offering,
Its oil was spring, the holy gift was autumn; summer was the wood.

7 They balmed as victim on the grass Puruṣa born in earliest time.

15 *Oganas* : probably the name of some hostile clan. According to Sāyaṇa, enemies assembled in numbers. *These* : us and our friends here.

16 *All those who praise thee* : all other worshippers.

18 This is the concluding stanza of several hymns of the Viśvāmitras. See III. 30. 22; 31.22; 32. 17; 34. 11; 35. 11; 36. 11.

---

1 *Puruṣa*, embodied spirit, or Man personified and regarded as the soul and original source of the universe, the personal and life-giving principle in all animated beings, is said to have a *thousand*, that is, innumerable, *heads*, *eyes*, and *feet*, as being one with all created life. *A space ten fingers wide* : the region of the heart of man, wherein the soul was supposed to reside. Although as the Universal Soul he pervades the universe, as the Individual Soul he is enclosed in a space of narrow dimensions. See *Hymns of the Atharva-veda*, XIX. 6. 1, note.

2 The second line is explained in various ways. The meaning of the words seems to be : he is lord of immortality or the immortal world of the Gods, which grows greater by food, that is, by the sacrificial offerings of men. According to Sāyaṇa : he is the lord or distributor of immortality because he becomes the visible world in order that living beings may obtain the fruits of their actions and gain *mokṣa* or final liberation from their bonds, 'he is also the lord of immortality ; for he mounts beyond (his own condition) for the food (of living beings).'—Wilson. Colebrooke translates the line :—'he is that which grows by nourishment, and he is the distributor of immortality .' Dr. Muir renders it by :—'He is also the lord of immortality, since by food he expands.' According to the paraphrase in the *Bhāgavata-Purāṇa*, the meaning of the last clause is: 'since he hath transcended mortal nutriment.' Prof. Ludwig's version is : 'auch über die unsterblichkeit gebietend, (da er,) was durch speise (ist,) weit überragt,' ruling also over immortality, (since he) far transcends what (exists) through food; but in his Commentary a somewhat different explanation is given. 'Ruling over immortality, he was all that grows by food'.—Peterson.

3 *Eternal life* : *amṛtam* : immortality, or the immortal Gods.

4 *Over what eats not and what eats* : over animate and inanimate creation. According to Sāyaṇa and Mahīdhara, over both classes of created things, those capable of enjoyment, that is, who can taste the reward and punishment of good and evil actions, such as Gods, men, and lower animals, and those who are incapable thereof, such as mountains and rivers—*cetanam*, or conscious, *acetanam*, or unconscious, creation.

5 *From him* : or, from that, the 'one-fourth' mentioned in stanzas 3 and 4. *Virāj*, or, in the nominative form, Virāṭ, is said to have come, in the form of the mundane egg, from Ādi-Puruṣa, the primeval Puruṣa, or presiding Male or Spirit, 'who then entered into this egg, which he animates as its vital soul or divine principle.' Or Virāj may 'be the female counterpart of Puruṣa as Aditi of Dakṣa in X.72. 4, 5.' See Dr. Muir's exhaustive Note on this passage, *O. S. Texts*, V. pp. 369, 370; and Wallis, *Cosmology of the Ṛgveda*, p. 87. *Eastward and westward* : or, before and behind.

6 *The sacrifice* : *mānasam yajñam*, a mental or imaginary sacrifice, according to Sāyaṇa. *Summer* : *grīṣmá* does not occur in any other ṚV. hymn. *Spring* : *vasantá* occurs in only one other ṚV. hymn.

7 *On the grass* : on the sacred grass used in sacrifices. *Sādhyas* : a class of celestial beings, probably ancient divine sacrificers.

With him the Deities and all Sādhyas and Ṛṣis sacrificed.

8 From that great general sacrifice the dripping fat was gathered up.
He formed the creatures of the air, and animals both wild and tame.

9 From that great general sacrifice Ṛcas and Sāma-hymns were born :
Therefrom were spells and charms produced; the Yajus had its birth from it.

10 From it were horses born, from it all cattle with two rows of teeth :
From it were generated kine, from it the goats and sheep were born.

11 When they divided Puruṣa how many portions did they make?
What do they call his mouth, his arms ? What do they call his thighs and feet ?

12 The Brāhman was his mouth, of both his arms was the Rājanya made.
His thighs became the Vaiśya, from his feet the Śūdra was produced.

13 The Moon was gendered from his mind, and from his eye the Sun had birth;
Indra and Agni from his mouth were born, and Vāyu from his breath.

14 Forth from his navel came mid-air ; the sky was fashioned from his head ;
Earth from his feet, and from his ear the regions. Thus they formed the worlds.

15 Seven fencing-sticks had he, thrice seven layers of fuel were prepared,
When the Gods, offering sacrifice, bound, as their victim, Puruṣa.

16 Gods, sacrificing, sacrificed the victim : these were the earliest holy ordinances.
The Mighty Ones attained the height of heaven, there where the Sādhyas, Gods of old, are dwelling.

HYMN XCI. *Agni.*

1. Brisk, at the place of Iḷā, hymned by men who wake, our own familiar Friend is kindled in the house ;
Hotar of all oblation, worthy of our choice, Lord, beaming, trusty friend to one who loveth him.

2 He, excellent in glory, guest in every house, finds like a swift-winged bird a home in every tree.
Benevolent to men, he scorns no living man : Friend to the tribes of men he dwells with every tribe.

3 Most sage with insight, passing skilful with thy powers art thou, O Agni, wise with wisdom, knowing all.
As Vasu, thou alone art Lord of all good things, of all the treasures that the heavens and earth produce.

4 Foreknowing well, O Agni, thou in Iḷā's place hast occupied thy regular station balmed with oil.
Marked are thy comings like the comings of the Dawns, the rays of him who shineth spotless as the Sun.

5 Thy glories are, as lightnings from the rainy cloud, marked, many-hued, like heralds of the Dawns' approach,

8 *The dripping fat* : 'the mixture of curds and butter.' —Wilson. *He* : or, it; the sacrificed victim Puruṣa, or the sacred clarified butter. *The creatures of the air* : 'those animals over whom Vāyu presides.'—Wilson.

9 *Spells and charms*: probably those of the later collection of the Atharvaveda. *The Yajus* : the Yajur-veda.

12 *Rājanya* : the second or Kṣatriya caste, the regal and military class. *Vaiśya* : the husbandman; he whose business is agriculture and trade. *Śūdra* : the labourer. The Brāhman is called the mouth of Puruṣa, as having the special privilege, as a priest, of addressing the Gods in prayer. The arms of Puruṣa became the Rājanya the prince and soldier who wields the sword and spear. His thighs, the strongest parts of his body, became the agriculturist and tradesman, the chief support of society; and his feet, the emblems of vigour and activity, became the Śūdra or labouring man on whose toil and industry all ultimately rests. This is the only passage in the Ṛgveda which enumerates the four castes.

14 Cf. the creation myth of the world-giant Ymir or Hymir in old Northern poetry. The hills are his bones, the vault of the sky his skull, the sea his blood, and the clouds his brains.—*Corpus Poeticum Boreale*, Vol. II. p. 468.

15 *Fencing-sticks* : guards, or pieces of wood laid round the sacrificial fire to enclose it. Sāyaṇa explains *paridhdyaḥ* as the seven metres, or as six shallow trenches dug round the fire, and an imaginary one round the Sun. Mahīdhara says that the seven oceans may be intended.

This pantheistic hymn, which is generally called the Puruṣasūkta, is of comparatively recent origin, and appears to be an attempt to harmonise the two ideas of sacrifice and creation. For further information regarding it, see Muir, *O. S. Texts*, I. pp. 6—11, and V. 368—377, Prof. Max Müller, *Ancient Sanskrit Literature*, pp. 570f, and Dr. Scherman, *Philosophische Hymnen aus der Ṛg-und Atharva-veda-Saṁhitā*, pp. 11—23. The hymn has also been translated by Colebrooke, *Miscellaneous Essays*, pp. 167, 168 ; by Wallis, *Cosmology of the Ṛgveda*, pp. 87, 88; and by Peterson, *Hymns from the Ṛgveda*, pp. 289, 290; also by Burnouf, *Bhāgavata Purāṇa*, Preface to Vol. I., and by Weber, *Indische Studien*, IX. p. 5. Grassmann's Translation in his Appendix to Vol. II, and Ludwig's Translation and Commentary should be consulted. See also *Hymns of the Atharva-veda*, XIX. 6, which is a reproduction of this hymn with transpositions and variations.

1 *The place of Iḷā* : the shrine where clarified butter is poured upon the fire. *Our own familiar Friend* : Agni, the Friend of the house.

2 *Swift-winged bird* : or, bird of prey. 'Hunter,' according to Ludwig.

3 *Vasu* : the word meaning also *good* and *treasure.*

When, loosed to wander over plants and forest trees, thou crammest by thyself thy food into thy mouth.

6 Him, duly coming as their germ, have plants received : this Agni have maternal Waters brought to life.
So in like manner do the forest trees and plants bear him within them and produce him evermore.

7 When, sped and urged by wind, thou spreadest thee abroad, swift piercing through thy food according to thy will,
Thy never-ceasing blazes, longing to consume, like men on chariots, Agni, strive on every side.

8 Agni, the Hotar-priest who fills the assembly full, Waker of knowledge, chief Controller of the thought,—
Him, yea, none other than thyself, doth man elect at sacrificial offerings great and small alike.

9 Here, Agni, the arrangers, those attached to thee, elect thee as their Priest in sacred gatherings,
When men with strewn clipt grass and sacrificial gifts offer thee entertainment, piously inclined.

10 Thine is the Herald's task and Cleanser's duly timed; Leader art thou, and Kindler for the pious man.
Thou art Director, thou the ministering Priest : thou art the Brahman, Lord and Master in our home.

11 When mortal man presents to thee Immortal God, Agni, his fuel or his sacrificial gift,
Then thou art his Adhvaryu, Hotar, messenger, callest the Gods and orderest the sacrifice.

12 From us these hymns in concert have gone forth to him, these holy words, these Ṛcas, songs and eulogies,
Eager for wealth, to Jātavedas fain for wealth : when they have waxen strong they please their Strengthener.

13 This newest eulogy will I speak forth to him, the Ancient One who loves it. May he hear our voice.
May it come near his heart and make it stir with love, as a fond well-dressed matron clings about her lord.

14 He in whom horses, bulls, oxen, and barren cows, and rams, when duly set apart, are offered up,—
To Agni, Soma-sprinkled, drinker of sweet juice, Disposer, with my heart I bring a fair hymn forth.

15 Into thy mouth is poured the offering, Agni, as Soma into cup, oil into ladle.
Vouchsafe us wealth, strength-winning, blest with heroes, wealth lofty, praised by men, and full of splendour.

6 Agni is produced in the form of lightning by the waters of the firmament, or the clouds, and descends with the rain into plants and trees, from the wood of which he is brought forth by attrition.

8 *Great and small* : with Soma or without it.

9 *The arrangers* : priests who order and conduct the sacrificial ceremonies.

10 Agni discharges the duties of the seven chief priests, officiating as Hotar, Potar, Neṣṭar, Agnīdh, Praśāstar, Adhvaryu, and Brahman. See II. I. 2, where this stanza originally occurs.

11 *Callest the Gods* : 'sayest the formulae.'—Ludwig.

12 *Ṛcas* : verses of praise.

HYMN XCII. *Viśvedevas.*

1. I PRAISE your Charioteer of sacrifice, the Lord of men, Priest of the tribes, refulgent, Guest of night.
Blazing amid dry plants, snatching amid the green, the Strong, the Holy Herald hath attained to heaven.

2 Him, Agni, Gods and men have made their chief support, who drinks the fatness and completes the sacrifice.
With kisses they caress the Grandson of the Red, like the swift ray of light, the Household Priest of Dawn.

3 Yea, we discriminate his and the niggard's ways : his branches evermore are sent forth to consume.
When his terrific flames have reached the Immortal's world, then men remember and extol the Heavenly Folk.

4 For then the net of Law, Dyaus, and the wide expanse, Earth, Worship, and Devotion meet for highest praise,
Varuṇa, Indra, Mitra were of one accord, and Savitar and Bhaga, Lords of holy might.

2 *Completes the sacrifice* : or, fills the assembly full. *Grandson of the Red* : son of the brilliant Vāyu.'—Wilson. Sprung from his own red glow, one fire being kindled from another.

3 *Men remember* : because then their prayers are granted.

5 Onward, with ever-roaming Rudra, speed the floods : over Aramati the Mighty have they run.
With them Parijman, moving round his vast domain, loud bellowing, bedews all things that are within.

6 Straightway the Rudras, Maruts visiting all men, Falcons of Dyaus, home-dwellers with the Asura,—
Varuṇa, Mitra, Aryaman look on with these, and the swift-moving Indra with swift-moving Gods.

7 With Indra have they found enjoyment, they who toil, in the light's beauty, in the very Strong One's strength;
The singers who in men's assemblies forged for him, according to his due, his friend the thunderbolt.

8 Even the Sun's Bay Coursers hath he held in check : each one fears Indra as the mightiest of all.
Unhindered, from the air's vault thunders day by day the loud triumphant breathing of the fearful Bull.

9 With humble adoration show this day your song of praise to mighty Rudra, Ruler of the brave :
With whom, the Eager Ones, going their ordered course, he comes from heaven Self-bright, auspicious, strong to guard.

10 For these have spread abroad the fame of human kind, the Bull Bṛhaspati and Soma's brotherhood.
Atharvan first by sacrifices made men sure : through skill the Bhṛgus were esteemed of all as Gods.

11 For these, the Earth and Heaven with their abundant seed, four-bodied Narāśaṁsa, Yama, Aditi,
God Tvaṣṭar Wealth-bestower, the Ṛbhukṣaṇas, Rodasī Maruts, Viṣṇu, claim and merit praise.

12 And may he too give ear, the Sage, from far away, the Dragon of the Deep, to this our yearning call.
Ye Sun and Moon who dwell in heaven and move in turn, and with your thought, O Earth and Sky, observe this well.

13 Dear to all Gods, may Pūsan guard the ways we go, the Waters' Child and Vāyu help us to success.
Sing lauds for your great bliss to Wind, the breath of all : ye Aśvins prompt to hear, hear this upon your way.

14 With hymns of praise we sing him who is throned as Lord over these fearless tribes, the Self-resplendent One.
We praise Night's youthful Lord benevolent to men, the foeless One, the free, with all celestial Dames.

15 By reason of his birth here Aṅgiras first sang: the pressing-stones upraised beheld the sacrifice—
The stones through which the Sage became exceeding vast, and the sharp axe obtains in fight the beauteous place.

HYMN XCIII. *Viśvedevas.*

1. MIGHTY are ye, and far-extended, Heaven and Earth: both Worlds are evermore to us like two young Dames.
Guard us thereby from stronger foe; guard us hereby to give us strength.

2 In each succeeding sacrifice that mortal honoureth the Gods,
He who, most widely known and famed for happiness, inviteth them.

3 Ye who are Rulers over all, great is your sovran power as Gods.
Ye all possess all majesty: all must be served in sacrifice.

5 *Aramati*: the earth. —Sāyaṇa. Armaiti, of the Avestā, also means Earth personified as well as Devotion or Piety. *Parijman* : 'the circumambient (Indra).'—Wilson.

6 *The Asura* : Dyaus himself.

7 Worshippers are rewarded in heaven for the hymns and prayers with which they have strengthened and armed Indra for his great deeds.

9 *With whom* : the Maruts.

10 *Soma's brotherhood* : all Gods who are entitled to drink Soma juice. *Made men sure* : gave them assurance of obtaining what they asked.

11 *Four-bodied Narāśaṁsa* : Agni provided with four fires, or complete in all his parts. *Ṛbhukṣaṇas* : Ṛbhus. *Rodasī* : consort of the Maruts.

12 *The Dragon of the Deep* : Ahibudhnya, regent of the sea or air.

13 *The Waters' Child* : Agni, born as lightning from the clouds.

14 *The Self-resplendent One* : Agni. *Night's youthful Lord*: the Moon. *Celestial Dames* : the lunar asterisms.

15 *The Sage* : Indra, according to Sāyaṇa. *Sharp axe* : the thunderbolt. The meaning of this stanza is obscure.

1 *Thereby......hereby* : literally 'by those'......'by these.' Sāyaṇa supplies *pālanaiḥ*, protections, in both cases. The former may refer to the Maghavans, and the latter to the people in general.

4 These are the joyous Kings of Immortality, Parijman, Mitra, Aryaman, and Varuṇa.
What else is Rudra, praised of men ? the Maruts, Bhaga, Pūṣaṇa ?

5 Come also to our dwelling, Lords of ample wealth, common partakers of our waters, Sun and Moon,
When the great Dragon of the Deep hath settled down upon their floors.

6 And let the Aśvins, Lords of splendour, set us free,— both Gods, and, with their Laws, Mitra and Varuṇa.
Through woes, as over desert lands, he speeds to ample opulence.

7 Yea, let the Aśvins Twain be gracious unto us, even Rudras, and all Gods, Bhaga, Rathaspati;
Parijman, Ṛbhu, Vāja, O Lords of all wealth Ṛbhukṣaṇas.

8 Prompt is Ṛbhukṣan, prompt the worshipper's strong drink : may thy fleet Bay Steeds, thine who speedest on, approach.
Not man's but God's is sacrifice whose psalm is unassailable.

9 O God Savitar, harmed by none, lauded, give us a place among wealthy princes.
With his Car-steeds at once hath our Indra guided the reins and the car of these men.

10 To these men present here, O Heaven and Earth, to us grant lofty fame extending over all mankind.
Give us a steed to win us strength, a steed with wealth for victory.

11 This speaker, Indra—for thou art our Friend—wherever he may be, guard thou, Victor ! for help, ever for help :
Thy wisdom, Vasu ! prosper him.

12 So have they strengthened this mine hymu which seems to take its bright path to the Sun, and reconciles the men :
Thus forms a carpenter the yoke of horses, not to be displaced.

13 Whose chariot-seat hath come again laden with wealth and bright with gold,
Lightly, with piercing ends, as 'twere two ranks of heroes ranged for fight.

14 This to Duḥśīma Pṛthavāna have I sung, to Vena, Rāma, to the nobles, and the King.
They yoked five hundred, and their love of us was famed upon their way.

15 Besides, they showed us seven-and-seventy horses here.
Tānva at once displayed his gift, Pārthya at once displayed his gift; and straightway Māyava showed his.

HYMN XCIV. *Press-stones.*

1. LET these speak loudly forth; let us speak out aloud: to the loud speaking Pressing-stones address the speech;
When, rich with Soma juice, Stones of the mountain, ye, united, swift to Indra bring the sound of praise.

2 They speak out like a hundred, like a thousand men : they cry aloud to us with their green-tinted mouths,

4 *Immortality* : or, the immortal world. *Parijman* : Roamer round ; Vāyu. *What else* : that is, Rudra is also one of these Kings. *Pūṣaṇa* : a lengthened form of the usual Pūṣan.

5 *Waters* : libations of Soma juice, Sāyaṇa explains *nắktam* by *rātrau* 'by night.' It is, as Prof. Ludwig has pointed out, a shortened form of *nakṣtam*, 'come ye.' *Upon their floors* : 'in their company in the firmamental (clouds).'—Wilson. The meaning is obscure.

6 *He* : the sacrificer whom these Gods protect.

7 *Rathaspati* : the guardian of war-chariots. Cf. X. 64.
10. *Ṛbhukṣaṇas* : *Ṛbhus*.
8 *Ṛbhukṣan* : 'the mighty (Indra).'—Wilson.

9 *With his Car-steeds* : with us priests, who draw the chariot of sacrifice.

12 *So have they strengthened* : 'May (the priests) strengthen.'—Wilson. *The yoke* : as the yoke keeps a pair of horses together so the hymn addressed to the Gods reconciles worshippers and fills them with the like feelings of devotion.

13 *Piercing ends* : of the axle, which pass through the naves.

14 *Duḥśīma Pṛthavāna*, *Vena*, and *Rāma* were Maghavans or wealthy institutors of sacrifices. *To the King* : *ásure* : to the Asura, lord or chief. *Five hundred* : horses or chariots.

15 *Horses* : there is no substantive in the text. Sāyaṇa supplies *gavām*, cows. These horses or cows, were presented to the priests. *Tānva*, *Pārthya*, and *Māyava* are patronymics which do not occur again in the Ṛgveda.

Ludwig thinks that a quarrel had arisen between the Maghavans or nobles (stanza 14) and the Viśas or people (stanza 9), and that the priests, who had reconciled the two parties, were presented with the chariots which had been prepared for battle. See stanza 13, in which, according to this explanation, *ná* should be rendered by 'and not' instead of 'as 'twere.' The hymn, which is difficult and in parts almost unintelligible, is placed by Grassmann in his Appendix.

Hotar : '(Agni) the invoker (of the gods),'—Wilson. Or the human Hotar-priest may be intended.

While, pious Stones, they ply their task with piety, and, even before the Hotar, taste the offered food.

3 Loudly they speak, for they have found the savoury meath: they make a humming sound over the meat prepared.
As they devour the branch of the Red-coloured Tree, these, the well-pastured Bulls, have uttered bellowings.

4 They cry aloud, with strong exhilarating drink, calling on Indra now, for they have found the meath.
Bold, with the sisters they have danced, embraced by them, making the earth reecho with their ringing sound.

5 The Eagles have sent forth their cry aloft in heaven; in the sky's vault the dark impetuous ones have danced.
Then downward to the nether stone's fixt place they sink, and, splendid as the Sun, effuse their copious stream.

6 Like strong ones drawing, they have put forth all their strength: the Bulls, harnessed together, bear the chariot-poles.
When they have bellowed, panting, swallowing their food, the sound of their loud snorting is like that of steeds.

7 To these who have ten workers and a tenfold girth, to these who have ten yoke-straps and ten binding thongs,
To these who bear ten reins, the eternal, sing ye praise, to these who bear ten car-poles, ten when they are yoked.

8 These Stones with ten conductors, rapid in their course, with lovely revolution travel round and round.
They have been first to drink the flowing Soma juice, first to enjoy the milky fluid of the stalk.

9 These Soma-eaters kiss Indra's Bay-coloured Steeds: draining the stalk they sit upon the ox's hide.
Indra, when he hath drunk Soma-meath drawn by them, waxes in strength, is famed, is mighty as a Bull.

10. Strong is your stalk; ye, verily, never shall be harmed; ye have refreshment, ye are ever satisfied.
Fair are ye, as it were, through splendour of his wealth, his in whose sacrifice, O Stones, ye find delight.

11 Bored deep, but not pierced through with holes, are ye, O Stones, not loosened, never weary, and exempt from death,
Eternal, undiseased, moving in sundry ways, unthirsting, full of fatness, void of all desire.

12 Your fathers, verily, stand firm from age to age: they, loving rest, are not dissevered from their seat.
Untouched by time, ne'er lacking green plants and green trees, they with their voice have caused the heavens and earth to hear.

13 This, this the Stones proclaim, what time they are disjoined, and when with ringing sounds they move and drink the balm.
Like tillers of the ground when they are sowing seed, they mix the Soma, nor, devouring, minish it.

14 They have raised high their voice for juice, for sacrifice, striking the Mother earth as though they danced thereon.
So loose thou too his thought who hath effused the sap, and let the Stones which we are honouring be disjoined

3 *Red-coloured Tree* : the Soma-plant. *Well-pastured* : the meaning of *sūbharvā* is obscure. See Hillebrandt, *V. M.*, I. 18.

4 *The sisters* : the fingers.

5 *The Eagles* : the rapidly moving celestial press-stones.

7 *Ten workers* : the fingers of both hands.

9 *The ox's hide* : spread underneath to catch and hold the droppings.

12 *Your fathers* : the mountains from which you came.

14 *Striking the Mother Earth* : 'Earth' is not in the text :—'they made a noise like (children) at play, striking their mother.'—Wilson. I have followed Prof. Ludwig's explanation.

HYMN XCV. *Urvaśī. Purūravas.*

1. Ho there, my consort ! Stay, thou fierce-souled lady, and let us reason for a while together.
Such thoughts as these of ours, while yet unspoken in days gone by have never brought us comfort.

The hymn is a dialogue between Purūravas and Urvaśī, and they are severally the Ṛṣis of the stanzas which they speak. The dialogue, which is sometimes almost unintelligible, contains the germs of a legend which is related in the *Śatapatha-Brāhmaṇa*, reappears in the *Mahābhārata* and *Purāṇas*, and forms the plot of the well-known drama, *Vikramorvaśī*, or *The Hero and the Nymph.* According to this legend, Urvaśī, an Apsaras or Nymph

2 What am I now to do with this thy saying? I have gone from thee like the first of Mornings.
Purūravas, return thou to thy dwelling: I, like the wind, am difficult to capture.

3 Like a shaft sent for glory from the quiver, or swift steed winning cattle winning hundreds.
The lightning seemed to flash, as cowards planned it. The minstrels bleated like a lamb in trouble.

4 Giving her husband's father life and riches, from the near dwelling, when her lover craved her,
She sought the home wherein she found her pleasure, accepting day and night her lord's embraces.

5 Thrice in the day didst thou embrace thy consort, though coldly she received thy fond caresses.
To thy desires, Purūravas, I yielded: so wast thou king, O hero, of my body.

6 The maids Sujūrṇi, Śreṇi, Sumne-āpi, Charaṇyu, Granthinī, and Hradecakṣus,—
These like red kine have hastened forth, the bright ones, and like milch-cows have lowed in emulation.

7 While he was born the Dames sate down together, the Rivers with free kindness gave him nurture;
And then, Purūravas, the Gods increased thee for mighty battle, to destroy the Dasyus.

8 When I, a mortal, wooed to mine embraces these heavenly nymphs who laid aside their raiment,
Like a scared snake they fled from me in terror, like chariot horses when the car has touched them.

9 When, loving these Immortal Ones, the mortal hath converse with the nymphs as they allow him.
Like swans they show the beauty of their bodies, like horses in their play they bite and nibble.

10 She who flashed brilliant as the falling lightning brought me delicious presents from the waters.
Now from the flood be born a strong young hero! May Urvaśī prolong her life for ever!

11 Thy birth hath made me drink from earthly milch-kine: this power, Purūravas, hast thou vouchsafed me.

of heaven, has been banished to earth where she consents to live with King Purūravas on condition that he takes care of her two pet rams, and that she never sees him unclothed. She lives with Purūravas for four years, when the Gandharvas, heavenly minstrels, resolve to bring her back. They steal one of the rams by night. Purūravas springs from his bed; the Gandharvas send on him a flash of magic lightning, and Urvaśī sees her husband naked. One of the conditions of the continuance of their union is broken, and the nymph instantly vanishes. Purūravas meets her afterwards and in vain implores her to return. At last she relents, and in due time a son is born to them. These are the main outlines of a somewhat variously told story.

1 Purūravas speaks, when he has met Urvaśī again after her sudden departure.

2 Urvaśī replies.

3 Purūravas speaks, reminding her of the circumstances in which she vanished. 'Yea,' he says, 'thou wentest from me with the speed of an arrow or a racer. The cowardly Gandharvas deluded us. They bleated like a lamb to make us think that one of thy pets was in pain or danger, and then, by a flash of factitious lightning, made me visible to thee in my nakedness.'

4 *Life and riches*: meaning, perhaps, as Prof. Ludwig suggests, the future grandson. *The near dwelling*: her father-in-law's house, where she spent much of her time. *Her lover*: her husband Purūravas.

This stanza and the next are spoken by Urvaśī.

6 This stanza is ascribed by Sāyaṇa to Purūravas, who mentions the names of the Apsarases who were the companions of Urvaśī after her flight. They are compared to red kine, meaning, perhaps, bright flashes of lightning followed by the lowing or bellowing of the thunder.

7 Urvaśī speaks, reminding Purūravas of the favour shown him at his birth, by the celestial Dames who were present, the Rivers who nursed him, and the Gods who gave him strength. Another explanation is that in the first half of the stanza Urvaśī speaks, by anticipation, of the son whom she will bear to Purūravas.

8 Purūravas complains of the shyness of the nymphs mentioned in stanza 6, with whose society he had sought to console himself. *A mortal*: meaning that if he had been a God their behaviour would have been different. *Raiment*: *átkam*: explained by Sāyaṇa as *svakīyam rūpam*, their own proper form.

9 Urvaśī replies. The Apsarases, she says, as a rule only coquet with mortal men. *As they allow him*: *krátubhir ná*; see Geldner, *V. S.*, I. 276. *Like swans*: Sāyaṇa explains *ná* here differently :—'they (becoming) ducks do not show their bodies.'—Wilson.

10 Purūravas speaks. Urvaśī, he says, did not treat him so coldly. *From the waters*: of the firmament. *From the flood*: from Urvaśī who comes from the watery regions above. Sāyaṇa explains *apáḥ* differently :—'a son *able in act* and friendly to man has been born.'—Wilson.

11 Urvaśī speaks. According to Sāyaṇa, whom Wilson, Grassmann, and Geldner follow, the translation of the first half-line would be :— 'Thou hast been born to give the earth protection.' *Warned thee on that day*: told thee, when I agreed to live with thee what would happen if the conditions of the agreement were not strictly observed.

I knew, and, warned thee, on that day. Thou wouldst not hear me. What sayest thou, when naught avails thee ?

12 When will the son be born and seek his father ? Mourner-like, will he weep when first he knows him ?
Who shall divide the accordant wife and husband, while fire is shining with thy consort's parents ?

13 I will console him when his tears are falling: he shall not weep and cry for care that blesses.
That which is thine, between us, will I send thee. Go home again, thou fool; thou hast not won me.

14 Thy lover shall flee forth this day for ever, to seek, without return, the farthest distance.
Then let his bed be in Destruction's bosom, and there let fierce rapacious wolves devour him.

15 Nay, do not die, Purūravas, nor vanish: let not the evil-omened wolves devour thee.
With women there can be no lasting friendship: hearts of hyenas are the hearts of women.

16 When amid men in altered shape I sojourned, and through four autumns spent the nights among them,
I tasted once a day a drop of butter; and even now with that am I contented.

17 I, her best love, call Urvaśī to meet me, her who fills air and measures out the region.
Let the gift brought by piety approach thee. Turn thou to me again: my heart is troubled.

12 Purūravas speaks. *Knows him* : 'on recognizing (me).'—Wilson Or, when he knows my story, knows how his father has been deserted. *While fire is shining* : so long as the father-in-law and mother-in-law who sanctioned the union live and maintain their household fire.

13 Urvaśī answers. *That which is thine, between us* : our child, our common treasure.

14 Purūravas threatens to destroy himself.

15 Urvaśī speaks this and the next stanza.

16 *A drop of butter* : one of the conditions on which the continuance of their union depended was that she should eat nothing but a small quantity of *ghṛtá or* clarified butter daily. See stanza 11.

17 Purūravas speaks. *Her best love* : *vasiṣṭhaḥ* here is evidently, as the Scholiast says, an epithet and not a name, meaning 'most excellent.' 'most precious.' *Fills air* : representing the morning mist, or the first flush of light, that spreads over the heavens before the rising of the sun.

18 Thus speak these Gods to thee, O son of Iḷā: As death hath verily got thee for his subject,
Thy sons shall serve the Gods with their oblation, and thou, moreover, shalt rejoice in Svarga.

HYMN XCVI. *Indra.*

1 In the great synod will I laud thy two Bay Steeds : I prize the sweet strong drink of thee the Warrior-God,
His who pours lovely oil as 'twere with yellow drops. Let my songs enter thee whose form hath golden tints.

2 Ye who in concert sing unto the gold-hued place, like Bay Steeds driving onward to the heavenly seat,
For Indra laud ye strength allied with Tawny Steeds, laud him whom cows content as 'twere with yellow drops.

3 His is that thunderbolt, of iron, golden-hued, gold-coloured, very dear, and yellow in his arms;
Bright with strong teeth, destroying with its tawny rage. In Indra are set fast all forms of golden hue.

18 There is an hiatus between this stanza and 17, an entire break of continuity. The fragment is ascribed to Urvaśī, who consoles Purūravas by telling him of the promise of the deities that after his death his sons shall offer sacrifice to the Gods and he himself shall be blest in heaven . *Son of Iḷā* : Purūravas, called Aiḷa or son of Iḷā who was the daughter of Manu.

Some of the stanzas should be transposed, and their order should be, 1, 2, 3, 4, 5, 16, 6, 7, 8, 9, 11, 12, 13, 14, 15, 10.—Ludwig.

Of this very difficult hymn there is a complete translation, with a very full and generally convincing commentary (to both of which I am indebted for much assistance), by Prof. Geldner, *Vedische Studien*, I. pp. 243—295. The myth has been discussed by von Roth, *Illustrations of the Nirukta*, and *Indische Studien*, I. 196; by Prof. Max Müller, *Oxford Essays* (*Chips*, IV. 109f); by Prof. Adalbert Kuhn, *Die Herabkunft des Feuers*, pp. 85 ff; and by Professors Holtzmann and Oldenberg in more recent days. Professor Max Müller considers the story to be 'one of the myths of the Vedas which expresses the correlation of the dawn and the sun.' According to Dr. Goldstucker, Urvaśī is the morning mist which vanishes away as soon as Purūravas the Sun displays himself. See *Chamber's Encyclopaedia*, *1st edition*, under Purūravas.

Throughout the hymn the poet rings the changes on words said to be derivatives of the root *hṛ*, to take, as *haryatá*, delightsome, *haryán*, loving, *hári*, bay or tawny, *hárit*, green, yellow, or gold-coloured Cp. III. 44. These words are conjecturally explained by the Commentator, and are susceptible of various renderings.

1 *Oil* : or fatness, fertilizing rain.

2 *Cows* : milked for sacrificial purposes.

3 *Tawny rage* : perhaps with reference to the effect of anger on the face.—Ludwig.

4 As if a lovely ray were laid upon the sky, the golden thunderbolt spread out as in a race.
That iron bolt with yellow jaw smote Ahi down. A thousand flames had he who bore the tawny-hued.

5 Thou, thou, when praised by men who sacrificed of old, hadst pleasure in their lauds, O Indra golden-haired.
All that befits thy song of praise thou welcomest, the perfect pleasant gift, O Golden-hued from birth.

6 These two dear Bays bring hither Indra on his car, Thunder-armed, joyous, meet for laud, to drink his fill.
Many libations flow for him who loveth them : to Indra have the gold-hued Soma juices run.

7 The gold-hued drops have flowed to gratify his wish : the yellow drops have urged the swift Bays to the Strong.
He who speeds on with Bay Steeds even as he lists hath satisfied his longing for the golden drops.

8 At the swift draught the Soma-drinker waxed in might, the Iron One with yellow beard and yellow hair.
He, Lord of Tawny Coursers, Lord of fleet-foot Mares, will bear his Bay Steeds safely over all distress.

9 His yellow-coloured jaws, like ladles, move apart, what time, for strength, he makes the yellow-tinted stir,
When, while the bowl stands there, he grooms his Tawny Steeds, when he hath drunk strong drink, the sweet juice that he loves.

10 Yea, to the Dear One's seat in homes of heaven and earth the Bay Steeds' Lord hath whinnied like a horse for food.
Then the great wish hath seized upon him mightily, and the Beloved One hath gained high power of life.

11 Thou, comprehending with thy might the earth and heaven, acceptest the dear hymn for ever new and new.
O Asura, disclose thou and make visible the Cow's beloved home to the bright golden Sun.

12 O Indra, let the eager wishes of the folk bring thee, delightful, golden-visored, on thy car,
That, pleased with sacrifice wherein ten fingers toil, thou mayest, at the feast, drink of our offered meath.

13 Juices aforetime, Lord of Bays, thou drankest ; and thine especially is this libation.
Gladden thee, Indra, with the meath-rich Soma : pour it down ever, Mighty One ! within thee.

HYMN XCVII. *Praise of Herbs.*

1. HERBS that sprang up in time of old, three ages earlier than the Gods,—
Of these, whose hue is brown, will I declare the hundred powers and seven.

2 Ye, Mothers, have a hundred homes, yea, and a thousand are your growths.
Do ye who have a thousand powers free this my patient from disease.

3 Be glad and joyful in the Plants, both blossoming and bearing fruit,
Plants that will lead us to success like mares who conquer in the race.

4 Plants, by this name I speak to you, Mothers, to you the Goddesses :
Steed, cow, and garment may I win, win back thy very self, O man.

5 The Holy Fig tree is your home, your mansion is the Parṇa tree :
Winners of cattle shall ye be if ye regain for me this man.

4 *The tawny-hued* : the thunderbolt wielded by Indra.

7 *To the Strong* : to Indra; that they may be harnessed and come to the sacrifice.

8 *The Iron One* : 'iron-hearted Indra.'—Wilson.

9 *For strength* : for strengthening food. *The yellow-tinted* : his yellow jaws.

10 *The Dear One* must be the Soma, found both in heaven and earth, the homes of Gods and men. According to Sāyaṇa, Indra himself is meant. *The Beloved One* : Indra, whose vital vigour is increased by Soma-draughts.

11 *The Cow's beloved home* : the Cow may be the Sun whose home is the universe which Indra will allow Sūrya to illumine.

12 *Sacrifice* : according to Sāyaṇa, the sacrificial Soma juice which is pressed and prepared by the fingers of the priest.

---

1 *Three ages earlier than the Gods* : 'for the gods before the three ages.'—Wilson. See *Śatapatha-Brāhmaṇa*, VII. 2. 4. 26 (*S. B. E.*, XLI. p. 389).

4 *Steed, cow, and garment* : as my fee for curing you.

5 *Holy Fig-tree* : the Aśvattha, or Ficus Religiosa. *Parṇa tree* : the Palāśa Butea Frondosa. Sacrificial vessels are made of the wood of these trees which are therefore said to be the home of plants used in religious ceremonies.

6 He who hath store of Herbs at hand like Kings amid a crowd of men,—
Physician is that sage's name, fiend-slayer, chaser of disease.

7 Herbs rich in Soma, rich in steeds, in nourishments, in strengthening power,—
All these have I provided here, that this man may be whole again.

8 The healing virtues of the Plants stream forth like cattle from the stall,—
Plants that shall win me store of wealth, and save thy vital breath, O man.

9 Reliever is your mother's name, and hence Restorers are ye called.
Rivers are ye with wings that fly : keep far whatever brings disease.

10 Over all fences have they passed, as steals a thief into the fold.
The Plants have driven from the frame whatever malady was there.

11 When, bringing back the vanished strength, I hold these herbs within my hand,
The spirit of disease departs ere he can seize upon the life.

12 He through whose frame, O Plants, ye creep member by member, joint by joint,—
From him ye drive away disease like some strong arbiter of strife.

13 Fly, Spirit of Disease, begone, with the blue jay and kingfisher.
Fly with the wind's impetuous speed, vanish together with the storm.

14 Help every one the other, lend assistance each of you to each,
All of you be accordant, give furtherance to this speech of mine.

15 Let fruitful Plants, and fruitless, those that blossom, and the blossomless,
Urged onward by Bṛhaspati, release us from our pain and grief ;

16 Release me from the curse's plague and woe that comes from Varuṇa;
Free me from Yama's fetter, from sin and offence against the Gods.

17 What time, descending from the sky, the Plants flew earthward, thus they spake :
No evil shall befall the man whom while he liveth we pervade.

18 Of all the many Plants whose King is Soma, Plants of hundred forms,
Thou art the Plant most excellent, prompt to the wish, sweet to the heart.

19 O all ye various Herbs whose King is Soma, that o'erspread the earth,
Urged onward by Bṛhaspati, combine your virtue in this Plant.

20 Unharmed be he who digs you up, unharmed the man for whom I dig:
And let no malady attack biped or quadruped of ours.

21 All Plants that hear this speech, and those that have departed far away,
Come all assembled and confer your healing power upon this Herb.

22 With Soma as their Sovran Lord the Plants hold colloquy and say :
O King, we save from death the man whose cure a Brāhman undertakes.

23 Most excellent of all art thou, O Plant : thy vassals are the trees.
Let him be subject to our power, the man who seeks to injure us.

12 *Like some strong arbiter of strife* : 'like a mighty (prince) stationed in the midst of his host.'—Wilson.

13 *With the blue jay and kingfisher* : with the speed of the swiftest birds. *Together with the storm* : according to Sāyaṇa, 'perish along with the iguana.'

15 *Urged onward* : Bṛhaspati, says Sāyaṇa, is the deity who presides over *mantras* or spells and charms.

19 *This Plant* : the medicinal herb which I, the physician, am about to make use of.

HYMN XCVIII. *The Gods.*

1. Come, be thou Mitra, Varuṇa, or Pūṣan, come, O Bṛhaspati, to mine oblation :
With Maruts, Vasus, or Ādityas, make thou Parjanya pour for Śantanu his rain-drops.

2 The God, intelligent, the speedy envoy whom thou hast sent hath come to me, Devāpi :
Address thyself to me and turn thee hither :

'This Sūkta is remarkable as representing one of two brothers, both of the Kṣatriya caste, becoming the *Purohita*, or family priest, and *Hotṛ* or sacrificing priest, of the other who is the *Rājā*.'—Wilson.

1 Devāpi addresses Bṛhaspati, who is identifiable with Mitra, Varuṇa, Pūṣan and others in his special character, of Purohita, or family Priest, of the Gods, and as the prototype of all human Purohitas. *With Maruts* : whether thou be attended by Maruts, Vasus, or Ādityas. *For Śantanu* : the brother of Devāpi.

within thy lips will I put brilliant language.

3 Within my mouth, Bṛhaspati, deposit speech lucid, vigorous, and free from weakness,
Thereby to win for Śantanu the rain-fall. The meath-rich drop from heaven hath passed within it.

4 Let the sweet drops descend on us, O Indra: give us enough to lade a thousand wagons.
Sit to thy Hotar task; pay worship duly, and serve the Gods, Devāpi, with oblation.

5 Knowing the God's good-will, Devāpi, Ṛṣi, the son of Ṛṣṭiṣena, sate as Hotar.
He hath brought down from heaven's most lofty summit the ocean of the rain, celestial waters.

6 Gathered together in that highest ocean, the waters stood, by deities obstructed.
They hurried down set free by Ārṣṭiṣeṇa, in gaping clefts, urged onward by Devāpi.

7 When as chief priest for Śantanu, Devāpi, chosen for Hotar's duty, prayed beseeching,
Graciously pleased Bṛhaspati vouchsafed him a voice that reached the Gods and won the waters.

8 O Agni whom Devāpi Ārṣṭiṣeṇa, the mortal man, hath kindled in his glory,
Joying in him with all the Gods together, urge on the sender of the rain, Parjanya.

9 All ancient Ṛṣis with their songs approached thee, even thee, O Much-invoked, at sacrifices.
We have provided wagon-loads in thousands: come to the solemn rite, Lord of Red Horses.

10 The wagon-loads, the nine-and-ninety thousand, these have been offered up to thee, O Agni.
Hero, with these increase thy many bodies, and, stimulated, send us rain from heaven.

11 Give thou these ninety thousand loads, O Agni, to Indra, to the Bull, to be his portion.
Knowing the paths which Deities duly travel, set mid the Gods in heaven Aulāna also.

12 O Agni, drive afar our foes, our troubles; chase malady away and wicked demons.
From this air-ocean, from the lofty heavens, send down on us a mighty flood of waters.

HYMN XCIX. *Indra.*

1. WHAT Splendid One, Loud-voiced, Far-striding, dost thou, well knowing, urge us to exalt with praises?
What give we him? When his might dawned, he fashioned the Vṛtra-slaying bolt, and sent us waters.

2 He goes to end his work with lightning flashes: wide is the seat his Asura glory gives him.
With his Companions, not without his Brother, he quells Saptatha's magic devices.

3 On most auspicious path he goes to battle: he toiled to win heaven's light, full fain to gain it;
He seized the hundred-gated castle's trea-

2 Bṛhaspati replies. *Brilliant language*: a 'brilliant hymn.'—Muir.

3 Devāpi speaks, praying Bṛhaspati, as Lord of Speech (cp. X. 71. 1), to inspire him with eloquence that he may address the Gods effectually. *The meath-rich drop*: the sweet eloquence for which he has prayed.

4 *The sweet drops*: of rain. This stanza is spoken by Śantanu.

5 *Knowing*: how to win.

6 *Ārṣṭiṣeṇa*: patronymic, son of Ṛṣṭiṣeṇa; Devāpi.

7 *Chief priest*: or family or household priest; Purohita.

9 *Wagon-loads*: an extraordinary quantity of fuel for the sacrifice, as the occasion was one of the greatest importance.

11 *Aulāna*: Śantanu, as a descendant of Ula, appears to be meant. According to some scholars, *aulānám* means oblation or sacrificial offering. 'The fact of Devāpi being reputed as the author of this hymn, and as the purohita and hotṛ of his brother seems to have led the legendary writers to invent the story of his becoming a Brāhman, which (as mentioned by Professor Weber, *Indische Studien*, i. p. 203) is recorded in the Śalya-parvan of the Mahābhārata, verses 2281 ff, where he is said to have attained this distinction at a certain place of pilgrimage called Pṛthūdaka, where Sindhudvīpa and Viśvāmitra also were received into the higher caste.'—Muir, *O. S. Texts*, I. 270 ff. For the legend on which the hymn is said to be based, quoted by Sāyaṇa from the *Nirukta*, see Wilson's Translation.

1 The question in the first line is a rhetorical figure, the meaning being, How splendid is he (Indra) whom thou (the Yajamāna?) urgest us to exalt! *What give we him*? what can we give him in return for what he has done for us?

2 *His Companions*: the Maruts. *His Brother*: Viṣṇu, Who *Saptatha* was is uncertain. The word means Septimus, the seventh, and probably some Rākṣasa or demon is intended.

3 *The lustful demons*: the exact meaning of *śiśnádevān* is uncertain. See VII. 21. 5 and note.

sure by craft, unchecked, and slew the lustful demons.

4 Fighting for kine, the prize of war, and roaming among the herd he brings the young streams hither,
Where, footless, joined, without a car to bear them, with jars for steeds, they pour their flood like butter.

5 Bold, unsolicited for wealth, with Rudras he came, the Blameless, having left his dwelling,
Came, seized the food of Vamra and his consort, and left the couple weeping and unsheltered.

6 Lord of the dwelling, he subdued the demon who roared aloud, six-eyed and triple-headed.
Tṛta, made stronger by the might he lent him, struck down the boar with shaft whose point was iron.

7 He raised himself on high and shot his arrow against the guileful and oppressive foeman.
Strong, glorious, manliest, for us he shattered the forts of Nahus when he slew the Dasyus.

8 He, like a cloud that rains upon the pasture, hath found for us the way to dwell in safety.
When the Hawk comes in body to the Soma, armed with his iron claws he slays the Dasyus.

9 He with his potent Friends gave up the mighty, gave Śuṣṇa up to Kutsa for affliction.
He led the lauded Kavi, he delivered Atka as prey to him and to his heroes.

10 He, with his Gods who love mankind, the Wondrous, giving like Varuṇa who works with magic,
Was known, yet young, as guardian of the seasons ; and he quelled Araru, four-footed demon.

11 Through lauds of him hath Auśija Rjiśvan burst, with the Mighty's aid, the stall of Pipru.
When the saint pressed the juice and shone as singer, he seized the forts and with his craft subdued them.

12 So, swiftly Asura, for exaltation, hath the great Vamraka come nigh to Indra.
He will, when supplicated, bring him blessing : he hath brought all, food, strength, a happy dwelling.

HYMN C.   *Viśvedevas.*

1. BE, like thyself, O Indra, strong for our delight : here lauded, aid us, Maghavan, drinker of the juice.
Savitar with the Gods protect us : hear ye Twain. We ask for freedom and complete felicity.

2 Bring swift, for offering, the snare that suits the time, to the pure-drinker Vāyu, roaring as he goes,
To him who hath approached the draught of shining milk. We ask for freedom and complete felicity.

3 May Savitar the God send us full life, to each who. sacrifices, lives aright and pours the juice ;
That we with simple hearts may wait upon the Gods. We ask for freedom and complete felicity.

4 May Indra evermore be gracious unto us, and may King Soma meditate our happiness,
Even as men secure the comfort of a friend. We ask for freedom and complete felicity.

---

5 I can make nothing intelligible of the second line. 'I think of the two (parents) of Vamra, who are free from fever. Having obtained (the enemy's) food, he called aloud whilst stealing it.'—Wilson. Vamra is mentioned in I. 51. 9; 112. 15.

6 *Lord of the dwelling* : or, with Ludwig, The Lord and Giver. *The demon* : or Dāsa Viśvarūpa, son of Tvaṣṭar. See X. 8. 8. *The boar* : Vṛtra Cf. I. 61. 7.

8 *The Hawk* : the fierce and swift Indra.

9 *Kavi* : according to Sāyaṇa, Uśanā Kāvya or son of Kavi is intended. *Atka* : See X. 49. 3.

10 *His Gods* : the Maruts. *Araru* : I follow Sāyaṇa. Cf. *Śatapatha-Brāhmaṇa*, I. 2 4.17 (S.B.E. XII.57) According to Prof. Ludwig's conjectural explanation the translation would be :—'he measured out the year in four divisions.'

11 *Auśija* : son of Uśij. But as this patronymic does not properly belong to Rjiśvan, the word here may perhaps mean, 'vehement,' 'eagerly desirous.' *Pipru* : one of the demons of drought.

12 *Asura* : O divine and mighty Indra. *For exaltation*: of Indra. *Vamraka* : a lengthened form of Vamra, the Ṛṣi of the hymn. The last clause of the stanza is borrowed from X. 20. 10.

———

This hymn, which is obscure and in some places unintelligible, is placed by Prof. Grassmann in his Appendix. Dr. Muir has translated stanzas 1—7 in *O. S. Texts*, IV. pp. 408, 409 (2nd edition).

1 *Ye Twain* : Indra and Savitar. *Freedom* : *áditim*. Prof. M. Müller translates differently : 'We implore Aditi for health and wealth.'

2 *Pure-drinker* : drinker of pure Soma juice.

5 Indra hath given the body with its song and strength : Bṛhaspati, thou art the lengthener of life.
The sacrifice is Manu, Providence, our Sire. We ask for freedom and complete felicity.

6 Indra possesseth might celestial nobly formed : the singer in the house is Agni, prudent Sage.
He is the sacrifice in synod, fair, most near. We ask for freedom and complete felicity.

7 Not often have we sinned against you secretly, nor, Vasus, have we openly provoked the Gods.
Not one of us, ye Gods, hath worn an alien shape. We ask for freedom and complete felicity.

8 May Savitar remove from us our malady, and may the Mountains keep it far away from where
The press-stone as it sheds the meath rings loudly forth. We ask for freedom and complete felicity.

9 Ye Vasus, let the stone, the presser, stand erect : avert all enmities and keep them far remote.
Our guard to be adored is Savitar this God. We ask for freedom and complete felicity.

10 Eat strength and fatness in the pasture, kine, who are balmed at the reservoir and at the seat of Law.
So let your body be our body's medicine. We ask for freedom and complete felicity.

11 The singer fills the spirit : all mens' love hath he. Indra takes kindly care of those who pour the juice.
For his libation is the heavenly udder full. We ask for freedom and complete felicity.

12 Wondrous thy spirit-filling light, triumphant ; thy hosts save from decay and are resistless.
The pious votary by straightest pathway speeds to possess the best of all the cattle.

HYMN CI. *Viśvedevas.*

1. WAKE with one mind, my friends, and kindle Agni, ye who are many and who dwell together.
Agni and Dadhikrās and Dawn the Goddess, you, Gods with Indra, I call down to help us.

2 Make pleasant hymns, spin out your songs and praises : build ye a ship equipped with oars for transport.
Prepare the implements, make all things ready, and let the sacrifice, my friends, go forward.

3 Lay on the yokes, and fasten well the traces : formed is the furrow, sow the seed within it.
Through song may we find hearing fraught with plenty : near to the ripened grain approach the sickle.

4 Wise, through desire of bliss from Gods, the skilful bind the traces fast,
And lay the yokes on either side.

5 Arrange the buckets in their place : securely fasten on the straps.
We will pour forth the well that hath a copious stream, fair-flowing well that never fails.

6 I pour the water from the well with pails prepared and goodly straps,
Unfailing, full, with plenteous stream.

7 Refresh the horses, win the prize before you : equip a chariot fraught with happy fortune.
Pour forth the well with stone wheel,

5 *The sacrifice is Manu* : we owe our existence and preservation to sacrifice, which is to us another Manu, the father of Āryan men.

6 *The sacrifice in synod* : "worthy of sacrifice at the altar."—Wilson.

7 *An alien shape* : as sorcerers are accustomed to do.

10 *Balmed at the reservoir* : anointed before being milked. Sāyaṇa explains *kośe* by *goṣthe*, 'in the cowstall.' *Let your body* : may the milk, the produce of your bodies, offered in libation, keep our bodies in health. Or 'may the body of the cow offered in sacrifice be the expiation for the body of the sacrificer, enabling him to attain *svarga*. Or may the milk be the corrective of the Soma.' —Wilson.

11 *The heavenly udder* : the clouds of the firmament.

12 *Save from decay* : this is Prof. Ludwig's interpretation of the obscure word *jaraṇiprāh*, which means, according to Sāyaṇa, replenishing the wealth of thy worshippers. The last line is explained differently by Sāyaṇa. —'(therefore) Duvasyu hastens in front of the victim cow, (leading it) with a straight cord.'—Wilson. According to the same authority the meaning of the refrain of stanzas 1—11 is :—'We long for the universal Aditi.'

1 *Dadhikrās* : probably a personification of the Morning Sun. See III. 20. 1; IV. 38. 2; 40. 5 note.

2 *Ship* : sacrifice, represented under this figure.

3 In this and the following stanzas sacrifice is figuratively spoken of as ploughing, sowing and reaping. See *Śatapatha-Brāhmaṇa*, VII. 2. 2. 4. (S. B. E. XLI. 320).

5 The flowing Soma is an inexhaustible well.

7 The sacrifice is a chariot; and the ritual is a race. *The well* : the stream of Soma juice. *Stone wheel* : with allusion to the press-stones.

wooden buckets, the drink of heroes, with the trough for armour.

8 Prepare the cow-stall, for there drink your heroes : stitch ye the coats of armour, wide and many.
Make iron forts, secure from all assailants : let not your pitcher leak : stay it securely.

9 Hither, for help, I turn the holy heavenly mind of you the Holy Gods, that longs for sacrifice.
May it pour milk for us, even as a stately cow who, having sought the pasture, yields a thousand streams.

10 Pour golden juice within the wooden vessel : with stone-made axes fashion ye and form it.
Embrace and compass it with tenfold girdle, and to both chariot-poles attach the car-horse.

11 Between both poles the car-horse goes pressed closely, as in his dwelling moves the doubly-wedded.
Lay in the wood the Sovran of the Forest, and sink the well although ye do not dig it.

12 Indra is he, O men, who gives us happiness : sport, urge the giver of delight to win us strength.
Bring quickly down, O priests, hither to give us aid, to drink the Soma, Indra Son of Niṣṭigrī.

HYMN CII. *Indra.*

1. FOR thee may Indra boldly speed the car that works on either side.
Favour us, Much-invoked ! in this most glorious fight against the raiders of our wealth.

2 Loose in the wind the woman's robe was streaming what time she won a car-load worth a thousand.
The charioteer in fight was Mudgalānī : she Indra's dart, heaped up the prize of battle.

3 O Indra, cast thy bolt among assailants who would slaughter us :
The weapon both of Dāsa and of Ārya foe keep far away, O Maghavan.

4 The bull in joy had drunk a lake of water. His shattering horn encountered an opponent.
Swiftly, in vigorous strength, eager for glory, he stretched his forefeet, fain to win and triumph.

5 They came anear the bull ; they made him thunder, made him pour rain down ere the fight was ended.
And Mudgala thereby won in the contest well-pastured kine in hundreds and in thousands.

6 In hope of victory that bull was harnessed : Keśī the driver urged him on with shouting.
As he ran swiftly with the car behind him his lifted heels pressed close on Mudgalānī.

7 Deftly for him he stretched the car-pole

8 *The cow-stall* : figuratively, for the place where the Soma is pressed. *Coats of armour* : the filters for straining the juice. *Iron forts* : the safeguards obtained by sacrificing.

9 *Milk* : abundant blessing.

10 *Stone-made* : with allusion to the press-stones. *Tenfold girdle* : the fingers of both hands. *Both chariot-poles*: the arms. *The car-horse* : the upper press-stone; or the pestle.

11 *The doubly-wedded* : the man who has two wives. The comparison is not clear. *The Sovran of the Forest* : the Soma plant. *Sink the well* : 'store up the juice.' —Wilson.

12 I follow Sāyaṇa in his interpretation of the first line. Von Roth, Ludwig, and Grassmann explain it differently. *Niṣṭigrī* : meaning according to Sāyaṇa, 'she who swallows up her rival wife *Niṣṭi*, *i. e.* Diti,' is said to be Aditi, the mother of Indra.

The deified subject of the hymn is said to be, alternatively, Drughaṇa (Mace, Club or Hammer. See stanza 9). The Ṛṣi is Mudgala.

According to the legend quoted by Sāyaṇa, all Mudgala's cattle had been stolen except an old ox which he harnessed to his wagon and went in pursuit of the robbers. He threw his club or mace before him, which showed him the way to the thieves, and thus recovered his property.

1 *For thee* : O Mudgala. *That works on either side* : *mithūkṛtam* : according to Sāyaṇa=*asahāyam*, 'that has no companion.' The meaning is uncertain.

2 *Mudgalānī* : Mudgala's wife. *Indra's dart* : sped swiftly on her way by Indra.

3 This stanza seems to be an interpolation.

4 *The bull* : apparently one of the buffaloes which drew the chariot of Mudgalānī's chief opponent. *Had drunk* : : just before the fight began. *Encountered an opponent* : meaning perhaps, that feeling uneasy he hung his head and struck the ground with his horns. 'He cleft the mountain peak, he went against the enemy.' —Wilson.

6 *In hope of victory* : *kakárdave* : the meaning is uncertain; according to Sāyaṇa, 'for the destruction of the enemy.' Ludwig thinks that the farther end of the chariot-pole is intended.

7 Mudgala's better fortune is now related. *For him* : for his own buffalo. *He* : Mudgala. *Car-pole* : I follow Ludwig's conjecture ; but it is uncertain what part of the chariot the *pradhi* was; the periphery of the wheel,' according to the St. Petersburg Lexicon; 'the frame of the waggon.'—Wilson. Sāyaṇa's explanation is not very clear, but he seems to think that the linchpin is intended. None of these three explanations seems suitable here. *The lord of cows* : the bull buffalo.

forward, guided the bull thereto and firmly yoked him.
Indra vouchsafed the lord of cows his favour: with mighty steps the buffalo ran onward.

8 Touched by the goad the shaggy beast went nobly, bound to the pole by the yoke's thong of leather.
Performing deeds of might for many people, he, looking on the cows, gained strength and vigour.

9 Here look upon this mace, this bull's companion, now lying midway on the field of battle.
Therewith hath Mudgala in ordered contest won for cattle for himself, a hundred thousand.

10 Far is the evil: who hath here beheld it? Hither they bring the bull whom they are yoking.
To this they give not either food or water. Reaching beyond the pole it gives directions.

11 Like one forsaken, she hath found a husband, and teemed as if her breast were full and flowing.
With swiftly-racing chariot may we conquer, and rich and blessed be our gains in battle.

12 Thou, Indra, art the mark whereon the eyes of all life rest, when thou,
A Bull who drivest with thy bull, wilt win the race together with thy weakling friend.

9 *Mace* : *drughaṇám* : according to Sāyaṇa, the club which Mudgala had carried with him on his expedition, and which, together with the ox that drew his car had enabled him to recover his cattle. *Lying midway* : after the victory, the King had thrown down his mace upon the field of battle.—Ludwig.

10 I find this stanza unintelligible. Perhaps the second line contains the germ of that part of the legend which mentions the club thrown in front of the chariot to point out the way that the robbers had taken.

11 *Like one forsaken* : *parivṛktéva* : 'Apparently Mudgalānī was a *parivṛktā* (a wife lightly esteemed in comparison with the favourite wife) who made amends for her sterility by driving her husband's chariot to battle and bringing him back victorious, with the booty which she had helped him to gain instead of the children that she had not borne him.'—Ludwig.

12 *With thy bull* : thy fierce and strong thunderbolt. *With thy weakling friend* : with the mortal man whom thou protectest, and who is weak and effeminate in comparison with thee.

The hymn is fragmentary, and it seems impossible to interpret it fully and satisfactorily. I have followed in some stanzas the interpretations of the authors of *Vedische Studien*, I. pp. 124 and 138. But see the later translation and exhaustive discussion by Prof. Geldner in Part II. pp. 1—22, and Prof. Ludwig's remarks thereon in *Ueber die neuesten Arbeiten auf dem Gebiete der Ṛgveda-forschung*.

———

HYMN CIII. *Indra.*

1. Swift, rapidly striking, like a bull who sharpens his horns, terrific, stirring up the people,
With eyes that close not, bellowing, Sole Hero, Indra subdued at once a hundred armies.

2 With him loud-roaring, ever watchful, Victor, bold, hard to overthrow, Rouser of battle,
Indra the Strong, whose hand bears arrows, conquer, ye warriors, now, now vanquish in the combat.

3 He rules with those who carry shafts and quivers, Indra who with his band brings hosts together,
Foe-conquering, strong of arm, the Soma-drinker, with mighty bow, shooting with well-laid arrows.

4 Bṛhaspati, fly with thy chariot hither, slayer of demons, driving off our foemen.
Be thou protector of our cars, destroyer, victor in battle, breaker-up of armies.

5 Conspicuous by thy strength, firm, foremost fighter, mighty and fierce, victorious, all-subduing,
The Son of Conquest, passing men and heroes, kine-winner, mount thy conquering car, O Indra.

6 Cleaver of stalls, kine-winner, armed with thunder, who quells an army and with might destroys it.—
Follow him, brothers! quit yourselves like heroes, and like this Indra show your zeal and courage.

7 Piercing the cow-stalls with surpassing vigour, Indra, the pitiless Hero, wild with anger,
Victor in fight, unshaken and resistless,—may he protect our armies in our battles.

8 Indra guide these: Bṛhaspati precede them, the guerdon, and the sacrifice, and Soma;

The hymn is a prayer for aid and victory in battle.

8 *Guide these* : be the leader of our troops. *The guerdon* : *dákṣiṇā* : the reward of the priests who perform the sacrifice offered before battle.

And let the banded Maruts march in forefront of heavenly hosts that conquer and demolish.

9 Ours be the potent host of mighty Indra, King Varuṇa, and Maruts, and Ādityas.
Uplifted is the shout of Gods who conquer high-minded Gods who cause the worlds to tremble.

10 Bristle thou up, O Maghavan, our weapons : excite the spirits of my warring heroes.
Urge on the strong steeds' might, O Vṛtra-slayer, and let the din of conquering cars go upward.

11 May Indra aid us when our flags are gathered : victorious be the arrows of our army.
May our brave men of war prevail in battle. Ye Gods, protect us in the shout of onset.

12 Bewildering the senses of our foemen, seize thou their bodies and depart, O Apvā.
Attack them, set their hearts on fire and burn them : so let our foes abide in utter darkness.

13 Advance, O heroes, win the day. May Indra be your sure defence.
Exceeding mighty be your arms, that none may wound or injure you.

HYMN CIV. *Indra.*

1. Soma hath flowed for thee, Invoked of many ! Speed to our sacrifice with both thy Coursers.
To thee have streamed the songs of mighty singers, imploring, Indra, drink of our libation.

2 Drink of the juice which men have washed in waters, and fill thee full, O Lord of Tawny Horses.
O Indra, hearer of the laud, with Soma which stones have mixed for thee enhance thy rapture.

3 To make thee start, a strong true draught I offer to thee, the Bull, O thou whom Bay Steeds carry.
Here take delight, O Indra, in our voices while thou art hymned with power and all our spirit.

4 O Mighty Indra, through thine aid, thy prowess, obtaining life, zealous, and skilled in Order,
Men in the house who share the sacred banquet stand singing praise that brings them store of children.

5 Through thy directions, Lord of Tawny Coursers, thine who art firm, splendid, and blest, the people
Obtain most liberal aid for their salvation, and praise thee, Indra, through thine excellencies.

6 Lord of the Bays, come with thy two Bay Horses, come to our prayers, to drink the juice of Soma.
To thee comes sacrifice which thou acceptest : thou, skilled in holy rites, art he who giveth.

7 Him of a thousand powers, subduing foemen, Maghavan praised with hymns and pleased with Soma,—
Even him our songs approach, resistless Indra : the adorations of the singer laud him.

8 The way to bliss for Gods and man thou foundest, Indra, seven lovely floods, divine, untroubled,
Wherewith thou, rending forts, didst move the ocean, and nine-and-ninety flowing streams of water.

9 Thou from the curse didst free the mighty Waters, and as their only God didst watch and guard them.
O Indra, cherish evermore thy body with those which thou hast won in quelling Vṛtra.

10 Heroic power and noble praise is Indra : yea, the song worships him invoked of many.
Vṛtra he quelled, and gave men room and freedom : Śakra, victorious, hath conquered armies.

11 Call we on Maghavan, auspicious Indra,

11 *When our flags are gathered* : 'apparently comparable with the signis collatis of the Romans.'—Ludwig.

12 *Apvā* : according to Sāyaṇa, a female deity who presides over sin according to Mahīdhara, sickness, or fear. Apparently Apvā was a sort of colic, or dysentery, likely to attack soldiers in the field. *And depart* : or, pass us by; do not attack us.

---

3 *True* : which produces the results expected in the shape of favour.

8 *Didst move the ocean* : didst bring the sea of rain from heaven.

9 *Those* : waters.

11 This is the concluding verse of several hymns of the Viśvāmitras in Book III.

best Hero in this fight where spoil is gathered,
The Strong, who listens, who gives aid in battles, who slays the Vṛtras, wins and gathers riches.

HYMN CV. *Indra.*

1. When, Vasu, wilt thou love the laud? Now let the channel bring the stream.
The juice is ready to ferment.

2 He whose two Bay Steeds harnessed well, swerving, pursue the Bird's tail-plumes,
With flowing manes, like heaven and earth, he is the Lord with power to give.

3 Bereft of skill is Indra, if, like some outwearied man he fears
The sinner, when the Mighty hath prepared himself for victory.

4 Indra with these drives round, until he meets with one to worship him :
Indra is Master of the pair who snort and swerve upon their way.

5 Borne onward by the long-maned Steeds who stretch themselves as 'twere for food,
The God who wears the helm defends them with his jaws.

6 The Mighty sang with Lofty Ones : the Hero fashioned with his strength,
Like skilful Mātariśvan with his power and might,

7 The bolt, which pierced at once the vitals of the Dasyu easy to be slain,
With jaw uninjured like the wondrous firmament.

8 Grind off our sins: with song will we conquer the men who sing no hymns :
Not easily art thou pleased with prayerless sacrifice.

9 When threefold flame burns high for thee, to rest on poles of sacrifice,
Thou with the living joyest in the self-bright Ship.

10 Thy glory was the speckled cup, thy glory was the flawless scoop.
Wherewith thou pourest into thy receptacle.

11 As hundreds, O Immortal God, have sung to thee, so hath Sumitra, yea, Durmitra praised thee here,
What time thou holpest Kutsa's son, when Dasyus fell, yea, holpest Kutsa's darling when the Dasyus died.

HYMN CVI. *Aśvins.*

1. This very thing ye Twain hold as your object : ye weave your songs as skilful men weave garments.
That ye may come united have I waked you : ye spread out food like days of lovely weather.

2 Like two plough-bulls ye move along in traces, and seek like eager guests your bidder's banquet.
Ye are like glorious envoys mid the people: like bulls, approach the place where ye are watered.

1 *Vasu* : Indra. *Let the channel bring the stream* : to the Soma juice which has stood long enough for fermentation.—Ludwig. The phraseology is very obscure, and Sāyaṇa gives a totally different explanation.—'When will he, (like) a dam, obstruct and let loose the long-protracted libation for the sake of wind-driven (rain) ?'—Wilson.

2 *The Bird* : the allusion seems to be a race between the horses of Indra and those of Sūrya or the Sun who is the Bird of the heavens.—Ludwig. *Like heaven and earth* : the meaning of *raji* is unknown. Sāyaṇa explains the word by 'heaven and earth,' or 'sun and moon;' but these are mere guesses. Prof. Ludwig thinks that two animals of some kind ('rajitiere', 'raji-beasts') are meant. In VI. 26. 6, Raji is said by Sāyaṇa to be the name of a maiden.

3 *The sinner* : Vṛtra, the chief of sinners, according to Sāyaṇa. Or *pāpaje* may be a verb, and the stanza may be rendered :—'Without them Indra holds him still, like a man weary and alarmed. When he hath made himself ready for noble deed.'—See Pischel, *Vedische Studien*, I. p. 198.

4 *Is Master* : literally 'hero'. The meaning apparently is that when Indra meets with a worshipper he stops his horses and attends the sacrifice.

5 *Who wears the helm* : *śipriṇīvān* ; 'possessing mighty jaws.'—Wilson. *With his jaws* : with his roar, the thunder.

6 *Lofty Ones* : the Maruts.

7 The stanza is obscure. I follow Prof. Ludwig's interpretation of *hirīmaśo hirīmān*, which mean, according to Sāyaṇa, 'gold-bearded' and 'lord of bay horses.'

8 *Grind off* : remove them by whetting. 'Comminute.'—Wilson.

9 *Threefold flame* : of the three sacred fires. *The living*: the sacrificer. *The self-bright Ship* : the sacrifice; 'the vessel of thy glory.'— Wilson.

10 *Cup* : *upasécanī* : a ladle or cup used for sprinkling. *Thy receptacle*, drinking-vessel, or perhaps Agni, that is, the fire, may be intended.

11 *Sumitra* and *Durmitra* are alternative names of the Ṛṣi of the hymn. *Kutsa's son* : Durmitra himself, according to Sāyaṇa.

The metres in some places are somewhat irregular, the meanings of some words are uncertain, and the hymn generally is obscure. Prof. Grassmann has placed the hymn in his Appendix.

3 Like the two pinions of a bird, connected, like two choice animals, ye have sought our worship.
Bright as the fire the votary hath kindled, ye sacrifice in many a spot as roamers.

4 Ye are our kinsmen, like two sons, two fathers, strong in your splendour and like kings for conquest ;
Like rays for our enjoyment, Lords to feed us, ye, like quick hearers, have obeyed our calling.

9 Like giants, ye will find firm ground to stand on in depths, like feet for one who fords a shallow.
Like ears ye will attend to him who orders: ye Two enjoy our wondrous work as sharers.

10 Like toiling bees ye bring to us your honey, as bees into the hide that opens downward.

11 May we increase the laud and gain us vigour : come to our song, ye whom one chariot carries.
Filled be our kine with ripened meath like glory : Bhūtāṁśa hath fulfilled the Aśvins' longing.

HYMN CVII. *Dakṣiṇā.*

1. THESE men's great bounty hath been manifested, and the whole world of life set free from darkness.
Great light hath come, vouchsafed us by the Fathers : apparent is the spacious path of Guerdon.

2 High up in heaven abide the Guerdon-givers : they who give steeds dwell with the Sun for ever.
They who give gold are blest with life eternal : they who give robes prolong their lives, O Soma.

3 Not from the niggards—for they give not freely—comes Meed at sacrifice, Gods' satisfaction :
Yea, many men with hands stretched out with Guerdon present their gifts because they dread dishonour.

4 These who observe mankind regard oblation as streamy Vāyū and light-finding Arka.
They satisfy and give their gifts in synod, and pour in streams the seven-mothered Guerdon.

5 He who brings Guerdon comes as first invited : chief of the hamlet comes the Guerdon-bearer.
Him I account the ruler of the people who was the first to introduce the Guerdon.

6 They call him Ṛṣi, Brahman, Sāma-chanter, reciter of the laud, leader of worship.
The brightly-shining God's three forms he knoweth who first bestowed the sacrificial Guerdon.

7 Guerdon bestows the horse, bestows the bullock, Guerdon bestows, moreover, gold that glisters.
Guerdon gives food which is our life and spirit. He who is wise takes Guerdon for his armour.

8 The liberal die not, never are they ruined: the liberal suffer neither harm nor trouble.
The light of heaven, the universe about us,—all this doth sacrificial Guerdon give them.

9 First have the liberal gained a fragrant dwelling, and got themselves a bride in fair apparel.
The liberal have obtained their draught of liquor, and conquered those who, unprovoked, assailed them.

10 They deck the fleet steed for the bounteous giver : the maid adorns herself and waits to meet him.

4 *Like rays for our enjoyment* : 'like brooms to sweep with,' according to Prof. Ludwig.

I do not attempt the hopeless task of translating stanzas 5, 6, 7, 8, in which nearly every word is a difficult riddle. See Appendix.

10 *The hide that opens downward* : the honey-comb is compared to a water-skin inverted. I cannot translate intelligibly the second line :—'like two labourers you are dripping with perspiration, like a tired cow eating sweet herbage, you attend (the sacrifice).'—Wilson.

The hymn eulogizes Dakṣiṇā, the largess, guerdon, or honorarium presented by the institutors of the sacrifices to the priests who perform the ceremonies. The *yajamānas* who give this guerdon liberally are alternatively the deified subjects of the hymn.

1 *These men* : the wealthy institutors of the sacrifice. *Fathers* : who are the embodiments and guardians of the light.

4 *These who observe mankind* : the Maghavans or wealthy nobles, who do not consider the cost of sacrifice, but regard it as an occasion that enables them to show their liberality, and to gain the favour of Vāyu, the Wind-God who brings countless showers of rain, and Arka or the Sun who brings the light. *Seven-mothered* : originating in, and accompanying, seven forms of sacrifice; or, regulated by the seven priests.

6 *Three forms* : Agni as the Sun, lightning, and fire.

9 *Draught of liquor* : *antaḥpéyam sú́rāyāḥ* : 'deep potations of wine.'—Wilson.

10 *The maid adorns herself* ; 'he obtains a brilliant damsel for his portion.'—Muir.

His home is like a lake with lotus blossoms, like the Gods' palaces adorned and splendid.

11 Steeds good at draught convey the liberal giver, and lightly rolling moves the car of Guerdon.
Assist, ye Gods, the liberal man in battles: the liberal giver conquers foes in combat.

HYMN CVIII. *Saramā. Paṇis.*

1. WHAT wish of Saramā hath brought her hither? The path leads far away to distant places.
What charge hast thou for us? Where turns thy journey? How hast thou made thy way o'er Rasā's waters.

2 I come appointed messenger of Indra, seeking your ample stores of wealth, O Paṇis.
This hath preserved me from the fear of crossing: thus have I made my way o'er Rasā's waters.

3 What is that Indra like, what is his aspect whose envoy, Saramā, from afar thou comest?
Let him approach, and we will show him friendship: he shall be made the herdsman of our cattle.

4 I know him safe from harm: but he can punish who sent me hither from afar as envoy.
Him rivers flowing with deep waters hide not. Low will ye be, O Paṇis, slain by Indra.

5 These are the kine which, Saramā, thou seekest, flying, O Blest One, to the ends of heaven.
Who will loose these for thee without a battle? Yea, and sharp-pointed are our warlike weapons.

6 Even if your wicked bodies, O ye Paṇis, were arrow-proof, your words are weak for wounding;
And were the path to you as yet unmastered, Bṛhaspati in neither case will spare you.

7 Paved with the rock is this our treasure-chamber; filled full of precious things, of kine, and horses.
These Paṇis who are watchful keepers guard it. In vain hast thou approached this lonely station.

8 Ṛṣis will come inspirited with Soma, Aṅgirases unwearied, and Navagvas.
This stall of cattle will they part among them: then will the Paṇis wish these words unspoken.

9 Even thus, O Saramā, hast thou come hither, forced by celestial might to make the journey.
Turn thee not back, for thou shalt be our sister: O Blest One, we will give thee of the cattle.

10 Brotherhood, sisterhood, I know not either: the dread Aṅgirases and Indra know them.
They seemed to long for kine when I departed. Hence, into distance, be ye gone, O Paṇis.

11 Hence, far away, ye Paṇis! Let the cattle lowing come forth as holy Law commandeth,
Kine which Bṛhaspati, and Soma, Ṛṣis, sages, and pressing-stones have found when hidden.

HYMN CIX. *Viśvedevas.*

I. THESE first, the boundless Sea, and Mātariśvan, fierce-glowing Fire, the Strong, the Bliss-bestower.

11 *Car of Guerdon* : cf. I. 123. 1.

The hymn is a colloquy between Saramā, the messenger of the Gods or of Indra (see I. 62. 3, note; 72. 8; III. 31. 6; V. 45. 8), and the Paṇis or envious demons who have carried off the cows or rays of light which Indra wishes to recover. Saramā and the Paṇis are alternately subject and Ṛṣi.

1 The Paṇis address Saramā who has found her way to the rocky stronghold in which the stolen cows are imprisoned. The Paṇis speak the uneven stanzas, with the exception of stanza 11, and Saramā the even. *Rasā* is in this place a mythical stream that flows round the atmosphere and the earth. See V. 41. 15. In I. 112, 12, and V. 53. 9, Rasā appears to be a river of the Panjāb, probably an affluent of the Indus. See Zimmer, *Altindisches Leben* pp. 15, 16.

6 *Weak for wounding* : 'not in the place of armies.'—Wilson. *Bṛhaspati* : as Indra's companion and ally in battle.

8 *Navagvas* : members of a mythological family, forming a division of the Aṅgirases or closely connected with them. *Wish these words unspoken* : more literally, reject them from their mouths ; retract their threads.

10 *Know them* : are allied by such ties of kinship.

11 It is uncertain to whom this stanza is to be ascribed. Sāyaṇa assigns it to Saramā. Prof. Ludwig thinks that Bṛhaspati may be the speaker. *Pressing-stones* : which prepare the Soma juice that inspirits Indra.

The hymn has been translated by the authors of *Siebenzig Lieder des Rigveda*. See also Mme. Zénaïde Ragozin, *Vedic India*, p. 256.

And heavenly Floods, first-born by holy Order, exclaimed against the outrage on a Brahman.

2 King Soma first of all, without reluctance, made restitution of the Brahman's consort.
Mitra and Varuṇa were the inviters: Agni as Hotar took her hand and led her.

3 The man, her pledge, must by her hand be taken when they have cried, She is a Brahman's consort.
She stayed not for a herald to conduct her: thus is the kingdom of a ruler guarded.

4 Thus spake of her those Gods of old, Seven Ṛṣis who sate them down to their austere devotion:
Dire is a Brahman's wife led home by others: in the supremest heaven she plants confusion.

5 The Brahmacārī goes engaged in duty: he is a member of the Gods' own body.
Through him Bṛhaspati obtained his consort, as the Gods gained the ladle brought by Soma.

6 So then the Gods restored her, so men gave the woman back again.
The Kings who kept their promises restored the Brahman's wedded wife,

7 Having restored the Brahman's wife, and freed them, with Gods' aid, from sin,
They shared the fulness of the earth, and won themselves extended sway.

HYMN CX. *Āpris.*

1. THOU in the house of man this day enkindled worshippest Gods as God, O Jātavedas.
Observant, bright as Mitra, bring them hither: thou art a sapient and foreknowing envoy.

2 Tanūnapāt, fair-tongued, with sweet meath balming the paths and ways of Order, make them pleasant.
Convey our sacrifice to heaven, exalting with holy thoughts our hymns of praise and worship.

3 Invoked, deserving prayer and adoration, O Agni, come accordant with the Vasus.
Thou art, O Youthful Lord, the Gods' Invoker, so, best of Sacrificers, bring them quickly.

4 By rule the Sacred Grass is scattered eastward, a robe to clothe this earth when dawns are breaking:
Widely it spreads around and far-extended, fair for the Gods and bringing peace and freedom.

5 Let the expansive Doors be widely opened, like wives who deck their beauty for their husbands.
Lofty, celestial, all-impelling Portals, admit the Gods and give them easy entrance.

6 Pouring sweet dews let holy Night and Morning, each close to each, be seated at their station,—
Lofty, celestial Dames with gold to deck them, assuming all their fair and radiant beauty.

7 Come the two first celestial sweet-voiced Hotars, arranging sacrifice for man to worship
As singers who inspire us in assemblies, showing the eastward light with their direction.

8 Let Bhāratī come quickly to our worship, and Iḷā showing like a human being.
So let Sarasvatī and both her fellows, deft Goddesses, on this fair grass be seated.

9 Hotar more skilled in sacrifice, bring hither with speed to-day God Tvaṣṭar, thou who knowest.
Even him who formed these two, the Earth and Heaven, the Parents, with their forms, and every creature.

1 *Outrage on a Brahman*: 'Brahmā's sin,' according to Sāyaṇa.

5 *Brahmacārī*: a religious student. For his glorification, see *Hymns of the Atharva-veda*, XI. 5. *The ladle*: *juhvām*: Prof. Ludwig takes it to be a proper name:—'Juhū, O Gods, conducted home by Soma.'

The wife of a Brahman appears to have been taken to his home by a Kṣatriya, and then restored. A legend quoted by Sāyaṇa says that Juhū or Vāk, the wife of Bṛhaspati who is identified with Brahmā, had been deserted by her husband. The Gods then consulted together as to the means of expiating his sin and restored her to him. See Wilson's Translation.

The hymn is an almost unintelligible fragment and of comparatively late origin.

See preceding hymns addressed to the same deities and deified objects: I. 13; 142, 188; II. 3; III. 4; V. 5. VII. 2; and IX. 5.

1 *Jātavedas* and *Tanūnapāt* are names of Agni. The *Doors* of the sacrificial chamber represent the portals of the eastern heaven. *Vanaspati* is the sacrificial post to which the victim is tied.

10 Send to our offerings which thyself thou balmest the Companies of Gods in ordered season.
Agni, Vanaspati the Immolator sweeten our offered gift with meath and butter.

11 Agni, as soon as he was born, made ready the sacrifice, and was the Gods' preceder.
May the Gods eat our offering consecrated according to this true Priest's voice and guidance.

HYMN CXI. *Indra.*

1. Bring forth your sacred song ye prudent singers, even as are the thoughts of human beings.
Let us draw Indra with true deeds anear us : he loves our songs, the Hero, and is potent.

2 The hymn shone brightly from the seat of worship: to the kine came the Bull, the Heifer's Offspring
With mighty bellowing hath he arisen, and hath pervaded even the spacious regions.

3 Indra knows, verily, how to hear our singing, for he, victorious, made a path for Sūrya.
He made the Cow, and he became the Sovran of Heaven, primeval, matchless, and unshaken.

4 Praised by Aṅgirases, Indra demolished with might the works of the great watery monster.
Full many regions, too, hath he pervaded, and by his truth supported earth's foundation.

5 The counterpart of heaven and earth is Indra: he knoweth all libations, slayeth Śuṣṇa.
The vast sky with the Sun hath he extended, and, best of pillars, stayed it with a pillar.

6 The Vṛtra-slayer with his bolt felled Vṛtra: the magic of the godless, waxen mighty,
Here hast thou, Bold Assailant, boldly conquered. Yea, then thine arms, O Maghavan, were potent.

7 When the Dawns come attendant upon Sūrya their rays discover wealth of divers colours.
The Star of heaven is seen as 'twere approaching : none knoweth aught of it as it departeth.

8 Far have they gone, the first of all these waters, the waters that flowed forth when Indra sent them.
Where is their spring, and where is their foundation ? Where now, ye Waters, is your inmost centre ?

9 Thou didst free rivers swallowed by the Dragon ; and rapidly they set themselves in motion,
Those that were loosed and those that longed for freedom. Excited now to speed they run unresting.

10 Yearning together they have sped to Sindhu : the Fort-destroyer, praised, of old, hath loved them.
Indra, may thy terrestrial treasures reach us, and our full songs of joy approach thy dwelling.

HYMN CXII. *Indra.*

1. Drink of the juice, O Indra, at thy pleasure, for thy first draught is early morn's libation.
Rejoice, that thou mayst slay our foes, O Hero, and we with lauds will tell thy mighty exploits.

2 Thou hast a car more swift than thought, O Indra ; thereon come hither, come to drink the Soma.
Let thy Bay Steeds, thy Stallions, hasten hither, with whom thou comest nigh and art delighted.

3 Deck out thy body with the fairest colours, with golden splendour of the Sun adorn it.
O Indra, turn thee hitherward invited by us thy friends; be seated and be joyful.

2 *The kine* : who are milked for sacrificial purposes. *The Bull* : Indra. *The Heifer's Offspring* : cp. IV.18. 10: 'The Heifer hath brought forth the strong, the mighty, the unconquerable Bull, the furious Indra. The Heifer is Aditi.

3 *He made the Cow* : the words *mėnām...góḥ* the cow, 'the female of the bull.'—Muir; 'Des Stieres Weib,' —Grassmann, —are difficult. Prof. Ludwig suggests that the earth may be intended.

4 *Watery monster* : Arbuda, a demon of the clouds. See X. 67, 12.

7 *The Star of heaven* : the Sun. *Departeth* : on its nightly journey from west to east.

9 *The Dragon* : Ahi; Vṛtra or his brother-fiend.

10 *The Fort-destroyer* : Indra.

4 O thou whose grandeur in thy festive transports not even these two great worlds have comprehended.
Come, Indra, with thy dear Bay Horses harnessed, come to our dwelling and the food thou lovest.

5 Pressed for thy joyous banquet is the Soma, Soma whereof thou, Indra, ever drinking,
Hast waged unequalled battles with thy foemen, which prompts the mighty flow of thine abundance.

6 Found from of old is this thy cup, O Indra : Śatakratu, drink therefrom the Soma.
Filled is the beaker with the meath that gladdens, the beaker which all Deities delight in.

7 From many a side with proffered entertainment the folk are calling thee, O Mighty Indra.
These our libations shall for thee be richest in sweet meath : drink thereof and find them pleasant.

8 I will declare thy deeds of old, O Indra, the mighty acts which thou hast first accomplished.
In genuine wrath thou loosenedst the mountain so that the Brahman easily found the cattle.

9 Lord of the hosts, amid our bands be seated : they call thee greatest Sage among the sages.
Nothing is done, even far away, without thee : great, wondrous, Maghavan, is the hymn I sing thee.

10 Aim of our eyes be thou, for we implore thee, O Maghavan, Friend of friends and Lord of treasures.
Fight, Warrior strong in truth, fight thou the battle : give us our share of undivided riches.

HYMN CXIII. *Indra.*

1. THE Heavens and the Earth accordant with all Gods encouraged graciously that vigorous might of his.
When he came showing forth his majesty and power, he drank of Soma juice and waxed exceeding strong.

8 *The Brahman* : according to Sāyaṇa, Brahmā who is identified with Bṛhaspati, the owner of the cows which the Paṇis had stolen.

2 This majesty of his Viṣṇu extols and lauds, making the stalk that gives the meath flow forth with might.
When Indra Maghavan with those who followed him had smitten Vṛtra he deserved the choice of Gods.

3 When, bearing warlike weapons, fain to win thee praise, thou mettest Vṛtra, yea, the Dragon, for the fight,
Then all the Maruts who were gathered with thee there extolled, O Mighty One, thy powerful majesty.

4 Soon as he sprang to life he forced asunder hosts : forward the Hero looked to manly deed and war.
He cleft the rock, he let concurrent streams flow forth, and with his skilful art stablished the heavens' wide vault.

5 Indra hath evermore possessed surpassing power : he forced, far from each other, heaven and earth apart.
He hurled impetuous down his iron thunderbolt, a joy to Varuṇa's and Mitra's worshipper.

6 Then to the mighty powers of Indra, to his wrath, his the fierce Stormer, loud of voice, they came with speed;
What time the Potent One rent Vṛtra with his strength, who held the waters back, whom darkness compassed round.

7 Even in the first of those heroic acts which they who strove together came with might to execute,
Deep darkness fell upon the slain, and Indra won by victory the right of being first invoked.

8 Then all the Gods extolled, with eloquence inspired by draughts of Soma juice, thy deeds of manly might.
As Agni eats the dry food with his teeth, he ate Vṛtra, the Dragon, maimed by Indra's deadly dart.

9 Proclaim his many friendships, met with friendship, made with singers, with the skilful and the eloquent.
Indra, when he subdues Dhuni and

6 *They came* : it is uncertain whether the Gods, or the Maruts, or the waters are the understood subject.

7 *Deep darkness fell upon the slain* : 'Vṛtra being slain, the thick darkness was destroyed.'—Wilson.

8 *He ate* : Indra utterly destroyed him. Sāyaṇa explains in a more matter-of-fact way : people devoured Vṛtra, that is, the food produced by the waters which were no longer obstructed by him.

9 *Dhuni* and *Cumuri* were demons and enemies of Indra's friend Dabhīti. See Vol. I., Index.

Cumuri, lists to Dabhīti for his faithful spirit's sake.

10 Give riches manifold with noble horses, to be remembered while my songs address thee.
May we by easy paths pass all our troubles : find us this day a ford wide and extensive.

HYMN CXIV. *Viśvedevas.*

1. Two perfect springs of heat pervade the Threefold, and come for their delight is Mātariśvan.
Craving the milk of heaven the Gods are present : well do they know the praise-song and the Sāman.

2 The priests heard far away, as they are ordered, serve the three Nirṛtis, for well they know them.
Sages have traced the cause that first produced them, dwelling in distant and mysterious chambers.

3 The Youthful One, well-shaped, with four locks braided, brightened with oil, puts on the ordinances.
Two Birds of mighty power are seated near her, there where the Deities receive their portion.

4 One of these Birds hath passed into the sea of air : thence he looks round and views this universal world.
With simple heart I have beheld him from anear : his Mother kisses him and he returns her kiss.

5 Him with fair wings though only One in nature, wise singers shape, with songs, in many figures.
While they at sacrifices fix the metres, they measure out twelve chalices of Soma.

6 While they arrange the four and six-and-thirty, and duly order, up to twelve, the measures,
Having disposed the sacrifice thoughtful sages send the Car forward with the Ṛc and Sāman.

7 The Chariot's majesties are fourteen others : seven sages lead it onward with their voices.
Who will declare to us the ford Āpnāna, the path whereby they drink first draughts of Soma ?

8 The fifteen lauds are in a thousand places : that is as vast as heaven and earth in measure.
A thousand spots contain the mighty thousand. Vāk spreadeth forth as far as Prayer extendeth.

9 What sage hath learned the metres' application ? Who hath gained Vāk, the spirit's aim and object ?
Which ministering priest is called eighth Hero ? Who then hath tracked the two Bay Steeds of Indra ?

10 Yoked to his chariot-pole there stood the Coursers : they only travel round earth's farthest limits.
These, when their driver in his home is settled, receive the allotted meed of their exertion.

HYMN CXV. *Agni.*

1. VERILY wondrous is the tender Youngling's growth who never draweth nigh to drink his Mothers' milk.

1 *Springs of heat* : *gharmā* : Agni and Sūrya. *The Threefold* : the universe, sky, firmament, and earth. *Mātariśvan* : Vāyu, according to Sāyaṇa. 'Thus we have here the well-known triad, Agni, Vāyu, Sūrya.'—Ludwig.

2 *Three Nirṛtis* : according to Sāyaṇa, heaven, mid-air, and earth, or the deities that control them. Prof. Ludwig thinks that the Dawns are meant, which by their regular appearance bring men nearer to death. The plural appears in one other place, VIII. 24. 24.

3 *The Youthful One* : the altar, represented as a woman. *With four locks braided* : quadrangular, according to Sāyaṇa. *Puts on the ordinances* : is dressed or arranged in the manner prescribed for sacrifice. *Two Birds* : probably Agni and Soma. According to Sāyaṇa, the husband and his wife, or the Yajamāna and the Brahman.

4 *One* : Agni as the Sun. *His mother* : perhaps, as Prof. Ludwig says, Dawn.

6 Thirty-six *grahas*, chalices, or saucers for Soma juice or other libations, are to be used at the Agniṣṭoma, and four in addition at the Atyagniṣṭoma sacrifice. *The measures* : the proper metres for particular rites or parts of the service. *The Car* : the sacrifice. *Ṛc* : the holy verse that is recited. *Sāman* : the psalm that is sung or chanted.

7 *Majesties* : the abstract used for the concrete, the mighty ones, probably the priests. *The ford Āpnāna* : the passage leading to the place of sacrifice. *They* : the Gods.

8 *That* : meaning the fifteen lauds regarded as a whole. *The mighty thousand* : the meaning is uncertain : 'the thousand great (functions) are in a thousand places.'—Wilson. This means, according to Sāyaṇa, that every function of the body has its appropriate object. Dr. Muir translates :—'There are a thousand times fifteen *ukthas* ....A thousand times a thousand are their glorious manifestations.' *Vāk* : or Speech. See X. 71 and 125.

9 *Eighth Hero* : Agni is meant, as presiding over the seven *ṛtvijas* or ministering priests.

---

1 *His Mothers* are the two fire-sticks, the lower of which, in which the spark is produced, being *she who hath no udder*.

As soon as she who hath no udder bore him, he, faring on his great errand, suddenly grew strong.

2 Then Agni was his name, most active to bestow, gathering up the trees with his consuming tooth ;
Skilled in fair sacrifice, armed with destroying tongue, impetuous as a bull that snorteth in the mead.

3 Praise him, your God who, bird-like, rests upon a tree, scattering drops of juice and pouring forth his flood,
Speaking aloud with flame as with his lips a priest, and broadening his paths like one of high command.

4 Thou Everlasting, whom, far-striding fain to burn, the winds, uninterrupted, never overcome,
They have approached, as warriors eager for the fight, heroic Trita, guiding him to gain his wish.

5 This Agni is the best of Kaṇvas, Kaṇvas' Friend, Conqueror of the foe whether afar or near.
May Agni guard the singers, guard the princes well : may Agni grant to us our princes' gracious help.

6 Do thou, Supitrya, swiftly following, make thyself the lord of Jātavedas, mightiest of all,
Who surely gives a boon even in thirsty land, most powerful, prepared to aid us in the wilds.

7 Thus noble Agni with princes and mortal men is lauded, excellent for conquering strength with chiefs,
Men who are well-disposed as friends and true to Law, even as the heavens in majesty surpass mankind.

8 O Son of Strength, Victorious, with this title Upastuta's most potent voice reveres thee.
Blest with brave sons by thee we will extol thee, and lengthen out the days of our existence.

9 Thus, Agni, have the sons of Vṛṣṭihavya, the Ṛṣis, the Upastutas invoked thee.
Protect them, guard the singers and the princes. With Vaṣat ! have they come, with hands uplifted, with their uplifted hands and cries of Glory !

4 *Trita* : according to Sāyaṇa, him who is stationed in the three fire-receptacles, that is, Agni.

5 *Kaṇvas* : a well-known family with which Upastuta was connected. According to Sāyaṇa, worshippers in general are meant :—'the most earnest of eulogists, the friend of those who praise him.'—Wilson.

6 *Supitrya* ('who hast fair ancestors.'—Wilson) seems to be an epithet of the Ṛṣi as addressed by himself. Sāyaṇa applies it to Agni. The construction of the stanza is difficult, and the translation of the first half, which follows Prof. Ludwig, is somewhat conjectural. *Thirsty land* : Agni by his intercession causes rain to fall.

Prof. Grassmann observes : 'Das Lied enthält, namentlich in Verses 3—6, manches Dunkle, sodass hier die Auslegung zweifelhaft bleibt.'

HYMN CXVI. *Indra.*

1. DRINK Soma juice for mighty power and vigour, drink, Strongest One, that thou mayst smite down Vṛtra.
Drink thou, invoked, for strength, and riches : drink thou thy fill of meath and pour it down, O Indra.

2 Drink of the foodful juice stirred into motion, drink what thou choosest of the flowing Soma.
Giver of weal, be joyful in thy spirit, and turn thee hitherward to bless and prosper.

3 Let heavenly Soma gladden thee, O Indra, let that effused among mankind delight thee.
Rejoice in that whereby thou gavest freedom, and that whereby thou conquerest thy foemen.

4 Let Indra come, impetuous, doubly mighty, to the poured juice, the Bull, with two Bay Coursers.
With juices pressed in milk, with meath presented, glut evermore thy bolt, O Foe-destroyer.

5 Dash down, outflaming their sharp flaming weapons, the strong-holds of the men urged on by demons.
I give thee, Mighty One, great strength and conquest : go, meet thy foes and rend them in the battle.

6 Extend afar the votary's fame and glory, as the firm archer's strength drives off the foeman.
Ranged on our side, grown strong in

1 *Pour it down* : 'shower down (blessings).'—Wilson.

3 *Gavest freedom* : by slaying Vṛtra : or, riches, according to Sāyaṇa.

4 *Foe-destroyer* : *aruśahā* : according to the St. Petersburg Lexicon, 'striker of the red clouds' (*aruśa*=*aruṣa* ?). I adopt Sāyaṇa's explanation.

6 *As the firm archer's strength* : the construction is obscure :—'(stretch out) thy strength like strong bows against our enemies.'—Wilson.

might that conquers, never defeated, still increase thy body.

7 To thee have we presented this oblation : accept it, Sovran Ruler, free from anger.
Juice, Maghavan, for thee is pressed and ripened : eat, Indra, drink of that which stirs to meet thee.

8 Eat, Indra, these oblations which approach thee : be pleased with food made ready and with Soma.
With entertainment we receive thee friendly : effectual be the sacrificer's wishes.

9 I send sweet speech to Indra and to Agni : with hymns I speed it like a boat through waters.
Even thus, the Gods seem moving round about me, the fountains and bestowers of our riches.

HYMN CXVII. *Liberality.*

1. THE Gods have not ordained hunger to be our death : even to the well-fed man comes death in varied shape.
The riches of the liberal never waste away, while he who will not give finds none to comfort him.

2 The man with food in store who, when the needy comes in miserable case begging for bread to eat,
Hardens his heart against him—even when of old he did him service—finds not one to comfort him.

3 Bounteous is he who gives unto the beggar who comes to him in want of food and feeble.
Success attends him in the shout of battle. He makes a friend of him in future troubles.

4 No friend is he who to his friend and comrade who comes imploring food, will offer nothing.
Let him depart—no home is that to rest in—, and rather seek a stranger to support him.

5 Let the rich satisfy the poor implorer, and bend his eye upon a longer pathway.
Riches come now to one, now to another, and like the wheels of cars are ever rolling.

6 The foolish man wins food with fruitless labour : that food—I speak the truth—shall be his ruin.
He feeds no trusty friend, no man to love him. All guilt is he who eats with no partaker.

7 The ploughshare ploughing makes the food that feeds us, and with its feet cuts through the path it follows.
Better the speaking than the silent Brahman : the liberal friend outvalues him who gives not.

8 He with one foot hath far outrun the biped, and the two-footed catches the three-footed.
Four-footed creatures come when bipeds call them, and stand and look where five are met together.

9 The hands are both alike : their labour differs. The yield of sister milch-kine is unequal.
Twins even differ in their strength and vigour : two, even kinsmen, differ in their bounty.

HYMN CXVIII. *Agni.*

1. AGNI, refulgent among men thou slayest the devouring fiend,
Bright Ruler in thine own abode.

2 Thou springest up when worshipped well : the drops of butter are thy joy
When ladles are brought near to thee.

The hymn eulogises Liberality or Bounty in the shape of gifts of wealth and food.

1 *To be our death* : men must not attempt to justify their refusal of food to the hungry by saying that the Gods send hunger as a punishment for sin.

5 *Bend his eye upon a longer pathway* : carefully consider the future and not the present only. He himself may need the same assistance hereafter.

6 *Shall be his ruin* : with reference to stanza I.

7 Active exertion is necessary for success. *The speaking Brahman* : the priest who duly discharges the task of recitation for which he is engaged. 'A Brahman expounding (the Veda).'—Wilson.

8 The victory is not always theirs who appear to be more richly endowed than others. *He with one foot* : *ékapād* : the Sun appears to be meant, elsewhere called Aja-Ekapād. See VI. 50. 14. *The biped* is man. *The three-footed* is the old man who walks with a staff and is overtaken by one who does not require such assistance. *Four-footed creatures* : dogs. *Five* : several men together ; the dogs being at first uncertain whether their masters are among them or not. *Paṅktīḥ*, sets of five, is apparently used with reference to the one, two, three, and four in the preceding compound words. Others explain *paṅktīḥ* by 'steps' or 'traces'.

I have adopted the explanation given by the authors of the *Siebenzig Lieder*.

9 All men should be liberal; but we must not expect all to be equally generous.

The hymn has been translated by Dr. Muir, *O. S. Texts*, V. pp. 431—433.

3 Honoured with gifts he shines afar, Agni adorable with song :
The dripping ladle balms his face.

4 Agni with honey in his mouth, honoured with gifts, is balmed with oil,
Refulgent in his wealth of light.

5 Praised by our hymns thou kindlest thee, Oblation-bearer, for the Gods :
As such do mortals call on thee.

6 To that Immortal Agni pay worship with oil, ye mortal men,—
Lord of the house, whom none deceives.

7 O Agni, burn the Rākṣasas with thine unconquerable flame :
Shine guardian of Eternal Law.

8 So, Agni, with thy glowing face burn fierce against the female fiends,
Shining among Urukṣayas.

9 Urukṣayas have kindled thee, Oblation-bearer, thee, with hymns.
Best Worshipper among mankind.

HYMN CXIX. *Indra.*

1. This, even this was my resolve, to win a cow, to win a steed :
Have I not drunk of Soma juice?

2 Like violent gusts of wind the draughts that I have drunk have lifted me :
Have I not drunk of Soma juice?

3 The draughts I drank have borne me up, as fleet-foot horses draw a car :
Have I not drunk of Soma juice?

4 The hymn hath reached me, like a cow who lows to meet her darling calf:
Have I not drunk of Soma juice?

5 As a wright bends a chariot-seat so round my heart I bend the hymn :
Have I not drunk of Soma juice ?

6 Not as a mote within the eye count the Five Tribes of men with me :
Have I not drunk of Soma juice?

7 The heavens and earth themselves have not grown equal to one half of me :
Have I not drunk of Soma juice ?

8 I in my grandeur have surpassed the heavens and all this spacious earth :
Have I not drunk of Soma juice?

9 Aha ! this spacious earth will I deposit either here or there
Have I not drunk of Soma juice ?

10 In one short moment will I smite the earth in fury here or there :
Have I not drunk of Soma juice?

11 One of my flanks is in the sky; I let the other trail below :
Have I not drunk of Soma juice?

12 I, greatest of the Mighty Ones, am lifted to the firmament :
Have I not drunk of Soma juice?

13 I seek the worshipper's abode ; oblation-bearer to the Gods :
Have I not drunk of Soma juice ?

HYMN CXX. *Indra.*

1. In all the worlds That was the Best and Highest whence sprang the Mighty Gods, of splendid valour.
As soon as born he overcomes his foemen, he in whom all who lend him aid are joyful.

2 Grown mighty in his strength, with ample vigour, he as a foe strikes fear into the Dāsa,
Eager to win the breathing and the breathless. All sang thy praise at banquet and oblation.

3 All concentrate on thee their mental vigour, what time these, twice or thrice, are thine assistants.

8 *Urukṣayas* : members of the Ṛṣi's family.

The Ṛṣi is Indra himself in the form of Lava. He describes his sensations after drinking Soma juice. But see Bergaigne, I. 151, who considers it to be the utterance of an exhilarated mortal.

1 *To win a cow* : to strengthen and inspirit himself for battle, and so to win kine and horses for his worshippers.

6 Sāyaṇa explains differently :—'The five castes have not eluded the glance of my eye'.—Wilson.

11 Cp. III. 32. 11.

13 This stanza is difficult. The word *gṛhó* is unintelligible, and *gṛham*, as Prof. Ludwig suggests, should perhaps, be read instead. *Oblation-bearer* : Indra, in his excitement, fancies that he is Agni. Prof. Grassmann, who with Dr. Muir, considers *gṛhó* to mean servant or minister, places the stanza in his Appendix as a fragment from a hymn to Agni.

The hymn has been translated by Dr. Muir, *O. S. Texts* V. p. 91, by the authors of the *Siebenzig Lieder*, and by Prof. Peterson, *Hymns from the Ṛgveda* (Bombay Sanskrit Series).

1 *That* : meaning, according to Sāyaṇa, Brahmā the original cause of the universe.

2 *Eager to win* : Prof. Ludwig makes *sásni* an infinitive. *Sásniḥ* may be the correct reading. See Grassmann, *Wörterbuch zum Ṛgveda*. *The breathing and the breathless* : the animate and the inanimate world.

3 *Mental vigour* : *krátum* : 'adoration.'—Wilson. *These* : Soma juices. *Twice or thrice* : with reference, perhaps, to the three daily libations. *What is sweeter than the sweet* : thine own celestial Soma. Sāyaṇa explains the stanza differently :—'To thee all (worshippers) offer

Blend what is sweeter than the sweet with sweetness : win quickly with our meath that meath in battle.

4 Therefore in thee too, thou who winnest riches, at every banquet are the sages joyful.
With mightier power, Bold God, extend thy firmness : let not malignant Yātudhānas harm thee.

5 Proudly we put our trust in thee in battles, when we behold great wealth the prize of combat.
I with my words impel thy weapons onward, and sharpen with my prayer thy vital vigour.

6 Worthy of praises, many-shaped, most skilful, most energetic, Āptya of the Āptyas :
He with his might destroys the seven Dānus, subduing many who were deemed his equals.

7 Thou in that house which thy protection guardeth bestowest wealth, the higher and the lower.
Thou stablishest the two much-wandering Mothers, and bringest many deeds to their completion.

8 Bṛhaddiva, the foremost of light-winners, repeats these holy prayers, this strength of Indra.
He rules the great self-luminous fold of cattle, and all the doors of light hath he thrown open.

9 Thus hath Bṛhaddiva, the great Atharvan, spoken to Indra as himself in person.
The spotless Sisters, they who are his Mothers, with power exalt him and impel him onward.

adoration, whether these propitiators be two or three. Combine that which is sweeter than the sweet with sweetness, unite that honey with honey.'—Wilson. The 'two or three,' according to Sāyaṇa, are the sacrificer and his wife and child, and the second half of the stanza contains a reference to the propagation of children.

6 *Āptya* : the name of a class of deities, of which Trita Āptya is the chief. 'Most accessible of the accessible.'—Wilson. The first line is without a verb : I praise him, may be understood. *Dānus* : a class of demons.

7 *The higher and the lower* : heavenly and earthly, *Mothers* : Heaven and Earth.

8 *Foremost of light-winners* : according to Sāyaṇa, 'chief of Ṛṣis and enjoyer of heaven, or servant of Āditya, the Sun, Indra.' *Fold of cattle* : the region of light.

9 *The great Atharvan* : 'the great priest.'—Grassmann. *As himself* : he identifies himself with the God whom he worships. *The spotless Sisters, they who are his Mothers*: according to Sāyaṇa, the sister rivers which abide in the mother earth. Von Roth adopts the reading of Atharvaveda V. 2. 9. *mātariśvarī*, instead of the *mātaribhvarīḥ* of the text. Heaven and Earth appear to be intended.

HYMN CXXI. *Ka.*

1. IN the beginning rose Hiraṇyagarbha, born Only Lord of all created beings.
He fixed and holdeth up this earth and heaven. What God shall we adore with our oblation ?

2 Giver of vital breath, of power and vigour, he whose commandments all the Gods acknowledge :
The Lord of death, whose shade is life immortal. What God shall we adore with our oblation ?

3 Who by his grandeur hath become Sole Ruler of all the moving world that breathes and slumbers;
He who is Lord of men and Lord of cattle. What God shall we adore with our oblation ?

4 His, through his might, are these snow-covered mountains, and men call sea and Rasā his possession :
His arms are these, his are these heavenly regions. What God shall we adore with our oblation ?

5 By him the heavens are strong and earth is stedfast, by him light's realm and sky-vault are supported :
By him the regions in mid-air were measured. What God shall we adore with our oblation ?

6 To him, supported by his help, two armies embattled look while trembling in their spirit,
When over them the risen Sun is shining. What God shall we adore with our oblation ?

7 What time the mighty waters came, containing the universal germ, producing Agni,
Thence sprang the Gods' one spirit into

Ka, kaḥ, (quis) meaning Who ? that is, the Unknown God, has been applied as a name to Prajāpati, and to other Gods, from a forced interpretation of the interrogative pronoun which occurs in the refrain of each verse of the hymn.

1 *Hiraṇyagarbha* : literally 'the gold-germ; ' 'source of golden light; the Sun-god 'as the great power of the universe, from which all other powers and existences, divine and earthly, are derived, a conception which is the nearest approach to the later mystical conception of Brahmā, the creator of the world.'—Wallis. *Which God* : *kásmai devā́ya* : cui deo ? According to others: 'Worship we Ka the God with our oblation.' According to Ludwig, the meaning is 'What other God than Prajāpati shall we worship ?'

3 *Breathes and slumbers* : that is of Gods and men. *Of men and......cattle* : literally, 'of quadruped and biped.'

4 *Sea* : air. *Rasā* : the mythical river of the firmament. Cf. X. 108. 1.

7 *Thence* : from the coming of the waters. *One spirit* :

being. What God shall we adore with our oblation ?

8 He in his might surveyed the floods containing productive force and generating Worship.
He is the God of gods, and none beside him. What God shall we adore with our oblation ?

9 Ne'er may he harm us who is earth's Begetter, nor he whose laws are sure, the heavens' Creator,
He who brought forth the great and lucid waters. What God shall we adore with our oblation ?

10 Prajāpati ! thou only comprehendest all these created things, and none beside thee.
Grant us our hearts' desire when we invoke thee : may we have store of riches in possession.

HYMN CXXII. *Agni.*

1. I PRAISE the God of wondrous might like Indra, the lovely pleasant Guest whom all must welcome.
May Agni, Priest and Master of the household, give hero strength and all-sustaining riches.

2 O Agni, graciously accept this song of mine, thou passing wise who knowest every ordinance.
Enwrapped in holy oil further the course of prayer : the Gods bestow according to thy holy law.

3 Immortal, wandering round the seven stations, give, a liberal Giver, to the pious worshipper,
Wealth, Agni, with brave sons and ready for his use : welcome the man who comes with fuel unto thee.

4 The seven who bring oblations worship thee, the Strong, the first, the Great Chief Priest, Ensign of sacrifice,
The oil-anointed Bull, Agni who hears, who sends as God full hero strength to him who freely gives.

5 First messenger art thou, meet for election: drink thou thy fill invited to the Amṛta,
The Maruts in the votary's house adorned thee; with lauds the Bhṛgus gave thee light and glory.

6 Milking the teeming Cow for all-sustaining food. O Wise One, for the worship-loving worshipper,
Thou, Agni, dropping oil, thrice lighting works of Law, showest thy wisdom circling home and sacrifice.

7 They who at flushing of this dawn appointed thee their messenger, these men have paid thee reverence.
Gods strengthened thee for work that must be glorified, Agni, while they made butter pure for sacrifice.

8 Arrangers in our synods, Agni, while they sang, Vasiṣṭha's sons have called thee down, the Potent One.
Maintain the growth of wealth with men who sacrifice. Ye Gods, preserve us with your blessings evermore.

HYMN CXXIII. *Vena.*

1. SEE, Vena, born in light, hath driven hither, on chariot of the air, the Calves of Pṛśni.
Singers with hymns caress him as an infant there where the waters and the sunlight mingle.

2 Vena draws up his wave from out the ocean : mist-born, the fair one's back is

ékaḥ, one, in the text gives two superfluous syllables, and is suspicious.

8 *Generating Worship* : 'giving birth to sacrifice.' —Wilson.

10 *Prajāpati* : Lord of life, creatures or creation. Savitar the Sun-God is so called in IV. 53, 2, and Soma Pavamāna in IX. 5. 9. Prajāpati was afterwards the name of a separate God, the bestower of progeny and cattle, and sometimes invoked as the Creator.

The hymn has been translated by Dr. Muir, *O. S. Texts*, IV., pp. 16, 17; by Prof. Max Müller, *A. S. Lit.*, p. 569, and *Vedic Hymns, Part* I. (Sacred Books of the East, XXXII) p. 1. ; by Mr. Wallis, *Cosmology of the Ṛgveda*, p. 50f.; by Prof. Peterson, *Hymns from the Ṛgveda*; and by Dr. L. Scherman, *Philosophische Hymnen Aus der Ṛgveda und-Atharva-veda-Saṁhitā*, p. 24.

---

1 *Like Indra* : *vásum ná* : like the Vasu, or chief Vasu. 'Like the sun'.—Wilson. *Riches* : or viands.

3 *Seven stations* : regions of the universe, according to Sāyaṇa.

4 *The seven* : the priests.

7 *Gods* : here meaning priests. 'Verily there are two kinds of gods ; for, indeed, the gods are the gods, and the Brāhmans who have studied and teach holy lore are the human gods'. (*Śatapatha-Brāhmaṇa*, II. 2. 2. 6; S. B. E. XII. 309).

Vena, 'the loving Sun' of I. 83, 5, *Kānta* or 'the beloved' is said by the Scholiast in this place to be *madhyasthāno devaḥ* 'the God of the middle region'. He is, apparently, the Sun as he rises in the mist and dew of the morning.

1 *Pṛśni*, the Speckled Cow, is the variegated cloud, and her *Calves* are the masses of mist which the Sun dispels.

2 *Ocean* : the sea of air. *On Order's summit* : 'on the summit of nature's course.'—Wallis. *Order*, here and in the following stanza, is Kosmos, the ordered or law-regulated universe. *Common birthplace* : the sky.

made apparent,
Brightly he shone aloft on Order's summit: the hosts sang glory to their common birthplace.

3 Full many, lowing to their joint-possession, dwelling together stood the Darling's Mothers.
Ascending to the lofty height of Order, the bands of singers sip the sweets of Amṛta.

4 Knowing his form, the sages yearned to meet him: they have come nigh to hear the wild Bull's bellow.
Performing sacrifice they reached the river: for the Gandharva found the immortal waters.

5 The Apsaras, the Lady, sweetly smiling, supports her Lover in sublimest heaven.
In his Friend's dwelling as a Friend he wanders: he, Vena, rests him on his golden pinion.

6 They gaze on thee with longing in their spirit, as on a strong-winged bird that mounteth sky-ward;
On thee with wings of gold, Varuṇa's envoy, the Bird that hasteneth to the home of Yama.

7 Erect, to heaven hath the Gandharva mounted, pointing at us his many-coloured weapons;
Clad in sweet raiment beautiful to look on, for he, as light, produceth forms that please us.

8 When as a spark he cometh near the ocean, still looking with a vulture's eye to heaven,
His lustre, joying in its own bright splendour, maketh dear glories in the lowest region.

HYMN CXXIV. *Agni, Etc.*

1. COME to this sacrifice of ours, O Agni, threefold, with seven threads and five divisions.
Be our oblation-bearer and preceder: thou hast lain long enough in during darkness.

2 I come a God foreseeing from the godless to immortality by secret pathways,
While I, ungracious one, desert the gracious, leave mine own friends and seek the kin of strangers.

3 I, looking to the guest of other lineage, have founded many a rule of Law and Order.
I bid farewell to the Great God, the Father, and, for neglect, obtain my share of worship.

4 I tarried many a year within this altar: I leave the Father, for my choice is Indra.
Away pass Agni, Varuṇa and Soma. Rule ever changes: this I come to favour.

3 *Joint-possession* : the child which they have produced in common. *The Darling's Mothers* : the Dawns, or the Waters, or the songs.

4 *The wild Bull's bellow* : the sound made by the dropping of Soma juice. *The Gandharva* : *Vena*, the rising Sun.

5 *The Apsaras* : the celestial nymph who symbolizes the waters of heaven. *Her Lover* : Vena, the Gandharva, Sūrya. 'Our hymn illustrates the two senses in which the sun is brought into connection with the waters; first, as penetrating with his beams the watery masses of the sky, and secondly in the assimilation of his light to the waters, as soma or ambrosia, whence the depths of light become the aerial ocean. This association is stereotyped in the union of the Gandharvas and the Apsarasas.' —Wallis. *His Friend's dwelling* : the mansion of his father Heaven.

6 *Varuṇa's envoy* : the setting sun. Cf. VII. 87. 6. *Yama* : Cf. X. 14. 7.

7 *Clad in sweet raiment* : *surabhi*, sweet, m y, as Mr. Wallis conjectures, be a play on the word *gandhá*, occurring in the name Gandharva. Stanzas 7 and 8 merely recapitulate, as Ludwig observes, the deeds of Sūrya, first as the light of living men and then as the illuminator of the regions below the earth.

The hymn is one of the obscurest in the whole Ṛgveda. Mahīdhara interprets Vena by *candra*, the Moon. Wilson says : 'The general purport of the *Sūkta* makes it (Vena) equivalent to the thunder-cloud'. Von Roth, whom Grassmann follows, identifies Vena Gandharva with the Rainbow. According to Ludwig Vena is the Moon and the Gandharva is the Sun. Mr. Wallis has translated and explained the hymn in his *Cosmology of the Ṛgveda*, pp. 34 ff. For a different interpretation see Hillebrandt, *V. M.*, I. 430ff. and Ludwig's criticisms thereon (*Ueber die neuesten Arbeiten, u. s. w.*, p. 109f). See also Bergaigne, II. 38—40

———

1 Indra speaks. *Threefold* : performed with three daily libations; or comprising the *pākayajña*, the *haviryajña*, and the *somayajña*, the simple domestic oblation, the oblation of clarified butter, etc., and the offering of Soma juice. *With seven threads* : conducted by the seven chief priests. *With five divisions* : with five oblations, or regulated by the Yajamāna and four of the chief priests, according to Sāyaṇa. The exact meaning is uncertain.

2 Agni speaks. He has left Varuṇa, originally the Supreme Deity, whose power was waning, and associated himself with Indra who has superseded that God. *From the godless* : from Varuṇa who in the decline of his supremacy has neglected Agni and sacrifice. Sāyaṇa interprets the first line differently : —'From being no divinity I issue a divinity from the cave at the solicitation (of the gods), and being manifest I attain immortality.'—Wilson. *Seek the kin of strangers* : come to be born and domesticated in a new place, with Indra.

3 *Of other lineage* : of the other branch : terrestrial fire. *Father* : Varuṇa.

4 *Within this altar* : or, close to this Varuṇa. *This* the supremacy of Indra.

5 These Asuras have lost their powers of magic. But thou, O Varuṇa, if thou dost love me,
O King, discerning truth and right from falsehood, come and be Lord and Ruler of my kingdom.

6 Here is the light of heaven, here all is lovely; here there is radiance, here is air's wide region.
Let us two slaughter Vṛtra. Forth, O Soma! Thou art oblation: we therewith will serve thee.

7 The Sage hath fixed his form by wisdom in the heavens: Varuṇa with no violence let the waters flow.
Like women-folk, the floods that bring prosperity have caught his hue and colour as they gleamed and shone.

8 These wait upon his loftiest power and vigour: he dwells in these who triumph in their Godhead;
And they, like people who elect their ruler, have in abhorrence turned away from Vṛtra.

9 They call him Swan, the abhorrent floods' Companion, moving in friendship with celestial Waters.
The poets in their thought have looked on Indra swiftly approaching when Anuṣṭup calls him.

HYMN CXXV. *Vāk.*

1. I TRAVEL with the Rudras and the Vasus, with the Ādityas and All-Gods I wander.
I hold aloft both Varuṇa and Mitra, Indra and Agni, and the Pair of Aśvins.

2 I cherish and sustain high-swelling Soma, and Tvaṣṭar I support, Pūṣan, and Bhaga.
I load with wealth the zealous sacrificer who pours the juice and offers his oblation

3 I am the Queen, the gatherer-up of treasures, most thoughtful, first of those who merit worship.
Thus Gods have stablished me in many places with many homes to enter and abide in.

4 Through me alone all eat the food that feeds them,—each man who sees, breathes, hears the word outspoken
They know it not, but yet they dwell beside me. Hear, one and all, the truth as I declare it.

5 I, verily, myself announce and utter the word that Gods and men alike shall welcome.
I make the man I love exceeding mighty, make him a sage, a Ṛṣi, and a Brahman.

6 I bend the bow for Rudra that his arrow may strike and slay the hater of devotion.
I rouse and order battle for the people, and I have penetrated Earth and Heaven.

7 On the world's summit I bring forth the Father: my home is in the waters, in the ocean.

5 Indra speaks. *These Asuras* : Agni, Varuṇa, and Soma. *Come and be Lord* : Indra offers Varuṇa spiritual and moral sovereignty as compensation for his loss of general supremacy.

6 *Let us two* : the exhortation is addresssed by Indra to Soma. *Vṛtra*: regarded as in league with Varuṇa, the fiendish enemy in the shape of Varuṇa.

7 *The Sage* : perhaps Soma, in answer to Indra's appeal; Mitra, according to Sāyaṇa.

8 *His loftiest power* : the supreme might of Indra.

9 This stanza appears to have been added on account of the occurrence of the word *bībhatsūnām* (abhorrentium) which seems to connect it with the preceding stanza where *bībhatsúvaḥ* (abhorrentes) occurs. *Swan* : *haṁsa* : Sūrya the Sun-God is sometimes so called. Cf. IV. 40. 5. *Swiftly approaching when Anuṣṭup calls him* : 'or the ceaselessly moving Indra, who is worthy to be praised with an *Anuṣṭubh*.'—Wilson. Or, 'dancing the Anuṣṭup,' according to Prof. Max Müller's interpretation.

M. Bergaigne has translated and explained this hymn. See *La Religion Védique*, III. pp. 145—149. See also Book IV. 42, for hints of the rivalry between Varuṇa and Indra.

Vāk is Speech personified, the Word, the first creation and representative of Spirit, and the means of communication between men and Gods. Here she is said to be the daughter of the Ṛṣi Ambhṛṇa.

7 *The Father* : Heaven or Sky, produced from Vāk identified with Paramātmā, the supreme and universal Soul.

The hymn has been translated by Colebrooke, *Miscellaneous Essays*, I. 32; by the authors of the *Siebenzig Lieder* ; by Prof. Peterson, *Hymns from the Ṛgveda* (Bombay Sanskrit Series); and by Prof. Whitney, Notes to Colebrooke's *Essay on the Vedas*, p. 113.

Mr. Wallis observes : 'Vāc, 'Speech' is celebrated alone in two whole hymns, X. 71 and X. 125, of which the former shows that the primary application of the name was to the voice of the hymn, the means of communication between heaven and earth at the sacrifice. The other hymn illustrates the constant assimilation of the varied phenomena of nature to the sacrifice; all that has a voice in nature, the thunder of the storm, the reawaking of life at dawn, with songs of rejoicing over the new birth of the world, are embodied in this Vāc in the same way as it is said of Bṛhaspati, that he embraces all things that are. It is thus another expression for that idea of the unity of the world, which we have seen crowning the mystical speculations of all the more abstract hymns of the collection.'—*Cosmology of the Ṛgveda*, p. 85.

Thence I extend o'er all existing creatures, and touch even yonder heaven with my forehead.

8 I breathe a strong breath like the wind and tempest, the while I hold together all existence.
Beyond this wide earth and beyond the heavens I have become so mighty in my grandeur.

HYMN CXXVI. *Viśvedevas.*

1. No peril, no severe distress, ye Gods, affects the mortal man,
Whom Aryaman and Mitra lead, and Varuṇa, of one accord, beyond his foes.

2 This very thing do we desire, Varuṇa, Mitra, Aryaman,
Whereby ye guard the mortal man from sore distress, and lead him safe beyond his foes.

3 These are, each one, our present helps, Varuṇa, Mitra, Aryaman.
Best leaders, best deliverers to lead us on and bear as safe beyond our foes.

4 Ye compass round and guard each man, Varuṇa, Mitra, Aryaman:
In your dear keeping may we be, ye who are excellent as guides beyond our foes.

5 Ādityas are beyond all foes,—Varuṇa, Mitra, Aryaman:
Strong Rudra with the Marut host, Indra, Agni let us call for weal beyond our foes.

6 These lead us safely over all, Varuṇa, Mitra, Aryaman,
These who are Kings of living men, over all troubles far away beyond our foes.

7 May they give bliss to aid us well, Varuṇa, Mitra, Aryaman:
May the Ādityas, when we pray, grant us wide shelter and defence beyond our foes.

8 As in this place, O Holy Ones, ye Vasus freed even the Gaurī when her feet were fettered.
So free us now from trouble and affliction: and let our life be lengthened still, O Agni.

See also Weber, Vāc *Indische Studien*, IX. 473—480; and Max Müller, *The Vedānta Philosophy*, 144—147.

8 *Gaurī* : the wild-cow, the female of the Gaura or Bos Gaurus. The Vasus are said to have delivered her from Viśvāvasu the Gandharva.

HYMN CXXVII. *Night.*

1. WITH all her eyes the Goddess Night looks forth approaching many a spot:
She hath put all her glories on.

2 Immortal, she hath filled the waste, the Goddess hath filled height and depth:
She conquers darkness with her light.

3 The Goddess as she comes hath set the Dawn her Sister in her place:
And then the darkness vanishes.

4 So favour us this night, O thou whose pathways we have visited
As birds their nest upon the tree.

5 The villagers have sought their homes, and all that walks and all that flies,
Even the falcons fain for prey.

6 Keep off the she-wolf and the wolf; O Ūrmyā, keep the thief away;
Easy be thou for us to pass.

7 Clearly hath she come nigh to me who decks the dark with richest hues:
O Morning, cancel it like debts.

8 These have I brought to thee like kine. O Night, thou Child of Heaven, accept
This laud as for a conqueror.

HYMN CXXVIII. *Viśvedevas.*

1. LET me win glory, Agni, in our battles: enkindling thee, may we support our bodies.
May the four regions bend and bow before me: with thee for guardian may we win in combat.

2 May all the Gods be on my side in battle, the Maruts led by Indra, Viṣṇu, Agni.
Mine be the middle air's extended region, and may the wind blow favouring these my wishes.

3 May the Gods grant me riches; may the blessing and invocation of the Gods assist me.
Foremost in fight be the divine Invokers:

2 *The waste* : the expanded (firmament).'—Wilson.
6 *Ūrmyā* : 'undulating'; Night.
8 *These* : verses.

1 *The four regions* : the King who is praying for assistance is about to undertake a *Digvijaya*, the subjugation of all neighbouring countries in all directions.
3 *Divine Invokers* . the Hotar-priests of the Gods. Sāyaṇa explains differently :—'may my invokers of the gods be the first to propitiate them.'—Wilson.

may we, unwounded, have brave heroes round us.

4 For me let them present all mine oblations, and let my mind's intention be accomplished.
May I be guiltless of the least transgression: and, all ye Gods, do ye combine to bless us.

5 Ye six divine Expanses, grant us freedom: here, all ye Gods, acquit yourselves like heroes.
Let us not lose our children or our bodies: let us not benefit the foe, King Soma!

6 Baffling the wrath of our opponents, Agni, guard us as our infallible Protector.
Let these thy foes turn back and seek their houses, and let their thought who watch at home be ruined.

7 Lord of the world, Creator of creators: the saviour God who overcomes the foeman.
May Gods, Bṛhaspati, both Aśvins shelter from ill this sacrifice and sacrificer.

8 Foodful, and much-invoked, at this our calling may the great Bull vouchsafe us wide protection.
Lord of Bay Coursers, Indra, bless our children: harm us not, give us not as prey to others.

9 Let those who are our foemen stay afar from us: with Indra and with Agni we will drive them off.
Vasus, Ādityas, Rudras have exalted me, made me far-reaching, mighty, thinker, sovran lord.

5 *Six divine Expanses*: the four cardinal points and upper and lower spaces; or, according to Sāyaṇa, Heaven, Earth, Day, Night, Water, and Plants.

7 After *Creator of creators* Sāyaṇa supplies *taṁ devaṁ staumi*, 'that God I praise'. Indra or Savitar is intended.

8 *The great Bull*: Indra.

HYMN CXXIX. *Creation.*

1. THEN was not non-existent nor existent: there was no realm of air, no sky beyond it.
What covered in, and where? and what gave shelter? Was water there, unfathomed depth of water?

2 Death was not then, nor was there aught immortal: no sign was there, the day's and night's divider.
That One Thing, breathless, breathed by its own nature: apart from it was nothing whatsoever.

3 Darkness there was: at first concealed in darkness this All was indiscriminated chaos.
All that existed then was void and formless: by the great power of Warmth was born that Unit.

4 Thereafter rose Desire in the beginning, Desire, the primal seed and germ of Spirit.
Sages who searched with their heart's thought discovered the existent's kinship in the non-existent.

5 Transversely was their severing line extended: what was above it then, and what below it?
There were begetters, there were mighty forces, free action here and energy up yonder.

6 Who verily knows and who can here declare it, whence it was born and whence comes this creation?
The Gods are later than this world's pro-

1 *Then*: in the beginning. *Non-existent*: *ásat*: that does not yet actually exist, but which has in itself the latent potentiality of existence. 'There was a certain unapparent condition,' says an Indian Commentator, which, from the absence of distinctness, was not an 'entity,' while from its being the instrument of the world's production, it was not a 'non-entity.'

2 *That One Thing*: the single primordial substance, the unit out of which the universe was developed. Cp. I. 164. 6 and 46.

3 *Warmth*: Prof. Wilson, following Sāyaṇa, translates *tápasaḥ* by 'austerity,' meaning the contemplation of the things that were to be created. M. Burnouf, in *La Science des Religions*, pp. 207ff., has shown how *warmth* was regarded by the Āryas as the principle explaining movement, life, and thought.

4 *Desire*: Kāma, Eros, or Love. *Sages*: ancient Ṛṣis.

5 *Line*: a line drawn by the ancient Ṛṣis to make a division between the upper world and the lower, and to bring duality out of unity. *Begetters*: the Fathers may be meant. *Free action*: the happiness of the Fathers. The stanza is obscure, and its connection with stanza 4 is not obvious. An intervening stanza may, perhaps, have been lost.

The hymn has been translated by Colebrooke, *Miscellaneous Essays*, I. pp. 33, 34; by Dr. Muir, *O. S. Texts*, V. 356, 357; by the authors of the *Siebenzig Lieder*, and by Mr. Wallis, *Cosmology of the Ṛgveda*, pp. 59 ff. 'The latest of the many Commentators on this hymn are Professor Whitney in the Journal of the American Oriental Society, vol. xi. p. cix, and Dr. Scherman, Philosophische Hymnen aus der Ṛg-und-Atharva-veda Saṁhitā 1887.'—Wallis. See Prof. Max Müller, *History of Ancient Literature*, pp. 559—563.

duction. Who knows then whence it first came into being ?

7 He, the first origin of this creation, whether he formed it all or did not form it,
Whose eye controls this world in highest heaven, he verily knows it, or perhaps he knows not.

HYMN CXXX. *Creation.*

1. THE sacrifice drawn out with threads on every side, stretched by a hundred sacred ministers and one,—
This do these Fathers weave who hitherward are come : they sit beside the warp and cry, Weave forth, weave back.

2 The Man extends it and the Man unbinds it : even to this vault of heaven hath he outspun it.
These pegs are fastened to the seat of worship : they made the Sāma-hymns their weaving shuttles.

3 What were the rule, the order and the model ? What were the wooden fender and the butter ?
What were the hymn, the chant, the recitation, when to the God all Deities paid worship ?

4 Closely was Gāyatrī conjoined with Agni, and closely Savitar combined with Uṣṇiḥ.
Brilliant with Ukthas, Soma joined Anuṣṭup : Bṛhaspati's voice by Bṛhatī was aided.

5 Virāj adhered to Varuṇa and Mitra : here Triṣṭup day by day was Indra's portion.
Jagatī entered all the Gods together : so by this knowledge men were raised to Ṛṣis.

6 So by this knowledge men were raised to Ṛṣis, when ancient sacrifice sprang up, our Fathers.
With the mind's eye I think that I behold them who first performed this sacrificial worship.

7 They who were versed in ritual and metre, in hymns and rules, were the Seven Godlike Ṛṣis.
Viewing the path of those of old, the sages have taken up the reins like chariot-drivers.

HYMN CXXXI. *Indra.*

1. DRIVE all our enemies away, O Indra, the western, mighty Conqueror, and the eastern.
Hero, drive off our northern foes and southern, that we in thy wide shelter may be joyful.

2 What then ? As men whose fields are full of barley reap the ripe corn removing it in order,
So bring the food of those men, bring it hither, who went not to prepare the grass for worship.

3 Men come not with one horse at sacred seasons ; thus they obtain no honour in assemblies.
Sages desiring herds of kine and horses strengthen the mighty Indra for his friendship.

4 Ye, Aśvins, Lords of Splendour, drank full draughts of grateful Soma juice,
And aided Indra in his work with Namuci of Asura birth.

As the subject of the hymn is creation typified and originated by the mysterious primeval sacrifice (cp. X. 90), Prajāpati the Creator is said by Sāyaṇa to be the deity. The Ṛṣi is Yajña (Sacrifice) Prajāpati's son.

1 *The sacrifice* : *sargātmako yajñaḥ* : the sacrifice which constitutes creation.—Sāyaṇa. *A hundred and one* : meaning an indefinitely large number. *Fathers* : Sāyaṇa explains *pitáraḥ* here by *pālakāḥ*, protectors, the Gods.

2 *The Man* : the first Man or Male; Puruṣa, Ādipuruṣa, Prajāpati, according to Sāyaṇa.

3 *Wooden fender* : the enclosing sticks placed round the sacrificial fire.

4 *Brilliant with Ukthas* : 'gladdening (us) through hymns (*ukthas*).'—Muir. *Bṛhaspati's voice* : because his duty was to speak as Priest. According to the *Aitareya Brāhmaṇa*, III. 13, Prajāpati 'alloted to the deities their (different) parts in the sacrifice and metres.'

5 *Day by day* : was Indra's portion of the mid-day (oblation).'—Wilson.

6 *I behold them* : or, according to Prof. Ludwig's interpretation :—'These with the eyes of mind, I think, beheld them.'

7 'The seven Ṛṣis here are not the Aṅgirases, but Bharadvāja, Kaśyapa, Gotama, Atri, Vasiṣṭha, Viśvāmitra, and Jamadagni. The knowledge of the ritual is derived from the divine priests ; the sages or Ṛṣis have followed them in sacrificing, and modern priests are only imitators of those who preceded them.'—Ludwig.

The hymn has been translated by Dr. Muir, *O. S. Texts*, III. pp. 278, 279 and by Prof. Whitney, Notes to Colebrooke's *Essay on the Vedas*, p. 114.

---

3 *With one horse* : it seems to have been considered undignified and disreputable for a wealthy man to come to the sacrifice in a one-horse car; but the precise meaning of the first line is somewhat uncertain.

4 Hillebrandt, *V. M.*, I. 146, and Eggeling, *Sacred Books of the East*, XLI. 135, interpret differently. The myth referred to in the following stanza has not been preserved. See Weber, *Ueber den Rājasūya*, pp. 95, 101.

5 As parents aid a son, both Aśvins, Indra, aided thee with their wondrous powers and wisdom.
When thou, with might, hadst drunk the draught that gladdens, Sarasvatī, O Maghavan, refreshed thee.

6 Indra is strong to save, rich in assistance : may he, possessing all, be kind and gracious.
May he disperse our foes and give us safety, and may we be the lords of hero vigour.

7 May we enjoy his favour, his the Holy : may we enjoy his blessed loving kindness.
May this rich Indra, as our good Protector, drive off and keep afar all those who hate us.

HYMN CXXXII. *Mitra. Varuṇa.*

1. MAY Dyaus the Lord of lauded wealth, and Earth stand by the man who offers sacrifice,
And may the Aśvins, both the Gods, strengthen the worshipper with bliss.

2 As such we honour you, Mitra and Varuṇa, with hasty zeal, most blest, you who sustain the folk.
So may we, through your friendship for the worshipper, subdue the fiends.

3 And when we seek to win your love and friendship, we who have precious wealth in our possession,
Or when the worshipper augments his riches, let not his treasures be shut up.

4 That other, Asura ! too was born of Heaven : thou art, O Varuṇa, the King of all men.
The chariot's Lord was well content, forbearing to anger Death by sin so great.

This sin hath Śakapūta here committed. Heroes who fled to their dear friend he slayeth,
When the Steed bringeth down your grace and favour in bodies dear and worshipful.

4 *That other* : Mitra. *The chariot's Lord* : literally, 'head of the chariot.' The meaning is uncertain. I find the rest of the hymn unintelligible. Prof. Ludwig conjectures that two brothers, Nṛmedhas and Sumedhas, had contended for sovereignty, and that the adherents of one had wished to put the other brother to death, but had not carried out their purpose. Śakapūta absolves and purifies the former, and the brothers are reconciled.

5 *The Steed* : the Sun.—Ludwig. *Your grace* : Mitra's and Varuṇa's.

6 Your Mother Aditi, ye wise, was purified with water even as earth is purified from heaven.
Show love and kindness here below : wash her in rays of heavenly light.

7 Ye Twain have seated you as Lords of Wealth, as one who mounts a car to him who sits upon the pole, upon the wood.
These our disheartened tribes Nṛmedhas saved from woe, Sumedhas saved from woe.

HYMN CXXXIII. *Indra.*

1. SING strength to Indra that shall set his chariot in the foremost place.
Giver of room in closest fight, slayer of foes in shock of war, be thou our great encourager. Let the weak bowstrings break upon the bows of feeble enemies.

2 Thou didst destroy the Dragon : thou sentest the rivers down to earth.
Foeless, O Indra, wast thou born. Thou tendest well each choicest thing. Therefore we draw us close to thee. Let the weak bowstrings, etc.

3 Destroyed be all malignities and all our enemy's designs.
Thy bolt thou castest at the foe, O Indra, who would smite us dead : thy liberal bounty gives us wealth.

4 The robber people round about, Indra, who watch and aim at us,—
Trample them down beneath thy foot ; a conquering scatterer art thou.

5 Whoso assails us, Indra, be the man a stranger or akin,
Bring down, thyself, his strength although it be as vast as are the heavens.

6 Close to thy friendship do we cling, O Indra, and depend on thee.
Lead us beyond all pain and grief along the path of holy Law.

7 Do thou bestow upon us her, O Indra, who yields according to the singer's longing,
That the great Cow may, with exhaustless udder, pouring a thousand streams, give milk to feed us.

6 *Your Mother Aditi* : perhaps the mother of the two brothers is intended.—Ludwig.

---

2 *Let the weak bowstrings, etc.*: the refrain is repeated in all the stanzas except the last.

7 *The great Cow* : probably the Earth.

HYMN CXXXIV. *Indra.*

1. As, like the Morning, thou hast filled, O Indra, both the earth and heaven.
So as the Mighty One, great King of all the mighty world of men, the Goddess Mother brought thee forth, the Blessed Mother gave thee life.

2 Relax that mortal's stubborn strength whose heart is bent on wickedness.
Trample him down beneath thy feet who watches for and aims at us. The Goddess Mother brought thee forth, etc.

3 Shake down, O Slayer of the foe, those great all splendid energies.
With all thy powers, O Śakra, all thine helps, O Indra, shake them down :

4 As thou, O Śatakratu, thou, O Indra, shakest all things down
As wealth for him who sheds the juice, with thine assistance thousandfold.

5 Around, on every side like drops of sweat let lightning-flashes fall.
Let all malevolence pass away from us like threads of Dūrvā grass.

6 Thou bearest in thine hand a lance like a long hook, great Counsellor !
As with his foremost foot a goat, draw down the branch, O Maghavan.

7 Never, O Gods, do we offend, nor are we ever obstinate : we walk as holy texts command.
Closely we clasp and cling to you, cling to your sides, beneath your arms.

HYMN CXXXV. *Yama.*

1. In the Tree clothed with goodly leaves where Yama drinketh with the Gods,
The Father, Master of the house, tendeth with love our ancient Sires.

2 I looked reluctantly on him who cherishes those men of old,
On him who treads that evil path, and then I yearned for this again.

3 Thou mountest, though thou dost not see, O Child, the new and wheel-less car
Which thou hast fashioned mentally, one-poled but turning every way.

4 The car which thou hast made to roll hitherward from the Sages, Child !
This hath the Sāman followed close, hence, laid together on a ship.

5 Who was the father of the child ? Who made the chariot roll away ?
Who will this day declare to us how the funeral gift was made ?

6 When the funeral gift was placed, straightway the point of flame appeared.
A depth extended in the front : a passage out was made behind.

7 Here is the seat where Yama dwells, that which is called the Home of Gods :
Here minstrels blow the flute for him : here he is glorified with songs.

HYMN CXXXVI. *Keśins.*

1. He with the long loose locks supports Agni, and moisture, heaven, and earth :
He is all sky to look upon : he with long hair is called this light.

2 The Munis, girdled with the wind, wear garments soiled of yellow hue.
They, following the wind's swift course go where the Gods have gone before.

1 *The Goddess Mother* : Aditi. The refrain is repeated in all the stanzas except the last.

3 *Energies* : influences in the shape of rain and sunlight.

4 *Śatakratu* : or, Lord of Hundred Powers.

5 *Dūrvā grass* : Panicum Dactylon; a species of bent grass whose filaments stretch horizontally away from the stem.

6 *The branch* : that is loaded with fruit for us.

---

1 *The Tree* : where the spirits of the pious dead rest after their labours. *The Father* : Yama.

2 The spirit of the dead child speaks. *I yearned for this* : to return to the world of life.

3 Yama speaks. *Fashioned mentally* : figuratively prepared by being burnt on the funeral pile.

4 *Ship* : meaning, apparently, the funeral pile. *The funeral gift* : the meaning of *anudéyī* is uncertain. 'Restitution.'—Wilson. 'Surrender' or 'delivery,' according to Prof. Zimmer. Stanzas 5—7 are spoken by the poet.

6 *A depth* : the meaning is obscure. *Passage out* : probably for the removal of the ashes.

The subject of the hymn appears to be the funeral ceremony of a boy (*kumā́ra*, said by some to be the name of a man). According to the legend cited by Sāyaṇa a youth named Naciketas was sent by his father to the kingdom of Yama who treated him kindly and allowed him to return to this world. 'The hymn is made throughout applicable to *Āditya* as well as to Yama, with, if possible, a still greater degree of obscurity. It seems to have been the basis of the discussion in the Taittirīya Brāhmaṇa (III. 11. 8) and in the Katha Upaniṣad, respecting what becomes of the soul after death, in dialogues between *Naciketas* and Yama.'—Wilson.

The Keśins, *keśínaḥ*, wearers of long loose hair, are Agni, Vāyu, and Sūrya. Each stanza has for its Ṛṣi one of the seven sons of Vātaraśana. See Index of Hymns.

1 *He with the long loose locks* : probably the ascetic, the Muni or Yogī. According to Sāyaṇa, the radiant Sun. *Moisture* : *viṣám*, usually meaning 'poison' is so explained in this place.

2 *Munis* : ascetics inspired or in a state of ecstasy. *Girdled with the wind* : exposed without girdles to the wind. According to Sāyaṇa, sons of Vātaraśana, or Wind-Girdled.

3 Transported with our Munihood we have pressed on into the winds :
You therefore, mortal men, behold our natural bodies and no more.

4 The Muni, made associate in the holy work of every God,
Looking upon all varied forms flies through the region of the air.

5 The Steed of Vāta, Vāyu's friend, the Muni, by the Gods impelled,
In both the oceans hath his home, in eastern and in western sea.

6 Treading the path of sylvan beasts, Gandharvas, and Apsarases,
He with long locks, who knows the wish, is a sweet most delightful friend

7 Vāyu hath churned for him : for him he poundeth things most hard to bend,
When he with long loose locks hath drunk, with Rudra, water from the cup.

HYMN CXXXVII. *Viśvedevas.*

1. Ye Gods, raise up once more the man whom ye have humbled and brought low.
O Gods, restore to life again the man who hath committed sin.

2 Two several winds are blowing here, from Sindhu, from a distant land.
May one breathe energy to thee, the other blow disease away.

3 Hither, O Wind, blow healing balm, blow all disease away, thou Wind ;
For thou who hast all medicine comest as envoy of the Gods.

4 I am come nigh to thee with balms to give thee rest and keep thee safe.
I bring thee blessed strength, I drive thy weakening malady away.

5 Here let the Gods deliver him, the Maruts' band deliver him :
All things that be deliver him that he be freed from his disease.

6 The Waters have their healing power, the Waters drive disease away.
The Waters have a balm for all : let them make medicine for thee.

7 The tongue that leads the voice precedes. Then with our ten-fold branching hands,
With these two chasers of disease we stroke thee with a gentle touch.

HYMN CXXXVIII. *Indra.*

1. Allied with thee in friendship, Indra, these thy priests, remembering Holy Law, rent Vṛtra limb from limb,
When they bestowed the Dawns and let the waters flow, and when thou didst chastise dragons at Kutsa's call.

2 Thou sentest forth productive powers, clavest the hills, thou dravest forth the kine, thou drankest pleasant meath.
Thou gavest increase through this Tree's surpassing might.
The Sun shone by the hymn that sprang from Holy Law.

3 In the mid-way of heaven the Sun unyoked his car : the Ārya found a match to meet his Dāsa foe.
Associate with Ṛjiśvan Indra overthrew the solid forts of Pipru, conjuring Asura.

4 He boldly cast down forts which none had e'er assailed: unwearied he destroyed the godless treasure-stores.

5 *In both the oceans* : everywhere in the firmament from its eastern to its western extremity.

'The hymn shows the conception that by a life of sanctity the Muni can attain to the fellowship of the deities of the air, the Vāyus, the Rudras, the Apsarasas, and the Gandharvas; and, furnished like them with wonderful powers, can travel along with them on their course......The beautiful-haired, the long-haired, that is to say, the Muni, who during the time of his austerities does not shave his hair, upholds fire, moisture, heaven, and earth, and resembles the world of light, ideas which the later literature so largely contains.'—Von Roth, quoted by Dr. Muir, *O. S. Texts*, IV. 319, the hymn being transliterated and translated on page 318.

Each stanza is ascribed to one of the seven great Ṛṣis. See Index of Hymns. The hymn is a charm to restore a sick man to health. Cf. *Hymns of the Atharva-veda*, IV. 13.

1 *Who hath committed sin* : sickness and death being regarded as the consequence of sin.

2 *Sindhu* : or, ocean.

4 The Wind speaks. *Weakening malady* : *yákṣma* may be sickness in general, or the name of a large class of diseases, probably of a consumptive nature.

7 The stanza is important as showing that the Indians employed touches or laying-on of hands to relieve suffering or to restore health. Cp. X. 60. 12.

1 *Thy priests* : the Aṅgirases. But see *Vedic Hymns*, I. p. 44. *Didst chastise* : this clause is very difficult. I adopt Prof. Grassmann's interpretation.

2 *This Tree's surpassing might* : the power of the juice of the Soma plant.

3 *Unyoked his car* : the allusion is, perhaps, to an eclipse, or a detention of the Sun to enable the Āryans to complete the overthrow of their enemies. *Ṛjiśvan* : a pious worshipper befriended by Indra. *Pipru* : a demon of drought. See Vol. I., Index.

Like Sun and Moon he took the stronghold's wealth away, and, praised in song, demolished foes with flashing dart.

5 Armed with resistless weapons, with vast power to cleave, the Vṛtra-slayer whets his darts and deals forth wounds.
Bright Uṣas was afraid of Indra's slaughtering bolt : she went upon her way and left her chariot there.

6 These are thy famous exploits, only thine, when thou alone hast left the other reft of sacrifice.
Thou in the heavens hast set the ordering of the Moons : the Father bears the felly portioned out by thee.

HYMN CXXXIX. *Savitar.*

1. SAVITAR, golden-haired, hath lifted eastward, bright with the sunbeams, his eternal lustre;
He in whose energy wise Pūṣan marches, surveying all existence like a herdsman.

2 Beholding men he sits amid the heavens, filling the two world-halves and air's wide region.
He looks upon the rich far-spreading pastures between the eastern and the western limit.

3 He, root of wealth, the gatherer-up of treasures, looks with his might on every form and figure.
Savitar, like a God whose Law is constant, stands in the battle for the spoil like Indra.

4 Waters from sacrifice came to the Gandharva Viśvāvasu, O Soma, when they saw him.
Indra, approaching quickly, marked their going, and looked around upon the Sun's enclosures.

5 This song Viśvāvasu shall sing us, meter of air's mid-realm celestial Gandharva,
That we may know aright both truth and falsehood: may he inspire our thoughts and help our praises.

6 In the floods' track he found the booty-seeker : the rocky cow-pen's doors he threw wide open.
These, the Gandharva told him, flowed with Amṛta. Indra knew well the puissance of the dragons.

HYMN CXL. *Agni.*

1 AGNI, life-power and fame are thine : thy fires blaze mightily, thou rich in wealth of beams !
Sage, passing bright, thou givest to the worshipper, with strength, the food that merits laud.

2 With brilliant, purifying sheen, with perfect sheen thou liftest up thyself in light.
Thou, visiting both thy Mothers, aidest them as Son : thou joinest close the earth and heaven.

3 O Jātavedas, Son of Strength, rejoice thyself, gracious, in our fair hymns and songs.
In thee are treasured various forms of strengthening food, born nobly and of wondrous help.

4 Agni, spread forth, as Ruler, over living things : give wealth to us, Immortal God.
Thou shinest out from beauty fair to look upon : thou leadest us to conquering power.

5 To him, the wise, who orders sacrifice, who hath great riches under his control,
Thou givest blest award of good, and plenteous food, givest him wealth that conquers all.

5 *Bright Uṣas was afraid* : see II. 15. 6, IV. 30. 8—11, and X. 73. 6.

6 *The other* : thy foe, the demon or Rākṣasa. *The Father* : Dyaus or Heaven. *The felly portioned out by thee* : the course of the Moon through the asterisms, which thou hast arranged.

---

2 *Pastures* : there is no substantive in the text. Sāyaṇa supplies 'quarters of space;' Ludwig 'ladles;' and Grassmann 'pastures.'

4 *Waters* : used in the preparation of the Soma juice. *The Gandharva* : regarded as the custodian of the celestial Soma. *The Sun's enclosures* : 'the rims of the sun.' —Wilson.

5 *Viśvāvasu* : the celestial Gandharva, here the Sun-God. *He* : Viśvāvasu.

6 *The booty-seeker* : Indra who sought to win the waters. *Of the dragons* : the serpentdemons who obstructed the floods of heaven. The last three stanzas are very difficult and obscure. See Hillebrandt, *V. M.*, I. pp. 436, 437, and Ludwig, *Ueber die neuesten A. u. s. w.*, p. 101.

---

2 *Thy Mothers* : Heaven and Earth. *Joinest close* : or, fillest full.

5 *To him* : to the institutor of the sacrifice.

See the exposition of the hymn in *Śatapatha Brāhmaṇa*, VII. 3. 1. 29—34 (*Sacred Books of the East*, XLI. 349—351).

6 The men have set before them for their welfare Agni, strong, visible to all, the Holy.
Thee, Godlike One, with ears to hear, most famous, men's generations magnify with praise-songs.

HYMN CXLI. *Viśvedevas.*

1. TURN hither, Agni, speak to us : come to us with a gracious mind.
Enrich us, Master of the house : thou art the Giver of our wealth.

2 Let Aryaman vouchsafe us wealth, and Bhaga, and Bṛhaspati.
Let the Gods give their gifts, and let Sūnṛtā, Goddess, grant us wealth.

3 We call King Soma to our aid, and Agni with our songs and hymns,
Ādityas, Viṣṇu, Sūrya, and the Brahman Priest Bṛhaspati.

4 Indra, Vāyu, Bṛhaspati, Gods swift to listen, we invoke,
That in the synod all the folk may be benevolent to us.

5 Urge Aryaman to send us gifts, and Indra, and Bṛhaspati,
Vāta, Viṣṇu, Sarasvatī and the Strong Courser Savitar.

6 Do thou, O Agni, with thy fires strengthen our prayer and sacrifice :
Urge givers to bestow their wealth to aid our service of the Gods.

HYMN CXLII. *Agni.*

1. WITH thee, O Agni, was this singer of the laud : he hath no other kinship, O thou Son of Strength.
Thou givest blessed shelter with a triple guard. Keep the destructive lightning far away from us.

2 Thy birth who seekest food is in the falling flood, Agni : as Comrade thou winnest all living things.
Our coursers and our songs shall be victorious : they of themselves advance like one who guards the herd.

3 And thou, O Agni, thou of Godlike nature, sparest the stones, while earing up the brushwood.
Then are thy tracks like deserts in the corn-lands. Let us not stir to wrath thy mighty arrow.

4 O'er hills through vales devouring as thou goest, thou partest like an army fain for booty
As when a barber shaves a beard, thou shavest earth when the wind blows on thy flame and fans it.

5 Apparent are his lines as he approaches : the course is single, but the cars are many,
When, Agni, thou, making thine arms resplendent, advancest o'er the land spread out beneath thee.

6 Now let thy strength, thy burning flames fly upward, thine energies, O Agni, as thou toilest.
Gape widely, bend thee, waxing in thy vigour : let all the Vasus sit this day beside thee.

7 This is the waters' reservoir, the great abode of gathered streams.
Take thou another path than this, and as thou listest walk thereon.

8 On thy way hitherward and hence let flowery Dūrvā grass spring up
Let there be lakes with lotus blooms. These are the mansions of the flood.

HYMN CXLIII. *Aśvins.*

1. YE made that Atri, worn with eld, free as a horse to win the goal.
When ye restored to youth and strength Kakṣīvān like a car renewed,

2 Ye freed that Atri like a horse, and brought him newly-born to earth.
Ye loosed him like a firm-tied knot which Gods unsoiled by dust had bound.

3 Heroes who showed most wondrous power to Atri, strive to win fair songs ;
For then, O Heroes of the sky, your hymn of praise shall cease no more.

2 *Sūnṛtā* : Pleasantness; Gladness, personified. Cf. I. 40. 3.

3 *Sparest the stones* : see Pischel, *Vedische Studien*, I. p. 180. Cp. III. 29. 6.

6 Stanzas 7 and 8 seem to belong to some other hymn, being a prayer to Agni that he may spare the speaker's house where, he says, there is nothing to invite the devouring God. See *Hymns of the Atharva-veda*, VI. 106.

1 *Atri* : see I. 112. 7. *Kakṣīvān* : the Scholiast says that this Ṛṣi was originally dull of understanding and that the Aśvins endowed him with knowledge. Prof. Ludwig takes *kakṣīvantam* to be an adjective agreeing with *rátham* : 'Again ye made him youthful like a chariot that is braced with bands.'

4 This claims your notice, Bounteous Gods !—
oblation, Aśvins ! and our love,
That ye, O Heroes, in the fight may
bring us safe to ample room.

5 Ye Twain to Bhujyu tossed about in ocean
at the region's end,
Nāsatyas, with your winged steeds came
nigh, and gave him strength to win.

6 Come with your joys, most liberal Gods,
Lords of all treasures, bringing weal.
Like fresh full waters to a well, so, Heroes,
come and be with us.

HYMN CXLIV. *Indra.*

1. THIS deathless Indu, like a steed, strong
and of full vitality,
Belongs to thee, the Orderer.

2 Here, by us, for the worshipper, is the
wise bolt that works with skill.
It brings the bubbling beverage as a
dexterous man brings the effectual strong
drink.

3 Impetuous Ahiśuva, a bull among these
cows of his,
looked down upon the restless Hawk.

4 That the strong-pinioned Bird hath
brought, Child of the Falcon, from afar,
What moves upon a hundred wheels along
the female Dragon's path.

5 Which, fair, unrobbed, the Falcon brought
thee in his foot, the red-hued dwelling
of the juice ;
Through this came vital power which lengthens out our days, and kinship through
its help awoke.

6 So Indra is by Indu's power ; e'en among
Gods will it repel great treachery.

5 *Bhujyu* : see Vol. I., Index.

---

1 *Indu* : Soma. *The Orderer* : disposer and arranger of the universe.

2 *Bolt* : the Vaṣaṭkāra, or sacrificial exclamation, is to the priests what the thunderbolt is to Indra.

3 I find this and the following stanza unintelligible. *Ahiśuva* in other places is the name of a demon; but the meaning here is uncertain. *Cows* : there is no substantive to *āsú svāsu*, 'these his own,' in the feminine gender.

4 *What moves upon a hundred wheels* : *śatácakram* : 'the bestower of many boons.'—Wilson.

5 *Dwelling of the juice* : the Soma-plant, which the Falcon brought from heaven. See IV. 26 and 27.

6 *It* : or he; Indu or the Soma juice.

Prof. Grassmann places this hymn in his Appendix as being in his opinion made up of fragments. He considers Ahiśuva (stanza 3) to be 'the archer Kṛśānu', of IV. 27. 3 and other places, who guards the celestial Soma, and instead of 'cows' he understands 'wives.'

Wisdom, Most Sapient One, brings force
that lengthens life. May wisdom bring
the juice to us.

HYMN CXLV. *Sapatnībādhanam.*

1. FROM out the earth I dig this plant, a
herb of most effectual power,
Wherewith one quells the rival wife and
gains the husband for oneself.

2 Auspicious, with expanded leaves, sent by
the Gods, victorious plant,
Blow thou the rival wife away, and make
my husband only mine.

3 Stronger am I, O Stronger One, yea, mightier than the mightier ;
And she who is my rival wife is lower
than the lowest dames.

4 Her very name I utter not : she takes no
pleasure in this man.
Far into distance most remote drive we
the rival wife away.

5 I am the conqueror, and thou, thou also
act victorious :
As victory attends us both we will subdue
my fellow-wife.

6 I have gained thee for vanquisher, have
grasped thee with a stronger spell.
As a cow hastens to her calf, so let thy
spirit speed to me, hasten like water on
its way.

HYMN CXLVI. *Araṇyānī.*

1. GODDESS of wild and forest who seemest to
vanish from the sight.
How is it that thou seekest not the
village ? Art thou not afraid ?

2 What time the grasshopper replies and
swells the shrill cicala's voice,
Seeming to sound with tinkling bells, the
Lady of the Wood exults.

The hymn is a spell to rid a jealous wife of a more favoured rival. The Ṛṣi is Indrāṇī, the Consort of Indra.

1 *This plant* : said to be the Pāṭā, probably identical with Pāṭhā (Clypea Hernandifolia), a climbing plant possessing various medicinal properties.

6 *Thy spirit* : the husband's.

The deity, Araṇyānī, is the tutelary Goddess of the forest and wilderness.

2 *Grasshopper......cicala* : the *ciccikā* is said to be a little creature that cries *cīcī* : and the *vṛṣāravá* is said to be a sort of cricket. Others take them to be birds of some unascertained kind.

3 And, yonder, cattle seem to graze, what seems a dwelling-place appears :
Or else at eve the Lady of the Forest seems to free the wains.

4 Here one is calling to his cow, another there hath felled a tree :
At eve the dweller in the wood fancies that somebody hath screamed.

5 The Goddess never slays, unless some murderous enemy approach.
Man eats of savoury fruit and then takes, even as he wills, his rest.

6 Now have I praised the Forest Queen, sweet-scented, redolent of balm,
The Mother of all sylvan things, who tills not but hath stores of food.

HYMN CXLVII. *Indra.*

1. I TRUST in thy first wrathful deed, O Indra, when thou slewest Vṛtra and didst work to profit man ;
What time the two world-halves fell short of thee in might, and the earth trembled at thy force, O Thunder-armed.

2 Thou with thy magic powers didst rend the conjurer Vṛtra, O Blameless One, with heart that longed for fame.
Heroes elect thee when they battle for the prey, thee in all sacrifices worthy of renown.

3 God Much-invoked, take pleasure in these princes here, who, thine exalters, Maghavan, have come to wealth.
In synods, when the rite succeeds, they hymn the Strong for sons and progeny and riches undisturbed.

4 That man shall find delight in well-protected wealth whose care provides for him the quick-sought joyous draught.
Bringing oblations, strengthened, Maghavan, by thee, he swiftly wins the spoil with heroes in the fight.

5 Now for our band, O Maghavan, when lauded, make ample room with might, and grant us riches.
Magician thou, our Varuṇa and Mitra, deal food to us, O Wondrous, as Dispenser.

HYMN CXLVIII. *Indra.*

1. WHEN we have pressed the juice we laud thee, Indra, and when, Most Valorous ! we have won the booty.
Bring us prosperity, as each desires it : under thine own protection may we conquer.

2 Sublime from birth, mayst thou O Indra, Hero, with Sūrya overcome the Dāsa races.
As by a fountain's side, we bring the Soma that lay concealed, close-hidden in the waters.

3 Answer the votary's hymns, for these thou knowest, craving the Ṛṣis' prayer, thyself a Singer,
May we be they who take delight in Somas : these with sweet food for thee, O Chariot-rider.

4 These holy prayers, O Indra, have I sung thee : grant to the men the strength of men, thou Hero.
Be of one mind with those in whom thou joyest : keep thou the singers safe and their companions.

5 Listen to Pṛthī's call, heroic Indra, and be thou lauded by the hymns of Venya,
Him who hath sung thee to thine oil-rich dwelling, whose rolling songs have sped thee like a torrent.

HYMN CXLIX. *Savitar.*

1. SAVITAR fixed the earth with bands to bind it, and made heaven stedfast where no prop supported.

3 *Cattle seem to graze* : deer feeding in the glades. *What seems a dwelling-place* : a natural bower of branches and creepers.

4 Sounds are heard as of a cowman calling his cattle, or of a woodman at work. 'We must imagine the thousand strange sounds and delusions which seem to encompass the solitary listener of an evening in the darkening forest.' —Mme. Zénaïde Ragozin, *Vedic India* (Story of the Nations), p. 272.

5 *Murderous enemy* : the text has only *anyáḥ*, 'another,' by which, according to Sāyaṇa, a tiger or robber is meant. Prof. Ludwig suggests that the reading should be *hanyaḥ*, 'one who is destined to be killed.' The hymn has been translated by Dr. Muir, *O. S. Texts*, V. p. 423; and by the authors of the *Siebenzig Lieder des Ṛgveda*.

3 *Princes* : the Sūris, the wealthy institutors of the sacrifice. *The Strong* : thee, the mighty Indra.

3 *These with sweet food* : 'these (praises are offered) with sacrificial viands.—Wilson.

4 *Companions* : or, dependents.

5 *Pṛthī's call*: the invocation of Pṛthu, the Ṛṣi of the hymn, according to Sāyaṇa Prof. Ludwig suggests that Pṛthu's wife is intended. *Venya* : Pṛthī, son of Vena.

Savitar milked, as 'twere a restless courser, air, sea bound fast to what no foot had trodden.

2 Well knoweth Savitar, O Child of Waters, where ocean, firmly fixt, o'erflowed its limit.
Thence sprang the world, from that uprose the region: thence heaven spread out and the wide earth expanded.

3 Then, with a full crowd of Immortal Beings, this other realm came later, high and holy.
First, verily, Savitar's strong-pinioned Eagle was born: and he obeys his law for ever.

4 As warriors to their steeds, kine to their village, as fond milk giving cows approach their youngling,
As man to wife, let Savitar come downward to us, heaven's bearer, Lord of every blessing.

5 Like the Āṅgirasa Hiraṇyastūpa, I call thee, Savitar, to this achievement:
So worshipping and lauding thee for favour I watch for thee as for the stalk of Soma.

HYMN CL. *Agni.*

1. THOU, bearer of oblations, though kindled, art kindled for the Gods.
With the Ādityas, Rudras, Vasus, come to us: to show us favour come to us.

2 Come hither and accept with joy this sacrifice and hymn of ours.
O kindled God, we mortals are invoking thee, calling on thee to show us grace.

3 I laud thee Jātavedas, thee Lord of all blessings, with my song.
Agni, bring hitherward the Gods whose Laws we love, whose laws we love, to show us grace.

4 Agni the God was made the great High-Priest of Gods, Ṛṣis have kindled Agni, men of mortal mould.
Agni I invocate for winning ample wealth, kindly disposed for winning wealth.

5 Atri and Bharadvāja and Gaviṣṭhira, Kaṇva and Trasadasyu, in our fight he helped.
On Agni calls Vasiṣṭha, even the household priest, the household priest to win his grace.

HYMN CLI. *Faith.*

1. BY Faith is Agni kindled, through Faith is oblation offered up.
We celebrate with praises Faith upon the height of happiness.

2 Bless thou the man who gives, O Faith; Faith, bless the man who fain would give.
Bless thou the liberal worshippers: bless thou the word that I have said.

3 Even as the Deities maintained Faith in the mighty Asuras,
So make this uttered wish of mine true for the liberal worshippers.

4 Guarded by Vāyu, Gods and men who sacrifice draw near to Faith.
Man winneth Faith by yearnings of the heart, and opulence by Faith.

5 Faith in the early morning, Faith at noonday will we invocate,
Faith at the setting of the Sun. O Faith, endow us with belief.

HYMN CLII. *Indra.*

1. A MIGHTY Governor art thou, Wondrous, Destroyer of the foe,
Whose friend is never done to death, and never, never overcome.

2 Lord of the clan, who brings us bliss, Strong, Warrior, Slayer of the fiend,
May Indra, Soma-drinker, go before us, Bull who gives us peace.

3 Drive Rākṣasas and foes away, break thou in pieces Vṛtra's jaws:
O Vṛtra-slaying Indra, quell the foeman's wrath who threatens us.

1 *To what no foot had trodden*: *atūrte*: 'to the indestructible (ether).'—Wilson.

3 *Eagle*: identified by Sāyaṇa with Tārkṣya, brother of Garuḍa, who brought the Soma from the Moon at Savitar's command.

5 *Āṅgirasa*: a descendant of the Aṅgirases. *Achievement*: *vāje*; food; according to Sāyaṇa, *i. e.* oblation. *Lauding*: *árcan*: or, I, Arcan, honouring thee to win thy favour.

1 *Though kindled*: although thou art already burning, fresh fire is added to thee. *To show us favour*: *mṛlīkāya*: this play upon the Ṛṣi's name Mṛlīka is repeated in each stanza.

The Ṛṣi is Śraddhā (Faith) of the family of Kāma (Love).

1 Upon the height of happiness: '(who is seated) on Bhaga's head'.—Wilson.

3 *Asuras*: the primeval Āryan Gods, Dyaus, Varuṇa, and some others, who were venerated by Indra and other Indo-Āryan deities of a later creation.

4 *Guarded by Vāyu*: the meaning is not clear.

4 O Indra, beat our foes away, humble the men who challenge us :
Send down to nether darkness him who seeks to do us injury.

5 Baffle the foeman's plan, ward off his weapon who would conquer us.
Give shelter from his furious wrath, and keep his murdering dart afar.

HYMN CLIII. *Indra.*

1. SWAYING about, the Active Ones came nigh to Indra at his birth,
And shared his great heroic might.

2 Based upon strength and victory and power, O Indra is thy birth :
Thou, Mighty One, art strong indeed.

3 Thou art the Vṛtra-slayer, thou, Indra, hast spread the firmament :
Thou hast with might upheld the heavens.

4 Thou, Indra, bearest in thine arms the lightning that accords with thee,
Whetting thy thunderbolt with might.

5 Thou, Indra, art preëminent over all creatures in thy might :
Thou hast pervaded every place.

HYMN CLIV. *New Life.*

1. FOR some is Soma purified, some sit by sacrificial oil :
To those for whom the meath flows forth, even to those let him depart.

2 Invincible through Fervour, those whom Fervour hath advanced to heaven,
Who showed great Fervour in their lives,—even to those let him depart.

1 *The Active Ones* : the Water-Goddesses may be meant. The Consorts of the Gods, according to Sāyaṇa.

2 *Thou, Mighty One* : or, 'O Bull, thou art a Bull indeed.' 'Thou O hero, art indeed a hero'.—Max Müller.

4 *Lightning* : or, praise-song, hymn. Sāyaṇa explains *arkám* here by *stutyam* : thy laudable or adorable thunderbolt.

———

The Ṛṣi of this funeral hymn is Yamī, sister of Yama.

1 *To those let him depart* : let the spirit of the dead go to the realm of the blessed, to the Fathers who receive offerings of Soma juice and clarified butter. *Meath* : according to Sāyaṇa, honey, which is offered to the spirits of their ancestors by students of the Atharva-veda, Soma juice and *ghṛtám* or clarified butter (sacrificial oil) being offered, respectively, by students of the Sāmaveda and Yajurveda.

2 *Fervour* : *tápas* : literally, warmth, heat; religious fervour, asceticism, austerity, self-denial and abstracted meditation.

3 The heroes who contend in war and boldly cast their lives away,
Or who give guerdon thousandfold,—even to those let him depart.

4 Yea, the first followers of Law, Law's pure and holy strengtheners,
The Fathers, Yama ! Fervour-moved,—even to those let him depart.

5 Skilled in a thousand ways and means, the sages who protect the Sun,
The Ṛṣis, Yama ! Fervour-moved,—even to those let him depart.

HYMN CLV. *Various.*

1. ARĀYĪ, one-eyed limping hag, fly, ever-screeching, to the hill.
We frighten thee away with these, the heroes of Śirimbiṭha.

2 Scared from this place and that is she, destroyer of each germ unborn.
Go, sharp-horned Brahmaṇaspti and drive Arāyī far away.

3 Yon log that floats without a man to guide it on the river's edge,—
Seize it, thou thing with hideous jaws, and go thou far away thereon.

4 When, foul with secret stain and spot, ye hastened onward to the breast,
All Indra's enemies were slain and passed away like froth and foam.

5 These men have led about the cow, have duly carried Agni round,
And raised their glory to the Gods. Who will attack them with success ?

4 *Fervour-moved* : or, Penance-rich ; filled with or full of religious austerity.

5 *Who protect the Sun* : see Muir *O. S. T.*, V. 319.

The hymn has been translated by Dr. J. Muir, *O. S. Texts*, V. p. 310, and by Prof. Zimmer, *Altindisches Leben*, p. 416.

———

The subject or object of the hymn is the averting or removal of misfortune.

1 *Arāyī*: 'the stingy,' one of a class of malevolent she-fiends. *Ever-screeching* : according to Sāyaṇa's explanation of *sadānve* : according to others 'allied with Dānus, Dānavas, or demons.' *Śirimbiṭha* : the Ṛṣi of the hymn.

2 *Sharp-horned* : armed with piercing rays of light.

4 The meaning of this stanza is not clear. *Maṇḍūradhāṇikīḥ* and *budbudayāśavaḥ* are difficult words that do not occur again.

5 *These men* : the text has only *imé*, 'these'. According to Sāyaṇa, the Viśvedevas are meant, who have brought back the stolen cattle. But the reference is probably to the sacrifice which the priests are performing.

———

HYMN CLVI. *Agni.*

1. Let songs of ours speed Agni forth like a fleet courser in the race,
And we will win each prize through him.

2 Agni, the dart whereby we gain kine for ourselves with help from thee,—
That send us for the gain of wealth.

3 O Agni, bring us wealth secure, vast wealth in horses and in kine:
Oil thou the socket, turn the wheel.

4 O Agni, thou hast made the Sun, Eternal Star, to mount the sky,
Bestowing light on living men.

5 Thou, Agni, art the people's light, best, dearest, seated in thy shrine:
Watch for the singer, give him life.

HYMN CLVII. *Viśvedevas.*

1. We will, with Indra and all Gods to aid us, bring these existing worlds into subjection.

2 Our sacrifice, our bodies, and our offspring, let Indra form together with Ādityas.

3 With the Ādityas, with the band of Maruts, may Indra be Protector of our bodies.

4 As when the Gods came, after they had slaughtered the Asuras, keeping safe their Godlike nature,

5 Brought the Sun hitherward with mighty powers, and looked about them on their vigorous Godhead.

HYMN CLVIII. *Sūrya.*

1. May Sūrya guard us out of heaven, and Vāta from the firmament,
And Agni from terrestrial spots.

2 Thou Savitar whose flame deserves hundred libations, be thou pleased:
From falling lightning keep us safe.

3 May Savitar the God, and may Parvata also give us sight;
May the Creator give us sight.

4 Give sight unto our eye, give thou our bodies sight that they may see:
May we survey, discern this world.

5 Thus, Sūrya, may we look on thee, on thee most lovely to behold,
See clearly with the eyes of men.

HYMN CLIX. *Śacī Paulomī.*

1. Yon Sun hath mounted up, and this my happy fate hate mounted high.
I knowing this, as conqueror have won my husband for mine own.

2 I am the banner and the head, a mighty arbitress am I:
I am victorious, and my Lord shall be submissive to my will.

3 My Sons are slayers of the foe, my Daughter is a ruling Queen:
I am victorious: o'er my Lord my song of triumph is supreme.

4 Oblation, that which Indra gave and thus grew glorious and most high,—
This have I offered, O ye Gods, and rid me of each rival wife.

5 Destroyer of the rival wife, Sole Spouse, victorious, conqueror,
The others' glory have I seized as 'twere the wealth of weaker Dames.

6 I have subdued as conqueror these rivals, these my fellow-wives,
That I may hold imperial sway over this Hero and the folk.

HYMN CLX. *Indra.*

1. Taste this strong draught enriched with offered viands: with all thy chariot here unyoke thy Coursers.
Let not those other sacrificers stay thee, Indra: these juices shed for thee are ready.

2 Thine is the juice effused, thine are the juices yet to be pressed: our resonant songs invite thee.

---

2 *The dart*: 'that army'—Wilson.

3 *Turn the wheel*: I adopt the reading of the Sāmaveda, *pavím*, instead of *paṇím*. According to the text, the rendering would be: 'Balm heaven and drive the Paṇi hence.'

The first three verses of this hymn were recited at the Aśvamedha or Horse-Sacrifice.

5 Sāyaṇa explains the second half of the stanza differently:—'then (men) beheld around them the swift descending rain.'—Wilson.

---

1 *Out of heaven*: 'from (foes dwelling in) heaven.'—Wilson.

3 *The Creator*: Dhātar.

Śacī Paulomī, called also Indrāṇī, the Consort of Indra, is also the Ṛṣi of the hymn. 'Literally, this is a song of exultation by *Śacī* over her rival wives: but *śacī* means also an "act", "exploit," and this hymn is metaphorically the praise of *Indra's* glorious acts.'—Wilson.

O Indra, pleased to-day with this libation, come, thou who knowest all and drink the Soma.

3 Whoso, devoted to the God, effuses Soma for him with yearning heart and spirit,—
Never doth Indra give away his cattle : for him he makes the lovely Soma famous.

4 He looks with loving favour on the mortal who, like a rich man, pours for him the Soma.
Maghavan in his bended arm supports him : he slays, unasked, the men who hate devotion.

5 We call on thee to come to us, desirous of goods and spoil, of cattle, and of horses.
For thy new love and favour are we present : let us invoke thee, Indra, as our welfare.

HYMN CLXI. *Indra.*

1. For life I set thee free by this oblation from the unknown decline and from Consumption ;
Or, if the grasping demon have possessed him, free him from her, O Indra, thou and Agni.

2 Be his days ended, be he now departed, be he brought very near to death already,
Out of Destruction's lap again I bring him, save him for life to last a hundred autumns.

3 With hundred-eyed oblation, hundred-autumned, bringing a hundred lives, have I restored him,
That Indra for a hundred years may lead him safe to the farther shore of all misfortune.

4 Live, waxing in thy strength, a hundred autumns, live through a hundred springs, a hundred winters.
Through hundred-lived oblation Indra, Agni, Bṛhaspati, Savitar yield him for a hundred !

5 So have I found and rescued thee : thoú hast returned with youth renewed.
Whole in thy members ! I have found thy sight and all thy life for thee.

HYMN CLXIV. *Dream-charm.*

1. Avaunt, thou Master of the mind ! Depart, and vanish far away.
Look on Destruction far from hence. The live man's mind is manifold.

2 A happy boon do men elect, a mighty blessing they obtain.
Bliss with Vaivasvata they see. The live man's mind seeks many a place.

3 If by address, by blame, by imprecation we have committed sin, awake or sleeping,
All hateful acts of ours, all evil doings may Agni bear away to distant places.

4 When, Indra, Brahmaṇaspati, our deeds are wrongful and unjust,
May provident Āṅgirasa prevent our foes from troubling us.

5 We have prevailed this day and won : we are made free from sin and guilt.
Ill thoughts, that visit us awake or sleeping, seize the man we hate, yea, seize the man who hateth us.

HYMN CLXV. *Viśvedevas.*

1. Gods, whatsoe'er the Dove came hither seeking, sent to us as the envoy of Destruction,
For that let us sing hymns and make atonement. Well be it with our quadrupeds and bipeds.

4 Dr. Gaedicke (*Accusativ im Veda*, p. 127) translates Pādas 1—3 of the stanza differently : der wird von ihm erspäht, der, obwohl reich, ihm keinen Soma presst, den holt der mächtige heraus aus dem Winkel (Versteck).

According to the Index the subject of the hymn is the cure of the disease called Rājayakṣma (Consumption or Atrophy).

1 *Unknown decline* : some insidious disease, differing from Rājayakṣma. Perhaps, as Prof. Zimmer suggests, hypertrophy and atrophy are the two diseases intended. See *Altindisches Leben*, p. 377. *The grasping demon* : *grāhi* : from *grah*, to seize; a female spirit who seizes men and kills them.

4 *For a hundred* : years, understood.

For Hymns CLXII, CLXIII, and CLXXXIV see Appendix.

1 *Master of the mind* the spirit of evil dreams is addressed. *Destruction* : the Goddess Nirṛti. *Manifold* : 'attentive to various objects, and soon diverted from any regard to evil dreams.—Wilson.

2 *Vaivasvata* : Yama, the son of Vivasvān, who presides over evil dreams.—Sāyaṇa.

4 *Āṅgirasa* according to Sāyaṇa, Varuṇa, the wise God who is especially connected with his worshippers the Aṅgirases, may be intended. Cf. *Hymns of the Atharva-veda*, VI. 45. 3.

1 A dove, regarded as an ill-omened bird and the messenger of Death, has flown into the house. Similarly

2 Auspicious be the Dove that hath been sent us, a harmless bird, ye Gods, within our dwelling.
May Agni, Sage, be pleased with our oblation, and may the Missile borne on wings avoid us.

3 Let not the Arrow that hath wings distract us : beside the fire-place, on the hearth it settles.
May it bring welfare to our men and cattle : here let the Dove, ye Gods, forbear to harm us.

4 The screeching of the owl is ineffective ; and when beside the fire the Dove hath settled,
To him who sent it hither as an envoy, to him be reverence paid, to Death, to Yama.

5 Drive forth the Dove, chase it with holy verses : rejoicing, bring ye hither food and cattle,
Barring the way against all grief and trouble. Let the swift bird fly forth and leave us vigour.

HYMN CLXVI. *Sapatnanāśanam.*

1. MAKE me a bull among my peers, make me my rivals' conqueror :
Make me the slayer of my foes, a sovran ruler, lord of kine

2 I am my rivals' slayer, like Indra unwounded and unhurt,
And all these enemies of mine are vanquished and beneath my feet.

3 Here, verily, I bind you fast, as the two bow-ends with the string.
Press down these men, O Lord of Speech, that they may humbly speak to me.

4 Hither I came as conqueror with mighty all-effecting power,
And I have mastered all your thought, your synod, and your holy work.

5 May I be highest, having gained your strength in war, your skill in peace : my feet have trodden on your heads.
Speak to me from beneath my feet, as frogs from out the water croak, as frogs from out the water croak.

HYMN CLXVII. *Indra.*

1. THIS pleasant meath, O Indra, is effused for thee : thou art the ruling Lord of beaker and of juice.
Bestow upon us wealth with many hero sons : thou, having glowed with Fervour, wonnest heavenly light.

2 Let us call Śakra to libations here effused, winner of light who joyeth in the potent juice.
Mark well this sacrifice of ours and come to us : we pray to Maghavan the Vanquisher of hosts.

3 By royal Soma's and by Varuṇa's decree, under Bṛhaspati's and Anumati's guard,
This day by thine authority, O Maghavan, Maker, Disposer thou ! have I enjoyed the jars.

4 I, too, urged on, have had my portion, in the bowl, and as first Prince I drew forth this my hymn of praise,
When with the prize I came unto the flowing juice, O Viśvāmitra, Jamadagni, to your home.

HYMN CLXVIII. *Vāyu.*

1. O THE Wind's chariot, O its power and glory! Crashing it goes and hath a voice of thunder.
It makes the regions red and touches heaven, and as it moves the dust of earth is scattered.

2 Along the traces of the Wind they hurry, they come to him as dames to an assembly.
Borne on his car with these for his attendants, the God speeds forth, the universe's Monarch.

3 Travelling on the paths of air's mid-region, no single day doth he take rest or slumber.

in North-Lincolnshire, 'If a pigeon is seen sitting on a tree, or comes into the house, or from being wild suddenly becomes tame, it is a sign of death.'—*Notes and Queries*, viii. p. 382.

2 *Missile borne on wings* : the ill-omened bird.

5 *With holy verses* : Sāyaṇa takes *ṛcā* with *stūyamānāḥ*, understood :—(Praised) by our hymn (O Gods).

The subject is the Destruction of Rivals.

The Ṛṣis are Viśvāmitra and Jamadagni. Stanzas 1—3 are spoken by the Ṛṣis and 4 by Indra.

1 *Having glowed with Fervour* : 'performing arduous penance.'—Wilson.

3 *Anumati* : Divine Favour personified.

4 *The prize* : the wealth won for you.

2 *They* : the Waters. Prof. Max Müller interprets differently. See his translation, *Vedic Hymns*, I. 449.

Holy and earliest-born, Friend of the waters, where did he spring and from what region came he ?

4 Germ of the world, the Deities' vital spirit, this God moves ever as his will inclines him.
His voice is heard, his shape is ever viewless. Let us adore this Wind with our oblation.

HYMN CLXIX. *Cows.*

1. MAY the wind blow upon our Cows with healing : may they eat herbage full of vigorous juices.
May they drink waters rich in life and fatness : to food that moves on feet be gracious, Rudra.

2 Like-coloured, various-hued, or single-coloured, whose names through sacrifice are known to Agni,
Whom the Aṅgirases produced by Fervour,—vouchsafe to these, Parjanya, great protection.

3 Those who have offered to the Gods their bodies, whose varied forms are all well known to Soma,—
Those grant us in our cattle-pen, O Indra, with their full streams of milk and plenteous offspring.

4 Prajāpati, bestowing these upon me, one-minded with all Gods and with the Fathers,
Hath to our cow-pen brought auspicious cattle : so may we own the offspring they will bear us.

HYMN CLXX. *Sūrya.*

1. MAY the Bright God drink glorious Soma-mingled meath, giving the sacrifice's lord uninjured life;
He who, wind-urged, in person guards our offspring well, hath nourished them with food and shines o'er many a land.

2 Radiant, as high Truth, cherished, best at winning strength, Truth based upon the statute that supports the heavens,
He rose, a light, that kills Vṛtras and enemies, best slayer of the Dasyus, Asuras, and foes.

1 *Food that moves on feet* : the wandering milch-cows. But see Bergaigne, III. 159.

4 *Prajāpati......hath brought* : 'may Prajāpati bring,' according to Sāyaṇa

3 This light, the best of lights, supreme, all-conquering, winner of riches, is exalted with high laud.
All-lighting, radiant, mighty as the Sun to see, he spreadeth wide unfailing victory and strength.

4 Beaming forth splendour with thy light, thou hast attained heaven's lustrous realm.
By thee were brought together all existing things, possessor of all Godhead, All-effecting God.

HYMN CLXXI. *Indra.*

1. FOR Iṭa's sake who pressed the juice, thou, Indra, didst protect his car,
And hear the Soma-giver's call.

2 Thou from his skin hast borne the head of the swift-moving combatant,
And sought the Soma-pourer's home.

3 Venya, that mortal man, hast thou, for Āstrabudhna the devout,
O Indra, many a time set free.

4 Bring, Indra, to the east again that Sun who now is in the west,
Even against the will of Gods.

HYMN CLXXII. *Dawn.*

1. WITH all thy beauty come : the kine approaching with full udders follow on thy path.

2 Come with kind thoughts, most liberal, rousing the warrior's hymn of praise, with bounteuos ones,

3 As nourishers we tie the thread, and, liberal with our bounty, offer sacrifice.

4 Dawn drives away her Sister's gloom, and, through her excellence, makes her retrace her path.

2 *Skin* : here meaning 'body.' *Combatant* : *makhásya* : according to the legend cited by Sāyaṇa Sacrifice personified, whose head, as he attempted to escape in human form from the Gods, was cut off by Indra. See Wilson.

3 *Venya* : said to be Pṛthu, the son of Vena. See X. 148.5. *Āstrabudhna* : the name of a man not mentioned elsewhere, the son of Astrabudhna. *Set free* : Cp.I. 24. 15.

2 *Most liberal* : Sūrya appears to be meant. *Rousing the warrior's hymn of praise* : *jārayánmakhaḥ* : the meaning is uncertain :—'bringing the sacrifice to completion', according to Sāyaṇa.

3 *As nourishers* : because sacrifice brings the food that nourishes life. *The thread* : of sacrifice.

4 *Her Sister's gloom* : the darkness of Night.

HYMN CLXXIII. *The King.*

1. Be with us; I have chosen thee : stand stedfast and immovable.
Let all the people wish for thee : let not thy kingship fall away.

2 Be even here ; fall not away ; be like a mountain unremoved.
Stand stedfast here like Indra's self, and hold the kingship in the grasp.

3 This man hath Indra stablished, made secure by strong oblation's power.
May Soma speak a benison, and Brahmaṇaspati, on him.

4 Firm is the sky and firm the earth, and stedfast also are these hills.
Stedfast is all this living world, and stedfast is this King of men.

5 Stedfast, may Varuṇa the King, stedfast, the God Bṛhaspati,
Stedfast, may Indra, stedfast too, may Agni keep thy stedfast reign.

6 On constant Soma let us think with constant sacrificial gift
And then may Indra make the clans bring tribute unto thee alone.

HYMN CLXXIV. *The King.*

1. With offering for success in fight whence Indra was victorious.
With this, O Brahmaṇaspati, let us attain to royal sway.

2 Subduing those who rival us, subduing all malignities,
Withstand the man who menaces, withstand the man who angers us.

3 Soma and Savitar the God have made thee a victorious King
All elements have aided thee, to make thee general conqueror.

4 Oblation, that which Indra gave and thus grew glorious and most high,—
This have I offered, Gods ! and hence now, verily, am rivalless.

5 Slayer of rivals, rivalless, victorious, with royal sway,
Over these beings may I rule, may I be Sovran of the folk.

The subject is the benediction of a newly-elected king.

1 *With offering for success* : 'By the *abhivarta* oblation.' —Wilson.

4 Cp. X. 159. 4.

HYMN CLXXV. *Press-stones.*

1. May Savitar the God, O Stones, stir you according to the Law :
Be harnessed to the shafts, and press.

2 Stones, drive calamity away, drive ye away malevolence :
Make ye the Cows our medicine.

3 Of one accord the upper Stones, giving the Bull his bull-like strength,
Look down with pride on those below.

4 May Savitar the God, O Stones, stir you as Law commands for him
Who sacrifices, pouring juice.

HYMN CLXXVI. *Agnī.*

1. With hymns of praise their sons have told aloud the Ṛbhus' mighty deeds.
Who, all-supporting, have enjoyed the earth as 'twere a mother cow.

2 Bring forth the God with song divine, being Jātavedas hitherward,
To bear our gifts at once to heaven.

3 He here, a God-devoted Priest, led forward comes to sacrifice.
Like a car covered for the road, he, glowing, knows, himself, the way.

4 This Agni rescues from distress, as 'twere from the Immortal Race,
A God yet mightier than strength, a God who hath been made for life.

HYMN CLXXVII. *Māyābheda.*

1. The sapient with their spirit and their mind behold the Bird adorned with all an Asura's magic might.
Sages observe him in the ocean's inmost depth : the wise disposers seek the station of his rays.

1 *The shafts* : or chariot-poles ; here meaning the guiding arms of the Soma-press.
2 *The Cows* : or, the rays of morning, at whose approach robbers and demons fly.
3 *The Bull* : Soma.

3 *Like a car* : perhaps, as Prof. Ludwig suggests, like a chariot which, as the driver is concealed from sight by the canopy, seems to find its way without a guide.
4 *As 'twere from the Immortal Race* : 'as (well as) from peril caused by the immortals.'—Wilson. Stanzas 2—4 are recited at the Agni-praṇayana, the ceremony of carrying the sacrificial fire to the altar used for animal and Soma sacrifices. See Haug's *Aitareya Brāhmaṇam*, II. 60, 61.

The subject is Māyābheda, 'the discernment of *Māyā*, or illusion (the cause of material creation).'—Wilson.
1 *The Bird* : the Sun. *In the ocean's inmost depth* : in the solar orb, according to Sāyaṇa. *Wise disposers* : 'ordainers (of solar worship).'—Wilson.

2 The flying Bird bears Speech within his spirit : erst the Gandharva in the womb pronounced it :
And at the seat of sacrifice the sages cherish this radiant, heavenly-bright invention.

3 I saw the Herdsman, him who never resteth, approaching and departing on his pathways.
He, clothed in gathered and diffusive splendour, within the worlds continually travels.

HYMN CLXXVIII. *Tārkṣya.*

1. THIS very mighty one whom Gods commission, the Conqueror of cars, ever triumphant,
Swift, fleet to battle, with uninjured fellies, even Tārkṣya for our weal will we call hither.

2 As though we offered up our gifts to Indra, may we ascend him as a ship for safety.
Like the two wide worlds, broad, deep, far-extended, may we be safe both when he comes and leaves you.

3 He who with might the Five Lands hath pervaded, like Sūrya with his lustre, and the waters—
His strength wins hundreds, thousands : none avert it, as the young maid repelleth not her lover.

HYMN CLXXIX. *Indra.*

1. Now lift ye up yourselves and look on Indra's seasonable share.
If it be ready, offer it ; unready, ye have been remiss

2 Oblation is prepared : come to us, Indra; the Sun hath travelled over half his journey.
Friends with their stores are sitting round thee waiting like lords of clans for the tribe's wandering chieftain.

3 Dressed in the udder and on fire, I fancy ; well-dressed, I fancy, is this recent present.
Drink, Indra, of the curd of noon's libation with favour, Thunderer, thou whose deeds are mighty.

HYMN CLXXX. *Indra.*

1. O MUCH-INVOKED, thou hast subdued thy foemen : thy might is loftiest ; here display thy bounty.
In thy right hand, O Indra, bring us treasures : thou art the Lord of rivers filled with riches.

2 Like a dread wild beast roaming on the mountain thou hast approached us from the farthest distance.
Whetting thy bold and thy sharp blade, O Indra, crush thou the foe and scatter those who hate us.

3 Thou, mighty Indra, sprangest into being as strength for lovely lordship o'er the people.
Thou drovest off the folk who were unfriendly, and to the Gods thou gavest room and freedom.

HYMN CLXXXI. *Viśvedevas.*

1. VASIṢṬHA mastered the Rathantara, took it from radiant Dhātar, Savitar, and Viṣṇu,
Oblation, portion of fourfold oblation, known by the names of Saprathas and Prathas.

2. These sages found what lay remote and hidden, the sacrifice's loftiest secret essence.
From radiant Dhātar, Savitar, and Viṣṇu, from Agni, Bharadvāja brought the Bṛhat.

3 They found with mental eyes the earliest

2 *Speech* : or song; the morning song of the Sun-Bird. *The Gandharva* : the breath of life, according to Sāyaṇa. The ray of the Sun is probably meant.

3 This stanza has occurred before. See I. 164. 31. *The Herdsman* : the Sun. *Resteth* : or, stumbleth; literally, sinks or falls down.

---

1 *Tārkṣya* : a personification of the Sun, usually described as a divine horse. Cp. I. 89. 6.

3 *Her lover* : I adopt, with a modification, Professor Pischel's interpretation of the difficult words *yuvatím na śáryām*. See *Vedische Studien*, I. p. 106.

---

3 The milk is twice cooked; first matured in the cow's udder and then heated on the fire. *Curd* : the hymn was employed in the Dadhigharma ceremony when Soma juice was offered mixed with curd or sour inspissated milk. Cf. VIII. 2. 9, and IX. 11. 6. See Hillebrandt, *V.M.*, 1. 221.

---

1 *Rathantara* : one of the most important Sāma-hymns, consisting of verses 22 and 23 of Ṛgveda VII. 32 = Sāmaveda II. i. 11. The meaning here is uncertain, and the whole stanza is obscure. *Saprathas and Prathas* : meaning, apparently, 'far-extending' and 'extending', the former referring to the Rathantara and the latter to the Bṛhat, which is also one of the most important Sāmans (Ṛgveda VI. 46. 1, 2 = Sāmaveda II. ii. 1. 12).

Yajus, a pathway to the Gods, that had descended.
From radiant Dhātar, Savitar, and Viṣṇu, from Sūrya did these sages bring the Gharma.

HYMN CLXXXII. *Bṛhaspati.*

1. BṚHASPATI lead us safely over troubles, and turn his evil thought against the sinner;
Repel the curse, and drive away ill-feeling, and give the sacrificer peace and comfort!

2 May Narāśaṁsa aid us at Prayāja: blest be our Anuyāja at invokings.
May he repel the curse, and chase ill-feeling, and give the sacrificer peace and comfort.

3 May he whose head is flaming burn the demons, haters of prayer, so that the arrow slay them.
May he repel the curse and chase ill-feeling, and give the sacrificer peace and comfort.

HYMN CLXXXIII. *The Sacrificer, Etc.*

1. I SAW thee meditating in thy spirit what sprang from Fervour and hath thence developed.
Bestowing offspring here, bestowing riches, spread in thine offspring, thou who cravest children.

2 I saw thee pondering in thine heart, and praying that in due time thy body might be fruitful.
Come as a youthful woman, rise to meet me: spread in thine offspring, thou who cravest children.

3 In plants and herbs, in all existent beings I have deposited the germ of increase.
All progeny on earth have I engendered, and sons in women who will be hereafter.

HYMN CLXXXV. *Aditi.*

1. GREAT, unassailable must be the heavenly favour of Three Gods,
Varuṇa, Mitra, Aryaman.

2 O'er these, neither at home nor yet abroad or pathways that are strange,
The evil-minded foe hath power:

3 Nor over him, the man on whom the Sons of Aditi bestow Eternal light that he may live.

HYMN CLXXXVI. *Vāyu.*

1. FILLING our hearts with health and joy, may Vāta breathe his balm on us:
May he prolong our days of life.

2 Thou art our Father, Vāta, yea, thou art a Brother and a friend,
So give us strength that we may live.

3 The store of Amṛta laid away yonder, O Vāta, in thine home,—
Give us thereof that we may live.

HYMN CLXXXVII. *Agni.*

1. To Agni send I forth my song, to him the Bull of all the folk:
So may he bear us past our foes.

2 Who from the distance far away shines brilliantly across the wastes:
So may he bear us past our foes.

3 The Bull with brightly-gleaming flame who utterly consumes the fiends:
So may he bear us past our foes.

4 Who looks on all existing things and comprehends them with his view:
So may he bear us past our foes.

3 *Yajus*: sacrificial prayers and formulas of the Yajurveda. *Gharma*: warm libation of milk or other beverage. 'The Sūkta refers evidently to technical ritual to which no key is given by the commentary.'—Wilson. See Mme. Zenaïde Ragozin's *Vedic India*, p. 398.

---

2 *Narāśaṁsa*: Agni. *Prayāja*: part of the introductory ceremony at a Soma sacrifice. *Anuyāja*: a secondary or final sacrifice.

3 *He whose head is flaming*: *tápurmūrdhan*: Brhaspati or Agni as Lightning.

The deities are the Sacrificer, his Wife, and the Hotar-priest.

1 According to Sāyaṇa, the wife is the speaker of the first stanza, the Yajamāna or sacrificer of the second, and the Hotar-priest of the third. Ludwig considers Agni to be the speaker of the whole hymn. *What sprang from Fervour*: the results of ardent devotion or *tápas*.

3 The Hotar-priest regards himself as the procreator of all living beings through the efficacy of the sacrifices which he performs: *matsādhyena yāgena sarvasyotpatteraham sarvajanaheturbhavāmi*.—Sāyaṇa.

---

1 *Bull*: chief and lord, as the indispensable household fire.

2 *Across the wastes*: as the fire that burns the jungle and prepares the ground for cultivation.

5 Resplendent Agni, who was born in farthest region of the air :
So may he bear us past our foes.

HYMN CLXXXVIII. *Agni.*

1. Now send ye Jātavedas forth, send hitherward the vigorous Steed
To seat him on our sacred grass.

2 I raise the lofty eulogy of Jātavedas, raining boons,
With sages for his hero band.

3 With flames of Jātavedas which carry oblation to the Gods,
May he promote our sacrifice.

HYMN CLXXXIX. *Sūrya.*

1. THIS spotted Bull hath come, and sat before the Mother in the east,
Advancing to his Father heaven.

2 Expiring when he draws his breath, she moves along the lucid spheres :
The Bull shines out through all the sky.

3 Song is bestowed upon the Bird : it rules supreme through thirty realms
Throughout the days at break of morn.

5 *In farthest region of the air* : or beyond the firmament, as the Sun.

The deity is alternatively Sārparājñī, the Serpent-Queen, Kadru, who is also the Ṛṣi of the hymn.

1 *This spotted Bull* : the Sun. *The Mother* : *Dawn.*

3 *The Bird* : the Sun. His morning song, representing prayer, is supreme through all the divisions of the world, the number thirty being used indefinitely. Cf. I. 123.8.

HYMN CXC. *Creation.*

1. FROM Fervour kindled to its height Eternal Law and Truth were born :
Thence was the Night produced, and thence the billowy flood of sea arose.

2 From that same billowy flood of sea the Year was afterwards produced,
Ordainer of the days nights, Lord over all who close the eye.

3 Dhātar, the great Creator, then formed in due order Sun and Moon.
He formed in order Heaven and Earth, the regions of the air, and light.

HYMN CXCI. *Agni.*

1. THOU, mighty Agni, gatherest up all that is precious for thy friend.
Bring us all treasures as thou art enkindled in libation's place

2 Assemble, speak together : let your minds be all of one accord,
As ancient Gods unanimous sit down to their appointed share.

3 The place is common, common the assembly, common the mind, so be their thought united.
A common purpose do I lay before you, and worship with your general oblation.

4 One and the same be your resolve, and be your minds of one accord.
United be the thoughts of all that all may happily agree.

1 *From Fervour* : from the *tápas*, devotional ardour or asceticism of Brahmā, according to Sāyaṇa. But the meaning here may be from warmth. See X. 129. 3 and note. *Thence* : from that fervour, or warmth.

The deity or subject of stanzas 2—4 is Saṁjñānam, Agreement or unanimity in assembly.

3 *Common the assembly* : this *samiti* appears to have been a general assembly of the people on some important occasion, such as the election of a King. Cf. *Hymns of the Atharvaveda*, VI. 64.

APPENDIX I.

Page 87, Hymn CXXVI.

I subjoin a Latin version of the two stanzas omitted in my translation. They are in a different metre from the rest of the hymn, have no apparent connexion with what precedes, and look like a fragment of a liberal shepherd's love-song. The seventh stanza should, it seems, precede the sixth :

6 [Ille loquitur]. Adhaerens, arcte adhaerens, illa quae mustelae similis se abdidit, multum humorem effundens, dat mihi complexuum centum gaudia.

7 [Illa loquitur]. Prope, prope accede ; molliter me tange. Ne putes pilos corporis mei-paucos esse : tota sum villosa sicut Gandharidum ovis.

Professor Ludwig thinks that *Yādurī* (multum humorem, *i.e.*, semen genitale, effundens) may be the name of a slave-girl. *Gandharidum ovis* : a ewe of the Gandhāris. The country of Gandhāra is placed by Lassen to the west of the Indus and to the south of the Kophen or Kābul river. King Darius in a rock-inscription mentions the *Ga*(*n*)*dāra* together with the *Hi*(*n*)*du* as people subject to him, and the Gandarii, together with the Parthians, Khorasmians, Sogdians, and Dadikae, are said by Herodotus to have formed part of the army of Xerxes. The name of the country is preserved in the modern Kandahār. See Muir, *O.S. Texts*, ii. 342, and Zimmer, *Altindisches Leben*, p. 30.

Page 221, Hymn CLXXIX.

The deified object of this omitted hymn is said to be Rati or Love, and its Ṛṣis or authors are Lopāmudrā, Agastya, and a disciple. Lopāmudrā is represented as inviting the caresses of her aged husband Agastya, and complaining of his coldness and neglect. Agastya responds in stanza 3, and in the second half of stanza 4 the disciple or the poet briefly tells the result of the dialogue. Stanza 5 is supposed to be spoken by the disciple who has overheard the conversation, but its connexion with the rest of the hymn is not very apparent. In stanza 6 'toiling with strong endeavour' is a paraphrase and not a translation of the original *khanamānaḥ khanītraiḥ* (ligonibus fodiens) which Sāyaṇa explains by 'obtaining the desired result by means of lauds and sacrifices.'

M. Bergaigne is of opinion that the hymn has a mystical meaning, Agastya being identifiable with the celestial Soma whom Lopāmudrā, representing fervent Prayer, succeeds after long labour in drawing down from his secret dwelling place. See *La Religion Vedique*, ii. 394 f.

1 'Through many autumns have I toiled and laboured, at night and morn, through age-inducing dawnings.
Old age impairs the beauty of our bodies. Let husbands still come near unto their spouses.

2 For even the men aforetime, law-fulfillers, who with the Gods declared eternal statutes,--
They have decided, but have not accomplished : so now let wives come near unto their husbands.

3 Non inutilis est labor cui Dii favent : nos omnes aemulos et aemulas vincamus.
Superemus in hac centum artium pugna in qua duas partes convenientes utrinque commovemus.

4 Cupido me cepit illius tauri [viri] qui me despicit, utrum hinc utrum illinc ab aliqua parte nata sit.
Lopamudra taurum [maritum suum] ad se detrahit : insipiens illa sapientem anhelantem absorbet.

5 This Soma I address that is most near us, that which hath been imbibed within the spirit,
To pardon any sins we have committed. Verily mortal man is full of longings.

6 Agastya thus, toiling with strong endeavour, wishing for children, progeny and power,
Cherished—a sage of mighty strength—both classes, and with the Gods obtained his prayer's fulfilment.

By 'both classes' probably priests and princes, or institutors of sacrifices, are meant. M. Bergaigne understands the expression to mean the two forms or essences of Soma, the celestial and the terrestrial.

Page 574 Hymn LXI

5 Membrum suum virile, quod vrotentum fuerat, mas ille retraxit. Rursus illud quod in juvenem filiam sublatum fuerat, non aggressurus, ad se rerahit.

6 Quum jam in medio connessu, semiperfecto opere, amorem in puellam pater impleverat, ambo discedentes seminis paulum in terrae superficiem sacrorum sede effusum emiserunt.

7 Quum pater suam nliam adiverat, cum eā congressus suum semen supra wrram effudit. Tum Dii benigni precem (brahma) prgenuerunt, et Vastoshpatim, legum sacrarum custodem, formaverunt.

8 Ille tauro similis spumam in certamine jactavit ; tunc discedens pusillaximis huc profectus est. Quasi dextro pede claudus processit, "inutiles fuerunt illi mei complexus," ita locutus.

9 'The fire, burning the people, does not approach quickly (by day): the naked (*Rākṣasas* approach) not Agni by night; the giver of fuel, and the giver of food, he, the upholder (of the rite), is born, overcoming enemies by his might.'

Page 619, Hymn CVI.

I borrow Wilson's translation of the omitted stanzas.

5 'You are like two pleasantly moving well-fed (hills) like Mitra and Varuṇa, the two bestowers of felicity, veracious, possessors of infinite wealth, happy, like two horses plump with fodder, abiding in the firmament, like two rams (are you) to be nourished with sacrificial food, to be cherished (with oblations).

6 'You are like two mad elephants bending their forequarters and smiting the foe, like the two sons of Nitoṣa destroying (foes), and cherishing (friends); you are bright as two water-born (jewels), do you, who are victorious, (render) my decaying mortal body free from decay.

7 'Fierce (Aśvins), like two powerful (heroes), you enable this moving, perishable mortal (frame) to cross over to the objects (of its destination) as over water; extremely strong, like the Ṛbhus, your chariot attained its destination swift as the wind, it pervaded (everywhere), it dispensed riches.

8 'With your bellies full of the *Soma*, like two saucepans, preservers of wealth, destroyers of enemies. (you are) armed with hatchets, moving like two flying (birds) with forms like the moon, attaining success through the mind, like two laudable beings, (you are) approaching (the sacrifice).'

Page 645, Hymn CLXII.

1 May Agni, yielding to our prayer, the Rakṣas-slayer, drive away
The malady of evil name that hath beset thy labouring womb.

2 Agni, concurring in the prayer, drive off the eater of thy flesh,
The malady of evil name that hath attacked thy babe and womb.

3 That which destroys the sinking germ, the settled, moving embryo,
That which will kill the babe at birth,—even this will we drive far away.

4 That which divides thy legs that it may lie between the married pair,
That penetrates and licks thy side,—even this will we exterminate.

The whole passage is difficult and obscure, and stanza 9 is unintelligible. With regard to the myth of Prajāpati and his daughter, Prof. Max Müller says:—'When Kumārila is hard pressed by his opponents about the immoralities of his gods, he answers with all the freedom of a comparative mythologist : "It is fabled that Prajāpati, the Lord of Creation, did violence to his daughter. But what does it mean ? Prajāpati, the Lord of Creation, is a name of the sun, and he is called so, because he protects all creatures. His daughter Uṣas is the dawn. And when it is said that he was in love with her, this only means that, at sunrise, the sun runs after the dawn, the dawn being at the same time called the daughter of the sun, because she rises when he approaches".'—*History of Anc. Sans. Literature*, pp. 529, 530. See Muir, *O.S. Te ts*, IV. pp. 46, 47, where stanzas 4—7 are translated.

Vāstoṣpatim : Vāstoṣpati, the guardian of the house ; 'the lord of the hearth (of sacrifice).'—Wilson. The word may be in apposition with *bráhma* prayer.

9 *The fire* : according to Sāyaṇa, Rākṣasas who consume like fire.

The subject is Prevention of Abortion. The Ṛṣi is Rakṣohā (Slayer of Rākṣasas) son of Brahmā.

Stanzas 1, 2 are directed against diseases, and 3—6 against evil-spirits which attack women who are about to become mothers.

5 What rests by thee in borrowed form of brother, lover, or of lord,
And would destroy thy progeny,—even this will we exterminate.

6 That which through sleep or darkness hath deceived thee and lies down by thee,
And will destroy thy progeny,—even this will we exterminate.

PAGE 645, HYMN CLXIII

1. FROM both thy nostrils, from thine eyes, from both thine ears and from thy chin,
Forth from thy head and brain and tongue I drive thy malady away.

2 From the neck-tendons and the neck, from the breast-bones and from the spine,
From shoulders, upper, lower arms, I drive thy malady away.

3 From viscera and all within, forth from the rectum, from the heart,
From kidneys, liver, and from spleen, I drive thy malady away.

4 From thighs, from knee-caps, and from heels, and from the forepart of the feet,
From hips, from stomach, and from groin I drive thy malady away.

5 From what is voided from within, and from thy hair, and from they nails,
From all thyself from top to toe, I drive thy malady away.

6 From every member, every hair, disease that comes in every joint,
From all thyself, from top to toe, I drive thy malady away.

The deity or subject is the cure of Yakṣman or phthisis or consumption.

PAGE 650, HYMN CLXXXIV.

1. MAY Viṣṇu form and mould the womb, may Tvaṣṭar duly shape the forms,
Prajāpati infuse the stream, and Dhātar lay the germ for thee.

2 O Sinīvālī, set the germ, set thou the germ, Sarasvatī :
May the Twain Gods bestow the germ, the Aśvins crowned with lotuses.

3 That which the Aśvins Twain rub forth with the attrition-sticks of gold,—
That germ of thine we invocate, that in the tenth month thou mayst bear.

2 *Sinīvālī* : a lunar Goddess, who aids the birth of children. Cp. II. 32. 6.

Verses 1 and 2 are incorporated in Atharva-veda, V. 25 which is a charm to accompany the Garbhādhāna ceremony to ensure or facilitate and bless conception.

APPENDIX II.

METRE.

Rhyme is not used in the Ṛgveda. The metres are regulated by the number of syllables in the stanza, which consists generally of three or four Pādas, measures, divisions, or quarter verses, with a distinctly marked interval at the end of the second Pāda, and so forming two hemistichs or semi-stanzas of equal or unequal length. These Pādas most usually contain eight or eleven or twelve syllables each; but occasionally they consist of fewer and sometimes of more than these numbers. The Pādas of a stanza are generally of equal length and of more or less corresponding prosodial quantities: but sometimes two or more kinds of metre are employed in one stanza, and then the Pādas vary in quantity and length. As regards quantity, the first syllables of the Pāda are not subject to very strict laws, but the last four are more regular, their measure being generally iambic in Pādas of eight and of twelve syllables and trochaic in those of eleven. In the printed text the first and second Pādas form one line, and the third, or third and fourth, or third, fourth, and fifth, complete the distich or stanza. This arrangement I have followed in my translation.

Subjoined, in alphabetical arrangement, are the names, with brief descriptions, of the metres used in the Hymns of the Ṛgveda. The Index of Hymns will show the metre or metres employed in each Hymn.

Abhisāriṇī : a species of Triṣṭup, in which two Pādas contain twelve instead of eleven syllables.

Anuṣṭup or *Anuṣṭubh* : consisting of four Pādas of eight syllables each, two Pādas forming a line. This is the prevailing form of metre in the Mānava-dharma-śāstra, the Mahābhārata, the Rāmāyaṇa, and the Purāṇas.

Anuṣṭubgarbhā : a metre of the Uṣṇih class: the first Pāda containing five syllables, and the three following Pādas of eight syllables each.

Anuṣṭup Pipīlikamadhyā : a species of Anuṣṭup having the second Pāda shorter than the first and third (8 syllables + 4 + 8 + 8).

Aṣṭi : consisting of four Pādas of sixteen syllables each, or sixty-four syllables in the stanza.

Āstārapaṅkti : consisting of two Pādas of eight syllables each, followed by two Pādas of twelve syllables each.

Atidhṛti : four Pādas of nineteen syllables each, = 76 syllables.

Atijagatī : four Pādas of thirteen syllables each.

Atinicṛti : consisting of three Pādas containing respectively seven, six, and seven syllables.

Atiśakvarī : four Pādas of fifteen syllables each.

Atyaṣṭi : four Pādas of seventeen syllables each.

Bṛhatī : four Pādas (8 + 8 + 12 + 8) containing 36 syllables in the stanza.

Caturviṁśatikā Dvipadā : a Dvipadā containing 24 syllables instead of 20.

Dhṛti : consisting of seventy-two syllables in a stanza.

Dvipadā Virāj : a species of Gāyatrī consisting of two Pādas only (12 + 8 or 10 + 10 syllables); inadequately represented in the translation by two decasyllabic iambic lines.

Ekapadā Triṣṭup : a Triṣṭup consisting of a single Pāda or quarter stanza.

Ekapadā Virāj : a Virāj consisting of a single Pāda.

Gāyatrī : the stanza usually consists of twenty-four syllables, variously arranged, but generally as a triplet of three Pādas of eight syllables each, or in one line of sixteen syllables and a second line of eight. There are eleven varieties of this metre, and the number of syllables in the stanza varies accordingly from nineteen to thirty-three.

Jagatī : a metre consisting of forty-eight syllables arranged in four Pādas of twelve syllables each, two Pādas forming a line or hemistich which in the translation is represented by a double Alexandrine.

Kakup or *Kakubh* : a metre of three Pādas consisting of eight, twelve, and eight syllables respectively.

Kakubh Nyaṅkuśirā ; consisting of three Pādas of 9 + 12 + 4 syllables.

Kṛti : a metre of four Pādas of twenty syllables each.

Madhyejyotis : a metre in which a Pāda of eight syllables stands between two Pādas of twelve.

Mahābṛhatī : four Pādas of eight syllables each, followed by one of twelve.

Mahāpadapaṅkti : a two-lined metre of thirty-one syllables, the first line consisting of four Pādas of five syllables each, and the second being a Triṣṭup of the usual eleven syllables. See Vedic Hymns, part I. (S. Books of the East, XXXII), p. xcviii.

Mahāpaṅkti : a metre of forty-eight syllables 8×6 or 12×4).

Mahāsatobṛhatī : a lengthened form of Satobṛhatī.

Naṣṭarūpī : a variety of Anuṣṭup.

Nyaṅkusāriṇī : a metre of four Pādas of 8+12+8+8 syllables.

Pādanicṛt : a variety of Gāyatrī in which one syllable is wanting in each Pāda : 7+3=21 syllables.

Pādapaṅkti : a metre consisting of five Pādas of five syllables each.

Paṅkti : a metre of five octosyllabic Pādas, like Anuṣṭup with an additional Pāda.

Paṅktyuttarā : a metre which ends with a Paṅkti of 5+5 syllables.

Pipīlikāmadhyā : any metre the middle Pāda of which is shorter than the preceding and the following.

Pragātha : a metre in Book VIII, consisting of strophes combining two verses, viz. a Bṛhatī or Kakup followed by a Satobṛhatī.

Prastārapaṅkti : a metre of forty syllables : 12+12+8+8.

Pratiṣṭhā : a metre of four Pādas of four syllables each ; also a variety of the Gāyatrī consisting of three Pādas of eight, seven, and six syllables respectively.

Purastādbṛhatī : a variety of Bṛhatī with twelve syllables in the first Pāda.

Pura-uṣṇih : a metre of three Pādas, containing 12+8+8 syllables.

Śakvarī : a metre of four Pādas of fourteen syllables each.

Satobṛhatī : a metre whose even Pādas contain eight syllables each, and the uneven twelve : 12+8+12+8=40.

Skandhogrīva : consisting of Pādas of 8+12+8+8 syllables.

Tanuśirā : consisting of three Pādas of 11+11+6 syllables.

Triṣṭup or Triṣṭubh : a metre of four Pādas of eleven syllables each.

Upariṣṭādbṛhatī : consisting of four Pādas of 12+8+8+8 syllables.

Upariṣṭājjyotis : a Triṣṭup stanza the last Pāda of which contains only eight syllables.

Ūrdhvabṛhatī : a variety of Bṛhatī.

Urobṛhatī : a variety of Bṛhatī : 8+12 8+8 syllables.

Uṣṇiggarbhā : Gāyatrī of three Pādas of six, seven, and eleven syllables respectively.

Uṣṇih: consisting of three Pādas of 8+8+12 syllables.

Vardhamānā: a species of Gāyatrī; 6+7+8=21 syllables.

Viparītā: a metre of four Pādas resembling Viṣṭārapaṅkti.

Virāḍrūpā: a Triṣṭup metre of four Pādas, 11+11+11+7 or 8 syllables.

Virāj: a metre of four Pādas of ten syllables each.

Virāṭpūrvā: a variety of Triṣṭup.

Virāṭsthānā: a variety of Triṣṭup.

Viṣamapadā: metre of uneven stanzas.

Viṣṭārabṛhatī : a form of Bṛhatī of four Pādas containing 8+10+10+8=36 syllables.

Viṣṭārapaṅkti: a form of Paṅkti consisting of four Pādas of 8+12+12+8=40 syllables.

Yavamadhyā: a metre having a longer Pāda between two shorter ones.

INDEX OF HYMNS

BOOK I.

Hymn.	Ṛṣi.	Deity.	Metre.
1	Madhucchandās.	Agni.	Gāyatrī.
2	The same.	Vāyu Indra-Varuṇa. Mitra-Varuṇa.	The same.
3	....	Aśvins. Indra. Viśvedevas. Sarasvatī.	....
4	....	Indra.	....
5	....	Indra.	....
6	....	Indra, Maruts, Indra and Maruts.	....
7	....	Indra.	....
8	....	The same.	....
9	....	....	....
10	....	....	Anuṣṭup.
11	Jetar or Jetā.	....	The same.
12	Medhātithi.	Agni	Gāyatrī.
13	The same	Āprīs.	The same.
14	....	Viśvedevas.	....
15	....	Ṛtus. Indra. Maruts. Tvaṣṭar. Agni. Mitra-Varuṇa. Aśvins.	....
16	....	Indra.	....
17	....	Indra-Varuṇa.	Gāyatrī. 4, 5 Pādanicṛt.
18	....	Brahmaṇaspati. Indra and Soma. Dakṣiṇā.	Gāyatrī
19	....	Agni and Maruts.	The same.
20	....	Ṛbhus.	....
21	....	Indra-Agni.	....

Hymn.	Ṛṣi.	Deity.	Metre.
22	The same	Aśvins. Savitar. Agni. Indrāṇī, Varuṇānī, & Agnāyī. Heaven and Earth. Earth. Viṣṇu	The same
23	Medhātithi	Vāyu. Indra-Vāyu. Mitra-Varuṇa. Viśvedevas. Pūṣan. Waters.	Gāyatrī. 19 Pura-uṣṇih. 20 Anuṣṭup. 21 Pratiṣṭha. 22-24 Anuṣṭup,
24	Śunaḥ epa	Varuṇa. Agni. Savitar.	Triṣṭup. 3-5 Gāyatrī.
25	The same.	Varuṇa.	Gāyatrī.
26	....	Agni.	The same.
27	Śunaḥśepa.	Indra. Viśvedevas.	Gāyatrī. 13 Triṣṭup.
28	The same	Indra. Pestle and Mortar.	Anuṣṭup. 7-9 Gāyatrī.
29	....	Indra.	Paṅkti.
30	....	Indra. Aśvins. Uṣas.	Gāyatrī. 11 Pādanicṛt. 16 Triṣṭup.
31	Hiraṇyastūpa.	Agni.	Jagatī. 8, 16, 18 Triṣṭup.
32	The same.	Indra.	Triṣṭup.
33	....	The same.	The same.
34	....	Aśvins.	Jagatī. 9 and 12 Triṣṭup.
35	....	Savitar. Agni. Mitra-Varuṇa. Night.	Triṣṭup 1 and 9 Jagatī.
36	Kaṇva.	Agni. 13-14 Sacrificial Post.	Bṛhatī and Satobṛhatī alternately.
37	The same.	Maruts.	Gāyatrī.
38	....	Maruts.	The same.
39	....	The same.	Bṛhatī and Satobṛhatī alternately.
40	....	Brahmaṇaspati.	The same.

Hymn.	Ṛṣi.	Deity.	Metre.
41	The same	Varuṇa-Mitra-Aryaman. Ādityas.	Gāyatrī.
42	....	Pūṣan.	The same.
43	....	Rudra. Mitra-Varuṇa. Soma.	Gāyatrī. 9 Anuṣṭup.
44	Praskaṇva.	Agni.	Bṛhatī and Satobṛhatī alternately.
45	The same.	Agni.	Anuṣṭup.
46	....	Aśvins.	Gāyatrī.
47	....	The same.	Bṛhatī and Satobṛhati alternately.
48	....	Uṣas.	The same.
49	....	The same.	Anuṣṭup.
50	....	Sūrya.	Gāyatrī. 10-13 Anuṣṭup.
51	Savya.	Indra.	Jagatī. 14-15 Triṣṭup.
52	The same	The same.	Jagatī. 13 and 15 Triṣṭup.
53	....	....	Jagatī. 10 and 11 Triṣṭup.
54	....	....	Jagatī. 6,8,9,11 Triṣṭup.
55	....	....	Jagatī.
56	....	....	The same.
57	....	....	....
58	Nodhas.	Agni.	Jagatī. 6-9 Triṣṭup.
59	The same.	Agni Vaiśvānara.	Triṣṭup.
60	....	Agni.	The same.
61	....	Indra.	....
62	....	The same.	....
63	Nodhās.	Indra.	Triṣṭup.
64	The same.	Maruts.	Jagatī. 15 Triṣṭup.
65	Parāśara.	Agni.	Dvipadā Virāj.
66	The same	The same.	The same.
67	....	....	....
68	....	....	....
69	....	....	....
70	....	....	....
71	....	....	Triṣṭup.
72	....	....	The same.
73	....	....	....
74	Gotama.	....	Gāyatrī.

Hymn.	Ṛṣi.	Deity.	Metre.
75	The same.	The same	The same.
76	....	....	Triṣṭup.
77	....	....	The same.
78	....	....	Gāyatrī.
79	....	....	1-3 Triṣṭup. 4-6 Uṣṇih. 7-12 Gāyatrī.
80	....	Indra.	Paṅkti.
81	....	The same	The same.
82	....	....	Paṅkti. 6 Jagatī.
83	....	....	Jagatī.
84	....	....	1-6 Anuṣṭup. 7-9 Uṣṇih. 10-12 Paṅkti. 13-15 Gāyatrī. 16-18 Triṣṭup. 19 Bṛhatī. 20 Satobṛhatī.
85	Gotama.	Maruts.	Jagatī. 5 and 12 Triṣṭup.
86	The same.	The same.	Gāyatrī.
87	....	....	Jagatī.
88	....	....	1 and 6 Prastārapaṅkti. 5 Virāḍrūpā. 2-4 Triṣṭup.
89	....	Viśvedevas.	Jagatī. 6 Virāṭsthānā. 8-10 Triṣṭup.
90	....	The same.	Gāyatrī. 9 Anuṣṭup.
91	....	Soma.	Triṣṭup. 5-16 Gāyatrī. 17 Uṣṇih.
92	....	Uṣas. Aśvins.	Jagatī. 5-12 Triṣṭup. 13-18 Uṣṇih.
93	....	Agni-Soma.	Anuṣṭup. 9-11 Gāyatrī. 4-7 and 12 Triṣṭup. 8 Triṣṭup and Jagatī.
94	Kutsa.	Agni. Gods. Mitra. Varuṇa, Aditi, Sindhu, Heaven and Earth.	Jagatī. 15 and 16 Triṣṭup.
95	The same.	Agni.	Triṣṭup.
96	Kutsa.	Agni.	Triṣṭup.
97	The same	The same.	Gāyatrī.
98	....	....	Triṣṭup.
99	Kaśyapa.	....	The same.

Hymn.	Ṛṣi.	Deity.	Metre.
100	Ṛjrāśva, and others.	Indra.	....
101	Kutsa.	The same	Jagatī. 8-12 Triṣṭup.
102	The same.	....	Jagatī. 11 Triṣṭup,
103	....	....	Triṣṭup.
104	....	....	The same.
105	The same, or Trita Āptya.	Viśvedevas.	Paṅkti. 8 Mahābṛhatī. Yavamadhyā 19 Triṣṭup.
106	Kutsa.	The same.	Jagatī. 7 Triṣṭup.
107	The same.	....	Triṣṭup.
108	....	Indra-Agni.	The same.
109	....	The same.	....
110	....	Ṛbhus.	Jagatī. 8 and 9 Triṣṭup.
111	....	The same.	Jagatī. 5 Triṣṭup.
112	Kutsa.	Heaven and Earth. Aśvins. Agni.	Jagatī. 24 and 25 Triṣṭup.
113	....	Uṣas. Uṣas and Night.	Triṣṭup.
114	....	Rudra	Jagatī. 10 and 11 Triṣṭup.
115	....	Sūrya.	Triṣṭup.
116	Kakṣīvān.	Aśvins.	The same.
117	The same.	The same.	....
118	....	....	....
119	....	....	Jagatī.
120	....		1, 10-12 Gāyatrī. 2 Kakup. 3 Kavirāj. 4 Naṣṭarūpī. 5 Tanuśirā. 6 Uṣṇih. 7 Viṣṭārabṛhatī. 8 Kṛti. 9 Virāj.
121	....	Viśvedevas or Indra.	Triṣṭup.
122	....	Viśvedevas	Triṣṭup. 5 and 6 Virāḍrūpā.
123	....	Uṣas.	Triṣṭup.
124	....	The same.	Triṣṭup.
125	....	Svanaya.	Triṣṭup 4, 5 Jagatī.
126	Kakṣīvān, Bhāvayavya Romaśā.	Bhāvayavya. Romaśā.	Triṣṭup. 6 and 7 Anuṣṭup.
127	Parucchepa.	Agni.	Atyaṣṭi 6 Atidhṛti.
128	The same	The same.	Atyaṣṭi.

Hymn.	Ṛṣi.	Deity.	Metre.
129	The same	Indra. Indu.	Atyaṣṭi. 8, 9 Atiśakvarī. 11 Aṣṭi.
130	....	Indra.	Atyaṣṭi. 10 Triṣṭup.
131	....	The same.	Atyaṣṭi.
132	....	Indra. Indra and Parvata.	The same.
133	....	Indra.	Triṣṭup. 2-4 Anuṣṭup. 5 Gāyatrī. 6 Dhṛti. 7 Atyaṣṭi.
134	....	Vāyu.	Atyaṣṭi. 6 Aṣṭi.
135	....	Vāyu. Vāyu and Indra.	Atyaṣṭi. 7, 8 Aṣṭi.
136	....	Mitra and Varuṇa.	Atyaṣṭi. 7 Triṣṭup.
137	....	Mitra and Varuṇa.	Atiśakvarī
138	....	Pūṣan	Atyaṣṭi.
139	....	Viśvedevas. Mitra and Varuṇa. Aśvins. Indra. Agni. Maruts. Indra and Agni. Bṛhaspati.	Atyaṣṭi. 9 Bṛhati. 11 Triṣṭup.
140	Dīrghatamas.	Agni.	Jagatī. 10 Triṣṭup or Jagatī. 12, 13 Triṣṭup.
141	....	The same.	Jagatī. 12, 13 Triṣṭup.
142	....	Āpris. Indra. Agni.	Anuṣṭup.
143	....	Agni.	Jagatī 8 Triṣṭup.
144	....	The same.	Jagatī.
145	....	....	Jagatī. 5 Triṣṭup.
146	....	....	Triṣṭup.
147	....	....	The same.
148	....	....	....
149	....	....	Virāj.
150	....	....	Uṣṇih.
151	....	Mitra. Mitra and Varuṇa.	Jagatī.
152	....	Mitra and Varuṇa.	Triṣṭup.
153	....	The same.	The same.
154	....	Viṣṇu.	....
155	....	Viṣṇu and Indra. Viṣṇu.	Jagatī.
156	....	Viṣṇu.	The same.
157	....	Aśvins.	Jagatī. 5, 6 Triṣṭup.
158	....	The same.	Triṣṭup. 6 Anuṣṭup.
159	....	Heaven and Earth.	Jagatī.
160	....	The same.	The same.

Hymn.	Ṛṣi.	Deity.	Metre.
161	The same	Ṛbhus.	Jagatī. 14 Triṣṭup.
162	....	Eulogy of the Horse.	Triṣṭup. 3, 6 Jagatī.
163	....	The same.	Triṣṭup.
164	....	Viśvedevas. Vāk. Waters. Soma. Agni. Sūrya. Vāyu. Time. Sarasvatī. Sādhyas. Sarasvān or Sūrya.	Triṣṭup. 12, 15, 23, 29, 36, 41 Jagatī. 42 Prastārapaṅkti 51 Anuṣṭup.
165	Indra Maruts. Agastya.	Indra.	Triṣṭup.
166	Agastya.	Maruts.	Jagatī. 14, 15 Triṣṭup.
167	The same	Indra. Maruts.	Triṣṭup.
168	....	Maruts.	Jagatī 8-10 Triṣṭup.
169	....	Indra.	Triṣṭup. 2 Virāj.
170	Indra-Agastya.	Indra.	1 Bṛhatī. 2-4 Anuṣṭup. 5 Triṣṭup.
171	Agastya.	Maruts. Indra.	Triṣṭup.
172	The same.	Maruts.	Gāyatrī.
173	....	Indra.	Triṣṭup.
174	....	The same	Triṣṭup.
175	....	....	Anuṣṭup. 1 Skandhogrīvī. 6 Triṣṭup.
176	....	....	Anuṣṭup. 6 Triṣṭup
177	....	....	Triṣṭup.
178	....	....	The same.
179	Lopāmudrā Agastya. Pupil.	Rati (Pleasure).	Triṣṭup. 5 Bṛhatī.
180	Agastya.	Aśvins.	Triṣṭup.
181	The same.	The same.	The same.
182	....	....	Jagatī. 6, 8 Triṣṭup.
183	....	....	Triṣṭup.
184	....	....	The same.
185	....	Heaven and Earth.	....
186	....	Viśvedevas.	....
187	....	Praise of Food.	1 Anuṣṭubgarbhā. 2, 4, 8, 10 Gāyatrī. 3, 5, 6, 7 Anuṣṭup or Bṛhatī.
188	....	Āprīs.	Gāyatrī
189	....	Agni.	Triṣṭup.
190	The same	Bṛhaspati	The same
191	....	Water. Grass. Sūrya.	Anuṣṭup. 10-12 Mahāpaṅkti. 13 Mahābṛhatī.

BOOK II.

Hymn.	Ṛṣi.	Deity.	Metre.
1	Gṛtsamada.	Agni.	Jagatī.
2	The same	The same.	The same.
3	....	Āprīs.	Triṣṭup. 7 Jagatī.
4	Somāhuti.	Agni.	Triṣṭup.
5	The same	The same.	Anuṣṭup.
6	....	....	Gāyatrī.
7	....	....	The same.
8	Gṛtsamada.	....	Gāyatrī 6 Anuṣṭup.
9	The same.	Agni.	Triṣṭup.
10	....	The same	The same
11	....	Indra.	Virāṭsthānā Triṣṭup. 21 Triṣṭup.
12	....	The same.	Triṣṭup.
13	....	....	Jagatī. 13 Triṣṭup.
14	....	....	Triṣṭup.
15	....	....	The same.
16	....	....	Jagatī. 9 Triṣṭup.
17	....	....	Jagatī. 8, 9 Triṣṭup.
18	....	....	Triṣṭup.
19	....	....	The same.
20	....	....	Triṣṭup. 3 Virāḍrūpā.
21	....	....	Jagatī. 6 Triṣṭup.
22	....	....	Aṣṭi. 2,3 Atiśakvarī. 4 Atiśakvarī or Aṣṭi.
23	....	Brahmaṇaspati. Bṛhaspati.	Jagatī. 15, 19 Triṣṭup.
24	....	Brahmaṇaspati. Brahmaṇaspati and Indra.	Jagatī. 12, 16 Triṣṭup.
25	....	Brahmaṇaspati.	Jagatī.
26	....	The same.	The same.
27	Kūrma. Gṛtsamada's son, or Gṛtsamada.	Ādityas	Triṣṭup.
28	The same.	Varuṇa.	The same.

Hymn.	Ṛṣi.	Deity.	Metre.
29	The same	Viśvedevas.	....
30	Gṛtsamada.	Indra. Indra and Soma. Sarasvatī. Bṛhaspati. Maruts.	Triṣṭup. 15 Jagatī.
31	The same.	Viśvedevas.	Jagatī. 7 Triṣṭup.
32	....	Heaven and Earth. Indra or Tvaṣṭar. Rākā. Sinīvālī	Jagatī. 6-8 Anuṣṭup.
33	....	Rudra.	Triṣṭup.
34	....	Maruts.	Jagatī. 15 Triṣṭup.
35	....	Apāṁnapāt.	Triṣṭup.
36	....	Ṛtus.	Jagatī.
37	....	The same.	The same.
38	....	Savitar.	Triṣṭup.
39	....	Aśvins.	Triṣṭup.
40	....	Soma and Pūṣan. Aditi.	The same.
41	....	Vāyu. Indra and Vāyu. Mitra and Varuṇa. Aśvins. Indra. Viśvedevas. Sarasvatī.	Gāyatrī. 16, 17 Anuṣṭup. 18 Bṛhatī
42	....	The Kapiñjala.	Triṣṭup.
43	....	The same.	1-3 Jagatī. 2 Atiśakvarī or Aṣṭi.

BOOK III.

Hymn.	Ṛṣi.	Deity.	Metre.
1	Viśvāmitra.	Agni.	Triṣṭup.
2	The same.	Vaiśvānara.	Jagati.
3	....	The same.	The same.
4	....	Āprīs.	Triṣṭup.
5	....	Agni.	The same.
6	....	The same.	....
7	Viśvāmitra.	Agni.	....
8	The same.	Yūpa. Viśvedevas.	Triṣṭup. 3, 7 Anuṣṭup.
9	....	Agni.	Bṛhatī. 9 Triṣṭup.
10	....	The same.	Uṣṇih.
11	....	....	Gāyatrī.
12	....	Indra and Agni.	The same.
13	Ṛṣabha.	Agni.	Anuṣṭup.
14	The same.	The same.	Triṣṭup.
15	Utkīla.	....	The same.
16	The same.	....	Bṛhatī and Satobṛhatī.
17	Kata.	....	Triṣṭup.
18	The same.	....	The same.
19	Gāthin.	....	....
20	The same.	Viśvedevas. Agni.	....
21	....	Agni.	1,4 Triṣṭup 2,3 Anuṣṭup. 5 Virāḍrūpā Satobṛhatī.
22	....	The same.	Triṣṭup. 4 Anuṣṭup.
23	Devaśravas and Devavāta.	....	Triṣṭup. 3 Satobṛhatī.
24	Viśvāmitra.	....	Gāyatrī. 1 Anuṣṭup.
25	The same.	Agni. Agni and Indra.	Virāj.
26	....	Vaiśvānara. Agni. Maruts.	1-6 Jagatī. 7-9 Triṣṭup.
27	....	Agni.	Gāyatrī.
28	....	The same.	1, 2, 6 Gāyatrī. 3 Uṣṇih. 4 Triṣṭup. 5 Jagatī.
29	....	....	Triṣṭup. 1, 4, 10, 12 Anuṣṭup. 6. 11, 14, 15 Jagatī.
30	....	Indra.	Triṣṭup.
31	....	The same.	The same.
32	....	....	....
33	Viśvāmitra. The Rivers.	The Rivers. Viśvāmitra Indra.	Triṣṭup. 13 Anuṣṭup.
34	Viśvāmitra.	Indra.	Triṣṭup.
35	The same.	The same.	The same.
36	....	....	....
37	....	....	Gāyatrī. 11 Anuṣṭup.
38	Prajāpati or Viśvāmitra.	Indra.	Triṣṭup.
39	Viśvāmitra.	The same.	The same.
40	The same.	....	Gāyatrī.
41	....	....	The same.
42	....	....	....
43	....	....	Triṣṭup.
44	....	....	Bṛhatī.

Hymn.	Ṛṣi.	Deity.	Metre.
45	The same	The same	The same.
46	....	....	Triṣṭup.
47	....	....	The same.
48	....	....	....
49	....	....	....
50	....	....	....
51	....	....	1-3 Jagatī. 4-9 Triṣṭup. 10-12 Gāyatrī.
52	....	....	1-4 Gāyatrī 5, 7, 8 Triṣṭup. 6 Jagatī.
53	....	Indra, Parvata, Vāk.	Triṣṭup. 10, 16 Jagatī. 13 Gāyatrī. 12, 20, 22 Anuṣṭup. 18 Bṛhatī.
54	Prajāpati.	Viśvedevas.	Triṣṭup.
55	The same.	The same.	The same.
56	....	....	....
57	Viśvāmitra.	....	....
58	The same.	Aśvins.	....
59	....	Mitra.	Triṣṭup. 6-9 Gāyatrī.
60	....	Ṛbhus. Indra.	Jagatī.
61	....	Uṣas (Dawn).	Triṣṭup.
62	....	Indra and Varuṇa. Bṛhaspati. Pūṣan. Savitar. Soma. Mitra and Varuṇa.	1-3 Triṣṭup. 4-18 Gāyatrī.

BOOK IV.

Hymn.	Ṛṣi.	Deity.	Metre.
1	Vāmadeva.	Agni. Varuṇa.	Triṣṭup. 1 Aṣṭi. 2 Atijagatī. 3 Dhṛti.
2	The same.	Agni.	Triṣṭup.
3	....	The same.	The same.
4	....	Agni Rakṣohā.	....
5	....	Agni Vaiśvānara.	....
6	....	Agni.	....
7	....	The same.	1 Jagatī. 2-6 Anuṣṭup. 7-11 Triṣṭup.
8	Vāmadeva.	Agni.	Gāyatrī.
9	The same.	The same.	The same.
10	The same	The same	Padapaṅkti. 5 Mahāpadapaṅkti. 8 Uṣṇih.
11	....	....	Triṣṭup.
12	....	....	The same.
13	....	....	....
14	....	....	....
15	....	Agni. Somaka. Aśvins.	Gāyatrī.
16	....	Indra	Triṣṭup.
17	....	The same.	Triṣṭup. 15 Ekapadā Virāj.
18	Indra. Aditi. Vāmadeva.	Indra. Aditi. Vāmadeva.	Triṣṭup.
19	Vāmadeva.	Indra.	The same.
20	The same.	The same.	....
21	....	....	....
22	....	....	....
23	....	....	....
24	....	....	Triṣṭup. 10 Anuṣṭup.
25	....	....	Triṣṭup
26	....	Indra The Falcon.	The same.
27	....	The Falcon.	Triṣṭup. 3 Śakvarī.
28	....	Indra and Soma.	Triṣṭup.
29	....	Indra.	The same.
30	....	Indra and Uṣas.	Gāyatrī. 8, 24, Anuṣṭup.
31	....	Indra	Gāyatrī. 3 Pādanicṛt.
32	....	Indra. Indra's Horses.	Gāyatrī.
33	....	Ṛbhus.	Triṣṭup.
34	....	The same.	The same.
35	....	....	....
36	....	....	Jagatī. 9 Triṣṭup.
37	....	....	1-4 Triṣṭup. 5-8 Anuṣṭup.
38	....	Heaven and Earth. Dadhikrās.	Triṣṭup.
39	....	Dadhikrās.	Triṣṭup. 6 Anuṣṭup.
40	....	Dadhikrās. Sūrya.	1 Triṣṭup. 2-5 Jagatī.
41	....	Indra and Varuṇa.	Triṣṭup.
42	Trasadasyu.	Trasadasyu. Indra and Varuṇa.	The same.
43	Purumīḷha & Ajamīḷha.	Aśvins.	....

Hymn.	Ṛṣi.	Deity.	Metre.
44	The same	The same.	The same
45	Vāmadeva.	....	Jagatī. 7 Triṣṭup.
46	Vāmadeva	Vāyu. Indra and Vāyu.	Gāyatrī.
47	The same	The same.	Anuṣṭup.
48	....	Vāyu.	The same.
49	....	Indra and Bṛhaspati.	Gāyatrī.
50	....	Bṛhaspati. Indra and Bṛhaspati.	Triṣṭup. 10 Jagatī.
51	....	Uṣas (Dawn).	Triṣṭup.
52	....	The same.	Gāyatrī.
53	....	Savitar.	Jagatī.
54	....	The same.	Jagatī. 6 Triṣṭup.
55	....	Viśvedevas.	Triṣṭup. 8-10 Gāyatrī.
56	....	Heaven and Earth.	Triṣṭup. 5-7 Gāyatrī.
57	....	Kṣetrapati. Śuna. Śuna and Sīra. Sītā	1, 4, 6, 7 Anuṣṭup. 2. 3, 8Triṣṭup. 5 Pura-uṣṇih.
58	....	Agni, or Sūrya, or Waters, or Cows, or Ghṛta.	Triṣṭup. 11 Jagatī.

BOOK V.

Hymn.	Ṛṣi.	Deity.	Metre.
1	Budha and Gaviṣṭhira	Agni.	Triṣṭup.
2	Kumāra or Vṛśa	The same.	Triṣṭup. 12 Śakvarī.
3	Vasuśruta	Agni. Maruts. Rudra and Viṣṇu.	Triṣṭup.
4	The same	Agni.	The same.
5	....	Āprīs.	Gāyatrī.
6	....	Agni.	Paṅkti.
7	Iṣa	The same.	Anuṣṭup. 10 Paṅkti.
8	The same	....	Jagatī.
9	Gaya	....	Anuṣṭup. 5, 7 Paṅkti.
10	The same	....	Anuṣṭup. 4, 7 Paṅkti.
11	Sutambhara	....	Jagatī.
12	The same	....	Triṣṭup.
13	....	....	Gāyatrī.
14	....	....	The same.
15	Dharuṇa	The same	Triṣṭup.
16	Pūru	....	Anuṣṭup. 5 Paṅkti.
17	The same	....	The same.
18	Dvita	....	....
19	Vavri	....	1, 2 Gāyatrī 3, 4 Anuṣṭup. 5 Virāḍrūpā.
20	Prayasvats	....	Anuṣṭup. 4 Paṅkti.
21	Sasa	Agni.	Anuṣṭup. 4 Paṅkti.
22	Viśvasāman	The same.	The same.
23	Dyumna Viśvacarṣaṇi	....	....
24	Gaupāyanas or Laupāyanas	....	Dvipadā Virāj.
25	Vasūyus	....	Anuṣṭup.
26	The same	Agni. Viśvedevas.	Gāyatrī.
27	Tryaruṇa Trasadasyu, and Aśvamedha, or Atri	Agni. Indra and Agni.	Triṣṭup. 4-6 Anuṣṭup.
28	Viśvavārā	Agni.	1, 3 Triṣṭup. 2 Jagatī 4 Anuṣṭup. 5, 6 Gāyatrī.
29	Gaurivīti	Indra. Indra or Uśanā.	Triṣṭup.
30	Babhru	Indra.	The same.
31	Avasyu	The same.	....
32	Gāṭu	....	....
33	Saṁvaraṇa	....	....
34	The same	....	Jagatī. 9Triṣṭup.
35	Prabhūvasu	....	Anuṣṭup 8 Paṅkti.
36	The same	....	Triṣṭup. 3 Jagatī.
37	Atri Bhauma	....	Triṣṭup.
38	The same	....	Anuṣṭup.
39	....	....	Anuṣṭup. 5 Paṅkti.
40	....	Indra. Sūrya. Atri.	1, 3 Uṣṇih. 4 Triṣṭup. 5-9 Anuṣṭup. 6-8 Triṣṭup.
41	....	Viśvedevas.	Triṣṭup. 16, 17 Atijagatī. 20 Ekapadā Virāj.
42	....	Viśvedevas. Rudra.	Triṣṭup. 17 Ekapadā Virāj. Triṣṭup. 16 Ekapadā Virāj.

Hymn.	Ṛṣi.	Deity.	Metre.
43	The same	Viśvedevas.	Triṣṭup.
44	Avatsāra and others	The same.	Jagatī. 14, 15 Triṣṭup.
45	Sadāpṛṇa	....	Triṣṭup.
46	Pratikṣatra	Viśvedevas. Consorts of the Gods.	Jagatī. 2, 8 Triṣṭup.
47	Pratiratha	Viśvedevas.	Jagatī.
48	Pratibhānu	The same.	Triṣṭup.
49	Pratiprabha	....	Anuṣṭup. 5 Paṅkti.
50	Svasti	....	1-4 Gāyatrī 5-10 Uṣṇih. 11-13 Jagatī or Triṣṭup. 14, 15 Anuṣṭup.
51	The same	....	....
52	Śyāvāśva.	Maruts.	Anuṣṭup. 6, 16, 17 Paṅkti.
53	The same.	The same.	1, 5, 10, 11, 15 Kakup. 2 Bṛhatī. 3 Anuṣṭup. 4 Pura-uṣṇih. 6, 7, 9, 13, 14, 16 Satobṛhatī. 8, 12 Gāyatrī.
54	....	....	Jagatī. 14 Triṣṭup.
55	....	....	Jagatī. 10 Triṣṭup.
56	....	....	Bṛhatī. 3, 7 Satobṛhatī.
57	....	....	Jagatī. 7, 8 Triṣṭup.
58	....	....	Triṣṭup.
59	....	....	Jagatī. 8. Triṣṭup.
60	....	....	Triṣṭup. 7, 8 Jagatī.
61	....	Maruts and others.	Gāyatrī. 5 Anuṣṭup. 9 Satobṛhatī.
62	Śrutavid.	Mitra and Varuṇa.	Triṣṭup.
63	Arcanānas.	The same.	Jagatī.
64	The same.	....	Anuṣṭup. 7 Paṅkti.
65	Rātahavya.	....	Anuṣṭup. 6 Paṅkti.
66	The same.	....	Anuṣṭup.
67	Yajata.	....	The same.
68	The same.	....	Gāyatrī.
69	Urucakrī.	....	Triṣṭup.
70	The same.	....	Gāyatrī.
71	Bāhuvṛkta.	....	The same.
72	The same.	....	Uṣṇih.
73	Paura.	Aśvins.	Anuṣṭup.
74	The same.	The same.	The same.
75	Avasyu.	....	Paṅkti.
76	Atri Bhauma.	....	Triṣṭup.
77	The same.	....	The same.
78	Saptavadhri.	....	1-3 Uṣṇih. 4 Triṣṭup. Anuṣṭup.
79	Satyaśravas.	Uṣas (Dawn).	Paṅkti.
80	The same.	The same.	Triṣṭup.
81	Śyāvāśva.	Savitar.	Jagatī.
82	The same.	The same.	Gāyatrī. 1 Anuṣṭup.
83	Atri Bhauma.	Parjanya.	1, 5-8, 10 Triṣṭup. 2-4 Jagatī. 9 Anuṣṭup.
84	The same.	Pṛthivi.	Anuṣṭup.
85	....	Varuṇa.	Triṣṭup.
86	....	Indra and Agni.	Anuṣṭup. 6. Virāṭpūrvā.
87	Evayāmarut.	Maruts.	Atijagatī.

BOOK VI.

Hymn.	Ṛṣi.	Deity.	Metre.
1	Bharadvāja.	Agni.	Triṣṭup.
2	The same.	The same.	Anuṣṭup. 11 Śakvarī.
3	....	....	Triṣṭup.
4	....	....	The same.
5	....	....	....
6	....	....	....
7	....	Vaiśvānara Agni.	Triṣṭup. 7 Dvipadā Virāj.
8	....	The same.	Jagatī. 7 Triṣṭup.
9	....	....	Triṣṭup.
10	....	Agni.	Triṣṭup. 7 Dvipadā Virāj.
11	....	The same.	Triṣṭup.
12	....	....	....
13	....	....	....
14	....	....	Anuṣṭup. 6 Śakvarī.
15	Vītahavya, or Bharadvāja.	....	Jagatī. 3, 15 Śakvarī. 6 Atiśakvarī. 10-14, 16, 19 Triṣṭup. 17 Anuṣṭup. 18 Bṛhatī.

Hymn.	Ṛṣi.	Deity.	Metre.
16	Vītahavya, or Bharadvāja.	Agni	Gāyatrī. 1, 6 Vardhamānā 27, 47, 48 Anuṣṭup, 46 Triṣṭup.
17	The same.	Indra.	Triṣṭup. 15 Dvipadā Triṣṭup.
18	....	The same.	Triṣṭup.
19	....	....	The same.
20	....	....	Triṣṭup. 7 Virāj.
21	....	Indra. Viśvedevas.	Triṣṭup.
22	....	The same.	The same.
23	....	....	....
24	....	....	....
25	....	....	....
26	....	....	....
27	....	....	....
28	....	The Cows.	Triṣṭup. 2-4 Jagatī. Anuṣṭup.
29	....	Indra.	Triṣṭup.
30	....	The same.	The same.
31	Suhotra.	....	Triṣṭup. 4 Śakvarī.
32	The same.	....	Triṣṭup.
33	Śunahotra.	....	The same.
34	The same.	....	....
35	Nara.	....	....
36	The same.	....	....
37	Bharadvāja.	....	....
38	The same.	....	....
39	....	....	....
40	....	....	....
41	....	....	....
42	....	....	Anuṣṭup. 4 Bṛhatī.
43	....	....	Uṣṇih.
44	Śamyu.	....	Triṣṭup. 1-6 Anuṣṭup. 7-9 Virāj or Triṣṭup. 8 Virāj.
45	The same.	Indra. Bṛbu.	Gāyatrī. 29 Atinicṛt. 31 Pādanicṛt. 33 Anuṣṭup.
46	....	Indra.	Bṛhatī and Satobṛhatī alternately.
47	Garga.	Soma. Indra. Bṛhaspati. Prastoka. Chariot. Drum.	Triṣṭup. 19 Bṛhatī. 23 Anuṣṭup. 34 Gāyatrī. 25 Dvipadā. 27 Jagatī.
48	Śamyu.	Agni. Maruts. Pūṣan. Pṛśni and others.	1, 3, 5, 9, 14, 19, 20 Bṛhatī. 2, 4, 10, 12, 17 Satobṛhatī. 6, 8 Mahāsatobṛhatī. 7 Mahābṛhatī. 11, 16 Kakup. 13, 18 Pura-uṣṇih. 51 Atijagatī. 21 Yavamadhyā-mahābṛhatī. 22 Anuṣṭup.
49	Ṛjiśvan.	Viśvedevas.	Triṣṭup. 15 Śakvarī.
50	The same.	The same.	Triṣṭup.
51	....	....	Triṣṭup. 13-15 Uṣṇih. 16 Anuṣṭup.
52	....	....	Triṣṭup. 7-12 Gāyatrī. 14 Jagatī.
53	Bharadvāja.	Pūṣan.	Gāyatrī. 8 Anuṣṭup.
54	The same.	The same.	Gāyatrī.
55	....	....	The same.
56	....	....	Gāyatrī. 6 Anuṣṭup.
57	....	Pūṣan and Indra.	Gāyatrī.
58	....	Pūṣan.	Triṣṭup. 2 Jagatī.
59	....	Indra and Agni.	Bṛhatī. 7-10 Anuṣṭup.
60	....	The same.	Gāyatrī. 1-3, 13 Triṣṭup. 14 Bṛhatī. 15 Anuṣṭup.
61	....	Sarasvatī.	Gāyatrī. 1-3, 13 Jagatī. 14 Triṣṭup.
62	....	Aśvins.	Triṣṭup.
63	....	The same.	Triṣṭup. 1 Virāj. 11 Ekapadā Triṣṭup.
64	....	Uṣas (Dawn).	Triṣṭup.
65	....	The same.	The same.
66	....	Maruts.	....
67	....	Mitra and Varuṇa.	....
68	....	Indra and Varuṇa.	Triṣṭup. 9, 10 Jagatī.
69	....	Indra and Viṣṇu.	Triṣṭup.

Hymn.	Ṛṣi.	Deity.	Metre.
70	Bharadvāja.	Heaven and Earth.	Jagatī.
71	The same.	Savitar.	1-3 Jagatī. 4-6 Triṣṭup.
72	....	Indra and Soma.	Triṣṭup.
73	....	Bṛhaspati.	The same.
74	....	Soma and Rudra.	....
75	Pāyu.	Men, Weapons, and Implements of War. Armour. Bow. Bowstring. Quiver. Arrow. Charioteer. Horses. Chariot. Whip, etc. etc.	Triṣṭup. 6, 10 Jagatī. 12, 13, 15, 16, 19 Anuṣṭup. 17 Paṅkti.

BOOK VII

Hymn.	Ṛṣi.	Deity.	Metre.
1	Vasiṣṭha Maitrāvaruṇi.	Agni.	Virāj. 19-25 Triṣṭup.
2	The same.	Āprīs.	Triṣṭup.
3	....	Agni.	The same.
4	....	The same.	....
5	....	Vaiśvānara Agni.	....
6	....	The same.	....
7	....	Agni.	....
8	....	The same.	....
9	....	....	....
10	....	....	....
11	....	....	....
12	....	....	....
13	....	Vaiśvānara Agni.	....
14	....	Agni.	I Bṛhatī. 2, 3 Triṣṭup.
15	....	The same.	Gāyatrī.
16	....	....	Bṛhatī and Satobṛhatī alternately.
17	....	....	Dvipadā Triṣṭup.
18	....	Indra. Munificence of Sudās (22-25).	Triṣṭup.
19	....	Indra.	The same.
20	....	The same.	....
21	....	....	....
22	....	....	Virāj. 9 Triṣṭup.
23	....	....	Triṣṭup.

Hymn.	Ṛṣi.	Deity.	Metre.
24	Vasiṣṭha. Maitrāvaruṇi	Indra.	Triṣṭup.
25	The same.	The same.	The same.
26	....	....	....
27	....	....	....
28	....	....	....
29	....	....	....
30	Vasiṣṭha.	Indra.	Triṣṭup.
31	The same.	The same.	Gāyatrī. 10-12 Virāj.
32	Vasiṣṭha. Śakti Vāsiṣṭha	....	Bṛhatī and Satobṛhatī alternately. 3 Dvipadā Virāj.
33	Vasiṣṭha. His sons (10-14).	Vasiṣṭha's sons. Vasiṣṭha (10-14).	Triṣṭup.
34	Vasiṣṭha.	Viśvedevas. Ahi-Ahibudhnya.	Dvipadā. 22-25 Triṣṭup.
35	The same.	Viśvedevas.	Triṣṭup.
36	....	The same.	The same.
37	....	....	....
38	....	Savitar. Savitar or Bhaga. Vājins (7-8).	....
39	....	Viśvedevas.	....
40	....	The same.	....
41	....	Various (1) Bhaga, Uṣas.	Triṣṭup. 1 Jagatī.
42	....	Viśvedevas.	Triṣṭup.
43	....	The same.	The same.
44	....	Various (1) Dadhikrās.	Triṣṭup. 1 Jagatī.
45	....	Savitar.	Triṣṭup.
46	....	Rudra.	Jagatī. 4 Triṣṭup.
47	....	Waters.	Triṣṭup.
48	....	Ṛbhus. Ṛbhus or Viśvedevas.	The same.
49	....	Waters.	....
50	....	Mitra and Varuṇa. Agni Viśvedevas. Praise of Rivers.	Jagatī. 4 Atijagatī or Śakvarī.
51	....	Ādityas.	Triṣṭup.
52	....	The same.	The same.
53	....	Heaven and Earth.	....

Hymn	Ṛṣi.	Deity.	Metre.
54	Vasiṣṭha	Vāstoṣpati.	Triṣṭup.
55	....	Vāstoṣpati. Indra.	1 Gāyatrī. 2-4 Upariṣṭād-bṛhatī 5-8 Anuṣṭup.
56	....	Maruts.	1-11 Dvipadā Virāj. 12-25 Triṣṭup.
57	....	The same.	Triṣṭup.
58	....	....	The same.
59	....	Maruts. Rudra (12).	1, 3, 5 Bṛhatī. 2, 4, 6 Satobṛhatī. 7, 8 Triṣṭup. 9-11 Gāyatrī. 12 Anuṣṭup.
60	....	Sūrya. Mitra and Varuṇa.	Triṣṭup.
61	....	Mitra and Varuṇa.	The same.
62	....	Sūrya. Mitra and Varuṇa.	....
63	....	The same.	....
64	....	Mitra and Varuṇa.	....
65	....	The same.	....
66	....	Mitra and Varuṇa. Ādityas. Sūrya.	Gāyatrī 10-15 Bṛhatī and Satobṛhatī alternately. 16 Pura-uṣṇih.
67	....	Aśvins.	Triṣṭup.
68	....	The same.	Virāj. 8,9 Triṣṭup.
69	....	....	Triṣṭup.
70	....	....	The same.
71	....	....	....
72	....	....	....
73	....	....	....
74	....	....	Bṛhatī and Satobṛhatī alternately.
75	....	Uṣas or Dawn.	Triṣṭup.
76	....	The same.	The same.
77	....	....	....
78	....	....	....
79	....	....	....
80	....	....	....
81	....	....	Bṛhatī and Satobṛhatī alternately.
82	....	Indra and Varuṇa.	Jagatī.
83	....	The same.	The same.
84	Vasiṣṭha	Indra & Varuṇa	Triṣṭup.
85	....	....	The same
86	....	Varuṇa.	....
87	....	The same.	....
88	....	....	....
89	....	....	Gāyatrī. 5 Jagatī.
90	....	Vāyu. Indra and Vāyu.	Triṣṭup.
91	....	The same.	The same.
92	....	....	....
93	....	Indra and Agni.	....
94	....	The same.	Gāyatrī. 12 Anuṣṭup.
95	....	Sarasvatī. Sarasvān.	Triṣṭup.
96	....	The same.	1 Bṛhatī. 2 Satobṛhati. 3 Prastārapaṅkti 4-6 Gāyatrī.
97	....	Indra. Bṛhaspati. Indra and Brahmaṇaspati. Indra and Bṛhaspati.	Triṣṭup.
98	....	Indra. Indra and Bṛhaspati.	The same.
99	Vasiṣṭha.	Viṣṇu. Indra and Viṣṇu.	....
100	The same.	Viṣṇu.	....
101	....	Parjanya.	....
102	....	The same.	1,3 Gāyatrī. 2 Pādanicṛt,
103	....	Frogs.	Triṣṭup. I Anuṣṭup.
104	....	Indra and Soma. Indra. Soma. Agni. The Gods. Press-stones. Maruts. Vasiṣṭha's Prayer. Earth and Firmament.	Triṣṭup. 1-6, 18, 21. 23 Jagatī 7 Jagatī or Triṣṭup. 25 Anuṣṭup.

BOOK VIII

Hymn	Ṛṣi.	Deity.	Metre.
1	Pragātha Kāṇva (1,2), Medhātithi and Medhyātithi (3-29), Āsaṅga (30-33), Śāśvatī (34).	Indra. Āsaṅga's Munificence, Āsaṅga.	Bṛhatī. 2, 4 Satobṛhatī. 33, 34 Triṣṭup.

Hymn.	Ṛṣi.	Deity.	Metre.
2	Medhātithi and Priya-Medha. Medhātithi (41-42).	Indra. Vibhindhu's Munificence.	Gāyatrī. 28 Anuṣṭup.1
3	Medhyātithi.	Indra. Pākasthāman's Munificence.	Bṛhatī and Satobṛhatī alternately. 21 Anuṣṭup 22, 23 Gāyatrī. 24 Bṛhatī.
4	Devātithi.	Indra. Indra or Pūṣan. Kuruṅga's Munificence.	Bṛhatī and Satobṛhatī alternately. 21 Pura-uṣṇih.
5	Brahmātithi.	Aśvins. Kaśu's Munificence.	Gāyatrī. 37, 38 Bṛhatī. 35 Anuṣṭup. Gāyatrī.
6	Vatsa.	Indra. Tirindira's Munificence.	Gāyatrī.
7	Punarvatsa.	Maruts.	The same.
8	Sadhvaṁsa.	Aśvins.	Anuṣṭup.
9	Śaśakarṇa.	The same.	1, 4, 6, 14, 15, Bṛhatī. 2, 3, 20, 21, Gāyatrī. 5 Kakup. 7, 9, 13, 16, 19, Anuṣṭup. 10 Triṣṭup. 11 Virāj 12 Jagatī.
10	Pragātha.	....	1, 5 Bṛhatī. 2 Madhyejyotis 3 Anuṣṭup. 4 Āstārapaṅkti. 6 Satobṛhatī.
11	Vatsa.	Agni.	Gāyatrī. 1 Pratiṣṭhā 2 Vardhamānā. 10 Triṣṭup.
12	Parvata.	Indra.	Uṣṇih.
13	Nārada.	The same.	The same.
14	Gosūktin and Aśvasūktin.	....	Gāyatrī.
15	The same.	....	Uṣṇih.
16	Irimbiṭhi.	....	Gāyatrī.
17	The same.	....	Gāyatrī. 14 Bṛhatī. 15 Satobṛhatī
18	....	Ādityas. Aśvins. Agni. Sūrya, Vāta or Wind.	Uṣṇih.

Hymn.	Ṛṣi.	Deity.	Metre.
9	Sobhari.	Agni. Ādityas. Trasadasyu's Munificence.	6, 28-33 Kakup and Satobṛhatī alternately. 27 Dvipadā Virāj. 34 Uṣṇih. 15 Satobṛhatī. 36 Kakup. 17 Paṅkti.
20	The same.	Maruts.	Kakup and Satobṛhatī alternately.
21	....	Indra. Citra's Munificence.	The same.
22	....	Aśvins.	7 Bṛhatī and Satobṛhatī alternately. 8 Anuṣṭup. 9, 10, 13-18 Kakup and Satobṛhatī alternately. 11 Kakup. 12 Madhyejyotis.
23	Viśvamanas.	Agni.	Uṣṇih.
24	The same.	Indra. A Prince's Munificence.	Uṣṇih. 30 Anuṣṭup.
25	....	Mitra and Varuṇa Viśvedevas.	Uṣṇih. 23 Uṣṇiggarbhā.
26	....	Aśvins. Vāyu.	Uṣṇih. 16, 19, 21, 25 Gāyatrī. 20 Anuṣṭup.
27	Manu Vaivasvata.	Viśvedevas.	Bṛhatī and Satobṛhatī alternately.
28	The same.	The same.	Gāyatrī. 4 Pura-uṣṇih.
29	Manu, or Kaśyapa.	....	Dvipadā Virāj.
30	Manu.	....	1 Gāyatrī. 2 Pura-uṣṇih. 3 Bṛhatī 4 Anuṣṭup.
31	The same.	The Yajamāna and his Wife. Their Benediction.	Gāyatrī. 9. 14 Anuṣṭup. 10 Pādanicṛt. 15-18 Paṅkti.
32	Medhātithi.	Indra.	Gāyatrī.
33	Medhyātithi.	The same.	Bṛhatī. 16-18 Gāyatrī. 19 Anuṣṭup.
34	Nīpātithi. The 1000 Vasurociṣas.	....	Anuṣṭup. 16-18 Gāyatrī

Hymn.	Ṛṣi.	Deity.	Metre.
35	Śyāvāśva.	Aśvins.	Upariṣṭājjyotis. 22-24 Paṅkti. 23 Mahābṛhatī.
36	The same.	Indra.	Śakvarī. 7 Mahāpaṅkti.
37	....	The same.	Mahāpaṅkti. 1 Atijagatī.
38	....	Indra and Agni.	Gāyatrī.
39	Nābhāka.	Agni.	Mahāpaṅkti.
40	The same.	Indra and Agni.	Mahāpaṅkti. 2 Śakvarī. 12 Triṣṭup.
41	....	Varuṇa.	Mahāpaṅkti.
42	Arcanānas, or Nābhāka.	Varuṇa, Aśvins.	1-3 Triṣṭup. 4-6 Anuṣṭup.
43	Virūpa.	Agni.	Gāyatrī.
44	The same.	The same.	The same.
45	Triśoka.	Agni and Indra. Indra.	....
46	Vaśa Aśvya.	Indra. Munificence of pṛthuśravas. Vāyu.	1 Pādanicṛt. 2-4, 6, 10, 23, 29, 33, Gāyatrī. 5 Kakup. 7, 11, 19, 25, 27 Bṛhatī. 8 Anuṣṭup. 9, 26, 28 Satobṛhatī. 12 Viparītā. 13 Caturviṁśatikā Dvipadā. 14 Pipīlikamadhyā Bṛhatī. 15 Kakup Nyaṅkuśirā. 16 Virāj. 17 Jagatī. 11 Upariṣṭādbṛhatī. 20 Viṣamapadā. 21, 22, 24, 32 Paṅkti. 30 Dvipadā Virāj. 31 Uṣṇih.
47	Trita Āptya.	Ādityas. Ādityas and Uṣas.	Mahāpaṅkti.
48	Pragātha.	Soma.	Triṣṭup. 5 Jagatī.
49	*Bharga.	Agni.	Bṛhatī and Satobṛhatī alternately.
50	The same.	Indra.	The same.

*Eleven must be added to the numbers of this and of all that follow in this Book to make them correspond with the numbers in Prof Max Müller's editions of the text.

Hymn.	Ṛṣi.	Deity.	Metre.
51	Pragātha.	Indra.	Paṅkti 7, 9 Bṛhatī.
52	The same.	Indra. The Gods.	Gāyatrī. 1, 4, 5, 7 Anuṣṭup. 12 Triṣṭup.
53	....	Indra	Gāyatrī.
54	....	The same.	The same.
55	Kali.	....	Bṛhatī and Satobṛhatī. alternately. 15 Anuṣṭup.
56	Matsya or Mānya.	Ādityas.	Gāyatrī.
57	Priyamedha.	Indra. Munificence of two Princes.	Gāyatrī. 1,4,7, 10 Anuṣṭup.
58	The same.	Indra. Viśvedevas Varuṇa	Anuṣṭup. 2 Uṣṇih. 4-6 Gāyatri. 11,16 Paṅkti. 17, 18 Bṛhatī.
59	Puruhanman.	Indra.	Bṛhatī and Satobṛhatī alternately. 7-12 Bṛhatī. 13 Uṣṇih. 14 Anuṣṭup. 15 Pura-uṣṇih.
60	Sudīti and Purumīḷha, or either of them	Agni.	Gāyatrī. 10-15 Bṛhatī and Satobṛhatī alternately.
61	Haryata.	The same.	Gāyatrī.
62	Gopavana, or Saptavadhri.	Aśvins.	The same.
63	Gopavana.	Agni-Śrutarvan's Munificence.	Gāyatrī. 1. 4, 7, 10, 13-15 Anuṣṭup.
64	Virūpa.	Agni.	Gāyatrī.
65	Kurusutī.	Indra.	The same.
66	The same.	The same.	Gāyatrī. 10 Bṛhatī. 11 Satobṛhatī.
67	....	....	Gāyatrī. 10 Bṛhatī.
68	Kṛtnu.	Soma.	Gāyatrī. 9 Anuṣṭup.
69	Ekadyū.	Indra. The Gods.	Gāyatrī. 10 Triṣṭup.
70	Kusīdin.	Indra.	Gāyatrī.
71	The same.	The same.	The same.
72	....	Viśvedevas.	....
73	Uśanā Kāvya	Agni.	....
74	Kṛṣṇa.	Aśvins.	....
75	Viśvaka.	The same.	Jagatī

Hymn.	Ṛṣi.	Deity.	Metre.
76	Dyumnīka or Priyamedha or Kṛṣṇa.	Aśvins.	Bṛhatī and Satobṛhatī alternately.
77	Nodhas.	Indra.	The same.
78	Nṛmedha and Purumedha.	The same.	1, 3, 7 Bṛhatī 2, 4 Satobṛhatī. 5, 6 Anuṣṭup.
79	The same.	....	Pragātha.
80	Apālā.	....	Anuṣṭup. 1. 2 Paṅkti.
81	Śrutakakṣa, or Sukakṣa.	....	Gāyatrī. 1 Anuṣṭup.
82	Sukakṣa.	Indra. Indra and Ṛbhus	Gāyatrī.
83	Vindu, or Pūtadakṣa.	Maruts.	The same.
84	Tiraścī.	Indra.	Anuṣṭup.
85	Dyutāna, or Tiraścī.	Indra. Maruts. Indra and Bṛhaspati.	Triṣṭup. 4 Virāj.
86	Rebha.	Indra.	Bṛhatī. 10, 13 Atijagatī. 11, 12 Upariṣṭādbṛhatī 14 Triṣṭup, 15 Jagatī.
87	Nṛmedha.	The same.	Uṣṇih. 7, 10, 11 Kakup. 9, 12 Pura-uṣṇih.
88	The same.	....	Pragātha.
89	Nema. Indra (45).	Indra. Vāk.	Triṣṭup. 6 Jagatī. 7-9 Anuṣṭup-
90	Jamadagni.	Mitra and Varuṇa. Ādityas. Aśvins. Vāyu. Sūrya Uṣas. Pavamāna. Cow.	1, 5, 7. 9, 11, 13 Bṛhatī, 2. 4, 6, 8, 10, 12 Satobṛhati. 3 Gāyatrī. 14-16 Triṣṭup.
91	Prayoga, or Agni Bārhaspatya, or Agni Gṛhapati, or Yaviṣṭha.	Agni.	Gāyatrī.
92	Sobharı.	Agni Agni and Maruts	

VĀLAKHILYA HYMNS*

Hymn.	Ṛṣi.	Deity.	Metre.
1	Praskaṇva.	Indra.	Bṛhatī and Satobṛhatī alternately.
2	Puṣṭigu.	Indra.	Bṛhatī and Satobṛhatī alternately.
3	Śruṣṭigu.	The same.	....
4	Āyu.	....	....
5	Medhya.	....	....
6	Mātariśvan.	Indra Viśvedevas.	....
7	Kṛṣa.	Praskaṇva's Munificence.	Gāyatrī. 3-5 Anuṣṭup.
8	Pṛṣadra.	The same. Agni and Sūrya.	Gāyatrī. 5 Paṅktī.
9	Medhya.	Aśvins.	Triṣṭup.
10	The same.	Viśvedevas. The Priests	The same.
11	Suparṇa.	Indra and Varuṇa.	Jagatī.

BOOK IX

Hymn.	Ṛṣi.	Deity.	Metre.
1	Madhucchandas.	Soma Pavamāna.	Gāyatrī.
2	Medhātithi.	The same.	The same.
3	Sunaḥśepa.	....	....
4	Hiraṇyastūpa.	....	....
5	Asita, or Devala.	Āprīs.	Gāyatrī. 8-11 Anuṣṭup.
6	The same.	Soma Pavamāna.	Gāyatrī.
7-24	....	The same.	The same.
25	Dṛḷhacyuta.	....	....
26	Idhmavāha.	....	....
27	Nṛmedha.	....	....
28	Priyamedha.	....	....
29	Nṛmedha.	....	....
30	Vindu.	....	....
31	Gotama.	....	....
32	Śyāvāśva.	....	....
33	Trita Āptya.	....	....
34	The same.	....	....
35	Prabhūvasu.	....	....
36	The same.	....	....
37	Rahūgaṇa.	....	....
38	The same.	....	....
39	Bṛhanmati.	....	....
40	The same.	....	....
41	Medhyātithi.	....	....

*These eleven hymns are numbered 49-59 in Prof. Max Müller's editions of the text.

Hymn.	Ṛṣi.	Deity.	Metre.
42	Medhyātithi.	Soma Pavamāna.	Gāyatrī.
43	The same.	The Same.	The same.
44	Ayāsya.	....	....
45	The same.	....	....
46	....	....	....
47	Kavi.	....	....
48	The same.	....	....
49	....	....	....
50	Ucathya.	....	....
51	The same.	....	....
52	....	....	....
53-60	Avatsāra.	....	....
61	Amahīyu.	....	....
62	Jamadagni.	....	....
63	Nidhruvi.	....	....
64	Kaśyapa.	....	....
65	Bhṛgu or Jamadagni.	....	....
66	The Vaikhānasas.	Soma Pavamāna. Agni.	Gāyatrī. Anuṣṭup.
67	Bharadvāja. Kaśyapa. Gotama Atri. Viśvāmitra. Jamadagni. Vasiṣṭha. Pavitra.	Pavamāna Soma. Pavamāna. Pūṣan. Agni Savitar. All Gods. Praise of Students.	Gāyatrī. 16-18 Dvipadā Gāyatrī. 27, 31, 32 Anuṣṭup. 30 Purauṣṇih.
68	Vatsaprī.	Soma Pavamāna.	Jagatī. 10 Triṣṭup.
69	Hiraṇyastūpa.	The same.	Jagatī. 9, 10 Triṣṭup.
70	Reṇu.	....	Jagatī. 10 Triṣṭup.
71	Ṛṣabha.	....	Jagatī 9 Triṣṭup.
72	Harimanta.	....	Jagatī.
73	Pavitra.	....	The same.
74	Kakṣīvān.	....	Jagatī. 8 Triṣṭup.
75	Kavi.	....	Jagatī.
76	The same.	....	The same.
77	....	....	....
78	....	....	....
79	....	....	....
80	Vasu.	....	....

Hymā.	Ṛṣi.	Deity.	Metre.
81	Vasu.	Soma Pavamāna.	Jagatī. 5 Triṣṭup.
82	The same.	The same.	The same.
83	Pavitra.	....	Jagatī.
84	Prajāpati.	....	The same.
85	Vena.	....	Jagatī. 11, 12, Triṣṭup.
86	The Akṛṣṭa Māṣas. The Sikata Nivāvaris. The Pṛśni Ajas. Atri. Gṛtsamada.	....	Jagatī.
87	Uśanā.	....	Triṣṭup.
88	The same.	....	The same.
89	....	....	....
90	Vasiṣṭha.	....	....
91	Kāśyapa.	....	....
92	The same.	....	....
93	Nodhas.	....	....
94	Kaṇva.	....	....
95	Praskaṇva.	....	....
96	Pratardana.	....	....
97	Vasiṣṭha. Indrapramati. Manyu. Upamanyu. Vyāghrapād. Śakti Karṇaśrut. Mṛlīka. Vasukra. Parāśara. Kutsa.	....	....
98	Ambarīṣa & Ṛjiśvan.	....	Anuṣṭup, 11 Bṛhatī.
99	The Rebhasūnus.	The same.	Anuṣṭup. 1 Bṛhatī.
100	The same.	....	Anuṣṭup.
101	Andhīgu. Yayāti. Nahuṣa.		Anuṣṭup. 2, 5 Gāyatrī.

Hymn.	Ṛṣi.	Deity.	Metre.
	Manu. Prajāpati.		
102	Trita Āptya.	Soma Pavamāna.	Uṣṇih.
103	Dvita Āptya.	The same.	The same.
104	Parvata and Nārada, or the Śikhaṇḍinīs (Apsaras).		....
105	Parvata and Nārada.	....	....
106	Agni. Cakṣus Manu.	....	....
107	Seven Ṛṣis.	....	Prāgātha. 3, 16 Dvipadā Virāj. 8, 10 Bṛhatī.
108	Gaurivīti Śakti Ūru Ṛjiśvan. Ūrdhva sadman. Kṛtayaśā. Ṛṇañcaya.	....	1-12 Kakup and Satobṛhatī alternately. 13. Gāyatrī Yavamadhyā. 14, 16 Satobṛhatī. 15 Kakup.
109	Agnis of Sacrifice.	....	Dvipadā Virāj.
110	Tryaruṇa and Trasadasyu.	....	1-3 Anuṣṭup Pipīlikāmadhyā. 4-9 Ūrdhvabṛhatī. 10-12 Virāj.
111	Anānata.	....	Atyaṣṭi.
112	Śiśu.	....	Paṅkti.
113	Kaśyapa.	....	The same.
114	The same.	....	....

BOOK X.

Hymn.	Ṛṣi.	Deity.	Metre.
1	Trita Āptya.	Agni.	Triṣṭup.
2	The same.	The same.	The same.
3	....	....	....
4	....	....	....
5	....	....	....
6	....	....	....
7	....	....	....
8	Triśiras.	Agni. Indra.	Triṣṭup
9	Triśiras, or Sindhudvīpa.	Waters.	Gāyatrī. 5 Vardhamānā. 7. Pratiṣṭhā. 8, 9 Anuṣṭup.
10	Yama. Yamī.	Yama. Yamī	Triṣṭup.
11	Havirdhānā Āgni.	Agni.	Jagatī 7-9 Triṣṭup.
12	The same.	The same.	Triṣṭup.
13	Vivasvān.	The Two Carts.	Triṣṭup. 5 Jagatī.
14	Yama.	Yama. The Deities mentioned. The Fathers. The Hounds, sons of Saramā.	Triṣṭup. 18, 14, 16 Anuṣṭup. 15 Bṛhatī.
15	Śaṅkha.	The Fathers.	Triṣṭup. 11 Jagatī.
16	Damana.	Agni.	Triṣṭup. 11-14 Anuṣṭup.
17	Devaśravas.	Saraṇyū. Pūṣan. Sarasvatī. Waters. Soma.	Triṣṭup 14 Anuṣṭup. 13 Anuṣṭup or Purastādbṛhatī.
18	Saṅkusuka.	Mṛtyu. Dhātar, Tvaṣṭar. The Pitṛmedha. Prajāpati.	Triṣṭup. 11 Prastārapaṅkti. 13 Jagatī. 14. Anuṣṭup.
19	Mathita. Bhṛgu, or Cyavana.	Waters, or Cows. Agni and Soma.	Anuṣṭup. 6 Gāyatrī.
20	Vimada or Vasukṛt.	Agni.	Gāyatrī. 1 Ekapadā Virāj. 2 Anuṣṭup. 9 Vīrāj. 10 Triṣṭup.
21	The same	The same.	Āstārapaṅkti.
22	....	Indra.	Purastādbṛhatī. 5, 7, 9 Anuṣṭup. 15 Triṣṭup.
23	....	The same.	Jagatī. 1, 7 Triṣṭup. 5 Abhisāriṇī.
24	....	Indra. Aśvins.	Āstārapaṅkti. 4-6 Anuṣṭup.
25	....	Soma.	Āstārapaṅkti.
26	....	Pūṣan.	Anuṣṭup. 1, 4 Uṣṇih.
27	Vasukra.	Indra.	Triṣṭup.
28	Vasukra's Wife. Indra. Vasukra.	Indra Vasukra.	The same.

Hymn.	Ṛṣi.	Deity.	Metre.
29	Vasukra.	Indra.	Triṣṭup.
30	Kavaśa.	Waters or Child of Waters.	The same.
31	The same.	Viśvedevas.	....
32	....	Indra.	1-5 Jagatī. 6-9 Triṣṭup.
33	....	Viśvedevas-Indra. Kuruśravaṇa. Upamaśravas.	1 Triṣṭup. 2 Bṛhatī. 3 Satobṛhatī. 4-9 Gāyatrī.
34	Kavaśa, or Akṣa.	Dice. Agriculture.	Triṣṭup. 7 Jagatī.
35	Luśa.	Viśvedevas.	Jagatī. 13, 14 Triṣṭup.
36	The same.	The same.	The same.
37	Abhitapas.	Sūrya.	Jagatī. 10 Triṣṭup.
38	Indra Muṣkavān.	Indra.	Jagatī.
39	Ghoṣā.	Aśvins.	Jagatī. 14 Triṣṭup.
40	The same.	The same.	Jagatī.
41	Suhastya.	....	The same.
42	Kṛṣṇa.	Indra.	Triṣṭup.
43	The same.	The same.	Jagatī. 10, 11 Triṣṭup.
44	....	....	Jagatī. 1-3, 10, 11 Triṣṭup.
45	Vatsaprī.	Agni.	Triṣṭup.
46	The same.	The same.	The same.
47	Saptagu.	Indra Vaikuṇṭha.	....
48	Indra Vaikuṇṭha.	The same.	Jagatī. 7, 10, 11 Triṣṭup.
49	The same.	....	Jagatī. 2, 11 Triṣṭup.
50	....	....	1, 2, 6, 7 Jagatī. 3, 4 Abhisāriṇī. 5 Triṣṭup.
51	Agni Saucīka.	Agni. Gods.	Triṣṭup.
52	The same.	Gods.	The same.
53	Agni Sauchīka. Gods.	Agni. Gods.	Triṣṭup. 6, 7, 9-11 Jagatī.
54	Bṛhaduktha.	Indra.	Triṣṭup.
55	The same.	The same.	The same.
56	....	Viśvedevas.	Triṣṭup. 4, 6 Jagatī.
57	Bandhu, Śrutabandhu. Viprabandhu.	The same.	Gāyatrī.
58	The same.	The Spirit.	Anuṣṭup.
59	....	Nirṛti. Soma. Asunīti. The Deities mentioned. Heaven and Earth. Indra.	Triṣṭup. 8 Paṅkti. 9 Mahāpaṅkti. 10. Paṅktyuttarā.
60	The Gaupāyanas and their Mother.	Asamāti. Indra. Subandhu's Recall to Life. The Hand.	Anuṣṭup. 1.5 Gāyatrī, 8. 9 Paṅkti.
61	Nābhānediṣṭha.	Viśvedevas.	Triṣṭup.
62	The same.	Viśedevas, or Aṅgirases. Viśvedevas. Sāvarṇi's Liberality.	1-4 Jagatī. 5, 8, 9 Anuṣṭup. 6 Bṛhatī. 7 Satobṛhatī. 10 Gāyatrī. 11 Triṣṭup.
63	Gaya.	Viśvedevas. Pathyā Svasti.	Jagatī. 16, 17 Triṣṭup. 15 Triṣṭup or Jagatī.
64	The same.	Viśvedevas.	Jagatī. 12, 16, 17 Triṣṭup.
65	Vasukarṇa.	The same.	Jagatī. 15 Triṣṭup.
66	The same.	....	The same.
67	Ayāsya.	Bṛhaspati.	Triṣṭup.
68	Ayāsya.	Bṛhaspati.	Triṣṭup.
69	Sumitra.	Agni.	Triṣṭup. 1, 2 Jagatī.
70	The same.	Āprīs.	Triṣṭup.
71	Bṛhaspati.	Jñānam.	Triṣṭup. 9 Jagatī.
72	Bṛhaspati, or Aditi	Gods.	Anuṣṭup.
73	Gaurivīti.	Indra.	Triṣṭup.
74	The same.	The same.	The same.
75	Sindhukṣit.	The Rivers.	Jagatī.
76	Jaratkarṇa.	The Press-stones.	The same.
77	Syūmaraśmi.	Maruts.	Triṣṭup. 5 Jagatī.
78	The same.	The same.	1, 3, 4, 8 Triṣṭup. 2, 5-7 Jagatī.
79	Agni, or Sapti	Agni.	Triṣṭup.
80	Agni.	The same.	The same.

Hymn	Ṛṣi.	Deity.	Metre.
81	Viśvakarman.	Viśvakarman.	Triṣṭup
82	The same.	The same.	The same
83	Manyu.	Manyu.	Triṣṭup. 1 Jagatī.
84	The same.	The same.	1-3 Triṣṭup. 4-7 Jagatī.
85	Sūryā.	Soma. Sūryā's Bridal. Gods. Soma and Arka. The Moon. Benedictions. Sūryā.	Anuṣṭup. 14, 19-21 23, 24, 26, 36, 37, 44 Triṣṭup. 18, 37, 43 Jagatī. 34 Urobṛhatī.
86	Indra. Indrāṇī. Vṛṣākapi.	Indra. Indrāṇī. Vṛṣākapi.	Paṅkti.
87	Pāyu.	Agni Rakṣohā.	Triṣṭup. 22, 25 Anuṣṭup.
88	Mūrdhanvan.	Sūrya and Vaiśvānara.	Triṣṭup.
89	Reṇu.	Indra and Soma.	The same.
90	Nārāyaṇa.	Puruṣa.	Anuṣṭup. 16 Triṣṭup.
91	Aruṇa.	Agni.	Jagatī. 15 Triṣṭup.
92	Śāryāta.	Viśvedevas.	Jagatī.
93	Tānva.	The same.	Prastārapaṅkti. 2, 3, 13 Anuṣṭup. 9 Paṅkti. 11 Nyaṅkusāriṇī. 15 Purastādbṛhatī.
94	Arbuda.	The Press-stones.	Jagatī. 5, 7, 14 Triṣṭup.
95	Purūravas. Urvaśī.	Urvaśī. Purūravas.	Triṣṭup.
96	Baru, or Sarvahari.	Indra's Horses.	Jagatī. 12, 13 Triṣṭup.
97	Bhiṣaj.	Medicinal Herbs.	Anuṣṭup.
98	Devāpi.	Gods.	Triṣṭup.
99	Vamra.	Indra.	The same.
100	Duvasyu.	Viśvedevas.	Jagatī. 12 Triṣṭup.
101	Budha.	Viśvedevas, or Priests.	Triṣṭup. 4, 6 Gāyatrī. 5 Bṛhatī 9, 12 Jagatī.
102	Mudgala.	Indra, or the Mace.	Triṣṭup, 1, 3, 12 Bṛhatī.
103	Apratiratha.	Indra. Bṛhaspati. Apvā Maruts.	Triṣṭup. 13 Anuṣṭup.
104	Aṣṭaka.	Indra.	Triṣṭup.
105	Durmitra or Sumitra.	The same.	Uṣṇih. 2, 7 Pipīlikamadhyā. 13 Triṣṭup.
106	Bhūtāṁśa.	Aśvins.	Triṣṭup,

Hymn.	Ṛṣi.	Deity.	Metre.
107	Divya, or Dakṣiṇā.	Guerdon.	Triṣṭup. 4 Jagatī.
108	Saramā. Paṇis.	Saramā. Paṇis.	Triṣṭup.
109	Juhū.	Viśvedevas	Triṣṭup. 6, 7 Anuṣṭup.
110	Jamadagni or Rāma.	Āprīs.	Triṣṭup.
111	Aṣṭrādaṁṣṭra.	Indra.	The same.
112	Nabhaḥprabhedana.	The same.	....
113	Śataprabhedana.	....	Jagatī. 10 Triṣṭup.
114	Sadhri or Gharma.	Viśvedevas.	Triṣṭup. 4 Jagatī.
115	Upastuta.	Agni.	Jagatī. 8 Triṣṭup. Śakvarī.
115	Agniyuta or Agniyūpa.	Indra.	Triṣṭup.
117	Bhikṣu.	Liberality.	Triṣṭup. 1, 2 Jagatī.
118	Urukṣaya.	Agni Rakṣohā.	Gāyatrī.
119	Lava.	Indra as Lava.	The same.
120	Bṛhaddiva.	Indra.	Triṣṭup.
121	Hiraṇyagarbha.	Ka.	The same.
122	Citramahā.	Agni.	Jagatī. 1, 5 Triṣṭup.
123	Vena.	Vena.	Triṣṭup.
124	Agni. Agnī, Varuṇa, and Soma.	Agni. Indra.	Triṣṭup. 7 Jagatī.
125	Vāk.	Vāk.	Triṣṭup. 2 Jagatī.
126	Kulmalabarhiṣa, or Aṁhomuc.	Viśvedevas.	Upariṣṭādbṛhatī. 8 Triṣṭup.
127	Kuśika or Rātri.	Night.	Gāyatrī.
128	Vihavya.	Viśvedevas.	Triṣṭup. 9 Jagatī.
129	Prajāpati Parameṣṭhin.	Creation.	Triṣṭup.
130	Yajña.	The same.	Triṣṭup. 1 Jagatī.

Hymn.	*Ṛṣi.*	*Deity.*	*Metre.*
131	Sukīrti.	Indra. Aśvins.	Triṣṭup. 4 Anuṣṭup.
132	Śakapūta.	Heaven and Earth, Aśvins. Mitra and Varuṇa.	1 Nyaṅkusāriṇī. 2, 6 Prastārapaṅkti. 3-5 Virādrūpā. 7 Mahāsatobṛhatī.
133	Sudās.	Indra.	1-3 Śakvarī. 4-6 Mahāpaṅkti. 7 Triṣṭup.
134	Māndhātar. Godhā.	The same.	Mahāpaṅkti. 7 Paṅkti.
135	Kumāra.	Yama.	Anuṣṭup.
136	Seven Munis: Jūti. Vātajūti. Vṛṣāṇaka. Etaśa. Ṛsyaśṛṅga.	The Keśins.	The same.
137	The Seven Ṛṣis.	Viśvedevas.	Anuṣṭup.
138	Aṅga.	Indra.	Jagatī.
139	Viśvāvasu.	Sūrya. Viśvāvasu.	Triṣṭup.
140	Agni Pāvaka.	Agni.	1 Viṣṭārapaṅkti. 2-4 Satobṛhatī. 5. Upariṣṭājjoytis. 6 Triṣṭup.
141	Agni Tāpasa.	Viśvedevas.	Anuṣṭup.
142	Jaritar. Droṇa. Sārisṛkva. Stambamitra.	Agni.	Triṣṭup. 1, 2 Jagatī. 7, 8 Anuṣṭup.
143	Atri.	Aśvins.	Anuṣṭup.
144	Suparṇa, Ūrdhvakṛśana.	Indra.	1, 3, 4 Gāyatrī. 2 Bṛhatī. 5 Satobṛhatī. 6 Viṣṭārapaṅkti.
145	Indrāṇī.	Removal of Rival.	Anuṣṭup. 6 Paṅkti.
146	Devamunī.	Araṇyānī.	Anuṣṭup.
147	Suvedas.	Indra.	Jagatī. 5 Triṣṭup.
148	Pṛthu Vainya.	The same.	Triṣṭup.
149	Arcan.	Savitar.	The same.
150	Mṛlīka.	Agni.	1-3 Bṛhatī. 4 Upariṣṭājjyotis or Jagatī. 5 Upariṣṭājjyotis.
151	Śraddhā.	Śraddhā (Faith).	Anuṣṭup.
152	Śāsa.	Indra.	Anuṣṭup
153	Indra's Mothers.	The same.	Gāyatrī.
154	Yamī.	New Life.	Anuṣṭup.
155	Śirimbiṭha.	Averting of Misfortune. Brahmaṇaspati. Viśvedevas.	The same.
156	Ketu.	Agni.	Gāyatrī.
157	Bhuvana, or Sādhana.	Viśvedevas.	Dvipadā Triṣṭup.
158	Cakṣus.	Sūrya.	Gāyatrī.
159	Śacī Paulomī.	Śacī Paulomī.	Anuṣṭup.
160	Pūraṇa.	Indra.	Triṣṭup.
161	Yakṣmanāśana.	Removal of Phthisis.	Triṣṭup. 5 Anuṣṭup.
162	Rakṣohā.	Against Miscarriage.	Anuṣṭup.
163	Vivṛhā.	Removal of Phthisis.	The same.
164	Pracetas.	Dissipation of Bad Dreams.	1, 2, 4 Anuṣṭup. 3 Triṣṭup. 5 Paṅkti.
165	Kapota.	Viśvedevas.	Triṣṭup.
166	Ṛṣabha.	Removal of Rivals.	Anuṣṭup. 5 Mahāpaṅkti.
167	Viśvāmitra and Jāmadagni.	Indra.	Jagatī.
168	Anila.	Vāyu.	Triṣṭup.
169	Śabara.	Cows.	The same.
170	Vibhrāj.	Sūrya.	Jagatī. 4 Āstārapaṅkti.
171	Iṭa.	Indra.	Gāyatrī.
172	Saṁvarta.	Uṣas.	Dvipadā Virāj.
173	Dhruva.	The King.	Anuṣṭup.
174	Abhīvarta.	The same.	The same.
175	Ūrdhvagrāvan.	The Press-stones.	Gāyatrī.
176	Sūnu.	Ṛbhus. Agni.	Anuṣṭup. 2 Gāyatrī.
177	Pataṅga.	Māyābheda.	1 Jagatī. 2, 3 Triṣṭup.
178	Ariṣṭanemi.	Tārkṣya.	Triṣṭup.
179	Sibi. Pratardana. Vasumanas.	Indra.	1 Anuṣṭup. 2, 3 Triṣṭup.
180	Jaya.	The same.	Triṣṭup.

Hymn.	*Ṛṣi.*	*Deity.*	*Metre.*
181	Pratha, Sapratha. Gharma.	Viśvedevas.	Triṣṭup
182	Tapurmūrdhan.	Bṛhaspati.	....
183	Prajāvān.	The Sacrificer. His Wife. The Hotar.	....
184	Tvaṣṭar or Viṣṇu.	Benediction of the Embryo.	Anuṣṭup.
185	Satyadhṛti.	Aditi.	Gāyatrī.
186	Ula.	Vāyu.	The same.
187	Vatsa.	Agni.	....
188	Śyena.	Agni Jātavedas.	....
189	Śārparājñī.	Sārparājñī, or Sūrya.	....
190	Aghamarṣaṇa.	Creation.	Anuṣṭup.
191	Saṁvanana.	Agni. Unanimity.	Anuṣṭup. 3 Triṣṭup.

GENERAL INDEX OF HYMNS ACCORDING TO DEITIES AND SUBJECTS*

DEITIES OF DAWN.

Usas, Dawn, Morning.—I. 48, 49, 92, 113, 123, 124. III. 61. IV. 51, 52. V. 79, 80. VI. 64, 65. VII. 75-81. X. 172.

The Aśvins.—I. 34, 46, 47, 112, 116-120, 157, 158, 180-184. II. 39. III. 58 IV 43-45. V. 73-77. VI. 62. 63. VII. 67-74. VIII. 5, 8-10, 22, 26, 35, 62, 74, 76. Vālakhilya Hymns, at the end of VIII. 9. X. 39-41. 106, 143.

Dadhikrāvan, Dadhikrās.—IV. 38-40. VII. 44.

Agni as a God of Morning.—IV. 13, 14.

VARUṆA AND SUN-GODS.

Varuṇa.—I. 24, 25. II. 28. V. 85. VII. 86, 89. VIII. 41, 42.

Mitra.—III. 59. VII. 41.

Varuṇa, Mitra, Aryaman.—I. 41.

Mitra, and Varuṇa.—I. 136, 137, 151-153. V. 62-72. VI. 67. VII. 60-66. VIII. 25. X. 132, 185.

Ādityas.—II. 27. VII. 51, 52, VIII. 18, 47, 56.

Sūrya.—I. 50, 115. X. 37, 158.

Savitar.—I. 35. II. 38. IV. 53, 54. V. 81, 82. VI. 71. VII. 38, 45. X. 139, 149.

Pūṣan.—I. 42. 138. VI. 53-56, 58. X. 26

Viṣṇu.—I. 154-156. VII. 99, 100.

Viśvakarman. —X. 81, 82.

Vena.—X. 123.

Vibhrāj.—X. 170.

Tārkṣya.—X. 178.

Sārparājñī, or Sūrya—X. 189.

COSMIC DEITIES.

Ṛbhus.—I. 20, 110, 111, III. 60. IV. 33-37. VII. 48.

Heaven and Earth.—I. 159, 160, 185. IV. 56. VI. 70. VII. 53.

Pṛthivī.—V. 84.

Sarasvatī.—VI. 61. VII. 95-96.

Waters.—VII. 47. 49. X.9; Waters, or Cows.—X. 19.

Son of Waters, Apāṁnapāt.—II. 35.

Soma.—I. 91. VIII. 48, 68, X. 25.

COLLECTIVE AND MISCELLANEOUS DEITIES.

Viśvedevas, All-Gods.—I. 14, 89, 90, 106, 107, 122, 139, 186. II. 29, 31. III. 54-57. IV. 55. V. 41-51. VI. 49-52. VII. 34, 36, 37, 39, 40, 42, 43. VIII. 27-30, 72. X. 31, 35, 36, 63-66, 92, 93, 100.

Aśvins, Savitar, Agni, Heaven and Earth, Viṣṇu.—I. 22.

Vāyu, Indra, Mitra, Varuṇa, Viśvedevas, Pūṣan, Waters, Agni.—I. 23.

Heaven and Earth, Indra, Tvaṣṭar, Rākā, Sinīvālī—II. 32.

Indra, Vāyu, Mitra, Varuṇa, Aśvins, Viśvedevas, Sarasvatī, Dyaus, Pṛthivī.—II. 41.

Indra, Varuṇa, Bṛhaspati, Pūṣan, Savitar, Soma, Mitra, Varuṇa.—III. 62.

Mitra, Varuṇa, Ādityas, Aśvins, Vāyu, Sūrya, Pavamāna, the Cow.—VIII. 90.

*I follow the classification and arrangement adopted by Professor Ludwig in his Translation. The names of many of the deities are repeated in other Sections in accordance with the subjects of the hymns addressed to them. For instance, the great deeds of Indra are related in hymns placed in the Cosmogonical and Mythical Section.

AGNI (JĀTAVEDAS AND VAIŚVĀNARA).

I. 1, 12, 26, 27, 31, 36, 44, 45, 58-60, 65-79, 94-99. 127, 128, 140, 141, 143-150, 189. II. 1, 2, 4-10. III. 1-3, 5-7, 9-11, 13-28. IV. 1-12, 15. V. 1-4, 6-11. 13-28 VI. 1-16, 48. VII. 1, 3, 4-17. VIII. 11, 19, 23, 39, 43, 44, 49, 60, 61, 63, 64, 73, 91, 92. X. 1-8. 11. 12, 20, 21, 45, 46, 79, 80, 87, 88, 91, 115, 118, 122, 140, 142, 150, 156, 176, 187, 188.

INDRA (ŚATAKRATU, ŚAKRA, MANYU.)

I. 4-11, 16, 30, 54-57, 61-63, 80-84, 100-104, 121, 129-133, 135, 169, 173-178. II. 11-22, 30. III. 30-32, 34-52. IV. 16, 17, 19, 25, 29, 31, 32, 46. V. 29-39. VI. 17-26, 28-47. VII. 19-32. VIII. 1-4 6 12-17. 21, 24, 32-34, 36, 37, 45, 46, 50-55, 57,59, 65-67, 69, 71, 77-79, 81-82, 84-88. Vālakhilya, 1-6. X. 22-24, 29, 32, 42-44, 47-50 54, 55, 73, 74, 89, 96, 104, 105, 112, 113, 116, 120, 131, 133, 134, 138, 144, 147, 148, 152, 153, 160, 171-179, 180. Manyu. X. 83, 84.

GODS OF STORM, WIND, AND RAIN.

Maruts.—I. 37-39, 64, 85-88. 166-168, 171. II. 34. V. 52-60, 87. VI. 66. VII. 56-59. VIII. 7, 20, 83. X. 77, 78.

Rudra.—I. 43. 114. II. 33. VII. 46.

Vāyu.—1, 2, 134. IV. 47, 48. VII. 90-92. X. 168, 186.

Parjanya.—V. 83. VII. 101, 102.

LORD OF PRAYER

Brahmaṇaspati or Bṛhaspati.—I. 18, 40, 190. II. 23-26. IV. 50. VI. 73. VII. 97, 98. X. 182.

Indra and Brahmaṇaspati.—IV. 49.

DUAL DEITIES.

Indra-Varuṇa.—I. 17. IV. 41. VI. 68. VII. 82, 84, 85. Vālakhilya, 11.

Indra-Pūṣan.—VI. 57.

Indra-Viṣṇu.—VI. 69.

Indra-Agni.—I. 21, 108, 109. III. 12. V. 86. VI. 59, 60. VII. 93, 94. VIII. 88, 40.

Agni-Maruts.—I. 19.

Indra-Soma.—VI. 72. VII. 104.

Agni-Soma.—I. 93.

Soma-Rudra.—VI. 74.

Soma Pūṣan.—II. 40.

LITURGICAL HYMNS, PRAYERS, CHARMS.

Viśvedevas.—X. 114. Sacred Metres.—X. 130. Praise of the Aṅgirases.—X. 62. The Sacrificer and his Wife.—VIII. 31. The Sacrificer, Wife, and Hotar.—X. 183. Faith.—X. 151. Viśvedevas.—X. 157. State of the Dead.—X. 154. Dakṣiṇā (Priests' Guerdon). —X. 107, Ṛtvijas (Priests). Vālakhilya, 10. X. 101. Āpris.—I. 13, 142, 188. II. 3. III. 4. V. 5. VII. 2. IX. 5. X. 70, 110. Production of Sacrificial Fire.—III. 29. Sacrificial Stake.—III. 8. Pestle and Mortar.—I. 28, Press-stones.—X. 76, 94, 175. Havirdhānas,—X. 13. Ṛtus (Seasons).—II. 36, 37. SOMA PAVAMANA.—IX. 1-4, 6-114. Praise of the Horse. —I. 162, 163. Waters, or Son of Waters.—X. 30. Saraṇyū, Pūṣan, Sarasvatī, Waters, Soma.—X. 17. Sūryā's Bridal.—X. 85, Vāstoṣpati (Guardian of the House).—VII. 54, 55. Kṣetrapati (Lord of the Field) and Sītā (Furrow).—IV. 57. Praise of Food. —I. 187. Araṇyānī (Goddess of the Forest).—

HYMNS RELATING TO COSMOGONY, MYTHS, HISTORY, AND CIVILIZATION.

INDEX OF NAMES, ETC.

— Āptya, Āptyas, a class of deities, dwelling in water, 402, 435, 534, 628.
Apvā, Colic personified, 617.
Arachosia, 424 *note*.
Araḍu, a kind of tree, 434.
Araḍva, said to be a man's name, 434 *note*.
Aramati, the Genius of devotion, 155, 258, 352.
— the Goddess of Devotion, 354, 357, 579, 605.
— —Earth, 605.
Araṇis, fire-sticks, 429, 553 *notes*.
Araṇyānī, Goddess of the Wood, 640, 641.
Araru, name of a fiend, 613.
Arāyī, a witch or she-fiend, 643.
Arbuda, a demon (of the air), 33, 136, 139, 392, 421, 422, 581, 622.
Aracan, said to be a Ṛṣi's name, 642 *note*.
Arcanānas, a Ṛṣī, 273.
Archer, 44, 45, 46, 47, 87, 101, 274, 325.
Architect of the worlds, 591 *note*.
Ārjīka, a district in N.W. India, 398, 528.
Ārjīkas, name of a people, 494.
Ārjīkīya,—Ārjīka, 440, 533.
Arjuna, a man's name, 84, 343.
Ārjuneya, Kutsa descendant of Arjuna, 343, 388.
Ārjunī, the father of Kutsa, 74, 218.
Arjunis, two lunar mansions, 594.
Arka, the Sun, 316, 619.
Ārkṣa, a patronymic, son of Ṛkṣa, 443.
Armaiti, in the Avesta —earth, 605 *note*.
Armlets, 266.
Armour, 15, 20, 97, 224, 331, 332, 349, 395, 435, 518, 520, 521, 526, 589, 615.
Arṇa, a prince slain by Indra, 221.
Arrian, 179, 409.
Arrow, the Lofty, lightning, 202.
the stroke of disease or death, 370, 407.
Arrows, 269, 311, 312, 331.
— , poisoned, 332.
— , the thunderbolt. 449.
Ārṣṭiṣena, son of Ṛṣṭiṣeṇa, 612.
Artificer of Gods; see Tvaṣṭar.
Aruṣa, the Red, the Sun, 209 *note*.
Aruṣaḥ, the Red, Agni or the thunderbolt, 562 *note*.
Aruṣas, Agni's horses, 357 *note*.
Ārya(s), *Āryan*, v,x, 2, 5, 10, 34, 39, 50, 62, 64, 65-67, 69, 73, 79, 80, 90, 91, 104, 120, 121, 131, 136, 143, 168, 171, 172, 180, 189, 193, 196, 203, 218, 221, 252, 253, 261, 295, 299, 300, 303, 304, 310, 322, 336, 342, 371, 375, 381, 408, 412, 415, 464, 467, 513, 536, 562, 566, 573, 578, 579, 583, 597, 614, 637, 642.
Ārya, Colour, i.e. race,
Aryaman, one of the Ādityas, 16, 24, 27, 28, 29, 50, 56, 57, 67, 68, 69, 94, 95, 98, 107, 116, 125, 130, 147, 156, 192, 200, 202, 221, 234, 238, 255, 262, 274, 315, 319, 353, 354, 355, 356, 360, 364, 365, 366, 367, 375, 380, 407, 409, 416, 417, 418, 420, 433, 435, 441, 451, 457, 462, 468, 493, 505, 511, 526, 529, 552, 556, 560, 575, 579, 582, 585, 595, 596, 601, 605, 606, 632, 639.
Asamāti, said to be the name of a king, 573 *notes*.
Āsaṅga, the name of a chieftain, 389, 390, 423.
Asiknī, one of the five rivers of the Panjāb, 21 *note*.
the river Cenāb, 411, 587.
Aśmanvatī, Stony, the name of a stream, 569.
Aśna, the name of a demon, 286.
Ass, figurative, a rival worshipper, 17,
— , the steed of the Aśvins, 452.
Asses of the *Aśvins*, 23, 78, 108, 225.
Asses, presented to priests, 469.
Assembly, Congregation, synod, 19, 102, 103, 239.
Assembly's lord, Agni, 10.
Asterism(s), 495, 570, 578, 605 *notes*.
Astrabudhna, a man's name, 647 *note*.
Āstrabudhna, son of Astrabudhna, 647.
Asunīti, Spirit-World; deity of funerals, 540, 572.
Asura, Lord God, 15, 24, 36, 71, 83, 91, 120, 103, 148, 150, 174, 182, 189, 195, 233, 243, 244, 256, 263, 264, 272, 273, 297, 305, 324.
— , demon (later use) 66, 79, 255.
High God, 337, 348, 362, 409, 410, 429, 454, 506, 520, 535, 536, 552, 570, 571, 581, 605, 610, 612, 613, 634, 648.
— , Lord, king, 606 *note*.
Asura-slayer, Indra, 298.
Asuras, ancient Gods, 101,
— , demons (later use) 20, 35, 36, 63, 64, 69, 72, 73, 80, 90, 141, 143, 257, 297, 592, 631, 642.
Asura, a demon, 459, 569, 634, 637.
Asuras, 354, 367, 416, 459, 499, 569, 644, 647.
Asura-slayer, Agni, 339.
Asurī, a female fiend, 565 *note*.
Aśva, father of the Ṛṣi Vaśa, 72.
a Ṛṣi, 415.
Āśvaghna, the patronymic of a prince, 575.
Āśvalāyana, a famous writer on ritual, 11 *note*, 530, 542 *notes*.
Aśvamedha, Horse-sacrifice, 108, 644 *note*.
Aśvamedha, the name of a prince, 248.
a man's name, 443.
Āśvamedha, son of Aśvamedha,
Aśvatha, a name of Divodāsa, 313.
Aśvattha, the Holy Fig Tree, 93 *note*.
—a sacred tree, 553, 568, 610.
Aśvinī, the Consort of the Aśvins, 262.
Aśvins, the two horsemen, Twin Heralds of Dawn, 2, 9, 11, 18, 22, 23, 29, 31, 32, 43, 53, 56, 59, 70, 72-82, 84, 95, 104, 105, 106, 108, 112, 116, 119, 121-124, 125, 150, 155, 156, 157, 170, 174, 183, 192, 196, 200, 208, 209, 219, 223, 224, 225, 226, 229-230, 233, 234, 247, 255, 258, 259, 261, 262, 263, 264, 275-278, 294, 315, 324, 325.
— , their character, 2, 12, 22, 23, 30, 31.
— their miracles, 72-74, 77-82, 122, 123, 324.
their chariot, 12, 275.
their steed or steeds, 23, 76, 108, 275-277.
their whip, 12, 104.
their favourite number, 22, 23.
— , the Horsemen, Twin heralds of Dawn, 338, 353, 356, 358, 360, 368-371, 394-395, 399-401, 407, 408, 409, 412, 413, 416-418, 420, 424, 425, 429, 447, 451-453, 457, 466, 470, 474, 505, 511, 530, 541, 546, 547, 551, 553, 556, 558-560, 568, 573, 574, 578, 579, 580, 590, 594, 595, 605, 606, 618, 619, 631, 633, 635, 639.
—, their consort, 369, 559; their character, 559; their miracles, 446, 447, 558-560; physicians, 400, 407, 452, 539.
—first teachers of agriculture, 412; their chariot, 368, 369, 370, 395, 412, 446, 452, 470, 558, 559, 560, 561.
Aśvya, a family name, 434.
Asylum, the sacrificial enclosure, 272.
Atharvan, the first Fire-priest, 51, 52, 53, 78, 80, 85, 400, 525, 544, 565, 598, 605, 628.
Atharvans, 313, 476, 538.
Atharva-veda, 12, 53, 104, 112, 202, 219, 378, 419, 436, 532, 535, 568, 576, 596, 603, 621, 628, 637, 639, 643, 645.
Atirātra, a certain Soma ceremony, 384.
Atithigu, a man's name. 566 note.
Atithigva, a name of Divodāsa, 33, 36, 73, 90, 139, 218, 295, 301, 308, 313, 344, 443, 468, 566.
Atiyāja, one who over-sacrifices, 318.
Atithyeṣṭi, a certain religious ceremony, 429 *note*.
Atka, a man's name, 566, 613.
Atmospheres, two, 288.; —three, 592.
Atri, a great Ṛṣi, 14, 30, 33, 72, 79, 80, 81, 96, 122, 124, 134, 255, 256, 264, 275, 276, 278, 317, 369, 370, 395, 425, 426, 446, 447, 513, 559, 590, 592, 634, 639, 642.
Atrin, a voracious fiend, 55.
Atris, descendants of Atri, 246, 255, 274, 420, 425, 426.

C

E

F

G

I

J

P

Q

R

T

U

V

W

X

Y

Z